FIFTH EDITION

What Is Psychology?

Foundations, Applications & Integration

Ellen Pastorino | Valencia College

Susann Doyle-Portillo | University of North Georgia

CENGAGE

Australia • Brazil • Canada • Mexico • Singapore • United Kingdom • United States

CENGAGE

What Is Psychology? Foundations, Applications, and Integration, **Fifth Edition**
Ellen Pastorino and Susann Doyle-Portillo

SVP, Higher Education & Skills Product: Erin Joyner

VP, Higher Education & Skills Product: Thais Alencar

Product Director: Laura Ross

Product Manager: Colin Grover

Product Assistant: Jessica Witzak

Learning Designer: Natasha Allen

Content Manager: Tangelique Williams-Grayer

Digital Delivery Lead: Allison Marion

Director, Marketing: Neena Bali

Marketing Manager: Tricia Salata

IP Analyst: Deanna Ettinger

IP Project Manager: Kelli Besse

Production Service: MPS Limited

Art Director: Chris Doughman, Bethany Bourgeois

Cover Image Source: © Getty Images/BlackJack3D

Library of Congress Control Number: 2020924185

ISBN: 978-0-357-37396-5

Cengage
200 Pier 4 Boulevard
Boston, MA 02210
USA

Cengage is a leading provider of customized learning solutions with employees residing in nearly 40 different countries and sales in more than 125 countries around the world. Find your local representative at **www.cengage.com.**

To learn more about Cengage platforms and services, register or access your online learning solution, or purchase materials for your course, visit **www.cengage.com.**

Printed at CLDPC, USA, 07-21

For Luca James
Dream big, be bold, and know that you are loved –
deeply and always.
—Nona

For my husband, Eulalio Ortiz Portillo. Eres mi mundo
y mi vida.
—Susann Doyle-Portillo

About the Authors

Ellen E. Pastorino (Ph.D., Florida State University, 1990) is a developmental psychologist who established her teaching career at Gainesville State College in Georgia. As a tenured professor, she created and developed the college's Teaching and Learning Center, working with faculty to promote student learning. For the past 22 years, she has been teaching at Valencia College in Orlando, Florida. Here, too, she has worked with faculty in designing learning-centered classroom practices. Ellen has won numerous teaching awards, including the University of Georgia Board of Regents Distinguished Professor, the NISOD Excellence in Teaching Award, and Valencia's Teaching and Learning Excellence Award. Ellen has published articles in the *Journal of Adolescent Research* and *Adolescence* and has participated in many regional and national teaching conferences. However, her main passion has always been to get students excited about the field of psychology. Ellen is a member of the Association for Psychological Science (APS) and she served for 10 years as the Discipline Coordinator of Psychological Sciences at Valencia's Osceola campus. She has authored test banks, instructor manuals, and student study guides. While working as a consultant for IBM Corporation, she developed numerous educational materials for teachers and students. Her current interests include reaching underprepared students and educating psychology undergraduate majors about potential job and career prospects. Ellen strives to balance her professional responsibilities with her love of physical fitness and family life.

Susann M. Doyle-Portillo (Ph.D. in Social Cognition, University of Oklahoma, 1994) is Department Head and Professor of Psychological Science at the University of North Georgia where she has taught for the past 26 years. She holds bachelor's degrees in engineering and psychology, and is a member of several professional organizations, including the *Association for Psychological Science (APS)* and the *Society for Personality and Social Psychology (SPSP)*. She has published articles in journals such as *Social Cognition, Contemporary Social Psychology*, the *American Journal of Health Education*, and *Personality & Individual Differences*, but the main focus of her career is teaching. During her career, Susann has twice been listed in Who's Who Among America's Teachers. In addition to her teaching and research activities, she has mentored many undergraduate researchers and authored several test banks, instructor manuals, and student study guides.

Brief Contents

Contents

Preface

Together, we have nearly 60 years of experience teaching Introductory Psychology. We have each spent the bulk of our careers teaching multiple sections of Introductory Psychology each semester—it is our bread and butter, so to speak. So, it's a good thing that Introductory Psychology is also our favorite course. Contrary to what many may think of professors teaching the same course over and over, it never grows old for us. Teaching Introductory Psychology allows us to touch on many different aspects of our fascinating field and to work with diverse students from all walks of life, such that no two classes are ever alike.

The uniqueness of each class is just one of the challenges that keeps us excited about teaching this course. There are others. Introductory Psychology classes are often full of students who are just beginning their college careers—some are fresh from high school; others are returning, nontraditional students who've been out of the classroom for several years. They come to us with the desire to learn about psychology, but often they face serious obstacles. Some are overworked in their personal lives. Some have lingering academic challenges. And most expect learning to be easier than we know it to be. A big part of our mission is to help students overcome these obstacles and obtain success.

Our Mission: Motivating Students to Read

Getting students to read their textbook in preparation for classes and exams is one of the biggest problems we face as instructors. Like many professors, our experience has been that few students read assigned chapters prior to class, and some even fail to read the chapters by the time they take exams. For years, we have tried various methods of motivating students to read—pop quizzes, reading quizzes, test questions from material in the book but not covered in class, and so on. None of these methods seemed to have much of an impact on students.

Students' free time is in short supply, and when they do have free time, reading a textbook doesn't always seem like an attractive option. Students often find their texts difficult to read, boring, and full of content that is far removed from the concerns of their daily lives. If we want students to read their textbooks, we will have to give them books that they will want to read, and that means giving them a book that they can understand and one that they find relevant enough to be worth the time it takes to read. Motivating students to read is our primary mission, and we wrote *What Is Psychology? Foundations, Applications and Integration* to give students a textbook that they would find interesting to read, easy to read, and memorable.

Our Mission: Giving Students an Integrated View of Psychology that Aligns with APA Guidelines

Another important goal is providing students with a comprehensive and integrated view of the field of psychology. We have long advocated for a "Big Picture" approach to the teaching of psychology, and our previous editions of *What Is Psychology?* emphasized the integrated nature of psychology as a field. Through the use of case studies that were woven throughout the chapters and through continually referring to material in other chapters, *What Is Psychology?* encouraged students to see psychology as a whole rather than as a sum of many parts.

The need to provide Introductory Psychology students with an integrated view of psychology has also been recognized by the American Psychological Association (APA, 2014) in their guidelines for strengthening the Common Core in the Introductory Psychology course. A prominent theme in these guidelines is that all Introductory Psychology courses should present students with a "big picture" view of psychology that integrates the different perspectives that psychologists take in examining mental processes and behavior. Furthermore, in presenting this integrated view of psychology, Introductory Psychology courses should highlight the common themes that tie the different perspectives or areas of psychology together—themes that include the scientific method of research, diversity and variations seen in human behavior, the applicability of psychology to real life, and the ethics that guide psychological research and practice.

This call for a Common Core in introductory courses places the Introductory Psychology course in line with the broader *APA Guidelines for the Undergraduate Psychology Major Version 2.0* (APA, 2013). These guidelines for the major contain the learning goals that students should attain by the time they complete an undergraduate degree in psychology. Each of these goals is broken down into a series of specific learning outcomes that are divided into two levels. The first level defines goals that students should attain during their first three or four "foundational" psychology courses, while the second level defines goals for what students should achieve by the completion of their degree program. Introductory psychology is clearly often the first foundation course taken by students who may take just a few psychology classes or decide to major in the field. These goals are numerically indexed; for example, the first learning outcome under Goal 1 is Learning Outcome 1.1.

A Summary of the Current APA Learning Goals

Goal 1: Knowledge Base in Psychology

Learning Outcomes 1.1–1.3 pertain to students' acquisition of the key concepts, domains, and applications of psychology.

1.1 Describe key concepts, principles, and overarching themes in psychology
1.2 Develop a working knowledge of psychology's content domains
1.3 Describe applications of psychology

Goal 2: Scientific Inquiry and Critical Thinking

Learning Outcomes 2.1–2.5 pertain to students' understanding and use of the scientific method, information literacy, integrative thinking, and use of sociocultural factors in scientific inquiry.

2.1 Use scientific reasoning to interpret psychological phenomena
2.2 Demonstrate psychology information literacy
2.3 Engage in innovative and integrative thinking and problem solving
2.4 Interpret, design, and conduct basic psychological research
2.5 Incorporate sociocultural factors in scientific inquiry

Goal 3: Ethical and Social Responsibility in a Diverse World

Learning Outcomes 3.1–3.3 pertain to students' understanding and use of ethical standards to build interpersonal relationships and communities.

3.1 Apply ethical standards to evaluate psychological science and practice
3.2 Build and enhance interpersonal relationships
3.3 Adopt values that build community at local, national, and global levels

Goal 4: Communication

Learning Outcomes 4.1–4.3 pertain to students' demonstration of effective writing, presentation, and interpersonal communication skills.

4.1 Demonstrate effective writing for different purposes
4.2 Exhibit effective presentation skills for different purposes
4.3 Interact effectively with others

Goal 5: Professional Development

Learning Outcomes 5.1–5.5 pertain to students' demonstration of the skills and knowledge necessary to meet their career goals in psychology, including self-management skills, project management skills, and the applicability of psychology to various professional pursuits.

5.1 Apply psychological content and skills to career goals
5.2 Exhibit self-efficacy and self-regulation
5.3 Refine project-management skills
5.4 Enhance teamwork capacity
5.5 Develop meaningful professional direction for life after graduation

As professors who also teach advanced courses in psychology, we firmly agree with the APA that students should be taught to see psychology as a unified whole rather than as a series of discrete areas of study. When students enter advanced courses with a unified understanding of Introductory Psychology, they are much more likely to be successful. And students who continue to build this big picture understanding of psychology throughout their coursework are the most successful in attaining their career goals at graduation. For this reason, we are very excited to introduce this new fifth edition of *What Is Psychology? Foundations, Applications, and Integration*. This edition retains the best features from our previous texts that have motivated thousands of students to actually read and learn psychology. Just as the fourth edition focused on strengthening the three themes represented in the subtitle: foundations, applications, and integration, this fifth edition is structured around the guidelines set forth in the *APA Guidelines for the Undergraduate Psychology Major Version 2.0*, and the recommendations made by the APA's Board of Educational Affairs (BEA) Working Group to Strengthen the Common Core. While the APA 2.0 guidelines suggest learning outcomes for college psychology courses, the Common Core proposes an optimal course structure to provide the best introduction to the field of psychology (APA, 2014).

What Is Psychology? Foundations, Applications, and Integration

What Is Psychology? Foundations, Applications, and Integration, 5e retains all the pedagogical features of our previous edition, as well as, new features designed to further strengthen students' mastery of the scientific methods that form the ultimate foundation of our field and help students of all majors see how psychology is relevant to their career development.

Foundations: Content Organized Around the Foundational Areas of Psychological Research

What Is Psychology? Foundations, Applications, and Integration, 5e is organized around the foundational areas of psychology emphasized by the APA in the Common Core discussions. The text opens with the ultimate foundation of psychology, the scientific research methods that inform all study of mental processes and behavior. An understanding of the research methods that psychologists use is essential to building a comprehensive understanding of psychology.

Unfortunately, all too often, students tend to forget the research methods they learn in the first chapter as they are reading and studying subsequent chapters. A common complaint in upper-division courses is that students don't seem to recall basic concepts such as independent and dependent variables, causation vs. correlation, and so on. This edition includes a couple of features that are designed to make the science of psychology salient for students as they read each of the subsequent chapters of the text and give students practice in applying their knowledge of research methods.

The scientific reasoning questions introduced in the fourth edition have been retained. These questions can be found periodically both in the quizzes that follow each section and in the end-of-chapter quizzes, where they are marked with this special icon ○. These questions are written using concepts relevant to the topics of the chapter, and they give the student the opportunity to review the research methods learned in Chapter 1. For example, a scientific reasoning question from Chapter 4 reads:

> The suprachiasmatic nucleus increases the release of melatonin as it gets darker outside. This represents a ______ correlation between amount of melatonin and amount of daylight.
>
> a. negative
> b. positive
> c. zero
> d. perfect

New to the fifth edition is the inclusion of a *Critical Thinking about the Science of Psychology* feature. At the end of each chapter, students are referred back to a study that was discussed in that chapter and asked to answer questions about the research methods used in that study. An example question from Chapter 6 reads:

> Recall the Bobo doll student conducted by Albert Bandura (1965) that you read about in Section 6.4.1. In particular, think about the first phase of the study, in which the children watched one of the films and were then simply left alone in the room with the Bobo doll. Then, see if you can answer these questions.
>
> 1. What type of research method did Bandura use in this study?
> 2. What was the independent variable in this study?
> 3. What was the dependent variable in this study?
> 4. How did Bandura control for confounding variables in his study?
> 5. Are there any potential ethical concerns with Bandura's study?

By continually reinforcing the content and application of research methods in psychology, these features help students to better understand the science of psychology and to better retain this knowledge as they move forward along their educational pathways.

In addition to understanding the scientific foundations of psychology, students must also master the schools of thought and content areas of psychology that have emerged in our field. Accordingly, the remaining chapters of the text are organized around four foundational content areas: the *biological, cognitive, developmental and social,* and *physical and mental health* areas of psychology. Content is divided to follow these topical sections of psychology while creating manageable chunks of related material, allowing professors to easily align their content with testing during the semester or quarter:

Chapter 1: The Science of Psychology

Part 1: Foundations in Biological Psychology
Chapter 2: Neuroscience
Chapter 3: Sensation and Perception
Chapter 4: Consciousness
Chapter 5: Motivation and Emotion

Part 2: Foundations in Cognitive Psychology
Chapter 6: Learning
Chapter 7: Memory
Chapter 8: Cognition, Language, and Intelligence

Part 3: Foundations in Developmental and Social Psychology
Chapter 9: Human Development
Chapter 10: Social Psychology
Chapter 11: Personality

Part 4: Foundations in Physical and Mental Health
Chapter 12: Health, Stress, and Positive Psychology
Chapter 13: Mental Health Disorders
Chapter 14: Mental Health Therapies

Applications: Integrating Psychology Through the Use of Case Studies

One of the best ways to motivate students to read is to capture their curiosity from the very beginning. If psychology is interesting for students, they will read. Each of our previous texts drew rave reviews from students for the use of attention-grabbing case studies at the opening of each chapter or part. In *Foundations, Applications, and Integration, 5e,* we continue this tradition. Each of the four foundational parts of the text opens with a case study that illustrates how the content covered in the chapters of that part helps us understand the behavior and mental processes of a real-life person. The case studies are compelling stories of people who have faced life's challenges with courage and grace. For example, the biological part opens with the case study of Jean-Dominique Bauby, a man who wrote a moving book that was later turned into a movie, *The Diving Bell and the Butterfly,* while in a state of locked-in syndrome that left him completely paralyzed save the ability to blink his left eye. The developmental and social psychology part begins with the story of Hongyong Baek, a woman who survived many challenges, including the Korean War and devastating personal losses, but still managed many triumphs in her lifetime. Each of the case studies is woven throughout all of the chapters of that part of the book, providing students with a view of the content that is both integrated and applied to real life. By using one case study to tie all of the related chapters together, students are encouraged to see the material as a whole rather than as a series of disparate parts; and in doing so, they begin forming an integrated "big picture" of psychology.

Integration: The Big Picture

To further facilitate the development of an integrated, "big picture" view of psychology in students, each chapter closes with a section called Integrating Psychology: The Big Picture. In this section, we revisit the part case study and use it as a vehicle for both reviewing the content of the chapter(s) of the section and previewing the content of the coming chapter(s). Through *Integrating Psychology: The Big Picture,* students begin to see that all of the material fits together—what has been learned informs what is yet to be learned.

Numerical Indexing Allows for Easy Cross-Referencing

Throughout the text, numeric indexing is used to help students quickly locate relevant information. All primary and secondary heads for the chapter are also numerically indexed with a sequential code. For example, here is the indexing for a portion of Chapter 2 content:

2.1 Billions of Neurons: Communication in the Brain
  2.1.1 The Anatomy of the Neuron
  2.1.2 Signals in the Brain: How Neurons Fire Up
  2.1.3 Jumping the Synapse: Synaptic Transmission

This numeric coding scheme allows for relevant material to be indexed back to the applicable section of the text, tying content to each section heading. Through numbering, the learning objectives, quizzes, review summaries, and visual summaries at the ends of each chapter are easy to reference to a specific location within the text. Numeric coding also makes it easy for instructors to assign specific portions of chapters, and for students to find that material across media, creating a smoother experience when moving around in the physical text or between the text and digital formats. Through the use of these numeric codes, students can quickly tie content from a variety of sources back to specific sections of the text.

Learning Objectives that Are Aligned with the APA Learning Goals and Outcomes

Each chapter opens with the Learning Objectives, which are numerically indexed to the appropriate Learning Goal and Learning Outcome in the *APA Guidelines for the Undergraduate Psychology Major Version 2.0* (APA, 2013). Learning Objectives are also numerically indexed to the section heading of the chapter in which the relevant material is covered. This allows both the instructor and the student to quickly assess which objectives are covered in each discrete section of the text, and which APA program outcomes are being addressed in that section. For example, here is a sample of the learning objectives for Chapter 8. The index numbers on the left refer to the relevant sections of the chapter. The codes on the right relate the learning objectives to the specific APA Learning Outcomes.

8.1 Describe how we represent knowledge in our memory. (APA 1.1, 1.2, 1.3)

8.1 Describe how we organize knowledge in our memory. (APA 1.1, 1.2, 1.3)

8.2 Describe the different types of problems we face in life and the ways in which we may try to solve them. (APA 1.1, 1.2, 1.3)

8.2 Describe common obstacles to problem solving. (APA 1.1, 1.2, 1.3)

Diversity: Making Psychology Relevant for All People

There is little doubt that students learn best when they become personally invested in the material they are reading and studying. However, for this to occur, students must actually find the material to be applicable to their lives. Given that today's college students are a diverse group of people, writing a text that is relevant to today's students means writing a text that embraces their diversity. Diversity and variations in human behavior are also themes that are emphasized in the APA Common Core guidelines and the *APA Guidelines for the Undergraduate Psychology Major.* Understanding psychology means understanding the behavior and mental processes of *all* people.

Appropriately, we wrote our book with inclusion in mind. Throughout the text we use examples of real people (such as those whose stories open each foundational section) who reflect the diversity seen in our classrooms. Where applicable, we have cited and highlighted research that reflects many aspects of diversity, including gender, racial diversity, sexual orientation, cultural diversity, age and generational differences, socioeconomic levels, and physical and/or mental health challenges. In all, we reference people from well over 120 countries and/or cultural groups.

An Engaging Narrative Writing Style Makes Difficult Material Easier to Understand

Motivating a student to read the text is, of course, a primary concern of professors. But reading the text does no good if the student does not understand what they have read. A major goal of this text is to bring psychology to the student by making it understandable, and to do so without sacrificing content. We believe that it is not necessary to condescend to students to get them to understand. Rather, you just have to explain difficult concepts thoroughly and clearly.

Throughout the text, we have adopted an engaging narrative writing style that will not intimidate students. Difficult concepts (such as neural transmission and classical conditioning) are given extended description, and many real-life examples are used to illustrate and clarify our points. The language we use in the text strongly reflects the way we speak to our students during class. We also include a pronunciation glossary so students will know how to correctly pronounce the more difficult, unfamiliar terms.

We attempted to use our prose to tell students the story of psychology, as opposed to a mere litany of theories and research findings. Throughout the text, we directly address students as "you" and refer to ourselves as "we" to help draw students into a conversation about psychology. And through that conversation, we provide students with an accessible and engaging story. Throughout the process of writing this text, many faculty reviewers and students have consistently praised our writing style for its clarity and accessibility. One reviewer commented that it was obvious that this text was written by authors who have spent much time in the classroom in front of students.

Enhancing Motivation and Learning by Making Psychology Practical and Personal

A key point in getting students to read a text and retain what they've read is making the material applicable to their lives. When information is associated with the self, it becomes more easily retrieved from memory. So, when students can see how psychology relates to their personal lives, they are much more likely to find it interesting and a lot less likely to forget it. Throughout the text, we have made a concerted effort to use practical, everyday examples to illustrate the concepts.

What Is Psychology? Foundations, Applications, and Integration 5th edition includes Psychology Applies to Your World, a feature that emphasizes the personal relevance of psychology by showing students that an understanding of psychology can help them to better understand their world. Topics for this feature include the opioid epidemic (Chapter 4), mindsets and motivation (Chapter 5), the modern face of racism (Chapter 10), and the role classical conditioning plays in our body's response to drugs (Chapter 6).

Personal relevance of the material also extends to students' career pathways. At many institutions, introductory psychology is a general education course, as well as, a major course. As such, many of our students are not psychology majors. Unsurprisingly, students often question the value and relevance of psychology to their chosen career pathways. To help students see the value in studying psychology, we have included a **new Psychology Works! feature in the fifth edition**. In each chapter, this boxed feature presents a photo and description of a career that utilizes psychological knowledge. These careers were specifically chosen to be for the most part outside of mainstream psychology and primarily require undergraduate degrees. Some of the Psychology Works! topics included are physical therapist assistants (Chapter 2), law enforcement personnel (Chapter 4), and advertising and marketing personnel (Chapter 10).

Enhancing Student Learning by Encouraging Active Learning and Self-Assessment

Many of our students learn best when they engage in active rather than passive learning. We have made a concerted effort to get students involved with the material as they read. By remaining engaged, students will be more motivated to read, and they will likely retain the information in memory much better. Several features aimed at encouraging active learning include:

Engage Yourself!

The Engage Yourself! active learning feature asks students to do hands-on activities to illustrate important chapter concepts. Active learning not only encourages students to see the personal relevance of the material, it also helps students elaborate the material in memory by connecting it to personal experience. Examples of Engage Yourself! activities include having students examine their attributional biases when making judgments about celebrities (Chapter 10), finding their own blindspot (Chapter 3), and an activity that demonstrates the brain's predisposition to perceive faces (Chapter 9).

Quiz Yourself

Another feature, Quiz Yourself, appears after each major section of the chapter. Quiz Yourself allows students to actively assess their learning by asking them to apply the material of the preceding section to answer several multiple choice questions. Most of the Quiz Yourself questions are application questions that apply the material to practical situations. For example, in Chapter 13, we use the following question to test the student's ability to apply the criteria for determining whether or not behavior is atypical:

Susan will only eat soup with a fork. By which criteria can Susan's behavior be considered atypical?

a. Danger to others
b. Violates social norms
c. Distress
d. All of the above

To answer this question, the student must not only understand the different criteria for judging behavior, but they must also be able to think analytically in applying these concepts to a behavioral scenario. Scientific reasoning questions can also be found sprinkled throughout the Quiz Yourself quizzes, serving to further help students integrate scientific reasoning into the big picture of psychology. These questions are marked with a circle for easy identification.

You Review

Each chapter features at least one You Review table that summarizes key points of a particular topic. For example, in Chapter 12, the transmission modes, symptoms, and treatments of sexually transmitted infections are summarized. In Chapter 8, the various theories of intelligence are summarized in this feature.

What Do You Know? Assess Your Understanding

In addition to the Quiz Yourself questions at the end of each major section of the chapter, we have included a more extensive self-assessment for students at the end of each chapter. This assessment, What Do You Know? Assess Your Understanding, includes a 20-question multiple choice practice test (with the answers provided) that allows students to evaluate their retention and understanding of the entire chapter. In most cases, these quizzes also contain scientific reasoning questions. By self-assessing, students can better judge which concepts and/or sections of the chapter they should target for further study.

Use It or Lose It: Applying Psychology Questions

In addition to the multiple choice section and the Critical Thinking about the Science of Psychology questions discussed previously, the end-of-chapter assessments also include Use It or Lose It: Applying Psychology, a series of essay or short-answer questions that require students to further elaborate and integrate their knowledge by applying what they have learned to a real-world problem or question. An example question from Chapter 2 reads:

1. Jean-Dominique Bauby was still able to think, feel, and remember the events of his life after a stroke left him in a permanent state of locked-in syndrome. Now that you know something about the brain, can you explain why he retained these abilities?

Are You Getting the Big Picture?

A visual summary of the chapter, entitled "Are You Getting the Big Picture?" is also included in the end-of-chapter material to allow students to grasp the big picture of the chapter. All of the major concepts and theories of the chapter are brought together in a graphical format in the visual summary that also uses thumbnail images as reminders. This tool will be especially helpful to students who prefer to learn through visual means.

Chapter-by-Chapter Changes to Content

As psychologists know, our field is dynamic and ever-changing. To stay abreast of current knowledge and offer our students the most accurate understanding of psychology possible, the research cited in *What Is Psychology? Foundations, Applications, and Integration, 5e* has been thoroughly updated. In addition, the new edition also includes key updates to some of the pedagogical features of the text. Here is a chapter-by-chapter summary of some of the important changes in this new text.

Chapter 1: The Science of Psychology

- added confirmation bias as a key term
- emphasized the importance of replication and addressed Psychology's replication crisis
- defined and added meta-analyses as a key term
- included operational definition in the discussion of forming a hypothesis
- mentioned the use of crowdsourcing platforms to recruit participants
- included survey results on Generation Z in discussion of generational differences
- added importance of not coercing possible participants to the ethics discussion
- identified review board for non-human subjects (IACUC)
- updated information on undergraduate degrees in psychology
- updated earning inequities for women and minorities in the field of psychology
- included discussion of licensed professional counselors (LPC) and applied behavioral analysis in discussion on careers in psychology
- included a discussion of COVID-19 pandemic and behavior

Chapter 2: Neuroscience

- added coverage of the opioid epidemic
- better integrated the Jean-Dominique Bauby case study into the chapter content
- terminology aligned with the APA dictionary of psychology
- added coverage of mindfulness and the hippocampus
- updated the research on the effects of Wifi exposure on the brain

Chapter 3: Sensation and Perception

- extended coverage of subliminal perception to include subliminal perception of faces in the processing of social cues of emotion
- added one new *Engage Yourself!* demonstration on finding your blindspot
- updated coverage of gender differences in color preference
- added coverage of signal detection theory
- updated coverage of theories of pitch perception to make the text more current and more precise
- updated coverage of taste to make the text more precise
- updated coverage on olfaction and included coverage of gender differences in sensory thresholds for smell
- added the key term of a perceptual set

Chapter 4: Consciousness

- all graphs and statistics updated with the most recent data
- included research on meditation and mindfulness-based practices
- discussed the influence of sleep deprivation on emotions
- explained why REM sleep is often referred to as paradoxical sleep
- included memory theory and continuity hypothesis of dreams as key terms
- discussed the difference between light and deep hypnosis
- New *Psychology Applies to Your World* box on the opioid epidemic
- prescription opiate drugs included in table on psychoactive drugs
- electronic nicotine delivery systems (vaping) included in nicotine discussion
- distinguished between CBD (cannabidiol) and THC (tetrahydrocannabinol)
- discussed COVID-19 syndrome and the benefit of sleep
- discussed vaping and increased risk of COVID-19 outbreak
- described EVALI respiratory disease and its association with vaping

Chapter 5: Motivation and Emotion

- added a new *Psychology Applies to Your World* box on mindsets and motivation
- updated coverage of self-determination theory of motivation
- added additional coverage of ghrelin and weight loss surgery
- increased coverage of sleep deprivation and weight
- updated statistics on the obesity epidemic
- updated information on prevalence of eating disorders
- updated information on basic emotions and facial feedback of emotion

Chapter 6: Learning

- added behavior modification, counterconditioning, instinctive drift, and delay of gratification as new key terms
- added a discussion of the purposiveness of behavior
- better explained the positive learning that can occur through videogame play

- updated the coverage on the Global Initiative to End All Corporal Punishment of Children
- updated research on the effects of viewing television and screen time in children
- added a new *Psychology Applies to Your World* box on the classical conditioning of compensatory responses to drugs

Chapter 7: Memory

- added a new *Engage Yourself!* box on the serial position curve
- added additional coverage on attention and multitasking
- added a new *Engage Yourself*! box on priming.
- extended the coverage on whether or not episodic and semantic memory are separate systems
- reworked our coverage of concussions and added coverage of chronic traumatic encephalopathy in professional football players
- added coverage of the SOAR method of learning, the purported benefit of handwritten notes, and self-testing to the tips for improving memory in the *Psychology Applies to Your World* box

Chapter 8: Cognition, Language, and Intelligence

- reworked and expanded the discussion of group differences in IQ to focus less on the specific differences seen and focus more on research examining the environmental influences on intelligence
- added discussion of the Raven's Progressive Matrices test of intelligence to the discussion of cultural bias in testing
- removed the discussion of gender differences in cognitive abilities from this chapter
- added discussion of biolinguistics and usage-based theories of language development
- added additional examples of possible language use in animals
- added neuroimaging evidence of visual images in memory
- added additional coverage on personality and creativity
- better connected heuristic processing with stereotyping and prejudice
- added coverage of interacting with the problem during problem solving

Chapter 9: Human Development

- distinguished between fetal alcohol spectrum disorder and fetal alcohol syndrome
- included research on infant processing of other-race faces
- included meta-analytic results on parenting styles and association with externalizing problems in children
- updated research on gender and education, and gender and the media
- added research on gender depictions in the video game industry
- updated dating and singlehood, cohabitation, and marriage statistical trends for heterosexual and same-sex couples
- included updated research on gender and marital satisfaction in different-sex and same-sex relationships
- added results from studies on blog posts of terminally ill and last words of death row inmates

Chapter 10: Social Psychology

- added a new *Engage Yourself!* demonstration on attitude similarity to close others
- reworked the *Psychology Applies to Your World* box on prejudice to include a discussion of police violence against people of color and the #Black Lives Matter movement
- included discussion of social psychological principles, such as conformity, and their relevance to the COVID-19 pandemic

Chapter 11: Personality

- thorough update of the literature

Chapter 12: Health, Stress, and Positive Psychology

- chapter retitled to include positive psychology as much of the chapter's content focuses as much on happiness and well-being as physical health
- expanded definition of stress
- expanded discussion of trauma
- included additional research on key factors in resilience
- modified Figure 12.3 on stress response to more accurately reflect biological pathway
- expanded discussion on mindfulness and meditation
- explained difference between hardiness and resilience
- vaping included in discussion of health-defeating behaviors
- expanded discussion of influence of social media on well-being in *Psychology Applies to Your World* box
- included cultural differences in value of happiness
- included how the appraisal process is influenced by culture
- included discussion on COVID-19 stress syndrome

Chapter 13: Mental Health Disorders

- moved away from term "abnormal"; all conditions referred to as mental health disorders

- included discussion of stigma and social stigma
- expanded discussion of gender differences in the prevalence of mental health disorders
- included influence of COVID-19 on mental health
- clarified the difference between normal and excessive anxiety
- included research on the cingulate cortex and anxiety
- added research on variables that put soldiers at risk for posttraumatic stress disorder (PTSD)
- specified criteria for a manic episode

Chapter 14: Mental Health Therapies

- added learning objective for emerging biomedical therapy techniques
- updated statistics on characteristics of people with mental health disorders who seek therapy
- expanded discussion of CBT
- included the key terms of mindfulness-based cognitive therapy (MBCT) and neurosurgery for mental disorder (NMD)
- added a new section on eclectic therapy types
- added a new section on cutting-edge biomedical treatments
- added a table on emerging biomedical therapy techniques
- SNRIs added to discussion of antidepressant medications

MindTap: Empower Your Students

MindTap is a platform that propels students from memorization to mastery. It gives you complete control of your course, so you can provide engaging content, challenge every learner, and build student confidence. Customize interactive syllabi to emphasize priority topics, then add your own material or notes to the eBook as desired. This outcomes-driven application gives you the tools needed to empower students and boost both understanding and performance.

Access Everything You Need in One Place

Cut down on prep with the preloaded and organized MindTap course materials. Teach more efficiently with activities, assignments, quizzes, and more. Give your students the power to read, listen, and study on their phones, so they can learn on their terms.

Empower Students to Reach their Potential

Twelve distinct metrics give you actionable insights into student engagement. Identify topics troubling your entire class and instantly communicate with those struggling. Students can track their scores to stay motivated towards their goals. Together, you can be unstoppable.

Control Your Course—and Your Content

Get the flexibility to reorder textbook chapters, add your own notes, and embed a variety of content including Open Educational Resources (OER). Personalize course content to your students' needs. They can even read your notes, add their own, and highlight key text to aid their learning.

Get a Dedicated Team, Whenever You Need Them

MindTap isn't just a tool, it's backed by a personalized team eager to support you. We can help set up your course and tailor it to your specific objectives, so you'll be ready to make an impact from day one. Know we'll be standing by to help you and your students until the final day of the term.

Instructor Resources

Additional instructor resources for this product are available online. Instructor assets include an Instructor's Manual, Educator's Guide, PowerPoint® slides, and a test bank powered by Cognero®. Sign up or sign in at www.cengage.com to search for and access this product and its online resources.

Acknowledgments

Writing a college textbook has been an exhausting yet rewarding experience. We are ordinary college professors who teach three to six classes every semester, so we are often writing in whatever free time we have—weekends, nights, and holidays. We are valued for our contributions to student learning and service to our institutions. And we have grown so much as educators and psychologists in tackling this project. This would not have been possible without the support of many people who deserve our acknowledgment.

We would like to thank Chris Jespersen at the University of North Georgia for his administrative support. Our deepest gratitude and thanks also go out to the great people who have helped with the development of *What Is Psychology?* throughout all of its previous editions: Jaime Perkins, Kristin Makarewycz, Shannon LeMay-Finn, Kim Russell, Liz Rhoden, Nicole Lee Petel, Mary Noel, Christy Frame, Vernon Boes, Paige Leeds, Jessica Alderman, Roman Barnes, Shelli Newhart, Jill Traut, Clayton Austin, Priya Subbrayal, Jennifer Levanduski, Andrew Ginsberg, and everyone else at Cengage and MPS Limited who helped make these texts the best possible learning tools for students everywhere.

For this new edition we are grateful for the invaluable contributions made by Colin Grover, Tangelique Williams-Grayer, Tricia Salata, Jennifer Bowes, Shelley Ryan, and Nisha Banu Beegum. We also would like to thank the reviewers for their insightful comments and expert guidance in developing this text.

We would also like to thank our friends and colleagues at the University of North Georgia and Valencia College for their support and latitude over the past 20 years. We would also like to thank the thousands of students we have worked with over the years. In your own way, each of you has helped us to become better teachers and better people. Our hope is that this book will touch many other students and foster an interest in and passion for psychology.

Finally, we would like to thank our families. Susann would like to thank her husband Eddie for his endless love and support. Ellen would like to thank her husband Dave for his technical assistance, his tireless rereading of material, and his patience and support through another edition.

What Is Psychology?

Foundations, Applications & Integration

Learning Objectives

- **1.1** Define psychology. (APA 1.1)
- **1.1** Identify common misconceptions about the field of psychology. (APA 2.1)
- **1.2** Identify the four goals of psychological research. (APA 1.1, 2.1)
- **1.2** Outline the steps of the scientific method and distinguish between predictive and causal hypotheses. (APA 2.1, 2.4)
- **1.2** Describe the advantages and disadvantages of observational, survey, correlational, and experimental research methods and the types of conclusions that can be drawn about behavior from each method. (APA 2.1, 2.2, 2.4, 2.5, 5.1)
- **1.3** Describe the main ethical principles that guide psychologists as they conduct research. (APA 3.1)
- **1.4** Distinguish among the seven modern perspectives of psychology and the eclectic approach and identify the major historical figures that influenced psychology's development. (APA 1.1, 1.2, 2.1, 2.5, 5.1)
- **1.4** Describe the training of a psychologist and compare and contrast the different specialty areas of the profession. (APA 1.3, 5.1, 5.5)
- **1.4** Describe how women and minorities have contributed to the field of psychology. (APA 1.2, 3.3)

1 The Science of Psychology

Chapter Outline

It was the first day of the semester. Parking, as usual, was a challenge. Christian finally found a spot, parked his car, and headed toward campus. While grabbing a coffee at the college café, he ran into his friend Andrew. "Hey, man, what's up?" he asked. "Not much," Andrew replied. "Just getting coffee before I head to class." "What are you taking?" Christian asked. "Well, I've got math and music appreciation tomorrow. Today, I've got oceanography and general psychology. I'm heading to the psych class now." Christian smiled and said, "Cool, I've got that psych class now, too." The two students grabbed their coffees and headed toward the psychology building, continuing their conversation. "What do you think the course will be about?" Andrew asked. "Probably how you feel about things. Ought to be an easy A—like being with a therapist all semester," Christian joked. Andrew laughed. "Yeah, I guess we'll see how screwed up we are and get a lot of therapy." "Speak for yourself," Christian kidded. "I figure it's just commonsense stuff, things your parents have been telling you since you were a kid. Shouldn't be too hard." Andrew nodded in agreement as they arrived at the classroom. "Let's take a seat in the back so we don't have to share our feelings too much," Christian whispered. The two found a seat in the back and waited for class to begin. ■

◀ Many students hold misconceptions about the field of psychology.

1.1 What Is Psychology?

psychology the scientific study of behavior and mental processes

scientific method a systematic process used by psychologists for testing hypotheses about behavior

Welcome to the world of **psychology**, the scientific study of behavior and mental processes. But what exactly does that include? Behavior includes actions, feelings, and biological states such as sleeping. Mental processes include problem solving, intelligence, and memory, to name just a few. Psychology is a science because psychologists conduct research in accord with the **scientific method**—a systematic process used to test ideas about behavior. Psychologists analyze the behavior of humans as well as other species.

Psychology is probably one of the few disciplines in which students come to the first class believing they already know much about the topic. We see psychologists and psychiatrists on talk shows and listen to them on the radio. We frequently see them depicted on television and in the movies. Many of these portrayals are quite entertaining, but they do not always represent psychology accurately. As a result, the public image of the discipline tends to be distorted.

The purpose of this textbook is to help you develop a deeper understanding of psychology as a science and how the results of psychological research apply to the real world and to your life. In this chapter, we explain what psychologists do, how they think, and where they work. It is a general overview of the field of psychology, an introduction to the more specific areas of psychology discussed in subsequent chapters. We describe how psychology is a science, the goals of psychological research, how psychologists study behavior, and what the field is like today.

Consider, for example, that in December 2019 a new coronavirus emerged causing COVID-19, an acute respiratory disease that quickly spread across the world creating a global pandemic. There was no vaccine or known therapies to treat or reduce its symptoms. As such, all the world *could* do was make significant shifts in behavior. New health norms emerged such as no longer shaking hands, hugging or kissing upon greeting, frequent handwashing and the use of face coverings in public to reduce transmission of the virus from person to person. People were encouraged to socially distance, shelter-in-place, or self-isolate, behaviors counter to humans' need to connect. So, people changed the nature of their social interactions by connecting online, through social media and video conferencing, or by drive-by car parades. Unemployment sky-rocketed. Others now worked from home. Students and teachers acclimated to online or distance learning. These shifts in work and school required family routines to readjust. Intimate relationships were tested as we were forced in close proximity to loved ones for an extended period of time. Mental health was challenged as health fears, self-isolation, and economic hardships increased anxiety, loneliness, and feelings of depression. The enormity of these stressors challenged all of us. Yet, these are all topics and behaviors that psychologists research and study. Psychological science can help us understand these behavioral changes and discuss possible solutions to deal with these changes.

JOHANNES EISELE/Getty Images

▲ Social-distancing became a new behavior in the wake of the COVID-19 pandemic.

This textbook follows the recommendations and guidelines of the American Psychological Association (APA, 2014) by emphasizing a common core structure of contemporary psychology. The chapters are arranged into four main parts representing foundational areas in the field of psychology: *biological, cognitive, developmental and social psychology,* and *physical and mental health.* Each part begins with a real-life story of a person whose life and experiences illustrate the concepts of the chapters that follow. Each chapter ends with an Integrating Psychology: The Big Picture section that ties together the person's story, the contents of the chapter, and the broader core of psychology. We hope that by reading these real-life stories, you will find psychological topics easier to understand and will be better able to apply psychological principles, concepts, and research to your own life. We also hope you will come to appreciate that understanding the mind and behavior is not a simple process but requires the integration of a multitude of perspectives to more fully comprehend humans' experiences and challenges.

1.1.1 Correcting Common Misconceptions About the Field of Psychology

You are probably reading this book because you have enrolled in a general psychology course. Your expectations of what you will learn have been influenced by your general impressions of psychology. Much of the psychological information presented in the media focuses on practitioners, therapy, and helping others, and you—like the students in the opening section—may have the impression that psychology is all about how you feel and how you can feel better. Although a large proportion of psychologists counsel or otherwise treat clients, most of these professionals hold a doctorate degree in psychology, which required that they study scientific methodology and complete a considerable amount of research (Wicherski, Michalski, & Kohout, 2009).

Psychology is rooted in scientific research. The information in this book is research based. Every idea put forward in the field is subject to scientific study. You will notice that many statements in this text are followed by names and years in parentheses, for example (Pastorino, 2020). These text citations refer to the scientific studies on which the stated conclusions are based, with the researchers' name(s) and date of the study. The complete research citations can be found in the References section at the end of this book. An example of a complete research citation is shown in ● FIGURE 1.1.

A psychologist's explanation of a particular behavior is generally presented as a theory. A **theory** is an explanation of why and how a behavior occurs. It does not explain a particular behavior for all people, but it provides general guidelines that summarize facts and help us organize research on a particular subject.

theory an explanation of why and how a behavior occurs

confirmation bias a tendency to interpret people's behavior in a way that supports our expectations

We all, at times, fancy ourselves as psychologists. We interact with people all the time, we observe others' behaviors, and we have our own personal experiences. Therefore, we might naturally think that we already know a lot about psychology. People often behave the way we think they will behave, so psychology seems as though it is just common sense. We are likely to interpret people's behavior in a way that confirms our expectations—a tendency referred to as the **confirmation bias**. However, we often overlook the examples of behavior or fail to seek out other sources of information that don't confirm our expectations or support our preexisting beliefs. Psychologists systematically test their ideas about behavior using the prescribed methods and procedures we will describe in the next section of this chapter.

APA Style:

Author, A. A., Author, B. B., & Author, C. C. (Year). Title of article:

Subtitle of article. *Title of Periodical or Journal, Vol #* (Issue #), pages. doi:

Example:

Whitton, S. W., & Whisman, M. A. (2010). Relationship satisfaction instability

and depression. *Journal of Family Psychotherapy, 24* (6), 791–794. doi: 10.1037/a0021734

FIGURE 1.1

Reference Citations in Psychology

The References section at the end of this book lists the complete source for each citation. Here is the APA style format for psychological references. The citation for this particular reference would appear in the text as (Whitton & Whisman, 2010).

Engage Yourself!

Take a look at ● TABLE 1.1 and answer the questions about behavior.

How many of the items did you mark as true? All the statements are false, yet many students have such misconceptions or believe such myths about human behavior despite unsupported or even contradictory psychological research. Psychological findings do *not* always confirm our everyday observations about behavior. Only by objectively measuring and testing our ideas and observations about behavior can we determine which ideas are more likely to stand up to scientific scrutiny. Behavior is much more complex than the simple statements as Table 1.1 suggest. (The chapter designation following each statement indicates where in the text each myth is addressed.)

TABLE 1.1 How Much Do You Know About Behavior?

Indicate whether you believe each statement is true (T) or false (F).	
1. We are either left-brain or right-brain thinkers. (Ch. 2)	T F
2. We have only five senses. (Ch. 3)	T F
3. During sleep, the brain rests. (Ch. 4)	T F
4. Dieting is an effective way to lose weight. (Ch. 5)	T F
5. Punishment is more effective than reinforcement in producing behavior change. (Ch. 6)	T F
6. Our memory works like a video recorder. (Ch. 7)	T F
7. Intelligence is primarily encoded in our genes. (Ch. 8)	T F
8. Most adults experience a midlife crisis in their 40s or 50s. (Ch. 9)	T F
9. Opposites attract. That is, we are most attracted to people who differ from us. (Ch. 10)	T F
10. Personality is set by our teenage years. (Ch. 11)	T F
11. Stress is caused by bad things that happen to you. (Ch. 12)	T F
12. Schizophrenia means you have multiple personalities. (Ch. 13)	T F
13. In order for therapy to be effective, you must confront issues from your childhood. (Ch. 14)	T F

Most students entering a general psychology class, like Christian and Andrew, expect to focus on diagnosing and treating mental health disorders. Although some psychologists specialize in mental health, many others work in academic settings, in the business world, in education, or in government agencies. Psychology is an extremely diverse field, and new specialties are appearing every year. Psychologists are interested in numerous topics, including neuroscience, learning, memory, aging, development, gender, motivation, emotion, sports, criminal behavior, and many other subjects. We cannot cover every area of psychology in this textbook, but we will give you an overview of the main areas of psychological research.

1.1.2 Psychology Will Teach You About Critical Thinking

Because behavior is so complex, psychological theories generally don't definitively explain the behavior of all people. To think like a psychologist, you must think critically, analyzing and evaluating information. You must be able to distinguish true psychological information from **pseudopsychology**. Pseudopsychological findings sound persuasive, but they are not necessarily based on scientific procedures. Their conclusions may go far beyond the scope of their actual data. For example, have you ever heard that people use only 10% of their brains? Many college students believe this false statement despite evidence that shows it is not true (Higbee & Clay, 1998; Lilienfeld, Lynn, Ruscio, & Beyerstein, 2011). To think like a psychologist, you must be skeptical rather than accepting about explanations of behavior.

pseudopsychology psychological information or conclusions that sound scientific but have not been systematically tested using the scientific method

critical thinking thought processes used to evaluate and analyze information and apply it to other situations

Critical thinking involves analyzing and evaluating information and applying it to other situations. Critical thinking also makes you an intelligent consumer of information. You will be encouraged to practice this skill throughout the book as you read the chapter and test your mastery of the material in the Quiz Yourself sections at the end of each main topic and in the What Do You Know? Assess Your Understanding questions at the end of each chapter. In the end-of-chapter material, we have also included Use It or Lose It questions. These short-answer questions ask you to apply your knowledge of psychological research to solve a problem or situation. Immediately following are Critical Thinking about the Science of Psychology questions that require you to analyze a research study to develop and enhance your ability to understand the research methods, concepts, and science underlying psychology.

Because we all engage in behavior, much of the information in this text will apply to your life. We all dream, remember, like or dislike others, are motivated, have high or low self-esteem, experience sadness, behave aggressively, help others, learn, perceive, and use our senses. Consequently, we recommend that you apply the material in this text to your own behavior as much as possible. This connection will increase your interest in the text, and you will study more effectively.

1.1 Quiz Yourself

1. Which of the following statements is *true*?
   a. Psychology is just common sense.
   b. Psychologists study only mental health disorders.
   c. Psychologists know why people behave the way that they do.
   d. Psychologists test ideas about behavior according to the scientific method.

2. Which of the following topics would a psychologist most likely study?
   a. Weather patterns in Africa
   b. Memory changes in adults
   c. Causes of the Vietnam War
   d. All of the above

3. Which of the following statements is *not* a pseudopsychology claim?
   a. Transplant organs carry personality traits that are always transferred from donors to receivers.
   b. Walking on hot coals without burning one's feet requires paranormal abilities.
   c. You can make a blood clot in your brain disappear by humming.
   d. Several studies show a relationship between academic achievement and self-esteem.

Answers 1. d; 2. b; 3. d

1.2 The Science of Psychology: Goals, Hypotheses, and Methods

Though psychologists study and emphasize different aspects of behavior, they all share similar goals. The main goals of psychology and psychological research are as follows:

- To describe behavior
- To predict behavior
- To explain behavior
- To control or change behavior

Description involves observing events and describing them. Typically, description is used to understand how events are related to one another. For example, you may notice that your fitness club or gym tends to get more crowded in the months of January, February, and March. It seems you have to wait longer to use the weight machines or there are more people in the fitness classes. This observation describes an event.

If you observe that two events occur together rather reliably or with a general frequency or regularity, you can make *predictions* about events or anticipate what events may occur. From your observations, you may predict that the fitness club will be more crowded in January. You may arrive earlier to make sure you get a parking spot or a place in the yoga class.

Although it may be known that two events regularly occur together, that doesn't tell us what *caused* a particular behavior to occur. Winter months do not cause fitness clubs to become crowded. These two events are related, but one event does not cause the other. Therefore, an additional goal of psychology is to *explain* or understand the causes of behavior. As stated previously, psychologists usually put forth explanations of behavior in the form of theories. A *theory* is an explanation of why and how a particular behavior occurs. We will detail seven types of explanations, or perspectives, later in the chapter. For example, how do we explain higher fitness-club attendance in the winter months? Is it a behavior that is influenced by the environment? Perhaps fitness clubs are more crowded because the weather makes outdoor exercise more difficult. Perhaps it is more influenced by motivation as many people at the start of a new year resolve to work out more. As these ideas are tested, more and more causes and predictors of behavior are discovered. Some of these explanations or theories will be modified, some will be discarded, and new ones will be developed.

The purpose behind explaining and understanding the causes of behavior is the final goal of psychology, *controlling* or *changing* behavior. It relates to the goal of explanation because one needs to understand what is causing a behavior in order to change or modify it. For example, let's say that the weather is a factor in fitness-club attendance. Fitness clubs could offer outdoor activities beginning in mid-March to prevent declining enrollment. Many psychologists go into the field in the hope of improving society. They may want to improve child care, create healthier work environments, or reduce discrimination in society. Such sentiments reflect the goal of control and underscore the potential impact of good research. • FIGURE 1.2 summarizes the goals of psychology.

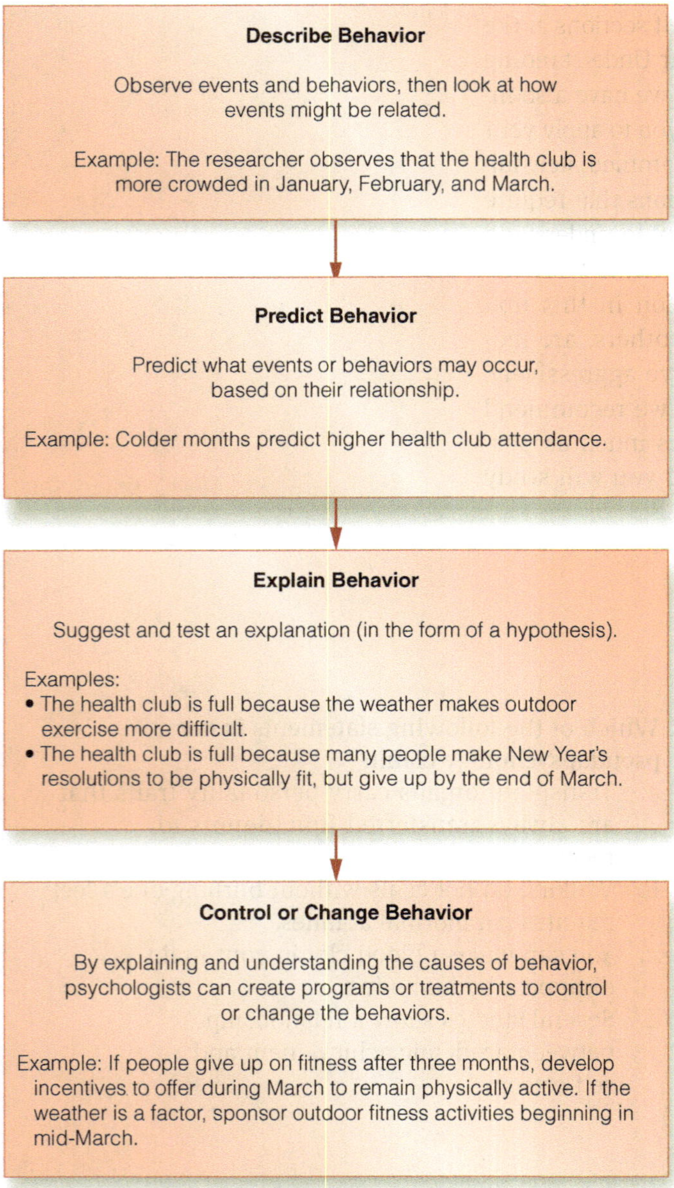

FIGURE 1.2

Goals of Psychology

Psychologists attempt to describe, predict, explain, and ultimately control or change behavior.

1.2.1 Psychologists Are Scientists: The Scientific Method

The purpose of psychological research is to test ideas about behavior. As previously stated, researchers use the *scientific method* when testing ideas about behavior. The scientific method is a set of rules for gathering and analyzing information that enables you to test an idea or *hypothesis*. All scientists adhere to these same steps even though they may use different techniques within each step. The decisions that scientists make at each step of the scientific method will ultimately affect the types of conclusions they can draw about behavior.

How can the scientific method be used to meet the goals of psychology? Let's say that you have an interest in understanding beer drinking among college students. You want to make some predictions (a goal of psychology) about beer drinking. You use the scientific method to test this idea, as outlined in ● FIGURE 1.3.

1. *Define and describe the issue to be studied.* You might hypothesize that college students who buy pitchers of beer tend to drink more than college students who purchase bottles of beer (a **prediction**). You study previous research in scientific journals on alcohol consumption and college students.

prediction an expected outcome of how variables will relate

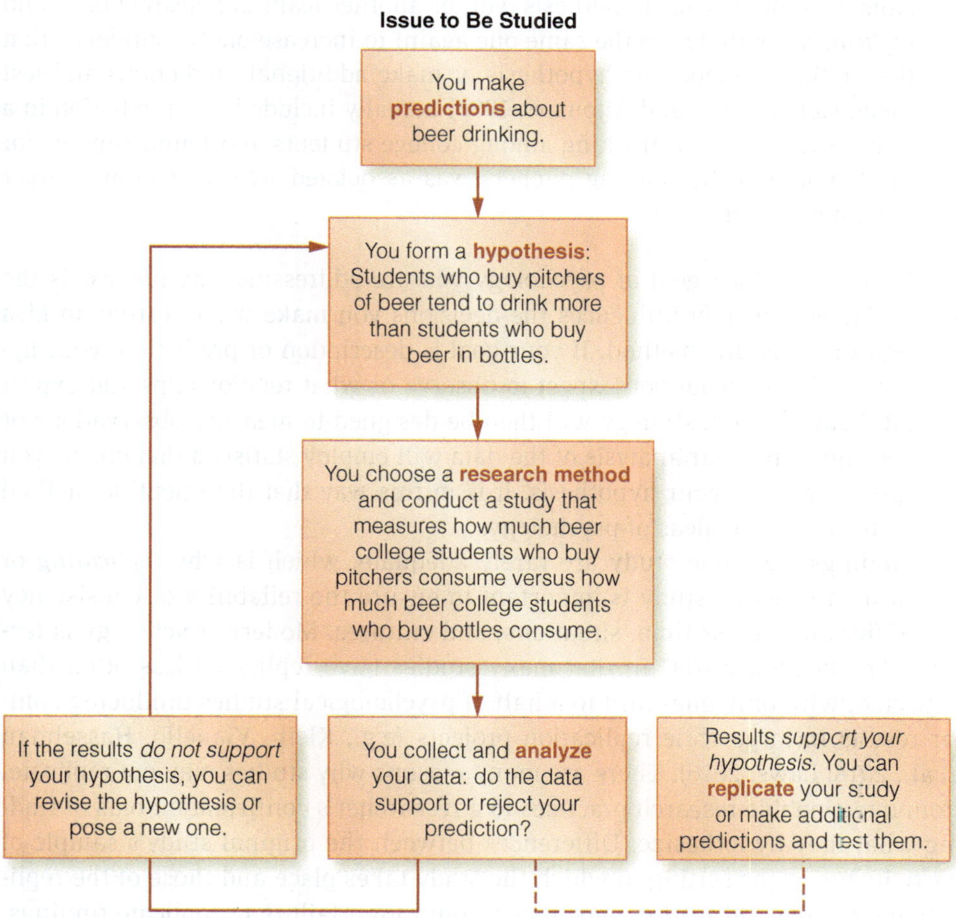

FIGURE 1.3

The Scientific Method

The scientific method enables researchers to test ideas about behavior.

hypothesis an educated guess

2. *Form a testable research hypothesis that states the relationship between the variables.* Students who buy pitchers of beer tend to drink more than students who buy beer in bottles. Your **hypothesis** *operationally defines* or specifies how your variables are being objectively measured—that is, in such a way that another person can test the same hypothesis to verify or replicate your results. In this example, we have operationally defined the method of purchase—bottles versus pitchers, and the second variable being the amount of beer consumed.
3. *Choose an appropriate research strategy.* You choose a group of people to observe (college students) and a research method that allows you to measure objectively how much beer students who buy pitchers drink versus how much beer students who buy bottles drink. You decide where your study will be conducted. Will it be in the environment where the behavior naturally occurs (such as the local college bar) or in a laboratory (a more controlled setting)? You decide who you will use as *participants*. Will you use animals or humans? If humans, how will they be selected? If animals, what species will you use?
4. *Conduct the study to test your hypothesis.* Run the study and collect the data based on the decisions in steps 1–3.
5. *Analyze the data to support or reject your hypothesis.* Researchers usually analyze their data using *statistics* (see Appendix A). If the results do not support your hypothesis, you can revise the hypothesis or pose a new one. If the results do support your hypothesis, you or another team of researchers should *replicate* your study (do the same one again) to increase one's confidence that the findings support the hypothesis or make additional predictions and test them. Geller, Russ, and Altomari (1986) actually included this prediction in a larger study on beer drinking among college students and found support for the hypothesis that buying pitchers was associated with consuming larger amounts of beer.

No matter which goal of psychology you are addressing, the process is the same. The goal merely influences the decisions you make when testing an idea through the scientific method. If your goal is description or prediction, your hypothesis will state what you expect to observe or what relationships you expect to find. Your research strategy will then be designed to measure observations or relationships, and your analysis of the data will employ statistics that enable you to support or reject your hypothesis. It is in this way that the scientific method allows us to test the ideas of psychology.

Findings from one study are rarely adequate, which is why *replicating* or repeating a research study is important to ensure the reliability or consistency of the findings across time, situations, and cultures. Modern psychology is facing a "replication crisis" in that many studies have replicated less often than expected, with only one-third to a half of psychological studies producing similar results in large-scale replication projects (e.g., Klein, Vianello, Hasselman et al., 2018; Laws, 2016). There are many reasons why studies may not replicate, from questionable research practices to a researcher's confirmation bias of finding what they hypothesize. Differences between the original study's sample of participants or the setting in which the study takes place and those of the replication's sample and setting may also account for a failure to replicate findings. Yet, there are also easy solutions such as sharing data for other researchers to analyze; funding, sharing, and publishing replication studies; and using larger samples that can be implemented. One scientific tool that has been particularly helpful to psychologists is the use of *meta-analyses* (Maxwell, Lau & Howard, 2015). **Meta-analyses** combine the findings from multiple scientific studies on the same question or topic to establish the reliability of the findings, observe any overall trends, and to resolve any discrepancies among the research studies. Both successful and nonsuccessful replications inform our knowledge about behavior and mental processes and are an integral step of the scientific process.

meta-analyses research procedures that combine the findings from a number of scientific studies on the same question or topic to establish the reliability of the findings, observe any overall trends, and to resolve any discrepancies among the research studies

predictive hypothesis an educated guess about the relationships among variables

causal hypothesis an educated guess about how one variable will influence another variable

1.2.2 Psychologists Ask Questions: Hypotheses

As you have seen, one of the first steps of the scientific method is to formulate a question or hypothesis about behavior. These hypotheses generally fall into one of two categories: *predictive hypotheses* and *causal hypotheses*.

A **predictive hypothesis** makes a specific prediction or set of predictions about the relationships among variables. Such hypotheses are used to address two goals of psychology: description and prediction. The previous example on beer drinking among college students illustrated a predictive hypothesis: The study predicted that students who buy pitchers of beer tend to drink more than students who buy beer in bottles. Predictive hypotheses are made when the researcher measures the variables of interest but does not manipulate or control the variables in the study. Because the researcher does not control the variables, conclusions of research studies that test predictive hypotheses are limited. The conclusions can only state what was observed or which variables appear to be related to one another. They cannot be used to draw cause-and-effect conclusions; that is, one cannot conclude that buying pitchers of beer causes a person to drink more beer. To determine the cause, you must form and test a *causal hypothesis*.

A **causal hypothesis** specifically states how one variable will influence another variable. Causal hypotheses can be tested only when the researcher is able to control or manipulate the main variables in a study. The researcher sets up different conditions in a study and then observes whether there is a change in behavior because of the different conditions. For example, suppose a researcher has developed a new strategy to teach children how to read. The researcher hypothesizes that this program will cause greater gains in reading than the standard method for teaching reading. This is a causal hypothesis. Some students are assigned to the new reading program, and others are assigned to the standard program. The researcher then measures the children's gains in reading at the end of the year to see whether there is a difference. As you will soon see, causal hypotheses can only be tested by means of an *experiment*. To test a causal hypothesis, a researcher must be able to conclude how one variable affects or causes a change in another variable.

1.2.3 Psychologists Strategize: Sampling and Research Methods

Once you have stated a hypothesis, the next step in the research process is to decide on a research strategy and a way of selecting participants. The type of hypothesis you make (predictive or causal) typically determines which research methods you can use. You are more likely to use some research methods to test predictive hypotheses and other methods to test causal hypotheses.

Naturalistic observations, case studies, surveys, and *correlational research* are used to test predictive hypotheses. All of these methods are used when the researcher cannot control or manipulate the main variables in the study. Each method has its advantages and disadvantages, which we will discuss in a moment.

population of interest the entire universe of animals or people that could be studied

sample the portion of the population of interest that is selected for a study

naturalistic observations research studies conducted in the environment in which the behavior typically occurs

Selecting Participants

In a perfect world, researchers would include every person they are interested in studying. This is termed the **population of interest**. For example, for a psychologist who studies infant development, all infants would be the population of interest. It is impossible to test everyone, however, so researchers select a portion, or subset, of the population of interest called a **sample**. Because the sample will be used to make inferences or judgments about the entire population, the sample should reflect the whole population as much as possible; that is, it should be a *representative sample*. Random sampling of participants helps ensure a representative sample. In a *random sample*, every member of the population has an equal chance of being selected to participate in the study; this avoids introducing *sampling bias* into the research.

The more representative the sample is, the more the results will generalize (or apply) to the population of interest. But random sampling is not always possible. Instead, psychological research often uses *samples of convenience*, or groups of people who are easily accessible to the researcher. The students in your psychology course are a sample of convenience. In fact, much psychological research relies on using college students as the sample of convenience! According to Current Population Survey results from the U.S. Census Bureau (2018) around 35% of people in the United States over the age of 25 have a college degree or higher, so samples of college students probably do not represent all types of people and groups. As such, these nonrepresentative samples limit a researcher's ability to generalize their findings to the population (Levenson, 2017).

In addition, online psychology labs at well-known universities across the United States as well as online crowdsourcing platforms, such as Amazon's Mechanical Turk (MTurk) and TurkPrime, are now much more common ways to recruit participants. On the plus side, researchers conducting online research have the distinct advantage of soliciting a larger and more diverse sample at a fraction of the cost, with improved efficiency and data storage (Gosling & Johnson, 2010; Litman, Robinson, & Abberbock, 2017). Thousands to millions of participants from all over the world may be gathered over the Internet as opposed to a few hundred that can be collected on-site. Several classic findings in psychology have been successfully replicated online, while other replications found a discrepancy between laboratory results and online results (Crump, McDonnell, & Gureckis, 2013; Miller, Crowe, Weiss, Maples-Keller, & Lynam, 2017). Recall that the people you get to participate in your study are very important to the conclusions of your study. However, Internet research does not ensure a representative sample. Some people do not have access to a computer or may not know how to use the Internet. Participants might be distracted or watching a movie while clicking answers on a survey. People who complete online research may be different in some way from people who are less willing to complete online research that presents an alternative explanation for one's results. Moreover, researchers may not be able to ensure that participants are who they say they are (Dance, 2015; Gosling & Mason, 2015; Ophir et al., 2020). People can more easily falsify their identity on the Internet than they can in person, calling into question the "true" characteristics of the sample that is generated.

Naturalistic Observations

Naturalistic observations are research studies that are conducted in the environment in which the behavior typically occurs. For example, Campos, Graesch, Repetti, and others (2009) wanted to investigate when and in what manner dual-earner families interact after work. The researchers measured interaction by observing and video-recording dual-earner couples and their children in their homes throughout two weekday afternoons and evenings. The researcher in a naturalistic study is a recorder or observer of behavior who then describes or makes predictions about behavior based on what they have observed. Because the researcher does not control events in a naturalistic study, it is not possible to pinpoint the causes of behavior. Therefore, naturalistic studies are predominately used to achieve the goals of description and prediction. In their observational study, Campos et al. found that although both mothers and fathers were likely to be greeted with positive behavior from family members, mothers spent more time with children, whereas fathers spent more time alone.

Jonathan Goldberg/Alamy stock photo

▲ A school playground could be an environment for naturally observing children's behaviors

While naturalistic observation can provide a picture of behavior as it normally occurs, researchers need to consider the influence of *reactivity*. Suppose you want to study childhood aggression by observing students on a school playground. What might happen if you were to simply enter the playground, sit down, and start writing about what you saw? The children might behave differently because of your presence and/or their awareness that they are being observed; as a result, your observations of aggression might not be reliable or true. When conducting a naturalistic observation, researchers attempt to minimize reactivity to ensure that they are observing the true behavior of their participants. Collecting unobtrusive (not noticeable) and objective records of naturalistic behavior can also be achieved through smart-home devices and mobile-sensing devices such as smartphones, smart watches, and fitness trackers (Nelson & Allen, 2018).

Case Studies

A **case study** is an in-depth observation of one or a few participants or settings. The participant may be a person, an animal, or even a setting, such as a business or a school. As with naturalistic observation, in case studies researchers do not control any variables but merely record or relate their observations. Case studies provide in-depth information on rare and unusual conditions that we might not otherwise be able to study. However, the main disadvantage of the case study method is its limited applicability to other situations. It is very difficult to take one case, especially a rare case, and say that it applies to everyone. In other words, case studies lack **generalizability**; therefore, the conclusions that are drawn from case studies are limited to the participant being studied.

Surveys

Often, psychologists want to study a whole group of people but in less depth. **Surveys** can accomplish this task by asking a large group of people about their attitudes, beliefs, and/or behaviors. A large group of people can quickly respond to questions or statements in their homes, online, over the phone, or out in public.

Survey data are used to make predictions and test predictive hypotheses. For example, knowing which people are more likely to buy a product enables a company to market its products more effectively and perhaps devise new strategies to

case study an in-depth observation of one or a few participants or settings

generalizability [jen-er-uh-lies-uh-BILL-uh-tee] how well a researcher's findings apply to other individuals and situations

surveys research methods that ask a large group of people about their attitudes, beliefs, and/or behaviors target individuals who are not buying them. Similarly, knowing which behaviors are related to a higher frequency of illness enables a psychologist to predict who is more at risk for physical illness or a mental health disorder. However, *who* you ask to complete a survey and *how* you ask them are critical elements in distinguishing good survey research from biased research. Recall that a random sampling of participants minimizes sampling bias. The more representative the sample is, the more the results will generalize to the population of interest.

A second critical element of the survey method is how the questions are worded. A respondent has to be able to understand the question and interpret it in the way the researcher intended. It is important to make questions clear and precise to obtain accurate estimates of people's feelings, beliefs, and behavior. For example, differences in survey question wording have been found to have an influence on rape estimates (Fisher, 2009), pornography use (Regnerus, Gordon, & Price, 2016), and estimates of adolescent sexual behaviors (Santelli et al., 2000).

In summary, surveys are advantageous in that they allow psychologists to ask a lot of questions to a large sample of people. Accurate information can be gathered in a relatively short period of time. Yet the survey's wording, the representativeness of the sample, and whether people choose to answer the questions honestly can bias the results.

For example, the Pew Research Center (2014) set out to compare the values, attitudes, and behaviors of Millennials (adults born between 1981 and 1996) with those of older adults by using the survey method, with a nationally representative sample of 1,821 adults. Not surprisingly, they reported differences among the groups in behaviors associated with the use of technology. For example, 55% of Millennials reported having posted a "selfie" on a social media site, compared to 24% of Generation Xers (those born between 1965 and 1980), 9% of Baby Boomers (those born between 1946 and 1964), and 4% of the Silent generation (those born before 1946). Eighty-one percent of Millennials had created a profile on a social media account.

Surveys on Generation Z or Gen Z (those born between 1997 and 2010) show similar attitudes to the Millennials with both generations more likely to support same-sex marriage and interracial marriage than older generations. However, Gen Zers are more likely than Millennials and older generations to report that they know someone who prefers gender-neutral pronouns (Pew Research Center, 2018). Gen Zers also are less likely to binge drink alcohol, date, or have had sex than Millennials did at that age. Yet, socially, Gen Zers spend less time interacting with their peers face-to-face and more time alone than any previous generation (Twenge, 2017).

What accounts for these reported differences? Survey research cannot explain the differences; it can be used only to describe and predict behavior. However, we can generate multiple hypotheses as to why these generational differences may occur. They could be due to the unique historical circumstances or social movements experienced by each generation, such as wars or technological advances. They could be due to changing social roles, longer life expectancies, varying economic factors, or to some combination of these factors. Also keep in mind that there are as many differences within generations as there are among them. Yet, from this survey research, we get a glimpse of the attitudes, values, and behaviors of the varying generations.

Correlational Studies

correlation [cor-ruh-LAY-shun] the relationship between two or more variables

Correlational studies test the relationship, or **correlation**, between two or more variables—television watching and violent behavior, or depression and gender, for example. The researcher does not control variables but rather measures them to see whether any reliable relationship exists between them. For example, if we were to measure your weight (one variable), what other variable might show a relationship to your weight? Your height? Your calorie consumption? The amount of exercise you engage in? Your age? Your life expectancy? If you were to measure all these variables, you might find that all of them vary in relation to weight. These relationships are correlations.

The strength of a correlation is measured in terms of a *correlation coefficient*—a statistic that tells us how strong the relationship between two factors is. Correlation coefficients range from −1.00 to +1.00. The closer the correlation coefficient is to −1.00 or +1.00, the stronger the correlation, or the more related the two variables are. A −1.00 or a +1.00 is a *perfect correlation;* the value of one variable always exactly predicts the value of the other variable. For example, every time people get angry, they hit something. The closer the correlation coefficient is to 0, the weaker the correlation—that is, one variable does not reliably predict the other. A *zero correlation* coefficient means that there is no linear relationship between the two variables—for example, how many movies you watch in a month and the color that your walls are painted. To illustrate correlation, let's look at a study by Hays and Roberts (2008) on eating behaviors and weight gain in older women. They found a +.25 correlation between weight gain and overeating in response to daily life circumstances. The correlation between weight gain and overeating in response to emotional states, such as anxiety and depression, was +.17. The higher correlation between weight gain and daily overeating opportunities suggests that ordinary environmental food cues such as television commercials, billboards, or available sweets are a better predictor of weight gain in older women than is "emotional eating." Generally, the stronger the correlation between two variables, the more accurate our predictions are, but perfect (+1.00 or −1.00) correlations rarely happen in psychology. Human behavior is too complex for such perfect relationships to occur.

The sign before the correlation coefficient tells us how the variables relate to one another (● FIGURE 1.4). A **positive correlation** means that as one variable increases, the other variable also tends to increase; or as one variable decreases, the other variable tends to decrease. In both cases, the variables are changing in the

positive correlation a relationship in which increases in one variable correspond to increases in the other variable

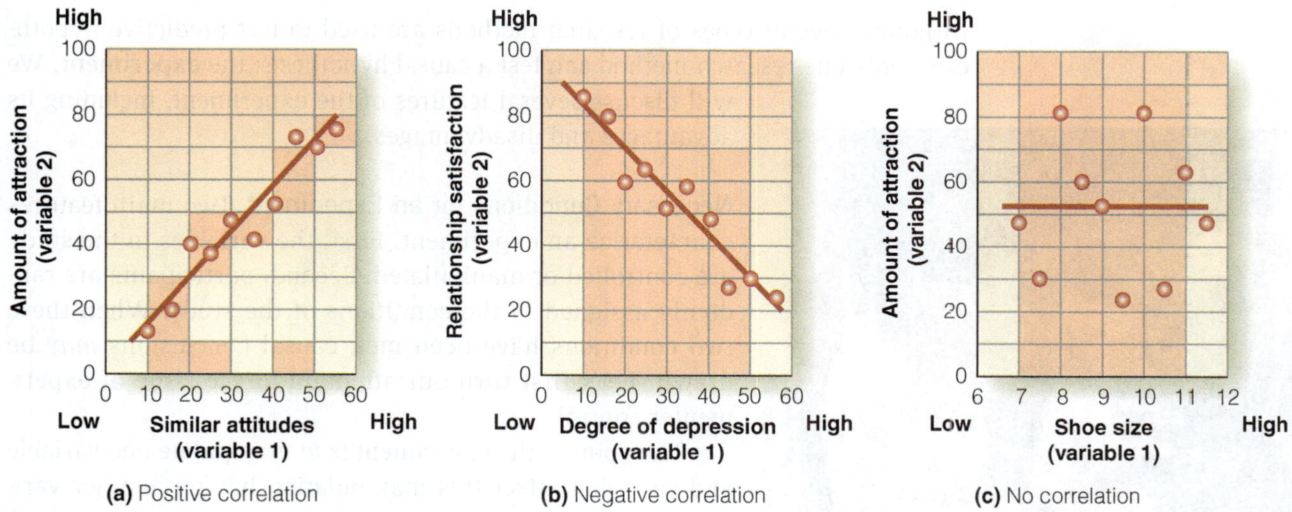

FIGURE 1.4

Correlation

Correlation, a research method used for description and prediction, shows how two variables are related.

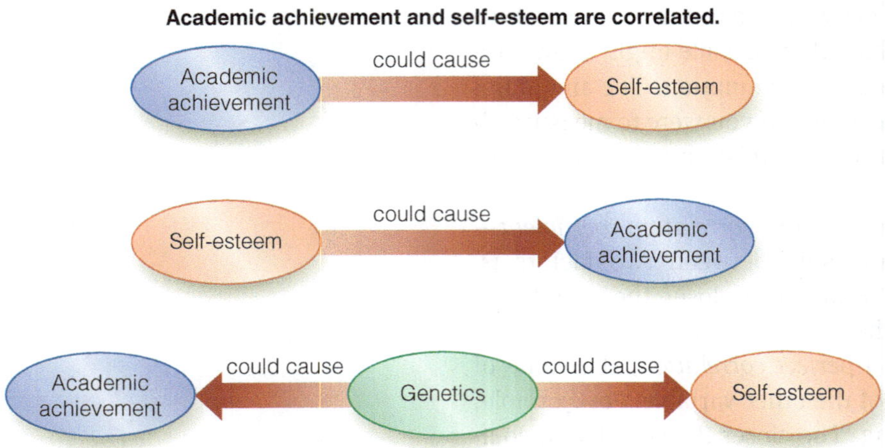

FIGURE 1.5

Correlation Does Not Mean Causation

When two variables are correlated or related, it does not mean that we know why they are related. It is possible that a third variable, not measured in the study, is the real cause of the relationship between the two measured variables. Correlation can only be used for making predictions, not for making cause-and-effect statements.

same direction. An example of a positive correlation is perceived stress and blood pressure. As perceived stress increases, so does one's blood pressure.

In a **negative correlation**, as one variable increases, the other variable tends to decrease in what is referred to as an *inverse* relationship. Notice that the variables are changing in *opposite* directions. An example of a negative correlation is video game playing and school competence. The more time children spend playing video games, the poorer their competence is at school (Hastings et al., 2009). Or consider the negative correlation between relationship satisfaction and depression. As relationship satisfaction increases, feelings of depression decrease (Whitton & Whisman, 2010).

Correlational studies enable researchers to make predictions about behavior, but they do *not* allow us to draw cause-and-effect conclusions (● FIGURE 1.5). For example, there is a positive correlation between academic achievement and self-esteem. Students who have high academic achievement also tend to have high self-esteem. Similarly, students who have low academic achievement tend to have low self-esteem. High academic achievement may cause an increase in self-esteem. However, it is just as likely that having high self-esteem causes one to do better academically. There may be a third variable, such as the parents' educational level or genetics, which actually causes the relationship between academic achievement and self-esteem. A correlational study does not tell us which of these explanations is correct. The only research method that may permit us to draw cause-and-effect conclusions is the experiment.

negative correlation a relationship in which increases in one variable correspond to decreases in the other variable

experiment a research method that is used to test causal hypotheses

independent variable the variable in an experiment that is manipulated

Experiments

Although several types of research methods are used to test predictive hypotheses, only one research method can test a causal hypothesis: the **experiment**. We will discuss several features of the experiment, including its advantages and disadvantages.

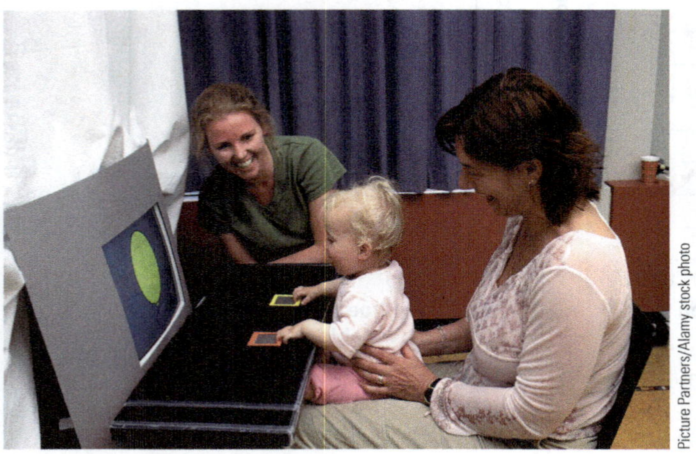

▲ By studying behavior in a lab environment, researchers are better able to control the variables in an experiment.

Necessary Conditions for an Experiment Two main features characterize an experiment. First, the variables in the study are controlled or manipulated. Second, participants are randomly assigned to the conditions of the study. When these two conditions have been met, causal conclusions *may* be drawn. Let's first turn our attention to the issue of experimenter control.

The point of the experiment is to manipulate one variable and see what effect this manipulation has on another variable (● FIGURE 1.6). These variables are termed the *independent* and *dependent variables*, respectively. The **independent variable** is the variable that the experimenter manipulates; it is the *cause* in the experiment, what the researcher is testing.

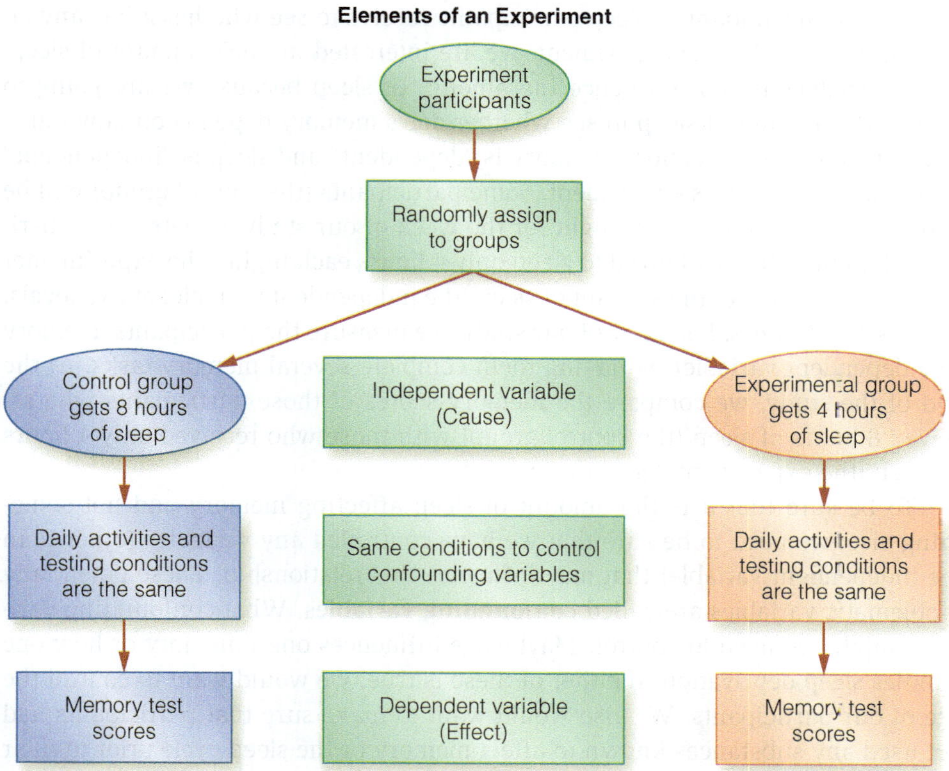

FIGURE 1.6

Elements of an Experiment

The two main ingredients of an experiment are (1) that the variables in the study are controlled or manipulated and (2) that participants are randomly assigned to the conditions of the study. When these two conditions have been met, causal conclusions *may* be drawn.

It is independent of or not being affected by the other variables in the study. The **dependent variable** measures any result of manipulating the independent variable; it is the *effect* in the experiment. It is dependent on or influenced by the other variables in the study.

The typical experiment divides participants into two types of groups: the *experimental group* and the *control group*. The **experimental group** includes those participants who receive the manipulation that is being tested. The **control group** includes those participants who do not receive the manipulation that is being tested; they serve as a baseline comparison for the experimental group. Both groups are then measured on the dependent variable to see whether there is a difference between the groups.

In some experiments, the control group receives a *placebo*, or inactive substance such as a sugar pill, rather than being given nothing. This procedure is to control for the *placebo effect*. The **placebo effect** occurs when participants show changes simply because they believe or expect a treatment to have certain effects. In **double-blind studies**, neither experimenters nor participants know who is receiving a placebo and who is receiving the actual treatment; they are *blind* to which group (experimental or control) a person has been assigned. In this way, neither the participant's nor the experimenter's expectations will bias the results.

Suppose, for example, that we want to study the effects of sleep deprivation. Specifically, we hypothesize that sleep deprivation causes deficits in memory. This is a causal hypothesis that can be tested with an experiment. We decide to

dependent variable the variable in an experiment that measures any effect of the manipulation

experimental group the group of participants who receive the manipulation that is being tested

control group the group of participants who do not receive the manipulation that is being tested

placebo effect a measurable change in participants' behavior due to the expectation or belief that a treatment will have certain effects

double-blind studies experiments in which neither the experimenters nor the participants know to which group (experimental or control) participants have been assigned manipulate the amount of sleep participants receive to see whether it has any effect on memory. In this experiment, we are interested in one's amount of sleep. Other variables do not influence the amount of sleep because we are going to control the amount of sleep to see whether one's memory depends on how much sleep one receives. Therefore, memory is "dependent" and sleep is "independent" for the purposes of this experiment. Some participants (the control group) will be allowed to sleep 8 hours per night for the week of our study. Others (the experimental group) will be allowed to sleep only 4 hours each night. The experimenter has set, or controlled, the amount of sleep (the independent variable) at two levels: 8 hours and 4 hours. Each day of our study, we measure the participants' memory (the dependent variable) by having them complete several memory tasks. At the end of the study, we compare the memory scores of those participants who received 8 hours of sleep (the control group) with those who received only 4 hours of sleep (the experimental group).

To be sure that it is the amount of sleep affecting memory and not something else, we need to be sure that we have controlled any variables (other than the independent variable) that may influence this relationship. These potentially problematic variables are called **confounding variables**. What confounding variables might we need to control? Maybe age influences one's memory or how one handles sleep deprivation. If either of these is true, we would want to control the age of our participants. We also would want to make sure that participants had not used any substances known to affect memory or the sleep cycle prior to their participation in the experiment. Consequently, we would control for this variable, too. Whereas independent variables are controlled by manipulating them to vary with at least two values, confounding variables are controlled by trying to hold them at a constant value so the outcomes of the study cannot be attributed to them.

confounding variables factors other than the independent variable that affect the dependent measure

random assignment a method of assigning participants in which they have an equal chance of being placed in any group or condition of the study

Both groups must be treated the same except for the amount of sleep they receive, so the researcher sets the conditions of the experiment to be the same for both groups. For example, every participant should complete the memory tasks at the same time of day, and every participant should complete the same memory tasks. The criteria for scoring the memory tasks must be the same as well. The instructions for completing the tasks must be the same. The lighting, temperature, and other physical features of the room in which the participants sleep and complete the memory tasks should be the same for all participants. Our purpose is to design a study in which we manipulate the independent variable to see its effect on the dependent variable. If we control any potentially confounding variables that might influence this relationship and we find a difference between our groups on the dependent variable, that difference is most likely due to the independent variable, and we have established a cause-and-effect relationship.

If the experimenter does not control a confounding variable, we now have more than one variable that could be responsible for the change in the dependent variable: the independent variable and the confounding variable. When this occurs, the researcher is left with an alternative explanation for the results. The change in the dependent variable could have been caused by the independent variable, but it also could have been caused by the confounding variable. Consequently, causal conclusions are limited.

Let's not forget the second condition necessary for an experiment—how participants are assigned to the conditions of the independent variable. We must be sure that there are no differences in the composition of our groups of participants. Psychologists eliminate this problem through **random assignment** of participants to the conditions of the study. In our example on sleep and memory, assigning all the males in the sample to the 4-hour sleep condition and all the females to the 8-hour sleep condition would create a confounding variable. Gender differences might have an effect on memory scores. It may be that gender (the confounding variable) rather than sleep deprivation (the independent variable) is the cause of a difference in memory. To eliminate the influence of such confounding variables, experimenters randomly assign participants to conditions. Each participant has an equal chance of being placed in either condition. Male participants are just as likely to be assigned to the 4-hour condition as they are to the 8-hour condition, and the same is true for female participants. In this way, any participant variable that has the potential to influence the research results is just as likely to affect one group as it is the other. Without random assignment, confounding variables could affect the dependent variable. This is typically what occurs in *quasi-experiments*.

A **quasi-experiment** is in some ways like an experiment. The researcher manipulates the independent variable and sets the other conditions to be the same for both groups. However, the second requirement for an experiment—randomly assigning participants to conditions—has not been met. Quasi-experiments use existing groups of people who differ on some variable. For example, suppose you want to see if vaping during pregnancy causes lower-birth-weight babies. For ethical reasons, you cannot assign some pregnant women to vape and prevent others from vaping. Instead, for your vaping condition, you must select pregnant women who already vape. These women may differ on other variables when compared to pregnant women who do not vape. For example, their eating habits may differ. As a result, a confounding variable (the diet of the mothers) rather than vaping could cause a difference in the dependent variable (the birth weight of the offspring). Because quasi-experiments do not meet the conditions necessary for a "true" experiment, causal conclusions based on these designs should be made cautiously (Shadish, Cook, & Campbell, 2002; West, 2009).

quasi-experiment a research study that is not a true experiment because participants are not randomly assigned to the different conditions

Advantages and Disadvantages of Using Experiments Experiments have several advantages. First, it is only through experimentation that we can approach two of the goals of psychology: explaining and changing behavior. An experiment is the only research method that enables us to determine cause-and-effect relationships. This advantage makes interpreting research results less ambiguous. In an experiment, we attempt to eliminate any confounding variables through experimenter control and random assignment of participants to groups. These techniques enable us to draw clearer conclusions from research results.

Experiments also have disadvantages. First, experiments do not address the first two goals of psychology: describing and predicting behavior. These are often the first steps in understanding behavior, and naturalistic observation, surveys, and correlational studies are quite useful for doing this. Second, in an attempt to control confounding variables, experiments conducted in laboratory settings may create an artificial atmosphere. It is then difficult to know whether the same result would occur in a more natural setting or whether the findings from a lab environment generalize to the real world. This may be another reason to conduct naturalistic observations or correlational studies. Third, sometimes employing the experimental method is simply not possible for ethical or practical reasons. As we mentioned in the case of quasi-experimental designs, we cannot force people to be randomly assigned to a condition that could harm them (such as vaping) or that does not pertain to them (such as having high blood pressure). Psychologists must follow certain ethical guidelines and practices when conducting research. We turn our attention to this topic next. You Review: Scientific Research Methods summarizes the strengths and weaknesses of the various research methods.

YOU REVIEW Scientific Research Methods

Method	Strengths	Weaknesses
Naturalistic Observation Observing behavior in the environment in which it typically occurs	Describes behavior as it typically occurs in the real world. May test predictive hypotheses.	Little control of variables. Reactivity can influence results. Cannot show cause and effect.
Case Study In-depth observation of one or a few participants or settings	Detailed information on one person or setting. May describe people or settings with special or rare abilities, qualities, or characteristics.	May not generalize to other people or settings. Cannot show cause and effect. Difficult to replicate.
Survey Asks a large group of people about their attitudes, beliefs, and/or behavior	Efficient collection of data with large samples. Can ask a lot of questions at once. Can test predictive hypotheses.	Participants may not answer truthfully. Question wording can bias results. Cannot show cause and effect.
Correlation Measures the relationship between two or more variables	Can measure the strength and direction of relationships between variables. Can test predictive hypotheses.	Does not randomly assign participants to conditions. Cannot show cause and effect.
Quasi-experiment Compare participants who are not randomly assigned on the manipulation of an independent variable	Allows comparisons of treatments. Can control some conditions of study. May test causal hypotheses.	Does not randomly assign participants to conditions. Causal conclusions are difficult to make.
Experiment Manipulate an independent variable to see changes in a dependent measure under controlled conditions	Allows random assignment of participants to conditions. May eliminate confounding variables. Can show cause and effect.	For ethical and practical reasons, may not be able to test some variables. Results may not apply to real-world settings.

1.2 Quiz Yourself

1. **When we know that two events regularly occur together, which goal of psychology can be met?**
   a. Predicting behavior
   b. Changing behavior
   c. Understanding behavior
   d. Explaining behavior
2. **Dr. Hincapie wants to test the hypothesis that stress increases one's blood pressure. What type of hypothesis is Dr. Hincapie interested in testing?**
   a. Predictive
   b. Causal
   c. Correlational
   d. Biological
3. **In an experiment on attitudes, participants are given either positive or negative information about a speaker and then asked to evaluate the effectiveness of the speaker. In this experiment, which is the independent variable?**
   a. The effectiveness of the speaker
   b. The type of information the participant is given
   c. Attitude change
   d. The speaker
4. **The more hours that students work, the less successful they are academically. This is an example of what type of correlation?**
   a. zero
   b. positive
   c. perfect
   d. negative
5. **Dr. Duarte is studying bullying behavior in children. Every day, Dr. Duarte goes to the local playground at 3 p.m., sits on the sidelines, and records the number of times one child bullies another, the sex of the children involved in the bullying, and the duration of the bullying. Dr. Duarte is using which research method in this study?**
   a. An experiment
   b. A case study
   c. A naturalistic observation
   d. A quasi-experiment

Answers 1. a; 2. b; 3. b; 4. d; 5. c

1.3 Ethical Principles of Psychological Research

Generally, psychologists associated with universities and colleges in the United States cannot conduct research unless their research proposal has passed review by an **Institutional Review Board (IRB)** (or human research ethics committees [HRECs] in other countries). The function of the IRB or HREC is to ensure that the research study being proposed conforms to a set of ethical standards or guidelines.

Institutional Review Board (IRB) a committee that reviews research proposals to ensure that ethical standards have been met

informed consent the ethical principle that research participants be told about various aspects of the study, including any risks, before agreeing to participate

confidentiality the ethical principle that researchers do not reveal which data were collected from which participant

1.3.1 Ethical Guidelines for Participants

The American Psychological Association (APA), one of the main professional organizations for psychologists, has taken the lead in establishing ethical guidelines, or professional behaviors that psychologists must follow. These guidelines, the "Ethical Principles of Psychologists and Code of Conduct" (APA, 2002), address a variety of issues, including general professional responsibility, clinical practice, psychological testing, and research. Here, we look at the guidelines psychologists must follow when conducting research with humans and animals. The ethical duties of psychologists who treat clients are discussed in Chapter 14.

One of the main concerns of the IRB is to ensure that the proposed research has met the ethical guideline of respect and concern for the dignity and welfare of the people who participate (APA, 2002). Researchers must protect participants from any potential harm, risk, or danger as a result of their participation in a psychological study. If such effects occur, the researcher has the responsibility to remove or correct these effects.

Another fundamental principle of ethical practice in research is **informed consent**. Researchers inform potential participants of any risks during the informed consent process, wherein the researcher establishes a clear and fair agreement with research participants prior to their participation in the research study (APA, 2002). This agreement clarifies the obligations and responsibilities of the participants and the researchers and includes the following information:

- The general purpose of the research study, including the experimental nature of any treatment
- Services that will or will not be available to the control group
- The method by which participants will be assigned to experimental and control groups
- Any aspect of the research that may influence a person's willingness to participate in the research
- Compensation for or monetary costs of participating
- Any risks or side effects that may be experienced as a result of participation in the study

Potential participants cannot be coerced or forced to take part in a study. Possible participants are also informed that they may withdraw from participation in the study at any time, and they are informed of any available treatment alternatives. In addition, the researcher agrees to maintain **confidentiality**. Personal information about participants obtained by the researcher during the course of the investigation cannot be shared with others unless explicitly agreed to in advance by the participant or as required by law or court order. It is also a good idea to obtain participants' consent for sharing data with other researchers, institutions, or other entities (Meyer, 2018).

Online research and data collection from mobile-sensing devices presents unique ethical challenges (Eynon, Schroeder, & Fry, 2009; Harari et al., 2016; Solberg, 2010). Psychologists have a duty to maintain the confidentiality and privacy of participants' data and personal information. When researchers collect information about users without their active participation (such as from social media profiles or smartphones), users must be adequately informed and give consent. Researchers may or may not consider security as part of their data collection plan or may not have the necessary training to implement electronic security. In such cases, researchers may need to consult technical experts to ensure the security of online information. Even with the best security, databases may still be compromised. Many universities and professional organizations have developed policies and procedures to address these issues.

It is not always possible to fully inform participants of the details of the research, as it may change their behavior. For this reason, psychologists sometimes use *deception* in their research. For example, suppose we wanted to research student cheating. If we tell participants we are studying cheating behavior, it will likely influence their behavior. If we tell participants we are investigating student-teacher behavior, we can measure student cheating more objectively. However, the use of deception must be justified by the potential value of the research results. Moreover, deception can be used only when alternative procedures that do not use deception are unavailable.

If participants have been deceived in any way during the course of a study, the researcher is obligated to *debrief* participants after the experiment ends. **Debriefing** consists of full disclosure by the researcher to inform participants of the true purpose of the research. Any misconceptions that the participant may hold about the nature of the research must be removed at this time.

debriefing the ethical principle that participants be fully informed of the nature of the study after participating in research involving deception

Consider the following classic research study. In the 1960s, Stanley Milgram (1963) set out to determine whether the average person could be induced to hurt others in response to orders from an authority figure. (You will read more about Milgram's research in Chapter 10.) Participants were deceived into believing that they were participating in a research study on learning rather than on obedience. Participants were told that they would be playing the role of a "teacher" in the experiment. Participants were introduced to a "learner" who was then led to a separate room. The teacher's job was to administer electric shocks to the learner every time the learner made a mistake in an effort to help the learner better retain a list of words. In reality, the participant was not actually shocking the learner. The learner's responses were prerecorded on a tape, but the participants did not know this and believed that they were, indeed, shocking the learner.

Despite the fact that participants believed the learner to be ill or worse, most of them continued to follow the experimenter's orders. A full 65% of the participants shocked the learner all the way up to the highest shock level! During the procedure, Milgram's participants exhibited emotional distress. Although Milgram debriefed the participants after the study, he still violated the ethical principle of psychological harm. He was criticized for exposing participants to the trauma of the procedure itself and for not leaving the participants in at least as good a condition as they were prior to the experiment (Baumrind, 1964). Because of these ethical problems, a study such as this would not be approved today.

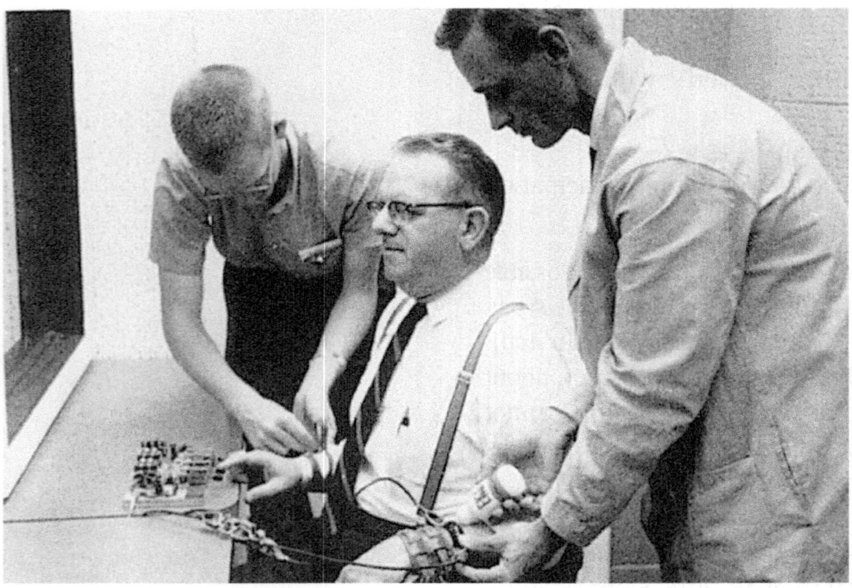

▲ Although Stanley Milgram debriefed his participants, he still caused them psychological harm. Such a study would violate current ethical standards of psychological research.

We should also note that for years the primary focus in research was on White males. Women and minorities were not only discouraged from becoming professionals in psychology but also were largely ignored or neglected when studying psychological issues. Many minority and female, as well as male, psychologists have contributed to the field of psychology by addressing these shortcomings and designing research that looks specifically at the behaviors of minorities and women.

1.3.2 Ethical Guidelines for Nonhuman Research

Animal studies have advanced our understanding of many psychological issues, including the importance of prenatal nutrition, our treatment of brain injuries, and our understanding of mental health disorders (Domjan & Purdy, 1995). Psychologists must meet certain standards and follow ethical guidelines when conducting research with nonhuman subjects. Whereas IRBs evaluate the ethics of research using human participants, psychological research using nonhuman subjects must also be approved by a review board called an *Institutional Animal Care and Use Committee* (*IACUC*). Animals must be treated humanely and in accord with all federal, state, and local laws and regulations. Researchers are responsible for the daily comfort, housing, cleaning, feeding, and health of nonhuman subjects. Discomfort, illness, and pain must be kept at a minimum, and such procedures can only be used if alternative procedures are not available. Moreover, harmful or painful procedures used on animals must be justified in terms of the knowledge that is expected to be gained from the study. Researchers must also promote the psychological well-being of some animals that are used in research, most notably primates (APA, 2002).

1.3 Quiz Yourself

1. **What is the rule for deceiving participants in a psychological research study?**
   a. Deception is never allowed in psychological research. It is against the law in every state.
   b. Deception is allowed only when using nonhuman subjects.
   c. Deception is allowed when alternative procedures are unavailable and when participants are debriefed at the end of the study.
   d. Deception can be used under any circumstances.

2. **Dr. Kwan is performing case study research. Dr. Kwan should be most concerned with which of the following ethical principles?**
   a. Deception
   b. Physical harm
   c. Debriefing
   d. Confidentiality

3. **Which of the following is *not* an ethical guideline that psychologists must follow when conducting research?**
   a. Paying participants for their participation
   b. Informed consent
   c. Freedom from harm
   d. Confidentiality

Answers 1. c; 2. d; 3. a

1.4 Psychology in the Modern World: Foundations and Growth

Psychology has been described as having "a long past but only a short history" (Ebbinghaus, 1910, p. 9). Traditionally, psychology's birth is linked with the first psychology laboratory, which was established by Wilhelm Wundt (1832–1920) in 1879 at the University of Leipzig, in Germany. Wundt wanted to know what conscious thought processes enable us to experience the external world. In particular, Wundt attempted to detail the *structure* of our mental experiences. Wundt's view that mental experiences were created by different elements is referred to as **structuralism**, a term coined not by Wundt but by his student Edward Titchener (1867–1927).

structuralism an early psychological perspective concerned with identifying the basic elements of experience

▲ The first woman to be awarded a doctorate in psychology was Margaret Washburn.

To identify the structure of thought, British psychologist Titchener used a process known as **introspection**, a self-observation technique. Trained observers were presented with an event and asked to describe their mental processes. The observations were repeated many times. From these introspections, Titchener identified three basic elements of all conscious experiences: sensations, images, and feelings.

Wundt's and Titchener's research went beyond introspection and structuralism to encompass a very broad view of psychology. They also conducted detailed studies on color vision, visual illusions, attention, and feelings, and influenced the field of psychology through their students, many of whom went on to establish psychology departments and laboratories in the United States. For example, Titchener's first graduate student, American Margaret Washburn (1871–1939), became the first woman to earn a doctorate in psychology. Washburn did not share Titchener's emphasis on structuralism, but she instead investigated the connection between motor movement and the mind and conducted extensive research on animal behavior.

1.4.1 Psychology's Roots and Modern Perspectives

introspection observing one's own thoughts, feelings, or sensations

biological perspective an approach that focuses on physical causes of behavior

neuroscience a field of science that investigates the relationships between the nervous system and behavior/mental processes

Like Washburn, other psychologists soon reacted against the limited view of the mind that structuralism presented. Such disagreement gave rise to other ways to explain behavior, which resulted in a very broad profession. Here we discuss seven perspectives or views on behavior and the historical figures that influenced their development (● FIGURE 1.7): *biological, evolutionary, psychodynamic, behavioral, sociocultural, humanistic,* and *cognitive*. We will also look at a combined perspective referred to as an *eclectic approach*.

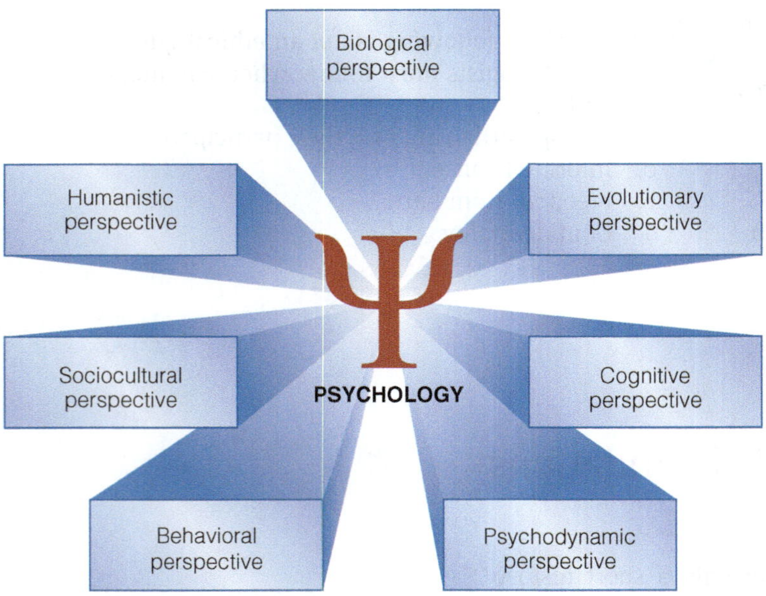

FIGURE 1.7

Psychological Perspectives

Just as a photograph or a piece of art can be examined from many different angles, so too, can mental processes and behavior. We call these angles *perspectives*. Each offers a somewhat different picture of why people behave as they do. Taken as a whole, these perspectives underscore the complex nature of behavior.

The Influence of Medicine

Because of the mind's association with the body, much of what we consider psychology today was at times part of the field of medicine. Hippocrates (460–377 BCE), the father of medicine, believed that personality was in part a reflection of the mix of chemicals in the body, and abnormal behavior was typically treated with medical procedures. The ancient Indian texts of knowledge, *The Vedas* (2000–600 BCE), describe *chakras* or energy processing centers within the body that govern physical, mental, emotional, and spiritual health.

Today, psychologists who adopt a **biological perspective** look for a physical cause for a particular behavior. Such psychologists examine genetic, biochemical, and nervous system (brain functioning) relationships to behavior and mental processes. The biological perspective is also a branch of science referred to as **neuroscience**. (We discuss the physical processes of the nervous system in Chapter 2.) For example, electroencephalographs (EEGs) and other brain imaging and computer technology have enabled neuroscientists to measure how a person's body movements cause nerve cells in the brain to fire. They can then use this information to design neuromotor prosthetic devices, such as robotic arms, that work in much the same way. These appliances can help replace or restore lost motor functioning in people with spinal cord injuries, stroke, and other severe motor deficits (Athanasiou et al., 2017).

From Functionalism to Evolution

American psychologist and philosopher William James (1842–1910) had visited Wundt's laboratory in Germany but did not share Wundt's focus on breaking down mental events into their smallest elements. Rather, James proposed a focus on the wholeness of an event and the impact of the environment on behavior. He emphasized *how* a mental process operates as opposed to the *structure* of a mental process. He came to believe that consciousness and thought evolved through the process of natural selection, to help the organism adapt to its environment (Nielsen & Day, 1999). *Evolution* and *natural selection* were ideas that were quite new at the time. Evolution refers to the development of a species—the process by which, through a series of changes over time, humans have acquired behaviors and characteristics that distinguish them from other species. Natural selection refers to how only the organisms best suited to their environment tend to survive and reproduce. James wanted to know how a particular behavior helps an organism adapt to its environment and thereby increases its chances of surviving and reproducing. James's perspective on psychology became known as **functionalism**. According to James, if human behavior is naturally selected, it is important for psychologists to understand the *function*, or survival value, of a behavior.

Today, psychologists may adopt an **evolutionary perspective**. The evolutionary perspective proposes that natural selection is the process that explains behaviors. Behaviors that increase your chances of surviving are favored or selected over behaviors that decrease your chances of surviving. Like James's functionalism, this approach analyzes whether a particular behavior increases a person's ability to adapt to the environment, thus increasing the chances of surviving, reproducing, and passing one's genes on to future generations (Buss, 2009).

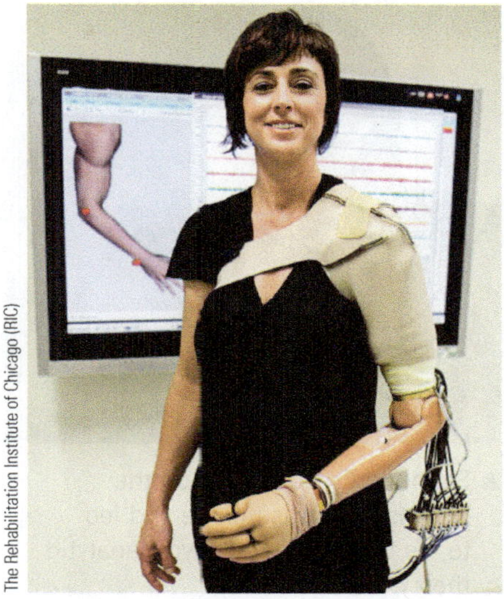

The Rehabilitation Institute of Chicago (RIC)

▲ By studying biological processes, neuroscientists can design neuromotor prosthetic devices such as robotic arms to help restore lost motor functioning.

An Emphasis on the Unconscious

Sigmund Freud (1856–1939) is probably the best-known historical figure in psychology, and his ideas can be found throughout Western culture in music, media, advertising, art, and humor—a testament to his influence and importance. Before creating theories of psychology, however, Freud studied medicine, focusing on neurology and disorders of the nervous system. He began studying people with all kinds of "nervous" disorders, such as an intense fear of horses or heights or the sudden paralysis of an arm. He began asking patients to express any and every thought that occurred to them, no matter how trivial or unpleasant. Freud theorized that encouraging patients to say whatever came to mind allowed them to recall forgotten memories that seemed to underlie their problems. This process, known today as *free association*, is one element of *psychoanalysis*, a therapy that Freud developed.

From these experiences, Freud came to believe that the *unconscious* plays a crucial role in human behavior. For Freud, the unconscious was that part of the mind that includes impulses, behaviors, and desires that we are unaware of but that influence our behavior. Until this time, much of psychology had focused on conscious mental processes. Freud's focus on the unconscious was unique and led to his formulation of **psychoanalytic theory**. According to this theory, humans are similar to animals in that they possess basic sexual and aggressive instincts that motivate behavior. However, unlike animals, humans can reason and think, especially as they mature. In childhood we learn to use these conscious reasoning abilities to deal with and to suppress our basic sexual and aggressive desires so

Bettmann/Contributor/Getty Images

▲ William James is associated with functionalism.

functionalism an early psychological perspective concerned with how behavior helps people adapt to their environment

evolutionary perspective an approach that focuses on how evolution and natural selection influence behavior

psychoanalytic theory Sigmund Freud's view that emphasizes the influence of unconscious desires and conflicts on behavior

Topham/The Image Works

▲ Sigmund Freud's focus on the unconscious was unique and led to his formulation of psychoanalytic theory.

that we can be viewed approvingly by others. For Freud, the conflict between the conscious reasoning part of the mind and the unconscious instinctual one was key to understanding human behavior.

Today, psychologists may adopt a **psychodynamic perspective**, a collective term that refers to those assumptions about behavior originally conceived by Freud, which have been modified by his followers. The psychodynamic view focuses on internal, often unconscious mental processes, motives, and desires or childhood conflicts to explain behavior. For example, many children lie to or manipulate parents to get what they want. The psychodynamic view might suggest that such behavior is an unconscious expression of feelings of powerlessness and lack of control that all children face from time to time.

A Focus on the Environment

In the 1920s, in the United States, a growing number of psychologists believed that in order for psychology to be taken seriously as a "true" science, it must focus on observable behavior and not on the mind, a school of thought referred to as **behaviorism**. You can't see the mind or what a person thinks; you can only see what a person does. Behaviorists believed that only overt, observable behaviors could truly be measured consistently from person to person. One of the most vocal proponents of this school of thought was American psychologist John B. Watson (1878–1958).

psychodynamic perspective an approach that focuses on internal unconscious mental processes, motives, and desires that may explain behavior

behaviorism a psychological perspective that emphasizes the study of observable stimuli, responses, and consequences

stimulus any object or event that is perceived by our senses

response an organism's reaction to a stimulus

Watson was influenced by Russian physiologist Ivan Pavlov's studies of digestion in dogs. While measuring and analyzing the first process of digestion (salivation), Pavlov (1849–1936) noticed that his dogs started to salivate *before* he gave them meat powder. When the experiments first started, the salivation had occurred only *after* the dogs were given the meat powder. To further study this curious change in response, Pavlov performed experiments to train the dogs to salivate to nonfood stimuli. (You will learn more about Pavlov's classic experiments in Chapter 6.)

Pavlov's experiments were important to Watson as examples of how behavior is the product of *stimuli* and *responses*. A **stimulus** is any object or event that is perceived by our senses. A **response** is an organism's reaction to a stimulus. To further his point, Watson and his associate, Rosalie Rayner, performed an experiment on a 9-month-old infant named Albert. Watson first presented "Little Albert" with the stimulus of a white rat. Albert played with the white rat and showed no fear of it (response). Knowing that infants fear loud noises, Watson paired the two stimuli, first presenting the rat to Albert and then presenting a loud gong sound behind Albert's head. Little Albert reacted to the loud noise with the startle, or fear, response. Over and over again, Watson repeated the procedure of pairing the two stimuli—presenting the rat followed by the loud gong. Then, when Watson presented the rat to Albert with no gong, the infant responded with the startle response. Watson had conditioned Little Albert to fear a white rat, a rat that Albert had played with earlier without fear. This demonstrated for Watson that observable stimuli and responses should be the focus of psychology. Unfortunately for Watson, a personal scandal resulted in his dismissal as the chair of the psychology department at Johns Hopkins University (Buckley, 1989).

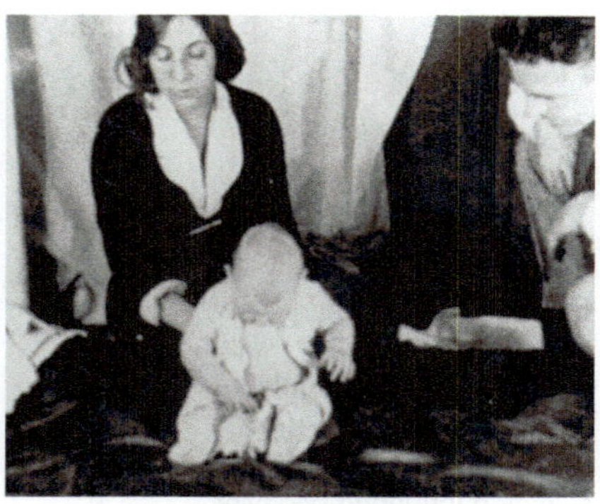

Archives of the History of American Psychology, University of Akron, Akron, Ohio

▲ John B. Watson and Rosalie Rayner showed how stimuli and responses could be studied in their experiment on Little Albert.

Although Watson was no longer operating within mainstream psychology, behaviorism remained strong in the United States, partially due to the work of B. F. Skinner (1904–1990). Skinner, like Watson, believed that psychology should focus on observable behavior. But Skinner added a dimension to Watson's framework: *consequences*. Skinner believed that psychologists should look not only at the stimuli in the environment that cause a particular response but also at what happens to a person or animal after the response—what Skinner called the consequences of a behavior. To illustrate consequences, let's look at Little Albert's behavior from Skinner's perspective. Once Albert was afraid of the rat, how would he act when he saw it? If Albert moved away from the rat, his behavior effectively reduced his fear. Feeling less fear or anxiety is a good (positive) consequence, or outcome. Whenever Albert saw the rat again, he probably moved away even faster. Skinner asserted that positive consequences, such as the reduction of Albert's anxiety, would lead him to engage in the same behavior again. Negative consequences, or outcomes that are not liked, would lessen Albert's desire to engage in the behavior again. We know these processes as *reinforcement* and *punishment*, topics that are explored further in Chapter 6.

Today, psychologists may adopt a **behavioral perspective** that focuses on external causes of behavior. It looks at how stimuli in our environment and/or the rewards and punishments we receive influence our behavior and mental processes. This approach suggests that behavior is learned and is influenced by other people and events. For example, if a student studies and then aces an exam, that reward may encourage them to study again the next time. If the student only gets an average score, merely passing the test may not be rewarding enough to encourage the student to study for future exams.

The **sociocultural perspective** adopts a wider view of the impact of the environment on behavior and mental processes. It suggests that your society or culture influences your actions. Like the behavioral perspective, it assumes that much of behavior is learned. However, it goes further to state that one cannot fully explain people's behavior without understanding their culture, gender identity, ethnic identity, and other important cultural factors. Consider, for example, that from 2008 to 2016 the United States teen birth rate has been steadily decreasing. However, it still remains one of the highest among developed countries (Mathews & Hamilton, 2018; Sedgh et al., 2015). The sociocultural perspective would attribute this phenomenon to aspects of society that may differ among these countries, such as sexual values, contraceptive availability and use, and exposure to sex education. Sociocultural views will be evident throughout this textbook when differences due to culture, age, income level, race, ethnicity, gender, and sexual orientation are highlighted.

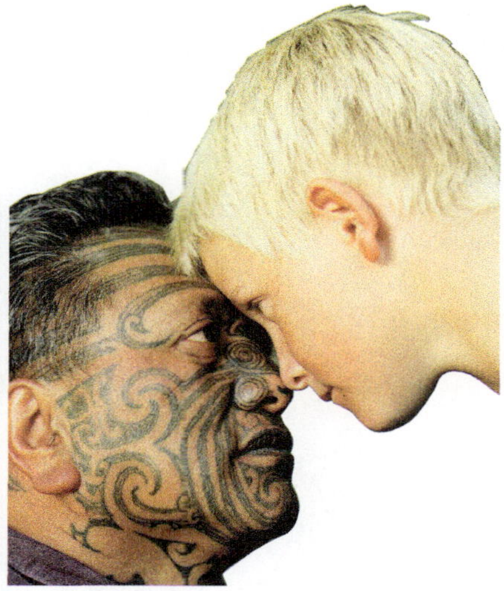
Wilfried Krecichwost/The Image Bank/Getty Images

▲ The sociocultural perspective suggests that one's culture influences behavior.

Beyond Behaviorism: Humanism, Cognitive Psychology, and the Birth of Positive Psychology

Behaviorism was a dominant force in American psychology until the 1960s. By that time, it became evident that this one theory could not account for all responses. For example, feelings and thoughts could not easily be reduced to stimuli and responses. This criticism, combined with the social climate of the time, led to a growing interest in an approach toward treatment called **humanism**. Many psychologists did not accept the behaviorists' view that humans were governed by stimuli and responses, with no will of their own to change their behavior. In the 1960s, societal values were rapidly changing, and the civil rights movement and the Vietnam War sparked widespread civil disobedience. Many young Americans were endorsing women's rights, free love, and free will. Psychology was changing too, and humanists emphasized that everyone possesses inner resources for personal growth and development. The goal of humanistic therapy, therefore, would be to help people use these inner resources to make healthier choices and thus lead better lives. Humanism stressed the free will of individuals to choose their own patterns of behavior. Two well-known humanists are Abraham Maslow and Carl Rogers.

behavioral perspective an approach that focuses on external, environmental influences on behavior

sociocultural perspective an approach that focuses on societal and cultural factors that may influence behavior

humanism a psychological perspective that emphasizes the personal growth and potential of humans

humanistic perspective an approach that focuses on how peoples' view of themselves and the world influence behavior

cognition mental processes such as reasoning and problem solving

cognitive perspective an approach that focuses on how mental processes influence behavior

positive psychology the study of factors that contribute to happiness, positive emotions, and well-being

Today, psychologists who adopt a **humanistic perspective** explain behavior as stemming from your choices and free will. These choices are influenced by your self-concept (how you think of yourself) and by your self-esteem (how you feel about yourself). This view of the self and these feelings toward the self will lead you to choose certain behaviors over others. For example, if you see yourself as a low achiever in school, you may be less likely to take challenging courses or to apply yourself in the courses that you do take. Humanistic views of behavior are explored in Chapters 5, 11, and 14.

While humanism was changing how psychologists were treating clients, changes were also occurring in research psychology. Some researchers were becoming disappointed with the limits of testing stimuli, responses, and consequences in the laboratory, and there was renewed interest in the study of mental processes. Research expanded to subjects such as memory, problem solving, and decision making. However, unlike the earlier functionalism and structuralism, this new study of mental processes was based on more objective experimental methods. Acknowledging that mental processes are not directly observable to the eye, scientists believed that reasonable inferences about mental processes could be made from performance data.

For example, in studying memory processes in children, a researcher can ask children what strategies or techniques they use to remember a list of items. If children using a particular strategy (Strategy A) remember more compared to children using a different strategy (Strategy B), then one can infer that there must be something about Strategy A that facilitates memory. This conclusion is reasonable even though we can't directly see the children use the techniques. Such reasoning led to much experimental research on mental processes, or **cognition**.

Today a **cognitive perspective** explains behavior with an emphasis on thoughts and interpretations based on memory, expectations, beliefs, problem solving, or decision making. A cognitive view focuses on how people process information and on how that process may influence behavior. For example, in explaining the mental health disorder of depression, a cognitive approach focuses on how people who are diagnosed with depression think and perceive the world differently from people who are not diagnosed with depression. You will learn more about cognitive processes in Chapters 7 and 8, when we discuss such topics as memory, problem solving, thinking, decision making, intelligence, and language.

▶ Positive psychology investigates those factors that contribute to happiness, positive emotions, and well-being.

Anne Ackermann/The Image Bank/Getty Images

Focusing on *how* we think, particularly whether our thoughts are pessimistic or optimistic in nature, soon led to a growing emphasis on human strengths and on how humans attain happiness, called **positive psychology**. Led by American psychologists Martin Seligman (b. 1942) and Ed Diener (b. 1946), positive psychology has produced an explosion of research over the past two decades investigating the factors that contribute to happiness, positive emotions, and well-being. By scientifically studying positive aspects of human behavior, the goal of positive psychology is to enable individuals, families, and communities to thrive (Seligman & Csikszentmihalyi, 2000).

YOU REVIEW Explaining Anxiety Using the Modern Perspectives

Perspective	Explanation
Biological	Anxiety is related to chemicals in the body and/or brain, or to genetics (heredity).
Evolutionary	Anxiety is an adaptive response that prepares one to respond to potential threats in the environment. This response helps humans survive, because it warns them of danger and thereby helps them avoid situations or people that may harm them. However, in modern times, these threats tend to be ongoing: traffic jams, crowding, and the hectic pace of consumerism.
Psychodynamic	Anxiety is the product of unresolved feelings of hostility, guilt, anger, or sexual attraction experienced in childhood.
Behavioral	Anxiety is a learned behavior much like Albert's fear of the white rat. It is a response that is associated with a specific stimulus or a response that has been rewarded.
Sociocultural	Anxiety is a product of a person's culture. In the United States, more females than males report being anxious and fearful, and this gender difference results from different socialization experiences. Males in the United States are raised to believe that they must not be afraid, so they are less likely to acknowledge or report anxiety. Females do not experience this pressure to hide their fears, so they are more likely to tell others that they are anxious and to seek treatment.
Humanistic	Anxiety is rooted in people's dissatisfaction with their real self (how they perceive themselves) as compared to their ideal self (how they want to be).
Cognitive	People who are anxious think differently than people who are not anxious. People who are anxious may engage in more pessimistic thinking or worry that everything will go wrong.
Eclectic	Anxiety stems from various sources depending on the individual. One person may be prone to anxiety because many people in their family are anxious and they have learned to be anxious from several experiences. Another person may be anxious because they are dissatisfied with themselves and believe that everything always goes wrong in their life.

Today, most psychologists do not rigidly adhere to just one of these perspectives but are likely to take what is referred to as an **eclectic approach** when explaining behavior. An eclectic approach integrates or combines several perspectives to provide a more complete and complex picture of behavior. You Review: Explaining Anxiety Using the Modern Perspectives illustrates these approaches and shows how a combined approach provides a more expansive understanding of behavior than any single approach could, using anxiety as an example.

eclectic [ee-KLECK-tic] approach an approach that integrates and combines several perspectives when explaining behavior

1.4.2 Specialty Areas in Psychology

In addition to the various approaches or perspectives psychologists take, they also study different aspects of behavior, which correspond to *specialty areas of psychology*. A number of these specialty areas are depicted in • TABLE 1.2, but keep in mind that there are many more. This diversity stems from the complexity of behavior and the interrelatedness of different areas. What a developmental psychologist studies, for example, is connected to and may have an impact on the work of social, clinical, and educational psychologists. If you are interested in becoming a psychologist, the Psychology Applies to Your World: Training to Be a Psychologist box details the educational requirements and potential career opportunities in the profession.

TABLE 1.2 Specialty Areas in Psychology

Specialty Area	Topics of Interest
Biopsychology/Neuroscience	Researches the biological processes that underlie behavior, including genetic, biochemical, and nervous system functioning.
Clinical psychology	Researches, assesses, and treats children, adolescents, and adults who are experiencing difficulty in functioning or who have a serious mental health disorder such as schizophrenia.
Cognitive psychology	Studies mental processes such as decision making, problem solving, language, and memory.
Community psychology	Seeks to understand and enhance the quality of life for individuals, communities, and society. Focuses on early intervention in and prevention of individual and community problems.
Counseling psychology	Researches, assesses, and treats children, adolescents, and adults who are experiencing adjustment difficulties.
Cross-cultural psychology	Investigates cultural similarities and differences in traits and behaviors and examines the cultural goals, values, and practices that underlie them.
Developmental psychology	Researches how we develop physically, cognitively, socially, and emotionally over the life span.
Educational psychology	Researches how people learn and how variables in an educational environment influence learning. May develop materials and strategies to enhance learning.
Environmental psychology	Examines the relationship between environments and human behavior. Focuses on designing, managing, protecting, and/or restoring the environment to enhance behavior. Also studies environmental attitudes, perceptions, and values to promote environmentally appropriate behavior.
Experimental psychology	Conducts research on sensation, perception, learning, motivation, and emotion.
Forensic psychology	Works with mental health issues within the context of the legal system. May study a certain type of criminal behavior such as rape or murder, or may be asked to determine a person's competence to stand trial.
Health psychology	Researches ways to promote health and prevent illness. May be concerned with issues such as diet and nutrition, exercise, and lifestyle choices that influence health.
Human factors psychology	Researches human capabilities as they apply to the design, operation, and maintenance of machines, systems, and environments to achieve optimal performance (e.g., designing the most effective configuration of control knobs in airplane cockpits for pilots).
Industrial/organizational (I/O) psychology	Examines the relationship between people and their work environments. May study issues such as increasing job satisfaction or decreasing employee absenteeism, or focus on understanding the dynamics of workplace behavior, such as leadership styles or gender differences in management styles.
Personality psychology	Researches how people differ in their individual traits, how people develop personality, whether personality traits can be changed, and how these qualities can be measured.
Positive psychology	Seeks to discover and promote those factors that contribute to happiness, positive emotions, and well-being.
School psychology	Assesses students' psychoeducational abilities (academic achievement, intelligence, cognitive processing) and shares test results with teachers and parents to help them make decisions regarding the best educational placement for students.
Social psychology	Researches how our beliefs, feelings, and behaviors are influenced by others, whether in the classroom, on an elevator, on the beach, on a jury, or at a football game.
Sports psychology	Investigates the mental and emotional aspects of physical performance.

Psychology Works!

MIND AND I/Shutterstock.com

Knowledge of psychological research and concepts is important to many college majors and career fields. For example, psychological research on the nature of motivation, reinforcement, and attention is critical to designing console-based and mobile video games that engage and excite players. Video game designers want to motivate people to keep playing their games rather than give up. They build rewards (reinforcement) and punishers into their games such as earning or losing a life, and need to understand how visual attention operates as many games require a player to simultaneously attend to a number of objects at one time. So, in addition to strong computer programming skills, understanding psychological concepts can help video game designers be successful in their field.

1.4.3 Gender, Ethnicity, and the Field of Psychology

In the early development of psychology, women and minorities were not allowed in many instances to receive graduate degrees, despite completing all the requirements for such degrees. In spite of these constraints and many other societal hurdles, several women and minority individuals contributed significantly to the field. As previously mentioned, Margaret Washburn became the first woman to be awarded a doctorate in psychology in 1894 (Furumoto, 1989). Mary Calkins (1863–1930) became the first female president of the American Psychological Association in 1905. She studied at Harvard University with William James and performed several studies on the nature of memory. Christine Ladd-Franklin (1847–1930) studied color vision in the early 1900s. Karen Horney (1885–1952) focused on environmental and cultural factors that influence personality development (see Chapter 11).

Few degrees were awarded to minority students in the early 1900s. Gilbert Haven Jones (1881–1966) was the first African American to earn a doctorate in psychology—in Germany in 1909. Francis Sumner (1895–1954) was the first African American to receive a doctorate in psychology from a university in the United States (in 1920) and is known as the father of

Archives of the History of American Psychology, University of Akron, Akron, Ohio

▲ Known as the father of African-American psychology, Francis Sumner, helped establish the psychology department at Howard University.

Psychology Applies to Your World

Training to Be a Psychologist

THE MAJORITY OF PSYCHOLOGISTS HOLD a doctorate in psychology—usually a Ph.D. (Doctor of Philosophy) or a Psy.D. (Doctor of Psychology). A Ph.D. program focuses more on research, whereas the Psy.D. focuses more on clinical training. To obtain either doctorate, psychologists must first complete a bachelor's and a master's degree. The road to a doctoral degree is long, usually 4–7 years after the undergraduate degree. Most doctoral programs require extensive study of research methods and statistics, and most require that students do some form of research.

Those who study psychology to the point of a bachelor's or master's degree aren't excluded from the profession. As you can see in ● FIGURE 1.8, psychology is a popular degree among undergraduate students. Those who graduate with a bachelor's degree in psychology can look forward to entry-level jobs in a variety of fields from business to social services to healthcare to government. In one study (American Psychological Association, 2016), nearly 62% of former psychology majors reported that their work was directly or somewhat related to psychology. The graduate may assist psychologists in mental

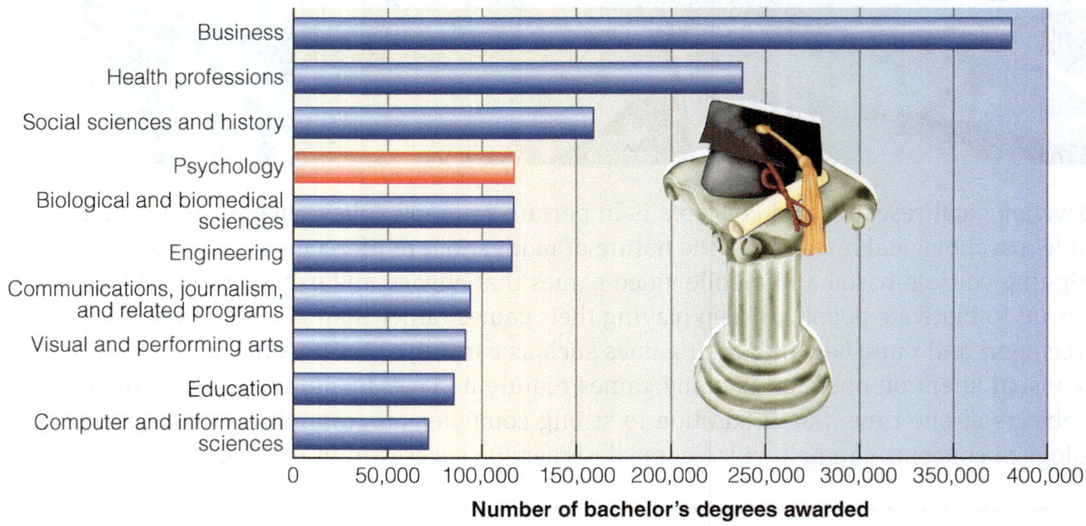

FIGURE 1.8
Undergraduate Degrees in Psychology
Psychology is a popular undergraduate degree. It ranked fourth following business, health professions, and social sciences and history in number of degrees awarded in 2016–2017.
Source: Data from U.S. Department of Education, National Center for Education Statistics, 2018.

African American psychology for his many contributions to the education of Black people. His research focused on equality between Blacks and Whites, disproving the idea that African Americans were inferior. He also helped establish an independent psychology department at Howard University, a historically Black college.

Two of Sumner's students, Kenneth Clark (1914–2005) and Mamie Phipps Clark (1917–1983), conducted research on the self-perceptions of Black children. The Clarks' experiments (Clark, 1950; Clark & Clark, 1950) found that Black children often preferred to play with white dolls over black dolls and attributed positive descriptors such as *good* and *pretty* to the color white and negative descriptors such as *bad* and *ugly* to the color black. The Clarks' findings were noted in the landmark 1954 case, *Brown v. Board of Education of Topeka,* in which the Supreme Court ruled that segregation of public schools was unconstitutional.

health, rehabilitation, or correctional centers; conduct market research analysis; or work in healthcare or management. Jobs in the business sector present the greatest earning opportunities, while jobs in nonprofit and social service sectors are going to be on the lower end of the compensation scale. Median starting and mid-career salaries for people with just a bachelor's degree are below average when compared to other liberal arts majors (Rajecki, 2012; Rajecki & Borden, 2011).

A master's degree typically requires 2–3 years of graduate work. Master's-level psychologists may administer tests, conduct research, or counsel patients under the supervision of a doctoral-level psychologist. In a few states, they may be able to practice independently. They may teach in high schools or community colleges, work in corporate human resource departments, or work as school psychologists or career counselors. Licensed professional counselors or LPCs are master's- or doctoral-level mental health and substance abuse service providers that are required to hold a graduate degree in counseling or a related field and must pass a licensing exam. Those interested in working with individuals on the autism spectrum or those with developmental disabilities may pursue a master's degree in applied behavior analysis found in psychology, special education, or social work departments.

A large percentage of psychologists affiliated with colleges and universities teach and do research, but not just in psychology departments. Psychological scientists can be found across disciplines such as computer science, law, hotel management, zoology, urban research, political science, and others (Association for Psychological Science [APS], 2016). Psychologists also work in school systems, hospitals, business, government, and other human services settings (Michalski et al., 2011; • FIGURE 1.9). Psychologists perform many functions in many different roles at varying institutions. Their job descriptions may include conducting research, counseling clients, and teaching college courses.

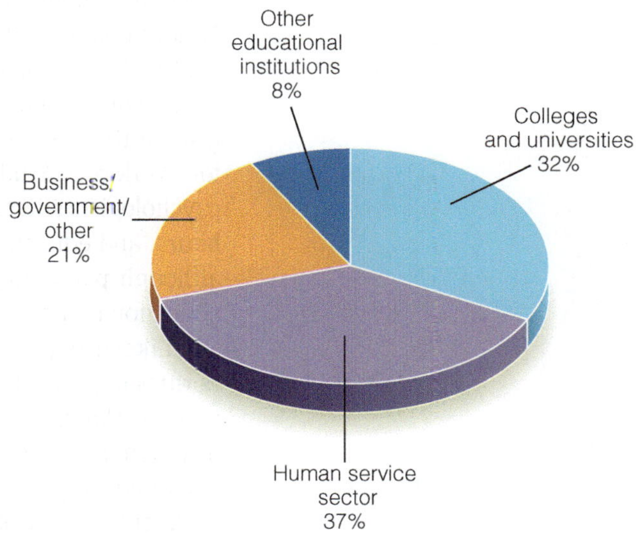

FIGURE 1.9

Work Settings of Psychologists

A large percentage of psychologists affiliated with colleges and universities teach and do research. Psychologists also work in school systems, business, and government, or are employed in health-related or other human services settings.

Source: 2009 Doctorate Employment Survey, APA Center for Workforce Studies.

A related profession is *psychiatry*. A psychiatrist holds a medical degree (M.D.) and then specializes in mental health. A psychiatrist's graduate work includes a medical internship and residency, followed by training in the treatment of mental health disorders. As medical practitioners, psychiatrists have extensive training in the use of therapeutic drugs; they may dispense or prescribe medication and order medical procedures such as brain scans.

Inez Prosser (1897–1934) was the first African-American woman to be awarded a doctorate in psychology, in 1933 (Benjamin, Henry, & McMahon, 2005). Her doctoral dissertation (Prosser, 1933) studied the self-perceptions of Black children. She compared the self-esteem of Black children attending a segregated school to that of Black children attending an integrated school. She found that the Black children at the segregated school fared better. The Black children at the integrated school were more likely to feel inferior and report less satisfactory school relations. Given the probable prejudicial attitudes of White people at the integrated school, it is not surprising that the Black children at the integrated school did not have positive experiences.

Have times changed for women and minorities in psychology? Women have indeed made great progress in the field of psychology. From 1920 to 1974, 23% of doctorates in psychology went to women (APA, 2000). Today, far more women than men earn graduate psychology degrees, with nearly 79% of master's degrees and 73% of doctorate degrees in psychology awarded to women (National Science Board [NSB], 2016). Educational gains have to some extent been followed by progress in the careers of women in the psychology workforce as the percentage of female psychologists in the workplace has also increased relative to male psychologists (APA Center for Workforce Studies, 2015; National Science Foundation, 2020). However, female psychologists still earn less than male psychologists do, after controlling for age, race, hours, and education (Goldin, 2014; National Science Foundation [NSF], 2015). Thus, although psychology has become more fully open to both men and women at the educational and professional levels, inequities in earnings still exist.

Likewise, progress has also been made in the numbers of racial and ethnic minorities in psychology. While minorities make up approximately 39% of the U.S. population (U.S. Census Bureau, 2017), a little over 26% of students in graduate schools in psychology are minorities (NSB, 2016). Between 1976 and 1993, about 8% of all doctorates in psychology were awarded to minorities (APA, 1997); whereas now that number has increased to almost 20% (NSB, 2016). Despite the increase in the number of advanced degrees awarded to minorities, they are still underrepresented in the psychology work force, accounting for approximately 16% of active psychologists (APA Center for Workforce Studies, 2015) and tend to earn less than White psychologists (NSF, 2015). To address this lack of minority representation, the APA has established several programs to attract more minorities to the field of psychology.

1.4 Quiz Yourself

1. **Javier wants to know how aggression helps a person adapt to the environment. Which historical approach is Javier emphasizing?**
   a. Structuralism
   b. Psychoanalysis
   c. Functionalism
   d. Humanism
2. **Which of the following persons would be least likely to emphasize the influence of stimuli and responses on behavior?**
   a. John Watson
   b. Carl Rogers
   c. Rosalie Rayner
   d. B. F. Skinner
3. **Which modern psychological perspective emphasizes the importance of thought processes for understanding behavior?**
   a. Behavioral
   b. Humanistic
   c. Sociocultural
   d. Cognitive
4. **Which of the following professionals is most likely to prescribe medication for a mental health disorder?**
   a. A clinical psychologist
   b. A psychiatrist
   c. A biopsychologist
   d. An experimental psychologist
5. **A psychologist who studies individual differences in shyness is probably from which specialty area?**
   a. Cognitive
   b. Human factors
   c. Developmental
   d. Personality

Answers 1. c; 2. b; 3. d; 4. b; 5. d

1.5 Integrating Psychology: The Big Picture

In the chapters that follow, we will describe in greater detail research in the main areas of psychology. The material has been divided into four roughly equal parts, covering the Common Core recommended by the American Psychological Association (2014). The first section, *foundations in biological psychology,* details the basic biological processes that underlie behavior. It includes chapters on neuroscience, sensation and perception, consciousness, and motivation and emotion. The second part, *foundations in cognitive psychology,* contains research on the mental processes that influence behavior. It includes chapters on learning, memory, and cognition. The third part, *foundations in developmental and social psychology,* examines how behavior varies across the life span, individuals, and social contexts. It includes chapters on human development, social psychology, and personality. The last part, *foundations in physical and mental health,* emphasizes those factors that influence our success or failure at achieving healthy behavior. It includes chapters on stress and health, mental health disorders, and mental health therapies. Each chapter will prepare you for mastering the concepts of the next chapter, and we frequently remind you of concepts presented in earlier chapters to help you connect and integrate the information.

Two features to help you study and master the material conclude each chapter: a 20-item quiz called "What Do You Know? Assess Your Understanding" and a visual summary, entitled "Are You Getting the Big Picture?" The former will help you assess your mastery and application of the material, and the latter will help you remember the topics and concepts that have been introduced and further your understanding of how these concepts relate to one another. Psychology is an integrated field. It is important not only to master the basic concepts of each chapter but also to understand how the information from the chapters ties together and applies to your life. It is in this way that a comprehensive explanation of behavior can be realized and that psychological knowledge can be used in practical ways to improve your daily life.

Studying the Chapter

Key Terms

behavioral perspective (27)
behaviorism (26)
biological perspective (24)
case study (13)
causal hypothesis (11)
cognition (28)
cognitive perspective (28)
confidentiality (21)
confirmation bias (5)
confounding variables (18)
control group (17)
correlation (14)
critical thinking (7)
debriefing (22)
dependent variable (17)
double-blind studies (17)
eclectic approach (29)
evolutionary perspective (25)
experiment (16)
experimental group (17)
functionalism (25)
generalizability (13)
humanism (27)
humanistic perspective (28)
hypothesis (10)
independent variable (16)
informed consent (21)
Institutional Review Board (IRB) (21)
introspection (24)
meta-analyses (11)
naturalistic observations (12)
negative correlation (16)
neuroscience (24)
placebo effect (17)
population of interest (12)
positive correlation (15)
positive psychology (28)
prediction (9)
predictive hypothesis (11)
pseudopsychology (7)
psychoanalytic theory (25)
psychodynamic perspective (26)
psychology (4)
quasi-experiment (19)
random assignment (18)
response (26)
sample (12)
scientific method (4)
sociocultural perspective (27)
stimulus (26)
structuralism (23)
surveys (13)
theory (5)

What Do You Know? Assess Your Understanding

Test your retention and understanding of the material by answering the following questions.

1. Which of the following is *not* true about psychology?
   a. Psychology is just common sense.
   b. Psychology is just the study of mental health disorders.
   c. Psychology has no connection with everyday life.
   d. All of the above are not true.

2. Which of the following topics would a psychologist have the *least* interest in?
   a. Learning
   b. Sexuality
   c. Employment trends
   d. Color perception

3. Which of the following is *not* a goal of psychology?
   a. To describe behavior
   b. To change behavior
   c. To explain behavior
   d. To practice behavior

4. Which of the following best defines the nature of a theory?
   a. An explanation of why a behavior occurs
   b. A statement of fact
   c. An untestable assumption
   d. A personal opinion

5. The hypothesis that the number of rapes will increase during the summer months is an example of a(n) _____ hypothesis.
   a. causal
   b. predictive
   c. untestable
   d. nonscientific

6. Dr. Vaz conducted an experiment in which participants were randomly assigned to one of two conditions. In the first condition, the participants were shown visual images of common objects and then 1 hour later asked to recall as many of the objects as they could remember. In the second condition, the participants heard the names of the same objects and then 1 hour later were asked to recall as many of the objects as they could. Dr. Vaz then compared the number of items recalled for these two groups of participants. In this experiment, the independent variable is _____.
   a. the number of items recalled
   b. whether the participants saw or heard the objects
   c. the sex of the participants
   d. the room in which the participants were tested

7. Dr. Pi wants to test the hypothesis that smoking ma impairs one's ability to remember information. Wha of hypothesis is Dr. Pi interested in testing?
   a. Predictive
   b. Causal
   c. Correlational
   d. Biological

8. Dr. Ling is studying helping behavior in children. E day, Dr. Ling goes to the local playground at 3 p.m., on the sidelines, and records the number of times o child helps another, the sex of the child who helps, the sex of the child who is helped. Dr. Ling is using research method in this study?
   a. An experiment
   b. A case study
   c. A naturalistic observation
   d. A quasi-experiment

9. A confounding variable _____.
   a. measures the effect of the independent variable
   b. is the variable that is manipulated by the experi
   c. has no effect on the dependent variable
   d. is any factor other than the independent variabl affects the dependent variable

10. The longer the commute for a student to a college ca the less likely they are to complete a degree. This is example of a _____.
    a. positive correlation
    b. negative correlation
    c. zero correlation
    d. case study

11. Dr. Eden tells potential participants of any risks they may experience prior to their participation i a research study. Dr. Eden is following the ethica guideline of _____.
    a. deception
    b. confidentiality
    c. informed consent
    d. debriefing

12. The _____ perspective in psychology stresses th importance of looking at the influence of uncons drives and motives on behavior and mental proc
    a. functionalism
    b. cognitive
    c. psychodynamic
    d. behavioral

13. Dr. Babar is a psychologist who studies how people's eating habits help them adapt to and survive in their environments. Dr. Babar is emphasizing which psychological perspective?

a. Evolutionary
b. Biological
c. Humanistic
d. Behavioral

14. Many modern psychologists follow the ______ approach to psychology, in that they do not adhere strictly to any one psychological perspective.

a. pragmatic
b. functional
c. commonsense
d. eclectic

15. Which of the following is the most likely educational attainment of the majority of psychologists?

a. Doctorate degree
b. Master's degree
c. Bachelor's degree
d. Associate's degree

16. Dr. Warren is a psychologist who studies chemicals in the brain. Dr. Warren is approaching psychology from the ______ perspective.

a. cognitive
b. eclectic
c. biological
d. sociocultural

17. Dr. Barrios is a psychologist who studies how people change over time. Dr. Barrios is most likely a ______ psychologist.

a. cognitive
b. biological
c. social
d. developmental

18. Dr. Grogan studies how psychological principles can be applied in the workplace. Dr. Grogan is most likely a(n) ______ psychologist.

a. industrial/organizational
b. clinical
c. social
d. health

19. The first African American to earn a doctorate in psychology was ______.

a. Karen Horney
b. Mary Calkins
c. Gilbert Haven Jones
d. Sidney Beckham

20. Today, who earns most of the doctorates in psychology?

a. Men
b. Women
c. African Americans
d. Asian Americans

Answers: 1. d; 2. c; 3. d; 4. a; 5. b; 6. b; 7. b; 8. c; 9. d; 10. b; 11. c; 12. c; 13. a; 14. d; 15. a; 16. c; 17. d; 18. a; 19. c; 20. b

Use It or Lose It: Applying Psychology

1. Explain how you can apply the scientific method to decide on a college major or a career choice. Could this method also be used as part of your decision-making process when purchasing a large item such as a car or a house? Explain how it could be used for these major purchases.
2. Design a research study to test the idea that listening to rock music while studying facilitates learning. What type of hypothesis would you make? Could this idea be tested by naturalistic observation? Could you set up a correlational study to test this idea? Could an experiment be designed to address this issue? What types of conclusions could you reach from these different research methods? What ethical considerations would you follow when conducting this study?
3. Suppose William James, Sigmund Freud, and John Watson had the opportunity to sit down and discuss the causes of behavior. What might this conversation sound like? On what issues might they agree? On what issues might they disagree?
4. Explain depression from each of the modern perspectives and using the eclectic approach. Use You Review: Explaining Anxiety Using the Modern Perspectives as a guide if you need help.

Critical Thinking About the Science of Psychology

We detailed in Section 1.3 of this chapter Stanley Milgram's classic study on obedience. Review the information given on his research and answer the following questions:

1. What was Milgram's hypothesis?
2. What research method did he use?
3. What was the dependent variable in his study?
4. Which ethical principles did Milgram follow and which ones did he not?

Are You Getting the Big Picture?

1.1 What Is Psychology?

Greg Hinsdale/Corbis

To think like a psychologist, you must be skeptical about explanations of behavior, rather than accepting of them.

Psychology is

- NOT simply giving advice
- NOT just "common sense"
- NOT limited to studying mental health disorders

1.2 The Science of Psychology: Goals, Hypotheses, and Methods

- The goals of psychological research are to:
  - describe behavior
  - predict behavior
  - explain behavior
  - control or change behavior
- Psychologists form **predictive** and **causal hypotheses** and then conduct research using the **scientific method**.
- Predictive hypotheses are tested by **naturalistic observation**, **case studies**, **surveys**, and **correlational studies**.
- Causal hypotheses are tested by **experiments** in which variables are controlled and care is taken to test a **random sample** of a **population of interest**. The **experimental group** is compared to the **control group** on the **dependent variable** to see whether the **independent variable** had an effect.
- In a **quasi-experiment**, participants are not **randomly assigned** to the different conditions, so causal conclusions should be made cautiously.

Picture Partners/Alamy Stock Photo

1.3 Ethical Principles of Psychological Research

- To ensure humane conduct of experiments, the American Psychological Association has established a set of strict ethical guidelines that must be followed when researchers study animals and humans.
- Key ethical guidelines for humans include **informed consent**, **confidentiality**, protecting the participant from harm, and **debriefing** to explain any deceptions used in research.

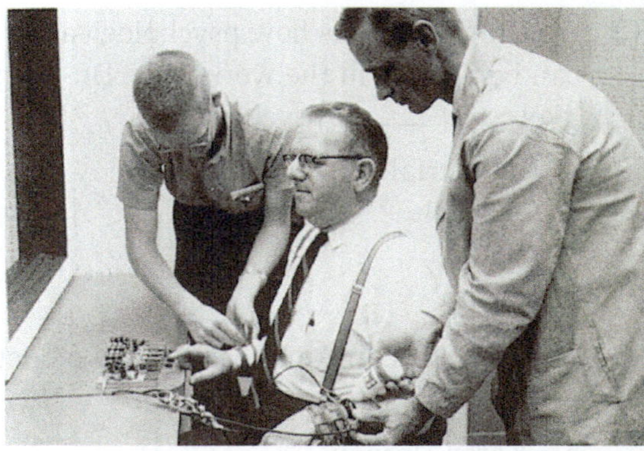
©Renewed 1993 by Alexandra Milgram

1.4 Psychology in the Modern World: Foundations and Growth

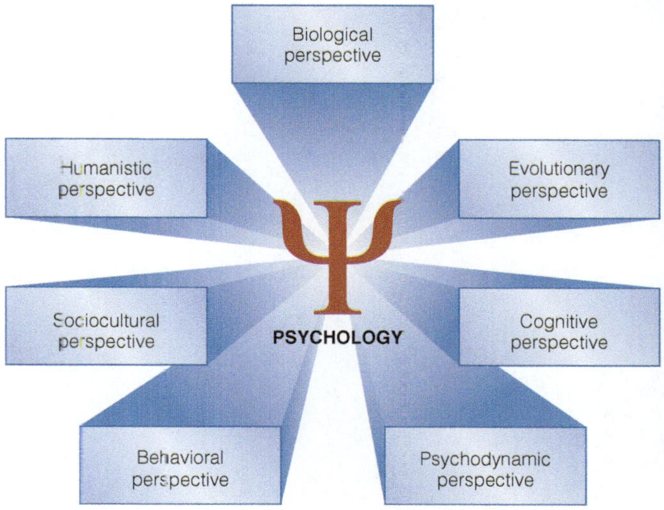

- Psychology became a distinct field of scientific study when Wilhelm Wundt established the first psychology laboratory, in Germany, in 1879.
- A **biological** or **neuroscience perspective**, stemming from the field of medicine, examines the physiological contributions to behavior.
- William James's focus was on how particular behaviors helped people adapt to their environment (**functionalism**). Today, an **evolutionary perspective** looks at how behaviors may be genetically programmed to help us adapt better for survival.
- Sigmund Freud, one of the most famous people to influence psychology, believed the key to understanding behavior was uncovering unconscious motivations (**psychoanalytic theory**). Today, the **psychodynamic perspective** focuses on internal, often unconscious, mental processes, motives, and desires or childhood conflicts to explain behavior.
- John B. Watson and B. F. Skinner emphasized the need to study observable behavior and the influence of the environment on behavior. Their research led to the **behavioral perspective**, which focuses on external causes of behavior, such as how **stimuli** in the environment and/or rewards and punishments influence our **responses**.
- The **sociocultural perspective** researches behaviors across societal groups and cultures (such as ethnicity, social class, or gender).
- The **humanistic perspective** explains behavior as stemming from choices and free will.
- The **cognitive perspective** focuses on how people process information and on how that process may influence behavior. Focusing on how we think led to the birth of **positive psychology**, which describes the factors that contribute to happiness, positive emotions, and well-being.
- Psychologists today embrace an **eclectic approach**, which integrates several perspectives when studying and explaining behavior.

Careers in Psychology

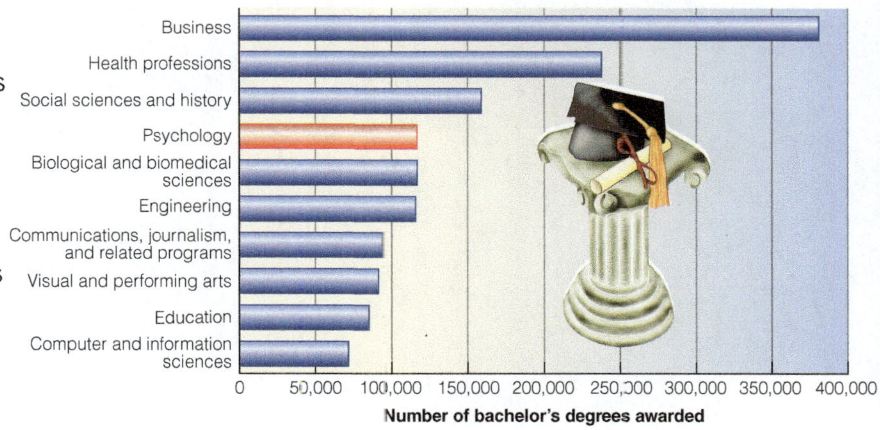

- Psychologists typically have a doctorate in psychology, which usually involves 4–7 years of postgraduate study and research beyond the undergraduate (bachelor's) degree.
- Psychology has numerous specialty areas, including these:
  - Developmental psychology (which studies child and adult development)
  - Social psychology (which examines ways in which we are influenced by others)
  - Industrial/organizational psychology (which looks at behavior in the workplace)
  - Experimental psychology (which performs research on sensation, perception, and learning)
  - Clinical or counseling psychology (which researches and treats people who are experiencing difficulty in functioning or who have a serious mental health disorder)
- Although the numbers of women and ethnic minorities in psychology have increased, inequities in the profession still exist.

Part 1

Foundations in Biological Psychology

Chapter 1 focused on the scientific method that forms the foundation of all areas of psychology. In this next part, we will discuss the biological foundations of psychology—the nervous and endocrine system functions (Chapter 2), sensation and perceptual processes (Chapter 3), states of consciousness (Chapter 4), and motivational and emotional functions (Chapter 5) that influence our mental processes and behavior. The fields of psychology and biology are intimately intertwined. Biology focuses on the body, its structures, and physiological functions. Our knowledge about the body helps inform psychology's study of mental processes and behavior. Without biological functioning, there would be no mental processes or behavior for psychologists to study. And changes in biological functioning, through taking drugs, injury, or illness, have the potential to affect our thoughts and behavior.

Despite its importance in our lives, we often pay little attention to our biological functioning. For example, when did you last stop to wonder how your brain works? For most of us, the answer to that question is probably never! Most of us lead our lives without giving our brain much thought. Every day we go about our business, taking for granted our ability to move, speak, feel, and breathe. We seldom, if ever, stop to think about the amazing internal systems that allow us to accomplish these tasks. Sometimes the best way to gain an appreciation for things we take for granted is to see what life would be like without them. In the case study for this part, we see what life was like for Jean-Dominique Bauby when he suddenly lost certain aspects of his brain function. After reading his story, you might just find yourself with increased respect for your own brain and the abilities that it provides you.

THE BIG PICTURE

THE IMPORTANCE OF A HEALTHY BRAIN

When Jean-Dominique Bauby began his day on December 8, 1995, his life was the essence of success. At age 43 he was editor-in-chief of the French fashion magazine *Elle*, the father of two loving children, a world traveler—a man who seemed to have everything. But all of this was about to change. As Bauby was driving that afternoon, he suddenly began to experience unusual neurological problems. As he drove along, Bauby began to feel as if he were moving in slow motion. His vision began to blur and double, and familiar landmarks along the road seemed only vaguely recognizable. Realizing that he was in trouble, Bauby pulled off the road and attempted to get out of the car, only to find that he was unable to walk. He collapsed and was rushed to a nearby hospital where he

In this Part:

lapsed into a coma that lasted nearly 3 weeks.

As you may have guessed, Bauby experienced a stroke on that December afternoon. Blood flow to the brainstem was disrupted, leaving Bauby with what physicians call "locked-in syndrome." People with locked-in syndrome remain conscious but are almost completely unable to move or speak. They are essentially trapped or "locked" inside their bodies, aware of the outside world, but unable to communicate with those around them in a typical fashion. Because people with locked-in syndrome have profound paralysis, locked-in syndrome is sometimes difficult to distinguish from a *persistent vegetative state*, a state in which consciousness is disrupted. In fact, on average it takes over 2.5 months for others to realize that people with locked-in syndrome have emerged from a coma and are aware of their surroundings (Laureys et al., 2005). Researchers are currently working on ways to use brain imaging techniques to distinguish locked-in syndrome from other states that involve disrupted consciousness, in hopes of producing faster, more accurate diagnoses (Roquet et al., 2016).

Paul Cooper/Shutterstock.com

▲ Jean-Dominique Bauby

When Bauby awoke from his coma, he was aware of his surroundings but unable to move any part of his body except for his left eyelid. He was also completely mute and half deaf; and because he was unable to blink his right eye, it had to be sewn shut to protect his cornea. For the remaining 15 months of his life, Bauby lived in this locked-in state, unable to move or speak but very aware of his surroundings and able to think, feel pain, and experience normal emotions and desires. Today, researchers are working on computer–brain interface technologies to help people with locked-in syndrome communicate with others (Bernat, 2018). However, in 1995 there was little technology to help Bauby let others know he was aware of his surroundings.

Yet, Bauby was not ready to give up, and there was to be more to Bauby's life than tragedy. The world would soon see the remarkable triumph of an intelligent and resourceful man. From his hospital bed, Bauby gradually learned to communicate with others by doing the only thing he could—blinking his left eye. Using an ingenious system, an assistant would read off the letters of the alphabet one at a time. When the assistant read the appropriate letter, Bauby would blink and the assistant would gradually compile the words and phrases that Bauby spelled out. Although it was painstaking, this system allowed Bauby to communicate with those who were patient enough to go through the process. Through blinking, Bauby was able to free himself to a small but meaningful degree from the prison of locked-in syndrome.

Not only did Bauby communicate with his family and friends, he also dictated a best-selling book that was later made into a major motion picture in 2007. It is estimated that Bauby had to blink his eye more than 200,000 times to dictate the manuscript (MacIntyre, 1998). *The Diving Bell and the Butterfly* (Bauby, 1997), published in France just days after his death on March 9, 1997, recounts Bauby's struggle to cope with the infirmities he suffered as a result of his devastating stroke, as well as his musings on the life he lost that December day. It also serves as a testament to the awesome complexity and power of the human brain.

Although it took a life-changing illness to make Bauby aware of his amazing biology, the same does not have to be true for us. In the chapters of this part, you will learn about the biological processes of the nervous and endocrine systems that underlie your thoughts and behavior (Chapter 2), the way you sense and perceive the world (Chapter 3), your awareness during altered states of consciousness (Chapter 4), and the motivations and emotions that guide your behavior (Chapter 5). As you read these chapters, we hope that you will begin to recognize the amazing intricacy and precision with which the systems within our bodies influence even our simplest behaviors. For as Bauby showed us, a glitch in our biological functioning can change our lives in profound ways. Keep in mind that as you read this page, *everything* you are doing—perceiving these words on the page, being conscious of the meaning of the words, being motivated to continue reading, and so on—originates in your wonderfully complex biology.

AF archive/Alamy stock photo

▲ Jean-Dominique Bauby blinked more than 200,000 times to write *The Diving Bell and the Butterfly* after having a stroke and ending up in a locked-in state. This book was later turned into a major motion picture.

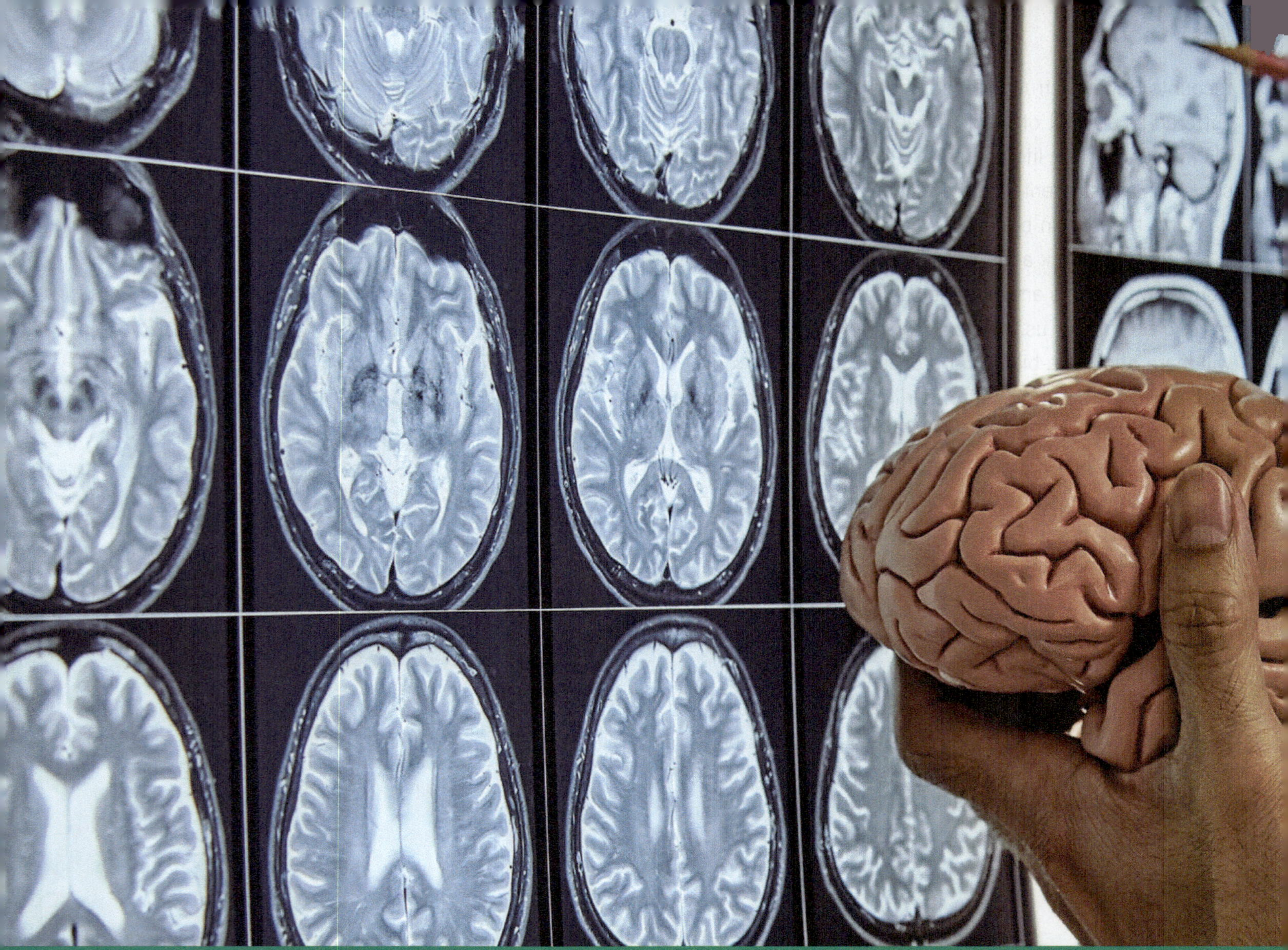

Learning Objectives

2.1 Describe the basic structure of a neuron, including the axon, dendrites, and synapse. (APA 1.1, 1.2)

2.1 Explain what an action potential is and how it moves down the axon and across the synapse. (AP 1.1, 1.2)

2.1 Explain the processes of excitation and inhibition at the synapse. (APA 1.1, 1.2, 1.3)

2.2 List the major neurotransmitters/neuromodulators, and describe the functions they may influence. (APA 1.1, 1.2, 1.3)

2.3 Describe the major parts of the nervous system and the types of information they process. (APA 1.1, 1.2, 1.3)

2.4 Be able to locate the hindbrain, midbrain, and forebrain; list their parts; and explain what they do. (APA 1.1, 1.2, 1.3)

2.4 Describe changes in the aging brain and what is known about protecting the brain as we age. (APA 1.1, 1.2, 1.3)

2.5 Describe brain-imaging techniques and other ways we can study the brain, and explain their advantages and limitations. (APA 1.1, 1.2, 1.3)

2.6 Explain how the endocrine system works and describe the function of the endocrine glands. (APA 1.1, 1.2, 1.3)

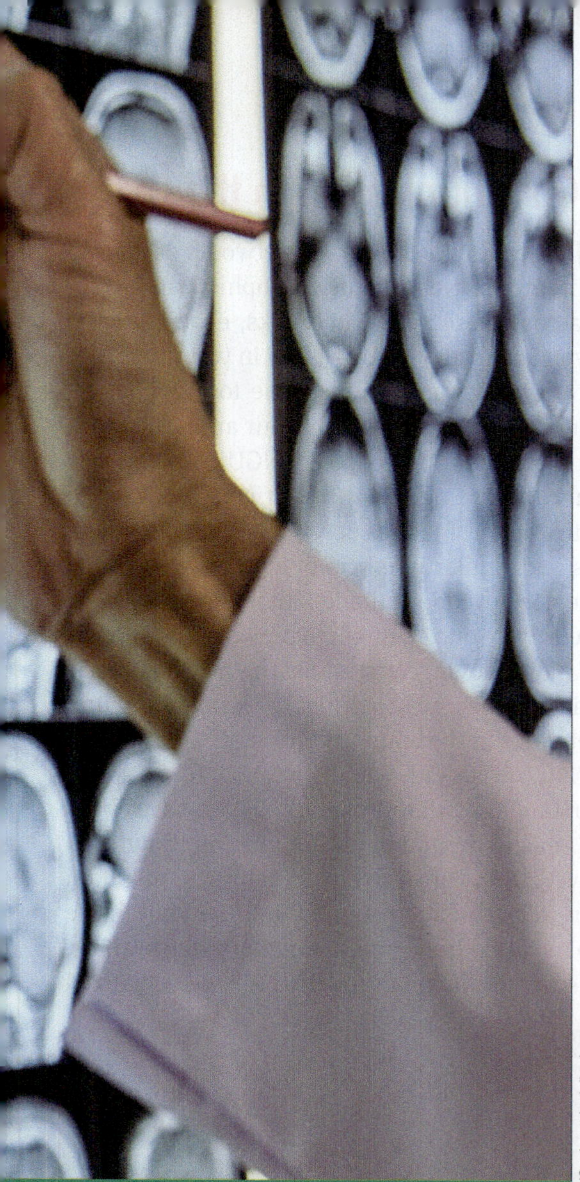

iStock.com/undefined

2 Neuroscience

Chapter Outline

As you read at the beginning of this part on foundations in biological psychology, the case of Jean-Dominique Bauby clearly highlights the importance of the brain and nervous system to our ability to control our bodies. When Bauby had his stroke, the lines of communication between his brain and body were severely damaged, resulting in *locked-in syndrome.* This left him a prisoner inside his own body. Modern psychologists are very interested in **neuroscience**—the study of how the brain and nervous system affect our mental processes and our behavior. This interest is well placed because we rely on our brains and nervous systems to enable us to perform all the tasks of daily life. Prior to his illness, Bauby took for granted the amazing things his nervous system did for him. Similarly, most of us do not question that our brain will somehow store the information we just learned in psychology class, and that on exam day it will retrieve that information. We take for granted that we will be able to walk, to talk, to write, and to maintain a constant body temperature and a steady heart rate. But psychologists want to know how such everyday miracles are accomplished. How does your brain know when you need to eat or sleep? How does your brain tell the muscles of your arm to contract so you can hold a pencil? In short, how does the brain communicate? This is one of the main questions we will examine in this chapter on *neuroscience.* ■

2.1 Billions of Neurons: Communication in the Brain

neuroscience [NUR-o-SCI-ence] the study of how the brain and nervous system affect mental processes and behavior

neurons [NUR-ons] cells in the nervous system that transmit information

glia [GLEE-uh] cells brain cells that provide important support functions for the neurons and are involved in the formation of myelin

myelin [MY-eh-lynn] a fatty, waxy substance that insulates portions of some neurons in the nervous system

The brain communicates with itself and the rest of the body over networks of specialized information-carrying cells called **neurons**. Neurons use a sophisticated communication system to conduct signals across these neural networks, enabling us to control our bodies. For example, when you touch a hot pot, neurons in your fingertips send information up your arm to your spinal column. In response to this possible threat, signals are sent back out from the spine to the muscles of your arm. The result is a quick, reflexive jerking of your arm away from the hot pot (● FIGURE 2.1).

Researchers have long believed that the average adult brain contains around 100 billion neurons. However, newer estimation techniques now suggest that the brain may contain roughly 86 billion neurons and similar numbers of another type of cell called **glia cells** (Azevedo et al., 2009; Lent, Azevedo, Andrade-Moraes, & Pinto, 2012; see also Herculano-Houzel, 2011). Glia cells were once thought to provide only support functions, such as providing nutrients and removing wastes, for the neurons of the brain. However, it is more likely that glia cells also play a critical role in both neural signaling and the formation of neural networks in the brain (Agnati et al., 2018; Eroglu & Barres, 2010; Lent et al., 2012; Logan, 2017; Volterra & Steinhauser, 2004).

Although scientists do not yet understand the full role of glia cells, we have abundant evidence of the importance of glia cells to normal brain functioning (Coutinho-Budd & Freeman, 2013; Logan, 2017; Nave, 2010). For starters, glia cells help maintain the chemical environment of the neuron, secrete cerebrospinal fluid (the fluid inside your brain and spinal column), and help repair neural damage after injuries. However, one of their most important functions is the formation of **myelin**. When specialized

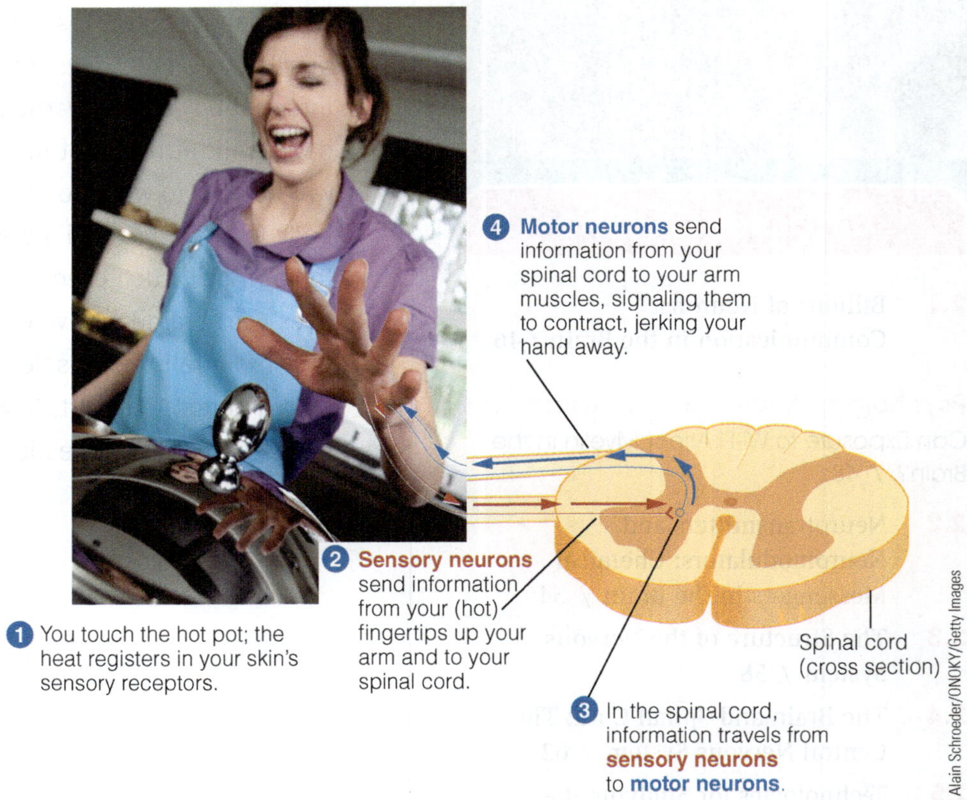

FIGURE 2.1

The Neurons Involved in a Reflex

When you touch a hot pot, neurons in your fingertips send information up your arm to your spinal column. In response to this possible threat, signals are sent out from the spine to the muscles of your arm. The result is a quick, reflexive jerking of your arm away from the hot pot.

glia cells wrap around a neuron, they form myelin. The result is a whitish, fatty, waxy coating that serves to protect the neuron and speed up the neural signals it sends. Myelin helps the signal get where it is going quickly. Myelinated neurons can conduct signals much faster than unmyelinated neurons. To appreciate what myelin does for neural communication, let's look at what happens when myelin is lost due to illness.

Multiple sclerosis (MS) is a disease that attacks and destroys the myelin insulation on neurons (Blanchard et al., 2013; Ozsvár et al., 2018; Rao et al., 2016). People with MS have difficulty controlling the actions of their body and have sensory problems, including numbness and vision loss. When myelin breaks down, neural signals are greatly slowed or halted altogether. Initially, movement becomes difficult; as the disease progresses, voluntary movement of some muscles may become impossible. Sensory systems such as vision may also fail because incoming signals from the eye do not reach the vision-processing parts of the brain. Life often becomes very challenging for people with MS as the "orders" sent to and from the brain are delayed or lost along the way.

Without myelin, our nervous system cannot function properly—our neurons cannot carry information efficiently from one point to another. As psychologists, we are particularly interested in understanding how healthy neurons send signals throughout the nervous system. Before we can examine how neurons transmit signals, however, we must first examine the anatomy of neural cells and how they connect with one another in the nervous system.

Tinseltown/Shutterstock.com

▲ Actress Selma Blair has multiple sclerosis, a disease that results in the destruction of myelin. As the myelin is destroyed, patients may experience a variety of neurological symptoms, including difficulty moving and sensory loss.

2.1.1 The Anatomy of the Neuron

Like any cell in the body, the neuron has a **cell body** that contains a nucleus (● FIGURE 2.2). The cell body is somewhat similar in shape to a fried egg, with

cell body the part of the neuron that contains the nucleus and DNA

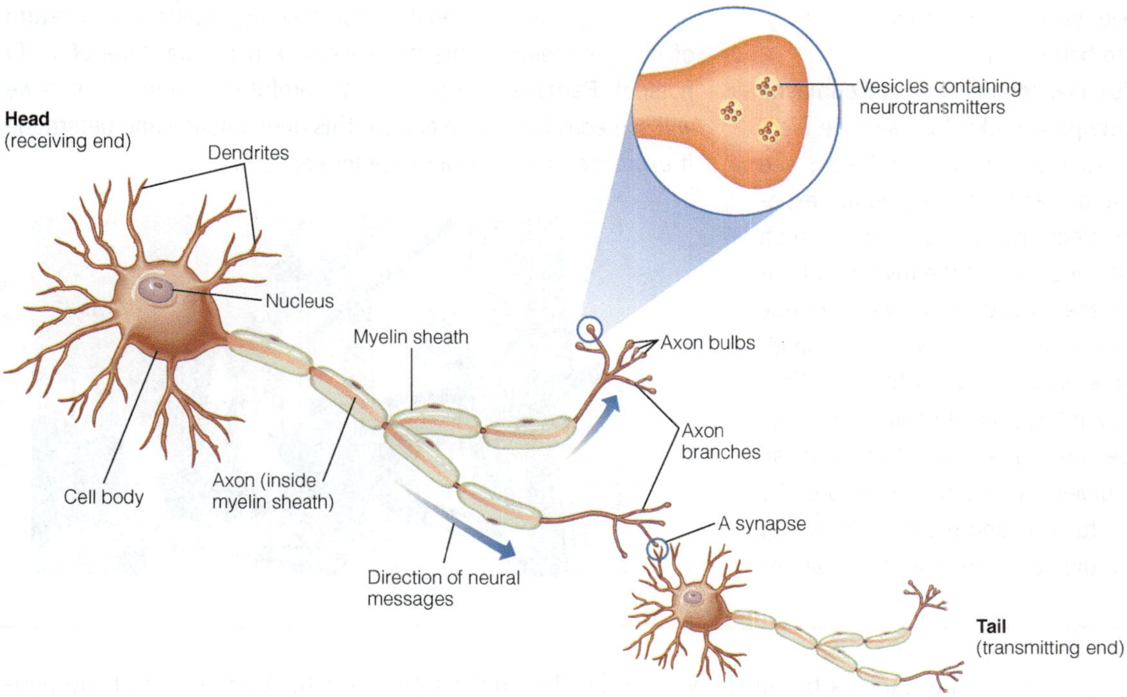

FIGURE 2.2

A Typical Neuron

The arrows indicate the flow of information from the dendrites on the head of the neuron to the axon bulbs at the tail of the neuron. Neurons may have many dendrites and axon branches, and some neurons are insulated with myelin, which helps speed up neural signals in the neuron.

Psychology Applies to Your World

Can Exposure to Wi-Fi Hotspots Affect Myelin in the Brain?

RESEARCHERS OLLE JOHANSSON and Mary Redmayne (2016) report an interesting case study that calls into question the safety of Wi-Fi hotspots for some individuals. The case describes a woman, JS, who survived an attack of West Nile virus in 2003. The virus attacked JS's nervous system, including her myelin, leaving her with paralysis and other neurological symptoms. With time, JS recovered from many of her neurological symptoms and resumed her life. However, in 2014 JS suddenly began to experience the same neurological symptoms she had experienced with West Nile virus—headaches, numbness, dizziness, localized seizures—even though tests suggested that she no longer had active West Nile virus in her body.

Curiously, JS felt better when she would go out for a while, only to get sick again upon returning home. After much investigation, JS deduced that her problems began when her neighbor installed a new Wi-Fi hotspot in his apartment. After speaking with her neighbor, he removed the hotspot and JS's symptoms quickly disappeared. Weeks later JS began to feel sick again when another nearby neighbor installed exactly the same type of hotspot. Again, when this hotspot was disabled, her symptoms disappeared. Subsequently, JS concluded that her symptoms are triggered by a particular type of hotspot because regular Wi-Fi routers, cellphones, microwave ovens, and other frequency-emitting devices do not seem to bother her.

After careful review of JS's case, Johansson and Redmayne suggest the possibility that some people like JS may have *electrohypersensitivity* (sensitivity to electromagnetic fields; see Carpenter [2015] for review) and that for these people, exposure to certain radio-frequency electromagnetic energies, such as Wi-Fi hotspots, may affect the integrity of the myelin in their nervous systems. As a result, these individuals may experience neurological symptoms such as seizures, dizziness, and headaches that are also seen in some diseases that attack myelin.

This case study is certainly interesting, but keep in mind that case studies by themselves are not sufficient to establish cause and effect. Likewise, survey studies that measure the amount of exposure people have to Wi-Fi and the symptoms they experience are not sufficient to rule out alternative explanations for participants' symptoms. To truly establish cause and effect, researchers would need to conduct *experiments* examining the effects of Wi-Fi on the brain. In such an experiment, some participants (the experimental group) would be exposed to the hotspot while others (the control group) would not be exposed. Then all participants' brains would be examined for damage.

For ethical reasons, such research cannot be conducted on human participants, but researchers have conducted similar experiments on rats. So far, many of these experiments have found that Wi-Fi exposure has no significant effect on the brains of rats (Aït-Aïssa et al., 2013; Poulletier de Gannes et al., 2012). However in one study, researchers found biochemical and behavioral impairments in rats exposed to Wi-Fi radiation in utero (Othman, Ammari, Sakly, & Abdelmelek, 2017), and others have found specific brain changes in rats that have been exposed to other types of electromagnetic radiation (e.g., mobile phone radiation; Narayanan et al., 2018). Seemingly contradictory results such as these are common in science, especially in the early years of research on a topic. Clearly, more research is needed to determine what effects, if any, Wi-Fi and exposure to other electromagnetic waves have on the brain. At this time, we do not have a clear explanation for why JS experiences a return of her symptoms in the presence of a particular type of Wi-Fi hotspot. Perhaps with continued, careful scientific research we will someday be able to explain this phenomenon and determine if exposure to Wi-Fi is a cause for concern.

themorningglory/Shutterstock.com

DNA the chemical found in the nuclei of cells that contains the genetic blueprint that guides development in the organism

dendrites [DEN-drights] branchlike structures on the head of the neuron that receive incoming signals from other neurons in the nervous system

the nucleus being the yolk. Like the nucleus of any cell, the nucleus of the neuron contains **DNA** (deoxyribonucleic acid), the chemical that contains the genetic blueprint that directs the development of the neuron. Growing out of the cell body are branchlike structures called **dendrites** (from the Greek word for tree branch). The dendrites receive incoming signals from other neurons. For ease of understanding, we will refer to the dendrite end of the neuron as the *head* of the cell.

Growing out of the other end of the cell body is a long tail-like structure called an **axon**, which carries signals away from the cell body. We will refer to the axon end of the neuron as the *tail* end of the cell. When a neuron is insulated with myelin, it is the axon that is covered, or myelinated. As you can see in Figure 2.2, myelin does not continuously cover the entire length of a neuron's axon. Rather, the myelin covers segments of the axon with a **myelin sheath**. Axons vary in length from a few hundred micrometers to many centimeters, depending on where in the nervous system they are located. Axons in the brain are typically very short (1 millimeter or less), whereas other axons in the body, such as those that extend down the legs, can be almost a meter in length (Purves et al., 1997).

The tail end of the axon splits into separate branches (Figure 2.2). At the end of each branch is an *axon bulb* that contains hundreds of small storage pouches called *vesicles* that hold **neurotransmitters**, the chemical messengers that carry signals across the synapse (Finnema et al., 2016; Tao et al., 2018). A **synapse** is the junction between two neurons where the axon bulb of one neuron comes into close proximity with specialized receptor sites on another neuron.

The neural structure of the brain is extremely complex, and synapses can occur at several places along a neuron (e.g., dendrites, axon, or cell body). However, for simplicity's sake we will discuss only a simple head-to-tail synapse. In this type of synapse, the axon bulb on the tail end of the first neuron is in close proximity to specialized *receptor sites* on the dendrites on the head of a second neuron (● FIGURE 2.3). You will notice that the first neuron, called the **presynaptic neuron**, does not physically touch the second neuron, called the **postsynaptic neuron**. At a synapse, there is a measurable distance, called the *synaptic gap*, between the presynaptic and postsynaptic neurons.

Adult humans have an extremely large number of synapses. Current estimates suggest we have more than 100 trillion synapses in our brain (Eroglu & Barres, 2010). Think about this for a moment. How is it possible for humans to have trillions of synapses but only around 86 billion neurons? It is possible because the neurons of the brain do not synapse in a one-to-one fashion. Rather, each neuron can synapse with up to 10,000 other neurons (Bloom, Nelson, & Lazerson, 2001). Look again at the neurons in Figure 2.3. Synapses can occur at any place along any of the dendrites of these neurons. The vast network of neurons that results from all of these synapses gives our

axon [AXE-on] a long tail-like structure growing out of the cell body of a neuron that carries action potentials that convey information from the cell body to the synapse

myelin sheath [MY-eh-lynn SHEEth] the discontinuous segments of myelin that cover the outside of some axons in the nervous system

neurotransmitters [NUR-oh-TRANS-mitt-ers] chemical messengers that carry neural signals across the synapse

synapse [SIN-aps] the connection formed between two neurons when the axon bulb of one neuron comes into close proximity with the dendrite of another neuron

presynaptic neuron [pre-sin-AP-tic NUR-on] the neuron that is sending the signal at a synapse in the nervous system

postsynaptic neuron [post-sin-AP-tic NUR-on] the neuron that is receiving the signal at a synapse in the nervous system

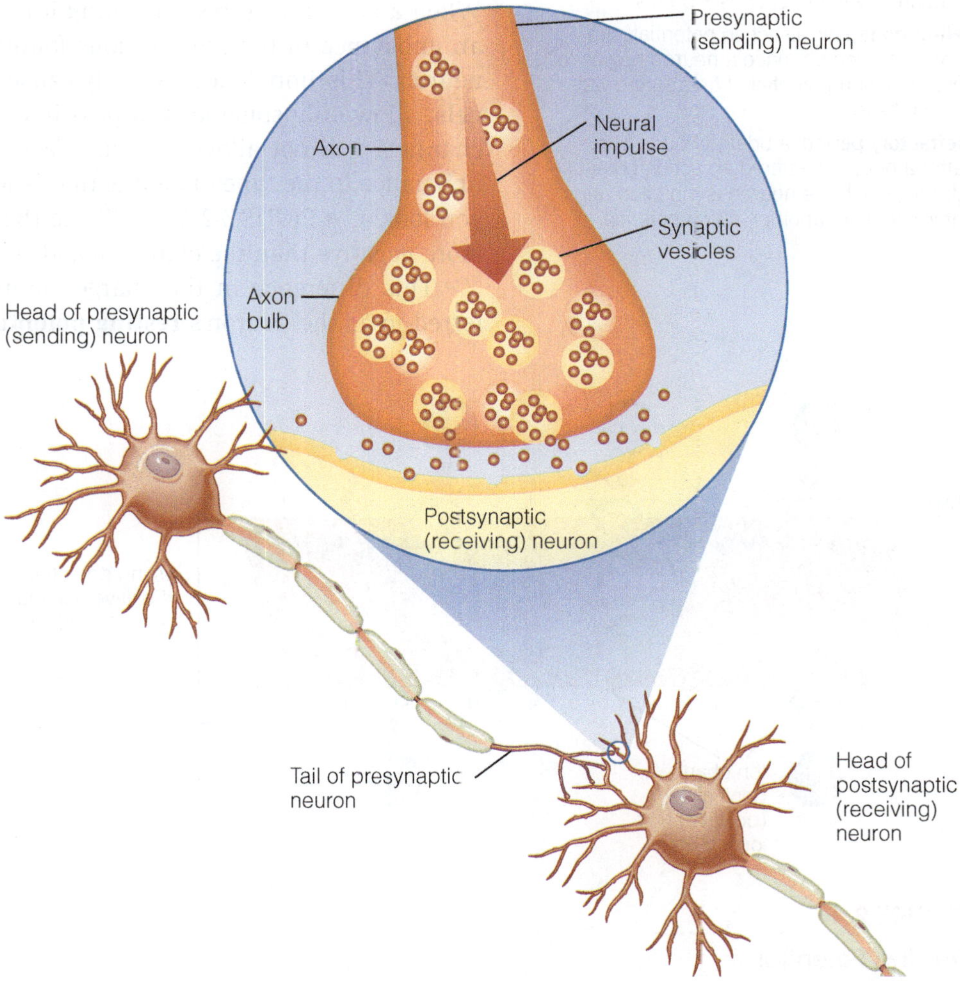

FIGURE 2.3

Detail of a Synapse

A synapse is formed when the axon bulb of one neuron comes in close proximity to the receptors on the dendrites of the postsynaptic neuron.

nervous system the ability to generate and send the messages that are necessary to govern our bodies. Let's take a closer look at how these signals are generated within the neuron and how the signals jump across the synapse as they travel through the nervous system.

2.1.2 Signals in the Brain: How Neurons Fire Up

Neural signals underlie much of the action in our bodies—breathing, movement, using our senses, and so on. To understand how these neural signals are generated within a neuron, we must first understand the chemical environment of the neuron.

Understanding brain chemistry is important because the brain uses *electrochemical* energy that is produced by charged particles called **ions** to send neural signals. Brain tissue is made up largely of densely packed neurons and glia cells. Brain tissue is surrounded by a constant bath of body fluid that contains many different ions. Some of these ions are positively charged, whereas others carry negative charges. Of all the different ions found in our body fluids, sodium (Na^+) and potassium (K^+) play a particularly important role in allowing our neurons to send signals.

ions [EYE-ons] charged particles that play an important role in the firing of action potentials in the nervous system

resting potential the potential difference that exists in the neuron when it is resting (approximately −70 mv in mammals)

threshold of excitation the potential difference at which a neuron will fire an action potential (−55 mv in mammals)

action potential a neural impulse fired by a neuron when it reaches −55 mv

all-or-none law all action potentials are equal in strength; once a neuron begins to fire an action potential, it fires all the way down the axon

refractory period a brief period of time after a neuron has fired an action potential during which the neuron is inhibited and unlikely to fire another action potential

The Neuron at Rest: The Resting Potential

When a neuron is at rest, meaning it is not actively conducting a signal, there is an imbalance in the types of ions found inside and outside the cell walls of the neuron. This imbalance exists because openings in the axon, called ion channels, allow only some ions to pass into and out of the neuron. At rest, these ion channels will not allow sodium (Na^+) to enter the neuron, which results in an imbalance in the type of charge that is found inside and outside of the neuron. If you look at ● FIGURE 2.4, you'll see that at rest, the charge inside the neuron is more negative than the charge outside of the neuron.

This difference in the charges found inside and outside the neuron is referred to as the neuron's **resting potential**. In mammals, the resting potential is about −70 millivolts (a millivolt, mv, is 1/1000th of a volt). This means that when resting, the inside of the neuron is about 70 mv more *negative* than the outside of the neuron. Although it is far less than 1 volt in magnitude, the resting potential is an important driving force in creating neural signals.

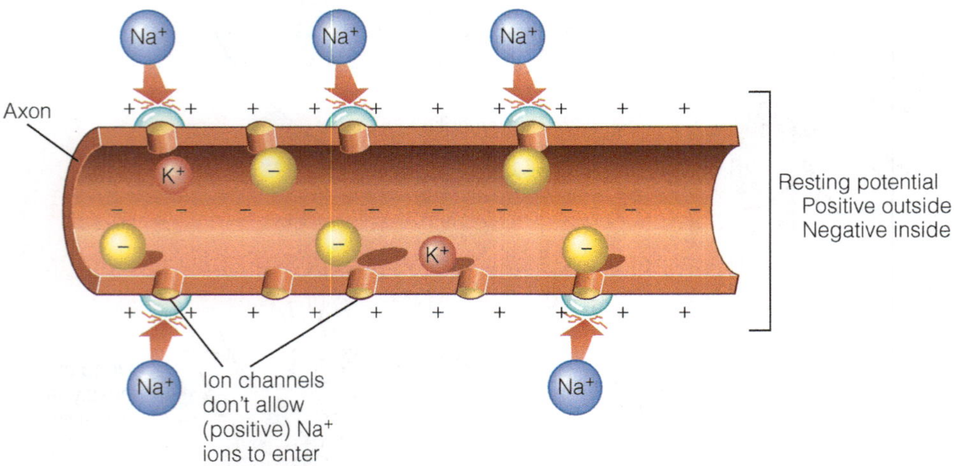

FIGURE 2.4

Resting Potential

When a neuron is at rest, the ion channels do not allow sodium ions (Na^+) to enter the cell. As a result of the high concentration of Na^+, the predominant charge on the outside of the neuron is positive. The predominant charge inside the neuron is negative because of the high concentration of negatively charged ions found there. This difference in charge between the inside and the outside of the cell is called the resting potential.

The Neuron in Action: Firing an Action Potential

When a neuron receives input from other neurons, these incoming signals enter at the dendrites and travel across the cell body to the axon. These signals can make the inside of the cell more positive or more negative. If the incoming signals make the inside of the neuron more positive, the inside of the neuron may become positive enough to reach the neuron's **threshold of excitation** (about −55 mv in mammals).

When the threshold of excitation is reached, the ion channels along the axon suddenly open and allow Na^+ ions to enter the cell. As Na^+ ions flood into the cell, the inside of the neuron rapidly becomes more and more positive. This is how a neuron fires. These firings or neural impulses within the neuron are called **action potentials** (● FIGURE 2.5a).

All neural impulses are equally strong. If a neuron reaches threshold and fires an action potential, the neural signal will reach the synapse. A neuron firing an action potential is like flipping a standard light switch. You either turn it on or you don't; and once you flip the switch, the light is going to turn all the way on! Because all action potentials are equally strong and because, once fired, they will reach the synapse, action potentials are said to fire according to the **all-or-none law**.

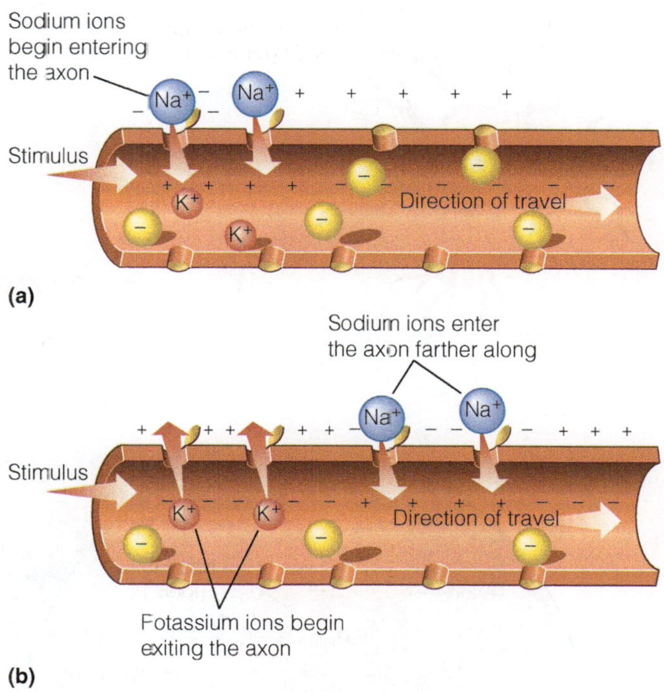

FIGURE 2.5

Action Potential

The action potential shown here (a) occurs all the way down the axon and is how we send neural signals in our nervous system. As the action potential travels down the axon (b), the sodium channels close and potassium (K^+) channels open, allowing potassium to leave the cell. As the K^+ leaves the cell, the inside of the cell becomes more negative. Potassium will continue to leave the cell until the neuron has returned to its resting potential.

Source: Modified from Starr, C., & Taggart, R. (1989). *Biology: The unity and diversity of life* (5th ed.). Pacific Grove, CA: Wadsworth.

Returning to the Resting Potential: The Refractory Period

As the action potential travels to the end of the axon, Na^+ floods into the neuron and the inside of the axon becomes more and more positive. As the inside of the neuron becomes increasingly positive, additional ion channels open along the axon and begin to pump positive potassium ions (K^+) *out* of the cell. This removal of potassium (K^+) from the neuron works to once again make the inside of the neuron more negatively charged (because *positive* ions are leaving the cell). Potassium will continue to leave the neuron until the neuron's original resting potential (−70 mv) is restored (Figure 2.5b). As the neuron is returning to its resting potential, it will experience a very brief (a few milliseconds) **refractory period** during which it is unable to fire another action potential (● FIGURE 2.6).

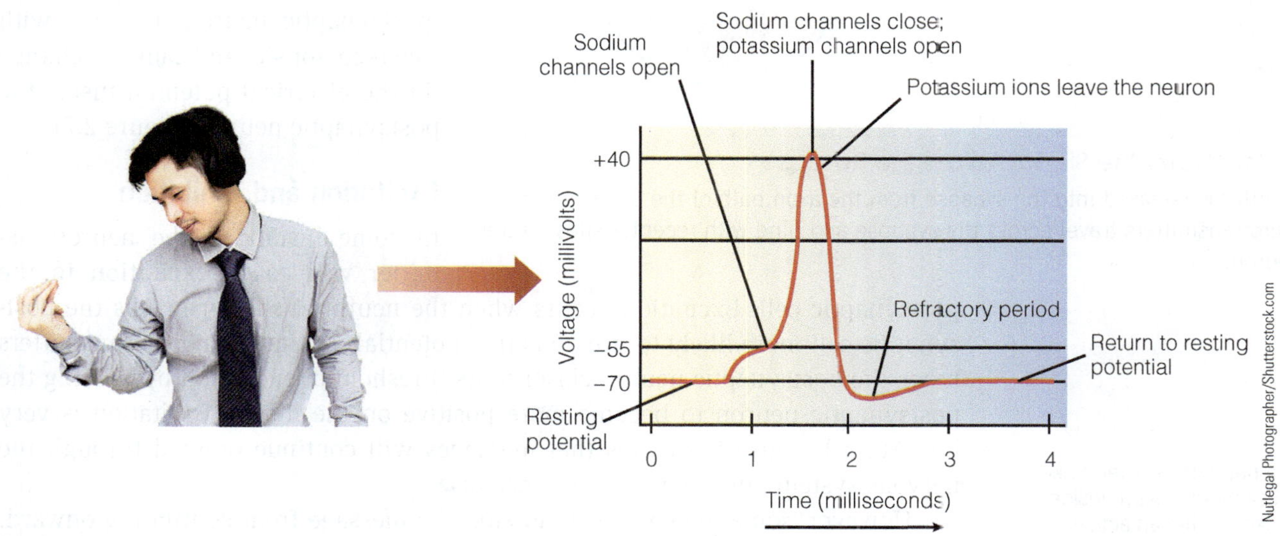

FIGURE 2.6

Electrical Changes in the Neuron As It Fires an Action Potential

Actions, such as snapping your fingers, require action potentials to be sent from your brain to your arms and hands. As each neuron fires, it will experience changes in the electrical charges inside its axon, as depicted in the graph to the right.

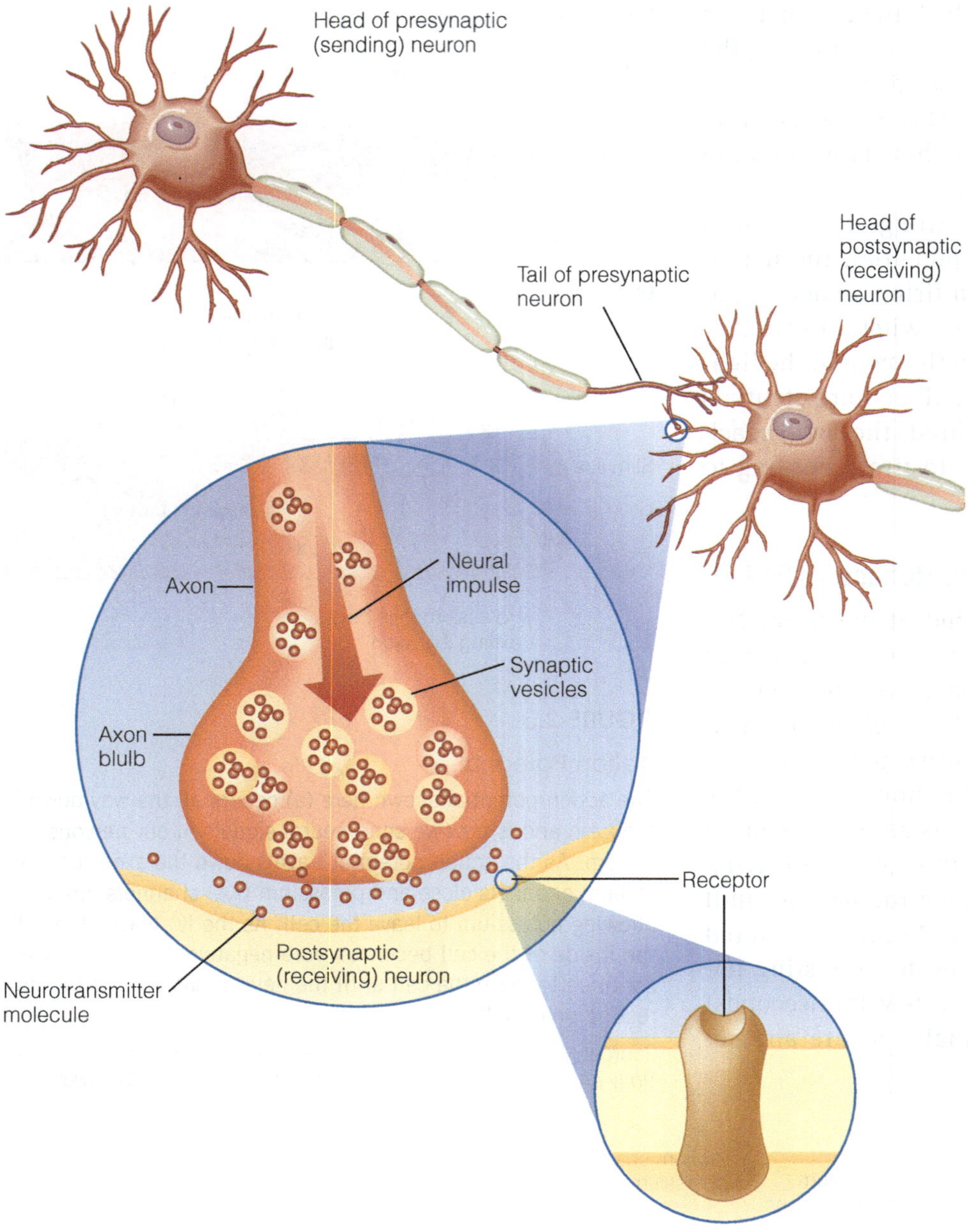

FIGURE 2.7

Neurotransmitters Carry the Signal Across the Synapse

The neurotransmitter is released into the synapse from the axon bulb of the presynaptic neuron. The neurotransmitters travel across the synapse and bind with receptor sites on the postsynaptic neuron.

So far, we've looked at how a neural signal travels down the axon, but what happens when the action potential hits the axon bulb at the end of the axon? How does the signal get across the synapse?

2.1.3 Jumping the Synapse: Synaptic Transmission

When the action potential reaches the axon bulb of the presynaptic (sending) neuron, it causes the release of neurotransmitters into the synapse. The neurotransmitter molecules float in the fluid-filled synapse (● FIGURE 2.7). Some of them will quickly drift across the synapse and come into contact with the tulip-shaped receptor sites lined up on the dendrites of the postsynaptic (receiving) neuron.

Each type of neurotransmitter has a specific molecular shape, and each type of receptor site has a specific configuration. Only certain types of neurotransmitters open specific receptor sites. Just as you must have the correct key to open a lock, a particular receptor site will be activated only by a specific neurotransmitter. When a neurotransmitter finds the correct receptor site on the postsynaptic neuron, it binds with the receptor site and causes a change in the electrical potential inside the postsynaptic neuron (Figure 2.7).

Excitation and Inhibition

In some instances, the neurotransmitter will cause **excitation** in the postsynaptic cell. Excitation occurs when the neurotransmitter makes the postsynaptic cell more likely to fire an action potential. Excitatory neurotransmitters move the postsynaptic neuron closer to its threshold of excitation by causing the postsynaptic neuron to become more positive on the inside. Excitation is very important because it ensures that messages will continue onward through the nervous system after they cross the synapse.

However, sometimes we need to stop the message from continuing onward. This process is called **inhibition**. Inhibition occurs when the neurotransmitter makes the postsynaptic cell less likely to fire an action potential. As you may have guessed, inhibitory neurotransmitters cause the inside of the postsynaptic cell to become more negative, moving it away from its threshold of excitation.

excitation when a neurotransmitter makes the postsynaptic cell more positive inside, it becomes more likely to fire an action potential

inhibition when a neurotransmitter makes the postsynaptic cell more negative inside, it becomes less likely to fire an action potential

Because of the complexity of the brain, a single postsynaptic cell can simultaneously receive excitatory and inhibitory signals from a great number of presynaptic neurons. So, how does the postsynaptic cell know whether to fire an action potential and send the signal down the line? All the incoming signals converge on the axon, which acts like an adding machine, summing up the excitatory and inhibitory signals. Only when the sum of the signals moves the resting potential at the axon to threshold (−55 mv) will the neuron fire an action potential. If the threshold is not reached, the signal simply does not go any farther at this time.

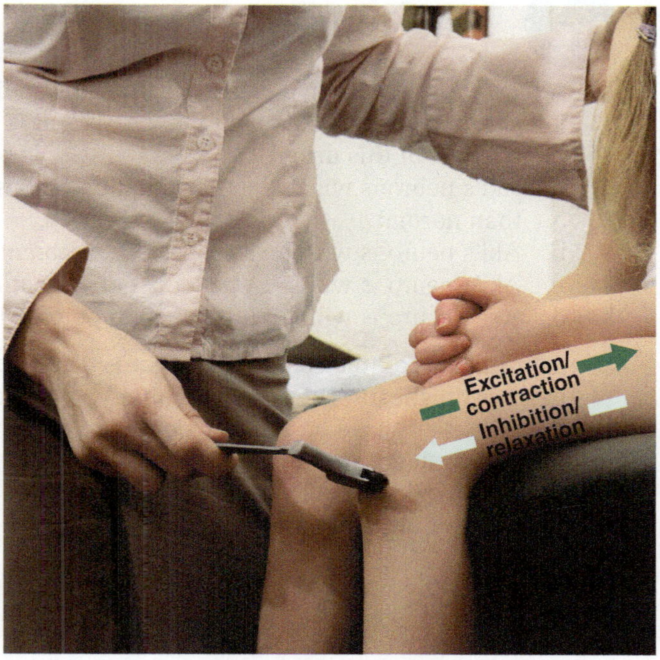

▲ When your knee is hit just below the kneecap, the quadriceps muscles on the top of the thigh are stretched. This stretching sets off a reflex in which the quadriceps receive excitatory impulses that contract them. At the same time, the hamstring muscles on the back of the thigh receive inhibitory impulses that cause them to relax. The result is the patellar reflex, and the leg kicks forward. This reflex, with its combination of excitatory and inhibitory impulses, helps us walk smoothly by automatically coordinating the contraction and relaxation of our thigh muscles.

2.1.4 Cleaning Up the Synapse: Reuptake

When neurotransmitters cross the synapse to bind with postsynaptic receptor sites, not all of these floating neurotransmitters will find available receptors to bind with. What happens to the neurotransmitters left in the synapse? Neurotransmitters are removed from the synapse and returned to the presynaptic neuron by a process called **reuptake**. Reuptake accomplishes two goals. First, it resupplies the presynaptic neuron with neurotransmitters so that the next signal sent by the neuron can also jump the synapse. Second, reuptake clears the synapse of neurotransmitters, thereby ensuring that just the right amount of excitation or inhibition occurs in the postsynaptic neuron.

When neurotransmitters bind with receptor sites, they cause either excitation or inhibition. Afterward, the molecules either dislodge from the receptor site or they are broken down by specialized chemicals called *enzymes*. If reuptake did not occur, once the receptor sites were cleared out, other unattached neurotransmitters in the synapse would bind with the sites, causing further excitation or inhibition. This duplication of signals could cause confusion or dysfunction in the nervous system. Therefore, reuptake is essential to healthy functioning of our brain and nervous system.

Later in this chapter, you will see that some beneficial drugs act on the body by altering this process of reuptake. In fact, as we will see in Chapter 4, most drugs have their effect in the body by altering the functioning of neurotransmitters in the nervous system. For now, let's turn our attention to the types of neurotransmitters and their basic influence on behavior.

reuptake the process through which neurotransmitters are recycled back into the presynaptic neuron

Engage Yourself!

The function of excitation in the nervous system is pretty clear. Excitation starts actions in the nervous system. But why do we need inhibition in the nervous system? Simply put, inhibition is required to slow down and shut off certain processes in the nervous system. Try this demonstration: Sit on the edge of a bed or table with both legs dangling freely. Reach down with the edge of your hand and strike your left leg just below the kneecap with moderate force. If done correctly, your leg should kick forward in what's called the patellar reflex. This reflex results in excitatory signals being sent to contract your quadriceps muscles (top of thigh) and inhibitory signals being sent to relax your hamstring muscles (back of thigh), causing your leg to kick. If you only had the capacity for excitation, your leg would tense but not kick. The interacting inhibition and excitation seen in this reflex are also at work when we walk, helping us balance and maintain posture.

2.1 Quiz Yourself

1. **Aki's dentist gave him a drug that froze the sodium ion channels along Aki's neural axons. What is the likely effect of this drug?**
   a. Aki's neurons will fire more action potentials than normal.
   b. Aki's neurons will fire stronger action potentials.
   c. Aki's neurons will fire weaker action potentials.
   d. Aki's neurons will fail to fire action potentials.

2. **Sabrina has contracted a disease that is destroying her myelin sheath. What effect would you expect this disease to have on the functioning of Sabrina's nervous system?**
   a. It will speed up the neural signals traveling through her nervous system.
   b. It will slow down the neural signals traveling through her nervous system.
   c. It won't affect the functioning of her nervous system in any measurable way.
   d. Her nervous system will speed up and slow down in a random fashion.

3. **Sara hypothesizes that taking a drug that increases a neurotransmitter, serotonin, in the brain will decrease anxiety. Sara's hypothesis would be *best* tested with a(n) ________.**
   a. naturalistic observation
   b. experiment
   c. correlational study
   d. case study

Answers 1. d; 2. b; 3. b

2.2 Neurotransmitters and Neuromodulators: Chemical Messengers in the Brain

neuromodulators [NUR-oh-MOD-yoo-lay-tors] chemicals in the nervous system that affect neural signaling without directly changing the resting potential of the postsynaptic cell

acetylcholine [uh-see-til-COE-leen] (ACh) a neurotransmitter related to muscle movement and perhaps consciousness, learning, and memory

Well over 100 different chemical compounds have been identified as neurotransmitters (Morrow et al., 2008), and many others have been identified as **neuromodulators** or substances that affect neural signaling without directly changing the resting potential of the postsynaptic cell. Neuromodulators affect neural signaling in less direct ways than neurotransmitters do, such as by protecting neurons from harmful substances (Zhao & Brinton, 2007) or affecting the release of other neurotransmitters in a synapse (Li et al., 2017). To complicate things, the same chemical can sometimes act as a *neurotransmitter, neuromodulator,* or even a *hormone* in different parts of the brain and body. For example, some forms of the female sex hormone *estrogen* have been shown to indirectly influence neurotransmission in the *hippocampus,* a part of the brain important to memory (Sárvári et al., 2015). Given the sheer number of neuroactive chemicals and the complex way in which they work together to influence the nervous system, a complete discussion of neurochemistry is well beyond the scope of this text. Instead, we will restrict our discussion to a small number of neurotransmitters/neuromodulators that are important to understanding mental processes and behavior.

2.2.1 Acetylcholine: Memory and Memory Loss

Acetylcholine (ACh) was the first neurotransmitter discovered. In the early part of the 20th century, ACh was found to inhibit the action of the heart and to excite skeletal muscles. Today, ACh is thought to also play a role in awareness or consciousness and in memory (Hasselmo, 2010; Perry et al., 1999). This hypothesized role in memory originated from the discovery that during the course of their disease, people with Alzheimer's experience both loss of neurons that release ACh into their synapses and progressive memory deficits (Martorana et al., 2009; Murray et al., 2013; Pepeu & Giovanni, 2017). In support of this conclusion, research has also shown that ACh plays an important role in the development of neural networks within one of the brain's chief memory centers, the *hippocampus* (Chung et al., 2016).

2.2.2 Dopamine, Serotonin, and Norepinephrine: Deepening Our Understanding of Mental Health Disorders

One group of neurotransmitters in particular, *dopamine, serotonin,* and *norepinephrine,* has proven to be very important to our understanding of a wide range of normal behaviors and mental health disorders. **Dopamine** appears to influence processes such as movement, learning, attention, motivation, and some aspects of social interaction (Homberg et al., 2016). Dopamine may influence motivation by making some activities, such as sex and eating, very pleasurable or rewarding. The reward produced by dopamine may even play a role in the development of certain types of substance abuse (Koob & Volkow, 2016; Neisewander, Cheung, & Pentkowski, 2014; Peng et al., 2013; see Chapter 4).

dopamine [DOPE-uh-mean] a neurotransmitter that plays a role in reward, movement, motivation, learning, and attention

serotonin [ser-uh-TOE-nin] a neurotransmitter that plays a role in many different behaviors, including sleep, arousal, mood, eating, and pain perception

norepinephrine [nor-ep-in-EF-rin] (NOR) a neurotransmitter that plays a role in regulating sleep, arousal, and mood

Parkinson's disease is associated with the loss of neurons in an area of the brain richest in dopamine. Drugs used to treat Parkinsonian symptoms work to indirectly increase the amount of dopamine in the brain. Care must be used in administering such drugs, though, because too much dopamine action in the brain produces some very troubling symptoms—in particular, symptoms similar to those of the mental health disorder *schizophrenia* (see Chapter 13), which is associated with too much dopamine action in the brain (Seeman, 2011; Veselinović et al., 2018). Drugs used to treat schizophrenia often block the action of dopamine at the synapse, and as you might imagine, prolonged use of dopamine-blocking drugs can cause Parkinsonian-like side effects. Think about it. Too little dopamine, and one has the symptoms of Parkinson's disease; too much dopamine, and the result is schizophrenic symptoms. It appears that healthy functioning requires just the right amount of dopamine activity in the brain.

Mental health may depend on having proper levels of other neurotransmitters as well. The neurotransmitter **serotonin** is thought to play a role in many different behaviors, including sleep, arousal, mood, eating, and pain perception. A lack of serotonin in the brain has been linked to several mental health and behavioral disorders (e.g., depression and anxiety). Drugs that increase the action of serotonin at the synapse by preventing its reuptake are called *selective serotonin reuptake inhibitors (SSRIs).* Prozac and other SSRIs have been used to successfully treat depressive disorders, eating disorders, compulsive behavior, and pain.

Another drug that affects serotonin is the illegal drug *MDMA,* commonly known as *molly* or *ecstasy.* Initially, MDMA causes an increase in serotonin action in the brain, but it may also lead to subsequent decreases in serotonin activity (Do & Schenk, 2013; Xie et al., 2006) that may account for reports of depression following molly highs in some users (see Chapter 4). Because MDMA causes a quick short-term increase in serotonin, some have suggested that it might be useful as a fast-acting treatment for *posttraumatic stress disorder* (PTSD; Feduccia, Holland, & Mithoefer, 2018; Pathania, 2015) and depression (Majumder, White, & Irvine, 2012). However, others point to the lack of scientific research examining the safety and effectiveness of MDMA as a therapeutic drug and urge caution (Parrott, 2014; Patel & Titheradge, 2015). Whether MDMA has any legitimate therapeutic role to play in treating such conditions is still being investigated.

▼ Actor Michael J. Fox has Parkinson's disease, and former boxer Mohammed Ali, who sadly passed away in 2016, had a related condition called parkinsonism. Parkinson's is a degenerative disease that results in decreased dopamine action in the brain, which causes tremors and other neurological symptoms.

STEPHEN JAFFE/AFP/Getty Images

Also related to mental health is **norepinephrine (NOR)**, a neurotransmitter thought to play a role in regulating sleep, arousal,

Dima Aslanian/Shutterstock.com

Joe Raedle/Getty Images News/Getty Images

▲ By inhibiting the reuptake of serotonin, Paxil increases the amount of serotonin activity in the synapse, which may reduce depressive symptoms in some people and allow them to once again enjoy pleasurable moments of their lives.

and mood. Some drugs that alleviate depression have an effect on NOR as well as on serotonin. NOR may also play a role in the development of synapses during childhood (Sanders et al., 2005) and recovery of functioning after traumatic brain injury (Armstead, Riley, & Vavilala, 2016). In addition to its function in the brain, NOR also plays a role in the functioning of the *endocrine system,* which we will discuss later in this chapter (see Section 2.6).

2.2.3 GABA and Glutamate: Regulating Brain Activity

gamma amino butyric [GAM-ma uh-MEAN-oh bee-you-TREE-ick] acid (GABA) the body's chief inhibitory neurotransmitter, which plays a role in regulating arousal and pain

glutamate [GLUE-tuh-mate] the chief excitatory neurotransmitter in the brain, found at more than 50% of the synapses in the brain

endorphins [in-DOOR-fins] neuromodulators that act as natural painkillers

Gamma amino butyric acid (GABA) is thought to regulate arousal, our general level of energy and alertness. GABA is the main inhibitory neurotransmitter in the brain (Augustine, 2012; Tao et al., 2018). It is estimated that one-third of all synapses, including most inhibitory synapses, in the brain use GABA as their neurotransmitter. Therefore, it appears that GABA plays an essential role in normal brain function. Loss of GABA in the brain can produce seizures because without GABA's inhibitory effects, arousal levels become too high. Some anticonvulsant drugs work by lessening the effects of enzymes that destroy GABA molecules (Rowlett et al., 2005). GABA may also play a role in anxiety (Nuss, 2015) and chronic pain (Reckziegel et al., 2016). Drugs that increase GABA action in the brain are often used to calm and sedate humans. These drugs include benzodiazepines (Valium), barbiturates (Phenobarbital), and alcohol (see Chapter 4). We will discuss the treatment of anxiety again in Chapter 14.

Whereas GABA is the chief inhibitory neurotransmitter, **glutamate** is the chief excitatory neurotransmitter in the brain (Augustine, 2012). More than 50% of all synapses in the brain use glutamate as a neurotransmitter, and without it many brain processes would not take place. Ironically, glutamate can also be a deadly force in the brain. When physical brain damage affects glutamate-bearing neurons, glutamate molecules may be released in large quantities from the damaged neuron. Large amounts of extracellular glutamate can cause brain cell death as the neurons literally become excited to death when the glutamate spreads to neighboring neurons and causes them to fire a frenzy of action potentials. It appears that in the brain too much excitation is a very bad thing!

TMI /Alamy stock photo

▲ Exercise can lead to the release of endorphins, producing feelings of pleasure and well-being that are sometimes called a "runner's high."

2.2.4 Endorphins: Pain and Pleasure in the Brain

Have you ever heard the term *endorphin*? If you have, what was the context? If you are like most people, your first exposure to endorphins was probably in the context of exercise or physical injuries. **Endorphins** are typically characterized as neuromodulators that are chemically very similar to the class of narcotic drugs called *opiates* (e.g., opium, heroin, morphine, and codeine) that are derived from poppy plants. Opiates are part of a larger class of drugs, *opioids*, which includes any drug that binds to the brain's *opioid receptors* and reduces pain. Both natural (e.g., heroin) and synthetic opioids (e.g., *fentanyl, oxycodone,* and *hydrocodone*) have great potential for abuse and have contributed to the American opioid crisis that began in the late 1990s and intensified in the first decades of the 21st century. The Centers for Disease Control and Prevention (CDC) reports that from 1999 to 2017 some 399,000 people died in the United States from opioid overdoses (Chapter 4; CDC, 2018).

In contrast to such drugs, endorphins are our body's natural painkillers. Endorphins are released in the central nervous system during times of stress, such as physical exertion or physical injury, to protect us from pain (Kavushansky et al., 2013). When endorphins bind with the brain's opioid receptors, they block pain messages by affecting the release of other neurotransmitters in the central nervous system (Sprouse-Blum et al., 2010). As a result we feel less pain and a mild sense of euphoria when they are released. Endorphins may be one of the reasons that physical activity makes us feel physically and mentally better (Fichna et al., 2007; Mikkelsen et al., 2017).

Endorphins may also play a role in making other activities, such as eating, pleasurable (Hayward et al., 2006). For example, research indicates that endorphins are released about 15 minutes after eating fat. The reward from endorphins may be one reason for the appeal of fatty foods (Mizushige, Inoue, & Fushiki, 2007).

We hope that you now have a basic understanding of the role that neurotransmitters play in allowing our neurons to communicate with one another (see You Review: Neurotransmitters and Neuromodulators). Our next step is to take a look at how this neural signaling fits into the structure of the nervous system.

YOU REVIEW Neurotransmitters and Neuromodulators

Neurotransmitter/Neuromodulator	Functions	Related Diseases and Mental Health Disorders
Acetylcholine	Excites skeletal muscles; inhibits heart action; memory	Alzheimer's disease
Dopamine	Movement; learning; attention; motivation and reward; social interaction	Parkinson's disease; schizophrenia; substance use disorders
Serotonin	Sleep; arousal; mood; eating; pain perception	Depressive disorders; obsessive compulsive disorder and other anxiety disorders; eating disorders; chronic pain
Norepinephrine	Sleep; arousal; mood	Depressive and bipolar disorders
GABA	Chief inhibitor; regulates arousal; may play a role in pain perception	Some anxiety disorders; some seizure disorders; perhaps some chronic pain conditions
Glutamate	Chief excitatory neurotransmitter; many diverse functions	Neural death following head injuries
Endorphins (typically neuromodulators)	Suppression of pain; eating; cardiovascular functioning	Depressive disorders

2.2 Quiz Yourself

1. Lakisha developed a disease that reduces the amount of dopamine in the brain. What symptoms would you expect Lakisha to have?
   a. Hallucinations
   b. Trouble with motor skills
   c. Loss of consciousness
   d. Seizures

2. Jackson is a normal, healthy adult. Jackson's brain likely contains more ________ than any other neurotransmitter.
   a. glutamate
   b. GABA
   c. dopamine
   d. acetylcholine

3. Acetylcholine is thought to play a role in memory processing in the brain. Sasha has half her research participants drink an herbal tea that boosts the body's ability to manufacture acetylcholine. The other half of the participants drink warm water. Later, Sasha measures all participants' memory. In this study, the type of drink is the ________ variable.
   a. independent
   b. dependent
   c. control
   d. confounding

Answers 1. b; 2. a; 3. a

2.3 The Structure of the Nervous System

nervous system an electrochemical system of communication within the body that uses cells called neurons to convey information

central nervous system (CNS) the brain and the spinal cord

peripheral nervous system (PNS) all of the nervous system except the brain and the spinal cord

sensory neurons neurons that transmit information from the sense organs to the central nervous system

motor neurons neurons that transmit commands from the brain to the muscles of the body

Our **nervous system** is the vast, interconnected network of all the neurons in our body. Every single facet of our body's functioning and our behavior is monitored and influenced by the nervous system. The nervous system is arranged in a series of interconnected subsystems, each with its own specialized tasks. At the broadest level, the nervous system is divided into the brain and spinal cord, known as the **central nervous system (CNS)**, and the remaining components of the nervous system, referred to collectively as the **peripheral nervous system (PNS)** (● FIGURE 2.8). We will discuss the function of the CNS later when we discuss the brain, but first let's take a closer look at the PNS.

2.3.1 Sensing and Reacting: The Peripheral Nervous System

The functions of the PNS are twofold. First, the PNS must ensure that the CNS is informed about what is happening inside and outside our body. To this end, the PNS is equipped with **sensory neurons** that convey information to the CNS from the outside world, such as sights and sounds, as well as information from our internal world, such as aches and pains. Once the information has reached the CNS, it is carried across *interneurons* as the brain processes the information. Then the second function of the PNS takes over as it acts out the directives of the CNS. The PNS is equipped with **motor neurons** that carry signals from the CNS to our muscles. For example, when you see a juicy apple, the sensory neurons of your eye send this information upward to the part of the brain that processes visual information. Here the brain recognizes the apple, and you decide to eat the apple. The brain then sends signals downward to the motor neurons of your hand and arm, which, in turn, direct you to reach out and grasp the apple with your hand

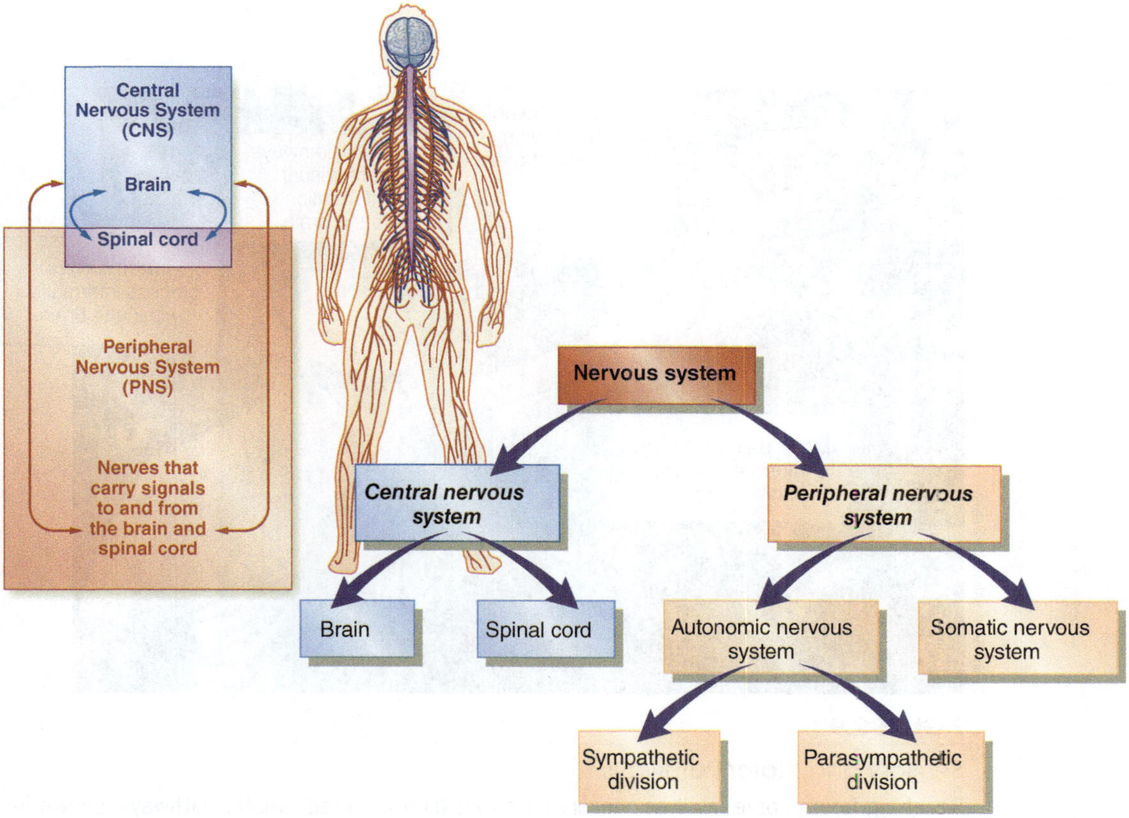

FIGURE 2.8

The Human Nervous System

The nervous system is divided into the central nervous system (CNS, shown in blue) and the peripheral nervous system (PNS, shown in red). Together the central and peripheral nervous systems affect virtually all of our bodily functions. The PNS can be further subdivided into the somatic nervous system (governs voluntary action and sensory functioning) and the autonomic nervous system (governs involuntary organ functioning). The autonomic nervous system can be further subdivided into the parasympathetic nervous system (governs organs in calm situations) and the sympathetic nervous system (governs organs during times of stress).

(● FIGURE 2.9). In this fashion, the sensory pathways send sensory information to the spinal cord and brain, and the motor pathways carry "orders" away from the brain and spinal cord to the rest of the body.

Although Bauby's brain damage was centered in the CNS, it still affected the functioning of his peripheral nervous system. The damage prevented certain parts of the brain from communicating with Bauby's peripheral nervous system. Most of the sensory information coming from the PNS was able to reach the sensory parts of Bauby's brain, allowing him to still perceive the world around him. However, the brain could no longer send signals down the motor pathways to his muscles, resulting in the loss of almost all of his motor functioning except for the blinking of his left eye. This loss of voluntary movement is a hallmark of locked-in-syndrome. However, Bauby's peripheral nervous system was still able to carry out some of the orders sent from the brain. His heart still beat on its own. His organs still functioned. Such involuntary actions were still possible because the functions of the PNS are

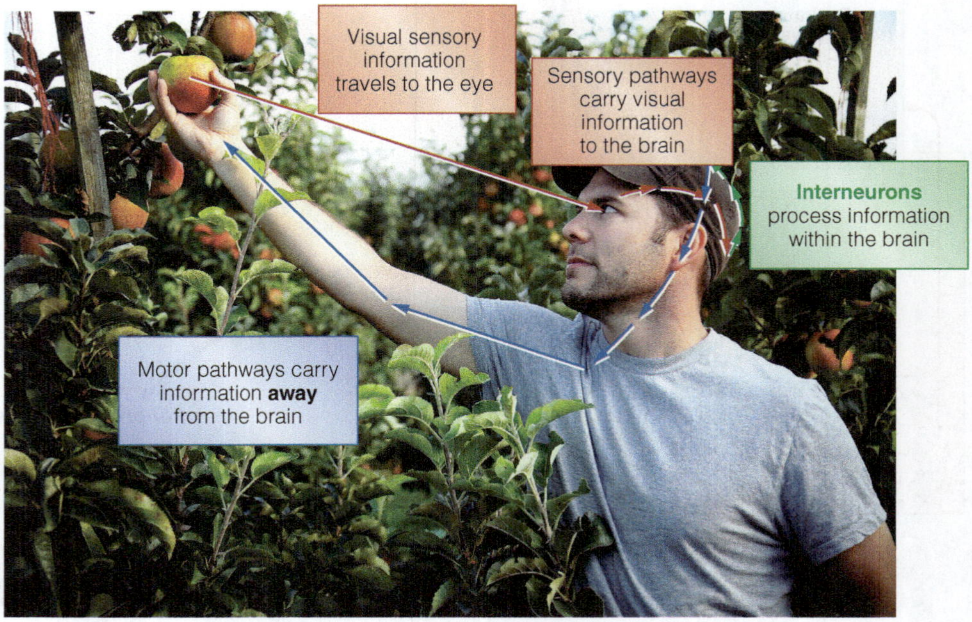

Design Pics Inc/Alamy Stock Photo

FIGURE 2.9

Sensory and Motor Pathways

Reaching for an apple involves sensory pathways (shown in red), motor pathways (shown in blue), and interneuron pathways (shown in green).

divided into two different branches, the *somatic nervous system* and the *autonomic nervous system*. The damage in Bauby's brain primarily impacted the function of the somatic branch of the PNS, which controls voluntary actions in the body.

2.3.2 Voluntary Action: The Somatic Nervous System

somatic nervous system the branch of the peripheral nervous system that governs sensory and voluntary motor action in the body

autonomic nervous system the branch of the peripheral nervous system that primarily governs involuntary organ functioning and actions in the body

The **somatic nervous system** includes those neurons that control the skeletal muscles of the body that allow us to engage in voluntary actions. For example, reaching for an apple requires the activation of the somatic nervous system. The brain makes the decision to reach for the apple; then this "order" is sent downward, across the motor neurons of the somatic nervous system that control the muscles of the arm. The arm muscles react to the orders from the CNS, and you reach for the apple. The functioning of the somatic nervous system enables us to control our bodies in a deliberate and flexible manner.

2.3.3 Involuntary Actions: The Autonomic Nervous System

Although controlling body movements is important, it is equally advantageous to have some processes in the body controlled automatically and involuntarily. The neurons of the **autonomic nervous system** control the smooth muscles of the internal organs, the muscles of the heart, and the glands. By automatically regulating organ functions, the autonomic nervous system frees up our conscious resources and enables us to respond quickly and efficiently to the demands placed

Psychology Works!

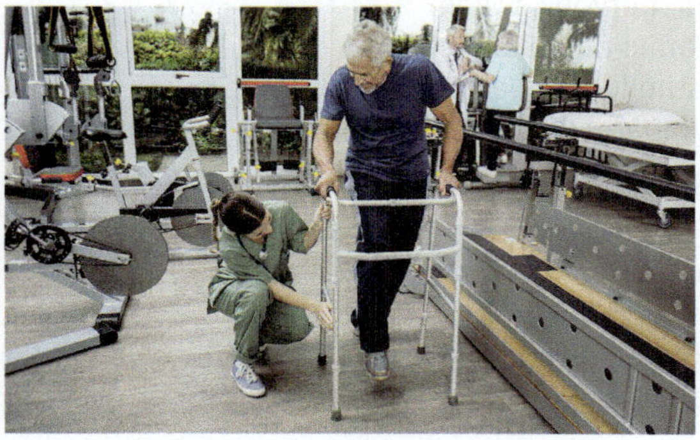
Tyler Olson/Shutterstock.com

Physical therapists and physical therapist assistants are just two of the many types of healthcare professionals who use knowledge of neuroscience in the workplace. For physical therapists and physical therapist assistants, knowledge of the nervous system and its functions allows them to tailor treatment plans to their clients' needs, helping them to regain their physical abilities and/or reduce pain after injury or illness.

on us by the environment. The autonomic nervous system has two divisions: the *parasympathetic nervous system* and the *sympathetic nervous system*.

The Parasympathetic Nervous System

The **parasympathetic nervous system** operates mainly under conditions of relative calm. As you read this text, it is very likely that your parasympathetic nervous system is primarily responsible for regulating the functions of your internal organs. When the parasympathetic nervous system is active, heart rate, blood pressure, and respiration are kept at normal levels. Blood is circulated to the digestive tract and other internal organs so that they can function properly, and your pupils are not overly dilated. Your body is calm, and everything is running smoothly. But if threat arises in the environment, this will quickly change. During times of stress, the sympathetic system takes over primary regulation of our organ functions from the parasympathetic system.

parasympathetic nervous system the branch of the autonomic nervous system most active during times of normal functioning

sympathetic nervous system the branch of the autonomic nervous system most active during times of danger or stress

The Sympathetic Nervous System

The **sympathetic nervous system** springs into action under conditions of threat or stress. The sympathetic nervous system evolved to protect us from danger. When it is activated, heart rate increases, breathing becomes more rapid, blood pressure increases, digestion slows, muscle tissue becomes engorged with blood, the pupils dilate, and the hair on the back of the neck stands up. All of these changes help to prepare us to defend our body from threat. For this reason, the actions of the sympathetic nervous system are often referred to as the *fight-or-flight response*. The increased cardiovascular activity quickly pumps oxygenated blood away from internal organs and to the muscles of the arms and legs so that the animal or person can swiftly attack, defend itself, or run away. Once the danger is past, the parasympathetic system resumes control, and heart rate, respiration, blood pressure, and pupil dilation return to normal. Because the sympathetic nervous system plays an important role in our response to stress, it also plays an important role in our health. We explore this connection in Chapter 12.

2.3 Quiz Yourself

1. **During a bad storm, Juanita saw what looked like a tornado forming in the sky above her home. Immediately *after* she saw the tornado, which division of the nervous system was most likely in control of Juanita's internal organ functions?**
   a. Parasympathetic
   b. Sympathetic
   c. Endocrine
   d. Spinal
2. **Moving your legs as you walk is an example of a behavior that is governed by which branch of the nervous system?**
   a. Somatic nervous system
   b. Autonomic nervous system
   c. Sympathetic nervous system
   d. Parasympathetic nervous system
3. **The sensory neurons in your fingertips are part of the ______ nervous system.**
   a. central
   b. peripheral
   c. autonomic
   d. sympathetic

Answers 1. b; 2. a; 3. b

2.4 The Brain and Spinal Cord: The Central Nervous System

hindbrain a primitive part of the brain that comprises the medulla oblongata, pons, and cerebellum

forebrain the brain structures, including the limbic system, thalamus, hypothalamus, and cortex, that govern higher-order mental processes

midbrain the brain structure that connects the hindbrain with the forebrain

medulla oblongata [meh-DOO-luh ob-LONG-ga-ta] a part of the hindbrain that controls basic, life-sustaining functions such as respiration, heart rate, and blood pressure

As we have discussed, the central nervous system is composed of the brain and the spinal cord. The structures of the brain are composed largely of neurons and glia cells. These structures are organized into three regions: the *hindbrain*, the *midbrain*, and the *forebrain*. The **hindbrain** sits directly above the spinal cord and is named for its position at the bottom of the brain (•FIGURE 2.10). The hindbrain is the most "primitive" part of the brain, involved in the most basic life-sustaining functions. The hindbrain makes up a good portion of the *brainstem*, a series of brain structures that are essential for life. Even small amounts of damage to the brainstem can be life threatening.

The **forebrain** resides in the top part of the skull and regulates complex mental processes such as thinking and emotional control. It is the largest region of the brain and includes structures that regulate many emotional, motivational, and cognitive processes. Without this well-developed forebrain, humans would not have mental abilities such as problem solving, thinking, remembering, and using language.

Between the hindbrain and the forebrain is the **midbrain**, which acts as a connection between the more basic functions of the hindbrain and the complex mental processes of the forebrain. Without the midbrain, the hindbrain could not supply the forebrain with the neural impulses it needs to remain active and keep us conscious.

Now that we have a feel for the overall organization of the brain, let's examine the components and functions of these structures.

2.4.1 The Hindbrain

Simply put, without the functioning of the hindbrain, we would die (Wijdicks, Atkinson, & Okazaki, 2001). The hindbrain consists of three structures: the *medulla oblongata*, the *pons*, and the *cerebellum*. The **medulla oblongata** sits at the top of the spinal column at the point where the spinal cord enters the base of the skull (● FIGURE 2.11). The medulla oblongata regulates heartbeat and respiration, and even minor damage to the medulla oblongata can result in death from heart or respiratory failure. It also plays a role in sneezing, coughing, vomiting, swallowing, and digestion.

The **pons** sits above the medulla oblongata, where the brainstem bulges inside the skull (Figure 2.11). Like the medulla oblongata, the pons is crucial to life. The pons plays a role in respiration, consciousness, sleep, dreaming, facial movement, sensory processes, and the transmission of neural signals from one part of the brain to another. The pons acts as a "bridge" for neural signals; in particular, sensory information coming from the right and left sides of the body crosses through the pons before moving on to other parts of the brain. If the pons becomes damaged, the "bridge" is out, and serious motor–sensory impairments can result. This is what occurred in Bauby's case. The stroke damaged areas of his brainstem most likely including areas of his pons, and this damage impaired his brain's ability to communicate with the nerves of his peripheral nervous system. Bauby's brain could no longer send motor signals to most of his body, resulting in almost total paralysis. But, the damage spared the sensory pathways in his pons, allowing him to still see, hear, and feel.

The final part of the hindbrain is the **cerebellum**. The cerebellum is the large, deeply grooved structure at the base of the brain (Figure 2.11). Amazingly, the cerebellum contains roughly 80% of the brain's cerebral neurons, but only accounts for 10% of the brain's total mass (Lent et al., 2012). The cerebellum is necessary for balance, muscle tone, and the performance of motor skills (Pool et al., 2013; Seidler et al., 2002). It may also play a critical role in the learning of motor skills (Ferrucci et al., 2013; Hikosaka et al., 2002) and the execution of certain behaviors (Walker, Diefenbach, & Parikh, 2007). Increasingly, research suggests that in addition to motor behaviors, the cerebellum also plays an important role in more cognitive functions, such as certain aspects of perception, memory, and emotion (Adamaszek et al., 2016; Steele & Chakravarty, 2018).

Given its functions, damage to the cerebellum can lead to substantial problems, including loss of balance and coordination. Alcohol impairs the functioning of the cerebellum (and some forebrain structures), producing the familiar symptoms of staggering, clumsiness, and slowed reaction time that make driving dangerous. Abnormalities in the cerebellum have also been linked to a number of mental health issues, including *depression, bipolar disorder* (Adamaszek et al., 2016; see Chapter 13), and *attention deficit hyperactivity disorder* (ADHD; Shaw et al., 2018).

2.4.2 The Midbrain

The midbrain structures connect the hindbrain with the more sophisticated forebrain. For psychologists, one of the most interesting midbrain structures is the **reticular formation**. The reticular formation, located near the pons, is a complex collection of neural networks that extend from the hindbrain region through the midbrain and into the forebrain. The neurons of the reticular formation serve

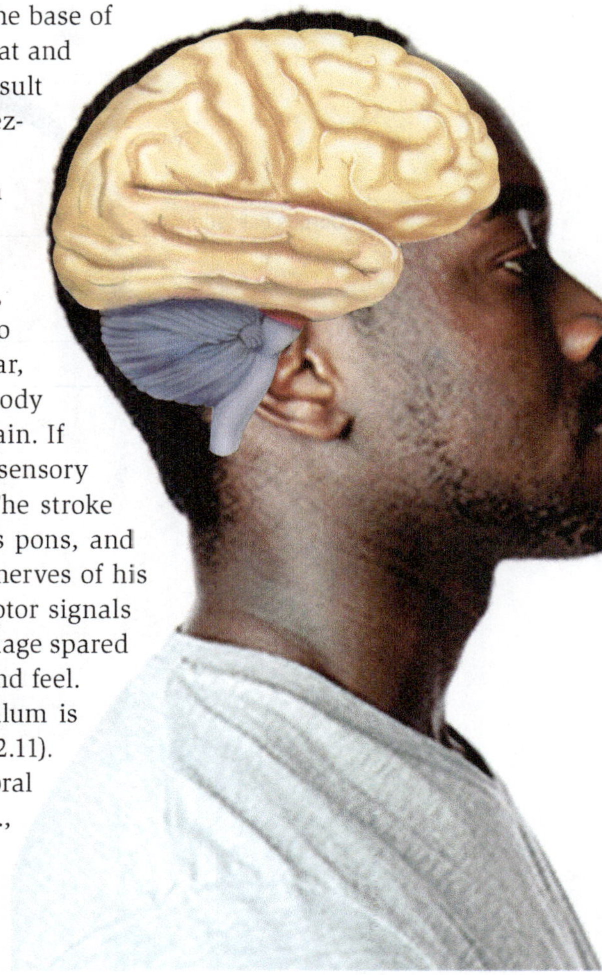

ESB Professional/Shutterstock.com

FIGURE 2.10

The Human Hindbrain, Midbrain, and Forebrain

The human hindbrain (shown in blue) governs basic and life-sustaining functions. The midbrain (shown in red) connects the lower structures of the hindbrain with the higher structures of the forebrain. The forebrain (shown in tan) governs complex processes such as cognition, sensory processing, and the planning and execution of behaviors.

pons a hindbrain structure that plays a role in respiration, consciousness, sleep, dreaming, facial movement, sensory processes, and the transmission of neural signals from one part of the brain to another

cerebellum a hindbrain structure that plays a role in balance, muscle tone, and coordination of motor movements

reticular formation a part of the midbrain that regulates arousal and plays an important role in attention, sleep, and consciousness

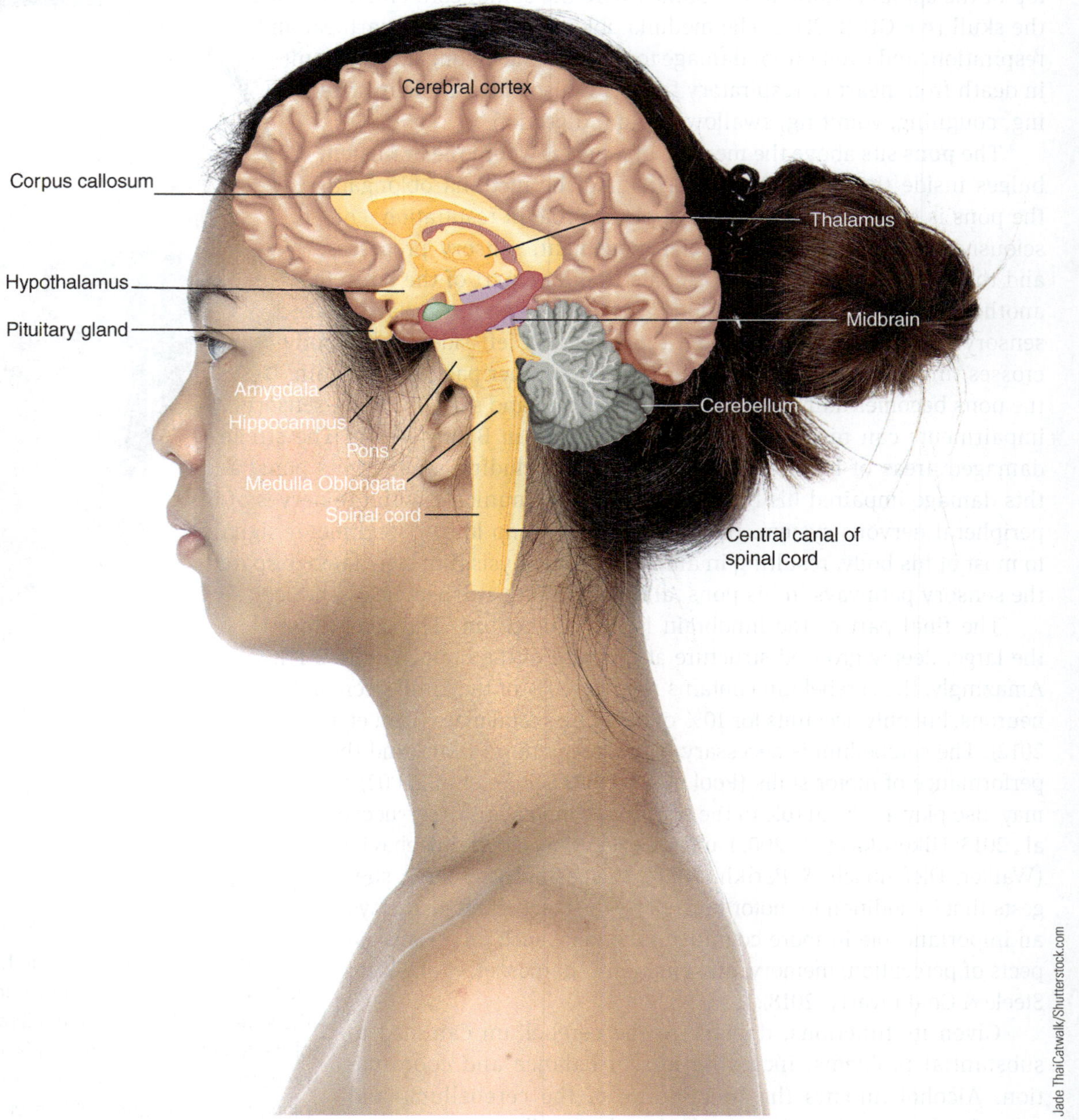

FIGURE 2.11

The Brain and Its Structures

This figure shows the cortex and the subcortical structures of the brain.

many functions, including regulating arousal levels (Kinomura et al., 1996), playing an important role in attention, sleep, and consciousness (Hudson, 2009; Izac, 2006; Vanini & Baghdoyan, 2013), regulating cardiovascular activity (White & Hall, 2012a), and body movement (White & Hall, 2012b).

2.4.3 The Forebrain

limbic system a system of structures, including the amygdala and hippocampus, that govern certain aspects of emotion, motivation, and memory

The forebrain contains several groups of structures that function as subsystems. The structures of the **limbic system** include the *amygdala* and the *hippocampus*. These structures govern emotional processes, and other forebrain structures govern sensory processing and motivation. The wrinkled and folded external surface of the brain, the **cerebral cortex**, governs high-level processes such as cognition and language. In ● FIGURE 2.12, you can see that the forebrain is divided into right and left **cerebral hemispheres**. For the most part, forebrain structures are duplicated in the right and left hemispheres.

The Limbic System

The series of forebrain structures collectively called the limbic system regulate some of our basic emotional reactions. Two limbic structures are located deep in the central region of the brain, above the hindbrain and beneath the cerebral cortex: the *amygdala* and the *hippocampus* (●FIGURE 2.13).

The **amygdala** is an almond-shaped structure located almost directly behind the temples. The amygdala governs the emotions of fear and aggression (Sah et al., 2003). More specifically, the amygdala may play a role in the way we perceive and respond to emotion-evoking stimuli (Adolphs, 2002; Isenberg et al., 1999). An example is how we process facial expressions of emotion in others (Sato et al., 2017). Studies have found that participants with damage to their amygdala have a difficult time making accurate judgments about others' mood states by looking at their facial expressions. This is especially true when participants are making judgments about other people's levels of fear and anger (Adolphs, Tranel, & Damasio, 1998; Graham, Devinsky, & LaBar, 2007). Research suggests that persons with *autism spectrum disorders (ASD)*, a mental health disorder characterized by deficits in social behavior, experience

Peter Hvizdak/The Image Works

▲ Without the cerebellum, we would not be able to accomplish tasks such as learning to ride a bicycle.

cerebral cortex the thin, wrinkled outer covering of the brain in which high-level processes such as thinking, planning, language, interpretation of sensory data, and coordination of sensory and motor information take place

cerebral hemispheres the right and left sides of the brain that to some degree govern different functions in the body

amygdala [uh-MIG-duh-luh] a part of the limbic system that plays a role in the emotions of fear and aggression

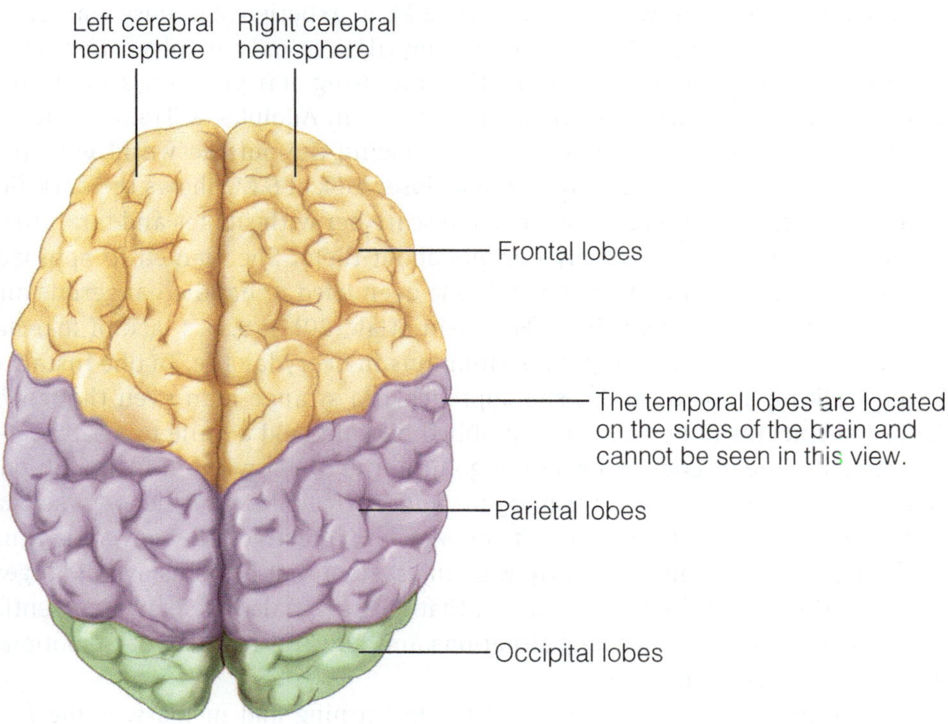

FIGURE 2.12

The Cerebral Hemispheres

The brain is divided into right and left hemispheres. The outside covering of the hemispheres, the cortex, is where the higher-order processing in the brain takes place.

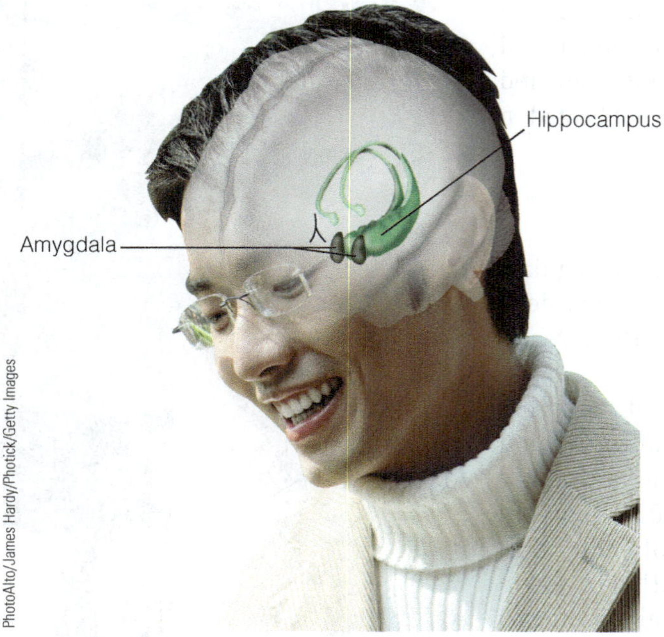

FIGURE 2.13

The Limbic System

Limbic system structures, including the amygdala and the hippocampus, process specific aspects of emotion and memory.

abnormal patterns of amygdala activation when perceiving fear in other people's faces (Aoki, Cortese, & Tansella, 2015; Ashwin et al., 2006). Furthermore, researchers have found that the severity of one's ASD symptoms is related to differences in both the size of the amygdala and the pattern of neural connections found between the amygdala and specific regions of the cortex (Gibbard et al., 2018). These findings suggest that dysfunction in the amygdala may prevent people with ASD from correctly perceiving people's emotions, frequently resulting in awkward social interactions with others. A complete lack of functioning in the amygdala can lead to even bigger problems.

Although we may admire people for being "fearless," the case of a woman known as S.M. (Feinstein et al., 2011) illustrates the important role that fear can play in our lives. S.M.'s amygdala was destroyed by a brain disease, leaving her unable to experience the emotion of fear when she encounters what most of us would consider frightening situations. In more than two decades of studying S.M., researchers have never documented a single instance in which, as an adult, she has been frightened by something she encountered. She is also unable to recognize fear in others' facial expressions. Yet, astoundingly, while S.M. cannot be frightened by things she experiences in the world, she can still experience fear that is caused by sensations emanating from inside her own body (e.g., feeling as if she cannot breathe). Such feelings actually cause S.M. to experience intense fear. S.M.'s case brings up the possibility that the amygdala is only involved in fear responses to the outside world and that the processing of frightening stimuli from inside the body bypasses the amygdala (Feinstein, Adolphs, & Tranel, 2016).

hippocampus [HIP-po-CAM-puss] a part of the brain that plays a role in the transfer of information from short- to long-term memory

▲ The amygdala plays a role in the experience of fear. Without a functioning amygdala, S.M. is unable to feel fear in most situations.

On the surface, you might think that facing the outside world with perpetual fearlessness is a good thing, but a closer look at S.M. shows the dark side of fearlessness. When researchers tried to scare her with snakes and tarantulas, she was unafraid and intensely curious about them. She wanted to approach animals that many of us would avoid. She even tried to handle dangerous animals despite repeated warnings (Feinstein et al., 2011). S.M.'s lack of fear has also led her to approach dangerous situations in everyday life. In one instance, while walking alone at night, she approached a strange man even though he looked suspicious to her. The man grabbed her and held a knife to her throat—yet she felt no fear. Luckily he let her go unharmed, but without fear, S.M. will likely find herself in harm's way again and again. S.M.'s case shows us that although fear may be unpleasant, it can also be protective. The amygdala functions as part of an emotional early warning system that helps us avoid dangers in the world. Studies like these suggest that the amygdala may play an essential role in helping us size up social situations and, in turn, regulate our emotional reactions to these situations.

The **hippocampus**, a structure related to learning and memory, is the final structure of the limbic system that we will describe (Figure 2.13). Much of what we know about the function of the hippocampus comes from case studies of people who have had damage to their hippocampus. One of the first of these studies dates from the early 1950s. Scoville and Milner (1957) reported the case of H.M., a young man with severe, uncontrollable epilepsy. H.M.'s epilepsy did not respond to medication and threatened his health as well as his lifestyle. In a last-ditch effort to reduce the severity of his seizures, doctors decided to take the drastic measure of destroying part of H.M.'s brain with surgically produced lesions. The doctors cut neurons in the limbic system, hoping to check the uncontrolled electrical current that occurs when a person with epilepsy has a seizure. The surgery performed on H.M. destroyed his hippocampus.

The surgery did reduce the intensity of H.M.'s seizures, but it also produced some unexpected and devastating side effects. Shortly after the surgery, it became apparent that H.M. had *anterograde amnesia,* the inability to store *new* memories (Chapter 7). He could hold information in consciousness the way we briefly hold a phone number in mind while we dial, and his memory for events that occurred prior to the surgery remained intact, but H.M. was unable to form new memories for concepts and events. He would forget conversations seconds after they occurred. For the rest of his life, H. M., who died in 2008, was unable to learn new facts. Oddly, though, he could store new motor skills (for example, he could learn new dance steps), but later he would have no recollection of having ever executed the new skill. Imagine waking up one day and knowing how to do a dance that you don't remember ever having danced!

Since H.M.'s surgery, a number of subsequent case studies, quasi-experimental studies, and controlled animal experiments have supported the hypothesis that the hippocampus is important to learning and memory, including tasks that relate to *autobiographical memory* (Bonnici & Maguire, 2018; Maguire, 2014; Chapter 7), imagining the future, and spatial navigation (Maguire & Mullally, 2013). In one important study, researchers used brain-imaging techniques to compare the hippocampi of London taxi drivers with those of London bus drivers. They found that certain areas of the hippocampus were enlarged in the taxi drivers but not in the bus drivers. Furthermore, the number of years a participant had been driving a taxi was positively correlated with the size of certain hippocampal areas. These data suggest that portions of the hippocampus enlarged as the taxi drivers memorized complicated maps of the entire city. For bus drivers, who only had to memorize a small number of bus routes, length of time driving did not correlate with the size of their hippocampus (Maguire, Woollett, & Spiers, 2006).

Researchers then compared the hippocampi of medical doctors, who also have to learn vast amounts of information, with those of people of similar intelligence who were not doctors. They found no difference in the size of the hippocampus between these two groups, suggesting that having a larger hippocampus is only associated with performing tasks that specifically involve spatial memory (Woollett, Glensman, & Maguire, 2008).

However, at least one study suggests that we may need to look more closely to see changes in the hippocampus during other types of learning. When medical students who underwent 14 weeks of intensive academic learning were compared to control participants over the same period of time, an increase in gray matter (unmyelinated neurons) was seen on the left side of the hippocampus, but not on the right side (Koch, Reess, Rus, & Zimmer, 2015). Collectively, such studies suggest

Dinendra Haria/Shutterstock.com

▲ Researchers (Maguire, Woollett, & Spiers, 2006) found that some regions of the hippocampus in London taxi drivers were larger than the same hippocampal regions in the brains of London bus drivers. These results suggest that certain regions of the hippocampus may enlarge as a cab driver uses their brain to memorize complicated street maps of an entire city such as London.

neuroplasticity [NUR-o-plas-TI-city] the nervous system's ability to rewire its structures as a result of experience

thalamus [THAL-uh-muss] a part of the forebrain that functions as a sensory relay station

hypothalamus [high-poe-THAL-uh-muss] a part of the forebrain that plays a role in maintaining homeostasis in the body, involving sleep, body temperature, sexual behavior, thirst, and hunger; also the point where the nervous system intersects with the endocrine system

homeostasis [hoe-mee-oh-STAY-suss] an internal state of equilibrium in the body

that the hippocampus exhibits **neuroplasticity**—the brain's ability to rewire its structures as a result of experience (see also Woollett & Maguire, 2012).

Unfortunately, the brain's ability to be changed by experience may not always be a good thing. Studies have shown that certain hormones released during times of stress can damage hippocampal tissue (Hawley & Leasure, 2012; Tata & Anderson, 2009) and that people who have experienced prolonged stress (such as combat or childhood abuse) have smaller hippocampi (Sapolsky, 2002). At first glance, the conclusion looked simple—stress shrinks the hippocampus. However, it's not that simple. One study found that combat veterans with *posttraumatic stress disorder* (Chapter 13) had smaller hippocampi—but so did their identical twin brothers who had never faced combat. This finding suggests that having a smaller hippocampus to begin with may predispose one to developing posttraumatic stress (Bonne et al., 2008; Childress et al., 2013; Gilbertson et al., 2002). In one study, relative to nonstressed animals, stressed animals exhibited a greater decrease in hippocampal volume throughout a 10-day period. Furthermore, animals that were the first to exhibit hippocampal shrinkage during the 10-day period were also the ones that exhibited the greatest memory problems at the end of the study. This led the researchers to suggest that smaller hippocampal volume earlier in life may be a risk factor for developing later stress-related mental health issues (Rahman et al., 2016). Given that life is often stressful and stress damages the hippocampus, possibly predisposing us to later mental health issues, how can we protect ourselves?

In one study, researchers found that people who practice meditation tend to have larger hippocampi than those of nonmeditators (Luders et al., 2013). In another study, memory improvements following 4 weeks of *mindfulness* training (a type of meditation when practiced formally) were found to be correlated with increases in the size of the left hippocampus (Greenberg et al., 2018). Because meditation is effective in relieving stress and having a small hippocampus is associated with mental health issues, studies like these bring up the question of whether meditation and mindfulness may protect us via their effects on the hippocampus. Clearly, more research is needed to answer this question, but, as we'll see in Chapter 12, meditation may be a beneficial activity to consider.

The Thalamus and Hypothalamus

The *thalamus* and *hypothalamus* of the forebrain may have similar names, but they have distinctly different functions. The **thalamus** plays a role in the attention we pay to things that stimulate our senses (Michael et al., 2001; Saalmann & Kastner, 2009), and it functions as a relay station for information coming from our senses to the brain (see Chapter 3).

The thalamus also plays a role in keeping specific areas of the cortex activated during rapid eye movement (REM) sleep, when much of our dreaming occurs (Miyauchi et al., 2009; Murillo-Rodriguez et al., 2009). The thalamus has also been shown to affect slow-wave activity during non-REM sleep (Connelly & Errington, 2012). We will discuss the process of sleep in more detail in Chapter 4.

Nestled below the thalamus is the **hypothalamus** (the prefix *hypo* means "below"). The hypothalamus maintains **homeostasis** in the body, a state of internal equilibrium across a variety of bodily systems (Makris et al., 2013). In maintaining homeostasis, the hypothalamus is responsible for monitoring and regulating body temperature, thirst, hunger, sleep, autonomic nervous system functioning, some sexual and reproductive functions, and can change hormone levels in the bloodstream. To maintain homeostasis, the hypothalamus must ultimately motivate us to engage in certain behaviors. For example, when our body needs fuel, the hypothalamus motivates us with hunger. When we need sleep, the hypothalamus makes us sleepy, and we are motivated to go to bed. No other part of the nervous system plays a more central role in physiological motivation, a topic we will return to in Chapters 4 and 5. Without the hypothalamus, we would not know when to engage in the behaviors that keep our bodily systems in balance.

frontal lobe the cortical area directly behind the forehead that plays a role in thinking, planning, decision making, language, and motor movement

parietal [puh-RYE-it-ull] lobe the cortical area on the top sides of the brain that play a role in touch and certain cognitive processes

occipital [ox-SIP-it-ull] lobe the cortical area at the back of the brain that plays a role in visual processing

temporal [TEM-por-ull] lobe the cortical area directly below the ears that plays a role in auditory processing and language

2.4.4 The Cortex

The most noticeable structure on the external surface of the brain is the *cerebral cortex*, or simply the cortex. The cortex is the thin (approximately 2 mm thick), wrinkled layer of tissue that covers the outside of the cerebral hemispheres, or the two sides of the brain (● FIGURE 2.14). The cortex is arguably the most sophisticated part of the brain and is responsible for the highest levels of processing: cognition and mental processes such as planning, decision making, perception, and language. It is the cortex that gives us our humanness. It is no coincidence that the human cortex is the most developed one among all known creatures and that humans also have the most highly developed cognitive skills of all known species. Compare the photographs in Figure 2.14. Notice that the human cortex is very folded and convoluted, whereas the cat's cortex is much less so. The folds allow for more cortical surface area within the confines of the skull cavity. A cat has proportionately less cortical area than a human does, and this smaller cortex translates into fewer cognitive abilities for the cat.

The Lobes of the Cortex and Lateralization in the Brain

The human cortex is divided into four distinct physical regions called *lobes*. These are the **frontal lobe**, the **parietal lobe**, the **occipital lobe**, and the **temporal lobe** (● FIGURE 2.15a). The lobes of the cortex are structurally symmetrical in the two hemispheres of the brain, meaning that the brain has both right and left frontal lobes, right and left temporal lobes, and so on. However, the functions of the right and left lobes are often somewhat different. Functions are lateralized, or found in only one hemisphere of the brain, for a couple of reasons. First, the lobes of the brain tend to be wired in a *contralateral* fashion, with the right side of the brain governing the left side of the body and the left side of the brain governing the right side of the body. Although contralateral wiring is the norm in the brain, some neural pathways carry information to and from the body to the same hemisphere of the brain.

Lateralization in the brain is also evident in that the right and left hemispheres process somewhat different types of information (Gotts et al., 2013; Stephan et al., 2003). For example, most people process language largely in the left hemisphere. Although some people have major language centers in the right hemisphere, and some have major language centers in both hemispheres, for the average person language is located in the left hemisphere. As a result, when people incur major damage to the left hemisphere (as from a stroke), their ability to use language often suffers, a condition known as *aphasia*.

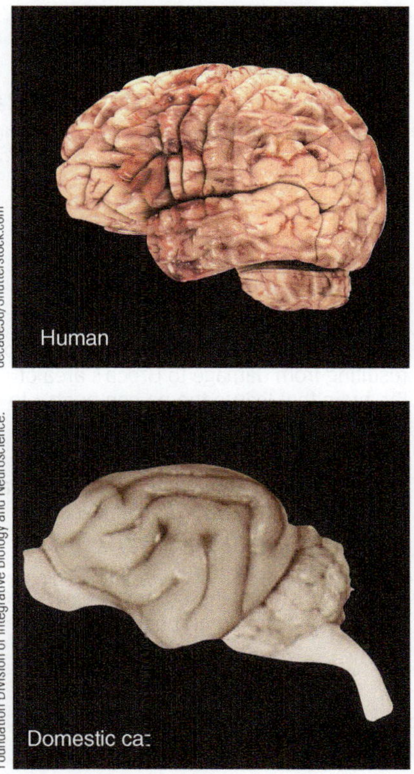

FIGURE 2.14

Cortex of a Human Brain and a Cat Brain

Note how much more convoluted, or folded, the human brain is compared to the cat brain. Many of the higher-order processes that humans engage in, such as language and thinking, are processed in the cortex.

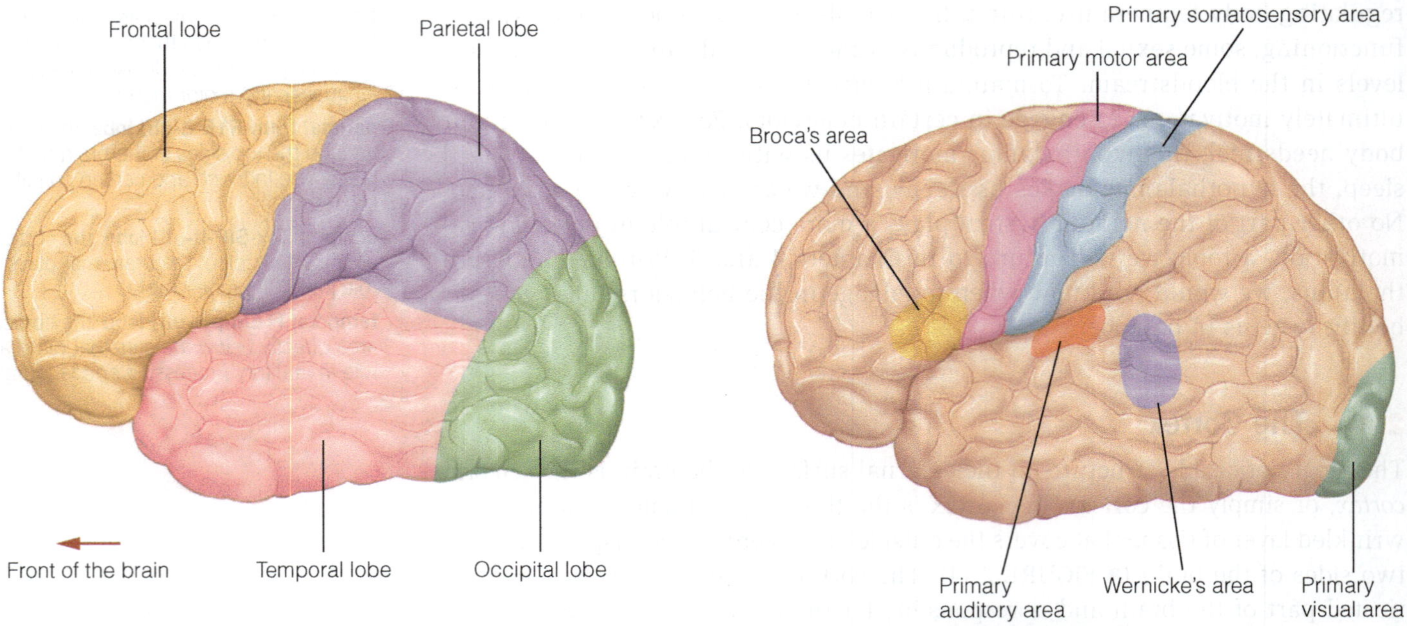

(a) Lobes of the brain (left hemisphere)

(b) Primary motor-sensory areas of the cortex

FIGURE 2.15

The Human Brain

(a) The lobes of the brain. (b) The language centers of the brain are generally found in the left hemisphere. Wernicke's area in the left temporal lobe allows us to comprehend speech. Broca's area in the left frontal lobe allows us to produce speech.

Broca's [BRO-kuz] area a region in the left frontal lobe that plays a role in the production of speech

Broca's aphasia [ah-FAYZ-yah] a condition resulting from damage to Broca's area of the brain that leaves the person unable to produce speech

Wernicke's [WURR-neh-kees] area a region of the left temporal lobe that plays a role in the comprehension of speech

Wernicke's aphasia [ah-FAYZ-yah] a condition resulting from damage to Wernicke's area of the brain that leaves a person unable to comprehend speech

Two examples illustrate this hemispheric specialization of language. When damage is severe in **Broca's area** in the left frontal lobe (Figure 2.15b), people are unable to produce understandable speech, a condition known as **Broca's aphasia** or *expressive aphasia* (Geschwind, 1975; Geschwind & Levitsky, 1968). When people have damage to **Wernicke's area** in the left temporal lobe (Figure 2.15b), the resulting **Wernicke's aphasia** (also called *receptive aphasia*) leaves them unable to understand spoken language. When the damage is confined to the right side of the brain, people usually remain able to understand and produce speech, but they have some difficulty processing certain types of spatial information, such as visually searching for a target stimulus on a computer screen or mentally constructing coherent visual scenes (Irish et al., 2017; Rastelli et al., 2013).

Overt differences in the linguistic and spatial processing of the left and right hemispheres once led scientists to conclude broadly that the hemispheres of the brain processed very different categories of information: They surmised that the left hemisphere processed verbal information and the right hemisphere processed spatial information. However, more recent studies have suggested that the left and right hemispheres of the brain may not divide up their functions as neatly as once thought. For example, early in life, language is processed in both hemispheres, and it is only as we mature that many language functions are relegated to the left hemisphere (Friederici, Brauer, & Lohmann, 2011). In fact, a review of the research suggests that hemispheric lateralization in general is a *graded* rather than an absolute process that emerges as the brain develops (Behrmann & Plaut, 2015). This gradation can be seen in the adult brain where much linguistic processing occurs in the left hemisphere, but subtle aspects of language, such as processing of certain metaphors, occur on the right side of the brain (Mashal & Faust, 2008; Segal, Mashal, & Shalev, 2017). In short, we are coming to understand that the two hemispheres accomplish tasks by working together and performing complementary functions.

Variations: Are Women's Brains Less Lateralized Than Men's Are?

Whether the hemispheres process different information or merely different aspects of the same information, they must have some means of coordinating the information they process. The **corpus callosum** is a dense band of neurons that sits just below the cortex along the midline of the brain (Banich & Heller, 1998; Figure 2.11). This band physically connects the right and left cortical areas and ensures that each hemisphere "knows" what the other hemisphere is doing. The corpus callosum passes information back and forth between the right and left hemispheres, allowing us to integrate these somewhat independent functions. Without the corpus callosum, the right and left cortices would function independently and in ignorance of each other.

corpus callosum [COR-puss cal-OH-sum] a thick band of neurons that connects the right and left hemispheres of the brain

Several studies suggest that even when taking into account the fact that women tend to have smaller overall brain volumes than men, they tend to have larger corpus callosa (plural of callosum) (Newman, 2016; Tanaka-Arakawa et al., 2015). Having a larger corpus callosum may allow for more connections between hemispheres, resulting in a brain that is less lateralized and more integrated (Reite et al., 1995). This interpretation is supported by the finding that the pattern of electrical activity in male brains tends to be more confined to one hemisphere than it is in female brains (Koles, Lind, & Flor-Henry, 2010; Tomasi & Volkow, 2012).

However, the implications of callosal size on brain lateralization are still being debated (for a review, see Ocklenburg et al., 2016). Some have argued that increased communication between hemispheres, such as may be facilitated by a larger corpus callosum, might actually *increase* lateralization in the brain (Kimura, 2000). Indeed, one study found that participants with damage to the corpus callosum exhibited *more* ambidextrousness (not being right- or left-handed), suggesting *less* lateralization of the hemispheres coinciding with *smaller* callosa (Ocklenburg et al., 2015).

Some have argued that we might be taking an overly simplistic view of the brain when looking for associations between the size of one's corpus callosum and the degree to which one's brain is lateralized. These researchers argue that the corpus callosum is just one of several influences on brain lateralization and that factors such as the efficiency of neural networks within the brain may also impact lateralization (Ocklenburg et al., 2016). Although a clear picture of sex differences in the corpus callosum and brain lateralization has not yet emerged, psychologists do have a much clearer understanding of what happens to the brain when the corpus callosum fails to do its job.

The Split Brain

Physicians have at times willfully disrupted communication between the hemispheres by destroying the corpus callosum in the human brain. Such a drastic measure is taken in cases where people have severe, uncontrollable epilepsy. In severe epilepsy, abnormal electrical activity can build up in one hemisphere and spread across the corpus callosum to engulf the opposite hemisphere. This short-circuiting of both hemispheres produces a severe, life-threatening seizure called a *grand mal seizure*. If drugs cannot control the seizures, surgery may be

split brain a brain with its corpus callosum severed; sometimes done to control the effects of epilepsy in people who do not respond to other therapies

performed to cut the corpus callosum and thereby contain the short-circuiting to one hemisphere only. The person still has seizures, but they are not as severe. People who have had this surgery are referred to as having a **split brain** because their hemispheres are no longer connected by neural pathways. People with split brains provide scientists with an opportunity to study the lateralization of the brain.

Working with people who have split brains, researchers have a chance to study the functioning of each hemisphere independent of the other. For example, split-brain research helped researchers conclude that the left hemisphere enables us to produce speech. Researcher Michael Gazzaniga (1967) briefly flashed pictures of familiar objects to the right and left visual fields of people with split brains and asked them to identify the objects (●FIGURE 2.16). When an object is briefly presented to the right peripheral field of vision, the resulting visual information is sent directly to the left hemisphere of the brain. Because Broca's area is in the left hemisphere for most people, Gazzaniga found that the average person with a split brain could verbally identify the object.

But what about an object presented to the person's left peripheral field of vision? When an object is briefly shown on the far left side, the resulting visual information is sent directly to the right hemisphere of the brain. Recall that most people do not have a Broca's area in their right hemisphere. In an intact brain, the information travels from the right hemisphere across the corpus callosum to the language centers in the left hemisphere. However, in individuals with split brains, this cannot happen. Without the corpus callosum, these people could not transmit the knowledge of what they were seeing to the language centers in their left hemisphere. The right brain knew what the objects were, but it could not inform the "speaking" left brain! Predictably, the people with split brains were unable to name the objects they saw in their left visual fields. Interestingly, in this situation, people with split brains were able to point to the objects in a drawing—provided they used their left hand (which is controlled by the right brain). Split-brain research

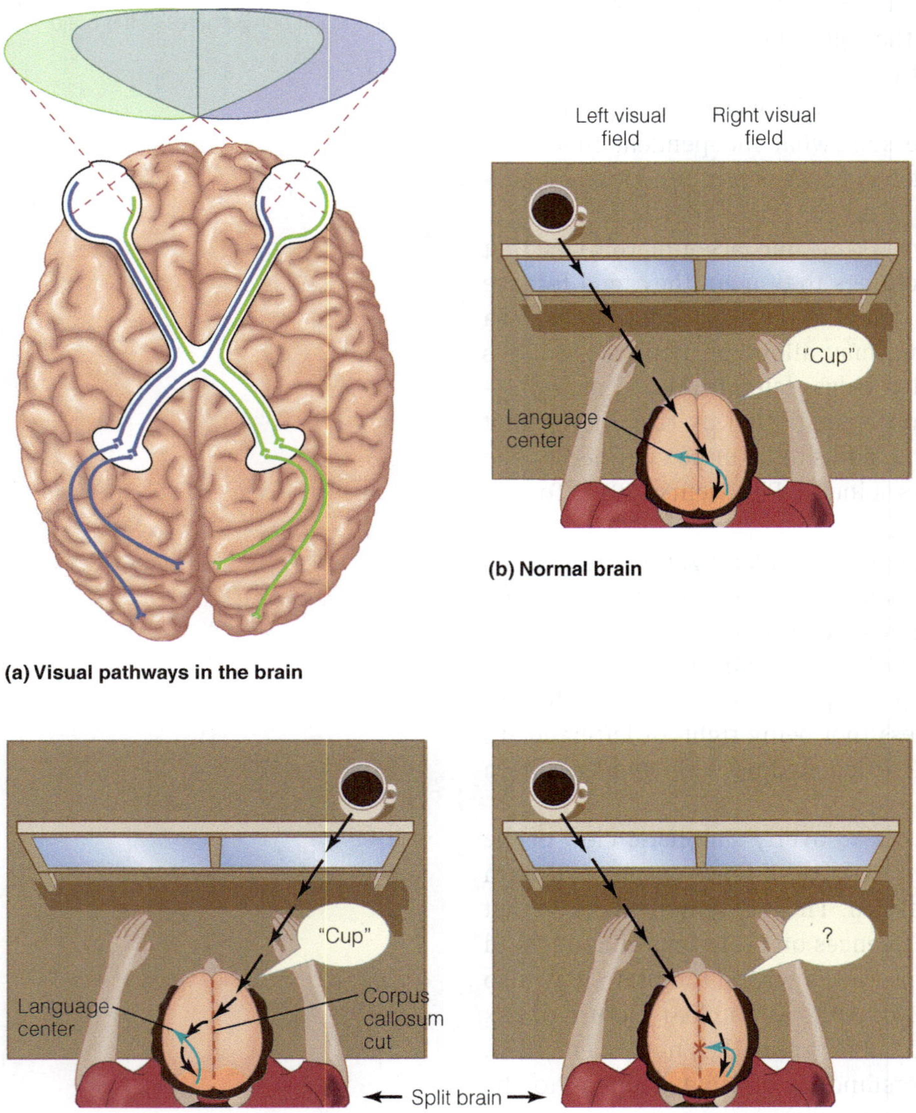

(a) Visual pathways in the brain

(b) Normal brain

(c) Split brain

FIGURE 2.16

A Typical Split-Brain Study

Visual pathways in the intact brain (a) send information to both hemispheres. As a result, when a person with an intact brain sees an object in either their right or left visual field, they will be able to name it (b). However, this is not true for people with split brains. In a typical split-brain experiment (c), an image is flashed to the right or left visual field of a person who has a split-brain, and they are asked to identify the object in the image. When the image is flashed to the person's right visual field, they are able to name it; but when it is flashed to their left visual field, they are unable to name it because the information cannot travel to the language centers in the left hemisphere.

has helped us begin to sort out the relative contributions that the right and left hemispheres make to everyday cognitive processes.

2.4.5 The Specialization of Function in the Lobes of the Cortex

Just as there is specialization in the hemispheres of the brain, there is also specialization within the different lobes of the brain. About 25% of the total surface area of the cortex is dedicated to motor and sensory functions such as vision, hearing, movement, and tactile sensation. Specific motor–sensory areas can be found in all the lobes of the brain (frontal, parietal, occipital, and temporal). The remaining 75% of the cortical area is thought to be devoted to higher-order processes that involve the integration of information, such as thinking, planning, decision making, and language. Collectively, this 75% is referred to as the **association cortex** because these areas are presumed to involve the association of information from the motor–sensory areas of the cortex.

association cortex areas of the cortex involved in the association or integration of information from the motor–sensory areas of the cortex

We do not yet have a complete understanding of the functions of specific areas of the association cortex. Often, damage to the association areas produces general changes and deficits in behavior. However, stimulation of specific areas of the association cortex does not usually lead to specific, predictable physical reactions. It is thought that the association cortex plays a role in general cognition, such as planning and decision making. Where applicable, we will discuss the known functions of the association areas for the specific lobes of the brain.

The Frontal Lobe

The frontal lobe is the area of the cortex that lies closest to the forehead (refer back to Figure 2.15a). Much of the frontal lobe is association cortex. We know more about the association areas of the frontal lobe than any other lobes. Broca's area in the association area of the left frontal lobe is, as previously mentioned, involved in the production of speech. It also appears that the frontal lobe association areas play a role in cognitive processes such as attention, problem solving, judgment, the planning and executing of behavior, and certain aspects of personality.

These cognitive functions are illustrated in a famous case study from the history of psychology. In 1848, a railway worker named Phineas Gage suffered severe trauma to his *prefrontal cortex* (the association area in the very front part of the frontal lobe) when a metal rod was shot through his head in an explosion. The rod entered his left cheek and shot out of the top of his head, damaging his left frontal cortex and profoundly altering communication within systems in his brain (Van Horn et al., 2012). Although he survived his injuries, they resulted in some dramatic personality changes (Harlow, 1868/1869). Although Gage had been a calm, responsible man prior to his injuries, he became impulsive, emotionally volatile, and irresponsible afterward. Because the prefrontal cortex is important for the regulation of emotion (Davidson, Putman, & Larson, 2000), the damage to Gage's brain robbed him of his ability to control his emotions, make good judgments, and execute planned behaviors (Damasio et al., 1994). The degree to which this disrupted his life is something of a historical debate. Some argue that Gage adjusted fairly well to his disabilities, citing evidence that Gage held a series of jobs after his accident, including working as a stagecoach driver in Chile (Macmillan & Lena, 2010), but other accounts suggest that lingering impairments caused substantial adjustment issues for Gage (Harlow, 1868/1869).

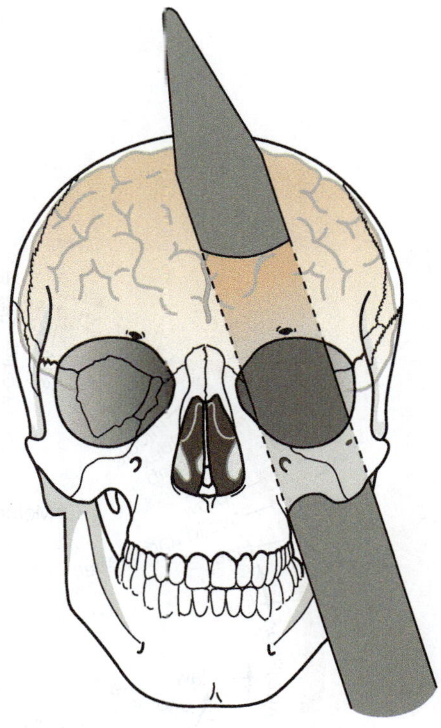

▲ Phineas Gage was a responsible, mild-mannered worker on a railway construction crew until a rod like this one was shot through his head in a freak accident. Gage survived, but he was never the same. The damage to Gage's prefrontal cortex coincided with dramatic changes in his personality. The once calm Gage became emotionally volatile and difficult. As a result, he was unable to perform his former job with the railroad.

primary motor area a strip of cortex at the back of the frontal lobe that governs the execution of motor movement in the body

At the back of the frontal lobe (behind the prefrontal cortex) lies the **primary motor area,** a narrow band of cortex that allows us to execute motor movements. The primary motor area on the right side of the brain affects movement on the left side of the body, and vice versa. Additionally, specific points along the primary motor area correspond to particular points on the body. • FIGURE 2.17a is a rendering of the motor *homunculus,* a humorous mapping of body parts onto their appropriate motor cortical points. If stimulation were applied to these points along the primary motor area, the result would be movement of the corresponding body part.

As you can see, the frontal lobe plays several roles in our daily functioning. Curiously, the frontal lobe is also an area of the brain that experiences changes across adulthood. We will discuss changes in the aging brain later in this section.

The Parietal Lobe

As with the frontal lobe, much of the parietal lobe is association cortex, but we know much less about the specific functions of these association areas. We do know that the motor–sensory areas of the parietal lobe play a role in sensation. A thin strip of the parietal lobe affects our sense of touch, pressure, and pain. This

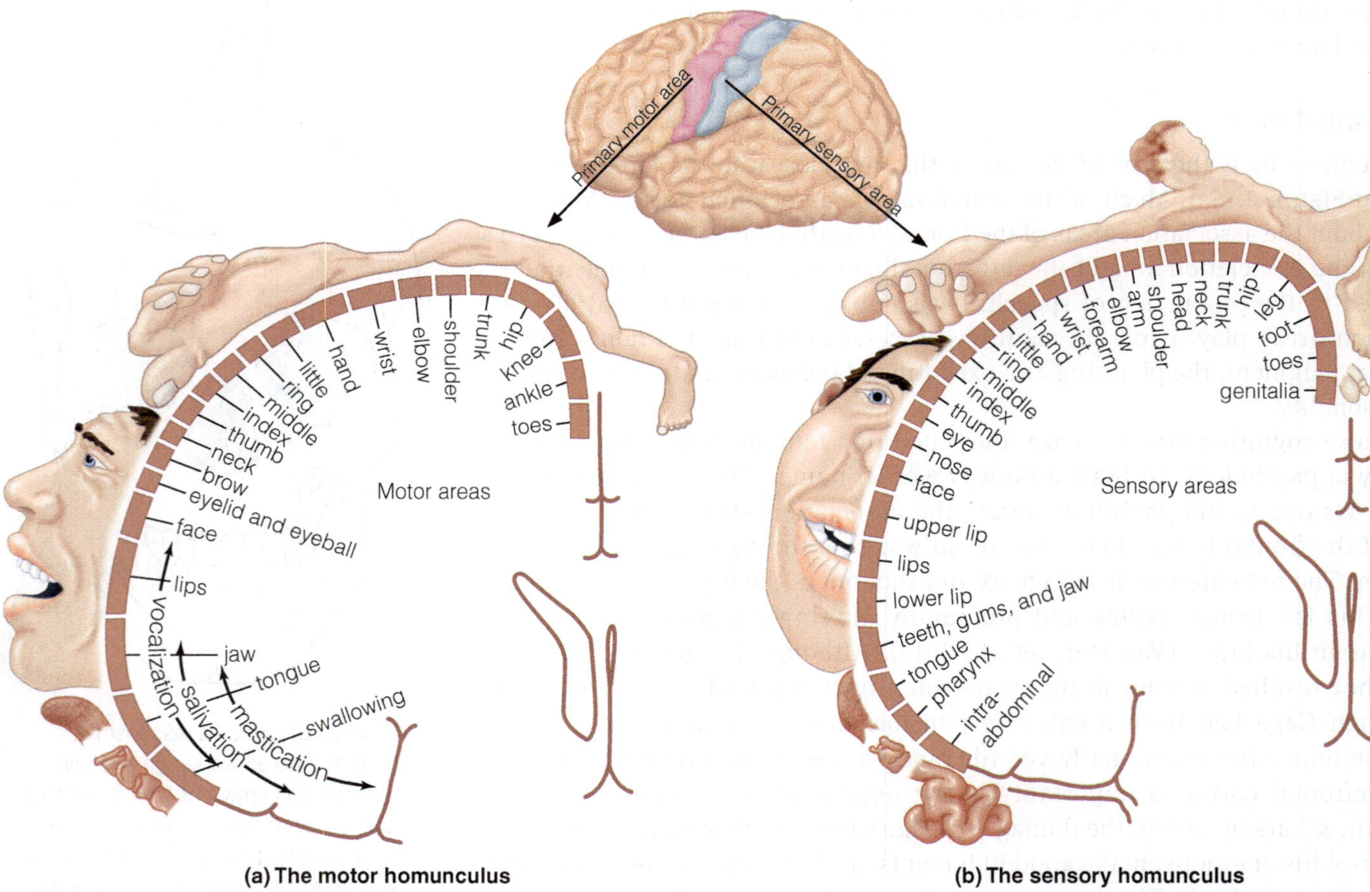

FIGURE 2.17

Motor and Sensory Homunculi

Homunculi are humorous depictions of the localization of function on the cortex.

From Penfield and Rasmussen, *The Cerebral Cortex of Man*, © 1950 Macmillan Library Reference. Renewed 1978 by Theodore Rasmussen.

strip, called the **primary somatosensory area,** lies directly behind the primary motor area, along the leading edge of the parietal lobe (Figure 2.15b). The primary somatosensory area is wired much like the primary motor area, and specific points along the primary somatosensory area correspond to particular points on the body (Figure 2.17b). Damage to the primary somatosensory area often results in numbness of the corresponding body part.

primary somatosensory [so-MAT-oh-SEN-sor-ee] area a strip of cortex at the front of the parietal lobe that governs the sense of touch

primary visual area a region of cortex found at the back of the occipital lobe that processes visual information in the brain

auditory cortex a region of cortex found in the temporal lobe that governs the processing of auditory information in the brain

The Occipital Lobe

The occipital lobe of the brain is located at the very back of the skull, above the cerebellum. Much of the occipital lobe is dedicated to processing visual information. The **primary visual area** (Figure 2.15b), of the occipital lobe is composed of layers of tissue that contain long axonal fibers. An action potential is stimulated in specialized cells of the primary visual area when our eyes receive specific types of visual stimuli from the outside world. For instance, some cells begin to fire only when we see lines, and other cells fire only when we see circular shapes. Like a computer, our brain integrates all the incoming neural impulses from these specialized cells in the primary visual area to enable us to perceive what we are viewing. Without the operation of the primary visual area, our brain could not make sense of what our eyes see and we would be functionally blind.

The Temporal Lobe

The temporal lobe is in front of the occipital lobe and just below the parietal and frontal lobes—roughly behind our ears inside the skull. Not surprisingly, one of the major functions of the temporal lobe is the processing of auditory information, or hearing. The temporal lobe area devoted to hearing is the **auditory cortex**, or *primary auditory area,* located on the upper edge of the temporal lobe (Figure 2.15b). In addition to the auditory cortex, the left temporal lobe of most people contains Wernicke's area. As we've already seen, Wernicke's area is responsible for the comprehension of speech. Persons who have major damage to Wernicke's area often cannot understand the meaning of spoken words. They hear the words, but they can't make sense of them.

Variations: The Aging Brain

As you just learned, the cortex of the brain is where some of our most important mental functioning takes place. Our ability to think, remember, and make sense of the world is due, in large part, to the cortex. However, many studies suggest that as we age, we tend to experience specific declines in our ability to do some mental or cognitive tasks (see Chapters 7, 8, and 9). For example, when compared to young adults, older adults tend to score lower on tests of *fluid intelligence,* the ability to process information rapidly and efficiently (Yu et al., 2009). Some capacities, such as the ability to learn new faces, can peak as early as our 30s (Germine, Duchaine, & Nakayama, 2011). But why do we perform more poorly as we age? What's happening in our brains?

A number of changes occur in our brains as we age. For example, certain brain structures shrink (Peng et al., 2016), lesions develop (Bohnen et al., 2009), and changes in neuronal functioning occur (Andrews-Hanna et al., 2007). Blood flow in the brain also changes as we age. Researchers compared the brains of

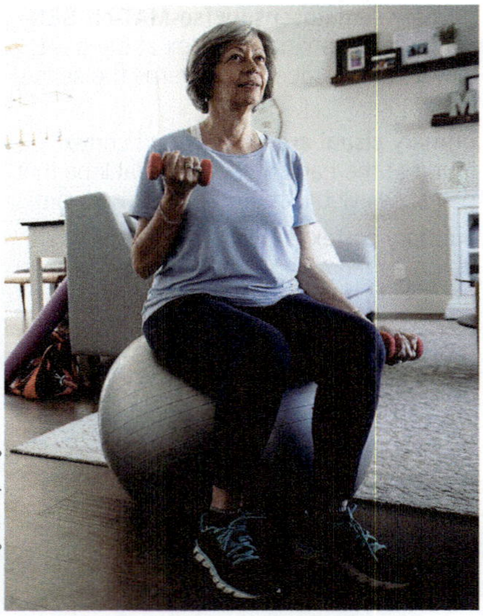

Hero Images/Getty Images

▲ Exercise helps to maintain blood flow in the brain, and it may be one way to help us retain as many of our cognitive abilities as we can in the future.

healthy people ages 20–80 and found that blood flow to the brain diminished about 1.38% per decade. The amount of oxygen carried in the blood also declined by about 1.4% per decade. Interestingly, some areas of the brain experienced more loss of blood flow than others did. Especially hard hit were the right frontal regions of the brain, including the prefrontal cortex (Lu et al., 2011). Better blood flow deep within the brain has also been shown to be associated with higher scores on tests of fluid intelligence (Angel et al., 2018).

Given that blood flow to the brain is fed by the same circulatory system that feeds the body, it is reasonable to expect that keeping our cardiovascular system in good shape may also help our brain. This may be especially true as we age because as the brain gets older, it needs more oxygen to function normally (Lu et al., 2011). Therefore, regular exercise may be one of our most powerful tools for protecting the aging brain (Anderson, Greenwood, & McCloskey, 2010) and maintaining our cognitive abilities (Duzel, van Praag, & Sendtner, 2016; Jedrziewski et al., 2010). So, if you haven't already done so, perhaps now would be a good time to develop an exercise program. Your physician can evaluate your situation and suggest an appropriate level of activity for your age and physical condition.

2.4 Quiz Yourself

1. **Damage to which of the following brain structures would be most likely to cause locked-in syndrome, such as seen in the case of Jean-Dominique Bauby?**
   a. Occipital lobe
   b. Amygdala
   c. Pons
   d. Hippocampus
2. **Billy had a stroke on the left side of his brain. Most of his left frontal lobe was destroyed. What symptoms would you most expect to see in Billy as a result of this damage?**
   a. Paralysis on the right side of his body and an inability to speak
   b. Paralysis on the right side of his body and an inability to understand speech
   c. Paralysis of his left leg, partial deafness, and stuttering
   d. Paralysis on the left side of his body and an inability to understand speech
3. **Isabel experienced a brain injury that left her with an inability to store new memories for events and concepts. Which part of Isabel's brain was most likely damaged?**
   a. Hippocampus
   b. Hypothalamus
   c. Thalamus
   d. Pons
4. **Bauby's story is an example of a(n) __________ and as such, it is of limited scientific usefulness because __________.**
   a. experiment; it has too many confounding variables
   b. correlational study; it lacks a dependent variable
   c. case study; it lacks generalizability
   d. experiment; it lacks an independent variable

Answers 1. c; 2. a; 3. a; 4. c

2.5 Technologies for Studying the Brain

Both physicians and psychologists use various technologies for studying the brain. Some of these procedures allow researchers to examine only the structure of the brain, whereas others indicate which areas of the brain are most active at a given moment. Because these techniques can be used on living brain tissue, they can give researchers important information about the specific behavioral functions that are governed by particular areas of the brain. ● TABLE 2.1 summarizes some of the most useful technologies available for helping us to better understand the inner workings of the brain: *CAT* or *CT scans, MRIs, PET scans, fMRIs, EEGs,* and *brain stimulation.*

TABLE 2.1 Common Techniques for Studying the Brain and Examples of Their Usage

Technique for Studying the Brain	Description	Aspect Measured
Computerized Axial Tomography (CAT or Computed Tomography [CT] Scan) 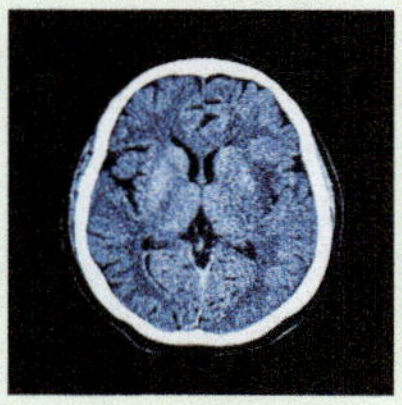 Puwadol Jaturawutthichai/ Shutterstock.com	Multiple X-ray beams are passed through the brain from different angles. A computer then analyzes the X-rays that exit the head and uses this information to build a very detailed picture of the brain and its structures. CAT scans can be used to diagnose tumors, strokes, certain diseases, and the structural features of the brain.	Brain structures
Magnetic Resonance Imaging (MRI) 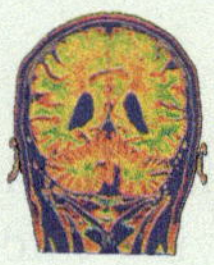 S&I/Science Source	A magnetic field is used to excite the atoms in the body, and the energy emitted by these atoms is used to construct a highly detailed computer-generated picture of the brain's structure.	Brain structures
Positron Emission Tomography (PET Scan) 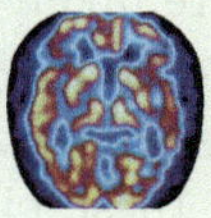 Tim Beddow/ Science Source	Radioactive glucose (the brain's fuel source) is injected into the bloodstream. The computer measures which areas of the brain are consuming the most glucose, meaning that they are most active.	Areas of activity in the brain
Functional MRI (fMRI) 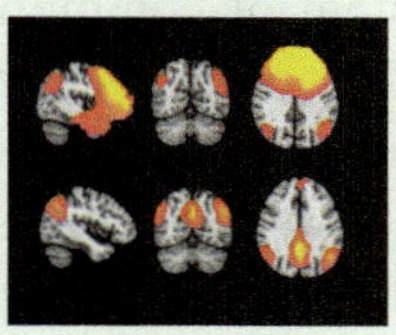 James King-Holmes/ Henry Luckhoo/Science Source	MRI technology tracks which neurons in the brain are most active at a given moment by examining the energy released by hemoglobin molecules in the bloodstream.	Areas of activity in the brain; brain structures
Electroencephalography (EEG) 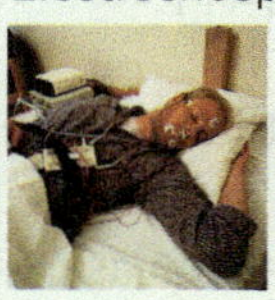 CC Studio/Science Source	Changes in electrical voltage are measured at points along the scalp, yielding information on gross patterns of brain activation.	Patterns of electrical activity in the lobes of the brain
Brain Stimulation 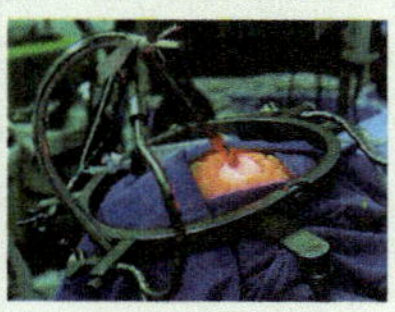 NASA/Hulton Archive/ Getty Images	By stimulating specific areas of the brain, researchers can see what effect this stimulation has on behavior. Doctors also use this technology to treat conditions such as depression. By implanting brain "pacemakers," doctors can stimulate areas of the brain that are not functioning properly.	Cognitive and behavioral reactions to stimulation of brain locations

2.5 Quiz Yourself

1. **Physicians and researchers often use EEGs on sleeping participants. What is this technology most likely to tell them about the participant's brain?**
   a. It will tell them whether or not some of the brain's structures are malformed.
   b. It will yield a highly detailed picture of the brain's structures.
   c. It will tell them where blood flow is greatest in the brain.
   d. It will show them the patterns of electrical activity in the brain's lobes.
2. **Which of the following technologies for studying the brain is most invasive and therefore used only when absolutely necessary in humans?**
   a. fMRI
   b. Brain stimulation
   c. PET scans
   d. CAT scans
3. **Which of the following techniques for studying the brain does not yield information on the activity that is taking place in the brain?**
   a. MRI
   b. fMRI
   c. PET scan
   d. EEG

Answers 1. d; 2. b; 3. a

2.6 The Endocrine System: Hormones and Behavior

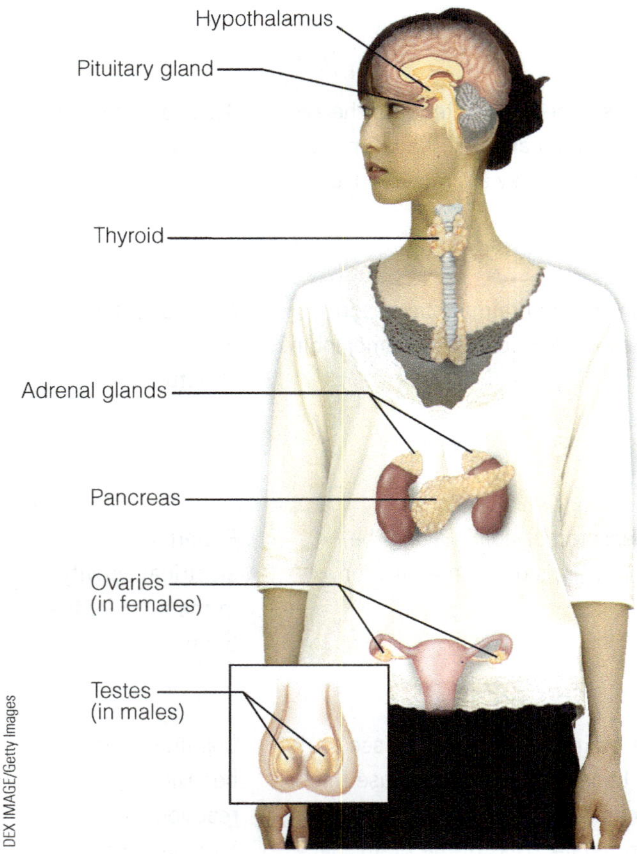

DEX IMAGE/Getty Images

FIGURE 2.18

Major Endocrine Glands of the Body

The glands of the endocrine system make and release hormones into the bloodstream.

We have seen that because of its electrochemical nature, the nervous system is especially good at quickly conveying information within the body. It is the speed of the nervous system that enables us to react quickly to changes in our environment. Messages are sent, decisions are made, and actions are taken—all accomplished with the speed of firing action potentials. At times, however, we require communication within the body that is slower and produces more long-lasting effects. In these circumstances, the **endocrine system** is called into action.

The endocrine system is a chemical system of communication that relies on the action of specialized organs called **endocrine glands**, which are located throughout the body (● FIGURE 2.18). When stimulated, endocrine glands release chemicals called **hormones** into the bloodstream. These hormones circulate through the bloodstream until they reach other organs in the body. Our internal organs are equipped with special receptor sites to accept these hormones.

The endocrine system is considerably slower than the nervous system in relaying messages because it relies on blood circulating through the veins and arteries of the cardiovascular system to transport hormones throughout the body. The stimulation created by hormones, however, tends to last longer than the stimulation caused by action potentials at the synapse. Some of the bodily processes that are heavily influenced by hormonal activity include sexual activity, eating, sleeping, general physiological arousal, and growth.

Communication between the nervous and endocrine systems takes place through the hypothalamus and its connection with the

pituitary gland. The pituitary gland, situated in the vicinity of the limbic system under the hypothalamus (Figure 2.18), is responsible for regulating hormone release in all the other endocrine glands. When the endocrine system is called into action, the hypothalamus sends a signal to the pituitary gland. The pituitary gland then releases hormones that travel through the bloodstream to the other endocrine glands, stimulating them to release the hormones they produce into the bloodstream. These hormones circulate to their target organs, where they bring about specific changes in the functioning of these organs.

Our bodies are equipped with a great number of peripheral endocrine glands (see Figure 2.18). Probably the best-known endocrine glands are the **gonads**, which are necessary for sexuality and reproduction. *Ovaries* are the female gonads, located in the abdominal cavity. Ovaries are directly responsible for the production of female eggs (ova) and the release of female sex hormones, or **estrogens**. *Testes* are the male gonads, located in the testicles. Testes produce male sex cells (sperm) and male hormones, or **androgens**.

The *adrenal glands* sit just above the kidneys in both males and females and are important for regulating arousal and sexual behavior, among many things. When the sympathetic nervous system becomes active during times of stress, the inside of the adrenal glands, or the **adrenal medulla**, releases norepinephrine and epinephrine (also known as *adrenaline*) into the body's bloodstream, where they function as hormones. The sudden flooding of the bloodstream with these hormones causes the familiar sympathetic reactions of fight or flight: increased heart rate, blood pressure, and respiration.

The outside of the adrenal glands, or the **adrenal cortex**, produces *adrenal androgens*, which are male sex hormones found in both males and females. These androgens control many aspects of our sexual characteristics and basic physiological functioning. The adrenal cortex also interacts with the immune system to help protect us from infection and disease.

Other important endocrine glands include the *thyroid*, which regulates how energy is used in our bodies; the *pancreas*, which regulates blood sugar levels in the body (see also Chapter 5); and the *pineal gland*, located in the brain, which may play a role in sexual maturation.

The nervous and endocrine systems are nothing short of amazing in their intricate structure and function. Without these systems we would not be able to control our bodies, think, feel, and interact with our environment. After studying this chapter, we hope you are impressed with the wonder of your own biology. In the next chapter, we will explore the areas of sensation and perception, the study of how we sense and perceive information from the outside world.

endocrine [EN-doe-crin] system a chemical system of communication in the body that uses chemical messengers, called hormones, to affect organ function and behavior

endocrine [EN-doe-crin] glands the organs of the endocrine system that produce and release hormones into the blood

hormones the chemical messengers of the endocrine system

pituitary [peh-TOO-uh-tare-ee] gland the master gland of the endocrine system that controls the action of all other glands in the body

gonads [GO-nads] endocrine glands that directly affect sexual reproduction by producing sperm (testes) or eggs (ovaries)

estrogens [ESS-tro-jens] a class of female sex hormones that regulate many aspects of sexuality and are found in both males and females

androgens [ANN-dro-jens] a class of male hormones that regulate many aspects of sexuality and are found in both males and females

adrenal [uh-DREEN-ull] medulla the center part of the adrenal gland that plays a crucial role in the functioning of the sympathetic nervous system

adrenal cortex the outside part of the adrenal gland that plays a role in the manufacture and release of androgens, and therefore influences sexual characteristics

2.6 Quiz Yourself

1. **The _____ releases male sex hormones in the body.**
   a. adrenal cortex
   b. adrenal medulla
   c. hippocampus
   d. ovary

2. **A malfunction in which of the following endocrine glands would be most disruptive to the overall functioning of the endocrine system?**
   a. Ovaries/testes
   b. Thalamus
   c. Pituitary
   d. Adrenal

3. **Alena was just frightened by a snake. Which of the following endocrine glands most likely played the biggest role in her response to stress?**
   a. Testes
   b. Adrenal cortex
   c. Ovaries
   d. Adrenal medulla

Answers 1. a; 2. c; 3. d

2.7 Integrating Psychology: The Big Picture

In this first chapter on foundations in biological psychology, we covered the field of neuroscience. Neuroscience is the study of the brain and nervous system and the manner in which they influence our mental processes and behavior. Understanding how the brain functions is one of the chief concerns of modern neuroscientists. One could argue that the brain is the most important organ in our bodies, because it is the organ that ultimately controls communication within our bodies via the nervous and endocrine systems. The case study of Jean-Dominique Bauby highlights just how important our brains are to our ability to function. When his brainstem was affected by a stroke, Bauby lost the ability to move most of his body at will. The only part he could still control was his left eye. Yet he managed to communicate with the outside world and to write a best-selling book—all by blinking his left eye.

The locked-in syndrome that Bauby endured for the rest of his life left him a prisoner in his own body. But it did not rob him of his ability to take in the world around him, his mind, the motivation to accomplish great things in life, or his ability to feel emotion. In the coming chapters of this part on foundations in biological psychology, we will continue to explore the biological processes that still allowed Bauby these pleasures in life. In Chapter 3, we will examine how sensation and perception allow us to interact with the world outside our bodies. In Chapter 4, we will look at levels of consciousness when you are not fully awake, alert, or aware. And, in Chapter 5, we will examine what motivates our behavior and makes us feel the emotions we all feel. As you read these chapters, think about your own life and the place these abilities play in it. And, think of Bauby and how even with the hand life dealt him he still lived life to its fullest.

Studying the Chapter

Key Terms

acetylcholine (ACh) (54)
action potential (51)
adrenal cortex (79)
adrenal medulla (79)
all-or-none law (51)
amygdala (65)
androgens (79)
association cortex (73)
auditory cortex (75)
autonomic nervous system (60)
axon (49)
Broca's aphasia (70)
Broca's area (70)
cell body (47)
central nervous system (CNS) (58)
cerebellum (63)
cerebral cortex (65)
cerebral hemispheres (65)
corpus callosum (71)
dendrites (48)
DNA (48)
dopamine (55)
endocrine glands (78)
endocrine system (78)
endorphins (56)
estrogens (79)
excitation (52)
forebrain (62)
frontal lobe (69)
gamma amino butyric acid (GABA) (56)
glia cells (46)
glutamate (56)
gonads (79)
hindbrain (62)
hippocampus (66)
homeostasis (68)
hormones (78)
hypothalamus (68)
inhibition (52)
ions (50)
limbic system (64)
medulla oblongata (62)
midbrain (62)
motor neurons (58)
myelin (46)
myelin sheath (49)
nervous system (58)
neuromodulators (54)
neurons (46)
neuroplasticity (68)

neuroscience (45)
neurotransmitters (49)
norepinephrine (NOR) (55)
occipital lobe (69)
parasympathetic nervous system (61)
parietal lobe (69)
peripheral nervous system (PNS) (58)
pituitary gland (79)
pons (63)
postsynaptic neuron (49)
presynaptic neuron (49)
primary motor area (74)
primary somatosensory area (75)
primary visual area (75)
refractory period (51)
resting potential (50)
reticular formation (63)
reuptake (53)
sensory neurons (58)
serotonin (55)
somatic nervous system (60)
split brain (72)
sympathetic nervous system (61)
synapse (49)
temporal lobe (69)
thalamus (68)
threshold of excitation (50)
Wernicke's aphasia (70)
Wernicke's area (70)

What Do You Know? Assess Your Understanding

Test your retention and understanding of the material by answering the following questions.

1. Neural impulses travel faster in neurons that have _____.
   a. myelin
   b. vesicles
   c. dopamine
   d. axon bulbs

2. When the potential of a neuron hits its threshold of excitation at _____, it will fire an action potential.
   a. −55 mv
   b. +55 mv
   c. −70 mv
   d. +70 mv

3. Neurotransmitters can be found in the _____ of the neuron.
   a. axon
   b. myelin
   c. axon bulb
   d. dendrites

4. Sara slipped and nearly fell while walking down the stairs. The increased heart rate and blood pressure that accompanied Sara's fear at almost falling were most likely due to activation of Sara's _____ nervous system.
   a. sympathetic
   b. parasympathetic
   c. somatic
   d. voluntary

5. There tends to be a(n) _____ of _____ in the brains of people with Alzheimer's disease.
   a. excess; dopamine
   b. lack; dopamine
   c. excess; acetylcholine
   d. lack; acetylcholine

6. Drugs that are used to treat depressive disorders often _____ the action of _____ in the brain.
   a. increase; serotonin
   b. decrease; serotonin
   c. increase; GABA
   d. decrease; GABA

7. Billy was in a car accident and sustained head injuries. Some of the injury occurred in areas of the brain that use glutamate. The damage caused the glutamate, the chief excitatory neurotransmitter in the brain, to spill out onto adjoining brain tissue. To their amazement, the doctors discovered that these areas of tissue died when exposed to the glutamate. The doctors concluded that the neurons in these regions were stimulated to death. This piece of research is best described as a(n) _____.
   a. experiment
   b. correlational study
   c. case study
   d. naturalistic observation

8. An inhibitory neurotransmitter makes the postsynaptic neuron _____ likely to fire an action potential by making the inside of the postsynaptic neuron more _____.
   a. more; positive
   b. less; positive
   c. more; negative
   d. less; negative

9. Rashid cut his finger while cooking. Which neurotransmitter/neuromodulator would be most useful in alleviating his pain?
   a. Dopamine
   b. Endorphin
   c. Norepinephrine
   d. GABA

10. The frontal lobe of the brain contains the primary ______ area.
   a. somatosensory
   b. auditory
   c. motor
   d. visual

11. Which part of the brain functions as a relay for sensory information?
   a. hippocampus
   b. amygdala
   c. thalamus
   d. hypothalamus

12. Walker has had too much alcohol to drink. As a result, he cannot walk without stumbling. Walter's problems with balance are likely due to the alcohol's effect on Walter's______?
   a. thalamus
   b. hippocampus
   c. cerebellum
   d. Broca's area

13. The ______ allows the right and left hemispheres of the brain to communicate.
   a. pons
   b. medulla oblongata
   c. corpus callosum
   d. limbic system

14. Yumiko was in a car accident in which she incurred massive damage to her left frontal lobe. What types of impairments would you most expect to see in Yumiko as a result of this damage?
   a. Paralysis on her right side
   b. Numbness on her right side
   c. An inability to comprehend speech
   d. Blindness in her right visual field

15. Damage to the left temporal lobe would likely produce what effect?
   a. An inability to produce speech
   b. Paralysis on the right side of the body
   c. Broca's aphasia
   d. Wernicke's aphasia

16. Which of the following techniques would tell us the *most* about the size of specific brain structures?
   a. PET scan
   b. fMRI
   c. EEG
   d. Brain stimulation

17. During times of stress, the endocrine system is most likely to release ______.
   a. GABA
   b. estrogens
   c. adrenaline
   d. dopamine

18. Male sex hormones are called ______.
   a. estrogens
   b. androgens
   c. endorphins
   d. adrenalines

19. A split-brain operation is done to control ______.
   a. seizures
   b. depression
   c. schizophrenia
   d. pain

20. Touch or somatosensory information is processed in the ______ lobe of the brain.
   a. temporal
   b. occipital
   c. parietal
   d. frontal

Answers: 1. a; 2. a; 3. c; 4. a; 5. d; 6. a; 7. c; 8. d; 9. b; 10. c; 11. c; 12. c; 13. c; 14. a; 15. d; 16. b; 17. c; 18. b; 19. a; 20. c.

Use It or Lose It: Applying Psychology

1. Jean-Dominique Bauby was still able to think, feel, and remember the events of his life after a stroke left him in a permanent state of locked-in syndrome. Now that you know something about the brain, can you explain why he retained these abilities?

2. Black widow spider venom causes a massive release of acetylcholine in the nervous system. Given what you know about the nervous system, what symptoms would you expect to see in someone who was bitten by a black widow spider?

3. Your best friend is interested in what you are learning in your psychology class. Your friend asks you to explain how the endocrine system differs from the nervous system. What would you tell your friend?

4. Your best friend's grandmother has just suffered a stroke. This stroke has left her with an inability to speak, but she can still understand what others say to her. She also has paralysis on the right side of her body. Your friend wants to know what part of her grandmother's brain was likely damaged by the stroke. Based on your understanding of the brain, what would you tell your friend?

Critical Thinking about the Science of Psychology

In this chapter, you read about a study conducted by Maguire, Woollett, & Spiers (2006) in which they compared the hippocampal regions of London taxi drivers to those of London bus drivers. Please review that study now in Section 2.4.3, and then answer these questions:

1. What type of research design did Maguire and colleagues use in this study?
2. What is/are the dependent variable(s) in this study?
3. What is/are the independent variable(s) in this study?

Are You Getting the Big Picture?

Neuroscience is the study of how the brain and nervous system affect mental processes and behavior.

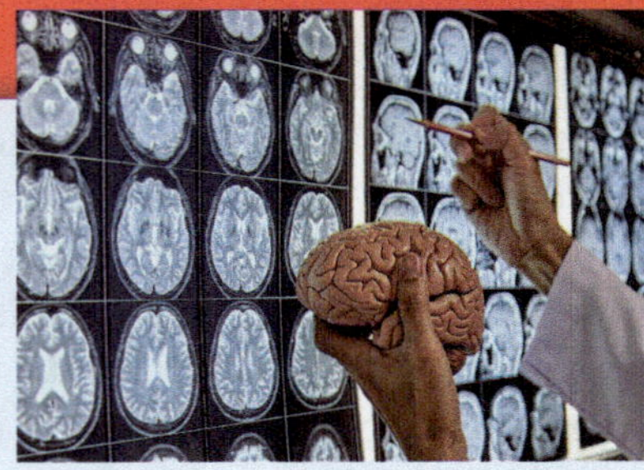

iStock.com/undefined

2.1 Communication in the Brain

- **Neurons** use electrochemical energy to generate **action potentials** that travel to the end of the neuron and cause the release of **neurotransmitters**.
- Action potentials or neural signals are fired when a neuron is depolarized enough to reach its **threshold of excitation** (–55 mv).

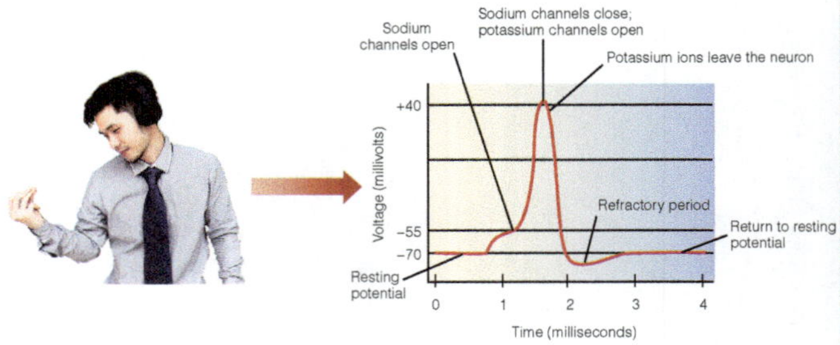

Nutlegal Photographer/Shutterstock.com

2.2 Neurotransmitters and Neuromodulators

- Neurotransmitters are chemical compounds that carry signals across neurons. Some of the key neurotransmitters are **acetylcholine**, **dopamine**, **serotonin**, **norepinephrine (NOR)**, **GABA**, and **glutamate**.
- **Neuromodulators**, such as **endorphins**, indirectly affect neural signaling in the brain, often by influencing the release of other neurotransmitters.
- Neurotransmitters play significant roles in regulating behavior and mood.
- Many drugs used to treat mental health conditions act on the functioning of neurotransmitters in the synapses of the brain. One such type of drug is selective serotonin reuptake inhibitors (SSRIs). SSRIs are used to treat many mental health conditions, including depressive disorders.

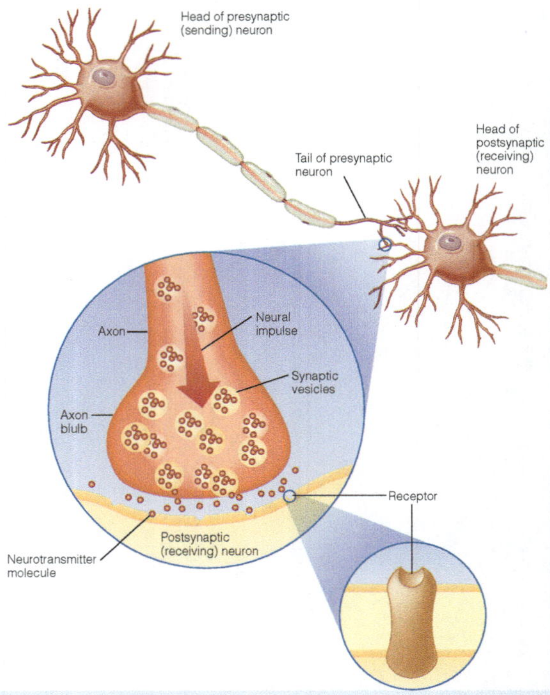

2.3 The Structure of the Nervous System

- The **nervous system** is arranged into a hierarchy of subsystems. The divisions of the nervous system include the **central nervous system**, **peripheral nervous system**, the **autonomic nervous system**, the **somatic nervous system**, the **sympathetic nervous system**, and the **parasympathetic nervous system**.

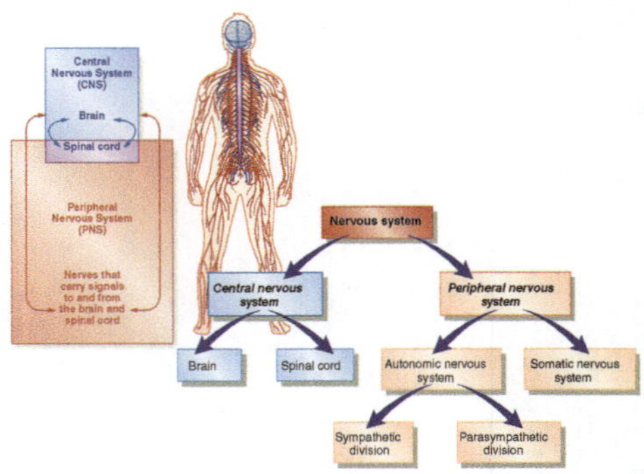

2.4 The Brain and Spinal Cord

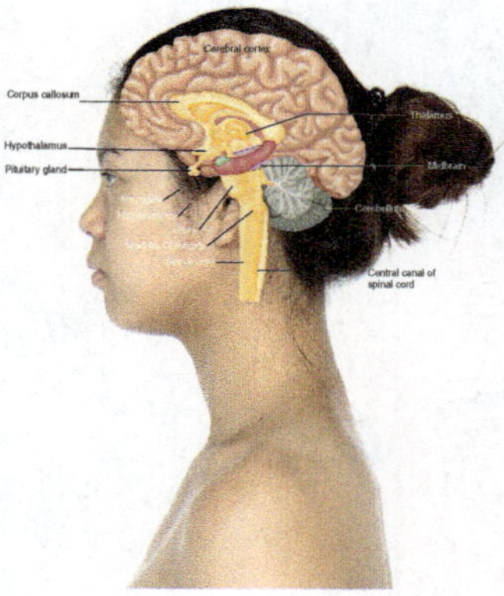

Jade ThaiCatwalk/Shutterstock.com

- The brain is divided into three key regions. The **hindbrain** governs basic and life-sustaining functions in the body. The **midbrain** connects the lower structures of the hindbrain with the more sophisticated structures of the **forebrain** that regulate higher-order processes such as thinking and emotional control.
- The brain regulates motor activity, sensation and perception, emotions, our ability to learn and remember, and all the other elements of human behavior.

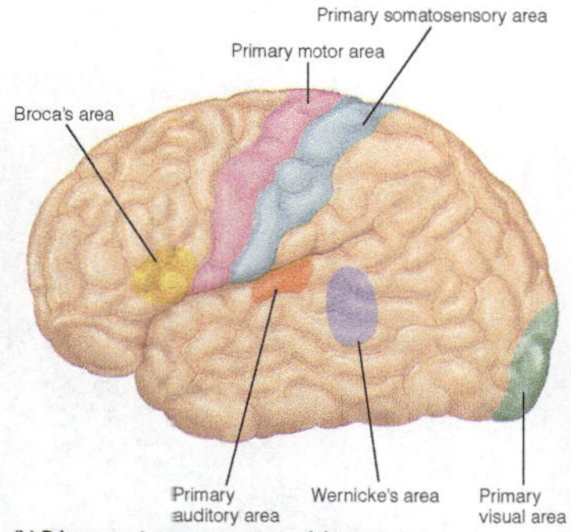

(b) Primary motor-sensory areas of the cortex

- The **cerebral cortex** is a thin layer of wrinkled tissue that covers the outside of the brain and is most responsible for the cognition, decision making, and language capabilities that are unique to humans.
- The brain is divided into right and left **cerebral hemispheres**. The left hemisphere generally governs the right side of the body, whereas the right hemisphere governs the left side of the body.

2.5 Technologies for Studying the Brain

- To assist in studying the brain and its functioning, technologies such as CAT scans, MRIs, fMRIs, PET scans, EEGs, and brain stimulation are all important tools.

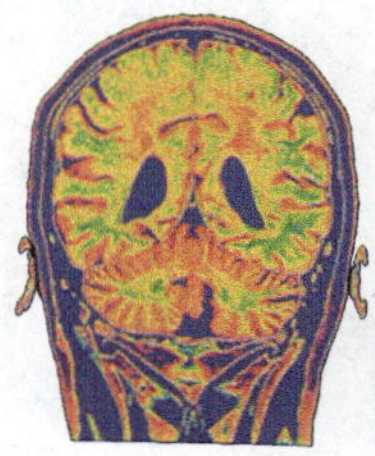

S&I/Science Source

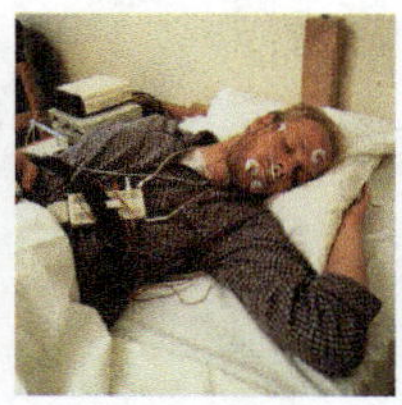

CC Studio/Science Source

2.6 The Endocrine System

- The **endocrine system** contains glands that release chemical messengers—**hormones**—into the bloodstream. Compared to the nervous system, the endocrine system is slower and more long-lasting in its effects.

MJTH/Shutterstock.com

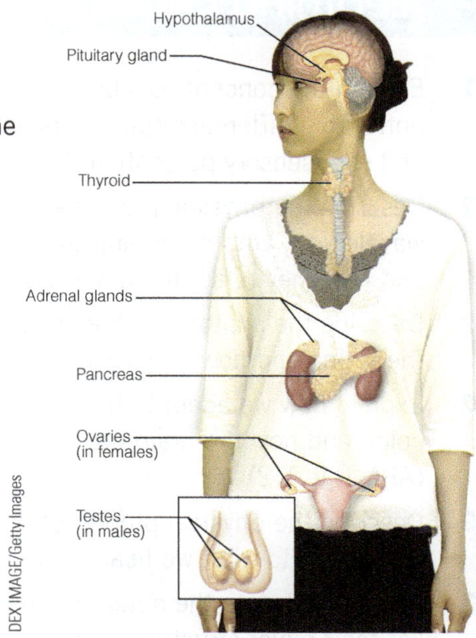

DEX IMAGE/Getty Images

Learning Objectives

- **3.1** Explain the concepts of absolute threshold, just noticeable difference (jnd), subliminal perception, and extrasensory perception. (APA 1.1, 2.1)
- **3.2** Describe the physical properties of light—wavelength, amplitude, and the visible spectrum—and how they relate to human vision. (APA 1.1, 1.2)
- **3.2** Describe the anatomy of the eye and the layers of the retina and how they function. (APA 1.1, 1.2)
- **3.2** Explain how we adapt to light and dark, how we see color, and how the brain processes what we see. (APA 1.1, 1.2)
- **3.3** Describe the physical properties of sound and how they relate to what we hear. (APA 1.1, 1.2)
- **3.3** Be able to locate the outer, middle, and inner ear; list their major structures; and describe their roles in hearing. (APA 1.1, 1.2)
- **3.4** Explain the processes involved in taste, smell, touch, and the body senses. (APA 1.1, 1.2)
- **3.5** Describe top-down and bottom-up perceptual processing, and explain the differences between them. (APA 1.1, 1.2, 2.1)
- **3.5** Give an overview of perceptual constancy theories and how we perceive depth. (APA 1.1, 1.2)
- **3.5** Describe the process of shape and form perception. (APA 1.1, 1.2)
- **3.6** Describe some of the common perceptual errors and illusions we experience, and explain their causes. (APA 1.1, 1.2, 2.1)
- **3.6** Explain how culture affects perception. (APA 1.1, 1.2, 2.5)

Dmytro Gilitukha/Shutterstock.com

3 Sensation and Perception

Unlike being in a vegetative state, when Jean-Dominique Bauby awoke from his coma, he was once again vividly aware of the world around him. He was able to focus his conscious awareness or **attention** on the people and equipment in his hospital room. He could feel pain in his body, and he was able to hear some of what was going on around him. Seeing, hearing, and feeling are examples of what psychologists call **sensation**. In sensation, sense organs of the body (for example, the eyes) convert environmental energy, such as the light that is bouncing off objects, into neural signals that the brain can then process. Sensation—in this case, seeing—is the first step to getting information into our minds. After sensation, you must understand the meaning of what you are seeing. **Perception** occurs when you interpret the meaning of the information gathered through your senses. Although Bauby's stroke did damage part of his hearing, Bauby's book documents, in part, his continued ability to sense and perceive the world. Although he lay motionless in bed, Bauby was just as aware of what was going on as you are aware right now that you are sensing and perceiving these words on this page. In this chapter, we will explore how sensation and perception take place in our bodies and the role that they play in our everyday lives. ■

Chapter Outline

attention conscious awareness; can be focused on events that are taking place in the environment or inside our minds

sensation the process through which our sense organs convert environmental energy such as light and sound into neural signals

perception the process through which we interpret sensory information

psychophysics the study of how the mind interprets the physical properties of stimuli

absolute threshold the minimum intensity of a stimulus at which participants can identify its presence 50% of the time

signal detection theory states that our ability to detect the presence of a stimulus is affected by more than just the intensity of that stimulus. Factors such as fatigue, motivation, and attention may also affect these judgments

just noticeable difference (jnd) the minimum change in intensity of a stimulus that participants can detect 50% of the time

3.1 Measuring Sensation and Perception: Psychophysics

Psychologists who study sensation and perception are most interested in understanding how we process sensory stimuli such as sights, sounds, and smells. How does your mind interpret the color of light bouncing off the surface of an apple? What physical properties of a food make it taste sweet or bitter? Questions like these are the focus of the branch of psychology called **psychophysics**.

3.1.1 The Limits of Sensation: Absolute Thresholds

One of the fundamental questions psychophysicists have sought to answer concerns the limits of human sensory capabilities. How faint a light can humans see? How soft a tone can we hear? Psychophysicists have conducted many experiments to answer these questions. These experiments typically involve presenting stimuli of gradually increasing or decreasing intensity (along with some trials in which the stimulus is not presented at all). Participants are asked to report whether they can detect the presence of the stimulus. In this way, psychophysicists establish an *absolute threshold*. **Absolute threshold** is defined as the minimum intensity of a stimulus that can be detected 50% of the time. This 50% mark is used because the level of the stimulus required for it to *just* be perceived varies from trial to trial, as well as from person to person, during an experiment. But why would this be true?

According to **signal detection theory** (Wixted, 2019), our ability to detect the presence of a stimulus is affected by more than just the intensity of that stimulus. Other factors, such as our level of attention, motivation, and fatigue can also play a role. For example, a fatigued air traffic controller may fail to perceive a beeping alarm on a computer screen, even though they had no trouble perceiving the same signal the day before when fully rested. On the other hand, motivation may also affect our sensory judgments. On a night of high air traffic, the air traffic controller may be so worried about missing an alarm that they think they hear the alarm even when they do not. In both of these scenarios, the intensity of the alarm has not changed, but the person's perception of it has, leading to errors (see ● FIGURE 3.1). For this reason, researchers define sensory thresholds in terms of intensities that can be detected 50% of the time, giving us the typical levels of stimulus intensity that can be detected across trials. ● TABLE 3.1 lists the approximate established absolute thresholds for our five senses, described in familiar descriptive terms.

	The alarm is going off (Signal present)	The alarm is not going off (Signal not present)
The air traffic controller thinks they hear the alarm (Signal detected)	Hit (Correct)	False Alarm (Error)
The air traffic controller does not hear the alarm (Signal not detected)	Miss (Error)	Correct Rejection (Correct)

FIGURE 3.1
The Possible Outcomes During Signal Detection

3.1.2 The Just Noticeable Difference and Weber's Law

In addition to establishing absolute thresholds for the senses, psychophysicists have tried to establish the minimum change in the intensity of a stimulus that can be detected 50% of the time. This barely noticeable change in the stimulus is referred to as the *difference threshold* or the **just noticeable difference (jnd)**. In the early 1800s, psychophysicist Ernst Weber (1795–1878) discovered an interesting characteristic of the jnd, known as **Weber's law**. According to this law, for each of our five senses, the amount of change in the stimulus that is necessary to produce a jnd depends on the intensity at which the stimulus is first presented. For example, if you add one additional teaspoon of salt to a very salty pot of soup, it will probably not be noticeable. But that same teaspoon of salt added to a less salty pot of soup may be very noticeable. Weber's law helps explain some of the subjectivity we experience in sensation. Under some conditions, a teaspoon of salt won't make a difference to our enjoyment of a recipe. Under other conditions, it might.

Weber's [VAY-bers] law a psychological principle that states that for each of our five senses, the amount of change in the stimulus that is necessary to produce a jnd depends on the intensity at which the stimulus is first presented

subliminal perception when the intensity of a stimulus is below the participant's absolute threshold and the participant is not consciously aware of the stimulus

3.1.3 Processing Without Awareness: Subliminal Stimulation of the Senses

Absolute thresholds and just noticeable differences describe the limits of our conscious awareness of sensations. But is sensation always a conscious experience? Or is it possible that we might be affected by sensory stimuli even when we are unaware of sensing them? **Subliminal perception,** the unconscious perception of stimuli, became a topic of many debates in the late 1950s when a man named James Vicary attempted to use subliminal messages to entice moviegoers at a public theater to buy more popcorn and soda without them knowing that they were being persuaded. Vicary flashed messages such as "Eat popcorn" and "Drink Coca-Cola" between the frames of a movie at a speed so fast that moviegoers did not have time to consciously perceive the messages. Because the messages were flashed so briefly, the moviegoers never consciously saw anything other than the movie.

Vicary reported that as a result of his "experiment," concession sales rose 18%. As it turns out, Vicary admitted in 1962 that he had not conducted a true experiment. The data that he collected were so few that they could not be used for scientific purposes (Epley, Savitsy, & Kachelski, 1999; Pratkanis, 1992). After Vicary's attempts at subliminal persuasion, researchers began to carefully examine the effects of subliminal perception both in the real world and in the laboratory. Many studies have failed to yield convincing evidence for the effectiveness of persuasive subliminal messages (Pratkanis et al., 2007). However, newer studies suggest that when certain criteria are met, subliminal persuasion can occur. For example, when subliminal messages specifically address the dimensions we are evaluating about the product, they *may* be effective (Loersch, Durso, & Petty, 2013). And when subliminal messages (e.g., *Red Bull*) coincide with relevant personality traits (e.g., being a risk taker) and situational factors (e.g., imagining staying up late), persuasion can occur (Bustin et al., 2015).

In addition to affecting persuasion, there is also evidence indicating that subliminal perception may play a role in our social interactions with others. Research findings suggest that we begin appraising threat-related stimuli (e.g., fearful and angry faces) before we are aware of having perceived the faces (Liddell et al., 2004).

TABLE 3.1 Descriptions of the Absolute Thresholds for Our Five Senses

Sense	Absolute Threshold
Vision  tiffanywickstrom/ 2 images/Pixabay	A candle seen from 30 miles away on a clear, dark night
Hearing  Vladimir Gjorgiev/ Shutterstock.com	A ticking watch that is 20 feet away in an otherwise quiet room
Smell  LightField Studios/ Shutterstock.com	One drop of perfume diffused in a three-room apartment
Taste  Digital Light Source/ Universal Images Group/ Getty Images	One teaspoon of sugar dissolved in 2 gallons of water
Touch  KITSANANAN/ Shutterstock.com	The wing of a bumblebee falling on one's cheek from a distance of 1 centimeter

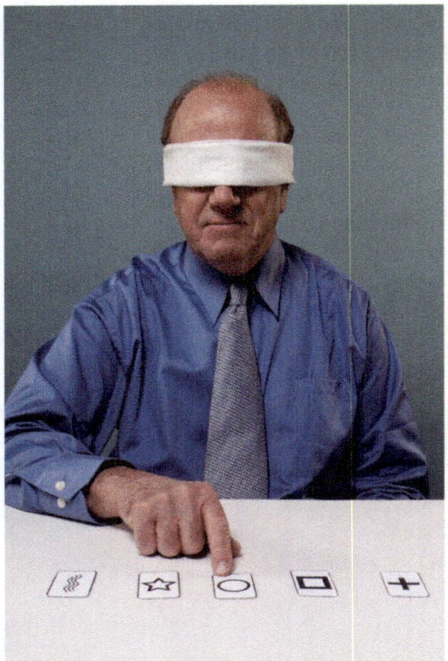

PM Images/The Image Bank/Getty Images

▲ Although researchers have been searching for evidence of ESP for a century, to date compelling evidence of its existence has not been found.

Furthermore, subliminal perception of angry faces tends to inhibit behavioral responses in people, making them less likely to react spontaneously (in this case, less likely to push a button on a computer keyboard). This suggests that subliminally perceiving an angry face makes us pause before reacting, perhaps giving us time to more carefully assess the situation before taking action (Parkinson et al., 2017). Taking a moment to consider the situation may be helpful as impulsively reacting to anger may not be in our best interest. By acting too quickly, we could engage in conflict unnecessarily and/or pick a fight that we cannot win.

The ability to subliminally perceive certain facial cues may begin very early in life. Infants as young as 7 months of age are able to detect trustworthiness in subliminally presented faces (Jessen & Grossmann, 2019). Detecting this ability so early in life suggests that subliminal processing of faces may hold some evolutionary survival advantage for us. Perhaps the ability to process facial cues before we are consciously aware of seeing a face allows us to make better judgments in social situations and aids in our survival. But, does our ability to sense without awareness also extend to other types of cognition? Proponents of *ESP* suggest that some of us can tell the future, read minds, and demonstrate other amazing abilities—but is this really true?

3.1.4 Extrasensory Perception: Can Perception Occur Without Our Five Senses?

extrasensory perception (ESP) also known as *psi*, the ability to acquire information about the world without using the known senses

Scientific research casts serious doubts on the existence of **extrasensory perception (ESP)**, sometimes also referred to as *psi*. ESP is the ability to acquire information about the world without using the known senses—for example, the ability to read people's minds or see the future (*precognition*). Most of the scientific tests of ESP involve the *Ganzfeld procedure*, in which one participant acts as a *sender* who tries to send a message to another participant acting as a *receiver* in another room. Although a few of these studies have suggested that some people may be better at sending and receiving such telepathic messages, the vast majority fail to support the existence of ESP (Milton & Wiseman, 2001).

Researchers have also used neuroimaging to investigate whether ESP exists. Researchers Samuel Moulton and Steven Kosslyn (2008) had participants engage in a modified version of the Ganzfeld procedure. During the experiment, the receiver had to guess which of two images on a computer screen was being sent by the sender in another room. As the receivers made these judgments, their brains were scanned using fMRI technology. Moulton and Kosslyn found that the receivers guessed the correct image only about 50% of the time (no better than chance alone). Furthermore, the fMRIs showed no differences in brain functioning between the trials resulting in correct and incorrect responses. Moulton and Kosslyn interpret these results as powerful evidence against the existence of ESP.

Now that we have a basic understanding of how psychologists measure the limits of our sensory abilities, we will examine how our bodies accomplish the process of sensation, starting with vision.

3.1 Quiz Yourself

1. **Jerry wants to sweeten his iced tea. He adds one teaspoon of sugar, but the tea does not taste sweet to him. When Jerry adds one more teaspoon of sugar, he finds that the tea now tastes sweet—but just barely. Two teaspoons of sugar seem to correspond to Jerry's ______________.**
   a. just noticeable difference (jnd)
   b. absolute threshold
   c. *k* value
   d. stimulus threshold

2. **If your tea already tastes sweet to you, the minimum amount of sugar that you would have to add to your tea to make it taste sweeter corresponds to your ______________.**
   a. just noticeable difference (jnd)
   b. absolute threshold
   c. *k* value
   d. stimulus threshold

3. **According to Weber's law, the amount of increase in the intensity of a stimulus needed to produce a just noticeable difference (jnd) is a function of the original intensity of the stimulus. To test the hypothesis that relative to starting with unsweet tea, starting with an already sweet tea causes one to have to add larger amounts of sugar to produce a jnd, you should use which of the following types of research designs?**
   a. An experiment
   b. A correlational design
   c. A case study
   d. All of the above designs would work equally well.

4. **In signal detection theory, if you don't hear the alarm clock when it goes off, you have just made a______________.**
   a. false alarm
   b. miss
   c. correct rejection
   d. hit

Answers 1. b; 2. a; 3. a; 4. b

3.2 Vision: Seeing the World

Our eyes are at the front of our skulls, so you might assume that vision is a direct transfer from object to eye to brain. Vision is more complicated than that however, and researchers have studied vision more than the other senses. To understand vision, we'll look at the properties of light that apply to vision, the anatomy of the eye, the layers of the retina, and how we process visual information in the brain.

3.2.1 How Vision Works: Light Waves and Energy

When we see an object, what we really see are the light waves that are reflected off the surface of the object. Thus, a blue shirt appears blue because blue is the only color of light that the shirt reflects. The shirt absorbs all other colors of light. As we'll see, the specific characteristics of the shirt's color and brightness are all determined by the physical characteristics of the particular light energy that is bouncing off the shirt.

Measuring Light: Wavelength and Amplitude

● FIGURE 3.2 depicts the *electromagnetic spectrum*, which includes visible light. Electromagnetic energies, including light, result from disturbances in the electrical and magnetic fields that exist in the universe. Like all electromagnetic

wavelength a physical property of some energies that corresponds to the distance between wave peaks

amplitude a physical property of some energies that corresponds to the height of wave peaks

visible spectrum the spectrum of light that humans can see

hue the color of light; it corresponds to the light's wavelength

brightness the intensity of light; it corresponds to the amplitude of the light waves

saturation the purity of light; light that consists of a single wavelength produces the richest or most saturated color

energies, light waves are characterized by their *wavelength* and *amplitude*. The **wavelength** of light is the distance between the peaks of consecutive waves. The **amplitude** of the light wave is the height of each wave peak. These distances are typically measured in nanometers (nm).

The human eye cannot sense all electromagnetic energy. In fact, the **visible spectrum** for humans is only a very narrow band of the electromagnetic spectrum that spans from about 360 nm to 750 nm (Figure 3.2). Other species can sense electromagnetic wavelengths that are beyond the human visible spectrum. Some snakes sense infrared rays, allowing them to sense other animals' body heat (Kaldenbach, Bleckmann, & Kohl, 2016). Other animals, such as spiders, butterflies, and rats, use their ability to sense ultraviolet (UV) light to help them hunt, find food, and navigate their environments (Bhaskara et al., 2009; Perry et al., 2016). If you are hiking through the woods, keep in mind that certain animals may be able to see you before you see them!

Although our eyes cannot sense much of the electromagnetic spectrum, we are capable of seeing millions of different combinations of color, richness, and brightness of light (Linhares, Pinto, & Nascimento, 2008). The wavelength of the light wave corresponds to the color or **hue** of the light we see. Shorter wavelengths correspond to cool colors such as blues and purples; longer wavelengths correspond to warmer colors such as yellows and reds (Figure 3.2). The amplitude of the light wave corresponds to its **brightness**. The higher the amplitude of the light wave, the brighter the color we perceive. One other characteristic of light, **saturation**, corresponds to the purity of the light. Light that consists of a single wavelength will produce the most saturated, or richest, color. Light that is a

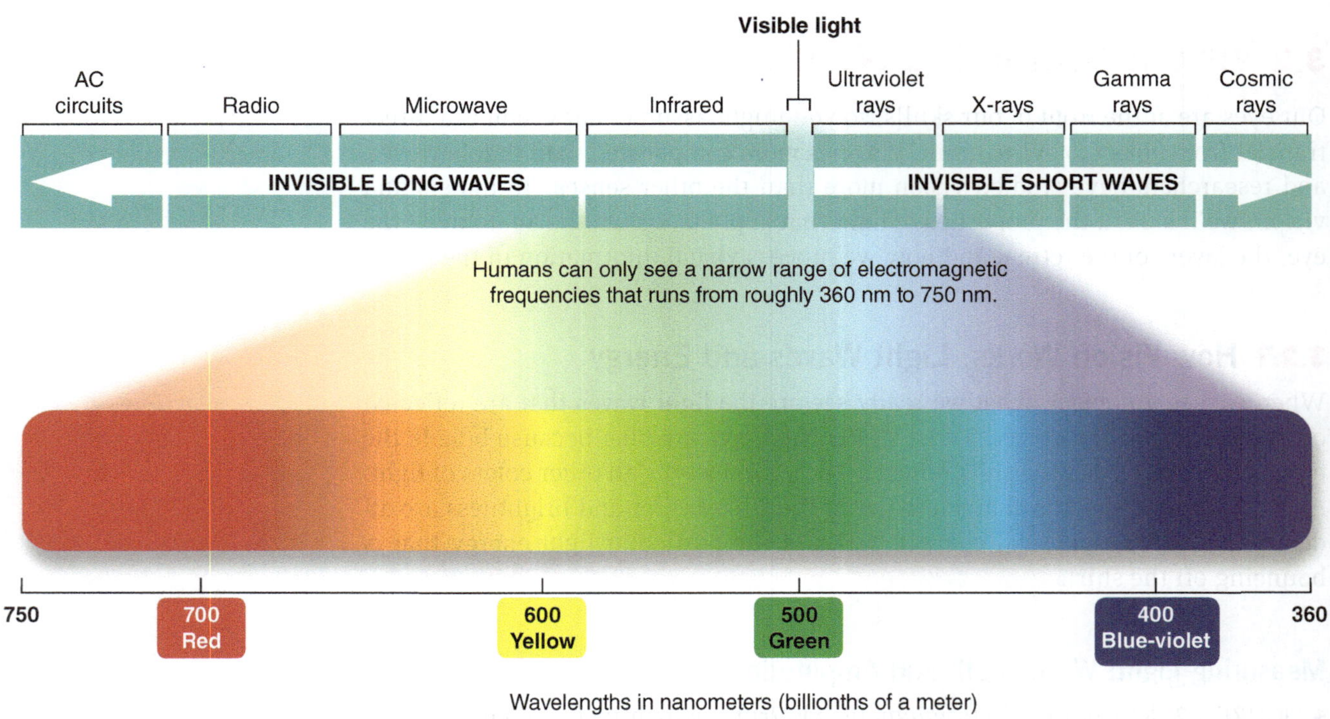

FIGURE 3.2

The Visible Spectrum of Light

The human visible spectrum comprises a narrow range of electromagnetic energies.

cornea [COR-nee-ah] the clear, slightly bulging outer surface of the eye that both protects the eye and begins the focusing process

pupil the hole in the iris through which light enters the eye

mixture of wavelengths produces less saturated colors. For example, pure blue light is high in saturation, but a mixture of blue and white light produces a less saturated blue light.

For vision to occur, our eyes must be able to convert the electromagnetic waves of the visible spectrum into neural signals that our brains can process. In the next section, we will look at the anatomy of the eye to get an idea of how this conversion occurs.

3.2.2 The Anatomy of the Outer Eye

The process of vision begins with the parts of the eye that we can readily see. The *cornea* is the clear outer structure that covers the *iris*, or the colored part of your eye. The *pupil*, which appears black, is merely the opening in the iris. After entering the eye through the pupil, light is eventually focused on the *retina* at the back of your eye. The white part, the *sclera*, is a supporting structure that doesn't play a part in the processing of visual information.

When light enters the eye, the first structure it passes through is the **cornea** (● FIGURE 3.3). The cornea is the clear, slightly bulging outer surface of the eye. It protects the eye and begins the focusing process. The light that is reflected from an object in the environment must eventually be focused on the rear surface of the eye if we are to see the object clearly. As light waves pass through the material of the cornea, they slow down and bend—just as they do when they pass through a camera lens. This bending of light waves plays an essential role in focusing images on the back of your eye. A damaged cornea can make it impossible for a person to see clearly.

Directly behind the cornea is the **pupil**. This black opening in the center of your eye is not really a structure. Rather, it is an opening, or aperture, through which light passes into the center of the eye. Light cannot pass through the white part of the eye, the sclera. Therefore, it must pass through the cornea and pupil to enter the eye. The iris, the colored part of the eye surrounding the pupil, is constructed of rings of muscles that control the size of the pupil. In dimly lit conditions, muscles in the iris pull outward to dilate the pupil, allowing the maximum

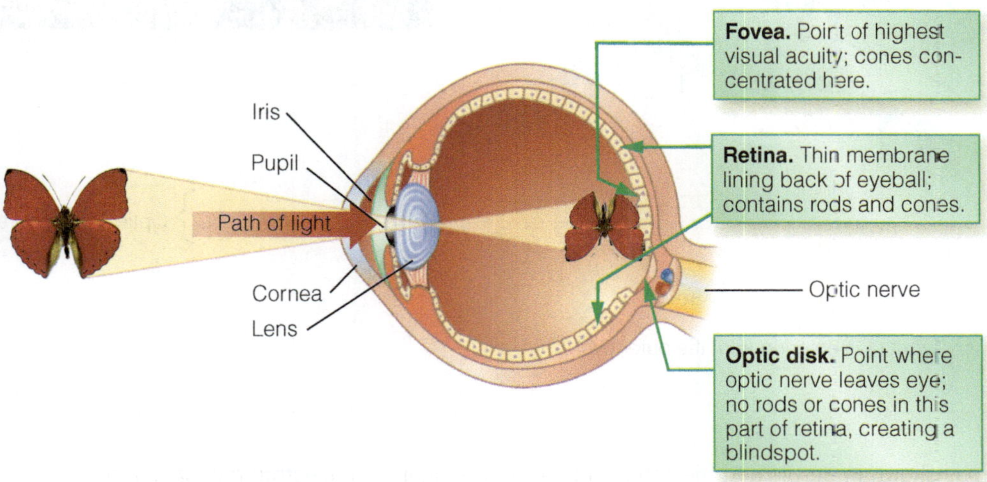

FIGURE 3.3
The Anatomy of the Eye

amount of light into the eye. In brightly lit conditions, the iris constricts to close the pupil, thus reducing the amount of light entering the eye so as not to overwhelm the light-sensitive cells in the eye.

lens the part of the eye that lies behind the pupil and focuses light rays on the retina

accommodation the process through which the lens is stretched or squeezed to focus light on the retina

Directly behind the iris and the pupil is the **lens** of the eye. The lens is a clear structure that is attached to the eye with strong ciliary muscles. The lens of the eye is rather like the lens of a camera—its job is to bring the light waves entering the eye into sharp focus on the back of the eye. The lens of the eye is somewhat soft and flexible. As the ciliary muscles stretch the lens, it changes shape, or undergoes **accommodation**, so that the image passing through it is focused properly.

3.2.3 The Retina: Light Energy to Neural Messages

Once the light waves have been focused on the back of the eye, conversion of light waves into neural impulses occurs in the retina, the surface that lines the inside of the

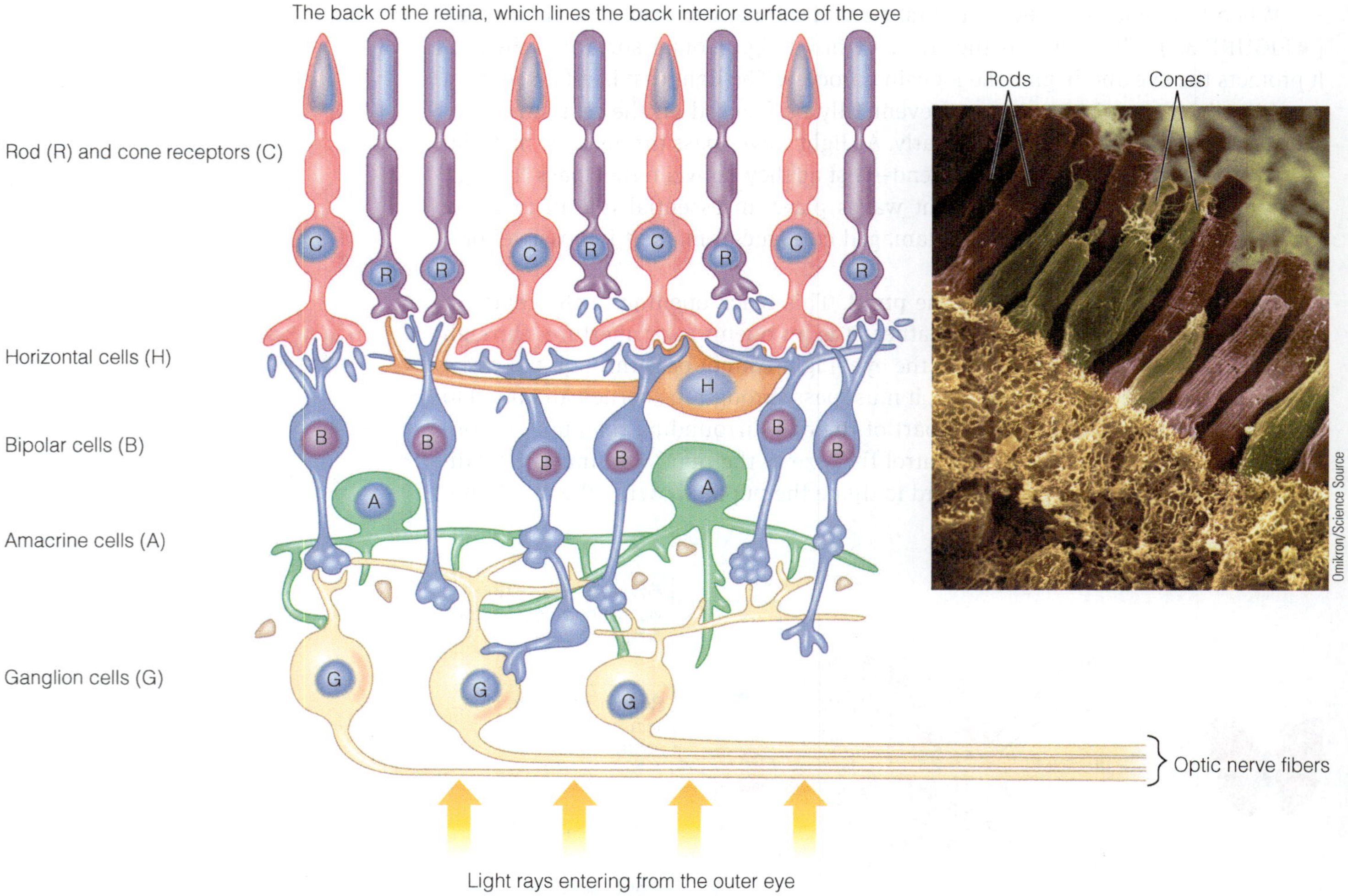

FIGURE 3.4

A Cross-section of the Retina

Above is a schematic of the retina with the rods shown in purple and the cones in pink. To the right is an electron micrograph of the retina showing the rods and cones.

Source: From "Organization of the Primate Retina," by J. E. Dowling and B. B. Boycott, in *Proceedings of the Royal Society of London, 16,* Series B, 80–111. Copyright © 1966 by the Royal Society.

back of the eyeball. In the **retina**, specialized cells called *rods* and *cones* convert light into neural signals. Without these cells, vision would not be possible.

The Anatomy of the Retina

The diagram in ● FIGURE 3.4 shows a cross-section of the layers in the human retina. The *ganglion cells* are on the surface of the retina, followed by successive layers of *amacrine, bipolar,* and *horizontal cells* and, finally, the light-sensitive rods and cones. Look closely at Figure 3.4 and you will see that the light entering the eye must filter through all the layers of the retina before finally striking the rods and cones.

Incoming light passes unimpeded through the transparent layers of the retina to reach the rods and cones, which convert the light energy into neural impulses. These signals travel back out to the ganglion cells on the surface of the retina. Along the way, the horizontal, bipolar, and amacrine cells funnel and consolidate the neural information from the rods and cones so that we can see a unified, coherent image. The signals that reach the ganglion cells in the top layer of the retina are to some degree summaries of the visual information from the rods and cones.

▲ Vision problems can strike at any age. Many people have *astigmatism*, or misshapen corneas or lenses, which can lead to blurred vision. Nearsightedness, or not seeing distant objects well, is common at all ages. Another condition, *presbyopia*, is more common after middle age. Presbyopia occurs when, as we age, the lens of the eye becomes more rigid and the eye is less able to accommodate to close objects. Because of presbyopia, many middle-aged and older adults need reading glasses or bifocals.

The Optic Nerve and the Blindspot

Once the neural impulses reach the ganglion cells, they exit the retina and travel to the brain via the **optic nerve**, which is composed of the axons of the ganglion cells (see Figures 3.3 and 3.4). The optic nerve actually exits the retina on the *surface* of the retina; there are no light-sensitive rods or cones at the point where the optic nerve leaves the retina. With no rods or cones at this spot, each of our eyes has a **blindspot**, which is a point in our visual field that we cannot see.

Luckily, however, our blindspots do not pose much of a problem. For one thing, the blindspot is at the side of our visual field, where we normally do not bring objects into focus in the first place (see Figure 3.3). If the blindspot were located at the *fovea* (the point directly behind the pupil), we might be much more aware of it. Another reason is that we have two eyes. Whatever part of the world we miss seeing because of the blindspot in our left eye we see with our right eye, and vice versa. Even though we are usually unaware that we have a blindspot, you can detect your own by trying this demonstration.

retina the structure at the back of the eye that contains cells that convert light into neural signals

optic nerve the structure that conveys visual information away from the retina to the brain

blindspot the point where the optic nerve leaves the retina (the optic disk) where there are no rods or cones

Engage Yourself!

Holding your book or screen approximately 18" from your face, close your right eye and look at the flower in ● FIGURE 3.5. Keeping your left eye fixed on the flower, notice that you can still see the smiley face in your peripheral vision. If you cannot see the smiley face, move your head further away from the page/screen until you can see it.

Now, keeping your eye fixated on the flower, slowly move your head closer to the page/screen. All the while, continue to notice if you can still see the smiley face. Continue to move closer to the page/screen until the smiley face disappears. You have found the *blindspot* in your left eye! In everyday circumstances, you are very unlikely to notice the blindspot, but under these tightly controlled circumstances, you should be able to locate it.

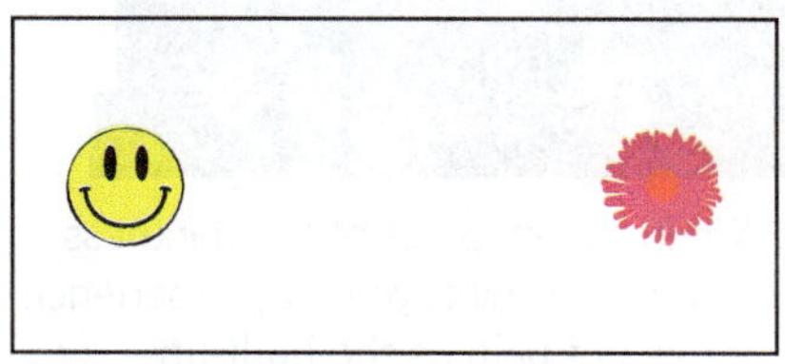

FIGURE 3.5

Follow the instructions in the text to find your blindspot.

rods the light-sensitive cells of the retina that pick up any type of light energy and convert it to neural signals

cones the cells of the retina that are sensitive to specific colors of light and send information to the brain concerning the colors we are seeing

photopigments light-sensitive chemicals that create electrical charges when they come into contact with light

The Rods and Cones

The rods and cones that line the inside layer of the retina play different roles in the process of vision. The **rods**, which are long and skinny, are sensitive to all colors of light, but they do not transmit information about color to the brain (see Figure 3.4). You can think of the rods as being black-and-white receptors. If you had only rods in your retina, you'd see everything in black and white. We see the world in color because of the cone cells in the retina. The **cones**, which are shorter and fatter than the rods, are responsible for transmitting information about color to the brain.

Relative to rods, the cones of the eye require a higher intensity of light to become activated. Because of this, we do not have good color vision in dimly lit situations. Think about driving at night. When light levels are not very intense, it may be possible to see objects in the distance, but impossible to discern their color. In each eye you have about 100 million rods but only about 5 million cones (Matlin & Foley, 1997). Having so many rods and so few cones in the retina indicates that perceiving shape and form takes precedence over perception of color. If you think about it for a minute, this arrangement makes sense. Which information would you need first: to see the shape of a car speeding toward you in the dark, or to see the color of the car? Your first concern would be seeing the car to avoid a collision!

In addition to being differentially sensitive to light energy, the rods and cones are not distributed evenly across the surface of the retina. The highest concentration of cones is at the fovea, where there can be as many as 247,000 cones per square millimeter of retinal area. However, the density of cones drops off quickly as you move outward toward the peripheral edges of the retina (Zhang et al., 2015). The density of rods follows the opposite pattern, with the highest concentration at the peripheral edges of the retina and fewer and fewer rods as you move toward the fovea. This arrangement means that our best color vision is for objects placed directly in front of us, whereas our color vision for objects seen out of the corners of our eyes (in our peripheral vision) is very poor.

Jack Wild/The Image Bank/Getty Images

▲ When you step out of the darkness into bright light, you may experience a flash of pain as the built-up photopigment in your eyes reacts all at once to the bright light.

Turning Light Energy into Neural Messages

The rods and cones of the eye are able to convert light into neural impulses because they contain light-sensitive **photopigments**, chemicals that are activated by light energy (Fitzpatrick & Mooney, 2012). When a rod is not receiving light input, its photopigment molecules are stable. However, when light strikes the rod, this incoming light energy splits the photopigments apart (Yau & Hardie, 2009). As the photopigments break up, they set off a complex chain of chemical reactions that change the rate at which the neurons of the visual system fire action potentials. The brain uses the pattern of these action potentials to interpret what we are seeing. Interestingly, research now suggests that photopigments may also play a role outside of visual imaging, for example in regulating sleep (see Chapter 4) and controlling pupillary reflexes (Jain et al., 2016), and that light-sensitive cells may even be found in areas of the nervous system outside of the retina (Matynia et al., 2016). These findings suggest that even in cases of blindness, light may still influence bodily function.

3.2.4 Adapting to Light and Darkness

Have you ever had to wait at the back of a dark movie theater for your eyes to adjust before you could find your seat? This type of adjustment is referred to as **dark adaptation**. It also takes our eyes a while to adapt to sudden increases in brightness, or undergo **light adaptation**.

dark adaptation the process through which our eyes adjust to dark conditions after having been exposed to bright light

light adaptation the process through which our eyes adjust to bright light after having been exposed to darkness

Dark and light adaptation are accomplished, in part, by changes in pupil size. Unfortunately, the amount of dilation and constriction that our pupils can provide is limited, and they alone cannot fully account for the adaptations we experience. Another mechanism of adaptation is found in the photopigments themselves. If you were to enter a completely darkened room, no light would enter your eyes and no photopigments would break down. After remaining in these darkened conditions for a period of time, the photopigment levels in your eyes would build up because they are not being broken down by light. This is what occurs when we sleep at night. With a large store of photopigments, your eyes are very sensitive to light. If someone were to suddenly turn on the lights in the bedroom, you would experience a bright flash of light and perhaps even pain as the large number of available photopigments makes your eyes very sensitive to the light. It would take about 1 minute for your eyes to adjust to the light (Hood & Finkelstein, 1986).

The process of dark adaptation is the opposite of what occurs during light adaptation. Under normal daytime lighting conditions, we constantly use our photopigments to see our surroundings. So, at any given moment during the day, a certain percentage of our photopigments is broken down. If you suddenly enter a darkened theater after being in bright daylight, you will not have enough photopigments to be able to see well. It will take approximately 30 to 45 minutes for your photopigment levels to build up completely (Poelman & Smet, 2010). This is why you may have to stand, popcorn in hand, at the back of the darkened theater for several minutes before you can find your seat.

monkeybusinessimages/iStock/Getty Images

▲ When suddenly entering dim conditions after leaving a brightly environment, such as occurs when you enter a darkened theater, it will take more than 30 minutes for your eyes to fully adjust to the darkness. In addition, because cones require more light energy than rods, it can be difficult to discriminate among colors in dim conditions.

3.2.5 How We See Color

Like the rods, the cones of the retina also contain photopigments. However, there is an important distinction between the photopigments in the rods and cones. All rods contain the same photopigment. In contrast, there are three different types of cones, each containing a slightly different photopigment. Having different types of photopigments in our cones is one reason we see color.

The Colors of Light

You may have learned in elementary school about three primary colors (red, yellow, and blue) from which all other colors can be made. This is true when you are talking about paint or crayons that actually reflect the color of light that we see. However, mixing colored light is different from mixing colors of paints or crayons. The primary colors of light are red, green, and blue. All other colors of light can be made from these three colors. If you mix all the primary colors of light together, you get white light. In contrast, if you mixed red, blue, and yellow paint together, you would get black paint (● FIGURE 3.6). When we describe color vision and combinations of colors, remember to think in terms of light, not in terms of paint.

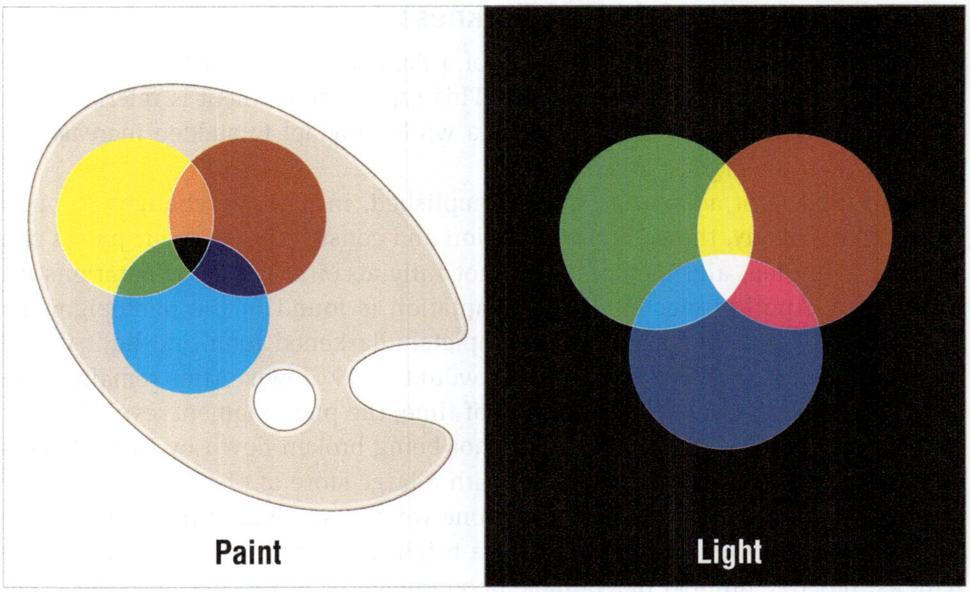

FIGURE 3.6

Primary Colors of Paint and Light

Mixing paint is not the same as combining colors of light.

The Trichromatic Theory of Color Vision

By now, we hope that some of you have made the connection between the three primary colors of light and the three different types of cones in our retinas. Could it be that each type of cone detects the presence of a different primary color of light? This is the central assumption of the **trichromatic theory of color vision**.

trichromatic [try-crow-MAT-ick] theory of color vision the idea that color vision is made possible by the presence of three different types of cones in the retina that react respectively to red, green, or blue light

color blindness a condition in which a person cannot perceive one or more colors because of altered cone activity in the retina

The exact origin of the trichromatic theory of color vision is not really known (Rushton, 1975; Wasserman, 1978). Most psychologists credit Hermann von Helmholtz (1821–1894) with proposing this theory in the mid 1800s. According to the trichromatic theory, we have three different types of cones, each of which contains a slightly different photopigment that makes the cell particularly sensitive to a certain wavelength of light. One type of cone is particularly sensitive to long wavelengths (red), another is very sensitive to medium wavelengths (green), and the third is most sensitive to short wavelengths (blue). Notice that these colors correspond to the primary colors of light.

These differentially sensitive cones give our brain a way of knowing what color of light we are seeing at any particular moment (B.R. Conway, 2009). For example, if the brain receives input that the red cones are very active and the green and blue are not very active, the brain knows you are seeing the color red. This same logic can be applied to seeing the colors green and blue, but how does it apply to seeing nonprimary colors? All colors of light are some combination of red, green, and blue light (see Figure 3.6). So, the brain processes the proportions of red, green, and blue cones that are firing intensely to know what color you are seeing (Schmidt et al., 2016).

Color Blindness: Do We All See the Same Colors?

Color blindness, or the inability to see one or more colors, results from altered cone activity in the retina. Color blindness can be caused by environmental factors such as exposure to chemicals (Beckman et al., 2016), but it is often the result of genetics. A particularly common type is red-green color blindness, a disorder that occurs in approximately 8% of males in the United States. Similar levels of color blindness have been seen in specific populations of males in Turkey and Greenland, whereas lower levels of color blindness have been found among males in Colombia, Spain, and Italy. The fact that rates of color blindness vary across genetically disparate populations suggests a genetic basis to the disorder (Citirik et al., 2005). Furthermore, the fact that red-green color blindness is seen much more often in men suggests a sex-linked genetic condition.

▲ If you were missing all of your cones, this piece of art would be perceived in grayscale instead of color.

Red-green color blindness can result from a lack of red or green cones in the retina. Without one of these types of cones, a person is unable to discriminate between red and green. At a stoplight, a person with such red-green color blindness must look at the position of the red and green lights because the lights appear to be the same color.

Yet some people who have all three types of cones also experience red-green color vision deficiencies. For these people (again mostly men), the issue is that the red or green cones are not sensitive to exactly the same ranges of wavelengths as the cones found in the average person. Therefore, these men experience difficulties in distinguishing among certain hues (Baraas et al., 2006). For example, a man with abnormally insensitive green cones may have trouble distinguishing small changes in color among orange hues. These deficiencies are sometimes more detectable in a laboratory where participants are asked to view samples of color under tightly controlled conditions than they are in the real world. In the natural environment, where colors and light levels are varied and mixed, some of these color deficiencies do not seem to be as problematic (Baraas et al., 2006).

Although trichromatic theory explains certain aspects of color vision, it does not explain all aspects of vision (Horiguchi et al., 2013). For example, trichromatic theory cannot explain *negative afterimages*. To understand what an afterimage is, try this demonstration.

Engage Yourself!

Get a blank sheet of paper and set it aside. Stare at the black dot in the center of ● FIGURE 3.7 without blinking or moving your eyes. Continue staring for 60–90 seconds. Then quickly move your gaze to the blank sheet of white paper. What do you see? You should see the image of a green shamrock with a yellow border on the blank sheet of white paper. The shamrock is a negative afterimage. Notice that the colors you see in the afterimage are different from the colors in the original. Why would you see different colors in your afterimage? Simply having different types of cones cannot explain this phenomenon. So, what does explain afterimages?

FIGURE 3.7

Negative Afterimages

See text for instructions.

The Opponent-Process Theory of Color Vision

The **opponent-process theory** proposes a different type of color-sensitive cell in the visual system, a cell that is sensitive to two colors of light. There are thought to be three types of opponent-process cells in our visual system: red/green, yellow/blue, and black/white. The key to opponent-process theory is that these

opponent-process theory the idea that we have dual-action cells beyond the level of the retina that signal the brain when we see one of a pair of colors cells can detect the presence of only one color at a time. The colors *oppose* each other so that the opponent-process cell cannot detect the presence of both colors at the same time. For example, a red/green cell can detect either red or green light at any one time. If you shine a red light in the eye, the red/green cells tell our brain that we are seeing red. If you shine a green light in the eye, the red/green cells tell our brain that we are seeing green. But these red/green cells cannot detect red and green at the same time. Opponent-process theory is consistent with the finding that if we simultaneously shine red and green lights into your eye, you will likely see a neutral shade that is neither red nor green (Hurvich & Jameson, 1957/2000).

Opponent-process theory can explain the phenomenon of negative after images. Recall the demonstration you tried with Figure 3.7. After staring at the red-and-blue shamrock, you saw a green-and-yellow afterimage. Opponent-process theory proposes that as you stared at the red-and-blue shamrock, you were using the red and blue portions of the opponent-process cells. After a period of 60 to 90 seconds of continuous staring, you expended these cells' capacity to fire action potentials. In a sense, you temporarily "wore out" the red and blue portions of these cells. Then you looked at a blank sheet of white paper. Under normal conditions, the white light would excite *all* of the opponent-process cells. Recall that white light contains all colors of light. But, given the exhausted state of your opponent-process cells, only parts of them were capable of firing action potentials. In this example, the green and yellow parts of the cells were ready to fire. The light reflected off the white paper could excite only the yellow and green parts of the cells, so you saw a green-and-yellow shamrock.

Trichromatic Theory or Opponent-Process Theory?

We've seen that trichromatic theory and opponent-process theory each explain certain aspects of color vision. So, which theory is correct? Both theories seem to have merit. It is generally believed that these two theories describe processes that operate at different places in the visual system (Hubel, 1995; Wade, 2010).

Trichromatic theory does a good job of explaining color vision at the level of the rods and cones. Opponent-process theory best explains the processing of color vision beyond the level of the rods and cones. Evidence suggests that opponent processing may occur at the level of the ganglion cells (B.R. Conway, 2009; DeValois & DeValois, 1975); the amacrine, horizontal, and bipolar cells of the retina; or even in the visual cortex (for review, see Schmidt et al., 2016). In the next section, we will trace the path that visual information takes as it leaves the retina and enters the brain.

3.2.6 The Visual Pathways of the Brain

Once the rods and cones of the retina convert light into neural signals, this information begins its journey to the visual cortex of the brain. Along the way, visual information is continually processed and combined to ultimately give us a coherent perception of what we see in the environment. The bipolar, horizontal, and amacrine cells gather the information from the rods and cones and funnel it to the ganglion cells. The ganglion cells join together to form the optic nerve, which carries visual information into the brain.

Visual information from the right side of the body travels to the left hemisphere, and information from the left side travels to the right hemisphere. The point at which the optic nerve from the left eye and the optic nerve from the right eye meet is called the **optic chiasm**. From the optic chiasm, most visual information travels to the thalamus before ultimately traveling to the visual cortex, where the meaning of the visual input is interpreted. We will discuss this interpretive process when we discuss perception later in the chapter (see • FIGURE 3.8).

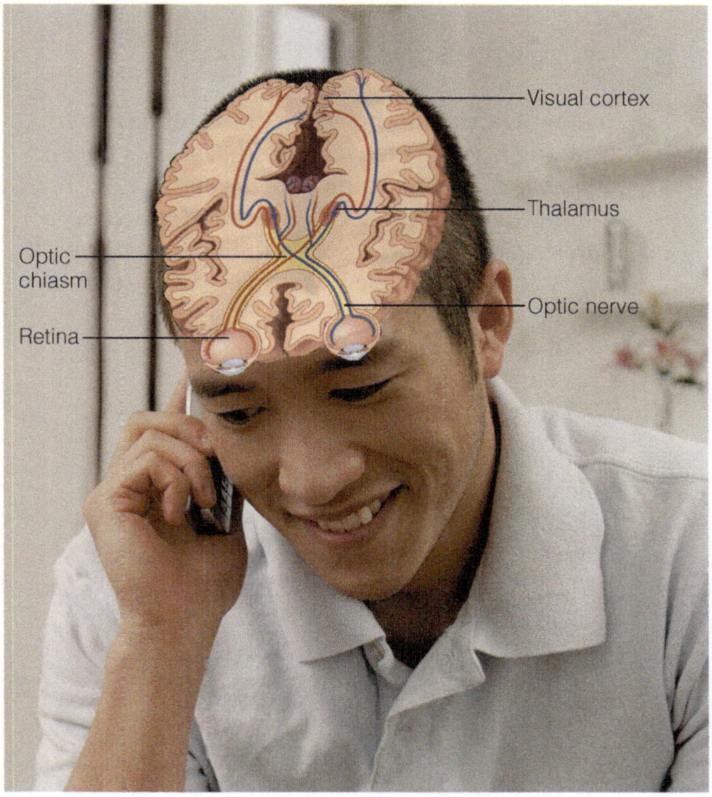

FIGURE 3.8

The Visual Pathways in the Brain

Visual information from your right side travels to the visual cortex on the left side of the brain, and information from your left side travels to the visual cortex on the right side.

Do Men and Women See the World Differently?

Evidence suggests that when it comes to processing visual information, men and women see things differently. Females tend to be better at discriminating one object from another (Overman et al., 1996), naming colors (Bornstein, 1985; Greene & Gynther, 1995), processing facial expressions accurately (Vassallo, Cooper, & Douglas, 2009), and perceiving colors (Jaint et al., 2010). In addition to having better color vision in general, females also tend to show a preference for using many colors and seem to prefer warm colors to cool ones, but this trend may be somewhat culturally dependent (Al-Rasheed, 2015; Witzel, 2015). Males tend to be better at processing moving objects (McGivern, et al., 2012), the spatial aspects of objects (Alexander, 2003), and the relative positions of places (De Goede & Postma, 2015). Differences in visual preferences appear at a very early age: female infants ages 3 to 8 months prefer to look at dolls, whereas male infants of the same age prefer to look at trucks (Alexander, Wilcox, & Woods, 2009). Other studies show that by age 2 ½ years girls tend to show a preference for pink and boys tend to show an avoidance of pink (LoBue & DeLoache, 2011).

optic chiasm the point in the brain where the optic nerve from the left eye meets the optic nerve from the right eye

Do these early gender differences indicate that color preferences are innate? Not necessarily. If such a characteristic were innate, we may expect to see it present from the time of birth rather than emerging during development (Franklin et al., 2010). In fact, newborn infants of both sexes have been shown to prefer the color blue to all others (Zemach, Chang, & Teller, 2007). Yet, school-aged children tend to prefer colors that are culturally associated with the gender with which they identify (Chiu et al., 2006). This pattern of similar color preference at birth with gender-specific color preference developing later suggests that our color preferences are at least partially shaped by cultural rules about color and gender. In many cultures, products marketed to girls are often colored with bright, warm colors. Worldwide, girls' toys often involve babies, fashion, cooking, nurturing, and other domestic themes, whereas toys marketed to boys frequently involve vehicles, weaponry, and darker, cooler colors. Thus, observed differences in gender roles and color preferences may reflect what we teach our children to prefer.

Our eyes are truly a window to the world. Now that you have learned about the amazing sense of vision, let's take a closer look at our other amazing senses. We will begin with our ability to hear.

3.2 Quiz Yourself

1. Juan was born with no cones in his retina. As a result, he is completely color-blind. Juan's doctor published a paper in which he discussed how Juan's complete color blindness seems to be related to Juan's academic success, social life, and personality. Juan's doctor conducted what type of research in this paper?
   a. An experiment
   b. A survey
   c. A quasi-experiment
   d. A case study

2. Which theory best explains why Sara would see flashes of red light after 8 hours of working on a computer monitor that has a green and black screen?
   a. The opponent-process theory
   b. The trichromatic theory
   c. The rod-and-cone theory
   d. The theory of red-green color blindness

3. You have just returned to a darkened theater after a trip to the concession stand. Now you have a problem—you can't find your seat in the dark. Knowing what you do about vision, which of the following would most likely help you find your seat?
   a. Stare straight ahead at the seats because rods are more sensitive to light
   b. Search for your seat out of the corner of your eye because rods are more sensitive to light
   c. Stare straight ahead at the seats because cones are more sensitive to light
   d. Search for your seat out of the corner of your eye because cones are more sensitive to light

Answers 1. d; 2. a; 3. b

3.3 Hearing: Listening to the World

Like vision, hearing is one of our most important senses; much of what we learn in life depends on these two senses. Additionally, hearing plays an important role in our ability to communicate with others. Sounds, such as a human voice, produce waves of compressed air that our ears convert to neural impulses. Like light waves, sound waves have their own psychophysical properties. A sound wave has both peaks and valleys (see ● FIGURE 3.9).

cycle a physical characteristic of energy defined as a wave peak and the valley that immediately follows it

frequency a physical characteristic of energy defined as the number of cycles that occur in a given unit of time

loudness the psychophysical property of sound that corresponds to the amplitude of a sound wave

decibels [DESS-uh-bells] (dB) the unit of measurement used to describe the loudness of a sound

pitch the psychophysical property of sound that corresponds to the frequency of a sound wave

A **cycle** includes the peak of the wave and the valley that immediately follows it (Figure 3.9a). Counting the number of cycles in a given time frame allows us to determine the **frequency** of a sound wave. Traditionally, the frequency of sound waves is measured in hertz (Hz), or the number of cycles completed per second. A sound wave with a frequency of 1,000 Hz would complete 1,000 cycles per second. The **loudness** of the sound we hear, measured in **decibels (dB)**, corresponds to the amplitude of a sound wave (Figure 3.9b). The higher the amplitude, the more pressure is exerted on the eardrum, and the louder the sound is.

The frequency of a sound wave corresponds to the **pitch** of the sound we perceive: the higher the frequency, the higher the pitch. The average young adult can perceive sounds that range from a low of 20 Hz to a high of 20,000 Hz (Gelfand, 1981). For example, we can hear the low pitch of a foghorn and the high pitch of a mosquito's wings. We lose some of this range as we age, however, particularly our ability to hear high pitches. Some young people have capitalized on this by downloading ultra-high-pitched "mosquito" ringtones for their cell phones so that parents and other adults will be unaware of incoming calls and text messages. Tones above 16,000 Hz go unheard by people as young as 24! Luckily, most of the everyday sounds we hear fall well below the 20,000-Hz level. In fact, unless the gradual deterioration impairs our ability to hear sounds at 1,800 Hz and below, our ability to comprehend speech should remain pretty much intact (Welford, 1987). Yet all of us would do well to protect our hearing. Threats to our hearing are all around us, and if we experience too much damage, we may find our hearing loss to be problematic.

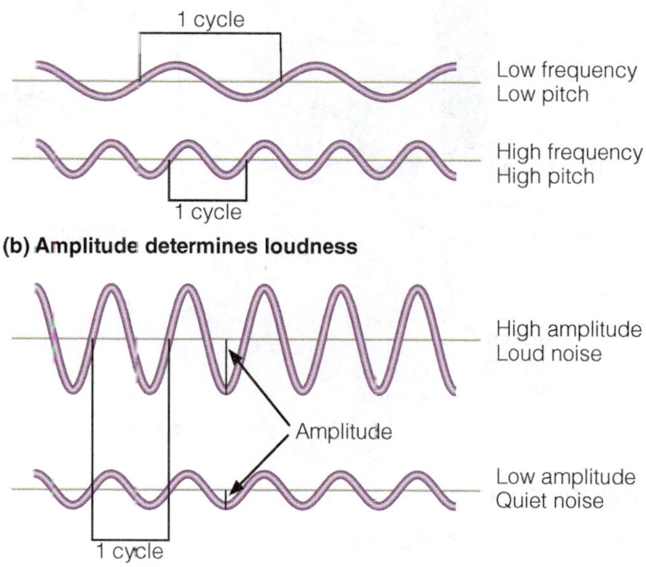

FIGURE 3.9

The Amplitude and Frequency of Sound Waves

The frequency, or number of cycles per second, determines the sound's pitch. The higher the wave's frequency, the higher the sound's pitch will be (a). The height, or amplitude, of a sound wave determines its loudness. Higher amplitudes correspond to louder sounds (b).

3.3.1 Environmental Noise and Hearing Loss

Living and working in noisy environments increase the likelihood of experiencing hearing loss as we age. For example, people living in North American urban areas experience greater age-related hearing loss than do people living in quiet rural areas of Africa (Bennett, 1990). In fact, roughly 10% of Americans between 20 and 69 have already experienced some level of permanent damage to their hearing as a result of overexposure to noise (Griest, Folmer, & Martin, 2007), and even in Africa, workers who are exposed to loud noises at work tend to experience greater age-related hearing loss than those who work in quieter settings (Strauss et al., 2014).

These numbers are not too surprising because today's world is full of noise-producing technologies (lawn mowers, power tools, loud headphones, and so on) that can be damaging to our hearing. For example, typical rock concert amplifier volumes of 120 dB can damage your hearing in as little as 15 minutes. A lawnmower can put out 90 dB, as can a noisy restaurant. Firearms can produce sounds in excess of 150 dB (Rasmussen et al., 2009), and past firearm use has been found to be correlated with hearing loss in men (Johnson et al., 2017). It is well-established that any sound over 85 dB has the potential to damage your hearing with prolonged exposure. However, some researchers (Johnson et al., 2017) now see reason to be concerned about workplace noise levels below 85 dB.

outer ear the outermost parts of the ear, including the pinna, auditory canal, and surface of the ear drum

middle ear the part of the ear behind the ear drum and in front of the oval window, including the hammer, anvil, and stirrup

Given these thresholds, a major concern is that many of us may be unknowingly damaging our hearing. For example, many people listen to loud music on cellphones or other personal listening devices (PLDs), some of which are capable of outputting more than 130 dB! Studies indicate that up to 25% of college students listen to their PLDs in violation of the so-called *60–60 rule*, which states that to avoid hearing damage, one should listen to a PLD for no more than 60 minutes a day at 60% of its maximum volume (Danhauer et al., 2009). Many of those who listen at unsafe levels are unaware of the risk involved to their hearing (Hutchinson et al., 2015). So, now that *you* know, think about turning down the volume and wearing ear protection when using any noisy machinery. You might just thank yourself later in life!

Rawpixel.com/Shutterstock.com

▲ Listening to personal listening devices (PLDs) at too high a volume and for too long a time can permanently damage your hearing. To protect your hearing, follow the 60–60 rule: listen to your PLD at no more than 60% of its maximum volume for no more than 60 minutes.

3.3.2 The Anatomy and Function of the Ear

The very outside of the **outer ear** is called the *pinna* (● FIGURE 3.10). This is the part of the body normally referred to as the ear and earlobe. The pinna acts as a funnel to gather sound waves. After being gathered by the pinna, sound waves are channeled through the *auditory canal*, where the sounds are amplified and then strike the membrane at the end of the auditory canal, the *eardrum*.

The eardrum, or *tympanic membrane*, is a very thin membrane that vibrates as the incoming sound waves strike it, much as the head of a drum vibrates when a drumstick strikes it. The three bones of the **middle ear** that are directly behind the eardrum are the *hammer, anvil*, and *stirrup* (Figure 3.10). These very small bones mechanically amplify the vibrations coming from the eardrum and transmit them to the

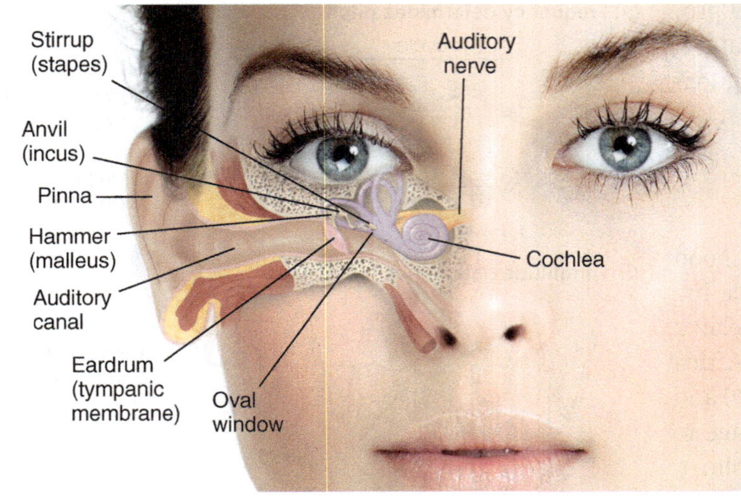

iStock.com/iconogenic

FIGURE 3.10

The Anatomy of the Ear

inner ear. The middle ear connects to the inner ear at the point where the stirrup rests against the *oval window* (Figure 3.10). The oval window is found on the outer end of the **cochlea**, one of the major components of the inner ear. The cochlea is a coiled, fluid-filled tube about 1.4 inches long that resembles a snail (Matlin & Foley, 1997). It is here that sound waves are turned into neural impulses.

If you were to uncoil the cochlea, you would see that it resembles a flexible tube that is closed off at the end. The inside of the tube contains a fluid-filled canal called the *cochlear duct* (● FIGURE 3.11). The floor of the cochlear duct is lined with the **basilar membrane**. Growing out of the basilar membrane are specialized **hair cells** that convert sound wave energy into neural impulses.

Incoming sound waves cause the bones of the middle ear to vibrate (Figures 3.10 and 3.11). The vibration of the stirrup against the oval window sets up a pressure wave inside the fluid-filled cochlea. As this wave travels through the cochlea, the cochlear duct begins to ripple. Inside the cochlear duct, the traveling wave ripples across the hair cells, causing them to begin sending neural impulses.

inner ear the innermost portion of the ear that includes the cochlea

cochlea [COCK-lee-uh] the curled, fluid-filled tube in the inner ear that contains the basilar membrane

basilar membrane the structure in the cochlear duct that contains the hair cells, which convert sound waves into neural impulses

hair cells neurons that grow out of the basilar membrane and convert sound waves into neural impulses

auditory nerve the nerve that carries information from the inner ear to the brain

place theory a theory that proposes that our brain decodes pitch by noticing which region of the basilar membrane is most active

3.3.3 The Auditory Pathways of the Brain

Once the hair cells convert sound into neural impulses, these impulses must be sent to the brain for further processing. Attached to the end of the cochlea is the **auditory nerve** (Figure 3.10). The bundled neurons of the auditory nerve gather the information from the hair cells and relay it to the brain. ● FIGURE 3.12 shows the path that auditory information takes from the ears to the brain. Notice that auditory information from each ear reaches both hemispheres of the cortex, after leaving the brainstem. It was in the brainstem that Jean-Dominique Bauby lost part of his hearing after the stroke damaged portions of his brainstem, including the *pons* (see Chapter 2).

The auditory cortex has the capacity to decode the meanings of the sounds we hear. Our next task is to examine how the brain perceives, or makes sense of, the auditory information it receives from the ears. We will begin by looking at several theories that explain our ability to perceive pitch.

Place Theory of Pitch Perception

Hermann von Helmholtz, who is credited by many with the trichromatic theory of color vision, also studied pitch perception. His **place theory** of pitch perception (Helmholtz, 1863/1930) proposes that sounds of different frequencies excite different hair cells at particular points along the basilar membrane. According to place theory, the brain receives information on pitch from the location, or place, on the basilar membrane that is being most excited by incoming sound waves. Evidence suggests that place theory may indeed explain some of our ability to perceive pitch.

In the late 1950s, Georg von Békésy conducted some important studies using pure tones made up of single sound waves, which revealed that different pitches caused the most vibration at different points along the basilar membrane (Békésy, 1960).

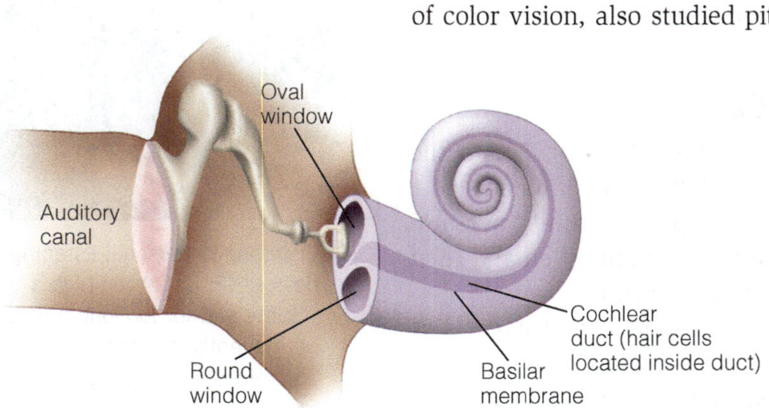

FIGURE 3.11

Enlarged Detail of the Inner Ear

Low-frequency sounds activate the far end of the basilar membrane the most. High-frequency sounds cause the most activation at the front part of the basilar membrane, near the oval window. Hair cells at the front of the basilar membrane are most vulnerable to damage, explaining why age-related hearing loss occurs first for high pitches (Waqas et al., 2018).

Although Békésy's research on place theory does describe some of our ability to perceive pitch, he only tested pure tones composed of a single frequency. He did not test tones of other *timbres*, meaning tones made up of multiple frequencies. This is important because most of the sounds we hear in life are a mixture of frequencies. When place theory is tested using complex sounds rather than pure tones, it does not fare as well as it does in explaining perception of pure tones (Matlin & Foley, 1997).

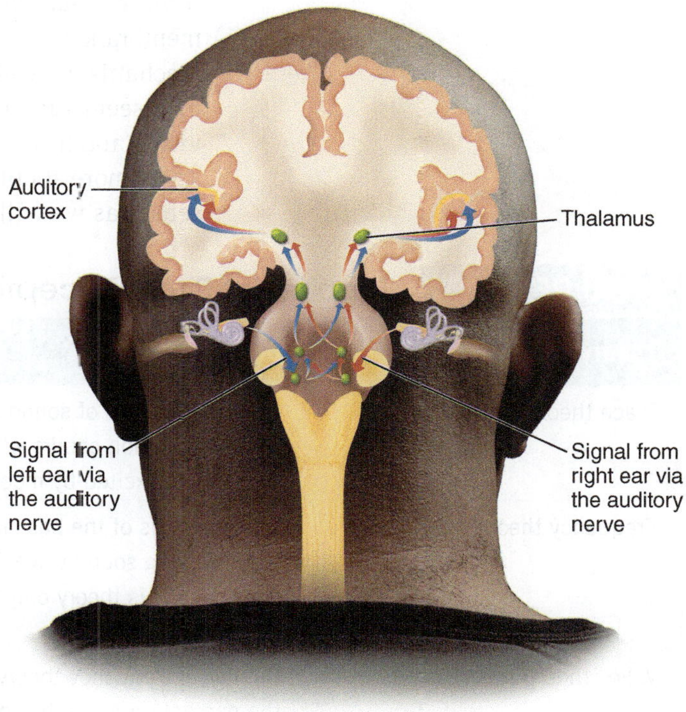

iStock.com/selimaksan

FIGURE 3.12

The Auditory Pathways in the Brain

Frequency Theory of Pitch Perception

Frequency theory proposes that our brain receives information about pitch directly from the frequency at which the hair cells are firing (Rutherford, 1886; Wever, 1949/1970). An incoming sound wave will cause the basilar membrane to vibrate and the hair cells to fire action potentials at a frequency that is relative to the frequency of the sound wave, a process called *phase locking* (Verschooten et al., 2019). For example, a sound wave at 500 Hz would cause the hair cells to fire more slowly than a 1000 Hz pitch would. A pitch of 20,000 Hz would result in a much higher rate of firing relative to the 1000 Hz pitch.

Frequency theory is a very simple concept, high-frequency pitches result in high rates of neural firing and low-frequency pitches result in low rates of neural firing. The brain knows which pitch we are hearing by examining the frequency at which the hair cells of the basilar membrane are firing. However, frequency theory has a major limitation. Hair cells can fire only at a maximum rate of 1,000 action potentials per second (1,000 Hz; Davis & Saul, 1930), yet we can hear sounds in the range of 20–20,000 Hz. How can frequency theory explain our perception of pitches well above the level of 1000 Hz?

Volley Theory of Pitch Perception

Volley theory is an updated version of frequency theory that seeks to explain perception of sounds over 1,000 Hz (Wever, 1949/1970). According to volley theory, "teams" of hair cells work together to give us the perception of sounds over 1,000 Hz. For example, let's say you hear a pitch that causes the basilar membrane to vibrate at 3000 Hz (a pitch higher than human speech). No single hair cell can fire at 3,000 Hz, but three hair cells, each firing at 1,000 Hz, can work together as a group to tell your brain that you are hearing this high-pitched tone.

Integrating Volley and Place Theories: A Dual Mechanism in Hearing

Volley theory seems adequate to explain pitch perception, but we still have to deal with place theory, which also seems to explain some aspects of our perception. Recall that Georg von Békésy (1960) found that different pitches excite different parts of the basilar membrane. Volley theory cannot explain why this would be the case. So, what is going on in our ears? Is it the place or the frequency of the excited hair cells that tells us what pitch we are hearing? It may well be *both*.

Today researchers widely believe that we perceive pitch through a combination of volley theory and place theory (Erfanian Saeedi et al., 2016;

frequency theory a theory that proposes that our brain decodes pitch directly from the frequency at which the hair cells of the basilar membrane are firing

volley theory a theory that proposes that our brain decodes pitch by noticing the frequency at which groups of hair cells on the basilar membrane are firing

Laudanski, Zheng, & Brette, 2014). The argument is that the brain uses information from the *dual mechanisms* of the *rate* of neural firing and the *place* on the basilar membrane that is most active in decoding pitch. However, exactly how these dual mechanisms work together is still being investigated (Verschooten et al., 2019). It may seem surprising to learn that we still don't fully understand the processes of vision and hearing, but sensory research is complex and challenging. However, we know more about how hearing and vision work than we do about some of our other senses as we will see as we explore *taste, touch, smell,* and the *body senses* next.

YOU REVIEW Theories of Pitch Perception

Theory	Description
Place theory	Different pitches of sound activate specific regions of the basilar membrane more than others. Pitch perception occurs when the brain notices which portions of the basilar membrane are being most excited by incoming sound waves.
Frequency theory	The hair cells of the basilar membrane fire action potentials at a rate relative to the frequency of the incoming sound wave. The brain determines pitch by noticing the rate at which the hair cells are firing. This theory only explains perception of pitches up to 1,000 Hz, the maximum firing rate of a hair cell.
Volley theory	Similar to frequency theory, this theory states that groups of hair cells fire as teams to give us the perception of pitches over 1,000 Hz. For example, three hair cells each firing at 1,000 Hz together yield the perception of a 3,000-Hz tone.
The dual mechanism approach	The dual mechanism approach proposes that a combination of frequency and place information is used in pitch perception. Exactly how these sources of information are integrated in the brain is still being investigated.

3.3 Quiz Yourself

1. In the United States, men have been shown to have greater age-related hearing loss than women have. One explanation for this is that men tend to work around noisy machinery more often than women do. To test the idea that, for humans, working around noisy machinery is related to age-related hearing loss, you would most want to use which of the following research designs?
   a. An experiment
   b. A correlational design
   c. A naturalistic observation
   d. A case study

2. By turning up the volume on your TV, you are changing the ________ of the sound waves being emitted by the TV.
   a. amplitude
   b. wavelength
   c. pitch
   d. width

3. ________ theory proposes that pitch is perceived when the brain locates the region of the basilar membrane that is firing the most action potentials.
   a. Frequency
   b. Basilar
   c. Place
   d. Volley

Answers 1. b; 2. a; 3. c

3.4 The Other Senses: Taste, Smell, Touch, and the Body Senses

3.4.1 Taste: Information from the Tongue

For most of us, the senses of taste and smell are interconnected. These two senses are called *chemical senses* because they require that certain chemicals come into direct contact with our sense organs. Vision and hearing don't require such direct contact; we can perceive visual and auditory stimuli at a distance. But for taste, or **gustation**, to occur, certain chemicals in foods and other substances must be dissolved in our saliva and come into direct contact with the sense organ commonly known as the tongue. For smell, chemicals in the nearby air—from food or other substances—must come into contact with cells in the nasal cavity.

gustation [gus-TAY-shun] the sense of taste

papillae [puh-PILL-ee] bumps on the tongue that many people mistake for taste buds

taste buds the sense organs for taste that are found between the papillae on the tongue

Sensing Flavor: The Five Basic Tastes

Traditionally, it was believed that humans could sense only four different types of tastes: *bitter, sweet, salty,* and *sour* (Bartoshuk & Beauchamp, 1994). However, it now appears that humans are also sensitive to a fifth taste called *umami,* or L-glutamic acid (Behrens & Meyerhof, 2018). Umami is a meaty, brothy flavor that is more common in Asian foods than it is in Western cuisine. Monosodium glutamate (MSG) is a combination of sodium and L-glutamic acid that is often added to Asian dishes. People who eat a Western diet are not as likely to be as familiar with umami's flavor as they are with the other basic tastes. Nonetheless, studies indicate that glutamate activates umami receptors on the tongue (Lopez Cascales et al., 2010), giving most people the ability to taste umami (Cecchini et al., 2019; Damak et al., 2003; Hodson & Linden, 2006). Interestingly, fMRI scans indicate that tasting both umami and salt, results in activation of the same brain areas. This suggests that the brain may use the same processing system for both umami and salty flavors (Han et al., 2018), which makes sense as people often use the adjective "salty" to describe how umami tastes (Cecchini et al., 2019).

Our tongues may have evolved to detect these five tastes because they are associated with certain types of foods that have implications for our survival (Scott & Plata-Salaman, 1991). For example, sweet flavors are associated with edible foods and bitter tastes with poisons. Salty flavors suggest the presence of sodium in a food. As you learned in Chapter 2, sodium is crucial to the function of our nervous system. Umami can make food taste better and stimulate our appetite (Stanska & Kreski, 2016); but it also may play a role in reducing overeating, especially in women who are prone to overeating (Magerowski et al., 2018). Because of the survival value found in the basic tastes, it seems likely that our sense of taste evolved to help us eat healthfully while still avoiding the numerous poisons that exist around us.

From Tongue to Taste: How Do We Experience Flavor?

When you look at your tongue in the mirror, you normally see a bunch of little bumps covering its surface. We'll guess that you were taught to refer to these visible bumps as taste buds. This is incorrect—the bumps you see are the **papillae** of the tongue. Your **taste buds** actually reside in the pits between the papillae (● FIGURE 3.13). Your taste buds are what convert the chemicals in the foods you eat into the neural impulses that convey taste information to your brain. Most people have between 2,000 and 5,000 taste buds on their tongue (Miller & Bartoshuk, 1991). Unlike some types of sensory cells, taste buds can regenerate. This is important because we damage our taste buds on a regular basis—for example, when we burn our tongues with hot food.

Many researchers believe that, like the cones of the eye, different taste buds are maximally sensitive to one of the basic

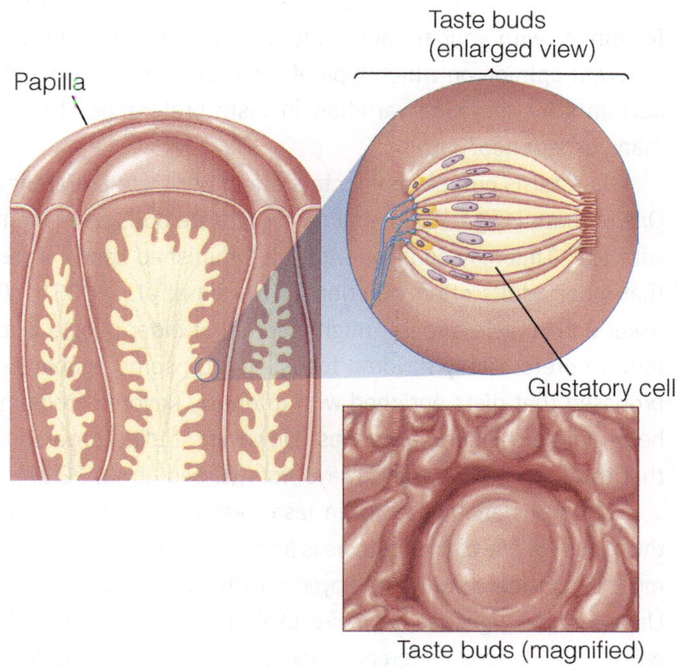

FIGURE 3.13

Papillae and Taste Buds

Taste buds are the sensory receptors for taste. Contrary to popular belief, the bumps on our tongues are not taste buds—they are papillae. Our taste buds are located next to the papillae on the tongue.

▲ If you burn your taste buds, you will experience temporary loss of taste sensation until the taste buds grow back.

flavors (Shallenberger, 1993). Thus, taste perception on the tongue appears to work very much like color perception in the retina. If the brain is informed that the "sweet taste buds" are very active, we taste a sweet flavor. If the "bitter taste buds" are most active, we taste something bitter. If all flavors are some combination of sweet, salty, sour, bitter, and umami, the presence of five types of taste buds is sufficient to explain our taste perception (Chandrashekar et al., 2006).

There is evidence that we can detect all of the five basic tastes across all regions of our tongues. However, once we do detect a flavor on our tongue, our sensitivity to it may depend to some extent on where the food is placed on our tongue and whether or not we swallow the food (Running & Hayes, 2017). Over the years, there has been significant disagreement as to whether or not these areas of sensitivity exist, and if they do, exactly where they are located. Some suggest that sweet flavors taste stronger at the front of the tongue and sour tastes are stronger on the sides. Salty tastes are thought to be more intense near the front of the tongue (Shallenberger, 1993); whereas, bitter and umami flavors may be most intense on the back of the tongue (Feeney & Hayes, 2014). Interestingly, researchers have discovered that lowering the temperature of the tongue and then allowing the tongue to rewarm prior to tasting led to increased taste sensitivity (Fujiyama & Toda, 2016). Perhaps having a cold drink of water a short time before eating will make your meal more enjoyable!

Psychology Applies to Your World

Why Don't We All Like the Same Foods?

HAVE YOU EVER FOUND YOURSELF discussing where to go for dinner with your friends, only to find that everyone has a different opinion on which type of food you should have? What accounts for the wide variation in taste preferences that humans experience?

As it turns out, several factors affect our taste preferences. One of these is age. We lose some of our taste buds permanently with age. This may contribute to the diminished sense of taste that older adults often experience (Nordin et al., 2003). With fewer active taste buds, it might seem that older people would tend to prefer richly flavored foods. In fact, some people have proposed that diets enriched with intensely flavored foods may help maintain elders' appetites. However, studies have shown that this strategy may not always work (Essed et al., 2007).

Culture is another factor in taste preferences. For example, the spouse of one of your authors is from El Salvador, where iguana meat is considered a treat enjoyed mostly by the wealthy. In the United States, iguanas are more likely to be kept as pets than eaten. Why do food preferences vary across cultures? One reason is that the availability of food sources dictates what a particular people can eat. Central Americans eat iguana meat today partly because their ancestors once ate the wild iguanas that roamed there. Every culture must take advantage of the food sources at its disposal, and hunger can make foods taste better, especially when those foods provide needed nutrients (Mobini, Chambers, & Yeomans, 2007).

Religious values and traditions also shape cultural food preferences. For example, observant Jews and Muslims will not eat pork, Hindus often do not eat beef, and Seventh Day Adventists frown upon the use of certain spices (Grivetti, 2000). These taste preferences are passed from generation to generation as parents teach children to follow their religious values.

▶ Our food preferences are a result of biological factors, our cultural background, and our personal experience with food.

Many of our individual food preferences develop through learning—some of it very early in life. Research shows that the foods a mother eats can affect the flavor of her breast milk, and

You may also be surprised to learn that the center of the tongue lacks taste buds. You won't taste flavors that are placed directly in the center of your tongue. In a sense, this region of the tongue is like the blindspot in the eye—no taste sensation can occur here (Matlin & Foley, 1997). Despite this taste blindspot, we still manage to taste the foods we eat because chewing distributes food across the tongue.

Of course, only after your brain has done its part can you become consciously aware of the flavor of your food. Each taste bud is connected to neurons that receive input from that taste bud. These neurons join together to form three nerves. One nerve gathers input from the front of the tongue, another from the back of the tongue, and a third from the throat. These nerves travel to the medulla oblongata and the pons of the brainstem before conveying the taste information to the thalamus. Like most sensory information, taste information travels from the thalamus to the "thinking" part of the brain, the cortex. Most of the taste information ends up in the somatosensory cortex of the parietal lobe, but some of the information is diverted to the limbic system before reaching the cortex. It's here in the cortex that we perceive the flavor of our food.

3.4.2 Smell: Aromas, Odors, and a Warning System

Olfaction, our sense of smell, has adaptive value. Smells can alert us to danger. The ability to smell smoke enables us to detect a fire long before we see flames.

olfaction the sense of smell

exposure to these flavors during breast-feeding can affect her child's later taste preferences (Mennella & Beauchamp, 1991). Being exposed to a variety of flavors in infancy tends to make infants more open to new and novel foods (Hausner et al., 2010).

Although the influence of learning on food preferences is strong, evidence also suggests that biological factors can influence our sense of taste. Prior to menopause, women's ability to taste fluctuates with hormone levels; and after menopause, the ability to taste declines (Prutkin et al., 2000). Ethnicity may also play a role in our ability to taste. For example, Hispanic and African-American subjects report having stronger taste sensations relative to non-Hispanic Whites. And, this ethnic difference is stronger for men than it is for women (Williams et al., 2016). Furthermore, certain flavors, such as sweet and umami, also seem to be particularly palatable to humans. This may help explain why sweeter vegetables (e.g., carrots) are often preferred to more bitter ones (e.g., broccoli; Dinnella et al., 2016).

There are also some genetic variations in our individual ability to taste certain flavors. Some people, called supertasters, have a higher-than-average number of taste buds and are able to strongly taste a bitter compound called 6-n-propylthiocuracil (PROP). In contrast, nontasters perceive very little or no bitterness from PROP (Bartoshuk, 2000). Nontasters have been shown to eat a wider variety of foods (Azar, 1998; Pasquet et al., 2002) and have higher body mass indexes (BMIs; Feeney et al., 2011) than supertasters do. Compared to nontasters, female PROP tasters tend to eat more fat and less fruit in their diets (Yackinous & Guinard, 2002). Supertasters may avoid some foods that are rich in cancer-fighting compounds but also have bitter flavors (such as Brussels sprouts), but masking the bitterness with a compound like aspartame (Nutrasweet) has been shown to increase liking for such foods (Sharafi, Hayes, & Duffy, 2013).

Bill Losh/The Image Bank/Getty Images

▶ The inability to smell also limits the ability to taste.

Being a supertaster may also allow a person to make finer discriminations among flavors. Connoisseurs of wine have been shown to be more likely to be supertasters or at least "medium" tasters. Their increased ability to perceive PROP may allow them to perceive nuanced flavors in the wine (Pickering, Jain, & Bezawada, 2013).

Finally, our sense of taste is not influenced solely by our culture, early learning, or taste buds. Our sense of taste is also heavily dependent on our sense of smell (Shepard, 2006). If you've ever tried to taste food when you've had a bad cold, you know that your sense of smell makes a significant contribution to taste and that clogged nasal passages tend to make food taste bland. Our food preferences are a result of biological factors, our cultural background, and our personal experience with food.

The rotten smell of spoiled food warns us not to eat it. Without such odoriferous warnings, we could easily find ourselves in harm's way.

Our ability to smell may play a role in our social relationships as well. Newborns use scent to recognize their mothers (Vaglio, 2009), which may facilitate both feeding and social bonding (Genva et al., 2019). Olfaction may also influence our selection of a mate and the development and breakdown of our romantic relationships (Mahmut & Croy, 2019). For example, women report that a man's smell is more important than how attractive he is when choosing a sexual partner (Herz & Inzlicht, 2002). Given the importance of smell in our daily lives, let's take a closer look at our olfactory sense.

Like the sense of taste, the sense of smell is a chemical sense. Odors come from airborne chemicals that are diffused in the air. When we inhale these molecules into our nose, we may experience smelling the substance. Compared with our other senses, our sense of smell is quite sensitive. Recall from our earlier discussion of sensory thresholds that we can detect the presence of a single drop of perfume in a three-room apartment (see Table 3.1). When compared to men, women perform slightly better on tests of olfaction, especially when it comes to their ability to detect the presence of odors (i.e., their *absolute thresholds*). This edge in performance may be related to hormonal differences in men and women (Sorokowski et al., 2019). Yet despite these impressive abilities, in daily life we typically pay attention only to odors that are quite strong (Sela & Sobel, 2010). For example, we are frequently unaware of the detectable smells of other people unless they are strong (for example, heavy cologne or strong body odor). In other words, smells have to make a big impact on us to capture our attention and make us consciously aware of them.

The Mystery of Smell

Researchers have not been able to determine precisely how our sense of smell works. Of the senses we have described to this point, smell is by far the least understood. What we do know is that we are able to smell because of a special piece of skin, the **olfactory epithelium**, that lines the top of the nasal cavity (● FIGURE 3.14). Estimates of the number of odors that humans can detect vary widely, but it is thought that we can detect at least 400,000 distinct odor molecules (Grabe & Sachse, 2018). Yet, the olfactory epithelium only contains roughly 400 different types of odor receptors (Block, 2018; Nimura, 2012). When we breathe in odor-laden air, the odor molecules reach the receptors in the olfactory epithelium and stimulate these cells. This stimulation accomplishes the conversion of odor into smell, but just how our brain understands what we smell is not well understood at this time (Trimmer et al., 2019). One theory, the **lock-and-key theory**, proposes that olfactory receptors are excited by odor molecules in much the same way that neurotransmitters excite receptor sites on the postsynaptic neuron (Amoore, 1970). According to lock-and-key theory, specific odor molecules have the power to "unlock" or excite certain olfactory receptors in the olfactory epithelium. However, research has shown that simple lock-and-key explanations are unable to fully explain our perception of odors (Triller et al., 2008). It appears that the activation of receptors in the olfactory epithelium is just one step in a series of neural processes that give rise to our perception of smell. The exact nature of these processes is still being investigated. Yet, despite our lack of understanding about *how* exactly the process of olfaction unfolds, we do have some understanding of the pathway that olfactory information travels through the brain.

olfactory epithelium [ole-FACT-uh-ree epp-ith-THEEL-ee-um] a special piece of skin at the top of the nasal cavity that contains the olfactory receptors

lock-and-key theory a theory that proposes that olfactory receptors are excited by odor molecules in a way that is similar to the way in which neurotransmitters excite receptor sites

Once the cells of the epithelium have converted odor into neural impulses, these signals travel across the *olfactory nerve* to the *olfactory bulb* of the brain.

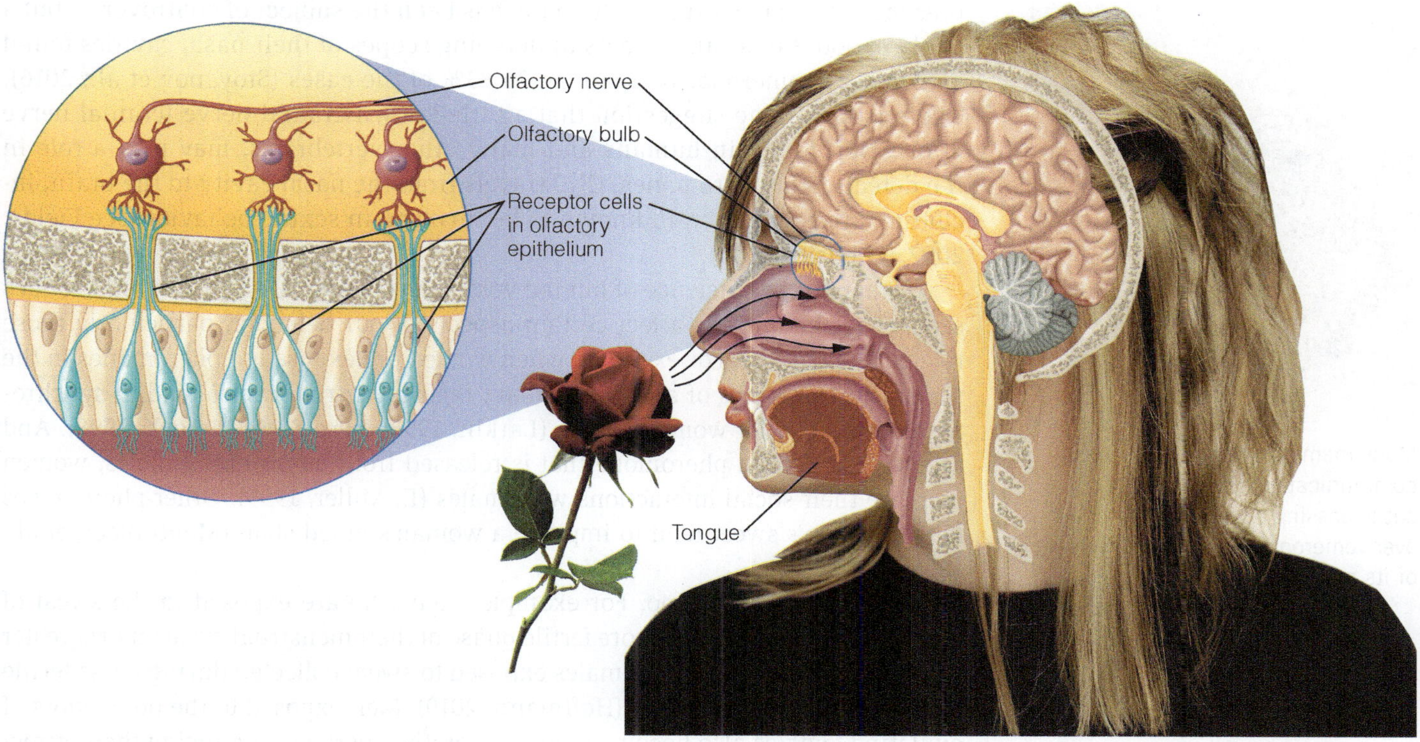

FIGURE 3.14

The Anatomy of the Nose

Odors in the form of airborne chemicals are inhaled into the nasal cavity, where sensory cells in the olfactory epithelium convert them into neural signals.

The olfactory bulb is located just below the bottom edge of the frontal lobe of the brain (see Figure 3.14). The olfactory bulb processes incoming information before sending it on to other parts of the brain. Unlike our other senses, olfactory information bypasses the thalamus as it travels to the cortex of the brain. Some olfactory information goes *directly* from the olfactory bulb to the primary smell cortex, in the temporal lobes of the brain. Other olfactory information is sent to both the cortex and the limbic system. Recall from Chapter 2 that the limbic system regulates emotional and motivational activity. The limbic system seems to be heavily involved in the processing of olfactory information. This may explain the strong emotional reactions we often have to certain smells. For example, the smell of one of your favorite childhood meals may conjure up beloved memories of your childhood. Are there particular smells that bring back emotionally charged memories for you?

Chemosignals: Pheromones and the Vomeronasal Sense

Some researchers believe that humans have yet another sense somewhat related to smell. This sense, the *vomeronasal sense*, is well documented in animals (Doty, 2001). Many animals communicate with each other via airborne *chemosignals* called **pheromones**. Pheromones are produced by glands in the animal's body and dispersed into the air, where other animals then inhale them. Such animals are equipped with vomeronasal organs that can detect the presence of inhaled pheromones. Perhaps you have seen a cat inhale deeply through its open mouth—a process called the *flehmen* response. The cat is passing pheromone-laden air over special organs, called Jacobson's organs, in the roof of its mouth. These organs can detect the presence of pheromones. The

pheromones [FAIR-uh-moans] airborne chemicals that are released from glands and detected by the vomeronasal organs in some animals and perhaps humans

NaturePL/NaturePL/Superstock

▲ Many mammals use pheromones to communicate with each other. This cat is passing pheromone-laden air over vomeronasal organs in the roof of its mouth.

presence of such an organ in humans has been the subject of controversy, but a study of 966 Bulgarian patients undergoing scopes of their nasal cavities found evidence of vomeronasal organs in 26.83% of the cases (Stoyanov et al., 2016). There is also some suggestion that a little-known cranial nerve (cranial nerve 0, or CN0), found in humans and many other vertebrates, may play a role in the detection of pheromones. CN0 travels from the nasal cavity to the brain, including areas of the brain known to be involved in sexual behavior (see Fields, 2007; Vilensky, 2014).

Although the existence of human vomeronasal organs is controversial, it does seem that pheromones affect certain aspects of our behavior, particularly those related to sexuality. For example, when women are exposed to pheromones in the underarm secretions of another woman, their menstrual cycles tend to synchronize with the other woman's cycle (Larkin, 1998; Stern & McClintock, 1998). And after exposure to a pheromone that is released from men's hair follicles, women increase their social interactions with males (E. Miller, 1999). Other pheromones found in men's sweat tend to improve a woman's mood state (Monti-Bloch et al., 1998).

Males are affected too. For example, men who are exposed to the sweat of women collected during a more fertile phase of their menstrual cycle report greater levels of sexual arousal than males exposed to sweat collected during a less fertile phase of the women's cycles (Hoffmann, 2019). Men exposed to the body odors of ovulating females also become more cooperative, perhaps enhancing their attractiveness as a potential mate (Oren & Shamay-Tsoory, 2019). Pheromones may also influence alcohol consumption. Humans often consume alcohol as a precursor to sexual activity, and men who are exposed to the pheromones of fertile women have been shown to consume more alcohol than men who are exposed to the pheromones of infertile women (Tan & Goldman, 2015).

On the other hand, pheromone signals may at times be capable of reducing sexual activity. When women cry, their tears contain chemosignals that may affect men's behavior. Shani Gelstein and colleagues (2011) collected women's tears in a vial as they watched a sad movie and later had men smell the tears without the women present. Compared to a control group that sniffed pure saline, the men who sniffed tears experienced decreased levels of testosterone (male sex hormones, see Chapter 2), and they reported lowered sexual arousal. Functional magnetic resonance imaging (fMRI) scans of the men's brains also showed reduced brain activity in areas of the brain related to sexual arousal, such as the hypothalamus and the left *fusiform gyrus* (Gelstein et al., 2011). These findings suggest that men may be biologically programmed to lose interest in sex when they encounter a crying woman. More research is needed to determine the significance of this effect. Also unclear is whether chemosignals are found in the tears of men and children and what, if any, effect they may have on others.

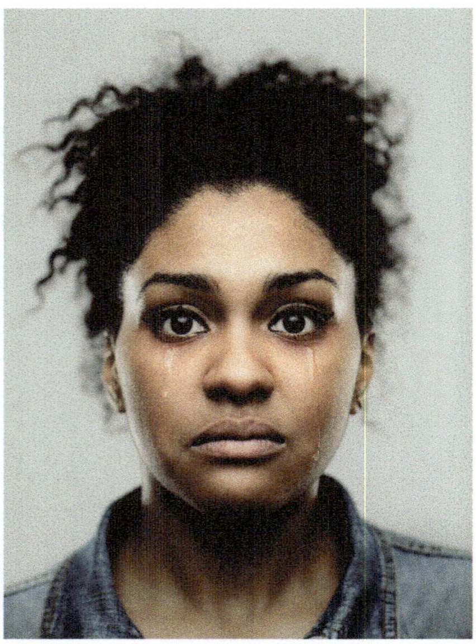

iStock.com/SensorSpot

▲ Research suggests that the tears of women contain chemosignals that impact men by reducing their level of testosterone production.

Whether or not a vomeronasal sense exists separately from our olfactory sense, it is clear that chemosignals affect our social behavior. For example, people born without a sense of smell have been shown to experience specific relationship difficulties. Specifically, males without a sense of smell exhibit fewer sexual relationships and females without the ability to smell exhibit a weaker sense of security with their partners (Croy, Bojanowski, & Hummel, 2013). One study also found that in people with bipolar disorder, having a poorer sense of smell was correlated with difficulties in recognizing facial expressions of emotion (Lahera, et al., 2016). Odd as it may sound, our sense of smell appears to facilitate our social interactions with others.

3.4.3 Touch: The Skin Sense

Touch is another sense that is important to social relationships. Touch is associated with many of life's pleasurable experiences. Feeling a friendly pat on the back can certainly enhance our social interactions. Sexual activity depends heavily on our ability to feel touch. But our ability to sense with our skin also affects our survival. Through our skin we feel touch, temperature, and pain.

Our keen sense of touch originates in our skin. The skin is composed of several layers that contain touch receptors. The inner layer, the **dermis**, contains most of the touch receptors (● FIGURE 3.15). The skin's outer layer is the **epidermis**, which consists of several layers of dead skin cells. The epidermis also contains touch receptors, especially in areas of the skin that do not have hair, such as the fingertips. Receptors in our fingertips are arguably the most important touch receptors in the body because we use our hands so much in interacting with the world (Martuzzi et al., 2014).

dermis the inner layer of the skin

epidermis the outer layer of the skin

gate control theory of pain a theory of pain that proposes that tiny neural networks in the spinal cord block pain signals from a particular part of the body when they receive additional neural signals from intense tactile stimulation being applied to the same part of the body

We have different types of receptors for touch, temperature, and pain (Figure 3.15). We know more about the function of the touch receptors than we do about the pain and temperature receptors. Pressure on the skin pushes against the axons of the touch receptors. This causes a change in the axonal membrane's permeability to positive ions, allowing them to enter the cell (Hu et al., 2010; Loewenstein, 1960). As you recall from Chapter 2, as positive ions enter a cell, the cell becomes more likely to fire an action potential. If the touch is intense enough to allow the receptors to reach threshold, neural impulses will be fired. These impulses travel to the spinal cord and then to the brain. In the brain, the signals enter the thalamus and then go on to the somatosensory cortex of the parietal lobe. Some signals, particularly those indicating the presence of threatening stimuli, go to the limbic system as well as the somatosensory cortex (Coren, Ward, & Enns, 1999). Once the signals reach the somatosensory cortex, our brain interprets the sensation and directs us to take the appropriate action.

For example, if you stub your toe getting out of bed, you might be motivated to rub your toe to ease the pain. But, why would this help? The answer may lie in what is known as the **gate control theory of pain** (Melzack & Wall, 1965; Ropero

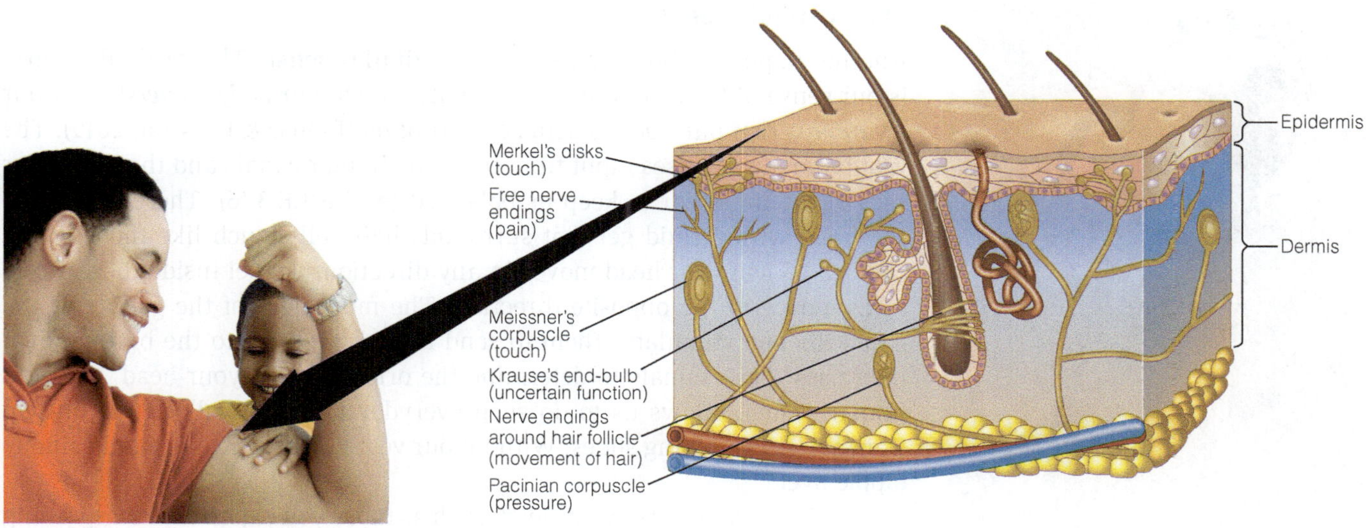

Jose Luis Pelaez Inc/Blend Images/Corbis

FIGURE 3.15

Anatomy of the Skin and Its Receptors

Different types of skin receptors pick up different types of stimulation.

kinesthesis [kin-ess-THEE-sis] the ability to sense the position of our body parts in relation to one another and in relation to space

vestibular [ves-STIB-you-lar] sense the sense of balance

Peláez, & Taniguchi, 2016). According to gate control theory, tiny neural networks in the spinal cord work to relieve pain when they receive signals from intense tactile stimulation (e.g., rubbing) being applied to the part of the body that hurts. It is as if a neurological gate closes, blocking the pain signals from reaching the brain, while allowing the signals from the rubbing sensation to travel onward to the brain. Modern medicine uses this idea in treating chronic pain. Perhaps you have seen advertisements for TENS (transcutaneous electrical nerve stimulation) units. These small electrical devices deliver mild electrical shocks to painful parts of the body, activating the gate control networks in the spinal cord and relieving pain.

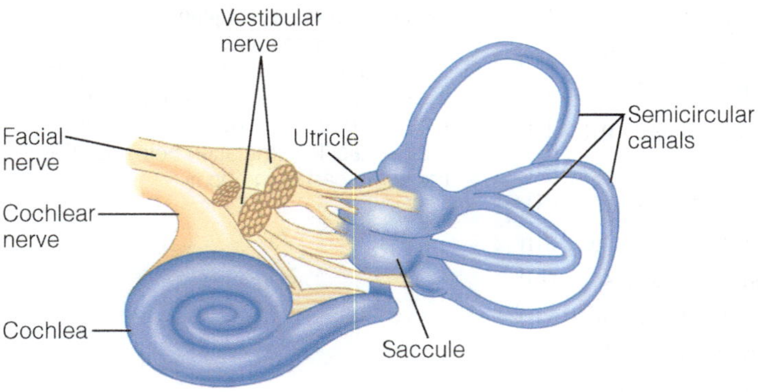

FIGURE 3.16

The Vestibular Organs

The vestibular system helps us balance our body by monitoring the position and acceleration of our head as we move. To accomplish this, a gel-like fluid in the semicircular canals, saccule, and utricle presses against hair cells much like those found in the cochlea of the inner ear. When the hair cells of the vestibular system are moved, they signal the brain with information about the orientation of our head in three-dimensional space.

3.4.4 The Body Senses: Experiencing the Physical Body in Space

So far, we have covered what are referred to as the five senses: vision, hearing, taste, smell, and touch. Do we possess other senses? The answer is yes, but this time, we're not talking about ESP. We are referring to the body senses, the senses that help us experience our physical bodies in space: *kinesthesis* and the *vestibular sense*.

Kinesthesis

Kinesthesis is the ability to sense the position of our body parts in space and in relation to one another. As you walk, you are aware of where your arms, legs, and head are in relation to the ground. Kinesthetic sense is important to athletes, especially to gymnasts and high divers. It allows them to know where their bodies are as they execute their routines and dives. Our kinesthetic sense uses information from the muscles, tendons, skin, and joints to keep us oriented at all times. The information from these sources is processed in the somatosensory cortex and the cerebellum of the brain (see Chapter 2).

Nick Laham/Getty Images

▲ Our vestibular sense keeps us balanced, and the kinesthetic sense allows this skateboarder to perform intricate moves without falling.

The Vestibular Sense

Another important body sense is our **vestibular sense**. The vestibular sense is our sense of balance. It may also contribute to our *body ownership*, or our awareness that our body is actually part of us (Preuss & Ehrsson, 2019). The vestibular system uses input from the semicircular canals and the vestibular sacs of the inner ear to keep us balanced (● FIGURE 3.16). These structures are filled with a fluid gel that surrounds hair cells much like those in the cochlea. When your head moves in any direction, the gel inside these structures moves in the opposite direction. The movement of the gel bends the hair cells and stimulates them to send neural impulses to the brain, which then uses these signals to determine the orientation of your head. Our vestibular system allows us to do such everyday tasks as walking, getting up from a desk, and tying shoes. Without our vestibular sense, we would simply topple over.

Rapid movements of your head, such as those you experience on spinning carnival rides, can overstimulate the vestibular system. Such movements can cause a violent wave action in the fluid gel of the vestibular system. When the gel crashes against the sensory cells, the result can be dizziness and nausea. People vary with respect to the degree of vestibular stimulation that they can comfortably tolerate.

You now have a working knowledge of how our sensory organs convert environmental energies into neural impulses. Our next topic is perception, or how we make sense of all of this sensory information.

3.4 Quiz Yourself

1. Which of the following is *not* thought to be a taste for which your tongue has receptors?
   a. Salty
   b. Sour
   c. Spicy
   d. Bitter
2. Spinning around and around on a carnival ride is most likely to affect which of your senses?
   a. Taste
   b. Hearing
   c. Smell
   d. Vestibular sense
3. Which of your senses would be least likely to be affected when you have a bad head cold?
   a. Taste
   b. Touch
   c. Smell
   d. Vestibular sense

Answers 1. c; 2. d; 3. b

3.5 Perception: Interpreting Your World

At the beginning of this chapter, we defined perception as the *interpretation of sensory information*. That's it in a nutshell. When you look at your friend, light bounces off their face. This light strikes your retina, and the rods and cones convert the light into neural impulses. Sensation is complete. But now your brain must interpret the meaning of the neural impulses so you will recognize your friend's face. The fact that you believe you are seeing your friend and not, say, a dog or your psychology instructor is the result of perceptual processes in your brain. But how does your brain know that you are seeing your friend's face?

top-down perceptual processing perception that is guided by prior knowledge or expectations

3.5.1 Using What We Know: Top-Down Perceptual Processing

Top-down perceptual processing occurs when we use previously gained knowledge to help us interpret a stimulus. Let's go back to the example of perceiving your friend's face. When you see a face that you recognize, what leads you to this recognition? Your memory helps you understand the meaning of the face you see. You know that faces usually contain two eyes, a nose, a mouth, and so on. Furthermore, you know how your friend's particular eyes, nose, and other features look. This stored knowledge allows you to quickly perceive the face of a friend.

Top-down perceptual processing can also fill in parts of a stimulus that are missing from our actual sensation of it. For example, look at ● FIGURE 3.17. You cannot see this woman's face, but you probably assume that she has one. Your knowledge of the human body tells you that the odds are slim that she is actually missing a face. Consequently, in perceiving this picture, you implicitly assume that the "missing" neck and face do, in fact, exist. This effect is so strong that later when you recall this picture, you might even remember having seen her face and neck—right down to the color of her eyes and the "necklace" she was "wearing."

Unfortunately, this "filling-in" of missing details can sometimes lead to mistakes in perception. Because people have different knowledge and expectations

JTSorrell/Getty Images

FIGURE 3.17

Top-Down Perceptual Processing

When you perceive the image in this photograph, your knowledge of the human body leads you to have certain expectations about the woman in this picture. Because of top-down processing, you do not perceive that this woman is missing her face and neck.

perceptual set a general readiness to perceive something in a particular manner

bottom-up perceptual processing perception that is not guided by prior knowledge or expectations

about the world, two people can witness the same event and yet perceive it differently. Sometimes this prior knowledge can even function as a **perceptual set**, creating a general readiness in us to perceive a stimulus in a certain way. For example, one's political ideology has been shown to be related to how they tend to perceive skin tone in racially ambiguous faces (Caruso, Mead, & Balcetis, 2009; Krosch et al., 2013). Stereotypes that we hold for specific groups of people can also affect how we perceive members of those groups (for review, see Bagnis et al., 2019). And, as you read "LOL" in this sentence, we bet you perceive the "O" to be a letter, rather than as a zero. Yet, you may have read the same character as a zero in the date that accompanies the "Krosch et al." reference a few lines up in this text. Did you? If you did, it was likely due to your perceptual sets for letters and numbers.

Keep in mind that many times the effects of perceptual sets and top-down perceptual processing are benign or even helpful. For example, you may be quicker to perceive a shape in the road in front of you as a pedestrian and slow down because you know that it is common to see people walking along the road. But, what if the correct identification of a suspect depended on accurately remembering what he was wearing? Or recalling the color of her eyes? This can be a real problem in eyewitness accounts of crimes (see also Chapter 7). In fact, one study showed that a majority of the falsely convicted people being studied had been mistakenly identified by eyewitnesses (Wells & Olson, 2003). Curiously, research suggests that compared to simply warning potential jurors about the weaknesses of eyewitness testimony, actually demonstrating the limitations of eyewitness testimony by having potential jurors experience firsthand an eyewitness identification procedure can make jurors place less faith in eyewitness testimony when making decisions (Duckworth et al., 2011). The hope is that such interventions may prove useful in reducing false convictions.

3.5.2 Building a Perception "from Scratch": Bottom-Up Perceptual Processing

What do we do when we have very little or no stored knowledge to help us perceive a stimulus? We use a different perceptual process, one that does not rely on stored knowledge or expectations of the stimulus. In **bottom-up perceptual processing**, the properties of the stimulus itself are what we use to build our perception of that stimulus.

Engage Yourself!

Look at ● FIGURE 3.18. What do you see? With few clues about what this stimulus is, you cannot easily use your knowledge to help you perceive it. The stimulus is too ambiguous. Without top-down processing, you are forced to use bottom-up processes to perceive the stimulus. You build your perception of the picture by piecing together your perceptions of the many different components that make up this stimulus. You perceive the lines, curves, dots, shaded areas, and shapes. You then try to fit these components together to figure out what the drawing means. Most people find it very difficult to figure out what Figure 3.18 is using only bottom-up perceptual processes!

If you are ready to give up and try top-down perceptual processing, look at ● FIGURE 3.21. Now turn back to Figure 3.18. You will likely find that you can now readily perceive the image in Figure 3.18. You now have knowledge of what to look for, so perception becomes much easier. Your knowledge of what the picture is guides the way you piece together the components of the stimulus. When you switch to top-down processing, the picture becomes almost obvious.

FIGURE 3.18

Top-Down Versus Bottom-Up Processing

What is this picture?

In the course of a typical day, we probably use both top-down and bottom-up perceptual processes continually. We use bottom-up processes to piece together perceptions of ambiguous stimuli and top-down processes to tell us what we can expect to perceive in certain situations. Perception can be complicated in a three-dimensional world that is full of shapes and forms. To make perception even more complicated, our bodies do not remain stationary during perception. We move. The objects we perceive sometimes move. As a result, the information our senses receive from our world is highly variable. Our perceptual processes must be able to deal with these dynamic conditions. So how do we organize and make sense of our perceptions?

3.5.3 Understanding What We Sense: Perceiving Size, Shape, and Brightness

One of the phenomena encountered in interpreting sensory data is *perceptual constancy* (Hatfield & Allred, 2012). When you look at a visual stimulus, the image it projects on your retina is highly influenced by the perspective from which you view the object. Yet your perception of the object is not as dependent on perspective as your sensation is. For example, if you view a friend from a distance of 3 feet, an image of a certain size is projected onto your retina. If you move away and view the same friend from a distance of 6 feet, a smaller image is projected on your retina. Your sensation has changed, but you will not perceive that your friend has shrunk. In this case, your brain appears to step in to correct your perception, to give you a constant perception of the objects that you see in the world. There is evidence that our brains correct not only for *size constancy*, but also for *shape constancy*, *brightness constancy*, and *color constancy* (● FIGURE 3.19).

(a) (b) (c) (d)

FIGURE 3.19

Perceptual Constancies

(a) The shape of the image this door projects onto the retina changes dramatically as the orientation of the door changes. Yet we still perceive that the door is rectangular because of shape constancy. (b) Even though the size of the image this person projects onto the retina shrinks as he walks away, because of size constancy, we do not perceive him as shrinking. (c) The coal may reflect more light in the sun than the paper does in the shade, yet we still perceive that the paper is brighter than the coal because of brightness constancy. (d) A photo of a dress like this one went viral in 2015 (#TheDress; Mahler, 2015) because some people saw it as blue and black while others saw it as being white and gold. One explanation for this phenomenon is that color constancy processes in the brain caused the differing perceptions (Hesslinger & Carbon, 2016). If people perceived that the dress was photographed in dim light, their brains may have compensated by removing the blue cast from their perception, resulting in the perception of a white/gold dress. If they perceived the dress to be photographed in bright light, they may have perceived an even slightly darker blue/black dress. In reality, the dress was blue and black.

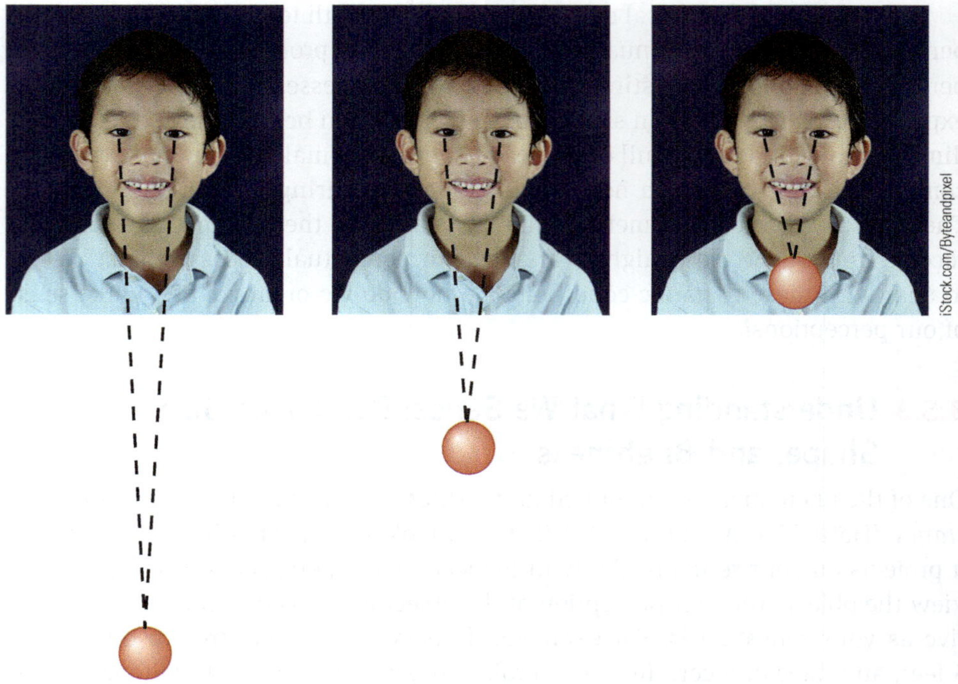

FIGURE 3.20

Binocular Depth Cues

The brain uses retinal disparity, or the degree to which the images projected on the right and left retinas differ from each other, to calculate how far away an object is. The farther away the object, the smaller the degree of retinal disparity.

binocular [bye-NOCK-you-lar] depth cues depth cues that utilize information from both eyes

retinal disparity a binocular depth cue that uses the difference in the images projected on the right and left retinas to inform the brain about the distance of a stimulus

monocular depth cues depth cues that require information from only one eye

FIGURE 3.21

Solution to the Problem in Figure 3.18

After looking at this picture, can you easily find the cow in Figure 3.18?

3.5.4 Depth Perception: Sensing Our 3-D World with 2-D Eyes

Another perceptual challenge is *depth perception*. The world we view is three-dimensional, but the image it projects onto our retina is two-dimensional, like a photograph. Somehow our brains must be able to determine depth from the information our eyes receive from the outside world. What makes this possible?

Binocular Depth Perception

One way that we perceive depth is through binocular depth cues. The term *binocular* means "two-eyed." **Binocular depth cues** rely on information from both eyes—specifically, information based on *retinal disparity*. **Retinal disparity** refers to the fact that, because our eyes are set a few centimeters apart, each eye sees a slightly different view of the world. Retinal disparity is greatest for objects that are close to us and less for objects that are distant (● FIGURE 3.20). Thus, the amount of retinal disparity we experience is a function of the distance from which we view an object. Our brain uses the amount of retinal disparity we experience to calculate how far the object is from us, enabling us to perceive depth in the world.

Monocular Depth Cues

Binocular disparity is an important depth cue, but it is not the only way we perceive depth. If it were, we would be in serious trouble if we lost the use of one eye. We also would not be able to perceive depth in paintings or photographs. Luckily, we have other means of depth perception that require the use of only one eye: **monocular depth cues**.

Many of you may have learned about monocular depth cues when you began drawing and painting as a child. Because a canvas has no depth, all parts of the painting are the same distance from the viewer's eyes, and retinal disparity does not help us perceive depth. So how do we perceive depth in paintings and photographs? We use cues such as the *relative size* of objects and *interposition* to tell us which objects are farther away. In fact, some people now believe that the famous Dutch painter Rembrandt had a visual problem that forced him to see the world using only monocular depth cues. Perhaps this helped him use monocular depth cues so effectively in his paintings (Dingfelder, 2010). In fact, established artists tend to have greater misalignment of their eyes (which would impede binocular depth perception) than non-artists have (Livingstone, Lafer-Sousa, & Conway, 2011), further suggesting that poor binocular depth perception is associated with increased artistic ability. Next time you want to draw a picture of a real world scene, try closing one eye to remove your retinal disparity. It might help. • TABLE 3.2 describes some of the most useful monocular depth cues.

TABLE 3.2 Monocular Depth Cues

Monocular Depth Cue	Description	Example
Interposition	More distant objects are partially hidden by closer objects.	 Robert Estall photo agency/Alamy stock photo
Height on the horizon	More distant objects are placed higher on the horizon than closer objects.	 Perati Komson/Shutterstock.com
Relative size	More distant objects are seen as smaller than closer objects of the same size.	 W. Cody/Getty Images
Texture gradient	More distant objects have less texture or detail than closer objects.	 68/Ocean/Corbis
Aerial perspective	More distant objects are hazier and blurrier than closer objects.	 Sylvain Grandadam/Getty Images
Linear perspective	Converging lines indicate distance or depth.	 Robert Glusic/Keepsake RF/Corbis
Motion parallax	More distant objects appear to move more slowly than closer objects as we pass by them.	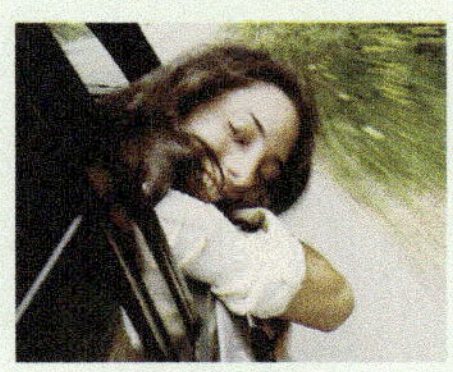 Steven Lam/Getty Images

Gestalt [gush-TALLT] approach a psychological school of thought originating in Germany that proposed that the whole of a perception must be understood rather than trying to deconstruct perception into its parts

figure-ground a Gestalt principle of perception that states that when we perceive a stimulus, we visually pull the figure part of the stimulus forward while visually pushing backward the background, or ground, part of the stimulus

FIGURE 3.22

Closure

According to the Gestaltists, we tend to mentally fill in, or close, solid forms during perception.

Perceptual constancy and depth perception are both important components of our perceptual processing. But how do we perceive the cylindrical shape of a soda can or the rectangular shape of a shoebox? To understand this level of perceptual processing, we will examine theories of *form perception*.

3.5.5 Perceiving Form: The Gestalt Approach

One influential approach to understanding form perception is the **Gestalt approach**. According to the Gestalt approach, the whole of a perception is greater than the sum of its parts. In fact, the word *Gestalt* is German for "whole form." According to the Gestaltists, when you look at your friend's face, the resulting perception is not merely a sum of the angles, curves, shapes, and lines that make up the face; rather, you perceive the stimulus *as a whole*. In this case, you perceive a face because your mind has implicitly grouped all of the stimuli that make up that face into a coherent whole.

One of the major contributions of Gestalt theory is a series of perceptual laws that attempt to explain how our minds automatically organize perceptual stimuli together to produce the perception of a whole form (Wertheimer, 1923). One of the most important Gestalt concepts of perceptual organization is **figure-ground**. When you look at your world, you see a multitude of objects or figures that seem to stand away from the background. For instance, your professor standing at the whiteboard is a *figure* against the whiteboard or *ground*. The photo in Psychology Works! shows figure-ground in action. You should have different perceptions of this picture, depending on what you visually pull forward as the figure and what you push back as the ground. For example, if you pull certain darker-colored parts forward, you will see a man's face or the crown of a sombrero rather than the pupil of the eye.

Psychology Works!

Patricia Aranda/Moment/Getty Images

Knowledge of psychology, especially in the areas of sensation and perception, is very useful to people who work in the areas of art and graphic design. To create effective pieces of art, artists must first understand how we sense and perceive the world. Here, artist Octavio Ocampo manipulates our perception through his clever use of the Gestalt rules of perception, top-down perceptual processes, monocular depth cues, and so on. What do you see in this painting?

Another Gestalt principle is **closure**. When we perceive a stimulus such as the one in • FIGURE 3.22, we tend to mentally fill in, or close, the object. The stimulus is not a complete triangle, but nearly everyone will perceive it as complete. According to the principle of closure, we have a preference for viewing solid shapes as opposed to lines.

The Gestalt principles of **proximity** and **similarity** help explain how we group objects together (cf. Pinna, Porcheddu, & Deiana, 2016). These rules state that we group together stimuli that are close to each other, or proximal, and also stimuli that are similar (• FIGURE 3.23). As you read this page, you are continually using proximity to discriminate between the words that make up the sentences. Without proximity, you would see a mass of letters, but you would not know where one word ends and another begins.

The final Gestalt principle that we will look at is **good continuation**. The principle of good continuation states that we prefer to perceive stimuli that seem to follow one another as part of a continuing pattern (• FIGURE 3.24). Camouflage works due to several of the Gestalt principles of perception, including good continuation. Can you see the hidden animal in Figure 3.24b? Or, does your eye *continue* right over the animal, unable to distinguish the *figure* of the animal from the back*ground*? In nature, this animal's survival depends on it!

closure a Gestalt principle of perception that states that when we look at a stimulus, we tend to see it as a closed shape rather than lines

proximity a Gestalt principle of perception that states that we tend to group close objects together during perception

similarity a Gestalt principle of perception that states that we tend to group like objects together during perception

good continuation a Gestalt principle of perception that states that we have a preference for perceiving stimuli that seem to follow one another as part of a continuing pattern

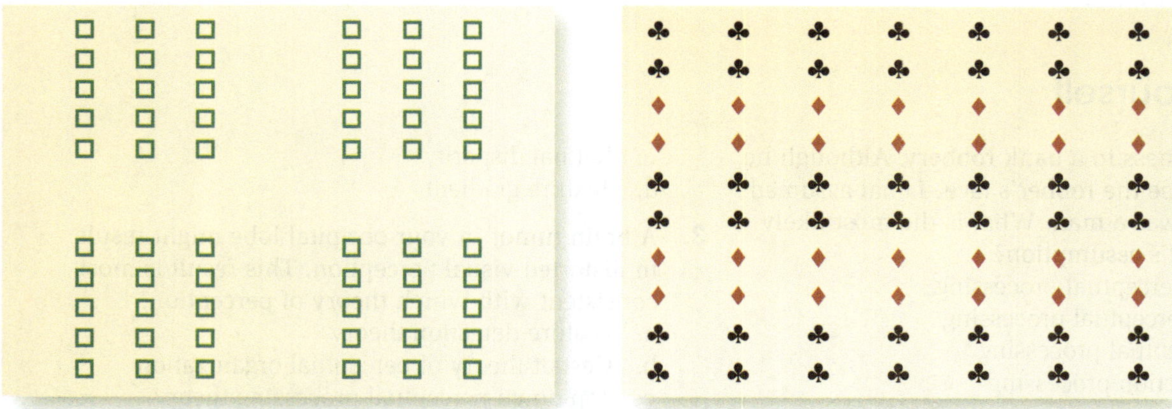

(a) Grouping based on proximity (b) Grouping based on similarity

FIGURE 3.23

The Gestalt Rules of Similarity and Proximity

(a) (b)

FIGURE 3.24

Two Instances of Good Continuation

Good continuation ensures that we perceive continuous patterns in the world. The survival of this animal may depend on the fact that you are unable to separate the figure of this animal from the background and your eye just continues uninterrupted across the scene (b).

3.5.6 Perceiving Form: Feature Detection Theory

feature detection theory a theory of perception that proposes that we have specialized cells in the visual cortex, feature detectors, that fire only when they receive input that indicates we are looking at a particular shape, color, angle, or other visual feature

Feature detection theory states that we have cells in our visual cortex that fire only in response to certain stimuli. These *feature detectors* fire only when they receive input that indicates we are looking at a particular shape, color, angle, or other visual feature. We have feature detectors for many different specific features of visual stimuli (Hulbert, 2003; Spillmann, 2014). The visual cortex and other parts of the brain gather information from our various feature detectors and combine it to help give us a coherent picture of whatever it is we are seeing (Jackson & Blake, 2010; Lumer, Friston, & Rees, 1998; Murray, Olshausen, & Woods, 2003; Neri, 2014).

The world is a complex place full of rich visual detail. Is it possible that all of our visual perception of the world results from feature detectors that respond to simple geometric shapes? Maybe not. Evidence is mounting to suggest that other areas of the brain may be organized to further process certain complex stimuli. For example, we have a region in the temporal lobe called the *fusiform face* area, which enlarges and specializes during childhood to selectively process the faces we see (Peelen et al., 2010). Likewise, other areas have been shown to selectively process body parts (Cross et al., 2010) and pictures of indoor and outdoor scenes (Kanwisher, 2003). At the moment, it seems that a simple feature detector explanation does not fully account for the complexity of human visual perception (Cheadle et al., 2015; Egner, Monti, & Summerfield, 2010; Jiang, Schmajuk, & Egner, 2012).

3.5 Quiz Yourself

1. **Jamal was a witness to a bank robbery. Although he did not clearly see the robber's face, Jamal assumed that the robber was a man. What is the most likely reason for Jamal's assumption?**
   a. Bottom-up perceptual processing
   b. Top-down perceptual processing
   c. Gestalt perceptual processing
   d. Feature detection processing
2. **If you went blind in one eye, which depth cue would you lose?**
   a. Motion parallax
   b. Interposition
   c. Retinal disparity
   d. Texture gradient
3. **A brain tumor in your occipital lobe might result in distorted visual perception. This result is most consistent with which theory of perception?**
   a. Feature detection theory
   b. Gestalt theory of perceptual organization
   c. Top-down perceptual processing theory
   d. Bottom-up perceptual processing theory

Answers 1. *b*; 2. *c*; 3. *a*

3.6 The Accuracy of Perception

One of our students once had a frightening experience in which he misinterpreted a visual stimulus. He was driving in the mountains of northern Georgia when he passed a bear on a distant hillside. The bear was standing on its hind legs, towering over the 20-foot-tall pine trees that surrounded it. The student knew this was very unlikely, so he turned his car around and went back for another look. On closer inspection of the scene, he saw that all of the pine trees on the mountainside were newly planted saplings, about 3 feet high. The bear that towered over them was only an average-sized Georgia black bear! Our student was able to go back and correct his perception, but this is not always the case. We may never discover that we have misperceived a situation. Why do we sometimes misperceive our world?

3.6.1 Errors Due to Top-Down Processing: Seeing What We Expect to See

Why do you think the student misperceived the size of the black bear? The key to his misperception of the bear was in his misperception of the size of the pine trees. We would explain this in terms of top-down processing. When driving through the mountains, most Georgians do not expect to see hillsides of baby trees. It's more typical to see mountainsides covered with mature pine trees that can be well over 20 feet tall. Because this is the normal expectation, the student simply took for granted that the trees were a mature height. It wasn't until he saw the pine trees up close that he realized that his top-down processing had failed him. Because he misperceived the trees, he also misperceived the height of the bear.

▲ Because of top-down processing, it would take a long time to accurately perceive this laptop computer in the road. We simply don't expect to see laptop computers in the middle of the highway; therefore, our perception is slowed down.

3.6.2 Errors Due to Perceptual Constancy: Tricks of the Brain

Errors that are caused by top-down processing relate to the knowledge and the expectations we have of our world. Misperceptions occur for other reasons, too. Sometimes we misperceive things when our brain's attempts to give us perceptual constancy go amiss.

The Moon Illusion

Have you ever noticed that the moon appears to be much larger as it rises over the horizon than when it is directly overhead? Many people think it is because the Earth is closer to the moon when it is at the horizon, but this is not true. Scientists are still trying to determine the exact cause of the *moon illusion* (Kim, 2012). A leading theory, *the apparent distance theory,* argues that the answer lies in our brain's attempt to correct for what it thinks is a mistake in perception. The moon projects the same size image on our retina when it is on the horizon as it does when it is directly overhead. But when the moon is on the horizon, many interposition cues, such as trees and buildings that stand between the moon and us, indicate distance to our brain. When we view the moon directly overhead, however, there are no interposition cues to indicate distance (Jones & Wilson, 2009). Consequently, our brain thinks the moon is farther away when it is on the horizon. The logic involved is this: If the moon is farther away on the horizon, but it still projects the same size image on the retina as the moon overhead, then the moon on the horizon must actually be bigger than the moon overhead. The brain tries to "fix" the inconsistency by inflating our perception of the size of the moon on the horizon (Kaufman & Rock, 1989; Weidner et al., 2014). Curiously, you can undo the moon illusion by facing away from the moon, bending over, and looking at the moon from between your legs. In this position, the brain does not try to fix the inconsistency, and the moon illusion disappears.

▲ One explanation for the moon illusion is that it occurs when our brain corrects for what it thinks is a perceptual error.

The Ponzo Illusion

This same logic underlies one explanation of the *Ponzo illusion,* in which lines of equal length that lie across converging lines appear to be unequal in length (● FIGURE 3.25).

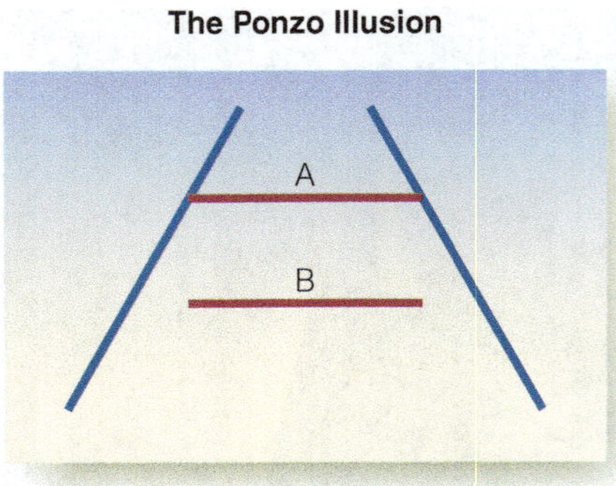

FIGURE 3.25

The Ponzo Illusion

Line segments A and B are both the same length, but we perceive that A is longer than B.

Although the exact cause of the Ponzo illusion is not yet known (Parks, 2013; Prinzmetal & Beck, 2001), some suggest that in the Ponzo illusion, linear perspective and height on the horizon cues tell the brain that the top line is farther away than the bottom one. Yet both lines project the same size image on the retina. In an attempt to maintain size constancy, the brain inflates our perception of the top line's length, thus causing the illusion that the top line is longer than the bottom line. This illusion occurs even though we do not consciously perceive the line on top as farther away (Gillam, 1980).

The Müller-Lyer Illusion

Size constancy probably also plays a role in the *Müller-Lyer illusion* (● FIGURE 3.26; Coren et al., 1988). In this illusion, our perception of the length of the vertical line segments changes, depending on the direction of the arrows at either end of the line. When the arrows extend away, the line looks longer (Figure 3.26b).

Although researchers are not quite sure why the Müller-Lyer illusion occurs, it is thought that the arrows serve as depth cues, much as we might find in the inside and outside corners of a building. If you look at Figure 3.26c, you can see that this type of corner produces a surface that is closer to the viewer than the recessed corner in Figure 3.26d. These depth cues may set off a process of compensation for size constancy that is similar to those found in the moon illusion and the Ponzo illusion.

3.6.3 Cultural Factors in Perception

As we've discussed, your beliefs and expectations of the world can influence your top-down perceptual processing. Given that culture and environment influence many of our beliefs and expectations (remember our student and the Georgia bear), it stands to reason that culture and environment also affect perception. The Müller-Lyer illusion is a good example of this type of influence.

People who live in "carpentered" environments, where many of the buildings are wood-framed rectangular structures, have much experience with the architectural angles that produce the Müller-Lyer illusion (e.g., right angles; Deregowski, 2013). Is it possible that these people also experience the Müller-Lyer illusion to a greater degree than those who have lived their lives in "noncarpentered" worlds (where rectangular structures are rare)? This seems to be the case. The Bashi people of Africa traditionally live in round dwellings. When compared to Europeans,

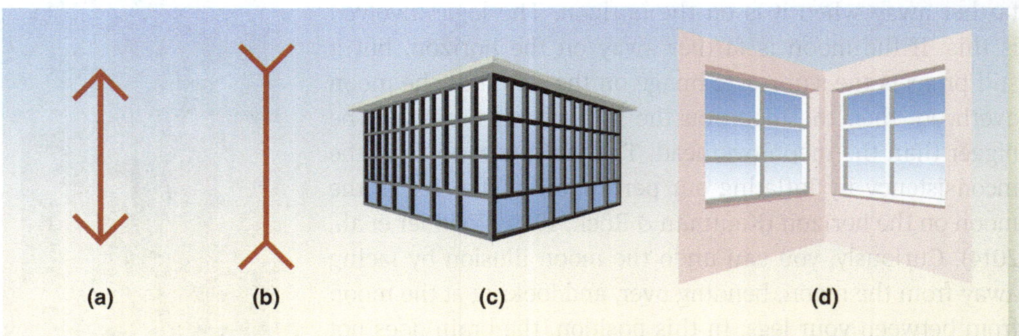

FIGURE 3.26

The Müller-Lyer Illusion

In the Müller-Lyer illusion, the line in (a) is perceived as being shorter than the line in (b), even though they are of equal length. The Müller-Lyer illusion is often seen in rectangular, "carpentered" buildings. The vertical line in the outside corner (c) looks shorter than the vertical line in the inside corner (d)—yet they are the same length. Architects use the Müller-Lyer illusion to create certain perceptions of their buildings.

the Bashi are often found to be less susceptible to the Müller-Lyer illusion (Bonte, 1962). A similar result has been found among the Navajos of the Southwestern United States. When traditional Navajos who live in round homes called *hogans* were compared to Navajos who grew up in rectangular buildings, the former were found to be less likely to experience the Müller-Lyer illusion (Pedersen & Wheeler, 1983). These studies suggest that our perceptions are influenced by elements in our culture that prepare us to see the world in a particular way.

3.6 Quiz Yourself

1. Leahannaba grew up in a culture where most of the structures were dome-shaped huts. Compared to someone from New York City, which optical illusion is Leahannaba less likely to experience?

a. Ponzo illusion
b. Müller-Lyer illusion
c. Moon illusion
d. All of the above

2. Last night, Samantha noticed that the moon looked huge as it rose above the horizon. Later, when the moon was overhead, it did not look nearly as large to her. Which of the following is thought to be a primary cause of this illusion?

a. Perceptual constancies
b. Top-down processing
c. Bottom-up processing
d. Binocular depth cues

3. When you look down the railroad tracks, the tracks appear to converge even though they are parallel. This illusion is the result of which perceptual process?

a. Monocular depth cues
b. Binocular depth cues
c. Top-down processing
d. Subliminal perception

Answers 1. b; 2. a; 3. a

Rob Crandall/The Image Works

People who grow up in noncarpentered environments, where structures tend to be like this round hogan, are less likely to experience the Müller-Lyer illusion

3.7 Integrating Psychology: The Big Picture

In the last chapter, we learned about our nervous and endocrine systems and how they influence our day-to-day functioning. In this chapter, we focused on the biological processes that underlie our ability to sense and perceive. After his stroke, Jean-Dominique Bauby's senses continued to give him a window through which to experience the world. For most of us, they do the same. Our senses are our connection with the outside world—for it is through our senses that environmental stimuli are converted into the neural language of our nervous system. If Bauby had lost his ability to sense and perceive, not only would he have been locked inside his own body, he would also have been completely alone. Take a moment to think about what life would be like if one or more of your senses failed to function. Would losing your sight or hearing affect your ability to learn, to interact with others, or even to survive? In what ways could you adapt, as Bauby did, if you lost one or more of your senses?

After our sense organs do their jobs, we must then make sense of what we are seeing, hearing, tasting, and so on. We accomplish this using a combination of top-down and bottom-up perceptual processes. Bottom-up processes help us piece together what we are sensing. Top-down processes use what we know about the world to help us create coherent perceptions of it. However, sometimes our attempts can lead to perceptual errors, such as those seen in perceptual illusions.

Our ability to sense and perceive is a crucial part of our lives. When we focus our attention on what we are sensing, we bring that information into our conscious awareness or *consciousness*. In our consciousness, this information is useful to us in a variety of ways, such as for problem solving, learning, and so on. In Chapter 4, we will take a closer look at our levels of consciousness and the role it plays when we are not fully awake or aware.

The information we acquire through sensation and perception can also help guide our behavior. We react to what our senses tell us about our bodies and the world. For example, if you saw the sky turning cloudy, you might be inspired to pack an umbrella in your backpack or book bag. If you sensed a rumbling in your stomach, you might be driven to find food to eat. Similarly, Bauby's perceptions of his life after the stroke led him to achieve his desire to write a book. In this manner, sensation and perception play a role in the *motivation* that guides our daily behavior. In Chapter 5, we will look at the motivational processes that drive our behavior and help us achieve our goals. As you read these coming chapters, keep in mind that much of life as you know it wouldn't be possible without the sensory, perceptual, and other biological processes at work inside your body.

Studying the Chapter

Key Terms

absolute threshold (88)
accommodation (94)
amplitude (92)
attention (87)
auditory nerve (104)
basilar membrane (104)
binocular depth cues (118)
blindspot (95)
bottom-up perceptual processing (116)
brightness (92)
closure (121)
cochlea (104)
color blindness (98)
cones (96)
cornea (93)
cycle (102)
dark adaptation (97)
decibels (dB) (102)
dermis (113)
epidermis (113)
extrasensory perception (ESP) (90)
feature detection theory (122)
figure-ground (120)

frequency (102)
frequency theory (105)
gate control theory of pain (113)
Gestalt approach (120)
good continuation (121)
gustation (107)
hair cells (104)
hue (92)
inner ear (104)
just noticeable difference (jnd) (88)
kinesthesis (114)
lens (94)
light adaptation (97)
lock-and-key theory (110)
loudness (102)
middle ear (103)
monocular depth cues (118)
olfaction (109)
olfactory epithelium (110)
opponent-process theory (99)
optic chiasm (101)
optic nerve (95)
outer ear (103)
papillae (107)
perception (87)
perceptual set (116)
pheromones (111)
photopigments (96)
pitch (102)
place theory (104)
proximity (121)
psychophysics (88)
pupil (93)
retina (95)
retinal disparity (118)
rods (96)
saturation (92)
sensation (87)
signal detection theory (88)
similarity (121)
subliminal perception (89)
taste buds (107)
top-down perceptual processing (115)
trichromatic theory of color vision (98)
vestibular sense (114)
visible spectrum (92)
volley theory (105)
wavelength (92)
Weber's law (89)

What Do You Know? Assess Your Understanding

Test your retention and understanding of the material by answering the following questions.

1. ______ is the conversion of environmental energies into neural impulses.
   a. Sensation
   b. Perception
   c. Absolute threshold
   d. The just noticeable difference (jnd)

2. Determining the qualities of light energy that are related to color would be most central to which of the following areas of psychology?
   a. Physiological psychology
   b. Perception psychology
   c. Psychophysics
   d. Psychodynamics

3. According to Weber's law, a teaspoon of sugar added to an already sweet glass of tea will be ______ noticeable than a teaspoon of sugar added to a glass of tea that has no sugar to begin with.
   a. less
   b. more
   c. equally
   d. Weber's law does not tell us what to expect in this situation

4. The average human would be able to see which of the following wavelengths?
   a. 950 nm
   b. 850 nm
   c. 789 nm
   d. 550 nm

5. The hue or color of a light we perceive corresponds to the ______ of the light wave.
   a. purity
   b. wavelength
   c. amplitude
   d. frequency

6. The eye's ______ undergoes ______ to focus an image of what we see on our retina.
   a. iris; constriction
   b. pupil; constriction
   c. lens; accommodation
   d. sclera; accommodation

7. ______ in the ______ of the retina allow us to see color.
   a. Neurotransmitters; cones
   b. Photopigments; cones
   c. Neurotransmitters; rods
   d. Photopigments; rods

8. According to the trichromatic theory of color vision, we have ______ for ______, ______, and ______ light.

a. cones; red; green; blue
b. cones; red; green; yellow
c. rods; red; green; blue
d. rods; red; green; yellow

9. The ______ of a sound corresponds to the ______ of a sound wave.

a. loudness; frequency
b. pitch; frequency
c. loudness; cycle
d. pitch; amplitude

10. When we hear a sound, ______ cells on the ______ convert sound waves into neural signals.

a. cone; tympanic membrane
b. rod; cochlear duct
c. hair; basilar membrane
d. hair; tympanic membrane

11. The ______ of the brain processes visual information before it travels to the cortex.

a. thalamus
b. hypothalamus
c. olfactory bulb
d. hippocampus

12. Jonas, a retired jet engine mechanic, is 65 years old. Lately he's been experiencing some hearing loss. From what you know about hearing and exposure to loud sounds, what would you predict about Jonas's hearing loss?

a. He will have the most trouble hearing low-pitched sounds.
b. He will have the most trouble hearing medium-pitched sounds.
c. He will have the most trouble hearing high-pitched sounds.
d. He will most likely be completely deaf.

13. In signal detection theory, if you think you hear your phone ringing, but it is not actually ringing, you have just experienced a ______.

a. miss
b. hit
c. correct rejection
d. false alarm

14. Researchers have argued that our ability to taste sweet flavors is best when the food is placed on the front of our tongues. To test this theory, a researcher randomly selects 20 males and 20 females. The researcher places a sweet food on the front of the males' tongues and on the sides of the females' tongues. The researcher then measures the participants' perception of the sweet flavor. In this study, gender is a(n) ______ variable.

a. independent
b. dependent
c. confounding
d. control

15. Ultimately, most taste information is processed in the ______ cortex of the brain.

a. somatosensory
b. occipital
c. temporal
d. motor

16. The fact that men who are exposed to fertile women drink more alcohol than males who are exposed to infertile women is most consistent with the notion that humans possess a(n) ______ sense.

a. vomeronasal
b. olfactory
c. vestibular
d. kinesthetic

17. Karina goes to a Halloween party where she meets a man who is wearing a monster mask that covers his entire face. Later, when her best friend asks her to describe the man, she describes him as being "good-looking" even though she never actually saw his face. Which of the following best explains Karina's perception of the man?

a. Good continuation
b. Closure
c. Bottom-up perceptual processing
d. Top-down perceptual processing

18. Mike was in an accident that injured his right eye. Although he'll recover, he must wear an eye patch for the next 2 weeks. During this time, Mike's doctor will not allow him to drive a car. Mike's doctor is most likely concerned with disturbances to Mike's ______.

a. vestibular system
b. binocular depth cues
c. monocular depth cues
d. kinesthetic system

19. In which of the following situations would you be most likely to use bottom-up perceptual processing?

a. When viewing a piece of abstract art composed of nothing but paint splatters on a canvas
b. When reading your best friend's bad handwriting

c. When trying to watch a movie in a crowded theater where your view of the screen is obstructed by the people sitting in front of you
d. When reading the daily news on the Internet

20. According to your text, we experience perceptual constancies for all of the following except which one?

a. Size
b. Texture
c. Shape
d. Brightness

Answers: 1. a; 2. c; 3. a; 4. d; 5. b; 6. c; 7. b; 8. a; 9. b; 10. c; 11. a; 12. c; 13. d; 14. c; 15. a; 16. a; 17. d; 18. b; 19. a; 20. b.

Use It or Lose It: Applying Psychology

1. Your younger sister listens to music at a very loud level through headphones nearly every day. What would you tell her to convince her to turn down the volume?
2. Because you are studying sensation in psychology, your uncle asks you to explain why he cannot distinguish red objects from green objects. What would you tell him?
3. Assume you work on the staff of an assisted-living home. Most of your clients are people in their 80s and 90s. How can you use your knowledge of sensation and perception to do your job better? In other words, what changes can you expect to see in your clients' sensory and perceptual abilities, and how can you accommodate those changes?
4. You have been charged with determining the additional amount of sugar one would have to add to a cup of coffee that already contained two teaspoons of sugar to produce a jnd. How would you go about determining this?
5. Find a picture of Vincent Van Gogh's painting *Starry Night*. What monocular depth cues are used in this painting? Provide specific examples of your choices.
6. Identify several species of animal that utilize camouflage. How do the Gestalt rules of perception help to explain how these types of camouflage work?

Critical Thinking About the Science of Psychology

In this chapter, you read about the famous study done by James Vicary in the 1950s, which examined the effectiveness of subliminal persuasion. Please review that study now in Section 3.1.3 and answer these questions:

1. What was Vicary's hypothesis in his study?
2. In Vicary's original study, what was the dependent variable?
3. In Vicary's original study, what was the independent variable?
4. Why should we not put much stock in Vicary's claims? Explain.
5. How could you design a study that would do a better job of testing Vicary's hypothesis?

Are You Getting the Big Picture?

Sensation occurs when our sense organs convert environmental energy into neural impulses. **Perception** is the process through which we interpret sensory information.

Dmytro Gilitukha/Shutterstock.com

3.1 Measuring Sensation and Perception

- **Psychophysics** is the branch of psychology that studies how we process sensory stimuli.
- Psychophysicists conduct experiments to determine the **absolute threshold** and **just noticeable difference (jnd)** of each of the five senses.
- **Signal detection theory** states that our ability to detect the presence of a stimulus is affected by more than just the intensity of that stimulus. Factors such as fatigue, motivation, and attention may also affect these judgments.

	The alarm is going off (Signal present)	The alarm is not going off (Signal not present)
The air traffic controller thinks they hear the alarm (Signal detected)	Hit (Correct)	False Alarm (Error)
The air traffic controller does not hear the alarm (Signal not detected)	Miss (Error)	Correct Rejection (Correct)

- **Weber's law** is the relationship between the original intensity of a stimulus and the amount of change that is required to produce a jnd.
- When sensory stimuli are too weak in intensity to reach absolute threshold, the stimuli are said to be **subliminal**.
- The existence of **extrasensory perception (ESP)** remains a controversial subject; however, to date there has not been convincing evidence of its existence.

3.2 Vision: Seeing the World

- Light is electromagnetic energy, measured primarily by **wavelength** and **amplitude**. Wavelength = **hue**; amplitude = **brightness**.
- The **visible spectrum** of light is the narrow band we are able to see. Some animals are able to see a much broader spectrum.
- In the **retina** of the eye, specialized cells known as **rods** and **cones** convert light into neural impulses, which eventually travel to the brain via the **optic nerve**.
- The **trichromatic theory of color vision** and the **opponent-process theory** are both used to explain how we process color.
- **Color blindness** is the inability to see certain colors and is the result of missing cones in the retina or having cones that are sensitive to atypical ranges of light wave frequencies.

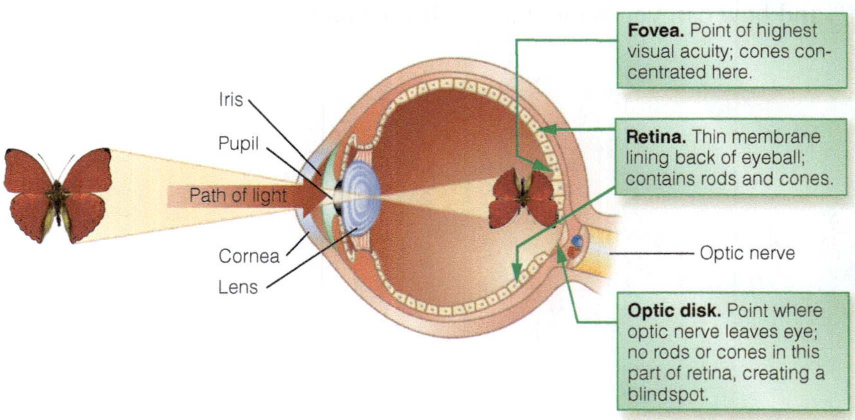

3.3 Hearing: Listening to the World

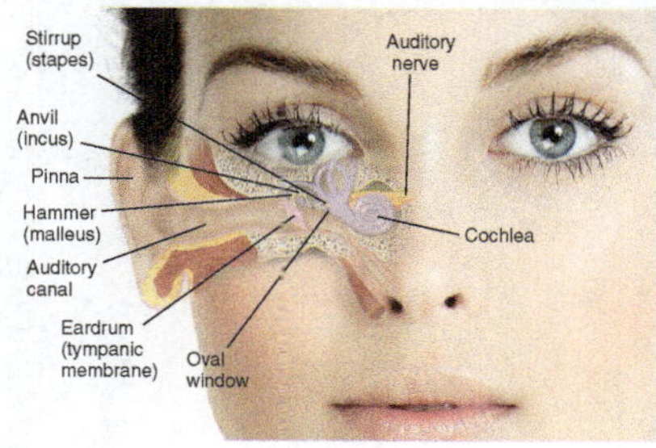

iStock.com/iconogenic

- Sounds are produced by waves of compressed air.
- **Frequency** = **pitch**; **amplitude** = **loudness**.
- The eardrum, or tympanic membrane, is a very thin membrane in the **middle ear** that vibrates to incoming sounds. It begins transmitting those sounds through the small bones to the **hair cells** of the fluid-filled **cochlea**, where neural impulses are generated.
- The **auditory nerve** carries the sounds we hear into the brain.
- The *dual mechanism* approach integrates **volley** and **place theories** of pitch perception by arguing that the brain uses a combination of frequency and place information to decode pitch.

3.4 The Other Senses: Taste, Smell, Touch, and the Body Senses

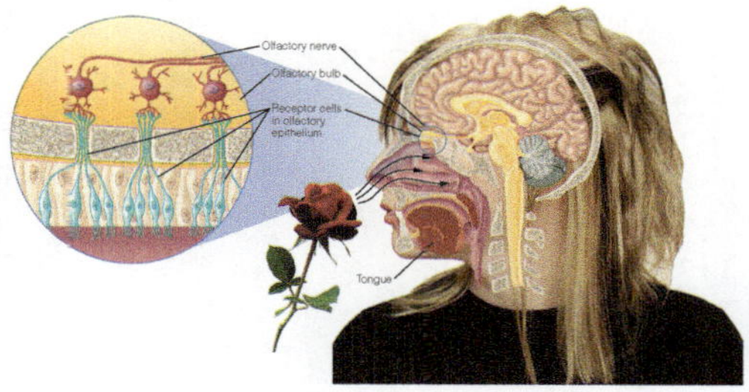

Margo Harrison/Shutterstock.com; Wayne Eardley/Masterfile

- Humans are sensitive to five tastes: bitter, sweet, sour, salty, and umami.
- The **taste buds**, which reside in the pits between the **papillae** on your tongue, convert the chemicals in the foods you eat into neural impulses.
- The sense of smell operates by converting odors captured by a special piece of skin, the **olfactory epithelium**, which lines the top of the nasal cavity, to neural impulses that travel via the olfactory nerve to the olfactory bulb in the brain.
- Many animals (and perhaps humans) have a vomeronasal system that allows them to communicate with other animals via airborne chemosignals known as **pheromones**. Chemosignals may impact some aspects of human social interaction and sexuality.
- The sense of touch originates in the skin, with the inner layer—the **dermis**—containing most of the touch receptors.
- The **gate control theory of pain** proposes that applying intense tactile stimulation to the same part of the body that hurts can alleviate pain.
- **Kinesthesis** is our ability to sense the position of our body parts in space and in relation to one another.
- **Vestibular sense** monitors the position of our head in space and helps us stay balanced.

3.5 Perception: Interpreting Your World

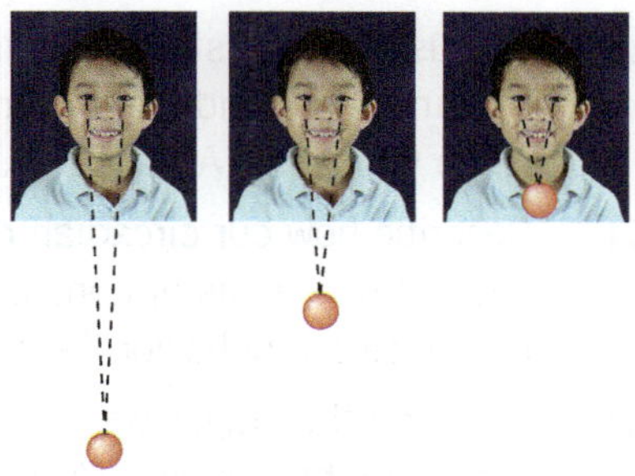
iStock.com/Byteandpixel

- **Top-down perceptual processing** refers to using previously gained knowledge to interpret a sensory stimulus. A **perceptual set** is a general readiness to perceive something in a particular manner.
- **Bottom-up perceptual processing** refers to using properties of the stimulus itself to form our perception of a stimulus.
- Perceptual constancies, **binocular** and **monocular depth cues**, and **feature detection** are among the mental shortcuts we automatically employ to assist in perceiving stimuli.

3.6 The Accuracy of Perception

The Ponzo Illusion

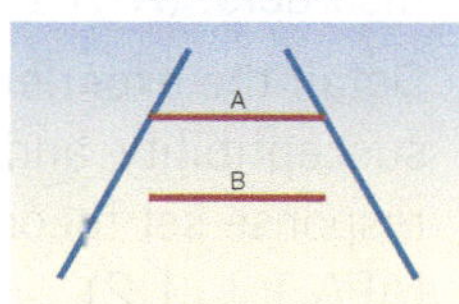

- Perceptual errors can occur for a variety of reasons. They are often due to misapplied expectations that lead us to think we have seen or heard something that we have not.

Learning Objectives

4.1 Discuss why we sleep and understand the variables that influence individual variations in the amount of sleep we need. (APA 1.1, 1.2, 1.3, 2.1, 2.5)

4.1 Describe how our circadian rhythm of sleep operates, and apply how disruptions in this circadian rhythm influence our behavior. (APA 1.1, 1.3)

4.1 Describe the stages we progress through during a typical night of sleep. (APA 1.1, 2.2)

4.1 Compare and contrast the different theories on dreaming. (APA 1.1, 1.2)

4.1 Describe and distinguish among the various sleep disorders. (APA 1.1, 1.3)

4.2 Detail the experience of hypnosis, describe hypnotic susceptibility, and apply the neodissociation and response set theories to how hypnosis occurs. (APA 1.1, 1.2)

4.2 Examine the scientific research to critically evaluate what hypnosis can and cannot do for you. (APA 2.1, 2.2, 5.1)

4.2 Distinguish between meditation and mindfulness and detail the research limitations in understanding the benefits of these practices.

4.3 Define tolerance and substance use disorder, and explain how one's biology, expectations, and culture influence how psychoactive drugs work. (APA 1.1, 1.2, 1.3, 2.2, 2.5, 3.2)

4.3 Identify depressants, opiates, stimulants, and hallucinogens, and describe the effects these types of drugs have on our health, cognition, and behavior. (APA 1.1, 1.3, 2.2, 3.3)

Baranov Dmitry/Shutterstock.com

4 Consciousness

Consciousness, in psychological terms, includes the feelings, thoughts, and aroused states of which we are aware. This chapter examines the levels or gradations of consciousness—when you are not fully awake, alert, aware, or perhaps of sound mind. Recall in the Part I case study how Jean-Dominique Bauby, after his stroke, went into a coma, a unique altered state that not many people experience. Yet, even during this state, Bauby still had some awareness of his surroundings. When he awoke from the coma, he was in a locked-in state. Although this dramatically affected his day-to-day living, Bauby's consciousness still functioned much like yours and mine. Psychologists have done quite a bit of research on various states of consciousness: *sleep, hypnosis, meditation,* and *mindfulness,* and the effects of various *psychoactive drugs.* By closely examining these states, we may better understand our behavior and the behavior of those around us. We will start with an altered state we all experience—sleep. ■

Chapter Outline

consciousness [CON-shis-nus] feelings, thoughts, and aroused states of which we are aware

microsleep a brief episode of sleep that occurs in the midst of a wakeful activity

4.1 Sleep, Dreaming, and Circadian Rhythm

Many of us never question what goes on in our bodies and minds as we sleep. But sleep offers plenty of behaviors for psychologists to explore. First, we will look at why we sleep and what occurs in our brains and bodies as we sleep. We will then explore the purpose of dreams and whether dreams have meaning. We will conclude by describing different types of sleep disorders. We caution you that just reading about sleep can make you drowsy!

4.1.1 Functions of Sleep: Why Do We Sleep, and What If We Don't?

What would happen if you tried to stay awake indefinitely? William C. Dement (1928–2020), a pioneer in sleep research, actually tried this experiment on himself. Although Dement's lack of sleep made him a danger to himself and others, he was not in danger of dying from lack of sleep. Eventually, he fell asleep. In the same way that you cannot hold your breath until you die, you cannot deprive yourself of all sleep. Sleep always wins. This is because we drift into repeated *microsleeps* (Innes, Poudel, & Jones, 2013; Poudel et al., 2014). A **microsleep** is a brief (3- to 15-second) episode of sleep that occurs in the midst of a wakeful activity. We are typically unaware of its occurrence unless we are behind the wheel of a car, steering a ship, or flying a plane. In such circumstances, microsleeps could cause a disaster. In general, though, microsleeps appear to help us survive by preventing total sleep deprivation.

Sleep ensures our continued physical and mental health in several ways:

- *Sleep restores body tissues and facilitates body growth.* Sleep allows your muscles, immune system, nervous system, and organs time to replenish lost reserves and energy and to repair any cellular damage. That is, sleep is intimately connected to the body's metabolic and hormonal processes. Sufficient sleep prepares the body for action the next day and ensures the continued health of the body. Adequate sleep optimizes athletic performance (Simpson, Gibbs, & Matheson, 2017). Lack of adequate sleep can affect energy levels, often making us feel drowsy and fatigued (Lekander et al., 2013; Murphy & Delanty, 2007; Oginska & Pokorski, 2006). Sleep loss impacts metabolic functioning, influencing one's risk of diabetes, weight gain, and cardiovascular disease (Depner, Stothard, & Wright, Jr., 2014; Sharma & Kavuru, 2010). Sleep also activates growth hormone, which facilitates physical growth during infancy, childhood, and the teen years (Szentirmai et al., 2007).
- *Sleep increases immunity to disease.* During sleep, the production of immune cells that fight off infection increases. Therefore, your immune system is stronger when you receive the appropriate amount of sleep (Ibarra-Coronado et al., 2015; Lange et al., 2006; Motivala & Irwin, 2007). When you deprive your body of sleep, your natural immune responses are reduced (Murphy & Delanty, 2007; Ruiz et al., 2012; Wright et al., 2015). This is in part why you are encouraged to sleep and rest when you are ill. This effect on immunity occurs after as few as 2 days of total sleep deprivation or several days of partial sleep deprivation (Ibarra-Coronado et al., 2015; Rogers et al., 2001; Ruiz et al., 2012). For college students, this may mean you are more susceptible to colds and flu at midterm and final exam time. You are

iStock.com/Manu1174

▲ It is estimated that more than 100,000 police-reported motor vehicle crashes each year are caused directly or in part by drowsy drivers.

likely to sleep less at these times, thereby decreasing your immune system's ability to combat illnesses. For those who contract COVID-19 or any virus, your body needs sleep to fight the infection. Sleeping truly is good medicine.

- *Sleep keeps your mind alert.* When people do not get enough sleep, they are more likely to be inattentive and easily distracted (Chengyang et al., 2017; Kahol et al., 2008; Short et al., 2013). Sleep makes your body more sensitive to norepinephrine—the neurotransmitter that keeps you alert during the day (Steriade & McCarley, 1990; Chapter 2).
- *Sleep enhances your mood.* Sleep activates many chemicals that influence your emotions and mood. Consequently, if you are deprived of sleep, you are more likely to be irritable, angry, cranky, hostile, and unhappy, in addition to being tired (Della Monica et al., 2018; Hisler & Krizan, 2017; Krizan & Herlache, 2016; Lemola, Ledermann & Friedman, 2013; Short et al., 2013). Insufficient or poor quality of sleep also makes it more difficult to control our emotions and accurately read others' emotions, particularly subtle ones (Christian & Ellis, 2011; Killgore et al., 2017; Mauss, Troy, & LeBourgeois, 2013; Van der Helm, Gujar, & Walker, 2010).
- *Sleep is intimately connected to cognition, learning, and memory.* When you sleep, emotional experiences as well as information that you have reviewed or rehearsed are more likely to be remembered (Gais, Lucas, & Born, 2006; Gaskell et al., 2014; Mazza et al., 2016; Paller, 2017; Payne & Kensinger, 2010; Scullin & Bliwise, 2015; Stickgold & Walker, 2013). Chapter 7 offers an in-depth look at memory processing, but a few simple statements here will help you understand the connection between sleep and memory.

  In order to get information into your memory, you must do something to remember the information. This may mean repeating the information over and over again, visualizing the information, or associating it with a personal experience. When information is thoroughly elaborated, it can be more easily transferred to long-term memory so that we can retrieve it later.

  Sleep allows you to better store material that was actually processed (that is, learned well enough) during studying. Information that you can't readily retrieve in the morning probably wasn't consolidated well enough, and you will need to study it again. You can see the advantage of a good night's sleep before an exam.

  Sleep's connection to memory processing may also explain why problem solving seems to improve after a night's sleep (Ellenbogen et al., 2007; Monaghan et al., 2015; Sanders et al., 2019). You may think about a problem repeatedly during the day, frustrated by your inability to find a solution. The next day you awaken with a solution in mind. This suggests that pertinent details about the problem are processed during sleep. The phrase "sleep on it" really has merit.

  Given sleep's connection to memory, recent human and animal research has been investigating the link between chronic sleep disruptions and the risk of Alzheimer's disease, the most common form of dementia. It is hypothesized that when a person is awake, extracellular levels of metabolites in the brain increase, most notably *amyloid beta* (Aβ), which contributes to the development of Alzheimer's disease. Sleep facilitates the removal of these metabolites from the brain. As such, insufficient sleep or disruptions in the sleep–wake cycle may be associated with one's risk of Alzheimer's disease (Cedernaes et al., 2017; Mander et al., 2016). Broadly speaking, maintaining good sleep quality in early and middle adulthood is associated with better cognitive functioning and may protect against age-related cognitive decline (Scullin & Bliwise, 2015).

Research suggests that sleep may have evolved as a necessary behavior for humans (Hirshkowitz, Moore, & Minhoto, 1997; Webb, 1983). When humans lived in caves, it was dangerous for them to go out at night to hunt for food because they had very little night vision and were relatively small compared to other species. If they did go outside at night, they were likely to be the food for larger predators. Humans who stayed inside the cave at night were more likely to survive and produce offspring. Over time, these offspring may have adapted to the pattern of nighttime sleeping and daytime hunting and gathering.

As you can see, sleep is a necessity, not a luxury. Sleep offers many benefits to our functioning and ensures that we will be healthy, alert, and happy.

4.1.2 Variations in How Much Sleep We Need

Some people brag about how little sleep they need. Yet research suggests that although the amount of sleep we need varies from person to person and depends on several factors, many of us are not getting enough. Here are some sleep factors and facts:

- *Age*. The older we get, the less sleep we need (● FIGURE 4.1). Babies require a lot of sleep, between 12 and 15 hours a day. Preschoolers require less sleep, about 10 to 13 hours a day, typically including a midday nap. Teenagers and young adults need less sleep than children, but they still require 8 to 10 hours of sleep a night (Hirshkowitz et al., 2015). While U.S. children may be getting the recommended amount of sleep, two-thirds to 70% of U.S. high school students report getting less than 8 hours of sleep per night (Centers for Disease Control, 2014; National Sleep Foundation, 2014; Wheaton et al., 2018). Adults between the ages of 18 and 64 are more likely to report less than 7 hours of sleep compared to people over the age of 65 (CDC, 2014). Adults in the United States, on average, sleep 6.9 hours a night on weekdays (National Sleep Foundation, 2015). According to sleep experts, most adults require at least 8 hours of sleep a night.
- *Lifestyle (environment)*. Our cultural beliefs, lifestyle habits, and bedroom environment also influence the amount of sleep that we need or get (Giannotti & Cortesi, 2009). If you were raised in a home in which everyone was up early on the weekends to do chores, you adapted to a different sleep schedule than someone who slept until 10 A.M. or noon on weekends. In one study of college students, good sleepers were more likely to have regular bedtime and rise time schedules than poorer sleepers (Carney et al., 2006). Sleeping with a light on in the bedroom or doing certain activities an hour before bedtime (such as watching television, reading, using a laptop or cell phone, or playing video or mobile games) also influence one's sleep quality and duration (National Sleep Foundation, 2014; Twenge, Krizan, & Hisler, 2017). In Jean-Dominique Bauby's case, noise and lights within the hospital setting, in addition to his brain injury, probably changed his sleep. Keep

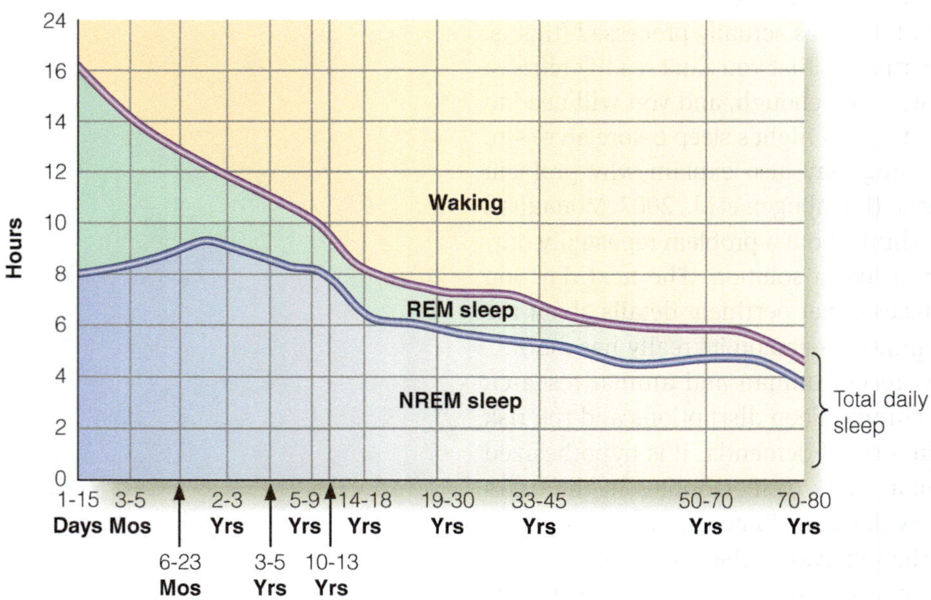

FIGURE 4.1

Age Differences in Sleep Needs

Newborns sleep an average of 16 hours a day. Preschoolers require less sleep, about 10 to 12 hours. Most teenagers and adults require 8 hours.

From "Ontogenetic Development of Human Sleep-Dream Cycle," by H. P. Roffwarg, J. N. Muzino, and W. C. Dement, *Science*, 1966, 152:604–609.

in mind, too, that stressors and responsibilities change as we get older. Living on one's own, parenting, and job responsibilities also bring about changes in our sleep schedule.

- *Genetics.* Genes may play a role in the amount of sleep that each of us requires (Crocker & Sehgal, 2010). For example, studies that measured the sleep patterns of identical twins compared to fraternal twins found more similar sleep needs and sleep behaviors among identical twins (Ambrosius et al., 2008; Dauvilliers et al., 2005; Hublin, Partinen, Koskenvuo, & Kaprio, 2013). Additional research also suggests that genes may influence our propensity to be either night owls or early birds. Some people may be genetically predisposed to get up early in the morning and go to bed earlier, whereas others may prefer getting up later and going to bed later (Mongrain et al., 2004; Novakova, Sladek, & Sumova, 2013). Learn your propensity toward morningness or eveningness by completing the brief scale in Engage Yourself!

Engage Yourself!

Answer the questions in the following table, and then add up the values to get your total score. Compare your total score with the key at the end to get an idea of your *chronotype*, or your propensity toward morningness or eveningness.

Question	Answer	Value
If you were entirely free to plan your evening and had no commitments the next day, at what time would you choose to go to bed?	8 P.M.–9 P.M. 9 P.M.–10:15 P.M. 10:15 P.M.–12:30 A.M. 12:30 A.M.–1:45 A.M. 1:45 A.M.–3 A.M.	5 4 3 2 1
You have to do 2 hours of physically hard work. If you were entirely free to plan your day, in which of the following periods would you choose to do the work?	8 A.M.–10 A.M. 11 A.M.–1 P.M. 3 P.M.–5 P.M. 7 P.M.–9 P.M.	4 3 2 1
For some reason you have gone to bed several hours later than normal, but there is no need to get up at a particular time the next morning. Which of the following is most likely to occur?	Will wake up at the usual time and not fall asleep again Will wake up at the usual time and doze thereafter Will wake up at the usual time but will fall asleep again Will not wake up until later than usual	4 3 2 1
You have a 2-hour test to take that you know will be mentally exhausting. If you were entirely free to choose, in which of the following periods would you choose to take the test?	8 A.M.–10 A.M. 11 A.M.–1 P.M. 3 P.M.–5 P.M. 7 P.M.–9 P.M.	4 3 2 1
If you had no commitments the next day and were entirely free to plan your own day, what time would you get up?	5 A.M.–6:30 A.M. 6:30 A.M.–7:45 A.M. 7:45 A.M.–9:45 A.M. 9:45 A.M.–11 A.M. 11 A.M.–12 P.M.	5 4 3 2 1
A friend has asked you to join him twice a week for a workout in the gym. The best time for him is between 10 P.M. and 11 P.M. Bearing nothing else in mind other than how you normally feel in the evening, how do you think you would perform?	Very well Reasonably well Poorly Very poorly	1 2 3 4

(Continued)

One hears about "morning" and "evening" types of people. Which of these types do you consider yourself to be?	Definitely a morning type	6
	More a morning than an evening type	4
	More an evening than a morning type	2
	Definitely an evening type	0

Morningness–Eveningness Scale	
Definitely morning type	32–28
Moderately morning type	27–23
Neither type	22–16
Moderately evening type	15–11
Definitely evening type	10–6

Adapted from "A Self-Assessment Questionnaire to Determine Morningness–Eveningness in Human Circadian Rhythms," by J. A. Horne and O. Ostberg, *International Journal of Chronobiology*, 1976, Vol. 4, 97–110.

circadian [sir-KAY-dee-un] rhythm changes in bodily processes that occur repeatedly on approximately a 24- to 25-hour cycle

suprachiasmatic [sue-pra-kigh-as-MAT-ick] nucleus (SCN) a group of brain cells located in the hypothalamus that signal other brain areas when to be aroused and when to shut down

melatonin [mel-uh-TONE-in] a hormone in the body that facilitates sleep

4.1.3 Circadian Rhythm and Its Application to Our Lives

A **circadian rhythm** is a built-in cycle of physical processes in living beings. In humans, circadian rhythms include core body temperature, alertness, hormone productions, and other biological processes. Our cycle of sleep is also greatly influenced by our biology. For example, if you were put in a cave and had no cues as to time—no watches, light, or clocks—your body would exhibit a natural rhythm of sleeping and waking that closely resembles a 24- to 25-hour cycle. This sleep circadian rhythm is programmed by a group of brain cells in the hypothalamus called the **suprachiasmatic nucleus (SCN)** (Zee & Manthena, 2007). The SCN works very much like an internal clock, signaling other brain areas when to be aroused (awake) to start the day and when to shut down (sleep) for the day. For Bauby, it is difficult to know if his SCN operated in this way, because circadian rhythms can vary in individuals who have brain damage.

How does the SCN know when it's time to be awake or asleep? The SCN is very responsive to light changes and takes its cues from your eyes. When your eyes transmit light information to the SCN, they are in essence telling it whether it is light or dark outside (● FIGURE 4.2). The light information helps the SCN direct the release of **melatonin**, the hormone that facilitates sleep. Hence, light information and melatonin regulate your sleep circadian rhythm and help you get to sleep or awaken (Burke et al., 2013). As darkness increases, so does the production of melatonin in your body (Arendt, 2006; Brzezinski, 1997). For this reason, it is called the "Dracula hormone," because it comes out at night.

A significant amount of research now suggests that a developmental change in our intrinsic sleep–wake cycle occurs during puberty, a phenomenon not specific to human adolescents, but perhaps common in mammals (Crowley, Acebo, & Carskadon, 2007; Darchia & Cervena, 2014; Hagenauer & Lee, 2012). Changes in melatonin secretion and light sensitivity alter the timing of our sleep–wake cycle. We are more likely to want to stay up later in the evening and sleep longer in the morning. Although teenagers' social calendars often strengthen this tendency, the finding that part of this change is developmental has serious implications for high school starting times and adolescent academic performance (Barnes & Drake, 2015).

"Weekend Lag" and Jet Lag

Unfortunately, many of us disrupt our sleep circadian rhythm on a weekly basis. We attempt to maintain a routine sleep schedule on weekdays, going to bed around the same time every night so that we can get up in the morning for work or school.

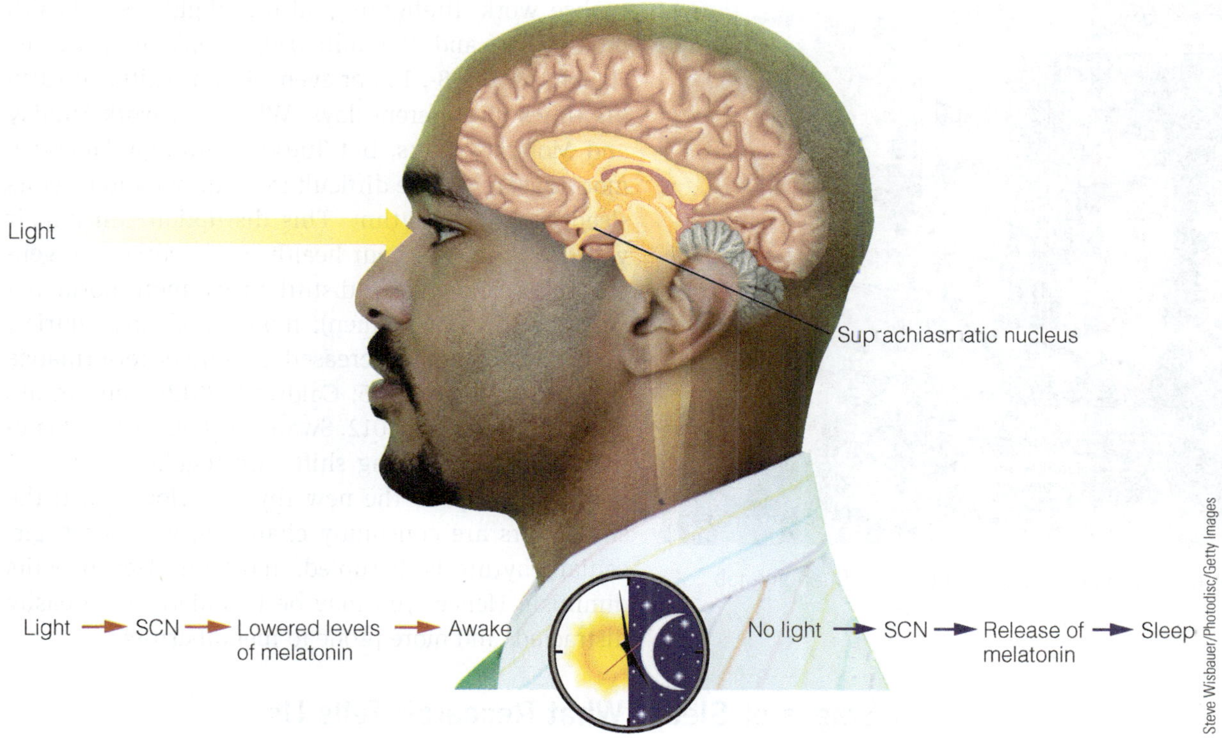

FIGURE 4.2

Circadian Rhythm, Sleep, and the Brain

The suprachiasmatic nucleus (SCN) takes its cues from the light that is transmitted to your eyes. The light information helps the SCN direct the release of melatonin, the "Dracula hormone" that helps you to get to sleep.

Adapted from Starr and McMillan, *Human Biology* (2nd ed.), p. 271, © 1997 Wadsworth.

Then the weekend comes, and many of us stay up later at night and sleep in the next morning, forcing our SCN to reset its cycle. Then Sunday night arrives. We may have the best intentions—getting to bed at a decent hour so that we'll get enough sleep to meet the demands of our Monday schedules. But instead, we toss and turn, look at the clock, and wonder when we are going to fall asleep. When Monday morning comes, we feel tired. We may hit the snooze button several times, oversleep, or take a long shower to help us wake up. Why? Because we just asked our internal clock to reset itself by 3, 4, or more hours! Disrupting our sleep circadian rhythm to this extent makes us irritable, tired, less attentive, and moody.

Our sleep circadian rhythm must also be reset to adapt to the 1-hour time change that takes place in the fall and spring in most parts of the United States and in many other countries. It must also be reset when we travel to different time zones, and we may experience *jet lag* as we adjust. On average, for each hour of time change, it takes 1 day to reset our sleep circadian rhythm.

▲ Sleeping on the plane may help reduce jet lag when traveling to other time zones.

Working the Night Shift

Our body's sleep circadian rhythm also has implications for the roughly 15% of full-time workers in the United States who do shift work. In many professions

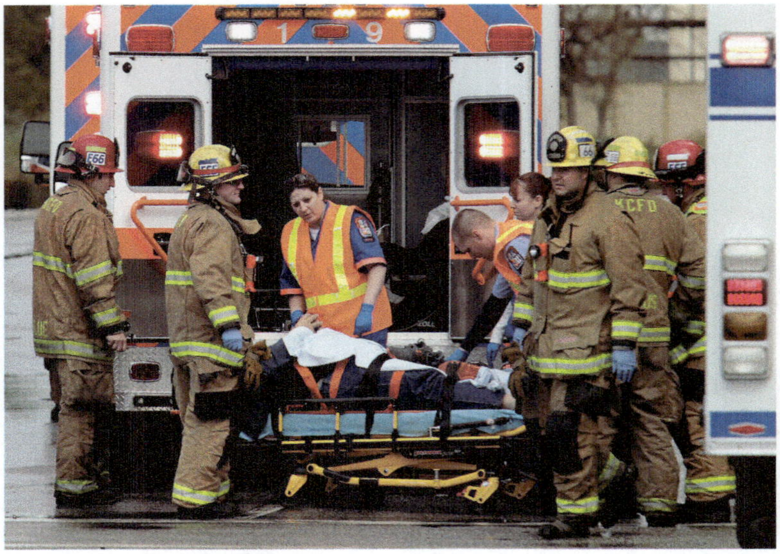

ZUMA Press Inc/Alamy stock photo

▲ Shift work may interfere with normal sleep patterns, influencing job performance.

(police work, firefighting, airline flight crew, health professions, and the military), people may be assigned to work 8-, 12-, or even 24-hour shifts, at varying times on different days. When you work Sunday and Monday nights, but Tuesday through Thursday mornings, it is more difficult for your body to reset its sleep circadian rhythm. This disruption can impair your thinking and your health. Shift workers in general report more sleep disturbances; more hormonal irregularities (for women); more accidents, injuries, and illnesses; and decreased cognitive performance (Barnes & Drake, 2015; Caldwell, 2012; Nena et al., 2018; Pirrallo et al., 2012; Swanson et al., 2010). If late-night or early-morning shifts are regular, then your body can adapt to the new rhythm. However, if the shift hours are constantly changing, your sleep circadian rhythm is disrupted, and your sleep benefits diminish. Hence, you may be less alert, more easily distracted, and more prone to mental errors.

4.1.4 Stages of Sleep: What Research Tells Us

Using *electroencephalogram* (EEG) technology, sleep researchers have identified five stages of sleep. Recall from Chapter 2 that EEGs examine the electrical activity of relatively large areas of the brain. These brain waves are then plotted on graph paper or a computer screen. The patterns the brain waves create give researchers an image of our brain activity when we are awake and when we are asleep (● FIGURE 4.3).

When we are awake and alert, our brain (as measured by an EEG) emits *beta* waves. Beta brain waves are rapid, with a high number of cycles per second. This indicates frequent impulses of electrical activity in the brain. When we are awake yet relaxed, our brain emits *alpha* waves. Alpha waves are somewhat slower and less frequent than beta waves. As we sleep, our brain-wave patterns change in a predictable sequence.

If you watch someone sleep, you will notice that at times the person's eyes move under the eyelids, showing rapid eye movement (REM). At other times during sleep, such eye movement is absent. From such observations, researchers have identified two distinct sleep patterns: **non-REM sleep** and **REM sleep**. When your eyes do not move during sleep, it is referred to as non-rapid eye movement, or non-REM sleep. The state in which our eyes do move is called rapid eye movement (REM) sleep. During these two states of sleep, our bodies and brains are experiencing very different activities.

non-REM sleep the relaxing state of sleep in which the person's eyes do not move

REM sleep the active state of sleep in which the person's eyes move

Non-REM sleep is a progressively relaxed state. In contrast, REM sleep is very active. During a night of sleep, our bodies and brains move back and forth between states of relaxation and activity until we wake up in the morning (Armitage, 1995; Dement & Kleitman, 1957). The sleep cycle begins with non-REM sleep.

The Four Stages of Non-REM Sleep

When we fall asleep, our bodies and brains progress through a series of four non-REM sleep stages:

- *Stage I sleep* is a light sleep and is characterized by *theta* waves. Notice in Figure 4.3 that theta waves are slower and less frequent than alpha waves.

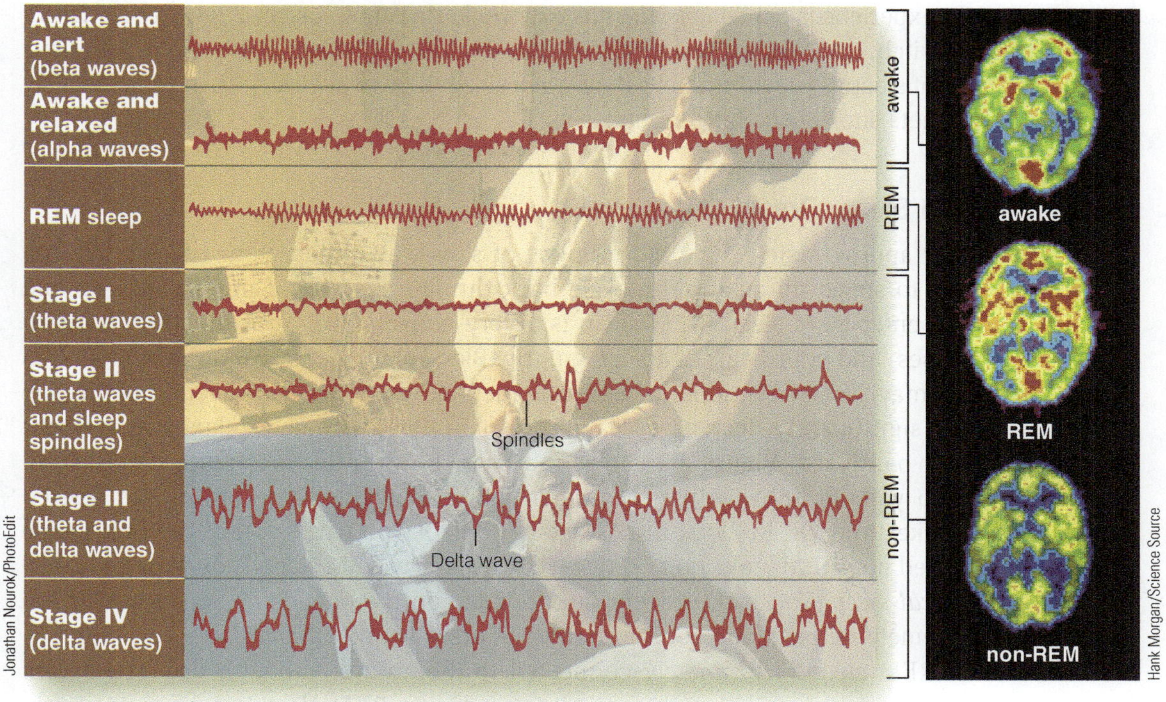

FIGURE 4.3

Brain Activity During Wakefulness and the Various Stages of Sleep

Electroencephalogram technology records brain-wave activity during wakefulness and the various stages of sleep. When fully awake and alert, the brain emits beta waves. When awake but relaxed, the brain emits alpha waves. Brain activity during non-REM sleep progressively slows from theta waves (stage I) to delta waves (stage IV). REM sleep is characterized by rapid brain waves. The brain slides also differentiate non-REM sleep, REM sleep, and wakefulness. Notice that your brain looks as though it is awake while you are in REM sleep. The brain slides labeled "awake" and "REM" look very similar, whereas the non-REM slide looks quite different.

During this stage, your breathing and heart rate slow down. You may experience sensations such as falling or floating. You can easily awaken from stage I sleep, which typically lasts from 1 to 7 minutes.

- *Stage II sleep* is characterized by the appearance of *sleep spindles* and lasts approximately 20 minutes. Sleep spindles (see Figure 4.3) are a pattern of slower theta waves sporadically disrupted by bursts of electrical activity. During stage II sleep, breathing, muscle tension, heart rate, and body temperature continue to decrease. You are clearly asleep and not easily awakened. Research suggests that stage II sleep spindles help us process both simple and complex motor skills that we have learned (Barakat et al., 2013; Fogel et al., 2017; Fogel & Smith, 2011; Tucker & Fishbein, 2009).
- *Stages III and IV* sleep are referred to as *slow-wave sleep*. In stage III sleep, you begin showing *delta* brain-wave patterns. Delta waves are large, slow brain waves. When a consistent pattern of delta waves emerges, you have entered stage IV sleep. Stage IV sleep is referred to as *deep sleep*. The body is extremely relaxed. Heart rate, respiration, body temperature, and blood flow to the brain are reduced. Growth hormone is secreted. It is difficult to awaken people from deep sleep. When they are awakened, they may be disoriented or confused. It is believed that during this deep sleep, body maintenance and restoration occur (Dang-Vu et al., 2010; Porkka-Heiskanen et al., 1997). For example, exercise increases the amount of slow-wave sleep (Driver & Taylor, 2000; Horne & Staff, 1983). Research findings also suggest a major role of slow-wave sleep for strengthening the long-term storage of specific events and

experiences called *episodic memory* (Ackermann & Rasch, 2014; Aly & Moscovitch, 2010; Inostroza & Born, 2013; Scullin & Bliwise, 2015). Your first hour of sleep is predominately slow-wave sleep. Slow-wave sleep then progressively gets shorter the longer you sleep.

REM Sleep: Dream On

After approximately 30 to 40 minutes of slow-wave sleep, your brain and body start to speed up again. You cycle back through stage II of non-REM sleep and then enter REM sleep. REM sleep is a very active stage. Your breathing rate increases, and your heart beats irregularly. Blood flow increases to the genital area and may cause erections in males (Somers et al., 1993). However, your muscle tone significantly decreases, leaving the muscles extremely relaxed and essentially paralyzed. Figure 4.3 shows that your REM brain-wave patterns are similar to your brain-wave patterns when you are awake. The brain slides labeled "awake" and "REM" look almost exactly alike! You can see that the brain slide labeled non-REM looks quite different. This is why REM sleep is often called *paradoxical sleep*. You look peaceful and relaxed on the outside as your muscles are extremely relaxed, and yet internally, the brain is quite active.

REM sleep is intimately connected to dreaming. Although you can dream in some form in all sleep stages, dreams during REM sleep are more easily recalled. More than 80% of people awakened from REM sleep report dreaming (Hirshkowitz et al., 1997). The body paralysis that occurs during REM prevents you from acting out your dreams. However, in rare instances, people do not experience the paralysis that normally accompanies REM sleep. This condition, which mainly occurs in older men, is referred to as **REM behavior disorder**. People with REM behavior disorder may thrash about while in REM sleep, causing harm to themselves or others (Gugger & Wagner, 2007; see Iranzo, 2018 for a review).

REM behavior disorder a condition in which normal muscle paralysis does not occur, leading to violent movements during REM sleep

REM rebound the loss of REM sleep is recouped by spending more time in REM on subsequent nights

Researchers are continuously questioning the purpose of REM sleep. Some studies suggest a connection between REM sleep and memory processing and storage. People who are deprived of REM sleep and dreaming are less likely to recall complex information learned earlier in the day than are people who were not deprived of REM sleep (Chollar, 1989; Karni et al., 1994). People who are REM-deprived also report having difficulty concentrating when they awaken. These findings have led researchers to speculate that REM sleep—and perhaps dreaming—facilitates the storage of memories as well as mental strategies (Della Monica et al., 2018; Diekelmann & Born, 2010; Rauchs et al., 2004). At the same time, REM appears to help us process recent emotional experiences (Ackermann & Rasch, 2014; Desseilles et al., 2011; Menz et al., 2013; Tempesta, Socci, De Gennaro, & Ferrara, 2018; Walker & van der Helm, 2009) and to "discard" information that is trivial or less important to us (Crick & Mitchison, 1995; Smith, 1995). Other research shows no relationship between time spent in REM sleep and memory problems (J. M. Siegel, 2001). Scientists continue to explore the exact connection between the various sleep stages and different memory processes (Poe et al., 2010).

Another curiosity of REM sleep is referred to as **REM rebound**. When people lose REM sleep because of medications, drugs, sleep deprivation, or due to sleep disorders (discussed shortly) they make up for it on subsequent nights (when not using the drugs/medication or when the sleep disorder is treated) by spending more time in REM sleep (Bougard et al., 2018; Dement, 1960; Koo, Wiggins, & Molina, 2012). Before we look at research on dreaming, let's review what happens during a typical night of sleep.

A Typical Night's Sleep

A typical night of sleep consists of cycling through non-REM stages and REM sleep. We progress through stages I, II, III, and IV of non-REM sleep. We revisit stages III and II of non-REM sleep. We then enter REM sleep. After a brief period in REM sleep, we begin the cycle again, starting with the non-REM stages. The pattern repeats throughout the night. One complete cycle of non-REM and REM sleep takes about 90 minutes. But notice from • FIGURE 4.4 that as the night progresses, we spend less time in slow-wave sleep and more time in REM sleep. This means that the body-restoring functions of slow-wave sleep take place early on, during the first few cycles of sleep. After these early cycles, we spend longer in REM sleep. So, if you are not getting enough sleep, you will miss out on the longest period of REM sleep. On average, we spend about 20% of our total sleep time in REM sleep. If you sleep 8 hours a night, you spend roughly 90 minutes of that time in REM sleep. That means each night you spend approximately 90 minutes having REM dreams. For Jean-Dominique Bauby, this typical pattern of sleep was likely altered. Studies on sleep in locked-in syndrome indicate disturbances in slow-wave sleep and a significant reduction in the amount of REM sleep (Cologan et al., 2010).

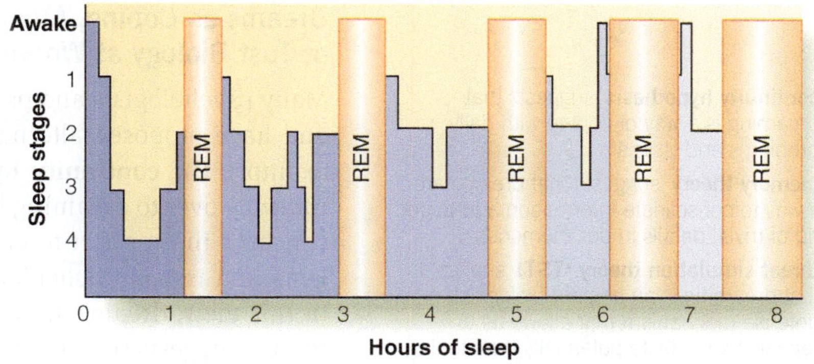

FIGURE 4.4

A Typical Night of Sleep

As the night progresses, we spend less time in slow-wave sleep (stages III and IV) and more time in REM sleep.

4.1.5 Dreaming: The Night's Work

Although not everyone reports remembering their dreams when they awaken, everyone, regardless of culture, progresses through dream states during sleep. When Jean-Dominique Bauby came out of his coma, he actually thought he was having a bad dream. Dreams do show some similarities in content from one culture to another. For example, dream themes that focus on basic needs or fears (sex, aggression, and death) seem to be universal. Other content seems to be specific to its presence in a culture. For instance, today's Alaskan natives may have dreams that include snowmobiles, but their ancestors of 100 years ago obviously did not. People dream about what they know, which is influenced by the culture in which they live (Price & Crapo, 2002).

Sigmund Freud's Interpretation of Dreams

One of the most controversial and best-known theories of dreaming is Sigmund Freud's. In his *Interpretation of Dreams* (1900/1980), Freud called dreams "the royal road to the unconscious." According to Freud, dreams allow us to express fears and sexual and aggressive desires without the censorship of our conscious thought processes. Having straightforward dreams about these "unacceptable" desires, he theorized, would cause us anxiety. Instead, we dream in symbols that represent our unconscious desires. For Freud, dreams contained both **manifest content** and **latent content**. The manifest content of a dream is what you recall when you awaken. The latent, or hidden, content of the dream is the symbolic interpretation. For example, a young student may dream of coming home from school one day to find the house deserted. They run from room to room, looking for their parents or some sign that they will be returning soon (manifest content). Such a dream among children may signify the anxiety of being left alone, deserted, uncared for, or unprotected (latent content).

manifest content according to Freud, what the dreamer recalls on awakening

latent content according to Freud, the symbolic meaning of a dream

continuity hypothesis suggests that dreaming is a way of coping with daily problems and issues

memory theory suggests that dreams are a way to consolidate information and to get rid of trivial details in our memories

threat simulation theory (TST) suggests that dreaming is an ancient biological defense mechanism that allows us to repeatedly simulate potentially threatening situations so that we can rehearse our responses to these events

activation-synthesis theory suggests that dreams do not have symbolic meaning but are the by-product of the brain's random firing of neural impulses during REM sleep

sleep disorder a disturbance in the normal pattern of sleeping

insomnia a sleep disorder in which a person cannot get to sleep and/or stay asleep

Dreams as Coping, Memory, Evolutionary Defense, or Just Biology at Work?

Many psychologists and psychiatrists have challenged Freud's theory of dreaming and have proposed alternative explanations or theories for why we dream. For example, the **continuity hypothesis** suggests that experiences from waking life *continue* over to dreaming life. We dream about everyday experiences and current concerns in an effort to emotionally process, cope with, and resolve daily problems and issues (Eichenlaub et al., 2018; Pesant & Zadra, 2006; Schredl, 2009). In this view, dreams are not as symbolic as Freud suggested. Similarly, **memory theory** suggests that dreams are a way to consolidate information and to get rid of trivial details in our memories (Eiser, 2005; Horton & Malinowski, 2015; Wamsley, 2014). From this viewpoint, dreams represent a function of memory.

The **threat simulation theory (TST)** suggests an evolutionary function of dreams. TST proposes that dreaming is essentially an ancient biological defense mechanism that allows us to experience potentially threatening situations so that we can rehearse our responses to these events. Although studies suggest that childhood trauma or recurrent dreams are associated with a greater number of threatening dream events, not all of our dreams involve themes of survival (Valli & Revonsuo, 2009; Zadra, Desjardins, & Marcotte, 2006).

A biologically based theory is the **activation-synthesis theory** (Hobson & McCarley, 1977), which suggests that dreaming is just a consequence of the highly aroused brain during REM sleep, when the brain shows activation of millions of random neural impulses. The cortex of the brain attempts to create meaning out of these neural impulses by synthesizing them into familiar images or stories based on our stored memories. These images and stories may reflect our past, our emotions, our personal perspectives, and information accessed during waking, but they have no hidden "Freudian" meaning. However, because we are the ones who integrate these images into a plot, the storyline may provide us with insights about ourselves (Hobson, Pace-Schott, & Stickgold, 2000; McCarley, 1998).

Obviously, our understanding of the purpose and meaning of dreaming is incomplete. Dreams aside, sleep research indicates that people do not always get a good night's sleep. Some of us exhibit sleep disturbances, our next topic of discussion.

4.1.6 Sleep Disorders: Tossing and Turning—and More

Not everyone sleeps soundly. An estimated 50 to 70 million adults in the United States experience a **sleep disorder**, or a disturbance in the normal pattern of sleep (Centers for Disease Control, 2011b). Sleep disorders also impact approximately 25% to 40% of children and adolescents (Meltzer & Mindell, 2006). Bauby and others in intensive care units often can experience sleep disruption due to noise from ventilators, activity from medical personnel, and exposure to light. Here, we will discuss several sleep disorders that influence behavior: *insomnia, narcolepsy, sleep apnea, restless legs syndrome, sleepwalking, night terrors,* and *enuresis*.

Insomnia: There is Help!

Insomnia, the most commonly reported sleep disorder, is the inability to get to sleep and/or stay asleep. Results from population-based surveys that estimate the prevalence of insomnia in U.S. adults range from 15% to 24% (Ford, Cunningham, Giles, & Croft, 2015; Roth et al., 2011). Insomnia is associated with a multitude of factors, including stress, coping with the loss of a loved one, a change in sleep schedule, obesity, chronic pain, drug abuse, anxiety, or depression (Roth, Krystal, & Lieberman, 2007).

Insomnia can be treated medically using antianxiety or sedative medications such as Xanax or Ambien, or by taking over-the-counter medications that contain antihistamines and pain relievers to induce sleepiness. However, long-term use of these drugs may lead to dependence and serious side effects, including memory loss, fatigue, and increased sleepiness. The prescription drug, Belsomra, was approved by the Food and Drug Administration (FDA) in 2014 to treat insomnia. Belsomra is an orexin receptor antagonist. *Hypocretin/orexins* are brain chemicals that play a role in keeping people awake. As an antagonist, Belsomra interferes with these brain chemicals, thereby promoting sleep (Chow & Cao, 2016). Chronic insomnia is best treated with a combination of taking medication for a limited time, cognitive-behavioral therapy (which focuses on changing thoughts and behaviors that interfere with restful sleep—discussed more in Chapter 14), and following several sleep guidelines that have evolved from our study of how we sleep (Morin et al., 2009; Riemann & Perlis, 2009; Roth, Krystal, & Lieberman, 2007):

iordani/Shutterstock.com

▲ The most commonly reported sleep disorder is insomnia. Insomnia can be reduced by changing one's thoughts and behaviors that interfere with restful sleep.

- Establish a regular sleep-wake cycle to work with your body's natural sleep circadian rhythm. Go to bed at the same time every evening and wake up at the same time every morning. Even if you have difficulty falling asleep at night, continue to get up at the same time each morning.
- Avoid long naps during waking hours. Naps can disrupt your sleep circadian rhythm. What about children who take daily naps and adults who take a "power nap" or siesta? Children's naps and siestas typically occur at the same time every day and thereby work with, rather than against, the sleep circadian rhythm. Power naps are short periods of rest (15–20 minutes) that are relaxing and that can reenergize the body and mind; because they are short, they generally do not interfere with our sleep cycles (Milner & Cote, 2009).
- Don't use your bed for anything other than sleeping. For example, people with insomnia should not eat, study, work, or watch television in bed. The bed should be associated only with sleeping.
- If you can't get to sleep after 15 minutes, get up and do something that you think will make you tired enough to get to sleep, such as reading (but not in your bed). Then try again to fall asleep.
- Avoid sleeping pills, alcohol, nicotine, and caffeine. These are all drugs that can interfere with your natural sleep cycle and disrupt sleep.
- Exercise during the day can promote good sleep (Reid et al., 2010; Yang et al., 2012). However, avoid physical workouts within an hour of bedtime. Your body should be relaxed prior to sleeping.
- Turn off your cell phone, tablet, video games, and computer prior to sleeping. Anticipating incoming text messages or calls, as well as the vibration or sound that occurs when a message or call is received, interrupts the natural sleep cycle and makes deep sleep less likely in adults and children (Dube et al., 2017; Van den Bulck, 2003, 2007). In one study, both cell phone usage and computer usage were positively correlated with insomnia (Fossum et al., 2014).
- Turn off the lights. Unnecessary light exposure, from the television, cell phone, LCD clock display, or a night light influences sleep quality. It is associated with increased stage I sleep and decreased slow-wave or deep sleep (Cho et al., 2013).

narcolepsy [NAR-co-lep-see] a rare sleep disorder in which a person falls asleep during alert times of the day

sleep apnea [APP-nee-uh] a sleep disorder in which a person stops breathing during sleep

Narcolepsy and Cataplexy

Narcolepsy, a rare sleep disorder that affects approximately 0.056% of Americans and an estimated 0.02% of Europeans, occurs when a person falls asleep during alert times of the day (Khatami et al., 2016; Longstreth et al., 2007). This condition is not the same as a microsleep, though. Narcolepsy is thought to stem from a loss of neurons in the hypothalamus of the brain. These neurons are responsible for producing the hypocretin/orexin chemicals that help control the sleep–wake cycle (Chow & Cao, 2016; Nishino, 2007; Zeitzer, Nishino, & Mignot, 2006). The person with narcolepsy experiences brief periods of REM sleep that may be accompanied by a sudden loss of muscle tone, a condition called *cataplexy*. Narcolepsy with cataplexy occurs in roughly 25–50 of every 100,000 persons (Longstreth et al., 2007). People with narcolepsy may fall down or otherwise injure themselves during these episodes. Those with the condition typically take *modafinil* to improve wakefulness (Nishino & Okuro, 2010; Roth, Schwartz et al., 2007) and *sodium oxybate*, the only FDA-approved medication for cataplexy (Thorpy, 2007).

Sleep Apnea

Sleep apnea is a disorder in which a person stops breathing while sleeping. In an attempt to get air, people with sleep apnea often emit loud snores or snorts that may awaken them or their partners. This pattern may occur hundreds of times during the night. People who experience sleep apnea may feel sluggish, tired, irritable, or unable to concentrate the next day because of the nighttime sleep disruption (Naegele et al., 1995). Obesity, being overweight, and the use of alcohol or sedatives increase one's chances of developing sleep apnea (Peppard et al., 2013; Pillar & Lavie, 2011). Sleep apnea is a risk factor for heart failure and stroke and is highly associated with heart disease, especially for middle-aged men (Butt et al., 2010; Chen et al., 2014; see Javaheri et al., 2017 for a review; Sanchez-de-la-Torre, Campos-Rodriguez, & Barbe, 2013).

Once diagnosed, sleep apnea may be treated in various ways. If obesity is a factor, a weight-loss program is the first treatment. In addition, a nasal mask (called a continuous positive airway pressure [CPAP] device) that blows air into the nose to facilitate continuous breathing can be worn at night. Wearing mouth retainers can help in some cases. There is also the Inspire® Upper Airway Stimulation (UAS) system, a surgically implanted device for moderate to severe sleep apnea for those unable to use a CPAP device. The device senses when a person stops breathing during sleep and stimulates muscles in the airway to keep it open. In severe cases, removing the tonsils or surgery to remove excess throat tissue can be performed (Saskin, 1997).

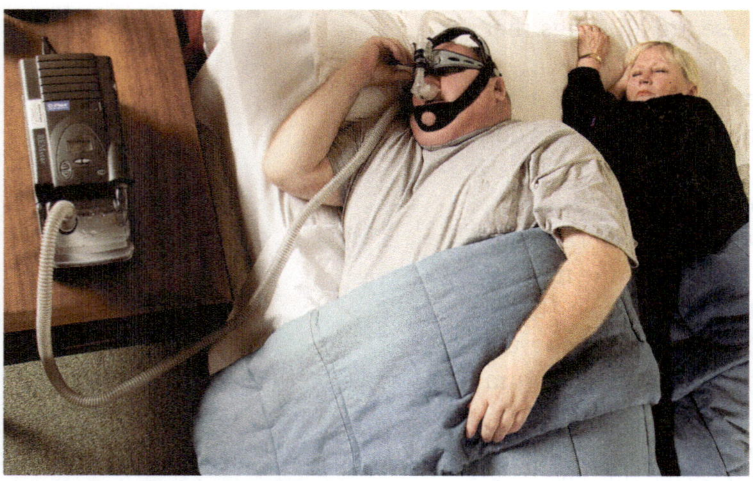

Custom Medical Stock Photo

▲ A continuous positive airway pressure, or CPAP, device blows air into the nose to facilitate continuous breathing for people who have sleep apnea.

Considerable evidence suggests a heritable basis for sleep apnea as it is known to surface strongly within families (Chiang, 2006; Polotsky & O'Donnell, 2007). However, its genetic basis is not well understood (Chen et al., 2018; Larkin et al., 2010). Moreover, the rate of sleep apnea in the United States has increased substantially over the last two decades, most likely due to the obesity epidemic. It is now estimated that 26% of U.S. adults between the ages of 30 and 70 years experience sleep apnea (Peppard et al., 2013). In a National Veteran Sleep Disorder study, sleep apnea was the most common sleep disorder indicated in medical records (Alexander et al., 2016).

Restless Legs Syndrome (RLS)

Restless legs syndrome (RLS) is a common sleep movement disorder in which a person has unpleasant sensations in the legs and an irresistible urge to move them to relieve the discomfort. Symptoms occur primarily at night. Estimates of RLS in the general population range from 5% to 25%, although the incidence is higher in adults with obesity and women (Lin et al., 2018; Nagandia & De, 2013).

The cause of RLS is unknown. Current hypotheses focus on a genetic component, abnormal metabolism of iron in the brain, and the role of the neurotransmitter dopamine, as dopamine is needed to produce smooth muscle activity and movement (Nagandia & De, 2013; Piao et al., 2017). Medications that influence dopamine functioning can lessen the discomfort and facilitate restful sleep (Garcia-Borreguero et al., 2016; Rios Romenets & Postuma, 2013). People with Parkinson's disease, another movement disorder of the dopamine pathways, can coexist with RLS, although the nature, development, and causes of these disorders may be different (Piao et al., 2017; Rijsman et al., 2014; Suzuki et al., 2015).

Some people with RLS also experience *periodic limb movement in sleep (PLMS)*. PLMS includes involuntary leg twitches or jerking movements during sleep that occur roughly every 15 to 40 seconds, sometimes throughout the night. The symptoms severely disrupt sleep. Although some people with RLS may develop PLMS, most people with PLMS do not experience RLS. PLMS risk increases with age and also may occur in people with narcolepsy, sleep apnea, REM sleep behavior disorder, and in those with no sleep disturbances (Haba-Rubio et al., 2016; Hornyak et al., 2006).

restless legs syndrome (RLS) a neurological movement disorder occurring primarily at night in which a person has unpleasant sensations in the legs and an irresistible urge to move them to relieve the discomfort

sleepwalking a sleep disorder in which a person is mobile and may perform actions during non-REM slow-wave sleep

night terrors very frightening non-REM sleep episodes

Sleepwalking: Wake Me Up!

Sleepwalking, or *somnambulism*, occurs during non-REM slow-wave sleep. People with this disorder get up and walk around during deep sleep, sometimes performing actions that make them appear to be awake. They may cook, eat, open doors, or engage in minimal conversation. Because sleepwalkers are asleep, they may injure themselves or others. What should you do if you come across a sleepwalker? Wake them up or guide them back to bed. They may be initially disoriented or confused, but you will not do harm by awakening them. Lifetime prevalence of sleepwalking is estimated to be between 4.6% and 10.3% of the general population and it is more common in children than in adults (Stallman & Kohler, 2016). Sleepwalking tends to run in families, suggesting a genetic basis (Horvath, Papp, & Szucs, 2016).

Night Terrors and Enuresis

During **night terrors**, people awaken in an apparent state of fear. Their heart rates and breathing are rapid, and they may scream loudly and sit up in bed, wide-eyed with terror. People rarely recall the incident in the morning (Moreno, 2015). Night terrors occur during non-REM slow-wave sleep, and an attack may last 5 to 20 minutes. Although they can occur any time in one's life, night terrors are more commonly reported by parents in children between the ages of 1½ to 13 years, and in older adults with various neurological and cognitive disorders such as Parkinson's disease and dementia (Abad & Guilleminault, 2004; Petit et al., 2015). In the United States, an estimated 1% to 6% of children experience night terror episodes. For adults, estimates are less than 1% (Owens, 2007).

Why night terrors occur is still a mystery, although the disorder does tend to run in families (Guilleminault et al., 2003; Owens, 2007). Keep in mind that people who are having night terrors do not know what is occurring. To help a

nightmares brief scary REM dreams that are often remembered

enuresis [en-your-REE-sus] a condition in which a person over the age of 5 shows an inability to control urination during sleep

person experiencing a night terror, simply reassure the person that everything is all right and to go back to sleep. Night terrors are different from *nightmares*. **Nightmares** are brief scary dreams that typically occur during REM sleep and are often recalled in vivid detail in the morning.

Enuresis is bedwetting, but it does not refer to the occasional nighttime bedwetting that is common among young children. Enuresis is diagnosed when a child who is at least 5 years old wets their bed or pajamas at least twice a week over a 3-month period. It is estimated that 5% to 10% of 5-year-olds are diagnosed with enuresis, but by adolescence the prevalence of enuresis decreases to about 1% (American Psychiatric Association, 2013). It is more common at younger ages, in males, and among African-American youth (Shreeram et al., 2009). Enuresis tends to run in families, suggesting that it may be inherited (Ondersma & Walker, 1998; von Gontard et al., 2001). However, the behavior may also occur during times of stress, such as when a new sibling is born or familial conflict is high, and may accompany night terrors. Scolding or punishing a child seldom has any effect on the bedwetting. In fact, scolding can potentially damage the child's self-esteem and the parent–child relationship. Several treatment methods are available, and most children outgrow the behavior (Berry, 2006; Sinha & Raut, 2016).

4.1.7 Gender, Ethnic, and Cultural Variations in Sleep

Sleep research has also investigated the degree to which gender, ethnicity, and culture influence sleep. Several studies have found that men report needing less sleep than women to function at their best, and that women are more likely than men to sleep 8 hours or more. Women are also more likely than men to report insufficient rest or sleep (Boerma et al., 2016; Della Monica et al., 2018), daytime sleepiness, and needing 30 minutes or more to fall asleep (National Sleep Foundation, 2005; Oginska & Pokorski, 2006). Working mothers also are two-and-a-half times more likely than working fathers to interrupt their sleep to take care of babies and small children (Burgard, 2011). In the area of sleep disorders, two consistent gender differences have emerged. Insomnia tends to be more frequent in women (Morlock, Tan, & Mitchell, 2006; Roberts, Roberts, & Chan, 2006; Suh, Cho, & Zhang, 2018), and snoring and sleep apnea are more common in men (Appleton et al., 2018; Jordan & McEvoy, 2003).

Only a limited number of studies have compared sleep variables across ethnic groups. Those that have suggest that African Americans sleep worse than European Americans. They report poorer sleep quality, more variation in sleep time, and taking longer to fall asleep (Carnethon et al., 2016; National Sleep Foundation, 2010). However, African Americans are more likely to live in urban areas, a variable that is also associated with poorer sleep quality (Haie & Do, 2007). Asian Americans were most likely of any ethnic group to say they get a good night's sleep and curiously also reported more daytime sleepiness compared to European Americans (Carnethon et al., 2016; National Sleep Foundation, 2010). European Americans report the highest rate of insomnia. African Americans, Native Americans, and Hispanic American adults are at high risk for sleep apnea, although these observed ethnic differences are mainly explained by high rates of obesity among these groups (Fiorentino et al., 2006; National Sleep Foundation, 2010).

Cultural variations in sleep habits also have been investigated. Japanese and U.S. adults report the least amount of sleep when compared to respondents from Canada, Germany, Mexico, and the United Kingdom. The most common sleep ritual reported across the six countries was television. Two-thirds of the adults in all countries surveyed watched television in the hour before bed (National Sleep Foundation, 2013).

In summary, sleep is as necessary to our survival as food and shelter. Sleep refuels our bodies and minds, preparing us for the challenges of the next day. When we skip sleep, change our sleep cycle, or experience disturbances in our sleep, we may feel irritable, tired, and less alert the next day.

4.1 Quiz Yourself

1. **Ronnie has a dream that he is being chased by a golden goose. He is told that this reflects his anxiety about impregnating women. This analysis represents the __________ of his dream.**
   a. manifest content
   b. latent content
   c. activation synthesis
   d. consolidation
2. **Hap is at a workshop and falls asleep. Hap's brain-wave pattern shows theta waves interrupted by short bursts of electrical activity. Hap is in what stage of sleep?**
   a. Stage I
   b. Stage II
   c. Stage IV
   d. REM
3. **Which of the following statements about sleep is *false*?**
   a. Sleep patterns change with age.
   b. Everyone needs at least 8 hours of sleep a night.
   c. Some people are night owls, whereas others are early birds.
   d. Circadian rhythms influence the sleep cycle.
4. **The suprachiasmatic nucleus increases the release of melatonin as it gets darker outside. This represents a ________ correlation between amount of melatonin and amount of daylight.**
   a. negative
   b. positive
   c. zero
   d. perfect
5. **Which of the following is poor advice to give to someone who is experiencing insomnia?**
   a. Avoid naps
   b. Exercise during the day.
   c. Go to bed when you feel tired and wake up when you feel rested.
   d. Do not watch television in bed.

Answers 1. b; 2. b; 3. b; 4. a; 5. c

4.2 Hypnosis, Meditation, & Mindfulness

Psychologists study other altered states of consciousness in which one is not fully awake or aware such as hypnosis, meditation, and mindfulness. **Hypnosis** is a method occasionally used by researchers and psychologists (and frequently by hypnotists) to create a state of relaxation and heightened suggestibility in others. **Meditation** is a practice whereby a person focuses their attention on a singular source such as a word, bodily sensation, or object for a period of time. There are many different types of meditation from Zen or chanting meditation to movement meditation such as yoga or tai chi. One particular type of meditation receiving increased research interest from psychologists is called mindfulness meditation. **Mindfulness meditation** is where a person intentionally focuses and pays attention to and experiences what is going on in the moment—their emotions, thoughts, and/or sensations—without judgment. This section describes these altered states and the research examining what they can and cannot do for you.

hypnosis a state of relaxation and heightened suggestibility

meditation a practice whereby a person focuses their attention on a singular source such as a word, bodily sensation, or object for a period of time

mindfulness meditation a practice where a person intentionally focuses and pays attention to and experiences what is going on in the moment—their emotions, thoughts, and/or sensations—without judgment

4.2.1 The Experience of Hypnosis

Typically, if you are undergoing hypnosis, you are asked to focus on an object, an image, or the hypnotist's voice. For several minutes, you are told that you are getting sleepy and becoming more relaxed (Druckman & Bjork, 1994). You don't fall asleep—though EEG brain-wave patterns of hypnotized people show an increase in alpha waves (light hypnosis) and theta waves (deep hypnosis)—and this condition isn't followed by the non-REM pattern of sleep stages discussed earlier (Graffin, Ray, & Lundy, 1995; Jensen, Adachi, & Hakimian, 2015). After inducing you into this relaxed hypnotic state, the hypnotist makes suggestions about what you are seeing, feeling, or perceiving. For example, one suggestion might be to lift your left arm over your head. A more complex suggestion might be that your eyelids feel as though they are glued shut and you cannot open them. Although accounts vary widely, many people who are hypnotized report that they feel as though they are floating or that their bodies are sinking. Under hypnosis, they remain in control of their bodies and are aware of their surroundings (Kirsch & Lynn, 1995).

4.2.2 Variations in Hypnotic Susceptibility

neodissociation [knee o dis-so-see-AYE-shun] theory Hilgard's proposal that hypnosis involves two simultaneous states: a hypnotic state and a hidden observer

Hypnotic susceptibility is the ability to become hypnotized. Some people have a low degree of susceptibility—they cannot easily be hypnotized. Others have a high susceptibility, meaning that they can be easily hypnotized. One well-known standard test for measuring the degree to which people respond to hypnotic suggestions is the *Stanford Hypnotic Susceptibility Scale*. The scale assesses your suggestibility to certain tasks while in a state of hypnosis with a trained hypnotist. The tasks range from pulling apart your interlocked fingers to hallucinating the presence of a buzzing fly. Contrary to what you may see on television or in the movies, research using such measures has found that not everyone can be hypnotized. About 25% of adults are difficult to hypnotize (Hoeft et al., 2012).

People who are easily hypnotized tend to be better able to focus their attention (Egner, Jamieson, & Gruzelier, 2005; Raz, 2005), have vivid imaginations (Silva & Kirsch, 1992; Spanos, Burnley, & Cross, 1993; Terhune, Cardena, & Lindgren, 2010), and have positive expectations about hypnosis (Barber, 2000). Neuroimaging studies even document differences in brain activation between people who are highly hypnotizable and those who are low in hypnotic susceptibility (Hoeft et al., 2012; Jensen et al., 2017; Jiang et al., 2016; Naish, 2010). Hypnotic suggestibility does not appear to be related to such factors as intelligence, gender, sociability, or gullibility (Kirsch & Lynn, 1995).

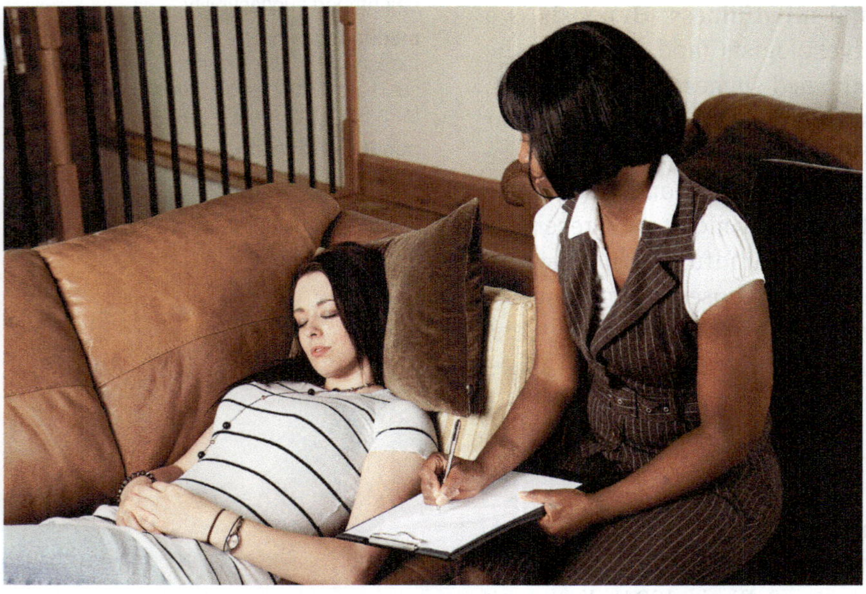

iStock.com/PaulaConnelly

▲ Not everyone can be hypnotized. You have to want to be hypnotized and believe it will work for you.

4.2.3 Explaining Hypnosis: Applying Neodissociation and Response Set Theories

Currently, two theories seek to explain hypnosis: *neodissociation theory* and the *response set theory*. Ernest Hilgard's (1977, 1992) **neodissociation theory** suggests that hypnosis is truly an altered state of consciousness: a person feels, perceives, and behaves differently than in a conscious state. To dissociate means to split or break apart. Hilgard maintains that under hypnosis, your consciousness divides into two states. One level of your consciousness voluntarily agrees to behave according to the suggestions of the hypnotist. However, at the same time, a *hidden observer* state exists. This hidden observer is aware of all that is happening.

We all engage in dissociation at times. Have you ever driven to a familiar location and realized when you arrived that you couldn't consciously remember driving there? Have you ever dissociated in a class—paying attention to the lesson while at the same time doodling or mentally organizing the rest of your day? If you have experienced any of these behaviors, then you are familiar with the concept of dissociation. Hilgard believes that hypnosis works in much the same way, allowing the person to attend to the hypnotist's suggestions while still being aware of what is happening through the hidden observer.

In a classic demonstration, Hilgard hypnotized participants and suggested that they would feel no pain. The participants were then instructed to submerge one arm in ice-cold water. When Hilgard asked them whether they felt pain, the participants replied, "No." However, when they were asked to press a key with their other hand if they felt pain, the participants did so. On one level, they agreed with the hypnotist that there was no pain, while at the same time a part of them—a "hidden observer"—indicated that there was pain (Hilgard, Morgan, & MacDonald, 1975).

Another view, the **response set theory of hypnosis** (Kirsch, 2000; Kirsch & Lynn, 1997; Lynn, 1997), asserts that hypnosis is *not* an altered state of consciousness. Rather, hypnosis is merely a willingness to respond appropriately to suggestions. Several studies suggest that people's response expectancies influence their responsiveness to hypnosis (Benham et al., 2006; Milling, Reardon, & Carosella, 2006). People who are highly hypnotizable enter hypnosis with the intention of behaving as a "hypnotized person" and hold the expectation that they will succeed in following the hypnotist's suggestions. Their intentions and expectations trigger their positive response to being hypnotized.

response set theory of hypnosis asserts that hypnosis is not an altered state of consciousness, but a cognitive set to respond appropriately to suggestions

Currently, theorists suggest that explaining hypnosis will require identifying the social, cultural, cognitive, and neurological variables that play a role in hypnosis and consider their possible interactions to understand the experience of hypnosis (Lynn, Laurence, & Kirsch, 2015). Unfortunately, hypnosis has acquired a reputation for doing some things that it cannot do. Let's look at these myths and realities of hypnosis.

4.2.4 Evaluating the Research: What Hypnosis Can and Cannot Do

In an attempt to separate fact from fiction, psychologists have researched the effects of hypnosis. To date, research suggests the following:

- *Relieving pain.* One of the best documented uses for hypnosis is pain relief (Adachi et al., 2014; Jensen et al., 2017; Kendrick et al., 2016). Under hypnosis, clients relax, which reduces pain, and/or distract themselves from the pain by focusing on more pleasing and pain-free scenarios. Hypnosis has been used to minimize pain in childbirth, to block pain during medical or dental treatments, and to relieve chronic pain stemming from various health conditions (Adachi et al., 2014; Jensen et al., 2011; Kendrick et al., 2016; Liossi, White, & Hatira, 2006; VandeVusse et al., 2007). This pain relief is more pronounced for people who have a high susceptibility to hypnosis (Bates, 1994). Hypnosis does not reduce the sensation of pain. The pain is still there, but hypnosis changes a person's subjective experience of pain so that it is more bearable (Rainville et al., 1997).
- *Curing addictions.* Posthypnotic suggestions have proven less successful for treating addictions or self-control behaviors, even in people with a high susceptibility to hypnosis. Although hypnosis has been used as a treatment to

stop smoking, nail biting, overeating, gambling, alcoholism, and other addictions, it has proven no more successful than other treatments at controlling these behaviors (Barnes et al., 2010; Bates, 1994; Green & Lynn, 2000). Self-control behaviors such as smoking and alcoholism are some of the most difficult behaviors to change, and hypnosis doesn't appear to have an advantage over other types of treatment (Barnes et al., 2019; Rabkin et al., 1984).

- *Enhancing physical performance.* Hypnosis does not create superhuman capacities. However, being in a relaxed state such as hypnosis can enhance physical performance (Barker, Jones, & Greenlees, 2010). The person can more readily visualize optimal performance and reduce self-doubt or nerves. This enhancement can also be achieved through other techniques, such as deep muscle relaxation and guided imagery (Druckman & Bjork, 1994; Newmark & Bogacki, 2005; see Chapter 12).
- *Decreasing anxiety and enhancing psychotherapy.* Hypnosis has proven useful in decreasing fears and anxieties for people with a high susceptibility to hypnosis (Saadat et al., 2006). Clinicians sometimes use hypnosis in therapy to help their clients solve problems or cope with bodily symptoms such as headaches or stomach pains that appear to be related to psychological stress (Hammond, 2010). Hypnosis also has been helpful in alleviating symptoms of *post-traumatic stress disorder* or PTSD (Rotaru & Rusu, 2016; see Chapter 13). Again, it is most effective for clients who have a high susceptibility to hypnosis (Kirsch, Montgomery, & Sapirstein, 1995; Pyun, 2013).
- *Enhancing or recovering memory.* One of the most controversial applications of hypnosis has been in the area of memory enhancement. Research in this area has focused on two key issues: age regression and recovered memories.
  - *Age regression* refers to a person reliving earlier childhood experiences. Numerous studies on age regression demonstrate that under hypnosis, adults act the way they *expect* children to behave (Spanos, 1996). They may write, sing, or behave like a child, but it is more like an adult playing the role of a child. Their behavior is not different from that of nonhypnotized people who are asked to behave like a child (Nash, 1987).
  - A *recovered memory* is one in which a person recalls forgotten traumatic events or information, such as events from a crime scene or from one's childhood. Being in a relaxed state may facilitate recall under certain circumstances. However, research reveals that people who are hypnotized may also recall untrue events. For this reason, information gathered under hypnosis is not permissible in a court of law in the United States, Canada, Australia, or Great Britain. People are more suggestible under hypnosis, and consequently their memories are more likely to be influenced by the suggestions, tone, hints, questions, and remarks of the hypnotist. They may recall just as many events that did *not* occur as events that did, and they may also be more prone to distort information (Geraerts et al., 2009; Patihis & Pendergrast, 2019; Patihis et al., 2014; Scoboria, Mazzoni, & Kirsch, 2006). For these reasons, the use of hypnosis in the area of memory enhancement should be viewed with skepticism.

To summarize, hypnosis does not endow us with superhuman strength, allow us to reexperience childhood events, or improve the accuracy of our memories. However, hypnosis may be of some benefit in decreasing pain, promoting relaxation, and perhaps enhancing therapy for *some* people. These benefits are not universal. The person must want to be hypnotized and have positive beliefs about hypnosis.

4.2.5 Research on Meditation & Mindfulness

Meditation methods are highly variable from Zen meditation to yoga to mindfulness meditation. In some cases, all these methods may be described as *mindfulness-based practices* as they all involve focusing one's attention or mind on the present without judgment. These practices have become increasingly popular, with 14% of U.S. adults reporting having used a meditation method in the last 12 months (Clarke, Barnes, & Black, 2018).

▲ Mindfulness-based practices that focus one's attention or mind on the present without judgment have become increasingly popular.

The purported benefits of meditation and mindfulness-based interventions have been widely publicized in the media and have ranged from better health outcomes, to stress reduction, to improved mood and decreased symptoms of anxiety and depression. However, the studies designed to evaluate these outcomes have major limitations that make such claims oversimplified. For example, studies have reported that meditation engages those parts of the brain that regulate attention and emotion (Lutz, Slagter, Dunne, & Davidson, 2008). Not surprising, given that this is what the various forms of meditation are designed to do. However, studies suggesting that long-term use of mindfulness-based practices *alters* the structure and function of the brain should be viewed with caution. Many of these studies involved a small number of participants, and were nonrandomized. That is, participants were not randomly assigned to the meditation versus control groups—a necessary condition of experiments that allows one to possibly make causal conclusions. In some cases, the participants in the meditation group had been practicing meditation for many, many years and may therefore differ substantially from people who had practiced mindfulness for weeks or months. Moreover, the various studies assessed different forms of meditation, decreasing one's ability to generalize to all forms of mindfulness-based practices (Levine, Lang, Bairey-Merz et al., 2017).

Studies suggesting that meditation and mindfulness reduce high blood pressure, anxiety, depression, or perceived stress also contain similar methodological flaws that make causal conclusions problematic (Breedvelt, Amanvermez, Harrer et al., 2019). However, considering the low costs and risks associated with mindfulness-based interventions, they are often recommended by healthcare and mental health professionals as a possible accompaniment (as opposed to a substitution) to other medications and therapies. Yet, the effects of these methods remain to be established and further research is warranted.

4.2 Quiz Yourself

1. **Research on hypnosis suggests that it is least helpful for which of the following?**
   a. Relieving pain
   b. Decreasing anxiety
   c. Curing addictions
   d. Enhancing physical performance
2. **Which of the following statements about hypnosis is *false*?**
   a. Everyone can be hypnotized.
   b. Hypnosis can promote relaxation.
   c. Memories recalled under hypnosis are not always accurate.
   d. Not all psychologists agree as to whether hypnosis is an altered state of consciousness.
3. **Cecilia has been hypnotized and told that she will not feel pain in her right hand. Her right hand is then immersed in freezing cold water. According to the dissociation theory of hypnosis, what part of Cecilia will report feeling pain?**
   a. The secret hypnotist
   b. The posthypnotic suggester

(Continued)

c. The conscious self
d. The hidden observer

4. Which of the following is the best description of mindfulness-meditation?
a. Focusing your attention on everything at once.
b. Focusing your attention on nothing at all.
c. Focusing your attention on what is going on in the moment.
d. Focusing your attention on what you did yesterday.

Answers: 1. c; 2. a; 3. d; 4. c

4.3 Psychoactive Drugs

psychoactive drugs substances that influence the brain and thereby the individual's behavior

tolerance a condition in which after repeated use, more of a drug is needed to achieve the same effect

Psychoactive drugs are substances that influence the brain and thereby a person's behavior. Despite widespread education programs, many misperceptions about drugs still exist. For example, can you name the three most widely used psychoactive drugs in American society? The three drugs most commonly used by Americans over the age of 12 are alcohol, nicotine, and caffeine (see • FIGURE 4.5)—substances that are all legal for adults to use (Center for Behavioral Health Statistics and Quality, 2018).

4.3.1 Variations in Drug Use

An estimated 30 million people (11.2%) in the United States ages 12 or older admitted to using an illegal substance in the past month. Illicit drug use is highest among young adults between the ages of 18 and 25, and is higher in males than in females (Center for Behavioral Health Statistics and Quality, 2018). Increasingly, young people are also engaging in nonmedical use of prescription drugs. Intentional abuse of prescription drugs is the second most common type of illegal drug use by young people (marijuana ranks first) (Center for Behavioral Health Statistics and Quality, 2018). Substance use in the United States also varies considerably by ethnic group (• FIGURE 4.6; Center for Behavioral Health Statistics and Quality, 2018). Multiracial and American Indian or Alaska Native groups have the highest rates of current illegal drug use, and Asians have the lowest.

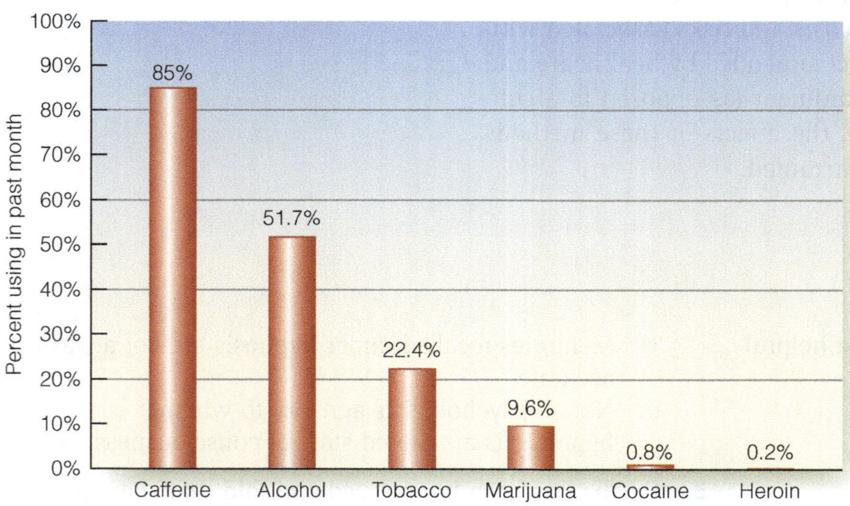

FIGURE 4.5

Current Drug Use in the United States, Ages 12 and Over

Caffeine, alcohol, and nicotine (the active ingredient in tobacco) are the three most commonly used psychoactive drugs in the United States.

Source: Center for Behavioral Health Statistics and Quality. (2018). *2017 National Survey on Drug Use and Health: Detailed Tables*. Rockville, MD: Substance Abuse and Mental Health Services Administration.

4.3.2 Drug Tolerance and Substance Use Disorder

In order to understand the effects of psychoactive drugs, it is important to establish the scientific meaning of two specific drug terms: *tolerance* and *substance use disorder*. Defining these terms will help you understand the effects of different psychoactive drugs.

Tolerance has to do with the amount of a drug required to produce its effect. After repeated use of a drug, it is usually the case that more and more of it is needed to achieve the same effect (American Psychiatric Association, 2013). For example, when someone first drinks alcohol, they may have one beer or one glass of wine and get a buzz from it. However, after drinking alcohol frequently, this person will require more beers or glasses of wine to achieve the same effect. This person has increased their tolerance for alcohol.

However, as tolerance develops, the difference between a safe dose and a potentially harmful dose, called the *margin of safety,* narrows. Some drugs (like barbiturates) have a very narrow, or small, margin of safety; that is, their too-high, toxic dose differs only slightly from their too-low, ineffectual dose. To obtain the same level of intoxication, a user who has developed tolerance may raise their dose to a level that may result in coma or death—the too-high, toxic dose.

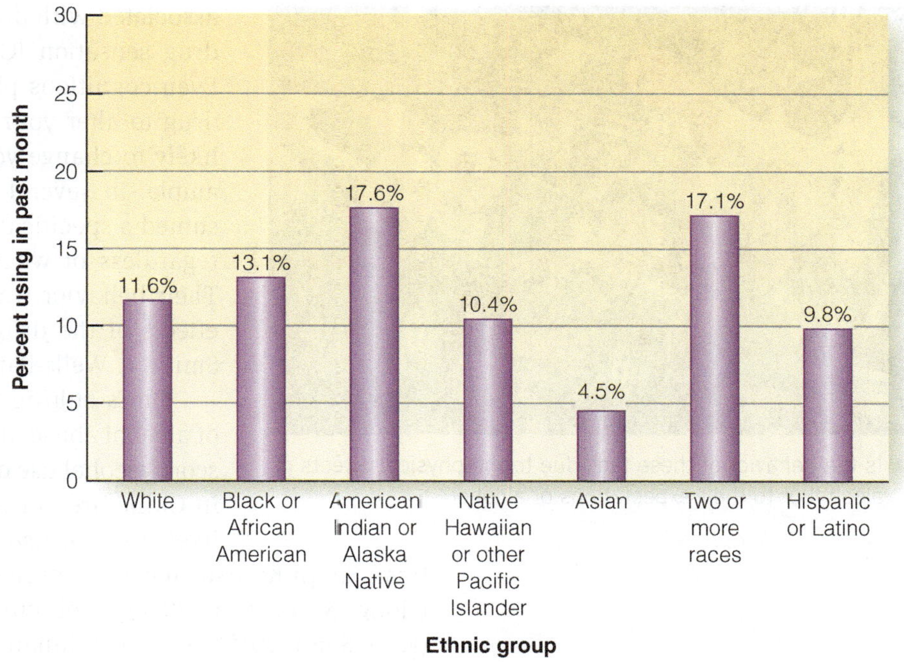

FIGURE 4.6

Ethnicity and Illicit Drug Use

Substance use in the United States varies considerably by ethnic group. American Indian or Alaska Native and multiracial groups have the highest rates of current illegal drug use; Asians have the lowest incidence.

Source: Center for Behavioral Health Statistics and Quality. (2018). *2017 National Survey on Drug Use and Health: Detailed Tables*. Rockville, MD: Substance Abuse and Mental Health Services Administration.

Related to tolerance is **substance use disorder**, which occurs when someone cannot control their drug use and continues to use a drug despite negative social, occupational, and health consequences, risky use, as well as evidence of tolerance or *withdrawal* (American Psychiatric Association, 2013). **Withdrawal symptoms** are physical and behavioral effects that occur when a person who has been using a drug heavily or for a long period of time stops or reduces its use. Withdrawal symptoms may include physical symptoms such as vomiting, shaking, sweating, physical pain, hallucinations, or headaches. People may also experience behavioral withdrawal symptoms when they are deprived of responses or rituals, such as injecting a drug or lighting a cigarette, that help them cope with negative emotions (Baker et al., 2006; S. Siegel, 2005). Not all drugs produce the same withdrawal symptoms. In many cases, people continue to use a drug just to ward off the unpleasantness of the withdrawal effects or emotional distress. We often hear the term *addiction* used to indicate that someone has lost control over their drug use.

substance use disorder a condition in which a person cannot control their drug use and continues to use a drug despite negative social, occupational, and health consequences, risky use, as well as evidence of tolerance or withdrawal

withdrawal symptoms physical or behavioral effects that occur after a person stops using a drug

4.3.3 How Drugs Work: Biology, Expectations, and Culture

Psychoactive drugs alter your state of functioning by interfering with the normal workings of the nervous system. Some drugs slow down normal brain activity, whereas others speed it up. Typically, drugs achieve these effects by interfering with or mimicking neurotransmitters in the brain (Chapter 2).

Psychological factors also influence a drug's effect. Exposure to stress or trauma (such as abuse, parental drug use, or poor parenting) increases a person's vulnerability to a substance use disorder (Parolin et al., 2016; Rohrbach et al., 2009; Taplin et al., 2014). Learning, specifically classical conditioning (Chapter 6), can also play a role. Environmental stimuli such as where a drug is taken or whether drug supplies and equipment such as a pipe or needle are present become

Blend Images/Alamy stock photo

▲ Is the behavior of these fans due to the physical effects of alcohol or to their expectations of alcohol?

associated with drug taking and later trigger the craving for the drug sensation (Crombag & Robinson, 2004; S. Siegel, 2005). Even cognitions play a role in a drug's effects. If you expect a drug to alter your behavior in a particular way, you are more likely to change your behavior to fit your expectations. For example, in several studies people who believed they had consumed a specific drug behaved in accord with the drug's effect, regardless of whether they had actually consumed the drug. Their behavior was influenced by their *expectations* about the effects of the drug (Fillmore, Roach, & Rice, 2002; McMillen, Smith, & Wells-Parker, 1989).

One's culture also influences drug use. For example, rates of alcohol abuse are very low in China, where traditional beliefs scorn alcohol use or being under the influence of alcohol. People in China are not only less likely to drink alcohol but also less likely to advertise the fact that they have been drinking. In contrast, South Koreans have higher rates of alcohol use than other Asian subgroups (Hong, Noh & Kim, 2017). Their culture encourages drinking in social situations (Ko & Sohn, 2018). As a Frenchman, Jean-Dominique Bauby often drank wine on a daily basis at mealtimes prior to his stroke.

The variety of psychoactive drugs in use today can be classified into four main groups: *depressants*, *opiates*, *stimulants*, and *hallucinogens*. You Review: Psychoactive Drugs and Their Effects provides a summary comparing the effects of these drugs. We'll begin with depressants.

4.3.4 Alcohol and Other Depressants

depressants drugs that inhibit or slow down normal neural functioning

Depressants interfere with brain functioning by inhibiting or slowing normal neural functioning. In *low* doses, depressant drugs often cause a feeling of well-being, or a "nice buzz." This may be why many people mistakenly believe that alcohol is an "upper." In *high* dosages, depressants can cause blackouts, coma, or death. Depressants are usually grouped into *alcohol, barbiturates*, and *sedatives*.

Health Effects of Alcohol

Alcohol affects the neurotransmitter GABA, which is related to anxiety levels. As noted earlier, in low dosages alcohol may make one feel more sociable and relaxed. Alcohol also depresses the functioning of the cerebral cortex. So, in addition to feeling calm and relaxed, we are more likely to shed our inhibitions in regard to our thoughts and behaviors (Giancola et al., 2010; Stahl, 1996). We are more likely to bond with unknown group members in a social setting (Sayette et al., 2012). When we drink alcohol, we are more willing to be silly or aggressive, share our emotions, or engage in behaviors that we would think twice about if we were sober.

Alcohol also inhibits the functioning of the brainstem, impairing motor functioning and coordination. Reaction time and reflexes are slowed. When your tolerance is exceeded, your speech becomes slurred and your judgment is impaired. It is also harder for your brain to sustain attention, process information, and form new memories (Givens, 1995; Sayette, Reichle, & Schooler, 2009).

Heavy drinking on college campuses across Europe and the United States has led to a growing concern about the effects of binge drinking. *Binge drinking* is excessive alcohol use over a short period of time that brings a person's blood alcohol concentration (BAC) to 0.08% or above. This often happens when males consume five or more drinks and when females consume four or more drinks

YOU REVIEW Psychoactive Drugs and Their Effects

The four groups of substances most often leading to substance use disorders are (1) depressants, (2) opiates, (3) stimulants, and (4) hallucinogens.

Substance	Trade Names; *Street Names*	Medical Uses	Routes of Administration	Main Effects
Depressants				
Alcohol 	Beer, wine, liquor	Antidote for methanol poisoning, antiseptic	Oral, topical	Relaxation; lowered inhibitions; impaired reflexes, motor coordination, and memory
Barbiturates	Nembutal, Seconal, Phenobarbital; *barbs, reds*	Anesthetic, anticonvulsant, sedative, relief of high blood pressure	Injected, oral	Anxiety relief, euphoria, severe withdrawal symptoms
Benzodiazepines	Librium, Rohypnol, Valium, Xanax; *roofies, tranks, bars, ladders*	Antianxiety, sedative, sleeping disorders	Injected, oral	Anxiety relief, irritability, confusion, depression, sleep problems
Opiates				
Codeine	Tylenol with codeine, *purple drank, sizzurp*	Pain relief, antitussive	Injected, oral	Euphoria, constipation, loss of appetite
Opioid prescription drugs	Hydrocodone, Oxycontin, Fentanyl, Vicodin, *Oxy, Hillbilly heroin, Captain Cody, Tango & Cash*	Pain relief	Injected, oral, transdermal, sniffed	Euphoria, pain control, drowsiness, slowed breathing, constipation, unconsciousness, nausea, coma
Heroin 	*Horse, smack, H, black tar, junk*	None	Injected, smoked, sniffed	Euphoria, pain control, constipation, loss of appetite
Methadone	Amidone, Methadose	Pain relief, treatment for opiate dependence	Injected, oral	Relief from withdrawal symptoms, constipation, loss of appetite
Morphine	Roxanol	Pain relief	Injected, oral, smoked	Euphoria, pain control
Opium	*Dover's powder, Aunti Emma, Dreams*	Pain relief, antidiarrheal	Oral, smoked	Euphoria, pain control
Stimulants				
Caffeine	Coffee, tea, soda, chocolate, energy drink	Treatment for migraine headaches	Oral	Alertness, insomnia, loss of appetite high blood pressure

(Continued)

Nicotine 	Nicorette gum, electronic nicotine delivery system, Nicotrol; *cigars, cigarettes, snuff, butts, dip, vape, hookah*	Treatment for nicotine dependence	Smoked, sniffed, oral, transdermal	Alertness, calmness, loss of appetite
Cocaine	*Coke, crack, rock, snow, blow, toot*	Local anesthetic; vasoconstrictor in Europe	Injected, smoked, sniffed	Increased energy, excitation, insomnia, loss of appetite, mood swings, delusions, paranoia, heart problems
Amphetamine	Dexedrine; Adderall; *black beauties, crosses, study buddies*	ADHD, obesity, narcolepsy	Injected, oral, smoked, sniffed	Increased alertness and energy, insomnia, loss of appetite, delusions, paranoia
Methamphetamine	*Crank, crystal, ice, meth, go fast*	ADHD, short-term aid for weight loss	Injected, oral, smoked, sniffed	Mood elevation, alertness, insomnia, loss of appetite, anxiety, paranoia
MDMA 	*Adam, Ecstasy, XTC, molly*	Trial treatment for PTSD	Oral, sniffed	Increased insight and emotion, muscle tension, sleep problems, anxiety, paranoia
Hallucinogens				
Marijuana/ Cannabis 	*Grass, herb, pot, reefer, weed, blunt, skunk, ganja*	Glaucoma, nausea from chemotherapy, pain relief, muscle spasms, seizure disorders, anxiety	Oral, smoked, topical	Relaxation, altered perceptions, sleep problems, paranoia, amotivation
Phencyclidine	PCP; *angel dust, hog*	Anesthetic (veterinary)	Injected, oral, smoked, sniffed	Euphoria, unpredictable moods, hostility
Lysergic acid diethylamide (LSD)	*Acid, microdot*	Trial treatment for addiction and severe anxiety in terminal diseases	Oral	Altered perceptions, distortion of senses, panic reactions, flashback effects

in 2 hours (National Institute of Alcohol Abuse and Alcoholism, 2004). Binge drinking is typically higher among males than females (Kanny, Liu, & Brewer, 2011; Patrick & Terry-McElrath, 2019) and puts one at risk for later developing an alcohol use disorder (Crabbe, Harris, & Koob, 2011). Binge drinking and alcohol use may cause *memory blackouts*—after a heavy night of drinking, you may not remember the events of the night before. Chronic alcohol use can lead to *Korsakoff's syndrome*, a memory disorder caused by a deficiency of vitamin B (thiamine). A person who chronically abuses alcohol often substitutes alcohol for more nutritious foods, which results in numerous vitamin deficiencies. Unfortunately, these memory deficits tend to be irreversible.

Because drinking alcohol results in reduced inhibitions, people are more likely to engage in sexual activity (K. C. Davis et al., 2009; Patrick & Maggs, 2009). However, alcohol impairs sexual performance. It makes it more difficult for a male to get and maintain an erection. The ability to achieve orgasm is also hampered

Psychology Works!

Corbis

Understanding the scope of how psychoactive drugs influence people's behavior is vitally important to law enforcement professions. Drug intoxication and criminal behavior are highly correlated, such that people who are under the influence of a drug are not only more likely to commit a crime but also are more likely to be a victim of a crime whether it be physical assault, property damage, intimate partner violence, or sexual assault (U.S. Department of Health & Human Services, 2000). Police officers perform sobriety tests to determine whether a person's use of alcohol or other substances meets the criteria for driving under the influence. Law enforcement is a high-risk job producing high levels of stress that also places these professionals at higher risk for substance use disorders (Cross & Ashley, 2004). These are just a few examples of how knowledge of psychoactive drugs can help people working in law enforcement.

by the effects of alcohol. We may think and feel that we are better lovers when under the influence of alcohol, but in reality, we are not.

Because ingested alcohol crosses the placenta, women who drink alcohol heavily during pregnancy put the fetus at risk for **fetal alcohol syndrome (FAS)**. Children born with FAS tend to have low birth weight; exhibit limb, head, and facial deformities; and have brain abnormalities that impair intellectual functioning and cause difficulties in learning, memory, problem solving, and attention (Ikonomidou et al., 2000; Kumada et al., 2007). Because of the potential negative effects of alcohol on prenatal development, even moderate drinking during pregnancy is not recommended.

fetal alcohol syndrome (FAS) a birth condition resulting from the mother's chronic use of alcohol during pregnancy; characterized by facial and limb deformities and intellectual impairment

Individual Variations in Alcohol's Effect

Does everyone experience the same effects from alcohol? No. The degree to which each of us experiences these effects depends on several factors. For example, alcohol has either more or less effect depending on your tolerance level: The higher your tolerance, the more alcohol you can consume before feeling its effects. Another factor is the rate of consumption. The faster you drink, the faster the alcohol is absorbed into the blood, increasing the alcohol's effect. Whether one's stomach is empty or full also influences one's level of intoxication (Brick, 2008). Gender influences alcohol's effect as well. Metabolic and weight differences between males and females make it easier for male bodies to tolerate higher levels of alcohol (York & Welte, 1994). Research also suggests that the social rewards associated with alcohol consumption are more pronounced for males (Fairbairn et al., 2015; Kuntsche et al., 2006). ● TABLE 4.1 describes the typical effects of alcohol at increasingly higher blood concentrations.

TABLE 4.1 Typical Effects of Blood Alcohol Concentrations (BAC)

Alcohol intoxication varies greatly among individuals. Some people become intoxicated at lower blood alcohol concentration levels.

BAC	Typical Effects
.02–.03	Slight euphoria and loss of shyness; light-headedness. Depressant effects of alcohol are not yet apparent
.04–.06	Feelings of well-being, relaxation, and lowered inhibitions; minor impairment of reasoning and memory; lowered alertness
.07–.09	Feelings of well-being; slight impairment of balance, speech, vision, reaction time, and hearing; reduced judgment and self-control; impaired reasoning and memory
.10–.125	Significant impairment of motor coordination; loss of judgment; slowed thinking; slurred speech; impairment of balance, vision, reaction time, and hearing
.13–.15	Gross motor impairment and lack of physical control; blurred vision and major loss of balance; severely impaired judgment. Feelings of well-being are reduced
.16–.20	Anxiety, restlessness, sadness; nausea and vomiting; feeling dazed and confused; blackouts
.25	Severely impaired physical and mental abilities; increased risk of injury by falls or accidents
.30	Stupor; little comprehension of whereabouts; loss of consciousness
.35	Possible coma
.40+	Onset of coma; possible death due to respiratory arrest

Alcohol: Genetics, Culture, and Learning

Research suggests a possible genetic influence in alcohol's effect (Stacey, Clarke, & Schumann, 2009; Wall, Luczak, & Hiller-Sturmhöfel, 2016). Studies of twins show that if one identical twin has an alcohol use disorder, the other twin has almost a 40% chance of developing a drinking problem. Rates for fraternal twins are much lower (Prescott et al., 1994). Research on sons of fathers who have alcohol use disorder also suggests a possible genetic predisposition to alcohol use disorder. The sons are likely to have an overall higher tolerance for alcohol, requiring more alcohol before feeling its effects, and are therefore at greater risk for abusing alcohol (Schuckit & Smith, 1997). Researchers also have located specific strands of genes that regulate the function of GABA. These genes vary across families with multiple members who have alcohol problems and may contribute to a person's vulnerability to alcohol use disorder (Edenberg & Foroud, 2006; Krystal et al., 2006; Soyka et al., 2008).

Cultural studies also support a possible genetic link. In some ethnic groups, such as Japanese and Chinese, drinking alcohol can cause facial flushing. This sudden reddening of the face is a genetic trait that rarely occurs in Europeans. The physical and social discomfort of facial flushing tends to reduce the rate of alcohol consumption and alcohol use disorder in these groups. People in ethnic groups that do not experience facial flushing are more at risk for alcohol use disorder (Helzer & Canino, 1992).

However, environmental factors such as learning also play a role. Children of parents who abuse alcohol have an increased risk of developing alcohol use disorder that cannot be attributed solely to genetics. As adults, they are more likely to cope with personal or work-related stress by imitating the behavior of the parent who abuses alcohol and avoiding conflict (Blane, 1988; Hall & Webster, 2007; Rivers, 1994). Similarly, the nature and quality (positive or negative) of an adolescent's environment influences alcohol use in teens that are genetically at risk for alcohol use disorder (Dick et al., 2011). Drinking alone, especially in response to negative emotions and conflict, also puts an adolescent at risk for alcohol problems (Creswell et al., 2014). In contrast, having parents who communicate clear and strict alcohol rules to young teenagers is related to the postponement of drinking (Van Der Vorst et al., 2006). Clearly, the effects of alcohol and whether one becomes an abuser of alcohol depend on the interaction among genetic, cultural, individual, and environmental factors.

Social Costs of Alcohol Use

Alcohol dependence is devastating to individuals, families, and society in general. According to the National Highway Transportation Safety Administration (NHTSA), 29% of all traffic deaths in the United States are alcohol-related (NHTSA, 2018). Alcohol-impaired driving is highest for people between the ages of 16 and 25, and more common for males than for females (Chou et al., 2006; SAMHSA, 2012). It is estimated that at least half of the sexual assaults on college campuses involve alcohol use by the perpetrator, victim, or both (Abbey, 2002). There is a strong correlation between alcohol and intimate partner violence (Abramsky et al., 2011; Quigley & Leonard, 2000; Testa, Quigley, & Leonard, 2003). Millions of children who live with parents who abuse alcohol are also seriously affected. High levels of conflict—as well as physical, emotional, and sexual abuse—are more likely in these households (Mathew et al., 1993; Taplin et al., 2014).

Alcohol abuse also has economic costs approximating $249 billion per year (Sacks, Gonzales, Bouchery, Tomedi, & Brewer, 2015). Alcohol abuse is associated with excessive absenteeism, lost productivity at work, higher rates of on-the-job injury, healthcare and legal costs, as well as property damage (Bouchery et al., 2011). Alcohol, contrary to the beer commercials, is indeed dangerous to our health and our society.

Barbiturates and Sedatives

Barbiturates, commonly called "downers," are a category of depressants that are typically prescribed to reduce anxiety or to induce sleep. Well-known barbiturate drugs include Nembutal and Seconal. Sedatives or tranquilizers are also prescribed to reduce anxiety. They include a class of drugs called the *benzodiazepines*, including Valium and Xanax. Both types of depressants have effects

AP Images/JACK KUSTRON

▲ Alcohol-impaired driving tragically affects families and friends.

similar to alcohol. In small dosages, they slow the nervous system, promoting relaxation. In high dosages, though, they severely impair motor functioning, memory, and judgment. Like alcohol, these drugs influence the functioning of the neurotransmitter GABA (Barbee, 1993). When these drugs are taken in combination with alcohol, they are potentially lethal. They can cause suppression of those brain areas that control breathing and heart rate, which can lead to unconsciousness, coma, or death.

You may have heard of the tranquilizer called Rohypnol ("roofies"), commonly known and used as a *date rape drug*. It is placed in a person's drink at a party or club without their knowledge or consent, and the combined effect of alcohol and Rohypnol renders them unconscious. In this state, the person is then sexually assaulted, raped, or physically harmed. In the morning, because of the drug's effects on memory, the person may not recall the event (Britt & McCance-Katz, 2005).

When used as prescribed, barbiturates and sedatives can be helpful in the short-term treatment of anxiety disorders and sleeping problems such as insomnia. However, over the long term, there is a risk of dependence. Long-term use of tranquilizers leads to memory loss and actually heightens anxiety (McKim, 1997). Withdrawal from these drugs can be brutal and includes convulsions, hallucinations, and intense anxiety.

4.3.5 Opiates (Narcotics): The Painkillers

opiates [OH-pee-ates] painkilling drugs that depress some brain areas and excite others

The **opiates**, or narcotics, are drugs that are used to treat pain by mimicking pain-inhibiting neurotransmitters in the body such as endorphins (Chapter 2). Opiates include morphine, codeine, fentanyl, Vicodin, hydrocodone, oxycodone, opium, and heroin, although heroin and opium are no longer prescribed as a medicine. Healthcare providers frequently use opiates to manage pain. While depressing some brain areas, these drugs create excitation in other brain areas. In addition to blocking pain, they produce an intense "rush" of pleasure that is almost like floating on a cloud or being in a dreamlike state (Bozarth & Wise, 1984). The opiates are extremely addictive, causing dependence within a few weeks. When you take opiates, your brain recognizes an abundance of pain inhibitors in the body and decreases its own production of endorphins. So, when the effect of the opiate wears off, you feel your earlier pain and the absence of pleasure, and you will want another, larger dose (Hughes et al., 1975; Zadina et al., 1997).

Physical withdrawal symptoms related to opiate use include hot and cold flashes, cramps, sweating, and shaking. These symptoms typically last from 4 to 7 days, but they are not life-threatening. What *is* life-threatening is the risk of overdose. Street concentrations of narcotic drugs such as heroin and opium can vary widely. In addition, a person's sensitivity to prescription and nonprescription opiates may fluctuate on a daily basis (Gallerani et al., 2001). The user never knows, therefore, if the concentration of drug they are taking will exceed the body's ability to handle it. The widespread misuse of, addiction to, and overdose from prescription and nonprescription opiates, persuaded the U.S. Department of Health and Human Services (HHS) in 2017 to declare a national opioid health crisis as detailed in the Psychology Applies to Your World box.

Currently, many heroin addicts are treated with the chemical *methadone* or buprenorphine. Each reduces the unpleasantness of the withdrawal symptoms yet does not produce the intense high of heroin. They are equally effective in treating heroin dependence (Fiellin, Friedland, & Gourevitch, 2006; Thomas et al., 2014; Vigezzi et al., 2006).

Psychology Applies to Your World

The Opioid Epidemic

IN 2018, NEARLY 47,000 PEOPLE IN the United States died from an opioid overdose and an estimated 1.7 million people had an opioid use disorder (Center for Behavioral Health Statistics & Quality, 2018; Wilson et al., 2020). People who are prescribed opioid prescription medication for pain management may after time misuse the drug because they miss or crave the good feelings produced by the release of endorphins which gives them relief from pain. However, once tolerance develops, increased doses are needed to keep feeling good and pain-free. Healthcare professionals may not renew a prescription or increase the dose, which may motivate some people to transition to cheaper illegal opioids such as heroin or *fentanyl*, a powerful synthetic opioid 50 times more potent than heroin. Because of its potency in low concentrations, fentanyl is often added to heroin or other illicit drugs to increase drug traffickers' profits and is a primary factor in the explosion of opioid-related deaths and overdoses.

Widespread media reports of emergency responders describing acute illnesses after being in proximity to powder believed to contain fentanyl has led to the belief that merely being near fentanyl can present a life-threatening hazard. The American College of Medical Toxicology (ACMT) and American Academy of Clinical Toxicology (AACT) state that the risk of exposure to emergency responders is extremely low and that dermal or skin exposure is unlikely to cause opioid toxicity. Nitrile or medical-grade gloves provide sufficient skin protection (Moss, Warrick, Nelson et al., 2017).

People misusing or dependent on opioids are at risk of overdose. Opioids in high doses (relative to one's tolerance level) cause respiratory depression or slow and ineffective breathing, which reduces oxygen and increases carbon dioxide in the body, which if left untreated can cause death. Nonfatal overdoses are much more common than fatal opioid overdoses. Nonfatal overdoses often result due to the timely administration of the opioid antagonist, *naloxone*. Recall that an antagonist blocks or reduces the effect of a drug. Consequently, Naloxone is a medication that completely reverses the effects of an opioid overdose if administered in time and it restores normal breathing (Doyon, Aks, & Schaeffer, 2014). *Narcan* is a generic naloxone nasal spray. It is increasingly being used by both first responders and nonemergency first responders to reverse opioid overdoses. In most states, people who are or who know someone at risk for opioid overdose can go to a pharmacy and get naloxone or Narcan without a prescription.

CREATISTA/Shutterstock.com

Additional risks of opioid use and dependence include infections and neonatal abstinence syndrome. There is an added risk of contracting HIV/AIDS and hepatitis C from using contaminated needles, because opiates are often injected into a vein. Infants born to mothers who used or misused opioids during pregnancy may experience *neonatal abstinence syndrome* (NAS), also called neonatal opioid withdrawal syndrome (NOWS), in the first days of life. Opioids pass freely through the placenta. Once the umbilical cord is cut, the supply of opioids to the newborn is abruptly terminated resulting in withdrawal symptoms such as body shakes, breathing problems, and excessive crying or fussiness. Morphine and methadone medications as well as a non-stimulating environment are used to manage infants with NAS (Gomez-Pomar & Finnegan, 2018).

4.3.6 Stimulants: Legal and Otherwise

The **stimulants** include drugs that interfere with brain functioning by speeding up normal brain activity. Five stimulant substances we will review are *caffeine, nicotine, cocaine, amphetamines*, and *MDMA* (*Ecstasy/Molly*).

stimulants drugs that speed up normal brain functioning

Caffeine: Java Jitters

Because many of us wake up each morning reaching for that cup of coffee or that energy drink to get us going, we may not even consider caffeine a mind-altering drug. Yet caffeine is a psychoactive drug because of its effects on the brain. It is perhaps the most frequently used psychoactive drug in the world. Caffeine is an active ingredient in coffee, tea, sodas, some energy drinks and shots, chocolate, migraine headache medications, and some diet pills. It stimulates the brain by blocking neurotransmitters (primarily adenosine) that slow down our nervous system and cause sleep (Julien, 1995). In small doses, caffeine gives us a boost, keeping us more alert and helping us focus. It helps problem solving and decreases reaction time (Warburton, 1995). However, in large doses caffeine can "wire" you, causing insomnia, upset stomach, racing heartbeat, nervousness, and irritability.

Regular caffeine use can lead to dependence. If you suddenly stop drinking coffee or kick your soda habit, you will likely experience headaches, irritability, tiredness, and flu-like symptoms (Schuh & Griffiths, 1997). These withdrawal symptoms, even if they aren't severe, can last a week. Excessive caffeine use increases the risk of high blood pressure and encourages the development of fibroid cysts in women's breasts. Pregnant women in particular should reduce caffeine intake because high amounts of caffeine are associated with an increased risk of miscarriage (Chen et al., 2016; Infante-Rivard et al., 1993).

Young people often mix energy drinks or shots with alcohol. Energy drinks and shots have about two to three times as much caffeine as a soda and include other energy-boosting ingredients such as guarana or taurine. Ingesting alcohol and energy drinks together decreases one's awareness of alcohol's impairment. In other words, people are more likely to perceive that they are not as intoxicated as they are. Yet motor coordination, reaction time, and driving performance are still impaired (Ferreira et al., 2006; Howland et al., 2011). Consuming energy drinks and alcohol also negatively influences cognitive functioning (Curry & Stasio, 2009). Moreover, the stimulant effects of the caffeine keep the person awake longer—a "wide-awake" drunk—which may allow them to consume even greater quantities of alcohol, increasing the chances of alcohol-related accidents, injuries, risk-taking behavior, and alcohol use disorder (M. C. O'Brien et al., 2008; Patrick & Maggs, 2014; Thombs et al., 2010). Yet caffeine may not be the sole reason for the excessive intoxication. It is possible that energy drinks and alcohol provide a novel context and unusual cues for drinking that enhance the alcohol's effect (Siegel, 2011).

Nicotine: A Really Bad Habit

Nicotine, the active ingredient in tobacco products such as cigarettes, cigars, and electronic nicotine delivery systems (ENDS), is a powerful stimulant. Tobacco use is the most preventable cause of death in the United States. More than 480,000 deaths result each year from tobacco use, at an annual price tag of more than $170 billion in direct medical care costs (U.S. Department of Health & Human Services, 2014). Tobacco use has been linked to lung cancer, throat cancer, chronic obstructive pulmonary disease (COPD; which includes emphysema and chronic bronchitis), stroke, and heart disease (U.S. Department of Health and Human Services, 2014).

Although the percentage of people in the United States who smoke cigarettes has decreased considerably over the last 50 years, 15.8% of adult men and 13.2% of adult women continue to smoke regularly (Wang, Asman, Gentzke et al., 2018). It is estimated that 3.7% of adults currently use electronic nicotine delivery systems, sometimes referred to as *vaping* (Schoenborn & Gindi, 2015). However, current use of these systems among teenagers is considerably higher with one in five high school students reporting their use in the past 30 days (Gentzke, Creamer, Cullen et al., 2019). While vaping may be perceived as less harmful than cigarettes, there are still many unknowns about vaping such as what chemicals are in the vapors and how they influence health in the long term. Yet, emerging evidence suggests that e-cigarette users are at increased risk of heart attack, COPD and other respiratory diseases such as COVID-19 (Alzahrani et al., 2018; Wills et al., 2019). What we do know is that many vaping devices include nicotine, a highly addictive chemical.

Aleksandr Yu/Shutterstock.com

▲ Nicotine is an addictive substance that makes it difficult for people to quit vaping or smoking once they have started.

Nicotine affects several neurotransmitters. It influences acetylcholine and glutamate such that, in low doses, nicotine improves attention and memory (McGehee et al., 1995). Nicotine also elevates dopamine levels, leading to feelings of pleasure and reward (Pidoplichko et al., 1997). In high doses, nicotine causes vomiting, diarrhea, sweating, and dizziness. Yet users quickly develop a tolerance to nicotine. Withdrawal from chronic nicotine use rivals withdrawal from other abused drugs such as cocaine, morphine, and alcohol (Epping-Jordan et al., 1998). Withdrawal symptoms, lasting anywhere from 2 to 6 weeks, include headaches, irritability, stomach upset, difficulty sleeping, and an intense craving for the drug. This indeed illustrates the power of dependence.

Cocaine and Crack

Cocaine and its derivative, crack, are powerful and dangerous stimulant drugs. Snorted, smoked, or injected, cocaine is quickly absorbed into the body and thus reaches the brain rapidly. Crack is powdered cocaine mixed with water and other additives that is then boiled until a solid mass forms. It is broken into rocks and smoked using a long glass tube called a *crack pipe*. Inhaling the smoke delivers large quantities of the drug to the lungs and produces an intense and immediate high.

Cocaine, in all its forms, blocks a protein called the dopamine transporter (DAT), which helps the reuptake of dopamine into the neuron (Chapter 2). Because reuptake is blocked, free dopamine in the brain increases (Hummel & Unterwald, 2002; Nestler & Carlezon, 2006; Williams & Galli, 2006). The buildup of dopamine produces an instant surge of arousal, a feeling of pleasure and optimism. Appetite decreases, but heart rate, blood pressure, and alertness increase. When the effect of the cocaine wears off, the person "crashes," showing decreased energy and depressed mood. This low creates an intense craving for the drug that sets up a cycle of continued use and dependence (Gawin, 1991). High doses of cocaine (relative to one's tolerance) can cause paranoia, sleeplessness, delusions, seizures, strokes, and potentially cardiac arrest (Lacayo, 1995). Users who are dependent on cocaine may lose interest in their usual friends and activities, lose weight, and have chronic sore throats and difficulty sleeping; their finances may also undergo a noticeable change.

Health effects of repeated use of cocaine include chronic nosebleeds, damage to nasal cartilage (from snorting), and respiratory and heart problems. Miscarriages are common for pregnant women who use cocaine. If the pregnancy continues, the infant is more likely to be born premature and, as a newborn, must be weaned from the effects of the drug. The long-term impact of prenatal exposure to cocaine shows a small but less favorable effect on language, cognitive ability, and academic functioning into adolescence. However, a poorer home environment and exposure to violence also play a role in a child's development (Ackerman, Riggins, & Black, 2010; Buckingham-Howes et al., 2013; Lewis et al., 2013). That is, children with poorer academic functioning were more likely to have come from less favorable home environments, regardless of prenatal cocaine exposure.

Amphetamines

Amphetamines, called "uppers" or "speed," have effects similar to those of cocaine. The high produced by these drugs is less intense but generally lasts longer (a few hours). One of the most abused forms of amphetamine is *methamphetamine*, commonly called crystal meth, ice, chalk, or crank. According to data from the National Survey on Drug Use and Health (NSDUH), about 5% of the U.S. population aged 12 or over has used crystal meth at least once (Center for Behavioral Health Statistics and Quality, 2018).

Methamphetamine, like cocaine, affects dopamine, serotonin, and norepinephrine levels in the brain (Volkow et al., 2001). The result is enhanced mood and pleasure, energy, alertness, and reduced appetite. Heart rate and blood pressure also increase. Like cocaine, methamphetamine leads to a crash involving low energy levels, paranoia, and depressed mood when the effects of the drug have subsided. However, methamphetamine remains present in the brain longer than cocaine. It not only blocks the reuptake of dopamine but also increases the release of dopamine, leading to a more toxic effect on the central nervous system (NIDA, 2006b). Continued use results in insomnia, paranoia, agitation, confusion, violent behavior, memory loss, and dependence. Methamphetamine use can also cause strokes, cardiovascular problems, and extreme anorexia. An overdose can cause coma and death. Users who inject the drug and share needles are also at risk for acquiring HIV/AIDS and hepatitis C (Bezchlibnyk-Butler & Jeffries, 1998).

MDMA (Ecstasy/Molly)

MDMA has become widely known as *Ecstasy*, referring to its pill form, but street Ecstasy, Adam, or XTC typically contains other drugs such as amphetamine, ketamine, caffeine, and ephedrine (Walters, Foy, & Castro, 2003). The term *molly* typically refers to a purer MDMA in powder or crystal form. MDMA was originally developed as an antibleeding medication in 1912 by a German pharmaceutical company (Freudenmann, Oxler, & Bernschneider-Reif, 2006). Before it was classified as a controlled substance in 1985, MDMA was used by some psychiatrists in the United States and Europe to enhance psychotherapy and couples counseling

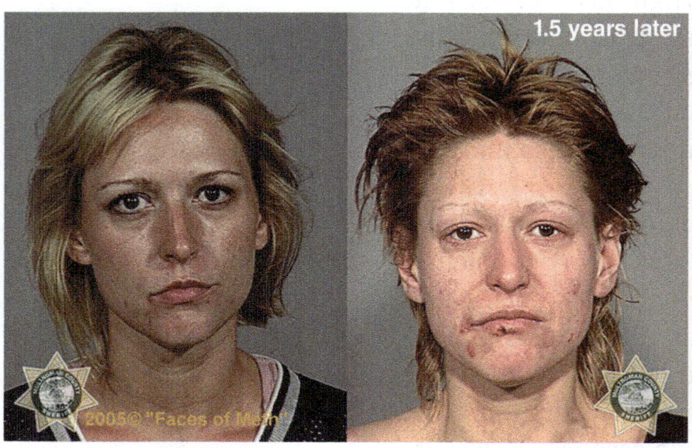

Multnomah County Sheriff/Splash/Newscom

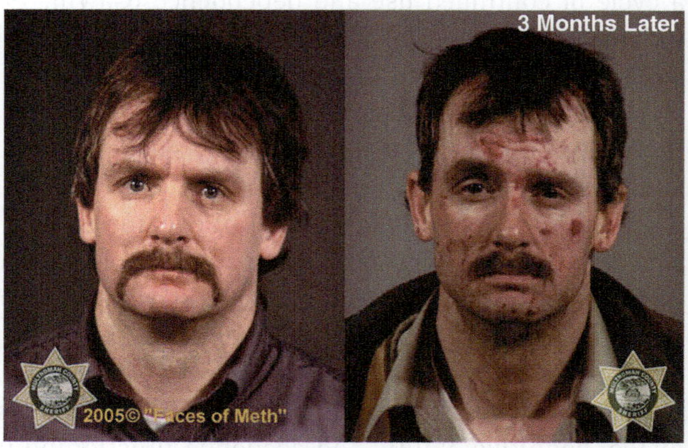

Multnomah County Sheriff/Splash/Newscom

▲ Methamphetamine abuse can radically alter one's physical appearance as it causes skin lesions and tooth decay.

(Greer & Tolbert, 1998). Nearly 7% of people in the United States over the age of 12 have reported using Ecstasy at some point in their lives (Center for Behavioral Health Statistics and Quality, 2017). Ecstasy and Molly enhance mood and energy levels and heighten users' sensations. Users report increased self-confidence, increased feelings of love and warmth toward others, emotional openness, and lack of inhibition (Fry & Miller, 2002). The effect begins within half an hour of consumption and lasts approximately 3 to 6 hours. Negative effects of MDMA use are insomnia, teeth clenching, nausea, increase in heart rate and blood pressure, fatigue, and blurred vision. Most of these negative effects subside within 24 hours. Paranoia, depression, drug craving, overheating, cardiac problems, kidney failure, seizures, strokes, and/or loss of touch with reality may also occur (Bezchlibnyk-Butler & Jeffries, 1998).

Although MDMA increases the activity of several neurotransmitters in the brain, it is the serotonin pathway that has received the most attention. MDMA binds to the serotonin transport protein so that the availability of free serotonin increases (Britt & McCance-Katz, 2005; Colado, O'Shea, & Green, 2004). Animal and human brain imaging studies suggest that heavy use of MDMA produces consistent alterations in serotonin receptors (Vegting, Reneman, & Booij, 2016 for review), but the long-term effects of MDMA on the human brain have not yet been determined. However, disrupted sleep patterns and subtle but persistent deficits in memory have been documented for both former and current users (McCann et al., 2009; Randall et al., 2009; Taurah, Chandler, & Sanders, 2014; Wagner et al., 2015). It is also unclear whether Ecstasy shares properties with the hallucinogens. Users regularly report hallucinations, but it is impossible to know whether they have really been using pure MDMA or have bought low doses of LSD instead.

Therapeutic use of MDMA, particularly for the treatment of posttraumatic stress disorder (PTSD), has been investigated with promising results (Amoroso & Workman, 2016; Mithoefer et al., 2011; Oehen et al., 2013; Ot'alora, Grigsby, Poulter et al., 2018; Sessa, Higbed, & Nutt, 2019). Although the research samples have been small, patients treated with MDMA psychotherapy have shown a greater decrease in PTSD symptoms compared to placebo psychotherapy control groups. In one study, the majority of MDMA-treated patients maintained symptom relief 17 to 74 months after the original study (Mithoefer et al., 2013). Replication of these results with larger samples will be needed to substantiate the efficacy of these results.

4.3.7 Hallucinogens: Distorting Reality

Hallucinogens are drugs that interfere with brain functioning by simultaneously exciting and inhibiting the nervous system. These contrasting effects often cause distortions in perception, or *hallucinations*. Hallucinogenic substances include *marijuana, synthetic marijuana, PCP,* and *LSD*.

hallucinogens [huh-LOO-sin-no-gens] drugs that simultaneously excite and inhibit normal neural activity, thereby causing distortions in perception

Marijuana

Marijuana, also known formally as *cannabis* or informally as pot or weed, is a mild hallucinogen. The majority of U.S. states have legalized medicinal and/or recreational use of marijuana for adults over the age of 21. Many states have also decriminalized possession of small amounts of marijuana. Canada has legalized marijuana federally. It has been recommended for medical conditions such as glaucoma, chronic pain, and nausea from cancer chemotherapy, and has been found moderately effective in clinical trials for muscle spasms and multiple sclerosis (Croxford, 2003; Iverson, 2003; Klein & Newton, 2007). It is also the most widely

Uriel Sinai/Getty Images News/Getty Images

▲ Although controversy continues over the medicinal and recreational use of marijuana, smoking weed does increase one's chances of respiratory problems and lung damage.

used illegal substance in the United States, with 45% of people over the age of 12 reporting having tried the drug (Center for Behavioral Health Statistics and Quality, 2018).

Cannabis produces compounds called cannabinoids. Two of the most well-known of these compounds are *CBD* (*cannabidiol*) and **THC (tetrahydrocannabinol)**. CBD does not have a psychoactive effect or cause a high, whereas THC is absorbed by the lungs and produces a high that lasts for several hours. THC binds to a neurotransmitter called *anandamide* that influences learning, short-term memory, motor coordination, emotions, and appetite—behaviors that are all affected when people are high on marijuana (Matsuda et al., 1990). In low doses, cannabis makes users feel good and experience vivid sensations. Cannabis affects cognition and motor coordination in ways that slow reaction time and increase risks of injury when driving a car or operating machinery. Marijuana use also interferes with memory, disrupting both the formation of memories and the recall of information (Nestor et al., 2008; Pope & Yurgelun-Todd, 1996; Ranganathan & D'Souza, 2006). Its stimulation of appetite and increased sensitivity to taste may result in an attack of the "munchies." In high doses, marijuana may produce panic reactions, disturbed thoughts, paranoia, and distortions in time and body image (Hanson & Venturelli, 1998; Morrison et al., 2009).

THC (tetrahydrocannabinol) [tet-rah-high-dro-can-NAH-bin-all] the active ingredient in marijuana that affects learning, short-term memory, coordination, emotion, and appetite

Because of these effects, interest in the relationship between marijuana and psychosis has increased dramatically over the last decade. *Psychosis* is when a person loses touch with reality and often experiences hallucinations and delusions. Psychosis is often associated with the mental health disorder called *schizophrenia*, although psychosis can occur separate from a diagnosis of schizophrenia. While a consistent association between marijuana use and psychotic symptoms has emerged, that does not mean that marijuana use *causes* psychosis or schizophrenia. Early and heavy use of marijuana may be more likely in individuals who have a vulnerability to a psychotic disorder, but so is early or heavy use of alcohol or tobacco (Ksir & Hart, 2016; McLaren et al., 2010; Minozzi et al., 2010). Remember, just because two variables are associated does not mean that a clear causal link is indicated.

Long-term marijuana use can lead to a substance use disorder. Many people report mild withdrawal symptoms when marijuana use is stopped, including irritability, sleeplessness, decreased appetite, anxiety, and drug cravings (Cooper & Haney, 2008; Grinspoon et al., 1997; Vandrey et al., 2008; Wickelgren, 1997). Studies on the long-term effects of marijuana use suggest cognitive deficits in attention, concentration, and memory; findings are mixed regarding its long-term effect on motor functioning and coordination (Ganzer et al., 2016; Pope & Yurgelun-Todd, 1996). Research investigating structural brain changes due to marijuana use has been inconclusive; some analyses suggest subtle effects on brain structure while others show no differences (Filbey et al., 2014; Orr, Paschall, & Banich, 2016; Quickfall & Crockford, 2006; Weiland et al., 2015). When smoked, marijuana users may experience respiratory problems such as bronchitis and lung damage

(Tashkin, 2005). Vaping products containing THC sometimes add vitamin E acetate to dilute the THC oil, which has been strongly linked to E-Cigarette, or Vaping Product, Use Associated Lung Injury (EVALI). EVALI is a potentially fatal respiratory disease characterized by shortness of breath, cough, fever, chills, diarrhea, vomiting, and rapid heartbeat (Chand et al., 2020).

Synthetic Marijuana: K2 and Spice

An increasing number of young people are turning to unregulated herbal smoking mixtures labeled as *K2* or *Spice* to get high. These products are sprayed with synthetic substances that attempt to mimic THC and claim to produce a marijuana-like high. Adverse side effects of synthetic THC include extreme paranoia, hallucinations, heart palpitations, racing thoughts, psychosis, and seizures (Fattore, 2016; Fattore & Fratta, 2011; Hudson & Ramsey, 2011; Wells & Ott, 2011). Citing these products as a threat to public health, many countries (including the United States) have banned the sale of these herbs and screen for synthetic THC during drug testing. Yet, new products can easily be accessed from online markets (Fattore & Fratta, 2011).

Phencyclidine (PCP)

In the 1950s, Parke, Davis and Company developed PCP (phencyclidine) as an anesthetic for surgery. However, following surgery, individuals showed worrisome side effects including hallucinations, delirium, and disorientation. Consequently, it was removed from the market (for humans) in 1965 and sold to veterinarians for use in animal surgery. Its use as a street drug spread significantly until 1978, when it was taken off the market completely (Rudgley, 1998). Today, PCP is manufactured illegally and sold on the street by such names as "angel dust" and "lovely." PCP also may be poured over cigarettes or marijuana joints. PCP can be eaten, snorted, smoked, or injected. Although the use of PCP has declined over the years, 2.2% of people over the age of 12 reported having tried PCP at some time in their lives (Center for Behavioral Health Statistics and Quality, 2018).

PCP has hallucinogenic properties as well as stimulant and depressant effects. These unpredictable effects often lead to distress, mood swings, and confusion. PCP inhibits the neurotransmitter *glutamate*, which is involved in the perception of pain, responses to the environment, and memory. In low doses, PCP produces a sudden increase in blood pressure, pulse rate, and breathing. Flushing, profuse sweating, and numbness of the limbs may also occur. Out-of-body experiences and the sensation of walking on a spongy surface are also reported. In higher doses, PCP causes a drop in blood pressure, pulse rate, and respiration. This reaction may be accompanied by nausea, vomiting, blurred vision, drooling, loss of balance, and dizziness. Hallucinations, confusion, paranoia, and garbled speech also result. Users may become severely disoriented or suicidal and may therefore be a danger to themselves or others. Seizures, coma, or death may also occur (Rudgley, 1998).

Using PCP can lead to dependence. Users often crave the feelings of strength, power, and invincibility and the escape from real life that PCP brings. Long-term use of PCP is associated with memory loss and difficulty in speaking and thinking, and may lead to permanent changes in fine motor abilities (NIDA, 2001).

Lysergic Acid Diethylamide (LSD)

Lysergic acid diethylamide (LSD), more commonly referred to as *acid*, is a potent perception-altering drug. First synthesized in 1938 and used in the 1950s and 1960s in psychiatric research, it became an illegal drug of abuse (Passie et al., 2008); 9.6%

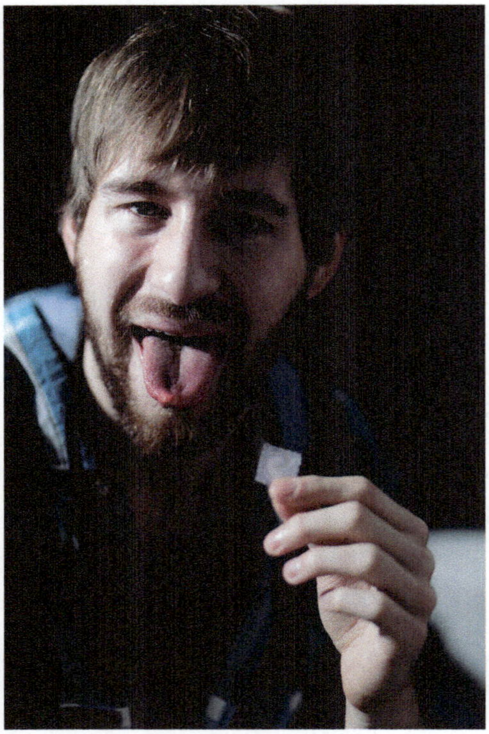

▲ LSD, commonly referred to as acid, is a powerful hallucinogen causing bizarre hallucinations, distortions in time and body image, and intense emotions.

of people over the age of 12 report having tried LSD at some time in their lives; males are more likely to have tried the drug than females (Center for Behavioral Health Statistics and Quality, 2018). LSD's effects typically begin 30 to 90 minutes after ingestion and can last from 6 to 12 hours.

Users of LSD may experience increased blood pressure and heart rate, dizziness, loss of appetite, and nausea, but the drug's main effects appear to be emotional and sensory. Even at very low doses, LSD causes bizarre hallucinations, distortions in time and body image, and intense emotions that together are often referred to as "tripping." Emotions may shift rapidly from fear to happiness, and the user may seem to experience several emotions at once. Colors, smells, sounds, and other sensory stimuli seem highly intensified and may even blend in what is known as *synesthesia*, in which a person seems to hear or feel colors and see sounds (Das et al., 2016). These effects are due to LSD's influence on the neurotransmitter serotonin (Aghajanian, 1994). LSD stimulates serotonin receptors, influencing perceptions, emotions, and sleep. However, whether one's "trip" is pleasant or unpleasant is unpredictable and depends on the user's expectations and mood. On good trips, users experience enjoyable sensations, but bad trips produce terrifying thoughts and feelings, including fears of insanity, death, or losing control. Although withdrawal symptoms from LSD have not been documented, users quickly develop tolerance, requiring a higher dosage to experience the mind-altering effects (Das et al., 2016; Miller & Gold, 1994).

There have been no documented human deaths from LSD overdose, but two rare yet serious documented long-term effects of LSD are *persistent psychosis* and *hallucinogen persisting perception disorder* (*HPPD*). Persistent psychosis is a long-lasting psychotic-like state after the trip has ended. It may include dramatic mood swings, visual disturbances, and hallucinations. These effects may last for years and can affect people who have no history or other symptoms of a mental health disorder. HPPD is a reexperiencing of the sensations originally produced by the LSD hours, weeks, or even years after its initial use, causing distress. It typically consists of visual disturbances, such as seeing bright or colored flashes and trails attached to moving objects (NIDA, 2001). Our knowledge of the causes and treatment for persistent psychosis and HPPD is very limited; further studies are needed (Halpern & Pope, 2003).

Recently, there has been renewed interest in the therapeutic use of LSD, particularly for the treatment of severe anxiety related to terminal diseases and in the management of drug addictions, that seems promising (Bogenschutz, 2013; Das et al., 2016; Pollan, 2018). Future research using carefully controlled studies may further our understanding of LSD's potential treatment applications.

4.3 Quiz Yourself

1. **Psychoactive drugs often have short-term and sometimes long-term effects on child development when mothers-to-be take the drug during pregnancy. Ethical guidelines on testing the effects of these drugs on children who are born to drug-using mothers would require which one of the following research methods?**
   a. Double-blind experiment
   b. Pseudo-experiment
   c. Quasi-experiment
   d. Single-blind experiment

2. **Rolanda takes a drug that raises her blood pressure and heart rate, makes her feel euphoric and excited, and suppresses her appetite. Rolanda in all likelihood has *not* taken ________.**
   a. cocaine
   b. alcohol
   c. methamphetamine
   d. crack

(Continued)

3. **The designer drug Ecstasy, or MDMA, produces effects similar to what two categories of drugs?**
   a. Stimulants and depressants
   b. Hallucinogens and depressants
   c. Stimulants and hallucinogens
   d. Opiates and depressants

4. **Mick, a successful author, has been drinking alcohol for 10 years. He feels that alcohol relaxes him and expands his mind, which makes him a more creative writer. In fact, he never attempts to write unless he has first had a drink. Mick has tried to stop drinking in the past, but he has always returned to it because he fears losing his creativity. Mick's behavior is best explained by ________.**
   a. substance use disorder
   b. withdrawal symptoms
   c. the margin of safety
   d. tolerance

5. **Deana takes a drug that blocks adenosine in her brain. This drug causes her to be more alert and enhances her ability to focus. If she takes too much, it causes irritability, nausea, and a racing heartbeat. Deanna is most likely taking ______.**
   a. nicotine
   b. cocaine
   c. methamphetamine
   d. caffeine

Answers: 1. c; 2. b; 3. c; 4. a; 5. d

4.4 Integrating Psychology: The Big Picture

This chapter examined several altered states of consciousness—when you are not fully awake, alert, aware, or perhaps of sound mind. We saw that sleep is a necessity, providing many benefits to our functioning and ensuring that we will be healthy, alert, and happy. Hypnosis is a state of relaxation and heightened suggestibility that may help *some* people decrease anxiety and manage pain. Meditation and mindfulness involve focusing one's attention or mind on the present without judgment. Psychoactive drugs alter our state of consciousness—in sometimes unpredictable and occasionally tragic ways. Although much is still unknown about many of these drugs, it is clear from the research cited here that the long-term negative effects outweigh the short-term high and feelings of well-being that they produce.

Our state of consciousness cannot easily be divorced from our general behavior, as this part's case study on Jean-Dominique Bauby clearly illustrated. Despite Bauby's severely limited physical abilities, he found a way to communicate his thoughts and awareness of his surroundings to others through the blinking of his one eye. These communications also allowed him to continue his social interactions with his family and medical staff. Jean-Dominique's case represents an extreme variation of human behavior, yet it still demonstrates how our biology, cognitions, and social interactions intertwine with our states of consciousness. His story also beautifully exemplifies the resilience of the human spirit and the need or *motivation* humans have to find purpose in our lives—our next chapter of study.

Studying the Chapter

Key Terms

activation-synthesis theory (144)
circadian rhythm (138)
consciousness (133)
continuity hypothesis (144)
depressants (156)
enuresis (148)
fetal alcohol syndrome (FAS) (159)
hallucinogens (167)
hypnosis (149)
insomnia (144)
latent content (143)
manifest content (143)
meditation (149)
melatonin (138)
memory theory (144)
microsleep (134)
mindfulness meditation (149)
narcolepsy (146)
neodissociation theory (150)
nightmares (148)
night terrors (147)

non-REM sleep (140)
opiates (162)
psychoactive drugs (154)
REM behavior disorder (142)
REM rebound (142)
REM sleep (140)
restless legs syndrome (RLS) (147)
response set theory of hypnosis (151)
sleep apnea (146)
sleep disorder (144)
sleepwalking (147)
stimulants (163)
substance use disorder (155)
suprachiasmatic nucleus (SCN) (138)
THC (tetrahydrocannabinol) (168)
threat simulation theory (TST) (144)
tolerance (154)
withdrawal symptoms (155)

What Do You Know? Assess Your Understanding

Test your retention and understanding of the material by answering the following questions.

1. Which of the following is *not* a benefit of sleep?
   a. Increased alertness
   b. Memory processing
   c. Decreased immunity to disease
   d. Enhanced mood

2. There is a negative relationship or correlation between sleep and age. This means that:
   a. the older we get, the more sleep we need.
   b. the older we get, the less sleep we need.
   c. the more you sleep, the faster you age.
   d. the less you sleep, the faster you age.

3. Alfred is just falling asleep. An EEG would most likely show Alfred exhibiting ______ brain waves.
   a. beta
   b. delta
   c. sleep spindle
   d. theta

4. Which of the following brain waves is most likely to occur during slow-wave sleep?
   a. Beta
   b. Alpha
   c. Delta
   d. Theta

5. Benita often wakes up in the morning feeling very tired, despite sleeping 9 to 10 hours. Her partner has noticed that she often emits loud snores and seems to have erratic breathing while she is sleeping. Benita most likely has which sleep disorder?
   a. Narcolepsy
   b. Sleep apnea
   c. Night terrors
   d. Enuresis

6. Recent research suggests a relationship between the sleep spindles of stage II sleep and ______.
   a. processing of motor skills
   b. body restoration
   c. storage of memories
   d. growth hormone

7. Dr. Surrell believes that dreaming evolved to help us rehearse potentially harmful events. Dr. Surrell is endorsing which dream theory?
   a. Freudian theory
   b. Activation-synthesis theory
   c. Continuity hypothesis
   d. Threat simulation theory

8. When Kaitlin wakes up in the morning, she recalls having a dream that toads were invading her room. According to Sigmund Freud, Kaitlin's recall is an example of ______.
   a. latent content
   b. manifest content
   c. activation-synthesis
   d. the continuity hypothesis

9. Why is melatonin referred to as the "Dracula hormone"?
   a. Because it increases during the day
   b. Because it increases at night
   c. Because it is in the blood
   d. Because it was first found in bats

10. EEG brain-wave patterns of people who are hypnotized show an increase in ______ waves.
    a. theta
    b. delta
    c. beta
    d. alpha

11. Which of the following is *not* a well-documented use of hypnosis?
    a. Decreasing anxiety
    b. Relieving pain
    c. Recovering memories
    d. Enhancing therapy

12. Which of the following is *true* in regards to meditation-mindfulness practices?
    a. They engage those parts of the brain that regulate attention and emotion.
    b. They change the structure of the brain.
    c. Research has definitely proven their positive effects on health.
    d. All of the above statements are true.

13. Which of the following drugs is a depressant?
    a. Ecstasy
    b. Nicotine
    c. PCP
    d. Alcohol

14. Paz now needs more alcohol to get high than she did when she first started drinking. Paz has developed ______ alcohol.
    a. an addiction to
    b. tolerance to
    c. a withdrawal from
    d. a margin of safety for

15. Howe has been using methamphetamine for several months now. If he stops taking the drug, which of the following is he most likely to experience?
    a. Paranoia
    b. Enhanced mood
    c. Skin lesions
    d. High energy

16. Which of the following variables influences a drug's effects?
    a. How much of the drug is taken
    b. Your tolerance to the drug
    c. Your expectations about the drug's effects
    d. All of the above

17. The feeling of well-being that results from nicotine or cocaine use is due to the activity of which of the following neurotransmitters?
    a. Dopamine
    b. Serotonin
    c. Acetylcholine
    d. Endorphins

18. Sven still experiences visual disturbances and dramatic mood swings after taking LSD several months ago. Sven is most likely experiencing ______.
    a. HPPD
    b. PTSD
    c. persistent psychosis
    d. tweaking

19. While at a nightclub one weekend, Aoki had a drug slipped into her drink that made her pass out and have no recall of the events of the evening. What type of drug was most likely put in Aoki's drink?
    a. Hallucinogen
    b. Sedative
    c. Stimulant
    d. Opiate

20. Which of the following drugs is most likely to be prescribed to reduce pain?
    a. Stimulant
    b. Depressant
    c. Hallucinogen
    d. Opiate

Answers: 1. c; 2. b; 3. d; 4. c; 5. b; 6. a; 7. d; 8. b; 9. b; 10. d; 11. c; 12. a; 13. d; 14. b; 15. a; 16. d; 17. a; 18. c; 19. b; 20. d.

Use It or Lose It: Applying Psychology

1. Given the numerous factors, such as age and lifestyle, that influence the amount of sleep a person needs, apply each of these factors to the amount of sleep that you get. How can you improve the quality of your sleep? What benefits might this change bring you?
2. Keep a dream log for a week. Applying the different theories on dreaming, interpret what your dreams mean. Which of these interpretations seems the most plausible, and why?
3. How would you rate your hypnotic susceptibility? Indicate under what circumstances you would consider using hypnosis as a therapy or treatment, and why.
4. How prevalent is drug use at your campus? Design a research survey to assess this issue at your school. Administer the survey to student volunteers following the ethical procedures for participants, and tabulate the results. What conclusions can you draw from your results? What factors may have influenced your results?

Critical Thinking About the Science of Psychology

In one of the studies discussed in Section 4.1.1 on the influence of sleep on memory Gais, Lucas, & Born (2006) had participants learn German vocabulary word lists in the evening at 8 P.M. and then tested them on their recall of the words. There were no significant differences between the two groups on the number of words remembered on this first test. Half of the participants, the "sleep condition," were then sent home to sleep, and half of the participants, the "sleep deprivation condition," stayed at the lab and were prevented from sleeping until 6 A.M. when they were allowed to go home and sleep. Recall of the vocabulary words was again tested for both groups 48 hours after their initial learning. Participants remembered more of the learned vocabulary when they had slept during the night following learning than when they had stayed awake. Given these specifics about the research study, answer the following questions:

1. What research method did Gais et al. use to test their hypothesis?
2. Identify the independent and dependent variables in this study.
3. What is the *best* way for Gais et al. to have determined whether a participant was a part of the "sleep condition" versus the "sleep deprivation condition"?
4. Name one potential confound in this study.

Are You Getting the Big Picture?

Baranov Dmitry/Shutterstock.com

Consciousness includes the feelings, thoughts, and aroused states of which we are aware. Altered states of consciousness occur when we sleep, are hypnotized, use meditation-mindfulness practices or take any psychoactive drug.

4.1 Sleep, Dreaming, and Circadian Rhythm

- When teenagers and adults get at least 8 hours of sleep, the benefits include restored body tissues, body growth, immunity to disease, an alert mind, processing of memories, and enhanced mood.
- The **circadian rhythm** of sleep is a natural rhythm of sleep and waking programmed by a group of brain cells in the hypothalamus called the **suprachiasmatic nucleus**.
- A typical night of sleep involves cycling through two states of sleep: **non-REM sleep**, which progressively relaxes the person; and **REM** (rapid-eye-movement) **sleep**, which is very active.
- Freud believed that dreams allow us to express fears and desires without conscious censorship. Many psychologists and psychiatrists dispute Freud's emphasis on sex and aggression in interpreting dreams.
- **Threat simulation theory** proposes that dreaming is an evolved defense mechanism that allows us to rehearse our responses to threatening situations.
- **Activation-synthesis theory** suggests that dreaming is just a consequence of the highly aroused brain during REM sleep.
- **Insomnia** is the inability to get to sleep or to stay asleep. It is the most common sleep disorder.
- Other sleep disorders include **sleep apnea**, in which a person stops breathing while asleep, and a more rare condition called **narcolepsy**, in which a person falls asleep during alert times of the day.

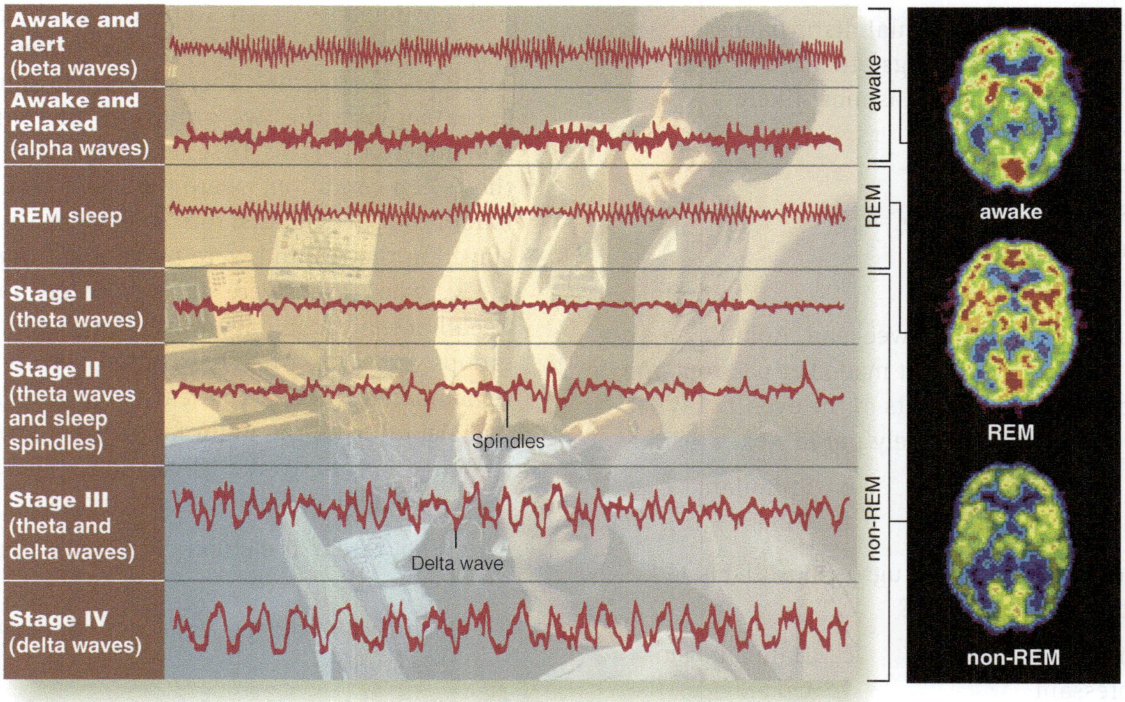

Jonathan Nourok/PhotoEdit
Hank Morgan/Science Source

4.2 Hypnosis, Meditation & Mindfulness

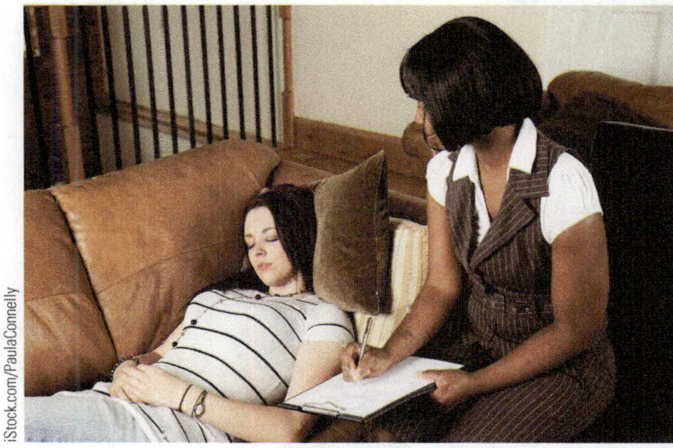

iStock.com/PaulaConnelly

- **Hypnosis** is a technique used to create a state of heightened suggestibility. Hypnosis usually involves being asked to mentally focus on an object, image, or the hypnotist's voice, thus inducing a deeply relaxed state.
- Hypnotic susceptibility varies greatly and does not seem to be related to intelligence, gender, or sociability. People who are easily hypnotized tend to be better able to focus their attention, have vivid imaginations, and have positive expectations about hypnosis.
- Hypnosis has been shown to be effective for *some* people in providing pain relief and decreasing anxiety. It has not been shown to be as effective in curing addictions or recovering accurate memories.
- The purported benefits of **meditation** and **mindfulness-meditation** have been widely publicized in the media from better health outcomes, to stress reduction, to improved mood and decreased symptoms of anxiety and depression. However, the studies designed to evaluate these outcomes have major limitations that make such claims oversimplified.

4.3 Psychoactive Drugs

- **Psychoactive drugs** are substances that influence the brain and therefore the behavior of a person.
- Drug **tolerance** refers to the amount of a drug required to produce its effects. After repeated use of a drug, more of it is usually needed to achieve its initial effect.
- **Substance use disorder** refers to when a person cannot control their drug use and continues to use a drug despite negative social, occupational, and health consequences; risky use; and evidence of tolerance or withdrawal.
- **Depressants** such as alcohol, sedatives, and barbiturate drugs interfere with brain functions by inhibiting or slowing normal neural function.
- **Opiates** such as morphine, codeine, and opium are used to treat pain by mimicking the effects of neurotransmitters such as endorphins.
- **Stimulants** are drugs such as caffeine, nicotine, cocaine, and amphetamines that interfere with brain functioning by speeding up normal brain activity.
- **Hallucinogens**, including marijuana and LSD, are drugs that interfere with brain functioning by simultaneously exciting and inhibiting normal neural activity. These contrasting effects often cause disruptions in perception or hallucinations.

Corbis

Learning Objectives

5.1 Describe how psychologists define motivation. (APA 1.1)

5.1 Describe the different theoretical ways of conceptualizing motivation. (APA 1.1, 1.2)

5.2 Describe the feedback our bodies use to regulate hunger. (APA 1.1, 1.3, 2.1)

5.2 Explain what is known about why some people become obese. (APA 1.1, 1.3)

5.2 Describe the prevalence of weight-based prejudice and the factors that affect it. (APA 1.1, 1.3, 3.3)

5.2 Describe bulimia, anorexia, and binge eating disorder and explain their possible causes. (APA 1.1, 1.3)

5.3 Explain the biological and psychological components of sexual desire. (APA 1.1, 1.3)

5.3 Describe the phases of the sexual response cycle in men and women. (APA 1.1, 1.3, 2.1)

5.3 Distinguish between sexual orientation and sexual behavior, and describe the research investigating the causes of sexual orientation. (APA 1.1, 1.3, 2.4, 3.3)

5.4 Describe the various theoretical perspectives on emotion. (APA 1.1, 1.3)

5.4 Describe how we express our emotional states through facial expressions. (APA 1.1, 1.3, 4.3)

Westend611/Getty Images

5 Motivation and Emotion

Chapter Outline

When Jean-Dominique Bauby awoke from his coma, his first reactions were predictable and understandable—he felt terror. *Emotions*, such as terror, can act as an early warning system, alerting us to danger, sometimes before we even become aware of what the danger is. Bauby's terror signaled that something was very wrong. During the 15 months that Bauby lived in a locked-in state, many more emotions followed. Sadness and fear—but also joy and contentment—punctuated his days. Bauby's emotions connected him to both his current and past life. They allowed him to feel human. Perhaps this is why Bauby was so *motivated* to capture his feelings in print—maybe he needed to let the world know that he was still a living human being despite the unresponsiveness of his body. Think about your own motivations and emotions. What goals do you want to accomplish? What emotions make you feel alive? In this chapter, we will examine the important roles that motivation and emotion play in our lives as they direct our behavior and signal our reactions to everyday experiences. ■

5.1 Theories of Motivation

motive a tendency to desire and seek out positive incentives or rewards and to avoid negative outcomes

instincts innate impulses from within a person that direct or motivate behavior

drive reduction theories theories of motivation that propose that people seek to reduce internal levels of drive

drive an uncomfortable internal state that motivates us to reduce this discomfort through our behavior

When we are motivated, we are driven to engage in some form of behavior. Just as something motivated you to start reading this chapter, every day we are motivated to do many different things. For example, we are motivated to eat, drink, attend school, go to work, interact with family and friends, and so on. In psychological terms, a **motive** is the tendency to desire and seek out positive incentives or rewards and to avoid negative outcomes (Atkinson, 1958/1983; McClelland, 1987). This means that we are motivated to avoid aversive states and to seek more pleasant states. When we experience the motive of hunger, we eat to avoid this aversive feeling. We are motivated to study because we want the feelings of pride and the opportunities for advancement that accompany academic success. Because we are generally motivated to avoid pain and other aversive states, our motives often serve to protect us. Without the motivation to eat, we could experience malnutrition or even starvation. As you can see, without motivation we would not engage in many behaviors that are necessary for good health and survival.

In an attempt to understand better what motivates us, psychologists have historically viewed motivation in several different ways: as *instincts* that direct our behavior; as uncomfortable biological states called *drives* that motivate us to find ways to feel better; as the desire to maintain an optimal level of *arousal* in our body; or as *incentives* that guide us to seek reward from the world. However, none of these theories seem to fully explain all aspects of motivation. Today psychologists do not expect any single theory to explain all our motivations. Instead, we recognize that each of these theories has its strengths and weaknesses. Let's take a closer look at these different theories of motivation.

5.1.1 Motivation as Instinct

One of the earliest views on motivation was one that was heavily influenced by the work of Charles Darwin and the theory of natural selection (Darwin, 1859/1936; see Chapters 1 & 8). Back in the 1800s, American psychologist William James proposed that motives are, in fact, genetically determined **instincts** that have evolved in humans because they support survival and procreation. According to James, instincts are impulses from within a person that direct or motivate that person's behavior. James proposed that we are motivated by more than 35 different innate instincts, including the impulse to love, fight, imitate, talk, and acquire things (James, 1890).

Over time, the idea that motives are inborn instincts gradually fell out of favor with psychologists. One problem with James's view was that the list of proposed instincts kept getting longer and longer, and it seemed unrealistic to argue that all behavior is due to instinct. Furthermore, it is impossible to determine whether many of the proposed instincts are truly inborn. Many of James's so-called instincts, such as being sympathetic or being secretive, may result from learning.

5.1.2 Motivation as a Drive

Instinct theory was followed by **drive reduction theories** of motivation. According to the drive reduction approach, motivation stems from the desire to reduce an uncomfortable, internal state, called a **drive**, that results when our needs are not fulfilled (Hull, 1943). For instance, when we do not have enough food in our system, we feel the uncomfortable state of hunger, which drives us to eat until we have taken in the food that our bodies require. Then, when we have taken in enough food, the hunger drive dissipates, and we stop eating. In this fashion, our drives can help us survive by creating what psychologists call a drive state, which ensures that we will be motivated to meet our biological needs.

Primary drives, such as needing food, water, and warmth, motivate us to maintain certain bodily processes at an internal state of equilibrium, or **homeostasis**. Obviously, it would be desirable for us to take in just the right amount of food and water, to sleep just enough, and to maintain our body temperature at 98.6 degrees. Without the motivation from drives, we would not keep our bodies at homeostasis because we would not know when to eat, sleep, drink, and so on. But what causes a drive state in the first place?

primary drives drives that motivate us to maintain homeostasis in certain biological processes in the body

homeostasis [hoe-mee-oh-STAY-suss] an internal state of equilibrium in the body

negative feedback loop a system of feedback in the body that monitors and adjusts our motivation level so as to maintain homeostasis

Primary drives begin in the body when the brain recognizes that we are lacking in some biological need. The brain recognizes need based on the *feedback* that it receives from the body's systems and organs. One type of feedback system is called a **negative feedback loop** (● FIGURE 5.1). Negative feedback loops are information systems in the body that monitor the level of a bodily process and adjust it up or down accordingly. A good analogy for a negative feedback loop is a thermostat. In your home, you set the thermostat at a desired level. The thermostat monitors the air temperature and compares it to that set level. If the room gets too cold, the heater turns on; if the room gets too warm, the heater turns off. Many primary drives in the body work in the same fashion.

The idea that motivation in the form of primary drives serves to maintain homeostasis makes a great deal of sense. Without primary drives, our

FIGURE 5.1

Negative Feedback Loops

Negative feedback loops maintain homeostasis in our bodies by monitoring certain physiological conditions (such as glucose levels and fluid levels). When levels drop too low, feedback from the body tells the brain to increase motivation (e.g., hunger or thirst). When levels are too high, feedback from the body tells the brain to decrease motivation.

biological needs would likely not be met, and we might not survive. But how well does the idea of drives explain some of our other motivations? For example, does drive reduction theory explain academic achievement motivation, or motivation to be loved? To help explain what motivates these kinds of behaviors, drive reduction theorists developed the notion of **secondary drives**—drives that motivate us to perform behaviors that are not directly related to biological needs.

secondary drives learned drives that are not directly related to biological needs

Secondary drives are presumed to have developed through learning and experience. Back in the 1930s, Henry Murray proposed that human behavior is motivated by a host of secondary motives such as *need for achievement, need for affiliation* (the need to be close to others), and *need for understanding* (the need to understand one's world) (Murray, 1938). According to some psychologists, the need to fulfill certain secondary drives differs from person to person, like any other personality characteristic. For example, some people have a higher need for achievement than others do.

The concept of motivation as a means of reducing drives seems to make more sense for primary drives than for secondary drives, but even here it is not without its faults. There are times when drive reduction theory cannot explain certain aspects of our biological motives. For example, what about overeating? Think about a typical holiday meal in your family. At holiday dinners, do you eat only enough food to satisfy your primary drive of hunger? We bet not. How many times have you eaten until you felt ill because it was a special occasion? If our sole motivation for eating were drive reduction, we would not "pig out" in instances like these.

Drive reduction theories also fail to account for times when we seem to be motivated to *increase* the tension or arousal levels in our bodies. For instance, when you decide to ride a roller coaster at an amusement park or to try skydiving, what possible drive could these behaviors lower? Activities such as these do not appear to reduce any of our primary drives. Rather, the sole purpose of these activities seems to be to *arouse* us physiologically. Clearly, we will have to conceptualize motivation in some other way to account for these types of behavior.

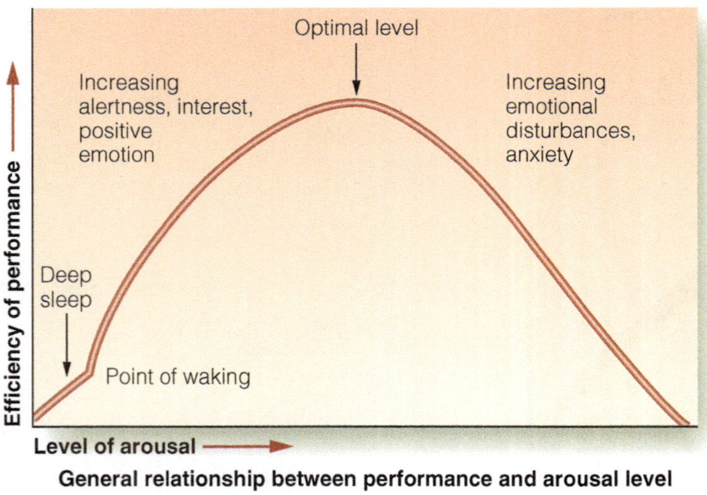

FIGURE 5.2

The Yerkes-Dodson Curve: Performance as a Function of Arousal

Our best performance often occurs at moderate levels of arousal. You would likely do your best on an exam if you were neither too sleepy nor too anxious. To ensure your best performance on your next exam, get a good night's sleep the night before and remain calm.

5.1.3 Arousal Theories of Motivation

In 1908, arousal theorists Richard Yerkes and John Dodson proposed that performance on a task is affected by the amount of physiological arousal in the body (Yerkes & Dodson, 1908). The relationship between arousal and performance is captured in the *Yerkes-Dodson curve* (● FIGURE 5.2). As you can see from Figure 5.2, we tend to perform best on tasks when we are moderately aroused. Too much or too little arousal generally weakens performance (Chaby et al., 2015; Hebb, 1955). For example, students who are either sleepy (underarousal) or experiencing test anxiety (overarousal) tend to perform poorly on exams. Students who are relaxed yet alert (moderate arousal) tend to perform better.

According to arousal theories of motivation, each of us is motivated to seek out arousal when we find ourselves underaroused and to reduce our arousal level when we are overaroused. This doesn't mean, however, that there is a

Psychology Works!

Pormezz/Shutterstock.com

Managers use knowledge of motivation every day in their work. To maximize the effectiveness of their businesses, managers must know how to apply principles of motivation, such as self-determination theory, to encourage their employees to be productive and reach their potential.

single level of arousal that is optimal for everyone. Just as we saw with secondary drives, individuals differ in how much arousal is optimal or right for them. Some people are motivated to seek out situations that elicit low arousal (such as going to the bookstore), whereas others tend to crave the excitement of more arousing activities (such as riding a roller coaster).

Animal studies suggest that our preferred level of arousal may be due in part to how much stress we experience during development. Compared to normal rats, rats that were raised in stressful, arousing environments were found to function better at higher levels of stress in adulthood (Chaby et al., 2015), suggesting that environmental factors may condition us to function best under certain conditions. Along with our preferred levels of arousal, situational factors also play a role in determining our performance levels. For example, performance on low-complexity tasks, such as driving in light traffic, might be improved at higher levels of arousal (Ünal et al., 2013). By contrast, performance on tasks of high complexity—such as those involving memorization and recall of new information—might suffer when we are aroused (Martinie, Olive, & Milland, 2010).

self-determination theory a theory of motivation that proposes that as we pursue the fulfillment of basic needs, we experience different types of motivation that come from both the self and the outside world

5.1.4 Self-Determination Theory of Motivation

The idea that humans are motivated by different things is part of a broad theory of motivation called *self-determination theory* (Deci & Ryan, 2008). According to **self-determination theory**, humans need to feel competent (skilled), autonomous (in control of our own behavior), and related (or connected) to others (Van den Broeck et al., 2016). As we try to meet these needs, we will at times experience *autonomous motivation* or *controlled motivation*. When we are autonomously motivated, we are self-motivated to engage in a behavior. For example, you might study for an exam because you want to do well on it. When we experience controlled motivation, we feel more compelled

Echo/Juice Images/Getty Images

▲ The self-determination theory of motivation states that many of us are motivated by extrinsic rewards such as money, material goods (such as cell phones), and praise from others.

Psychology Applies to Your World

Mindsets and Motivation

DO YOU BELIEVE THAT PEOPLE ARE able to change their traits and abilities? For example, is intelligence something that can change with time? Can we develop intelligence? Or, is the level of intelligence that you possess today the same level that you will have for the rest of your life? According to psychologist Carol Dweck, your answers to these questions may have important implications. Dweck (2006) pioneered the idea that our beliefs about the world, or our *mindset*, impact our motives, the goals we choose to pursue, and our persistence in pursuing these goals. In particular, Dweck proposed that the beliefs we hold about intelligence have importance for our levels of motivation and achievement in school (for review, see Dweck & Yeager, 2019).

Some of us have a *growth mindset* about intelligence. People with a growth mindset believe that intelligence is something that develops and changes over time. They believe it is possible to grow and improve one's intelligence. On the other hand, some of us hold a *fixed mindset* about intelligence. People who hold a fixed mindset see intelligence as an unchangeable characteristic. They believe that intelligence cannot be improved or developed. Whether you see your intelligence as fixed or open to growth has big implications for how you approach challenges in life— especially academic challenges.

If you believe that intelligence is fixed, then verifying that you are intelligent becomes an important goal. People with fixed mindsets may avoid challenging tasks where the chance of failure is high because failure would suggest a lack of intelligence that cannot be changed. Meanwhile, people with growth mindsets tend to seek out challenging tasks in the hopes that such tasks will lead to improvements in their intelligence.

For example, in one study conducted in Hong Kong, students for whom English was a second language were tested on their English proficiency, mindset about intelligence, and willingness to take a high quality remedial English class to improve their English skills. Students with a fixed mindset were less willing to take the course, even if their English skills were poor. Presumably taking the course would have lowered their self-esteem because it would indicate that their English skills were fixed at a low level of proficiency. In contrast, students with a growth mindset who were also low in English proficiency were more willing to take the course, presumably because they believed that it would lead to improved levels of proficiency. For the growth mindset students, taking the class seemed less of a threat to their self-esteem and more of a chance to improve their abilities (Hong et al., 1999). The implications are clear, having a growth mindset may lead people to actually develop their own abilities better. Having a fixed mindset is less likely to do so.

So, what happens when people with these different mindsets actually do fail? As you might expect, failure affects people with growth and fixed mindsets differently. Students with a fixed mindset find failure to be more of a threat to their self-esteem than do students with a growth mindset. This leads students with a fixed mindset sometimes to develop *helplessness* responses to failure (Diener & Dweck, 1978). A helplessness response is one that places the blame for one's failure either on their own inability or on some external cause over which they have no control. For example, "I failed because I am not smart" or "I failed because the test was unfair," are both helplessness types of responses. They are helplessness oriented because they offer the student no hope of improvement in the future. On the other hand, a student with a growth mindset may blame their own failure on the fact that they did not study hard enough. After all, students do have control over how much they study, giving them hope for improvement in the future. This type of response has been called a *mastery-orientation* response (Diener & Dweck, 1978). Unsurprisingly, researchers have found that growth

---

to engage in certain behaviors. For example, you may study for an exam because you want to please your parents or because you feel that you should work hard in school.

incentives goals or desires that we are motivated to fulfill

These examples show the power that **incentives** have to motivate us into action (Atkinson, 1958/1983). You can think of incentives as goals or desires that you wish to satisfy or fulfill. For example, someone who desires money will be motivated to engage in behaviors that will likely lead to obtaining money, such as taking a job or buying lottery tickets. Incentives can be either *intrinsic* (coming from within us) or *extrinsic* (coming from outside us). Intrinsic incentives, such mindset is a predictor of academic success in junior high and high school students (Blackwell, Trzesniewski, & Dweck, 2007; West, Buckley, Krachman, & Bookman, 2018).

So, how do these mindsets develop in the first place, and can one's mindset be changed? It appears that mindsets develop in much the same fashion as other beliefs that we hold about the world. Our past experiences and our interpretation of these events play a role, as does the feedback that we receive from people around us (for review, see Dweck & Yeager, 2019). The *attributions* (see Chapter 10) that we make for our own behavior play a key role in this process. Attributions are the causes that we assign to behavior. If you make an "A" on an exam, why did you make that grade? Was it due to your ability? Was it due to your effort? Or was it due to luck? Often our answers to these questions are influenced by feedback that we get from others (e.g., parents, teachers). Research suggests that praise that encourages one to assign a success to their ability (*person praise*) is related to developing a fixed mindset, but praise that encourages one to assign a success to their level of effort (*process praise*) is related to developing a growth mindset (Mueller & Dweck, 1998). The same is true for attributions about failures (Kamins & Dweck, 1999). It is more empowering to attribute failure to a lack of effort than it is to attribute it to a lack of ability.

SchubPhoto/Shutterstock.com

▲ If this child attributes their academic success to their hard work, this may help the child develop a growth mindset. A growth mindset may help them achieve their goals in life.

Since mindsets are related to the attributions we make about behavior, is it possible to change them? Perhaps it is. In one study, college students in a growth mindset condition were taught that intelligence is like a muscle—the more that you exercise it, the more it grows. They were then asked to write letters to future students in which they encouraged these students to adopt a growth mindset. When compared to college students in a control condition, those who wrote the letters encouraging a growth mindset later themselves earned higher grades. Furthermore, compared to White students, the benefits of the growth mindset were even more pronounced for African-American students. Not only did their grades improve, but they also experienced increases in their enjoyment of school and their academic identification (Aronson et al., 2002).

In another study, students heard statistics lectures that were framed with either a growth mindset, fixed mindset, or control condition perspective. As a result, students who heard the growth mindset lectures developed more of a growth mindset than did those in the fixed mindset condition. The growth mindset students also performed better on quizzes relative to the students in the control condition (Smith et al., 2018). Studies such as these suggest that growth mindset can be developed, and that doing so increases academic performance.

So, how do you view intelligence? If you have a growth mindset, great! If not, are you willing to develop one? If so, you might try writing a letter to your future self. In it, take the position that you can improve your intelligence and encourage yourself to keep trying to do so. Think of times when you have tried to master challenges and have succeeded. Argue for the possibility of change. The science suggests that you can grow, but first you have to believe it.

as wanting to make a good grade to please yourself, provide **intrinsic motivation** for behavior. Extrinsic incentives, such as wanting to please others or desiring monetary rewards, provide **extrinsic motivation** for behavior (Deci & Ryan, 1985).

intrinsic motivation motivation that comes from within the person

extrinsic motivation motivation that comes from outside the person

All of us are motivated at times by both intrinsic and extrinsic rewards. For example, in a study of firefighters, researchers found that a combination of intrinsic (e.g., wanting to be fit) and extrinsic (e.g., not wanting to let down fellow firefighters by not being fit enough to do the job) motives pushed the firefighters to engage in regular physical exercise (Long, Readdy, & Raabe, 2014).

Although all of us can be either intrinsically or extrinsically motivated, we do differ with respect to what types of motives tend to motivate us the most. Some of us tend to be more motivated by intrinsic rewards, such as a sense of accomplishment and pride. Others tend to be more motivated by extrinsic rewards, such as grades and money. Which motivates you more? Some studies suggest an advantage for having more of an intrinsic orientation. For example, studies have found that intrinsically motivated college students are less likely to use drugs and alcohol (Rockafellow & Saules, 2006; Shamloo & Cox, 2010) or cheat on a task (Ozdemir Oz, Lane, & Michou, 2016). Intrinsic motivation has also been shown to predict success in learning in school (Núñez & León, 2016) and sticking to an exercise program (Teixeira et al., 2010). For example, people who exercise using exercise video games (e.g., fitness games for the Wii) tend to engage in greater activity when compared to those who exercise in traditional ways, such as on a treadmill. One of the reasons this seems to be true is due to participants' increased enjoyment of the games (Bock et al., 2019). It appears that intrinsic rewards, such as a sense of enjoyment for the task, are more likely to keep us working hard for success.

5.1.5 Maslow's Hierarchy of Needs

hierarchy of needs Maslow's theory that humans are motivated by different needs, some of which take precedence over others

Imagine that you have to miss lunch because you don't have time to stop and eat. On this particular day, you have a paper to write, an exam to study for, and a long list of algebra problems to finish. As you sit down to study, you find that several different motives are all trying to direct your behavior at the same time. You need to study, you are hungry, you are sleepy because you did not sleep well last night, and you really want to go to the movies with your friends. Which of these motives will win? What will your first course of action be in this situation? Will you eat, study, go to the movies, or fall asleep?

Abraham Maslow, a prominent figure in humanistic psychology (Chapters 1 and 11), recognized that in certain circumstances, some motives have greater influence over our behavior than others do. Maslow conceptualized both our physiological and psychological motives as different classes of *needs* to which we assign different levels of priority. These different classes form a **hierarchy of needs**, in which the lower-level needs have the first priority (Maslow, 1970). Maslow's hierarchy of needs is usually presented as a pyramid, as shown in • FIGURE 5.3.

The lowest level of Maslow's hierarchy—the base of the pyramid—is our *physiological needs*. Maslow theorized that we seek to satisfy such basic needs as hunger and need for warmth before we are motivated to satisfy any of our other needs. If our physiological needs are met, then our next level of concern is satisfying *safety needs*, such as having a safe place to live. At the next level, Maslow identified *belongingness* and *love needs*, the motivation to be with

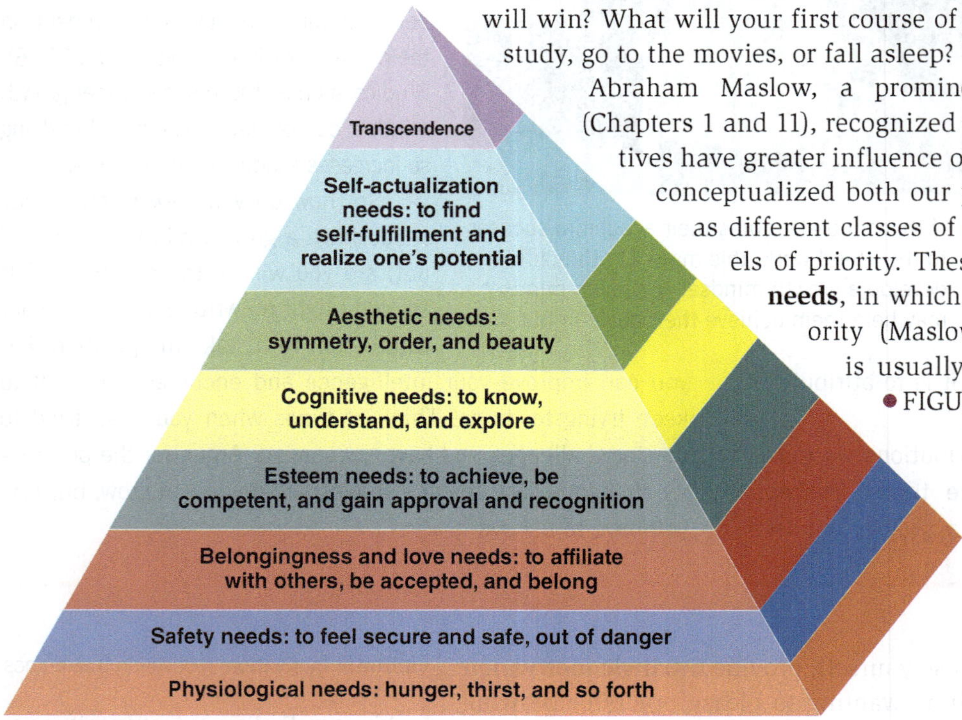

FIGURE 5.3

Maslow's Hierarchy of Needs

Source: Maslow, Abraham H.; Frager, Robert D. (Editor); Fadiman, James (Editor), *Motivation and Personality*, 3rd, © 1987.

Tim Graham/Hulton Archive/Getty Images

Phillip Massey/FilmMagic/Getty Images

▲ According to Abraham Maslow, few of us will ever fulfill enough of our lower-level needs to actually reach the level of self-actualization. During her lifetime, Mother Teresa appeared to have reached the levels of self-actualization and need for transcendence. Similarly, singer Bono of the group U2 appears to be striving for self-actualization, spending much of his time engaged in humanitarian causes.

others, to be loved, and to be appreciated by others. At the next levels we seek to successively satisfy our *esteem needs, cognitive needs*, and *aesthetic needs* (see Figure 5.3 for descriptions).

If we meet our aesthetic needs, we may seek to move to even higher levels, toward self-fulfillment. At these levels, motives include *self-actualization needs*, or the motivation to reach our full potential, and the *need for transcendence*, the motivation to achieve spiritual fulfillment. Maslow had little hope that the average person would actually reach the self-fulfillment level. He believed that most people are unable to fulfill enough of the needs at the lower and middle levels of the pyramid, but that some of us do satisfy enough of our lower-level needs at least to try for self-actualization and transcendence. For example, Mahatma Gandhi, Martin Luther King Jr., and Mother Teresa all appeared to be motivated by these higher levels of Maslow's hierarchy.

At first glance, Maslow's hierarchy seems to make sense. If you are starving, you will probably be less concerned with whether people love you and more concerned with finding food. Indeed, a recent study conducted in China found that the degree to which a need was satisfied correlated positively with the degree to which the need at the next higher level of the hierarchy was satisfied as well (Taormina & Gao, 2013). This finding is consistent with Maslow's predictions that lower-level needs must be fulfilled before moving on to higher-level needs. Due to its commonsense approach to motivation, Maslow's theory has had considerable influence in the business world, such as in management (for review, see Lussier, 2019) and in advertising (Hackley, 2007; Soper, Milford, & Rosenthal, 1995).

However, much of the work on Maslow's hierarchy of needs has failed to generate strong support for his theory (Soper, Milford, & Rosenthal, 1995). In fact, we often seem to behave in ways that contradict Maslow's notion that we must fulfill lower level needs before we can be concerned with higher-order needs. For instance, have you ever gone without lunch to pursue some other activity, such as studying for an exam? In that case, you were motivated by esteem needs even though your physiological needs had not been met. Maslow's theory cannot account for such discrepancies.

We have seen that there are many different ways to look at motivation. However, whether we view motivation as an instinct, a drive, a need, or an incentive, one thing is certain: motivation is what spurs our behavior and moves us into action.

5.1 Quiz Yourself

1. Which of the following approaches to motivation is most closely aligned with Darwin's theory of natural selection?
   a. Drive theory
   b. Instinct theory
   c. Self-determination theory
   d. Maslow's hierarchy of needs
2. Which of the following approaches to motivation assumes that motivation can come from outside the person?
   a. Instinct theory
   b. Drive theory
   c. Self-determination theory
   d. None of the above
3. Which of the following is the best example of intrinsic motivation?
   a. Engaging in your favorite hobby
   b. Staying late at work to earn overtime
   c. Cleaning your house because you have company coming
   d. Dressing up for a job interview because you want to make a good impression
4. Believing that you failed an exam due to a lack of studying is a(n)____________that is associated with having a ___________mindset.
   a. extrinsic motive; fixed
   b. extrinsic motive; growth
   c. attribution; fixed
   d. attribution; growth

Answers *1. b; 2. c; 3. a; 4. d*

5.2 Hunger and Eating

Lying in his hospital bed, being fed through a feeding tube, Jean-Dominique Bauby still fantasized about eating delectable gourmet meals. This shouldn't surprise us, given the importance of food in our daily lives. Food is part of one's culture. Eating is one of our most fundamental activities, basic to survival. But what is it that initiates the hunger that motivates us to eat?

5.2.1 The Origins of Hunger

The hunger motive is one of the primary drives that helps us maintain homeostasis in the body. The goal of hunger is to motivate us to eat when our bodies need fuel. Thus, we should feel hungry when we are lacking fuel and nutrients, but we should *not* feel the motivation to eat when we have enough fuel and nutrients in our bodies. Like a thermostat, hunger works on a *negative feedback loop* in the body that allows us to maintain homeostasis in our bodies.

set point a particular weight that our body seeks to maintain

Homeostatic regulation of hunger explains why we seem to have an individual **set point**, or a weight that our body naturally attempts to maintain

(Levin, 2010). Having a set point may be one reason that the vast majority of people who lose weight tend to regain it. When the body loses weight, the person's hunger increases, the person eats more, and the weight is regained. Although having a set point makes dieting very difficult, experiencing increased hunger when we fall below our set point also protects us from starvation. In environments where people struggle to find enough to eat, this extra motivation may make them work harder to obtain enough food to survive.

To motivate us to eat enough food to maintain homeostasis and thereby our set point, our brain must receive accurate and reliable feedback from the rest of our body. Where in the body does this feedback about the current status of our body's fuel supply originate?

Hunger Feedback from the Body

One of the first places psychologists looked for clues to hunger was the stomach, and some evidence suggests that one part of the feedback that initiates hunger is an empty stomach. When our stomachs become empty, the walls of the stomach contract, and these contractions appear to stimulate hunger. Additionally, the stomach appears to release a hormone called **ghrelin** that sends strong hunger signals to the brain (Suzuki et al., 2010). Studies done on rats suggest that ghrelin is a powerful hunger stimulant that can induce eating even when the body is not in need of additional energy (Bake et al., 2019). When people undergo a type of weight loss surgery called a *laproscopic sleeve gastrectomy,* one of the effects seems to be a reduction in the amount of ghrelin released by the stomach. This reduction in ghrelin has been shown to be associated with weaker reactions to food cues and reduced appetite. This could be one of the reasons that such weight loss surgeries are effective in reducing obesity (Li et al., 2019).

ghrelin [GRELL-in] a hunger-stimulating hormone produced by the stomach

Just as the stomach signals hunger, it may also play a role in telling the brain when it is time to stop eating. When we eat, our stomach's walls must distend to increase the volume of the stomach and allow room for the food we eat. This distention of the stomach has been suggested as one source of feedback that signals to the brain that it is time to stop eating (Deutsch, 1990; Xu et al., 2008). However, the role it plays may be complex. One study found that distending the stomach by means of an inflatable balloon placed in the stomach had no effect on subsequent food intake, but it did reduce feelings of hunger while the balloon was in place (Oesch et al., 2006). Failure of an inedible balloon to reduce subsequent eating may be explained by the fact that receptors in the walls of the stomach may actually be able to measure the nutritive value of the food we eat. Researchers have shown that the degree to which we feel hungry is directly correlated with the balance of proteins, carbohydrates, and fats we have consumed (El Khoury et al., 2010; Lomenick et al., 2009). When the stomach is filled with a non-nutritive balloon, ghrelin levels are unchanged, but when the stomach is filled with a nutritive substance, ghrelin levels drop (Ly et al., 2016). This reduction in ghrelin curbs the hunger signals being sent to the brain, resulting in *satiety,* or feeling full.

Ghrelin may also play a role in emotional eating. Obese women who exhibited a normal reduction in ghrelin after eating also exhibited less anxiety and stress compared to participants who had abnormally high postmeal ghrelin levels (Sarker, Franks, & Caffrey, 2013). In non-obese women, postmeal ghrelin levels were higher in lonely women than they were in non-lonely women (Jaremka et al., 2015). Furthermore, stress can cause the release of ghrelin, but this increase in

TABLE 5.1 The Liver's Role in Hunger

	The Liver Detects That Glucose Is Converting to Glycogen	The Liver Detects That Glycogen Is Converting to Glucose
Hungry		X
Not Hungry	X	

glucose the form of sugar that the body burns as fuel

glycogen [GLIE-co-jen] a starchy molecule that is produced from excess glucose in the body; it can be thought of as the body's stored energy reserves

insulin [IN-suh-lin] a hormone produced by the pancreas that facilitates the movement of glucose from the blood into the cells of the body

cholecystokinin [coe-lih-cyst-oh-KYE-nin] (CCK) a hormone released by the small intestines that plays a role in hunger regulation

ghrelin is only associated with increased intake of highly palatable foods in those who are overweight (Sinha et al., 2019). These findings suggest that certain emotional states may be related to still feeling hungry after eating, which may contribute to further emotional eating and weight gain, especially in those who are overweight.

Although the stomach is an important source of feedback in the hunger process, it is not the only source. Surprisingly, even people who have had their stomachs completely removed because of cancer usually still feel hunger (Janowitz & Grossman, 1950). The liver is another source of feedback for hunger. Our liver has the capacity to help regulate hunger by monitoring the levels of *glucose* and *glycogen* in our body (see ● TABLE 5.1). **Glucose** is the form of sugar that our bodies burn for energy, and **glycogen** is the form of starch that we store along with fatty acids. When we have excess glucose in our body, we convert it into glycogen and then store it for future use. The liver determines what our energy requirements are by monitoring our levels of glucose and glycogen. When the liver detects that we are converting glucose into glycogen, indicating that we have too much fuel in our bodies, it will send signals to the brain to shut off hunger. But, when the liver notices that glycogen is being turned back into glucose, indicating that we are dipping into our energy reserves, it will send signals to the brain to initiate hunger.

The endocrine system (see Chapter 2) also plays a role in regulating hunger. The hormone **insulin** can increase feelings of hunger (see Grossman & Stein, 1948). Made in the pancreas, insulin facilitates the movement of glucose from the blood into our cells, where it is metabolized. When glucose moves into the cells, blood levels of glucose drop, so we begin to dip into our glycogen reserves, and hunger is initiated. In this indirect way, insulin can produce feelings of hunger.

Foods that tend to cause a rapid increase in blood sugar, called *high glycemic foods*, do not keep our hunger satisfied for very long. This is because the body pumps out a large amount of insulin to counteract the rapid increase in blood sugar, resulting in a subsequent drop in blood glucose levels that sets off hunger (Bornet et al., 2007). Keep in mind, however, that glycemic index alone does not necessarily predict exactly how your body will respond to the foods you eat. Other factors, such as your individual insulin response and how much protein you have consumed, can also impact postmeal blood sugar levels (Eleazu, 2016) and your later intake of food (Nepocatych et al., 2019). So although your diet should be tailored to your individual needs, in general, an apple is likely to be a better snack for weight management than a piece of candy is.

Other hormones affect hunger even more directly. When we eat, the small intestines release the hormone **cholecystokinin (CCK)** into the bloodstream. CCK appears to shut off the urge to eat (Kaelberer & Bohórquez, 2018; Lassman et al., 2010; May et al., 2016). However, the level of hunger that we experience is due to more than just the amount of CCK in our bloodstream. How much food we have recently eaten also seems to influence hunger. If we have not taken in enough food, CCK by itself may not be enough to stop our hunger and our eating (Muurahainen et al., 1991). This may be because CCK appears to work with the insulin that is released after a meal when signaling satiety to the brain (May et al., 2016).

Fat cells may provide yet another source of feedback for hunger regulation. Fat cells make and secrete a chemical called **leptin**. When fat cells release leptin into the bloodstream, it travels to the brain, where it is picked up by receptors near the brain's *ventricles* (the fluid-filled cavities in the brain) and in the *hypothalamus* (the part of the brain that maintains homeostasis) (McGregor et al., 1996; Sohn et al., 2016). Leptin is thought to inform the brain about the level of fat reserves available. When the brain senses high leptin levels, this may indicate that a large number of fat cells are full of fat reserves. Therefore, we do not need to take in more fuel, and our hunger may be reduced. In support of this hypothesis, researchers have found that mice that are bred to be genetically fat will lose weight if they are given injections of leptin (Pelleymounter et al., 1995).

leptin a hormone released by fat cells in the body that plays a role in hunger regulation

lateral hypothalamus (LH) a region of the hypothalamus once thought to be the hunger center in the brain

Unfortunately, we do not yet understand the exact role of fat cells and the leptin they release in motivating human eating. For example, researchers are still investigating the role that *dopamine* (see Chapter 2; Burdakov, Karnani, & Gonzalez, 2013) and *melatonin* (see Chapter 4; Buonfiglio et al., 2019) play in mediating leptin action in the brain, and how leptin, CCK, and other digestive tract chemicals interact to regulate hunger (Blevins & Baskin, 2010; Woods, 2013). Furthermore, it is now known that in addition to leptin, fat cells release other chemicals that impact the functioning of our bodily systems. The picture is so complex that some now view fat or *adipose* tissue in the body as an *endocrine organ* rather than a mere energy storage system (Guo et al., 2017; Kotnik, Fischer Posovszky, & Wabitsch, 2015).

Hunger Regulation in the Brain

The brain, of course, plays a significant role in our eating behavior. It receives and processes signals from the stomach about contractions and distention, from the liver about the glucose-glycogen balance, and from leptin. The brain may also directly monitor our energy supplies. Evidence suggests that the brain, like the liver, monitors the level of glucose in the blood (Chaput & Tremblay, 2009). There appear to be specialized *glucoreceptors* in the hypothalamus that measure glucose levels in the bloodstream (Burdakov, Luckman, & Verkhratsky, 2005). If an animal is given a substance that makes its hypothalamus unresponsive to glucose, the animal goes on an eating binge (Miselis & Epstein, 1970). Disabling the hypothalamus's glucoreceptors tricks the brain into thinking that the body is critically low on fuel. The brain then signals extreme hunger to quickly replenish the body's glucose.

Further clues about the role of the hypothalamus in hunger regulation come from animal studies in which surgical lesions are made in the brain. By destroying part of the hypothalamus and observing the effect that this destruction has on behavior, psychologists have uncovered some clues about the role that the different parts of the hypothalamus play in both initiating and stopping eating.

One part of the hypothalamus, the **lateral hypothalamus (LH)**, seems to function as an "on switch" for hunger. When the LH is destroyed in a rat, the rat stops eating. As a result, the rat loses weight and eventually dies. Without the LH, the rat simply starves to death (Teitelbaum & Stellar, 1954), which seems to indicate that the LH turns on hunger. However, further investigation has shown that the LH is not the only "on switch" for hunger. Curiously, if a rat is force-fed for long enough after having had its LH destroyed, the rat will eventually get some of its appetite back. Its appetite will not be as great as it was prior to losing its LH, but the rat will eat, particularly very tasty foods (Teitelbaum & Epstein, 1962).

neuropeptide Y a powerful hunger stimulant

ventromedial [ven-tro-MEE-dee-al] hypothalamus (VMH) a region of the hypothalamus that plays an indirect role in creating a feeling of satiety

Another bit of evidence that suggests an "on switch" for hunger outside the LH comes from studies using **neuropeptide Y**, a powerful hunger stimulant (Gibbs, 1996). When an animal is injected with neuropeptide Y, its strongest effect occurs outside the LH (Leibowitz, 1991). It stands to reason that if the LH were the primary "on switch" for hunger, then this powerful stimulant would have its strongest effect in the LH. That this does not appear to be the case suggests that there is an even more important "on switch" for hunger elsewhere in the brain. To date, the research suggests that the LH plays an important role in hunger, but it is not the only brain structure involved in motivating us to eat (Petrovich, 2013).

The hypothalamus is also thought to play a role in shutting off hunger. Some evidence suggests that a part of the hypothalamus, the **ventromedial hypothalamus (VMH)**, plays a role in creating a feeling of *satiety*. When we are sated, we feel full and do not wish to eat more. Rats who have had their VMH destroyed will begin to eat ravenously and will gain enormous amounts of weight (● FIGURE 5.4). If the VMH were the rat's only satiety center, or hunger "off switch," then destroying its VMH should make the rat eat continuously until it dies. But this doesn't happen. A rat without a VMH will eat a great deal of food and gain a great deal of weight, but after a certain amount of weight gain, its appetite will level off and the rat will then eat only enough food to maintain its new, higher weight. It's as if losing the VMH changes the rat's set point. In other words, the weight that the rat's body tries to maintain through homeostatic regulation has been shifted upward to a new, higher weight.

Richard Howard Photography

FIGURE 5.4

A Mouse with a Lesion in the Ventromedial Hypothalamus (VMH)

This mouse had its ventromedial hypothalamus damaged. As a result, the mouse has eaten more than normal and gained a great deal of weight. But this mouse will not eat itself to death. Rather, it will now eat just enough to maintain this new, higher set point weight.

So, although the VMH may not be the only "off switch" for hunger, it does appear to play a role in obesity (see King, 2006; Levin & Routh, 1996). When the VMH is damaged surgically in a rat, the endocrine system's control over insulin release is disturbed. The result is an increased release of insulin into the bloodstream, which produces greater hunger and subsequent increases in eating (Valensi et al., 2003). Loss of the VMH doesn't remove the satiety center, but rather causes disturbances in the endocrine system that result in increased eating. Most of us, however, have not had our VMH surgically removed or damaged. Why might the system fail us under conditions seen in everyday life?

Recent research suggests that chronic challenges to the hunger-regulating centers of the brain can disrupt its ability to sense and respond to insulin, thereby damaging its ability to regulate hunger and metabolic functioning. One of these challenges seems to be eating a high-fat diet. Mice fed a high-fat diet were shown to develop less activity in certain neural pathways of the VMH as a result of increased insulin activity in the brain. This reduction in neural activity was also related to weight gain in the mice and lessened ability to control blood sugar in their bodies (Klöckener et al., 2011). Some studies further suggest that a high-fat diet is

YOU REVIEW Mechanisms of Hunger

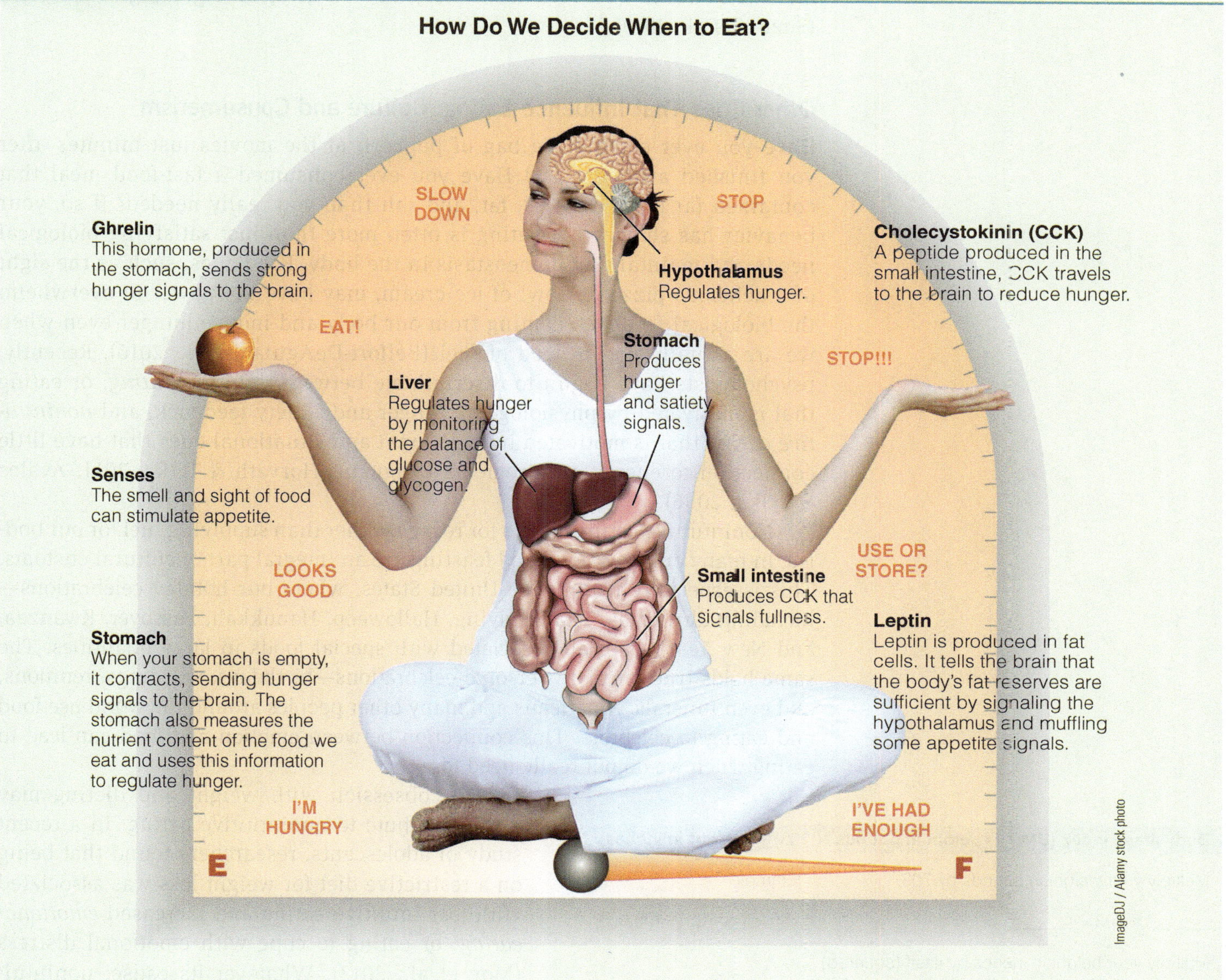

particularly damaging to insulin function when it is preceded by a diet that is insufficient in protein (Leite et al., 2016).

Sleep deprivation may also affect the functioning of the hypothalamus in ways that increase the likelihood of one overeating. In one study, a single night of sleep deprivation was associated with changes in the functioning of neural circuits between the hypothalamus and amygdala that are associated with the reward value that we place on food. In other words, when we are sleep-deprived, food may look better to us, causing us to overeat (Rihm et al., 2019). This could be one reason that chronic sleep deprivation is often associated with obesity and overeating, especially in children (Lombardo et al., 2019).

What we have learned from studies of the hunger motive is that many mechanisms turn on and shut off feelings of hunger (for review, Carreiro et al., 2016). There does not appear to be a single on or off switch for hunger (King, 2006).

overweight having a body mass index of 25–29.9

Rather, hunger seems to be regulated by a complex network of feedback to the brain from various sources in the body, as well as direct signaling in the brain (Suzuki et al., 2010)

Other Cues That Influence Eating: Culture and Consumerism

Have you ever eaten a big bag of popcorn at the movies just minutes after you finished a large meal? Have you ever consumed a fast-food meal that contained far more calories, fat, and salt than you really needed? If so, your behavior has shown that eating is often more than just satisfying biological needs and maintaining homeostasis in the body. Food cues, such as the sight of a delicious pizza or bowl of ice cream, may have the power to overwhelm the biological feedback coming from our body and induce hunger even when we are actually not in need of fuel (Belfort-DeAguiar et al., 2016). Recently, psychologists have begun to discriminate between *intuitive eating*, or eating that is motivated by physiological hunger and satiety feedback, and *nonintuitive eating* that is motivated by emotional and situational cues that have little connection to energy requirements (Augustus-Horvath & Tylka, 2011; Avalos & Tylka, 2006).

Nonintuitive eating occurs for reasons other than supplying fuel for our bodies. In many cultures, food and feasting are an integral part of cultural customs. This is especially true in the United States, where our holiday celebrations—including Christmas, Thanksgiving, Halloween, Hanukkah, Passover, Kwanzaa, and New Year's—are all associated with special foods in large quantities. The same holds true for more personal celebrations—birthdays, weddings, reunions, and even funerals. Americans and many other peoples around the world use food and eating to celebrate. This connection between emotion and food can lead to eating when we do not really need to.

Our obsession with weight and dieting may also contribute to nonintuitive eating. In a recent study of adolescents, researchers found that being on a restrictive diet for weight loss was associated with less intuitive eating and increased *emotional eating*, or eating to cope with emotional distress (Moy et al., 2013). Whatever its cause, nonintuitive eating can lead to unwanted weight gain. In contrast, intuitive eating is associated with lower body mass index (BMI; Herbert et al., 2013). In one study, for every 1-point score increase on a measure of intuitive eating, participants had a 34% *decrease* in their odds of being overweight (Cole et al., 2016). Higher levels of intuitive eating are also associated with less weight gain during pregnancy (Paterson et al., 2019). Clearly eating that is not motivated by internal hunger cues is one reason for the obesity epidemic.

Body mass index (BMI) = (weight in pounds × 703) + (height in inches)^2	
Multiply your weight in pounds by 703	Example
______ × 703 = ______	155 lbs × 703 = 108,965
Multiply your height in inches by itself (squared)	
______^{2} = ______	68 × 68 [inches] = 4,624
Divide the first number by the second:	
______ ÷ ______ = ______ Weight × 703 Height squared BMI	$\frac{108{,}965}{4{,}624}$ = 23.6 BMI

BMI	Weight status
below 18.5	Underweight
18.5–24.9	Normal
25.0–29.9	Overweight
30.0 and above	Obese

FIGURE 5.5

Calculating your BMI

This chart shows how to calculate your body mass index (BMI). To do so, you will need a calculator, your weight in pounds, and your height in inches.

5.2.2 The Obesity Epidemic

One way to define overweight and obesity is to look at the *body mass index* (*BMI*; • FIGURE 5.5). A BMI of 25–29.9 indicates **overweight**, and a BMI of 30 or

obesity having a body mass index of 30 or over

more indicates **obesity** (NIH, 2016). BMIs over 30 are correlated with higher incidences of many diseases, including type 2 diabetes, heart disease, and some cancers (Kopelman, 2000). Clearly, we have reason to be concerned about weight.

Americans are clearly obsessed with weight. Collectively we spend millions of dollars each year on diets, exercise equipment, diet pills, gym memberships, and surgeries, yet roughly 35.2% of all Americans are considered to be *overweight*, having BMIs between 25 and 29.9 (CDC, 2016c), and 39.8% are *obese*, having BMIs of 30 or higher (Hales et al., 2017; ● FIGURE 5.6). Sadly, among children ages 2–19, 18.5% are considered overweight (Hales et al., 2017). Similar figures are now seen in other cultures as well. In England, the national health authority, Public Health England, reports that 68.5% of men and 63.3% of women in England are considered overweight or obese (PHE, 2017). The World Health Organization (WHO) (2019) maintains datasets showing that in European Union (EU) countries, overweight and obesity rates range from 30 to 70% of adults. In Southeast Asia, the percentage of overweight adults ranges from 7.6% of males in Bangladesh to 53% of females in the Maldives. In the Americas, some 62% of adults are overweight or obese, and in the Middle East, 74% to 86% of women and 69% to 77% of men are overweight or obese. Numbers like these suggest that the obesity epidemic is a global issue.

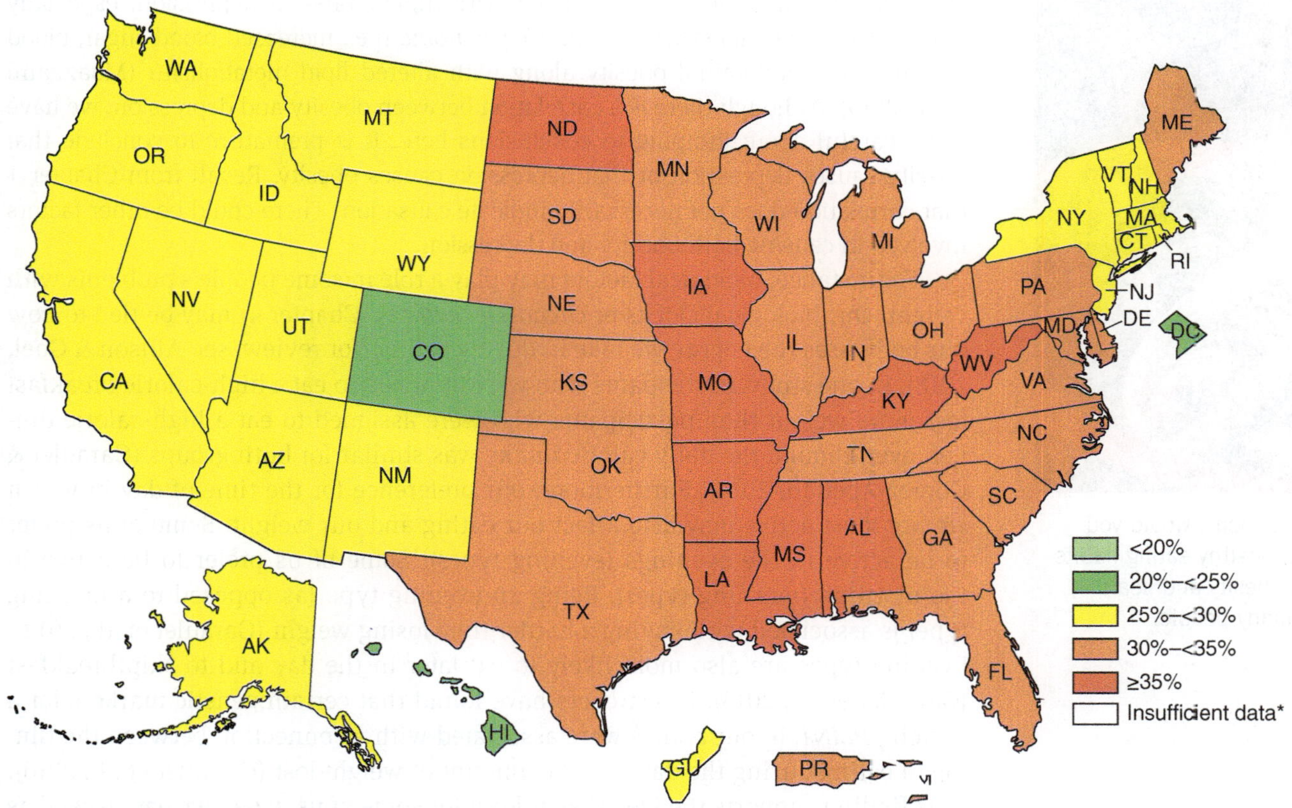

*Sample size <50 or the relative standard error (dividing the standard error by the prevalence) ≥ 30%.

FIGURE 5.6

The Obesity Epidemic in the United States

In the United States, almost one-third of all adults are obese. This map shows the percentage of people who are obese across the United States. The highest concentrations of people with obesity (shown in dark red) seem to be primarily in the South, the Mississippi River Valley, and portions of Appalachia. The reasons for this epidemic are the subject of much debate, but it is likely that several causes are at work—including genetic, lifestyle, and diet factors.

Source: Centers for Disease Control and Prevention, www.cdc.gov.

Elenadesign/Shutterstock.com

Atsushi Hirao/Shutterstock.com

▲ Which of these meals would you rather eat? Unhealthy eating habits contribute to obesity and health problems in many people.

In light of these problems, the U.S. government–funded Medicare program began considering obesity a disease in the mid-2000s (Centers for Medicare and Medicaid Services (CMMS) 2004), and in 2011 it announced that it would begin funding obesity prevention services (Kennedy & Hellmich, 2011). Despite our great concern over the issues of weight and health, why did obesity take such a hold in the United States and other countries?

Poor diet is one reason that some people gain weight. One culprit is the high-fat diet common in many Western cultures. A typical fast-food lunch can contain a whole day's worth of fat and calories. Coupled with a lack of exercise, this diet leads to weight gain in many people. Another factor comes from the way our society views food. As we mentioned earlier, we tend to eat for reasons that have little to do with maintaining homeostasis. Many of us engage in emotional eating when we experience either negative emotions (e.g., feeling lonely, sad, or stressed) or positive emotions (happiness or joy; Reichenberger et al., 2018). Furthermore, being higher in emotion-driven impulsiveness is associated with having a higher BMI (Coumans et al., 2019).

Researchers have also discovered links between obesity and certain problematic emotions. For example, abdominal obesity (fat stored around the midsection) has been linked to some aspects of depression—namely, the somatic or body-centered symptoms of depression (e.g., fatigue, sleep disturbances, dizziness; Wiltink et al., 2013). Obesity in general is associated with higher rates of depression, especially when obesity is coupled with *metabolic syndrome* (i.e., increased blood sugar, blood pressure, and abdominal obesity along with altered lipid metabolism) (Moazzami et al., 2019). Although there is a correlation between obesity and depression, we have to be careful about jumping to conclusions here. It is premature to conclude that obesity causes depression or that depression causes obesity. Recall from Chapter 1 that correlation does not necessarily indicate causation. There could be other factors involved in causing both obesity and depression.

For instance, biological factors may play a role in some people's problems with weight. Our biological clocks or *circadian rhythms* (Chapter 4) may be tied to how our body uses the energy we take in during eating (for review, see Allison & Goel, 2018). In one study, participants who were assigned to eat a high-calorie breakfast lost more weight than participants who were assigned to eat a high-calorie dinner, even though the daily caloric intake was similar for both groups (Garaulet & Gómez-Abellán, 2014). Furthermore, our preference for the time of day in which we are most active may also affect our eating and our weight. Some of us prefer to be active in the evenings (evening types). Some of us prefer to be active in the morning (morning types). Being an evening type (as opposed to a morning type) is associated with having a harder time losing weight (Garaulet et al., 2012). Evening types are also more likely to eat later in the day and to skip breakfast (Garaulet et al., 2013). Researchers have found that certain genetic markers for a protein, *PLIN1*, in our bodies were associated with a connection between the timing of eating during the day and the amount of weight lost (Garaulet et al., 2016). This finding supports the idea that at least for some of us, *when* we eat, as well as *what* we eat, may influence our waistline.

Another biological factor that contributes to obesity is having a low *resting metabolic rate*—the rate at which we burn energy in our bodies when resting. People differ with respect to how much energy is required to run their bodies. Some people have high metabolic rates and require large amounts of fuel; others have low metabolic rates and require relatively little energy to survive. A person with a very low metabolic rate who eats the same number of calories and exercises just as much as a person with a normal metabolic rate will still gain more weight than the normal person will. Over time, this weight gain could lead to obesity (Friedman, 1990).

Ironically, having a low metabolic rate isn't always a disadvantage. In fact, across our evolutionary history, a low metabolic rate was probably a decided advantage. Our ancestors had to hunt and forage for enough food to eat. During times of scarce food and starvation, those early humans who required less energy to survive probably had an easier time finding enough food to meet their needs. Therefore, those with low metabolic rates probably survived better and procreated more than their counterparts with high metabolic rates. This advantage could have led to some members of our modern society having "thrifty genes" that conserve energy, but it may have also led to obesity in a world in which hunting and gathering high-calorie foods is as simple as a trip to the grocery store or fast-food drive-through. So far, scientists have not found direct genetic evidence to support the thrifty gene hypothesis (Genné-Bacon, 2014) and the theory has many critics (Gosling et al., 2015).

However, researchers are currently honing in on chemicals in the nervous system, *endocannabinoids*, that seem to be able to alter our food intake and energy expenditures to conserve energy in the body (Choromanska et al., 2015). The presence of such mechanisms in the body would be consistent with the thrifty gene hypothesis (DiPatrizio & Piomelli, 2012). Researchers have also identified variants of the PPARGCIA gene that may constitute a thrifty gene in some Pacific Islanders (Myles et al., 2011).

Cross-cultural studies, particularly of Pacific Islanders, have long been used to support the notion of thrifty genes. The typical American diet is far different from that of our ancestors. Americans today consume large amounts of red meat, fat, eggs, and dairy products, but few fruits and vegetables. In contrast, the diets of some cultures, such as the Japanese and certain Mediterranean cultures, are much lower in red meat and contain significantly larger proportions of fruits and vegetables.

By examining cultural groups that have recently adapted to the American high-fat diet, we can see more clearly the impact of that diet on health. As a group, ethnic Hawaiians show high rates of high blood pressure, type 2 diabetes, obesity, and high cholesterol. One reason for these health problems appears to be the fat-heavy American diet they have adopted. When ethnic Hawaiians return to their native diet of sweet potatoes, taro root, breadfruit, fish, chicken, and vegetables for just 21 days, their health improves significantly (Shintani et al., 1991). Perhaps thrifty genes make many native Hawaiians biologically unsuited to eat the American diet.

On the other hand, critics of the thrifty gene hypothesis point out that such cross-cultural studies do not provide direct support of the thrifty gene hypothesis. They also argue that the archaeological and anthropological record of the Pacific Islands does not provide clear evidence of the past starvation conditions that would have led to the development of thrifty genes in its populations (Gosling et al., 2015). Whether or not some of us inherited "thrifty genes" from ancestors who faced starvation, it is quite clear that today many of us struggle to maintain a healthy weight. But, why is dieting so hard?

5.2.3 The Battle of the Bulge: Why Is Losing Weight So Hard?

Many people try to lose weight by going on diets that restrict their eating to varying degrees. Unfortunately, depriving yourself of food is also one reason that most diets fail. When we reduce our caloric intake to the point that we begin to lose weight, our bodies try to counteract the diet. Recall that our motivation to eat is designed to keep us from starving. When we begin to draw on our fat reserves while dieting,

resting metabolic rate the rate at which we burn energy in our bodies when resting

our body takes steps to avoid "starvation." At first, we may feel increased hunger as our body tries to avoid burning up fat reserves by urging us to eat. Later, our **resting metabolic rate** may drop, a phenomenon called *metabolic adaptation*, as the body tries to avoid burning up its fat reserves. Metabolic adaptation has been shown to also occur after certain types of weight loss surgery (i.e., gastric bypass and gastric sleeves), but not others (i.e., gastric banding; Tam et al., 2016). Metabolic adaptation can make lasting weight loss difficult. Our bodies appear inclined to fight against weight loss and to maintain our typical weight, or *set point*.

There are psychological factors in dieting, too. Depriving yourself of food often leads to bingeing. It appears that when dieters stray from their diet program, they feel as if they might as well *really* go off the diet. In one study that illustrated this reaction, dieters and nondieters were given a liquid drink. Half of each group was told that the drink was very high in calories; the other half was told that the drink was very low in calories. In reality, all the drinks had the same caloric and nutritional content. After the drink, all participants were allowed to eat as much ice cream as they wanted. The nondieters ate the same amount of ice cream regardless of whether they thought they had just consumed a high- or low-calorie drink. This was not true, however, for the dieters. The dieters who thought they had had a high-calorie drink were more likely to eat more ice cream than the dieters who thought their drink had been low-calorie. It appears that the dieters felt that having already "ruined" their diet with the high-calorie drink, there was little point in restraining themselves when it came to the ice cream (Spencer & Fremouw, 1979).

Recall that intuitive eating is less likely when one is on a restrictive diet and eating to ease emotional distress is more likely (Moy et al., 2013). Therefore, people who restrain their eating are most at risk for this bingeing when they are emotionally aroused. Emotional distress can make dieters more likely to cheat on their diet (Ruderman, 1985), but so can positive emotions (Cools, Schotte, & McNally, 1992). Whether one is happy or sad, it seems that dieting makes eating binges more likely.

The recipe for dieting success involves two factors. First, you have to make permanent changes in your eating behavior. Dieting is forever, and it is probably a mistake to think of losing weight as dieting. Successful weight loss is more related to permanent changes in eating habits than to restrictive dieting. Perhaps becoming more of an intuitive eater is a better strategy. In one study, researchers found that teaching people to chew their food for a longer period of time, slow down their eating, and be *mindful* (see Chapter 4) of their bodily sensations while eating was associated with increases in intuitive eating, and decreases in poor eating habits and body mass (Schnepper et al., 2019).

The second aspect of successful weight loss is exercise. Weight loss by restrictive dieting alone has been shown to increase appetite more than weight loss by exercise alone (Cameron et al., 2016). This could lead to failure. Exercise also increases your metabolism. Recall that weight loss leads to metabolic adaptation. You can help keep your metabolism higher by exercising, which will lead to a more permanent weight loss as your set point moves to a lower weight. Exercise, especially strength training, can also ensure that you don't lose too much muscle mass while dieting. If you diet by caloric reduction alone, you run the risk of losing beneficial muscle along with the fat (Parr, Coffey, & Hawley, 2013).

Sadly, there are no quick fixes when it comes to shedding pounds. Even people who undergo *gastric bypass surgery* to drastically reduce the size of their stomach must adhere to a strict diet regimen and make lifestyle changes to achieve and sustain long-term weight loss (Powell, Calvin, & Calvin, 2007). Unfortunately, many people continue to struggle with unwanted weight that can threaten one's health and make one the target of discrimination and prejudice.

5.2.4 Culture and Weight-Based Prejudice

People who are overweight are often ridiculed, socially isolated, and even discriminated against both inside and outside of the workplace (Puhl, 2018). Social media has created a platform for *fat-shaming, body-shaming,* and other forms of bullying. Blogger Melissa McEwan created the hashtag #FatMicroaggressions to start a conversation about prejudice against the overweight (Bahadur, 2013). A recent search of the hashtag on Twitter found many who shared personal stories of their experience with weight-based prejudice, as well as several people using the hashtag to actually engage in weight-based prejudice against others. A survey of 2,866 people in the United States, Canada, Iceland, and Australia found that two-thirds of participants felt it is time for their governments to pass laws prohibiting weight-based discrimination (Puhl et al., 2015).

Weight-based discrimination occurs in many settings, including the workplace, education, the media, and health care (Puhl, 2018). For example, people are less willing to support a charity whose spokesperson is overweight compared to a charity with a spokesperson who is of average weight (Randall et al., 2017). Even children are not immune to such prejudice. Elementary school-aged children exhibit weight-based discrimination against other children (Rex-Lear, Jensen-Campbell, & Lee, 2019). Students with obesity may also face prejudice in the classroom. In one study, eighth graders, community college, and university students with obesity tended to earn lower grades relative to normal weight students, despite the fact that they showed no difference in ability or standardized test scores (MacCann & Roberts, 2013).

Yet tragically, such abuse does not always come at the hand of strangers. Parents have been shown to exhibit weight bias against their own children. Parents are less likely to help their overweight children finance a car (Kraha & Boals, 2011) or their college tuition (Crandall, 1991; Incollingo Rodriguez et al., 2019). Even health care professionals who specialize in the treatment of obesity sometimes demonstrate negative attitudes toward the overweight. In one study, health care professionals, including psychologists, were found to have used words such as lazy and stupid to refer to overweight persons (Schwartz et al., 2003). Similarly, researcher Kristen Davis-Coelho and her colleagues (2000) found that some members of the American Psychological Association displayed a negative bias in their perceptions of overweight versus normal-weight women. This tendency to perceive overweight people less favorably was most evident in younger and less experienced mental-health care professionals (Davis-Coelho et al., 2000). Why would some people exhibit such prejudices?

Researchers have begun to examine the individual characteristics of people who hold anti-fat prejudices. One factor that seems to be important is *fear of negative appearance evaluations* (Bissell & Hays, 2011). Likewise, having a *tendency to compare one's appearance to that of others', having a poorer body image,* and *placing greater importance on physical appearance* were correlated with having greater prejudice against the overweight (O'Brien et al., 2007).

Exposure to stigmatizing media depictions of overweight people may also work to exacerbate weight-based prejudice. Participants who viewed stigmatizing depictions of people who are obese were subsequently more likely to endorse a policy that discriminated against the obese. But subjects who viewed nonstigmatizing depictions of people with obesity were less likely to endorse prejudicial policies aimed at the overweight (Brochu et al., 2014). These data suggest that eliminating stigmatizing media depictions of obesity may help reduce weight-based prejudice. Our cultural fear of fat exacts a heavy toll on the many people who experience weight-based prejudice (Danielsdottir, O'Brien, & Ciao, 2010). Our attitudes about weight may also play a role in the development of certain eating disorders—our next topic.

5.2.5 Eating Disorders: Bulimia Nervosa, Anorexia Nervosa, and Binge Eating Disorder

Obesity is not the only problem that involves eating. Some people also experience the devastating toll that eating disorders, or mental health disorders that are associated with eating, can take on a person's health and life. Of particular interest are *bulimia*, *anorexia nervosa*, and *binge eating disorder*.

Bulimia Nervosa

bulimia nervosa an eating disorder in which a person alternately binges on large quantities of food and then engages in some inappropriate compensatory behavior to avoid weight gain

Bulimia nervosa is an eating disorder that is characterized by alternating bouts of *bingeing* and inappropriate compensatory behaviors such as *purging*, fasting, or excessive exercise (American Psychiatric Association, 2013). People who are bulimic gorge on large quantities of food, sometimes as much as 20,000 calories at a time; then they either go on a very rigid starvation diet or purge the food from their system (Schlesier-Stropp, 1984). Purging is achieved by self-induced vomiting or the abuse of laxatives (in the mistaken belief that laxatives prevent weight gain after overeating).

The typical person with bulimia is a young female who is of average to slightly above average weight. Within a given 12-month period, approximately 1% to 1.5% of young females will have bulimia nervosa (American Psychiatric Association, 2013), and an American woman has roughly a 0.5 to 1% chance of developing the disorder across her lifetime (Udo & Grilo, 2018; Williams, Goodie, & Motsinger, 2008). Bulimia is much less likely among males; at any point in time, approximately 10 times more females than males have the disorder (American Psychiatric Association, 2013).

Bulimia is especially likely among college-age females, almost 4% of whom are estimated to have the disorder (Anorexia and Related Eating Disorders, 2008). Not surprisingly, bulimic behavior is particularly common among female college students (Cain et al., 2010). Bulimia can be a socially isolating disorder. A college student who spends evenings gathering up large quantities of food and bingeing and purging usually does so alone. Aside from its social toll, bulimia can sometimes be fatal. The frequent purging of food can lead to dehydration and electrolyte imbalances, which can lead to serious cardiac problems as well as other problems such as holes and erosions in the esophagus. In a long-term study of women with eating disorders, women with bulimia were 2.33 times more likely to die than women in a control group (Franko et al., 2013).

Given the toll that bulimia can take on one's life, what would motivate anyone to engage in bulimic behavior? At this time, no one can say for sure why people become bulimic. However, many people with bulimia are troubled by low self-esteem and depression (Perez, Joiner, & Lewisohn, 2004). They tend to be perfectionists who have negative views of their bodies (La Mela et al., 2015). People with bulimia also tend to have grown up in families that were troubled somehow (Bardone et al., 2000; Spanou & Morogiannis, 2010). For some, bingeing and purging become a means of coping with negative emotions such as anxiety and a sense that one has no control over the events of one's own life. Indeed, in people with any eating disorder, anxiety has been shown to be one of the strongest triggers for binge eating (Rigaud et al., 2014).

Fairfax Media/Getty Images

▲ Anorexia nervosa is a devastating disorder in which people are motivated to drastically restrict their eating. Some people with anorexia also increase their level of exercise. The result is extreme weight loss, but this weight loss is never enough to please the person with anorexia. This woman with anorexia may look in the mirror and feel that she needs to lose more weight.

Anorexia Nervosa

Anorexia nervosa is an eating disorder that is characterized by self-starvation, intense fear of gaining weight, and a distorted body image. Unlike in cases of bulimia nervosa, the first diagnostic criterion for anorexia nervosa is that the client be significantly below normal weight (American Psychiatric Association, 2013). People with anorexia can get down to astonishingly low weights (as low as 50 pounds), and 5% to 10% of them die as a result of the disorder (Wilson, Grilo, & Vitousek, 2007). A person with anorexia's risk of premature death is also a function of several factors, including how long one has been ill, alcohol use, BMI, and social adjustment (Franko et al., 2013). The most bizarre aspect of anorexia is that even at a life-threateningly low weight, a person with anorexia can look in the mirror and see themself as fat (Grant & Phillips, 2004). Compared to people without anorexia, people with anorexia tend to have a negative bias when it comes to information about their bodies. This bias cannot be attributed to levels of depression and may be one of the reasons behind the extreme weight loss efforts seen in this condition (Brockmeyer et al., 2018).

anorexia [an-or-EX-ee-uh] nervosa an eating disorder in which a person has an intense fear of gaining weight, even though they are actually underweight; this irrational fear motivates the person to lose unhealthy amounts of weight through self-starvation

Within a given 12-month period of time, approximately 0.4% of females have anorexia nervosa (American Psychiatric Association, 2013). Across their lifetimes, females have at least a 1.42% chance of developing anorexia (Udo & Grilo, 2018). Worldwide, most cases are females from middle- and upper-class families in industrialized countries. Anorexia is rarely found in males. For every male with anorexia, there are approximately 10 females with the disorder (American Psychiatric Association, 2013). However, eating disorders are not unheard of in males, and when males are diagnosed with eating disorders, their symptoms are no less severe than those seen in females (Gorrell & Murray, 2019). Eating disorders among males may also be a bigger problem in the gay community, where body image concerns appear to be heightened (Russell & Keel, 2002), and among males with gender-identity confusion (Crosscope-Happel, 2000). Confusion about one's sexual orientation may be another risk factor. A recent study of adolescent male sexual minorities (gay/bisexual/sex with another male) found highest levels of anorexia among boys who did not identify as either gay or bisexual, but had had sex with other males (Burns et al., 2015). As cultural pressures result in males of all sexual orientations becoming increasingly concerned with having lean and muscular body types, the incidence of male anorexia and other body-image-related disorders may increase (Griffiths, Murray & Touyz, 2013; Murray & Touyz, 2012; Strübel & Petrie, 2020).

Anorexia is also less common in cultures that hold a fuller-figured woman up as the standard of beauty. It appears that one of the contributing factors in the development of anorexia is societal pressure on young women to be very thin—unrealistically thin. If you pick up just about any American fashion magazine or

FIGURE 5.7

Too Thin?

Many models and actresses are very thin. The steady parade of these women in the media may have contributed to the increase in eating disorders seen in the 1980s and 1990s.

watch just about any American television show, you will find that most of the females depicted are extremely thin. Sometimes they actually look anorexic (● FIGURE 5.7). Many television stars and models wear size 0 or 2 clothes, whereas many American women wear size 10 or 12 (or larger)! If you do the math, you'll see that many American women fall short of the standard of beauty depicted in the media. What do you do if you are a young girl who aspires to look like the actors you see on TV, and a healthy diet and exercise do not allow you to meet your goals? Some girls take drastic steps to reach their "ideal" body image, and anorexia may be the result.

Researchers have found wide cultural variations in women's perceptions of their ideal body image. For example, in one study that compared U.S., Israeli, Spanish, and Brazilian women, the American women were found to be the least satisfied with their bodies. The American women also reported that they felt the most pressure to be thin (Joliot, 2001). A recent study of Mexican American college women also found that the degree to which these women had internalized American standards of female beauty was related to their levels of dissatisfaction with their own bodies (Poloskov & Tracey, 2013). This finding is also mirrored in female members of deaf culture in the United States, in that greater internalization of mainstream media depictions of beauty is associated with having a more negative body image and engaging in disordered eating (Aldalur & Schooler, 2019). This is significant because in cultures that portray beautiful women as being somewhat plumper—for example, in Jamaica (Smith & Cogswell, 1994) or even in American culture prior to the 1970s—anorexia is uncommon. Pre-1970, women who were considered beautiful were considerably heavier than those who are considered beautiful today. For example, Marilyn Monroe was considered to be the standard of beauty in the 1950s and early 1960s, and before her, Mae West—these two women were not the ultrathin models of today (● FIGURE 5.8). Still, despite being bombarded with images of very thin women, most American girls do not become anorexic. Why is it that some do?

At one time, anorexia was thought to be correlated with ethnicity. Because the thin standard of female beauty is most frequently portrayed as a White woman in American culture, many predicted that White women would experience greater pressure to be unrealistically thin and therefore have higher rates of anorexia. Indeed, studies conducted in the 1980s seemed to confirm this hypothesis. Today the picture is different. Some studies have shown that relative to White women, minority women are equally susceptible to risk factors for eating disorders such as dissatisfaction with one's body and disordered eating behaviors (e.g., fasting, purging, diet pill use) (Beccia et al., 2019; Shaw et al., 2004; see also Wade, 2007). Although anorexia is clearly no longer just an issue for White women, racial differences may still exist. For example, relative to White and Hispanic women, Black college women have been shown to experience fewer appearance concerns about their bodies and less disordered eating behaviors (Schaefer et al., 2015).

Other characteristics that seem to be correlated with anorexia include perfectionism, low self-esteem, depression (Egan et al., 2013; Hartmann et al., 2014), faulty thinking about food (e.g., thinking one should never eat carbohydrates; Steinhausen & Vollrath, 1993), and higher levels of persistence and constraint (Wagner & Vitousek, 2019). Biochemical differences (D'Andrea et al., 2012; Young, 2010) and dysfunction in specific brain circuits are also seen in people

binge eating disorder (BED) an eating disorder characterized by recurrent episodes of binge eating, as in bulimia nervosa, but without regular use of compensatory measures to avoid weight gain with anorexia (Jiang et al., 2019). And finally, many people with eating disorders also have *personality disorders*—characteristic, maladaptive ways of dealing with the world (Himmerich et al., 2019; Marañon, Echeburúa, & Grijalvo, 2004; Sansone & Sansone, 2011a), substance use disorders, or depressive disorders (Himmerich et al, 2019, see Chapter 13). We do not yet know if these are *causal* factors or merely factors that *correlate* with eating disorders.

Another piece of the puzzle may be genetics (Keel & Klump, 2003; Trace et al., 2013). Some scholars have argued that genes for anorexia evolved to allow our ancestors to survive famine by helping them ignore food while migrating to better environments (Guisinger, 2003). Indeed, evidence supports the idea of a genetic basis for anorexia (Bulik et al., 2019). If one identical twin is anorexic, the other twin's chances of becoming anorexic are drastically increased. However, having a fraternal twin who is anorexic only modestly increases one's chances of becoming anorexic (Holland, Sicotte, & Treasure, 1988). This pattern of results supports the existence of a genetic predisposition to anorexia. It is also common to see family members, particularly mothers and daughters, who both have eating disorders (Strober et al., 2000). However, this doesn't necessarily indicate a genetic basis for the disorders as family members also tend to have shared environmental influences. At present, it appears that both bulimia and anorexia may result from a complex mix of cultural factors, personality characteristics, environmental issues, and biological factors.

Dan Kosmayer/Shutterstock.com

L. J. Willinger/Getty Images

Hulton Archive/Getty Images

FIGURE 5.8

Standards of Female Beauty

Standards of beauty in the United States have changed over time, and they also differ across cultures. In the 1930s, Mae West (bottom) was considered an icon of feminine beauty. In the 1950s and early 1960s, it was Marilyn Monroe (above). Today, women like Keira Knightly (above left) are the standard of beauty.

Binge Eating Disorder

Binge eating disorder (BED) is an eating disorder characterized by recurrent episodes of binge eating, such as those seen in bulimia nervosa, but without regular use of the inappropriate compensatory measures that people with bulimia employ to avoid weight gain (American Psychiatric Association, 2013). Because binge eaters do not compensate for their overeating, they may be overweight. As we've already seen, obesity and being overweight are at epidemic levels in the United States. Current estimates suggest that within a 12-month period, 1.6% of adult females and 0.8% of adult males have BED (American Psychiatric Association, 2013). The lifetime risk of developing BED is estimated to be approximately 1.25% to 2.6%, making BED the most common eating disorder (Citrome, 2015; Udo & Grilo, 2018).

Phil Noble-PA Images/Getty Images; Alexander Tamargo/Getty Images Entertainment/Getty Images; dbimages/Alamy Stock Photo

▲ In cultures like Tonga, Mexico, and Mauritania the standard of beauty leans toward heavier women. Cultures such as these have far lower rates of eating disorders than the United States.

YOU REVIEW *DSM-5* Criteria for Eating Disorders

Bulimia Nervosa

A. Recurrent episodes of binge eating. An episode of binge eating is characterized by both of the following:
   1. Eating, in a discrete period of time (e.g., within any 2-hour period), an amount of food that is definitely larger than what most individuals would eat in a similar period of time under similar circumstances.
   2. A sense of lack of control over eating during the episode (e.g., a feeling that one cannot stop eating or control what or how much one is eating).

B. Recurrent inappropriate compensatory behaviors in order to prevent weight gain, such as self-induced vomiting; misuse of laxatives, diuretics, or other medications; fasting; or excessive exercise.

C. The binge eating and inappropriate compensatory behaviors both occur, on average, at least once a week for 3 months.

D. Self-evaluation is unduly influenced by body shape and weight.

E. The disturbance does not occur exclusively during episodes of anorexia nervosa.

Anorexia Nervosa

A. Restriction of energy intake relative to requirements, leading to a significantly low body weight in the context of age, sex, developmental trajectory, and physical health. Significantly low body weight is defined as a weight that is less than minimally normal or, for children and adolescents, less than minimally expected.

B. Intense fear of gaining weight or of becoming fat, or persistent behavior that interferes with weight gain, even though at a significantly low weight.

C. Disturbance in the way in which one's body weight or shape is experienced, undue influence of body weight or shape on self-evaluation, or persistent lack of recognition of the seriousness of the current low body weight.

Binge Eating Disorder

A. Recurrent episodes of binge eating. An episode of binge eating is characterized by both of the following:
   1. Eating, in a discrete period of time (e.g., within any 2-hour period), an amount of food that is definitely larger than what most individuals would eat in a similar period of time under similar circumstances.
   2. A sense of lack of control over eating during the episode (e.g., a feeling that one cannot stop eating or control what or how much one is eating).

B. The binge eating episodes are associated with three (or more) of the following:
   1. Eating much more rapidly than normal.
   2. Eating until feeling uncomfortably full.
   3. Eating large amounts of food when not feeling physically hungry.
   4. Eating alone because of feeling embarrassed by how much one is eating.
   5. Feeling disgusted with oneself, depressed, or very guilty afterward.

C. Marked distress regarding binge eating is present.

D. The binge eating occurs, on average, at least once a week for 3 months.

E. The binge eating is not associated with the recurrent use of inappropriate compensatory behavior as in bulimia nervosa and does not occur exclusively during the course of bulimia nervosa or anorexia nervosa.

American Psychiatric Association, 2013

As a relatively new disorder, not much is known about the causes of BED. People with BED have been shown to be more impulsive, especially when it comes to food (Schag et al., 2015). But they also exhibit a motivational ambivalence about food. People with BED self-report more positive feelings about food than controls, while at the same time their nonverbal facial movements suggest negative feelings toward food. The meaning of this conflict over food in the development of BED is not known (Leehr et al., 2016). BED may also be linked to how people respond to negative moods. In one study, engaging in *rumination*, or extended focus on one's distress and its causes, predicted the onset of a bingeing episode. On the other hand, employing successful emotional regulation techniques to curb one's negative mood predicted that one would avoid a subsequent bingeing episode (Svaldi et al., 2019). Such a finding suggests that bingeing on food may be a maladaptive way of coping with one's distress.

5.2 Quiz Yourself

1. A friend of yours was recently in a car accident and experienced severe damage to their lateral hypothalamus. As a result, you should expect that your friend will_________.

a. likely stop eating.
b. lose a great deal of weight, but then their weight loss will level off at a new, lower set point.
c. likely gain a great deal of weight.
d. likely gain a great deal of weight, but then they will lose the pounds and return to their normal weight.

2. In a study examining the effects of CCK on eating, fasting participants are randomly assigned to get either an injection of CCK or a saline injection. Thirty minutes after the injections, all participants are allowed to eat as much ice cream as they want. The results show that both groups eat the same amount of ice cream. This piece of research is an example of a ________ and it ____________ previous research on the role that CCK plays in hunger and eating.

a. true experiment; supports
b. true experiment; contradicts
c. correlational study; supports
d. correlational study; contradicts

3. Mona's liver is converting glycogen into glucose. As a result, Mona will likely feel which of the following?

a. Not hungry
b. Hungry
c. Nauseous
d. We cannot predict from the information given.

4. Hannah is 23 years old, 5' 2'' tall, and weighs 185 lbs. Hannah routinely eats large amounts of food when stressed. Afterward, she feels awful, but she continues to deal with stress in this fashion. Given what you know, Hannah would most likely be diagnosed with which eating disorder?

a. Anorexia nervosa
b. Bulimia nervosa
c. Binge eating disorder
d. A & B

Answers 1. *a*; 2. *a*; 3. *b*; 4. *c*

5.3 Sexual Motivation

Another fundamental motive is the motivation to engage in sexual activity. Even locked inside his own body, Jean-Dominique Bauby no doubt felt sexual desire as he remembered intimacies from his past and lamented the loss of future ones. For most of us, sexuality is a healthy and important part of our lives. And, although sexual motivation is not necessary for life in the same manner that hunger is, sexual motivation does help ensure survival of the species through procreation.

5.3.1 Sexual Desire: A Mixture of Chemicals, Thoughts, and Culture

Sexual desire is our motivation and interest in engaging in sexual activity. It is the first step in experiencing **sexual arousal**, a heightened state of sexual

sexual desire one's motivation and interest in engaging in sexual activity

sexual arousal a heightened state of sexual interest and excitement interest and excitement. Like many other behaviors that we have discussed, sexual desire is influenced by our biology as well as our learning experiences and cultural expectations.

libido [leh-BEE-doe] one's physical desire, or drive, to have sex

estrogens a class of female hormones that regulate many aspects of sexuality

estrus [ESS-truss] in most mammals, a period of "being in heat" in which the female is receptive to males' attempts to mate with her

ovaries the organs in a female's body that produce eggs, or ova

testosterone a male hormone that plays a role in many aspects of sexuality, including sexual desire

testes the organs in a male's body that produce both sperm and testosterone

Biological and psychological processes influence sexual desire. The physical desire to have sex, or **libido**, is affected by both the hypothalamus and certain hormones of the endocrine system. As discussed in Chapter 2, the brain's hypothalamus works with the master gland of the body, the pituitary gland, to release hormones into the bloodstream. In this way, the hypothalamus plays a key role in regulating sexual behavior. The hypothalamus continually monitors the level of sex hormones in the bloodstream and directs the endocrine system to either increase or decrease the release of these hormones as required.

In mammals, **estrogens** are female hormones that regulate the female animal's desire to mate. Female animals' estrogen levels increase dramatically during a period called **estrus** ("being in heat"), in which the female is receptive to males' attempts to mate with her. Estrus coincides with ovulation in the female. During ovulation, the female's egg (or eggs) matures, so that it can be fertilized by the male sperm during mating. If fertilization does not occur, the female will pass out of estrus, and she will shed the egg along with the lining of her uterus during menstruation. If a pregnancy is going to occur, estrus is when it will happen. Therefore, it is in both the male and female animals' best interest to mate during estrus. To ensure that mating will occur, estrus is usually marked by some physical change in the female that signals to males of the species that she is in estrus and ready to mate. For example, many female chimpanzees have sexual swelling, or engorgement, of the external female genitals that indicates to male chimpanzees that it is time to mate.

Humans are a bit different from other mammals in that a human female has no defined period of estrus. Human females can mate at any time in the menstrual cycle, and although female estrogen levels do fluctuate during the menstrual cycle, estrogen is not closely related to human female libido. Evidence for the limited role of estrogen in sexual desire comes from cases of women who have had hysterectomies that involved removal of their ovaries. **Ovaries** are organs that produce eggs and estrogen in a woman's body. Without ovaries, a woman's estrogen levels plummet. Despite the drastic loss of estrogen, some women do not experience a loss of sexual desire after a hysterectomy (Sherwin & Gelfand, 1987). And for those women who do experience loss of desire, taking estrogen alone does not always increase desire or improve sexual response (Santoro et al., 2016).

In humans, **testosterone** is a hormone that plays a major role in regulating libido. Testosterone is part of a class of male hormones called *androgens*. Although testosterone is a male hormone, it is also found in females (likewise, males have estrogen). In males, the **testes** produce testosterone (in addition to sperm). In women, it is produced by the *adrenal glands* that sit above the kidneys. Adequate testosterone levels seem to be important in maintaining sexual desire. If testosterone levels fall too low, both males and females experience disinterest in sex (Gannon & Walsh, 2016; Meyer, 2016).

Gallo Images/Getty Images

▲ Some female mammals show visible signs when they are receptive to mating.

Testosterone may not be the only hormone that drives our desire, however. In females, estrogen also plays a role in sexual desire (Cappelletti & Wallen, 2016), and *oxytocin*, a hormone that plays a role in adult social bonding or attachment, may also be linked to libido (Seshadri, 2016). Oxytocin is released during sexual activity and may contribute to the feeling of closeness we feel toward our partner during sexual activity (Fisher, 2004). *Dopamine*, a neurotransmitter associated with pleasure and reward (Chapter 2), also influences sexual desire (Pfaus, 2009; Seshadri, 2016).

Are chemicals the sole cause of sexual desire? No. Although hormones and neurotransmitters play a significant role in our libido, sexual desire is not merely a function of chemicals in our bodies (Baumeister, 2004; Brotto et al., 2011; Chadwick et al., 2017). Our senses, our thoughts, and our culture also influence human sexual desire. Visual cues can increase or decrease sexual desire. For example, just fixating one's gaze on the chest or pelvic region of another can increase physiological arousal (Nummenmaa et al., 2012). Erotic photographs or movies may be a sexual turn-on for some people, but not for others (Gola et al., 2016). Seeing a lover nude or in sexy lingerie may be stimulating for some. Such visual stimulation seems to have a greater effect on men than on women (Reinisch, 1991). Sounds, such as a lover's voice or romantic music, may be appealing to some. Research also suggests that our sense of smell may play a role in sexual arousal (Stern & McClintock, 1998). For some it may be the scent of a particular cologne or perfume, whereas for others it may be natural body scents such as sweat. When fertile or at midcycle, women prefer the scent of males who have more masculine-looking faces. Similarly, men find the scent of women who are ovulating especially attractive (Gangestad, Thornhill, & Garver-Apgar, 2005), and they release more testosterone when exposed to the scent of ovulating women (Miller & Maner, 2010).

Juanmonino/E+/Getty Images

▲ Human sexual desire is more than just a matter of hormones.

Our sense of touch plays an even more direct role in sexual desire. Because nerve endings are unevenly distributed throughout the body, some areas of the skin are more sensitive to touch than others. These areas, called **erogenous zones**, include the genitals, buttocks, breasts, armpits, ears, navel, mouth, and the inner surfaces of the thighs. However, areas that may be highly stimulating to one person may produce a negative reaction in another; hence, our preferences in reaction to touch differ.

erogenous [eh-ROJ-en-ous] zones areas of the skin that are sensitive to touch

Many of the differences in our reactions to sensory cues exist because we all think differently about what should or should not be sexually stimulating. Such expectations may be learned or reflect the larger influence of gender roles and culture on our behavior. For instance, in the United States, we emphasize cleanliness and the masking of natural body odors with perfumes and deodorants. As a result, Americans may learn to consider perfumes and deodorants more sexually appealing than body sweat. In a culture where perfume and deodorant are not commonly used, people may find natural body odors more appealing.

Body chemicals, sensory cues, as well as, past personal experiences and cultural influences can all influence our sexual desire. But once we are willing to engage in sexual activity, a predictable cycle of physical responses occurs, as described in the next section.

5.3.2 The Sexual Response Cycle

In the 1960s, William Masters, a gynecologist, and Virginia Johnson, a nurse, were the first researchers to directly observe and measure the sexual responses of men and women engaged in a variety of sexual activities. Electronic sensors were placed on the bodies of the participants to directly measure physical responses. The participants were also interviewed in detail about their experiences. The information gathered in this study, subsequently published in Masters and Johnson's *Human Sexual Response* (1966), described the common physical

▲ Masters and Johnson pioneered field research on the sexual response of males and females.

changes that we experience in our sexual encounters. The model includes four successive phases: *excitement, plateau, orgasm,* and *resolution* (● FIGURE 5.9). Men and women were remarkably similar in their physical responses.

During the **excitement phase**, men and women experience an increase in heart rate and blood pressure. The nipples may become erect and blood flow is increased to the genital area. Males experience penile erection, and the scrotal sac thickens. Females produce vaginal lubrication, and the inner two-thirds of the vagina expands. The clitoris, the female sex organ that is extremely sensitive to sensation, swells. During the **plateau phase**, excitement peaks and remains somewhat constant. Breathing becomes rapid, and blood pressure and heart rate continue to rise. Men experience a full penile erection and fully elevated testes. A few droplets of fluid that can contain sperm may appear at the tip of the penis. In women, the inner part of the vagina expands fully and the uterus becomes elevated. The clitoris shortens and withdraws.

During the **orgasm phase**, breathing, blood pressure, and heart rate peak. Brain imaging studies suggest that in women, at least 80 different brain structures play a role in orgasm (Komisaruk & Whipple, 2011; Komisaruk et al., 2011). In the body, contractions of the pelvic muscles and the anal sphincter produce the sensation of orgasm. And other muscles throughout the body may also spasm during orgasm. In the male, the internal bodily contractions propel seminal fluid through the penis, causing ejaculation. Hence, in the male, the orgasm phase consists of two processes: orgasm and ejaculation. However, males' and females' subjective experiences of orgasm are actually quite similar (Mah & Binik, 2002; Vance & Wagner, 1976). Men and women describe the experience in much the same way.

The sexual response cycle concludes with the **resolution phase**, in which the body returns to its prearoused state. Breathing, heart rate, and blood pressure return to normal. The male loses his erection, and in the female the vagina, clitoris, and uterus return to their normal size and position. Yet a distinct gender difference occurs in sexual response during the resolution phase. Unlike women,

excitement phase the first stage of the sexual response cycle, in which males get erections and females produce vaginal lubrication

plateau phase the second stage of the sexual response cycle, in which excitement peaks

orgasm phase the third stage of the sexual response cycle, in which the pelvic and anal muscles contract

resolution phase the final stage of the sexual response cycle, in which the body returns to homeostasis

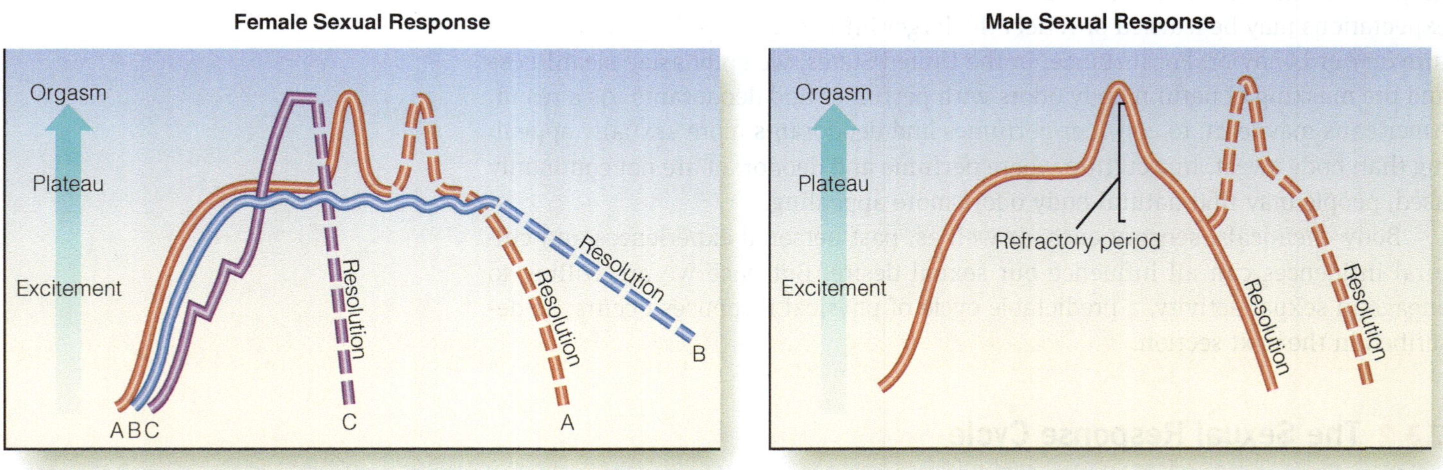

FIGURE 5.9

The Sexual Response Cycle

Masters and Johnson identified three basic patterns of response in females. A female may experience one or more orgasms (A), an extended plateau with no orgasm (B), or a rapid rise to orgasm with a quick resolution (C). Males show less variability in their sexual responses because of the refractory period.

Source: From *Human Sexual Response* by W. H. Masters and V. E. Johnson. Copyright © 1966 Little, Brown & Co.

men experience a **refractory period**, or a time during which they are physically incapable of experiencing another orgasm or ejaculation. This measure of time increases as men age. For an adolescent male, the refractory period may last only a few minutes, whereas for men over age 50, it may last from several minutes to a day. Because women do not undergo a refractory period, they can more easily be rearoused after orgasm, leading some women to experience repeated or multiple orgasms. Hence, compared to males, who experience refractory periods of varying lengths, there is greater variability in the female sexual response pattern (Figure 5.9; Masters, Johnson, & Kolodny, 1993).

refractory period a time during the resolution phase in which males are incapable of experiencing another orgasm or ejaculation

5.3.3 Variations in Sexuality: Generational, Age, Gender, and Sexual Orientation Differences

Although the experience of orgasm is similar for males and females, how we express our sexuality and the attitudes we hold about sex tend to vary more across generations and genders. Yet despite the central role that sex plays in our lives, large-scale studies of these sexual trends in society are not as common as you might think. In fact, only a handful of good studies have ever been conducted.

In one of these studies, researchers asked 27,500 men and women aged 40 to 80 years from 29 different countries questions about their sexual behavior. The results indicated that across the world sexuality is an important part of people's lives. Over 80% of the males and 65% of the females surveyed indicated that they had engaged in sexual intercourse in the past year (Nicolosi et al., 2004). These data suggest that contrary to popular myths about sexuality, middle-aged and older adults are very much interested in sex! But what factors influence sexuality in later life? Good health, maintaining regular sexual activity throughout the lifespan, feeling close to one's partner during sex, and the duration of one's relationship seem to be important factors in determining whether or not couples will still be enjoying a healthy sex life in later adulthood (Traeen et al., 2018).

There are, however, some interesting age and generational differences in sexuality. In 2010, London's Lloyds Pharmacy commissioned a survey of 3,000 British women. They found generational differences in the number of sexual partners women had had by age 24. Women who came of age between 2000 and 2009 reported having 5.65 partners by age 24. In contrast, young women of the 1970s reported having 3.72 by the same age, and women of the 1960s reported an average of 1.67 partners (Pinedo, 2010). These data suggest that women are taking more partners at a younger age than in the past—an especially important finding in light of the threat posed by HIV/AIDS and other sexually transmitted infections (see also Chapter 12).

An ABC News survey of American sexuality also revealed some generational differences in attitudes about sex (ABC News, 2004). This survey examined participants ranging from 18 to over 65 years of age, ensuring that participants came from several different generations: the Millennial Generation (those adults born after 1980), Generation X (those born between 1965 and 1980), Baby Boomers (those born between 1946 and 1964), and the Silent Generation (those born before 1946). • TABLE 5.2 summarizes some of the sexual differences seen across these generations.

As you can see from Table 5.2, the more recent generations tend to have more open and accepting attitudes about sexuality. It also appears that the attitudes of the Silent Generation (those born before 1946) differ the most from those of the other generations. However, a bit of caution in interpreting these data is in order. Remember that these data were collected in 2004, when the participants were at very different stages of life. It is possible that some of the differences seen are due more to the

TABLE 5.2 Generational Differences in Attitudes About Sexuality

Age (in 2004)	18–29 (Millennials & Gen X)	30–39 (Gen X)	40–49 (Baby Boomers)	50–64 (Baby Boomers & Silent Generation)	65+ (Silent Generation)
Discusses sexual fantasies with their partner	71%	55%	49%	37%	22%
Describes self as being sexually adventurous	55%	46%	41%	29%	19%
Feels that premarital sex is acceptable	71%	66%	69%	60%	30%
Feels that homosexuality is acceptable	65%	55%	55%	56%	40%

participants' stage of life than to the generation from which they come. This difficulty in interpreting data is very common when people of different ages or cohorts are tested at a single point in time.

Likewise, the National Survey of Sexual Health and Behavior (NSSHB), an ongoing project at the University of Indiana that has surveyed over 20,000 people aged 14–102 over a period of years, has revealed age-related differences in sexuality (Center for Sexual Health Promotion, 2019). However, it is hard to say whether these differences are due to age-related changes, generational influences, or a combination of the two. Among the more interesting findings was that 80.4% of the men 70 and older and 58.3% of women 70 and older reported having ever engaged in masturbation. Higher percentages of participants from the Millennial, Gen X, and Baby Boomer generations reported having engaged in masturbation at some point. Perhaps surprisingly, among male and female participants ages 18–69, the lowest levels of reported experience with masturbation came from Millennials aged 18–19 years (86.1% of males; 66% of females). However, Millennials ages 25–29 years reported the highest levels of experience with masturbation (94.3% of males, 84.6% of females; Herbenick et al., 2010). The fact that Millennials report both the lowest and highest levels of experience with masturbation may reflect both the sexual growth that occurs in late adolescence and the openness of the Millennial generation's attitudes about sex.

NSSHB participants were also asked to report whether they had had vaginal intercourse in the last month. As you might expect, the rates increased across early adulthood (up to age 29) and then began to decrease across young, middle, and late adulthood. This trend was seen for both males and females (Herbenick et al., 2010). Interestingly, respondents under age 30 were less likely to report kissing their partners during sex. The reason given for this was that kissing was seen as being too intimate an act (Herbenick et al., 2018). People over the age of 40 were least likely to report condom usage, and reports from participants of all ages suggest that the nature of sexual encounters varies widely across individuals (Center for Sexual Health Promotion, 2019). Although there may be age-related differences in the frequency and character of sexual behavior, don't take this to mean that sex is just for the young. Consistent with what was seen in the global study of adults (Nicolosi et al., 2004), American men and women also expressed interest in sex later in life. In fact, a full 42.9% of the men aged 70+ and 21.6% of the women aged 70+ reported having had vaginal intercourse within the last year (Herbenick at al., 2010).

▲ For many people, sexuality remains an important part of life well into late adulthood.

Engage Yourself! Sex is a fundamental part of life, but sex (especially unprotected sex) can expose us to sexually transmitted infections. Did you know that when you have sex with someone, you may be exposing yourself to infections that this person might have picked up from previous sexual partners? For this reason, the U.S. Centers for Disease Control and Prevention (CDC) recommends that all people aged 13–64 be tested at least once for HIV. Additional screening measures are recommended for sexually active women, pregnant women, men who have sex with other men, and all adults who have had unprotected sex and/or share drug injection equipment (CDC, 2016b). You can find a free and confidential testing center near your home by going to the CDC *GetTested* website. On this website, you can also explore links to information on STIs, risk factors, and protecting yourself from infection.

Although large-scale studies of sexuality across the life span and across generations are infrequently conducted, they do provide interesting information on our sexuality. One fact is clear: Despite the age and generation differences seen, sexuality is a vital and important aspect of our lives. For many people, sexuality remains an important part of life well into late adulthood.

5.3.4 Whom Do We Desire? Sexual Orientation

As we have seen, sexual desire and sexual arousal are states that most of us experience. Yet there are individual differences in sexuality. Some people experience higher levels of sexual desire than others, and there is great variability in whom we desire to have sex with. **Sexual orientation**—one's sexual attraction for members of the same and/or other sex—is one of the factors that influences our choice of sexual partners.

sexual orientation one's sexual attraction for members of the same and/or other sex

heterosexuals people who are sexually attracted primarily to members of the other sex

homosexuals people who are sexually attracted primarily to members of the same sex

bisexuals people who are sexually attracted to members of both sexes

Many people never question their sexual orientation, whereas others may be in doubt as they grapple with the developmental task of establishing their identity in adolescence (see Chapter 9). Traditionally people have classified sexual orientation into three categories. **Heterosexuals** are attracted to members of the other sex, **homosexuals** are attracted to members of the same sex, and **bisexuals** are attracted to members of both sexes. However, sexual orientation is not as fixed as these three terms suggest. Heterosexuality and homosexuality more often represent end points on a broad spectrum of behaviors that Kinsey and his colleagues (Kinsey, Pomeroy, & Martin, 1948) identified as a continuum of sexual orientation (● FIGURE 5.10). Moreover, sexual orientation may change over time, with women reporting greater change in orientation than men (Dickson et al., 2013; Kinnish, Strassberg, & Turner, 2005). The commonly used acronym LGBTQ (Lesbian, Gay, Bisexual, Transgender, Queer/Questioning) demonstrates the fact that people self-identify in many different ways, and there are some who would argue that these categories are not inclusive enough to truly capture sexual orientation.

Sexual Orientation and Sexual Behavior

When speaking of sexual orientation, one must be careful to distinguish between attraction and behavior. Sexual orientation is not simply a matter of whether you have sex with men or women. A man could be married to a woman, never have had sex with a man, but still identify as gay because he is attracted to men. A woman could have sex with other women but still consider herself to be heterosexual.

In the late 1940s, Alfred Kinsey (Kinsey et al., 1948, 1953) began a series of studies on sexual behavior in which he surveyed people on many aspects of their sexuality. Kinsey found that 37% of men and 13% of women had had at least

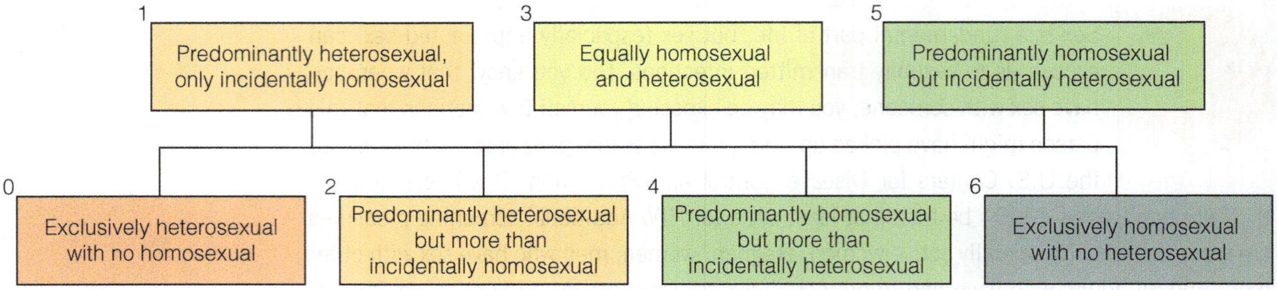

FIGURE 5.10

Kinsey's Continuum of Sexual Orientation

Sexual orientation may be expressed along a continuum of behaviors.

Source: Adapted from Kinsey, A. C., Pomeroy, W. B., & Martin, C. E. (1948). *Sexual behavior in the human male.* Philadelphia: Saunders., 1948, p. 638.

one same-sex sexual encounter, but not all of these people identified themselves as gay or lesbian. If this sounds confusing, it is. When trying to determine just how many people are homosexual, bisexual, or heterosexual, researchers have had some problems (Savin-Williams, 2006). Kinsey and his colleagues (1948) estimated that roughly 3% of the general population are exclusively homosexual.

In a more recent study of 12,287 young adults, the data support the notion that sexual orientation does not fall neatly into the traditional three categories. Approximately 1.7% of males and 0.9% of females identified as 100% homosexual; 0.7% of males and 0.8% of females identified as *mostly* homosexual; 0.5% of males and 2.3% of females identified as bisexual; 3.5% of males and 15.8% of females identified as being *mostly* heterosexual; and 93.6% of males and 80.2% of females identified as being 100% heterosexual (Savin-Williams, Joyner, & Rieger, 2012). Meanwhile data collected by the NSSHB indicated that 8% of males and 7% of females identified as being gay, lesbian, or bisexual (Center for Sexual Health Promotion, 2019).

It's hard to know how accurate any self-reported measures of sexual orientation are. The negative attitudes that some people hold about homosexuality make it difficult to get accurate data. It could well be that some people are reluctant to admit their true sexual feelings because they fear reprisals or feel personally stigmatized by their sexuality.

Variations: Attitudes Toward Gays and Lesbians Across the World

American attitudes toward gays and lesbians have become somewhat less negative over the last few decades. A search of Wikipedia found at least 88 dramatic television and online platform shows that premiered during 2018–2019 that had at least one character who engaged in same-sex sexual activity (Wikipedia, 2019). These numbers suggest that the public is becoming more comfortable with homosexuality.

In 1973, the American Psychiatric Association eliminated homosexuality from its list of mental illnesses and in 1980 dropped it from its *Diagnostic and Statistical Manual* (*DSM;* discussed in Chapter 13). Moreover, based on evidence that gay and lesbian relationships are influenced by the same set of variables that influence heterosexual marriages, the American Psychological Association passed a resolution declaring it unfair and discriminatory to deny same-sex couples legal access to civil marriage (APA, 2004).

As attitudes become more accepting of homosexuality, societal change is clearly occurring. As of 2019, at least 27 countries have legalized same-sex marriage (Pew Research Center, 2019).

Although societal change is taking place, **homophobia**, or prejudice against homosexuals, has not disappeared. In 2017, there were 1,130 victims of hate crime offenses that were based on sexual orientation (FBI, 2017). Approximately 80% to 90% of gay, lesbian, bisexual, and transgender youth report having experienced verbal abuse in a school setting (Mueller et al., 2015). Compared to heterosexual teens, lesbian, gay, and bisexual youth face higher rates of dating violence (Dank et al., 2014). Gay, lesbian, and bisexual adults also report higher levels of domestic abuse, sexual assault, and childhood abuse than heterosexuals (Balsam, Rothblum, & Beauchaine, 2005; Sweet & Welles, 2012).

Red Umbrella and Donkey/Shutterstock.com

Thinkstock/Getty Images

▲ Gays, lesbians, and bisexuals face many prejudices in today's society. Yet their relationships are influenced by the same variables that influence heterosexual relationships.

homophobia prejudicial attitudes against homosexuals and homosexuality

As of 2019, 31 states and the District of Columbia had enacted laws against hate crimes motivated by sexual orientation (Human Rights Campaign, 2019). Many religions condemn homosexual behavior as immoral (Kashubeck-West et al., 2017). Others see homosexuality as a mental illness that should be cured. Some studies do suggest that lesbian, gay, and bisexual persons are more likely to report having mental health problems (Kuyper & Fokkema, 2011; Oswalt & Wyatt, 2011). However not all studies show such a trend. For example, one study of people in U.S. urban environments indicated that only individuals who identify as bisexual are at increased risk of psychological distress (Nam et al., 2019). Furthermore, when sexual minorities experience increased psychological distress, it could be the result of *minority stress* (see Chapter 12), or being forced as a minority member to live in an environment where majority members hold negative stereotypes and prejudices against one's group (Kuyper & Fokkema, 2011). Research further suggests that mostly heterosexual adults, who still harbor internal feelings of negativity about their same-sex attraction, may be most at risk for mental health issues (Kuyper & Bos, 2016).

Despite lingering sexual orientation-based prejudice, homosexual and heterosexual relationships tend to be similar in some important ways. Homosexuals are just as committed and satisfied in their romantic relationships as heterosexuals (Roisman et al., 2008). Furthermore, decades of research show that children of gay and lesbian parents do not differ in adjustment or development when compared to children raised by heterosexual couples (Patterson, 2006).

The negative attitudes that some Americans hold toward gays and lesbians are not shared by all cultures. In fact, many cultures openly accept homosexuality as a natural part of life. One study of 190 societies across the world found that approximately two-thirds of them accepted homosexuality (Ford & Beach, 1951). Why do some people abhor homosexuality or see it as a mental illness, whereas others see it as a normal variation of human sexuality? Perhaps these differing points of view stem from beliefs about what causes sexual orientation (Mucherah, Owino, & McCoy, 2016).

What Causes One's Sexual Orientation?

One common mistake that people make when trying to answer this question is to confuse sexual orientation with gender. *Gender* is the collection of personality traits that your society typically associates with either males or females. Gender is not the same thing as sexual orientation. For instance, a gay male may be very masculine or very feminine. Likewise, a heterosexual woman may be either masculine or feminine. In other words, not all feminine men are gay, and not all masculine women are lesbians.

Having said that, there is some indication in the research that early gender-related behavior may be a predictor of later sexual orientation *for some*. Some studies have shown that gender-nonconforming behavior (masculine behavior in girls, feminine behavior in boys) during childhood is correlated with later homosexuality in both men and women (Rieger, Gygax, & Bailey, 2008). Be careful about how you interpret these findings, though. Not all boys who prefer feminine activities become gay, nor do all girls who prefer masculine activities become lesbian. In fact, in one study, approximately half of the adult gay male participants had a preference for traditionally masculine activities in childhood (Bell, Weinberg, & Hammersmith, 1981). Also, even if some gays and lesbians showed a preference for gender-nonconforming activities in childhood, this does not indicate that the activities made them homosexual. It is just as likely that their homosexuality stemmed from other causes. In fact, in less stereotyped cultures in which children are not pressured to be masculine or feminine, there is less tendency for gay males to have exhibited feminine behavior in childhood (Ross, 1980).

Genetics is another possible cause of sexual orientation. A genetic link for homosexuality has been investigated in the traditional ways—by examining pairs of identical and fraternal twins who are gay and by examining familial rates of homosexuality. Such studies find a higher *concordance rate* (percentage of pairs in which both twins are homosexual) among identical twins than fraternal twins. This trend holds true for both male and female participants. Overall, the causes of male sexual orientation have received more research attention than female sexuality has. A review of this research suggests that male sexual orientation is at least moderately heritable (Chaladze, 2016; Dawood, Bailey, & Martin, 2009). Although the picture is less clear for females, the preliminary evidence also suggests that genetics plays a role in determining female sexual orientation (Dawood et al., 2009).

Other investigations have found that gay men have a greater number of older brothers than heterosexual men—a phenomenon called the *fraternal birth order effect* (Blanchard, 2008; Schwartz et al., 2010; Swift-Gallant et al., 2019). Discovery of this phenomenon led to development of the *maternal immune hypothesis*, which suggests that some mothers may become increasingly immune to prenatal male hormones as they bear sons. In other words, their bodies may produce more antibodies to male hormones, creating a different prenatal hormonal environment that may affect subsequent male fetuses (Bogaert & Skorska, 2011).

Similarly, research has found that homosexuals have a greater chance of being left-handed than heterosexuals, an attribute that is believed to be established prior to birth (Lippa, 2003; Swift-Gallant et al., 2019). Such findings suggest that prenatal factors are related to sexual orientation (Rahman, 2005).

In conclusion, data indicate a strong biological role in sexual orientation. However, as of this moment, no one can say for sure just what causes our sexual orientation. The continuum of sexual orientation is in all likelihood related to the interaction among biological, psychological, and environmental forces that results in different pathways for every person.

5.3 Quiz Yourself

1. **Which is true of animals, but not of humans?**
   a. Testosterone regulates sex drive.
   b. Menstruation follows ovulation.
   c. Mating occurs only during estrus.
   d. Hormones influence sexual behavior.
2. **While dancing with his girlfriend, Malik notices that he has an erection. He is in which stage of the sexual response cycle?**
   a. Excitement
   b. Plateau
   c. Orgasm
   d. Resolution
3. **Paul has been married for 5 years to Lisa. However, he is primarily sexually attracted to men and not to women. What is Paul's sexual orientation?**
   a. Heterosexual
   b. Homosexual
   c. Bisexual
   d. Both a and b

Answers 1. c; 2. a; 3. b

5.4 Theories and Expression of Emotion

If you ask people to define emotion, you will get a variety of answers. Most people will probably say that emotions are *feelings*. Some people will give examples, such as *happiness, sadness,* or *anger,* but few will be able to produce a good definition of what an emotion actually is. Even psychologists have had trouble defining what is meant by an emotion.

One definition is that an **emotion** is a complex reaction to some internal or external event that involves physiological reactions, behavioral reactions, facial expressions, cognition, and affective, or emotional, responses (Lazarus, 1991). For example, let's imagine that you are walking through the woods and you hear some rustling up ahead. You look up and see a large bear in your path. This event would likely cause an emotional reaction of *fear.* Your experience of fear would have several aspects to it:

emotion a complex reaction to some internal or external event that involves physiological reactions, behavioral reactions, facial expressions, cognition, and affective responses

- *Physiological reactions*: Your heart rate would increase, your respiration would increase, your pupils would dilate, and your muscles would tense.
- *Behavioral reactions*: You might freeze in your tracks. You might run (an unwise choice in this situation). You might yell at the bear.
- *Facial expressions*: Fear would show on your face. If someone were to observe you at this moment, they would likely recognize that you were afraid.
- *Cognition*: You might think about the TV show you saw on bears last week and what the experts said that you should do in this situation. You might think about what you will do if the bear charges.

- *Affective responses*: You would have some subjective reaction to this situation. For example, "I am scared," or—if you are an animal lover—"I'm thrilled!"

As you can see, emotions are complex. Perhaps that is why psychologists have had a difficult time defining exactly what an emotion is. Another confusing aspect of emotion is that emotion is very similar to motivation. In fact, emotions can produce motivation (Mega, Ronconi, & De Beni, 2014; Zaalberg, Manstead, & Fischer, 2004). In our previous example, your fear of the bear might motivate you to run or to yell at the bear. So what separates emotions from motivation? What makes fear different from hunger? One unique element is the **affective component of emotion**, the subjective experience of what you are *feeling* that fills your consciousness during the emotion. When you are scared, you *know* that you are scared because you *feel* the affective state of fear. This affective quality of emotion allows us to clearly know when we are feeling an emotion.

affective component of emotion the subjective experience of what you are feeling during the emotion

James-Lange theory a theory of emotion that defines an emotion as a unique pattern of physiological arousal

Emotions can also be distinguished from motivation in that they are usually (but not always) sparked by things outside our bodies. For instance, when we see a depressing movie, we may feel sad. Or when we see a baby, we may feel happy. Motivation, in contrast, often comes from some internal source—hunger may be initiated by low blood sugar or an empty stomach. Motives tend to be sparked by a specific need or goal, but emotions can be elicited by many stimuli. For instance, many things can make us happy, but only a few conditions will lead to hunger.

Although psychologists have struggled with the concept of emotion, several notable theories of emotion have been set out over the years. Let's take a look at some of them now.

5.4.1 The James-Lange Theory of Emotion

American psychologist William James and Danish physiologist Carl Lange each proposed one of the earliest theories of emotion at approximately the same point in history (James, 1884). Their theory, now called the **James-Lange theory** of emotion, states that emotion is *equal* to the pattern of physiological arousal that the person experiences during an emotion. In short, emotion is a physiological response to some stimulus. In our example of meeting the bear in the woods, from the James-Lange point of view, the emotion you feel is the pattern of physiological reactions you have as you see the bear. Your physiological reactions—the increased heart rate and the increased respiration—are the emotion of fear that you would experience in this situation. In the James-Lange view, emotion is a purely physiological event.

Renee Lynn/Corbis/VCG/Getty Images

▲ How would you feel if you came across a bear while hiking in the woods?

Cannon's Criticisms of the James-Lange Theory

The James-Lange view of emotion has had many critics. One important critic was Walter Cannon, who noted that for the James-Lange theory to adequately explain emotion, there would have to be a *different* bodily response for each emotion we experience. If emotion is simply a physiological and bodily response, the only way to discriminate among emotions would be if there were different physical reactions for each emotion. Cannon doubted that this was true and, in fact, offered three good reasons to doubt the James-Lange view (Cannon, 1927). His first criticism, which we just mentioned, is that the physiological experience of emotion does not appear to vary from emotion to emotion to the degree that would be necessary to distinguish one emotion from another based purely on our physiological reaction. For example, the physiological experience of anger is not very different from that of terror—both involve increased heart rate, muscle tension, and so forth.

Second, Cannon argued that the physiological, bodily aspect of emotion sometimes follows our subjective experience of the emotion. For example, we may know that we are afraid *before* we feel our heart pounding and our muscles tensing. In the James-Lange view, there can be no emotion before there is a physiological response.

Cannon's third criticism was that artificially created physiological responses do not give rise to emotions. For example, drinking a lot of coffee may increase your physiological arousal, but it does not cause you to experience fear, excitement, love, or any other emotion. If emotion were nothing more than a physiological response, it would stand to reason that artificially caused physiological responses would also cause emotional responses.

In light of these criticisms, Cannon proposed that emotion does not originate in the body; rather, it originates in the brain. According to Cannon, when you see a bear in the woods, your fear is not due to the increased heart rate and rapid breathing you experience. Instead, when you see the bear, your brain causes you to feel fear. You may even be aware that you are afraid before you become aware of your rapidly beating heart and your panting breath. Cannon's explanation of emotion was later extended by a man named Philip Bard, and today this theory is called the **Cannon-Bard theory** of emotion.

Cannon-Bard theory a theory of emotion that states that emotions originate in the brain, not the body

Modern Support for the James-Lange Theory

Of Cannon's three criticisms, by far the most problematic was the first one—that physiological responses are too similar to allow us to adequately discriminate among the many emotions we feel. For many years this criticism was seen as a fatal blow to the James-Lange theory. Things change, however, and in the 1990s, some new evidence gave the James-Lange theory new life. By the 1990s, psychologists had new tools for studying bodily reactions. In addition to precisely measuring heart rate, researchers could now measure minute changes in skin temperature and in the electrical conductivity of the skin that indicates small changes in the moisture of the skin. With these measurement techniques, it is now possible to examine the physiological response that accompanies emotions in greater detail than was possible in Cannon's time.

Using measures such as these, researchers have been able to show that some emotions do indeed involve different bodily reactions (Kreibig, 2010; Kreibig, Samson, & Gross, 2015). For example, when participants were asked to make facial expressions for the emotions of fear, anger, happiness, disgust, sadness, and surprise, and to hold these expressions for 10 seconds, just as the James-Lange theory predicts, there were slight but noticeable differences in heart rate, skin temperature, and other physiological reactions for the different emotions. Although all of the emotions caused changes in heart rate and skin temperature, it was the degree of change that separated the emotions from one another (● FIGURE 5.11) (Levenson, Ekman, & Friesen, 1990). Likewise, watching film

Yellowj/Shutterstock.com

▲ According to the James-Lange theory of emotion, this woman is experiencing joy because her body has reacted with a characteristic pattern of physiological changes in response to this event. In contrast, the Cannon-Bard theory proposes that this woman's joy originated in her mind rather than in her body.

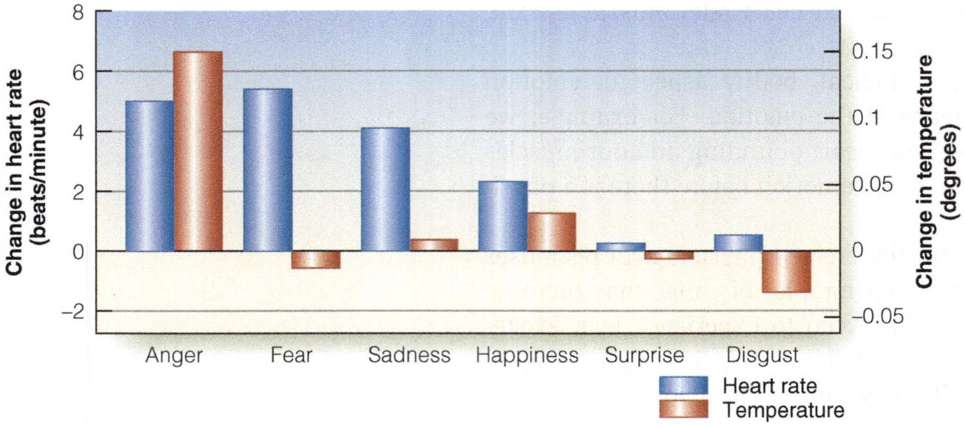

FIGURE 5.11

Physiological Changes for Six Different Emotions

Note the varying degrees of change for these different emotions.

Source: Levenson, R. W., Ekman, P., & Friesen, W. V. (1990). Voluntary facial action generates emotion-specific nervous system activity. *Psychophysiology*, 27, 363–384.

clips that induce amusement, disgust, or mixed emotions, has been shown to elicit differing patterns of physiological arousal (Keribig, Samson, & Gross, 2015).

These results indicate that there may be some merit to the James-Lange approach, but they do not necessarily support the entire theory. They do not address Cannon's other two criticisms—that physiological reactions sometimes follow our awareness of emotions and that artificially created arousal does not seem to directly cause the experience of emotion. Even if patterns of physiological arousal do help us discriminate among emotions, other factors may still be involved in the experience of emotion. One of these factors could be feedback from our faces.

5.4.2 The Facial Feedback Hypothesis

facial feedback hypothesis a theory that states that our emotional state is affected by the feedback our brain gets from facial muscles

You may have noticed that in the experiment we just described, the researchers induced the different emotions in an unusual way (Levenson et al., 1990): having the participants make and hold facial expressions of the desired emotion for 10 seconds. In other words, they induced the emotional state through the facial expression of the emotion. How does this work? Doesn't the emotion come *before* the facial expression? Well, maybe not entirely, according to the **facial feedback hypothesis** (McIntosh, 1996). This theory proposes that our experience of an emotion is affected by the feedback our brain gets from our facial muscles. Thus, smiling can influence us to feel happy, and frowning can influence us to feel bad. In one study, participants were asked to smell and rate a series of odors while either smiling or frowning. Consistent with the facial feedback hypothesis, they rated the smells more positively when they were smiling and less positively when they were frowning (Kraut, 1982). In another study, participants who experienced involuntary frowning as a result of facing the sun while walking reported increased feelings of aggressiveness (Marzoli et al., 2013). Based on a metanalysis of 138 studies, the configuration of your facial muscles does seem to influence your mood (Coles, Larsen, & Lench, 2019). But why would this be true?

One possibility is that the configuration of your facial muscles affects the blood flow to your brain, which in turn affects the temperature of your brain. Certain configurations, such as frowns, may change blood flow to the brain in a way that increases the temperature of the brain. Other facial configurations, such as smiles, may result in blood flow changes that decrease the brain's temperature. Brain temperature, in turn, may affect the release of certain neurotransmitters that affect mood. As wild as this sounds, some evidence suggests that it might be true.

Researchers have been successful in detecting participants' emotions of joy, disgust, anger, fear, and sadness from the temperature patterns on their faces (Cruz-Albarran et al., 2017). In a study of drivers, feelings of power were successfully detected using facial temperature (Zhang, Ihme, & Drewitz, 2019). And, participants who read stories that contained words that forced them to repeatedly hold their mouths in a position that was similar to smiling rated their story more positively than the other participants who read a story that was equally positive in emotional tone, but did not contain words that forced them to approximate a smile. Furthermore, when researchers looked at the participants' forehead temperatures, those who read the story that forced them to approximate a smile had lower forehead temperatures. It appears that when we smile, we hold our facial muscles in such a way as to promote blood flow that reduces brain temperature, which somehow improves mood (Zajonc, Murphy, & Inglehart, 1989). Studies such as these suggest that there may actually be something to being a "hothead" or keeping a "cool head"!

GoGo Images Corporation /Alamy stock photo

Dean Drobot/Shutterstock.com

▲ The facial feedback hypothesis maintains that feedback from facial muscles sent to the brain can affect our emotional state. Therefore, these men are experiencing different emotions, in part, because their brains are receiving very different messages from their faces.

5.4.3 The Schachter-Singer Two-Factor Theory of Emotion

All the theories of emotion we have looked at so far see emotion in primarily physiological terms. Certainly physiological responses and facial expressions are part of an emotional experience—but what about cognition? Do our thoughts play a role in our emotions? Some theorists, including psychologists Stanley Schachter and Jerome Singer, believe that they do. Their **two-factor theory of emotion** states that emotions are a product of both physiological arousal *and* cognitive interpretations of this arousal. Schachter and Singer agreed with Cannon that we do not have a separate pattern of physiological arousal for each emotion we experience; rather, when we experience an emotion, we experience a nondistinct, general physiological arousal. We then use the situational context to help us cognitively interpret the meaning of this arousal. This cognitive interpretation leads to the experience of an emotion. Going back to our example of the bear in the woods, when we see the bear, we become aroused and our heart begins to beat faster. Next, we interpret why we are reacting this way, given the context of the situation. Because we are faced with a potentially dangerous wild animal, our arousal is likely to be interpreted as stemming from fear. Therefore, we label our emotional experience as fear.

In one of their studies, Schachter and Singer (1962) gave participants an injection of epinephrine, a stimulant that causes increased heart rate, respiration, and nervousness. Some of the participants were accurately informed about what to expect from the injection. Others were told that the injection was a harmless shot that would produce no symptoms. After receiving the injection, all of the participants were asked to sit in a waiting room with another participant. But the "participants" they were sent to wait with were *confederates*, or actors playing a part in the experiment. In one condition, the confederate acted angry. He complained, stomped his feet, and eventually left the waiting room in a huff. In the other condition, the confederate acted happy. He appeared joyful, tossed paper airplanes, and generally acted a bit silly.

The dependent variable in the experiment was the mood of the participants after their time in the waiting room with the confederate. Schachter and Singer reasoned that the mood of the informed participants would not be influenced by the mood of the confederate. Because the informed participants would interpret their arousal as being due to the drug and not due to some emotional state, there was no reason for their mood to be influenced by the confederate. At the same time, Schachter and Singer predicted that the mood of the uninformed participants would indeed be influenced by the mood of the confederate. Because they did not have a ready (cognitive) explanation for their arousal, the uninformed participants would look to the situation to help them interpret their reactions. If the confederate was happy, the participants interpreted their arousal as part of a positive

two-factor theory of emotion a theory that states that emotions result when we cognitively interpret our physiological reactions in light of the situation emotional state. If the confederate was angry, then the participants interpreted their arousal as part of a negative emotional state.

The results confirmed Schachter and Singer's predictions. The mood of the informed participants was not influenced by the confederate's mood, but the confederate did influence the mood of the uninformed participants. The uninformed participants who waited with the angry confederate reported feeling angrier than did the informed participants. The uninformed participants who waited with the happy confederate reported feeling happier than did the informed participants. It appears that the uninformed participants used the situation to help them figure out their own emotions.

Although Schachter and Singer and others (Brown & Curhan, 2013) have produced experimental evidence to support the notion that arousal can affect our emotional states, the two-factor theory has not stood the test of time well. Decades of research on the two-factor theory show that there is little reason to believe that emotions *require* physiological arousal or that emotions necessarily come from labeling unexplained physiological arousal. For example, people who've been given beta-blocking drugs that prevent autonomic nervous system arousal (i.e., a fight or flight reaction) still report experiencing emotions that are relevant to their current environment (Reisenzein, 1983). Despite doubts about the two-factor theory, Schachter and Singer's contribution to the study of emotion is significant. They introduced the idea that cognition plays an important role in emotion, and many theorists recognize that thoughts are part of the emotional experience.

5.4.4 Lazarus's Cognitive-Mediational Theory of Emotion

cognitive-mediational theory a theory of emotion that states that our cognitive appraisal of a situation determines what emotion we will feel in the situation

According to Richard Lazarus (1995), cognition is the most important part of emotion. Unlike Schachter and Singer, who thought that emotion results from the cognitive interpretation of preexisting physiological arousal, Lazarus's **cognitive-mediational theory** of emotion states that our initial *cognitive appraisal* of a situation determines what emotion we will feel in the situation. Going back to the bear example, if you see a bear in the woods one day after having seen a show on TV about some hikers who were killed by a bear, you would likely feel a lot of fear! On the other hand, you might feel less fear on encountering the bear if your only knowledge of bears came from a TV show about a boy and his pet bear. According to cognitive-mediational theory, your appraisal of the situation determines your specific emotion.

Differing appraisals are one reason different people react with different emotions in the same situation (see also Chapter 12). Cognitive-mediational theory also suggests that the best way to control our emotions is by controlling how we perceive situations in life. For instance, a student who perceives that they received a poor grade because the teacher doesn't like them will likely get angry. A calmer student may simply see the grade as a challenge to work harder and not get mad. Teaching yourself to appraise events like this as opportunities and not as threats may help you become a happier, more successful student.

Variations: Gender Differences in Emotional Regulation

Even if your initial appraisal of a situation is such that it leads to negative emotions, research shows that we can still regulate our emotions by reappraising the situation in a more positive light (Song et al., 2019). For example, a woman might initially assume that a man bumped into her on purpose, leading her to feel angry. She then quickly reappraises the situation, realizing that he probably bumped into her by accident. This reappraisal is likely to lessen or even eliminate her anger. Developing the ability to regulate our emotions helps us to function well in many everyday situations (McRae, 2016). Do males and females differ in their ability to regulate their emotional reactions?

Kateri McRae and colleagues (2008) found that although males and females did not differ with respect to how they reacted emotionally to an event, they did show different patterns of brain activity during reappraisal of these events. As the participants attempted to reduce their negative emotional reactions to upsetting pictures through reappraisal (e.g., by reminding themselves that disturbing scenes were just pictures and not real), activity levels in their prefrontal cortex, amygdala, and ventral striatal (a reward center in the brain) were monitored. Relative to the male participants, the females seemed to engage these parts of the brain more during the reappraisal process (● FIGURE 5.12).

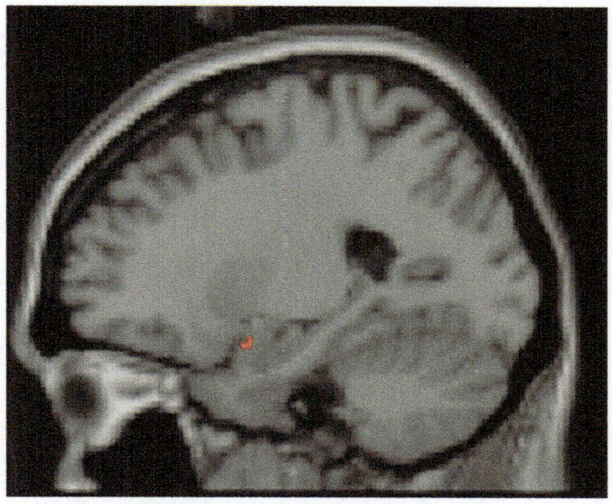

FIGURE 5.12

Gender Differences in Brain Functioning During Cognitive Reappraisal

In this fMRI scan, you can see the left amygdala in red. Relative to male participants, female participants used the amygdala, prefrontal cortex, and ventral striatal more as they attempted to reappraise an emotional situation in order to reduce their negative emotions.

McRae, K., Ochsner, K. N., Mauss, I. B., Gabrieli, J. J. D., & Gross, J. J. (2008). Gender differences in emotion regulation: An fMRI study of cognitive reappraisal. *Group Processes & Intergroup Relations, 11,* 143–162. Reprinted with permission.

The meaning of these brain differences is not yet clear, but McRae and colleagues speculate that relative to women, men may not need to expend as much cognitive effort to control their negative emotions (i.e., less prefrontal and amygdala activity for men). It is also possible that during reappraisal, women must work to initiate positive emotions to help counteract their own negative emotions (i.e., more ventral striatal activity for females). Nonetheless, it is important to note that although male and female participants initiated different brain processes to control their emotion, they were equally able to do so. The stereotype that women are more emotional and less able to control their emotions was not supported in this study (McRae et al., 2008).

Is Cognition Essential to Emotion?

Although it is clear that cognitive appraisals do influence our emotional states (McRae et al., 2012; van Reekum et al., 2004), not everyone agrees that cognition is an essential part of emotion. Robert Zajonc has argued that we can have an emotional reaction to something that is completely independent of our thoughts. In one study, Zajonc (1980) showed English-speaking participants Japanese ideographs (the symbols of the Japanese language). Each ideograph was presented either frequently or infrequently. Later, the participants were asked to rate their preference for ideographs. Despite having no knowledge about the meaning of the ideographs, the participants showed a clear preference for some of them. They preferred the ideographs that they had seen more frequently to the ones they had seen infrequently. Zajonc called this phenomenon of preferring things to which we have had the most exposure the **mere exposure effect**. He reasoned that because the participants did not know the meaning of the ideographs, their emotional reactions to them could not have been influenced by cognition. Rather, their emotions were purely physiological. We will examine the mere exposure effect again in Chapter 10 when we look at its implications for romantic attraction.

mere exposure effect the idea that the more one is exposed to something, the more one grows to like it

5.4.5 Communicating Emotions: Culture, Gender, and Facial Expressions

Imagine that you have traveled to a place where you do not understand the local language. How will you communicate with these people? Perhaps you will try to use gestures to communicate with someone, but how will you choose which person? How will you tell if a particular person is likely to react kindly to your attempts at communication? One way would be to read the emotional expression on the person's face. Do they look happy? Do they look angry? This could be a crucial source of information for you. But what about the cultural differences in this situation? Can we read the emotional expressions of someone from an unfamiliar culture? This is another question psychologists have tried to answer.

basic emotions a proposed set of innate emotions that are common to all humans and from which other higher-order emotions may derive

Engage Yourself!

Before you read any further, look at the pictures in FIGURE 5.13. Can you identify the emotions that these people are feeling? These pictures represent the facial expressions of what psychologists call basic emotions. **Basic emotions** are defined as emotions that all humans are thought to have, regardless of cultural background. The idea behind basic emotions is that the capacity for these emotions is genetically programmed in us as a result of evolution. Many psychologists believe that *anger*, *happiness*, *fear*, and *sadness* are basic emotions, but there is disagreement about what other emotions might be basic. Some add disgust, shame, interest, surprise, and anxiety to the list (Turner & Ortony, 1992). But others do not. Furthermore, some believe that basic emotions can blend together to give us more complex emotions (e.g., guilt, pride; Plutchik, 1984) or compound emotions (happy-surprise, angry-surprise; Du & Martinez, 2015). More recently, researchers have recognized that emotional displays are *multimodal*. We do not just display emotion in our faces, but also in our body language, tone of voice, and so on. Nonetheless, much of the early work on basic emotions generally focused on facial expressions of emotion (Ekman, 1973). When studies examine the multimodal display of emotion, the studies suggest that humans are able to display over 20 distinct emotions using some combination of facial, bodily, vocal, etc., displays (Keltner et al., 2019). So, were you able to accurately identify the facial expressions? From left to right, top to bottom, they are *happiness*, *anger*, *sadness*, *surprise*, *disgust*, and *fear*.

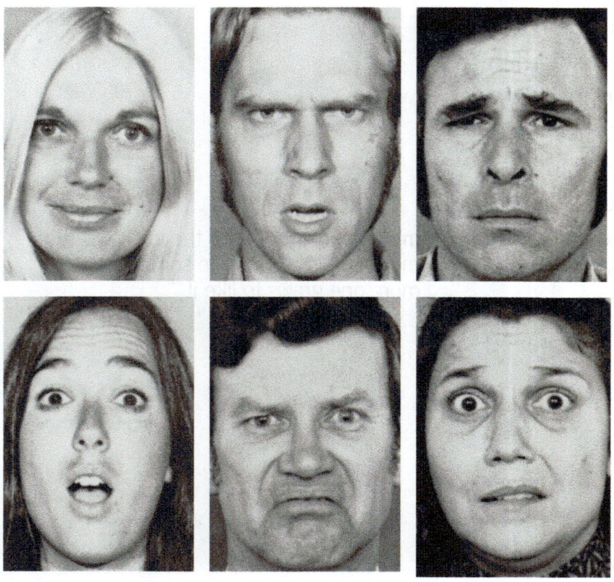

FIGURE 5.13

Can You Identify These Emotions?

P. Ekman & W. Friesen, *Unmasking the Face,* 2nd Edition 1984. Used by permission of Ekman.

Paul Ekman (1973) showed pictures like those in Figure 5.13 to people from Argentina, Brazil, Chile, Japan, and the United States and asked participants to identify the emotions being expressed. He found that people were generally able to identify the emotions regardless of their culture, although some emotions appeared to be more universal than others. Happiness appeared to be the easiest emotion to identify (Recio, Schacht, & Sommer, 2013). People from the different cultures disagreed the most when identifying fear and anger. Other studies have shown that fear and surprise are easily confused, but that women are better than men at discriminating between these emotions. In general, women have been shown to be faster than men in identifying others' facial expressions of emotion, but they are not always found to be more accurate than men. Gender differences in the ability to recognize facial expressions depends on other factors, such as the sex of the person displaying the emotion, the emotion, and the age of the person displaying the emotion (Parmley & Cunningham, 2014).

In addition to facial expression, we also seem to be able to discern the basic emotions from the sounds that people make. Ekman and colleagues found that Western and Namibian participants were both good at detecting basic emotions in each other's nonverbal vocalizations, such as laughs and screams that transcend language barriers (Sauter et al., 2010). Further support for the notion of basic emotions comes from research using neuroimaging technologies to show that specific and distinct patterns of neural activity in the brain are linked to the basic emotions (Duan et al., 2010; Vytal & Hamann, 2010).

However, researchers have found that people from different cultures have different **display rules** governing when it is and isn't appropriate to display certain emotions. For example, in the United States, it would be considered inappropriate for a person to display fear or sadness during a business meeting. And if an Arab man is insulted, he must respond with a display of extreme anger to avoid dishonor (Heine, 2008). People from different cultures may also have slightly different ways of displaying emotions through facial expressions—somewhat similar to how speakers of the same language can have different accents or dialects (Elfenbein et al., 2007). It is also possible that in addition to cultural display rules, we may learn to regulate our emotional reactions themselves so as to avoid the possibility of violating the rules for displaying emotion in our culture (De Leersnyder, Boiger, & Mesquita, 2013). For example, an American business-person may adjust their cognitive appraisal of the events in a business meeting so as to avoid feeling sadness, because they feel it is inappropriate.

display rules cultural rules governing when it is and isn't appropriate to display certain emotions

So, does the fact that at least some emotions (e.g., happiness) translate fairly well across cultures guarantee that these emotions are basic emotions? Perhaps not. Some cultures list "basic" emotions that may be recognizable to people from other cultures but would not be considered basic emotions in those other cultures. For example, Hindus list *peace, wonder, amusement,* and *heroism* as basic emotions (Hejmadi, Davidson, & Rozin, 2000). Americans may be able to feel these emotions and recognize them in others, but may not consider them to be basic emotions. For reasons like these, some people have begun to question whether basic emotions truly exist (Ortony & Turner, 1990). Regardless of whether basic emotions exist, emotions are powerful tools of communication. A smile can signal friendliness to many people—regardless of background or culture.

5.4 Quiz Yourself

1. **Which of the following is not traditionally thought of as a basic emotion?**
   a. Fear
   b. Sadness
   c. Pride
   d. Happiness

2. **Derrick and Monique each went out on blind dates. Derrick took his date to dinner. Monique took her date to a football game. According to the two-factor theory of emotion, who is more likely to go out on a second date with their partner?**
   a. Derrick
   b. Monique
   c. Monique and Derrick are equally likely to go out on a second date.
   d. Two-factor theory makes no predictions about this situation.

3. **Mohammed and Betty are each stuck in a traffic jam. Mohammed remains calm, but Betty begins to get very angry. Which theory of emotion best explains Mohammed's and Betty's different emotions in this situation?**
   a. Cognitive-mediational theory
   b. Two-factor theory
   c. Facial feedback theory
   d. James-Lange theory

Answers 1. c; 2. b; 3. a

5.5 Integrating Psychology: The Big Picture

When Jean-Dominique Bauby had his stroke, the loss of portions of his brainstem left him in a permanent state of locked-in syndrome. For the remainder of his life, he was unable to voluntarily move most of his body. The only part of his body that was still under his conscious control was his left eyelid, which he could blink at will. A relatively small disruption in Bauby's biological functioning had profound effects on his ability to function, changing the course of his development for the remainder of his life.

But not all of Bauby's abilities were devastated by the stroke. His ability to sense and perceive the world was left primarily intact. His conscious mind was untouched, leaving him able to process information in a normal fashion. Through blinking, he could still use language to maintain social relationships with those around him. As for many of us, social interaction was important to Bauby, for he still felt emotions and he still had needs. Like most of us, Bauby felt normal emotions, including fear, sadness, love, and happiness. He also experienced normal human motivations, including hunger, sexual desire, and the need to achieve. The desire to express himself and connect with others provided Bauby with the intrinsic motivation to blink the some 250,000 times needed to write *The Diving Bell and the Butterfly.* Writing a bestselling book is a rare achievement—even for a healthy person—but then again, Bauby was a remarkable man. Where many of us would give up, Bauby was still motivated to live life to its fullest.

Bauby's story shows the crucial role that our biology plays in our ability to function in everyday life. The biological functioning of the nervous and endocrine systems underlies our ability to sense and perceive our conscious awareness, and our motivational and emotional processes. All aspects of our mental processes and behavior are affected by our biology.

In our next part, we will turn our attention to the *cognitive* dimension of psychology—the mental processes that guide our behavior and allow us to function in the world. Like our biology, our cognitive processes can have profound effects on our ability to function. In Chapter 6, we will examine how we learn. In Chapter 7, we will examine how we process information in the memory systems of our minds. And in Chapter 8, we will examine the cognitive processes that underlie our daily functioning, including the language we use to communicate with one another and the intelligence that allows us to solve the problems we face in life. As you read these chapters, keep in mind the story of Jean-Dominique Bauby and recall how your own biological processes make everything you do possible.

Studying the Chapter

Key Terms

affective component of emotion (214)
anorexia nervosa (199)
basic emotions (220)
binge eating disorder (BED) (201)
bisexuals (209)
bulimia nervosa (198)
Cannon-Bard theory (215)
cholecystokinin (CCK) (188)
cognitive-mediational theory (218)
display rules (221)
drive (178)
drive reduction theories (178)
emotion (213)
erogenous zones (205)
estrogens (204)
estrus (204)
excitement phase (206)
extrinsic motivation (183)
facial feedback hypothesis (216)
ghrelin (187)

glucose (188)
glycogen (188)
heterosexuals (209)
hierarchy of needs (184)
homeostasis (179)
homophobia (211)
homosexuals (209)
incentives (182)
instincts (178)
insulin (188)
intrinsic motivation (183)
James-Lange theory (214)
lateral hypothalamus (LH) (189)
leptin (189)
libido (204)
mere exposure effect (219)
motive (178)
negative feedback loop (179)
neuropeptide Y (190)
obesity (193)
orgasm phase (206)
ovaries (204)
overweight (192)
plateau phase (206)
primary drives (179)
refractory period (207)
resolution phase (206)
resting metabolic rate (196)
secondary drives (180)
self-determination theory (181)
set point (186)
sexual arousal (203)
sexual desire (203)
sexual orientation (209)
testes (204)
testosterone (204)
two-factor theory of emotion (217)
ventromedial hypothalamus (VMH) (190)

What Do You Know? Assess Your Understanding

Test your retention and understanding of the material by answering the following questions.

1. According to William James, motives are best characterized as ______.
   a. drives
   b. instincts
   c. desires
   d. needs
2. Which of the following is most likely to be a primary drive?
   a. Feeling sleepy and wanting to go to bed
   b. Longing to be loved by others
   c. Wanting a good job
   d. Need for achievement
3. The Yerkes-Dodson Law predicts that most people perform best at a moderate level of arousal. Dr. Wills conducts a study to examine the relationship between arousal and performance. She has 300 participants come to her lab and perform a task while she measures both their arousal and their performance levels. Dr. Wills is conducting what type of research?
   a. True experiment
   b. Correlational
   c. Case study
   d. Naturalistic observation
4. Which of the following is an example of a negative feedback loop?
   a. Scratching a mosquito bite, making it itch more
   b. Sexual arousal, leading one to desire more stimulation
   c. Drinking water when you are dehydrated
   d. All of the above
5. Which of the following is the *best* example of extrinsic motivation?
   a. Working on your favorite hobby in your free time
   b. Doing a good deed in keeping with your own moral code
   c. Working hard to earn good grades to keep your scholarship
   d. Being nice to your grandmother because you love her
6. According to Abraham Maslow, which of the following is the highest level of motivation we experience?
   a. Belongingness
   b. Safety needs
   c. Aesthetic needs
   d. Physiological needs
7. A person with a high level of CCK in their bloodstream would likely ______.
   a. feel intense hunger
   b. have just finished a large meal
   c. also have a large amount of ghrelin in their bloodstream
   d. be on the brink of starvation

8. If you injected a hungry rat with ghrelin, what would likely happen?
   a. The rat would become even hungrier.
   b. The rat would stop eating immediately.
   c. The rat would stop eating only if it had already ingested sufficient food.
   d. The rat would slow down its eating, but it would continue to eat.

9. Damage to which area of the brain would most likely result in weight gain in a rat?
   a. The ventromedial hypothalamus (VMH)
   b. The lateral hypothalamus (LH)
   c. The thalamus
   d. The hippocampus

10. Being obese is defined as ______.
   a. being at least 20 pounds overweight
   b. having a BMI of at least 30
   c. being at least 100 pounds overweight
   d. having a BMI of at least 50

11. Belinda often binges by eating large quantities of food. After these binges, she feels bad about herself but does little to change her eating behavior. As a result of these binges, Belinda is overweight. Belinda most closely meets the criteria for which eating disorder?
   a. Anorexia nervosa
   b. Bulimia nervosa
   c. Binge eating disorder
   d. Obesity

12. For men, which of the following is not correlated with having a homosexual orientation?
   a. Being Native American
   b. Being the youngest of four brothers
   c. Being left handed
   d. All of the above are correlated with homosexuality in men.

13. When a female mammal is receptive to sexual intercourse, she is said to be in ______.
   a. estrus
   b. resolution
   c. the refractory period
   d. the plateau phase

14. In humans, sexual desire is *not* influenced by which of the following chemicals?
   a. Testosterone
   b. Oxytocin
   c. Dopamine
   d. Acetylcholine

15. Male and female sexual response cycles differ most significantly in which stage?
   a. Excitement phase
   b. Orgasm phase
   c. Plateau phase
   d. Resolution phase

16. Sabrina is married with two kids. What do we know about Sabrina's sexual orientation?
   a. She's homosexual.
   b. She's bisexual.
   c. She's heterosexual.
   d. We cannot tell from this information.

17. Which theory of emotion best explains why one student panics before an exam and another remains calm?
   a. James-Lange theory of emotion
   b. Cannon-Bard theory of emotion
   c. Cognitive-mediational theory
   d. Two-factor theory

18. Which theory of emotion best explains why someone would feel more sexual attraction to their partner while at a concert than with the same partner in a library?
   a. James-Lange theory of emotion
   b. Cannon-Bard theory of emotion
   c. Cognitive-mediational theory
   d. Two-factor theory

19. Which of the following theories of emotion defines emotion as a pattern of physiological response in the body?
   a. James-Lange theory of emotion
   b. Cannon-Bard theory of emotion
   c. Cognitive-mediational theory
   d. Two-factor theory

20. The fact that women are discouraged from expressing anger in a given culture is an example of ______.
   a. the two-factor theory of emotion
   b. a reappraisal
   c. a display rule
   d. a primary appraisal

Answers: 1. b; 2. a; 3. b; 4. c; 5. c; 6. c; 7. b; 8. a; 9. a; 10. b; 11. c; 12. a; 13. a; 14. d; 15. d; 16. d; 17. c; 18. d; 19. a; 20. c.

Use It or Lose It: Applying Psychology

1. Assume that you are a scientist who is trying to develop a new appetite suppressant pill for weight loss. Given your understanding of hunger, what kind of an effect would you want your pill to have on a person's body?
2. What would life be like if humans did not have the capacity for emotion?
3. Sabina was cut off in traffic on the way home from work, nearly causing her to have a serious accident. Immediately on arriving home, Sabina finds that her partner has left a dirty towel on the bathroom floor, something Sabina dislikes. What predictions would Schachter and Singer make about Sabina's emotional reaction to finding the dirty towel? Explain.
4. Pretend that you are in charge of developing a campaign to prevent eating disorders in teenage girls. What type of campaign would you develop?

Critical Thinking about the Science of Psychology

In this chapter, you read about Schachter & Singer's (1962) study on the two-factor theory of emotion in which they injected participants with epinephrine to examine the role that arousal plays in emotion (see section 5.4.3). After reviewing this study, answer these questions:

1. In this study, what was the independent variable?
2. How did Schachter and Singer measure their dependent variable in this study?
3. What type of research method did Schachter and Singer employ?
4. What could Schachter and Singer legitimately conclude from their research findings?
5. What ethical considerations are present in this study?

Are You Getting the Big Picture?

A **motive** is the tendency to desire and seek out positive incentives and rewards and to avoid negative outcomes.

Westend611/Getty Images

5.1 Theories of Motivation

- William James believed that motives tend to be inborn **instincts**.
- According to the **drive reduction theory, primary drives** maintain **homeostasis**.
- **Arousal theories** of motivation suggest that each of us has an optimal level of arousal.
- According to **self-determination theory,** as we pursue the fulfillment of basic needs, we are motivated by both **intrinsic** and **extrinsic motives**.
- Having a *growth* or a *fixed mindset* about intelligence has implications for one's goals and one's level of motivation to achieve these goals.
- Abraham Maslow proposed a **hierarchy of needs** in which some needs take priority over others.

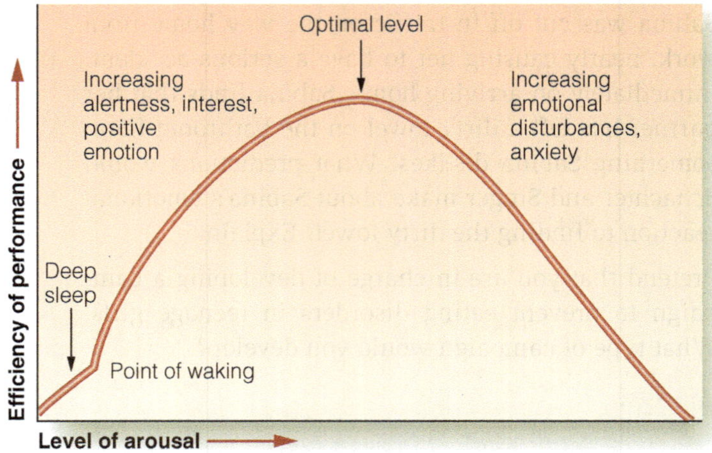

General relationship between performance and arousal level

5.2 Hunger and Eating

- Receptors in the stomach monitor the intake of food and contractions of the stomach, and signal the brain when to make us hungry or to shut off hunger.
- Liver cells, hormones, fat cells, and glucoreceptors in the hypothalamus all play a role in signaling hunger or shutting it off.
- External cues such as advertisements and the sight or smell of food can also trigger hunger.
- **Obesity** can be caused by biological factors, such as a slow metabolism and a number of behavioral factors, including a poor diet, excessive food intake, and emotional eating.
- **Bulimia nervosa** involves bingeing on food followed by purging or drastic reduction in caloric intake to rid the body of the extra calories.
- **Anorexia nervosa** is a serious eating disorder that involves extreme concern about gaining weight and reduction in caloric intake that leads to drastic weight loss.
- **Binge eating disorder (BED)** involves bingeing on food without compensatory measures to rid the body of extra calories.

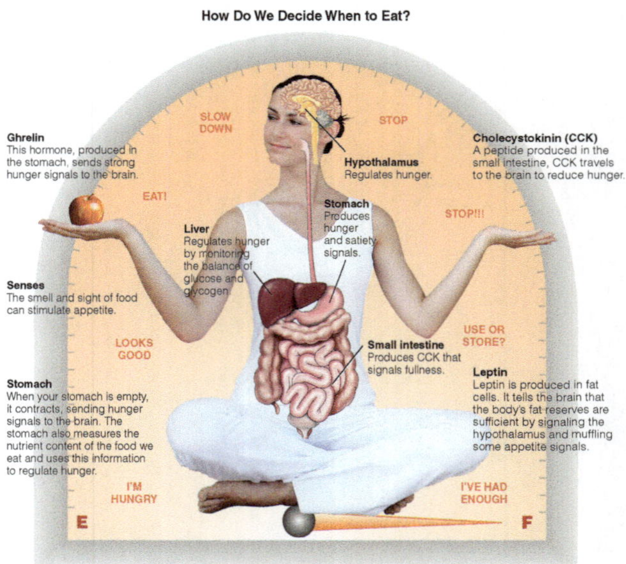

ImageDJ/Alamy stock photo

5.3 Sexual Motivation

Juanmonino/E+/Getty Images

- **Sexual desire** is influenced by neurotransmitters, hormones, sensory cues, and cultural attitudes about what is sexually appealing.
- Masters and Johnson's research examined the physiological changes that men and women undergo during sexual activity. Their results indicate that the sexual response cycle involves **excitement**, **plateau**, **orgasm**, and **resolution phases**.
- Although there are age and generational differences in sexuality, interest in sexual activity is an important part of life across the lifespan for many people.
- **Sexual orientation** is not just a matter of whether you have sex with men or women. Surveys show that some people may have some same-sex encounters but not consider themselves gay or lesbian.
- Sexual orientation falls along a continuum from **heterosexual** (attracted to the other sex) to **bisexual** (attracted to both sexes) to **homosexual** (attracted to the same sex).
- **Homophobia**, prejudice against homosexuals and bisexuals, is still a big problem in some cultures, including the United States.

5.4 Theories and Expression of Emotion

- Components of **emotion** include physiological reactions, behavioral reactions, facial expressions, cognition, and affective response.
- The **James-Lange theory** of emotion proposes that emotion can be understood as a physiological response to some stimulus.
- The **Cannon-Bard theory** of emotion holds that emotion is the brain responding to some stimulus or situation, then prompting an emotional reaction.
- In the **facial feedback hypothesis**, the experience of an emotion is affected by the feedback the brain receives from muscles in the face. Thus, smiling can influence us to feel happy, and frowning can influence us to feel bad.
- The Schachter-Singer **two-factor theory of emotion** states that emotions are a product of both physiological arousal and cognitive interpretations of this arousal.
- **Cognitive-meditational theory** states that our cognitive appraisal of a situation determines what emotion we will feel in the situation; thus, different people react with different emotions in the same situation.
- **Basic emotions**, including happiness, sadness, anger, and fear, have been found to be present across cultures. However, there is considerable debate as to how many basic emotions exist.
- **Display rules** determine the appropriate expression of emotion in a culture.

GoGo Images Corporation /Alamy stock photo

Dean Drobot/Shutterstock.com

Part 2

Foundations in Cognitive Psychology

In previous parts, we covered the scientific foundation of psychology and the biological systems that influence our mental processes and behavior. By now, we hope that you have developed an appreciation for the complexity and importance of our biological systems, especially our remarkable brains. Many psychologists compare the brain and the mental processes of the mind to a computer (the brain) running a software program (the mind). Like a computer, we process, store, and retrieve countless bits of information as we go about our days learning, thinking, speaking, solving problems, and so on. Collectively, these mental processes of the mind are referred to as cognition, or the ways in which we store and use information. We engage in some form of cognition virtually every moment of our day. We store new information as we learn new concepts and behaviors. We use information that we have previously stored when solving problems in our lives. We use stored knowledge in the form of language to communicate with others. Cognition underlies much of our behavior, making an understanding of cognition an essential second foundation of the field of psychology.

As we explore cognitive psychology in this part, we will examine what decades of scientific research have taught us about cognition and its influence on our behavior. Chapter 6 describes how our experiences lead to **learning** that then affects our behavior. In Chapter 7, we will look at **memory**, the storage, processing, and retrieval of information in the mind. And in Chapter 8, we examine the role **cognition**, **language**, and **intelligence** play in our daily lives. Cognitive abilities such as these play a critical role in our ability to function in life. Well-developed cognitive abilities may pave the way for success in life, whereas cognitive inabilities may make it difficult to meet some of life's challenges. Both of these situations are illustrated in our case study for this part.

THE BIG PICTURE

THE POWER OF THE MIND

Our case study for Part 2 tells the story of a remarkable man, Kim Peek, the real-life "Rain Man" portrayed by Dustin Hoffman in the Oscar-winning movie of that name. As you read Kim's story, think about your own cognitive processes. How do your cognitive abilities (and inabilities) measure up to his? Would you like to have Kim's cognitive abilities? Why or why not?

Kim, who passed away in December 2009 from a heart attack, was different from the moment of his birth. His head was 30% larger than normal. He did not respond normally to stimulation. His eyes moved independently of one another, and he had a large blister-like growth across the back of his head that doctors could not identify.

In this Part:

At age 3, the growth on Kim's head suddenly began to relocate, growing into the back of his skull, and exploding the right half of his cerebellum into many separate pieces. Later it was discovered that Kim had no corpus callosum and that the two hemispheres of his brain were fused into one large mass (see Chapter 2). Despite these brain abnormalities, Kim excelled at certain aspects of memory. At age 6, Kim was memorizing parts of encyclopedias, and his ability to memorize information continued to become more impressive as he aged. By adulthood, he exhibited extraordinary mental abilities in more than a dozen topic areas. Kim spent most of his time voraciously reading—phone books, maps, history books, album covers—all with near total recall. In fact, he could simultaneously read two passages at the same time—one with his left eye and one with his right eye! If you told Kim your date of birth, he could *immediately* tell you the day of the week you were born on and the year and date when you could retire at age 65. If you told him your hometown, he could tell you your ZIP code, telephone prefix, and most likely the history of your town. He could also hum almost any piece of music on demand and do mental mathematics at an astounding level. These mathematical skills allowed Kim to do the payroll for a nonprofit organization without the use of a calculator or computer. He did all the calculations in his head! It appeared that Kim's mind was able to store and process factual information with the same efficiency as a personal computer. In fact, in tribute to his son's amazing talents, Kim's father affectionately nicknamed Kim the *Kimputer.*

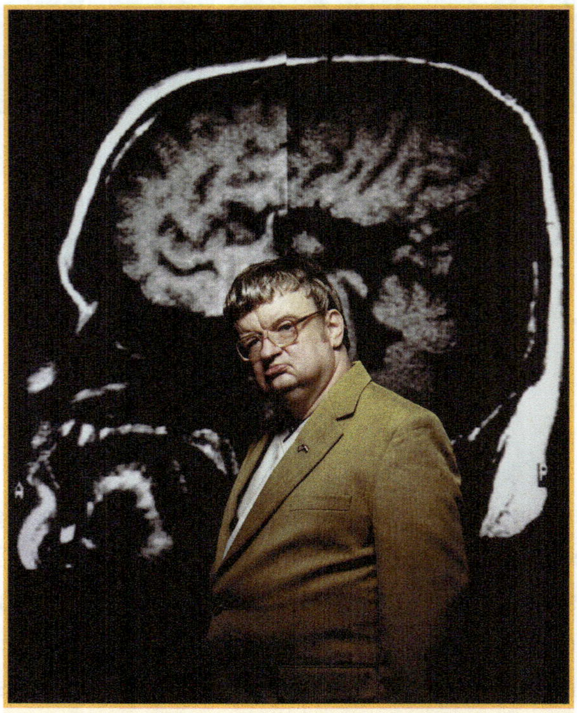
Ethan Hill/Contributor/Getty Images

▲ Kim Peek

Yet, Kim's genius did not extend to all types of cognitive functioning. He had extreme difficulty with certain types of learning. In particular, Kim found it impossible to learn many motor skills, most likely because of his damaged cerebellum. Despite the fact that his father showed him how to do many personal tasks on a daily basis, Kim never learned to brush his teeth or dress without assistance. By age 14, Kim completed his high school requirements at home, but he couldn't attend public school because of his extreme hyperactivity. Kim's mind constantly jumped from idea to idea, and he could not concentrate on one task at a time. He was quite poor at cognitive tasks that involve analytical reasoning or conceptual thought. For example, he could memorize a history book, but had difficulty discussing the meaning of *democracy*. Kim's score on traditional intelligence tests was approximately 74, in the range that indicates intellectual disability. On tests that only measure knowledge, he scored around 175—*way* above average.

For unknown reasons, Kim's damaged brain seemed to give him the amazing ability to process massive amounts of factual information. The price for this ability seemed to be that Kim's mind was constantly besieged by its own mental connections. His mind wandered along a meandering sequence of related facts, exhausting Kim's cognitive resources and leaving him with little capacity for higher-order cognitive processes (e.g., reasoning and problem solving).

So, think about it once again. Which would you value more—the ability to memorize every word of this textbook, or the ability to understand and apply the knowledge it contains? We would certainly choose the latter. While it's true that most of us have to put much more effort into our memory than Kim did, most of us are self-sufficient in our daily tasks, and most of us are able to use reason to tackle life's challenges.

Kim's story is one of remarkable contrasts in cognition. On the one hand, he excelled at learning some tasks; on the other hand, he was also unable to learn how to execute some important skills involved in daily living. His ability to memorize information was phenomenal, yet he could not use the information he stored in memory in novel ways. In short, Kim's unusual cognitive abilities could be viewed as both a sign of genius-level intelligence or a sign of cognitive disability.

Although Kim was a study in the extremes of human behavior, most of us exhibit cognitive abilities that fall squarely between these extremes. In the next part, we will examine what psychologists have discovered about the cognitive abilities of the average person. As you read the chapters in this part, you will gain a deeper understanding of how you learn; how you process information in memory; and how you use stored knowledge to reason, solve problems, communicate, and, in general, exhibit intelligence in daily life. As you are on this journey, think about Kim and think about your own abilities. How might gaining insight into how your own mind works help you to better achieve your goals in life? We hope that as you learn about cognition in the coming chapters, you'll come to better appreciate the power of your mind and find ways to apply what you are learning to the improvement of your own cognitive abilities.

Everett Collection

▲ Kim Peek was the remarkable man who inspired the character of the Rain Man in the Oscar-winning movie of the same name.

Learning Objectives

6.1 Define learning. (APA 1.1, 1.2)

6.1 Define and give examples of orienting reflexes, habituation, and dishabituation. (APA 1.1, 1.2, 1.3)

6.2 Describe Pavlov's studies of classical conditioning. (APA 1.1, 1.2, 2.1)

6.2 Define classical conditioning and describe the factors that affect it. (APA 1.1, 1.2)

6.2 Explain how classical conditioning occurs in humans. (APA 1.1, 1.2, 1.3)

6.2 Describe the process through which classically conditioned responses are removed. (APA 1.1, 1.2, 1.3)

6.2 Describe how classical conditioning can be used to help people. (APA 1.3, 3.1)

6.3 Explain Thorndike's law of effect and the experiments that led to its discovery. (APA 1.1, 1.2, 1.3, 2.1)

6.3 Describe the contributions that B. F. Skinner made to the study of operant conditioning. (APA 1.1, 1.2, 2.1)

6.3 Describe the phases of operant conditioning, including acquisition and extinction. (APA 1.1, 1.2)

6.3 Describe the factors that affect the process of operant conditioning, including schedules of reinforcement. (APA 1.1, 1.2)

6.3 Describe discrimination, generalization, and shaping as they relate to operant conditioning. (APA 1.1, 1.2)

6.3 Describe the decisions that must be made when applying operant conditioning in the real world. (APA 1.1, 1.2, 1.3, 3.1)

6.3 Describe the evidence supporting the idea that cognition plays an important role in learning. (APA 1.1, 1.2, 2.1)

6.4 Describe Albert Bandura's Bobo doll experiments and their implications for real-world behavior. (APA 1.1, 1.2, 1.3, 2.1, 3.1)

6.4 Describe the process of observational learning and the role that cognition plays in observational learning. (APA 1.1, 1.2)

iStock.com/FluxFactory

6 Learning

Kim Peek's story at the beginning of Part 2 illustrates the extremes of human learning abilities. On the one hand, Kim could learn factual information with a genius-like ease. On the other hand, he found learning simple tasks such as brushing his teeth to be impossibly difficult. Most of us find that our ability to learn falls somewhere in between these extremes of genius and disability. In this chapter, we will explore the learning processes that mold and shape our behavior. ■

Chapter Outline

6.1 Learning from the First Days of Life: Habituation

cognition the way in which we use and store information in memory

learning a relatively permanent change in behavior, or behavior potential, as a result of experience

memory the storage, processing, and retrieval of information in the mind

language a well-developed, syntactical verbal system for representing the world

intelligence abilities that enable you to adapt to your environment and behave in a goal-directed way

orienting reflex the tendency of an organism to orient its senses toward unexpected stimuli

Let's begin by taking a formal look at what learning is. *Learning* can be defined as a relatively permanent change in behavior, or the potential for behavior, that results from experience. Learning results from many experiences in life. We learn concepts and skills in school. We learn from watching others. And we learn certain skills, like riding a bike, by doing them. Learning may show up in our behavior (as when we ride a bike), or it may not (as when we get a speeding ticket even though we've learned that speeding is wrong). Learning may stay with us for years (as with riding a bike), or it may only linger for a while (as when we observe the speed limit for only a few weeks after getting a ticket). Either way, learning is one of life's most important activities. In this chapter, we will look at four common types of learning—*habituation*, *classical conditioning*, *operant conditioning*, and *observational learning*. We will begin with what is widely thought to be the simplest form of learning—*habituation*.

6.1.1 Paying Attention and Learning to Ignore: Orienting Reflexes and Habituation

Suppose you are sitting in class, listening to your psychology professor and taking notes. All of a sudden there is a loud banging noise directly outside your classroom. What would your very first reaction to the unexpected noise be? If you are like most people, you would immediately stop listening to the lecture and turn your head in the direction of the noise. This very normal response is called an **orienting reflex** (Pavlov, 1927/1960). Orienting reflexes occur when we stop what we are doing to orient our sense organs in the direction of unexpected stimuli.

In our example, the stimulus was auditory, but this doesn't have to be the case. If you were standing in line to buy coffee and someone poked you in the back, you would most likely turn to see what the person wanted. If you were having dinner in a restaurant and someone started taking pictures using a flash camera, you would likely look in the direction of the flashes of light. In short, we exhibit the orienting reflex to any type of novel stimulus.

Engage Yourself!

Your course syllabus probably contains some warning about coming to class on time. Here's one reason why: Notice what happens to you and your classmates the next time a student comes in late to class. Does everyone automatically look toward the door as the student comes through it? This is also an orienting reflex—one that distracts from your ability to learn the course material. Orienting reflexes are part of everyday life. To see how common they are, tomorrow as you go about your daily routine, record as many examples of orienting reflexes in yourself (or others) as you can. Keep in mind that orienting reflexes can occur in response to any unexpected sight, sound, touch, smell, or even taste.

mediaphotos/Getty Images

Why do you think we exhibit orienting reflexes? What is the benefit of automatically paying attention to novel stimuli? If you said "self-protection," you are correct. Orienting reflexes allow us to quickly gather information about stimuli that could potentially be threatening. For instance, that banging noise in the hallway could be a student dropping their books, or it could be a fight. In the case of a fight, you may want to take steps to ensure that the fight doesn't affect you in a negative way. Recall from Chapter 2 that the sympathetic branch of our nervous system is behind the *fight or flight response* that helps us survive in dangerous situations. If we perceive danger, our sympathetic system will be engaged. By orienting your senses toward the event, you can quickly assess what, if any, action is needed to protect yourself.

The benefit of having orienting reflexes is limited, though. Suppose that after looking up at the sound of the banging, you see that it is only a worker hammering as they install a new bulletin board in the hallway. You would likely return your attention to the psychology lecture. If the banging noise continues, your tendency to look up at the noise in the hall would steadily decrease. In other words, your orienting reflex would diminish over time. This decrease in responding to a stimulus as it is repeated over and over is called **habituation**.

Jed Leicester/Shutterstock.com

▲ After people live in these houses for a while, habituation will ensure that they barely even notice the sounds of jets like this one as they take off and land.

habituation [huh-bit-chew-AYE-shun] the tendency of an organism to ignore repeated stimuli

Despite its name, habituation does not refer to forming a habit. Instead, habituation ensures that we do not waste our energy and mental resources by responding to irrelevant stimuli. In our previous example, after you have established that the noise in the hallway is not threatening, there is no reason to keep looking. If you did keep exhibiting the orienting reflex, you would needlessly miss part of your psychology lecture and waste energy that could be spent more usefully.

Almost all creatures, including those with very simple nervous systems, seem to have the capacity for habituation (Harris, 1943). This universality implies that habituation is the simplest type of learning seen in living things (Davis & Egger, 1992). Habituation can be seen in newborn infants (Cortesa, Hudac, & Molfese, 2019; Lavoie & Desrochers, 2002; Rose, Slater, & Perry, 1986) and even in fetuses (Leader, 2016; Van Heteren et al., 2000). Studies have shown that certain neural networks in the brain may undergo habituation when we experience repetitive stimuli. For example, participants who repeatedly viewed pictures of painful events while having an functional magnetic resonance imaging (fMRI) scan of their brain showed greater decreases in neural activity in parts of the cerebellum and several other brain structures than participants who viewed neutral pictures (Preis et al., 2015). Other studies have also linked behavioral habituation to decreased activity in neural networks of the brain (Nickel et al., 2014). Habituation has also been seen in some patients who are receiving *deep brain stimulation* for certain neurological disorders. After a period of responding favorably to the electrical stimulation of their brains, all of a sudden the therapy seems to lose its effectiveness and their symptoms return (Su, Kim, & Martinez, 2020). Studies like these suggest that habituation can occur at both the behavioral and the neural levels.

6.1.2 Possible Benefits of Habituation: Protecting the Brain

To get a better feel for the value of habituation, imagine what life would be like if you could not habituate. Without habituation, you would reflexively respond to every sight, sound, touch, taste, and smell you encountered, every time you encountered it. You would not be able to ignore these stimuli. Think of how this would limit your ability to function. Every time the worker hammered the bulletin board in the hall, your attention would move away from the lecture and toward the hall. You certainly would not learn much psychology under these circumstances! With habituation, you get the best of both worlds. You can respond to novel stimuli that may pose a danger, and you can also ignore stimuli that have been checked out and deemed to be harmless. Habituation gives you flexibility in that you don't have to continue to respond to a stimulus.

▲ Some researchers have suggested that migraines may result from the inability to sufficiently habituate to environmental stimuli, leading to overstimulation of the brain and migraine symptoms.

Habituation may also serve to protect our brains from overstimulation. Many people experience intense headaches called *migraines*. These debilitating headaches are frequently characterized by severe pain on one side of the head and can be associated with sensitivity to light, nausea, or vomiting. Some people with migraines also experience visual disturbances, called *auras*, which signal the impending onset of a migraine. In searching for the causes of migraines, researchers have uncovered some interesting information. First, having a specific genetic marker called the MTHFR C677T is correlated with a higher likelihood of having migraines, especially migraines with auras. This genetic marker is also associated with having higher levels of a chemical called *homocysteine* in the body (de Tommaso et al., 2007). Second, researchers have discovered that people with migraines often appear to have a lessened ability to habituate to stimuli perhaps at a neuronal level (Buonfiglio et al., 2019; de Tommaso et al., 2016; Restuccia et al., 2013; Reyngoudt et al., 2011). For example, people with migraines showed less ability than people without migraines to habituate to a stressful sound (Huber, Henrich, & Gündel, 2005). People with migraines may have impaired ability to habituate to visual stimuli (for review, see Brighina, Cosentino, & Fierro, 2016). Studies like these suggest that people with migraines may have less ability to tune out stressful stimuli, which may lead to hyperactivity in the brain that results in migraine pain. In fact, when people with migraines are taught to increase their levels of habituation to environmental stimuli, they tend to experience fewer migraine attacks (Kropp, Siniatchkin, & Gerber, 2002). Perhaps one function of habituation may be to protect our nervous system from sensory overload.

6.1.3 Dishabituation

dishabituation [DIS-huh-bit-chew-AYE-shun] re-responding to a stimulus to which one has been habituated

Habituation may protect us from unwanted stimulation, but a permanent state of habituation would not likely be in our best interest. Imagine never again being able to attend to the sounds around you after having habituated so that you could study. Thankfully, you don't have to worry. We have the flexibility to stop habituating when the circumstances warrant it. **Dishabituation** occurs when an organism begins to respond more intensely to a stimulus to which it has previously habituated. Let's return to our example of the worker in the hallway. Although you find the hammering distracting at first, you soon habituate to the sound. Then, after several minutes of ignoring the steady hammering, you hear a new sound. The worker has turned on some music at a rather high volume. Will you ignore this sound, too? No, you likely will not. Because the quality of the stimulus has changed dramatically, you will dishabituate. You will again find yourself orienting toward the hallway. This new sound is too dissimilar to the hammering, and you have to check it out. Once you recognize that it is the worker's music (and that it poses no threat), you will likely habituate to this new sound as well as to the hammering.

A change in the quality of the stimulus is not the only thing that can cause dishabituation. So can the passage of time. For instance, if the worker took an hour-long lunch break and then went back to hammering, you might briefly dishabituate to the hammering. This would not last long, however—after just a few bangs of the hammer, you would reenter habituation and return your attention to the lecture. As you can see, adaptive functioning is a balance of responding—habituating and dishabituating at the appropriate time.

6.1.4 Practical Applications of Habituation

One practical application of habituation is the use of habituation training for people who experience chronic motion sickness, or *vertigo*. For some people with vertigo, simple tasks like working at a computer may be impossible. Physical therapists often use habituation techniques to help people overcome chronic motion sickness. By repeatedly exposing clients to the stimulation that produces motion sickness, the therapist can gradually train these clients to habituate, or stop responding, to some of the visual and *vestibular signals* (Chapter 3) that would normally cause them to feel sick (Childs, 2011; Walak et al., 2013; Yardley & Kirby, 2006). Similar techniques have been used to train figure skaters (Tanguy et al., 2008), pilots, and astronauts to do their jobs without experiencing motion sickness (Bagshaw, 1985). Habituation-based therapies may also be useful in treating mental health issues.

Prolonged Exposure Therapy is a habituation-based therapy that is used to treat people with *post-traumatic stress disorder* (PTSD; see Chapter 13). By repetitively exposing clients to fear-producing stimuli, therapists are able to help them habituate to these anxiety-producing triggers and improve the quality of their lives (Sripada & Rauch, 2015). Both *mindfulness-based stress reduction* and *cognitive behavioral therapies* have been shown to enhance habituation in the *hypothalamic-pituitary-adrenocortical (HPA) axis* (see Chapters 12 and 14), suggesting they may be helpful in treating people with anxiety disorders because they tend to lessen one's physiological response to stressors (Manigualt et al., 2019).

Habituation is quite important to everyday life, but it is still a very simple type of learning. Habituation does not explain the bulk of the learning that we engage in during our lifetime, such as learning to play tennis or ride a bike. Nor does habituation explain how we come to associate certain emotions and physiological reactions with certain stimuli, such as learning to fear snakes or feeling happy when we smell Grandma's perfume. For explanations of these more complex events, we will have to turn our attention to more sophisticated and complex types of learning. We will begin with *classical conditioning*.

6.1 Quiz Yourself

1. Which of the following is an example of habituation?

a. Juan was teasing the family dog when it bit him. Because of the pain of the bite, Juan learned not to tease the dog again.
b. Teresa was trying to learn to knit. At first, she had to consciously think about what she was doing, but after practicing for 3 hours, Teresa could knit without thinking about it.
c. Janel just bought a new puppy. At first, the dog's barking was distracting to Janel as she tried to watch TV, but after a while Janel did not notice the puppy's barking.
d. Kerry loved her partner very much. Now that they have broken up, every time she hears their favorite song on the radio, Kerry starts to cry.

2. Fido the puppy tilts his head up and sniffs the air as he smells his owner cooking dinner in the kitchen. Fido is exhibiting _____.

a. habituation
b. dishabituation
c. an orienting reflex
d. a & c

3. Which of the following would likely have the capacity for habituation?

a. A 3-month-old human baby
b. An adult monkey
c. An adult dog
d. All of the above

Answers 1. c; 2. c; 3. d

6.2 Classical Conditioning: Learning Through the Association of Stimuli

The discovery of classical conditioning was something of an accident. Around the turn of the 20th century, a Russian physiologist named Ivan Pavlov (1849–1936) was doing research on the digestive processes of dogs (for which he would eventually win a Nobel Prize). Pavlov was investigating the role that salivation plays

FIGURE 6.1

Pavlov's Original Experiment

The dog was held in the harness and food was placed before it. The presence of the food (unconditioned stimulus, or US) caused the dog to salivate (unconditioned response, or UR). After a while, cues in the laboratory situation (lights, sounds, or sights) became conditioned stimuli (CS) that also caused the dog to salivate (conditioned response, or CR).

in digestion. He had surgically implanted devices in the cheeks of dogs so that he could measure how much saliva they produced. His experimental method was to place the dog in a harness, present the dog with some food, and then measure the amount of saliva the dog produced (see • FIGURE 6.1).

While conducting these studies, Pavlov noticed that sometimes the dogs began to salivate *before* the food was presented to them. Sometimes the mere sight of the food dish or the sound of the approaching experimenter was enough to produce salivation. So what was going on? Why would a dog start to salivate when it heard footsteps or saw an empty food bowl? Pavlov reasoned that the dog had learned to associate certain cues or stimuli with the presentation of food. To the dog, the approach of footsteps had come to mean that food was soon going to appear. Consequently, the dog had become *conditioned*, or taught, to respond to the footsteps the same way that it responded to the food—by salivating. Accidently, Pavlov had discovered a learning process, one that would become extremely influential in psychology.

Pavlov began to investigate the learning process itself. He systematically paired different stimuli with food to see which could be conditioned to produce the reflexive response of salivation. In one of these investigations, Pavlov sounded a buzzer just before he gave the dog some food. He repeated these trials several times while measuring the amount of saliva the dog produced. After repeated pairing of the buzzer and the food, the dog soon began to salivate on hearing the buzzer—even on trials in which the food was not presented after the buzzer sounded. The dog had become conditioned to associate the buzzer with the presentation of food. As a result, the buzzer had taken on the same power as food to cause the dog to salivate.

6.2.1 The Elements of Classical Conditioning

The process of learning that Pavlov discovered is commonly referred to as *classical conditioning*, or Pavlovian conditioning. We will formally define it in a minute, but first let's look at the process that produces a conditioned response:

unconditioned stimulus (US) a stimulus that naturally elicits a response in an organism

1. *The unconditioned stimulus and response.* To classically condition a person or animal, you must begin with a stimulus that naturally and reliably causes some response in the organism. Because this stimulus naturally causes the reflexive response, it is referred to as an **unconditioned stimulus (US)**, and the response

it evokes is called an **unconditioned response (UR)**. The term *unconditioned* refers to the fact that the association between the stimulus and the response is not learned. In Pavlov's studies, the food was the unconditioned stimulus, and salivation was the unconditioned response. You do not need to teach a dog to salivate when food is presented. Instead, salivation occurs naturally when a dog sees food. ● TABLE 6.1 gives some more examples of US-UR pairs that could be used in classical conditioning.

2. *The neutral stimulus.* The next step is the selection of a **neutral stimulus (NS)** that does not naturally elicit the unconditioned response. In Pavlov's case, the neutral stimulus used was a buzzer. Prior to training or conditioning, a dog would not be likely to salivate when it heard a buzzer. If anything, the

unconditioned response (UR) the response that is elicited by an unconditioned stimulus

neutral stimulus (NS) a stimulus that does not naturally elicit the unconditioned response in an organism

TABLE 6.1 Some Examples Of US-UR Pairs

Unconditioned Stimulus (US)	Unconditioned Response (UR)	
A puff of air to the eye	Eye blink	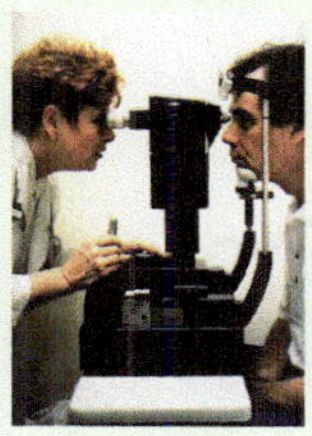 Michael L. Abramson/Getty Images
Ingestion of a toxin	Nausea	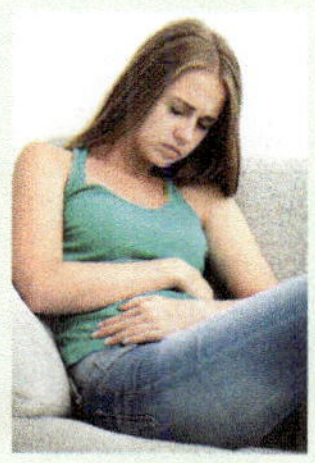 Alexandra Daltis/Shutterstock.com
Being stuck with a needle	Flinching away from needle	 Tatevosian Yana/ Shutterstock.com
Sour food placed on the tongue	Salivation	 Lapina/Shutterstock.com
A light shone in the eye	Pupil constricts	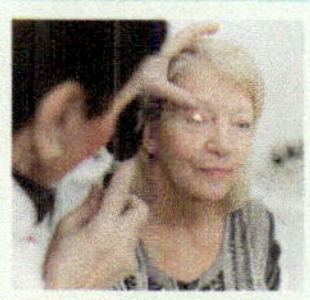 iStock.com/zoranm
A firm tap to the knee	Knee-jerk reflex	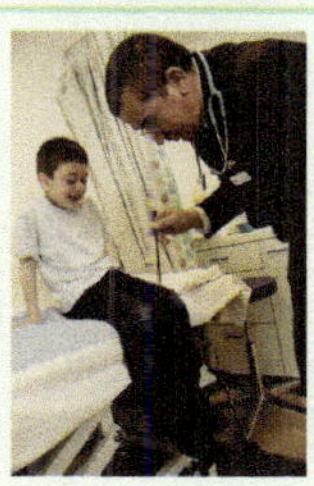 Michael Donne/Science Source

conditioned stimulus (CS) a stimulus that elicits a conditioned response in an organism

conditioned response (CR) the response that is elicited by a conditioned stimulus

dog would be more likely to exhibit an *orienting reflex*. Therefore, the buzzer is said to be neutral. It has no power to naturally cause the UR of salivation.

3. *Pairing the neutral stimulus and the unconditioned stimulus*. The third step is to systematically pair the neutral stimulus with the unconditioned stimulus. Pavlov accomplished this by repeatedly sounding the buzzer (NS) just prior to presenting the dog with the food (US). Through this repeated association of the US and the NS, the NS eventually loses its neutrality. In Pavlov's case, the dog began to salivate when the buzzer was presented without the food. At this point, classical conditioning had occurred because the buzzer was no longer neutral. The buzzer had become a **conditioned stimulus (CS)** that had the power to produce the **conditioned response (CR)** of salivation (● FIGURE 6.2).

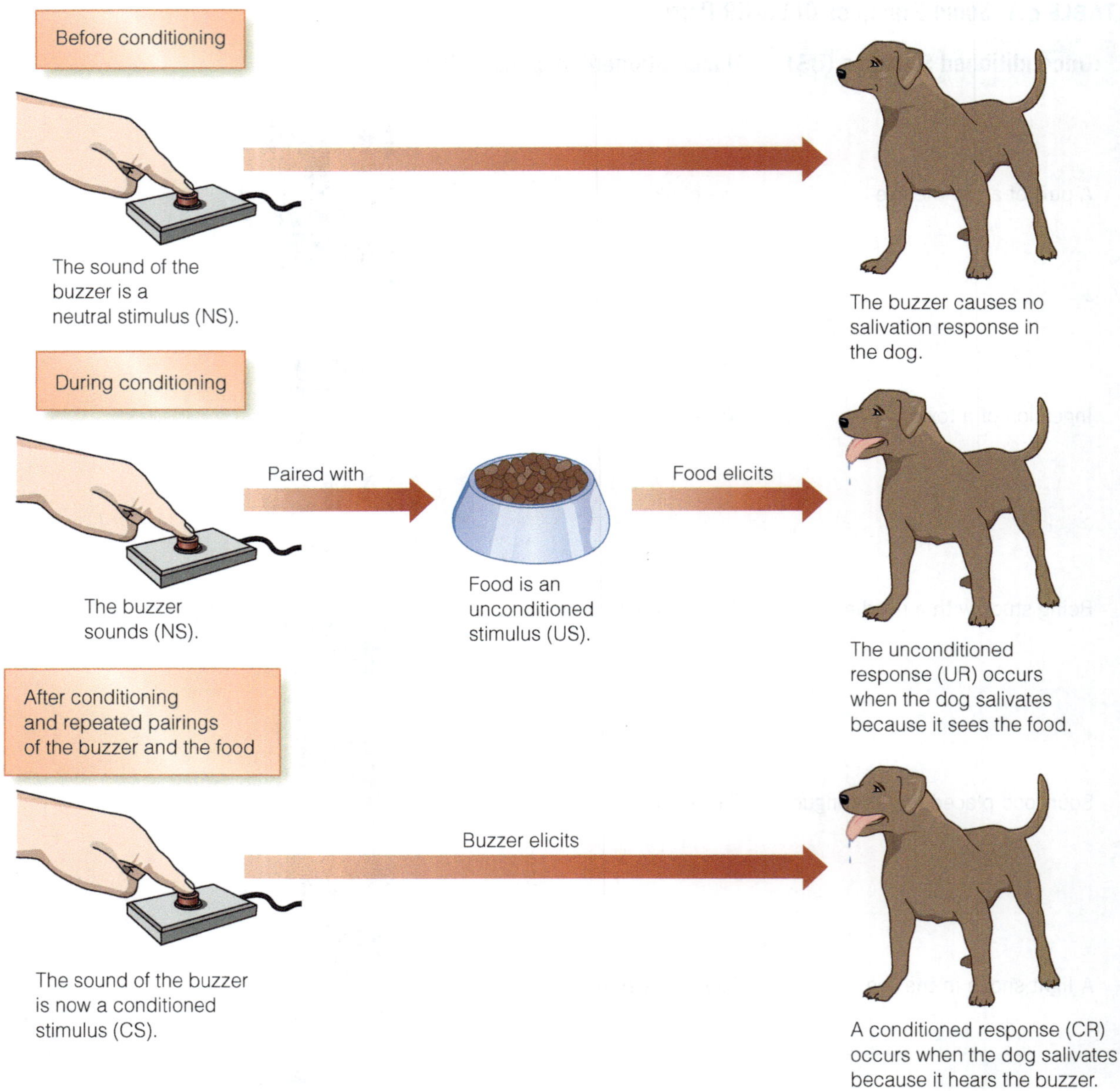

FIGURE 6.2

Pavlov's Classical Conditioning Procedure

Before conditioning, the neutral stimulus has no power to cause the response. After repeated pairings of the neutral stimulus with an unconditioned stimulus, which naturally elicits an unconditioned response, the neutral stimulus becomes a conditioned stimulus with the power to elicit the response—now called the conditioned response.

Summing up classical conditioning in a nice, neat definition is a bit awkward but nonetheless extremely important. Once, when one of your authors asked a student to define classical conditioning, she replied, "What Pavlov did with his dogs." This isn't, of course, a definition of classical conditioning. It does reflect the student's difficulty in trying to understand the concept of classical conditioning apart from Pavlov's particular demonstration of it, however. Keep in mind that to truly understand a concept, you must be able to define it in abstract terms as well as give an example of it. So here goes. We would define **classical conditioning** as *learning that occurs when a neutral stimulus is paired with an unconditioned stimulus that reliably causes an unconditioned response; and because of this association, the neutral stimulus loses its neutrality and takes on the same power as the unconditioned stimulus to cause the response.* This definition may seem a bit complex, but classical conditioning is actually a fairly simple process. It merely involves learning to associate two stimuli, the unconditioned stimulus and the neutral stimulus. Through this association, the neutral stimulus becomes a conditioned stimulus (You Review: Classical Conditioning). In the next section, we will examine some of the factors that affect the strength of the association.

classical conditioning learning that occurs when a neutral stimulus is repeatedly paired with an unconditioned stimulus; because of this pairing, the neutral stimulus becomes a conditioned stimulus with the same power as the unconditioned stimulus to elicit the response in the organism

contiguity [con-teh-GYU-eh-tee] the degree to which two stimuli occur close together in time

6.2.2 Factors Affecting Classical Conditioning

Exactly what is being learned in classical conditioning? We said that the organism learns to associate the NS/CS with the US. This is true, but what is the nature of this association? Why do these two particular stimuli become associated? Why did Pavlov's dog associate the buzzer with the food instead of associating other stimuli from the situation with the food? After training, why did the dog no longer begin to salivate when it heard the laboratory door open, or when the laboratory lights turned on? Why did it wait for the buzzer? To answer these questions, psychological researchers have experimentally examined different facets of the relationship between the NS/CS and the US.

Relationship In Time: Contiguity

Contiguity refers to the degree to which the NS/CS and US occur close together in time. Generally speaking, for classical conditioning to occur, the NS/CS and the US must be separated by only a short period of time (Bangasser et al., 2006; Wasserman & Miller, 1997). If the interval between the presentation of the NS/CS and the US is too long, the two stimuli will not be associated, and conditioning will not occur.

YOU REVIEW Classical Conditioning

Abbreviation	Term	Definition
US	Unconditioned stimulus	A stimulus that naturally and reliably evokes a response in the person or animal
UR	Unconditioned response	The response that is naturally and reliably elicited by the unconditioned stimulus
NS	Neutral stimulus	A stimulus that does not initially elicit the unconditioned response in the person or animal
CS	Conditioned stimulus	A stimulus that was once neutral but, through association with the unconditioned stimulus, now has the power to elicit the response in the animal or person
CR	Conditioned response	After conditioning has occurred, the response that is elicited in the person or animal by the conditioned stimulus

contingency [con-TINGE-en-see] the degree to which the presentation of one stimulus reliably predicts the presentation of the other stimulus

The interval of time between the CS and US is thought to play a pivotal role in learning to associate the CS with the US in classical conditioning (Díaz-Mataix, Tallot, & Doyére, 2014). If Pavlov had sounded the buzzer 2 hours before presenting the food to the dog, the dog would not have noticed a temporal connection between these two events and conditioning most likely would not have occurred.

Studies have shown that in most cases, if the US lags behind the NS/CS by more than a few seconds, conditioning will not be as strong as it could have been (Church & Black, 1958; Noble & Harding, 1963; Smith, Coleman, & Gormezano, 1969). The exact length of the optimal time interval varies depending on what response is being conditioned, but in general the longer the interval, the weaker the learning (Kryukov, 2012).

Another aspect of contiguity is the relative placement of the NS/CS and the US in time—in other words, whether the NS/CS precedes the US or follows it. Imagine if Pavlov had first given the dog the food and then sounded the buzzer. In that case the dog would not have been as likely to associate the food with the buzzer. ● FIGURE 6.3 shows the five major ways to place the NS/CS and the US in classical conditioning. Of these placements, forward (delayed) conditioning produces the strongest conditioning, and backward conditioning produces the weakest conditioning (Klein, 1987).

Consistency and Reliability: Contingency

Although contiguity is necessary for conditioning, it alone does not guarantee that conditioning will occur. Conditioning also requires **contingency**, which refers to the degree to which the NS/CS reliably signals that the US is going to be presented, resulting in the NS/CS becoming associated with the US (Díaz-Mataix et al., 2014). If the NS/CS does not reliably predict the onset of the US, then conditioning may be weak or not occur at all (Bolles, 1972; Rescorla, 1967; for a review, see Wheeler & Miller, 2008). For example, if Pavlov had sometimes fed the dog after sounding the buzzer and other times did not feed the dog after sounding the buzzer, conditioning would have been weakened. This inconsistency would not send the dog a clear message that the buzzer meant food was coming. Therefore, the dog would be less likely to salivate on hearing the buzzer, because it would not have made a strong association between the buzzer and the food. Given that both contiguity and contingency are necessary for strong classical conditioning, the best way to ensure strong conditioning is to consistently present only one NS/CS immediately before presenting the US.

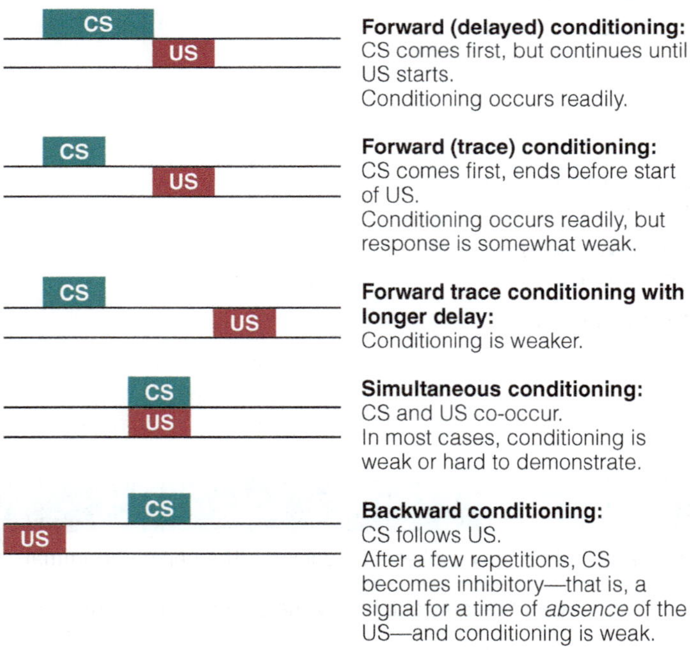

FIGURE 6.3

Possible Placements of the CS and the US in Classical Conditioning

Relative positions of the CS and US are shown for five different versions of classical conditioning: forward delayed, forward trace, forward trace with longer delay, simultaneous, and backward conditioning.

6.2.3 Real-World Applications of Classical Conditioning

The process of classical conditioning seems a bit complex, doesn't it? It also seems as if it could occur only in a laboratory (where stimuli could be systematically paired)—but this is not true. Classical conditioning occurs frequently in everyday life. In fact, each of us has probably felt the effects of classical conditioning many times. For example, we have been classically conditioned to have certain emotional reactions in our lives. You may feel happy when you smell a perfume that reminds you of your mother. You may feel fear when you see a snake.

As you will recall, the starting point for classical conditioning is a preexisting US-UR relationship. Table 6.1 lists some unconditioned stimuli that naturally and reliably evoke unconditioned responses without prior training. These US-UR pairs can be used to produce an initial or *first-order* level of classical conditioning in a person. However, in the real world, sometimes classical conditioning occurs on top of preexisting classical conditioning. This is called *higher-order* classical conditioning. For example, if a snake bites you, the bite (US) may cause a fear (UR/CR) of snakes (CS_1). This is first-order conditioning. Later, if you tend to see snakes (now a CS_1 that elicits fear) when hiking in the woods (NS), you may become conditioned to fear (UR/CR) going into the woods (the new CS_2). Higher-order conditioning occurs when these two stimuli (CS_1 and CS_2) are associated, resulting in a new, conditioned fear of the woods.

Because of the nature of most unconditioned stimulus–unconditioned response relationships, the types of responses that can be classically conditioned usually fall into two categories: *emotional responses* and *physiological responses*.

Classical Conditioning of Emotional Responses

The classical conditioning of emotional responses was clearly demonstrated in a famous—now infamous—set of experiments conducted by John B. Watson and his student Rosalie Rayner in the early 1900s (Chapter 1; Watson & Rayner, 1920). Watson set out to show that classical conditioning could be used to condition fear responses in a child. Because Watson used an 11-month-old boy named Albert, the experiments are now commonly referred to as the "Little Albert" experiments.

In the Little Albert experiments, Watson classically conditioned Albert to fear a white rat. To do this, Watson first gave Albert a white rat and allowed him to play with it. Prior to conditioning, the rat was an NS for Albert because it did not cause him to be afraid. A few minutes after giving Albert the rat, Watson made a very loud noise by striking a piece of metal with a hammer. As with most 11-month-olds, a loud noise such as this was a US for Albert that reliably produced the UR of frightening Albert and making him cry. Over and over, Watson repeated this sequence of presenting the rat (NS), then making the noise (US), with the result that Albert would become afraid and cry (UR).

Can you see the parallels here between what Watson and Rayner were doing to Albert and what Pavlov did with his dogs? In the same way that Pavlov conditioned his dogs to salivate at the sound of the buzzer, Watson conditioned Albert to fear a white rat by associating the rat with a frightening noise. After several trials of pairing the noise and the rat, all Watson had to do to get Albert to cry was to show him the rat. Because the rat had been paired with the noise, the rat lost its neutrality and became a CS that was able to evoke the CR of fear.

Emotional reactions such as fear are also classically conditioned outside of the laboratory. For example, one of us once had a professor who had an intense fear of bees because earlier in his life, several bees had stung him after he accidentally disturbed a beehive. In this case of classical conditioning, the multiple bee stings were a US that elicited the UR of fear. The bees were initially an NS, but because they were paired with the bee stings, they became a CS that could produce the CR of fear. From that day onward, all the professor had to do was to see a bee to feel intense fear.

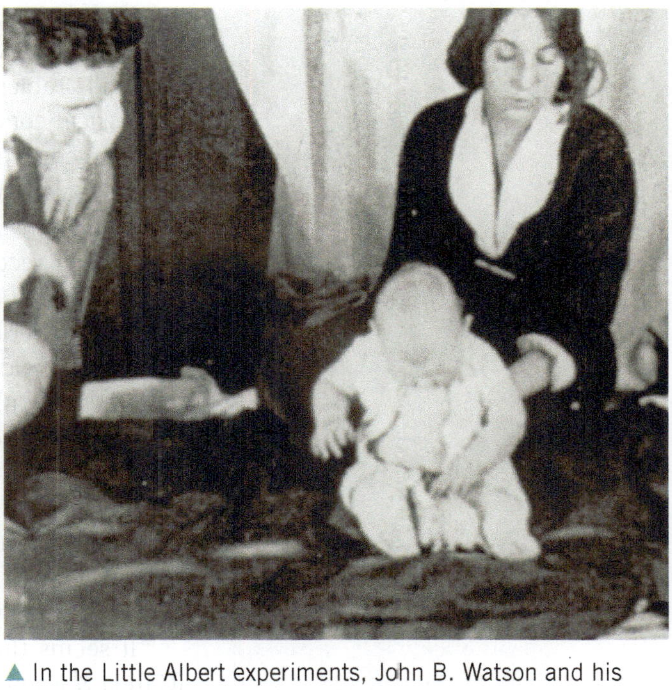
Archives of the History of American Psychology, University of Akron, Akron, Ohio

▲ In the Little Albert experiments, John B. Watson and his assistant, Rosalie Rayner, classically conditioned Albert to fear a white rat.

Rick Friedman/Getty Images

▲ Phobias are classically conditioned responses. A fear-producing encounter with a dog can result in the stimulus—the dog—becoming a conditioned stimulus that elicits fear.

stimulus generalization responding in a like fashion to similar stimuli

stimulus discrimination responding only to a particular stimulus

taste aversion classical conditioning that occurs when an organism pairs the experience of nausea with a certain food and becomes conditioned to feel ill at the sight, smell, or idea of the food

In fact, the professor's fear of bees was so great that it spread to other insects as well. Not only was he afraid of bees, he was also afraid of wasps, yellow jackets, and any other flying insect that could sting. In psychological terms, his fear had undergone **stimulus generalization**, which occurs when stimuli that are similar to the CS have the same power to elicit the CR even though they have never been paired with the US. The professor had never been stung by a wasp, yet he feared them because they are similar to bees.

Stimulus generalization also occurred in the Little Albert experiments. After being conditioned to fear the rat, Albert also exhibited fear when presented with a dog, a rabbit, a fur coat, and a fake white Santa Claus beard. His fear of white rats had generalized to several furry things (Watson & Rayner, 1920). This may leave you wondering what happened to Little Albert. Did he suffer through life as a result of his conditioned phobias? Unfortunately, Albert's identity and his fate have not yet been conclusively determined (Griggs, 2014b; Harris, 2020). We do know that Albert was withdrawn from the study before Watson and Rayner could remove the fear they had conditioned in Albert—leaving future psychologists to debate the ethics of Watson and Rayner's research.

Unlike what happened to Little Albert, not all classically conditioned responses necessarily generalize. The opposite process, **stimulus discrimination**, often occurs. In stimulus discrimination, the conditioned response occurs in response to a particular conditioned stimulus, but it does not occur in response to other stimuli that are similar to the conditioned stimulus. For instance, a person who works in the reptile house at the zoo is probably not afraid of most snakes, but if they found themself face to face with a poisonous king cobra, they would likely feel afraid. Sometimes, knowing when to discriminate and when to generalize is important to survival!

Classical Conditioning of Physiological Responses: Taste Aversion

Emotions are not the only responses that can be classically conditioned. Pavlov's original demonstrations of classical conditioning show a physiological response, salivation. But what other kinds of physiological responses can be classically conditioned? Table 6.1 lists some of the US-UR relationships that could form the basis of classical conditioning. Of these, one of the most important and common is the classical conditioning of nausea.

Have you ever eaten a food that you liked and soon after became sick to your stomach with the flu, food poisoning, motion sickness, or some other ailment? Then, after recovering from your sickness, did you find the sight, smell, or even the idea of that food nauseating? If you answered "yes" to both of these questions, you have experienced what psychologists call classically conditioned **taste aversion** (Garcia, Kimeldorf, & Koelling, 1955; Lin, Arthurs, & Reilly, 2017).

One of your authors can vividly remember going through this type of conditioning as a child. After she ate a big dessert of peppermint ice cream, she came down with a severe case of tonsillitis that was accompanied by nausea and vomiting. After she recovered from the tonsillitis, it was years before she could even think about peppermint ice cream without feeling queasy. The same author regularly holds an informal contest in her classes to see who has had the longest-running taste aversion. The current record stands at more than 20 years!

It seems that taste aversion is something that we learn with particular ease (Garcia & Koelling, 1966). Taste aversion is unique in two ways. First, it often occurs with only one pairing of the NS/CS and the US. Unlike most cases of classical conditioning, in taste aversion, a single pairing of the food (NS/CS) and the agent that initially causes the nausea, in this case a virus (US), is usually sufficient to cause strong conditioning. The second difference is that in taste aversion, the interval between the NS/CS and the US can be very long. Intervals as long as 24 hours can result in conditioning in nonhuman animals (Garcia, Ervin, & Koelling, 1966; Logue, 1979). In humans, intervals of up to 7 hours between the NS/CS and US can still produce strong taste aversions (Logue, Ophir, & Strauss, 1981). Because taste aversion is an exception to some of the rules of conditioning, some psychologists believe that our genes give us a **biological preparedness** to learn taste aversion easily (Seligman, 1970).

LTim/Shutterstock.com

▲ Eating a food and then becoming ill can result in a conditioned taste aversion. The food becomes a conditioned stimulus that results in the conditioned response of nausea.

biological preparedness a genetic tendency to learn certain responses very easily

aversion therapy a type of therapy that uses classical conditioning to condition people to avoid certain stimuli

By being biologically prepared to learn taste aversion, we are better able to avoid certain poisonous plants and substances (Lin et al., 2017). Once something has made us sick, we want no part of it in the future. No doubt the ability to learn taste aversion quickly, and consequently to avoid poisonous substances, has survival value. Therefore, through natural selection, genes that enabled our ancestors to learn taste aversion quickly would have been retained, because animals with those genes—human and nonhuman—would have lived, whereas those slower to learn taste aversion would have been more likely to die. Taste aversion is widely seen in many species of animals (Garcia, 1992).

In fact, because many other species are also susceptible to taste aversion, it can be used to help control the pesky nature of some animals. In the western United States, coyotes like to sneak into sheep pastures and kill sheep rather than hunt for food in the wild. In the past, frustrated sheep ranchers would be very tempted to either shoot the coyotes on sight or lethally poison them. But thanks to psychologists, ranchers now have a more humane and ecologically sound alternative—using taste aversion to condition the coyotes to dislike sheep as a food source. They slaughter a few sheep and treat their carcasses with a chemical that causes nausea in coyotes. These tainted carcasses are then left out for the coyotes to eat. Because the coyotes can't pass up a free meal, they eat the sheep and get very sick to their stomachs. After they recover, they want nothing to do with sheep because of conditioned taste aversion (Gustavson & Garcia, 1974). The ranchers' problem is solved. Since the groundbreaking work on coyotes, taste aversion has been used to help train other species of animals to avoid conflict with humans—for example, in training monkeys to avoid human crops (Pebsworth & Radhakrishna, 2020).

Taste aversion can also be used to control problem behaviors in humans. One such application is in the treatment of alcoholism. The idea behind this **aversion therapy** is to condition a taste aversion to alcohol (see Chapter 14). The client takes the drug *disulfiram*. If they then drink alcohol, the result is intense nausea and headache, which often leads to conditioned taste aversion for alcohol.

Aversion therapy has been shown to be modestly helpful in motivating people with alcoholism to remain abstinent (Smith, Frawley, & Polissar, 1997) or significantly reduce their alcohol intake (Higuchi & Saito, 2013). However, it does not represent a "cure" for alcoholism. In one study, only 20% of the people with alcoholism remained abstinent for 1 year after being treated with aversion therapy alone (Landabaso et al., 1999). Even with strong motivation (see Chapter 5) to stop drinking, clients often relapse and often must stay on disulfiram to remain sober (Kristenson, 1992). But, disulfiram has many side effects and it cannot be used at all by certain people (Caputo et al., 2014; PDR.net, 2016). So, although aversion therapy with disulfiram may be a useful part of a comprehensive treatment program, it should not be the only treatment used for alcoholism (Finn, 2003; Hunt, 2002).

However, researchers may have found a promising new use for disulfiram. Disulfiram may intensify the negative effects of cocaine (e.g., anxiety), therefore motivating users to avoid it (Kosten et al., 2013). But some studies found no increase in such symptoms in participants taking disulfiram, despite the fact that the drug seemed to reduce their use of cocaine (Schottenfeld et al., 2014).

Psychology Applies to Your World

Can Classical Conditioning Help Us Understand How Our Bodies Respond to Drugs?

In Chapter 4, we discussed the use and misuse of substances, such as opiates and alcohol. Now that you have some understanding of classical conditioning, you may be surprised to learn that conditioning plays a role in how our bodies respond on a physiological level to these substances.

In a 1986 paper, Shepard Siegel and Delbert Ellsworth reported a case study of a man with cancer who died unexpectedly of a morphine overdose. The man had been receiving regular injections of morphine to reduce his cancer pain. Over the previous month, his son had always administered the morphine in his dimly lit bedroom. Under these conditions, the man tolerated the dosage well. Then one day, his son administered the usual dose of morphine, but in a different room of the home—the brightly lit living room. Almost immediately, the man began to show signs of morphine overdose. Even with medical intervention, sadly the man died hours later from a presumed overdose of morphine. Unfortunately, this sort of perplexing "overdose" has been seen in other cases and has been replicated in laboratory animals (Siegel, 1984; Siegel & Ellsworth, 1986). Why would someone suddenly overdose from taking their *usual* dosage of the drug?

Classical conditioning seems to play a role in these cases. One possible explanation is that these people had developed *conditioned compensatory responses* to cues associated with taking the drug in a particular and typical setting. The idea is that the physiological effects of the drug (i.e., central nervous system [CNS] depression in the case of morphine) act as a US that causes the UR of compensatory responses in the body (i.e., CNS arousal in the case of morphine). These compensatory responses are part of developing *tolerance* to the drug (see Chapter 4). Due to the compensatory response, your body requires more of the drug to get the desired effect because the compensatory response counteracts the effect of the drug on the body. Then, when a person habitually takes the drug in a particular setting, environmental cues in that setting (e.g., dim light) can serve as a CS that comes to evoke the conditioned compensatory responses, the CR, in the body (i.e., central nervous system or CNS *arousal*). Once this conditioning has occurred, if the person takes the same dose of the drug in a different, novel situation (e.g., a brightly lit room), the CS is missing, and the body does *not* respond with the conditioned compensatory response. Without the compensatory increase in CNS arousal to counteract the drug, the body may react much more strongly to this dosage of the drug (see Figure 6.4). In other words, there

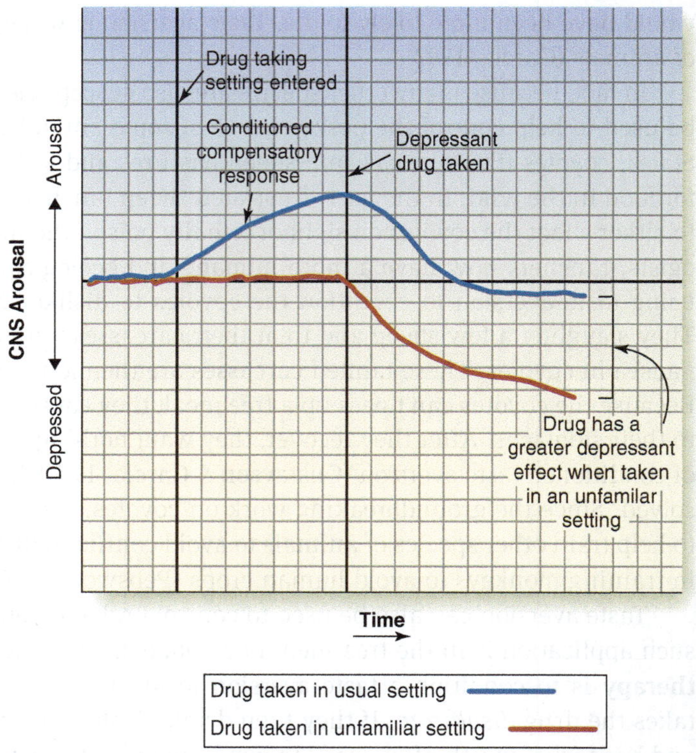

FIGURE 6.4

Conditioned Compensatory Responses to Taking the Same Dosage of a Depressant Drug in Typical and Atypical Settings.

These hypothetical data show changes in central nervous system arousal when taking one's usual dosage of a depressant drug such as morphine in a typical setting (shown in blue) and in an atypical setting (shown in red). As you can see, due to the initiation of a conditioned compensatory response in the typical setting, the net depressant effect of the drug is far less than what is seen when the same dosage of the drug is taken in a novel setting.

Disulfiram is also being investigated as a possible treatment for methamphetamine abuse (deMoura, Kohut, & Bergman, 2018).

In addition to its use in therapy for substance use disorders, classical conditioning may also help us better understand both the addiction process and the therapeutic use of drugs, a topic explored in *Psychology Applies to Your World.*

has been a sudden decrease in tolerance for the drug in this novel setting, possibly leading to an overdose (Siegel, 1989).

Sometimes conditioned compensatory responses are less dramatic and dire. Alcohol is sometimes referred to as a "social lubricant" because it tends to disinhibit us. To counteract this tendency, our body responds with the compensatory response of behavioral inhibition. People who have been conditioned to drink alcohol in a specific context tend to subsequently show greater behavioral disinhibition when they drink in a novel context (Birak, Higgs, and Terry, 2011). This could mean that drinking in an unfamiliar context may make one more likely to behave impulsively.

Drinking alcohol in social settings has been shown to enhance tolerance for alcohol but also increase craving for alcohol in these familiar settings (McKusker & Brown, 1990). The idea here is that for habitual social drinkers, the conditioned compensatory responses kick in when they are in social settings. As their body attempts to counteract the alcohol that it expects will be forthcoming, their tolerance increases, but they also begin to feel an increased need for the alcohol—perhaps because they begin to feel inhibited (a compensatory response) and feel they need the alcohol to relax. This could potentially help explain how some people progress from social drinking to alcohol addiction. However, other factors are mostly likely involved in this process as well. Before we move on, just a word of caution here—heavy drinking can and does lead to death due to alcohol poisoning, accidents, increased aggression, etc. (Fagan, Lyons, & Smyth, 2014; Gawryszewski & Monteiro, 2014; Hingson et al., 2002). Although we are unaware of studies showing increased overdose risk for people drinking in novel settings, you should always drink responsibly.

All of this may sound far-fetched, but there are a substantial number of human and animal studies that indicate that our bodies can become classically conditioned to respond to certain environmental cues with a variety of physiological reactions. For example, our bodies can be conditioned to release hormones, such as insulin and growth hormone (for review see, Skvortsova et al., 2019; Stockhorst, de Fries, Steingrueber, & Scherbaum, 2004; Stockhorst et al., 2004). Even the reactions of our immune system can be classically conditioned (Wirth et al., 2011).

For example, *cyclosporine A* is an immunosuppressant drug that can be used to treat certain autoimmune disorders, such as allergies, and to inhibit organ rejection in people with organ transplants. It is thought to work by dampening the function of *lymphocytes* (a type of white blood cell) in the body. In one study, both human men and rats were classically conditioned to associate a novel flavor (NS/CS) with an injection of cyclosporine A (US) that caused immunosuppression (UR/CR). For the rats, the novel flavor was saccharin, and for the men, it was a lavender-scented strawberry milk drink. After conditioning, both the rats and the men experienced immunosuppression (CR) when they were presented with the flavored drink alone (CS). Furthermore, this conditioned response was shown to last 6 days for the rats and 11 days for the men (Wirth et al., 2011). These findings raise the hope that doctors may be able to harness the power of classical conditioning to train the body to emit therapeutic responses on its own, with less frequent doses of medication needed. So, as you can see, classical conditioning is not just about Pavlov's dog. It is an important source of learning that may hold the keys to helping scientists find potentially lifesaving treatments.

Jacob Lund/Shutterstock.com

Social drinkers who tend to do their drinking in specific social settings may develop conditioned compensatory responses to the cues in these familiar settings. These cues may become conditioned stimuli that later cause an increase in behavioral inhibition when these people drink in the familiar settings and disinhibition of behavior when they drink in unfamiliar settings.

Engage Yourself! Psychologists have classically conditioned children to like healthful vegetables by pairing new vegetable flavors with the flavor of sugar to produce liking. After repeated pairings of the vegetables (NS/CS) with pleasant-tasting sugar (US), the children were conditioned to also like the vegetables (UR/CR). After conditioning, the children exhibited liking for the vegetables even when sugar was not present (Havermans & Jansen, 2007). Similar approaches have also been shown to work in children with autism spectrum disorder, getting them to accept foods that they had refused to eat in the past (Meier, Fryling, & Wallace, 2012). So, if you ever find yourself struggling with a child who doesn't want to eat healthy foods, try pairing them with a food that they do like—perhaps even a little sugar!

On the other hand, you may not have to go so far as to pair disliked foods with flavors that they already like. Some studies suggest that merely exposing children to disliked foods over and over is good enough to increase their taste preference for these foods. For example, Dutch children were exposed to vegetable crisps that they dipped into either ketchup (Conditioned trials) or a neutral white sauce (Unconditioned trials) over a period of 7 weeks. At the end of the trials, the children showed increased liking for the vegetables, regardless of whether they had been dipped into ketchup or the neutral white sauce (de Wild, de Graaf, & Jager, 2015). It appears that simple exposure was effective in increasing liking.

Studies like these suggest that exposure and classical conditioning are tools that parents can use to increase children's desire to eat a healthier diet full of vegetables (Wadhera, Capaldi Phillips, & Wilkie, 2015). Perhaps you can try such a strategy on yourself. Find a healthy food that you wish you liked better. Pair it with a food that you already like over a number of meals. You might just find yourself with a taste for healthier eating!

As you continue to read and study this chapter, keep in mind the general definition of classical conditioning and try to generate your own examples of real-world classical conditioning (perhaps even some of taste aversion). By doing this, you will increase your understanding and retention of this material—both of which will help you on exam day!

6.2.4 Removal of Classically Conditioned Responses: Extinction and Counterconditioning

Let's assume that you had the misfortune of developing a classically conditioned taste aversion to your favorite food because you ate this food just before you became ill with the flu. Furthermore, let's assume that you wanted to be able to eat your favorite food again without feeling sick to your stomach. How would you go about ridding yourself of your acquired taste aversion?

extinction the removal of a conditioned response

In classical conditioning, **extinction**, or removal of the conditioned response, can be brought about by presenting the conditioned stimulus to the participant without also presenting the unconditioned stimulus. In our example, extinction would begin when you ate your favorite food (CS) and you did not have the flu (US). When the CS is presented alone, it no longer predicts the onset of the US, and the CR decreases.

The degree to which a conditioned response can be extinguished is affected by several factors, such as the context in which extinction takes place (Claassen et al., 2016). Happily, your author finally got over her taste aversion to peppermint ice cream years later after she took a job in a restaurant that sold a great deal of it. After scooping many scoops of peppermint ice cream, she found that the sight and smell of it no longer made her feel sick. It wasn't long before she was even able to eat peppermint ice cream without a problem.

Pavlov's experiments with dogs also included extinction trials with the dogs. ● FIGURE 6.5 shows the **acquisition**, or learning curve, for the CR and the extinction curve for the CR in Pavlov's experiment. As you can see from this figure, the CR of salivation to the buzzer was acquired over several trials in which the CS and the US were paired. In the extinction trials, the buzzer was sounded but no food was presented, and there was a fairly steady decrease in the CR. In other words, the dog became less and less likely to salivate when it heard the buzzer.

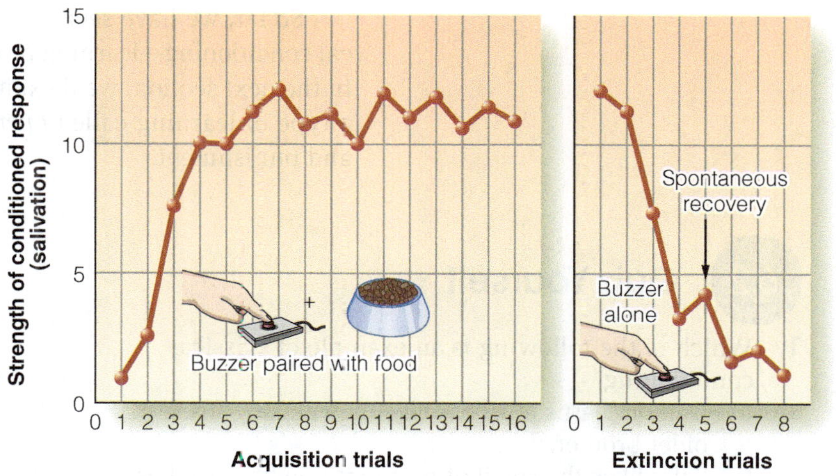

FIGURE 6.5

The Phases of Classical Conditioning

These plots show the number of conditioning trials on the *x*-axis and the strength of the conditioned response on the *y*-axis. During acquisition, the response increases in strength as a function of the number of times the CS and US have been paired together. During extinction, the CS is presented without the US, which leads to a decrease in the strength of the CR. Note that during extinction, sometimes there is a temporary increase in the strength of the CR even though the CS has not been recently presented with the US. This is called *spontaneous recovery*.

Does this mean that once a response has been extinguished, it is gone forever? Note that the extinction curve in Figure 6.5 does not show a completely continuous pattern of decrease in the CR. Sometimes, after a response has been extinguished, there will be a temporary increase in the CR. This phenomenon, called **spontaneous recovery**, can occur at any point during extinction (Troisi, 2003) and may be especially likely if a response is extinguished immediately after it is originally learned (Huff et al., 2009). Let's go back to our example of taste aversion to peppermint ice cream. Today, although your author does not have an active, ongoing taste aversion to peppermint ice cream, every now and again when she thinks of peppermint ice cream, she will feel a bit sick. Thankfully, her spontaneous recovery doesn't last long. She soon reenters extinction, and she can think of peppermint ice cream and even eat it without a trace of nausea.

acquisition the process of learning a conditioned response or behavior

spontaneous recovery during extinction, the tendency for a conditioned response to reappear and strengthen over a brief period of time before re-extinguishing

counterconditioning removing a classically conditioned response by conditioning a new, incompatible response to the unconditioned stimulus

What do you suppose would happen if she happened to eat some peppermint ice cream on a hot day and suffered from a small amount of heat-induced nausea? Do you think her taste aversion to peppermint ice cream would return? It is likely that it would. In fact, responses that are extinguished are usually reacquired more easily than they were acquired in the first place. Extinction does not mean that we forget that there once was a connection between the CS and the US; it simply means that the CR is less likely to occur when the CS is presented.

Another method of removing a conditioned response would be to condition the person or animal to have a different, incompatible response to the unconditioned stimulus. This technique is called **counterconditioning**. Recall the story of Little Albert (Chapter 1 and Section 6.2.3 of this Chapter). One way to remove Albert's fear of the white rat would be to repeatedly pair the rat with a US that elicits a positive emotional response, for example a piece of candy. By presenting the rat and then giving Albert candy, he may come to associate the rat with the candy, producing happiness rather than fear. Since it is difficult to simultaneously be happy and distressed, Albert's fear might be reduced as a result of this counterconditioning.

So far, we have seen that learning can occur through habituation and classical conditioning—learning processes that both result in rather simplistic behaviors. In the next section, we'll examine how we learn more complex responses through a type of learning called *operant conditioning*, which depends on reinforcement and punishment.

6.2 Quiz Yourself

1. Which of the following is an example of classical conditioning?
- a. Damon learns to ride a bike by watching his older brother.
- b. Sally likes the smell of rose perfume because her ex-partner used to wear rose scented cologne.
- c. After 20 minutes in the day-care center, Ralph barely notices the squealing of the children at play.
- d. Ted never speeds after receiving a $500 fine for speeding.

2. Which of the following is the *best* example of a US-UR pair in first-order classical conditioning?
- a. Receiving money—happiness
- b. An electric shock to the finger—jerking one's finger away
- c. Receiving a promotion—working overtime
- d. Seeing a snake—fear

3. Janna, a real estate agent, desperately wants to sell a home. Janna tells the owner to place a pan of vanilla extract in the oven and heat it just before the prospective buyers arrive to look at the house. Janna knows that the smell of vanilla in the house will increase the chance that the buyers will like the house because they have been classically conditioned to respond favorably to the smell of vanilla. In this example, what is the CR?
- a. The pleasant emotions evoked by the smell of vanilla
- b. The smell of vanilla
- c. The memory of Grandma baking cookies
- d. The house

4. Jamal was eating a hotdog *on* a Ferris wheel, and *while on* the ride Jamal became ill from motion sickness. Afterward, Jamal developed a conditioned taste aversion to hotdogs. Jamal's story best illustrates the fact that classically conditioned taste aversions can be learned even when there is a lack of _____.
- a. contingency
- b. contiguity
- c. both a and b
- d. None of the above

5. Wanda developed a conditioned taste aversion to pickles as a child. Today at age 30, Wanda can once again eat pickles without experiencing nausea. Wanda's ability to now eat pickles is likely due to _____.
- a. dishabituation
- b. classical conditioning of a new taste aversion
- c. extinction
- d. an orienting reflex to pickles

Answers 1. b; 2. b; 3. a; 4. a; 5. c

6.3 Operant Conditioning: Learning from the Consequences of Our Actions

Suppose you are sitting in your psychology class, listening to a lecture, when your professor asks the class a question. For some reason, you raise your hand to answer the question even though you have never made a comment in this class before. The professor calls on you, and you give the correct answer. In response to your answer, the professor smiles broadly and praises you for giving such an accurate and insightful answer.

How do you think this scenario would affect you? As a result of the professor's reaction, would you be more or less likely to raise your hand in the future when they asked a question? If you are like most people, this type of praise would encourage you to raise your hand in the future. But what would happen if, instead of praising you, they frowned and said that your answer was one of the stupidest they had ever heard. How would this reaction affect your behavior? Obviously, after such a cruel response, many of us would be very unlikely to answer any more questions in that professor's class!

Both of these examples illustrate another type of learning, called **operant conditioning**. In operant conditioning, we learn from the consequences of our behavior. In our example, being praised for answering a question makes one more likely to answer questions in the future; being called stupid makes one less likely to answer future questions. We will see that operant conditioning is a powerful means of learning that explains how we learn many of the important lessons in our lives. But first, we will begin by looking at how operant conditioning was discovered.

operant conditioning a type of learning in which the organism learns through the consequences of its behavior

law of effect a principle discovered by E. L. Thorndike, which states that behaviors that lead to positive consequences will be strengthened and behaviors that lead to negative consequences will be weakened

6.3.1 E. L. Thorndike's Law of Effect

At about the same time that Ivan Pavlov was developing his theories about learning in Russia, American psychologist E. L. Thorndike (1874–1949) was busy conducting experiments on operant conditioning in New York. Thorndike was working with cats in specially constructed puzzle boxes. A puzzle box is a box with a lid or door that locks into place so that an animal can be placed inside. Once inside the box, the animal must activate some type of unlatching device to win its release. The device that unlatches the lid may be a rope pull, a pedal that needs to be pushed, or a switch that needs to be flipped. ● FIGURE 6.6 shows a typical puzzle box with a foot-pedal release.

Unlocking the Puzzle of Learning

In his research, Thorndike (1898) locked a hungry cat in one of these puzzle boxes and placed some food outside the box. Then he recorded how long it took the cat to figure out how to get out of the box. Once the cat activated the device and got out of the box, Thorndike would take the cat and place it back in the puzzle box. Over and over, Thorndike repeated this procedure of imprisoning the cat and measuring the time it took the cat to win its release.

Thorndike observed in these studies that when the cat was first placed in the puzzle box, it thrashed around randomly until, by accident, it tripped the mechanism and got out of the box. After several more trials, however, the cat's behavior became less random, and the time it took to get out of the box declined. This decrease in the amount of time it took the cat to get out of the box indicated to Thorndike that learning was taking place: The cat was learning to associate its behavior with the consequences that its behavior brought about.

Based on what he observed in his puzzle box studies, Thorndike developed a principle of learning that he called the **law of effect**. The law of effect states that in a given situation, behaviors that lead to positive, satisfying consequences will be strengthened, such that the next time the situation occurs, the behavior is more likely to be repeated. A corollary to the law of effect also states that in a given situation, behaviors that lead to negative, discomforting consequences will be weakened, such that the next time the situation occurs, the behavior will be less likely to be repeated (Thorndike, 1905).

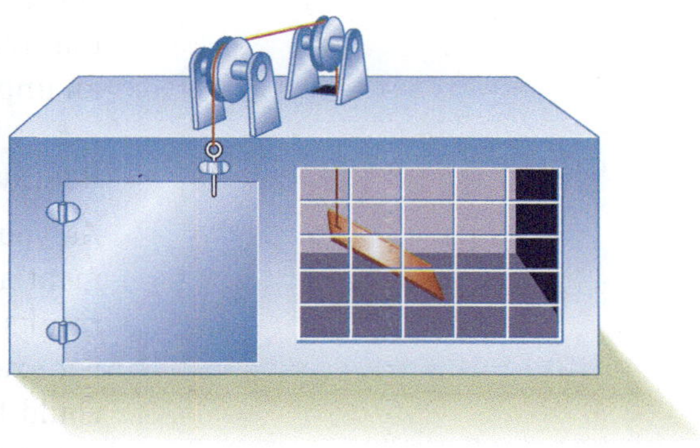

FIGURE 6.6

Puzzle Box

This is an example of a puzzle box like those used by Thorndike. To get out of the box, the cat would have to pull the string or step on the pedal.

Random Actions and Reinforcement

Let's examine the law of effect in terms of a hungry cat in a puzzle box. When the cat is first trapped in the box, it will likely perform many random behaviors. For instance, it may claw, hiss, bite at the bars, or meow. But none of these behaviors will open the box. The cat's early responses to being stuck in the box are random or via trial and error. After some time, let's say that the cat happens to step on the foot pedal that opens the puzzle box and is able to get out to where the food is waiting. This particular random behavior has led to a consequence that is far more rewarding than any of the other random behaviors the cat has tried. The law of effect states that this particular response is strengthened, or *reinforced*, because it results in a pleasant consequence. This process of **reinforcement** means that the behavior will become more likely in the future. The next time the cat is locked in the box, it will be more likely to step on the pedal than to try the other behaviors that did not lead to release on prior trials. Over many trials, the law of effect results in the cat's becoming more and more likely to step on the pedal and less and less likely to use other behaviors that were not reinforced in the past. The behaviors that were not reinforced are likely to die out.

reinforcement the strengthening of a response that occurs when the response leads to a pleasant consequence

positive reinforcement strengthening a behavior by adding something pleasant to the environment of the organism

negative reinforcement strengthening a behavior by removing something unpleasant from the environment of the organism

punishment the weakening of a response that occurs when a behavior leads to an unpleasant consequence

positive punishment weakening a behavior by adding something unpleasant to the organism's environment

negative punishment weakening a behavior by removing something pleasant from the organism's environment

Positive and Negative Reinforcement

The two types of reinforcement are *positive reinforcement* and *negative reinforcement* (see You Review: The Four Consequences of Behavior). In **positive reinforcement**, the behavior leads to the addition of something pleasant to the organism's environment. For instance, Thorndike positively reinforced the cat for stepping on the pedal by giving the cat food when it got out of the puzzle box.

In **negative reinforcement**, the behavior is reinforced by the removal of something unpleasant from the organism's environment. In Thorndike's case, the cat was negatively reinforced for stepping on the pedal because this behavior led to the removal of its imprisonment in the puzzle box. (We are, of course, assuming that the hungry cat did not enjoy being trapped in the box.)

The difference between punishment and negative reinforcement is a point that gives many students great trouble because they tend to think that negative reinforcement is a type of punishment. This is not true! The "negative" in negative reinforcement refers to the fact that negative reinforcement removes something from the organism's environment; it does not refer to a negative or unpleasant consequence of the behavior. When you see the term *reinforcement*, keep in mind that reinforcement leads to an increase in behavior. **Punishment**, in contrast, is an unpleasant consequence that leads to a decrease in behavior.

Positive and Negative Punishment

As you can see from You Review: The Four Consequences of Behavior, punishment also comes in two varieties. **Positive punishment** occurs when a behavior results in the addition of something unpleasant to the organism's environment. For example, if we wanted to stop the cat from pressing the pedal, the puzzle box could be rigged to electrify the floor of the cage every time the cat stepped on the pedal. The cat would then be positively punished every time it stepped on the pedal because the resulting shock would add pain to the cat's environment.

In **negative punishment**, the behavior leads to the removal of something pleasant from the organism's environment. A puzzle box could be designed so that when the cat presses the pedal, a drape falls over the cage, and the cat can no longer see outside the cage. If the cat enjoys seeing outside the cage, then stepping on the pedal would lead to negative punishment because it leads to the loss of a

YOU REVIEW **The Four Consequences of Behavior**

Reinforcement increases the likelihood of a behavior; punishment decreases it.

	Positive	Negative
Reinforcement The consequence increases the behavior	**Positive Reinforcement** Something pleasant is added to the environment  Nils Jacobi/Shutterstock.com Example: Your cat learns to use the cat door, so you give it a kitty treat.	**Negative Reinforcement** Something unpleasant is removed from the environment  Dorling Kindersley ltd/Alamy Stock Photo Example: Your cat, who hates to be wet, uses its new cat door to come in out of the rain.
Punishment The consequence decreases the behavior	**Positive Punishment** Something unpleasant is added to the environment  Juniors/Juniors/Superstock Example: Every time your cat gets on the table, you squirt it with a water bottle.	**Negative Punishment** Something pleasant is removed from the environment  blickwinkel/Alamy stock photo Example: Your cat misbehaves, so you put it outside away from its toys.

pleasant privilege for the cat. The effect of punishment is to decrease a behavior, regardless of whether the punishment is positive or negative.

6.3.2 B. F. Skinner and the Experimental Study of Operant Conditioning

Although E. L. Thorndike is generally credited with discovering the law of effect, American psychologist B. F. Skinner (1904–1990) is more commonly associated with the scientific study of operant conditioning. Skinner began to formally study operant conditioning in the late 1920s when he was a graduate student at Harvard University. During his long career—from the 1920s through the 1980s—Skinner made many significant contributions to our understanding of operant conditioning (Schultz & Schultz, 2016). One of his most obvious contributions was to introduce new terminology and technology to the study of this type of learning.

It was Skinner who introduced the term *operant conditioning* to the study of the law of effect. Skinner felt that using the term *operant* was a good way to distinguish this type of learning from classical conditioning. Skinner wanted to emphasize the fact that in classical conditioning, the organism does not actively choose to operate on the environment to produce some consequence; rather, the response is forced from the animal. Thus, Skinner referred to classically conditioned behavior as *respondent* behavior. In contrast, Skinner wanted to emphasize that in operant conditioning, the animal makes a choice to respond to its environment in a certain way. In this type of learning, behavior operates on the environment to produce some consequence, hence the term *operant* (Skinner, 1938).

Another of Skinner's contributions to the study of operant conditioning was the development of a new device that allows researchers to condition animals in less time than is required to condition an animal in a puzzle box. This device, now called a **Skinner box**, is a chamber large enough to house a small animal, typically a rat or a pigeon. When rats are used, the chamber contains a lever or bar that the rat can press. When the rat depresses the lever or bar, it receives reinforcement in the form of a pellet of food from an automatic feeding device attached to the chamber. When pigeons are used, the pigeon receives a food reinforcer by pecking at a disk on the side of the box.

Skinner box device created by B. F. Skinner to study operant behavior in a compressed time frame; in a Skinner box, an organism is automatically reinforced or punished for engaging in certain behaviors

To study operant behavior, Skinner would place a hungry rat in the Skinner box and wait for the rat to accidentally press the bar (which tends to happen rather quickly given the Skinner box's small size and simplicity). Once the rat pressed the bar, a pellet would drop into the chamber to reinforce this operant behavior. The rat was free to press the bar as often as it wanted and whenever it wanted. By recording the number of bar presses and when they occurred, Skinner could get a good picture of the acquisition of the operant behavior. Using the Skinner box, researchers have been able to learn a great deal about the different aspects of operant conditioning. This advance in the methodology and apparatus for studying animal learning is one of B. F. Skinner's major contributions to psychology.

Science Source

Science Source

▲ In these operant chambers, the animals can be reinforced with food for pressing the bar or pecking the disk. Skinner boxes such as these allow researchers to efficiently gather data on operant conditioning.

Applying Skinner Box Technology In The Real World

In 1958, B. F. Skinner wrote an article entitled "Teaching Machines" in which he argued that psychologists and educators should apply their understanding of operant conditioning to develop devices that would allow children to learn at their own pace (Skinner, 1958). In Skinner's view, these teaching machines would present the learner with a question or task to answer or complete. If the learner's answer was correct, the machine would allow them to advance to the next question, thereby reinforcing the learner for getting the correct answer. If the learner's answer was incorrect, they would not be allowed to advance until they provided the right answer, thus withholding reinforcement for the incorrect response. In essence, the devices functioned as Skinner boxes for humans.

Before advanced computer technology became part of everyday life, such teaching machines were elaborate and cumbersome to construct. The personal computer changed all this. Today, we have abundant examples of these "teaching machines," although we rarely refer to them as such. They are now known as Leap Pads, Nintendo Switch, Xbox One X, Wii U, PlayStations, smartphone/tablet apps, and so on. Some of these products were developed with the specific goal of being educational, teaching machines. Others were not.

In playing electronic games, players are reinforced for their behavior in various ways. A child selecting a correct answer on a Leap Pad hears a reward tone and is congratulated. A gamer scores points for shooting the villain, gets to see the next level after successful play, receives feedback on their exercise form from a Nintendo Switch, and so on. Players can also be punished. If you make a bad decision, your character might be killed or you may lose points or resources. You may hear a disappointed failure tone if you spell a word incorrectly, and so on.

Research has indicated that these devices can have both positive and negative impact on behavior. For example, college students who played video games in which women are portrayed as sex objects exhibited increased tendencies to treat women inappropriately (Yao, Mahood, & Linz, 2010). In another study, male (but not female) college students exhibited increased acceptance of attitudes supporting rape after playing a game that objectified women (Beck et al., 2012). Young men randomly assigned to play the video game *Grand Theft Auto III* were also found to exhibit more uncooperative behavior and more permissive attitudes about alcohol and drugs than did a control group that played a low-violence game (Brady & Matthews, 2006). In a study of Flemish adolescents, violent video game play (e.g., *Call of Duty* and *Tomb Raider*), but not nonviolent video game play (e.g., *Tetris*), was found to be a small but significant risk factor for engaging in delinquent behavior (e.g., inappropriate sexual behavior, threatening others with weapons, etc.; Exelmans, Custers, & Van den Bulck, 2015). And, in another study, violent video game play was found to impair one's recognition of anger in other's facial expressions, increase one's perception that they themselves are a good fighter, and reduce one's perception of another man's toughness (Denson et al., 2020). In other words, playing a violent video game seemed to change one's perceptions in a way that made players feel like more competent fighters. Whether or not this increased feeling of competence would lead to future conflicts with others remains to be seen.

Yet psychologists are somewhat divided on the issue of whether or not violent video games are really harmful. In examining the body of research on this issue, some researchers argue that violent video games are not harmful and only slightly (if at all) increase aggression in players (Ferguson, 2015; Furuya-Kanamori & Doi, 2016). Other researchers argue that the available research suggests that violent video games are likely to increase aggression and other harmful effects in players (Boxer, Groves, & Docherty, 2015; Gentile, 2015; Rothstein & Bushman, 2015; Valkenburg, 2015). At present, the argument is a complex, mathematical one that centers on how to most accurately summarize and analyze the results of many studies examining the link between violent game play and subsequent aggressive behavior.

Whether or not violent video games tend to increase problematic behavior in players, there is evidence to suggest that computer games and other interactive technologies may sometimes have the power to condition us in positive ways. For example, playing a violent video game in a cooperative manner may increase subsequent prosocial behaviors. In one study, playing a violent role-playing game with someone from a different university as a teammate (i.e., cooperating with an *out-group* member—see Chapter 10) led to less willingness to use physical aggression (Velez et al., 2014). Another study showed that habitual players of violent video games had shorter reaction times when playing a police officer's dilemma game in which they had to quickly determine whether or not to shoot a target. Most interestingly, this quicker reaction time was not related to increased errors of shooting the wrong target (Greitemeyer, 2020). Video game play in general may also have the power to increase the psychological, social, and physical well-being of players in certain ways, such as, in fulfilling *self-determination* needs (Chapter 5), providing friendship, and developing teamwork skills (for review, see Halbrook, O'Donnell, & Msefti, 2019; Johnson, Wyeth, & Sweetser, 2014).

Interactive technologies have also been shown to increase motivation for learning and cognitive skill building. For example, kindergarteners who used a Leap Pad experienced an increase in reading enjoyment, reading proficiency, and reading engagement (Munson, 2006). Older people using Nintendo DS to play "brain training" games that exercise cognitive function were more engaged in the games and enjoyed them more than doing the same sorts of exercises in a paper and pencil format (Nacke, Nacke, & Lindley, 2009). Given that numerous studies suggest that exercising cognitive function in adulthood may help us keep our cognitive abilities longer (Valenzuela & Sachdev, 2009), having engaging devices like the Nintendo DS to encourage such exercise is a good thing. Even more exciting are gaming systems

▲ Computer and video games are examples of modern technologies that are similar to Skinner boxes, in that they are programmed to reinforce players for certain behaviors, while punishing them for others.

such as the Wii Fit and the newer Nintendo Switch that combine the cognitive aspects of gaming with physical exercise. Use of these so-called *exergames* has been shown to improve the cognitive *and* physical functioning of both older adults (Maillot, Perrot, & Hartley, 2012) and children with *attention deficit hyperactivity disorder (ADHD)* (Benzing & Schmidt, 2019). And, playing an exergame in which you play an avatar of yourself may offer additional motivation to continue exercising (Li & Lwin, 2016). The well-documented link between physical fitness and cognitive decline (e.g., Brown, Peiffer, & Martins, 2013; Köbe et al., 2016) makes the use of these technologies especially promising for warding off age-related cognitive decline and improving overall health. The good news is that even light levels of physical activity may provide us with some cognitive benefits (e.g., Gothe, 2020). So, think about that next time you are looking for some new entertainment. An exergame might just be a fun way to strengthen both your body and your brain.

6.3.3 Acquisition and Extinction

Although Skinner was ahead of his time in recognizing the real-world potential of the Skinner box, his main purpose for developing the device was to use it to better research the process of operant conditioning. Two areas that Skinner explored with the Skinner box were the *acquisition* and *extinction* of behavior. You may recall from our discussion of classical conditioning that acquisition refers to the conditioning of a response and extinction refers to the loss of a conditioned response. As in classical conditioning, it is possible to plot acquisition and extinction curves for operantly conditioned behaviors. The rat learns that pressing the bar leads to obtaining food, and its tendency to press the bar increases. The frequency with which the rat presses the bar continues to increase until it reaches some maximum strength. For example, the rat can eat the pellets only so fast. Therefore, the number of times the rat will press the bar in a given time frame is limited by the speed at which it eats (● FIGURE 6.7).

Extinction also occurs in operant conditioning, but it is caused by

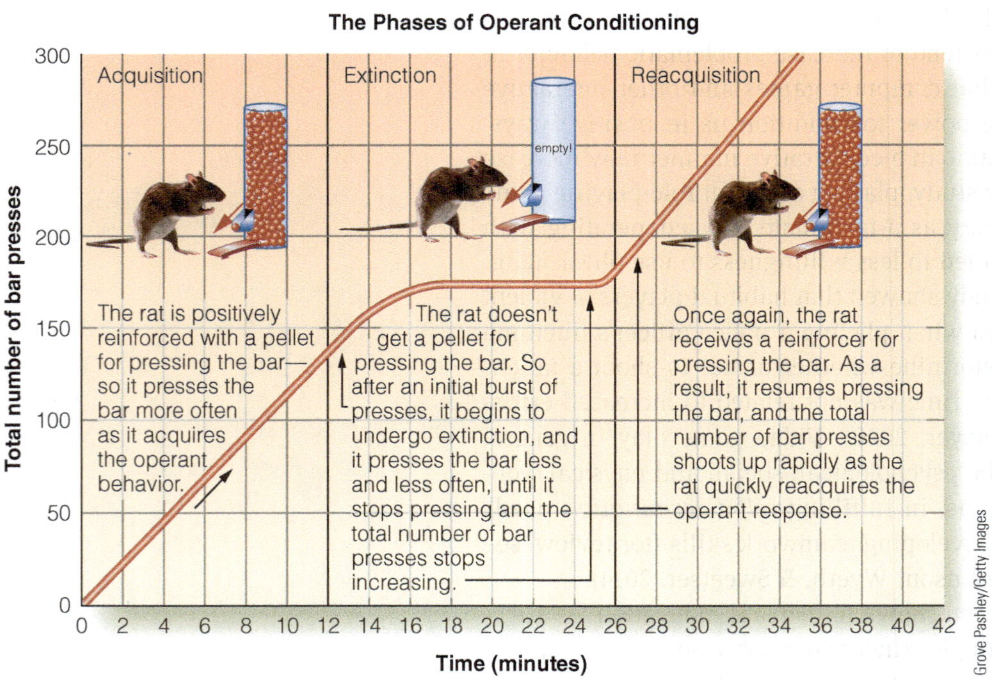

FIGURE 6.7

Acquisition and Extinction in Operant Conditioning

Just as we saw in classical conditioning, operant responses can also undergo acquisition, extinction, and reacquisition.

circumstances that differ from those that cause extinction in classical conditioning (Lattal & Lattal, 2012). In classical conditioning, extinction occurs when the CS is presented without the US. In operant conditioning, extinction occurs because the behavior is no longer reinforced (see Figure 6.7). Many of us hold jobs, and going to work is an example of an operantly conditioned response. We go to work because we expect to be reinforced for this behavior on payday. What would it take to extinguish your going-to-work behavior? The answer is simple, isn't it? All it would take is the removal of your reinforcement. If your boss stopped paying you, you would likely stop going to work! In operant conditioning, withholding the reinforcement that maintains the behavior causes the extinction of that behavior.

Like acquisition, extinction does not typically happen in one trial. Even if your boss failed to pay you on payday, you might very well return to work for a few days. In fact, you might even experience a temporary **extinction burst**, during which you worked harder in an attempt to obtain reinforcement immediately after your boss withholds your pay (Galensky et al., 2001). At the very least, you probably would not entirely abandon work until it became very clear that reinforcement would no longer be forthcoming. Extinction tends to occur over a number of trials. Each time the organism emits the operant response without being reinforced, its tendency to repeat the response diminishes (see Figure 6.7).

Because extinction removes responses, it has many practical applications. One way to stop someone from engaging in an annoying behavior is to extinguish it by removing the reinforcement for that behavior. Take the example of a parent and child shopping together in a department store. The child sees a toy that they want, but their parent refuses to buy it. At this refusal, the child begins to whine and cry, but instead of punishing the child for this behavior, the parent ignores the child. By not reinforcing the whining and crying, the parent begins to extinguish this annoying behavior. Once the child learns that crying and whining do not lead to reinforcement, the child will stop using this behavioral strategy to get what they want.

The trick to using extinction to reduce unwanted behaviors is figuring out what is actually reinforcing the behavior, removing that reinforcement, and then making sure that no other reinforcement of the unwanted behavior is occurring (Martin & Pear, 2007). If one parent ignores the child's tantrums when they take the child shopping but the other gives in and buys the child toys, then the behavior will not be completely extinguished.

iStock.com/FangXiaNuo

▲ By ignoring this child's tantrum, the parent is placing the child on an extinction schedule. If the parent does not reinforce the child for this behavior, the behavior should be less likely to occur in the future, at least for this parent.

6.3.4 Schedules of Reinforcement

Acquisition and extinction of operant behavior seem simple enough, but numerous Skinner box studies have taught us that many factors can affect the rate at which responses are acquired or extinguished. One extremely important factor is the **schedule of reinforcement**—the timing and the consistency of the reinforcement. Schedules of reinforcement include both *continuous* and *partial reinforcement* of behavior. Let's take a closer look.

Continuous Reinforcement

Conceptually, the simplest type of reinforcement schedule is **continuous reinforcement**, in which each and every instance of the desired behavior is reinforced. In a Skinner box study, every time the rat presses the bar, a pellet of food is delivered to the rat. In real life, many simple behaviors are reinforced on a continuous schedule. One example is when we reach for objects. The act of

extinction burst a temporary increase in a behavioral response that occurs immediately after extinction has begun

schedule of reinforcement the frequency and timing of the reinforcements that an organism receives

continuous reinforcement a schedule of reinforcement in which the organism is reinforced for every instance of the desired response reaching is reinforced when we actually grasp the object we were trying to get. Except in unusual circumstances, such as reaching for an object on a shelf that is too high, reaching is reinforced every time we reach (Skinner, 1953).

Unfortunately, continuous schedules of reinforcement are often not very helpful when using operant conditioning to modify behavior. Continuous reinforcement is often not very helpful for two main reasons. The first drawback is a practical one. Let's say that you were going to use continuous reinforcement to change a child's behavior. You want your child to be polite when speaking to others, so you decide to use a continuous schedule and reinforce your child with praise every time they are polite. Would this be a realistic goal? We doubt it. A continuous schedule of reinforcement would mean that you would have to be around your child every time they were polite, and you would have to praise or otherwise reinforce them for this politeness. This just isn't practical or possible.

The second problem is that continuously reinforced behaviors are vulnerable to extinction. What happens when your children are not in your presence, and you are not there to continually reinforce their good behavior? As we have already seen, when reinforcement is withheld, behavior often starts to extinguish. The problem with using continuous schedules of reinforcement is that they lead to behaviors that extinguish very quickly once the reinforcement ceases (Nevin, 2012; Nevin & Grace, 2005). Research suggests this may be especially true in situations where acquisition of the response happens quickly (Gradari et al., 2016).

Why would this be true? When a behavior has been continuously reinforced, there is a very clear contingency between the behavior and the reinforcement. The organism learns that the behavior should always lead to a reinforcer. When the reinforcement stops, a clear signal is sent that the contingency no longer holds true, and extinction occurs relatively rapidly.

Partial Reinforcement

However, let's say the behavior is reinforced only some of the time. What is likely to happen then? The child or animal is less likely to see the lack of reinforcement as a sign that the contingency is no longer operating. Schedules of reinforcement that reinforce a behavior only some of the time are called **partial reinforcement** schedules. *Ratio schedules* of partial reinforcement are based on the number of responses, whereas *interval schedules* are based on the timing of the responses.

partial reinforcement a schedule of reinforcement in which the organism is reinforced for only some instances of the desired response

fixed ratio schedule a schedule of reinforcement in which the organism is reinforced for every *x*th instance of the desired response

variable ratio schedule a schedule of reinforcement in which the organism is reinforced on average for every *x*th instance of the desired response

Ratio Schedules of Reinforcement There are two types of ratio schedules of reinforcement, *fixed* and *variable*. In a **fixed ratio schedule**, a set number of responses must be emitted before a reinforcer is given. For example, suppose every third response is reinforced. A rat in a Skinner box would have to press the bar three times to get a food pellet. In the real world, some people are paid on fixed ratio schedules. A person who works in a manufacturing plant and is paid a bonus for every 100 parts assembled is being reinforced on a fixed ratio, as are agricultural workers who are paid per bushel of fruit picked, garment workers who are paid per piece sewn, and so on.

Besides producing slower extinction than continuous reinforcement, fixed ratio schedules also lead to fairly high response rates (● FIGURE 6.8a). High rates of responding are especially likely if it takes many responses to get a reinforcer (Collier, Hirsch, & Hamlin, 1972; Stephens et al., 1975). If your goal is to produce many instances of the behavior, such as many filled boxes of raspberries, in a short time frame, a fixed ratio schedule may just do the trick.

The second type of ratio schedule is the **variable ratio schedule**, in which the exact number of responses that are required to receive a reinforcer varies around some average. For example, the rat may have to press the bar two times to receive

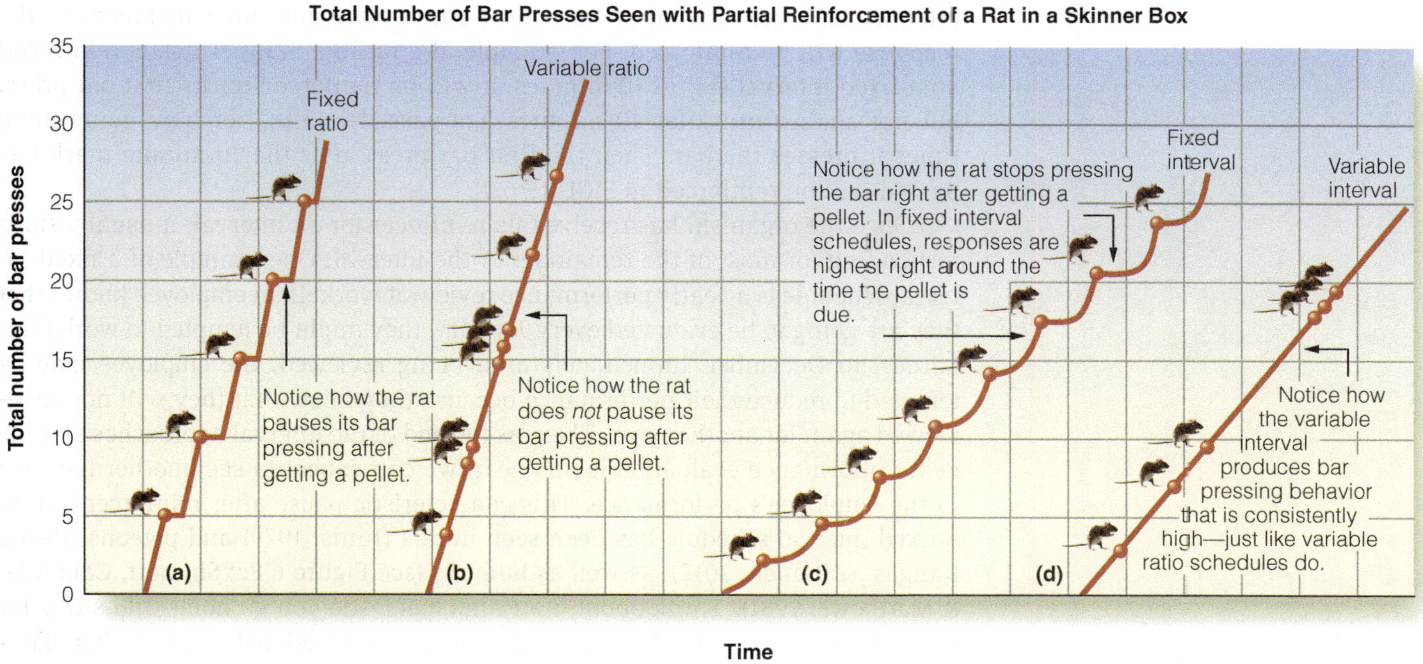

FIGURE 6.8

Partial Reinforcement of a Rat in a Skinner Box

This graph plots the rates of response for different schedules of reinforcement and the points at which the rat is reinforced. Notice how the rat's bar-pressing behavior changes before and after it receives a pellet on the different schedules of reinforcement. Which schedule would you use if you were going to use positive reinforcement to train your dog?

the first reinforcer, one time to receive the second reinforcer, and then six times to receive the third reinforcer.

Variable ratio schedules of reinforcement yield higher rates of response (Figure 6.8b) and even slower rates of extinction than fixed ratio schedules. A good example of this resistance to extinction comes from a real-world example of variable ratio reinforcement. Slot machines pay off on a variable ratio schedule of reinforcement. You never know how many pulls of the handle it will take to lead to the reinforcement of a payoff. Consequently, people will play slot machines for long periods of time, even when they haven't hit the jackpot (Schreiber & Dixon, 2001). To further enhance this effect, some slot machines are programmed to reinforce players with celebratory sounds and images, even when they have *lost* money (Dixon et al., 2015). One of your authors once knew a student who lost $2,000 in an evening playing slots. They don't call slot machines one-armed bandits for nothing!

Interval Schedules of Reinforcement Ratio schedules of reinforcement are based on the number of responses emitted by the organism. In interval schedules of reinforcement, the organism is reinforced only once per some interval of time. There are two types of interval schedules of reinforcement, *fixed* and *interval*. In a **fixed interval schedule**, the organism is reinforced for the first instance of the desired response,

fixed interval schedule a schedule of reinforcement in which the organism is reinforced for the first desired response in an *x*th interval of time

▲ Slot machines pay off on a variable ratio schedule of reinforcement. Because it is hard to predict when the next reinforcer is due, people playing the machine are likely to show high rates of responding and very slow rates of extinction. This translates into big profits for the casinos!

after which a set interval of time must pass before any other instances of the response will be reinforced. For example, if a rat in a Skinner box is reinforced on a fixed interval (FI) of 10 minutes, it will be reinforced for its first bar press, but not again until after 10 minutes has passed—no matter how many more times it presses the bar. Then the first bar press after the 10-minute mark has passed will be reinforced (● FIGURE 6.9).

Once the organism has received its reinforcer for an interval, it usually stops responding for most of the remainder of the interval. One example of a fixed interval schedule is a yearly performance review at work. If an employee knows that they are going to be evaluated every January, they might be tempted to work their hardest in December. Immediately after being reviewed, the employee may be tempted to reduce their performance because they know that they will not be reviewed again for another year. Then, as the end of the interval approaches and the next performance evaluation looms near, we can expect to see another increase in the employee's performance. This characteristic pause after reinforcement on a fixed interval schedule has been seen in rats (Innis, 1979) and pigeons (Berry, Kangas, & Branch, 2012), as well as humans (see Figure 6.8c; Shimoff, Cantania, & Matthews, 1981). Think about it for a moment—do you go home and study for your psychology course the night after you take a scheduled exam in that class? Or, do you procrastinate and put off reading your next assignment? The research on schedules of reinforcement predicts that you will procrastinate.

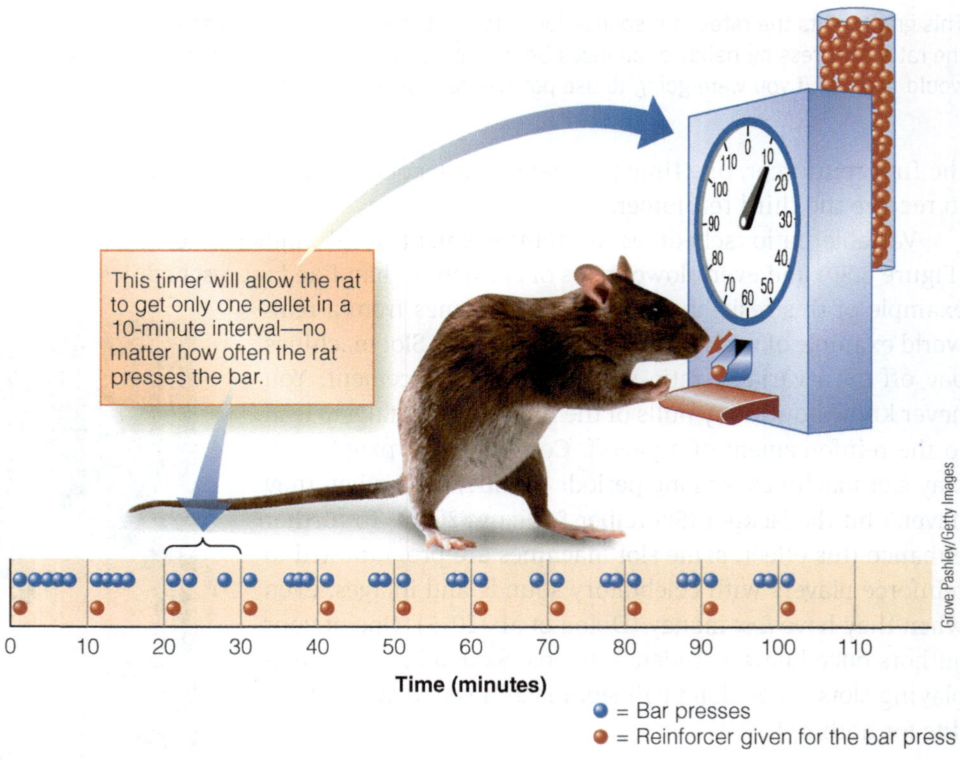

FIGURE 6.9

Fixed Interval Schedule of Reinforcement

This is an example of an FI 10-minute schedule of reinforcement for a rat in a Skinner box. The blue dots indicate when the rat pressed the bar, and the red dots indicate when the rat was reinforced for its bar-pressing behavior. On an FI of 10 minutes, the rat will receive a maximum of one reinforcement during any 10-minute interval—no matter how often the rat presses the bar. The rat learns to press the bar only when reinforcement is due—right around the 10-minute interval mark. Yes, rats do have some sense of time!

One way to avoid this pause in the behavior immediately after reinforcement is to make the interval variable. Similar to what we saw in the variable ratio schedule, in a **variable interval schedule**, the length of the interval varies. What if our employee from the previous example did not know when to expect their next evaluation? What if they could be evaluated during any month of the year? Under these circumstances, their only choice would be to always perform well—assuming, of course, that they wanted to do well on their evaluation. Pop quizzes also reinforce students on a variable interval schedule for keeping up with their reading and studying. As unpopular as pop quizzes are with students, they do serve a psychological purpose. As you can see from Figure 6.8d, variable interval schedules produce steady rates of responding in rats. Another benefit of variable interval schedules is that they produce behaviors that are more resistant to extinction than those produced with fixed interval schedules.

variable interval schedule a schedule of reinforcement in which the organism is reinforced for the first desired response in an average *x*th interval of time

In summary, when it comes to the effects that these different schedules have on operant conditioning:

- Continuous reinforcement leads to high rates of responding but the quickest extinction.
- Ratio schedules of reinforcement lead to higher rates of responding than do interval schedules of reinforcement.
- Variable schedules of reinforcement lead to behaviors that are the most resistant to extinction.

6.3.5 Discrimination and Generalization

Just as classically conditioned responses undergo discrimination and generalization, so do operantly conditioned responses. In operant conditioning, discrimination occurs when the organism learns to distinguish among similar stimulus situations and to offer a particular response only in those specific situations in which reinforcement will be forthcoming. For example, at work we learn to do our job because it leads to reinforcement in the form of pay, but this doesn't mean that we will also do a coworker's job for which we do not expect pay.

Equally important is our ability to generalize our operant responses. Generalization occurs when the same operant behavior is emitted in response to different but similar stimuli. For example, if studying in a particular manner leads to a lot of learning in your psychology class, you may also try this study method in your history class, where it may also pay off.

In the previous examples, discrimination and generalization led to positive outcomes. Unfortunately, this is not always the case. One example of the negative aspects of discrimination and generalization is found in prejudice and discrimination against certain groups of people (see Chapter 10). In prejudice, one's negative feelings about a few members of a group generalize to most or all members of that group. Similarly, one may discriminate by treating members of some groups in a kind manner and treating all or most members of a disliked group in an unkind manner. Here what we commonly refer to as discrimination in the social sense is also an example of what psychologists refer to as discrimination in learning.

6.3.6 Shaping New Behaviors

Before a behavior can be operantly conditioned, the organism must first engage in the behavior spontaneously. Before Thorndike's cat learned to quickly receive reinforcement by stepping on the foot release in the puzzle box, it first had to accidentally or spontaneously step on the pedal and open the box. Learning occurs only after the behavior has occurred and the organism has been either punished or reinforced. Given this, how can operant conditioning explain the development of novel behaviors? For example, how could an animal trainer use operant conditioning to teach a dog to do a trick that involves walking on its hind legs? If you wait for a dog to spontaneously stand up on its hind legs and begin to walk so that you can reinforce this behavior with a treat, you are going to be waiting for a long time!

shaping using operant conditioning to build a new behavior in an organism by reinforcing successive approximations of the desired response

Animal trainers use an operant conditioning technique called **shaping**, in which a novel behavior is slowly conditioned by reinforcing *successive approximations* of the final desired behavior. In the case of training the dog, the trainer will reinforce any spontaneous behavior that is in the direction of the final desired behavior. The trainer may start by reinforcing the dog for looking at them. Once the dog learns to pay attention, it may expand on this behavior by sitting up. This will also lead to a treat. Then the dog must sit up to get the treat. Once the dog learns to sit up, it may go a bit further and rear up a bit on its hind legs. This will also earn the dog a treat. Now that the dog can rear up, it must do so to get a treat. After rearing up for a time, the dog may spontaneously go up all the way onto its hind legs. The trainer responds with more treats. Soon the dog will progress to standing on its hind legs, and the trainer will reciprocate with more treats every time the dog stands up on its hind legs. The final step comes when the dog spontaneously takes its first steps after being conditioned to stand on its hind legs. At this point, all the trainer has to do is reinforce the dog for walking on its hind legs.

Animal trainers and animal owners have long used operant conditioning to shape the behavior of many species of animals. For example, many pet owners take their dogs to obedience classes. The film industry regularly hires animal actors of all types who have been specially trained to perform various behaviors on command. The U.S. military has trained animals, such as dolphins, to detect underwater explosives (Lekic, 2013), and service and support animals have to be trained to perform any number of novel behaviors in support of their human companion (Tedeschi, Pearson, & Bayly, 2015).

Training animals to perform such complex and important tasks is time consuming, and it requires patience on the part of the trainer. One issue that might

Psychology Works!

Justin Baker/WireImage/Getty Images

There are many professions that utilize the principles of learning theory on a daily basis. Pretty much any job that involves molding the behavior of another person or an animal requires some knowledge of learning theory. Animal trainers, such as Jackson Galaxy from *My Cat from Hell*, apply the principles of conditioning to shape new behaviors in animals. Sometimes these efforts are aimed at decreasing problematic behaviors in our pets. Other times, the trainer may seek to get the animal to engage in noninstinctive behaviors, as in animal trainers who train animals to work in the entertainment or marketing industries. Perhaps one of the most valuable applications of learning theory in training animals can be seen in cases where trainers hope to train the animal to perform important services (e.g., service animals for people with disabilities, police dogs, animals trained to detect drugs, explosives, and so on.)

be encountered is a phenomenon called **instinctive drift**, or the tendency for an animal who has been conditioned to perform a certain behavior to abandon this learned behavioral response in favor of a more instinctive response. For example, my attempt to operantly condition my cat, Juaquin, to stop scratching on the couch is likely to fail in the long run. In the short-run, I may succeed in getting him to stop scratching the furniture when he sees me with the squirt bottle that I use to punish him. However, as scratching is a cat's instinctive way of marking its territory, he will likely return to scratching the furniture despite the conditioning I have used to modify his behavior. In other words, the conditioning cannot fully override his instinctive behavioral patterns. As a result, his behavior will likely "drift" towards his instincts. Instinctive drift may be one reason why cats are not used as service animals in the United States, but they can be used as emotional support animals, which requires less conditioning (U.S. Service Animals, 2020).

instinctive drift the tendency for an animal who has been conditioned to perform a certain behavior to abandon this learned behavioral response in favor of a more instinctive response

behavior modification using the principles of learning to modify problematic behaviors

Shaping can also be used to condition human behavior. A parent could use shaping to help a child become more successful in school. At first the parent could reinforce the child for any study-related behavior, such as doing reading assignments or homework. Then the parent could progress to reinforcing the child for earning good grades on individual assignments, followed by reinforcement only for good grades on individual exams. Then the parent could reinforce the child for making good grades in individual courses. Finally, the parent could reinforce the child only for making good grades in all courses. By slowly reinforcing closer and closer approximations of the final desired behavior, the parent can shape a behavior in the child that would, perhaps, have never occurred on its own.

These last examples point to the usefulness of operant conditioning in the real world. If used correctly, operant conditioning can be very effective in modifying a child's behavior. This is not to say that operant conditioning can be used only with children. Operant conditioning can be used with any person or animal. In fact, the principles of learning, including operant conditioning, are often used as a therapeutic tool to help modify problematic behavior. This practice, called **behavior modification**, has been used in many different situations. For example, reinforcement, such as a person allowing themself to buy a new piece of clothing after weight loss, may help them stick to a diet. Reinforcing a person for dealing with their frustration in a nonaggressive manner may help them develop healthier responses to frustration (see Chapter 14). However, the use of operant conditioning as a parental tool provides a nice backdrop for discussing some of the choices one must make before implementing an operant conditioning program of behavior modification with any person or animal.

6.3.7 Decisions That Must Be Made When Using Operant Conditioning

One of the first decisions that has to be made when using operant conditioning to change behavior is which type of consequence to use. Recall that there are two basic types of consequences that follow behavior—reinforcement and punishment. When designing an operant conditioning program of behavior modification, one must first decide whether to punish or reinforce the behavior. Sometimes this choice will be a very clear one, but often it will not be.

Punishment or Reinforcement?

At times, a parent will have a choice either to reinforce a child's good behavior or to punish the child's undesired behavior. For example, suppose your child is not studying. You can punish the child for not studying, or you can reinforce the child for studying. Which of these methods do you think will be more successful and cause fewer problems? If you guessed that reinforcement is the safer, more effective route, you guessed correctly. In fact, one of the most effective ways of controlling children's behavior is to show them how you want them to respond and then reinforce them for behaving that way (Kochanska, 1995; Zahn-Waxler & Robinson, 1995). So, what makes punishment riskier and less effective?

- *Punishment doesn't teach the correct behavior in a given situation.* Think about it for a moment. Let's say you hear your child getting frustrated with the family dog and swearing at the dog. As a result, you immediately yell at them. What have you taught them? You have taught them not to use whatever swear word they uttered at the dog. What you have not taught them, however, is how they should have responded in this situation. The next time they are frustrated with the dog, they will not know how to express their frustration appropriately. Because punishment does not teach the correct response, any use of punishment should include a discussion of appropriate behavior and reinforcement of that behavior (Martin & Pear, 2007).
- *Harsh punishment, especially physical punishment, has the capacity to teach aggressive behavior.* Physical punishment provides an aggressive model for the child. When a parent spanks a child, the parent is teaching the child two things: first, that the child's behavior has had aversive consequences; and second, that being aggressive is a powerful means of controlling other people's behavior. In later sections of this chapter, we will see that children often imitate the behavior of others (Bandura, 1977; McGuigan, 2013). Therefore, while physical punishment may stop an unwanted behavior in the short-term, it may also teach the child to be aggressive. The next time the child feels frustrated or upset with another person, they may try using aggression to express those feelings. This is rarely the goal most parents have in mind!
- *Punishment is often ineffective at producing behavior change* (see Romano, Bell, & Norian, 2013; Strassberg et al., 1994). When punished, children often stop engaging in the undesired behavior, but only for as long as their parents are around. When the parents are out of sight—and the threat of immediate punishment is gone—the undesired behavior returns. Because the goal is usually to ensure that the child behaves even when the parents are not around, punishment is not always effective.
- *Punishment often leads to negative emotional reactions* (Skinner, 1953). These negative reactions include anger, fear, and anxiety. If a child experiences fear and anxiety when a parent punishes them, they may come to fear the parent. Just as Little Albert came to associate the white rat with loud, frightening noises, a child can come to associate a parent with pain and humiliation. Through classical conditioning, the parent can become a conditioned stimulus that evokes negative emotions in the child. This conditioned fear can lead to a psychologically unhealthy, fear-based parent–child relationship in which the child seeks to avoid the parent and the parent becomes resentful toward the child.

Punishment, especially if harsh, is riskier and less effective than reinforcement. Especially problematic is the use of physical punishment or spanking, which should be avoided. Years of research have shown us that children who experience physical punishment are more likely to be aggressive, exhibit fewer prosocial behaviors, and experience lower levels of mental health than children who are not physically punished (Cuartas et al., 2020; Gershoff, 2002, 2010). Harsh physical punishment in childhood is also linked to poorer physical health in adulthood (Afifi et al., 2013).

Furthermore, having experienced physical punishment as a child is correlated with relationship problems in college students (Leary et al., 2008). Parents who use physical punishment have been shown to be more hostile and to have higher levels of conflict in their marriages (Kanoy et al., 2003). In one study, mothers who experienced intimate partner violence were more likely to use harsh methods of punishment on their children, and they reported that their children engaged in higher levels of disruptive behavior (Grasso et al., 2016).

Monkey Business Images/Shutterstock.com

▲ Even though a parent may only intend to use punishment when spanking a child, it is possible that the child may also experience classical conditioning. Because the parent is delivering the punishment, the parent can become a conditioned stimulus that elicits fear or other negative emotions in the child.

The Cultural Debate over the Ethics of Physical Punishment Decades ago, the potential risks associated with the use of physical punishment led the American Psychological Association (APA) to issue a policy statement discouraging the use of physical punishment on children (APA, 1975). However, societal change is often slow to occur. In a 2006 study, 91% of a sample of U.S. college students reported having been hit by their parents during childhood; even more troubling, 62% reported being hit with an object (Chang, Pettit, & Katsurada, 2006). By 2013, 86% of respondents in a national poll reported having been spanked, and 81% of respondents stated that they agreed that spanking children was sometimes appropriate (The Harris Poll, 2016). A recent cross-cultural study on data recorded between 2010 and 2013 found that in low and middle-income countries, having lower household wealth was positively correlated with an increased tendency to use physical punishment on children. Physical punishment use was also related to having heightened levels of stressors in one's country (Beatriz & Salhi, 2019).

However, some declines in parental use of physical punishment in the United States have been seen. Elizabeth Gershoff (2010) reports that only about 50% of U.S. parents still regularly use physical punishment on toddlers, while 65% to 68% use it on preschoolers. Although these numbers represent a decline, they are still high. Furthermore, Gershoff and colleagues report that the use of physical punishment in school is still legal in 19 states and nearly 200,000 American schoolchildren are physically punished each year in school (Gershoff, Purtell, & Holas, 2015). Gershoff attributes the persistence of physical punishment in the United States in part to cultural values that are passed from generation to generation. Because we learn much of what we know about parenting from our own parents, viewing physical punishment as a successful parenting tool has been passed from parent to child for generations.

Yet change is taking place. The debate over the dangers of physical punishment has gone global, leading the Council of Europe to launch a campaign to end physical punishment of children in Europe. According to the multinational Global Initiative to End All Corporal Punishment of Children (2020), whose aims have been endorsed by United Nations Children's Fund (UNICEF) and United Nations Educational, Scientific and Cultural Organization (UNESCO), some 60 countries worldwide have banned physical punishment of children. To date, Albania, Andorra, Argentina, Austria, Benin, Bolivia, Brazil, Bulgaria, Cabo Verde, Costa Rica, Croatia, Cyprus, Denmark, Estonia, Finland, France, French Guiana, Georgia, Germany, Greece, Greenland, Honduras, Hungary, Iceland, Ireland, Israel, Japan, Kenya, Kosovo, Latvia, Liechtenstein, Luxembourg, New Zealand, Malta, Mongolia, Montenegro, Nepal, the Netherlands, Nicaragua, Norway, Paraguay, Peru, Poland, Portugal, Republic of Moldova, Republic of Congo, Romania, San Marino, Seychelles, Slovenia, South Africa, South Sudan, Spain, Sweden, Togo, TFYR Macedonia, Tunisia, Turkmenistan, Ukraine, Uruguay, and Venezuela have all enacted total bans on physical punishment of children. Many more countries have enacted partial bans and are committed to working to enact full bans in the future. Perhaps someday, future generations will also commit to eliminating the use of physical punishment on children in the United States where there is currently no federal ban on the use of physical punishment in the home, alternative care, daycare, schools, or prisons.

Practical Alternatives to Physical Punishment The strong case we have made against physical punishment does not mean that children should not be disciplined at all. Effective parenting means teaching children to behave in socially acceptable ways, and discipline is sometimes needed to teach children appropriate self-control. Sometimes situations call for some form of punishment. Luckily, a number of alternatives to physical punishment are possible, many of which are listed in ● TABLE 6.2. If used properly, these techniques will most likely prove effective. Here are a few tips for making punishments like the ones in Table 6.2 more effective in general:

- Tell the child what the appropriate behavior is, and then reinforce that behavior.
- Minimize situations that tempt the child to engage in undesired behavior.

TABLE 6.2 Alternatives to Physical Punishment

Method	Example
Nonphysical Punishment Methods	
Timeout: The child is sent to sit in a quiet place.	Devon, 5 years old, is sent to sit in the laundry room for 5 minutes after hitting another child. There are no toys, friends, or other reinforcements present.
Restitution: The child has to give up something.	Sabina broke a friend's toy on purpose. Now Sabina has to give one of her own toys to them.
Fines: The child has to pay a fine.	Every time a family member uses inappropriate language, they have to put 50 cents in the "swear jar."
Loss of privileges: The child loses a privilege.	Giorgio is grounded for 2 weeks for breaking curfew and talking back to his parents.
Nonpunishment Methods	
Empathy training: Teach the child to empathize with others. If the child hurts another, they are encouraged to imagine what that person might have felt as a result of being hurt. The ability to empathize reduces the motivation to hurt others.	Suzy intentionally breaks Jimmy's toy. To teach Suzy empathy, Suzy's mother asks her to think about how she felt when Bobby broke her toy last week. Then Suzy is asked to think about whether Jimmy might be feeling the same way now that Suzy broke his toy. This should make Suzy feel bad about having hurt Jimmy's feelings.
Differential reinforcement of incompatible responses (DRI): The child is reinforced for engaging in a desirable behavior that cannot be performed at the same time as the undesirable behavior.	Marya's parents reinforce her for being quiet in church as opposed to punishing her for being loud in church.

- Use a punishment that really is punishing. If the child does not find the punishment aversive, it will fail to control the behavior.
- Punishment must occur immediately after the undesired behavior occurs.
- Punishment must occur each and every time the undesired behavior occurs. Otherwise, the undesired behavior is partially reinforced when the child escapes the punishment.
- Remain calm while you are punishing a child. This will help ensure that you do not abuse the child.

Although nonphysical punishment may be necessary at times to reduce undesirable behavior, when you have a choice, it is much safer and often more effective to use reinforcement of good behavior to control behavior. However, there are things to consider if you want to be sure your program of reinforcement has the desired effect on the behavior you are trying to change.

Choosing a Reinforcer That Is Reinforcing

It may seem like a trivial issue, but the first consideration in developing a program of reinforcement is to choose a reinforcer that is actually reinforcing for the person you are trying to condition. If the reinforcer is not something the person likes or values, it will not work. For example, if your significant other cleans the whole house, and you reinforce them by cooking a meal that they do not like, then they will not be more likely to clean the house again. Your attempt at operant conditioning will have failed. When in doubt, it's a good idea to discuss with the person the consequences that they would find reinforcing before conditioning begins.

Primary and Secondary Reinforcers

Reinforcers can be categorized as either *primary* or *secondary*. A **primary reinforcer** is one that is directly reinforcing. Examples of primary reinforcers are food, water, a warm bed, and sexual pleasure. These reinforcers are primary because they are pleasurable in and of themselves. If you are hungry, then food will reinforce you by removing your hunger.

primary reinforcer a reinforcer that is reinforcing in and of itself

secondary reinforcer a reinforcer that is reinforcing only because it leads to a primary reinforcer

token economy a system of operant conditioning in which participants are reinforced with tokens that can later be cashed in for primary reinforcers

In contrast, a **secondary reinforcer** is reinforcing only because it leads to a primary reinforcer. A wonderful example of a secondary reinforcer in Western society is money. By itself, a dollar bill is not reinforcing. What makes a dollar reinforcing is what you can buy with it—food, water, shelter, and other primary reinforcers. When you get right down to it, you don't go to work for money per se. You go to work to ensure that you will be able to purchase an adequate supply of primary reinforcers.

One method of secondary reinforcement is to use a *token economy*. A **token economy** reinforces desired behavior with a token of some sort (e.g., a poker chip or a gold star) that can later be cashed in for primary reinforcers (Martin et al., 1968). Token economies are often used to control the behavior of groups of people such as schoolchildren (Salend, 2001), preschoolers (Jowett Hirst, Dozier, & Payne, 2016), children receiving treatment for intellectual disabilities (Matson & Boisjoli, 2009), or inmates (Holmqvist, Hill, & Lang, 2009). Token economies can also be used in the context of a family (Kazdin, 1977) or in the workplace (Schumacher et al., 2013).

To set up a token economy, the first step is to draw up a list of desired and undesired behaviors that you will try to control. The next step is to decide how many tokens to give (or take away) for each of the behaviors, and to develop some sort of recordkeeping system to keep track of each participant's tokens. One recordkeeping approach is to draw a chart like the one shown in • FIGURE 6.10 and hang it on the wall in a prominent place.

Mrs. Alvarez's Class

Students	Paying attention in class, +5 tokens	On time for class, +3 tokens	Homework completely done, +7 tokens	B or better on daily quiz, +10 tokens	Talking in class, −5 tokens	Fighting, −10 tokens	Calling people names, −10 tokens
Franco							
Mary							
Louisa							
Billy							
George							
Eddie							
Latesha							

Token values
25 tokens = 1 sticker, eraser, or pencil
50 tokens = 1 small toy
75 tokens = 1 medium-size toy
100 tokens = 1 coupon for a phone/tablet app
125 tokens = 1 download of a computer game

FIGURE 6.10

A Sample Point System from a Token Economy

Using token economies has three main advantages. One is that a token economy is effective when trying to simultaneously modify a number of behaviors in a group of people. For example, a token economy can be used with an entire class, which is easier than trying to develop an individual operant conditioning program for each student.

The second major advantage is that token economies allow for immediate reinforcement with a token, even when it is not practical to immediately present the primary reinforcer. For example, it's disruptive for a teacher to stop the class to give a child a toy as a reinforcer. However, the teacher can immediately hand the child a token that can be used at week's end to purchase a toy. The use of tokens helps to bridge the gap between the behavior and the eventual primary reinforcement of the behavior. A third benefit of token economies is that they force participants to practice **delay of gratification**, in that the real reinforcement for their behavior only comes when they are able to later cash in their tokens. Delay of gratification is an important ability in everyday life, as often the rewards of our behavior are not immediate. For example, the ultimate reward for your hard work in school today will not be realized for some time. If you were unable to delay gratification, your ability to make it through to graduation would be less certain. Yet, token economies also have their drawbacks.

delay of gratification learning to forego immediate reinforcement in favor of waiting for a later, sometimes larger, reinforcement

A potential problem with token economies is that they often place the behavior on a continuous schedule of reinforcement. As we saw in previous sections, continuous reinforcement can lead to behavior that is vulnerable to extinction. It is possible that a token economy may lessen a person's desire to engage in a behavior when the behavior is not likely to lead to a token or some other reinforcer. This potential problem may be outweighed, however, by the usefulness of the token economy in controlling the immediate behavior of the people in the program. For instance, in a prison you may be more worried about controlling the immediate, day-to-day behavior of the prison population. Facilitating the future motivation of the inmates to behave in a particular way once they are out of the token economy is likely to be less of a concern.

6.3.8 The Role of Cognition in Learning

So far in this chapter, we have discussed three major types of learning—habituation, classical conditioning, and operant conditioning—that have some important things in common. One common feature is that all of these types of learning require that the person or animal *do something* before learning can occur. In habituation, the organism must emit an orienting reflex. In classical conditioning, the organism must have an unconditioned response. In operant conditioning, the organism must first engage in some random behavior that is either reinforced or punished.

Another common feature of these learning theories is that they do not emphasize the role that mental or cognitive processes play in learning. Researchers such as Ivan Pavlov, John B. Watson, E. L. Thorndike, and B. F. Skinner did not discuss thoughts and feelings and how these may affect the learning process. Skinner, in particular, argued that psychology should not seek to study the cognitive aspects of behavior because he believed that these things could not be studied scientifically and objectively. Skinner did not deny that humans and animals had thoughts and feelings; he simply held that they could not be studied adequately. Skinner subscribed to the psychological perspective of **behaviorism** (see Chapter 1), which states that the only aspect of living things that can and should be studied scientifically is behavior. Therefore, Skinner tried to explain behavior without discussing cognitive or mental processes (Skinner, 1953).

behaviorism a school of thought in psychology that emphasizes the study of observable behavior over the study of the mind

insight a sudden realization about how to solve a problem that occurs after an organism has studied the problem for a period of time

Because strict behaviorism totally ignores the influence of cognitive processes, it does not explain some of the learning we see in the real world, or in the lab. In the early 1900s, some researchers, including Wolfgang Köhler (1887–1967), became aware that cognitive processes must play a role in learning. Köhler observed that chimpanzees did not always attempt to solve problems in a trial-and-error fashion as predicted by the law of effect. Rather, they often seemed to study a problem for a long time as if formulating a mental plan—before attempting to solve it. In one experiment, Köhler placed a banana just out of reach outside a chimpanzee's cage, and he placed a stick inside the cage. The law of effect would predict that the chimpanzee would try many random behaviors—like shaking the bars and jumping up and down—before picking up the stick and using it to reach the banana. But this is not what Köhler observed. Instead, the chimpanzee studied the situation and then appeared to suddenly come up with the solution. After this flash of **insight** into how to solve its dilemma, the chimpanzee picked up the stick and used it to scoot the banana to a point where it could be reached (Köhler, 1925). This act illustrates the *purposiveness* or goal-directed nature of behavior. The chimpanzee was not simply engaging in a pattern of behavior that had been reinforced in the past. Rather, the chimpanzee was using its behavior as a strategy aimed at achieving the *goal* of getting something to eat. If we were to think of behavior solely in terms of one's past history of reinforcement, we would be overlooking an important aspect of behavior—the *motivation* (Chapter 5) behind the behavior. For example, let's take a look at going to work. Does a person simply go to work because they have been reinforced for working in the past? Or, do they go to work because they hope to achieve their goal of not only surviving, but also having nice clothes, an active social life, and so on? Clearly, people tend to think of their own behavior in terms of their own goals and desires, even if hardcore behaviorists do not.

Penny Tweedie/Alamy stock photo

▲ Wolfgang Köhler found that chimpanzees like this one can acquire insight into how to solve problems by watching and studying situations before acting. This type of problem solving suggests that cognitive processes can play an important role in learning.

Köhler's work also deviates from strict behaviorism in that it shows that learning can be a purely cognitive task. The chimpanzee did not have to wait for the consequences of its behavior to rule out behavioral strategies that would not accomplish the goal of obtaining the banana. Rather, the chimpanzee appeared to reason its way to a solution before acting.

In the 1930s, Edward Tolman (1886–1959) found additional support for the idea that cognition plays a role in learning. He discovered that rats would learn to run through a maze even when they were not reinforced for doing so (Tolman & Honzik, 1930). In Tolman's experiment, one group of rats was allowed to wander through the maze, and they were reinforced with food if they found their way to the end of the maze. Another group of rats was also allowed to explore the maze, but they were not reinforced even if they found their way to the end. As you might expect, after 10 days of training in the maze, the group that was reinforced could run through the maze more quickly than the unreinforced group could. On the 11th day, Tolman began to give rats in both groups a reinforcer at the end of the maze. After just a few reinforced trials, the previously unreinforced rats could run through the maze just as fast as the rats that had been reinforced all along. This rapid learning in the previously unreinforced rats indicates that these rats had been learning even when they were not being reinforced.

latent learning learning that cannot be directly observed in an organism's behavior

cognitive map a mental representation of the environment that is formed through observation of one's environment

Tolman's findings cannot be explained by operant conditioning alone because learning occurred *without* reinforcement. Tolman interpreted his results as being evidence that the rats had engaged in **latent learning**, or learning that cannot be directly observed through behavior. He proposed that while the unreinforced rats were wandering through the maze, they were developing a **cognitive map**, or mental representation, of the maze in their heads. Once the reinforcer was presented, they used this map to help them get to the reinforcer more quickly.

Although Tolman's experiments pointed to cognitive processes at work during learning, many psychologists ignored the impact of cognition on learning because of behaviorism's dominance in psychology at the time. It was not until the 1960s that learning researchers really began to look at the role of cognition in learning and behavior.

6.3 Quiz Yourself

1. Denzel wants to increase his son Mario's tendency to mow the yard on Saturday mornings without having to repeatedly ask him. To do this, Denzel tells Mario that he will pay him $5 when he mows the yard without first having been told to do so. Denzel is using which schedule of reinforcement?
   a. Fixed interval
   b. Variable interval
   c. Variable ratio
   d. Continuous

2. Which of the following is an example of operant conditioning?
   a. Byron doesn't go to the dentist because the last time he did, it was very painful.
   b. Byron is afraid of dentists because the last time he went to the dentist, it was very painful.
   c. Byron wants to go to the dentist because when his friend Gina went to the dentist, the dentist gave Gina a toy.
   d. All of the above are examples of operant conditioning.

3. John's operantly conditioned his dog, Rover, to shake paws. However, lately John has noticed that when he asks Rover to shake paws, instead of doing so, Rover just sits and barks at John. This failure to perform the conditioned response is most likely due to _____.
   a. shaping
   b. instinctive drift
   c. spontaneous recovery
   d. all of the above

4. When Kim Peek performed his feats of memory for people, they usually reacted with surprise and laughter. These reactions served as _____ that encouraged Kim to continue performing his displays of memory for others.
   a. positive reinforcement
   b. negative reinforcement
   c. token reinforcers
   d. b and c

5. Credit card points, earned by using the card to make purchases, are an example of _____ and they help card users develop _____.
   a. conditioned stimuli; delay of gratification
   b. primary reinforcers; spontaneous recovery
   c. tokens; delay of gratification
   d. operants; spontaneous recovery

Answers 1. d; 2. a; 3. b; 4. a; 5. c

6.4 Observational Learning or Modeling: Learning by Watching Others

As we saw in the previous discussion, learning can occur without reinforcement, but even Tolman's unreinforced rats had at least engaged in the behavior of moving through the maze. Does all learning require that we actually engage in the behavior? As it turns out, we can learn by simply observing the behaviors of others. In this type of learning, called **observational learning**, we *observe* others and imitate, or *model*, their behavior. For that reason, observational learning is sometimes referred to as *social learning* or *modeling*. One example of observational learning comes from the life of Kim Peek. Due to the damage to his brain, Kim had a very difficult time learning certain motor skills. Every day Kim's father had to show him how to brush his teeth and button his shirt, by modeling the behavior for him. When you were a child, it is likely that you also learned how to perform these tasks by watching someone else do them.

observational learning learning through observation and imitation of others' behavior

As you read the following sections, keep in mind that observational learning departs from the behaviorism that Skinner so forcefully advocated on two major points. First, it acknowledges that learning can occur without an overt change in behavior; second, it takes into account the role of cognition in the learning process.

6.4.1 Albert Bandura and the Bobo Doll Experiments

In the 1960s, psychologist Albert Bandura (b. 1925) conducted several experiments on observational learning, now considered classic psychological experiments, that contributed to his development of *social learning theory*. Collectively, these experiments are referred to as the *Bobo doll experiments*, because the experimental procedure used an inflated plastic "Bobo" doll, a popular children's toy at the time.

In the Bobo doll experiments, children watched films in which a woman beat up the Bobo doll. She hit him with a mallet, sat on him, threw him in the air, and so on (Bandura, Ross, & Ross, 1961). After the children viewed the films, Bandura and his colleagues placed them in a room alone with the Bobo doll and observed their behavior without their knowledge. If the children imitated the characteristic behaviors of the model, then Bandura knew that learning had occurred (● FIGURE 6.11).

In one of the Bobo doll experiments (Bandura, 1965), children were randomly assigned to watch one of three different films. In the *reward* film condition, the model was reinforced after beating up on Bobo. In the *punishment* film condition, she was punished after beating up on Bobo. In the *no consequences* film condition, nothing happened to the model after she beat up Bobo.

After viewing one of these films, the children were observed with Bobo, and their aggressive behaviors were recorded. As you

Albert Bandura

FIGURE 6.11

Bandura's Bobo Doll Experiments

These photos, taken from the Bobo doll experiments, clearly show the children (panels B and C) modeling what they saw the model (panel A) doing to Bobo.

might expect, the children who had seen the model reinforced for beating up Bobo were most likely to beat up on him themselves. However, an unexpected finding of the study was that the children who had seen the no consequences film were equally likely to beat up on Bobo. This means that seeing someone merely get away with aggressive behavior is just as likely to lead to modeling as seeing aggression reinforced. The only thing that deterred the children's aggression toward Bobo was having seen the film in which the model was punished for treating Bobo badly. Only these children were more hesitant to beat up on Bobo when they were left alone with him in the observation room.

By leaving the children alone with Bobo and recording their aggressive behavior, Bandura was able to assess how willing the children were to beat up on Bobo as a function of the consequences they expected would follow such aggression. But what had they actually learned about how to be aggressive toward Bobo? Is it possible that some of the children who did not beat up Bobo had still learned *how* to beat up Bobo? To test the children's level of *learning*, Bandura (1965) asked the children to show him exactly what they had seen in the films. Here, the children were free to model the behavior without fear of any type of punishment. Under these conditions, Bandura found that there were no significant differences across the three groups. All of the groups exhibited equal levels of learning when it came to knowing how the model had beat up Bobo.

The Bobo doll experiments show us two things. First, you don't have to engage in a behavior or experience reinforcement for learning to occur. Second, just as Tolman discovered with his rats in the mazes, learning can be latent. The children who viewed the punishment film had learned how to beat up Bobo, but they were reluctant to beat him up because they feared there would be negative consequences for them if they did. We hope that the Bobo doll experiments make you think about the potential impact that violent movies, video games, and television may have on the children who view them, because more recent research seems to underscore the notion that kids do not merely watch TV—rather, they can learn from TV (Pinto da Mota Matos, Alves Ferreira, & Haase, 2012; Zack et al., 2009). Like it or not, TV is likely to be an important source of learning for children in the United States, given that parents reported 2.07 hours of television viewing a day for children (ages 6–11) in 2011–2012 and 1.79 hours a day for preschoolers (ages 2–5) during the same period (Loprinzi & Davis, 2016). Of course, the United States is not the only country where children are exposed to television. In Bulgaria, researchers found that exposure to television advertising in children was related to increases in materialism and consumerism, a trend that some in this former Soviet culture find disturbing (Opree, Petrova, & Rozendaal, 2019). A cross-cultural study of children in six countries (Brazil, China, India, Nigeria, Pakistan, and Russia) found that exposure to Western advertising on T.V. and other media predicted higher levels of preference for Western food items, such as *Coca-Cola* and *McDonald's* hamburgers (Borekowski & Pires, 2018).

Given the evidence that children can learn from watching television, at what age do parents need to begin thinking about how television and other media are impacting their children? Perhaps at a younger age than you may think. Researchers Donna Mumme and Anne Fernald (2003) have found that children as young as 12 months old pay attention to how a televised model reacts to certain stimuli, and they model their own reaction to the stimulus after the model's reaction. In this study, 12-month-old infants watched a televised actress interacting with certain toys. The actress responded positively, neutrally, or negatively to certain toys. Later, the infants were allowed to play with the same toys. The results showed that the infants were most likely to react favorably to the toys that the actress had either been neutral about or liked. Conversely, the infants were less likely to want to play with the toys to which the actress had reacted negatively. It seems that the infants disliked these toys simply because they had seen the actress reacting negatively toward them. Thus, the observational learning that occurs when watching TV may have the power to influence the attitudes that even very young children hold about the objects in their world. Subsequent research has suggested that infants are even more likely to pay attention to televised information when their parents also pay attention to it (Demers et al., 2013). In essence, if they are in the room, our children are likely to be watching what we are watching on TV.

Furthermore, studies have linked screen time to poorer performance in some, but not all, aspects of *executive functioning* in children (Jusiene et al., 2020; McHarg et al., 2020). Executive functioning refers to the cognitive skills that allow us to use our minds in a flexible manner, for example, controlling one's attention, holding information in memory, speed of mental processing, and so on. We will discuss these skills more in Chapter 7. Concerns about the potential impact of television and other electronic media on developing infants has prompted the American Academy of Pediatrics (AAP) to develop a policy statement discouraging parents from allowing children younger than 18 months to view television and other electronic media. Although parents may find it difficult to disconnect from media in the presence of their infant children, the AAP suggests that other activities such as reading to children and playing with them may be much better uses of parental time with their children (AAP, 2016).

Does this mean that children of all ages should be prohibited from watching television and using electronic devices? Of course not. The AAP recommendation on screen time is for very young children. Furthermore, media presentations are not all violent and potentially detrimental. Television, tablets, computers, and video games can also be beneficial educational tools. So, perhaps the best advice for older children is not to ban their use, but rather to place appropriate limits on the amount of time children spend in front of screens and to regulate what types of content they have access to on them.

6.4.2 Observational Learning and Cognition

Classical and operant conditioning theories, which form the basis of behaviorism, cannot explain why a child would act out scenes from their favorite superhero cartoon on the playground hours or days *after* seeing the cartoon. Likewise, they cannot explain why children learned how to be aggressive toward Bobo *before* they were actually aggressive toward him. Because of such realities, Bandura concluded that cognitive processes must play a role in learning that is somewhat separate from the actual behavior. Let's take a closer look at this idea.

Rawpixel.com/Shutterstock.com

▲ For better or worse, we learn from watching others. Media depictions of behavior have the power to teach us from a very young age. Whether or not this is a good thing depends, in part, on the behaviors we are exposed to via these media.

According to Bandura (1986), modeling is a four-step process as follows:

1. *Attention.* The observer must first pay attention to the model's behavior before they can model it. Research shows that children tend to model their behavior after people who are warm, nurturant, or powerful (Bandura, 1977). For example, a child may pay attention to the behavior of loving parents, a nurturant teacher, or a popular and seemingly powerful classmate. As we have already seen, another type of model that is particularly good at grabbing attention is a televised

model (Bandura, Grusec, & Menlove, 1966). It is quite common to see children on the playground modeling the behavior of their favorite TV cartoon character. As we age and mature, however, we tend to seek out models that seem similar to us in some way (Bandura, 1986). For example, we may model our behavior after people of the same sex, ethnicity, or occupation.

2. *Retention in memory.* The observer must retain a cognitive representation or memory of the model's behavior. For children on the playground to model the behavior of TV characters, they must have memories of what they have previously seen on TV.
3. *Reproduction of the behavior.* The observer must have a mental representation of the behavior stored in memory that can be retrieved and used to reproduce the behavior. Of course, the person must have the physical abilities to actually reproduce the behavior if modeling is to occur. For instance, a child may remember seeing a cartoon superhero flying. Although the child may be able to model an approximation of this behavior, they will not be able to model the behavior precisely.
4. *Motivation.* After retrieving the memory of the behavior and figuring out how to produce the behavior, the observer must be motivated to actually execute the behavior. As we saw in the Bobo doll experiments, the observer may sometimes not want to execute the behavior. This is especially true if the observer believes that execution of the behavior may lead to punishment.

Bandura's observational learning theory brings an additional element to the study of learning, in that it addresses the role of cognition in the learning process. In the next two chapters, we will look more carefully at cognitive processes, examining how memory works in Chapter 7 and the cognitive processes involved in solving problems and making decisions and judgments in Chapter 8.

6.4 Quiz Yourself

1. **When Kim Peek's father attempted to teach Kim how to brush his teeth by modeling for him the process of brushing teeth, he was attempting to teach Kim through ____.**
   a. operant conditioning
   b. classical conditioning
   c. observational learning
   d. All of the above
2. **How do observational learning and operant conditioning differ?**
   a. In observational learning, the person is less aware that learning is taking place.
   b. In operant conditioning, the person is less aware that learning is taking place.
   c. In observational learning, the person does not have to engage in the response.
   d. In operant conditioning, the person does not have to engage in the response.
3. **Albert Bandura's studies with the Bobo doll can best be described as being ____.**
   a. correlational studies
   b. true experiments
   c. case studies
   d. quasi-experiments
4. **Tyrone watches a violent TV show, but he has never imitated any of the behaviors he has seen on the show. Which of the following statements is true regarding Tyrone's learning?**
   a. Tyrone has not learned anything from watching the show.
   b. Tyrone has definitely learned something from watching the show.
   c. Tyrone may have learned something from watching the show.
   d. At some point in time, Tyrone's behavior will definitely change as a result of watching the show.

Answers 1. c; 2. c; 3. b; 4. c

6.5 Integrating Psychology: The Big Picture

In this chapter, we explored the process of *learning,* a relatively permanent change in behavior, or potential for behavior, as a result of experience. We learn to ignore repetitive stimuli when we *habituate. Classical conditioning* explains how we come to have particular physiological and emotional responses to certain stimuli. And *operant conditioning* occurs when our behavior is shaped by the consequences it elicits from the environment. We also have the ability to engage in *observational learning* by observing the actions of others and later modeling these actions in our own behavior.

All of us have some capacity for learning. Learning is an important process through which we adapt our behavior to meet the demands of our environment. Recall the case of Kim Peek. Kim illustrated the extremes of human behavior, having both an extraordinary capacity for learning and serious learning difficulties. On the one hand, he learned to keep the payroll at his job without the use of a computer or calculator. On the other hand, no matter how many times his father demonstrated how to brush his teeth and button a shirt, Kim had great difficulty modeling these tasks. In fact, he had difficulty learning many motor-skill tasks. Most of us will fall somewhere between the extremes of Kim's learning abilities.

In our next chapter, we will continue to explore the cognitive aspect of psychology as we delve deeper into the learning process by taking a look at how we process information in memory. As you read Chapter 7, recall both the extraordinary cognitive abilities of the "Kimputer" and the difficulties Kim had with conceptual thought. Then think about your own learning and your own memory. Which types of learning come easily to you? Which types of learning are more difficult for you? And how can you apply what you are learning about psychology to improve your learning?

Studying the Chapter

Key Terms

acquisition (249)
aversion therapy (245)
behaviorism (269)
behavior modification (263)
biological preparedness (245)
classical conditioning (241)
cognition (229)
cognitive map (270)
conditioned response (CR) (240)
conditioned stimulus (CS) (240)
contiguity (241)
contingency (242)
continuous reinforcement (257)
counterconditioning (249)
delay of gratification (268)
dishabituation (236)
extinction (248)
extinction burst (257)
fixed interval schedule (259)
fixed ratio schedule (258)
habituation (235)
insight (269)
instinctive drift (263)
intelligence (229)
language (229)
latent learning (270)
law of effect (251)
learning (229)
memory (229)
negative punishment (252)
negative reinforcement (252)
neutral stimulus (NS) (239)
observational learning (271)
operant conditioning (251)
orienting reflex (234)
partial reinforcement (258)
positive punishment (252)
positive reinforcement (252)
primary reinforcer (267)
punishment (252)
reinforcement (252)
schedule of reinforcement (257)
secondary reinforcer (267)
shaping (262)
Skinner box (254)
spontaneous recovery (249)
stimulus discrimination (244)
stimulus generalization (244)
taste aversion (244)
token economy (267)
unconditioned response (UR) (239)
unconditioned stimulus (US) (238)
variable interval schedule (261)
variable ratio schedule (258)

What Do You Know? Assess Your Understanding

Test your retention and understanding of the material by answering the following questions.

1. Sasha is sitting in class, trying to listen to her professor's lecture, but she finds herself very distracted by the student next to her who is talking to another student. Sasha is exhibiting a(n) ______.
   a. orienting reflex
   b. habituation
   c. dishabituation
   d. conditioned response

2. After 2 days working at a day-care center, Roman no longer snaps to attention every time a child screams. The change in Roman's behavior is most likely due to habituation. Sally, who has only been working at the center for 2 hours, still exhibits an orienting reflex every time a child screams. In a study examining the effects of time spent around children on habituation of one's orienting reflex to children's screams, what would be the independent variable?
   a. Orienting reflexes
   b. Habituation
   c. The screaming children
   d. Time spent around children

3. ______ is responding to a stimulus to which you have previously learned to ignore.
   a. Habituation
   b. Classical conditioning
   c. Dishabituation
   d. Operant conditioning

4. Getting an injection causes Marla to flinch. In classical conditioning terms, the needle stick is a(n) ______.
   a. conditioned stimulus
   b. conditioned response
   c. unconditioned response
   d. unconditioned stimulus

5. Which of the following types of learning does not require that the person or animal do anything in order for learning to occur?
   a. Habituation
   b. Classical conditioning
   c. Operant conditioning
   d. Social learning

6. In Pavlov's original studies, the unconditioned stimulus was ______.
   a. the buzzer
   b. salivation
   c. food
   d. the tube inserted into the dog's salivary gland

7. Tyra is trying to condition a dog to not fear thunderstorms. To do this, Tyra uses the following approach. When the forecast calls for storms, Tyra brings a dog inside and allows it to sit on the couch with Tyra. While the dog is on the couch, Tyra pets it and gives it treats as the thunderstorm begins. Tyra seems to be using which principle of learning to help the dog?
   a. Habituation
   b. Counter conditioning
   c. Extinction
   d. Observational learning

8. Amelia was in a car accident recently. Just prior to the crash, a certain song was playing on the radio. Now, whenever Amelia hears this song, she feels uneasy. This example shows that classical conditioning can sometimes occur even with low levels of ______.
   a. contiguity and contingency
   b. contiguity
   c. contingency
   d. similarity

9. Classical conditioning best explains the conditioning of what type of responses?
   a. Behavioral
   b. Emotional
   c. Physiological
   d. b & c

10. The law of effect was developed by ______.
    a. Ivan Pavlov
    b. E. L. Thorndike
    c. B. F. Skinner
    d. Albert Bandura

11. Which of the following processes best explains why a child may pretend to spank their teddy bear?
    a. Habituation
    b. Classical conditioning
    c. Operant conditioning
    d. Observational learning

12. Thelma reinforces her son for making his bed by telling him that he doesn't need to mow the grass. Thelma is using ______ with ______ to condition her son's behavior.
    a. classical conditioning; positive reinforcement
    b. operant conditioning; positive reinforcement
    c. classical conditioning; negative reinforcement
    d. operant conditioning; negative reinforcement

13. ______ is responding to only a particular stimulus.
    a. Stimulus generalization
    b. Stimulus discrimination
    c. Extinction
    d. Shaping

14. A therapist is reinforcing successive approximations of the final desired behavior to help a client with developmental disabilities learn a complex job task. The therapist is using ______.

   a. extinction
   b. shaping
   c. secondary reinforcement
   d. primary reinforcement

15. Points earned for shopping at a particular store are an example of ______.

   a. primary reinforcers
   b. secondary reinforcers
   c. fixed interval reinforcers
   d. continuous reinforcers

16. Oscar is working in a manufacturing plant where he is paid $50 for every 1,000 units he produces. Oscar is being reinforced on a ______ schedule of reinforcement.

   a. continuous
   b. fixed interval of $50
   c. fixed ratio of 1,000 units
   d. variable ratio of 50 to 1,000 units

17. In question number 7, Tyra's attempt to train the dog not to fear thunderstorms could be considered to be ______.

   a. secondary reinforcement
   b. a token economy
   c. behavior modification
   d. all of the above

18. Which of the following is *not* a true statement about using physical punishment on children?

   a. Physical punishment may teach children to be aggressive.
   b. Physical punishment may teach children correct behaviors.
   c. Physical punishment is often less effective than positive reinforcement.
   d. Physical punishment may result in classical conditioning of negative emotions in children.

19. Sally studies the children in her preschool class to see if they will pretend to make a pizza after watching the Cookie Monster make a pizza on TV. What type of learning is Sally studying, and what research method is she using?

   a. Habituation; case study
   b. Classical conditioning; case study
   c. Operant conditioning; naturalistic observation
   d. Observational learning; naturalistic observation

20. Which of the following learning theorists would be most likely to acknowledge the role that memory plays in learning?

   a. John B. Watson
   b. B. F. Skinner
   c. Albert Bandura
   d. Ivan Pavlov

Answers: 1. a; 2. d; 3. c; 4. c; 5. d; 6. c; 7. b; 8. c; 9. d; 10. b; 11. d; 12. d; 13. b; 14. b; 15. b; 16. c; 17. c; 18. b; 19. d; 20. c.

Use It or Lose It: Applying Psychology

1. Identify a situation in which you were classically conditioned. Then identify the NS/CS, US, and UR/CR.
2. Think about two different environments that you frequently experience (e.g., school, work, hanging with your friends). What behaviors are likely to be reinforced in these environments? What behaviors are likely to be punished? Are some behaviors reinforced in one environment but punished in the other? How will these reinforcements and punishments affect your future behavior? Explain.
3. Describe how you use classical conditioning, operant conditioning, and social learning (intentionally or not) to modify the behavior of someone in your life.
4. If you were an employer who wanted to maximize employee productivity, which schedule of reinforcement would you use when creating a timetable for performance reviews of your employees? Defend your choice.

Critical Thinking about The Science of Psychology

Recall the Bobo doll study conducted by Albert Bandura (1965) that you read about in Section 6.4.1. In particular, think about the first phase of the study, in which the children watched one of the films (i.e., the reward, punishment, or no consequences film) and were then simply left alone in the room with the Bobo doll. Then, see if you can answer these questions:

1. What type of research method did Bandura use in this study?
2. What was the independent variable in this study?
3. What was the dependent variable in this study?
4. How did Bandura control for confounding variables in his study?
5. Are there any potential ethical concerns with Bandura's study?

Are You Getting the Big Picture?

iStock.com/FluxFactory

Learning is a relatively permanent change in behavior or the potential for behavior that results from experience.

6.1 Learning from the First Days of Life: Habituation

Jed Leicester/Shutterstock.com

- **Orienting reflexes** allow us to respond to unexpected stimuli.
- **Habituation** allows us to stop responding to stimuli that are repeated over and over.
- **Dishabituation** allows us to re-respond to a stimulus to which we were previously habituated.

6.2 Classical Conditioning: Learning Through the Association of Stimuli

- Ivan Pavlov discovered classical conditioning while studying salivation in dogs.
- **Classical conditioning** occurs when a **neutral stimulus** is paired with an **unconditioned stimulus** that reliably causes an **unconditioned response**, and because of this association, the neutral stimulus loses its neutrality and becomes a **conditioned stimulus** that elicits the **conditioned response**.
- Classical conditioning is most effective when the NS/CS and US are separated by only a brief period of time (**contiguity**), and the pairing must reliably predict the response (**contingency**).
- In the Little Albert experiments, John B. Watson and Rosalie Rayner studied how emotional responses could be classically conditioned in humans.
- **Stimulus generalization** occurs when we respond to similar stimuli with the same conditioned response.
- **Stimulus discrimination** occurs when the conditioned response is only elicited by a particular CS.
- **Taste aversion** occurs when a particular food is associated with some other ailment or condition that causes nausea and the food becomes a conditioned stimulus for nausea.
- Conditioned responses can be removed using **extinction** or **counterconditioning** techniques. Extinction trials present the CS without the US. In counterconditioning, the goal is to get the subject to associate the CS with a new US that produces a response that is more desired and incompatible with the previous US. For example, training Little Albert to associate the rat with candy rather than with the loud and scary noise.

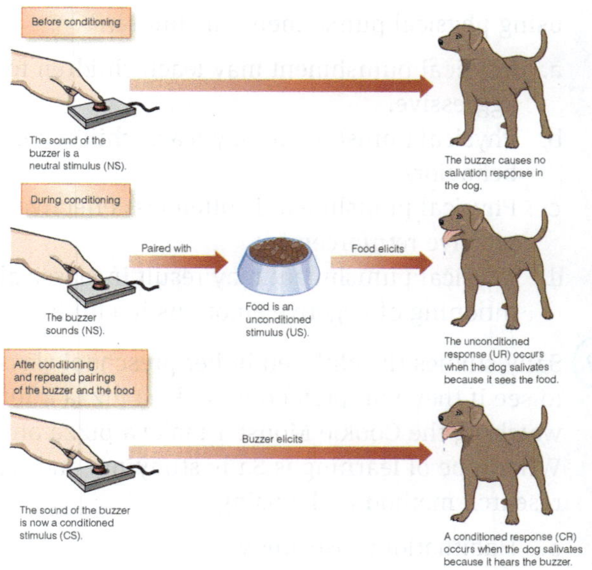

6.3 Operant Conditioning: Learning from the Consequences of Our Actions

- In **operant conditioning**, we learn from the consequences of our actions.
- E. L. Thorndike developed the **law of effect**, which emphasized the negative and positive consequences of behavior.

	Add to Environment	Remove from Environment
Increase Behavior	+ Reinforcement	– Reinforcement
Decrease Behavior	+ Punishment	– Punishment

Jon Feingersh Photography Inc/DigitalVision/Getty Images

- B. F. Skinner, a strong proponent of **behaviorism**, coined the term operant conditioning to refer to how a certain behavior operates on the environment to produce some consequence. The **Skinner box** is a chamber used to study animal learning.
- Five schedules of **reinforcement—continuous**, **fixed ratio**, **variable ratio**, **fixed interval**, and **variable interval**—describe the timing and number of responses required to receive reinforcement.
- **Behavior modification** is the use of learning principles (e.g., classical conditioning, operant conditioning, and social learning) to purposely change behavior in people or animals.
- In **shaping**, a novel behavior is slowly conditioned by reinforcing successive approximations of the final desired behavior.
- Due to **instinctive drift**, it is common to see previously conditioned responses replaced with more instinctive behavioral responses in certain species.
- **Punishment** is often less effective than reinforcement in controlling behavior. Harsh punishment, especially physical punishment, can have several unintended negative consequences.
- **Primary reinforcers** are reinforcing in themselves. **Secondary reinforcers** are reinforcing because they lead to primary reinforcers.
- A **token economy** reinforces desired behavior with a token of some sort that can later be cashed in for primary reinforcers. One of the benefits of token economies is that they also teach **delay of gratification**, the ability to forego immediate reinforcement in favor of waiting for a later, sometimes larger, reinforcement.

6.4 Observational Learning or Modeling: Learning by Watching Others

- **Observational learning** is learning that occurs by observing others and modeling their behavior.
- Albert Bandura's Bobo doll experiments showed that you do not have to engage in a behavior or experience for learning to occur, and that learning can be **latent**.
- In contrast to behaviorists such as Skinner, social learning theorists emphasize the role that cognitive processes (attention and retention in memory), reproduction of the behavior, and motivation play in learning.

Rawpixel.com/Shutterstock.com

Learning Objectives

7.1 Explain the functions of memory. (APA 1.1)

7.1 Explain the difference between implicit and explicit use of memory, and give examples of each. (APA 1.1, 1.3)

7.2 Describe the three-stages model of memory, including the function and characteristics of sensory, short-term, and long-term memory. (APA 1.1, 2.1)

7.2 Describe the newer conception of working memory and how it relates to the three-stages model's concept of short-term memory. (APA 1.1)

7.3 Explain how information is organized in long-term memory. (APA 1.1)

7.3 Describe the different types of long-term memory and their characteristics. (APA 1.1)

7.3 Describe the different types of amnesia and what case studies of amnesia have taught us about memory. (APA 1.1, 1.2, 1.3, 2.1)

7.3 Describe age- and gender-related differences in memory. (APA 1.1, 1.2, 1.3, 2.1, 3.3)

7.4 Explain retrieval processes in memory, and give real-world examples of them. (APA 1.1, 1.3)

7.4 Describe and give examples of the various theories of forgetting in long-term memory. (APA 1.1, 1.3)

7.4 Describe some of the practical measures you can take to improve your memory. (APA 1.3, 5.2)

7.5 Describe the accuracy of memory and its implications for eyewitness memory. (APA 1.1, 1.3, 3.3)

7.6 Describe what is known about the biology of memory. (APA 1.1, 1.2)

iStock.com/Fly View Productions

7 Memory

Kim Peek's father affectionately referred to Kim as the "Kimputer." Kim's amazing ability to process and store large quantities of factual information, such as phone numbers, ZIP codes, and encyclopedia entries, certainly brings to mind the workings of a computer. This notion that our minds function as computers is not unusual in psychology, either. In fact, many cognitive psychologists have adopted an *information-processing approach* to understanding the mind, which assumes that the mind functions like a very sophisticated computer. A computer accepts input—the information you type into it—stores and processes the information, and allows you to go back and retrieve the same information. In essence, this is also what your mind does with information. ■

Chapter Outline

7.1 The Functions of Memory: Encoding, Storing, and Retrieving

encoding the act of inputting information into memory

memory traces the stored code that represents a piece of information that has been encoded into memory

storage the place where information is retained in memory

retrieval the process of accessing information in memory and pulling it into consciousness

consciousness an organism's awareness of its own mental processes and/or its environment

attention an organism's ability to focus its consciousness on some aspect of its own mental processes and/or its environment

explicit memory the conscious use of memory

implicit memory the unconscious use of memory

As you read this chapter, you are inputting, or **encoding**, information into your memory in the form of **memory traces**, which are stored bits of information in memory. Your mind will process this information and put it into memory **storage**. Then, on test day or some other day when the information is needed, you will use **retrieval** processes to recall and output the information from memory. Without memory, we would not be able to learn.

However, there are important differences between computers and the human mind. One difference is the human capacity for **consciousness**, the awareness of our own thoughts and the external world. When we focus our **attention** on something, we bring the stimulus into our consciousness—we become consciously aware of it. If we turn our attention inward, we become conscious of our own thoughts. If we focus our attention outward, we become conscious of the outside world. A computer does not have such awareness. But, is all memory conscious? Not necessarily, as we will talk about in our next section.

7.1.1 Explicit and Implicit Memory

Psychologists define **explicit memory** as the conscious use of memory (Bush & Geer, 2001; Graf & Schacter, 1985). We use explicit memory when we consciously search our memory for a previously stored bit of information. For example, try to answer the following question: "What part of the brain's cortex processes visual information?" To answer, you must consciously search your memory for the information you learned in Chapter 2. We hope your search led you to the correct answer, the occipital lobe! As you can see, explicit memory relies heavily on language. When using memory explicitly, the information retrieved is typically in the form of words (i.e., "occipital lobe") that symbolize the concepts you have encoded in memory. Furthermore, while you were probing your memory for this answer, you were fully aware that you were searching your memory for an answer to the question. In this respect, you were utilizing your memory explicitly (Ward, Berry, & Shanks, 2013). But do we always know what's going on inside our own memory?

Psychology Works!

iStock.com/scyther5

Computer programmers who work in the area of *artificial intelligence (AI)*, which seeks to develop computer software that is capable of mimicking human intelligence, use their knowledge of cognitive psychology on a routine basis. After all, you must understand how the human mind processes information to write software that mimics this process. Jobs that utilize AI and cognitive science skills include data analytics, software analysis and development, user experience positions, medical robotics, and many more.

Not always. Sometimes we access and retrieve memories without having consciously tried to do so. For example, have you ever pulled into your driveway, only to realize that you don't recall the last few miles of your trip home? How did you find your way home without being consciously aware of driving the car? This example illustrates the phenomenon of **implicit memory**, or the unconscious use of memory (Graf & Schacter, 1985; Reder, Park, & Kieffaber, 2009). During the trip home, you were using stored knowledge of how to drive your car, how to find your home, how to read street signs, and so on. The trick is that you did all of these things without conscious awareness. Every day, we execute many behaviors at the implicit level of memory. Unlike explicit memory, implicit memory is typically nonverbal in nature. If you are a seasoned driver, you don't usually recall a list of verbal instructions on how to drive your car while you are driving it. Rather, you just execute the behaviors necessary to drive. As we will shortly see, our cognitive resources for conscious memory are quite limited. We simply have to rely on implicit memory for many everyday tasks. If we had to execute everything explicitly, using our conscious and verbal cognitive resources, we would literally not be able to think and walk at the same time! Some important examples of implicit memory that help us function on a daily basis include *motor skills, habits, classical conditioning, priming* (see Engage Yourself!), and *perceptual learning*.

Engage Yourself!

You just learned that *priming* is an example of implicit memory, but what is it? Priming is the unconscious activation of memory. To demonstrate it, try this activity. Before reading on, answer these questions? *How much does a stamp cost? Where do you go to mail a letter? What are envelopes used for? What does the word "seal" mean?*

When you answered the last question, did you say something along the lines that "seal" means to lick an envelope before closing it? If so, that was in part the result of priming. You could have also defined a "seal" as an animal—why didn't you? Because in answering the mail-related questions, your memory was being implicitly activated or *primed*. In particular, your memories of "seal" as a verb were being activated. Your memories of the animal, "seal", were not being activated. Try this demonstration on a few friends—do they also show evidence of priming?

7.1 Quiz Yourself

1. **Your friend asks you to repeat the word "silk" 5 times. Then they ask you the question, "What do cows drink?". When you answer with "milk", they laugh and tell you that of course cows drink water. Which of the following *best* explains why you answered incorrectly?**
   a. Explicit memory
   b. Priming
   c. A lack of attention
   d. None of the above
2. **Which of the following *best* illustrates the use of explicit memory?**
   a. Forgetting to get eggs at the grocery store
   b. Trying to remember the name of a woman you once met at a party
   c. Automatically thinking of a cat when you see a dog on TV
   d. Guessing the correct answer on a multiple-choice test
3. **Which of the following *best* illustrates the use of implicit memory?**
   a. Knowing the correct answer on a multiple-choice test
   b. Trying to remember where you left your car keys
   c. Forgetting where you left your car keys
   d. Tying your shoe while talking on your cell phone

Answers 1. b; 2. b; 3. d

7.2 The Development of New Memories

As you may recall from Chapter 1, the study of cognition grew in psychology from the 1960s to the 1980s. As it did, the *information-processing approach* to understanding memory also became more prominent as psychologists began to develop theories of memory that described memory using a computer analogy for the mind. In this section, we'll look at two of these models—the *three-stages* and *working memory models* of memory.

7.2.1 The Traditional Three-Stages Model of Memory

Traditionally, memory has been explained as having three distinct stages of storage (Atkinson & Shiffrin, 1968). When information enters memory, its first stop is **sensory memory**. In sensory memory, information that comes in from our eyes, ears, and other senses is briefly stored in a sensory form, such as a sound or a visual image. If we pay attention to the information in our sensory memory, the information is sent on to the second stage, **short-term memory (STM)**, for further processing. Short-term memory functions as a temporary holding tank for a limited amount of information. We can hold information in short-term memory for only a few seconds before we must act either to send it further on in the memory system or to keep it in short-term memory by refreshing it. If we decide to further process the information, we can move it from temporary storage in short-term memory to the permanent storage system of **long-term memory (LTM)** (● FIGURE 7.1). Let's look at each of these stages of memory in a bit more detail.

sensory memory a system of memory that very briefly stores sensory impressions so that we can extract relevant information from them for further processing

short-term memory (STM) a system of memory that is limited in both capacity and duration; in the three-stages model of memory, short-term memory is seen as the intermediate stage between sensory memory and long-term memory

long-term memory (LTM) a system of memory that works to store memories for a long time, perhaps even permanently

Sensory Memory: Iconic and Echoic Memory

All of the information that enters our memory from the outside world must first pass through our senses. The information we receive from our sense organs lasts for a very brief time after the sensory stimulation has ended. As noted earlier, this holding of sensory information after the sensory stimulus ends is sensory memory. Perhaps you have noticed your sensory memory at work. Have you ever asked a friend to repeat what they just said in conversation, only to realize as they began to speak that you did know what they said after all? If so, you just caught your sensory memory at work.

Of all our senses, sight (*iconic memory*) and hearing (*echoic memory*), the two most studied by psychologists, are also the primary means through which we acquire information. But they are not the only useful senses. We also learn through our senses of taste, smell, and touch (*haptic memory*). Psychologists assume that we have sensory memories for each of the senses.

The function of sensory memory is to hold sensory information just long enough for us to process it and send it on to short-term memory for further processing. The amount of information that we can process in sensory memory at one time tends to be rather large. However, at least with respect to iconic memory, this capacity seems to vary, being affected by things such as our emotional state (Kuhbandner, Lichtenfeld, & Pekrun, 2011). For example, in one study, participants experiencing negative emotion showed reduced capacity, but increased precision, in iconic memory (Spachtholtz, Kuhbandner, & Pekrun, 2014). It also appears that we are faster to recognize images that we associate with either positive or negative emotion, indicating that we pay more attention to emotional images in sensory memory.

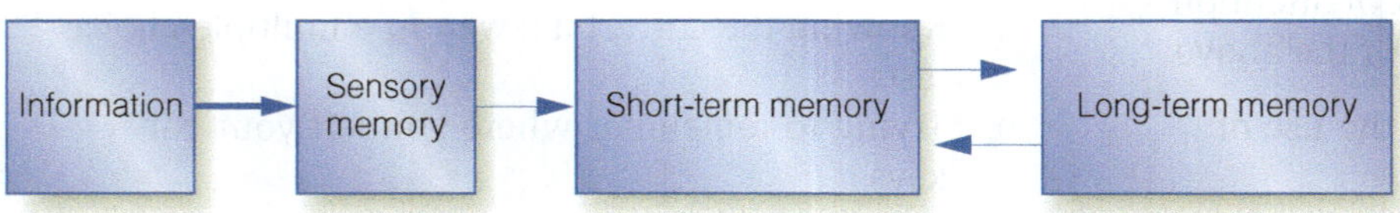

FIGURE 7.1

The Traditional Three-Stages Model of Memory

The traditional three-stages model of memory proposes that in forming new memories, information passes sequentially from sensory memory to short-term memory to long-term memory.

Furthermore, images associated with negative emotion are retained for a longer period of time in iconic memory (Kattner & Green, 2019). If you think about it, it makes sense that we would prioritize emotional images as these images may have survival value for us (e.g., threats and rewards).

Although the capacity of sensory memory is typically large, its duration is short. In the case of iconic memory, the information stays in sensory memory for merely a fraction of a second (Rensink, 2014). Although still very brief, the exact duration of echoic (hearing) memories seems to vary across situations (Demany & Semal, 2005). In the end, if we do not send sensory information on to short-term memory within seconds (or less), it will be lost forever as our sensory memories decay (see • FIGURE 7.2).

So, how do we transfer information from sensory memory to short-term memory? It's simple, actually. To transfer information from sensory memory to short-term memory, all we have to do is pay attention to the sensory information. In paying attention to a sensory stimulus, we focus our consciousness on that stimulus. For example, as your professor tells the class about the due date for an assignment, you pay attention to the date and bring it into your consciousness. As you do this, you ensure that the date will be transferred from echoic memory into short-term memory (see • FIGURE 7.3, a and b). If you are distracted or unmotivated, you may listen without paying attention to the information. In that case, the date will be lost as it decays from echoic memory. As you can see, if you don't pay attention to what you are hearing, you are wasting your time!

Larry Marano/Shutterstock.com

Asia Images/Getty Images

FIGURE 7.2

Sensory Memory

As this man watches a concert video, he stores brief sensory images of what he is seeing in his iconic memory. At the same time, he stores a brief sensory image of the sound he is hearing in his echoic memory. The resulting sensory memories may last for only a fraction of a second, but in that time he will extract the information he wants to keep and send it on to short-term memory for further processing.

Unfortunately, attention is a limited cognitive resource. As much as we might want to, we cannot attend to everything going on around us at once. Our attention is *selective*, in that, we can focus our attention on the thing that seems most important at the time (e.g., the page you are now reading). However, our attention can also be *automatically selected* by things that capture our attention (e.g., someone yelling your name across the room). We often find ourselves in situations where multiple things are competing for our attention. *Divided attention* is the term used to describe these situations. Divided attention can occur in a variety of situations, for example when we engage in *multitasking* or doing two or more tasks at once. Multitasking forces us to try to pay attention to multiple things at the same time. For example, when texting in class, you are trying to pay attention to the lecture, to your phone screen, to the notes you are taking, to what you want to type in your next text, etc. Your attention is being divided in many directions, and your cognitive resources are being strained. As a result, your ability to process incoming information in memory is likely to falter. In one study, even gifted students learned less when they were asked to multitask by texting while watching an instructional video. Non-gifted students fared even worse (Mercimek, Yavuz, & Dönmez, 2020). When attention is divided between two or more tasks, memory functioning can suffer. Protecting your ability to learn is one reason why your professor may ban or discourage cellphone use in class, and why you should study in a quiet, distraction free place!

As we have seen, attention is a necessary step in encoding memories, but there is more to it than that. Once information makes it to your short-term memory, you still have to take active steps to keep this information in memory.

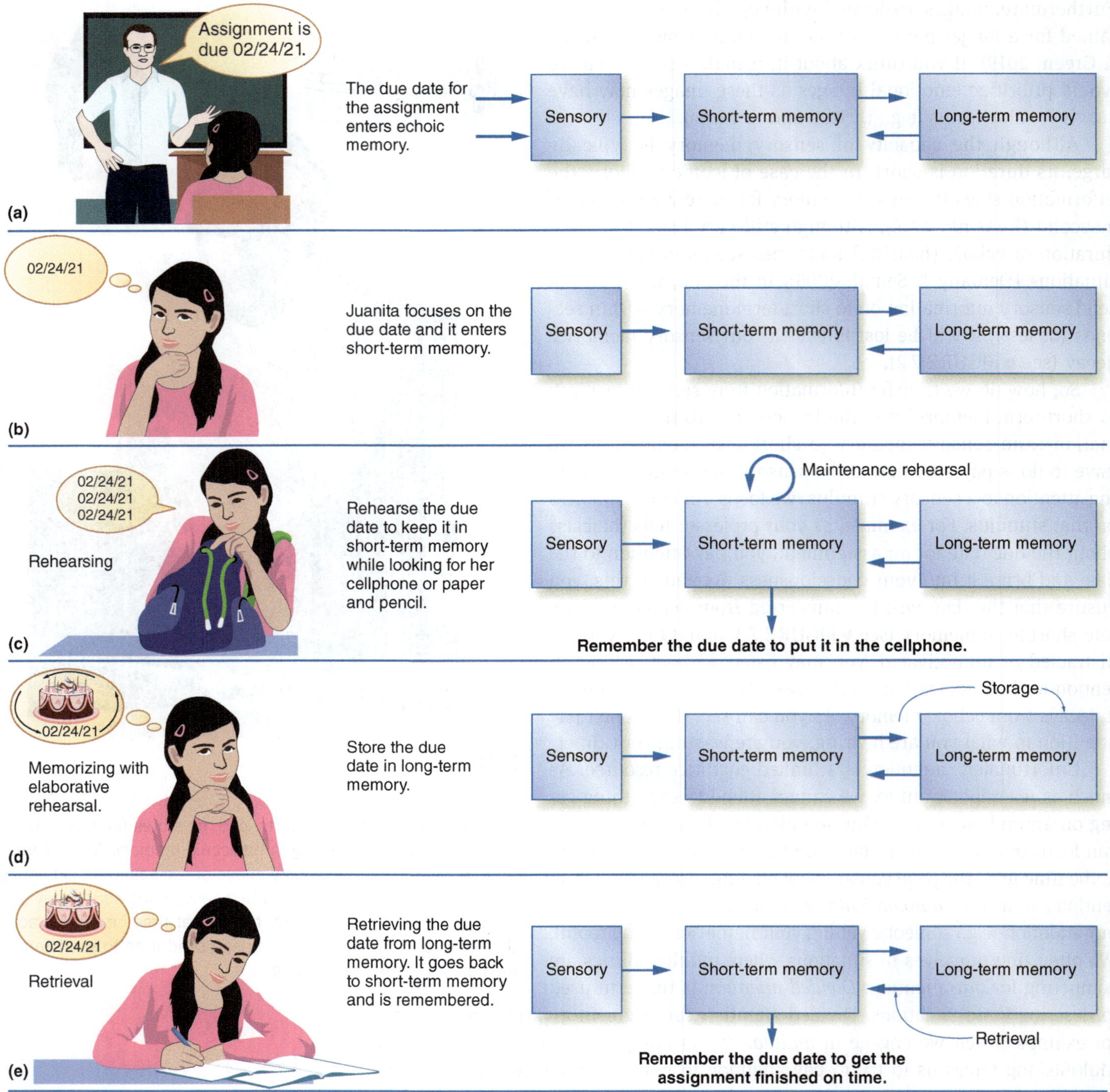

FIGURE 7.3

The Three Stages Model of Memory

(a) Juanita's professor verbally gives the class details about an assignment and its due date. This information enters Juanita's echoic memory. (b) As she focuses her attention on the details of the assignment, the information now moves to her short-term memory. (c) To keep the details, such as the due date in mind while she looks for her phone, Juanita uses maintenance rehearsal, repeating the date over and over to herself. (d) As Juanita continues to think about the date, she engages in elaborative rehearsal by associating the date with details of the dates of other events in her life, such as the birthday party that will happen on the same day the assignment is due; as a result, the information is now stored in her long-term memory. (e) Later, when Juanita wants to remember the due date, she retrieves information about the party from long-term memory and does not need to check her phone's calendar.

Short-Term Memory: Where Memories are Made (and Lost)

The three-stages view of memory conceptualizes short-term memory as a temporary holding tank for information that has been transferred in from sensory memory. Short-term memory uses multiple **coding systems** in which memories can be encoded visually, acoustically (with sound), verbally, or semantically (in terms of meaning) in memory (Henry et al., 2012; Lewis-Peacock, Drysdale, & Postle, 2015; Paivio, 1982). Although short-term memory serves us well, it is another point in the system where we can lose information. Because short-term memory is designed for temporary storage, both its capacity and its duration are limited. It can hold only a small amount of information, and only for a short time. If you've ever tried to hold the homework instructions your professor gave the class in your head while digging your laptop out of your bookbag, you know just how limited short-term memory is and how susceptible it is to forgetting!

coding system a system of encoding in which memories can be stored in memory using a visual, acoustic (with sound), verbal, or semantic (in terms of meaning) format

chunking a means of using one's limited short-term memory resources more efficiently by combining small bits of information to form larger bits of information, or chunks

7.2.2 The Capacity of Short-Term Memory: Seven (Plus or Minus Two)

In 1956, psychologist George Miller published a landmark paper on the capacity of short-term memory. In this research, Miller had participants try to remember as many items from a list as they could. He found that the average person could hold about seven, plus or minus two, items in short-term memory. Ever since, psychologists have referred to the "magic number seven" when speaking of the capacity of short-term memory. This 7 ± 2 capacity applies to small bits of information such as single digit numbers, letters, words, and other small bits of information.

However, more recent research has suggested that the actual capacity of short-term memory also depends on the size of the bits of information being stored. For example, a number sequence of 8, 1, 5 is relatively difficult to compress in memory as there is no inherent association among the numbers, but the number string 1, 2, 3 can be easily compressed into one unit or *chunk* in memory due its familiar sequential nature. As such, 1, 2, 3 should take up less short-term memory space than 8, 1, 5 would. This process of compressing information into small, meaningful units is called **chunking** (Bor & Seth, 2012; Simon, 1974). When taking into account the ease with which information can be compressed into chunks, researchers have discovered that we can only hold 4 ± 1 chunks of information in memory (Cowan, 2001; Mathy & Feldman, 2012).

The limited capacity of short-term memory may be due to the way that neurons in the hippocampus code and store information (Migliore, Novara, & Tegolo, 2008; von Allmen et al., 2013; von Allmen, Wurmitzer, & Klaver, 2014). Given this limitation, it is in our best interest to utilize chunking as often as we can in everyday life. In fact, many of the important numbers in our culture—Social Security numbers, software keys, computer-generated passwords, license plates, credit card numbers, and so on—are usually presented in a prechunked form so as to facilitate our remembering them. It would be harder to recall your Social Security number as nine separate digits rather than three chunks.

7.2.3 The Duration of Short-Term Memory: It's Yours for 30 Seconds

Duration is the second major limitation of short-term memory. Once information passes into short-term memory, it can only be kept there for around 30 seconds without some type of rehearsal or refreshing of the material (Brown, 1958; Peterson & Peterson, 1959).

What if you have to keep some information in short-term memory for more than 30 seconds? Suppose your professor tells the class the due date for your next assignment, and you have to remember it while you search in your backpack for your cellphone. If you can't write the date down, you need to find a way to keep it in your short-term memory for longer than 30 seconds. What do you think you would do in this situation? One simple solution would be to repeat the date over and over out loud as you look for your phone or paper and pencil (Figure 7.3c). This repetition of the material in short-term memory, called **maintenance rehearsal**, is useful for extending the duration of short-term memory (Nairne, 2002). When you repeat the information over and over again, you resupply it to short-term memory before it can decay, extending its retention for another 30 seconds or so before you must repeat the number to yourself again. You can keep this up all day, as long as no one interrupts or distracts you!

maintenance rehearsal repeating information over and over again to keep it in short-term memory for an extended period of time

Technology, Distraction, and Memory in the Classroom

Today, students have unprecedented access to technology in the classroom and beyond. For some of us, our cell phone is vital to everyday life, and cell phones can even be used as a tool in the classroom, such as when professors incorporate cellphone-based clicker systems into their courses (Terrion & Aceti, 2012). But, what about unauthorized uses of technology in the classroom? Can technology sometimes distract us and impede our learning?

As we have seen, attention plays a key role in memory processing (Allen, Baddeley, & Hitch, 2014; Carlisle & Woodman, 2013). Achieving our learning goals depends in part on our ability to focus our attention on relevant information. When technology disrupts our ability to pay attention, memory and learning can suffer. This can happen to students who misuse technology in class (e.g., texting unrelated material, receiving texts, and using social media) (Kuznekoll, Munz, & Titsworth, 2015; Mendoza et al., 2018; Wood et al., 2012), but it can also happen when *other* students' use of technology is distracting. How many times have you been in class when another student's cell phone began to ring? Has this ever happened during an exam? Aside from being annoying, research suggests that a ringing cell phone can impair memory.

In a classroom setting, Christian End and colleagues (2010) randomly assigned some students to watch a video during which the researchers called a classmate's phone twice, letting it ring for five seconds each time. In the control condition, students watched the video uninterrupted. Later, all students were given a multiple-choice test on the content of the video. The results showed that relative to the control group, students in the cell phone condition performed more poorly on the exam. They were also more likely to have incomplete class notes on the video content. These results indicate that ringing cell phones affect students' attention and later memory for course content. It appears that muting your cell phone is more than just a matter of politeness. Your classmates' and your own academic success may depend on it.

Transferring Information from Short-Term to Long-Term Memory

Assuming that we can pay attention well enough to get information into short-term memory, we still need to move this information into long-term memory if we wish to keep it for an extended period of time. Maintenance rehearsal may be useful for keeping information in short-term memory. However, you will likely have to do more than merely repeat the information if you want to store it permanently in long-term memory. Maintenance rehearsal accomplishes only a weak transfer of information into long-term memory (Glenberg, Smith, & Green, 1977; Lockhart & Craik, 1990). Memories encoded using maintenance rehearsal are easily forgotten with time.

• FIGURE 7.4 illustrates what psychologists refer to as a **forgetting curve**, or the amount of information forgotten as time passes. As you can see from Figure 7.4, when maintenance rehearsal is used to learn material, nearly 75% of the information will be lost in only two days. You may have learned this lesson the hard way if repetition is your primary means of studying material for exams. If you simply repeat information over and over in your head, or repeatedly read over the information in your text and notes, your studying will not accomplish strong transfer of information into long-term memory, and you may find yourself in trouble on test day. To really learn new material, you'll have to use a more effective rehearsal strategy.

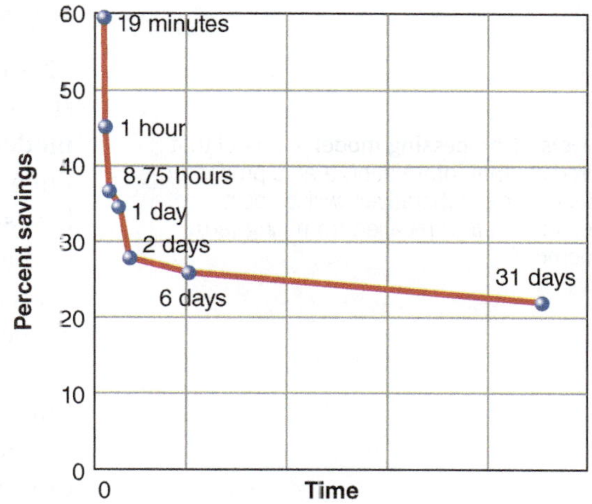

FIGURE 7.4

Retention After Maintenance Rehearsal

Psychologist Hermann Ebbinghaus learned lists of nonsense syllables (such as NID) using maintenance rehearsal and then calculated how much of this learning was retained over various periods of time—a factor he called savings in learning. A savings score of 100% would mean that no learning was lost with time. As you can see, memory for the syllables dropped off very quickly over time. After only 2 days, nearly 75% of the learning was lost. These data clearly indicate that maintenance rehearsal is a relatively poor means of storing information in long-term memory. If you want to really retain what you have learned, you should use elaborative rehearsal. (Based on data from Ebbinghaus, 1885/1913.)

7.2.4 Elaborative Rehearsal: Making Memories Stick

As we just saw, the main function of maintenance rehearsal is to keep information in short-term memory—and information in short-term memory is only temporary. To really get information into your long-term memory, you have to use another technique, called **elaborative rehearsal** (Craik & Lockhart, 1972). Elaborative rehearsal (Figure 7.3d) involves forming associations, or mental connections, between the information in short-term memory that you want to store and information you already have stored in your permanent long-term memory. To get customers to recall a business's name or phone number, for example, advertisers often use jingles. Associating the company's name with the melody serves to elaborate it in memory. This approach is how many of us in the United States were taught to learn our alphabet letters—we sang the letters to the well-known tune of *Twinkle Twinkle Little Star!*

Another powerful type of elaboration, called the *self-reference effect (SRE)*, is to generate personally relevant examples of the material you are learning. Every time you generate an example from your own life that demonstrates a psychological principle, you are engaging in elaborative rehearsal and increasing the chances of retrieving the material later (Figure 7.3e). For example, thinking about how you used repetition to memorize your multiplication tables in grade school as an example of maintenance rehearsal will help you retain this concept in long-term memory. If you find it difficult to connect the material to yourself, you may try connecting it to a friend of yours as these types of elaborations have also been shown to improve memory (Yamawaki et al., 2017).

forgetting curve a graph of the amount of learned information that is forgotten over time

elaborative rehearsal forming associations or links between information one is trying to learn and information already stored in long-term memory so as to facilitate the transfer of this new information into long-term memory

Engage Yourself!

To illustrate the power that elaborative rehearsal has on memory, try this quick demonstration. Get a blank sheet of paper and try to write the lyrics to a song you have in your music collection without playing or singing the song. How well did you do? If you're like most of us, you probably found this task challenging. Now, play the song and try to sing along. Is it easier to recall the lyrics while singing? For most of us it would be. We have elaborated the lyrics by associating them with the tune in our long-term memory. Recalling the tune helps us recall the words. Elaborative rehearsal leads to better memory, and connecting words to a familiar tune can help us integrate the words deeper into our memory (see Tamminen et al., 2017).

7.2.5 Levels of Processing

levels-of-processing model a model that predicts that information that is processed deeply and elaboratively will be best retained in and recalled from long-term memory

This notion that the more thoroughly or deeply you process information, the more strongly you transfer it to long-term memory is referred to as the **levels-of-processing model** of memory (Baddeley & Hitch, 2017; Craik & Lockhart, 1972; Ekuni, Vaz, & Bueno, 2011). When Fergus Craik and Robert Lockhart (1972) first proposed the levels-of-processing approach, it was assumed that the only way to get information into long-term memory was to use elaborative rehearsal. Subsequent research has shown that this isn't necessarily the case. Although maintenance rehearsal is a shallow form of processing that doesn't involve much elaboration of the material, it does allow for some transfer of information into long-term memory (Lockhart & Craik, 1990).

For example, you may eventually remember your college id number if you have to write it, and thus repeat it, frequently enough. However, the type of transfer to long-term memory that occurs with maintenance rehearsal doesn't really help students pass an exam in which they actually have to understand what they are talking or writing about. One study found that if you increase the amount of maintenance rehearsal by nine times (900%), you increase your recall of the information by only 1.5% (Glenberg et al., 1977). Elaborative rehearsal, in contrast, involves a very deep level of processing. To elaborate material, you must access information stored in long-term memory and associate it with the new information you are trying to learn (Rudner et al., 2013). This requires much more effort and thought than merely repeating the information over and over. The good news is that this effort pays off in terms of better memory for the information. Elaborative rehearsal is clearly your best bet if you want to successfully master material, whether in a course or in life.

As an example, let's say that you attend a multicultural fair at your school in which students bring foods from their native cultures for everyone to try (one of the author's schools regularly holds such an event). You sample a West African dish called a puff-puff, a type of slightly sweet fried bread that is often eaten with kidney bean stew. Finding the puff-puff delicious, you decide to commit its name and characteristics to memory so that you can later find some means of obtaining more—trust us, they're that good!

If you want to commit information about the puff-puff to long-term memory, you must associate it with what you already know. You might think about how a puff-puff looks very much like an American donut hole. You may note that the puff-puff contains nutmeg, which reminds you of drinking eggnog with nutmeg during the winter. You might associate the puff-puff with similar fried breads in other cultures, such as Native American fry bread or beignets from New Orleans. Or you might associate puff-puffs with your friend Denis from West Africa. Do you see what we're doing here? We are finding ways to associate and link the puff-puff to concepts that you already have stored in long-term memory, such as donuts, nutmeg, and a friend. This is what elaborative rehearsal is all about. You go beyond simply repeating information to actually thinking about the information, and in doing so, you process the information deeply enough to efficiently transfer it to long-term memory.

▲ If you want to commit information about the puff-puff to long-term memory, you must use elaborative rehearsal. In other words, you must associate the puff-puff with what you already know.

When you use elaborative rehearsal as you learn, you will retain the information in the permanent storage system of long-term memory in a way that maximizes the chances of being able to retrieve it when you need it—whether on test day or when searching online for West African recipes. By the way, we found one version of a puff-puff recipe on the website *Immaculate Bites*. You might want to give it a try!

Does Short-Term Memory Really Exist?

Recall that the three-stages model proposes short-term memory as a separate, intermediate stage of memory that is limited in capacity and duration (see Figure 7.1). As you learned in Chapter 1, any scientific theory must be supported by the results of scientific experiments before we place much stock in it. As you will shortly see, not all of the available research supports the three-stages model, particularly in its conception of short-term memory. Let's take a look at the evidence supporting and calling into doubt this model.

7.2.6 The Serial-Position Curve and Age-Related Changes in Memory

Some support for the three-stages model comes from *serial-position experiments*. In a typical experiment, participants listen to a list of around 20 words slowly read aloud by the experimenter, after which they immediately try to *recall* the words in any order they can. The experimenter then plots the *serial-position curve*, or the tendency for participants to recall each word correctly plotted as a function of the position of the word in the original list. ● FIGURE 7.5 shows a typical serial-position curve. You will notice in Figure 7.5 that not all of the words in the list have an equal chance of being recalled. Rather, words at the beginning and the end of the list are recalled better than words in the middle of the list.

The overall shape of the serial-position curve fits well with the three-stages view of memory. In fact, the model predicts that you will obtain a curve like that shown in Figure 7.5. The tendency for words at the beginning of the list to be better recalled, called the **primacy effect**, can be explained in terms of long-term memory. As participants listen to the list of words, they spend considerable time rehearsing the words at the beginning of the list in their short-term memory. While they are doing this, they have no short-term memory capacity left to rehearse the words in the middle of the list. Therefore, words in the middle of the list are lost from short-term memory, but the words at the beginning of the list are moved to long-term memory and thus are remembered well at recall.

primacy effect the tendency for people to recall words from the beginning of a list better than words that appeared in the middle of the list

Interestingly, diminished primacy effects have been seen in adults with Alzheimer's disease and *mild cognitive impairments (MCI)* that are likely to progress on to become Alzheimer's disease (Cunha et al., 2012). Diminished primacy effects may also help predict who is progressing from normal age-related changes in cognition to having MCI (Talamonti et al., 2020). Presumably, having a diminished primacy effect suggests a person is having difficulty transferring information from short-term memory to long-term memory.

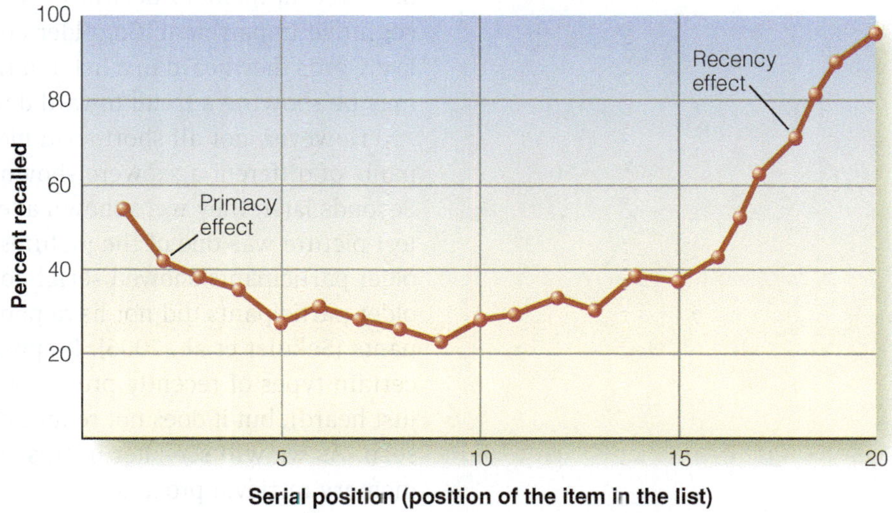

FIGURE 7.5

Serial-Position Curve

In a serial-position experiment (Murdoch, 1962), participants are asked to remember a list of words that are read aloud to them. In such experiments, words at the beginning of the list (primacy effect) and words at the end of the list (recency effect) are remembered best.

recency effect the tendency for people to recall words from the end of a list better than words that appeared in the middle of the list

Primacy is not the only phenomenon seen in serial position experiments. A **recency effect** is also seen, in that, the words at the end of the list are also well remembered. The recency effect is thought to occur because participants still have these words in short-term memory at the time they are asked to recall the list. Therefore, all the participants have to do is dump these words from their short-term memory before going on to retrieve the other words (i.e., those from the beginning of the list) from long-term memory. In the serial-position experiment, participants should be able to recall the last two or three words they heard (Glanzer & Cunitz, 1966). The recency effect does not extend to the full capacity of short-term memory because some of the capacity of short-term memory is taken up in rehearsing the words from the start of the list and in continuing to process incoming words. To see these serial position effects in action, take a moment and try this Engage Yourself! activity.

Engage Yourself!

Try this demonstration on one or more of your friends. Read the following list of words to your friend(s) at a rate of about 1 second per word. Immediately after you finish the list, ask your friend(s) to write down the words in any order on a sheet of paper. When comparing their answers to the original list, do you see evidence of the primacy and recency effects? Do they have better recall for the words at the beginning and end of the list?

Words: *fad, dog, ant, tea, cab, fan, cat, man, sea, fat, car, tin, ram, art, mat, dam, can, lad, rat, far, gin.*

Interestingly, recency memory is one of the aspects of memory that is most affected by normal aging (Wingfield & Kahana, 2002). As we get older, our short-term memory tends to suffer more than our distant long-term memories. As we saw with the primacy effect, changes in memory for recently encoded information can also predict eventual cognitive impairment in people. In particular, the more one's recent memory declines over time, the greater the likelihood of developing cognitive impairment. So, older adults who can immediately recall many of the last words they heard in a list, but then quickly forget these words as time goes on, may be showing a trend toward developing MCI (Bruno et al., 2016, 2018).

However, not all short-term memory suffers as we age. In one study, participants of different ages were shown a series of three pictures in rapid succession. Seconds later, they were shown a test picture and asked to determine whether the test picture was one of the pictures they had just seen. In this case, younger and older participants showed serial-position curves that were strikingly similar. The older participants did not have poorer recency memory than the younger participants (Sekuler et al., 2006). It appears that aging may reduce our ability to *recall* certain types of recently processed information (e.g., verbal information that we just heard), but it does not reduce our ability to *recognize* things we have recently seen. As we will see later in this chapter, recalling and recognizing are different memory retrieval processes.

Another positive finding is that older adults appear to compensate for poorer recency memory by becoming more strategic in their memory processing. Older adults tend to focus their memory processing more on the most important information, and they have been shown to restudy information strategically just before it needs to be recalled (Castel et al., 2013). Strategies such as these may help ensure that older adults remain as functional as younger people despite the normal age-related changes in memory they face.

Although numerous serial-position experiments support the three-stages model of memory, some scientists still express doubts about the model, especially its conception of short-term memory (Baddeley, Hitch, & Allen, 2019; Plancher & Barrouillet, 2020). One potential problem with the three-stages model has to do with how we process information in memory. The three-stages model proposes that the only route by which information can reach long-term memory is through the short-term memory stage. Furthermore, in this model, short-term memory is conceptualized as only being able to engage in a single process at a time. There is some doubt as to whether these assumptions are true (Logie, 1999). If information must pass from sensory memory into short-term memory without having made contact with long-term memory, then long-term memory is activated only *after* information is processed in short-term memory. The problem is that this is not always the case. If you are given a list of seven words to remember, you will likely use maintenance rehearsal (repeating the words over and over to yourself) to keep these words in short-term memory. To do so, however, you will have to know how to pronounce the words, which you can only know by accessing your knowledge (from long-term memory) of how to pronounce the words. As you pronounce the words, you may also be aware of the meaning of the words. For these things to be possible, you must access and retrieve information in long-term memory *before* you have processed the information held in short-term memory into long-term memory (Logie, 1999). As you are doing all of this, you are also processing multiple aspects of the information at the same time—its sound, the meaning of the words, perhaps even how to spell the word.

The three-stages model cannot easily account for this simultaneous activity. Furthermore, the case of a man, K.F., with brain damage from an accident, also brought some aspects of the three-stages model into question. If short-term memory is the gateway to long-term memory as the three-stages model predicts (see Figure 7.1), then it seems that having a very small short-term memory capacity would coincide with poor long-term memory performance. Deficits in short-term memory should act like a roadblock to reduce the efficiency of getting information into and out of long-term memory. However, in the case of K.F., this was not what happened. K.F.'s long-term memory performance was fairly normal despite his ability to only hold approximately one to two items in short-term memory at a time (Baddeley, Hitch, & Allen, 2019; Shallice & Warrington, 1970). Failure of the model to fully account for cases like K.F.'s, as well as our everyday use of memory led researchers to develop alternative views of memory. One of the most influential alternatives to the three-stages model is the *working memory view* of memory (Baddeley, 1986, 2012; Baddeley & Hitch, 1974; Baddeley, Hitch, & Allen, 2019).

7.2.7 The Working Memory Model: Parallel Memory

Today, many researchers reject the notion that information passes sequentially through the three stages of memory and instead propose a new type of memory called **working memory** (Baddeley, 2002, 2012; Baddeley, Hitch, & Allen, 2019). The working memory model views the memory stages in more of a parallel fashion as opposed to a serial fashion. In other words, the working memory model assumes that we process different aspects of memory at the same time, rather than in a series of stages as predicted by the three-stages model. As you read the following example, notice how information is stored temporarily in working memory while several different aspects of the information are processed simultaneously (● FIGURE 7.6). Also notice how information is moved into and out of long-term memory at the same time that information is being held in working memory.

working memory a multifaceted component of long-term memory that contains a central executive, an episodic buffer, a phonological loop, and a visuospatial sketchpad; the function of working memory is to access, move, and process information that we are currently using

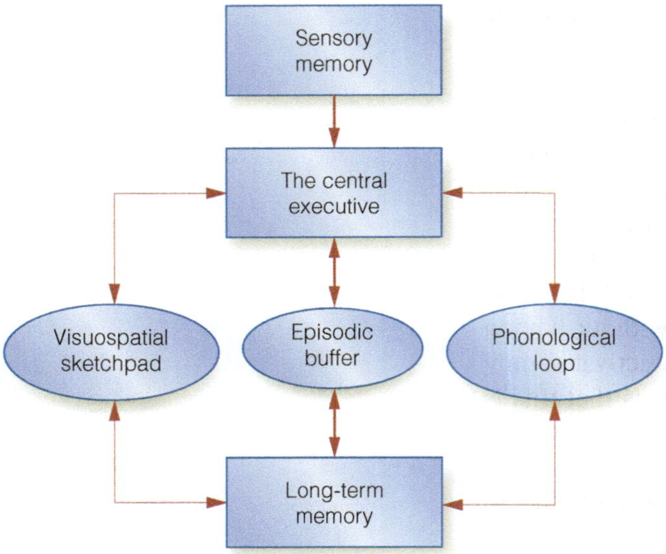

FIGURE 7.6

The Working Memory Model

Working memory is an alternative view of short-term memory that proposes that while information is temporarily stored, several aspects of the information are processed in a parallel fashion by a multicomponent working memory system. The central executive of working memory controls the action of several subordinate systems, including the visuospatial sketchpad (processes visual information), phonological loop (processes verbal/auditory information), and episodic buffer (connects the information to long-term memory).

Suppose a bee stings you. Your haptic (touch) sensory memory registers the pain of the sting, and your visual sensory memory captures the sight of the bee. These sensory impressions are then sent to working memory, where they are combined into an integrated memory representation of being stung by the bee (Kessler & Meiran, 2006). At the same time, your working memory may activate a long-term memory of what you learned in first-aid class about the dangers of allergic reactions to bee stings. Working memory accesses this information on allergic reactions, and you now consciously think about the signs of an allergic reaction as you check to see whether you are having one. You conclude that you are not having an allergic reaction, so you cease to think about it, and working memory transfers the new knowledge that you are not allergic to bee stings to long-term memory.

As you can see, in this view of memory, information does not flow sequentially from sensory to short-term to long-term memory. Rather, working memory plays several roles. Much like short-term memory, working memory acts as a temporary storage system for information that is currently being used. However, at the same time, other parts of working memory act to retrieve information, process new information, and send new and revised information on to long-term memory. The order in which the different memory stages are activated can vary depending on the circumstances.

One advantage of the working memory model is that it can explain why we sometimes seem to access long-term memory before we process information in short-term memory. For instance, as you read this page, you must access information that you have stored in long-term memory about the English language in order to pronounce and understand the words. As the words on the page enter your short-term memory, you already know what they mean and how they sound. The working memory view of memory can explain this, but the three-stages model cannot. In the working memory model, you can go to your long-term memories to help you process perceptual information in a *top-down* fashion, meaning that your perception is guided by your knowledge of the world (Logie, 1999; see Chapter 3).

The Central Executive and Deficits in Memory Functioning

central executive the attention-controlling component of working memory

One of the more prominent theories of a multicomponent working memory proposes that working memory contains a *central executive* component and several subordinate systems: the *phonological loop,* which processes and stores verbal and auditory information (such as the buzzing of a bee), the *visuospatial sketchpad,* which processes visual and spatial information (the sight of a bumblebee), and an *episodic buffer* that connects information in working memory to information found in long-term memory (such as knowing that bees can sting) (Baddeley, 1992, 2012; Baddeley, Allen, & Hitch, 2010; Baddeley & Hitch, 1974; Baddeley, Hitch, & Allen, 2019). The episodic buffer may also integrate information coming from different sources in working memory (Baddeley, 2012; Bahrami Balani, 2020). These systems are called subordinate systems, because they fall under the control of the central executive (● FIGURE 7.7).

The **central executive** functions as an attention-controlling mechanism within working memory. The central executive must coordinate the actions of the

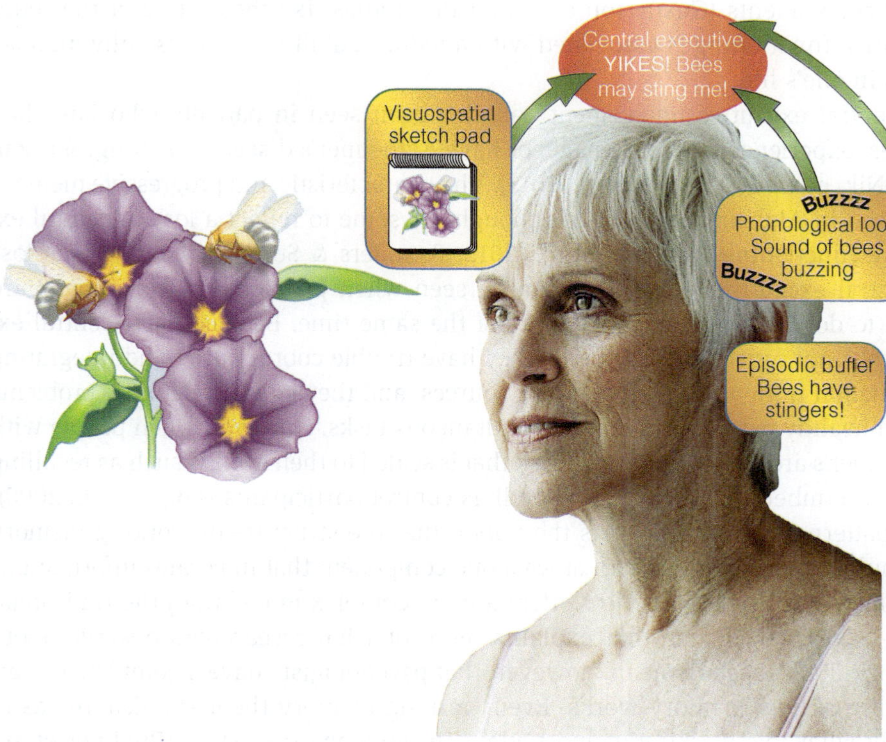

FIGURE 7.7

Baddeley's Central Executive Model of Working Memory

In Baddeley's model of working memory, the central executive integrates visual information from the visuospatial sketchpad, auditory information from the phonological loop, and semantic information from long-term memory via the episodic buffer. The integration of information that the central executive provides is crucial when we are engaged in activities that require us to use both visual and auditory information—as in deciding how to react when you both see and hear nearby bumblebees.

subordinate systems and integrate information that comes in from these systems (e.g., directing you to pay attention to how close a bee gets to your arm). This makes the central executive component especially important when we are engaged in tasks that require attention and the coordination of visual and auditory information, such as when playing a video game (Baddeley, 1992). Furthermore, it appears that some aspects of central executive functioning are affected by our motivation for processing information in a given situation (Sanada et al., 2013). Being motivated to win the video game may facilitate your working memory function and help you achieve your goals. However, despite their best efforts, some people still have difficulties with memory processing.

Some researchers have proposed that faulty executive functioning—an inability to direct one's attention while using working memory—may be one of the underlying mechanisms in attention deficit hyperactivity disorder (ADHD) in both children (Dovis et al., 2013; Rinsky & Henshaw, 2011) and adults (Silverstein et al., 2020). Furthermore, it seems that the ability to integrate information from multiple sources in working memory is essential to our ability to function well in everyday life. One recent study found that executive function impairment was correlated with poorer coping strategies and increased anxiety in a sample of young adults (O'Rourke, Halpern, & Vaysman, 2020). Lower levels of executive functioning have also been shown to correlate with a general tendency to worry in college students (Gustavson et al., 2020). Studies like these suggest that poor executive functioning is associated with a reduced ability to successfully manage stress in one's life.

Central executive impairment has also been seen in patients who have had strokes, experienced brain damage, or have Alzheimer's disease (Li, Tang, & Chen, 2016; Niki et al., 2020; Yang et al., 2013). The characteristic and progressive memory loss seen in Alzheimer's disease is thought by some to reflect a loss of central executive functioning (Gibbons et al., 2012; Saunders & Summers, 2011). This loss of central executive functioning can be seen when people with Alzheimer's are asked to do visual and auditory tasks at the same time. Because their central executive is not functioning properly, they have trouble coordinating and integrating information from visual and auditory sources, and they experience more problems than a healthy person does on the simultaneous tasks. However, when people with Alzheimer's are tested on a single task that is scaled to their ability, such as recalling a list of numbers, they perform as well as control participants (Logie et al., 2000). This pattern of results supports the notion that the structure of working memory has multiple components, with at least one component that integrates information.

The working memory view offers a more complex model than the traditional three-stages model, one that explains more of what researchers observe about memory. This does not mean, however, that psychologists have a complete understanding of how memory works. Even working memory theorists disagree as to exactly what role working memory plays in the memory system (Buehner et al., 2005). Theorists also disagree as to whether working memory is separate from long-term memory. Not all researchers are convinced that working memory is composed of multiple components, and those who are convinced of its multiplicity do not agree on the number of components. Clearly, our understanding of working memory is still developing (Hurlstone, Hitch, & Baddeley, 2014; Repovs & Baddeley, 2006; Sepp et al., 2020). Still, relative to the three-stages model, the working memory model represents a better explanation of memory (see You Review: The Three-Stages and Working Memory Models of Memory).

YOU REVIEW The Three-Stages and Working Memory Models of Memory

Comparison	Three-Stages Model	Working Memory Model
What are the components of the memory system?	Memory consists of three separate stages: sensory memory, STM, and LTM.	Memory consists of several interacting components: sensory memory, working memory, and LTM.
What is the relationship between short-term memory and long-term memory?	STM is a single component of memory that is separate from LTM.	Working memory is a multicomponent temporary memory store that interfaces with LTM in an ongoing fashion. While information is in working memory, the central executive directs the action of the phonological loop, visuospatial sketchpad, and episodic buffer in processing different aspects of the information.
How does memory operate?	Memory operates in a serial fashion.	Memory operates in a parallel fashion.
To what degree does the model explain real-world behavior?	The three-stages model cannot easily explain some cognitive processes such as top-down perceptual processing.	Because the working memory model is a parallel model of memory, it can better account for processes such as top-down perceptual processing.

7.2 Quiz Yourself

1. **Which of the following views of memory can best explain our ability to simultaneously process the music of a video and the images of the video in short-term memory?**
   a. The three-stages model of memory
   b. The working memory view of memory
   c. Procedural memory processing
   d. Semantic memory processing
2. **When you are listening to and watching a music video on your computer, which component(s) of memory are you likely to be using?**
   a. The phonological loop
   b. The central executive
   c. The visuospatial sketchpad
   d. All of the above
3. **Which of the following is the best example of elaborative rehearsal?**
   a. Reading a chapter in your text three times
   b. Relating the material to your personal experiences
   c. Using flashcards of key concepts in the chapter
   d. Rewriting your lecture notes
4. **You are trying to study your psychology notes, and at the same time you are trying to listen to music online. Which component of working memory is *most* at work, attempting to divide your attention among these tasks?**
   a. The phonological loop
   b. The central executive
   c. Short-term memory
   d. The episodic buffer
5. **You are at a very noisy party, but instead of listening to the background noise, you are having a serious conversation with a friend. The fact that you are able to do this *best* illustrates ______.**
   a. encoding
   b. memory storage
   c. divided attention
   d. selective attention

Answers 1. b; 2. d; 3. b; 4. b; 5. d

7.3 Long-Term Memory: Permanent Storage

According to the memory models we've explored—the three-stages model and the working memory model—long-term memory is our largest and most permanent memory storage system (Figures 7.3 and 7.6). Long-term memory is where we store information that we wish to keep for a long period of time. It is in long-term memory that we store all of our knowledge of ourselves and of the world. Information stored in long-term memory is not conscious until we activate it and call it into working memory or short-term memory. Let's begin our quest to understand how we store memory for the long haul by getting a better understanding of the capacity, encoding, organization, and types of long-term memory.

7.3.1 The Capacity of Long-Term Memory

For all practical purposes, long-term memory seems to have a limitless capacity. To date, psychologists have not found any reason to believe that long-term memory has a limited capacity, as short-term memory and working memory do. It is safe to say that you are unlikely to ever run out of room in your long-term memory. It may sometimes feel as though your brain is full, but you still have the capacity to store more information in long-term memory. What you are feeling is more likely to be a problem in focusing your attention or a lack of available capacity in short-term or working memory. If you can pay enough attention to move the information through sensory memory to short-term/working memory, and then rehearse the material enough to get it to long-term memory, you will find that you have ample storage space for the information.

moodboard/SuperStock

▲ Although you may sometimes feel as if your long-term memory is "full," you always have the capacity to store information—provided that you are not too tired, distracted, or unmotivated to rehearse and elaborate the material you wish to learn.

7.3.2 Encoding in Long-Term Memory

Information is encoded in long-term memory in several forms. As in the other parts of memory storage, information in long-term memory can be stored in both acoustic (sound) and visual forms (Paivio, 1986; Tozios & Fukuda, 2020). However, we more often encode long-term memories semantically, in terms of the meaning of the information. **Semantic encoding** stores the gist, or general meaning, of the stimulus rather than storing all of the sensory details (Anderson, 1974; Gernsbacher, 1985; Purser & Jarrold, 2010; Wanner, 1968).

Semantic encoding offers some distinct advantages over acoustic and visual encoding in long-term memory (Cherry et al., 2012), even though it sacrifices a lot of the details because all of the features of the original stimulus are not stored in memory. For example, if you read a description of a West African puff-puff in a cookbook, you could store information about the sound of the word *puff-puff* or the visual image of a puff-puff in your long-term memory, but this wouldn't really help you make a puff-puff. In fact, you could memorize an exact picture of a puff-puff and still not know what it is. On the other hand, if you stored semantic information about the puff-puff—that it is a West African food consisting of a fried ball of dough made of flour, eggs, sugar, nutmeg, shortening, milk, and baking powder—you would potentially have enough understanding of a puff-puff to actually make one. A picture couldn't give you that.

7.3.3 Organization in Long-Term Memory

One aspect of encoding information in long-term memory is how we organize it. Over the years, psychologists have proposed various means by which we organize our knowledge categorically (i.e., by category; for a review, see Anderson, 2000). One of these strategies involves the use of a generalized knowledge structure called a **schema** (Bartlett, 1932; Rumelhart, 1980). We have schemas for people, places, concepts, events, groups of people, and just about everything else we know.

Schemas can be thought of as filing systems we use for knowledge about particular concepts. Schemas contain general information on the characteristics of the concept's category, its function, and so on. For each of these general characteristics, the schema has slots for information specific to the concept. For example, let's look at a portion of a hypothetical schema for a puff-puff. On the left are the names of the slots in the schema found for breads. On the right are the specific bits of information that would be placed in these slots for the puff-puff.

Puff-Puff	
Is a:	bread
Contains:	flour, sugar, shortening, eggs, etc.
Method of preparation:	fried
Uses:	energy source; eaten with kidney bean stew
Appearance:	small, donut hole–sized
Origin:	West Africa

These slots can also have default values that are used when information is missing from our perception. For instance, if you did not read that the puff-puff is fried, you might assume that because a puff-puff is bread, it must be baked. One of the default values for the slot "method of preparation" may be "baked."

semantic encoding encoding memory traces in terms of the meaning of the information being stored

schema [SKEE-ma] an organized, generalized knowledge structure in long-term memory

We probably rely on these default values in schemas when we engage in *top-down perceptual processing* (see Chapter 3).

Obviously, breads are not the only objects for which we have schemas. In fact, we have schemas for many different types of information. In addition to schemas for objects, we have schemas for abstract *concepts* such as love, hate, and psychology. We also have schemas to categorize our social world. We use *person schemas* for specific people, such as best friend, mother, or brother; *stereotypes* for groups of people, such as Asians, Catholics, football fans, or artists; and *scripts* for events, such as going to the doctor, eating at a fancy restaurant, or going on a date. In Chapter 9, we will take a closer look at how these schemas develop and change. For now, let's take a look at the different types of long-term memory.

7.3.4 Declarative and Procedural Long-Term Memories

Most research on memory has concerned itself with a type of explicit memory called **declarative memory**. Declarative memory is memory for knowledge that can be easily verbalized: names, dates, events, concepts, and so on. This is the type of memory that Kim Peek excelled so well at, memorizing phone books, textbooks, and so on. Declarative memory can be divided into two subtypes: **semantic memory**, which is memory for concepts, and **episodic memory**, which is memory for the recent events in one's life.

declarative memory a type of long-term memory encompassing memories that are easily verbalized, including episodic and semantic memories

semantic memory long-term, declarative memory for conceptual information

episodic [epp-uh-SOD-ick] memory memory for the recent events in our lives

autobiographical memory memory for our past that gives us a sense of personal history

Semantic memories tend to be conceptual and lacking in detail. For example, think about an "icicle" right now. As you think about an icicle, you probably know what an icicle is and what characteristics it possesses. However, you probably don't have an extremely detailed mental image of a specific icicle that you have seen in mind right now. You are thinking of a *concept* rather than a particular icicle.

As you read this chapter, you are adding to your semantic memory by increasing your knowledge of psychology and memory processes. In doing this, you will add to the schemas you have stored in long-term memory for these (and other) concepts in the chapter. For example, you may think of semantic and episodic memories from your own life and tie your growing knowledge of psychology to the well-formed schemas you have for the world. By building and strengthening these schemas, you are helping to build a knowledge base for psychology that will later enable you to apply this information to problems that require some understanding of psychology, including the exam on test day.

As you attend school and go about the business of your everyday life, you are also adding to your episodic memory (Pause et al., 2013; Staniloiu, Kordon, & Markowitsch, 2020; Tulving, 1972; Wheeler, Stuss, & Tulving, 1997). Episodic memory contains fairly detailed memories of the recent events in your life (Conway, 2009). You store memories of your conversations with others, events you have attended, and your activities in your episodic memory. Episodic memories are associated with a unique sense of personal awareness (Wheeler et al., 1997). Later, when you remember reading this chapter, you'll think, "I was there; I remember reading that chapter." This self-awareness makes episodic memory a very personal part of our long-term memory.

Our lives are a series of events. Once encoded, our episodic memories are quickly integrated into **autobiographical memory**, our more general memory of our unique personal history (Burt, Kemp, & Conway, 2008; Nelson & Fivush, 2004). As episodic memories are integrated into autobiographical memory, some of the details are lost (Conway, 2009) and some errors, such as incorporating

▲ Autobiographical memory gives us our past—such as these childhood memories.

the details of one event into the memory of another, occur (Devitt et al., 2016). So, although you can probably recall a great deal about what you did an hour ago, you probably cannot recall many of the details of what you did last week. Our cherished memories of the past are, to some degree, abstractions of the original events. Nonetheless, these memories are extremely important to us. Without autobiographical memory, we would lose an important part of our selves (Rathbone et al., 2012).

Gender and Autobiographical Memory

Take a moment now to recall some of your own episodic memories. What comes to mind when you think of your past? Is it easy to recall the events of your life, or is it a struggle? Interestingly, researchers have found that your ability to recall specific types of episodic memories may be a function of your gender (Colley et al., 2002; Grysman et al., 2016; Grysman & Hudson, 2013; Niedzwienska, 2003; Pillemer et al., 2003). Penelope Davis (1999) found that compared to men, women are better at recalling emotional childhood memories, such as a happy birthday party or an angry conflict with a childhood friend. Davis hypothesized that gender differences are evident only for emotional memories because females' greater tendency to elaborate is particular to emotional event memories.

To test this notion, Davis first had all participants retrieve emotion-laden childhood memories. Then they were asked to sort their memories into categories of memories that seemed to go together—for example, happy memories, memories associated with school, memories associated with family, and so on. The participants were free to use as many or as few categories as they chose. As predicted, the females sorted their memories into significantly more categories than the males did. From these data, Davis concluded that females' enhanced autobiographical memory for emotional events is due to their tendency to organize these memories into more diverse categories. In other words, women have been socialized to do more elaborative processing of emotion-laden autobiographical memories, and this processing pays off in terms of better recall.

▲ Research suggests that relative to males, females are better at recalling emotionally charged episodic memories. Later in life, this girl may recall this happy graduation day better than her male classmates do.

In line with this conclusion, relative to men, women have been shown to express more emotion, connectedness with others, and factual elaboration in their episodic memories. Furthermore, the more feminine someone's gender is, the greater her tendency to describe episodic memories that involve being connected to others. These findings led the authors to suggest that reminiscing about one's life is more of a feminine gender-typed activity, meaning that women tend to be socialized toward it more than men are (Grysman et al., 2016; Grysman, Merrill, & Fivush, 2017).

The connection among gender, emotion, and episodic memory has also been examined by looking at events that disrupt episodic memory, such as binge drinking. In one study, females who engaged in binge drinking had a tendency to remember more emotionally negative words than positive words on a memory task. However, for males, binge drinking was not associated with differential recall of the emotional words. These findings suggest that female binge drinkers may have a hard time ignoring negative emotional cues (Carbia et al., 2020). Studies such as these also suggest that for females, emotion plays a particularly important role in memory.

Are Semantic and Episodic Memory Separate Systems?

Given that semantic and episodic memory are both enhanced by elaborative rehearsal, does this mean that they are stored in the same fashion in the brain? Currently, there is some debate on this issue. A number of studies suggest that episodic and semantic memory may indeed be separate memory systems (Graham et al., 2000; Murphy et al., 2008; Renoult et al., 2016; Wheeler et al., 1997). Some of the most persuasive research on this issue comes from studies using the positron emission tomography (PET) and functional magnetic resonance imaging (fMRI) scan technologies that you learned about in Chapter 2. These scans allow researchers to see which parts of the brain are most active while the participant is engaged in certain activities. By scanning participants' brains while they perform semantic and episodic memory tasks, researchers can get an idea of which parts of the brain are involved in these two types of memory.

These studies suggest that processing semantic and episodic memory tasks produces activation in some common areas of the brain, such as the prefrontal cortex, but also some unique patterns of activation (Beaty et al., 2020; Levine et al., 2004; Nyberg et al., 2003; Renoult et al., 2016, 2019). If episodic memory and semantic memory tasks involve activity in different parts of the brain, it is not a far leap to presume that they may be separate memory systems. Additionally, researchers have found that people with certain brain disorders experience more impairment in storing long-term episodic/autobiographical memories than they do in storing semantic memories (Gao et al., 2020; Tramoni et al., 2011).

Studies such as these support the notion of separate systems in memory. However, there also appears to be considerable overlap and intertwining of semantic and episodic memory function. For example, many of the same regions of the brain are active during both episodic and semantic memory tasks (for review, see Renoult et al., 2019). Retrieved episodic memories often also contain conceptual or semantic content (e.g., when recalling an episodic memory of being at school yesterday, you will likely also recall the meaning of the concepts covered in lecture). And, as episodic memories convert to more distant autobiographical memories, they tend to have some of the characteristics of both episodic and semantic memories. For example, my autobiographical memory of junior high math class contains personally relevant information that is tied to certain events (e.g., a memory of listening to a lecture on mathematical proofs). Yet, this memory also lacks detail and is very conceptual, as are semantic memories (e.g., I no longer recall specific details such as the teacher's name or his face, but I recall the general idea that he was a blonde, white male).

To attempt to reconcile both the similarities and dissimilarities of episodic and semantic memory, some researchers have proposed the existence of a memory system that has features of both semantic and episodic memory, a system called *personal semantics* (Renoult et al., 2012, 2016). Personal semantic memory is thought to encompass *knowledge* about oneself (e.g., I like peanuts), whereas episodic memory is memory for events or episodes from one's life (e.g., I ate peanuts last night). Some researchers propose that personal semantics are actually a part of semantic long-term memory (Klein & Markowitsch, 2015; Staniloiu, Kordon, & Markowitsch, 2020).

So, where does this leave us? Are episodic and semantic memory separate systems? Currently, much of the evidence suggests that they are separate, but inextricably intertwined systems in memory. Recalling a memory of your past most likely draws on both your episodic and semantic memories (Renoult et al., 2019). However, more research will need to be done to confirm or disconfirm this notion and to examine exactly how these systems may work together in memory.

Procedural Memory: Memory for Skills

procedural memory long-term memory for skills and behaviors

Regardless of whether semantic and episodic memory are part of the same memory system, they share the characteristics of being *explicit* and *declarative* or easily verbalized. This is not true of all of our knowledge. **Procedural memory**, our memory for skills, is typically implicit and not as readily put into words as our declarative (semantic and episodic) memories are. To illustrate the differences between declarative and procedural memories, take a moment to try the following demonstration.

Engage Yourself!

Use your procedural memory to think of a skill that you know how to execute very well, such as walking, riding a bike, or driving a car; then attempt to tell someone else how to execute that skill without showing them how to do it. You can only use words to describe the skill. Now choose something about which you have declarative memory—the directions to your favorite café or the plot of your favorite movie—and try to communicate that using only words.

Which task did you find to be more difficult? We bet that you found the first task to be much harder than the second. The first task asked you to verbalize a procedural memory, whereas the second asked you to verbalize a semantic memory. As we said before, procedural memories are not easily verbalized, and we've demonstrated just how hard it can be to find words to describe even everyday skills.

Another defining characteristic of procedural memory is that it is often *implicit* memory (Cohen, 1984; Reber, 2013; Squire, Knowlton, & Musen, 1993). Recall that implicit memory is memory that is used unconsciously. We use information stored in memory without being aware that we are doing so. For the most part, the skills we execute every day are done in an unconscious, implicit fashion. As you walk to your classes, are you consciously aware of what you need to do to get your body to walk? When you take notes in class, are you aware of what you need to do to get your hand to write? Of course not! We walk, write, drive a car, and perform many other skills without thinking about them. The fact that procedural memories are implicit may also help explain why we have a difficult time verbalizing them. How can you verbalize your execution of a behavior when you are not aware of how you do it? You can't.

A final aspect of procedural memory that separates it from declarative memory is its longevity. Unlike declarative memory abilities, which continue to develop throughout childhood and adolescence, our procedural memory abilities are largely developed by age 10 (Finn et al., 2016). These procedural memory skills allow us to learn tasks in childhood that will remain in long-term memory for a long time. You've probably heard the saying "It's like riding a bike. You never forget how to do it." There is a great deal of truth in this folk wisdom—once we have mastered a skill, it does stay with us for a long time. An adult can jump on a bike after years of not riding and pick right back up where they left off in childhood. Declarative memory, on the other hand, does not enjoy the same longevity as procedural memory. If you put aside your study of psychology and never thought about it, how much psychology do you think you would be able to recall 10 years from now? Probably not much.

As you can see, procedural memory seems to differ substantially from declarative memory. The degree of disparity between these two types of memory brings up the question of whether they are separate memory systems. Strong evidence to support the notion that procedural memory is a separate memory system comes from studies done on people with *amnesia*.

7.3.5 Amnesia: What Forgetting Can Teach Us About Memory

Amnesia is a condition in which a person cannot recall certain declarative memories. Amnesia can be classified as *retrograde* or *anterograde* (● FIGURE 7.8). **Retrograde amnesia** is an inability to recall previously stored declarative memories; **anterograde amnesia** is an inability to store new declarative memories in long-term memory. In short, retrograde amnesia is amnesia for one's past, and anterograde amnesia is amnesia for one's present and future.

retrograde amnesia an inability to recall previously stored declarative memories from long-term memory

anterograde [an-TARE-oh-grade] amnesia an inability to store new declarative memories in long-term memory

Amnesia has several causes, but of most interest to us here is amnesia that is caused by brain injury or illness (for review, see Matthews, 2015). In particular, studies of people with anterograde amnesia have taught us much about the distinction between declarative and procedural memory. One of the most famous cases of anterograde amnesia involved H.M. (Henry Molaison; Corkin, 1968), who had a severe form of epilepsy that was centered in the vicinity of his hippocampal regions in the temporal lobe (see Chapter 2) and did not respond to medication. In an effort to curb H.M.'s seizures, doctors removed large parts of the hippocampus in both hemispheres of his brain along with portions of the amygdala and adjacent cortical areas (Augustinack et al., 2014; Squire, 1992). The surgery was successful in that H.M.'s seizures were drastically reduced. However, in another sense, the operation was a serious failure. After H.M. recovered from the surgery, it became apparent that he could no longer store new declarative memories. He could not remember seeing his doctor seconds after the doctor left the room. He was also unable to read an entire magazine article. By the time he got to the end of a long paragraph, he would have forgotten what he'd just read. It was clear that H.M. had severe anterograde amnesia, a condition he lived with for the next 55 years until his death in 2008 at age 82 (Augustinack et al., 2014; Carey, 2008).

Interestingly, however, H.M. did not completely lose his ability to store new long-term memories. After the surgery, he could still store procedural memories. For instance, H.M. could learn to do certain perceptual-motor tasks, such as tracing a stimulus while looking at its image in a mirror. Furthermore, he was seen to improve on these tasks with time (Milner, Corkin, & Teuber, 1968). Results similar to those found in H.M. have also been found in other people with amnesia (see, for example, Cermak et al., 1973; Mulligan & Besken, 2013). The fact that H.M. and other people with amnesia can still learn new skills indicates that procedural memory is not stored in long-term memory in the same way as declarative memory.

For people with amnesia, the ability to learn new skills is very fortunate. They can still use their procedural memory to learn new skills that may allow them to perform certain jobs, such as making furniture or knitting sweaters, although they will not remember where they acquired these new skills. If they also lost their ability to encode procedural memories, they would be even more impaired. They would not be able to add anything to their long-term memory.

FIGURE 7.8

Amnesia Affects a Person's Memory in Dramatic Ways

Amnesia in Everyday Life: Concussions in Sports

Most of us will never face amnesia to the degree that H.M. did. However, amnesia may be more common than you think. Head injuries are a common occurrence. In 2014, there were 2.53 million patients with head injuries that were either seen in emergency rooms, hospitalized, or died from their injuries (CDC, 2020a). Furthermore, each year, in the United States, over 200,000 people are treated for nonfatal sport- and recreation-related brain injuries, many of which are concussions (CDC, 2011a). In one study, 15.1% of high school students in a particular school reported having had at least one concussion from playing sports or being active in the last 12 months (DePadilla et al., 2018).

Studies of injured athletes show that many will suffer at least mild temporary amnesia (Chrisman et al., 2013; Collins et al., 2003). In fact, temporary amnesia is so common after head injury that its presence is sometimes used as an indication that a concussion has occurred (Gasquoine, 2019). High school athletes with a history of two or more concussions have significantly more cognitive, physical, and sleep difficulties compared to athletes with histories of one or fewer concussions (Schatz et al., 2011). Newer studies of collegiate athletes with concussions have found abnormalities in the *white matter* (myelinated areas) of the brain one month post-injury (Meier et al., 2016). Reductions in brain blood flow levels were also found in young athletes eight days after injury and after the athletes appeared to have physically and behaviorally recovered from their injuries (Wang et al., 2016). Even more worrisome is the fact that the research is beginning to establish that a history of concussions in athletes is related to later mental health problems, especially depressive symptoms (Finkbeiner et al., 2016).

NEIL BRAKE/AFP/Getty Images

▲ Studies have indicated that repeated injury to the brain can result in *Chronic Traumatic Encephalopathy (CTE)*. Symptoms of CTE include cognitive difficulties in processing information, feelings of depression, and perhaps suicidal thoughts.

Chronic traumatic encephalopathy (CTE) is a condition that seems to develop in people who have experienced repeated trauma to the brain, such as professional football players (Omalu et al., 2010). CTE is characterized by cognitive difficulties in processing information, feelings of depression, and perhaps suicidal thoughts—although the link between repeated damage to the brain and suicide has been recently debated (see Burley, 2020). Brain scans of both players and military personnel with a history of brain injury show a buildup of *tau protein* in many areas of the brain (Chen et al., 2018; Omalu et al., 2010). In a study that involved the examination of deceased American football players' brains (they had been donated to science), 223 of the 266 brains showed signs of CTE. Furthermore, the longer the player had been an active player in life, the higher the chances of finding CTE-related changes in his brain after death (Mez et al., 2020). Given the seriousness of CTE and the overall rates of concussions seen each year, it appears that we should focus on finding ways to better protect all people who are at increased risk of brain injury.

Even without brain injury or amnesia, you may still encounter mild problems with your memory from time to time. Normal, everyday forgetting can be an annoyance. In the next sections, we will discuss how we retrieve information from long-term memory and theories of why we sometimes forget the information we have encoded in memory.

7.3 Quiz Yourself

1. Remembering the definition of elaborative rehearsal is an example of a(n) ______ memory.
   a. semantic
   b. episodic
   c. procedural
   d. sensory
2. You know how to behave when you go to a fast-food restaurant because you have a(n) ______ stored in long-term memory for this event.
   a. episode
   b. icon
   c. schema
   d. proposition
3. Which of the following is the best example of semantic encoding in long-term memory?
   a. Remembering how to play the tune to your favorite song on a guitar
   b. Remembering the name of the artist who sings your favorite song
   c. Remembering having pancakes for breakfast this morning
   d. Remembering your first day of high school

Answers 1. a; 2. c; 3. b

7.4 Retrieval and Forgetting in Long-Term Memory

We store memories so that we can later retrieve them. Remember that retrieval is the act of moving information from long-term memory back into working memory or consciousness. Retrieval occurs when we send a *probe* or *cue* into long-term memory in search of memory traces, or encoded memories, that we have stored there. A probe or cue can be many things—a test question, the sight of a playground, the sound of a roller coaster, or even a particular smell. For example, the smell of a pumpkin pie in the oven may remind you of a particularly joyous holiday event with loved ones. Or the sight of a calculator may remind you of a test you took in a high school math class. Memories such as these can be recalled into consciousness many times throughout a given day. The ability to retrieve information from long-term memory also serves important practical applications. For example, the ability to retrieve instructions on how to execute a mathematical problem comes in very handy on a math exam. Recalling how to cook your favorite dish allows you to have a nice dinner. And retrieving information that you have stored about your friends facilitates your social interactions with them by giving you things to talk about. These are just some of the many examples of how we use retrieval in everyday life. Now let's take a closer look at how retrieval occurs in memory and explore ways to improve our use of memory.

recall a type of retrieval process in which the probe or cue does not contain much information

Jupiterimages/Stockbyte/Getty Images

▲ Many things can function as memory probes—test questions, sights, sounds, smells, and so on. These probes have the power to retrieve memories and bring them to consciousness. For example, smelling your mother's perfume may bring a host of pleasant memories to mind.

7.4.1 Recognition and Recall

Think for a moment about the types of exams you have had in the past—for example, multiple-choice, essay, fill-in-the-blank, and true/false. An essay question is an example of a **recall** task. In a recall task, the probe is relatively weak; it does not contain a great deal of information to go on as you search your memory for the answer. You can't guess your way through an essay test. You must really know the information to answer the question. If you have not elaborated the material in long-term memory, you will likely find it difficult to recall.

recognition a type of retrieval process in which the probe or cue contains a great deal of information, including the item being sought

decay theory a theory of forgetting that proposes that memory traces that are not routinely activated in long-term memory will degrade

A multiple-choice question, on the other hand, is an example of a **recognition** task. In recognition, the probe is stronger and contains much more information than does a recall cue. Several researchers have proposed theories to explain why recognition is typically easier than recall (Gillund & Shiffrin, 1984; Tulving, 1983). One theory proposes that recognition is easier because of the overlap between the content of the probe and the content of the memory trace (Tulving, 1983). Think about it for a minute: In a multiple-choice question, the answer is actually part of the probe. Because recall is the harsher test of memory, you should always study as if you are going to take an essay exam. This way, you'll be sure to be prepared for your professor's questions. See Psychology Applies to Your World: Tips on Improving Memory.

7.4.2 Forgetting: Why Can't I Remember That?

Unfortunately, despite your best efforts at studying, there will always be instances when retrieval is difficult. We've all known times when the probes and cues we sent into long-term memory were not successful in retrieving the desired information. For a memory to actually be retrieved from long-term memory, two conditions must be met: the memory must be both *available* and *accessible*. A memory is available when it has been encoded in long-term memory and the memory trace is still present in long-term memory. Obviously, if you never encoded the memory in long-term memory, you won't be able to retrieve it later.

However, availability by itself is not enough to ensure retrieval. Accessibility of the memory trace is also important. If the probe cannot reach the memory trace in long-term memory, the memory will not be retrieved, even if it is available. As we will see in the next section, there are a variety of circumstances in which the probe fails to retrieve an available, but inaccessible, memory.

Masterfile

▲ On exam day, you really hope that your retrieval methods work!

Decay Theory: If You Don't Use It, You Lose It

What student hasn't asked themself this question: "I studied that material, so why did I forget it on the test?" Forgetting occurs when we cannot, for some reason, retrieve information from long-term memory. One theory of forgetting, **decay theory**, maintains that once a memory trace is stored in long-term memory, it must be routinely activated to keep it there (Ebbinghaus, 1885/1913). If we store a memory and then fail to recall it periodically, the memory trace weakens and decays. If the decay is not stopped by recalling the memory, the memory trace will be lost forever.

Memories are thought to be stored in long-term memory through a process called *long-term potentiation*, in which biochemical changes at the synapse affect the sensitivity of the postsynaptic neuron to incoming signals, changing the ease with which signals can travel over that specific neural pathway. Some research now suggests that processes that affect functioning of the synapse may also explain how memories are lost through decay (Sachser et al., 2017).

Although decay theory seems to make sense, there are some good reasons to doubt that memory traces always decay from disuse. One is that memories seem to last a very long time, even when we do not routinely access them. For example, in one study, participants' recognition of English-Spanish vocabulary words was tested anywhere from 1 to 50 years after they had studied Spanish. The results showed that recognition memory for these vocabulary words had declined little over the years (Bahrick, 1984).

Interference: Temporary Forgetting

Have you ever found yourself unable to answer a test question, only to remember the answer later, after the test is over? Sometimes we know that we know information, even though we cannot recall it at the moment, something psychologists refer to as the **tip of the tongue phenomenon**. This frustrating experience is often due to *interference,* a condition in which the memory trace is still available but has become temporarily inaccessible. There are two types of interference, *proactive* and *retroactive interference,* that can block the retrieval of memories. **Proactive interference** occurs when older information inhibits our ability to retrieve other, newer information from memory. For example, one of your authors spells her first name in an unusual way that often causes proactive interference in others. Her name is pronounced "Suzanne," but it is spelled *Susann*. Because of its spelling, people often pronounce her name as "Susan" when they first see it in print. Then, no matter how many times she corrects them, they seem to always want to call her Susan. This example is one of proactive interference because the *older* (people's original) pronunciation of her name inhibits the *newer* (correct) pronunciation in people's memory. (It's also the reason she started going by Sue early in childhood!)

tip of the tongue phenomenon knowing that you know a piece of information, even though you cannot recall it at the moment

proactive interference a type of forgetting that occurs when older memory traces inhibit the retrieval of newer memory traces

retroactive interference a type of forgetting that occurs when newer memory traces inhibit the retrieval of older memory traces

cue-dependent forgetting a type of forgetting that occurs when one cannot recall information in a context other than the context in which it was encoded

We can also experience **retroactive interference**, in which *newer* information inhibits the retrieval of *older* information in memory. Suppose you move to a new home and work very hard to memorize your new address. Chances are, you will soon find it hard to recall your old address. This is an example of retroactive interference, because the new address interferes with your ability to retrieve the old address from long-term memory.

Unfortunately, our susceptibility to both proactive (Dulas & Duarte, 2016; Jacoby, Debner, & Hay, 2001) and retroactive (Hedden & Park, 2003) interference may increase as we age. One explanation for why interference increases with age is that our central executive function tends to decline with advancing age. As the central executive becomes less efficient, it is also less able to suppress interfering memory traces (Adólfsdóttir et al., 2016; Biss, Campbell, & Hasher, 2013; Hedden & Yoon, 2006). Other factors such as sleep deprivation (Riontino & Cavallero, 2020) and our baseline level of cognitive functioning or *cognitive reserve* (Gajewski et al., 2020) also affect how well we can combat interference in memory as we age. As we discussed in Chapter 2, exercise helps protect our brains. Perhaps keeping your body and brain as healthy as possible is one way to help retain your memory function over time. For example, one preliminary study of young adults indicated that exercise may help to lessen the effects of retroactive interference in memory (Loprinzi, Frith, & Crawford, 2020).

Context and Forgetting

Interference theory does seem to describe one way in which we forget information, but there is reason to suspect that interference may not occur as often in the real world as it does in laboratory experiments (Slameka, 1966). **Cue-dependent forgetting** may be a better explanation of forgetting in the real world. The theory of cue-dependent forgetting (Tulving, 1974) is that the amount of information we can retrieve from long-term memory is a function of the type of cue or probe we use. If the memory cues we use are not the right ones, we may experience forgetting.

The cue-dependent forgetting theory is part of the *encoding specificity principle* developed by Endel Tulving (b. 1927; Wiseman & Tulving, 1976). According to this principle, we encode aspects of the context in which we learn information,

Psychology Applies to Your World

Tips for Improving Your Memory

ALTHOUGH SOME PEOPLE, such as Kim Peek, have remarkable memories, most of us find that storing large amounts of new information requires hard work. As students, much of your academic performance relies on your ability to store and remember information. Now that you have learned a bit about how your memory works, you can apply this knowledge to your own life. To be a successful student, you have to study in a way that works with these processes, not against them. We'll outline some strategies that will help maximize your memory.

Single-Task—Don't Multitask

Attention is the first step in getting information into memory. If you are distracted by other tasks (e.g., participating in social media) while studying, your attention will be divided and you won't be able to devote your full attention to the information you are trying to learn, and your ability to recall the information later may be affected (Iidaka et al., 2000; Zeamer & Fox Tree, 2013). Therefore, you should study when and where you can focus your full attention on the single task of studying the material you are trying to learn. Try studying in a quiet, distraction-free environment.

Do Not Cram for Exams

Cramming is one of the worst ways to study for an exam. Unfortunately, many students procrastinate and then try to make up for it by pulling an all-nighter right before the exam. If this is the way you approach your studies, you are asking for failure. Even if you manage to pass the exam, the information you stored in long-term memory is likely to become inaccessible shortly after the exam. In short, you waste your time when you cram.

Studies have shown that *massed practice*—when you try to learn a great deal of information in one study session—results in poor recall of the information. Recall suffers because massed practice results in fatigue, which leads to a lack of attention, and the shortened time frame does not give you time to adequately rehearse information. Without adequate attention and elaborative rehearsal, information will not be efficiently stored in long-term memory. A better way to study is to use *distributed practice,* distributing your study time across several days rather than bunching it up on one day (or night). The beauty of distributed practice is that you don't necessarily have to study longer; you just need to space out the time you spend studying.

wavebreakmedia/Shutterstock.com

▲ You can't learn well if you don't pay attention!

Use Elaborative Rehearsal

To study efficiently, you must process the information at a deeper level, finding ways to elaborate on the meaning of the material in your memory. This means you must form connections or associations among the bits of information you are trying to learn and the information you already know. Outlining is one way to do this. Take all of the material you are trying to learn and organize it into an outline. When you create an outline, you must elaborate the material because you have to think about the relationships among concepts. It also helps to come up with your own original examples of the concepts you are learning—a technique we've encouraged you to use throughout this text. By generating examples, you once again elaborate the material. Taking examples from your own life is even better as it capitalizes on the *self-reference effect* to improve memory (Carson et al., 2019; Symons & Johnson, 1997).

Another way to potentially enhance elaboration of the material is to go "old school" and handwrite your notes as opposed to typing them on a keyboard of some kind. There is some evidence to suggest that handwriting forces us to elaborate the material more because we are more likely to try to condense and synthesize the material when writing by hand. When typing, we tend to just copy information in a more passive fashion (Mueller & Oppenheimer, 2014). However, not all studies support this notion, and a meta-analysis of the available studies on this issue did not find that paper and pencil notes were substantially better than typed ones (Morehead, Dunlosky, & Rawson, 2019). So, while it may not make a large difference, taking thorough handwritten notes of the important concepts is not likely to harm your learning. Furthermore, adding some hand-drawn pictures or diagrams to your notes may also help your learning a bit (van der Meer

& van der Weel, 2017). One thing we know for sure is that taking no notes in class is a very bad idea if you want to be academically successful!

Use Overlearning

Overlearning is a technique in which you learn the material until you feel that you have mastered it, and then you continue to study it some more. By doing this, you help ensure that you will be able to retrieve it at a later date because every time you activate information in long-term memory, you help to make it more available for retrieval. Overlearning can also make you feel more confident as you sit down to take an exam. Knowing that you really know the material, as opposed to "sort of" knowing it, can lessen the anxiety that you feel during an exam, which in turn can improve your performance.

Test Yourself Often

Another helpful strategy when studying is to repeatedly test yourself on the material that you are trying to learn. Studies show that repeated self-testing of one's knowledge can lead to improved learning and retention of material. One way this seems to work is by reducing the amount of interference we experience in memory (Bufe & Aslan, 2018).

Use the SOAR Method

SOAR is an acronym for *select*, *organize*, *associate*, and *regulate* (Jairam et al., 2013). When using this method to study, you first must *select* what is important and take notes on this information. The goal is to create a complete set of notes containing all of the important information. The goal is not a verbatim transcript, but a summary of the important points and concepts. The next step is to re*organize* these notes into a framework that condenses the information (e.g., an outline or graphic depiction). Next comes *association*, you must think about how the different concepts fit together and also fit with what you already know about the world. If this sounds like elaboration, that's because it is! Finally, you must *regulate* your own learning. This is best done through testing yourself on the material that you are studying. Are you learning? Do you need to adjust your study methods? How close are you to being ready for the exam? The only way to know is to test your own learning *before* your professor does in class!

Mnemonics Make Your Memory Mighty

If you find it difficult to elaborate the material, you might try using *mnemonic devices,* memory tricks that help you recall information. A few that you might try include acronyms, taking the first letter of each word you want to remember and use these first letters to form a word; and acrostics, creating a rhyme or saying in which each word starts with the first letter of each of the to-be-remembered words. For example, ESR could be an *acronym* for the three memory processes of encoding, storage, and retrieval. And "Warren plants violets on every corner" could be an *acrostic* to help you remember the components of the working memory model: working memory, phonological loop, visuospatial sketchpad, episodic buffer, and central executive.

Get Enough Sleep, Eat Well, and Exercise

Many studies suggest that maintaining a healthy lifestyle via eating well, exercising, and getting enough sleep should be an important goal for anyone wishing to have a long and healthy life. But did you know that these behaviors are also related to maintaining good memory? For example, a recent study of university students found that exhibiting aerobic fitness was related to better long-term and implicit memory performance (Pontifex et al., 2014). Preliminary evidence also suggests that diet can affect memory. Eating a diet high in fat and sugar during adolescence may set the stage for later obesity, which a number of rodent studies suggest may lead to deficits in learning and memory (Reichelt, 2016). On the other hand, a healthy diet may have the power to stave off memory problems. Studies have found that a diet high in *flavanols* (found in cocoa, tea, etc.) improved brain function and memory in older adults (Brickman et al., 2014) and the consumption of chocolate is associated with improved performance across a number of cognitive tasks (Crichton, Elias, & Alkerwi, 2016). Finally, as you learned in Chapter 4, sleep, especially REM sleep, is thought to play an essential role in the processing of memory. In healthy research participants, experiencing slow-wave sleep (deep sleep) was found to enhance declarative memory (Atherton et al., 2016), and getting a full night's sleep has been shown to facilitate the consolidation of associations and links among bits of information in memory (Ribeiro, Gounden, & Quaglino, 2020). Getting enough sleep between learning sessions has also been shown to substantially cut down on the amount of practice needed to learn and to increase long-term retention of the material (Mazza et al., 2016).

Studies like these suggest that one way to improve your memory is to take care of yourself. Eating unhealthily, not getting enough sleep each night, and skipping the gym may be affecting your grades as well as your health.

▲ Studies show that we remember information best when we retrieve it in the same context in which it was learned. Godden and Baddeley (1975) found that divers who learned a list of words while under water recalled more of the words while submerged than they did on the dock. Studies like these suggest that a change in context may be one of the reasons we sometimes forget.

later using these contextual aspects as cues to help us retrieve the information from long-term memory. If the encoding specificity principle is correct, then we should have better memory when we retrieve information in the same setting that we learned it.

In one distinctive study, researchers asked divers to learn a list of words while they were either on shore or 20 feet under water (Godden & Baddeley, 1975). Later, researchers tested the divers' recall for the words in either the context in which they had studied the words or the context in which they had not studied the words. Consistent with the encoding specificity principle, the researchers found that when the divers recalled the words in the same context in which they had learned the words, their recall was better.

Encoding specificity has also been shown to hold true for mood states and states of consciousness. People can recall information they learned while drinking alcohol better when they have been drinking (Eich et al.,1975). Information learned while smoking marijuana is better recalled while smoking marijuana (Eich, 1980). And information learned while in a bad mood is better recalled in a negative mood state than when one is happy (Teasdale & Russell, 1983). These findings do not mean that it is better to learn while in these states, however. For example, alcohol can reduce one's ability to encode information in the first place (Parker, Birnbaum, & Noble, 1976).

Repression: Motivated Forgetting

The final type of forgetting we will discuss is forgetting on purpose. Have you ever had a memory—perhaps a memory of an embarrassing moment—that you wish you didn't have? Most of us have. When we encounter such memories, is it possible to forget them on purpose?

This question is one that Sigmund Freud (1915, 1943) dealt with in his comprehensive theory of personality (see Chapter 11). In this theory, Freud proposed that the emotional aspects of a memory can affect our ability to retrieve it. According to Freud, when we experience emotionally threatening events, we push or *repress* these memories into an inaccessible part of our mind called the *unconscious*. This **repression** results in amnesia for this information.

repression a type of forgetting proposed by Sigmund Freud in which memories for events, desires, or impulses that we find threatening are pushed into an inaccessible part of the mind called the unconscious

Over the years, repression of memories has become a very controversial subject because of its relationship to cases of childhood sexual abuse. Some people have claimed that they suddenly "remembered" abuse that had occurred many years before. After many years have passed, there is often no corroborating evidence to support such claims. Furthermore, the content of recalled memories for events can be affected by, among other things, the stress the child was under during the event (Klemfuss et al., 2013), and some experiments indicate that the details of children's memories for past events can often be incorrect (Brainerd & Reyna, 2002; Howe, 2000). In one study, researchers found that preschool children could not distinguish memories for fictitious events from memories for real events after 10 weeks of thinking about the events. Even more alarming, the children were able to give detailed accounts of the fictitious events, and they seemed to really believe that the fictitious events had happened (Ceci, 1995). The frequent lack of corroborating evidence for recovered memories, along with experimental evidence that questions the accuracy of memory, has led some to charge that these are in fact *false memories* (Loftus & Davis, 2006).

Another issue is that trauma does not always seem to lead to forgetting. For example, some people who have experienced trauma go on to develop *post-traumatic stress disorder* (PTSD; Chapter 13). People with PTSD are often disturbed by frequent memories of their traumatic event (Meyer, Ikani, & Morina, 2019). Even people without PTSD often remember the details of traumatic events in their lives (Meígas et al., 2007).

The debate is further fueled by the lack of experimental data to support the notion that repression can occur under emotional duress. To test the Freudian notion of repression, researchers would have to traumatize participants and then see whether they repressed their memories of the trauma. Obviously, this type of study cannot be done for ethical reasons. So, for now, psychologists cannot say for sure whether Freud's conception of the unconscious and repression is correct.

Whether or not Freud's ideas are valid, modern neuroscience has given us evidence to suggest that humans are at least capable of temporarily pushing specific memories from our conscious mind (i.e., explicit working memory). This process, called *motivated forgetting*, has been demonstrated in a variety of studies (Anderson & Hanslmayr, 2014; Cano & Knight, 2016; Dalton & Huang, 2014). Memory suppression seems to work by intentionally blocking the retrieval of the unwanted memories into working memory (Anderson & Huddleston, 2012). This newer research on motivated forgetting, especially the research on the neurological underpinnings of such forgetting, is bound to perpetuate the debate on whether or not forgetting can be a tool for coping with distressing memories.

YOU REVIEW Theories of Forgetting

Theory	Definition	Example
Decay	Memory traces that are not routinely activated erode and disappear over time.	You haven't thought of your best friend from kindergarten in 15 years. When you meet them, you cannot recall their name.
Proactive interference	Older memory traces inhibit the retrieval of newer memory traces.	You can't seem to remember your friend's new, married name, but you can recall her maiden name.
Retroactive interference	Newer memory traces inhibit the retrieval of older memory traces.	You can't recall your old address, but you can recall your new address.
Cue-dependent forgetting	Memories are not as easily retrieved when the retrieval cues do not match the cues that were present during encoding.	You run into a classmate at the grocery store, and you can't recall their name. But you do recall their name when you see them at school.
Repression	Threatening memories are pushed into the inaccessible unconscious part of the mind.	You are in a horrible car accident in which other people are seriously injured. Although you are uninjured, you later cannot recall details of the accident.
Motivated forgetting	Unwanted memories are temporarily blocked from being retrieved into working memory.	Every time you start to remember the embarrassing things you did at the party last week, you push the thoughts from working memory and concentrate on something else.

7.4 Quiz Yourself

1. You meet an old friend on the street and search your memory for their name. This is an example of which type of retrieval task?
   a. Recall
   b. Recognition
   c. Implicit retrieval
   d. Encoding specificity

2. Decay theory states that forgetting is due to a lack of _____, whereas interference theory states that forgetting is due to a lack of _____.
   a. availability; accessibility
   b. accessibility; availability
   c. encoding; accessibility
   d. encoding; availability

3. Mary was married 6 months ago. Much to her dismay, her friends continue to call her by her maiden name even though she has legally taken her partner's name. Mary's friends are experiencing which memory phenomenon?
   a. Encoding specificity
   b. Repression
   c. Proactive interference
   d. Retroactive interference

4. Jack doesn't want to remember the blind date he went on last week because it didn't go well. Every time he starts to think of the date, Jack pushes the memory from his mind, and he focuses his attention on something else. Which type of forgetting best describes what Jack is experiencing?
   a. Proactive interference
   b. Retroactive interference
   c. Repression
   d. Motivated forgetting

Answers 1. a; 2. a; 3. c; 4. d

7.5 The Accuracy of Memory

flashbulb memory an unusually detailed and seemingly accurate memory for an emotionally charged event

Even when we are successful in retrieving memories, a lingering question is just how accurate they are. Many people report experiencing **flashbulb memories**, or unusually detailed memories for emotionally charged events (Brown & Kulik, 1977; Hirst & Phelps, 2016). For example, some people can remember what they were doing when they heard that terrorists had attacked the World Trade Center (WTC) on September 11, 2001. Do you or your parents recall watching the live TV coverage as the tragedy was taking place? If so, answer this question: How long after the plane hit the first tower did it take for both towers to fall?

Researchers interviewed 690 people 7 weeks after the attack and asked them this question. On average, the participants reported that it took 62 minutes for the towers to collapse—when in reality it took almost 2 hours. On the day of the attack, do you remember watching news coverage of the first plane hitting the towers? If so, you are not alone—despite the fact that this video footage did not air until the next day (Perina, 2002). So how did you do on this task? How accurate (or inaccurate) is your memory or your parent's memory of that day?

Interestingly, some researchers now suspect that stress hormones that act on the amygdala (see Chapter 2) may be responsible for certain aspects of flashbulb memories. A current theory is that when you experience an emotional event, such as watching a horrific terrorist attack, your body releases stress hormones that direct your brain's amygdala to initiate storage of a long-term memory of that event. However, these stress hormones also seem to block the formation of accurate memories for what was happening immediately before the emotional event. Therefore, you may end up with a memory for the emotional event that is not entirely accurate because you have something of a "gap" in your memory (Bower, 2003; Hirst et al., 2009).

Flashbulb memories are also subject to forgetting over time, especially for older adults (Kopp, Sockol, & Multhaup, 2020). In a 10-year follow-up study of the WTC attacks, researchers found the greatest amount of forgetting of event details and flashbulb memories (e.g., where you were during the attacks) occurred within the first year after the attacks and then leveled off over the remainder of the decade. Interestingly, however, participants' confidence in their memories did not change across the 10-year period (Hirst et al., 2015).

Steve McCurry/Magnum Photos

▲ Do you or your parents remember what you were doing when you heard about the September 11th attacks?

7.5.1 Memory Is Not Like a Video Camera

Does it surprise you to know that memory is often inaccurate? But think about it: Even when we store memories of the everyday events in our lives, we do not store memory traces for every detail. Memory does not work like a video recorder. It's more like a construction project. We store the gist of the information in long-term memory with the help of schemas, but we do not store all of the details. This means that when we retrieve a memory, we do not recall all of the details and then use them to *reconstruct* the event. Memory is more than just **reconstructive**, or based on actual events; it is also *constructive*.

reconstructive memory memory that is based on the retrieval of memory traces that contain the actual details of events we have experienced

constructive memory memory that utilizes knowledge and expectations to fill in the missing details in retrieved memory traces

misinformation effect the distortion of memory that occurs when people are exposed to misinformation

Memory is **constructive** in that we use the knowledge and expectations that we have stored in our schemas to help us fill in the missing details in our stored memories (Schacter & Addis, 2007). It is very possible that many people have filled in the gaps in their memory of September 11, 2001—such as what they were wearing that day, the setting in which they first heard the news, or specific details of the news coverage that they watched that day. Most of the time, it makes little difference whether we recall such details accurately. But sometimes the details of our recollections can be extremely important, even a matter of life and death, such as in the case of eyewitness memory.

7.5.2 Eyewitness Memory

Psychologist Elizabeth Loftus (b. 1944) has spent a good part of her career showing that eyewitness memory can be manipulated by the expectations we hold about the world. For example, in one experiment (Loftus & Palmer, 1974), Loftus showed participants a film of a car accident. After viewing the film, the participants were randomly divided into several groups and questioned about their memory of the film. In one group, the participants were asked, "About how fast were the cars going when they *smashed* into each other?" In another group, the participants were asked, "About how fast were the cars going when they *hit* each other?" In the control group, the participants were not asked to estimate the speed of the cars. The results showed that the verb used in the question affected participants' estimates of the speed of the cars. Participants in the "smashed into" group estimated the speed of the cars, on average, at 41 mph; the average estimate for participants in the "hit" group was 34 mph.

The participants exhibited the **misinformation effect**, or the distortion of memory that occurs when people are exposed to misinformation. In this case, the words *smashed* and *hit* activated different expectations that were used to fill in the missing details in the participants' memories of the film, and the result was that they remembered the film differently. Imagine how a lawyer's choice of words might influence a witness's memory on the witness stand.

Even more dramatic is the fact that our memories can be permanently altered by things that happen *after* we encode the memories. In another study (Loftus & Zanni, 1975), Loftus showed participants a film of a car crash and then asked them a series of questions about the accident. The participants in one group were asked, "Did you see *a* broken headlight?" In a second group, the participants were asked, "Did you see *the* broken headlight?" Although there had been no broken headlight in the film, of those who were asked about *a* broken headlight, 7% reported that they had seen a broken headlight in the film. Of the participants who were asked about *the* broken headlight, 17% said they had seen it. Subtly suggesting to these participants that there *had* been a broken headlight caused more of them to remember seeing something that they had not seen. That simple suggestion caused a false memory in these participants.

These false memories do not seem to be motivated by a participant's desire to please the researcher. In another study, Loftus offered participants $25 if they could recall an event accurately. Even with this motivation to be accurate, the participants could not prevent their memories from being distorted by the misleading information they heard after viewing the incident (Loftus, 1979).

Although it is clear that eyewitness memory is susceptible to errors, there is some disagreement as to why these errors occur. According to Loftus (2000), we accept subsequent misinformation as being correct, and this information becomes part of our memory for the original event when our memory of the event is *reconsolidated* or stored once again after having been retrieved from long-term memory. Others propose that eyewitness memory becomes faulty when we make errors in identifying the source of information we have stored in long-term memory (Carpenter & Schacter, 2017; Johnson, Hashtroudi, & Lindsay, 1993). According to this view, when we retrieve a memory for a particular event from long-term memory, we also retrieve information from other sources relevant to the event. For instance, we might retrieve information from times when we discussed the event with others, from comments others made about the event, from things we read about the event in the media, and so on. Because there is considerable overlap between our memory for the original event and our memories of information related to the event, it is easy for us to get confused about the source of these bits of information. We might misattribute the source of a particular detail to our memory of the original event, when we actually encoded it in another situation. Regardless of which interpretation is correct, after we witness the original event, the more information we are faced with, the more likely it is that our memory will become faulty.

Do these research findings mean that all of our long-term memories are faulty in some fashion? Of course not. Our memories of the past can also be very accurate. In fact, the accuracy of our long-term memory for things that we see frequently has been shown under certain conditions to be just as accurate as the new memories we store in our working memory (Miner, Schurgin, & Brady, 2020). It's when memories are not well encoded to begin with (such as when briefly witnessing a crime) or when they are repeatedly retrieved and reconsolidated (such as when repeatedly recounting past events) that they are especially likely to become inaccurate. The problem lies in the fact that it is difficult for us to tell whether or not one of our own memories is accurate or not. Perhaps someday when we better understand how memories are stored in the brain, we will have a better understanding of the accuracy and inaccuracy of memory. In our next section, we will take a look at what is known about the role the brain plays in memory.

7.5 Quiz Yourself

1. **In recalling his date from last Saturday night, Juan assumes that his date was wearing shoes, even though he did not encode the details of what the shoes looked like. Juan's memory is an example of _____.**
   a. constructive memory
   b. reconstructive memory
   c. procedural memory
   d. encoding specificity
2. **In question number 1, Juan's recollection of his date is *most* likely to be the result of _____.**
   a. reconstructive memory
   b. constructive memory
   c. constructive and reconstructive memory
   d. memory that is like a videotape—an exact copy of what he experienced on the date
3. **Which of the following events is *most* likely to produce a flashbulb memory?**
   a. Taking a difficult math test
   b. Being in a serious car accident
   c. Having a heated discussion with your best friend
   d. Going to a very scary movie on a date

Answers 1. a; 2. c; 3. b

7.6 The Biology of Memory

Much of what we know about the role that the brain plays in memory comes from studies of people with amnesia. People with amnesia often experience severe memory problems that can be traced to damage or disease in particular parts of the brain. Recall the case of H.M., discussed earlier in this chapter. H.M.'s hippocampal regions were removed in an attempt to control his epilepsy; as a result of the surgery, he could no longer achieve **memory consolidation** (the stabilization and long-term storage of memory traces in the brain). In short, he lost the ability to move new declarative memories from short-term to long-term memory (● FIGURE 7.9). Other amnesic cases, too, have supported the notion that the hippocampus plays a significant role in the consolidation of declarative memories (Parkin & Leng, 1993).

memory consolidation the stabilization and long-term storage of memory traces in the brain

Scientists also use brain-imaging technology, discussed in Chapter 2, to study the function of the brain during memory tasks (Finn, 2004). These studies indicate that the hippocampus plays an important role in the declarative memory function of people without amnesia. For instance, PET scans show that blood flow in the normal brain is higher in the right hippocampal region during declarative memory tasks, but not during procedural memory tasks (Schacter et al., 1996; Squire et al., 1992).

Using fMRI technology, researchers have found that the anterior (back) part of the hippocampus is active during tasks such as recalling autobiographical memories, perceiving scenes, remembering previously seen scenes, and imagining the future (Zeidman & Maguire, 2016). Compared to control participants, people with hippocampal damage have also been shown to be less able to form coherent mental representations of scenes that they have seen (McCormick et al., 2017). Likewise, numerous studies have documented memory problems in animals that have had lesions (areas of damage) made in their hippocampal regions (see Franklin & Grossberg, 2017; Winocur, Moscovitch, & Sekeres, 2013).

Research on both animals (Iso, Simoda, & Matsuyama, 2006) and humans (Clemenson & Stark, 2015; Clemenson et al., 2020; Woollett, Glensman, & Maguire, 2008) suggests that the degree to which we use our memory may have implications for the structure of our brains, particularly in the area of the hippocampus.

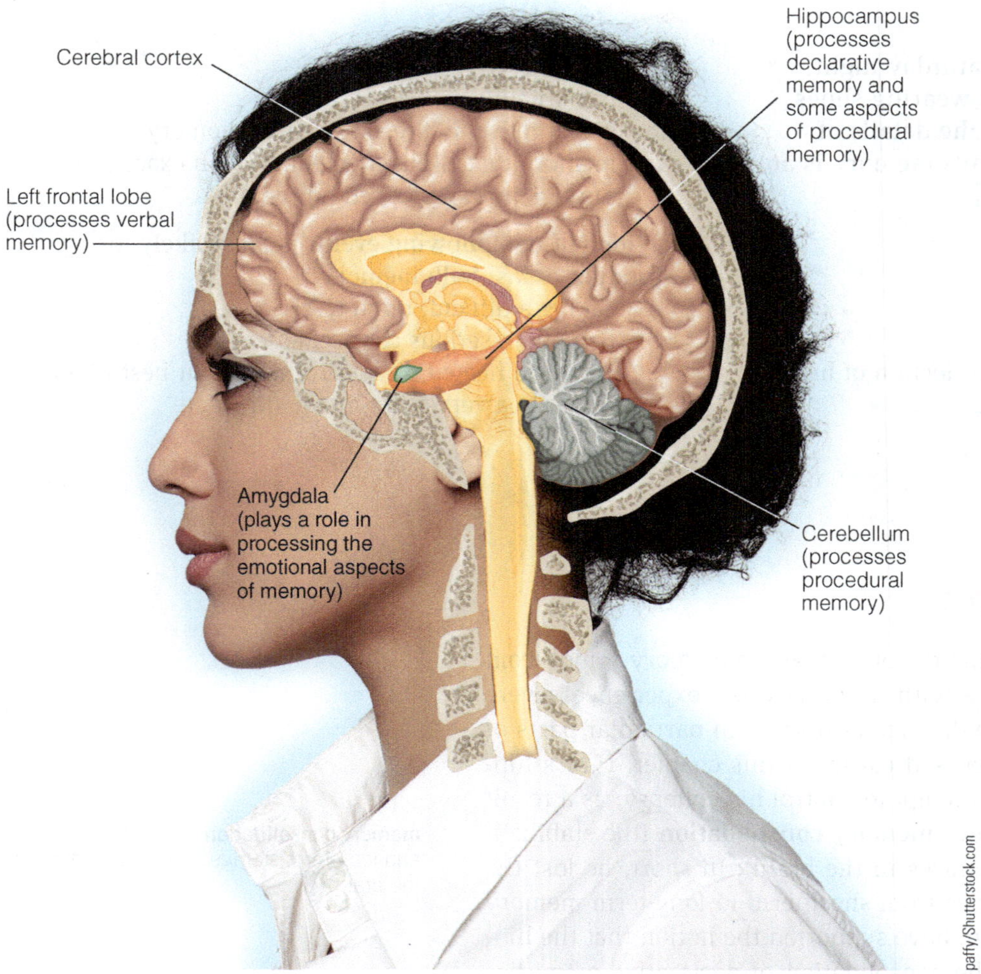

FIGURE 7.9

Some Brain Structures That Are Important to Memory

The hippocampus plays a significant role in the consolidation of declarative memories, but it may also process some aspects of procedural memories. The left frontal lobe processes verbal memories, and the cerebellum processes procedural memories. The amygdala and striatum (not pictured) are also important to processing certain types of memory.

Do you recall the study of London taxi drivers from Chapter 2? That study used magnetic resonance imaging (MRI) technology to show that London cab drivers have specific hippocampal regions that are larger than those found in London bus drivers. London's street system is old and complicated, and taxi drivers must memorize the entire city, not just a single bus route, in order to be licensed. Is it possible that these drivers experienced greater hippocampal development because they relied on their memory so much in doing their job? No one can say for sure at this time, but consistent with this notion, the researchers did find that the taxi drivers who had been driving the longest tended to have the biggest hippocampal regions (Maguire, Woollett, & Spiers, 2006). Furthermore, research on non-taxi drivers has correlated the size of specific areas of the hippocampus with the ability to clearly recall episodic memories (Chadwick, Bonnici, & Maguire, 2014).

Because the hippocampus appears to play an important role in memory, researchers are currently investigating whether or not certain interventions such as drug therapy or mental exercises may help protect our memory by strengthening the hippocampus. For example, leisure activities such as playing immersive 3D video games (i.e., *Super Mario or Angry Birds*), results in improved performance on memory tasks known to involve the hippocampus in both young and older adults (Clemenson & Stark, 2015; Clemenson et al., 2020). In addition to behavioral interventions, researchers are also investigating whether or not certain drugs may help preserve memory function by slowing hippocampal degeneration. Scientists hope this research will lead to new treatments for people who have memory robbing diseases, such as Alzheimer's disease (Chen et al., 2020; Lee et al., 2019).

Like the hippocampus, areas of the frontal lobe also seem to play a significant role in the processing of declarative memory. Evoked response potential (ERP) recordings have revealed that the left frontal lobe is very active during the processing of verbal information, and electrical stimulation of specific areas of the left frontal lobe can enhance verbal learning (Nikolin et al., 2015).

fMRI scans of the brain in action, also indicate that areas of the left frontal lobe are also involved in naming and *semantic recognition* or understanding of things we see (Xu et al., 2020). This makes sense because one of the language centers of the brain, Broca's area (see Chapter 2), is in the left frontal lobe (Anderson, 2000). Similarly, PET scans of the brain in action have revealed that the amount of left frontal lobe activation seems to be related to the degree to which the participant is processing the material. Left frontal lobe activity is especially likely to occur when participants are deeply processing the material. In fact, the more activation there is in the participants' left frontal lobe, the better they tend to recall the information (Kapur et al., 1994). Findings like these seem to suggest that the levels-of-processing approach to memory may have some biological correlate.

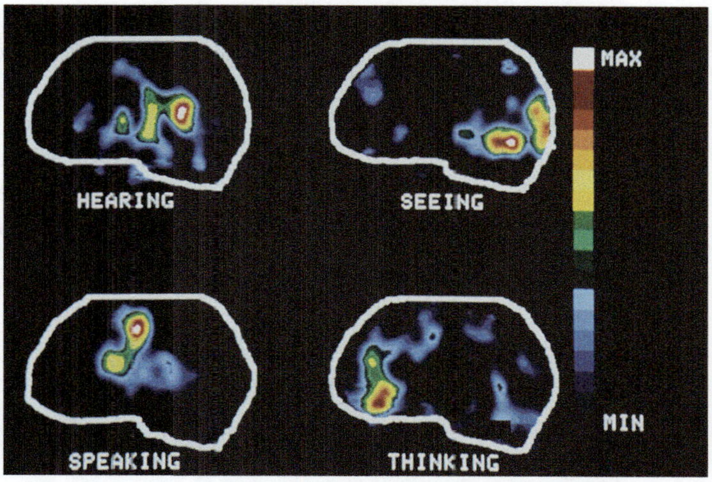

▲ This PET scan shows that regions of the left frontal lobe, shown in red, are very active during thinking (lower right). When listening, the brain shows high activity in the temporal lobe (upper left). When a person is speaking, high activity is seen in the left frontal lobe along the motor cortex and in Broca's area (lower left). When seeing something, the brain shows high levels of activity in the occipital lobe (upper right).

It appears that the hippocampus and the frontal lobes play a crucial role in the processing of declarative memory, but what about procedural memory? How is it that a person with severe hippocampal damage, like H.M., can still learn new skills? Declarative memory is usually explicit, but procedural memory is typically executed in an implicit, unconscious manner. Therefore, we may gain some insight into how the brain processes procedural memory by examining the brain function that underlies implicit memory.

To examine brain function during implicit memory processing, researchers took PET scans of participants while they completed implicit and explicit memory tasks. As expected, the explicit memory task was associated with increased blood flow in the hippocampal regions of the brain. However, when the participants used their implicit memory, all of the blood flow changes that occurred were outside the hippocampal regions of the brain (Schacter et al., 1996).

Other brain-imaging studies have shown that implicit memory is linked to brain structures outside the hippocampus. For instance, motor skill (procedural) memory seems to rely, in part, on the *cerebellum* (Sanes, Dimitrov, & Hallett, 1990; Figure 7.9) and the *striatum* (Censor, Dayan, & Cohen, 2014). Other forms of implicit, nondeclarative memory such as classical conditioning (Zhang et al., 2019) and habit formation (Liljeholm & Simon, 2015) have also been linked to areas of the brain outside of the hippocampus. For example, the *amygdala* seems to play a role in the conditioning of fear responses and the striatum and cerebellum play a role in habit formation (Bernabe et al., 2020; Liljeholm & Simon, 2015; Squire & Dede, 2015). The discovery that the brain processes different types of memory in different locations explains why someone like Kim Peek, who had cerebellar damage, would have problems learning new motor skills, but another person like H.M., who had hippocampal damage, would still be able to acquire new procedural memory skills.

Although the role of the hippocampus in processing declarative memories has been well established and damage to the hippocampus does not eliminate the ability to store new procedural memories, exactly how procedural memories are stored is still under investigation. Some recent studies suggest that the hippocampus may play some role in processing procedural memories after all (Gheysen et al., 2010). For example, activity in the hippocampus has been shown to coincide with the overnight memory consolidation of newly learned motor skills (Albouy et al., 2008, 2013), and other brain regions may play a role in maintaining the procedural memories over time (Albouy et al., 2013; Squire & Dede, 2015). Studies like these suggest that we still have more to learn about the role that the hippocampus and other brain structures play in memory.

7.6 Quiz Yourself

1. Which of the following tasks would be most difficult for an adult with anterograde amnesia?
a. Learning to jump rope
b. Learning to play a new video game
c. Recalling their fifth birthday party
d. Learning psychology

2. Sarah is learning a list of new words. If you took a PET scan of Sarah's brain during completion of this task, where would you expect to see the greatest brain activity?
a. The cerebellum
b. The hypothalamus
c. The hippocampus
d. The right frontal lobe

3. After his death, a postmortem examination was performed on H.M.'s brain to examine which specific structures had been damaged by the earlier surgery that doctors performed to curb his epilepsy. This postmortem examination is best characterized as what type of research?
a. An experiment
b. A correlational study
c. A case study
d. A quasi-experiment

4. José was in a car accident and he damaged his cerebellum. Which of the following tasks would be most difficult for José after his accident?
a. Learning to play the piano
b. Learning psychology
c. Recalling his childhood
d. Remembering what he had for breakfast

Answers 1. d; 2. c; 3. c; 4. a

7.7 Integrating Psychology: The Big Picture

In Chapter 6, we discussed processes of learning (*habituation, classical* and *operant conditioning,* and *observational learning*) that occur throughout daily life and how this learning affects our behavior. In the current chapter, we further explored the cognitive aspect of psychology by examining the memory processes of encoding, storage, and retrieval that underlie much of our learning in life.

The case of Kim Peek, the real-life *Rainman,* illustrates the extremes of human abilities for learning and memory. On the one hand, Kim had a computer-like ability for learning. On the other hand, Kim exhibited great deficiencies in learning. Both Kim's abilities and inabilities for learning likely reside in the manner in which he processed information in memory. Kim's unique brain seemed to foster an amazing ability to encode, store, and retrieve vast quantities of factual information in his declarative memory. But it was also because of his unique brain that Kim was unable to efficiently encode, store, and retrieve procedural memories, such as how to brush his teeth each day.

Unlike Kim, you most likely cannot memorize a book chapter simply by reading it. For you (and for most of us) committing information to long-term memory requires careful encoding and elaboration of the material in working memory. As you read this chapter, your central executive directed your working memory to process the visual, auditory, and meaning aspects of what you were reading. You then elaborated the material by thinking about how this information fits with what you already know about psychology and the world. As you elaborated the material, the information became encoded in your long-term semantic memory, where you will continue to elaborate it as you study in preparation for retrieval at some point in the future—such as on exam day! So, although it takes effort, your memory most likely serves you well when you use it properly.

In our next and final chapter in this part, "Cognition, Language, and Intelligence," we will further explore our cognitive abilities and the implications they have for our ability to survive and thrive in a challenging world. As we prepare to complete our discussion of cognition in the next chapter, think again about Kim Peek. Did Kim's unique abilities help him solve problems in his daily life? Or, did they hinder his ability to function? Would you consider someone like Kim to be intelligent? Was he a genius? Or did he have a disability? How do your own memory abilities stack up against Kim's? Are your abilities more or less advantageous than Kim's when it comes to living everyday life?

Studying the Chapter

Key Terms

anterograde amnesia (303)
attention (282)
autobiographical memory (299)
central executive (294)
chunking (287)
coding system (287)
consciousness (282)
constructive memory (313)
cue-dependent forgetting (307)
decay theory (306)
declarative memory (299)
elaborative rehearsal (289)
encoding (282)
episodic memory (299)
explicit memory (282)
flashbulb memory (312)
forgetting curve (289)
implicit memory (283)
levels-of-processing model (290)
long-term memory (LTM) (284)
maintenance rehearsal (288)
memory consolidation (315)
memory traces (282)
misinformation effect (313)
primacy effect (291)
proactive interference (307)
procedural memory (302)
recall (305)
recency effect (292)
recognition (306)
reconstructive memory (313)
repression (310)
retrieval (282)
retroactive interference (307)
retrograde amnesia (303)
schema (298)
semantic encoding (298)
semantic memory (299)
sensory memory (284)
short-term memory (STM) (284)
storage (282)
tip of the tongue phenomenon (307)
working memory (293)

What Do You Know? Assess Your Understanding

Test your retention and understanding of the material by answering the following questions.

1. Bits of information that are encoded into memory are known as ______.
   a. memory probes
   b. memory cues
   c. memory traces
   d. attentional foci

2. Brushing your teeth, combing your hair, and tying your shoes are all most likely to involve use of which type of memory?
   a. Explicit
   b. Implicit
   c. Declarative
   d. Semantic

3. As you read a book, which is the first stage of memory into which the information that you are reading is processed?
   a. Short-term
   b. Working memory
   c. Iconic memory
   d. Phonological loop

4. Which of the following types of memory has the shortest duration?
   a. Long-term memory
   b. Short-term memory
   c. Sensory memory
   d. Working memory

5. To test the idea that the average person should be able to hold approximately seven items in short-term memory, a researcher has participants listen while an assistant reads off a list of words. Some participants listen to a list of three words. Others hear a list of 5, 7, 10, or 15 words. Later, all participants are asked to recall as many of the words as they can, and the researcher calculates the percentage of words they were able to recall from the list they heard. In this study the independent variable is the ______.
   a. number of words recalled by the participants
   b. percentage of words recalled by the participants
   c. number of words heard by the participants
   d. type of words heard by the participants

6. The available research evidence suggests that the ______ may play a role in the learning of habits.
   a. hippocampus
   b. amygdala
   c. striatum
   d. b and c

7. Which of the following would be the *best* example of maintenance rehearsal?
   a. Reading your notes over and over as you study for an exam
   b. Thinking about how the material you are studying relates to chapters that you have previously studied
   c. Developing mnemonics to help you remember the material
   d. Thinking about how the material relates to your own life

8. According to the working memory model, which of the following is not a component of working memory?
   a. The episodic buffer
   b. The phonological loop
   c. The central executive
   d. Iconic memory

9. The working memory model is to ______ as the three-stages model is to ______.
   a. serial processing; explicit memory
   b. parallel processing; explicit memory
   c. serial processing; parallel processing
   d. parallel processing; serial processing

10. As you read the words on this page, which component of working memory is likely controlling the manner in which you process this information?
    a. The episodic buffer
    b. The phonological loop
    c. The central executive
    d. The visuospatial sketchpad

11. Your knowledge of animals is most likely stored in ______.
    a. short-term memory as acoustic memory traces
    b. short-term memory as semantic memory traces
    c. long-term memory as acoustic memory traces
    d. long-term memory as semantic memory traces

12. Glenn experienced a concussion in a terrible car accident, after which he could no longer store new episodic or semantic memories. Glenn seems to be have ______.
    a. retrograde amnesia
    b. anterograde amnesia
    c. repression
    d. cue-dependent forgetting

13. Your knowledge of psychology is an example of ______ memory.
    a. long-term
    b. semantic
    c. declarative
    d. All of the above

14. Which one of the following is not an example of implicit memory?
   a. Knowing your best friend's name
   b. Knowing how to jump rope
   c. Being classically conditioned to fear snakes after experiencing a snake bite
   d. Being able to tie your shoes without looking

15. In ______, the memory probes and cues are stronger and contain more information.
   a. recall
   b. recognition
   c. short-term working memory
   d. long-term memory

16. When you first met your classmate, he was introduced to you as Calvin. However, Calvin never uses his first name and goes by just his initials (C.D.). Now, after a few years, you find that you cannot recall C.D.'s first name. This is most likely an example of ______.
   a. retroactive interference
   b. proactive interference
   c. memory trace decay
   d. repression

17. According to the available research, which of the following is *not* a true statement about flashbulb memories?
   a. They are emotionally charged memories.
   b. They are in part a function of the stress hormones that are released at the time the memory trace is encoded.
   c. They are more accurate in their detail than normal memories are.
   d. Many people experience flashbulb memories at some point in their lives.

18. Recalling the actual details of your first day in college in an accurate manner would be an example of ______ memory.
   a. reconstructive
   b. constructive
   c. semantic
   d. procedural

19. The phrase "Please excuse my dear aunt Sally," used as a tool to help people recall the order of mathematical operations, is an example of ______.
   a. an acronym
   b. a mnemonic
   c. massed practice
   d. All of the above

20. Research suggests that athletes who experience concussions may be predisposed to later experiencing ______.
   a. schizophrenia
   b. depression
   c. brain hemorrhages
   d. b & c

Answers: 1. c; 2. b; 3. c; 4. c; 5. c; 6. c; 7. a; 8. d; 9. d; 10. c; 11. d; 12. b; 13. d; 14. a; 15. b; 16. a; 17. c; 18. a; 19. b; 20. b

Use It or Lose It: Applying Psychology

1. If you were going to design a computer that "thinks" like a human does, what would you have your computer do?
2. Your best friend tells you about a very detailed memory of their first day of kindergarten 16 years ago. They claim to recall all of the details of that special day—everything from what they had for breakfast to the color and design of the clothes they wore. After telling you of their memory, your friend asks you how it is possible that they can remember that day in such detail. Given what you know about memory, what would you say to your friend about their childhood memory?
3. Assume that you are a psychologist who is called to testify in court. The defense attorney asks you to describe for the jury how humans store memories for everyday events. What would your testimony be about the accuracy of memory?
4. Your grandmother thinks she is having some problems with her memory. However, her doctor has assured her that her forgetting is normal and that she does *not* have Alzheimer's disease. How would you explain to her why she sometimes forgets things that she meant to buy at the store and the names of old friends that she hasn't seen in years?

Critical Thinking about the Science of Psychology.

In the study done by Mez et al. (2020), the researchers found an association between how long a man had played football and the degree of chronic traumatic encephalopathy (CTE) seen in his brain after death (See section 7.3.5). After reviewing this study, answer these questions:

1. What type of research design was used in this study?
2. What was the dependent variable in this study?
3. What was the independent variable in this study?
4. What can be concluded from this study?

Are You Getting the Big Picture?

Memory traces are the stored code that represents a piece of information that has been encoded into memory for later retrieval.

iStock.com/Fly View Productions

7.1 The Functions of Memory: Encoding, Storing, and Retrieving

- The human brain **encodes**, stores, and processes information. We can use memory both **explicitly** (consciously) and **implicitly** (unconsciously).

7.2 The Development of New Memories

- The **three-stages model of memory: sensory memory, STM,** and **LTM**
- Many researchers today reject the rigid three-stages model of memory and suggest a different type of memory, called **working memory**. Like **short-term memory (STM)**, working memory temporarily stores information before moving it to **long-term memory (LTM)**. Unlike STM, working memory is a multifaceted memory system that processes different aspects of the information in a parallel, rather than a serial, fashion.

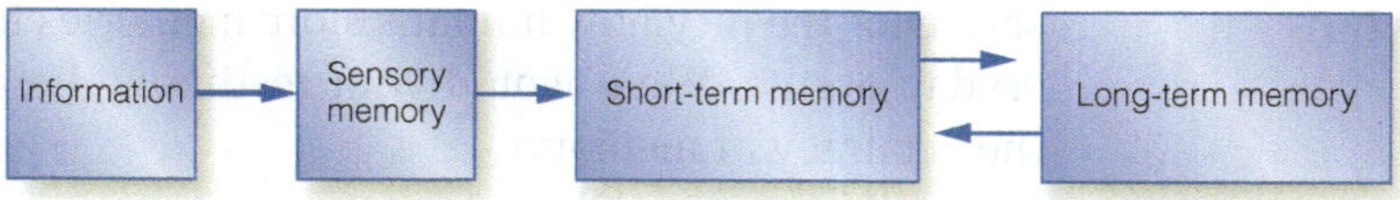

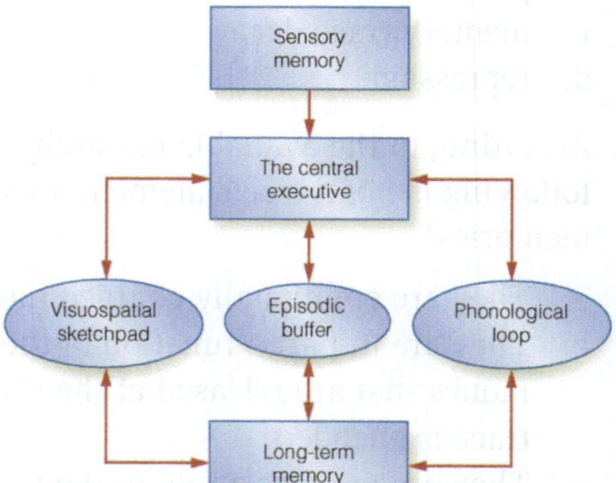

7.3 Long-Term Memory: Permanent Storage

- Long-term memory includes **declarative** and **procedural memory.** Declarative memory comprises **semantic**, **episodic**, and **autobiographical memory.**
- Long-term memory is organized into **schemas**, which allow us to quickly and efficiently use our memory. In a sense, schemas are like a filing system for the library of knowledge we have stored in our long-term memory.

Masterfile

7.4 Retrieval and Forgetting in Long-Term Memory

- Despite our best efforts to retain information, sometimes forgetting occurs. Forgetting may be due to **decay** of memory traces, **interference**, **cue-dependent forgetting**, *motivated forgetting*, or perhaps even **repression**.

To improve your memory:

- Don't multitask! Pay **attention** to what you are trying to remember; avoid distractions that may cause divided attention.
- Do not cram for exams!
- Use **elaborative rehearsal** to reinforce retention of information.
- Use overlearning.
- Test yourself on the material often.
- Use the SOAR method: Select, Organize, Associate, & Regulate
- Use mnemonics to make your memory mighty
- Take care of yourself: Eat right, exercise, and get enough sleep.

wavebreakmedia/Shutterstock.com

7.5 The Accuracy of Memory

- **Flashbulb memories** are unusually detailed memories for emotionally charged events—memories that are quite powerful but not always accurate.
- In general, we are prone to many memory errors, including the **misinformation effect**. In cases of eyewitness testimony, these errors can have serious consequences.

Steve McCurry/Magnum Photos

7.6 The Biology of Memory

- **Memory consolidation** is the stabilization and long-term storage of memory traces in the brain.
- Brain-imaging research shows that people who use their memory a great deal may have structural differences in their hippocampal regions. The hippocampus and frontal lobe seem to play significant roles in processing declarative memory.
- The hippocampus may also play some role in the memory consolidation of procedural memories.
- Studies suggest that procedural memory is linked to the cerebellum and the striatum.
- Other forms of implicit, nondeclarative memory are also processed in the amygdala and striatum.

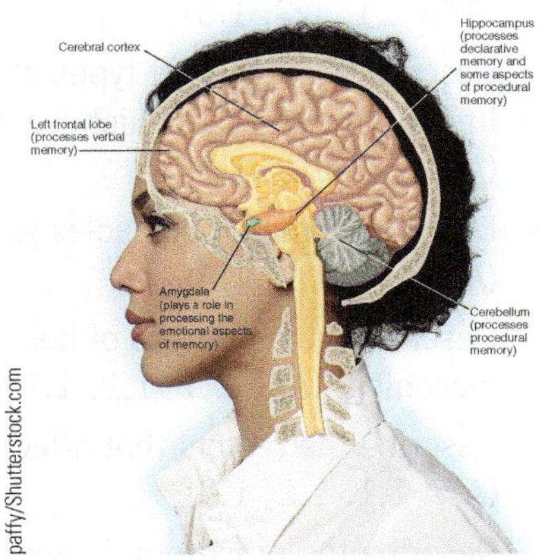

paffy/Shutterstock.com

Learning Objectives

8.1 Describe how we represent knowledge in our memory. (APA 1.1, 1.2, 1.3)

8.1 Describe how we organize knowledge in our memory. (APA 1.1, 1.2, 1.3)

8.2 Describe the different types of problems we face in life and the ways in which we may try to solve them. (APA 1.1, 1.2, 1.3)

8.2 Describe common obstacles to problem solving. (APA 1.1, 1.2, 1.3)

8.3 Describe the processes of deductive and inductive reasoning. (APA 1.1, 1.2, 1.3, 2.1)

8.3 Describe the factors that affect decision making. (APA 1.1, 1.2, 1.3)

8.3 Describe the process of judgment and the heuristics that affect our judgments. (APA 1.1, 1.2, 1.3, 3.3)

8.4 Explain how children acquire language. (APA 1.1, 1.2, 1.3, 2.1)

8.4 Describe the concept of linguistic relativity. (APA 1.1, 1.2, 1.3, 2.1, 3.3)

8.4 Describe current research on the issue of nonhuman language. (APA 1.1, 1.2)

8.5 Describe historical and modern attempts to measure intelligence, and explain some of the advantages and disadvantages of these methods. (APA 1.1, 1.2)

8.5 Describe the various ways that psychologists have conceptualized intelligence. (APA 1.1, 1.2)

8.5 Describe the diversity seen in intelligence and discuss potential reasons for this diversity. (APA 1.1, 1.2, 1.3, 3.3)

iStock.com/RossHelen

8 Cognition, Language, and Intelligence

In the last two chapters, we covered the cognitive aspect of psychology in terms of how we learn from our experiences, and how we encode, store, and retrieve information about these experiences in memory. In the final chapter of this part, we will examine how we put the results of our learning and memory to good use in everyday life by engaging in *cognition* (e.g., thinking, reasoning, and so on), using *language*, and exhibiting *intelligence*. After all, what good would learning and memory be to us, if we weren't able to use the products of these processes to help us survive in the world? Recall again the case of Kim Peek. Would you consider Kim to be a genius because he could memorize entire phone books? Or, would you consider him to have a disability because he could not use his memory in practically important ways, such as to live independently? Think about your own cognitive abilities. Would you be willing to trade places with Kim, or would you prefer to remain as you are? Although you may not be able to memorize entire books, we are betting that you can still use your cognitive abilities to do some pretty remarkable things, such as choosing a major; balancing the demands of school, work, and/or family; managing your budget; and many more great feats of daily life. In this chapter, we will examine how we use cognitive processes, such as thinking, problem solving, language, and intelligence, to help us cope with the challenges of everyday life. ■

Chapter Outline

8.1 Thinking: How We Use What We Know

cognition the way in which we use and store information in memory

thinking the use of knowledge to accomplish some sort of goal

knowledge information stored in our long-term memory about the world and how it works

mental representations memory traces that represent objects, events, people, and so on that are not present at the time

We engage in some sort of **cognition** during every waking moment. Each day, we do a lot of thinking, but most of us would have difficulty defining what it is that we actually *do* when we think. Psychologists define **thinking** as the use of **knowledge**, the information we have stored in long-term memory, to accomplish some sort of goal. Thinking includes the ability to perceive and understand our world, to communicate with others, and to solve the problems we encounter in our lives (Mayer, 1983).

Thinking involves the use of all types of knowledge. We store our knowledge in long-term memory as **mental representations**—bits of memory that represent objects, events, people, and so on that are not actually present now. For instance, most of us can close our eyes and think about what our best friend looks like, the smell of their cologne and their likes and dislikes. To do this, we call on the many mental representations of our friend that we have stored in long-term memory.

In general, thinking involves the use of two broad classes of mental representations: those based on *sensory* aspects of the object, such as its visual appearance, smell, taste, and so forth; and those based on the *meaning* of the object, such as its name, definition, and properties. We will now turn our attention to a discussion of the best-studied forms of these mental representations: *visual images* and *concepts*.

8.1.1 Visual Images: How Good Is the Mental Picture?

The ability to "see" a friend's face in our mind or to visualize a map of our hometown in our head can be very useful in everyday life, but do we really store "pictures" in our memory? Over the years, psychologists have studied this question by examining how people perform on certain tasks in which they must mentally manipulate visual images (Denis & Cocude, 1999; Kosslyn, Ball, & Reiser, 1978/2004).

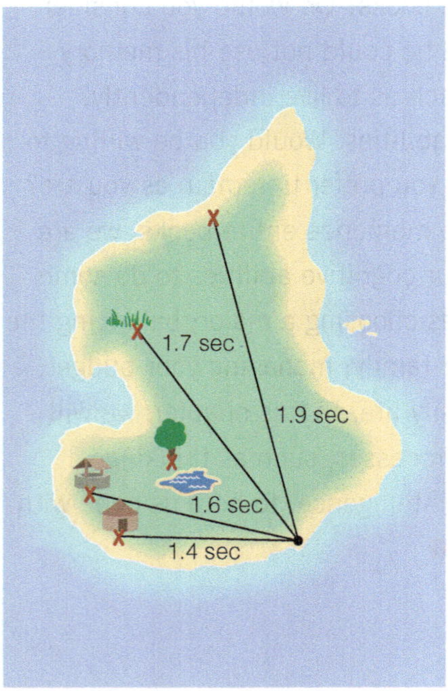

FIGURE 8.1

An Image-Scanning Task

In this task, participants were asked to imagine a black dot moving across the map to the points indicated by the *X*s. The average amount of time to do this was proportionate to the distance between the starting point and the ending point on the map.

Source: © Stephen Kosslyn 1978

In a typical image-scanning experiment, like the one done by Stephen Kosslyn and colleagues (Borst & Kosslyn, 2008; Kosslyn et al., 2004), participants are asked to memorize a map of a fictitious island with several objects depicted on it (see • FIGURE 8.1). After the participants have memorized the map, they are asked to mentally scan the path that a black dot would take as it travels from one point on the map to another. Because the points are at various distances from one another, researchers can correlate the time it takes participants to mentally scan the image with the distance between the points on the actual map. If the participants' visual images of the map are copies of the actual map, the time it takes to scan longer distances should be longer than the time it takes to scan shorter distances on the map. This is exactly what Kosslyn found: the time it took to scan distances increased proportionately with the increase in the actual distances on the map. The results of this and numerous other experiments (see Jolicoeur & Kosslyn, 1985; Pylyshyn, 2006; Shepard, 1978, for a review) suggest that visual images may have all of the spatial properties of the real stimulus. In other words, the visual image we store is essentially a copy of the stimulus we see in the world.

Interestingly, researchers have found that when trying to recall previously seen images, participants' gazes (the position of their eyes) tended to move to the same position they were in when they first saw the picture. Furthermore, participants whose gazes at recall matched their gaze at encoding exhibited better memory for the images. And asking the participants to look in a different location while trying to recall pictures they had previously seen reduced the accuracy of their memory. These findings suggest that recalling visual images relies in part on recreating the original gaze from which we saw the image in the first place (Laeng et al., 2014). As convincing as such experiments are in supporting the argument that visual images have spatial properties that mimic those of the actual stimulus, the question still remains: do we actually store photographic images of the things that we see? As it turns out, there are reasons to suspect that we generally do not. For example, try the following demonstration.

Engage Yourself!

Let's look at your ability to answer questions about a visual stimulus that you have seen many times, a map of North America.

Which is farther east: Reno, Nevada, or San Diego, California?

Which is farther north: Montreal, Canada, or Seattle, Washington?

Which is farther west: the Atlantic or the Pacific entrance to the Panama Canal?

The answers seem obvious, but researchers have found that most people answer them incorrectly (Stevens & Coupe, 1978). The correct answers are San Diego, Seattle, and the Atlantic entrance. Are you surprised? Take a look at ● FIGURE 8.2, which shows that these are the correct answers.

FIGURE 8.2

A Map of North and South America

Most people answer questions about this map incorrectly even though they have seen it many times before. It is highly unlikely that we have an exact visual image of this map stored in our long-term memory.

So where does all of this research leave us with respect to visual images? Isn't it a bit contradictory? Some studies suggest that visual images are precise mental copies of the actual stimuli (Shepard, 1978), but other studies show that visual images may deviate significantly from the actual stimuli (Boden, 1988; Chambers & Reisberg, 1992; Pylyshyn, 2003, 2006).

According to Stephen Kosslyn (1994; Pearson & Kosslyn, 2015), our mental representation of visual stimuli relies on both visual images *and* verbal knowledge. In other words, we use both types of mental representations—sensory (pictures) and meaning (words)—to fully represent visual stimuli. The pictures represent parts of the stimulus, and the words describe the stimulus and tell us how the pieces of the picture fit together. For example, when you look at a flower, you might store, among other things, a visual image of the shape of a petal, the stem, and the center, along with words describing the fact that the petals are placed around the center and the stem descends from the bottom of the flower. In Kosslyn's view, we do not store an exact copy of the flower. Instead, we use this mixture of verbal and pictorial pieces to construct our visual image of the flower.

In keeping with this view, brain imaging studies have revealed similarities in the patterns of neural activity seen in certain areas of the *visual cortex* during both the visual perception of stimuli and the mental imaging of stimuli (Pearson et al., 2015). In other words, certain patterns of brain activity are similar whether we are seeing something or conjuring up a mental image of it. Findings like these have led researchers to conclude that certain low-level features of the image (e.g., edges and angles) are indeed stored in memory (Naselaris et al., 2015; Pearson & Kosslyn, 2015). So although we have evidence that certain features of images are stored in memory, we do not yet have evidence that the complete details of images are encoded in memory.

Recall from Chapter 7 that memory is, after all, constructive. Unfortunately, the constructive nature of memory does sometimes lead to inaccuracies. So don't feel bad if you thought Reno was east of San Diego!

8.1.2 Concepts: How We Organize What We Know

concepts mental categories that contain related bits of information

As we saw in Chapter 7, we have a tendency to organize our knowledge in long-term memory. We store mental representations for related objects together in the same mental category. For example, we would store our knowledge of cats, dogs, and elephants together in the category for *animals,* and apples, oranges, and grapes together in the category for *fruits*. This tendency to organize information based on similarity shows the *conceptual* nature of human cognition. **Concepts**, the mental categories that contain related bits of knowledge, are organized around the meaning of the information they represent. For instance, animal is a concept. In our mind we know what it means to be an animal. Animals must be animate, but we also distinguish animals from humans.

Conceptual information is encoded in a variety of formats in long-term memory. At times, concepts are stored in a semantic or meaning-based form (Collins & Quillian, 1969; Hawco, Armony, & Lepage, 2013). For example, we may store certain facts about an orange—it's round, orange-colored, a fruit, and so on—in our memory. However, we also appear to store some of our perceptual experiences of objects in memory as well (see, for instance, Lanska, Olds, & Westerman, 2014; Pearson & Kosslyn, 2015). When we see, smell, and taste an orange, specific patterns of neural activity arise in our brains. We capture and store information on these unique patterns of neural activity and later use this information to recreate the perceptual experience of seeing, smelling, and tasting an orange (Barsalou, 2008; Marques, 2010).

We use this stored semantic and perceptual information to perceive, think about, and deal with our world. Conceptually organizing our knowledge helps us use that knowledge more efficiently. Concepts can be viewed as a type of mental shorthand that both organizes and saves space in our cognitive system. For example, close your eyes and picture an orange in your mind's eye. Can you see it clearly? Most of us can do this easily for something as familiar as an orange. Now look carefully at your mental orange. Is this concept that you have stored in your mind a particular orange that you have seen? Not likely! Instead, your concept of an orange is an abstraction, or a general idea, of what an orange is. You don't have to store mental representations for each and every orange you have seen. Rather, you only need to store a generalized concept of what an orange is and what it looks like. This is a great cognitive space-saver when you think about all of the oranges you'll see in your lifetime.

Organizing Concepts into Categories

Another benefit of mental concepts is that we can organize them into hierarchical categories (Markman & Ross, 2003). We have a natural tendency to group things together in memory based on their sameness and their differences. For example, fruits and vegetables are similar (they are both edible), but they are also different (fruits tend to be sweeter than vegetables). The manner in which we conceptualize these items in memory will reflect these relationships. Carrots are more likely to be associated with vegetables and apples with fruits.

Our tendency to categorize information in memory based on such conceptual relationships is similar to the organizational scheme used to arrange products in a grocery store by aisles (e.g., the produce, pet food, & frozen foods aisles) so that you can quickly find the item you need. However, unlike a grocery store where it is rare to find the exact same item in multiple aisles, your mind's hierarchical system of organization freely allows for items to be placed in multiple, interrelated categories. For example, the concept of "orange" could be found in the mental category for *citrus*, *fruit*, or *food*. Likewise, we can use multiple search strategies to find the information in memory, such as searching by meaning (fruits high in vitamin C), image (orange citrus fruits), personal relevance (foods I love), and so on (Unsworth, 2017).

Psychologists have found that we tend to organize our knowledge into three levels of categorization (Rosch et al., 2004). The highest, most general level is called the **superordinate category**. The superordinate level contains concepts that are broad and general in their description. For example, fruit would be considered to be a superordinate category. The intermediate level of categorization is the **basic level category**. The concept orange is a basic level category. And the lowest level, the **subordinate category**, is the most specific and detailed category (e.g., naval orange, blood orange, or Valencia orange).

superordinate category the highest, most general level of a concept

basic level category the intermediate level of categorization that seems to be the level that we use most to think about our world

subordinate category the lowest level of categorization, which contains concepts that are less general and more specific than those at the basic level

The basic level seems to be the level that we most often use to think about our world. For example, when we write out a shopping list, we probably list basic level concepts, such as oranges rather than fruit or naval oranges. The basic level is also the first level of knowledge young children acquire (Quinn & Tanaka, 2007; Rosch et al., 2004). Accordingly, people tend to be faster in naming and categorizing objects at the basic level, a phenomenon called the *basic level effect*. For example, determining that an animal is a *dog* should take less time than determining that an animal is a *schnauzer* or an *animal* (Mack & Palmeri, 2015; Wu & Mo, 2011).

▲ The basic level category *pear falls* under the superordinate category *fruit*. The label *Bosc pear* is a subordinate category of the basic level category *pear*.

Indeed, Michael Mack and Thomas Palmeri (2015) found that participants were typically able to judge that pictures of dogs belonged to the category *dog* faster than they could judge whether or not they belonged at the superordinate level (*animal*) or subordinate level (e.g., *German Shepherd*). An interesting exception to this finding was that when participants were given very little time to perceive the dog before making a judgment (e.g., 25 milliseconds), they were quicker to make category judgments at the superordinate level (i.e., *animal*). So, it appears that when we see category members under many circumstances, we are quickest to judge their membership at the basic level (e.g., *dog*), but when we only have time for the briefest glance at the category member, we are quicker to judge that we saw an *animal* (superordinate level) than we are to judge that it was a *dog* (basic level). In the real world, this may mean that you would be able to tell that the thing that darted past your car as you were driving was an animal before you could tell what type of animal it was.

Formal and Natural Categories

formal concepts concepts that are based on learned, rigid rules that define certain categories of things

natural concepts concepts that develop naturally as we live our lives and experience the world

We acquire concepts from an early age as we observe and learn from our world. We acquire **formal concepts** as we learn the rigid rules that define certain categories of things. For example, for an animal to be considered a member of the formal category *female,* it must possess certain attributes or characteristics. All females are genetically designed to produce either offspring or eggs. If an animal does not have this attribute, it cannot be a female. The lines that define formal categories are very clear-cut.

Unfortunately, life is not always so neat and tidy as to provide us with formal rules for everything, and much of our knowledge of the world does not fit cleanly into only one category. For example, do you consider a tomato to be a fruit or a vegetable? Many people consider tomatoes to be vegetables, whereas others—including botanists—categorize them as fruits. Why the confusion? Perhaps because we associate fruits with sweetness, we tend not to classify tomatoes as fruit even though they do contain seeds, which is a defining attribute of fruit. Most of us are aware of the rules for membership as a female but are not aware of the botanical definition of a fruit. We have organized our fruit and vegetable concepts in a less distinct and orderly fashion based on our own experiences with them.

Concepts that develop naturally as we experience the world are referred to as **natural concepts**. We do not learn formal rules for these concepts; rather, we create the rules as we learn about our world. As a result, the boundaries defining natural concept categories are often blurry, or "fuzzy" (Rosch, 1973; Rosch et al., 2004). Our example of the tomato is a good illustration of this. You can classify the tomato as a vegetable, a fruit, or both, depending on your experience. Because many of us see tomatoes in the vegetable section of the supermarket, we include them in the vegetable category. However, botanists scientifically classify tomatoes as fruits. How do you see them?

Because natural concepts are a by-product of our day-to-day experience, they develop in a relatively effortless and natural manner. Curiously, when researchers try to force people to develop new natural concepts in the laboratory, people have a lot of trouble doing so (Makino & Jitsumori, 2007). In such situations, we may overthink and try to develop clear-cut rules for concepts that are inherently fuzzy. Even when we try to define the boundaries of preexisting natural concepts, we can have trouble. For example, if you were asked to define the criteria for identifying real-world examples of "love," you would likely find this to be a very difficult task.

Engage Yourself!

Natural categories are learned as a consequence of everyday life. No one sits us down and formally educates us about the rules that define membership in natural categories. For example, it is unlikely that anyone ever taught you the formal definition of an *animal*. Yet you probably feel that you know what an animal is. Perhaps because of this we tend to do better with the fuzzy boundaries of natural concepts in the real world than we do in the laboratory. However, we are not perfect. The difficulty involved in deciding which items to include and which to exclude from a category varies considerably across situations. Sometimes it's an easy task, and other times it's not. For example, take a look at ● FIGURE 8.3, and answer the questions as quickly as you can. Which of the questions were you able to answer quickly? Which ones took longer? Why do you think some of them were easier than others?

FIGURE 8.3

Natural Concept Categories

Answer these questions as fast as you can.

prototypes our concepts of the most typical members of categories

exemplars [ig-ZEM-plar] a mental representation of an actual instance of a member of a category

Most people find it easier to decide that a robin is a bird than that a penguin is a bird. Why? One possibility is that a robin is a more typical example of the category bird than a penguin is. According to some researchers, we form what are called **prototypes** for natural concept categories, much like the mental image of the orange we discussed earlier. A prototype is our concept of the most typical member of the category—in essence, a summary of all the members of the category. When we judge whether something belongs in a natural concept category, we compare it to the prototype of the category (Minda & Smith, 2002). The more similar the object is to the prototype, the faster we judge it to be a member of the concept category.

Interestingly, prototypes may be one of the reasons we waste so much food in the United States. Consumers are often reluctant to purchase fruits and vegetables that are misshapen, have blemishes, or are generally less than ideal. This may be because these food items fail to sufficiently match their prototypes for these items, even though they are perfectly nutritious and edible. One recent study found that people who have experience growing their own produce are less likely to reject produce items based on superficial flaws. This may be because compared to non-gardeners, gardeners' prototypes for produce are more realistic and less idealized (Hingston & Noseworthy, 2020).

However, prototypes may not be the only standard by which we judge category membership. Some researchers argue that we judge category membership by comparing an item to the memories we have stored for actual specific examples, or preexisting **exemplars**, of that concept category (Nosofsky & Zaki, 2002; Rehder & Hoffman, 2005; Voorspoels, Vanpaemel, & Storms, 2008). In this view, you would determine that the robin in your backyard is a bird by comparing this robin to the memories or exemplars of the *actual* birds you have seen in your lifetime. Unless you live where penguins are common, you are likely to have many more songbird exemplars than penguin exemplars available in your memory. Because robins resemble the songbird exemplars that quickly come to mind more closely than penguins do, you are quicker to decide that a robin belongs in the category of birds.

The debate over whether we use prototypes or exemplars to judge category membership is ongoing (Habibi, Kemp, & Xu, 2020; Leliévre-Desmas et al., 2015). Some argue that we may even use both (Ashby & Maddox, 2005; Storms, DeBoeck, & Ruts, 2001) or that our categories may be based on idealized representations of concepts rather than what is most prototypical or most real (Voorspoels, Vanpaemel, & Storms, 2011). Regardless of how we go about making category judgments, these judgments are crucial to our ability to think about our world. In the next section, we will see just what we can accomplish with all of our thinking as we discuss problem solving.

8.1 Quiz Yourself

1. **Which of the following is evidence indicating that our visual images contain all the properties of the actual stimulus?**
   a. Memory for images is near perfect in children.
   b. The time it takes to mentally scan an image of an object is related to the actual size of the object.
   c. Most people can visualize familiar objects in great detail.
   d. Our mental maps of the world are perfect in their detail.
2. **Which of the following would be a superordinate concept for the category car?**
   a. Prius
   b. Truck
   c. Vehicle
   d. Red sports car

(Continued)

3. In an experiment, Dr. Kelly asks participants to name the first example of an "animal" that comes to mind. Based on what you know about concepts, which of the following would the average participant be most likely to name?

a. Dog
b. Tramp
c. German shepherd
d. Bat

4. In an experiment, Dr. Bay presents participants with category members such as *dog, Fido, German Shepherd*, etc., and measures the time it takes participants to determine whether or not the word is a member of the category *animal*. In this study, what is the dependent variable?

a. The type of word presented
b. The category level of the word presented
c. Whether or not the participants answer the question correctly
d. The time it takes the participants to answer the question

Answers 1. b; 2. c; 3. a; 4. d

8.2 Problem Solving: Putting Our Thinking to Good Use

Imagine that you get into your car one morning only to find that it won't start. It's 7:30 and you have an 8:00 class. Today of all days you don't need this, because you have a final exam in your psychology class. You have a problem! What would you do in this situation? Use a ride-hailing app? Walk to school? Or, call your professor and arrange to take a makeup final? In general, when we solve problems, we go through a series of six stages (Hayes, 1989), outlined in ● TABLE 8.1.

Although the prospect of missing a final exam is frightening, there are a number of obvious solutions to this problem. This is not the case for all problems, however. If it were, we would have ended hunger, war, disease, and pollution long ago. Why do some problems seem to have obvious possible solutions whereas others do not? The answer lies in the type of problem we are facing, specifically whether it is *well-* or *ill-structured*.

TABLE 8.1 The Steps to Problem Solving

Problem-Solving Step	Example
Identify the problem.	The car won't start, and I have a final exam.
Represent the problem.	If I miss this exam without permission, I'll fail the course.
Plan a solution.	I will use a ride-sharing service, such as Uber or Lyft.
Execute the plan.	Use the Lyft app.
Evaluate the plan.	The ride will get me to school, but I will be late. Maybe I should also have called my professor?
Evaluate the solution.	I did make it to school, and I took the exam. My professor was a bit angry that I didn't call to say I'd be late, but I did pass the exam. I handled this situation adequately, but next time I'll call my professor.

Adaptive from: Hayes, 1989.

▲ Deciding how much paint to buy for a home improvement project is an example of a task that can be most accurately solved using an algorithm.

Kinga/Shutterstock.com

8.2.1 Well-Structured and Ill-Structured Problems

Well-structured problems are problems for which there is a clear pathway to the solution. We face well-structured problems every day. Learning to use your new cell phone or finding the cheapest hotel at your vacation destination are examples of well-structured problems. When we solve well-structured problems, we tend to go about it in one of two ways. We use either an *algorithm* or a *heuristic* to achieve a solution.

An **algorithm** is a method of solving a particular problem that always leads to the correct solution; a **heuristic** is a shortcut or rule of thumb that may or may not lead to a correct solution. Imagine that you're going to paint your bedroom, but you don't know how much paint to buy. The algorithmic solution to this problem is to measure the height and width of all your walls, calculate the area, and look up how many gallons of paint are required to cover the area. This algorithm will lead to the correct answer, and as a result, you will buy just the right amount of paint. However, this strategy also takes considerable time. You must measure the walls, find the formula for paint coverage, and calculate the required figures. If you are in a hurry (or impatient), this strategy may not be your first choice. Instead, you might use a heuristic, such as simply guessing how much paint you will need to do the job. Guessing is quick, but you do run the risk of not buying the right amount of paint. *Guessing* and repeated guessing, or *trial and error,* are two very common heuristics.

As you consider this example, you may think that it seems foolish to guess at the amount of paint to buy when a clear algorithm exists for this problem. Why would anyone approach a problem in this seemingly haphazard fashion? One might choose a heuristic over an algorithm for at least two reasons. First, as noted earlier, heuristics can save time. You might guess correctly that you need two gallons of paint to cover your room. Second, we do not always know the correct algorithm for the problem we are facing. What if you lack the mathematical knowledge to calculate the surface area of your bedroom walls? Even though a formula for calculating the surface area and paint coverage exists, if you don't know what it is, you cannot implement the algorithm, and you would have to use a heuristic.

In contrast, when attempting to solve an *ill-structured problem,* we have no choice but to use a heuristic. **Ill-structured problems** are problems for which there is no known algorithm, such as trying to end global warming or effect world peace. **Intuition**, simply believing that something is true independent of any reasoning process, is a common strategy for solving ill-structured problems. Often we go with a hunch or feeling that a particular strategy will lead us to solve a problem without having a logical reason for believing this. For example, you might have a hunch that taking a particular side road that you've never been on will get you around a traffic jam and to school on time, but it might not. The problem with intuition is that it is frequently wrong.

Although intuition can fail us, it and other heuristics do sometimes lead to viable solutions to problems. For example, a person lost at sea might randomly plug a hole in their boat by shoving a shoe in the hole. Of course, to implement this problem-solving strategy, they would first have to think about trying the shoe. The danger is that we may not even think of certain possible solutions to our problems.

This is often the case with ill-structured problems. Often we get stuck in particular ways of trying to solve problems, and we lack the *insight* required to find a true solution. **Insight** occurs when we find a new way of looking at the problem

well-structured problems problems for which there are clear pathways to the solutions

algorithm [AL-go-rih-thum] a method of solving a particular problem that always leads to the correct solution

heuristic [hyur-RISS-tick] a shortcut or rule of thumb that may or may not lead to a correct solution to the problem

ill-structured problems problems for which algorithms are not known

intuition believing that something is true independent of any reasoning process

insight a new way of looking at a problem that leads to a sudden understanding of how to solve it that leads to a sudden understanding of how to solve it (Dominowski & Dallob, 1995; Kizilirmak et al., 2016; Qiu et al., 2010). Because of its perceived suddenness, insight is often referred to as the "Aha!" experience. Insight often feels as if a lightbulb has turned on, illuminating the answer for us. But current research indicates that insight isn't such a sudden process. Insight often occurs only after we have thought about the problem for a while (Kaplan & Simon, 1990). Truly understanding a problem and how to solve it often occurs only as the result of much thought and gradual acquisition of knowledge about the problem (Hamel & Elshout, 2000). Insight is also affected by a person's level of motivation and emotion in a given situation (Li et al., 2013).

Recently, some have called for examination of another aspect of problem solving that is often overlooked by researchers in laboratory studies—the manner in which a person interacts with the problem itself (Vallée-Tourangeau & Vallée-Tourangeau, 2020). For example, when playing the board game, *Scrabble*, players who rearrange their tiles are more likely to generate a larger amount of words (Ross & Vallée-Tourangeau, 2020). So, if you are stuck on a problem, you might try looking at it from a different perspective, rearranging the pieces of the problem, and so on.

8.2.2 Creativity: Overcoming Obstacles to Problem Solving

We do not need to tell you that some problems in life are more difficult to face than others. At times, all of us may encounter problems that challenge even our best problem-solving skills. Solving difficult problems often requires *creativity*.

For more than 50 years, psychologists have been trying to define exactly what creativity is and what abilities or traits creative people possess (Mumford, 2003). To date, the major agreement among researchers has been that **creativity** involves the ability to combine mental elements in new and useful ways (Sternberg, 1999; Vartanian, Martindale, & Kwiatkowski, 2003). Creativity may mean finding a novel solution to a problem or coming up with a unique approach to creating some new product—a piece of music, a painting, or a scientific theory that is widely recognized as being creative (Gelade, 2002).

creativity the ability to combine mental elements in new and useful ways

Certainly all of us can think of people we believe are creative. But what makes one person more creative than another? Are there special traits or abilities that creative people possess? Over the years, psychologists have proposed several variables that may be related to creativity, including certain aspects of intelligence and executive functioning (Kandler et al., 2016; Nusbaum & Silvia, 2011), and specific personality traits, such as openness to experience and the degree to which one is extraverted (Hughes, Furnham, & Batey, 2013; Kandler et al., 2016).

Having personality traits that make one socially effective (i.e., extraversion, openness to experience, emotional stability, conscientiousness, and agreeableness; see Chapter 11) has been shown to be related to how well one generates ideas. Being able to effectively critique ideas is an important part of being creative (Gibson & Mumford, 2013). When compared to people with lower levels of these traits, people with higher levels of socially effective personality traits tend to be better at critiquing the ideas of others. However, this advantage isn't seen when critiquing their own ideas. In fact, they are worse at critiquing their own ideas. This may suggest that people high in socially effective traits may engage in greater levels of self-enhancement at the expense of carefully evaluating their own ideas (Rodriguez et al., 2020). These findings suggest that having a socially

▲ Creativity requires us to think divergently. In creating this piece of art, the artist has found a new use for these common items.

effective personality may be associated with greater creativity, but only when one is working with others.

Given that personality is related to creativity, is it possible to change your level of creativity? The good news is that it might be. Robert Epstein and Victoria Phan (2012) conducted a large-scale study of people, measuring their levels of trainable competencies and their self-reported degree of creativity. They found that *capturing* new ideas so they are not forgotten, *challenging* oneself with difficult tasks, *broadening* one's skills and knowledge through continued learning, and *surrounding* oneself with a stimulating environment were all predictors of how creative the person reported themselves to be. These data suggest that learning to stimulate and challenge oneself are characteristics that coincide with creativity. However, is thirsting for knowledge and stimulating experience enough to guarantee creativity? Probably not. Obviously, not everyone who visits an art museum is a creative artist. What individual cognitive skills might explain why some of us turn knowledge and inspiration into feats of creativity and some of us do not?

One cognitive trait that has received a great deal of research attention is a skill called *divergent thinking* (Vartanian et al., 2003). Divergent thinking is the ability to generate many ideas quickly in response to a single prompt (Eysenck, 1995). For example, a divergent thinker can quickly come up with many different ways to tie a scarf or many different uses for an ink pen. Divergent thinking aids creativity because it allows you to come up with many different ideas about how to solve a problem. As we will see, when you can think quickly to generate many different ideas, you are less likely to be blocked by some of the common obstacles to problem solving, including *functional fixedness* and *mental sets*.

When we attempt to solve problems, we often rely on well-used strategies. We look at the tools that we have at our disposal, and we evaluate them in terms of their common, everyday uses. We think of a hammer as a tool for pounding and a box as an object for holding other objects. We often cannot conceive of using these tools in new, novel ways. This limitation of being able to see objects only in their familiar roles is called **functional fixedness**. Functional fixedness can prevent us from solving problems that otherwise could be solved.

functional fixedness being able to see objects only in their familiar roles

mental set the tendency to habitually use methods of problem solving that have worked for you in the past

incubation [in-cue-BAY-shun] a period of not thinking about a problem that helps one solve the problem

Recent research has suggested that certain types of meditation (see Chapter 12) may increase your cognitive flexibility (Müller, Gerasimova, & Ritter, 2016) and help you to achieve better divergent thinking, which may help you avoid another obstacle to problem solving called a *mental set*. A **mental set** is a tendency to habitually use the methods of problem solving that have worked for you in the past. Mental sets become an obstacle when we persist in trying solutions that may have worked in the past but are not working in the current situation. If you find yourself having little success in solving a problem, stop working on the problem for a while and let it *incubate*.

Incubation, or a period of not thinking about the problem, sometimes helps us solve a problem (Hélie & Sun, 2010; Sio & Ormerod, 2009). When we incubate, unproductive strategies recede from memory, and we are better able to attack the problem from a fresh, more productive perspective when we return to it (Penaloza & Calvillo, 2012). Incubation may also help us overcome fixation on mental sets by allowing other relevant strategies to be activated in memory during the incubation period (Sio, Kotovsky, & Cagan, 2017). This is especially true if after an incubation period, we re-attempt to solve the problem in a new context (Smith & Beda, 2020). If we are locked in a mental set, incubation and a change of scenery may be just what are needed to solve the problem.

As we've seen in this section, problem solving is a matter of generating possible solutions and then selecting the one that will ultimately solve the problem. If your car broke down tomorrow, how would you decide which course of action to take? Would you call in absent to school? Take an Uber? Many times, choosing the best solution from among all the possibilities is the real task. In the next section, we take a closer look at the cognitive processes that we engage in when we reason, make decisions, and make judgments.

8.2 Quiz Yourself

1. **Which of the following is the *best* example of an ill-structured problem?**
   a. Solving an algebra problem
   b. Filling out a job application
   c. Choosing a major in college
   d. Fixing your favorite meal for dinner
2. **Incubation sometimes aids problem solving because it _____.**
   a. reduces fatigue
   b. improves deductive reasoning
   c. allows us to forget unproductive strategies
   d. improves inductive reasoning
3. **Sue used a chair with wheels to carry a big load of books to her car. She piled the books in the seat of the chair and pushed it to her car. Trina made several trips carrying books by hand, even though she also had a chair with wheels in her office. Trina was most likely experiencing the effects of _____.**
   a. functional fixedness
   b. an ill-structured problem
   c. heuristic thinking
   d. divergent thinking
4. **Based on what you know about Kim Peek, which of the following cognitive tasks would likely be easiest for him to accomplish?**
   a. Using creativity to solve a problem
   b. Solving a well-structured problem
   c. Breaking out of a mental set
   d. Using divergent thinking

Answers 1. c; 2. c; 3. a; 4. b

8.3 Reasoning, Decision Making, and Judgment

Reasoning, decision making, and judgments are cognitive processes that use some of the same strategies as problem solving. We engage in *reasoning* when we draw conclusions based on certain assumptions about the world. For example, you might reason that your friend is a nice person because they have many friends. *Decision making* is choosing among several options, as in our example of what you might do if your car breaks down. *Judgments* are also related to solving problems, often using two particular heuristics that we'll discuss.

8.3.1 Deductive and Inductive Reasoning

We engage in **reasoning** when we draw conclusions that are based on certain assumptions about the world. In contrast to relying on our *intuition* to draw conclusions, reasoning tends to be a slower, more deliberative and logical process. For example, you might reason that your friend has money because they wear nice clothes. Or, based on your experiences, you might reason that studying leads

reasoning drawing conclusions about the world based on certain assumptions to better grades. You may recall that reasoning was one skill that Kim Peek had trouble with. Although Kim could memorize well, he was unable to use this information to draw new conclusions about the world.

deductive reasoning reasoning from the general to the specific

inductive reasoning reasoning from the specific to the general

dialectical reasoning or thinking an advanced type of reasoning that emerges, in part, from cultural influences. When examining opposing or contradictory statements, dialectical reasoning does not assume that one statement is necessarily true and the other is therefore necessarily false. Rather, both statements are assumed to have the potential to be at least partially true, and logic, reason, and discourse are used in an attempt to fully understand the opposing views.

Psychologists who study reasoning have traditionally looked at two types of reasoning processes: *deductive reasoning* and *inductive reasoning*. **Deductive reasoning** involves reasoning from the *general* to the *specific*. In other words, you start with a general rule (studying leads to good grades) and apply it to particular cases (my friend makes good grades, so they must study hard).

Inductive reasoning is the opposite approach. When using inductive reasoning, we reason from the *specific* to the *general*. Here the object is to begin with specific instances (several friends who get good grades are often busy studying), and then discover what general rule fits all of these instances (studying hard seems to be the factor that leads to good grades). When we use specific instances to arrive at a general rule, we are employing inductive reasoning.

We hope you see the parallels between reasoning and the scientific method that psychologists use to conduct research (see Chapter 1). When conducting studies to test theories, psychologists try to induce the general rules that explain mental processes and behavior. Once these rules have been induced, they can then be applied to individual situations to help deduce, or predict, how people and animals are likely to behave. This, of course, does not mean that reasoning is just for scientists. Deductive and inductive reasoning are equally important to the decisions we make in everyday life. However, engaging in effective reasoning can sometimes be challenging as we will see in our next section.

8.3.2 Dialectical Reasoning or Thinking

Often in life, we are faced with bits of information that seem to contradict one another. Consider the following two hypothetical examples:

- *Researchers from University X have evidence that humans are causing climate change.*
- *Researchers from University Y have evidence that humans are not responsible for global warming.*

When you encounter conflicting statements like these, how do you resolve the apparent conflict? Researchers Kaiping Peng & Richard Nisbett (1999) argue that you have four options. (1) You can ignore or deny the contradiction. (2) You can discount both statements as being suspicious and likely untrue. (3) You can evaluate both statements and decide that one is correct and one is incorrect. (4) You can reason that there is some truth to both positions, even if this means that you cannot fully reject either statement.

Which option did you choose as you were reading? If you chose option 3, you exhibited a more Western style of reasoning. If you chose option 4, you demonstrated a more Eastern style of reasoning (Peng & Nisbett, 1999). How we reason about such contradictions is influenced by our cultural upbringing. Western culture emphasizes a dichotic reasoning in which we seek to categorize things as being good/bad, true/untrue, etc. On the other hand, some Eastern cultures emphasize reasoning in which contradictions are tolerated and truth is seen as being more relative in nature (e.g., theft may be both moral and immoral). Although a stronger tolerance for ambiguity and contradiction is seen in Eastern cultures, people from both the East and West are capable of engaging in what is known as *dialectical reasoning*. **Dialectical reasoning or thinking** is a mature or advanced type of reasoning skill (Basseches, 1980) that emerges, in part, from cultural influences.

In dialectical reasoning, one does not assume that one statement is necessarily true and the other is therefore necessarily false. Rather, one assumes that both statements have the potential to be at least partially true and uses logic, reason, and discussion in an attempt to fully understand the opposing views. In Western dialectical reasoning, the task is not to necessarily discard one statement, but to use reasoning and logic to reconcile the two statements, thereby synthesizing a coherent understanding of the world (Liu, Wang, & Yang, 2015). For example, a possible solution to the contradiction in our example could be that perhaps human activity and natural forces are both harming the earth. In East Asian dialectical reasoning, there is less pressure to remove contradiction as these cultures accept contradiction and the coexistence of opposites as being part of the world (see Liu et al., 2015). In this view, perhaps seeing human activity as simultaneously harmful and benign would be acceptable. Keep in mind that these hypothetical examples are merely illustrative. We are psychologists, not climate change scientists!

Whether deductive, inductive, or dialectical, reasoning is one of our most important cognitive skills. Reasoning plays a crucial role as we choose different courses of action in life, a topic we will now turn to as we examine *decision making*.

8.3.3 Decision Making: Outcomes and Probabilities

Decision making involves choosing from several alternatives. We must first choose a course of action before we can implement a solution to a problem. Two factors that influence our decisions are the perceived *outcomes* of our decisions and the *probability* of achieving these outcomes. For example, when you consider a major, you weigh the expected outcomes of choosing that major. What kind of job will it lead to? What is the pay like in this field? You also temper these judgments with your perception of how likely it is that these outcomes will actually occur. There may be high-salaried jobs in your major area, but if you see little chance of actually getting one of them, then you will be less likely to choose that major.

decision making making a choice from among a series of alternatives

judgment the act of estimating the probability of an event

Logically, we would seek to make decisions that we believe have a good chance of leading to favorable outcomes. However, our decision-making processes are a bit more complex than this. Another factor that affects our decisions is how the possible courses of action are presented, or *framed* (Cooper, Blanco, & Maddox, 2017; Jain et al., 2020; Kahneman & Tversky, 1984; Tversky & Kahneman, 2004). For example, which of the following options would you choose? Would you choose to take a class that you had a 60% chance of passing? Or one that you had a 40% chance of failing? Many people would choose the first option because it is framed positively, even though the chance of succeeding in the course is the same in both cases. Whether you prefer a positively framed option or a negatively framed one depends on your orientation. Sometimes we exhibit *loss aversion*, or a tendency to focus on what a certain decision could cost us in terms of potential gain—for example, worrying that your choice of major may limit your future employment opportunities. Other times, we exhibit *risk aversion*, or concern over losing what we already have—for example, worrying that the time you need to devote to your chosen major may force you to give up your current job. When making decisions, such as which major to choose, we sometimes have to also make *judgments*, our next topic.

8.3.4 Judgments: Estimating the Likelihood of Events

Judgment can be seen as a type of problem solving in which we estimate the probability of an event. If you don't know what the probability of a certain event is, and you need to have this probability to make a decision, what do you do?

As with all problems, you can solve this one using either an algorithm or a heuristic. An algorithm would involve somehow looking up or calculating the exact probability that a given event will occur. This is often neither possible nor practical, as in the case of trying to figure out what the stock market will do in the coming months. So, as we saw before, we tend to rely on heuristics when we make judgments.

The Availability Heuristic

Many people are afraid to fly, even though commercial air travel is statistically safer than traveling by car (National Safety Council, 2011). In fact, commercial air travel is getting safer. According to the National Transportation Safety Board (NTSB), the accident rate for commercial air carriers decreased by 80% in the 10 years leading up to 2012 (Weener, 2012). The most recent data available from the Federal Aviation Agency (2016) show that there were no deaths on commercial flights from November 2015 to July 2016 in the United States. So why would people be afraid to choose a safer form of travel? The answer lies in the manner in which we make judgments about the frequency of events. When we estimate the frequency of events, we heuristically base our judgments on the ease with which we can recall instances of the event in memory. The more easily we can recall a memory for an event, the more frequent we estimate the event to be. This memory shortcut is called the **availability heuristic** (Tversky & Kahneman, 1974).

availability heuristic a heuristic in which we use the ease with which we can recall instances of an event to help us estimate the frequency of the event

The availability heuristic explains the previous example of fearing air travel more than driving. Although fatal car accidents occur every day, they are not as widely covered by the media as plane crashes are. A fatal car crash may result in one or a few deaths, but a plane crash usually involves a larger number of fatalities. Therefore, when a plane goes down, the news coverage is graphic, horrifying, and prolonged. This leaves us with a strong, easily accessible memory for the plane crash. The result is that when we think of ways to travel, we more readily recall memories of plane crashes, and we may mistakenly overestimate the risk associated with air travel (Bahk, 2006). The result is that many people fear flying, when they really ought to be more afraid of traveling by car (see • FIGURE 8.4).

Milkovasa/Shutterstock.com

▲ According to the availability heuristic, the ease with which we can retrieve memories of events from long-term memory biases our judgments of how frequently the event occurs in real life. Seeing news coverage of air disasters leaves us with vivid memories of plane crashes that cause us to overestimate the probability of a plane crash occurring in the future. As a result, air traffic often falls off immediately following a crash, although in general flying is still safer than driving to your destination.

The availability heuristic may also play a role in the development of *stereotypes* we hold for groups of people and the *attitudes* that we hold for particular individuals (see Chapter 10; Wyman, Shiovitz-Ezra, & Parag, 2019). For example, if one has had recent or frequent exposure to older adults who are in poor health, these memories may be relatively available in memory when thinking of older adults in general. This can lead one to overestimate the probability any older person will be in ill-health. For example, one may automatically assume that their new next-door neighbor is incapable of mowing their own lawn, simply because they are a senior. Obviously, this judgment may prove to be unfair and prejudicial, as your neighbor, like many older adults, may be very able to take care of this everyday task.

To recap, use of the availability heuristic ensures that we tend to overestimate the *frequency* of events that are easily brought to mind. Next, we will look at heuristics that are often used to judge whether or not a person, event, or thing *belongs* in a certain category.

The Representativeness and Affective Heuristics

We also make heuristic judgments when deciding whether an object, event, or person belongs in a particular category by relying on the degree to which the person or thing in question is representative of the category. This tendency, called the **representativeness heuristic**, explains some of the mistakes we make in judgment (Tversky & Kahneman, 1974).

For instance, we often ignore the true probability, or *base rate*, of events in favor of our heuristic judgments. In one experiment on the representativeness heuristic, participants were told that a group of 100 people contained 70 engineers and 30 lawyers. They were also given a description of one of the group members—a man—that included the following traits: conservative, ambitious, nonpolitical, likes carpentry, and enjoys solving mathematical puzzles. Then they were asked to judge the probability that he was an engineer or a lawyer. If we were to approach this question logically, we would base our judgment on the base rate and say that there is a 70% chance that the man is an engineer and a 30% chance that he is a lawyer. The participants, however, did not approach this task logically. Instead, they based their judgments on the representativeness of the description that they were given and ignored the base rate information. As a result, the participants judged that there was a 90% chance that the man was an engineer (Kahneman & Tversky, 1973). Clearly, we often place more confidence in irrational judgments based on heuristics than in rational ones based on more factual probabilities (Tversky & Kahneman, 1980).

A Comparison of Accidental Death Risk
United States 2018

Type	Deaths in 2018*	General Population Risk**
Trucks, Buses, Cars	23,625	1 out of 13,845
Motorcycles	4985	1 out of 65,616
Rail Transit	169	1 out of 1,935,481
Bicycles	857	1 out of 381,676
Commercial Air Carriers and Commuter Flights	1	1 out of 327,096,265

*Source: NTSB (2020). *U.S. Transportation fatalities in 2018-By mode.* Retrieved from ntsb.gov/investigations/data/SiteAssets/Pages/Data_Stats/US-Transportation-fatalities-2018.pdf

**A figure of 327,096,265 people was used for the population of the USA in 2018. Source: Worldometer (2020). *United States population (live).* Retrieved from https://worldometers.info/world-population/us-population/

FIGURE 8.4

Although Many People Fear Flying, Other Modes of Transportation Are Actually Much Riskier

Heuristics like representativeness can also contribute to serious problems like prejudice (Chapter 10). For example, one of your authors once met a man who had little personal contact with African Americans. His exposure to African Americans was mostly limited to watching episodes of true crime shows on TV (e.g. *Cops, The First 48*), in which he saw many African Americans being arrested for crimes. This left the man with the false impression that most African Americans are representative of the category criminal. As a result, the man grew uneasy when he encountered any African American—a clear and unfortunate expression of racial prejudice (see Chapter 10). Media depictions of people can interact with our tendency to use heuristics like representativeness, making them powerful influences on our judgments of others.

Another way that such media depictions can affect us is through the use of another heuristic called the *affective heuristic* (Slovic et al., 2002). The **affective heuristic** suggests that we will make quick judgments about people and things based on whether or not we have an immediate positive or negative emotional reaction to them. For example, if one has an immediate negative emotional reaction when meeting a minority member because they have learned to

representativeness heuristic a heuristic in which we rely on the degree to which something is representative of a category, rather than the base rate, to help us judge whether or not it belongs in the category

affective heuristic a heuristic in which we make quick judgments about people and things based on whether or not we have an immediate positive or negative emotional reaction to them associate minorities with crime, this immediate emotional reaction is likely to influence the judgments they make about this person. As you might imagine, use of the affective heuristic frequently leads to making incorrect judgments about others, because the judgment is not based on the person's actual traits and behaviors.

If all of this sounds as though humans are incapable of making good judgments, don't despair. This is not the case. Often heuristics do lead to correct judgments. In addition, we do not always behave in a heuristic way. Sometimes we do pay attention to probabilities (Cosmides & Tooby, 1996; Costello & Watts, 2014; O'Brien & Hess, 2020). Whether we make judgments algorithmically or heuristically is a product of both the situation (Cosmides & Tooby, 1996) and the characteristic way that we as individuals tend to think (Stanovich & West, 1998). When the conditions are right, we do make good and logical judgments. This is especially true when we are making judgments in everyday, real-life situations (Anderson, 2000).

8.3 Quiz Yourself

1. You made an "A" on your last psychology exam and a "A-" on your last algebra exam. When asked to predict the likelihood that you will make an "A" on an upcoming English mid-term, you are likely to ______ this probability because of the ______.
- a. underestimate; affective heuristic
- b. overestimate; availability heuristic
- c. underestimate; algorithm
- d. overestimate; representativeness heuristic

2. Jonas is hesitant to take a calculus class even though it would help him after graduation because he is afraid of lowering his 4.0 GPA. Jonas is exhibiting ______.
- a. loss aversion
- b. risk aversion
- c. the representativeness heuristic
- d. the affective heuristic

3. Of the 100 people in Harry's psychology class, 60 are education majors and 40 are psychology majors. Yet when Harry first met a classmate named Sally, he guessed that there was a 90% chance that she was a psychology major because she had a poster of Sigmund Freud on her dorm room wall. Harry likely based his judgment on ______.
- a. the affective heuristic
- b. an algorithm
- c. the representativeness heuristic
- d. the availability heuristic

4. Which of the following is an example of ***deductive*** reasoning?
- a. Because Jared received a traffic ticket, he must have broken a traffic law.
- b. Because your psychology professor is friendly, professors tend to be friendly.
- c. Because it was cold this winter, winters are growing colder.
- d. b and c

5. Based on his observations of the world, Dr. Ali develops the hypothesis that older people are more difficult to persuade than younger people are. In formulating hypotheses such as this one, scientists are using ______ reasoning.
- a. deductive
- b. inductive
- c. algorithmic
- d. none of the above

Answers 1. b; 2. b; 3. c; 4. a; 5. b

8.4 Language: Communication, Thought, and Culture

language a well-developed, syntactical verbal system for representing the world

Our capacity for **language** is one of the most spectacular human abilities. No other species has such a well-developed, syntactical verbal system (i.e., one that has rules for sentence structure) for representing its world (see Psychology Applies to Your World box for more on this issue). As you learned in Chapter 2, Broca's and Wernicke's areas are specialized structures in the left hemisphere of the human brain that help us produce and comprehend speech. We put these brain areas to good use in that we use words in just about every aspect of our lives. As we have seen, much of our knowledge is represented in memory using words. Language, be it verbal or gestural (as in sign language), is an essential tool of cognition. As early as 16 months of age, we are already using language to help us both adjust our mental representations of the world and form new ones as we experience new things (Ganea et al., 2016). Without language, our ability to mentally represent our world, solve problems, and make decisions would be drastically altered.

8.4.1 How Humans Acquire Language

Some researchers have proposed that humans are born with an innate tendency to acquire language (Cattell, 2006; Chomsky, 1957). The linguist Noam Chomsky (b. 1928) proposed that we are born with a *language acquisition device (LAD)*, or a biological makeup that gives us an innate knowledge of the syntax or sentence structure of a language (Chomsky, 1965). Chomsky's theory is part of a larger group of theories, *biolinguistic theories*, which propose that language is only possible when a species has evolved a genetic make-up that allows language to develop (Pleyer & Hartmann, 2019). Many supporters of biolinguistic theories argue, among other things, that children across the world are not uniformly exposed to enough language and language coaching to account for the speed and consistency with which they learn language. This argument for the innateness of language is called the *poverty of stimulus (POS)* argument (Berwick et al., 2011).

However, *usage-based* language theorists argue that POS supporters significantly underestimate children's true exposure to language in early life (Behme & Deacon, 2008; King, 2016), and reject the notion that language is innate (Helmuth, 2001). Rather, they argue that we learn language by exercising general cognitive abilities and interacting with others (Pleyer & Hartmann, 2019).

These theoretical perspectives seem to take opposite sides in a debate over whether our traits and abilities are the result of genetic influences (nature) or environmental influences (nurture), a topic we will discuss in greater detail in section 8.5.3. Deciding which perspective is correct has challenged psychologists for decades (Pleyer & Hartmann, 2019). A complicating factor in settling this debate is that it is practically impossible to isolate the effects that our biology and our environment have on language development. How can we determine whether children are born with innate knowledge of language, when nearly all children in the world are exposed to language immediately after birth? When children begin speaking (at about 1 year), it may be the result of some innate, biological mechanism; it could be that they learned to develop language; or it could be that while they were biologically prepared to learn language, interaction with others was necessary for them to do so.

In typical children, it is impossible to tell exactly why language develops, but what if we could find children who were never exposed to spoken language? What could these children teach us about the development of human language? During the 1970s, researchers documented such a case of children with deafness in Nicaragua who had never been exposed to sign language and were unable to hear spoken Spanish. The children's teachers did not know sign language, so they tried to teach the children to read and write in Spanish. However, when left to their own devices, such as on the playground, the children began to develop their own spontaneous form of sign language. Their language, Nicaraguan Sign Language (NSL),

Psychology Applies to Your World

Are Humans the Only Animals to Use Language?

FOR CENTURIES, HUMANS BELIEVED that they alone had the ability to use language. It was assumed that only the advanced human mind was capable of dealing with the complexities of a language. Remarkably, this assumption has been called into question. Although it is very controversial, today some researchers believe that some other animals may possess linguistic abilities (Pepperberg, 2017; Shanker, Savage-Rumbaugh, & Taylor, 1999).

In looking at the linguistic abilities of other species, we first have to make a distinction between *language* and *communication*. Language is a system of communication that has a set vocabulary and a set structure, or grammar. For instance, English sentences generally follow a subject-verb-object pattern. Though many languages reverse the order of the verb and the object, most of the world's languages place the subject at the beginning of the sentence—for example, *Mike ran home* (Ultan, 1969). Languages also differ with respect to the placement of adjectives and adverbs. English places the adjective before the noun, *blue dress*; Spanish places it after, *vestido azul*. As you can see, each language has its own set of rules.

In contrast to the structure and order of language, communication can be very unstructured. All that is required in a communication system is that your meaning be conveyed to others. There is little argument that animals can communicate. For example, a rooster will emit an alarm cry to warn other chickens of danger (Marler, Duffy, & Pickert, 1986), whales communicate through vocalizations and song (Dunlop, 2016), and domestic dogs respond to specific play signals of their owners (Rooney, Bradshaw, & Robinson, 2001). But does this ability of some animals to communicate mean they have the capacity for language?

Some of the best evidence for animal language comes from studies done on Bonobo chimpanzees. Bonobos, also known as pygmy chimpanzees, are perhaps our closest genetic relatives, even more closely related to us than the common chimpanzee. During the 1980s, researcher Sue Savage-Rumbaugh and others attempted to teach English to a Bonobo named Matata. Because Bonobos do not have vocal cords that produce humanlike speech, they cannot actually speak. To get around this problem, the researchers used a special computer keyboard during the language training. On the surface of the keyboard were pictures, and when a picture was pressed, a computer-generated voice spoke the name of the object in the picture. Using this keyboard, Savage-Rumbaugh tried to teach Matata the meaning of certain words, but Matata did not catch on well (Wise, 2000, p. 223). However, Matata's infant stepson, Kanzi, had been observing his mother's lessons. Although Savage-Rumbaugh and her colleagues never attempted to teach Kanzi to use the keyboard, he picked up this skill on his own (Savage-Rumbaugh et al., 1986). By age 2½, Kanzi had begun to use some of the symbols his mother was trying to learn on the keyboard. When experimenters gave up trying to teach Matata to use the keyboard, they separated her from Kanzi. The day Matata left, Kanzi approached the keyboard and began to use it to make requests and express himself. In fact, he used it a total of 120 times on that first day (Wise, 2000).

Much like a young child, Kanzi appeared to have learned some vocabulary just by observing language being used around him. Kanzi's acquisition of language seemed to occur quite naturally (Shanker et al., 1999). For example, a patch of wild strawberries grew outside Kanzi's laboratory, and when he discovered them, Kanzi began to eat them. He overheard researchers referring to them by the word *strawberries* and soon appeared to understand what the word *strawberries* meant. After apparently learning the meaning of the word *strawberries,* Kanzi would head for the berry patch whenever he heard someone speak the word (Savage-Rumbaugh, 1987).

MICHAEL NICHOLS/National Geographic Image Collection

▲ As an infant, Kanzi learned to use a language keyboard like this one to communicate with humans just by watching researchers who were working with his mother, Matata.

Overall, Kanzi's use of language is quite impressive. He uses the keyboard to make requests, such as to visit a chimpanzee named Austin. If he is told that he cannot visit because it's too cold to go outside, Kanzi modifies his request to ask to see a picture of Austin on TV (Savage-Rumbaugh, 1987). Furthermore, Kanzi seems to be able to respond to very unusual and novel requests, such as "Put the pine needles in the refrigerator" or "Put the soap on the ball."

Language abilities have been shown in species other than the Bonobos as well. Researcher Irene Pepperberg (1993, 1999) had some success in training an African grey parrot named Alex to speak some English. Unlike the Bonobo, a parrot has the physical ability to produce speech as well as comprehend it. Before his death in 2007, Alex was able to speak some words in English and identify the shape, color, and material of many objects (Pepperberg, 1991). Alex was also able to answer the question "how many?" suggesting that he was able to conceptualize the meaning of some words. To answer the question, "how many?", one has to mentally draw connections between number and the objects that one is supposed to be counting (Nelson, 2019). For example, in asking "how many cats" you see in a picture, you must understand both the concepts of *quantity* and *cat* to get the right answer.

Attempts to train other African grey parrots to use words to refer to objects in laboratory settings have yielded mixed results (Giret et al., 2010). However, one study conducted in an animal's home environment found that a pet African grey parrot (Cosmo) tended to utter phrases such as "Cosmo wanna talk" when her owner was in the same room and "Where are you" when her owner was out of sight. These results suggest that the parrot's speech, which she learned from her owner, was influenced by specific social contexts (Colbert-White, Covington, & Fragaszy, 2011). Furthermore, Cosmo appeared to be able to tell the difference between situations when her owner ignored her verbal requests (e.g., not responding to a request to "Come here") and when her owner flat-out denied these requests (e.g., verbally saying "No" to Cosmo's request to "Come here"). Cosmo's vocalizations immediately following ignored and denied requests were systematically different. This suggests that Cosmo understood that these situations, although similar in that she was not being rewarded, were still somehow different (Colbert-White, Hall, & Fragaszy, 2016).

Rick Friedman/Corbis Historical/Getty Images

▲ Although controversial, studies of animals like Alex, the African grey parrot, challenge the presumption that language is a solely human attribute.

Dolphins have also shown some linguistic promise. Researcher Louis Herman and his colleagues have had some success in training dolphins to understand a language that the researchers created. This created language is based on gestures, but it has a set vocabulary in which certain gestures stand for certain words, and a specific set of grammatical rules dictate how gestures can be combined into phrases. (Herman & Uyeyama, 1999). There is also evidence of language-like behaviors in wild dolphins. Wild dolphins tend to have unique signature whistles. When researchers recorded these whistles and then played them back to the dolphins, individuals were found to only call back when hearing their own unique whistle (King & Janik, 2013). This is similar to responding to the sound of your own name, and it suggests that dolphins learn to label certain objects with specific vocalizations—much as humans use words to label objects.

As impressive as the linguistic abilities of Kanzi, Alex, and Cosmo are not everyone is convinced that animals truly have the capacity for language. Some argue that these animals are merely highly trained (Pinker, 1994) and that animals really aren't capable of truly learning words or grammar (Terrace, 2019). Skeptics propose that rather than actually using language, the animals are engaging in trained behaviors that they hope will lead to some reward. Certainly, Alex and Cosmo were trained to use language, but what about Kanzi, who was never trained to use language? He learned it on his own during his early years, just as children do (Shanker et al., 1999).

Another criticism of animal language research directly questions the linguistic abilities of animals. Some argue that animal language researchers have not adequately demonstrated that animals can follow all of the grammatical and syntactical rules of human language (Kako, 1999). Animal language researchers counter that their critics have unfairly focused on the linguistic abilities that animals lack and have largely ignored the linguistic abilities that animals do have (Shanker et al., 1999). At this time, we simply do not have enough information to determine whether or not animals have grammatical abilities that closely match our own (ten Cate, 2017).

▲ The speed and uniformity with which infants learn language across the world suggests to some that humans have a biological preparedness to learn language.

is today recognized as a true language complete with gestural vocabulary and its own syntactical and grammatical rules (Senghas & Coppola, 2001) that continue to evolve across generations (Kocab, Senghas, & Snedeker, 2016). Cases like this one are consistent with the notion that the drive to develop some form of language is innate.

But what about spoken language? Is there any evidence that children who can hear also have an innate capacity for language? Yes, there is. Evidence for the innate nature of language also comes from cross-cultural studies on language development in hearing children. These studies show that regardless of the culture, language seems to develop in children at about the same age and in the same sequence of stages. This similarity in the developmental process, which occurs despite cultural differences, argues for some biological mechanism that underlies language (Bornstein et al., 2015).

Nonetheless, it is hard to imagine that a child would fully develop language if they were never allowed to interact with others. Even if we are biologically prepared to learn language, environmental influences may still affect the process. For example, it is likely that children must hear a spoken language to develop that language themselves. Some type of social interaction with others is necessary. Typical parents attempt to communicate with their children through shared attention and using words to refer to objects (e.g., noticing the child is looking at their father and telling the child that is "Daddy"). Through such attempts at communication, children begin to learn that spoken words refer to objects in the real world. Even the Nicaraguan children had to interact with each other in order to develop their language. In our next section, we will take a look at the sequence of language development children go through as they interact with others.

Cooing and Babbling: Baby Steps to Learning One or More Languages

cooing the vowel sounds made by infants beginning at 2 months

babbling the combinations of vowel and consonant sounds uttered by infants beginning around 4 months

Most of us acquire our first language beginning in the first couple of years of life. Exposure to language begins while we are still in utero. Although we cannot discern actual words from inside the amniotic sac, we do perceive the tone and rhythm of language (Abboub, Nazzi, & Gervain, 2016). Newborn infants from birth to 1 month are capable of perceiving vowel sounds in an adult-like manner (Aldridge, Stillman, & Bower, 2001), and by about 2 months, infants begin **cooing**. Cooing involves making vowel sounds such as "ooo" and "ah." By 4 months, infants begin to engage in **babbling**, which adds consonant sounds to the vowel sounds they emitted during cooing. For example, an infant might repeat the sound "ka, ka, ka" over and over. Infants' first babbles are very similar across cultures, but this soon changes (Stoel-Gammon & Otomo, 1986). By 7 months, infants begin to emit babbles that contain sounds that are part of the language they have been exposed to in their environment. In this fashion, the infant's language system apparently tunes itself to the language or languages that the infant hears on a regular basis (Feldman et al., 2013). By 1 year, children's babbling contains the sounds and intonations of their native language (Levitt & Utmann, 1992).

Perhaps because the infant's language system appears to tune itself to the sounds of the language the child hears, children who grow up in bilingual households, where adults speak two languages to the children, tend to acquire both languages at high levels of proficiency (Petitto, 2009). But this does not mean that a child cannot learn a second language later in life. A child who is not exposed to a second language until elementary school can still develop near-native proficiency in the language (Hakuta, 1999). However, from childhood to adulthood, it seems to become steadily more difficult for us to become bilingual. For example, an adolescent who is just beginning to learn Spanish may never speak Spanish as fluently as a child who began learning Spanish in elementary school (Hakuta, Bialystok, & Wiley, 2003). Therefore, if true bilingualism is desired, it is best to begin learning the second language as early as possible.

Once a child achieves the stage of babbling the basic sounds, or **phonemes**, of their native tongue, the next step in language development is learning to communicate. At around 12 months, children begin trying to communicate in earnest with others. This communication is often based on gestures before it is based on words. For example, a child may point at a toy that they want. When parents learn to interpret these *preverbal gestures*, communication is achieved. As they catch on to their child's preverbal gestures, parents often verbalize the meaning of the gesture for the child. Parents say things like, "Oh, do you want this toy?" This verbalization of the child's intention allows the child to begin to learn **morphemes**, or the smallest sounds in a language that have meaning. As a result, by the end of the first year or so, children begin to speak their first words.

phonemes [FOE-neem] the smallest units of sound in a language

morphemes [MORE-feem] the smallest units of sound in a language that have meaning

overextension when a child uses one word to symbolize all manner of similar instances (e.g., calling all birds *parakeet*)

underextension when a child inappropriately restricts the use of a word to a particular case (e.g., using the word *cat* to describe only the family pet)

telegraphic speech two-word sentences that children begin to utter at 20 to 26 months

grammar the rules that govern the sentence structure in a particular language

From "Mama" and "Dada" to Full Conversations

A child's first words are usually the names of familiar objects, people, actions, or situations, ones with which they have had a great deal of contact. Typically, these words are *Dada, Mama, hi, bye,* and the like. Between 12 and 18 months of age, children usually utter only one word at a time, and often they convey tremendous meaning with these one-word sentences. For example, the utterance "Milk!" may stand for "I want some milk, please!"

As young children begin to speak, they may exhibit **overextension** in their language, using one word to symbolize all manner of similar instances. For instance, the word dog may be used to symbolize any animal. During this period, the opposite problem may also occur when children exhibit **underextension** of language. In this situation, children inappropriately restrict their use of a word to a particular case, such as when a child uses the word dog to refer only to the family pet.

By the time children reach 20 to 26 months, they begin to combine words into two-word sentences in what is called **telegraphic speech**. Telegraphic speech is often ungrammatical, but it does convey meaning, such as "Doggie bad," meaning "The dog was bad." From here, children rapidly acquire both vocabulary and **grammar**, or the rules that govern sentence structure in their language, such as word order and verb tenses. From the simple subject-verb combinations of telegraphic speech, English-speaking children progress to more complex subject-verb-object sentences between ages 2 and 3. Children who speak other languages adopt the relevant grammatical patterns of their native language. As children develop throughout the preschool years, their knowledge and use of grammar becomes increasingly complex. Interestingly, just as sleep aids in adult cognition (see Chapter 4), it also seems to facilitate language development during infancy and toddlerhood. Infants and toddlers who nap frequently throughout the day have been shown to have better language acquisition and larger vocabularies (Horváth & Plunkett, 2016). By age 6, the average child has an impressive vocabulary of around 10,000 words and a fairly competent mastery of grammar (Tager-Flusberg, 2005).

As children develop better vocabularies and acquire the grammatical rules of language, they exercise these abilities during social interactions with

pragmatics the rules of conversation in a particular culture

Whorfian [WORE-fee-un] hypothesis or the **linguistic relativity hypothesis** the theory that one's language can directly determine or influence one's thoughts

others. It's during these social interactions with peers and adults that children begin to learn **pragmatics**, or the rules of conversation operating in their culture. Pragmatics may include rules about turn taking, eye contact, tone of voice, and other aspects of conversation.

These hard-earned linguistic abilities will be very valuable to the child, as they are to us all. Let's take a closer look at what, exactly, language does for us.

8.4.2 The Function of Language in Culture and Perception

It is not difficult to see that language affects us in many ways. Obviously, one of language's main functions is to facilitate communication. We use language to describe our world, our thoughts, and our experiences to others. Without language, we would lead lives of social isolation.

Language and the Development of Culture

Because language brings us together and allows us to share ideas and experiences, language also plays a role in the development of culture. Russian psychologist Lev Vygotsky (1896–1934) noted the influence of language in the development of culture in his *sociocultural theory* (Vygotsky, 1934/1987) (see Chapter 9). According to sociocultural theory, older and more knowledgeable members of a society pass on the values, beliefs, and customs of their culture to children by telling the children stories and by engaging in conversations with them. The children store these dialogues in their memory and later use this knowledge to guide their behavior. Just as you learned from the stories of your elders, someday you too will pass down elements of your culture as you converse with younger people. Exchange of ideas via discussion of controversial and contradictory points of view is also essential to dialectical reasoning and to the development of cultural values over time. No doubt, some of the values and traditions of our current culture will change over time as we continue to talk to one another.

Language may facilitate the development and transmission of culture from generation to generation, but does the language we speak also affect the way we view the world? In the next section, we'll take a look at this interesting issue.

Linguistic Relativity: The Influence of Language on Thought

One of the most intriguing theories about language came from an unlikely source. Benjamin Whorf was a Connecticut fire insurance inspector whose unusual hobby was *linguistics*, or the study of language. After intensive studies of the languages of Native Americans, Whorf became convinced that one's language could directly determine or influence one's thoughts (Whorf, 1956). This notion has since come to be called the **Whorfian hypothesis** or the **linguistic relativity hypothesis** (for a review, see Tohidian, 2009).

In its strongest form, the linguistic relativity hypothesis states that one's language actually determines one's thoughts and one's perception of the world. According to this view, people who have different native languages think differently and perceive the world in a different light. For example, Whorf argued that Native Alaskans would understand "snow" differently than Europeans because the Native Alaskan's language has more words for snow than English has. Whorf claimed that differences among languages make it impossible to express all thoughts equally in all languages. Therefore, you can think and see the world only in terms of the language that you know. According to Whorf, your language *determines* what you think and how you perceive the world.

To date, the bulk of the evidence does not support the strong form of Whorf's linguistic relativity hypothesis (see ● TABLE 8.2). However, there is reason to think that a modified, or weaker, interpretation of the Whorfian hypothesis may hold true. The weaker version states that instead of language determining thought processes, language merely *influences* them. For example, a study that compared Spanish speakers to Mayan speakers found differences in their ability to remember colors. These memory differences were related to how easy it is to verbally label colors in Spanish and Mayan (Stefflre, Castillo-Vales, & Morley, 1966). It appears that how easily you can label a color in your language does affect your memory for that color.

TABLE 8.2 Different Words for Snow

Contrary to Whorf's hypothesis, like Native Alaskans, English speakers do have several words for snow.

Native Alaskan	English
qanuk: "snowflake"	snowflake
qanir: "to snow"	snow
kanevvluk: "fine snow/rain particles"	snowfall
muruaneq: "soft deep snow"	powder
pirta: "blizzard, snowstorm"	blizzard, snowstorm
nutaryuk: "fresh snow"	powder
qengaruk: "snow bank"	snowbank

It is also likely that language can influence our visual perception of the world (Athanasopoulos & Casaponsa, 2020). In one study involving the sorting of color samples, participants who spoke Setswana were more likely to group blues and greens together than were those who spoke English or Russian. This finding was attributed to the fact that in Setswana, one word describes both blue and green colors (Davies, 1998). The idea that humans do not all categorize color the same way is an important premise of the linguistic relativity hypothesis.

Language may also influence how we perceive both ourselves and others. In one interesting study of bilingual Chinese/English speakers, participants were found to exhibit more dialectical thinking about themselves and others when they were using Chinese relative to when they were using English (Chen, Benet-Martínez, & Ng, 2014). This finding and others suggest that when using Chinese, Chinese cultural values favoring dialectical thinking are activated in memory, producing more varied perceptions of self and others as a result (see also Boucher & O'Dowd, 2011).

Whether or not humans are the only species to have language, it is very evident that language is one of our most important cognitive abilities. Language is one of the skills that allow us to function in and adapt to our ever-changing social world. It is part of what makes us *intelligent* beings, a topic we will discuss next.

8.4 Quiz Yourself

1. **Babies begin _____ when they begin to make _____ sounds.**
   a. cooing; consonant
   b. babbling; vowel
   c. cooing; vowel and consonant
   d. babbling; vowel and consonant

2. **Which of the following people would be the most likely to agree with the statement "Language facilitates the development of culture"?**
   a. Lev Vygotsky
   b. Benjamin Whorf
   c. Sue Savage-Rumbaugh
   d. Eleanor Rosch

3. **One's language can influence one's _____.**
   a. speech
   b. memory
   c. perception
   d. All of the above

Answers 1. d; 2. a; 3. d

8.5 Defining and Measuring Intelligence

intelligence abilities that enable you to adapt to your environment and behave in a goal-directed way

mental age the age that reflects the child's mental abilities in comparison to the average child of the same age

What makes a person intelligent? Is it being able to memorize large amounts of information like Kim Peek could? Knowing how to survive in the wilderness? Having good social skills? Today, many psychologists view **intelligence** broadly as having abilities that allow you to adapt to your environment and behave in a goal-directed way. But over the years, psychologists have found that developing a precise definition of intelligence is not as easy as it may seem, and our conception of intelligence has undergone several revisions. Equally challenging has been finding ways of measuring intelligence.

8.5.1 Measuring Intelligence by Abilities and IQs

One of the first people to study the measurement of intelligence was British psychologist Sir Francis Galton (1822–1911). Galton claimed that intelligence is an inherited trait that is correlated with having superior physical abilities. As such, he believed that intelligence could be measured by measuring traits like reaction time, eyesight, and so on. However, early studies failed to find much support for Galton's ideas (Schultz & Schultz, 2012), and they soon fell out of favor.

Alfred Binet: Measuring Intelligence by Measuring Cognitive Abilities

The modern intelligence test is credited to Alfred Binet (1857–1911). In 1904, the French government appointed Alfred Binet and psychiatrist Théodore Simon to a commission charged with developing a means of measuring the intelligence of French schoolchildren so that the government could identify children who would not likely profit from traditional education.

Binet saw intelligence as the capacity to *find and maintain a purpose, adopt a strategy to reach that purpose, and evaluate the strategy so it can be adjusted as necessary* (Terman, 1916). In essence, Binet suggested that having intelligence makes one a good problem solver. As such, he developed an intelligence test that assessed general cognitive abilities such as the individual's attention, judgment, and reasoning skills (Binet & Simon, 1905).

Binet prepared a set of 30 tasks that measured these skills and arranged them in order of difficulty, with the easiest questions first and the hardest questions last. Not surprisingly, the brighter students could answer more of the questions than the not-so-bright students could. Also, not surprisingly, the older children tended to answer more questions correctly than the younger children. In fact, Binet noticed that the brighter younger children could sometimes answer correctly as many questions as the average child of an older age. For example, a very smart 6-year-old might be able to answer as many questions as the average 10-year-old child could. So Binet began to quantify children's intelligence in terms of **mental age**, or the age that reflects a child's mental abilities in comparison to the "average" child. In Binet's scheme, a mental age that exceeds one's chronological age indicates above-average intelligence, and a mental age that is below a child's actual age indicates a below-average level of intelligence. Binet's concept of mental age became the foundation for the IQ score, and his test became the basis for modern intelligence tests.

Lewis Terman: The Intelligence Quotient and the Stanford-Binet

In 1916, Stanford psychologist Lewis Terman (1877-1956) completed an American revision of the intelligence test that Binet and Simon had developed. He named his version of the test the Stanford Revision of the Binet-Simon Scale, which became known as the *Stanford-Binet*. The Stanford-Binet is an example of a **standardized test**—a test that uses a standard set of questions, procedures, and scoring methods for all test takers. In standardizing the Stanford-Binet, Terman gave the test to a large number of people and calculated the average test scores that people of different ages made on the test. These norms allowed Terman to establish mental age scores for people taking the Stanford-Binet.

standardized test a test that uses a standard set of questions, procedures, and scoring methods for all test takers

intelligence quotient (IQ) one's mental age divided by one's chronological age times 100

Perhaps Terman's most significant contribution to the test was to popularize the use of an **intelligence quotient (IQ)**, as the measure of an individual's intelligence. An IQ score is calculated as follows:

$$IQ = (MA/CA) \times 100$$

where

$$MA = \text{mental age}$$

and

$$CA = \text{chronological, or actual, age}$$

Using the concept of an IQ, a person of average abilities has, by definition, an IQ of 100 or, in other words, a mental age equal to their actual age. IQs over 100 indicate above-average intelligence, and IQs below 100 indicate below-average intelligence. For example, Kim Peek had an IQ score of 74 (Peek, 1996, p. 121). Although he could memorize with ease, he was relatively unable to perform cognitive tests that involved reasoning, resulting in him having a relatively low IQ score.

The Stanford-Binet has undergone four major revisions since 1916 and is still in wide use today. The most recent edition, the Stanford-Binet Intelligence Scales, Fifth Edition (SB5), was released in 2003. However, a modern IQ test developed by psychologist David Wechsler (1896–1981) and first released in 1939 has greatly challenged the popularity of the Stanford-Binet.

David Wechsler's Intelligence Scales

Wechsler (1939) developed his intelligence test in response to shortcomings he saw in the Stanford-Binet. Wechsler objected to the fact that the Stanford-Binet test tried to sum up intelligence in a single score. He believed that one number could not adequately express something as complex as intelligence. Furthermore, Wechsler objected to the use of the mental age concept for adults (Kaplan & Saccuzzo, 1989). After all, would you necessarily expect a 40-year-old to correctly answer more questions than a 35-year-old? The concept of mental age doesn't apply as well to adults as it does to children because adults do not change as much from year to year as children do. Therefore, mental age has little significance in adulthood.

To correct these problems, Wechsler developed an intelligence test that yields scores on individual subscales that measure different mental abilities. Furthermore, instead of using mental age to determine IQ, Wechsler's tests compare a participant's performance to the average person's performance to determine IQ. The Wechsler tests are standardized tests that are devised so that an average person's performance on the test results in an IQ of 100. Using this number as a benchmark, people who score above average on the test are given IQ scores above 100, and people who perform below average are given IQ scores below 100. Most people can expect to score near this average IQ, somewhere in the range of 85–115 (● FIGURE 8.5).

Today there are three separate Wechsler intelligence tests. The Wechsler Preschool and Primary Scale of Intelligence, Fourth Edition (WPPSI-IV), is administered to children ages 2½ to 7. The Wechsler Intelligence Scale for

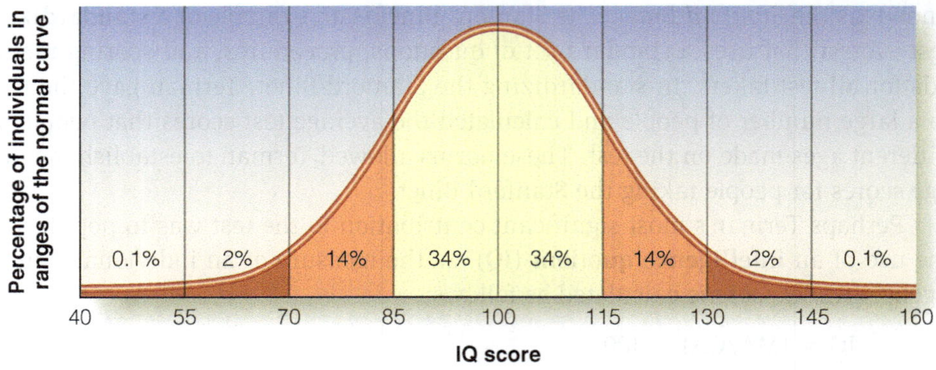

FIGURE 8.5

The Normal Distribution of IQ Scores

IQs tend to be normally distributed across the population. This means that when a frequency distribution of IQ scores is plotted, it forms a bell-shaped curve, with most people scoring near the average of 100 on the IQ test and very few scoring extremely high or low.

Children, Fifth Edition (WISC-V), is used for children ages 6–16. And the Wechsler Adult Intelligence Scale, Fourth Edition (WAIS-IV), is used for people ages 16–90.

The WAIS-IV consists of 10 subtests that measure various verbal and performance abilities (● TABLE 8.3). Performance on these subtests is used to calculate an overall IQ score as well as separate index scores for *verbal comprehension, perceptual reasoning, working memory,* and *processing speed*. The design of the WAIS-IV makes it flexible. Testers can administer any of the indexes alone (e.g., measuring only perceptual reasoning) or all of them together to obtain an overall IQ score.

Testing the Test: What Makes a Good Intelligence Test?

So far, we have looked at two widely accepted tests that psychologists and educators use to measure intelligence. These are but two of a great many tests that have been devised to measure intelligence and other psychological traits. When choosing which test to administer or when interpreting the scores yielded by these tests, we have to ask, "Is this a good test?" If psychologists never worried about the quality of their measurements, they could well find themselves making many faulty judgments about the people they measure.

reliability the degree to which a test yields consistent measurements over time

validity the degree to which a test measures what it claims to measure

Before a test is used to make decisions about anyone's life, the test itself must be tested and evaluated. Psychologists must be assured that the test is both *reliable* and *valid* before it can be put into widespread use. The **reliability** of a test refers to the degree to which the test yields consistent measurements over time. Although intelligence can change over time, it usually does so very slowly. In general, if you are intelligent today, you will be intelligent 6 months from now. So, if we use a test to measure your IQ today and then again in 6 months, the scores should be comparable. This doesn't mean that the test has to yield exactly the same score, but the scores should be close.

Establishing the reliability of an intelligence test is very important, but the **validity** of the test is an equally important characteristic. Validity is the degree to which the test measures what it was designed to measure. In the case of an intelligence test, one must show that the test actually measures intelligence!

TABLE 8.3 The Wechsler Adult Intelligence Scale (WAIS-IV) and Its Subscales

NOTE: The test items shown are examples—they do not appear in the actual test.

Content Area	Explanation of Tasks/Questions	Examples of Possible Tasks/Questions
	Verbal Comprehension	
Vocabulary	Define the meaning of the word.	What does *persistent* mean? What does *archaeology* mean?
Information	Supply generally known information.	Who is Kamala Harris? What are six New England states?
Similarities	Explain how two things or concepts are similar.	In what ways are an ostrich and a penguin alike? In what ways are a lamp and a heater alike?
	Perceptual Reasoning	
Block design	Use patterned blocks to form a design that looks identical to a design shown by the examiner.	Assemble the blocks on the left to make the design on the right. 
Matrix reasoning	Fill in the missing cell in a matrix with a picture that would logically complete the matrix.	Which of these figures would complete the logical sequence in this matrix? 
Visual puzzles	Construct a figure from a series of puzzle pieces.	Which three of these pieces go together to make this puzzle? 
	Working Memory	
Digit span	Listen to a series of digits (numbers), then repeat the numbers either forward, backward, or both.	Repeat these numbers backward: 9, 1, 8, 3, 6.
Arithmetic	Mentally manipulate arithmetical concepts.	How many 52-cent candy bars can you buy with a 5-dollar bill?
	Processing Speed	
Symbol search	When given an array of symbols, find the specified symbol and circle it.	Circle the ♣ in the following array: ♣ ψ Δ λ ♦ ⊗ ℑ ♣ θ ♣ θ Δ λ ♥ ⊕ Σ ℑ • Δ ♣ λ ♦ ♥ ℑ ≅ ψ ♦
Digit symbol	When given a key matching particular symbols to particular numerals, copy a sequence of symbols, transcribing from symbols to numerals, using the key.	Look carefully at the key. In the blanks, write the correct numeral for the symbol below each symbol. 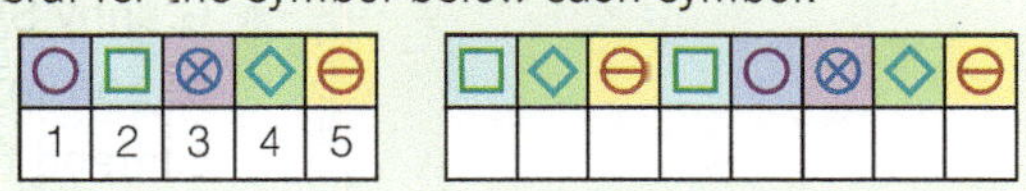

Psychology Works!

iStock.com/monkeybusinessimages

Many jobs require knowledge of cognition, language, and intelligence. Some of these include, psychometrists working in schools who assess the cognitive and intellectual abilities of students, afterschool program workers, school counselors, disabilities services professionals, paraprofessional workers, and developers of academic games and educational materials.

One way to establish a test's validity is to show that scores on the test reliably predict future behavior. For example, if we expect that intelligence is related to doing well in school, then scores on a valid IQ test should predict who does well in school and who does not. If the test is valid, IQ and grade point average (GPA) should correlate. Students with higher IQ scores should tend to also have higher GPAs and students with lower IQ scores should tend to have lower GPAs. If they do not, the IQ test is not a valid predictor of academic success, and it should not be used as such.

Engage Yourself!

You might be thinking that validity seems like a trivial issue. After all, if you create an IQ test that asks people questions that seem to require intelligence to answer, won't the test tell you who is smart and who is not? As it turns out, it is quite easy to devise tests that are invalid. For example, questions that require specific cultural knowledge may not assess the intelligence of people unfamiliar with that culture—even though they may be very intelligent. This validity problem is referred to as **cultural bias**. Some people have argued that intelligence tests are often biased and invalid for cultural minority members (Reynolds & Brown, 1984). To illustrate this point, try to answer the following sample IQ test question.

cultural bias the degree to which a test puts people from other cultures at an unfair disadvantage because of the culturally specific nature of the test items

Choose the term that best completes this analogy:

Granny Smith is to apple as chayote is to_________.

a. knife

b. animal

c. squash

d. clothing

Was the answer immediately apparent to you? If you are from a culture that is not familiar with the word *chayote*, which is a type of squash eaten in some Latin American cultures, you might not realize that chayote is a type of squash the way Granny Smith is a type of apple. Does this mean you are unintelligent? Of course not—but an incorrect answer would count against you if it were on an IQ test. Some people contend that IQ tests can't help reflecting the cultural values, language, and knowledge of the people who develop them, and therefore all IQ tests carry some form of cultural bias (Greenfield, 1997). Others provide data suggesting that test takers' proficiency with the language of the test may be a more important biasing factor than mere cultural bias is (te Nijenhuis, Willigers, Dragt, & van der Flier, 2016). This has led some to develop nonverbal measures of ability, such as Raven's Progressive Matrices (RPN) (Raven & Raven, 2003). On the RPN, test takers are shown a sequence of pictures and asked to determine which picture from a list of options is the next most logical picture in the sequence (● Figure 8.6). Tests such as this may be less susceptible to cultural bias because they avoid the use of language. They can also be administered to people who are nonverbal or are speakers of another language.

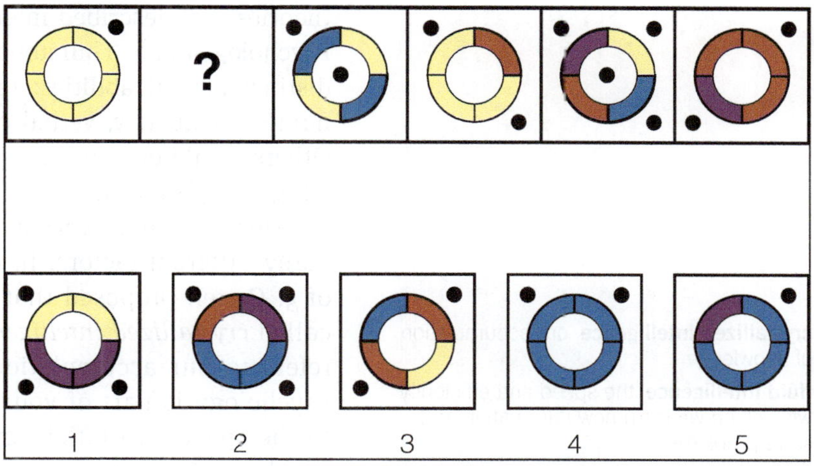

FIGURE 8.6

Raven's Progressive Matrices

Measures, such as the Raven's Progressive Matrices (RPN) may be less prone to cultural bias as such measures do not rely on language. Can you determine which item belongs in the space marked with a question mark?

Aside from the items on the test itself, another concern is the practice of population-based norming of tests (adjusting how a test is scored for a particular population to ensure that people with average intelligence score an IQ score of 100). This practice does not take into account subgroups of people living within a country and therefore introduces further bias in IQ scores (Shuttleworth-Edwards, 2016). Furthermore, we should always keep in mind that IQ tests do not measure all human intellectual abilities, and our cultural environment can affect our performance on these tests (Sternberg, 1997a).

8.5.2 The Nature of Intelligence: The Search Continues

Back in the early 1900s, psychological historian E. G. Boring noted that "intelligence is what the tests test" (quoted in Gardner, 1999, p. 13). By this, Boring meant that psychologists had placed a great deal of emphasis on developing tests to measure intelligence, but they had not spent adequate time exploring what intelligence actually is. Since then, numerous ideas have been proposed as we discuss here—from intelligence as a single ability to the idea that intelligence encompasses multiple abilities that interact with one another. We will begin with the notion that intelligence is a single or unidimensional ability.

Intelligence as a Single Factor

A century ago, British statistician Charles Spearman (1863–1945) argued that because test scores of separate mental abilities (such as verbal skills, mathematical ability, deductive reasoning skills) tend to correlate, there must be one general level of intelligence that underlies these separate mental abilities (Spearman, 1904). Spearman referred to this **general intelligence** as *g*. In Spearman's view, one's level of *g* would determine how well they functioned on any number of cognitive tasks. The idea that intelligence is a single, unitary factor helped lead to the rapid expansion of intelligence testing in schools, the workplace, and the military. But the notion of *g* would soon be challenged.

general intelligence *(g)* a general level of intelligence that underlies our separate abilities

Intelligence as a Collection of Abilities

Is intelligence really a single factor? Can't a person be smart in some areas, but not in others? By the 1930s, some theorists were beginning to challenge the idea of a single intelligence. The notion of *g* fell from favor as psychologists proposed theories that described intelligence as a set of abilities rather than a single trait. Psychologist L. L. Thurstone (1938) argued that intelligence was made up of seven distinct mental abilities: reasoning, associative memory, spatial visualization, numerical fluency, verbal comprehension, perceptual speed, and word fluency. Others would eventually propose as many as 120 different factors underlying intelligence (Guilford, 1967).

However, not everyone was convinced that intelligence was made up of many different factors. In the 1960s, Raymond Cattell (1963) revived the idea of *g*. Cattell proposed that *g* does exist, but in two different forms, which he called *crystallized intelligence* and *fluid intelligence*. **Crystallized intelligence** refers to our accumulation of knowledge. For example, your knowledge of psychology is part of your crystallized intelligence. **Fluid intelligence** refers to the speed and efficiency with which we learn new information and solve problems. For instance, the higher your fluid intelligence, the more quickly you will learn the material in this chapter. As a result, both fluid and crystallized intelligence are related to educational attainment across the lifespan (Kaufman et al., 2009).

crystallized intelligence our accumulation of knowledge

fluid intelligence the speed and efficiency with which we learn new information and solve problems

There is both good and bad news when it comes to our levels of fluid and crystallized intelligence over a lifetime. The evidence shows that crystallized intelligence can continue to grow well into late adulthood (Horn, Donaldson, & Engstrom, 1981), but fluid intelligence tends to decrease across adulthood (Buczylowska & Petermann, 2016; Schaie, 1994). The degree to which we retain these abilities throughout life is affected by our environment (Horn, 1982), our personality traits (Ziegler et al., 2015), our physical health (Bergman & Almkvist, 2013), and perhaps even our diet (Zamroziewicz et al., 2016).

When researchers compared middle-aged and older adults who were healthy (healthy group) with middle-aged and older adults who had high blood pressure and/or vascular disease (vascular risk group) over a 5-year period (Raz et al., 2007), they found that relative to the healthy group, the vascular risk group experienced more negative brain changes. For example, the vascular risk group experienced more brain lesions and increased shrinkage in the prefrontal cortex and hippocampus of the brain relative to the healthy participants. Recall from Chapters 2 and 7 that the hippocampus and prefrontal cortex play important roles in the processing of memories. The vascular risk group also experienced more decline in their *working memory*, an important aspect of fluid intelligence. Engaging in health-promoting behaviors that reduce cardiovascular risk may be one way to help reduce the level of age-related declines in fluid intelligence you experience later in life. For example, one study found that yoga, meditation, and mindfulness practitioners experienced less age-related decline in fluid intelligence (Gard et al., 2014). We will have more to say about health-defeating and health-promoting behaviors in Chapter 12.

So far, we have seen that there has been some disagreement among psychologists as to exactly what intelligence is. Disagreement among scientists is a normal part of the scientific process. Although many psychologists, especially those who focus on the measurement of intelligence, still favor the idea of a general intelligence, others have gone on to develop newer theories that conceptualize intelligence as a multifaceted set of abilities or intelligences (Gardner, 1999).

Howard Gardner's Multiple Intelligences

In the early 1980s, Harvard psychologist Howard Gardner (b. 1943) proposed a theory of intelligence that views humans as possessing many different intelligences (Gardner, 1983). According to Gardner, an intelligence is "a biopsychological potential to process information that can be activated in a cultural setting to solve problems or create products that are of value in a culture" (Gardner, 1999, pp. 33–34). This definition emphasizes the fact that intelligence allows us to function efficiently in our own environment, and it also highlights the fact that different cultures and environments place different demands on our intelligence.

For example, in the United States today, we might consider the ability to understand and predict fluctuations in the stock market as a sign of intelligence. In an unindustrialized, nomadic culture, however, the ability to seek out a source of water may be a more highly valued intelligence. After carefully considering the different human abilities that allow us to function in our environment, Gardner developed a strict set of criteria for identifying an intelligence (Gardner, 1999). Using these criteria, Gardner has identified nine different intelligences and allowed for the possibility that more may someday be identified (Gardner, 2004; Gardner, Kornhaber, & Chen, 2018). Gardner's theory of **multiple intelligences** is summarized in ● TABLE 8.4.

multiple intelligences the idea that we possess different types of intelligence rather than a single, overall level of intelligence

As you look at Table 8.4, can you see that you have more of some types of intelligence and less of others? Most of us do not possess equal levels of all types of intelligence. Rather, we each have our own strengths and weaknesses. Therefore,

TABLE 8.4 Gardner's Multiple Intelligences

Intelligence	Description	Examples
Linguistic	The ability to learn and use languages	An author has a good command of language and can express ideas well in written form.
Spatial	The ability to recognize and manipulate patterns of space	A surveyor is very good at judging distances. A fashion major designs a pattern for a jacket.
Logical-mathematical	The ability to attack problems in a logical manner, solve mathematical problems, and in general exhibit scientific thought	A psychologist can develop and test theories in a scientific manner. A physician examines a patient and makes a diagnosis.
Musical	The ability to perform, compose, and appreciate music	A songwriter can create unique melodies and perform them.
Bodily-kinesthetic	The ability to use one's body to solve problems and create products	A gymnast can perform intricate maneuvers on the balance beam.
Interpersonal	The ability to understand the intentions, motivations, and desires of others	A manager is good at working with others and can inspire others to perform at their optimal level of performance.
Intrapersonal	The ability to understand oneself	A student knows what they want in terms of their career and uses this information to choose an appropriate major.
Naturalistic	Paying attention to nature and understanding environmental issues	A person recycles their trash and avoids using household cleaners and insecticides that are harmful to the environment.
Existential	Being concerned with "ultimate" issues; seeking higher truths	A philosophy student ponders the meaning of life.

Source: *Intelligence Reframed: Multiple Intelligences for the 21st Century* by Howard Gardner (New York: Basic Books/Perseus, 1999). Reprinted by permission of BASIC BOOKS, a member of Perseus Books Group.

Gardner doesn't have much use for tests that seek to measure general intelligence. For Gardner, it is far more important to look at a person's intelligence profile—their level of ability across the different types of intelligence.

Robert Sternberg's Triarchic Theory of Intelligence

Psychologist Robert Sternberg (b. 1949) has taken an approach somewhat similar to Howard Gardner's. Like Gardner, Sternberg rejects the usefulness of trying to measure a single, general intelligence. However, Sternberg doesn't subscribe to the idea that we possess many separate intelligences. Sternberg considers some of Gardner's intelligences as talents that some people possess. For example, it's hard to see why musical intelligence would be important in many cultures. Even if you have little or no musical ability, you could still function very well in many cultures, including American society. However, in the United States and many other cultures, the ability to think logically would be very important to your survival and well-being.

Sternberg suggests that *successful intelligence,* or intelligence that helps us function in our world, is composed of three types of cognitive abilities (Sternberg, 2015). Accordingly, Sternberg calls his theory the **triarchic theory of intelligence** (Sternberg, 1985, 1997b). According to the triarchic theory, intelligence is composed of analytical, practical, and creative abilities that help us adapt successfully to our environment.

triarchic [tri-ARK-ic] theory of intelligence a theory that proposes that intelligence is composed of analytical, practical, and creative abilities that help us adapt to our environment

Analytical intelligence is seen in our ability to use logic to reason our way through problems—for example, finding a way to fix your car when it breaks down. Analytical intelligence is also important as we implement and evaluate problem-solving strategies, allowing us to evaluate whether a particular problem-solving strategy is working well.

Practical intelligence is our ability to adapt to our environment. This is the type of intelligence that we see in people who have a great deal of common sense. People who are high in practical intelligence exhibit savvy. They know how to function efficiently within their environment. For example, a Central American farmer may be able to predict the weather by noticing changes in the environment. Or someone who lives in New York City may be very good at finding the quickest way across town during rush hour. Both of these people, although they possess very different skills, exhibit practical intelligence. Keep in mind that behaviors and skills may be intelligent in some environments, but not in others.

Creative intelligence is our ability to use our knowledge of the world in novel situations. For example, suppose you found yourself in a foreign culture where you did not know the language or the customs. Would you be able to function? People who are high in creative intelligence can adapt what they know about the world to meet the unique demands of new situations. In this case, you might use gestures learned while playing charades, Heads Up, or some other pantomime game to help you communicate without words.

iStock.com/FamVeld

▲ Having good emotional intelligence allows one to remain calm and effective during life's challenging moments.

Daniel Goleman's Theory of Emotional Intelligence

Yet another way of conceptualizing intelligence comes from psychologist Daniel Goleman (b. 1946). In his best-selling book *Emotional Intelligence,* Goleman (1995) argues that a concept of intelligence that is based solely on cognitive abilities is too limiting. He notes that even people with relatively high IQs can fail to succeed in life and sometimes do things that appear to be downright unintelligent. For example, a gifted student with a perfect score on the SAT may turn out to be an unsuccessful college student who fails most of their classes (Goleman, 1995). According to Goleman, the reason for this is that many times our actions are guided not by our intellectual abilities but by our emotions. Goleman contends that just as some of us are intellectually gifted, some of us are endowed with emotional expertise—an ability he calls *emotional intelligence*.

In Goleman's view, emotional intelligence includes awareness of your own emotional states, accurate assessment of your own abilities, self-confidence, self-control, trustworthiness, conscientiousness, the ability to adapt to changes, innovation or creativity, achievement motivation, commitment to completing goals, initiative or self-motivation, and a sense of optimism (Goleman, 1998; Petrides, Furnham, & Martin, 2004). In other words, an emotionally intelligent person is a confident self-starter who is ethical and adaptable—the kind of person who sets a goal and works toward it without letting minor obstacles derail their progress. With this sort of determination, confidence, and ability to adapt, a person with only an average IQ might be able to go far. Likewise, a bright person with low emotional intelligence might become overwhelmed with self-doubt or lack of motivation and, as a result, fail to perform well in life.

For example, when compared to general intelligence, emotional intelligence has been found to be a better predictor of quality of life and lower distress levels in children who have aged-out of the foster care system. This suggests that emotional intelligence is more related to resiliency in children than general intelligence is (Kennedy et al., 2019), but does this mean that emotional intelligence and general intelligence are unrelated?

Although emotional intelligence and general intelligence are separate abilities, they may be connected. A recent meta-analysis of studies examining emotional intelligence among gifted and non-gifted students suggested that relative to non-gifted students, gifted children are higher in emotional intelligence. Furthermore, female gifted students tended to have the highest levels of emotional intelligence (Abdulla Alabbasi, A. Ayoub, & Ziegler, 2020).

If having emotional intelligence is related to intelligence and to better success in life, what role does it play in the workplace? Goleman and his colleagues have suggested that one way to increase effective leadership in the corporate world is to teach personnel to achieve higher levels of emotional intelligence (Goleman, Boyatzis, & McKee, 2002). A recent study found that leadership skills were positively related to both emotional and general intelligence (Sánchez, Pérez, & Aránega, 2020). Higher levels of emotional intelligence may also offset some of the negative effects of bullying in the workplace (Nel, 2019), and higher levels of emotional intelligence are associated with less occupational stress and greater use of effective coping strategies (Mazzella et al., 2019).

Given that emotional intelligence seems to be a useful ability, some have questioned whether or not it can be learned. There is some evidence to suggest that emotional intelligence is a learned skilled that can be taught in both children (Idogho & Osuya, 2020) and adults (Tuyakova, Baizhumanova, & Alekeshova, 2020). In our next section, we will address whether or not the same can be said for general intelligence. Do we learn to be intelligent?

8.5.3 Nature, Nurture, and IQ: Are We Born Intelligent, or Do We Learn to Be?

The issue of what intelligence is has stimulated debate among researchers (see You Review: The Nature of Intelligence), but another issue has captured the attention of the public even more. Where does intelligence come from? Are we born with a predestined level of intelligence, or do we acquire intelligence as we develop (Gardner, 1999)?

YOU REVIEW The Nature of Intelligence

Theorist	View of Intelligence
Charles Spearman	Intelligence → is → Generalized Intelligence (*g*)
L. L. Thurstone	Intelligence → is → Reasoning; Associative Memory; Spatial Visualization; Numerical Fluency; Verbal Comprehension; Perceptual Speed; Word Fluency
Raymond Cattell	Generalized Intelligence (*g*) → has two forms → Crystallized Intelligence; Fluid Intelligence
Howard Gardner	Multiple Intelligences → are → Linguistic; Spatial; Logical-mathematical; Musical; Bodily-kinesthetic; Interpersonal; Intrapersonal; Naturalistic; Existential
Robert Sternberg	Successful Intelligence → comprises → Cognitive Abilities: Analytical Intelligence; Practical Intelligence; Creative Intelligence
Daniel Goleman	Emotional Intelligence → coexists with → Traditional Intelligence

Nature Versus Nurture and Interactionism

nature-nurture debate the age-old debate over whether we are mostly a product of our genes or of environmental influences

Explaining how and why we develop as we do is the central issue in the age-old **nature-nurture debate**. On the nature side of this debate is the claim that individual characteristics (such as intelligence) are largely determined by one's genes and are not learned. On the nurture side, individual characteristics are thought to be molded by environmental influences such as parents, the educational opportunities you have, and the TV shows you watch. From the nurture point of view, our traits and characteristics are acquired totally by experience.

There is little doubt that genes exert a powerful influence on the development of an organism. All living organisms develop according to a "blueprint" or plan contained in the *genes* that an organism inherits from its parents. **Genes** are strands of deoxyribonucleic acid (DNA) that are found in the nuclei of all living cells and direct the development of the organs and systems of the body. In 2003, scientists working on the *Human Genome Project,* a large-scale scientific project aimed at identifying the entire set of genes that are found in the DNA of the human body, completed this mapping. One of the most surprising findings of the project was that the total number of genes in the human genome is about 30,000. Originally, scientists had predicted that they would find approximately 100,000 genes. The fact that a mere 30,000 genes direct the development of something as complex as humans was a surprise (U.S. Department of Energy, 2007). So, why do humans possess these specific 30,000 genes and the characteristics that they govern? To answer this question, think back to a concept we discussed in Chapter 1—natural selection.

genes strands of DNA found in the nuclei of all living cells

natural selection the cornerstone of Darwin's theory of evolution, which states that genes for traits that allow an organism to be reproductively successful will be selected or retained in a species and genes for traits that hinder reproductive success will not be selected and therefore will die out in a species

genotype [JEAN-oh-type] inherited genetic pattern for a given trait

phenotype [FEEN-oh-type] an actual characteristic that results from interaction of the genotype and environmental influences

interactionism the perspective that our genes and environmental influences work together to determine our characteristics

In 1859, Charles Darwin published *On the Origin of Species by Means of Natural Selection* (Darwin, 1859/1936), in which he outlined the process of natural selection. **Natural selection** is a simple but powerful process that can change, kill, or create a species over time. The central principle of natural selection is that for characteristics to be retained in a species, genes for these traits must be passed on to offspring. If an organism does not reproduce, its genes die with it. If a specific trait is maladaptive and tends to prevent an organism from surviving and procreating, then the genes for this trait are not as likely to be passed on to offspring. Over time, these maladaptive genes should die out in the species. In contrast, adaptive genes, which give rise to traits that help an organism reproduce, will be passed on to future generations. Through natural selection, these adaptive genes will become more widespread in the species over time. From this perspective, the genes of the human genome are present in us today because they aided our ancestors' ability to thrive and reproduce.

Even though our human genes direct our bodies to develop as human bodies, we are not all the same. As individuals, we have unique characteristics because we inherited a particular mix of genes for specific traits from our parents. At conception, we get half of our genes from each of our parents. From this combination of genes, we develop our characteristics. The genetic code that we inherit for a particular trait is called the **genotype**. But the genotypes we inherit, such as genes for dark hair, only partly determine the traits we actually acquire. The environment plays a role as well. The actual trait or characteristic we develop is referred to as the **phenotype**. The phenotype is a product of the genotype an organism inherits and the environment in which it lives. For example, the exact shade of your hair, the level of your intelligence, the speed with which you run—all are phenotypes, which are the expression of inherited genotypes and environmental influences.

Today, the dominant perspective on the nature-nurture debate is **interactionism**. Most psychologists now believe that genetic influences interact with environmental influences to produce our traits and behavior. For example, a child can inherit very "smart" genes, but if education is not provided, the child will not be as smart as they could have been. Interactionism does not end the nature-nurture debate, however. Today, some psychologists are attempting to understand the relative contributions of nature and nurture to specific traits, asking whether a trait such as intelligence is mostly genetic or mostly environmental. Researchers are also interested in explaining the exact manner in which genes and environmental influences interact to produce traits.

Blend Images/Shutterstock.com

▲ Identical twins have been very useful in helping researchers to determine the relative heritability of traits, such as intelligence.

Genetic Studies

The same technology that made the Human Genome Project possible has also opened new doors to researchers studying the origins of intelligence and other traits. Today, researchers are able to collect blood samples from people and then, using DNA analyses, correlate the presence of particular genes in the person's genome (genotype) with their particular levels of traits, such as intelligence (phenotype). In one of the first studies to use this approach, researchers in Scotland were able to show that intelligence is *polygenetic* or based on many genes and that an identified collection of genetic markers accounted for 40% of the variation seen in the participants' crystallized intelligence scores and 51% of the variation seen in participants' fluid intelligence scores (Davies et al., 2011). This study strongly suggests that genetics do influence intelligence. However, notice that the genetic markers they tested did not account for 100% of the variability in intelligence. Therefore, the researchers' data do *not* rule out environmental influences on intelligence.

Twin Studies

Twin studies are another way to answer questions about the relative contributions of nature and nurture to intelligence. Twin studies compare specific traits between pairs of *identical twins* (twins who share 100% of their genetic code) and pairs of nonidentical or *fraternal twins* (twins no more genetically related than other siblings). If identical twins share a similar trait more often than fraternal twins do, then a genetic basis for the trait is implied. If, on the other hand, identical twins are no more similar on a trait than fraternal twins, there is less support for a genetic influence (if the trait were genetic, we would expect the genetically identical twins to be more alike). Other studies compare identical twins raised in different environments to identical twins raised in the same household. Dissimilarities between identical twins reared together and identical twins raised apart would be a powerful argument for environmental influence on the trait being measured. Through such comparisons, psychologists can isolate the influence of nature and nurture on the development of specific traits.

Across a wide variety of such studies, *heritability* estimates (the proportion of variability in a trait accounted for by genetics) have been shown to range from about 0.4 to 0.8 for intelligence (Nisbett et al., 2012). Findings such as these leave little doubt that intelligence is influenced by genetics. But once again, such findings do not negate the importance of environmental factors. For example, one interesting wrinkle is that heritability estimates for intelligence seem to vary from population to population. In particular, intelligence seems to be more heritable in upper socioeconomic status (SES) children and less heritable in lower SES children (for a review, see Nisbett et al., 2012). This suggests that environments associated with lower SES may exert more influence on intelligence, perhaps preventing some children from reaching their full genetic potential.

Environmental Predictors of Intelligence

As we begin to dig into the research examining the environmental and genetic factors that predict levels of intelligence, we feel it is important to caution you about a few things. First, to conduct research on the bases of intelligence, scientists must inevitably compare the intelligence levels of *groups* of people. This means separating people into categories that have meaning in society (e.g., race, gender, income levels, age, education level) and that can be a divisive and emotional process. Some have argued that it is impossible to study the genetic and environmental bases of intelligence in a socially neutral fashion (Roberts, 2015), and the research on the nature-nurture bases of intelligence has been one of the most controversial and emotional debates seen in both the scientific community and in society. So, as you read the following sections, you may find yourself feeling a bit uneasy. We understand, and that leads us to our second caution.

It is crucial that you keep a few things in mind while interpreting the meaning of these studies. When looking at the practical relevance of group differences in intelligence, it is *very* important to note that there is more variability in intelligence *within* groups than there is *between* groups. For example, the range of IQ scores among European Americans or among African Americans is wider than the average difference between these groups. Furthermore, keep in mind that group characteristics do *not* predict individual characteristics. We cannot assume to know an individual's level of IQ (or any other characteristic) based solely on knowing their group membership. For example, knowing that the class average on your last psychology exam was 73 does not mean that you made a 73. You may have scored above or below average. To automatically assume that someone is less intelligent based on their race, age, gender, etc. would be an example of *prejudice*, a topic we will cover in Chapter 10. So, with these cautions in mind, let's take a look at the research.

In 1994, the publication of a book, *The Bell Curve*, brought the debate over the origins of intelligence into the public eye (Herrnstein & Murray, 1994). The title of this book refers to the fact that IQ scores tend to follow a normal distribution, which is shaped like a bell (see Figure 8.5). In *The Bell Curve*, the authors argued that intelligence is primarily encoded in our genes and that environmental influences do little to change it. This extreme position was largely denounced by scholars (Gardner, 1999), but the public became engaged in heated discussions about the merits of this position, as well as the implications of the authors' claims. Of particular concern was the implication that some minority groups may be genetically inferior with respect to intelligence. Though the authors never stated that particular minorities were genetically inferior, this conclusion appeared to follow from their arguments and the data that have been collected on IQ differences across racial groups.

Generally speaking, *average* IQ scores have varied across racial groups in the United States. As a group, Asian Americans tend to outscore European Americans, who in turn tend to outscore African Americans and Hispanic Americans (Dickens & Flynn, 2006; Nisbett, 1995; Nisbett et al., 2012; Rushton, 2012). If we are to believe the message of *The Bell Curve*, the inference would be that these differences exist mostly because of genetic inheritance. Furthermore, some may be tempted to conclude that if these differences are genetically based, then any attempt to raise children's IQ scores by improving their environment would be a waste of time and money. It is this sort of offensive assertion that has kept the debate on race, genetics, and intelligence ignited for decades (Flynn, 2018; Rushton & Jensen, 2005; Winegard, Winegard, & Anomaly, 2020; see also Sternberg, Grigorenko, & Kidd, 2005, for thorough reviews of the research from opposing points of view).

Overall, the results of twin studies (and other studies) on the inheritance of traits in families have not supported the strong nature claims made in *The Bell Curve*. Rather, these studies support an *interactionist* perspective that intelligence seems to stem from both our genes and our environment (Chipuer, Rovine, & Polmin, 1990; Nisbett et al., 2012; Polmin, 1994). Some even argue that newer studies, employing cutting-edge techniques, such as studies of interracial children and molecular genetics, suggest that genetics contribute little to the Black-White

IQ gap (Colman, 2016). Rather it is more likely that environmental and cultural factors are related to the bulk of these group differences (Flynn, 2019). Furthermore, evidence suggests that improving a child's environment is associated with attaining higher IQ scores.

One study (Moore, 1986) showed that African-American middle-schoolers who had been placed in affluent European American families as infants had average IQs that were not only above average for African-American children but also above average for European American children. Nisbett and colleagues (2012) review several studies showing that being adopted into a higher SES family is associated with a 12- to 18-point increase in IQ score. These studies support the notion that the environment in which one grows up contributes significantly to one's IQ. But, exactly what types of environmental influences might be important here?

Compared to European Americans, a disproportionate number of minority group members live in poverty. Poverty or a lack of money by itself is not likely to lead to lower levels of intelligence in children. Rather, it is more likely that the environmental factors that tend to coincide with poverty are predictive of differences in intelligence. But which specific environmental factors are important here? Some researchers have attempted to answer this question.

It's true that compared to richer parents, poorer parents often cannot afford the same toys, computers, electronics, and so on for their children. Yet, some studies indicate that having possessions, such as television, electronics, cell phones, etc. either isn't correlated with the intelligence of one's children, is weakly correlated with their intelligence, or may even be negatively associated with their intelligence (Rindermann & Baumeister, 2015). In other words, it is not just about having money and possessions. A more important factor may be that more affluent parents are better able to provide their children with *educational influences* in the home that enhance cognitive development. For example, research has indicated that parents who use many words, a positive tone of voice, use language that refers to relationships among things and events, ask children what to do rather than telling them what to do, and are verbally more responsive to their children are more likely to raise children with higher levels of intelligence and verbal ability (Hart, Risley, & Kirby, 1997). Furthermore, these educational influences predict the intelligence levels of children far better than simply how much money the parent has (Rindermann & Baumeister, 2015).

So why might more affluent parents be better able to provide such educational influence? Perhaps because the parents are more highly educated themselves and have better linguistic skills, they have more free time to interact with their children, they are less stressed by life circumstances, or some other reason. Research is needed to answer this question. For now, the important message is that having parents who provide high-quality verbal environments for their children is predictive of higher levels of intelligence in children, and poverty is associated with parents providing fewer of these positive influences.

Of course, SES and educational influences in the home are but two of the many environmental factors that could affect intelligence. SES has received the most research attention, in part because it is easy to measure. Other environmental factors that may influence intelligence include exposure to environmental toxins, nutritional differences, influences outside the home, and so on. For example, prenatal exposure to fluoride (Bashash et al., 2011) and phthalates (Li et al., 2019) have been linked to lower IQs in childhood. Having been breastfed in infancy is also associated with developing greater intelligence (Boutwell, Young, & Meldrum, 2018).

Breast milk contains Omega-3 fatty acids. Infants who received Omega-3 supplements or whose mothers' diets were enriched with Omega-3s during pregnancy or breastfeeding showed subsequent increases in IQ (Protzko, Aronson, & Blair, 2013).

Child-rearing practices and formal education also matter. Parents of higher-IQ children tend to be more positive and affirming when interacting with their children (Flynn, 2019). Parents who read with their children in an interactive manner by asking the children questions about what they are reading contribute to IQ increases in their children (Protzko et al., 2013). Having musical training as a child (Schellenberg, 2011) is also related to higher IQ. Perhaps the most predictable finding is that having quality schooling is associated with higher intelligence (Nisbett, 2013). After all, much of our educational system is specifically designed to increase students' intelligence. Unfortunately, not all school environments are equal in quality. Schools located in poorer areas of the United States tend to be funded less than schools in more affluent areas, and lower-income districts tend to have higher-proportions of minority students (Owens, 2018). There is some evidence to suggest that students who attend lower-income schools perform more poorly than students who attend more affluent schools (Reardon, 2016). Furthermore, when lower-income students attend more affluent schools, they tend to have higher levels of achievement (Schwartz, 2012), and giving disadvantaged children access to quality preschool has been shown to increase IQ scores substantially (Protzko et al., 2013).

▲ It is very important to correctly interpret the meaning of group differences in abilities, such as IQ. Group averages tell us *nothing* about individual levels of traits.

In addition to these factors, it is likely that there are other environmental influences on intelligence that have not yet been studied by psychologists. Some of these potential influences, such as societal *prejudices* and cultural *norms* and *attitudes* can be challenging to quantify and measure in scientific studies (see Chapter 10), which is why so many studies have focused on things like SES.

Happily, there is reason to suspect that the general environment may be changing for the better when it comes to intelligence. In the United States, average IQ scores have been rising from generation to generation over much of the 20th century and into the 21st century (Flynn, 2012). On average, the gain is about 3 IQ points per decade (Pietschnig, 2016). Similar trends have also been seen in many other countries (Pietschnig & Voracek, 2015). This effect has been named the *Flynn Effect* in recognition of the person who first documented this trend (Flynn, 1999).

The Flynn effect is not particular to a single societal group. There does not appear to be a gender difference in the Flynn effect (Pietschnig et al., 2011), and non-white racial groups have also shown IQ gains over time. The IQ gap between Black and White students has reduced by more than 5.5 points since the 1970s, suggesting that Blacks are catching up to Whites in terms of educational and intellectual attainment (Flynn, 2018, 2019; Nisbett et al., 2012). Such a change in just a few decades would be hard to explain in terms of genetic differences, leaving the explanation that the narrowing of the IQ gap may be due to environmental factors such as increased access to better educational environments.

Researchers are currently debating the meaning of such IQ score shifts in society. Do they reflect increases in general intelligence, g, or do they simply reflect better development of discrete abilities and skills, in people? Do these gains in average IQ across societal groups show that environment is more important than genetics in determining intelligence (Flynn, 2018; Pietschnig, 2016; Rushton, 2012)? The debate over the origins of intelligence continues (Winegard et al., 2020).

8.5 Quiz Yourself

1. Which psychologist would be most likely to agree with the following statements: "Intelligence is not a single ability. We do not possess intelligence. We possess many intelligences."
   a. Robert Sternberg
   b. Francis Galton
   c. Howard Gardner
   d. Daniel Goleman

2. Gilbert recently developed a new intelligence test that he plans to administer to second-grade children, but when he wrote the questions, he used an adult-level vocabulary. Based on your understanding of intelligence tests, what would you predict the test to be?
   a. Valid and reliable
   b. Unreliable
   c. Invalid
   d. Valid, but not reliable

3. One day, your front door starts squeaking at the hinges. You are out of the spray lubricant that you would normally use for this purpose, so you go to the kitchen and get a bottle of cooking oil. You dab a bit of the cooking oil on the hinge, and the squeak goes away. This best exhibits a high level of _____ intelligence.
   a. analytical
   b. existential
   c. practical
   d. creative

4. On which of Sternberg's types of intelligence would Kim Peek likely have scored highly?
   a. Analytical
   b. Practical
   c. Creative
   d. None of the above

5. Jared is a 14-year-old African-American male. Jonah is a 14-year-old White male. Based on this information, we can assume that _____.
   a. Jared has a lower IQ than Jonah
   b. Jonah and Jared have the same IQ
   c. Jared has higher emotional intelligence than Jonah
   d. None of the above

Answers 1. c; 2. c; 3. d; 4. d; 5. d

8.6 Integrating Psychology: The Big Picture

In this final chapter on the cognitive aspects of psychology, we explored the cognitive processes commonly referred to as *thinking*. Thinking involves the use of *knowledge* to attain our goals. Some of the goals that we strive to attain include solving the *well-structured* and *ill-structured problems* that we face in life, *reasoning, decision making,* making *judgments,* and using *language* to communicate with others. Most of us are able to engage in these cognitive processes, but some of us accomplish them better than others do. For example, although Kim Peek was easily able to memorize large amounts of information, he was not particularly good at reasoning, decision making, or solving ill-structured problems. On the other hand, you might be very skilled at such tasks, perhaps demonstrating high levels of *creativity* or *dialectical reasoning* skills. Or perhaps you are very skilled at expressing your thoughts through language. How well we engage in such cognitive tasks determines to some degree how well we function in life. Possessing well-developed cognitive skills is conducive to exhibiting *intelligence* or adapting to your environment and behaving in a goal-directed manner. Because life challenges us in many different ways, some psychologists have argued that rather than being a single trait, intelligence is best conceptualized as a series of *multiple intelligences* or collections of domain-specific abilities. So while Kim Peek may have demonstrated very high levels of knowledge, he did not score highly on traditional tests of *generalized intelligence* (*g*). Think about your own intelligence. What are your intellectual strengths? What are your weaknesses? Whatever they may be, your own unique levels of intelligence are likely due to an *interaction* between the genes you inherited from your parents and the environments in which you have lived. It is this interplay of *nature* and *nurture* influences that makes you the unique individual you are.

In our next part, we will explore the sociocultural and individual variations in our traits and behaviors that form the third foundation of psychology. In Chapter 9, we will examine how we develop across our lifetimes as a result of nature and nurture influences. In Chapter 10, we will explore how we understand and interact with other people in our environment and how these interactions vary across cultures. And, in Chapter 11, we will look at how psychologists explain and measure personality or our characteristic patterns of behavior across situations. As you read these coming chapters, think about your own unique cognitive abilities, the influences that helped these abilities develop in you, and how these abilities affect your interactions with others and the world.

Studying the Chapter

Key Terms

affective heuristic (341)
algorithm (334)
availability heuristic (340)
babbling (346)
basic level category (329)
cognition (326)
concepts (328)
cooing (346)
creativity (335)
crystallized intelligence (356)
cultural bias (354)
decision making (339)
deductive reasoning (338)
dialectical reasoning or thinking (338)
exemplars (332)
fluid intelligence (356)
formal concepts (330)
functional fixedness (336)
general intelligence (*g*) (355)
genes (361)
genotype (361)
grammar (347)
heuristic (334)
ill-structured problems (334)
incubation (336)
inductive reasoning (338)
insight (334)
intelligence (350)
intelligence quotient (IQ) (351)
interactionism (361)
intuition (334)
judgment (339)
knowledge (326)
language (342)
mental age (350)
mental representations (326)
mental set (336)
morphemes (347)
multiple intelligences (357)
natural concepts (330)
natural selection (361)
nature-nurture debate (360)
overextension (347)
phenotype (361)
phonemes (347)
pragmatics (348)
prototypes (332)
reasoning (337)
reliability (352)
representativeness heuristic (341)
standardized test (351)
subordinate category (329)
superordinate category (329)
telegraphic speech (347)
thinking (326)
triarchic theory of intelligence (358)
underextension (347)
validity (352)
well-structured problems (334)
Whorfian hypothesis or the **linguistic relativity hypothesis** (348)

What Do You Know? Assess Your Understanding

Test your retention and understanding of the material by answering the following questions.

1. ______ is the information we have stored in our long-term memory about the world.
   a. Thinking
   b. Memory
   c. Cognition
   d. Knowledge

2. The idea of what a giraffe is, is an example of a(n) ______.
   a. mental representation
   b. judgment
   c. image
   d. heuristic

3. The available evidence most strongly suggests that we store mental representations of stimuli that are ______ of what we see.
   a. exact visual copies
   b. only verbal descriptions
   c. both verbal descriptions and visual images
   d. only prototypes

4. Given the concepts fish, seafood, catfish, and swordfish, which one represents the basic level category?
   a. Fish
   b. Seafood
   c. Catfish
   d. Swordfish

5. Which of the following is most likely an example of a natural concept?
   a. Furniture
   b. Sofa
   c. Wing-back chair
   d. Housewares

6. Using a formula to calculate the gas mileage on your car is an example of a(n) ______.
   a. algorithm
   b. heuristic
   c. exemplar
   d. judgment

7. Determining the best location for the family vacation is most likely an example of a(n) ______.
   a. well-structured problem
   b. ill-structured problem
   c. judgment
   d. insight

8. Which of the following is *not* an aid to problem solving?
   a. A mental set
   b. Incubation
   c. Creativity
   d. Insight

9. Reasoning that because many larger cars and trucks get poorer gas mileage, a Jeep SUV must get very poor mileage is an example of ______.
   a. inductive reasoning
   b. deductive reasoning
   c. dialectical reasoning
   d. b & c

10. After watching a show about people who became rich and famous after dropping out of college, Mitch overestimates the likelihood of having a successful career after dropping out of college. Mitch's error is most likely due to ______.
    a. the availability heuristic
    b. the representativeness heuristic
    c. framing
    d. poor decision making

11. The English prefix *pro-* is an example of a(n) ______.
    a. phoneme
    b. morpheme
    c. pragmatic
    d. overextension

12. Lamond is 5 months old. At which stage of language development would you most expect Lamond to be?
    a. Cooing
    b. Babbling
    c. One-word speech
    d. Telegraphic speech

13. Who would most agree with the statement "A Spanish-speaking person and an English-speaking person will necessarily have different perceptions of the world"?
    a. Lewis Terman
    b. Noam Chomsky
    c. Benjamin Whorf
    d. Alfred Binet

14. According to the text, which of the following species has not been shown to possibly possess linguistic skills?
    a. Parrots
    b. Horses
    c. Chimpanzees
    d. Dolphins

15. ______ is credited with being the father of the modern intelligence test.
    a. Francis Galton
    b. Alfred Binet
    c. Robert Sternberg
    d. Lewis Terman

16. Six-year-old Tasha scores as well as the average 10-year-old on an intelligence test. Tasha's IQ score is approximately ______.

a. 100
b. 134
c. 167
d. 182

17. David Wechsler did which of the following?

a. He developed the first intelligence test.
b. He moved psychologists away from using the concept of mental age to calculate IQ scores.
c. He introduced the idea that humans possess multiple intelligences as opposed to a general level of intelligence, or *g*.
d. All of the above

18. An intelligence test must be ______ to be of use to psychologists.

a. reliable
b. valid
c. culturally biased
d. a and b

19. As we age, ______ intelligence tends to decline, but ______ intelligence tends to increase.

a. fluid; crystallized
b. crystallized; fluid
c. practical; analytical
d. analytical; practical

20. Your specific level of intelligence is due to your ______.

a. genotype
b. genotype and nurture influences
c. genotype and nature influences
d. nature influences

Answers: 1. d; 2. a; 3. c; 4. a; 5. b; 6. a; 7. b; 8. a; 9. b; 10. a; 11. b; 12. b; 13. c; 14. b; 15. b; 16. c; 17. b; 18. d; 19. a; 20. b.

Use It Or Lose It: Applying Psychology

1. What abilities define our concept of an intelligent person in the United States? What abilities do you think would define the concept of an intelligent person in rural Africa?
2. Make a case for why one would want to use heuristics for solving problems and making decisions and judgments.
3. Give an original example of an ill-structured and a well-structured problem.
4. Describe the stages that children go through as they develop language and give an example of each. If you wanted to raise a child who is bilingual, how do you think you could best accomplish this?
5. Examine the theories of multiple intelligences that you read about in this chapter. Are there any types of intelligence that you feel were overlooked in these theories? Why or why not?

Critical Thinking about the Science of Psychology

In section 8.1.1, you learned about Stephen Kosslyn and colleagues' visual imagery study in which participants memorized a map and then mentally scanned from point to point on the map. Answer the following questions about this study.

1. What is the independent variable in this study?
2. What is the dependent variable in this study?
3. What is the hypothesis that is being tested in this study?
4. Is this an ethical study? Defend your answer.

Are You Getting the Big Picture?

iStock.com/RossHelen

Cognition is the way in which we store and use information.

8.1 Thinking: How We Use What We Know

- Our **knowledge** comprises the mental representations of the world that we have stored in long-term memory.
- **Thinking** is the use of knowledge to accomplish a goal.
- Visual images are powerful **mental representations** that allow us to remember a person's face or a map.
- **Concepts** are mental categories that contain related bits of knowledge and are organized around the meaning of the information they represent.
- We tend to organize our knowledge into three levels of categorization: the general, broad **superordinate category**; the **basic level category**; and the **subordinate category**, which is the most specific.

RTimages/Alamy stock photo

Ann Pics/Shutterstock.com

Charles Mistral/Alamy stock photo

- We acquire **formal concepts** as we learn the rigid rules that define certain categories of things, but **natural concepts** develop naturally as we live our lives and experience the world.
- A **prototype** is our concept of the most typical member of a category—in essence, a summary of all members of that category.
- **Exemplars** are stored representations of actual category members we have experienced.

8.2 Problem Solving: Putting Our Thinking to Good Use

- An **algorithm** is a method of solving a **well-structured problem** that always leads to the correct solution. A **heuristic** is a shortcut, or rule of thumb, that may or may not lead to the solution of a problem. **Ill-structured problems** must be solved with heuristics.
- **Insight**, **creativity**, and **incubation** help us overcome common obstacles to problem solving like **functional fixedness** and **mental sets**.

James D. Morgan/Getty Images

8.3 Reasoning, Decision Making, and Judgment

Milkovasa/Shutterstock.com

- We engage in **reasoning** when we draw conclusions that are based on certain assumptions about the world. **Deductive reasoning** involves reasoning from the general to the specific, whereas **inductive reasoning** involves reasoning from the specific to the general. **Dialectical reasoning or thinking** is a type of reasoning in which contradictions are reconciled or accepted.
- **Decision making** involves choosing among several alternatives and is often part of the problem-solving process.
- Framing, or how possible courses of action are presented, can affect our decisions.
- Three mental shortcuts that can be useful but that can also lead to mistakes are the **availability, affective,** and **representativeness heuristics**.

8.4 Language: Communication, Thought, and Culture

Masterfile

- Human **language** is a well-developed, syntactical, verbal system for representing the world.
- *Biolinguistic theories* argue that humans have evolved linguistic abilities. One such theory states that humans are born with an innate language acquisition device (LAD), or a programmed capacity for language. *Usage-based* theories argue that rather than being innate, language develops out of our social interactions and the exercise of general cognitive abilities.
- Research indicates that infants generally proceed from **cooing** to **babbling** to **morphemes** on their road to language skills. By age 2, most children exhibit **telegraphic speech**. Soon after, children learn the rules of **grammar** and **pragmatics** for their language.
- One theory, known as the **Whorfian hypothesis** or the **linguistic relativity hypothesis**, suggests that one's language actually determines one's thoughts and perceptions of the world. A more widely held view is that language *influences*, rather than determines, our thoughts.
- Although animals communicate, it is hotly debated whether they have the capacity for language.

8.5 Defining and Measuring Intelligence

- Many modern psychologists broadly view **intelligence** as those abilities that allow you to adapt to your environment and behave in a goal-oriented way.
- Alfred Binet established the measurement of **mental age** that reflected a child's mental abilities compared to those of the "average" child at a specific age.
- Stanford psychologist Lewis Terman revised Binet's testing procedures and introduced the **intelligence quotient**, or **IQ**, which is a score obtained by dividing one's mental age by one's chronological age.
- The adult version of David Wechsler's test (WAIS-IV) yields several separate index scores and an overall score.
- Intelligence tests are frequently criticized for having a **cultural bias**. Tests that rely less on language, such as Raven's Progressive Matrices, may be less culturally biased.
- The idea of mental ability as a single unitary factor is known as **general intelligence**, or *g*.
- **Crystallized intelligence** refers to our accumulation of knowledge, whereas **fluid intelligence** refers to the speed and efficiency with which we learn new information and solve problems.
- Some theorists argue that we have **multiple intelligences**. Examples are Robert Sternberg's **triarchic theory of intelligence** and Howard Gardner's theory of multiple intelligences.
- Daniel Goleman's theory of emotional intelligence argues that emotions are also an important component of successful living.
- Although a heated debate continues over whether intelligence is inherited, most research suggests that an interaction of heredity (**nature**) and environment (**nurture**) contributes to our intellectual capabilities.
- Over the last century, average IQ scores have increased—a phenomenon called the *Flynn effect*.

Part 3

Foundations in Developmental and Social Psychology

The two previous parts included chapters that focused on specific psychological processes such as neuroscience, consciousness, learning, and memory. This third part expands on these topics by illustrating how a person's behavior is better understood by evaluating individual variability and the sociocultural environment. This part includes three chapters: human development, social psychology, and personality. **Development** consists of changes in our behavior and abilities over our lifetime. **Social psychology** examines how we think and behave in the company of others. **Personality** is our unique collection of attitudes, emotions, thoughts, habits, impulses, and behaviors that define how we behave across situations. The Part 3 case study powerfully illustrates these mutually influential forces. It is the life story of Hongyong Baek, as told by her granddaughter, Helie Lee, in *Still Life with Rice* (1996). As you read about the challenges she faced, think about how her development, personality, and social environment may have influenced her behavior, as sometimes it is easier to see these patterns and influences in others than it is in ourselves. Then examine how these same areas may be influencing your own behavior. At the same time, consider and imagine what challenges may still be ahead of you.

THE BIG PICTURE

THE CHANGES AND CHALLENGES OF LIFE

Hongyong Baek was born in Korea in 1912, the second of four children and the first daughter of wealthy parents. She was strong and willful and curious to conquer life, behaviors that were not in line with acceptable gender roles for Korean females at that time. So, as was the custom for Korean girls, at the age of 9, Hongyong began daily lessons in virtue, womanhood, and managing a household. She preferred the household lessons as they were "something I could touch, see, and use freely," but her headstrong temperament often incurred her mother's wrath and discipline. She understood obedience, but the idea of chastity was difficult to grasp. For example, when her mother told her to protect her "private parts," she thought her mother meant her knees, because she was constantly being told to keep her knees covered. At age 12 when she started to menstruate, her mother told her it was a woman's curse. Ashamed, she hid in her room fearing that everyone would know.

Unwed at 22, Hongyong feared she was too plain and clumsy to marry. She prayed to Buddha for a husband; without one she was considered a burden on her family. A marriage was arranged, to 19-year-old Dukpil Lee. Hongyong now belonged to another man's family. To her surprise, Hongyong's husband encouraged her to share her ideas and opinions, and her affection for him grew. She gave birth to a boy, Yongwoon, fulfilling her most important wifely duty by giving her husband a son. Over the next 15 years, Hongyong bore four more children, two daughters and two sons.

In 1939, as Hongyong gloried in the role of wife and mother, civil unrest in her country, long occupied by the Japanese, grew. Not wanting to lose their Korean heritage, the Lee family went to China, leaving behind all that was familiar. At Hongyong's suggestion, they started a sesame oil business. The business prospered, but Hongyong grew bored. Against her husband's wishes (which at that time and place was considered uncommon for a wife), she began to smuggle opium. Soon they had more money than they could spend. However, her husband spent more time away from her and had affairs with other women. Hongyong's insecurities about her appearance resurfaced. To keep her husband's attention, they opened a restaurant to entertain the most prominent and powerful people in China.

© Terace Greene

▲ Helie Lee recounts the eventful life of her Korean grandmother, Hongyong Baek, in her memoir, *Still Life with Rice.*

In her 30s, Hongyong was plagued with health problems. She discovered the ancient art of *ch'iryo,* a healing technique in which the flesh is pinched and slapped in order to improve blood circulation. Hongyong used ch'iryo to improve her health and treated herself and her children daily.

In 1945, Americans dropped the atomic bombs on Japan, and the Japanese surrendered Korea. Thousands of Koreans boarded trains for their homeland, the Lee family among them. The Lee family returned to North Korea, which was quickly occupied by Korean communists. Most of the family's land and money were confiscated. As her husband turned to alcohol, Hongyong converted to Christianity and developed a thirst for religious knowledge. She questioned her reason for living, learned how to read and write, and gave away what little riches they had left.

In 1950, the Korean War erupted at the 38th parallel. Because of her religion, Hongyong was imprisoned for "treasonous" activities. She spent 30 days in an overcrowded prison cell. Her daughter Dukwah dodged bombs and gunfire to bring her baby sister Dukhae to be breastfed by Hongyong every day. Once she was released, Hongyong knew her family would not be safe unless they went to South Korea.

Hongyong watched her husband leave for South Korea, and then she bid farewell to her eldest son. Unable to bear the waiting, Hongyong packed up her children to cross the Taedong River. Thousands of other refugees had the same idea. During the crossing, Hongyong and her baby were trampled. Once across, Hongyong prepared to bury her baby. Miraculously, Dukhae was still breathing, although barely. With frozen feet, empty bellies, and little energy, the family continued to walk, hoping to find shelter and peace. At one point, Hongyong was so exhausted that she wanted to leave Dukhae under a tree to die. Because the baby was practically dead, Hongyong thought to sacrifice her in hopes that the rest of the family would survive. But Dukwah refused to leave her sister, and the two women took turns carrying her.

Amid exploding bombs, throngs of people, and piles of wreckage, the Lee family made it to Seoul, 2 weeks before the South Korean borders closed. Hongyong found her husband in a refugee camp, but her eldest son, Yongwoon, never appeared. The agony was too much for Hongyong. For 8 months, she was a living ghost, ignoring her husband and children, forgetting to pray. She sat on a crate all day, staring into space, barely eating or sleeping. Her husband took care of the children and made money by selling gum and cigarettes. Finally, Hongyong's two sisters found her and took in the entire family.

Just as their lives were returning to some sort of normalcy, Hongyong's husband contracted diphtheria and quickly died. Hongyong vowed to find her way back to God. Just shy of 40 years old, she was now a widow. For the first time in her life she would have to make decisions on her own without anyone's approval. She again questioned her purpose in life and turned back to her ch'iryo. As her patients' health improved, more clients came looking for her services. Her hands could not keep up with the demand, so she developed an internship program to train other women in the art of ch'iryo.

As Hongyong's practice expanded, her children grew, went to college, married, and had children. She enjoyed being a grandmother and doted on her grandchildren with affection. As her 60th birthday approached, Hongyong waved good-bye to her daughter and granddaughters, who emigrated to the United States. Eight years later, Hongyong left Korea and emigrated to America herself, but she never stopped searching for her eldest son. After 40 years, she finally received news. He was alive! He had been caught behind the lines in North Korea. At 80 years of age, Hongyong finally achieved peace of mind.

Hongyong's story illustrates the sometimes dramatic turning points that shape our behavior. A multitude of forces help or hinder our development: the love or ridicule of others, our ability to deal with death, our quest to find personal meaning in our lives, to name just a few. Every person is also influenced by a multitude of social environments: family, school, friends, neighborhoods, religion, and culture. Hongyong followed the prescribed social roles for her time and for her culture. Her parents arranged her marriage. As a female, her role was to be a good wife and mother. Yet, Hongyong's natural curiosity and strong personality violated cultural expectations of how a female should behave. Fortunately, her husband accepted her despite her willfulness, allowing Hongyong to explore her talents as an entrepreneur through the sesame oil business, as an opium madam, and as a restaurant owner.

Consider how learning about development, social psychology, and personality will help you appreciate the sociocultural forces and individual experiences that make each person unique—just as Hongyong's journey makes her tale one of a kind. We hope this understanding will lead to a deeper appreciation of why you behave the way you do and to more productive and enjoyable interactions with the people around you. ■

Learning Objectives

9.1 Explain the nature-nurture issue and how it leads to diversity in behavior. (APA 1.2, 2.1)

9.1 Identify and describe the three stages of prenatal development, and explain the importance of a positive prenatal environment. (APA 1.1, 1.3, 2.2, 5.1)

9.2 & 9.5 Describe major physical changes across the life span and how they impact cognitive and psychosocial development. (APA 1.1, 1.3, 5.1)

9.3 Describe infant perceptual abilities and explain how they relate to cognitive development. (APA 1.1, 1.3)

9.3 Compare and contrast Piaget's and Vygotsky's theories of cognitive development, and apply these theories to children's behavior. (APA 1.1, 1.2, 2.1, 2.5, 5.1)

9.3 Compare and contrast Kohlberg's and Gilligan's theories of moral reasoning, and apply these theories to moral decisions. (APA 1.1, 1.2, 2.1, 2.5)

9.4 Define temperament, and distinguish among the three infant temperamental styles. (APA 1.1)

9.4 Describe behaviors that indicate that an attachment has been formed, and distinguish among different attachment patterns. (APA 1.1, 1.3, 2.1, 2.4, 2.5, 5.1)

9.4 & 9.7 Describe the parenting styles that Baumrind researched, and explain the new roles and responsibilities of being a parent. (APA 1.1, 1.3, 2.1, 2.2, 4.1)

9.4 & 9.7 Detail Erikson's theory of psychosocial development, and indicate the possible positive and negative outcomes at each stage. (APA 1.1. 1.2)

9.4 Explain gender-schema theory, and describe how nature and nurture influence gender-role behavior and gender identity. (APA 1.1, 1.2, 1.3, 5.1)

9.6 Compare and contrast formal operations and postformal thought in adolescence and adulthood. (APA 1.1, 1.2)

9.6 Describe changes in mental abilities in adulthood. (APA 1.1, 1.3, 2.2, 4.1)

9.7 Define and describe the transitional phase of development called emerging adulthood. (APA 1.1, 2.5)

9.7 Describe the varieties of social relations in adolescence and adulthood. (APA 1.1, 1.3, 2.2, 2.5, 4.1)

9.7 Explain the predictable changes people experience in career development. (APA 1.1, 1.3)

9.8 Describe and apply the emotional reactions that characterize dying people, according to Kübler-Ross' research. (APA 1.1, 1.2, 1.3, 5.1)

9.8 Describe and apply the three phases of grief. (APA 1.1, 1.3)

Masterfile

9 Human Development

This chapter outlines the processes of development. **Development** consists of changes in behavior and abilities over our lifetime. As we saw in the opening story in Part 3 about Hongyong Baek, and may understand from our own experiences, human development is complicated. Physical changes are occurring along with emotional, social, and mental (or cognitive) development. At the same time, social forces (such as people around us) and our environment also influence these processes. We hope that by understanding the physical, cognitive, and social aspects of development, you will be able to appreciate the many forces that make each child, teenager, and adult unique. ■

Chapter Outline

development changes in behavior or abilities or both

nature-nurture issue the degree to which biology (nature) or the environment (nurture) contributes to a person's development

9.1 Human Development: How Does It All Begin?

Psychologists study development in order to understand the changes that humans experience from conception to the end of life. Because development covers such a long time span, developmental psychologists typically specialize by limiting their investigations to a particular stage of life, such as infancy, childhood, adolescence, or adulthood. Within any one of these age stages, psychologists may focus on different aspects of development: physical, mental, social, or personality development. One developmental psychologist may study how language develops in infants while another may research how peer pressure influences drug use in adolescents.

Recall from Chapter 1 that psychology seeks to *describe, predict, explain,* and *control* behavior. If psychologists can accomplish these goals, then we can promote healthy development and prevent or alter maladaptive patterns of development. For example, if we understand how children think, we can then create appropriate educational environments, thus maximizing each child's potential. Understanding the dynamics of peer pressure during adolescence may suggest strategies to reduce drug use, delinquency, and teen pregnancy. Stories like Hongyong's illustrate the importance of understanding more fully how experiences such as war, imprisonment, or alcoholism influence people's development. Knowing about developmental processes, therefore, has numerous real-world applications. However, as we'll read about next, explaining developmental changes is not easy. Part of the difficulty is that some but not all of human development is predictable, and it is the combinations of life events that add to the complexity and uniqueness of each person's story.

9.1.1 Nature-Nurture Revisited: How Biology and Culture Lead to Diversity

Think about all the variables that can potentially influence how a person grows and changes. In addition to a unique biological foundation (genetics), every person is also influenced by a multitude of environments: family, school, friends, neighborhoods, religion, and culture. The potential contribution of these biological and environmental factors to development has become a central issue for developmental psychologists. Recall from Chapter 8 that this is referred to as the **nature-nurture issue** or debate. Psychologists are interested in how much one's biology, or *nature*, contributes to a person's development versus how much one's environment and culture, or *nurture*, influence this process.

Genes—or *nature*—influence almost every aspect of development, from personality and physical development to cognitive processes such as language development and intelligence (Bouchard, 2004; Davis, Haworth, & Plomin, 2009; Gottlieb, Wahlsten, & Lickliter, 1998). *Nurture* is the total effect of all the environmental events and circumstances that influence your development. It includes your family, friends, how others perceive and behave toward you, events that happen to you, television programs that you watch, music that you listen to, the customs and rituals of your ethnic background, your gender, your culture, your schooling, and so on.

Recall that it is not really a case of nature *or* nurture. Rather, it is the *interaction* of these two forces that influences behavior. Genes may moderate the influence of environmental forces; likewise, gene expressions may be altered by the environment (Avinun, 2020; Champagne, 2010; Champagne & Mashoodh, 2009; Eagly & Wood, 2013; Tucker-Drob, Briley, & Harden, 2013). As you read about the various types of development that we experience, keep this nature-nurture issue in mind, as the influences of nature and nurture interact in a complex fashion.

9.1.2 Prenatal Development

From the outside, all we see is a woman with a swollen belly who walks with a waddle. We may even have the opportunity to see or feel movement occurring inside her belly. Any woman who has been pregnant has experienced having some people want to touch her stomach or to treat her more delicately because of her "condition." Both tendencies speak to our fascination with the developments going on inside.

All the genetic material for development is inherited from your biological parents at the time of conception. The male sperm cell, containing 23 single chromosomes, fertilizes the female ovum, also containing 23 single chromosomes, to create a fertilized egg, called a **zygote** that has 23 pairs of chromosomes. Over the next 38 to 40 weeks, the average gestation period for a human, the zygote will experience dramatic changes as it evolves. So many changes occur during this time that scientists divide the prenatal period into three stages: the *germinal* or *zygotic stage*, the *embryonic stage*, and the *fetal stage*.

The first 14 days after conception are the **germinal stage** of development. The major characteristic of this stage is cell division. Following conception, the zygote starts to replicate itself and divide. This process ensures that all the cells of the organism contain the same genetic material. The zygote divides into 2 cells, which then replicate and divide again, creating a 4-cell organism. The cells continue replicating and dividing, and around the 5th day after conception the zygote has become a 100-cell organism, called a *blastocyst*. During this process of cell division, the mass of cells also travels down the fallopian tube to the uterus. On approximately the 9th day after conception, the blastocyst implants itself in the lining of the uterine wall. Cell division continues through the 2nd week.

The **embryonic stage** covers development of the organism, now called an *embryo*, from the 3rd through the 8th week. After the blastocyst attaches to the uterine wall, its outside cells develop into the support structures: the *placenta*, *umbilical cord*, and *amniotic sac*. The inner cells become the embryo.

The major characteristic of the embryonic period is the formation and development of the major organs and systems. Cells start to specialize into bone, muscle, and body organs. All the major biological systems—the cardiovascular system, the digestive system, the skeletal system, the excretory system, the respiratory system, and the nervous system—are forming. Given the importance of these systems for survival and well-being, the embryonic stage is perhaps the most precarious stage of prenatal development. Most miscarriages occur and genetic defects surface during this stage. The embryo's development may also be harmed by outside environmental factors, producing devastating effects. We will return to these topics in a moment.

By the end of the embryonic stage, all basic bodily structures and systems have formed. About 4 weeks after conception, the heart is beating, the spinal cord is forming, the liver is producing red blood cells, and ovaries or testes have formed (but the embryo's sex is not apparent by ultrasound until between 12 and 18 weeks). Although only an inch long, the embryo already looks human. Facial features, such as the eyes, lips, nose, and jaw, have taken shape. Short stubs represent arms and legs, and the beginnings of fingers and toes are apparent.

The third prenatal development period, the **fetal stage**, begins the 9th week after conception. From now until birth, the organism is referred to as a *fetus*. The major characteristic of the fetal stage is continued growth and maturation. The fetus grows larger and starts to move. By 14 weeks, the fetus can kick, open its mouth, swallow, and turn its head. Its lungs and external sex organs have

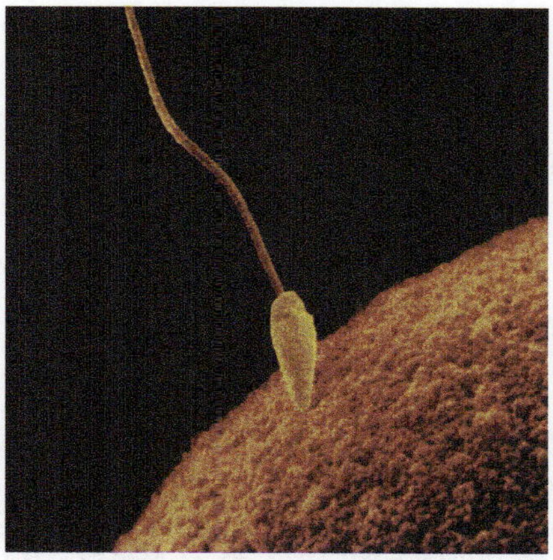

Don W. Fawcett/Science Source

▲ Human sperm and egg at the moment of penetration. The sperm cell fertilizes the female ovum to create a zygote.

zygote [ZIE-goat] a fertilized egg

germinal stage the first stage of prenatal development, from conception to 14 days

embryonic [em-bree-AH-nik] stage the second stage of prenatal development, lasting from the 3rd through the 8th week

fetal stage the third stage of prenatal development, from the 9th week through the 9th month

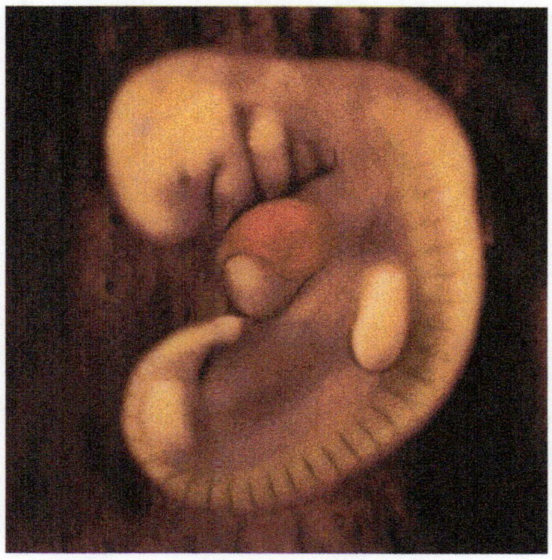

Anatomical Travelogue/Science Source

▲ Micro-MRI, reconstructed with 3-D imagery, actual size of embryo 4.0 mm. The image depicts a human embryo during its 4th week of development. Age is calculated from the day of fertilization. In this image, the fusing tubes of the heart are highlighted in red. Early growth of the cardiovascular system begins during the 3rd week, when blood vessels form, and continues into the following weeks of development. Image from the book *From Conception to Birth: A Life Unfolds.*

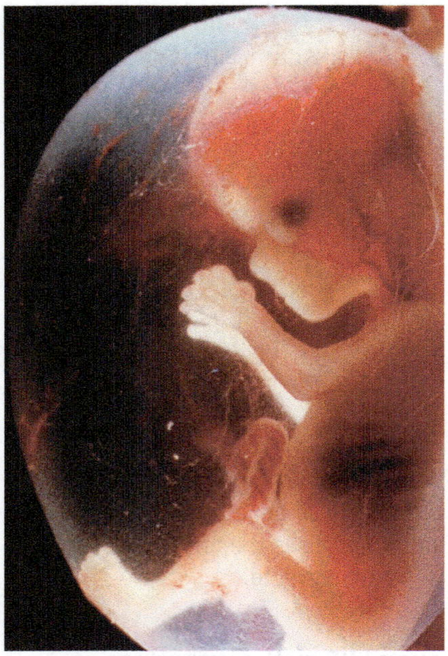

Claude Edelmann/Science Source

▲ At 14 weeks, the fetus's lungs and external sex organs have developed.

developed. By the end of the 6th month (24 weeks), the organs are sufficiently formed that the fetus has reached *viability*—the possibility of surviving outside the womb (but only in a neonatal intensive care unit). During the last 3 months, the fetus is responsive to sound, light, and touch.

From the union of a single sperm cell and egg, the fetus has undergone significant and complex changes over the course of 40 weeks. However, not all zygotes experience these changes. About half of all fertilized eggs die and are miscarried, usually before the woman knows she is pregnant. Of pregnancies that the female knows about (because of a missed menstrual cycle), approximately 15% to 20% end in miscarriage (American College of Obstetricians and Gynecologists, 2002).

9.1.3 Application: The Importance of a Positive Prenatal Environment

The support structures of the intrauterine environment are designed to protect the developing organism. However, internal and external forces can still interfere with this natural defense system and cause birth defects.

When internal chromosomal abnormalities are present at conception, their effects typically arise during the embryonic stage. For example, **Down syndrome** results from an extra 21st chromosome. Babies with Down syndrome are characterized by distinct facial features (such as almond-shaped eyes or a flat nose) and are more likely to experience heart defects and varying degrees of intellectual disability. Medical tests can identify the presence of Down syndrome and other inherited genetic disorders so that couples can discuss their options (Rappaport, 2008). This possibility highlights the importance of regular prenatal consultations with a physician.

Birth defects may also be caused by outside environmental forces. Any environmental agent that has the potential to harm the embryo is referred to as a **teratogen**. It may be a drug that the mother takes, such as cocaine or alcohol; a disease, such as German measles (rubella); or chemicals that the mother inhales, such as certain cleaning fluids. All these substances have the potential to cause birth defects. The critical factor seems to be *when* the mother is exposed to these agents. These **sensitive periods** emphasize the complex interplay of nature and nurture on development. Certain organs and systems are more vulnerable to the effects of teratogens during particular stages of prenatal development (● FIGURE 9.1). Notice from Figure 9.1 that the most severe effects are most likely to occur during the embryonic stage of development. Because a woman usually does not discover that she is pregnant until the embryo is already formed and developing, she may unknowingly expose the embryo to harm.

Women who use any type of drug during pregnancy can potentially influence prenatal development. Women who smoke during pregnancy reduce the flow of oxygen to the fetus; their babies tend to be irritable, have respiratory problems, and have lower birth weight (Banderali et al., 2015; Lester, Andreozzi, & Appiah, 2004; Shea & Steiner, 2008). Maternal consumption of alcohol during pregnancy puts the fetus at risk for *fetal alcohol spectrum disorder (FASD)* and includes the severe disorder called **fetal alcohol syndrome (FAS)**. Children with FAS tend to have low birth weight, brain abnormalities, and lowered intellectual functioning, and tend to exhibit limb, head, and facial deformities (Dalen et al., 2009; Drew & Kane, 2014; Ikonomidou et al., 2000; Ornoy & Ergaz, 2010).

Illegal drugs also produce damaging effects. If the mother is a heroin addict, the baby will be born addicted and have to undergo withdrawal. Crack or cocaine babies are often born premature, underweight, and irritable, and tend to have poor feeding habits (Frank et al., 2002; Gouin, Murphy, & Shaw, 2011).

Down syndrome a genetic birth disorder resulting from an extra 21st chromosome, characterized by distinct facial features and a greater likelihood of heart defects and intellectual disability

teratogen [tur-RAH-tuh-jun] an environmental substance that has the potential to harm the developing organism

sensitive periods in prenatal development, times when genetic and environmental agents are most likely to cause birth defects

fetal alcohol syndrome (FAS) a birth condition resulting from the mother's chronic use of alcohol during pregnancy, characterized by facial and limb deformities and intellectual disability

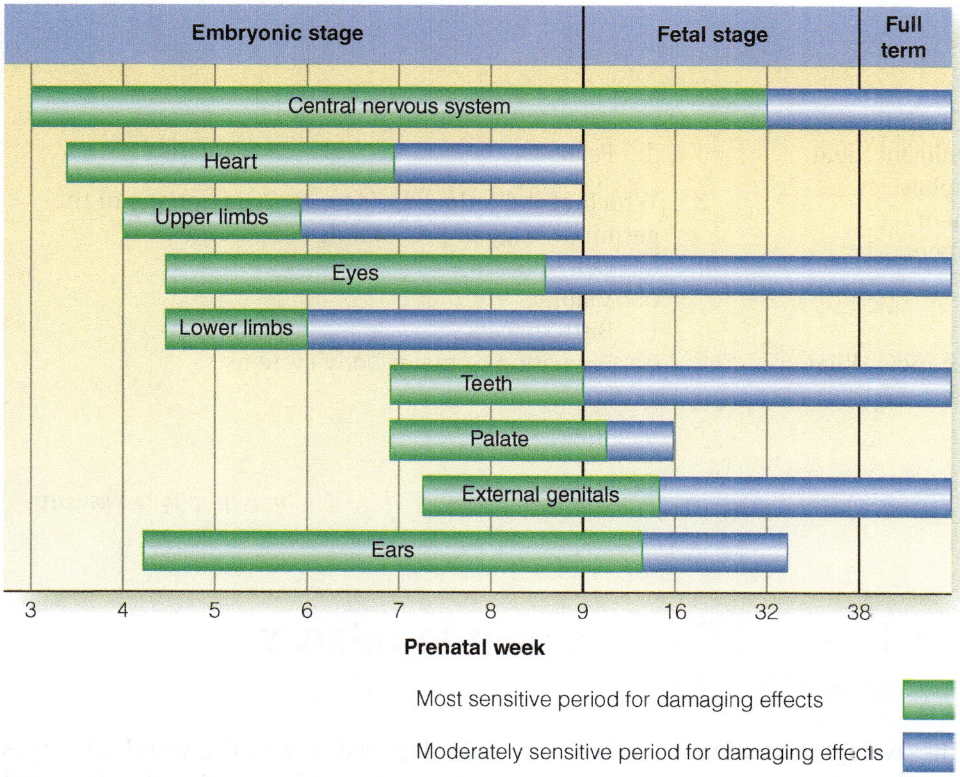

FIGURE 9.1

Sensitive Periods and Prenatal Development

The darker bars indicate the most sensitive period for certain organs and structures; the lighter bars indicate lessened vulnerability. Sensitivity is greatest during the embryonic period, although some structures remain vulnerable throughout the prenatal period.

Source: Adapted from K. L. Moore and T. V. N. Persaud, *Before We Are Born: Essentials of Embryology and Birth Defects*. Philadelphia: Saunders. Copyright © 1998 Elsevier Science (USA).

Prenatal exposure to teratogens may also have long-term effects. Children exposed to the previously mentioned drugs during pregnancy tend to be more impulsive, less adaptable, and evidence more behavioral problems later in life than children not exposed to these drugs during pregnancy (Espy, Riese, & Francis, 1997; Morie, Crowley, Mayes, & Potenza, 2019; Richardson et al., 2011). There is also increasing evidence that maternal stress and anxiety during pregnancy may influence the offspring's development. High levels of maternal stress hormones during pregnancy increase the risk of preterm birth and autism spectrum disorder symptoms among males, and are associated in childhood with higher blood pressure, behavioral and emotional problems, and a higher risk of obesity (Christian, 2015; Coussons-Read, 2012; Harris & Seckl, 2011; Ram et al., 2019; Reynolds, 2013; Rinaudo & Wang, 2012). Fetal exposure to abnormal lipid (fat) levels may also contribute negatively to children's psychological health (Manczak & Gotlib, 2019).

Prescription and over-the-counter (OTC) medicines may also influence fetal development. Read the warning labels on any OTC medication and you will see that pregnant and nursing women are cautioned to seek a doctor's advice before using any medicine. Much of what the mother takes in during pregnancy or breastfeeding can be transmitted to the fetus or baby. Proper nutrition and a healthy lifestyle are paramount for a pregnant woman. They increase the chances of producing a healthy newborn who is better prepared to face the developmental and life challenges ahead. These challenges include the enormous changes that occur in infancy and childhood—our next topic of discussion.

9.1 Quiz Yourself

1. Dr. Newhart is investigating if mental stimulation in infancy can impact childhood intelligence and behavior. Dr. Newhart's research emphasizes ______.
   a. nature's influence on development
   b. nurture's influence on development
   c. the influence of teratogens
   d. viability and development
2. Loretta is in her 5th month of pregnancy. What stage of development is the organism in?
   a. Germinal
   b. Zygote
   c. Embryonic
   d. Fetal
3. Which of the following is ***most*** characteristic of the germinal stage of prenatal development?
   a. Cell division
   b. Viability
   c. Birth defects
   d. Formation of major body systems

Answers 1. b; 2. d; 3. a

9.2 Physical Development in Infancy and Childhood

neonate a newborn during the first 28 days of life

The average **neonate**, or newborn up to 28 days old, enters the world 20 inches long, weighing 7 pounds. One year later, the average infant is 29 inches long and will have tripled in weight, emphasizing how rapidly babies grow during infancy. Physical growth and developmental changes result from the complex interaction of the forces of nature and nurture. Our genes lay the foundation for how tall we grow and how our body fat is distributed. The environmental factors of nutrition, health care, and lifestyle also influence our height and build. A similar interplay of nature and nurture is seen in brain and motor development.

9.2.1 Brain Development

What is your very first childhood memory? How old were you then? Most people do not recall events in infancy or before 3 years old. This lack of memory may be related to the development of the nervous system. At birth, an infant's brain has billions of neurons, but the connections between the neurons are very limited, and myelin (see Chapter 2) is incomplete. Experience and learning mix with heredity to shape brain development. Neural pathways grow rapidly. A 2-month-old has very few neural connections compared to the billions a 2-year-old has. More experience plus increased activity equals more neural connections.

During childhood and early adolescence, the brain prunes and discards unnecessary connections, reducing the total number of synapses (Cook & Cook, 2005; Thompson et al., 2000). Those connections that are used repeatedly become permanent, whereas those that are used infrequently or not at all are unlikely to survive (National Scientific Council on the Developing Child [NSCDC], 2007). This discovery has altered researchers' thinking on infant care and early education. Providing stimulating age-appropriate activities fosters and strengthens brain development. Impoverished environments weaken neural connections—fewer connections are made, and unexercised connections are likely to be discarded.

A young child's brain is highly *plastic,* or changeable, and very dense with neurons when compared to adults' brains. If a certain area of the brain is damaged in infancy, other areas of the brain can compensate by reorganizing neural connections (Xiong, Mahmood, & Chopp, 2010). As children age, the brain is less able to change and adapt because neural connections have already been formed, and in some cases discarded, although some plasticity remains throughout adulthood (Huttenlocher, 2002; Kelsch, Sim, & Lois, 2010). The plasticity and density of the brain ensure a child's best chance of adapting to their environment. This adaptation is also evident in the development of children's motor skills.

9.2.2 Reflexes and Motor Development

Infants are born relatively helpless creatures. They cannot feed themselves and are unable to walk. Infants do have certain sensory abilities, a good set of lungs that enable them to cry, and a set of *reflexes*, all of which biologically prepare them to get the help they need to survive.

A **reflex** is an *automatic* response to a particular stimulus. Reflexes enable infants to learn about their environment, thus establishing important neural connections for *voluntary* motor behaviors. Hence, reflexes serve as the foundation for behaviors such as walking, eating, crying, smiling, and grasping. For example, infants are born with a *sucking reflex*. They will automatically suck on any object that touches their lips. Infants also have a *rooting reflex*. When you touch the side of infants' cheeks, they will turn in that direction and open their mouth. These two reflexes teach infants how to use their mouths to get food. Infants are also born with a *grasping reflex*. When an object is placed on their palm, they will automatically grasp it. The grasping reflex is the foundation of *prehension*, when infants learn to handle items with their hands. Their brains and bodies learn, through grasping, the necessary skills that will later be used to write with a pen, play a musical instrument, tie their shoes, or give a parent a hug.

reflex an automatic response to a specific environmental stimulus

gross motor skills motor behaviors involving the large muscles of the body

Infants are also biologically prepared to communicate, despite lacking formal language skills. A *crying reflex*—automatically crying when distressed—alerts the caretaker to the infant's needs. In a matter of weeks, the baby learns to use crying to get the caretaker's attention. Luckily, infants are also born with a *smiling reflex* to use when they are pleased (which also serves as positive reinforcement for their caregivers). This reflex evolves into a *social smile* during the second month of life, when the infant smiles at everybody. Infants' smiles then become more discriminating; by 6 months of age, they reserve their smiles for familiar voices and faces.

Reflexes also initiate *locomotive* ability, or the ability to move around. *Crawling* and *stepping reflexes* prepare the brain and body for motions involved in pulling oneself up, crawling, and walking. These abilities develop in much the same sequence for all infants around the world, evidence of our genetic heritage. However, cross-cultural research suggests that child-rearing practices and variations in the environment may speed up or slow down this process (Keller, 2017). For example, despite living in poverty and poor sanitary conditions, Ugandan infants sit independently on average at 4 months compared to 6 months for U.S. infants. This advantage is lost when Ugandan infants are raised in Western culture—evidence of a nurture influence (Adolph, Karasik, & Tamis-Lemonda, 2009).

By age 2, most infants are walking, running, and getting into everything. However, motor development, the changes in a child's body activities, does not end there. As children age, *gross motor skills* become more proficient. **Gross motor skills** refer to behaviors that involve large muscle groups such as the biceps or quadriceps. These include running, walking, jumping, and hopping. This proficiency is apparent when you watch a toddler, a preschooler, and an 8-year-old run. The toddler waddles and is unsteady on their feet. The preschooler is more coordinated compared to the toddler, but less fluid and not as fast as the 8-year-old.

fine motor skills motor behaviors involving the small muscles of the body

Similar changes occur in **fine motor skills**, which involve small muscle groups. Fine motor skills include such activities as writing, using utensils, and playing a musical instrument. Toddlers and preschoolers are less adept at tasks involving fine motor skills, but as the school years approach, children become much more proficient. ● TABLE 9.1 shows average age ranges for specific gross and fine motor skills achieved in infancy and early childhood in the United States. Notice that the achievement of a particular task lays the foundation for attaining the subsequent, more difficult, task. In other words, babies must be able to sit up before they can crawl. Children must walk before they learn to jump rope.

Enormous changes occur in physical development through the infancy and childhood years. The same magnitude of change characterizes cognitive development, or how children think, which we'll turn to next.

TABLE 9.1 Motor Milestones in Infancy and Early Childhood

Age	Photo	Milestones
3 mos	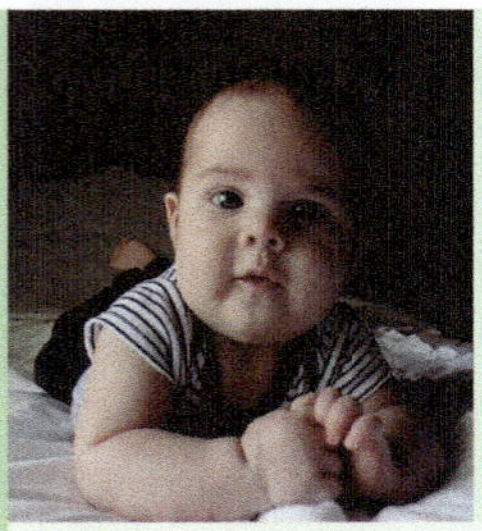 Carmen Compton	• Lifts head and chest when lying on stomach • Grasps rattle • Waves arms • Kicks legs
6 mos		• Reaches for and grasps objects • Helps hold a bottle • Shakes a rattle • Sits with little support • Rolls over
1 yr	 Monkey Business Images/Shutterstock.com	• Sits alone • Crawls and pulls self up • Uses finger to point • Grasps object with thumb and index finger
18 mos		• Pulls and pushes objects • Turns pages in a book • Scribbles • Stacks a few blocks • Walks and runs stiffly
2 yrs	 Ami Parikh/Shutterstock.com	• Drinks from a straw • Tosses a ball • Feeds self with a spoon • Bends over without falling
3 yrs		• Puts on shoes • Dresses self with help • Kicks a ball • Hops on one foot • Pedals • Climbs
4 yrs	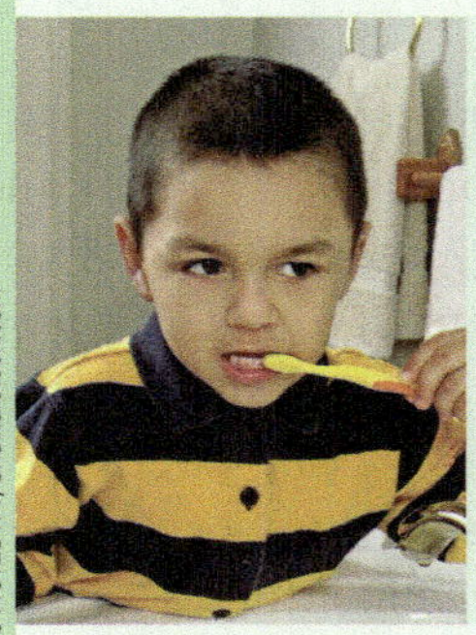 3445128471/Shutterstock.com	• Runs, jumps, hops, and skips • Brushes teeth • Jumps over objects • Catches, bounces, and throws a ball
5 yrs		• Rides a bicycle with training wheels • Balances on one foot • Cuts with scissors • Jumps rope • Copies simple designs • Capable of swimming and skating

9.2 Quiz Yourself

1. **Which of the following infants is *most* likely to have the fewest neural connections?**
   a. A 1-month-old
   b. A 4-month-old
   c. A 1-year-old
   d. A 2-year-old
2. **The rooting reflex is to eating as the grasping reflex is to ____.**
   a. locomotion
   b. crawling
   c. gross motor skills
   d. prehension
3. **Children in preschool learn how to use scissors in order to help develop their ____ skills.**
   a. gross motor
   b. fine motor
   c. reflex
   d. locomotive

Answers 1. a; 2. d; 3. b

9.3 Cognitive Development in Infancy and Childhood

Television shows, movies, and comics capitalize on the unique way in which children develop mentally (their *cognitive development*). What is it about children's thinking that makes adults laugh? This section reviews psychological research into how infants first learn to conceptualize the world and how this thinking changes as they proceed through childhood. We will start with perceptual development.

9.3.1 Perceptual Development: Gathering Information from the Environment

Infants are hard to study. They sleep most of the time, and they can't talk much. We can't remember what it's like to be an infant. Researchers must therefore study infants when they are awake and active, and devise clever ways to measure what infants know. The best way to gather information about what infants can and cannot perceive seems to be to measure certain behaviors and see how those behaviors change under particular conditions. For example, researchers may measure how long an infant spends looking at a stimulus or how long an infant sucks when exposed to different sounds. As researchers create more precise ways of measuring infant behavior, we are discovering that infants know a lot more than we once believed.

Vision

Babies are very nearsighted at birth. Objects need to be close in order for babies to see them, and even then, the objects look blurry. In addition, a baby's eyes lack *convergence,* or the ability to focus both eyes on an object. This may be why newborns typically look cross-eyed in photos. However, as the structure of the eyes and the neural connections in the brain mature, babies attain visual convergence.

Newborns show a preference for looking at complex, high-contrast stimuli. If given a choice among various complex visual stimuli, infants will spend most of their time looking at faces (Frank, Amso, & Johnson, 2014; Pascalis & Kelly, 2009; Turati, 2004). This preference is adaptive, as it helps foster a social bond with the primary caretaker. By 3 months old, a baby can tell the difference between its primary caretaker's face and that of a stranger and more easily recognizes faces from its own race (Bar-Haim et al., 2006; Kelly et al., 2007; Sangrigoli & de Schonen, 2004). However, by 9 months, infants look significantly longer at other-race faces perhaps to explore less familiar faces (Liu et al., 2015). Infants also have more difficulty processing male faces than female faces (Ramsey-Rennels & Langlois, 2006).

Engage Yourself!

Our brains are predisposed to recognize a face, and this predisposition is present in babies. Look closely at the upside-down image on this page before looking at it right side up. Notice anything? Even when presented with an inverted portrait, we ignore the distortions and recognize that it is a face. When you look at the portrait right side up, you notice all the distortions.

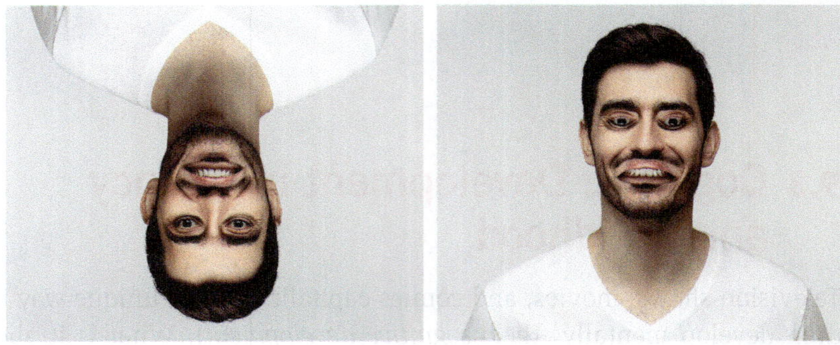
Damir Khabirov/Shutterstock.com

We also have the tendency to see faces in random patterns that strongly resemble the configuration of a face, a psychological phenomenon referred to as *pareidolia* (Hadjikhani et al., 2009; Voss, Federmeier, & Paller, 2012). Have you ever seen the "person in the moon" or faces in arrangements of food or clouds even though there is not a literal face visible? Face perception develops quite early and may even be "hard-wired" at birth, bestowing an evolutionary advantage in quickly detecting friend or foe that enhances human survival (Leopold & Rhodes, 2010).

Depth Perception

During their first year, infants develop *depth perception*. In a classic experiment conducted in 1960, researchers Eleanor Gibson and Richard Walk created an apparatus called a "visual cliff" (see drawing). They then observed at what age infants would or would not cross over the surface where it appeared to drop off. Infants as young as 6 months of age hesitated when approaching this perceived cliff. Again, we see that biology prepares us for developmental challenges. Babies acquire depth perception at about the same time they become mobile. Because depth perception and body coordination may not yet be developed in some infants, it is extremely important never to leave a baby unattended on a bed, a changing table, or any other elevated surface. Immature depth perception and inadequate body control make it more likely that infants will fall and hurt themselves.

Mark Richards/PhotoEdit

▲ Eleanor Gibson and Richard Walk's visual cliff apparatus tests depth perception in infants.

Hearing

Fetuses react to sounds in the intrauterine environment at around the 20th week. A mother's voice is one of those sounds, which may explain why babies are likely to recognize their mothers' voices soon after birth (L. S. Black et al., 2004; DeCasper & Fifer, 1980). Infants can locate the direction of sounds. They readily learn the difference between similar consonant sounds, such as /d/ and /p/, and appear to remember simple speech sounds a day after hearing them (Gerken, 2002). Research suggests that these abilities to discriminate sounds and familiar voices from unfamiliar ones may also be present in fetuses (Draganova et al., 2007; Kisilevsky et al., 2003; Lecanuet, Manera, & Jacquet, 2002).

Babies prefer soft and rhythmic sounds, which explains why they enjoy lullabies so much. They prefer most to listen to voices, specifically *motherese* or baby talk, the drawn-out vowels, exaggerated syllables, and rhythmic, up-and-down inflection used by people across the world (Piazza, Iordan, & Lew-Williams, 2017; Pool, 2005). Infants do not like loud noises, which may explain why some children become classically conditioned to fear thunderstorms (see Chapter 6).

The Other Senses

Taste, touch, and smell are other ways that infants gather meaning from their environment. Infants' taste buds are functional at birth, and infants prefer sweet tastes. Infants are also born with an acute sense of smell. As soon as 3 days after birth, breastfed infants can discriminate the smell of their own mother from that of an unfamiliar female (Cernoch & Porter, 1985; Porter, 1999).

Infants are also very responsive to pleasant touch. Touching and caressing infants stimulates their growth, promotes social development, and can improve brain development and cognitive development (Diamond & Amso, 2008; Fairhurst, Loken, & Grossman, 2014). In one study, two groups of premature infants were given the same neonatal care with one exception—half the infants were routinely massaged, and the other half were not. Those receiving the massages gained weight faster, developed faster neurologically, and were therefore able to leave the hospital sooner than those in the control group (Field et al., 1986). Today, it is standard practice to encourage parents to hold their babies often. Holding and touching infants also fosters their social development.

Infants' perceptual abilities allow them to gather much needed information from the environment—how their caretakers look, sound, and smell, where the food is, and what sounds contribute to language. From these beginnings, infants develop the abilities to know, think, and remember, a process called *cognition* (see Chapter 8). Perhaps no one has advanced our understanding of children's thinking more than Jean Piaget, whose ideas and research are presented next.

9.3.2 Piaget's Theory of Cognitive Development

Swiss psychologist Jean Piaget (1896–1980) interviewed and observed infants and children, including his own, to discover and describe the changes in thinking that occur in childhood. Piaget gave children certain tasks to perform, observed their problem-solving strategies, and then asked them how they came to their conclusions.

▲ Piaget observed children's problem-solving strategies to discover and describe the changes in thinking that they experience.

From these observations and interviews, Piaget (1929, 1952) developed a theory about how children acquire their mental abilities. His theory traces the shifts in thinking from infants' reflexes to a teenager's reasoning abilities. He believed that cognition advances in a series of distinct stages, and that how a preschooler thinks differs dramatically from how an elementary school student thinks. Three concepts central to his theory are *schemas, assimilation*, and *accommodation*.

Schemas, Assimilation, and Accommodation

To Piaget, any mental idea, concept, or thought is a **schema**. We form these schemas based on our experiences of the world. For example, a baby may have a sucking schema, "Is this object suckable?" or a parent schema, "Does this person fit with my cognitive framework of parent?" A preschooler may have the schema "The sun follows me wherever I go." Adults' schemas may be very simple—"Pressing this button will start the car"—or more complex, such as individual ideas of justice, morality, or love.

Piaget believed that our brains are biologically programmed to seek understanding of our world. So, we form schemas to fit with our perceptions of the world. When we achieve this fit, so that our cognitions correspond with the environment, we have *mental equilibrium*. For example, an infant may grab a pacifier, put it in their mouth, and suck it—an experience that confirms the schema that a pacifier is suckable. When there is not a fit between our schemas and the world, we experience *mental disequilibrium*, an uncomfortable state that we are motivated to get rid of so our mental harmony can be restored. For example, an infant may grab a fistful of sand at the beach, put it in their mouth, and determine it is not suckable; therefore, the infant will not suck on sand in the future. The processes of assimilation and accommodation explain how we use existing schema and create new ones to fit our experiences and, therefore, maintain mental equilibrium.

schema [SKEE-ma] a mental idea, concept, or thought

assimilation [uh-sim-uh-LAY-shun] the process by which an existing schema is used to understand something new in the environment

accommodation [uh-com-muh-DAY-shun] the process by which a schema is changed, modified, or created anew in order to understand something new in the environment

Assimilation is the process by which we apply an existing schema to our understanding of the environment. For example, a young child is traveling in a car with their parents. As they pass an open field, the child sees some cows. The only schema the child has for a four-legged animal is dog. So the child points and says, "Doggies!" The parents may correct the child—"No, those are called cows"—but the child may persist in calling them "doggies" because that is their framework for understanding four-legged animals. The child has *assimilated* the experience of "cow" into the existing schema of "dog." However, many times our existing schema will not fit our new experiences. At times like these, the process of accommodation takes center stage.

Accommodation is the process we use to change or modify our existing schema—or even create new ones—to adapt to some change in the environment. For example, suppose the child in the previous example sees a dog and a cow side by side. The differences in the animals cannot be ignored and will create disequilibrium in the child's mental state. In this situation, the child may come to call the new animal "cow." The existing schema for four-legged animals has now been modified. The child will go through the same process when they see a horse, a cat, or a hippopotamus.

Piaget's Stages of Cognitive Development

According to Piaget, assimilation and accommodation create shifts in mental processing that allow the child to progress through four stages of cognition: *sensorimotor, preoperational, concrete operations*, and *formal operations* (1952; summarized in

YOU REVIEW Piaget's Stages of Cognitive Development

Sensorimotor (birth–2 yrs)	Preoperational (2–6 or 7 yrs)	Concrete Operations (6 or 7–11 or 12 yrs)	Formal Operations (12 yrs–adult)
Reflexes	Symbolic thinking	Conservation	Abstract reasoning
Object permanence	Illogical thinking	Logical thinking	
	Centration	Decentration	
	Egocentrism		

Bill Anderson/Science Source

You Review: Piaget's Stages of Cognitive Development). Each stage has characteristics that permit the child to conceptualize the world in a unique fashion.

Sensorimotor Stage During the first cognitive stage, the **sensorimotor stage**, from birth to 2 years, Piaget suggested that infants acquire knowledge through their senses and through their motor abilities—hence the name *sensorimotor*. For example, infants quickly recognize and prefer to look at their mothers' faces. Similarly, infants use their hearing to form schemas of what certain sounds mean, establishing the foundation for language. Taste, touch, and smell are also used to gather information and to form schemas as infants explore objects with their hands, mouths, and feet. We also saw that infant reflexes help establish schemas for later voluntary behaviors such as grasping, sitting, crawling, and walking.

sensorimotor stage Piaget's first stage of cognitive development, in which infants form schemas through their senses and motor abilities

object permanence the understanding that an object continues to exist even when it is not present

Piaget believed that during this stage, infants can only form schemas of objects and actions that are in their immediate perception—in other words, what they currently see, hear, or touch. They learn by doing and by acting on objects. They lack the ability to represent an object when it is not present. For infants, it is truly "out of sight, out of mind," according to Piaget. The baby thinks of a pacifier when it is present by manipulating it with their mouth or hands. An infant can think about their "blankie" only when it is present. If these objects are not present, they no longer exist for the infant. However, as the infant grows and the brain matures, babies begin to have mental representations. One sign of this milestone is *object permanence.*

Object permanence is the understanding that an object continues to exist even when it is not present. We can see this in infants' behavior when they start to search for hidden objects. For example, Piaget would show a baby an interesting toy and then cover it. Before the age of 6 months, infants would not search for the toy, lacking the understanding that the toy still existed. It seemed as if the infant could not keep a mental representation of the object and its location in mind. However, by 8 months, infants will begin to search for the toy, suggesting the beginnings of object permanence. This ability steadily improves through 24 months, when infants will search long and hard for hidden objects, indicating that they have fully achieved object permanence.

Although Piaget accurately described the process of object permanence in infancy, he may have underestimated infants' abilities. Current research suggests that infants as young as 3 to 6 months old have a basic understanding of object permanence and that they gradually develop stronger mental representations of objects through experience (Bremner, Bryant, & Mareschal, 2006; Kibbe & Leslie, 2011; Ruffman, Slade, & Redman, 2005; Shinskey & Munakata, 2005; Wang, Baillargeon, & Brueckner, 2004).

symbolic thinking the understanding that objects can be represented with symbols such as bodily gestures or language

preoperational stage Piaget's second stage of cognitive development, characterized by the use of symbols and illogical thought

centration the act of focusing on only one aspect or feature of an object

Once infants acquire object permanence, they are on their way to **symbolic thinking**. This is the understanding that an object can be represented with symbols such as gestures or language (Ganea et al., 2007). For example, a toddler may imitate the sound or walk of a monkey even when there is no monkey in sight. This ability to use symbols propels the child to the second stage of cognitive development: the *preoperational stage*.

Preoperational Stage During the **preoperational stage**, from about age 2 to age 6 or 7, preschoolers and young schoolchildren are actively acquiring and using symbols (DeLoache, 2001). Being able to use symbols opens up a new world to the preschooler. It is the foundation of a child's language development. A word symbolizes or stands for an object that may or may not be present. A child's vocabulary and understanding of language dramatically increase during these years. Recall from Chapter 8 that children progress from one-word utterances at 12 to 18 months to two-word sentences at 20 to 26 months, and that by age 6, the average child has a vocabulary of around 10,000 words. So, when a parent asks, "Do you want some juice?" the preoperational child knows what juice is and may even go to the refrigerator to get it. Young children's pretend play also demonstrates their use of symbols, such as using a stick to represent a sword or taking on family roles when they play "house." However, the child's new ability to symbolize objects is still illogical and does not always make sense to adults. For example, a child may believe that a switch turns on ocean waves or that there are monsters hiding under the bed.

The illogical thinking of preschoolers is due to cognitive limitations that include *centration* and *egocentrism*. **Centration** occurs when the child focuses on only one feature or aspect of an object. For instance, a child who sees a man with long hair may conclude that the man is a woman. The child focuses on one feature, the man's hair length, and this man's hair length fits with their schema for females. For preschoolers, if it looks like a duck, it is a duck; they have difficulty distinguishing between appearance and reality. Centration so dominates

Jenny Sturm/Shutterstock.com

▲ Pretend play indicates advancement in cognition as children acquire the ability to think symbolically.

children's thinking at this stage that they do not realize that something can remain the same if its appearance changes, an ability called **conservation**.

In classic experiments, Piaget tested preschoolers and school-age children's conservation abilities (see photos). Children were shown two identical glasses containing the same amount of liquid. In front of the child, Piaget poured the liquid from one of these glasses into a taller, thinner glass. Children were then asked whether the glasses had equal amounts of liquid or whether one glass had more liquid than the other. Children in the preoperational stage were most likely to reply that the tall, thin glass had more because they were focused on the height of the liquid in the narrower glass. It looked as though it had more, so it must have more. For preschoolers at a party, then, adults should be aware that it must *look* as though the children all have the same amount of cake or punch. Otherwise the preschoolers will think they are receiving different amounts—which can create havoc!

An additional limitation to the preschooler's thinking is **egocentrism**, or the belief that everyone else thinks as you do. For example, when one of your authors was playing hide-and-seek with her then 3-year-old son, he hid in his room in the corner. His face was turned to the wall, much like a child who is sent to stand in a corner for misbehaving. On entering the room, your author said, "I see you." Her son replied, "No, you don't." From her son's perspective, he could not see his mother; therefore she could not see him. Preschoolers believe that others see things as they do, and therefore think as they do, a finding that has been repeatedly replicated using a range of different research methods (Wellman, Cross, & Watson, 2001).

Although adults may find it frustrating, the illogical thinking of a preschooler lends an almost magical quality to their thought processes. For example, they believe in monsters, bad-dream catchers over their beds to prevent nightmares, the tooth fairy, imaginary friends, and fantasy. However, current research suggests that here, too, Piaget's ideas probably underestimate children's thinking abilities. Egocentrism, centration, and the inability to tell the difference between appearance and reality do not *always* characterize preschoolers' thoughts and may to some degree be a result of the testing method used (Deak, 2006; Jenkins & Astington, 1996). Rather, these limitations are *sometimes* present in children's thinking and gradually fade as the child matures and develops more logical thought processes.

Marmaduke St. John/Alamy Stock Photo

Marmaduke St. John/Alamy Stock Photo

▲ Lacking the ability of conservation, young children are likely to believe that the amount of liquid has changed when it is poured into the taller, thinner glass. Centering on the height of the liquid, they believe the taller, thinner glass has more.

Concrete Operations Stage During Piaget's third cognitive stage, **concrete operations**, from about age 6 or 7 through age 11 or 12, schoolchildren become logical thinkers. They no longer center on one feature or facet of an object as the preschooler did, and their conservation abilities improve (● TABLE 9.2). By age 11 or 12, children realize that although the tall, thin glass looks as though it has more liquid, in reality the glasses have equivalent volume. Changes in these abilities force the child to recognize that previous beliefs may be mistaken, so accommodation occurs. It also brings about a reduction in egocentrism as the child can now consider the perspectives of others. This enables empathy, persuasion, and a sense of humor to grow.

Although the concrete operational child thinks more logically, these schemas are limited to actual experience or concrete objects and situations. School-age children have difficulty reasoning abstractly about what may be or what could be without being able to test their ideas in an observable way. This is why hands-on activities and class demonstrations of abstract ideas for school subjects such as math and science are often necessary in elementary and middle school and

conservation the understanding that an object retains its original properties even though it may look different

egocentrism [ee-go-SEN-trih-zum] the belief that everyone thinks as you do

concrete operations Piaget's third stage of cognitive development, characterized by logical thought

TABLE 9.2 Piaget's Conservation Experiments

Mastery of conservation tasks begins gradually during the concrete operations stage. Children typically master conservation of number by age 6 or 7. Conservation of area may not be grasped until age 8 or 9.

Typical Tasks Used to Measure Conservation		Typical Age of Mastery
	**Conservation of number** Two equivalent rows of objects are shown to the child, who agrees that they have the same number of objects.	6–7
	One row is lengthened, and the child is asked whether one row has more objects.	
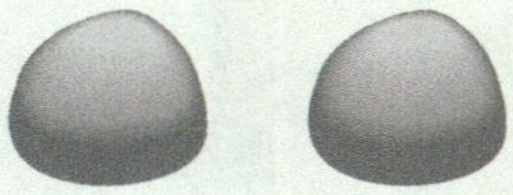	**Conservation of mass** The child acknowledges that two clay balls have equal amounts of clay.	7–8
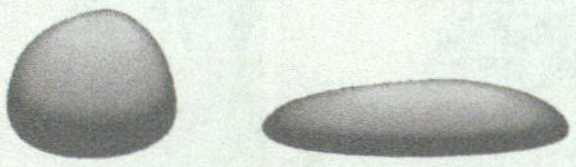	The experimenter changes the shape of one of the balls and asks the child whether they still contain equal amounts of clay.	
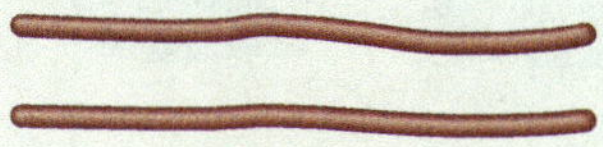	**Conservation of length** The child agrees that two sticks aligned with each other are the same length.	7–8
	After moving one of the sticks to the left or right, the experimenter asks the child whether the sticks are of equal length.	
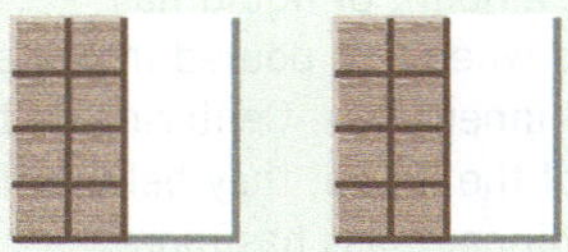	**Conservation of area** Two identical sheets of cardboard have wooden blocks placed on them in identical positions; the child confirms that the same amount of space is left on each piece of cardboard.	8–9
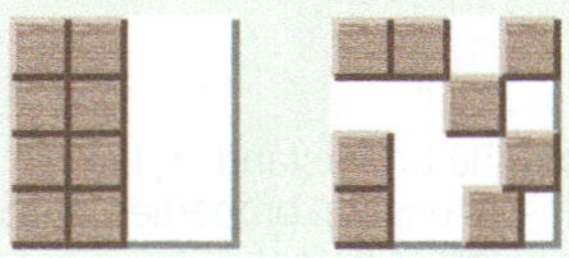	The experimenter scatters the blocks on one piece of cardboard and again asks the child whether the two pieces of cardboard have the same amount of unoccupied space.	

actually help children learn abstract concepts (Novack et al., 2014). Notice that Hongyong preferred the household lessons as they were "something I could touch, see, and use freely." When told to protect her "private parts," Hongyong thought her mother meant her knees because she was constantly being told to keep her knees covered. Being able to think about situations that are not present or easily brought to mind occurs in the final stage of Piaget's theory, *formal operations.*

Formal Operations Stage According to Piaget, as children approach their teenage years, they may achieve the final cognitive stage, **formal operations**. They are no longer limited to concrete objects and situations; they can now engage in abstract reasoning. Teenagers can imagine and hypothesize what *could* be. This ability expands their horizons. They are able to understand more abstract,

formal operations Piaget's final stage of cognitive development, characterized by the ability to engage in abstract thought scientific, and mathematical concepts. They can imagine potential careers and envision future consequences for current behavior.

Piaget's Influence on Cognitive Development Research

Piaget's theory revolutionized our understanding of children's thinking abilities and stimulated much research in cognition. The changes in thinking that Piaget proposed do not always proceed according to the precise stages and timetable he originally suggested (Haith & Benson, 1998). Children's mental abilities develop at different ages. Nurture, culture, or experience can facilitate growth and change in these abilities. However, Piaget very accurately described the *sequence* in which these changes occur, even in diverse societies (Dasen, 1994; Lourenco & Machado, 1996). One final criticism of Piaget's theory is that it overlooks the important influence of culture on cognitive development. The ideas of Lev Vygotsky explore this connection between culture and cognition.

9.3.3 Vygotsky's Theory of Cognitive Development: Culture and Thinking

Lev Vygotsky (1896–1934) was a Russian psychologist whose ideas have influenced how psychologists and educators think about children's cognitive development, and have provided an alternative to Piaget's theory (John-Steiner & Mahn, 1996). In contrast to Piaget's emphasis on the internal origin of schemas, Vygotsky (1978, 1986) emphasized that mental processes begin externally with our social interactions with others. For example, babies smile at caretakers or toddlers raise their arms to signal that they want to be picked up. A child internalizes these mental processes to create a cognitive framework for understanding the world.

private speech Vygotsky's term describing the behavior of young children who talk to themselves to guide their own actions

Young children often talk to themselves as they play, a behavior Vygotsky called **private speech**. For Vygotsky, private speech represents an internal monitor that guides the child's actions. Private speech, or *self-talk*, as it is sometimes called, is common among preschoolers and peaks around 5 to 7 years of age. Around 9 years of age, children internalize these spoken words as silent lip movements. Eventually, children just think the thoughts rather than saying them. However, private speech can return at any age when we are confused or having difficulties in problem solving or learning new skills. Such inner speech guides our thinking and can help regulate our behavior. Self-talk strategies that support Vygotsky's ideas on private speech have been developed to help children who are deaf use sign language, help students with emotional and behavioral disorders, and to enhance sports performance and healthier eating in adults (Berk & Spuhl, 1995; Furman, Kross, & Gearhardt, 2020; Hatzigeorgiadis et al., 2011; Kelman, 2001). It makes sense, therefore, to allow and even encourage children and adults to use self-talk when problem solving or learning new skills.

According to Vygotsky, because cognition is so intimately tied to our social interactions, culture has a profound influence on our mental processing. The language, measurement systems, rituals, beliefs, and technology of a culture both limit and support certain ways of thinking (Tomasello, 2000). For instance, if your language does not have a word to capture an idea or expression, it is difficult to imagine or understand that concept. Similarly, children who have the opportunity to read books, use the Internet, travel, and attend cultural events will be more capable of conceptualizing ideas than will children without such tools. According to Vygotsky, cognitive development does not occur in fixed stages as Piaget theorized. Rather, cognitive development may proceed in any number of directions, depending on our culture, social interactions with others, and the environment we live in.

Representing concepts is not achieved simply by having these tools. Conceptual thinking is taught to children by parents, teachers, siblings, coaches, and other important people in their lives. This instruction is most helpful when it is within a child's **zone of proximal development (ZPD)**—the gap between what a child can already do and what they are not yet capable of doing without help. Through collaborative interaction, the adult initially guides and supports the child's efforts to master a task. The less able a child is to do a task, the more direction and guidance an adult must give. The adult then gradually minimizes the guidance and support until the child can do the task alone, in a process called **scaffolding**. For example, when teaching a child how to dress, an adult first supports the child by holding the shirt out as the child puts their arms into the sleeves and then buttons the shirt for the child. When the child seems ready, less and less support is given until the child is putting the shirt on by themselves and buttoning it on their own. It is through these interactions with others that children internalize strategies, reasoning skills, and problem-solving abilities. For this reason, Vygotsky believed that a child's cognitive development benefits most from interactions with people who are more capable or advanced in their thinking than the child.

zone of proximal development (ZPD) according to Vygotsky, the gap between what a child is already able to do and what they are not yet capable of doing without help

scaffolding [SKAH-fol-ding] a process in which adults initially offer guidance and support in helping a child to reason, solve a problem, or master a task; as the child becomes more proficient and capable, the adult helps less and less until the child can master the task on their own

Piaget's and Vygotsky's theories detail the ways in which children develop their thinking and reasoning skills. Yet, other developmental psychologists wanted to understand how children develop a specific type of thinking called *moral reasoning*—a topic we turn to next.

Psychology Works!

weedezign/Shutterstock.com

Educators play an important role in influencing and shaping the cognitive and social skills of young people around the world. Educators are often required to take several psychology courses, most notably one in human or child development, so that they can learn how to maximize each student's potential. Understanding cognitive theories of development such as Piaget's and Vygotsky's help teachers design and adjust lessons and activities to the developmental age and abilities of their students. Understanding the psychosocial development of children and teens also helps educators foster positive social classroom environments for young people's social, emotional, and academic learning. Understanding typical patterns of cognitive and social development also helps teachers recognize when their students may be in need of additional resources for developmental delays or enrichment. Educators' developmental knowledge helps students thrive!

9.3.4 Moral Reasoning: How We Think About Right and Wrong

moral reasoning how you decide what is right and what is wrong

Consider the following situation: An automatic teller machine (ATM) dispenses $10,000 to you, and there is no way that this error would ever be discovered. You keep the money, but you donate half of it to the local food bank. Should you have kept the money? How did you decide what to do? Your answer to this situation would provide clues to psychologists about your level of **moral reasoning**, or how you distinguish right from wrong. Two well-known theories on moral development are Lawrence Kohlberg's *stages of moral reasoning* and Carol Gilligan's *ethic of care*.

Kohlberg's Theory of Moral Development

Lawrence Kohlberg (1927–1987) developed hypothetical moral dilemmas or situations like the one we posed to you, and then asked participants to describe what the main character should do and why. After analyzing data from thousands of participants, Kohlberg created a theory of how people morally reason and the changes in this reasoning that occur as they develop (Kohlberg, 1969; Kohlberg, Levine, & Hewer, 1983). He proposed that our moral reasoning develops in six stages, which he arranged in three levels: preconventional, conventional, and postconventional (● TABLE 9.3).

At the *preconventional level* of reasoning, children make decisions about right or wrong based on their ability to avoid punishment or to gain rewards. For example, it is wrong to take the money because you may get caught and then punished. It is right to take the money because you can use it and no one will find out about it. Recall that at this age, children are egocentric and have difficulty

TABLE 9.3 Kohlberg's Stages of Moral Reasoning

Preconventional Level (Most Children)
Stage 1: Obedience and Punishment Orientation. Children obey rules to avoid punishment. "Taking a cookie without asking is wrong because you get a timeout."
Stage 2: Naively Egoistic Orientation. Children view morally right action as that which increases their personal rewards and meets their needs. "You scratch my back, and I'll scratch yours."
Conventional Level (Most Adolescents and Adults)
Stage 3: Good Boy/Good Girl Orientation. Moral rightness is based on maintaining the approval and/or avoiding the disapproval of others such as family and friends. "I will return the rest of the money so my parents won't be disappointed in me."
Stage 4: Law and Order Orientation. Moral rightness is based on following the rules or laws of the society. Exceptions to the rules are not allowed. "Stealing is wrong because it is against the law."
Postconventional Level (Some but Not All Adults)
Stage 5: Contractual/Legalistic Orientation. Exceptions to rules can now be considered, as the protection of individual rights is emphasized over societal laws. "I confessed to the crime, but I was not told I had a right to remain silent, so the confession is not valid."
Stage 6: Universal Principles Orientation. Individuals develop their own set of universal principles that guide their judgments of right and wrong across all situations and all societies. "All people, regardless of skin color, should have access to education."

understanding the nature of rules. Consequently, children are centered on the immediate consequences of their actions.

With the ability to think logically and to understand another person's perspective, children at the *conventional level* of reasoning can now understand rules and expectations that others may have for them. Therefore, their moral reasoning is based on the standards of the group or society. They believe behaviors are right or wrong because they gain the approval or avoid the disapproval of parents, teachers, or peers. You may not take the money because you are afraid your parents would find out and be disappointed in you, or you may take the money to gain acceptance from your friends. At this level, children can appreciate society's rules or laws for moral behavior. However, because they lack the ability to reason abstractly, children apply these laws to every situation and every person very rigidly. Exceptions based on circumstances are not considered.

At the *postconventional level* of moral reasoning, people base their judgments of right or wrong on contractual or universal principles of morality. The person can appreciate extenuating circumstances and realizes that external standards handed down from society cannot always be applied to all situations in the same manner. The person develops internal standards of right and wrong to guide moral behavior. These abstract principles may include the "Golden Rule" (Do unto others as you would have them do unto you) or values such as respecting the dignity of all persons regardless of race, creed, or culture. You may not take the money because you did not earn it and you may be financially hurting someone else.

Kohlberg's theory has stimulated much research—as well as much criticism and controversy (Narvaez, 2010). Kohlberg-like studies in 27 cultures support his stage sequence of moral reasoning. People typically move through these stages in the way that Kohlberg proposed (Damon, 1999; Helwig, 1997; Walker & Taylor, 1991). By adulthood, most people have progressed to conventional moral reasoning, but few people move on to postconventional reasoning, especially the highest stage. Postconventional reasoning emphasizes the individual rights that each person in a society should be afforded. Such reasoning may apply more to people from Western cultures. In other parts of the world, moral systems tend to emphasize the well-being of the group in regulating values (Haidt, 2008; Snarey, 1995). Another perspective from which Kohlberg's theory has been criticized is that of gender, a controversy initiated by one of his students, Carol Gilligan.

▲ Carol Gilligan's classic work *In a Different Voice* challenged Kohlberg's theory of moral reasoning.

Gilligan's Theory: Gender and Moral Reasoning

Carol Gilligan (b. 1936) hypothesized that males and females do not judge right and wrong in the same manner. She believed that Kohlberg's model emphasized the male perspective on moral reasoning more than the female view. In her book *A Different Voice* (1982), Gilligan speculated that males and females focus on different principles for deciding what is right and wrong. Males tend to be more focused on concepts of fairness and justice. Females are more likely to emphasize concern, care, and relations with others in making judgments about right and wrong. Gilligan asserts that women's focus on caring is a different, but not a less valid, basis for moral reasoning.

Research evaluating gender differences in moral reasoning has not strongly supported Gilligan's claims. On hypothetical dilemmas, *both* males and females emphasize themes of justice and caring in their responses (Jadack et al., 1995; Jaffee & Hyde, 2000; Walker, 1995). Thus, moral reasoning may be based on justice or caring independent of gender (Jorgensen, 2006).

9.3 Quiz Yourself

1. **Which of the following statements about infants' sensory abilities is *false*?**
   a. Infants prefer looking at complex, high-contrast stimuli.
   b. Infants have functioning taste buds at birth.
   c. Infants prefer to listen to voices.
   d. Infants perceive depth at birth.
2. **Simone sees a military tank on the highway and confidently calls it a "truck." According to Piaget, which process is Simone engaged in?**
   a. Disequilibrium
   b. Private speech
   c. Assimilation
   d. Accommodation
3. **Pedro has four nickels in his pocket. His sister has a dollar. Pedro thinks he has more than his sister because it looks like and feels like more. Pedro is *most* likely in Piaget's _____ stage of development.**
   a. sensorimotor
   b. preoperational
   c. concrete operations
   d. formal operations
4. **Zahara can pull her pants on but has not yet mastered how to button them. Zahara's behavior best exemplifies which developmental concept?**
   a. Private speech
   b. Zone of proximal development
   c. Egocentrism
   d. Scaffolding
5. **Kayla, a 4-year-old, believes it's right to share her toys with June so that June will also share her toys. At what level of Kohlberg's theory is she operating?**
   a. Preconventional
   b. Formal operations
   c. Conventional
   d. Postconventional

Answers 1. d; 2. c; 3. b; 4. b; 5. a

9.4 Psychosocial Development in Infancy and Childhood

A close connection between nature and nurture also influences a child's social and personality development. Children come into the world with a biological tendency to behave in a certain way. How parents and others respond to these behaviors can influence the child's personality as well as the relationships the child develops with others. We explore these issues as we look at the topics of *temperament, attachment, parenting styles*, Erik Erikson's theory of *psychosocial development*, and *gender-role development*.

9.4.1 Temperament: The Influence of Biology

Babies come into the world showing a general disposition to behave in certain ways in response to their surroundings. These differences are believed to be due more to the child's biological makeup than to their environment, especially because the child has not yet been exposed to any environment other than the womb. These differences at birth in behavioral style are referred to as **temperament**. In pioneering research, Stella Chess and Alexander Thomas (Chess & Thomas, 1984;

temperament a person's general pattern of attention, arousal, and mood that is evident at birth

attachment an emotional bond between an infant and someone or something; an infant's first attachment with their caretaker is typically established by 8 or 9 months

separation anxiety the fear an infant expresses when separated from the primary caretaker

Thomas & Chess, 1977, 1986) gathered information on numerous infant behaviors such as these:

- General activity level
- General mood
- Ability to establish a regular pattern of eating and sleeping
- Likelihood of approaching or withdrawing from new people and new situations
- Ability to adapt to changes from their normal routine

From observing babies' behaviors on these variables, these researchers described three temperamental styles: easy infants, difficult infants, and slow-to-warm-up infants.

As the label implies, *easy infants* are generally in a good mood, establish a regular pattern of eating and sleeping, readily approach new objects and people, and adapt readily to changes in their routines. *Difficult infants,* in contrast, show more intense negative emotions such as crying. They have a more irregular pattern of eating and sleeping and are not as likely to approach new people and situations. Parents may even call such babies "colicky." *Slow-to-warm-up infants* are in between these two extremes. They are not as negative in response as difficult infants, but it takes them some time to adapt to new situations.

A child's temperament and the parents' responses to this temperament influence the parent-child bond called *attachment.*

Courtesy of Harlow Primate Lab, University of Wisconsin-Madison

Courtesy of Harlow Primate Lab, University of Wisconsin-Madison

▲ Harlow's studies showed that while the infant monkeys went to the wire "surrogate mother" for food, they clung to and spent most of their time with the cloth-covered "surrogate mother."

9.4.2 Attachment: Learning About Relationships

Attachment, the emotional bond between the infant and the primary caretaker, is usually firmly established by 8 to 9 months. Initially, psychologists believed that feeding provided the basis for building the attachment relationship: the baby feels connected to the primary caretaker because the parent satisfies the infant's hunger. However, animal research by Harry Harlow (1905–1981) in the 1950s changed the way we view the attachment process today.

The Origins of Attachment

In a classic study, Harlow and Zimmerman (1959) wanted to investigate the nature of attachment. They used infant rhesus monkeys as subjects because ethical principles would prohibit such a study with human infants. They designed two artificial monkeys to act as surrogate mothers for the babies. One of the "surrogate mothers" was covered with a soft terry cloth fabric. The other "surrogate mother" was made of wire and had a feeding tube attached. The researchers wanted to see which surrogate mother the infants preferred. The data showed that while the infant monkeys went to the wire surrogate mother for food, they clung to and spent most of their time with the cloth-covered surrogate mother. This showed that feeding was not the reason the monkeys attached; rather, it was the close, warm contact that facilitated this bond. Establishing close, warm contact through holding and caressing facilitates attachment. Human infants can thus easily attach to multiple people and objects, including fathers, grandparents, siblings, and teddy bears.

The attachment bond is readily seen in specific infant behaviors by the end of the first year. For example, most babies reserve certain behaviors for their parents and caretakers. Infants smile when a parent approaches them, raise their hands toward the parent to be picked up, and nestle closer when the parent holds them. Two additional signs of attachment include *separation anxiety* and *stranger anxiety.* **Separation anxiety** is a fear the infant expresses when separated from the primary caretaker. This distress normally appears at about 6 or 7 months of age, and peaks at about 14 to 18 months. Separation anxiety gradually becomes less frequent and less intense throughout the toddler and preschool years. However, it is not uncommon for even older children to become anxious or homesick when separated from their parents for a long period (Thurber & Walton, 2007).

In **stranger anxiety**, the infant becomes distressed when approached by unfamiliar people. Stranger anxiety typically appears between 8 and 10 months of age. It may intensify through the end of the first year, but usually subsides over the second year. Therefore, it is not unusual for a 1- or 2-year-old to cry or cling to a parent when approached by a doctor, an unfamiliar relative, or a new babysitter.

stranger anxiety the distress an infant expresses when faced with unfamiliar people

Variations in Attachment Patterns

Although most infants establish an attachment with a caregiver by the end of the first year, the quality of these attachments is not necessarily the same from infant to infant. Mary Ainsworth (1913–1999) and her colleagues (Ainsworth et al., 1978) designed a research technique called the *strange situation* procedure to try to measure qualitative differences in infant attachments. In the strange situation, infants and their parents are placed in an unfamiliar playroom. The infant's behavior is observed and measured as certain events occur. For example, does the infant explore the new situation and the toys when left in the playroom with the parent? How does the infant behave when a stranger enters the room? What is the baby's response when the parent leaves the room? What is the infant's reaction when the parent returns?

Observations of infants under these circumstances uncovered several patterns, or *styles of attachment*. Ainsworth and others (Ainsworth et al., 1978; Hesse & Main, 2006; Main & Solomon, 1990) described four patterns of attachment: secure, avoidant, resistant, and disorganized/disoriented.

- *Secure attachment.* Infants who are securely attached use the parent as a supportive base from which to operate and explore. They explore the toys while in the new situation, paying attention to any new strangers who may enter the room. They may or may not cry when the parent leaves, but this emotional upset is quickly over once the parent returns.
- *Avoidant attachment.* Infants who show avoidant attachment appear to ignore the parent. They pay the parent little attention. They do not appear to be distressed when the parent leaves, and they show little emotional response when the parent reappears.
- *Resistant attachment.* Infants who display resistant attachment resemble a "clinging" baby. They remain close to the parent and do not actively explore the new situation. They show extreme distress when the parent leaves and appear to be angry when the parent returns. They may hit and push at the parent and are less easily soothed when the parent returns.
- *Disorganized/disoriented attachment.* Infants showing disorganized attachment seem confused or disoriented. They look away from the parent while being comforted and have a blank facial expression after being calmed by the parent.

Although most children worldwide appear to have secure attachments to their caretakers, we must be cautious in interpreting the other three "insecure" patterns of attachment. Different child-rearing practices and cultural attitudes influence how we interact with our children, and these interactions as well as the larger social context appear to influence attachment (Keller, 2013). In some countries, children's independence is encouraged; in other countries, a closeness with the caretaker is emphasized. Moreover, individual differences in attachment may have evolved to promote survival. For example, individuals who are resistant and anxious about being separated from a caregiver may be quicker than infants with the other attachment styles to notice danger in the environment and warn others—an important survival skill that has evolutionary value (Ein-Dor & Hirschberger, 2016). Perhaps this is why these same styles of attachment have generally emerged across cultures, suggesting that these styles of attachment are common worldwide (van Ijzendoom & Sagi-Schwartz, 2008).

Many psychologists endorse the notion that the quality of this first attachment relationship lays the foundation for the quality of all other relationships with friends and romantic partners. Research supports this reasoning to a certain degree. Securely attached infants are more likely to become curious, resilient, and self-controlled preschoolers. Such children are more likely to persist in problem-solving tasks, do well in school, interact more skillfully with their peers during the school years, and recover from conflict better in romantic relationships in young adulthood (Dindo et al., 2017; Kerns et al., 2007; Orina et al., 2011; Salvatore et al., 2011; Simpson, Collins, & Salvatore, 2011).

However, being securely attached at an early age does not guarantee an absence of problems later. Moreover, research has not been able to consistently document a negative or unfavorable picture of development for the insecure attachment patterns. Some studies suggest that insecurely attached infants are more prone to behavioral and adjustment problems in their social relations with others, whereas other studies do not (Hamilton, 2000; Hill-Soderlund & Braungart-Rieker, 2008; Rothbaum et al., 1995b). Bonds with individuals other than the caretaker can compensate for insecure attachments at home. Moreover, given the number of variables that can influence attachment, an early pattern of insecure attachment does not guarantee a lifelong pattern of insecure relationships. As family circumstances improve, so too may the quality of the attachment. Similarly, social relationships *after* infancy must also be considered when we evaluate children's psychological adjustment.

9.4.3 Variations in Parenting Styles

Parents' responses to their infants and children also influence the parent-child relationship. Clinical and developmental psychologist, Diana Baumrind (1927–2018; 1967, 1971) investigated these responses by observing parents' interactions with their children. From her observations, three styles of parenting emerged: *authoritarian*, *authoritative*, and *permissive*.

authoritarian [ah-thor-uh-TARE-ee-an] parent a parenting style characterized by high levels of control and low levels of affection

authoritative [ah-thor-uh-TAY-tive] parent a parenting style characterized by moderate levels of control and affection

Authoritarian parents tend to exhibit a high level of control and a low level of affection toward their children. They set high expectations for their children but without communicating the reasons behind their expectations. "It's my way or the highway" would be a characteristic attitude of authoritarian parents. The children are not included in discussions of family issues, rules, or roles. They are to do what they are told. If they do not obey, force and physical punishment are used to ensure compliance. Baumrind found that children from authoritarian households tended to be more withdrawn, anxious, and conforming than other children. A meta-analysis of 1,435 studies on parenting behaviors and styles found authoritarian parenting style and harsh parental control associated with higher levels of externalizing problems in children (Pinquart, 2017). Externalizing behaviors include disobeying rules, losing one's temper and verbal and physical aggression. Less parental warmth has also been found to be associated with poorer self-esteem in the United States, Spain, Germany, and Brazil (Garcia et al., 2019).

Authoritative parents tend to exhibit moderate control and are warm toward their children. Authoritative parents are least likely to spank or hit their children. Rules—and the consequences for violating them—are established in a democratic manner, and children are included in family discussions. Reasonable expectations and demands are made of the children, and the children respond accordingly. Baumrind found that parents who use this style of parenting tended to have competent, happy, and self-confident children. It appears to be the most effective approach to parenting. Although Baumrind's sample was predominantly restricted to European Americans, these benefits of authoritative parenting have also been found to apply to several U.S. ethnic groups, including African Americans, Korean Americans, Chinese Americans, and Hispanic Americans (Abar, Carter, & Winsler, 2009; Cheah et al., 2009; Kim & Chung, 2003; Querido, Warner, & Eyberg, 2002; Steinberg et al., 1992).

Permissive parents have very little control over their children. Discipline is lax. Children make their own decisions even when they may not be capable of doing so. Very few demands are made of the children in terms of rules or chores. Permissive parenting includes two distinct types: indulgent and neglectful. *Permissive-indulgent* parents are very warm, affectionate, and involved with their children but still make few demands on their children, hence the name "indulgent." *Permissive-neglectful* parents make few demands and show little affection or warmth toward their children; they are uninvolved with parenting and neglect the emotional needs of their children. Children of permissive-indulgent parents tend to be impulsive, disobedient, yet emotionally secure, whereas children of permissive-neglectful parents tend to have the poorest outcomes in terms of social skills, self-esteem, and academic achievement.

Do parents always *cause* children to act a certain way? Perhaps not. Recall that these are correlations, and causal connections cannot be made from correlational data (Chapter 1). A parent-child relationship is not a one-way street. Children's temperaments influence the way parents treat them just as much as a parent's responsiveness influences the development of a child (Raby et al., 2012). Moreover, other variables such as the quality of the parents' relationship or the level of family functioning can influence how parents and children interact (Caldera & Lindsey, 2006; Schoppe-Sullivan et al., 2007). How a child develops socially and emotionally will depend in part on the *goodness of fit* between the child's temperament and their surrounding social relationships, including those with parents (Bradley & Corwyn, 2008; Chess & Thomas, 1984; Newland & Crnic, 2017; Stright, Gallagher, & Kelley, 2008).

Simon Marcus/Getty Images

▲ Parents who are warm and moderate in discipline are more likely to have competent and happy children.

permissive parent a parenting style characterized by low levels of control or discipline

9.4.4 Erikson's Stages of Psychosocial Development: The Influence of Culture

After studying child-rearing practices in several cultures, Erik Erikson (1902–1994) believed that children and adults progress through eight stages, or *developmental crises* (Erikson, 1963, 1968, 1980). At each stage, the environment and the person's responses to the environment influence the development of either a healthy or an unhealthy personality characteristic. At each stage, the person incorporates a new quality into their personality. Resolving earlier stages with healthy outcomes makes it easier to resolve later stages with positive outcomes. An unhealthy resolution of a stage can have potential negative effects throughout life, although damage can sometimes be repaired at later stages. Four of Erikson's eight stages pertain to the childhood years and are discussed here. The other four stages focus on the adolescent and adult years and are discussed later in the chapter. You Review: Erikson's Stages of Psychosocial Development summarizes all eight stages.

1. *Trust versus mistrust.* This stage occurs during the first year of life, when infants are totally dependent on others in their environment to meet their needs. An infant whose needs are met is more likely to develop trust in others

▲ For Erikson, the child-rearing practices of a culture fulfill basic psychological and emotional needs to influence healthy personality development.

than one whose needs are not met. Developing a sense of trust also fosters the development of a secure attachment.

2. *Autonomy versus shame and doubt*. From 1 to 3 years of age, toddlers struggle with separating from their primary caretaker. They must negotiate an appropriate balance between autonomy, or independence, and dependence. If people in the toddler's environment belittle the child's efforts at independence or encourage dependence by being overly protective, then Erikson believed the child will be more likely to develop shame and doubt.
3. *Initiative versus guilt*. Erikson believed that during the preschool years (ages 3–6), children's environments encourage the development of either initiative or guilt. When children develop initiative, they are motivated to take the first step, to start something on their own, and to be ambitious. Preschoolers are actively exploring their environments through trial and error. At the same time, they start to understand that others have expectations for their behavior, and they learn to read people's reactions to their explorations. From these explorations and observations, they begin to develop schemas of what they "ought to do." If these schemas conflict with what others in their environment expect from them, guilt may develop. Hongyong's curious nature encouraged a sense of initiative. Yet this initiative at a later age was discouraged because it violated cultural expectations of how a female should behave.
4. *Industry versus inferiority*. During the elementary school years (ages 6–12), children receive a great deal of feedback on their performance. They are in school usually 6 hours a day, where they receive a steady stream of information on their abilities. Their assignments may have stars, red marks, or numbers on them. Children may be grouped according to ability. Because children this age can think logically, they can compare their performance on a task with that of their peers. In this way, they form opinions about which activities make them feel industrious, masterful, or competent, as well as ideas about activities or tasks that make them feel inferior or less capable of performing.

According to Erikson, by the time children approach adolescence, their personality has been shaped by the resolution of each of these developmental challenges. How the child resolves these issues has encouraged the development of either a healthy or a not so healthy personality.

YOU REVIEW Erikson's Stages of Psychosocial Development

Age	Stage	Developmental Challenge
Birth–1 year	Trust versus mistrust	Sense of security
1–3 years	Autonomy versus shame and doubt	Independence
3–6 years	Initiative versus guilt	Trying new things
6–12 years	Industry versus inferiority	Sense of mastery and competence
Adolescence	Identity versus role confusion	Sense of self, personal values, and beliefs
Early adulthood	Intimacy versus isolation	Committing to a mutually loving relationship
Middle adulthood	Generativity versus stagnation	Contributing to society through one's work, family, or community services
Late adulthood	Ego integrity versus despair	Viewing one's life as satisfactory and worthwhile

9.4.5 Gender-Role Development

By 2 or 3 years old, children know whether they are a boy or a girl and can label the gender of others. These labels then provide a framework for understanding what clothes, toys, colors, jobs, and behaviors are "appropriate" for each sex. Thus, children at a very early age are processing and developing schemas about **gender roles**, or society's expectations for how a female and a male should behave (Leaper & Friedman, 2007).

Gender permanence, or *gender constancy*, is the knowledge that our assigned gender will not change. Typically, children under the age of 6 years do not yet understand that their gender is permanent (De Lisi & Gallagher, 1991; Szkrybalo & Ruble, 1999). Although young children lack gender permanence, they are especially rigid in gender stereotyping even across ethnic groups (Bussey & Bandura, 1999; Halim et al., 2013; 2014; Ruble et al., 2006). Recall that at this age children focus on only one aspect of a situation or an object. If one of your features or behaviors looks like that of a boy, then you are a boy. If the feature fits with the child's concept of a girl, then you are a girl. Consequently, if a little boy puts on his mother's dress, he may believe that he is now a girl.

Ellen Pastorino

▲ Young children lack gender permanence, the knowledge that our assigned gender does not change. Playing dress-up allows them to explore the gender roles of the other sex.

Bem's Gender-Schema Theory: Integrating Learning and Cognition

The process by which a child develops gender roles and comes to label specific behaviors and activities as either masculine or feminine is not completely understood. Psychologists currently endorse Sandra Bem's (1944–2014) **gender-schema theory**, a perspective that combines elements of social learning theory and cognitive development. Gender-schema theory suggests that the learning processes of modeling and reinforcement work together with a child's developing mental abilities to facilitate the child's understanding of gender (Bem, 1981; Crane & Markus, 1982; Markus et al., 1982; Martin & Halverson, 1981, 1987).

From a very early age, children are keen observers of their environment. They see which behaviors men and women engage in, and which of those behaviors are reinforced or punished. With these observations, children actively construct schemas on gender-appropriate behaviors. These schemas then guide children's decisions about how they and others should behave (Martin & Ruble, 2004).

The schemas for gender-role behavior are culturally defined and vary from society to society. In many cultures, traditional gender roles are emphasized for children (Shiraev & Levy, 2010). Males are seen as aggressive, unemotional, and dominant, whereas females are seen as passive and emotional. These traditional gender roles were evident in Hongyong's culture. Yet within U.S. society, one's ethnic background may convey different gender stereotypes (Markus, 2013). For example, traditional Hispanic American gender roles stress the faithful, self-giving female who is subordinate to her husband and is seen as the preserver of family and tradition. The male is strong, dominant, and the head of the household who is responsible for the safety and honor of the family (McNeill et al., 2001; Reid & Bing, 2000). Among African Americans, females often assume the dominant role in the family. Females are independent, emotionally strong, and obliged to help others (Abrams et al., 2016; Woods-Giscombé, 2010). Strong extended family bonds and high levels of adaptability in gender roles are emphasized (Reid & Bing, 2000). Asian Americans tend to value group solidarity. Often, for females, family obligations are expected to be of higher priority than individual achievement, and males are seen as dominant (Abrams et al., 2016; Pyke & Johnson, 2003).

gender roles society's expectations for how males and females should behave

gender permanence the understanding that one's gender will not change

gender-schema theory the idea that gender roles are acquired through modeling and reinforcement processes that work together with a child's mental abilities

Paul Bradbury/Getty Images

Fuse/Getty Images

▲ Parents' interactions with their children influence their developing schemas of gender roles.

Nature and Nurture Influences on Gender-Role Behavior

Psychologists have explored the extent to which gender-role behavior is due to nature and nurture. For example, research suggests that many gender differences appear across cultures and in other species, such as the preference to develop same-sex friendships, the higher level of activity and physical aggression in males, and gender-specific toy preferences (Hassett, Siebert, & Wallen, 2008; Martin & Ruble, 2010). For example, Hassett et al. (2008) found that male rhesus monkeys showed consistent preference for wheeled toys, whereas female rhesus monkeys tended to show a broader range of toy preferences. These findings suggest that gender differences may in part be influenced by genetic or hormonal differences, particularly during prenatal development. Females prenatally exposed to high levels of male hormones show increased male-typical play and aggression (Auyeung et al., 2009; Drea, 2009; Hines, Constantinescu, & Spencer, 2015). At the same time, a child's environment is filled with messages about gender. These messages come from parents, teachers, peers, and the larger society and suggest the powerful impact of nurture on gender behavior (Bussey & Bandura, 1999).

Parents are the first source of information for babies on gender. In many ways, sons and daughters are treated similarly. Parents encourage both sons and daughters to be independent and are equally warm to their children regardless of gender. Parents also have high educational aspirations for their children and value achievement in both their sons and daughters (Paulson & Sputa, 1996; Spera, Wentzel, & Matto, 2009). Yet daughters experience more parental involvement with their education than do sons, and girls perceive their parents as more encouraging of higher education than do sons (Carter & Wojtkiewicz, 2000; Reynolds & Burge, 2008). However, in the area of science achievement (a traditionally male-stereotyped activity), parents were more likely to believe that science was less interesting and more difficult for their daughters, even when there were no differences in the children's interest or science grades (Tenenbaum & Leaper, 2003).

In addition, most parents expect their children to play with gender-appropriate toys. Boys play with guns, cars, blocks, and balls. Girls are expected to play with dolls and tea sets and to enjoy activities such as playing dress-up, house, and school. Parents often assign different household chores to their sons and daughters. Girls wash the dishes and do chores inside the house such as vacuuming and dusting. Boys take out the trash and do outdoor chores such as mowing the lawn, washing cars, and cleaning out the garage. Younger parents, parents with lower educational levels, and fathers are much more likely to hold to these gender stereotypes and tend to be less accepting of cross-gender behaviors, especially in their sons (Kollmayer et al., 2018; Lytton & Romney, 1991; O'Bryan, Fishbein, & Ritchey, 2004; Paul Halpern & Perry-Jenkins, 2016).

Parents who are less likely to hold these gender expectations tend to have children who are less gender-typed (Paul Halpern & Perry-Jenkins, 2016; Warner & Steel, 1999). Moreover, children who *see* their parents behave in a less stereotypical fashion—moms taking out the trash or dads mopping the floor—also tend to be less gender-typed (Croft et al., 2014; Hupp et al., 2010; Paul Halpern & Perry-Jenkins, 2016). Parents, however, are not the only ones who influence children's gender schemas. Once children begin school, teachers and peers influence them as well.

Research suggests that *gender bias* exists in many classrooms (Leaper & Brown, 2014; Stromquist, 2007). Gender bias is the favoring of one gender over the other because of different views of male and female roles. Boys tend to receive both more positive and more negative attention from teachers, and are called on more often (Einarsson & Granstrom, 2004; Jones & Dindia, 2004; Swinson & Harrop, 2009). Teachers are also more likely to accept wrong answers from girls, encourage boys to try harder when they make errors, and see boys as more clever (Horgan, 1995; Skelton, 2006). Teachers also tend to rate girls as less proficient than boys in math, even when boys and girls perform similarly (Brown & Stone, 2016; Keller, 2001; Robinson-Cimpian et al., 2014; Tiedemann, 2002). As early as second grade, U.S. children are more likely to endorse the cultural stereotype that math is for boys (Cvencek, Meltzoff, & Greenwald, 2011). When it comes to career counseling, boys are more likely to be encouraged to pursue careers in math and science, such as engineering, whereas girls are encouraged to pursue education, nursing, and social work (Brown & Stone, 2016; Halpern et al., 2007; Sadker, 2000).

Children's notions about gender are also reinforced within their peer groups, starting as early as age 3. Same-sex peers praise the child for engaging in gender-appropriate behaviors. Children who engage in gender-inappropriate behavior may be teased, laughed at, and even isolated from the group. Boys are particularly critical of same-sex peers who engage in "girlish" behavior, resulting in harsher punishment for their activities (Levy, Taylor, & Gelman, 1995; Rose & Smith, 2009).

Society in general also contributes to children's gender stereotypes. Some toy stores still have aisles marked "Boys" and "Girls." Male names are much more prevalent than female names within fiction novels, nonfiction books, and subtitles from television and film (Johns & Dye, 2019). Many prime-time television shows still hold to traditional gender stereotypes (Aucoin, 2000; Ellithorpe & Bleakley, 2016; Smith et al., 2012). For example, males appear more frequently and tend to be the dominant characters. Male characters are more likely than female characters to engage in active tasks such as climbing or riding a bike. When men are portrayed in traditionally female occupations such as nursing, the man's masculinity, sexuality, and career choice are questioned (Weaver et al., 2014). Female television characters are more often depicted as passive, dependent, and emotional. Many of the female characters on television are not employed. When they do have jobs, they are less likely to be shown in leadership positions or in computer or engineering professions.

Studies analyzing television advertisements across the globe echo these findings. Women are more likely to be the user of the product, whereas men are more often portrayed as the wise, knowledgeable expert. Women appear more often in domestic roles selling body care and household cleaning products and appear less often in occupational settings. Men are more likely to be associated with products related to technology and cars and are less likely to be shown in private residences or with children in the background (Furnham & Paltzer, 2010; Matthes, Prieler, & Adam, 2016; Nassif & Gunter, 2008). Children who watch television frequently may adopt these gender-role stereotypes.

Gender portrayals in film paint a similar picture. In 100 of the top-grossing family films of 2017 (not including animated films), male lead characters outnumbered female lead characters two-to-one. Male lead characters also had significantly more screen time and speaking time. Yet, in a positive trend, the number

Anna Stowe/Alamy stock photo

▲ Society encourages stereotypical gender schema by prescribing what are appropriate "girl" and "boy" toys, as indicated by this obviously girl-oriented display.

of female lead characters had significantly increased over the previous 4 years (The See Jane 100, 2018).

Sexist depictions of women are even more prevalent in the video game industry. Female characters are often depicted as sexual objects, wearing low-cut clothing, and as visions of beauty. They are shown as passive, needing rescue or help, or as a trophy to be won (Dill & Thill, 2007; Downs & Smith, 2010). Males who spend a significant time playing video games with such sexist content may be more likely to endorse sexist attitudes toward women (Bègue, et al., 2017; Stermer & Burkley, 2015).

9.4 Quiz Yourself

1. **As a child Hongyong was described as willful and strong. If as a baby she had difficulty adapting to new situations and showed intense negative emotions, her temperament would best be described as _____.**
   a. easy
   b. difficult
   c. slow-to-warm-up
   d. sensitive

2. **In the strange situation procedure, a baby who clings to the mother while she is present and who shows extreme distress when the mother leaves would be exhibiting which style of attachment?**
   a. Secure
   b. Avoidant
   c. Disorganized
   d. Resistant

3. **Of the different styles of parenting, _____ parenting seems to result in the best developmental outcomes for most children.**
   a. authoritative
   b. authoritarian
   c. permissive-indulgent
   d. permissive-neglectful

4. **Jose is a very active toddler who prefers to do things by himself. According to Erikson, Jose appears to be successfully resolving which developmental crisis?**
   a. Trust versus mistrust
   b. Autonomy versus shame and doubt
   c. Initiative versus guilt
   d. Industry versus inferiority

5. **Which of the following statements about gender-role development is *false*?**
   a. At 3 years old, toddlers can label their gender.
   b. At 4 years old, preschoolers have gender permanence.
   c. At 6 years old, children have gender roles.
   d. At 8 years old, children have gender constancy.

Answers 1. b; 2. d; 3. a; 4. b; 5. b

9.5 Physical Changes in Adolescence and Adulthood

Development is not limited to the childhood years; changes continue during the adult years, too. In adulthood, however, these changes are much more variable than in childhood. In this section, we describe the physical changes that characterize adolescence and adulthood. As in childhood, both nature and nurture influence our development.

During adolescence and adulthood, we both peak and decline in terms of our physical development. How much and how rapidly we decline are very much influenced by both nature and nurture. Genes affect how we age, but so do the degree to which we exercise mind and body and the experiences we have as we age. What we think of as aging is an incremental and gradual process, but growing into our sexual maturation can be abrupt and actually quite dramatic. We are referring, of course, to the onset of *puberty*.

9.5.1 Puberty: Big Changes, Rapid Growth, and Impact on Behavior

puberty [PEW-bur-tee] the process of sexual maturation

menarche [MEN-ar-kee] a female's first menstruation

Puberty is the process of sexual maturation. These developmental changes involve overall body growth and maturation of sex characteristics that enable people to sexually reproduce. Puberty generally occurs 2 years earlier in females than in males, with an average onset at age 10 in females and age 12 for males, but the timing of puberty varies greatly from one person to another and from one culture to another (Parent et al., 2003). Over the past 100 years, the age at which puberty begins has dropped in the United States, Western Europe, and Japan. Even within the United States, ethnic variations exist, with African American and Hispanic females entering puberty a year earlier, on average, than European American females (Butts & Seifer, 2010; Mendle, 2014).

A growth spurt shortly after age 10 for females and after age 12 for males adds almost 10 inches in height and about 40 pounds in weight to the average body through adolescence. Females' hips broaden relative to their shoulders, and males' shoulders widen relative to their hips. Both sexes gain muscle and fat during puberty; however, females gain more fat and males gain more muscle. Because these changes are abrupt and uneven at times, early adolescence is regarded as an especially awkward phase of development (Malina, 1990).

In addition to overall growth, puberty includes internal and external signs of sexual maturity, caused by the release of sex hormones. In females, sex hormones cause the breasts, ovaries, uterus, and vagina to mature, and initiate the start of their first menstrual cycle, or **menarche**. Pubic hair and underarm hair also develop. In males, sex hormones cause the penis, scrotum, and testes to mature. These changes are accompanied by the growth of body hair and a deepening of the voice as the larynx enlarges. On average, males and females complete the process of puberty within 4 to 5 years (Rogol, Roemmich, & Clark, 2002).

Puberty has a definite emotional and psychological impact, particularly on the adolescent's self-image and mood. Typically, adolescents' reactions to these physical changes are mixed, but if they are prepared for the upcoming changes and have a supportive family, psychological adjustment to puberty is better (Mrug et al., 2008; Omar, McElderry, & Zakharia, 2003). As we saw in this part's case study, Hongyong's lack of knowledge and understanding of these changes made puberty confusing for her. Many adults attribute teenagers' moodiness to "raging hormones." Although higher hormone levels may influence teenagers' moods, it is also likely that teenagers' emotions influence hormone levels (Adam, 2006; Nottelmann et al., 1990). Teenagers often juggle multiple activities such as school, sports, clubs, band, or part-time work while interacting with varying groups of people—teachers, peers, family, coworkers, or coaches. Regulating their emotions and expectations within these different interactions and activities can be stressful and result in moodiness.

The timing of puberty also may influence the self-image of an adolescent. The majority of studies suggest that adolescents who mature earlier than their peers display higher levels of both depression and anxiety during adolescence and early adulthood (Hamlat et al., 2019; Mendle, 2014; Mendle & Ferrero, 2012). Early-maturing males display greater levels of delinquent acts such as vandalism, property damage, and speeding; are more likely to drink alcohol and use tobacco and marijuana; and are more likely to engage in sexual activity and view Internet porn than those who mature later (Mendle & Ferrero, 2012). Early-maturing females are more likely to use tobacco and drink alcohol during adolescence, develop disordered eating, be sexually victimized, and do less well in school than those who mature later (Ge et al., 2006; Graber, Brooks-Gunn, & Warren, 2006; Mendle, 2014; Tanner-Smith, 2010). Adolescents who develop early may find the attention they receive hard to cope with and feel fraught with pressures to become sexually active or rebellious when they may not be ready cognitively and emotionally to do so. Adolescents who develop later are better adjusted to these changes because the demand to "be adult" or to become sexually active occurs at an older age, when their cognitive abilities are better able to handle such pressures. However, keep in mind that the social context of the adolescent may moderate the effect of early maturation. A supportive family environment may serve as a protective mechanism, whereas deviant peers may encourage rule breaking (Mendle & Ferrero, 2012).

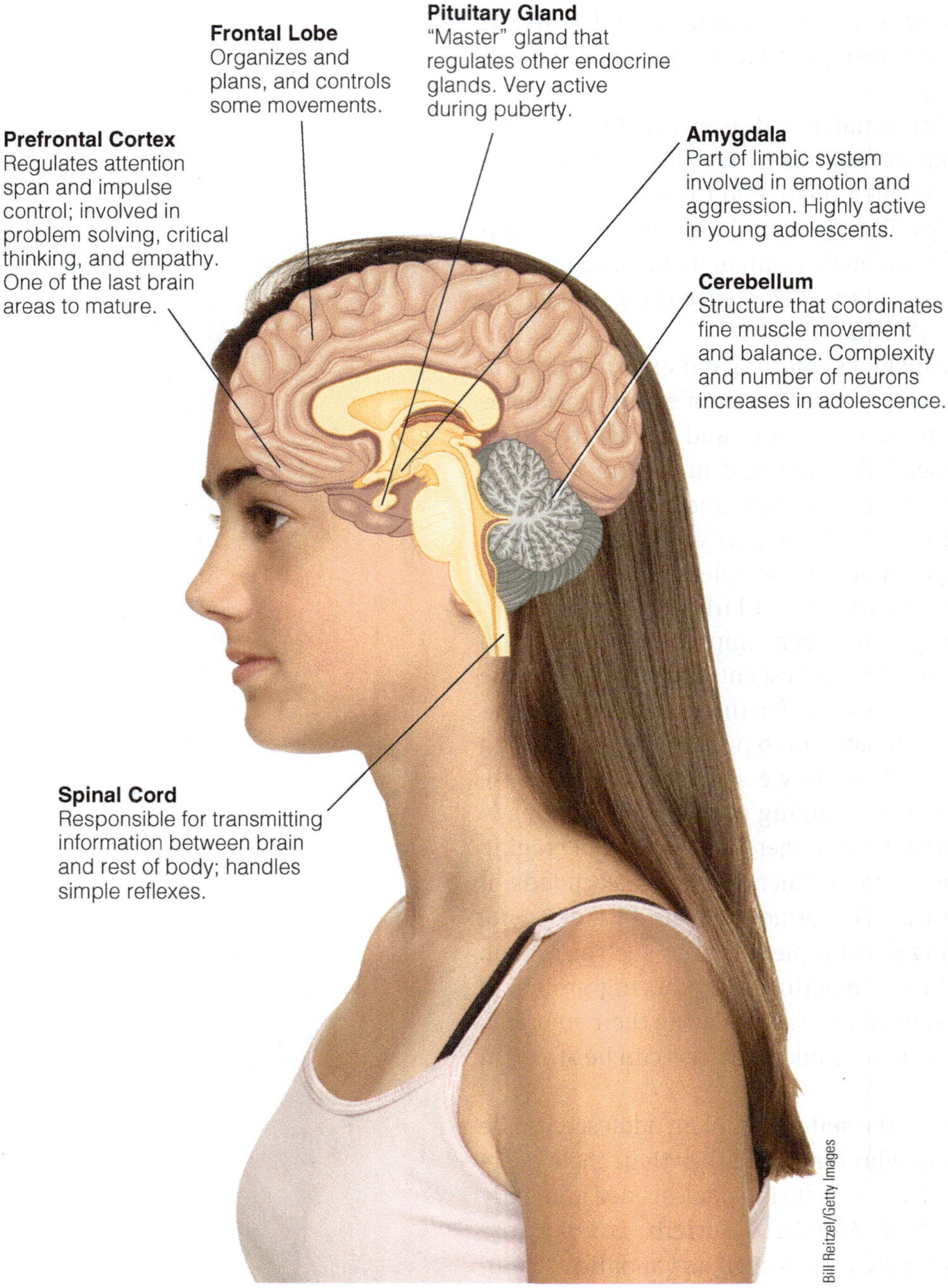

FIGURE 9.2

Changes in the Adolescent Brain

Changes in the adolescent brain generally start at the back of the brain and move toward the front. Hence, the areas of the brain that are most involved in problem solving, planning, and critical thinking are the last areas to mature.

9.5.2 Brain Changes in Adolescence and Adulthood

In addition to pubertal changes, a tremendous amount of brain development takes place during adolescence and into early adulthood. Medical technology such as magnetic resonance imaging (MRI and fMRI; see Chapter 2) has allowed researchers to examine people's brains. These studies indicate dynamic changes in brain anatomy into early adulthood (Ashtari et al., 2007; Galvan et al., 2007; Porter et al., 2011). These changes appear to start at the back of the brain and move toward the front (● FIGURE 9.2). The number of neurons and the complexity of their connections increase in the cerebellum. Recall that the cerebellum is necessary for balance, muscle tone, and performance of motor skills. The amygdala is more active in teens than in adults, and is larger in males (Koolschijn & Crone, 2013; Scherf, Smyth, & Delgado, 2013). As we saw in Chapter 2, the amygdala regulates our emotional reactions. Nerve fibers in the corpus callosum—the band of nerves that connects the two cerebral hemispheres—also thicken before and during puberty (Porter et al., 2011; Thompson et al., 2000).

Just prior to puberty there appears to be a second wave of overproduction of cortical gray matter—the tissue that covers the outside of the cerebral hemispheres that appears gray because of the absence of myelin on the axons (Durston et al., 2001; Krongold, Cooper, & Bray, 2017). The brain then prunes these connections as it did earlier in life—keeping the connections that are used while those that are not used wither away (see ● FIGURE 9.3). This gray matter growth spurt predominates in the prefrontal cortex—the area that plays a major role in cognitive processes such as problem solving, judgment, reasoning, impulse control, and the planning and execution of behavior. This is among the last brain areas to mature, not reaching adult dimensions until the early 20s (Casey, Giedd, & Thomas, 2000; Cohen et al., 2016; Giedd, 2004).

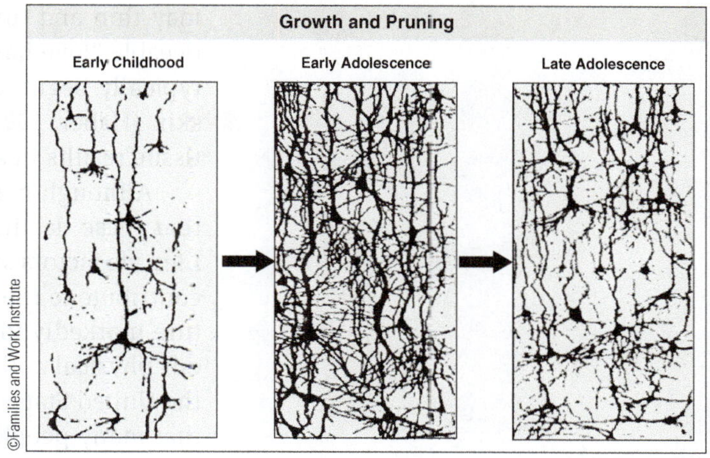

FIGURE 9.3

Neural Growth and Pruning

During early adolescence, new neural connections are formed. In a process called pruning, those that are used are strengthened, whereas those that are not wither away. Hence, engaging in stimulating and interesting activities during adolescence is good for our brains.

Do these brain changes *cause* teenagers' behavior? Changes in the cerebellum *may* explain why young teens tend to be more physically uncoordinated and awkward than older teens and adults. The immaturity of the prefrontal cortex *may* explain why teenagers' judgment and reasoning are not always sound. However, although structural changes in the brain *correlate* with teenage behavior, that does not mean they *cause* the behavior. Adolescent brain research does not take into account other aspects of development, such as cognitive abilities and the psychosocial challenge of forming an identity (discussed later). Moreover, adolescent behavior is also influenced by other environmental and cultural factors that contribute to brain processing, such as parenting, peer pressure, and the influence of school and the media. Adolescents all over the world experience roughly the same process of brain development, yet teenagers in different cultures and environments do not all behave the same way. Attributing a specific teenager's behavior solely to brain changes ignores variations among individuals and across development. Yet we do know that teenagers have continued opportunities to develop their brains through activities in which they participate (Brant et al., 2013). Exercising their minds by reading, doing mathematics, and playing sports or music can strengthen neural connections.

Is the brain completely developed at adolescence? No. Under normal conditions, stem cells in some regions of the brain continuously generate neurons throughout life and neural networks reorganize (Park & McDonough, 2013; Schmidt-Hieber, Jonas, & Bischofberger, 2004; Shors, 2014). The brain remains *plastic*—able to adapt in response to new experiences such as new jobs, marriage, divorce, children, new friends, and financial responsibilities.

9.5.3 Physical Changes from Early to Later Adulthood

We hit our biological prime during early adulthood, when all major biological systems reach full maturation. Both females and males peak during their late 20s and early 30s in terms of physical strength, stamina, coordination, dexterity, and endurance (Whitbourne, 1996). These abilities gradually decline in middle and late adulthood.

A similar process occurs in our sensory abilities. Visual acuity, or the ability to focus vision, peaks in our early 20s and remains fairly high until middle adulthood. As we age, we lose the ability to focus on close objects (*presbyopia*), so that reading glasses or bifocals may become necessary in middle or late adulthood. Age-related hearing loss is also common among older adults, especially for high-pitched tones such as a distant telephone or a doorbell. However, people's senses of taste, smell, and touch remain fairly stable until late adulthood.

We see additional signs of the aging process in people's physical appearance as they approach their 40s and 50s. The skin starts to show wrinkles, and the hair may thin and turn gray. Weight gain is likely as metabolism slows, causing noticeable "love handles" or a "pot belly." Then, as people approach their 60s, they typically begin to lose weight and muscle, which may result in a sagging of the skin (Haber, 1994). The compression of vertebrae combined with a loss of bone tissue results in a loss of height as people age.

Although many physical abilities decline over the adult years, it is not clear that these declines are inevitable. As we discuss in more detail in Chapter 12, lifestyle factors such as poor diet, smoking, drinking alcohol, and lack of exercise contribute to the decline in physical functioning for some people. Moreover, culture markedly influences the way we think about aging and our expectations of our physical abilities in middle and later adulthood. In Western cultures such as the United States, becoming old is associated with being frail, useless, and ill, so that many people attempt to push back the aging process. Yet in countries such as Brazil, China, Japan, and Russia, where older people are more valued, aging is viewed more positively and is perceived as a time to look forward to rather than to dread (Gardiner, Mutter, & Kosmitzki, 1998; Lockenhoff et al., 2009). People with positive perceptions of aging engage in more preventive health behaviors, such as exercising, and tend to live longer (Levy & Myers, 2004; Levy et al., 2002). Across the world, many older people, despite changes in physical functioning, still lead active lifestyles (Baltes, 1997). As people age, they can usually continue their daily activities by making some adjustments and allowing themselves more time.

9.5.4 Gender and Reproductive Capacity

Our reproductive capacity also changes during the adulthood years. Female fertility steadily decreases from age 15 to age 50 (McFalls, 1990; Rowe, 2006). Sometime around age 50, on average, women undergo changes associated with the process of **menopause**. Menopause signals the end of a female's childbearing years. The body produces less and less estrogen, affecting the number of eggs that are released from the ovaries. Eventually, as she ages, ovulation and menstruation stop altogether. Decreasing levels of estrogen also cause the breasts and the uterus to shrink. The vaginal walls produce less lubrication, which may make sexual intercourse painful.

menopause the period when a female stops menstruating and is no longer fertile

Although males do not experience a "male menopause," they, too, undergo hormonal changes after age 60, termed *andropause* (Finch, 2001; Mohr et al., 2005; Whitbourne, 2001). They gradually produce fewer male hormones as they age, which lowers the concentration of sperm in the semen and results in hair loss on the legs and face. However, males are still capable of producing offspring into their 70s, 80s, and 90s. Despite these reproductive changes, older adults continue to remain sexually active through their 80s (Lee et al., 2016; Lindau et al., 2007).

Rawpixel.com/Shutterstock.com

▲ Regular physical exercise in older adults is beneficial for one's cardiovascular, metabolic, and cognitive functioning.

Because many cultures equate "looking old" with being unattractive, especially for females, middle age and later life may not seem very appealing. However, despite the effects of aging, 40% of noninstitutionalized people over 65 report being in very good to excellent health compared to 65% for persons 18 to 64 years old (Administration on Aging [AOA], 2011). Although older adults may not be pleased with certain aspects of physical aging, they are no less content with their lives. Several studies show that older adults often report high levels of well-being and are generally satisfied and happy with their lives (Blanchflower & Oswald, 2008; Cacioppo et al., 2008; Charles & Carstensen, 2010; Dolan, Kudrna, & Stone, 2017; Stawski et al., 2008). Happiness and contentment perhaps have more to do with people's ability to adjust to these changes rather than with the changes themselves.

9.5 Quiz Yourself

1. Research suggests that early maturation during puberty may show a negative association with males' and females' self-image. Which of the following conclusions can be drawn from this finding?

a. Early maturation causes a negative self-image in adolescence.
b. A negative self-image in adolescence causes early maturation.
c. There is a relationship between the timing of puberty and an adolescent's self-image.
d. Both a and b

2. Andre, a 65-year-old male, is likely to experience all of the following as the result of aging except _____.

a. weight loss
b. andropause
c. loss in visual acuity
d. hearing loss for low-pitched tones

3. Which of the following lists the brain structures in the correct order in which they change (from earliest to latest) in adolescence?

a. Cerebellum, prefrontal cortex, amygdala
b. Cerebellum, amygdala, prefrontal cortex
c. Prefrontal cortex, cerebellum, amygdala
d. Amygdala, prefrontal cortex, cerebellum

Answers 1. c; 2. d; 3. b

9.6 Cognitive Changes in Adolescence and Adulthood

Adolescence and adulthood are also marked by changes in the way that we think. Consider how Hongyong's thoughts and focus changed over time. Initially, as a young adolescent, her concerns and thoughts predominantly centered on herself. With her marriage, her focus expanded to include her spouse and her family's views on herself. Then, as she grew older, she became more accepting of others. This section examines these changes in cognition.

9.6.1 Formal Operations Revisited: Applying Cognition to Adolescent Behavior

As we saw earlier in this chapter, children think and reason in ways that are qualitatively different from the thinking of adolescents and adults. Similarly, teenagers do not necessarily think like adults, but they are beginning to practice the reasoning skills and the ability to think outside themselves that characterize later cognitive development.

Recall that Piaget (1952) proposed that teenagers begin to think abstractly during the formal operations stage. This ability to reason abstractly allows them to imagine what could be and to hypothesize about future events and future outcomes. As a result, adolescents experience what they believe are—and indeed sometimes are—tremendous insights into how things could be rather than how they are. This phenomenon is often labeled the *idealism of youth* (Elkind, 1998). Adolescents believe that they have the answers to problems such as world hunger or conflicts. This mental ability also helps adolescents in discovering who they are as individuals—a topic that will be discussed later in this chapter.

Michael J. Doolittle/The Image Works

▲ The ability to reason abstractly allows teenagers to successfully tackle complex academic topics.

imaginary audience the belief held by adolescents that everyone is watching what they do

personal fable the belief held by adolescents that they are unique and special

Formal operational thinking also allows teenagers to tackle more challenging academic subjects (science, geometry, calculus) that rely on abstract visualization and reasoning powers. It also enables adolescents to argue more effectively, a power that may not be seen positively by their parents! They are more capable of suggesting hypothetical scenarios ("What if...") to justify their position, making them more effective debaters (Elkind, 1998). However, along with this ability to think abstractly comes the return of *egocentrism*.

Egocentrism in adolescence involves teenagers' imagining what others must be thinking. However, teens believe that other people are concerned with the same things they are. Because adolescents' ideas focus mainly on themselves, they believe that others are equally concerned about them (Elkind & Bowen, 1979). For example, a teen with a pimple on their face may imagine that their peers and teachers are thinking only about the pimple on their face. Recall how Hongyong hid in her room ashamed that everyone would know that she was menstruating. Teenagers may not ask or answer questions in class because they are so sure that everyone is talking about them and thinking about them. They are newly and acutely aware of their own being, and self-consciousness peaks. Because teens believe that others are focused on them, they behave as if they are on stage—playing to an audience—a phenomenon referred to as the **imaginary audience** (Elkind, 1998). They may laugh especially loudly or behave dramatically because of their belief that they are being constantly watched. Neuroimaging research and adolescent self-reports support this heightened sensitivity to others' evaluation in adolescence (Somerville, 2013; Somerville et al., 2013). Although the imaginary audience and egocentrism are most associated with the teenage years, they may still be somewhat present later in life as young adults choose clothing, jobs, or interests to impress an audience that is largely imaginary (Frankenberger, 2000; Schwartz, Maynard, & Uzelac, 2008).

Another feature of adolescents' thought that relates to egocentrism is the **personal fable** (Elkind, 1998). Teenagers develop the "personal fable" that they are special and unique, that their thoughts and feelings cannot be adequately understood by others (Elkind, 1994). Reflect back on your first love. When that relationship ended, you may have felt as if no one in the world could identify with what you were feeling. The story you tell yourself is that this person, who is the only person in the world for you, has now gone away, and your life will never be happy again. This is one personal fable of adolescence.

Personal fables may contribute to adolescent risk taking. Because teenagers feel that they are special and unique, they often feel that their own risks are less than those of their peers. For example, they may engage in unprotected sexual intercourse, believing that they won't be the ones to contract a sexually transmitted infection or get pregnant. They may experiment with drugs, believing that they will not become addicted. In their minds, addiction happens to other people. However, some research suggests that this *optimistic bias* is no more prevalent in adolescents than it is in adults (Reyna & Farley, 2006). Moreover, adolescent risk-taking behavior is much more likely in emotionally charged situations than in cool, less emotional ones (Casey & Caudle, 2013; Figner & Weber, 2011).

Although formal operational thinking is often perceived as the hallmark of adolescent thinking, this does not mean that *all* adolescents think abstractly in this way. Cross-cultural research (Hollos & Richards, 1993; Rogoff & Chavajay, 1995) suggests that the development of formal operational thinking is very much influenced by experience and culture. If abstract thought is necessary to "get by" in one's society or for a particular task, then humans may learn it. This thinking is more likely to be found in youths who are formally educated and in societies with more specialized and technical occupations (Flieller, 1999; Kuhn & Crowell, 2011). Beyond Piaget's stage of formal operations, research has documented that adolescents think in other ways that are qualitatively different from adults. One such discovery is from research studies on *postformal thought*.

Jerzyworks/Masterfile

▲ The physical changes of puberty and the cognitive ability to think abstractly often make teenagers self-conscious about their appearance.

9.6.2 Postformal Thought: Developing Adult Reasoning

Suppose you were in the same situation as Hongyong. You are traveling in the middle of a war with a baby strapped to your back and three young children. Your baby's survival is questionable because she has been crushed by the crowds, and all of you are tired, hungry, and cold. Her added weight makes it difficult for you to walk, especially because you have been traveling for days with little food or water. What do you do? Would you, like Hongyong, consider leaving the baby under a tree in the hope of ensuring the survival of the rest of your family? Or would you, like Dukwah, insist that the baby continue to be carried? Is there a right or a wrong answer?

When situations like this are presented to adolescents and adults, differences emerge in their thinking. Adolescents often reason in terms of black or white, right or wrong, good or bad—what is called **dualistic thinking** (Perry, 1981). They tend to believe that there is only one solution. However, as people enter adulthood, they are more capable of **relativistic thinking**, the idea that in many situations there is not necessarily one right or wrong answer. As adults we become aware that sometimes solutions and answers are relative to the situation or to the people in the situation. In Hongyong's dilemma, for example, adults typically would consider additional situational aspects such as how much farther the family has to travel, whether the younger children can help carry the baby, and the likelihood of the mother's surviving if she continues to carry the baby. The adolescent, thinking dualistically, may still believe the adult must do everything—carry the baby, lead the family, and reach safety.

Numerous research investigations support the notion that relativistic thinking represents a qualitative change beyond formal operations (Sinnott, 1998; Yang, Wan, & Chiou, 2010). In this context, it has been termed a type of **postformal thought**, characterized by the appreciation that a correct solution or answer may vary from situation to situation and that there may be multiple solutions, all equally viable, to a given problem (see dialectical reasoning, Chapter 8). As adults age, their experiences truly do help them reason, resolve conflicts, and make decisions in a more pragmatic way (Grossmann et al., 2012; Worthy et al., 2011).

9.6.3 Changes in Mental Abilities

Adults not only reason differently from adolescents but also show changes in other mental abilities. The most comprehensive research to date, undertaken by Schaie (1983, 1994, 1996; Schaie & Willis, 2000), reveals that patterns of aging differ for different mental abilities. Recall from Chapter 8 that there are two broad categories of mental abilities, called *fluid intelligence* and *crystallized intelligence*.

dualistic [do-uhl-LIS-tik] thinking reasoning that divides situations and issues into right and wrong categories

relativistic [rell-uh-tah-VIS-tik] thinking the idea that in many situations there is not necessarily one right or wrong answer

postformal thought the idea that a correct solution (or solutions) may vary, depending on the circumstances

fluid intelligence abilities that rely on information-processing skills such as reaction time, attention, and working memory

crystallized intelligence abilities that rely on knowledge, expertise, and judgment

Fluid intelligence, which develops during early childhood, relies heavily on processing skills such as reaction time, attention, and working memory. It is presumed to be based primarily on nature or biology, peaking when brain maturity has been reached (Li et al., 2004). Within the category of fluid intelligence, some mental abilities remain stronger than others. For example, perceptual speed and numeric ability tend to decline in one's late 20s and early 30s. Other fluid skills such as spatial orientation and inductive reasoning remain strong and steady through one's 50s, declining after that (Bucur & Madden, 2010; Salthouse, 2012; Schmiedek, Lovden, & Lindenberger, 2013; Spreng & Turner, 2019).

Crystallized intelligence, in contrast, involves the use of knowledge, expertise, and good judgment. Crystallized intelligence depends more on nurture or experience, such as educational background and occupational expertise. These abilities increase into adulthood and then decline somewhat after one's 70s (Ackerman, 2014; Hartshorne & Germine, 2015; Salthouse, 2012; Spreng & Turner, 2019; van Hooren et al., 2007). Crystallized skills include vocabulary, verbal memory, and responses to social situations. These age-related trends in mental abilities are summarized in ● FIGURE 9.4.

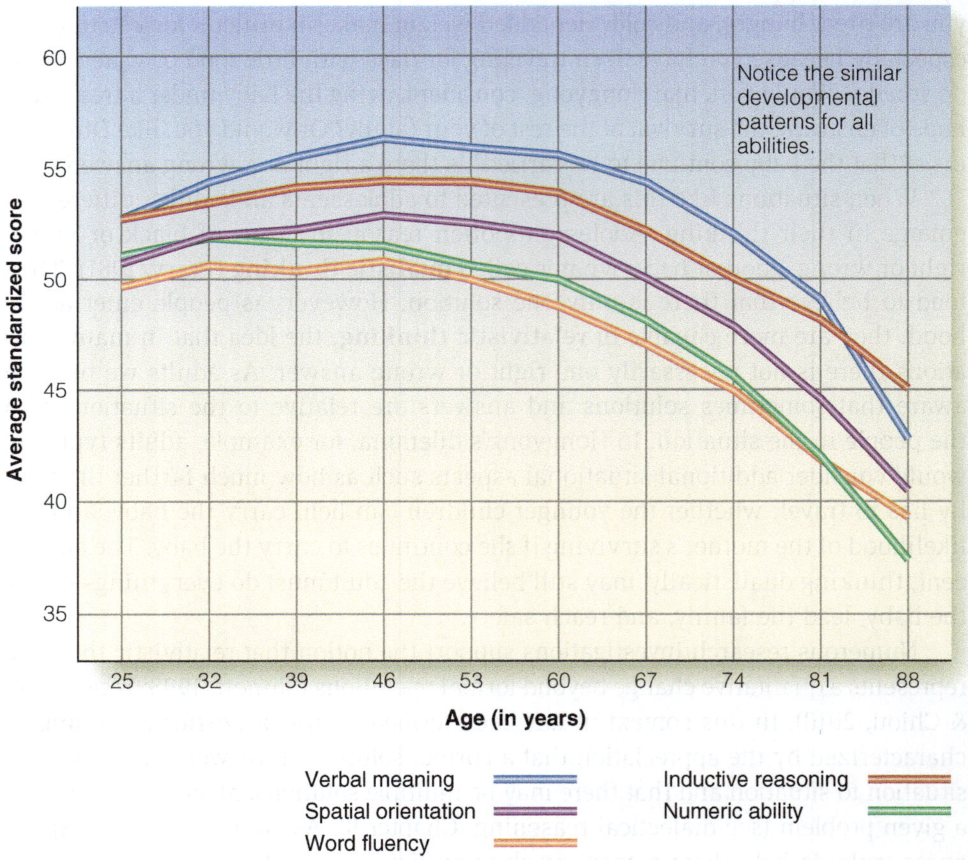

FIGURE 9.4

Age Trends in Mental Abilities

In his ongoing study of mental abilities, Schaie (1983, 1994, 1996) has documented that most mental abilities remain strong through early and middle adulthood. Eighty percent of his participants showed no declines by age 60, and almost two-thirds were still stable through age 80.

Source: "The Course of Adult Intellectual Development," by K. W. Schaie, 1994, *American Psychologist, 49*, 304–313. Copyright © by the American Psychological Association.

Many factors other than age shape how well we function mentally. Poor health, diseases, and some prescription medications may contribute to a rapid decline in mental abilities. Older adults can benefit cognitively from regular physical exercise (Emery, Finkel, & Pedersen, 2012; Jackson et al., 2016; Kramer & Colcombe, 2018). A mentally inactive lifestyle is also a potential factor in cognitive decline and Alzheimer's disease (Leung et al., 2015; Schaie, 1996; Wilson & Bennett, 2003). The motto "Use it or lose it!" seems most appropriate in this context. Doing crossword puzzles, playing trivia games, and continuing to read, travel, or participate in educational pursuits are all activities that help sustain cognitive functioning (Hertzog et al., 2008; Stine-Morrow et al., 2007).

9.6 Quiz Yourself

1. **The idea that a correct solution (or solutions) may vary depending on the circumstances is called ______.**
   a. dualistic thinking
   b. egocentrism
   c. postformal thought
   d. formal operations
2. **When at the mall with her friends, Maria acts as if everyone is watching her. Maria's behavior is an example of ______.**
   a. egocentrism
   b. an imaginary audience
   c. idealism
   d. a personal fable
3. **Which one of the following mental abilities shows the *least* amount of decline after age 25?**
   a. Inductive reasoning
   b. Numeric ability
   c. Perceptual speed
   d. Reaction time

Answers 1. c; 2. b; 3. a

9.7 Psychosocial Changes in Adolescence and Adulthood

How people's individuality and character develop and change in adolescence and adulthood, and how people navigate their social environments, are challenging research areas in contemporary psychology. Erik Erikson saw adolescence and adulthood as a process of building, modifying, and sustaining a personal identity. This identity is influenced by our social relationships as well as the world of work.

9.7.1 Erikson's Psychosocial Stages of Adolescence and Adulthood

Recall Erikson's psychosocial stages of development (You Review), in which children, adolescents, and adults face developmental crises that establish their individuality. Successfully mastering each stage strengthens the person's capacity to confront and negotiate the next stages. Here we examine the four stages Erikson attributed to the adolescent and adult years.

Identity versus Role Confusion: Know Who You Are

For Erikson (1956, 1958, 1959), adolescence represents the integration and summation of the previous crises of childhood into an appropriate *identity*. Adolescents must figure out who they are and what they believe in, what their values are, and how they may be similar to or different from peers and parents. This search for personal identity is thought to be very much influenced by both the biological changes of puberty and the newly acquired cognitive ability of abstract reasoning (Grysman & Hudson, 2010). Adolescents begin to imagine what they want to be and experiment with new roles and responsibilities as they figure out their personal identity. For example, adolescents may try out different styles of clothing or listen to many types of music. They may join different peer groups or try out different college courses to explore various career options. Sometimes adolescents and young adults become so involved in constantly trying out new roles that they fail to form a stable identity. Erikson referred to this condition as *role confusion*.

Even when an adolescent fully attains an identity, this identity is not permanently etched in stone. Rather, adolescence represents a time when the core of our identity is established. We continue to refine and modify our identity as we transition to adult roles and responsibilities (Marcia, 2002). Think back to Hongyong's identity. Although headstrong, she adopted the values specified for her as a Korean female. Yet given a spouse who valued her opinions, she was able to explore her potential as a businessperson.

Intimacy versus Isolation: Connect with Others

In Erikson's theory, successful resolution of the identity crisis prepares the young adult for the next developmental crisis: *intimacy versus isolation*. Having formed a stable identity, the person is now prepared to make a long-term commitment to a partner. Intimacy requires that people refine and modify their identity to accommodate the values and interests of another. In successfully meeting this challenge, neither partner's identity would be sacrificed. For Erikson, *intimacy* is characterized by cooperation, tolerance, and an acceptance of others' different views and values. This secure sense of intimacy may be expressed through marriage or long-term romantic partnerships, through close friendships, or through work relationships. Some people may lose their sense of identity—or fear losing it—and therefore be reluctant to connect with others. Erikson referred to this state as *isolation*. Isolated individuals are easily threatened by close relations with others and hesitate to establish close ties. They are more defensive in the relationships they do form, and they have less tolerance for the varying views and opinions of others.

Consider Hongyong and her husband Dukpil's relationship. They met for the first time when they were joined in marriage, but were fortunate to build an intimate relationship. They confided in one another and valued each other's opinions. They each deferred to the other when the other had more interest or expertise on the subject. Hongyong forgave Dukpil and accepted him despite his infidelities and drinking. He accepted her despite her willfulness and conversion to Christianity. They were tolerant of one another in a manner consistent with their culture.

▼ According to Erikson, young adults with stable identities are prepared to make a commitment to a partner.

Marisa Rios

Generativity versus Stagnation: Make the World a Better Place

According to Erikson, resolving the intimacy versus isolation stage prepares adults for the developmental crisis of the middle adulthood years: *generativity versus stagnation*. This stage of development has to do with our feeling that we have made significant and meaningful contributions to our society. Middle adulthood is often the time when people become aware of their mortality. They recognize that their time here on Earth is limited. As a result, they begin to think about their accomplishments and their effect on society. Erikson believed that if middle-aged adults feel that they have contributed something worthwhile to society, then a sense of *generativity* has been achieved. Marriage, long-term relationships, child rearing, career accomplishments, and service to the community may all contribute to this sense of having lived a productive life (Westermeyer, 2004). On the one hand, generativity is associated with positive personality characteristics, psychological well-being, and life satisfaction (McAdams & Guo, 2015; Peterson & Duncan, 2007). On the other hand, middle-aged adults who conclude that they have contributed very little to society will experience *stagnation,* a sense of failure, and an absence of meaningful purpose in life.

People cope with feelings of stagnation in a variety of ways. Some remain disenchanted and bitter. Others attempt to change their lives to regain a sense of generativity and identity. Society often perceives such attempts as a *midlife crisis.* However, the number of people who actually experience such dramatic shifts in their life structure is actually quite small (Lachman, Teshale, & Agrigoroaei, 2015; Wrightsman, 1994). For example, in a 12-year study of people over age 40, Sadler (2000) found that a significant number of middle-aged adults are productive, enjoy their close relationships, and have begun to take risks. They experience what Sadler calls a "second growth" in midlife, characterized by enjoyment of life as Hongyong did with her ch'iryo practice.

Integrity versus Despair: No Regrets

Near the end of the life span, adults begin to review their lives and judge their satisfaction with the choices they have made and the direction that their lives have taken. Erikson believed that the issue facing people in their 60s and beyond was one of *integrity versus despair.* When this evaluation is generally positive and satisfying, individuals have achieved a sense of *integrity,* which allows them to face their eventual death without fear or regret. However, if this life review results in dissatisfaction and a sense of regret over roads not taken, the person is more likely to experience *despair* or hopelessness stemming from the knowledge that one cannot relive one's life. In such a case, the person may become fearful of death.

emerging adulthood the transitional period between late adolescence and the mid-20s when young people have left adolescence but have not yet assumed adult roles and responsibilities

9.7.2 Emerging Adulthood

In developed nations such as the United States, the time between the teenage years and when one assumes adult responsibilities is not as short as it used to be. This added length has resulted in a new transitional phase of development from one's late teens to one's mid-20s referred to as **emerging adulthood** (Arnett, 2007).

More young people are attending college, especially women. The median age of marriage has risen and parenthood is often delayed such that emerging adulthood prolongs identity development as young people pursue education, travel, explore various career paths, and experiment with varying love relationships (Arnett, 2010). Unfortunately, substance and behavioral addictions may also take hold during this time (Sussmann & Arnett, 2014). Even at a subjective level, young people don't feel like they have assumed adult responsibilities. For example, in one large diverse sample of college and noncollege young

▼ For older adults, reminiscing about their experiences provides a sense of integrity and life satisfaction.

John Henley/Getty Images

Jeffrey Isaac Greenberg 20+/Alamy Stock Photo

▲ Emerging adults may participate in career fairs to further explore their identity options.

adults between the ages of 18 and 35, 56% reported feeling "somewhat like an adult" (Lowe et al., 2013).

However, emerging adulthood does not occur for all young people. In many non-Western cultures, there is no delay between the teen years and adult roles; young people work, get married, and raise families in adolescence or soon after (UNICEF, 2009). Even in Western nations like the United States that have postponed adult roles, a transitional period of emerging adulthood is not possible for young people with limited economic resources or little education or for those who experience early parenthood (P. Cohen et al., 2003).

9.7.3 Variations in Social Relations in Adolescence and Adulthood

Hongyong followed the prescribed social roles for her time and for her culture. She did not socialize with boys or date, and her parents arranged her marriage. Despite her husband's infidelities, she never considered divorce. She and her husband expected to have children. If they did not, they would have been viewed as abnormal. Although in many cultures such prescribed social roles may still be the norm, in Western cultures, today's adolescents and adults express intimacy in relationships in a wide range of lifestyles, including dating, marriage, cohabitation, divorce, and parenthood.

Dating and Singlehood

Most teens date at some point in adolescence, but regular dating has declined in recent years with 49% of high school seniors reporting that they have never dated, or been otherwise romantically involved with another person (Child Trends, 2019). However, this decline could reflect a change in teens' language. Nowadays, young people more often talk of "hanging out" or "hooking up" rather than dating. Interestingly, teens of the iGen generation (those born between 1995 and 2012) are not only less likely to date but are more likely when they do go out of the house to be in the company of their parents (Twenge, 2017). When they do date, young people look for social support, affection, and someone who has similar interests (B. B. Brown, 2004; Collins & van Dulmen, 2006). Males rate the attractiveness of a potential partner as especially important, whereas females rate the attractiveness and social status of a potential partner as important factors in whom to date (Ha, Overbeek, & Engels, 2010).

Dating serves several functions for teenagers. Besides being an outlet for fun and recreation, dating gives teenagers a chance to learn how to cooperate and compromise with people in a variety of situations (Lambeth & Hallett, 2002). For example, choosing a movie or a restaurant entails listening to the other person's wishes and then resolving any differences. Teens can discover more about themselves and how others' needs may differ from their own. Flirting via social media and texting, and sexual experimentation may also be involved (Lenhart et al., 2015; Smetana, Campione-Barr, & Metzger, 2006). Dating and romantic relationships during adolescence pave the way for establishing adult intimate relationships.

Maria Teijeiro/Getty Images

▲ Dating gives teenagers a chance to learn how to cooperate and compromise with people in a variety of situations

It is typical to start one's adulthood as unmarried—and the number of young adults who are single is growing. Currently, an estimated 28% of all U.S. residents 18 and older had never married (U.S. Census Bureau, 2018). In the United States, the median age for first marriages is 29.8 for men and 27.8 for women (U.S. Census Bureau, 2018). Delaying marriage appears to be a global trend as the average age of first marriage has increased in many countries. However, international differences exist with Indonesia and India having lower average ages for first marriage (21.9 and 22.8 years respectively) compared to Spain (33.4 years) and Sweden (34.8 years) (United Nations, 2017). Being single allows young adults a chance to explore different types of friendships and relationships as well as to continue refining and defining their identities. Young single adults also may be moving or traveling as part of building careers, which can make it harder to start or maintain a relationship.

Cohabitation

Some adults choose to live together, or *cohabit*, with an intimate partner, one with whom they enjoy a sexual relationship. Cohabitation rates have been increasing steadily in the United States, and these unions typically last longer than in the recent past. Currently, 48% of women ages 15–44 had cohabited before marriage. About 33 percent of people living together got married within the first five years, while 22 percent continued to live together. The median duration for cohabitation was about 2 years (Copen, Daniels, & Mosher, 2013; Lamidi, Manning, & Brown, 2015). Similar statistics characterize same-sex couples (Manning, Brown, & Stykes, 2016). The increased rate of cohabiting couples is not unique to the United States—an even higher level exists in many other countries, such as Sweden, Canada, France, Finland, Denmark, Peru, Colombia, Chile, and the Dominican Republic (Loveless & Holman, 2007; Yim, Alkema, & Kantorova, 2017). However, cohabitation is rarer in more traditional societies. It is frowned on in Asian societies and discouraged in Islamic societies.

Couples cohabit for various reasons. Delaying marriage and childbearing is now the norm as many young people extend their educations and emerge into adulthood (Lundberg, Pollack, & Stearns, 2016). Many couples may feel that cohabiting before marriage will give them the opportunity to see whether they are truly compatible before undertaking the serious commitment of marriage. Some couples cohabit after divorce as an alternative to remarriage (Brown, Lee, & Bulanda, 2006). Older couples may cohabit with a new partner after the divorce/death of a spouse to preserve financial resources such as alimony, a pension, or social security benefits.

Michael Doolittle /Alamy stock photo

▲ More than 90% of people in the United States choose to get married at some point in their lives.

Marriage: Adaptation, Satisfaction, and Gender

More than 90% of Americans choose to get married at some point in their lives (U.S. Census Bureau, 2015). Marriage, like any other lifestyle choice, involves adaptation. A new role as spouse has been added and people must adjust to living as a couple rather than as individuals. Researchers have found that many aspects of the marital relationship change after the first year. The "I love you's" become less frequent, sexual activity becomes less frequent, and couples spend more time performing daily chores and tasks together rather than talking and having fun. Despite these changes, many couples continue to report satisfaction in their marital relationships.

Research has discovered many factors that are related to *marital satisfaction* or a person's perception of the overall quality and happiness with the marriage. For example, when both people are similar in family background, social class, education, and religion, couples report more satisfying relationships (Gaunt, 2006). Couples who wait to marry until their mid- to late-20s are more likely to report happier marriages than those who marry before then (Glenn, Uecker, & Love, 2010). Warm and positive family relationships (before and during marriage), supportive spouse behavior, a willingness to sacrifice, viewing one's partner positively or as an ideal mate, and secure financial circumstances also increase the chances of a satisfying marital or romantic relationship (Ackerman et al., 2013; Clark et al., 2010; Kogan et al., 2010; McNulty, Olson, Jones, & Acosta, 2017; Murray et al., 2011; Waldinger & Schulz, 2016). On the other hand, boredom, negative comments, contempt, defensiveness, and criticism are more likely to harm the chances of a satisfying long-term relationship (Gottman, 1999a, 1999b; Helland et al., 2014; Lavner & Bradbury, 2010; Robles & Kiecolt-Glaser, 2003).

Meta-analytic studies indicate no significant gender differences in marital satisfaction among heterosexual couples in the general population (Jackson et al., 2014). Although married people in different-sex and same-sex relationships report greater life satisfaction and well-being than single people, lesbians, in contrast, report higher well-being cohabitating (Chen & van Ours, 2018; Holt-Lunstad, Birmingham, & Jones, 2008; Myers, 2000). In one study using participants from 166 nations, married people had slightly higher life satisfaction compared to unmarried people over the whole life span (Jebb, Morrison, Tay & Diener, 2020). On average, being married, especially happily married, is associated with better physical and mental health. Men appear to receive more physical health benefits from a happy marriage whereas women appear to be more psychologically and physically vulnerable to marital strain and conflict (Donoho, Crimmins, & Seeman, 2013; Liu & Waite, 2014; Read & Grundy, 2011; Revenson et al., 2016; Wanic & Kulik, 2011). Health advantages for married women are more likely when the marriage is characterized as highly satisfying (Gallo, Troxel, Kuller et al., 2003; Gallo, Troxel, Matthews et al., 2003). While these findings may suggest that marriage makes you healthy and happier, keep in mind that they are just correlations. As you learned in Chapter 1, correlation does not mean causation. It could be that a close, stable, and satisfying partnership protects one physically and emotionally from the stresses of life. However, it is just as likely that people who are already physically and mentally healthy are more likely to get and stay married. Notice too that these results pertain more to marriages rated high in satisfaction. Not all marriages are satisfying which may lead to divorce—our next topic of discussion.

Divorce

About 1 in 5 adults will at some time in their lives experience divorce. Divorce rates are higher among couples who do not have children, have lower levels of education, who marry at a young age, or whose parents divorced (Amato & DeBoer, 2001; Aughinbaugh, Robles, & Sun, 2013; Goodwin, Mosher, & Chandra, 2010; Shulman et al., 2001). Divorce rates are also higher among African Americans and European Americans than among Hispanic Americans and Asian Americans, and higher among lower-income couples than higher-income couples (Aughinbaugh et al., 2013; Lin, Brown, Wright, & Hammersmith, 2018; U.S. Census Bureau, 2010).

Like other lifestyle changes, divorce brings with it stresses and adaptations that the couple and the family must negotiate. Typically, divorce is preceded by a period of conflict and dissatisfaction (Lucas, 2005). Emotional, economic, legal, and practical difficulties follow. What was once one household must now be divided into two. If there are children involved, custody arrangements must be made. Identities are reshaped and redefined as the couple mentally shifts from thinking in terms of "us" to "me." Friendships with other couples may fade. Simultaneously, each member of the couple is resolving feelings of anger, rejection, disappointment, or loneliness (Amato, 2000). Given these changes, it is not surprising that at least *initially* divorced people are more likely to report higher levels of psychological distress or experience physical health problems (Hughes & Waite, 2009; Lorenz et al., 2006; Sbarra, 2015). Over time, however, most people are resilient and adjust to their new lives (Amato, 2010; Mancini, Bonanno, & Clark, 2011; Sbarra, Hasselmo, & Bourassa, 2015). Many divorced adults, especially young people, choose to marry again. However, it is more common for men to remarry than for women (Wang & Parker, 2014).

Divorce also affects the family. Previous styles of parenting may change, as the custodial parent must assume more responsibility for disciplining the children. The noncustodial parent may become more permissive because they spend less time with the children. Children experience many of the same emotions as their parents, such as loss, grieving for the family that was, and anger that their parents were not able to make the marriage work. As a result, they are more likely to misbehave. Children of divorce may be more aggressive, disrespectful, disobedient, withdrawn, or moody, and school performance may deteriorate, at least over the short term (Lansford, 2009; Weaver & Schofield, 2015). Their misbehavior makes it even more difficult for parents to be effective. Studies suggest that it is this breakdown in parenting and children's exposure to marital conflict both prior to and following a divorce that are most harmful to a child's development (Amato, 1993; Amato & Booth, 1996; Cummings & Miller-Graff, 2015). Hence, a two-parent household filled with conflict and disharmony is as difficult for a child as the experience of divorce (Booth & Amato, 2001; Lansford, 2009).

9.7.4 Parenting

At one time, marriage was synonymous with becoming a parent, but that is not necessarily the case today. With increasing numbers of birth control options available, parenthood is more of a choice today than it used to be. About 14% of U.S. women ages 40–44 had never had a child (U.S. Census Bureau, 2018). At the

▲ Parenting may bring changes in gender roles and the division of labor in the home. Such changes may increase or decrease marital satisfaction.

same time, more single adults, cohabitating couples, and gay couples are having or adopting children (U.S. Census Bureau, 2018). For those who do have children, parenthood becomes another life transition that includes adaptation to new roles and responsibilities.

Although most prospective parents look forward to the birth of their child, children radically change people's lives. With the joy and elation of a newborn baby comes less sleep, leisure time, and time spent together as a couple. Life satisfaction typically decreases (Luhmann et al., 2012). Financial planning is a must; it will cost about $230,000 to raise one child from birth through age 17—and that's not including college expenses (Lino et al., 2017). Life becomes a juggling act as the couple tries to keep an eye on all the responsibilities of work and family at the same time. Although fathers today are more involved in child care and housework than ever before (Coley, 2001), most heterosexual couples become more traditional in their gender roles following the birth of a child (Baxter et al., 2015; Katz-Wise, Priess, & Hyde, 2010). Mothers, even working mothers, are more likely to become the primary caregiver of the child as the father intensifies his role as provider (Baxter, Hewitt, & Haynes, 2008; Cowan & Cowan, 2000; Deutsch, 2001).

Other variables also influence life satisfaction following the birth of a baby. For example, the baby's temperament (discussed previously) may create more or less stress on new parents (Schoppe-Sullivan et al., 2007; Slagt et al., 2016). Difficult babies who cry all the time are more of a challenge than babies who are quiet or who are generally cheerful. The parent makes a difference too. Generally, older parents who have waited longer after marrying to have children are better able to adjust to parenthood (Belsky & Rovine, 1990; Umberson et al., 2005). Younger couples who have children right away are adjusting to marriage at the same time that they are coping with being new parents. The levels of income, spousal support, and support from extended family and friends also increase or decrease the amount of stress that comes with parenting (Conger et al., 2013; Levy-Shiff, 1994).

As the child grows older, the demands of parenting do not ease up. Parents adjust their styles of discipline to meet the new challenges their children pose as they grow older and become established (O'Brien, 1996). As the child enters middle school, parenthood may become even more stressful, and marital satisfaction tends to decrease (● FIGURE 9.5; Cui & Donnellan, 2009; Hirschberger et al., 2009; Kurdek, 1999; Waldron-Hennessey & Sabatelli, 1997). Parent-child conflicts increase as adolescents achieve formal operational abilities and begin defining their own identity (Steinberg & Morris, 2001). At the same time, parents, who are typically middle-aged at this time, may also be evaluating and questioning the direction of their own lives. As a result of this conflict and tension, parents may relinquish some control and move toward more shared decision making with their teenagers.

Once the last child has left the family home for college or an independent life, parents are left with what is referred to as the *empty nest*. Parents may be lonely at times and feel that a major chapter in their family life is over. The parents are also aware of their own aging. Yet this stage presents lots of opportunity, too. Most parents, especially women, enjoy the changes brought about by the empty nest. Marital satisfaction tends to increase, and women generally feel better about themselves as the stress and responsibilities of parenthood decrease (Gorchoff, John, & Helson, 2008; White & Edwards, 1990).

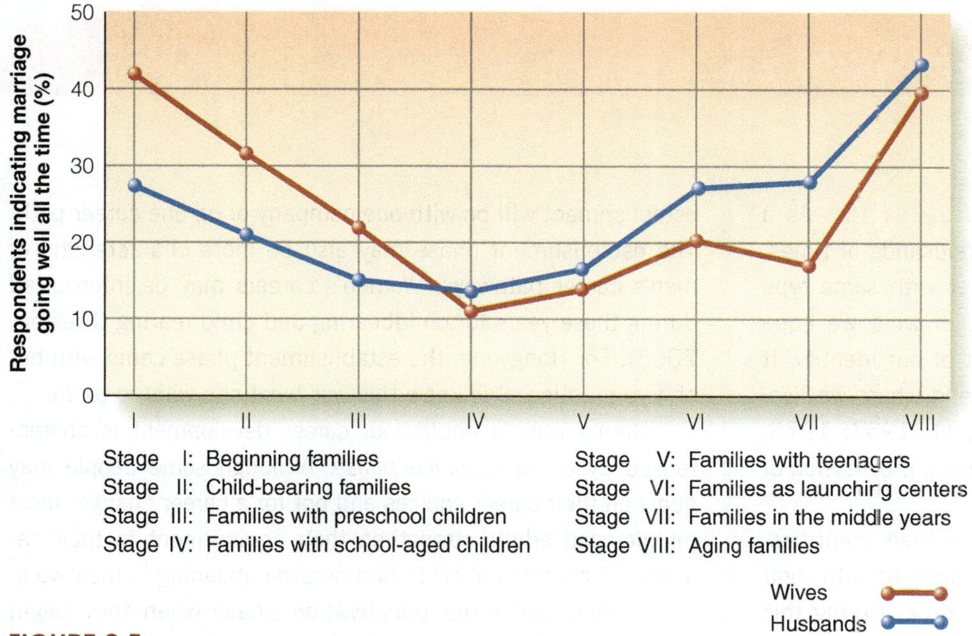

FIGURE 9.5

Marital Satisfaction and Stages of Parenting

First documented by Rollins and Feldman (1975) and later replicated in many studies, the graph shows the percentage of males and females who said their marriage was going well "all the time" at various stages while raising children.

Source: Adapted from Boyd C. Rollins and Harold Feldman, "Marital Satisfaction over the Family Life Cycle," *Journal of Marriage and the Family, 32* (February), 25. Copyrighted 1975 by the National Council on Family Relations, 3989 Central Ave., N.E., Suite 550, Minneapolis, MN 55421.

What happens to parents if their children don't leave—or if they come back because of divorce, limited finances, or extended schooling? This situation is more common today, with over half of U.S. young adults ages 18 to 24 and 16% of 25- to 34-year-olds living with their parents (U.S. Census Bureau, 2018). This phenomenon is referred to as the *full nest* or the *boomerang generation*. It is more common among Hispanic Americans, African Americans, and Asian Americans, perhaps due to economic resources and the greater emphasis on family closeness in these ethnic groups (Arnett, 2004; Lei & South, 2016). Some parents gladly support their emerging adults. If these young adults act responsibly, going to school or working, parents appear to adjust well (Igarashi et al., 2013). However, some parents do find living with their young adult children stressful, which may be detrimental to parental marital quality (Davis, Kim, & Fingerman, 2018; Gitelson & McDermott, 2006). Parents and adult children need to redefine their roles and expectations to reduce conflict and live harmoniously (Burn & Szoeke, 2016).

We see, then, that children complicate the lives of adults. Parenthood tends to correlate with lower rates of marital satisfaction and higher levels of stress. Despite these negative effects, most parents don't regret the experience and report higher levels of happiness, positive emotion, and meaning in life than do nonparents (Nelson et al., 2013). Children bring many joys and experiences that enrich their parents' lives. However, the association between parenthood and well-being varies by age and gender. Compared with nonparents, male and middle-aged parents evidence greater well-being, while young and single parents evidence lower well-being (Nelson et al., 2014).

Psychology Applies to Your World

Career Development

WHAT DO YOU WANT TO BE WHEN YOU GROW UP? As a child, you have been asked this question thousands of times, with the expectation that you will answer it with some type of career choice. What we do for a living, or what we hope to do for a living, becomes an integral part of our identity. It may also determine who we socialize with and where we live. For four decades, Donald Super (1910–1994; 1957, 1976, 1980, 1991) addressed such issues, outlining a progression of career development.

In early adolescence, as teenagers form their identities, they experiment with how various career options fit with their ideas of who they are and what they want to be. During this *crystallization phase,* potential career options are reduced to a few choices. For example, a teenager who views themselves as outgoing, quick thinking, and motivated may imagine themselves in a marketing or law career. Teenagers and young adults further explore career options by testing out prospective career choices in the *specification phase*. For example, a young person who is considering becoming a doctor may volunteer at a hospital or take a part-time job in a physician's office to determine whether medicine fits their interests and abilities. Although somewhat older, Hongyong explored her talents as an entrepreneur through the sesame oil business, as an opium madam, and as a restaurant owner.

Young people enter the workforce and begin to learn about jobs firsthand in the *implementation phase*. The young adult learns both the actual tasks of the job and job-related skills such as getting along with coworkers, getting to work on time, and responding to authority figures. The reality of the work may not meet the person's initial expectations. For example, a teacher's aide may discover that working with children 6 hours a day is not what they expected it to be. Everyone experiences this sort of *reality shock* in some form. However, it is the degree of reality shock that typically determines our willingness to stay on a particular career path. For this reason, the implementation phase can be quite unsettling and unstable. Young adults may find themselves changing positions frequently as they attempt to adjust their expectations to the realities of a particular career.

When young adults decide on a specific occupation, they enter the *establishment phase*. Career expectations continue to be adjusted as the person settles into an occupation and advances in their career. Today, however, it is unlikely that this establishment will be with one company or on one career path. The establishment phase may also be more characteristic of men's career pathways. Women's careers may be interrupted during these years for childbearing and child rearing (Preston, 2005). For Hongyong, the establishment phase came with her ch'iryo practice. She knew this was what she wanted to do.

During middle adulthood, career development is characterized by a *maintenance phase*. Although some people may question their career choices and opt for a career change, most middle-aged adults strengthen their commitment to their careers and are more likely to find personal meaning in their work.

Workers enter the *deceleration phase* when they begin planning for their upcoming retirement. Older adults consider such things as finances, where they want to live, and how they want to spend their retirement years. When people stop working full-time, the *retirement phase* begins. Most Americans choose to retire sometime in their 60s and look forward to retirement living. As with other developmental processes that we have discussed, retirement is a process of adjustment that is influenced by many factors such as health, finances, one's control over the decision to retire, and the ability to maintain social ties with others (Lowis, Edwards, & Burton, 2009; Price & Balaswamy, 2009; van Solinge & Henkens, 2005).

Peter Garrard Beck/Getty Images

▲ During the establishment phase, young adults settle into an occupation or a career.

9.7 Quiz Yourself

1. **According to Erikson, feeling that you have made important contributions to society will lead to a sense of _____.**
   a. integrity
   b. generativity
   c. industry
   d. identity
2. **Which of the following statements is *false*?**
   a. Emerging adulthood occurs for all young people.
   b. Emerging adulthood prolongs identity development.
   c. Emerging adulthood typically occurs in one's late teens to one's mid-20s.
   d. Emerging adulthood is when young people have not yet assumed adult roles and responsibilities.
3. **Which of the following is *false* in regard to social relations in adulthood?**
   a. Cohabitation rates have increased over the past decade.
   b. Among heterosexual couples, more males than females report being happily married.
   c. Worldwide, young adults are delaying marriage.
   d. Divorced people are more likely to experience physical health problems.
4. **Parents' marital satisfaction tends to _____ when their children enter middle school.**
   a. increase
   b. decrease
   c. marginally get better
   d. stay the same
5. **"Reality shock" is most likely to happen during which phase of career development?**
   a. Specification phase
   b. Establishment phase
   c. Implementation phase
   d. Deceleration phase

Answers 1. b; 2. a; 3. b; 4. b; 5. c

9.8 Death and Dying

Hongyong Baek witnessed many people's deaths due to war, disease, and starvation. She also personally grieved for her husband. What do people experience psychologically at times like these? Psychologists are also interested in these issues of the last life stage.

Death is a process rather than a point in time. Decades ago it was a process that took place at home, with family members present. Today, it is more likely to occur in a hospital or medical facility, surrounded by doctors, nurses, and machines. In our society, death is more removed from our everyday experiences. As a result, when we face death, we and our families are often unprepared for it. Nevertheless, loss is an inevitable part of our development. Knowing what happens when a loved one is dying and how people respond to the death of a loved one may better prepare us for this final journey.

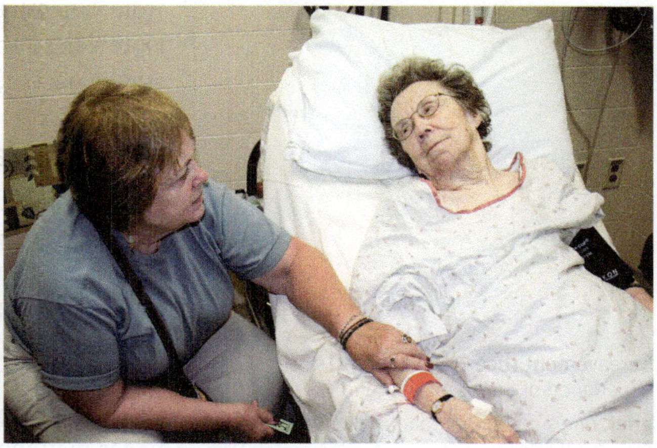

▼ Terminally ill patients experience a variety of emotional reactions to their deaths, according to Elisabeth Kübler-Ross's research on death and dying.

Steve Skjold/Alamy stock photo

9.8.1 Emotional Reactions to Death: Kübler-Ross's Stages

If you were told today that you only had 6 months to live, how would you react? Elisabeth Kübler-Ross (1926–2004; 1969, 1974), a pioneer researcher on death and dying, interviewed more than 200 terminally ill people to address this question. She wanted to investigate any predictable emotional and psychological changes that people might experience as they confront their own death. From her research, she identified five reactions that may characterize dying people: denial, anger, bargaining, depression, and acceptance.

When people first learn that they have a terminal illness, a typical reaction is *denial*. They behave as if they have not just been told that they are going to die. For example, they may insist on a second or third medical opinion. Others may continue in their normal activities, behaving as if they had never received this news. Denial is an effective coping strategy that allows the person time to come to terms with impending death.

As denial dwindles, it is replaced by the emotional reaction of *anger*. People lash out at loved ones and medical personnel over the unfairness of death. "Why me?" may be a common response during this stage. Looking for others to blame may also be an expression of this anger.

Following denial and anger, some dying people may also express emotions indicative of *bargaining*. They attempt to strike a deal for more time with the doctors, a supreme being, or the universe. For example, a person may want to live just long enough to see their child graduate from college. Another person may bargain to make it through a particular holiday. These bargains may be unrealistic and impossible to fulfill.

People who are dying may become *depressed* or extremely sad when denial, anger, and bargaining fail to delay the progress of their illness. They may lose interest in their usual activities or refuse to participate. This depression may be one way for those who are near the end of life to mourn their own death.

The final emotional state described by Kübler-Ross is *acceptance*. A peace and calm characterize the dying as they face the end of life. They may separate themselves from all but a few of their loved ones as they prepare for life's ending. For example, in one study (Goranson et al., 2017) blog posts of terminally ill patients and the last words of death-row inmates tended to become more positive and less negative as death approached.

Research confirms the legitimacy of Kübler-Ross's reaction stages (Kalish, 1985; Samarel, 1995). However, not every dying person experiences all these reactions. Moreover, not all dying persons go through these reactions in the same order. Death, like many other developmental processes, is influenced by a variety of factors, including one's personality and coping style, the type of support received from family members and health professionals, and the nature of the terminal illness (Stroebe & Schut, 2015). Yet Kübler-Ross's model is useful for understanding the emotions of dying people and for supporting anyone suffering from loss. People may also experience similar reactions when they face a divorce, unemployment, or the impending death of a loved one.

Hongyong experienced many of these emotions as she wondered over the fate of her son and watched her husband die. At first, she denied the possibility that her son was dead or that her husband's illness was fatal. She turned away in anger from her religion when her son did not appear at the refugee camp. Her depression was so intense that she ignored her living children. But as time went by, she slowly accepted her husband's death as well as not knowing the fate of her son.

9.8.2 Bereavement and Grief: How We Respond to Death

When a loved one dies, *bereavement* and *grief* follow. **Bereavement** is the experience of losing a loved one; **grief** is our emotional reaction to that loss. Just as death is a highly personal experience, so too is grief. However, research on bereaved people has identified common themes and emotional reactions within three phases: impact/shock, confrontation, and accommodation/acceptance (Bowlby, 1980; Parkes, 1986, 1991; Rando, 1995).

Most people's first reaction to the loss of a loved one is shock. This *impact phase* may include disbelief on hearing that a loved one has died. It may feel as if a

bereavement [bee-REEVE-munt] the experience of losing a loved one

grief one's emotional reaction to the death of a loved one numbness has settled within one's body or mind. This numbness is adaptive, dulling the painful emotions of loss. People in this stage may perform such actions as picking out a casket, making arrangements for a funeral or a burial, and even calling friends and relatives to inform them of the death, as if in a dream. This shock is particularly intense if the person's death was sudden. Think about the emotional numbness and body aches that Hongyong experienced when she thought that her son was dead. She operated as if she were in a fog, a living ghost.

RichLegg/E+/Getty Images

▲ Shock, disbelief, and numbness are common emotional reactions to the loss of a loved one.

Deep despair and agony may soon follow the numbness and shock in the *confrontation phase*. Uncontrollable weeping, anxiety, and feelings of guilt and anger are not uncommon as the grieving person yearns for the loved one to return. The survivor must confront the reality of the loss, and this can be especially painful. The person may have difficulty concentrating, sleeping, and eating. By confronting each wave of despair, the person moves closer to realizing that the loved one is gone.

As the pain of the confrontation phase subsides, the survivors begin to accept the death of the loved one in the *accommodation phase*. The survivors reengage with life, and the memories of the deceased are internalized. People are now able to refocus their emotional energies on normal daily events and relationships with the living.

How long does this grieving process take? A definitive answer is not possible. The course and intensity of these phases differ from person to person. Personality traits, cultural background, and the circumstances surrounding the death of the loved one are all factors that influence one's grief responses. Some people function considerably better after a year or two; others may take several years. Some may never recover, especially from the death of a child (Murphy, 2008). This may explain Hongyong's 40-year search for her son. Research also suggests that men and women may cope differently with grief, as women are more likely than men to seek social support and express their feelings more openly (Rando, 1995; Stroebe, 2001). Family dynamics may also influence the grief process, either helping or hindering the individual's and/or family's adjustment (Stroebe & Schut, 2015). There also are different cultural norms when it comes to grieving and bereavement. Views on death, dying, and grief are influenced by our cultural upbringing and influence how one expects to grieve and the customs and rituals of the death process (Rosenblatt, 2008).

9.8 Quiz Yourself

1. **Caryn has just started chemotherapy to treat breast cancer. Each day she prays that she will be a better person if she is given a second chance and recovers from her illness. Which Kübler-Ross stage is Caryn most likely in?**
   a. Acceptance
   b. Bargaining
   c. Anger
   d. Denial
2. **Our emotional reaction to the loss of a loved one is called _____.**
   a. bereavement
   b. grief
   c. bargaining
   d. reality shock
3. **The most intense emotional reactions to the loss of a loved one typically occur during which grief phase?**
   a. Impact
   b. Shock
   c. Confrontation
   d. Accommodation

Answers 1. b; 2. b; 3. c

9.9 Integrating Psychology: The Big Picture

In this chapter, we examined the many different ways in which people develop. We hope that as you read this chapter, you were able to see how Hongyong Baek's development contributed to the unique person she became. Although the chapter separately outlined physical, cognitive, and social aspects of development, it is only by integrating these forces that we can truly appreciate and understand Hongyong's life story.

For example, Hongyong's difficult temperament (biology) did not help her conform to the prescribed social roles for her gender and culture. This may have been a factor in why she married at a later age than other Korean females and in why she was imprisoned. Her culture and gender roles, in turn, influenced her cognitions and psychosocial development. She thought she was ugly and that her value was in being a good wife and mother. Her internal conflict between what she thought she should be and what she wanted to do resulted in role confusion as she searched for meaning in her life through a variety of careers. Her relationships with her husband and children were at times complicated and at times nurtured this quest for meaning. Her morality and beliefs were tested not only by these relationships but also by the political environment of her time. As you can see, development is quite complex and requires an understanding of physical, cognitive, and social variables to fully comprehend how it leads to variations in human behavior. Keep these concepts in mind, as many of them will be reinforced in the next two chapters as we explore how social psychology and personality also contribute to variations in behavior.

Studying the Chapter

Key Terms

accommodation (388)
assimilation (388)
attachment (398)
authoritarian parent (400)
authoritative parent (400)
bereavement (426)
centration (390)
concrete operations (391)
conservation (391)
crystallized intelligence (414)
development (377)
Down syndrome (380)
dualistic thinking (413)
egocentrism (391)
embryonic stage (379)
emerging adulthood (417)
fetal alcohol syndrome (FAS) (380)
fetal stage (379)
fine motor skills (384)
fluid intelligence (414)
formal operations (392)
gender permanence (403)
gender roles (403)
gender-schema theory (403)
germinal stage (379)
grief (426)
gross motor skills (383)
imaginary audience (412)
menarche (407)
menopause (410)
moral reasoning (395)
nature-nurture issue (378)
neonate (382)
object permanence (389)
permissive parent (401)
personal fable (412)
postformal thought (413)
preoperational stage (390)
private speech (393)
puberty (407)
reflex (383)
relativistic thinking (413)
scaffolding (394)
schema (388)
sensitive periods (380)
sensorimotor stage (389)
separation anxiety (398)
stranger anxiety (399)
symbolic thinking (390)
temperament (397)
teratogen (380)
zone of proximal development (ZPD) (394)
zygote (379)

What Do You Know? Assess Your Understanding

Test your retention and understanding of the material by answering the following questions.

1. Enrique believes that genes are primarily responsible for development. Enrique is emphasizing the ______.
   a. nurture side of the nature-nurture issue
   b. nature side of the nature-nurture issue
   c. influence of the environment
   d. influence of unconscious desires

2. Organs and systems form during the ______ stage of prenatal development.
   a. zygote
   b. germinal
   c. embryonic
   d. fetal

3. ______ are environmental factors, such as alcohol or cleaning fluids, that may cause birth defects.
   a. Chromosomes
   b. Teratogens
   c. Sensitive periods
   d. Myelins

4. ______ serve as the foundation for behaviors such as walking, eating, crying, smiling, and grasping.
   a. Temperaments
   b. Attachments
   c. Formal operations
   d. Reflexes

5. Learning how to skip, jump on a trampoline, or ride a bike are examples of ______ motor skills.
   a. gross
   b. fine
   c. big
   d. scaffolding

6. Which of the following stimuli do infants prefer to look at?
   a. Circles
   b. Colors
   c. Faces
   d. Machines

7. Pablo sees a dolphin for the first time and exclaims, "Fishy, Daddy!" Pablo is engaging in the cognitive process of ______.
   a. assimilation
   b. accommodation
   c. scaffolding
   d. formal operations

8. Ms. Lucy, the kindergarten teacher, tries her best to coach her students by making each task somewhat more difficult than the last and modeling how best to approach each task. Ms. Lucy's practice is consistent with ______.
   a. assimilation
   b. accommodation
   c. scaffolding
   d. sensorimotor thought

9. Some students think it is wrong to cheat because they could get caught and punished. Such students are operating at Kohlberg's ______ level of moral reasoning.
   a. preconventional
   b. conventional
   c. postconventional
   d. preoperational

10. Jamal sees two differently shaped glasses filled with liquid. Jamal recognizes that even though they look different, the glasses hold the same amount of liquid. Piaget would say that Jamal is operating at the ______ stage of cognitive development.
    a. sensorimotor
    b. preoperational
    c. concrete operations
    d. preconventional

11. As a baby, Reece did not cry a lot, regularly approached new people and situations, and had a regular pattern of eating and sleeping. Reece's temperament is best described as ______.
    a. easy
    b. slow-to-warm-up
    c. difficult
    d. avoidant

12. While at the state fair, Cicily remains close to her parent and does not explore the games or rides. She shows extreme distress if her parent leaves her side. Cicily most likely has a(n) ______ attachment style.
    a. avoidant
    b. resistant
    c. secure
    d. disorganized

13. Which part of the brain is among the last to fully develop during adolescence and young adulthood?
    a. Cerebellum
    b. Amygdala
    c. Pituitary gland
    d. Prefrontal cortex

14. Older adults evaluate how satisfying their lives have been in Erikson's psychosocial crisis of ______.
    a. identity versus role confusion
    b. intimacy versus isolation
    c. generativity versus stagnation
    d. integrity versus despair

15. Consuelo dresses and acts like a girl. She feels that she is a female. This describes Consuelo's ______.
    a. gender role
    b. gender identity
    c. gender typing
    d. gender bias

16. Tomas believes that there is only one right answer or single solution to a situation. Tomas is engaging in ______.
    a. dualistic thinking
    b. relativistic thinking
    c. postformal thought
    d. All of the above

17. The development of one's personal values and character is referred to as ______.
    a. industry
    b. integrity
    c. generativity
    d. identity

18. As she was studying the chapter on development, Ellie had to learn several interrelated ideas that would help her explain and make predictions about development. Ellie was learning ______.
    a. hypotheses
    b. models
    c. theories
    d. scientific methods

19. Marital satisfaction is associated with ______.
    a. similar educational background
    b. warm and positive extended family relationships
    c. secure financial circumstances
    d. All of the above

20. Pilar's partner died a week ago and she is in the impact stage of grief. What emotions is Pilar most likely feeling?
   a. Numbness and shock
   b. Deep despair and agony
   c. Anxiety and feelings of guilt
   d. Acceptance and reengagement with her daily living

Answers: 1. b; 2. c; 3. b; 4. d; 5. a; 6. c; 7. a; 8. c; 9. a; 10. c; 11. a; 12. b; 13. d; 14. d; 15. b; 16. a; 17. d; 18. c; 19. d; 20. a

Use It or Lose It: Applying Psychology

1. At what age would you introduce your child to the following games and toys? Defend your reasoning by considering physical, cognitive, and psychosocial aspects of development.
   A board game
   Building blocks
   Constructing a model spaceship
   Hide-and-seek
   A chemistry set
2. Analyze your parent(s)' style of discipline during your childhood. How would Baumrind classify their parenting style? How well did their style complement your temperament? What impact do you think your parent(s)' style of discipline had on your cognitive, psychosocial, and emotional development? Be specific, and cite examples to support your answer.
3. For each of Erikson's psychosocial stages, detail what specific behaviors may suggest that an individual is having difficulty resolving that particular stage.
4. Imagine that you have just been told that you are going to have a baby. Use your knowledge about infant physical, cognitive, and psychosocial development to design a nursery for your baby. Create a list of items you'd like to include, such as furniture, toys, and bedding, and describe how you would decorate the walls and the types of toys you would purchase. Explain your choices in terms of developmental processes.
5. Describe what you feel are benefits to aging into middle and later adulthood and give examples to support your arguments.
6. Spend an hour watching television shows aimed at children, playing children's video or online games, listening to children's music, or using computer programs developed for children. What messages, schemas, or concepts will children acquire from these sources? How might these messages influence their ideas about gender? In your opinion, are these messages appropriate for children? Explain.

Critical Thinking About the Science of Psychology

In this chapter, you read about Harlow's and Zimmerman's (1959) classic study on the nature of attachment. Please review that study now in section 9.4.2, and then answer these questions:

1. What type of research method did Harlow and Zimmerman use in this study?
2. What is/are the dependent variable(s) in this study?
3. What is/are the independent variable(s) in this study?

Are You Getting the Big Picture?

Development includes changes in physical, emotional, social, and cognitive behavior and abilities over time through an interaction of **nature** (one's biology) and **nurture** (one's environment and culture).

Masterfile

9.1 Human Development: How Does It All Begin?

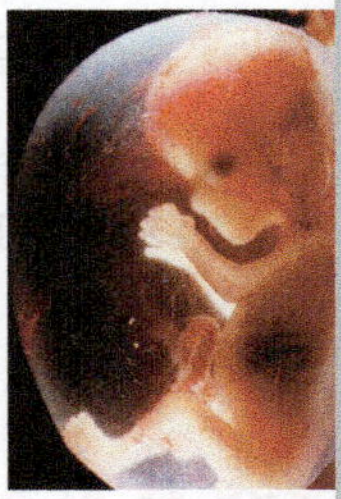

Claude Edelmann/Science Source

- **Germinal stage** (0–14 days): The **zygote** undergoes rapid cell division and duplication.
- **Embryonic stage** (3–8 weeks): Major organs and organ systems form.
- **Fetal stage** (week 9–birth): Body organs and systems more fully develop.

9.2 Physical Development in Infancy and Childhood

- Infants' and children's brains are highly *plastic*, or changeable.
- **Reflexes** such as sucking, rooting, and grasping help the infant survive.
- **Gross motor skills** (behaviors that involve large muscle groups) allow the child to run, walk, jump, and hop. **Fine motor skills** (involving small muscle groups) aid in activities such as writing, using utensils, and playing a musical instrument.

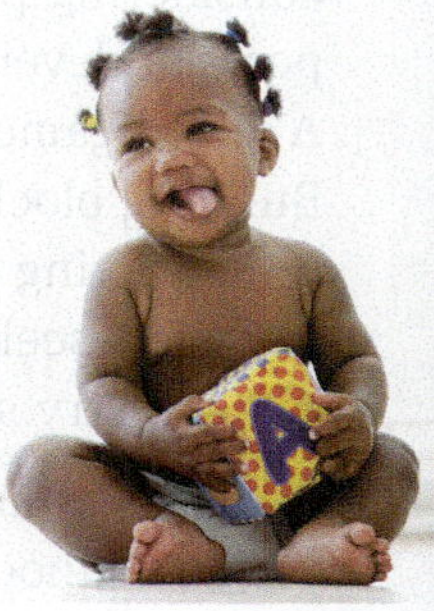

Monkey Business Images/Shutterstock.com

9.3 Cognitive Development in Infancy and Childhood

- According to Jean Piaget, infants and children apply **schemas (assimilation)** to understand their environment and adapt to change through **accommodation** when existing schema are changed or modified in four stages of cognitive development: **sensorimotor**, **preoperational**, **concrete operations**, and **formal operations**.
- Lev Vygotsky stressed the importance of culture and social interactions in cognitive development.
- Lawrence Kohlberg's research on **moral reasoning** suggests that children's understanding of right and wrong develops progressively from a focus on the self to the external world.

Monkey Business Images/Shutterstock.com

9.4 Psychosocial Development in Infancy and Childhood

Monkey Business Images/Shutterstock.com

- An infant's **temperament** can influence their first **attachment** or emotional bond with their primary caregiver.
- Diana Baumrind identified three styles of parenting: **authoritarian**, **authoritative**, and **permissive**. Permissive parenting may be *indulgent* or *neglectful*.
- Psychologist Erik Erikson proposed that the environment and the child's responses to the environment influence the development of either a healthy or an unhealthy personality as children navigate the crises of *trust vs. mistrust, autonomy vs. shame and doubt, initiative vs. guilt*, and *industry vs. inferiority*.
- At a very early age, children process and develop schema about **gender roles**, or society's expectations for how a female and a male should behave.

9.5 Physical Changes in Adolescence and Adulthood

Jerzyworks/Masterfile

- **Puberty** involves maturation of sex characteristics that enable us to reproduce. At around age 50, females experience **menopause** and hormonal changes that eventually bring an end to reproductive capacity. Males undergo hormonal changes after age 60, termed *andrcpause*.
- During adolescence and throughout life, the brain remains highly plastic, allowing us to adapt to changing conditions.

9.6 Cognitive Changes in Adolescence and Adulthood

- Teenagers tend to be **egocentric**, believing that others are concerned with the same things that they are.
- **Postformal thought** is characterized by **relativistic thinking**, an appreciation that the correct solution or answer may vary from situation to situation. Remaining cognitively active helps adults avoid declines in mental abilities.

9.7 Psychosocial Changes in Adolescence and Adulthood

Michael Doolittle /Alamy stock photo

- Erik Erikson considered adolescence the key stage for developing an *identity*, but he believed adults continue to develop when they establish *intimacy*, *generativity*, and *integrity*.
- Adolescent and adult relationships are expressed in a wide range of lifestyles, including dating, cohabitation, marriage, divorce, and parenthood.
- Finding satisfying work and holding a job are part of adult development.

9.8 Death and Dying

RichLegg/E+/Getty Images

- Death is a process rather than a point in time and is an inevitable part of our development.
- Researcher Elizabeth Kübler-Ross identified five reactions that may characterize people who know they are dying: *denial, anger, bargaining, depression*, and *acceptance*.

Learning Objectives

10.1 Describe attitudes, how they develop, and how they affect behavior. (APA 1.1, 1.3)

10.1 Describe cognitive dissonance theory and explain the role of dissonance in attitude change. (APA 1.1, 1.2, 1.3)

10.1 Describe the major theories of persuasion and how the communicator, the message, and the audience affect persuasion. (APA 1.1, 1.2, 1.3, 2.1)

10.2 Explain how we form impressions about ourselves and others by making attributions. (APA 1.1, 1.3, 3.2)

10.2 Describe the common heuristics and biases that affect the attribution process. (APA 1.1, 1.3)

10.3 Define and distinguish among prejudice, stereotypes, discrimination, and stereotype threat. (APA 1.1, 1.3, 3.2, 3.3)

10.3 Explain how prejudice develops. (APA 1.1, 1.2, 1.3, 3.2, 3.3)

10.3 Describe ways to reduce prejudice. (APA 1.1, 1.2, 1.3, 3.2, 3.3)

10.4 Describe the factors affecting attraction: proximity, exposure, similarity, and physical attractiveness. (APA 1.1, 1.3, 3.2)

10.5 Describe how cohesiveness and norms function within groups. (APA 1.1, 1.2, 1.3, 3.2)

10.5 Describe the factors that affect our tendency to conform to the norms of a group. (APA 1.1, 1.2, 1.3, 3.2)

10.5 Describe how working in a group can affect both performance and decision making within the group. (APA 1.1, 1.3, 3.2)

10.6 Describe the process of compliance and commonly used compliance techniques. (APA 1.1, 1.3)

10.6 Describe obedience, destructive obedience, and the factors that affect our tendency to obey. (APA 1.1, 1.2, 1.3, 3.3)

10.7 Define aggression and its different types. (APA 1.1, 1.3)

10.7 Describe how biology, learning, and situational factors affect aggression. (APA 1.1, 1.3, 3.2, 3.3)

10.8 Describe the steps involved in deciding whether to help another. (APA 1.1, 1.3, 3.2, 3.3)

10.8 Describe the factors that influence helping. (APA 1.1, 1.3, 3.2, 3.3)

monkeybusinessimages/iStock/Getty Images

10 Social Psychology

Chapter Outline

The story of Hongyong Baek illustrates how those around us affect our thoughts and behaviors. Hongyong's feelings about her body were influenced by both her mother's teachings and the cultural values placed on women in Korea at the time. As a result, she felt ashamed and inadequate. In the presence of her mother, she tried to behave as her mother expected her to behave—as a chaste and obedient woman—but often failed. Then when Hongyong's parents arranged for her marriage to Dukpil Lee, it was through his encouragement that she learned to become more assertive and independent. If Hongyong had married a more domineering man, who never let her speak her mind, it is possible that she might not have developed the independence that ultimately allowed her to survive the challenges she faced during the Korean War.

Similarly, Hongyong's own behavior likely had influence on the thoughts and behaviors of those around her. Her decision to smuggle opium resulted in her husband's decision to spend more time away from home. Hongyong's change of career influenced her husband to spend more time with her. As you can see, in the social world each of us is capable of being both influenced by others *and* being an influence that changes others. The **social influence** goes both ways. This influence affects not only our behavior, but also our **social cognition**, or the way that we think about ourselves and others. Take a moment to reflect: In what ways have others influenced your thoughts and behaviors? In what ways have you influenced the thought and behavior of others? These are the questions that we will explore in this chapter on *social psychology*. ■

social influence social pressures that serve to modify our thoughts and/or behavior

social cognition the area of social psychology that deals with the ways in which we think about other people and ourselves

social psychology the branch of psychology that studies how we think and behave in social situations

attitudes evaluative beliefs that we hold about things in our world

10.1 Evaluating the World: Attitudes

Social psychology is the study of how we think and behave in the vast array of social situations that we experience. One area of social psychology, *social cognition*, investigates the ways in which we think (cognition) about ourselves and others—for example, studying how we develop **attitudes**, our liking or disliking for the people, places, and things in our world. We all have attitudes about a multitude of things that represent the evaluative beliefs we hold about the contents of our world (e.g., liking country music or disliking lazy people). But how do we acquire these attitudes?

10.1.1 Acquiring Attitudes Through Learning

As with many of our beliefs, we learn to have many of the attitudes we hold. One learning process that affects our attitudes about the world is *classical conditioning* (Chapter 6). Recall that classical conditioning is often responsible for the development of certain learned *emotional* and *physiological* responses in humans (● FIGURE 10.1). Because classical conditioning has the power to change the way we feel about certain stimuli, it also has the power to influence our attitudes toward these stimuli. For example, in one study examining techniques for preventing child abuse, researchers found that seeing a picture of a child (NS/CS) right before seeing a smiley face emoji (US) that produced a positive emotion (UR/CR) resulted in participants later having more positive reactions to seeing the children (Wagner et al., 2020). In short, classical conditioning can often explain the gut-level emotional and physiological aspects of our attitudes (Grossman & Till, 1998). Similarly, if a celebrity (US) makes us feel positive emotion (UR), then seeing this celebrity marketing a product (NS/CS) may condition us to have a positive emotional reaction (CR) when we encounter the product (Chen et al., 2013; Till, Stanley, & Priluck, 2008).

FIGURE 10.1

Classically Conditioning a Negative Attitude Toward Dogs

For a young child, a fear response in a parent (US) will naturally cause fear in the child (UR). On the other hand, the sight of a dog will not reliably elicit fear in a small child. Therefore, the dog is initially a neutral stimulus (NS). When the sight of the dog (NS) is repeatedly paired with a fear response in the parent (US), the child can easily acquire a conditioned fear of dogs (CR) that is elicited by the mere sight of a dog (CS).

Operant conditioning, or learning through the consequences of our behavior (see Chapter 6), also affects our attitudes. If you are rewarded for having certain attitudes, the attitude will be strengthened. But if you are punished for having certain attitudes, they will be weakened. For example, if your friends applaud your efforts to "go green" and recycle your trash, then your pro-green attitude is likely to strengthen. However, if you tell a prejudicial joke and your friends become angry rather than laughing, your prejudicial attitude may begin to weaken.

Operant conditioning can also influence our attitudes through the consequences of our direct interaction with the objects of our attitude. For example, despite the many negative health effects of smoking, nicotine produces physiological responses that are rewarding for some people. The reinforcement derived from smoking is one reason why some smokers continue to exhibit pro-smoking attitudes and behavior.

At times, we also model the attitudes of others. Recall that in *observational learning* we learn by watching the actions of others and storing mental representations of their behavior in memory (see Chapter 6). For example, Hongyong Baek's early attitudes about the role of women in society were very similar to the attitudes held by her mother. Because she spent a lot of time with her mother, she may have simply modeled the attitudes that she saw her mother and other women in her culture express. Take a minute to think about your attitudes and the attitudes of those closest to you. Are your views on the roles of men and women in society similar to those of your closest loved ones? If so, the similarity may be due to observational learning. If you are like most people, you will find that overall, your attitudes are quite similar to those of your parents (Rohan & Zanna, 1996) and those around you (Kowalski, 2003). For example, a study of adolescents conducted in Finland and Russia found that adolescents' attitudes toward smoking were significantly correlated with both their own smoking behavior and the smoking behavior of their best friend (Aura et al., 2016). And in another study, the anti-immigrant attitudes of parents and friends were shown to be significantly related to levels of anti-immigrant attitudes in children (Miklikowska, 2017). Like it or not, our attitudes do tend to align with those close to us.

As you can see, we learn attitudes the way that we learn everything in life—through experience. Once we form our attitudes about the world, they then have the power to affect what we know, how we feel, and how we behave toward just about everything we encounter in our lives.

Jim West/Alamy stock photo

▲ We often take on the attitudes of our parents through observational learning. This child is likely to adopt the pro–public education attitudes of these adult models.

Engage Yourself!

Get a sheet of paper and write down 10 attitudes that you hold about the world. Choose 5 subjects for which people typically hold strong attitudes, such as political figures, religion/spiritual issues, moral values, conservation/sustainability, and choose 5 subjects about more everyday types of things (for example, favorite foods, activities). Then have a conversation with someone who you know well and spend a good deal of time with—for example a parent, relative, or good friend. Ask them to share their attitudes on the same 10 topics (be sure to do this in a nonjudgmental manner). How well do their attitudes match your own? Did the degree of agreement vary for the strongly held attitudes versus the more commonplace ones? We often share similar attitudes with those closest to us. Did you find this to be true?

10.1.2 Attitude-Behavior Consistency

Do you ever find yourself behaving in a manner that contradicts your attitudes? For example, have you ever laughed at a joke you didn't find very funny because everyone else was laughing? Do you sometimes engage in behavior that you know is harmful to you because others are doing it too? If so, your behavior is not unusual. We often behave in ways that go against our attitudes, especially when social pressures direct us to do so. This lack of *attitude-behavior consistency* has intrigued researchers because it seems so counterintuitive and illogical (LaPiere, 1934).

If social pressures can make it difficult for us to behave consistently with our attitudes, what factors make it more likely that we will behave in ways that are consistent with our attitudes? Answers to this question have great practical value in society. For instance, under what circumstances might people's positive attitudes toward safer sex actually lead them to engage in protected sex? When might political attitudes accurately predict voting behavior? And in which situations can a company assume that consumer attitudes toward their products will actually translate into sales? Researchers have been diligently trying to answer such questions. ● TABLE 10.1 describes some of the variables that have been shown to influence attitude-behavior consistency.

TABLE 10.1 Factors That Affect Attitude-Behavior Consistency

Factor	Example
If your attitude about the object is low in ambivalence (having both positive and negative feelings about something), the attitude will be a better predictor of behavior (Cooke & Sheeran, 2004; Jiang et al., 2016).	Feeling completely positive about spinach (rather than having mixed feelings about spinach) increases your chance of eating it.
If the cognitive and affective aspects of the attitude are both positive (or both negative), the attitude will be a better predictor of behavior (Cooke & Sheeran, 2004; Zhou et al., 2009).	Both enjoying spinach (affective) and knowing that it is good for you (cognitive) increase the chances that you will eat it.
Attitudes that are quickly and automatically retrieved from long-term memory are better predictors of behavior (Cooke & Sheeran, 2004; Fazio, 1989; cf. Meyer & Schoen, 2014).	If the first thing you think of when ordering dinner is your love of spinach, you are more likely to order it.
Attitudes that have been stable over time are likely to be better predictors of behavior (Cooke & Sheeran, 2004).	If you have loved spinach since early childhood, you are more likely to continue eating it than you would be if you only recently developed a liking for spinach.
Attitudes that are certain are better predictors of behavior (Cooke & Sheeran, 2004).	If you are very sure about your love of spinach, you are more likely to eat it than you would be if you were not very certain about liking spinach.
Attitudes that are learned through direct experience with the attitude object are likely to be better predictors of behavior (Cooke & Sheeran, 2004).	If you first learned to love spinach by actually eating it, you are more likely to eat it again.
Being in a negative mood has been shown to enhance attitude-behavior consistency (Elen et al., 2013).	You have loved spinach since childhood. Today, you had a bad day and are in a bad mood. When your friend offers you corn at the picnic today, instead you eat the spinach.
Attitudes best predict behavior when the attitude and behavior have the same level of attitude-relevant action activity (Paulson et al., 2012).	You love spinach and believe in promoting spinach as a healthy food (active attitude). When planting your garden, you choose to grow spinach (active behavior).
When the subject of an attitude holds personal importance for us, meaning we have a vested interest in the outcome of the acting on the attitude, it is more likely to predict our behavior (Donaldson, Siegel, & Crano, 2020).	You are a spinach farmer, who believes that spinach should be consumed by all people. Spinach consumption helps you stay in business, and it is good for people. You serve spinach regularly at your own table, especially when you have guests for dinner.

Given that our attitudes develop through experience and that once in place they influence our behavior at least part of the time, many psychologists are interested in how attitudes can be changed. This information also has great practical value. If we knew how to change attitudes, we might be able to reverse social problems such as prejudice and prescription drug abuse. These and other pragmatic concerns have fueled a great deal of research on attitude change.

cognitive consistency the idea that we strive to have attitudes and behaviors that do not contradict one another

cognitive dissonance theory a theory that predicts that we will be motivated to change our attitudes and/or our behaviors to the extent that they cause us to feel cognitive dissonance, an uncomfortable physical state

10.1.3 Cognitive Consistency and Attitude Change

Throughout our lifetimes, our attitudes will change as we acquire new knowledge and have different experiences. For example, Hongyong converted to Christianity during a difficult period in her life. Once her attitude about religion changed, so did her attitudes about her possessions and her lifestyle. This led her to give away many of her remaining belongings and to learn to read and write. Some of her old attitudes were discarded in favor of attitudes that were more consistent with her new religious convictions. In this example, the attitude change was motivated from within the attitude holder. The change was not the result of a concerted effort on the part of others. It was motivated more by a desire to maintain what psychologists refer to as **cognitive consistency**, or the desire to avoid contradictions in our attitudes and behaviors (Festinger, 1957). Cognitive consistency theories (Festinger, 1957; Heider, 1946) propose that humans find it uncomfortable when there is inconsistency among their attitudes or between their attitudes and their behavior. Most of us believe that we are intelligent, logical beings. This attitude about being intelligent and logical would be inconsistent with the attitude that an unhealthy restaurant is a good place to eat. So we adjust one of our attitudes (the one concerning the restaurant) to avoid such an inconsistency. But why does inconsistency make us uncomfortable and therefore motivate attitude change?

One explanation of how cognitive inconsistency motivates attitude change is **cognitive dissonance theory** (Festinger, 1957). According to this theory, inconsistencies among attitudes or between attitudes and behavior cause an unpleasant physical state called *cognitive dissonance*. Think of dissonance as a state of unease much like being anxious. It stems from the realization that we have behaved in a way that is contrary to our self-concept (Aronson, 1998). Because dissonance makes us feel bad, we are motivated to stop this unpleasant feeling, which can lead to attitude and/or behavior change (Joule & Azdia, 2003; Martinie, Milland, & Olive, 2013; Powers & Jack, 2013). For example, dissonance can be used to help treat certain eating disorders in women (see Chapter 5; Kant et al., 2019). One treatment program, Succeed Body Image Programme (SBIP; Becker & Stice, 2011) has participants actively criticize the idea that the ideal female body type is the ultra-thin body type often portrayed in Western media. Participants are asked to do this via role-playing exercises, group discussions, writing letters, etc. The idea is that repeatedly stating attitudes that are inconsistent with believing that one should strive to meet an ultra-thin standard of beauty will produce dissonance in women who had up to that point held this standard of beauty (Kant et al., 2019). Most of us do not believe ourselves to be dishonest, hypocritical, or liars. To overtly and repeatedly state

LightField Studios/Shutterstock.com

▲ The ultra-thin standard of beauty frequently portrayed in Western magazines and other media is a contributing factor to the development of certain eating disorders (e.g., anorexia and bulimia nervosa). Dissonance-based interventions, such as the Succeed Body Image Programme, use dissonance to move participants' attitudes about their body in a healthier direction.

agreement with attitudes that do not reflect our true feelings is not something honest, truthful people do. Therefore, the SBIP intervention will likely produce cognitive dissonance.

In general, there are three ways to remove the inconsistencies that cause dissonance in this case. First, a person could change their behavior (refuse to participate in the SBIP). Second, they could change their attitude (decide that an ultra-thin body type is not desirable). Or third, they could remove the inconsistency by bringing new beliefs and attitudes to bear on the situation (convince themself that participating in the SBIP is just for fun, and it doesn't mean that they are being dishonest). Any of these three methods would reduce their dissonance and restore a state of *consonance* or consistency among their attitudes and behavior. Which method did the women use? Kant and colleagues (2019) found that after participating in SBIP, heterosexual women were less likely to agree that an ultra-thin body type is desirable. Furthermore, both heterosexual and homosexual women had fewer attitudes in favor of disordered eating after finishing the program. Both these findings suggest that SBIP may be useful in reducing maladaptive attitudes about body image.

10.1.4 Persuasion and Attitude Change

Cognitive dissonance theory can explain certain aspects of how we change and grow as human beings, but dissonance is not the only means through which our attitudes change. We also encounter frequent **persuasion** situations in which others directly attempt to change our attitudes. Every day we face persuasive attempts from friends, family members, politicians, the media, and advertisers. Some marketing experts estimate that most people in the United States are exposed to somewhere between 4,000 and 10,000 ads each day, many of them online (Simpson, 2017). With all of these persuasive attempts being hurled at us on a daily basis, an understanding of how persuasion occurs becomes almost a necessity.

persuasion a type of social influence in which someone tries to change our attitudes

central route to persuasion a style of thinking in which the person carefully and critically evaluates persuasive arguments and generates counterarguments; the central route requires motivation and available cognitive resources

peripheral route to persuasion a style of thinking in which the person does not carefully and critically evaluate persuasive arguments or generate counterarguments; the peripheral route ensues when one lacks motivation and/or available cognitive resources

Obviously, not all of the persuasive attempts we are subjected to actually produce attitude change. We do not become loyal to every product we see advertised on TV. We do not vote for every political candidate we hear speak. So just what makes persuasion successful—or what makes it fail?

One very important factor in the effectiveness of persuasion is the type of cognitive processes that we engage in during the persuasive attempt. There are two general styles of thinking that affect persuasion. These styles are characterized by the degree to which we analyze persuasive arguments, influencing whether those arguments are effective in changing our attitudes (Petty & Cacioppo, 1986; Wegener & Carlston, 2005). When we process on the **central route to persuasion**, we carefully and critically evaluate the logic of the persuasive arguments we encounter. When we process on the **peripheral route to persuasion**, we do not attempt to critically evaluate the arguments and are instead persuaded by superficial aspects of the arguments such as the likability of the person making them or the attractiveness of the ad. For example, when viewing job ads online, participants who were motivated to carefully evaluate the ad's content (central route processing) developed attitudes toward the company that were less affected by the aesthetics of the website. In contrast, if the participants were motivated to focus on superficial aspects of the ads rather than carefully evaluating their content (peripheral route processing), they developed attitudes toward the company that were more affected by the aesthetics of the website (Gregory, Meade, & Thompson, 2013).

Generally, we are likely to process persuasive arguments on the central route when we are involved with the issue at hand, and we have the cognitive resources to think carefully about the arguments. If we are uninvolved or if our cognitive resources are depleted, then we will likely process persuasive arguments on the peripheral route.

Whether or not persuasion is successful depends in large measure on the cognitive processing we employ. However, other variables can also affect our chances of being persuaded. These variables fall into three categories: variables associated with the *communicator* of the message (the person or entity trying to persuade us), variables associated with the persuasive *message* itself, and variables associated with the *audience* that receives the persuasive message.

Communicator Variables

We tend to be most persuaded when the communicator is attractive (Eagly & Chaiken, 1975; Evans & Clark, 2012), appears to be credible or have relevant knowledge (Hovland & Weiss, 1951; Tormala, Briñol, & Petty, 2007; Wasike, 2017), or appears to be an expert (Evans & Clark, 2012; Petty, Cacioppo, & Goldman, 1981). We are also most persuaded when the communicator does not appear to be trying to persuade us—unless they are attractive, in which case persuasion is not reduced by the awareness that the communicator is trying to persuade us (Messner, Reinhard, & Sporer, 2008). This is one reason that advertisers hire well-respected, attractive actors and actresses to sell their products. They know that we will be more likely to be persuaded because we place our trust in such people—especially if we are processing on the peripheral route (Petty et al., 1981; Shavitt et al., 1994). This trust can sometimes even override the effects of having a weak argument. One study showed that receiving weak arguments from a credible source can increase persuasion over time, if the recipient is focused on the communicator's credibility rather than being focused on the strength of the arguments themselves. This effect is diminished, however, when participants are instructed to focus on the arguments themselves (Albarracín, Kumkale, & Poyner-Del Vento, 2017). Findings like these suggest that perceived communicator credibility can be a powerful force when it comes to persuasion—especially if we fail to focus on what they are saying.

Message Variables

The logic of the persuasive argument has its greatest impact when we are processing on the central route, for it is here that we can truly appreciate the goodness of the argument (Petty & Briñol, 2008). Superficial cues such as the ease of navigation on a website and the attractiveness of a print ad are more likely to be persuasive to people processing on the peripheral route. However, at times, peripheral cues can indirectly affect persuasion, such as when viewers become more involved with an issue because they find a website covering the issue to be attractive or they become less likely to attend to a website's content because they find the site difficult to navigate (Cyr et al., 2018).

We are also more likely to be persuaded if the communicator effectively presents both the pros (why we should accept the arguments) and cons (why we might not accept the arguments) of the proposal. Two-sided arguments generally work best because we tend to trust a communicator who is willing to openly discuss the drawbacks of a proposal (Eisend, 2007). This approach is especially effective when the communicator successfully argues against objections that audience members have to accepting the proposal (Crowley & Hoyer, 1994).

AP Images/John Bazemore

▲ Attractiveness of a communicator can be one factor that makes you more likely to accept an argument. This is especially true when you are processing on the peripheral route to persuasion.

Psychology Works!

Leonardo Patrizi/E+/Getty Images

Advertisers and marketers must know how persuasion works and the factors that influence its effectiveness. Often times, students in marketing and advertising majors will take psychology courses to help them gain this knowledge. By using their knowledge of social psychology, advertisers can develop ad campaigns that will actually work to change the public's attitudes about the products they represent. Successfully persuading the public to hold positive attitudes about these products may translate into increased sales for their clients. Happy clients may then lead to more accounts for the advertising firms!

Audience Variables

Effective persuasion is heavily dependent on who is being persuaded. In general, all of us are easier to persuade on the peripheral rather than the central route to persuasion. However, individual differences among us can also influence whether we are persuaded. Variables such as intelligence (Rhodes & Wood, 1992), age (Mueller et al., 2020), self-esteem (Petty, Fabrigar, & Wegener, 2003), self-monitoring (our tendency to change our behavior to meet other's expectations; Evans & Clark, 2012), self-concept clarity (how well we know ourselves; Koller et al., 2013), emotional intelligence (see Chapter 8; Mueller et al., 2020), and mood (Sanaktekin & Sunar, 2008) can all affect our tendency to be persuaded. Yet after decades of research, it is still impossible to make blanket statements about the effect these variables have on persuasion, because our individual differences interact in a complex fashion with other variables, such as the route we are processing on (Petty & Briñol, 2008). For example, under the right circumstances, either high or low levels of intelligence, self-esteem, or positive emotion can all lead to high or low persuasion.

10.1 Quiz Yourself

1. If Mike wishes to make the best possible decision about how to vote in the upcoming presidential election, Mike should watch the presidential debates while processing on the ______________.
   a. central route
   b. algorithmic route
   c. peripheral route
   d. shortest route

2. A politician is attempting to persuade people to vote for them in an upcoming election. With which of the following types of arguments would you expect to have the most success in winning over a skeptical audience?
   a. A short argument that lacks great detail
   b. A very long and detailed argument
   c. A one-sided argument explaining why voters should vote for them
   d. A two-sided argument explaining why voters should vote for them, as well as some concerns they may have about voting for them

(Continued)

3. **Luca recently discovered that his favorite actress supports a radical political group that Luca despises. According to cognitive dissonance theory, what is most likely to happen in this situation?**
   a. Luca will begin to like the actress more.
   b. Luca will begin to like the actress less.
   c. Luca will begin to dislike the political group more.
   d. Luca's attitudes toward the actress and the group will not change.

4. **The hypothesis: "The effectiveness of a persuasive argument depends on the style of thinking used by audience members" is an example of a _______ hypothesis.**
   a. null
   b. predictive
   c. causal
   d. correlational

Answers 1. *a*; 2. *d*; 3. *b*; 4. *c*

10.2 Forming Impressions of Others

One of the most important aspects of social cognition is **impression formation**, or how we understand and make judgments about others. When we meet someone for the first time, we usually attempt to determine what type of person they are. Is this person kind, smart, aggressive, or untrustworthy? We want to know. Why do we want to know what other people are like? In short, if we have a good understanding of other people's traits and abilities, we think we can predict how they will behave in certain situations. This allows us to guide our own behavior in social situations. Without some understanding of others, social interactions would be much more awkward and uncertain.

impression formation the way that we understand and make judgments about others

attribution the act of assigning cause to behavior

trait attribution an attribution that assigns the cause of a behavior to the traits and characteristics of the person being judged

situational attribution an attribution that assigns the cause of a behavior to some characteristic of the situation or environment in which the behavior occurs

10.2.1 The Attribution Process

One of our basic social cognitive tendencies is to try to explain the behavior of ourselves and others, but how do you determine the traits and characteristics of someone you've just met? If you're thinking that we pay attention to what the person says and does, you're correct. When we judge a person, we observe their behavior, and then we attempt to determine the cause of this behavior (Heider, 1958). This process of assigning cause to behavior is called **attribution**. For example, imagine that you enter a local café and see a person yelling at an employee at the counter. Witnessing their outburst, you would likely try to determine why the person is yelling. Is it because they are an aggressive person? Or did the employee somehow provoke this type of outburst in an otherwise kind person? Questions like these may pass through your mind as you watch the scene unfold.

In this example, we can attribute the person's behavior to one of two types of causes. We can attribute the behavior to their traits, abilities, or characteristics, in which case we are making a **trait attribution**. Or we may attribute the behavior to something in the environment, in which case we are making a **situational attribution**. If we make a trait attribution about the yelling person, we may assume that they are yelling because they are an aggressive person. If we make a situational attribution, we assume that something happened in the environment that caused the person to yell—perhaps the employee accidently spilled hot coffee on them. Note that when we make a situational attribution, we do not attribute the person's behavior to their personality.

▼ If you witnessed this scene, what attributions would you make about this person's behavior? Would you assume that their behavior reflects their personality traits? Or would you assume that the situation must have elicited their behavior?

PR Image Factory/Shutterstock.com

10.2.2 Heuristics and Biases in Attribution

Ideally, we would weigh all the available evidence before making either a trait attribution or a situational attribution. Unfortunately, the realities of the world do not always allow us to make careful, analytic attributions. Humans are *cognitive misers*, meaning that we try to conserve our cognitive resources whenever we can (Fiske & Taylor, 2013; Sherman, Gawronski, & Trope, 2014). As we saw in Chapter 8, when we have to quickly solve a problem, we often use shortcuts, or heuristics, in hopes of finding a solution. Heuristics may lead to quick answers, but they do not always lead to accurate answers. People have been shown to employ several time-saving heuristics while making attributions, and these shortcuts often lead to errors and biases in the attribution process.

Engage Yourself!

Try the following demonstration. Look at the photos in ● FIGURE 10.2 and follow the instructions. What type of personality traits did you list for these people? How confident were you in these judgments? Now ask yourself this question: What evidence do I have that these people actually possess these personality traits? If you're like most people, your perceptions of these celebrities are based on the roles they play on TV or in the movies. Most of us assume that their behavior on TV is indicative of their personality traits in real life. Did you? If so, what situational explanations for these people's TV behavior did you fail to take into account? Did you take into account that on TV, these celebrities are acting? Did you think about the fact that even reality shows and talk shows involve someone directing the actors' behavior and the actors are aware that they are being watched by millions of people? Probably not. The bottom line is that unless you've spent time with these celebrities in real life, you've never really seen their natural

DFree/Shutterstock.com; DFree/Shutterstock.com; lev radin/Shutterstock.com; Robin Marchant/Getty Images Entertainment/Getty Images

Donald Glover (AKA Childish Gambino) of *Atlanta*.	Taraji P. Henson of *Empire*.	Jennifer Lopez of *Hustlers*.	Mark Harmon of *NCIS*.
Trait:	Trait:	Trait:	Trait:
Trait:	Trait:	Trait:	Trait:
Trait:	Trait:	Trait:	Trait:
Confidence rating:	Confidence rating:	Confidence rating:	Confidence rating:

FIGURE 10.2

What Do You Think About These Celebrities?

Take a look at these celebrities. Would you like to be friends with these people? What kind of people do you think they are? In the spaces below each photo, write down some of the traits you think this person possesses. Then rate your confidence in the accuracy of your judgments on a scale from 1 to 10, where 1 = not at all confident that your judgment is correct and 10 = very confident that your judgment is correct.

behavior; therefore, it's somewhat illogical to draw firm conclusions about their personality traits. If you did just that, don't feel bad. This tendency to rely on trait attributions and to discount situational explanations of behavior is a common heuristic known as the **fundamental attribution error** or *correspondence bias.*

fundamental attribution error our tendency to overuse trait information when making attributions about others

individualistic cultures a culture, like many Western cultures, in which individual accomplishments are valued over group accomplishments

collectivistic cultures a culture, like many Asian cultures, in which group accomplishments are valued over individual accomplishments

Fundamental Attribution Error

Why we tend to engage in the fundamental attribution error is not entirely clear. Perhaps it reflects our preference to know more about a person's traits than about a person's environment. After all, the goal of forming attributions is to understand the person, not the environment (Jones, 1979). It may just be easier to assume that most behavior stems from people's traits. It is also possible that we engage in the fundamental attribution error because we are less aware of situational influences on behavior. For example, in one study participants were found to make negative *trait* attributions about the author of an e-mail that contained spelling and grammatical errors. However, when they were given *situational* information that indicated that the author was from a different culture, the participants formed less negative impressions of the author (Vignovic & Thompson, 2010).

Another explanation for the fundamental attribution error is that when we view someone in a social setting, we tend to focus our attention on the person and their behavior, paying less attention to the situation. If we don't pay much attention to the situation, we are unlikely to give situational factors much weight when making our attributions. This effect seems to be enhanced when we are under stress, suggesting that our tendency to focus on trait information at the expense of also examining situational information has heuristic value for us (Kubota et al., 2014).

Engaging in the fundamental attribution error also varies with the degree to which our culture emphasizes individual behavior over group behavior. Some cultures, such as those in North America and Western Europe, are **individualistic cultures**, emphasizing the behavior and success of individuals rather than groups. Some other cultures, such as those in India and Japan, are **collectivistic cultures**, emphasizing the behavior and success of groups more than individuals (Triandis, 1994). Research has shown that people from individualistic cultures are more likely to engage in the fundamental attribution error (Choi & Nesbitt, 1998), but people from collectivistic cultures are less likely to engage in this bias (Morris & Peng, 1994). Presumably, the Western focus on the individual accounts for this difference in attribution, but more research needs to be done to pinpoint the exact causes of the fundamental attribution error and its connection to culture (Lien et al., 2006).

One piece of good news is that education in social psychology, such as you are getting right now, can reduce our tendency to engage in the fundamental attribution error (Stalder, 2012). Practicing *mindfulness,* a meditative state of being in the moment without being judgmental, has also been shown to reduce the fundamental attribution error (Hopthrow et al., 2017). It seems that being aware of our own potential biases can help us behave in a less biased fashion when making attributions and forming impressions of others.

Actor/Observer Bias

What kind of attributions do we make when we are examining our own behavior? What if you found yourself yelling at an employee in a coffee shop? Would you be as likely to label yourself as a mean person as you would the person in the previous example? Probably not. When we observe our own behavior, we tend to take situational factors more into account than we do for others. This tendency

actor/observer bias our tendency to make the fundamental attribution error when judging others, while being less likely to do so when making attributions about ourselves

self-serving bias our tendency to make attributions that preserve our own self-esteem—for example, making trait attributions for our successes and situational attributions for our failures

has been called the **actor/observer bias** because we make different attributions as *actors* than we make as *observers* of others (Choi & Nesbitt, 1998; Jones & Nesbitt, 1971). The actor/observer bias predicts that you are likely to attribute your own yelling to some situational factor. Perhaps the employee angered you, or you had a bad day. The explanation you would likely use for others, being a mean person, would be low on your list of attributions for your own behavior.

The actor/observer bias may seem self-serving, but this is not always the case. You would also be more likely to attribute a classmate's unexpected A on an exam to their traits than you would your own unexpected A. In this case, the actor/observer bias predicts that you would consider situational causes, such as an easy exam, more for yourself than for others. So why do we treat ourselves differently from others when it comes to attribution?

One potential reason for the actor/observer bias is that when we are the actor, we cannot literally see our own behavior, and our attention is generally focused outward on the environment. But when we are the observer, our attention is generally focused on the other person's behavior. Therefore, because we are relatively unaware of our own behavior and very aware of the environment, we are more likely to consider situational factors in making attributions for ourselves (Hennessy & Jakubowski, 2007; Storms, 1973).

The actor/observer bias may also stem from the different knowledge we have about ourselves and other people (Eisen, 1979). When we are making attributions about our own behavior, we are usually very aware of the way in which the environment influences it. Because we do not typically know other people's thoughts, we usually do not know how other people perceive the situation and whether it indeed influences their behavior.

Self-Serving Bias

Although the actor/observer bias does not stem from a desire to enhance one's self-esteem, this does not mean that we never seek to make ourselves look better. Often we do make self-esteem-boosting attributions. The **self-serving bias** refers to our tendency to make trait attributions for our successes and situational attributions for our failures (Miller & Ross, 1975). If you were to earn an A on your next psychology exam, you would likely attribute this grade to your ability or your study habits. However, if you were to fail your next psychology exam (and we hope that you do not!), you would be more likely to attribute your grade to some situational factor, such as your professor's teaching or the fact that your roommate interfered with your studying.

Most people, regardless of age, gender, or culture, engage in the self-serving bias (Mezulis et al., 2004). Even in collectivistic cultures, such as China, this tendency can be found (Hu, Zhang, & Ran, 2016). The major reason for the self-serving bias appears to be our desire to feel good about ourselves (Brown & Rogers, 1991; Trafimow, Armendariz, & Madsen, 2004). For example, in a study in India, parents attributed their own children's negative behavior to situational factors not related to parenting. However, they attributed the negative behaviors of other people's children to personality factors and parenting factors (Montemayor & Ranganathan, 2012). Attributions such as these presumably allowed the parents to still think of themselves as good parents, despite negative behavior in their own children. In this manner, self-serving bias may help us cope with information that may threaten our self-esteem.

Curiously, self-serving bias is seen less in people with major depressive disorder (see Chapter 13) than it is in people without depressive symptoms. This tendency to avoid self-serving attributions is correlated with abnormal activity in the prefrontal cortex of people who have major depressive disorder (Cui et al., 2020). This may suggest that self-serving bias is a somewhat normal process for us.

Although the self-serving bias may help us protect our self-esteem, it can also cause problems if we become too self-serving. For instance, not taking responsibility for our failures can lead others to like us less (Carlston & Shovar, 1983). Engaging in the self-serving bias to a great extent is also associated with high levels of *grandiose narcissism*, or having excessive self-admiration, self-importance, and needing to be adored by others. Narcissists devalue others while demanding that others value them and support their needs. Unsurprisingly, narcissism is associated with having difficulties in social relationships across a variety of settings (Selle, Brown, El-Alayli, & Ewert, 2019).

As we have seen in this section, we often take shortcuts, or heuristics, when making attributions about others. Heuristics may save time, but often they lead to incorrect attributions and judgments. Our tendency to use mental shortcuts can also lead to bigger problems, including prejudice and discrimination, our next topic of discussion.

10.2 Quiz Yourself

1. **Our tendency to overuse trait attributions and to ignore the situational influences on behavior is known as the ____________.**
   a. fundamental attribution error
   b. self-serving bias
   c. social desirability bias
   d. actor/observer bias

2. **Which of the following people would be *least* likely to exhibit the fundamental attribution error?**
   a. Henri from Canada
   b. Hongyong from Korea
   c. Lamont from the United States
   d. Greta from Germany

3. **You were quick to assume that a classmate is intelligent when you saw that they earned an A on the last psychology exam. However, when you earned an A on your history test, you were not so quick to assume that you are intelligent. Which of the following biases in social cognition *best* explains your behavior?**
   a. The fundamental attribution error
   b. The self-serving bias
   c. The social desirability bias
   d. The actor/observer bias

Answers *1. a; 2. b; 3. d*

10.3 Prejudice: Why Can't We All Just Get Along?

Across history, *prejudices* or unfair negative beliefs about members of certain groups have caused many people great harm. Today, prejudices based on race, gender, sexual orientation, age, religion, country of origin, and other perceived differences still hamper many people's ability to live a productive and happy life. People have been harassed and belittled, lost jobs, and even been killed because of prejudice. In 2018, the Federal Bureau of Investigation (FBI) reported a total of 7,036 incidents of hate crimes. Most of these incidents were motivated by prejudice based on race, ethnicity, or ancestry (57.5%), with prejudice based on religion (20.2%) and prejudice based on sexual orientation (17.0%) being the next most frequent motives for hate crimes (FBI, 2018a).

Besides violent crimes and crimes against property, discrimination can also manifest in subtler forms. In 2017, there were 8,186 complaints involving discrimination in housing in the United States. Of these, the largest proportion (59.4%) were based on alleged discrimination against people with disabilities and the second largest (26%) alleged discrimination based on race (HUD, 2017). Since the 1970s, the U.S. Department of Housing and Urban Development (HUD) has conducted several large-scale studies of discrimination in housing. To date, these studies have indicated that overt housing discrimination against minority members (e.g., refusing to rent to qualified minority candidates) has declined since the 1970s. However, they also indicate that more subtle forms of discrimination still exist. For example, when Black renters and prospective homebuyers contact housing providers about available properties, they are typically told about and shown fewer apartments and houses than their White counterparts are (Quillian, Lee, & Honoré, 2020). Similar trends are seen for Asian homebuyers and Latino or Asian renters. Same-sex couples are also more likely to have their email requests for information about housing opportunities go unanswered by housing providers. This trend is especially true for male same-sex couples (HUD, 2012). On average, members of racial minorities also pay higher mortgage costs and are denied for mortgages at higher rates compared to White buyers (Quillian, Lee, & Honoré, 2020). These forms of discrimination suggest that prejudice is still an issue in the housing market.

Discrimination also extends to other groups and other areas of life. Despite gains in equal rights over the last several decades, women have still not achieved equal status in the workforce, academia, or the government (Blackwell, Snyder, & Mavriplis, 2009; Chapman & Benis, 2017; Cheung & Halpern, 2010; Reilly et al., 2016; Sanchez-Hucles & Davis, 2010; Stephens & Levine, 2011). Prejudice remains a serious social problem.

Because prejudice poses a threat to all of us, understanding what it is and where it comes from is essential. Although people frequently use the words *prejudice, stereotypes,* and *discrimination* in everyday conversation, psychologists have very specific definitions for these concepts. Let's take a look at how psychologists conceptualize these terms.

10.3.1 Stereotypes, Prejudice, and Discrimination

Although prejudice is incredibly destructive, it can also be viewed as an extension of normal cognitive processes in that prejudices are attitudes that develop like all other attitudes. You will recall from Chapter 7 that as we acquire knowledge about the world, we store that information in generalized knowledge structures called schemas. *Schemas* reside in our long-term memory and allow us to more efficiently encode, store, and retrieve information (Fiske & Taylor, 2013). When we form a schema for a particular group of people, that schema is referred to as a **stereotype**. All of us have stereotypes for the various groups of people—such as professors, children, or females—we encounter in life. Our stereotypes allow us to make assumptions about others and to have certain expectations about how others will behave.

stereotype a schema for a particular group of people

prejudice a largely negative stereotype that is unfairly applied to all members of a group regardless of their individual characteristics

Although stereotypes are generally helpful to us, they are related to the prejudices that cause untold difficulties for humankind. One way to conceptualize a **prejudice** is as a stereotype gone awry. A stereotype can be thought of as the *cognitive* component of an attitude (Aronson, Wilson, & Akert, 2005) or the knowledge you have stored in memory about some group of people. Stereotypes become problematic when we generically apply them to all members of a group without regard to those individuals' unique characteristics. Furthermore, when a stereotype contains biased and negative information about a particular group of people, the stereotype begins to look like a prejudice (Chory-Assad & Tamborini, 2003). For example, in a study of stereotypes held in the United States, United Kingdom, and Australia, researchers found similarities between the stereotypes participants held for people with low-socioeconomic standing and the stereotypes they held for apes. These results suggest that many people in these cultures hold stereotypes about the poor that are dehumanizing (Loughnan et al., 2014). Finally, when a biased, negative stereotype becomes coupled with a negative *affective* or emotional reaction toward all (or most) people belonging to that group, a prejudice results.

In the mind of the prejudiced person, members of a particular group are disliked and labeled as having negative characteristics, regardless of their individual qualities. Additionally, prejudice can affect how the prejudiced person behaves toward others. All too often, prejudice motivates people to treat others poorly. **Discrimination** is the behavioral expression of a prejudice. For example, not considering a person for a job as a forklift operator simply because they are female would be an act of discrimination.

Discrimination doesn't always take such an obvious form. It can be much more subtle. Psychologists Samuel Gaertner and John Dovidio (1986, 2005) have argued that modern-day racial prejudice in the United States takes the form of **aversive racism**. According to this theory, European Americans who outwardly support equality and fairness may still feel negative emotions in the presence of African Americans (Dovidio, Gaertner, & Pearson, 2017; Hodson, Dovidio, & Gaertner, 2010). These negative or *aversive* emotions may motivate the person to discriminate against or avoid interaction with minority members. In fact, aversive emotions may even be better predictors of people's refusal to help minority members than racist attitudes are (McManus, Saucier, & O'Dea, & Bernard, 2019).

Aversive racism may also impact the decisions we make about others. In one study examining verdicts in a mock-trial situation, European American jurors were more likely to convict defendants depicted as being undocumented Latino immigrants from Mexico than they were immigrants who had attributes such as being from Canada, Caucasian, or documented immigrants. Latino jurors, on the other hand, showed no such bias, despite the fact that the details of the defendants' cases were held constant (Minero & Espinoza, 2016).

Aversive racism may be more likely when stressful situations heighten such aversive feelings. For example, European Americans were found to be slower to help African Americans than they were to help other European Americans during a severe emergency, but equally likely to help members of either group during a minor emergency (Kunstman & Plant, 2008). These results suggest that under stress, hidden prejudices can surface and give rise to discrimination. For a closer look at this form of prejudice, see Psychology Applies to Your World: The Modern Face of Racism.

Jack Hollingsworth/Photodisc/Getty Images

▲ Studies suggest that bias and discrimination still exist in the U.S. housing market. Members of racial minorities, such as this couple, are often shown fewer houses and apartments when seeking new homes. Same-sex couples are also more likely to have their email inquiries about available properties go unanswered.

discrimination the behavioral expression of a prejudice

aversive racism a proposed form of subtle racism in which European Americans feel aversive emotions around African Americans, which may lead them to discriminate against African Americans

stereotype threat a phenomenon in which fears of being discriminated against elicit stereotype-confirming behaviors

10.3.2 Stereotype Threat: Prejudice Can Be a Self-Fulfilling Prophecy

Many people live with the fear that others may harbor prejudices about them. Psychologist Claude Steele proposes that some victims of prejudice actually end up reinforcing certain aspects of the prejudices held against them because of a phenomenon called **stereotype threat**. Stereotype threat exists when a person fears that others will judge them not on their own qualities but rather on prejudicial stereotypes held about the group(s) to which they belong (Steele, 1997). Understandably, this fear can lead to considerable anxiety in people from marginalized groups because of the negative nature of the prejudices they face. For example, women often experience stereotype threat when performing mathematical and scientific tasks (Good, Woodzicka, & Wingfield, 2010). Widespread negative stereotyping of women in the workplace also leads women to expect that coworkers will give them less credit for successes and more blame for failures (Heilman & Kram, 1983).

Studies have shown that stereotype threat can actually inhibit performance on a task. For example, normally high-achieving females tend to score less well on mathematics problems but not on verbal tasks when they are asked to perform these tasks in an environment where they are outnumbered

Psychology Applies to Your World

The Modern Face of Racism

SINCE THE EARLY 2010s, growing anger over the disproportionate killing of unarmed blacks by law enforcement personnel and civilians claiming to be protecting their neighborhoods has raised awareness of ongoing racial prejudice in the United States. This awareness has led to widespread protests, activism, and at times civil unrest. Groups arguing many sides of the issue have emerged and taken to the streets to debate the causes of these killings and the scope of racism in our society. One of the most visible of these groups has been the #Black Lives Matter movement founded in 2013 in the wake of the killing of Trayvon Martin and the subsequent acquittal of his killer (Blacklivesmatter.com, 2020). So, how can psychology help us understand what is going on? Are prejudice and racism still a big problem in our society?

One of the complicating factors involved in studying prejudice is the fact that humans process information on different levels of consciousness (recall Chapter 7). Part of the time, we process information at the conscious, *explicit*, level, where we tend to carefully evaluate information and use logic to make decisions. But, the other part of the time, we process information below a level of conscious awareness, using *implicit* memory processes. When we are processing on the implicit level, we behave less rationally and more intuitively. The fact that we are capable of processing on these two levels has led some social psychologists to refer to the human mind as being *"a duplex mind"* (Baumeister & Bushman, 2017, p. 51). Part of the mind is conscious, deliberate, and rational. Although rational and systematic in its processing of information, it is also comparatively slow. The other part of the mind is unconscious, automatic, intuitive, and emotional. Due to its heuristic nature, it is not systematic and rational in processing information, but it is comparatively fast. We are most likely to rely on the deliberate part of the mind when we have the cognitive resources required to engage in careful processing. When we are in a hurry, stressed, disinterested, or distracted our unconscious, automatic, and intuitive cognitive processes are likely to exert more influence—simply because we may not have (or choose not to use) the cognitive resources needed to exert more conscious control.

▲ In the United States, Blacks are killed by law enforcement personnel at rates disproportionate with the percentage of Blacks living in the U.S. Growing anger over the killing of unarmed Blacks by police has led to many protests calling for an end to these shootings. The #BlackLivesMatter movement has been one of the most visible and active protest groups.

As such, it is likely that all social cognitive processes, such as person perception, judgment, persuasion, and attribution, are affected by the workings of the duplex mind. Prejudice is one of these processes. Some acts of prejudice and discrimination are examples of *explicit bias*. They are conscious and deliberate thoughts and actions aimed at devaluing *out-group members* or people that belong to groups other than our own. Other acts of prejudice and discrimination may be more subtle and not so deliberate. These prejudices, called *implicit biases*, may operate without us even knowing they are guiding our actions (de Houwer, 2019). Implicit bias can be measured using a test called the *Implicit Associations Test (IAT)* (Greenwald & Krieger, 2006; Greenwald, McGhee, & Schwartz, 1998). Instead of asking participants to answer questions about their attitudes toward groups of people as measures of explicit bias do, the IAT uses reaction time to determine how closely we associate certain positive and negative words or images with specific people. By analyzing the pattern of reaction times, the

by males (Inzlicht & Ben-Zeev, 2000). In this situation, females presumably become aware of the inaccurate stereotypes that many people hold—that males are better at math—and the fear of being perceived to be mathematically inept (stereotype threat) then impairs their math performance. Females are not stereotyped as being poor at verbal tasks, so there is no stereotype threat for verbal tasks, and females exhibit no impairment in performance test can detect signs of implicit bias. So, when measuring both explicit and implicit bias, what trends have psychologists seen?

For decades, explicit racial prejudice and discrimination have been diminishing in the United States. However, this does not mean that prejudice and discrimination (even the overt, explicit kind) have ceased to exist in our society (Bonilla-Silva, 2015). Yet for the most part, prejudice and discrimination have changed face. The majority of White Americans today do not consciously think of themselves as being prejudiced and racist. For most White people, the idea of purposely holding prejudicial beliefs and engaging in discrimination against minority members is considered wrong and immoral. But what happens when these same people rely on the implicit, unconscious parts of their minds to help them make social judgments? Is it possible to consciously think of yourself as being egalitarian, but still act as if you are prejudiced? Unfortunately, the answer seems to be yes (Dovidio, Gaertner, & Saguy, 2015).

For example, between the years of 1989 and 1999, researchers studied prejudice in White college students at a specific college. First, they surveyed the students' overt, explicit expressions of racial prejudice and found that self-reported levels of racial prejudice declined during this 10-year period. Second, they studied more subtle forms of prejudice using the following paradigm. Students were presented with descriptions of Black and White job candidates applying for a specific job on campus and asked to choose who should be hired. Half of each race of candidate was depicted as having very strong credentials and half was depicted as having ambiguous credentials for the position. In the case where candidates of both races had strong credentials, the participants did not discriminate by choosing the White candidates more often than the Black candidates. However, when examining the candidates that had the more ambiguous credentials, participants showed a clear bias toward hiring the White candidates over the Black. It appears that when the judgment was more difficult and less clear-cut, taxing their cognitive resources, participants relied more on their unconscious biases to guide their decisions. When looking at the rates of this more subtle and implicit form of prejudice, the researchers saw no decline over the 10-year period, despite the fact that rates of overt, explicit prejudice did decline (Dovidio & Gaertner, 2000). Similar findings have also been found in human resource professionals (Dovidio & Gaertner, 2007) and in participants' judgments in mock college admissions scenarios (Hodson, Dovidio, & Gaertner, 2002). Could it be that lingering implicit bias also plays a role in the disproportionate number of police shootings of minority members?

Perhaps. Some studies have found that in a modified version of the IAT, *both* Black and White police officers are more likely to exhibit implicit bias toward Black suspects. Specifically, officers of both races were quicker to choose "shoot" over "don't shoot" when seeing Black faces, regardless of whether a weapon was present or not (Correll et al., 2007; Sadler et al., 2012). Some have concluded that implicit bias against ethnic and racial minorities is the norm among police officers (Price & Peyton, 2017). However, not all data supports this conclusion. In one small study, James and colleagues (2017) found that compared to armed White suspects, police officers were less likely to shoot an armed suspect who was Black.

Others argue that the problem goes beyond the scope of implicit biases exhibited toward individual suspects. They argue that the issue is more a problem of *structural or systemic racism* (Siegel, 2020). According to Siegel, structural racism is the result of decades of overt, explicit racism against Blacks and other minorities. Due to a long history of disadvantage, many Blacks still live today in segregated neighborhoods with higher rates of poverty, unemployment, and crime. Siegel argues that when police enter these neighborhoods, they respond differently than they would in richer, less segregated areas of town. Because they implicitly (or explicitly) expect more danger and crime, they respond with a higher level of aggression. Furthermore, because a higher percentage of people living in the area are members of minorities, the targets of this aggression are often people of color. According to Siegel, solving the issue of police violence against Blacks and other people of color must go beyond training police to limit the effects of implicit bias. It must also involve societal change that addresses the inequities that still exist for members of racial minorities.

even when they are outnumbered by males. Stereotype threat can thus become a *self-fulfilling prophecy* in which a woman behaves in a manner that actually reinforces negative stereotypes about females (Keller & Dauenheimer, 2003). Similarly, stereotype threat has been shown to impede learning in women (Grand, 2017) and weaken academic performance of students with disabilities (Desombre, Anegmar, & Delelis, 2018).

The effect of stereotype threat may be due to increased physiological arousal that results when we perceive that others expect us to perform poorly. As such, the effects of stereotype threat appear to be especially strong when the task being performed is a difficult one (Hively & El-Alayli, 2014) or one that is being learned (Grand, 2017). Recall from Chapter 5 that high or low levels of arousal can degrade performance on tasks (Yerkes & Dodson, 1908). When a task is difficult, the amount of arousal needed to impair performance is lower than the level needed to impair performance on easy tasks (Martinie, Olive, & Milland, 2010). As a result, when stereotype threat is experienced while performing a difficult task, performance is more likely to suffer (Keller, 2007). Unfortunately, stereotype threat may discourage some people from attempting certain challenges in life.

For example, stereotype threat has been shown to impair African Americans' academic performance (Steele & Aronson, 1995), and it may contribute to some African Americans' experiencing *disidentification* with certain aspects of European American culture. If young African Americans experience stereotype threat in school (they perceive that others expect them to fail), one way they may protect themselves emotionally is by devaluing education. If one does not feel that academic achievement is important, then if one fails at academics, it is not damaging to their self-esteem (Nadler & Komarraju, 2016; Steele, 1997). Unfortunately, this not only prevents some African Americans from achieving academically, but it may also place pressure on those African Americans who do wish to pursue academic success. Recall that our need for cognitive consistency is strong. If your friends devalue your dreams, you must either abandon your plans or distance yourself from your friends—both of which can be painful.

Our long-term goal should be to eliminate stereotype threat at its source by ridding the world of prejudice. In the meantime, there may be other ways to reduce the negative effects of stereotype threat on young people. In an interesting study, seventh grade Latino and African American students who engaged in an ongoing program of self-affirmation showed a significant improvement in their academic performance relative to their Asian and White counterparts. They also showed improved on-time graduation rates (Borman, Choi, & Hall, 2020). Until we can remove the damaging prejudices that cause stereotype threat, such interventions may provide some relief. Given the destructiveness of prejudice, you might ask why it is part of the human condition? In our next section, we will begin to examine this issue.

10.3.3 Learning to Be Prejudiced

Like other attitudes, prejudices can develop through the learning processes of classical conditioning, operant conditioning, and observational learning (Duckitt, 1992). For example, children who witness adults sending negative nonverbal signals toward members of a specific group begin to develop biased feelings toward that group (Skinner, Olson, & Meltzoff, 2020). As you can see in You Review: The Learning of a Prejudice Against People Who Are Homeless, these learning experiences allow prejudices to develop and also to be passed from person to person within a culture (Kowalski, 2003).

How easily prejudices can be learned was dramatically demonstrated in one of the most famous classroom exercises ever done on prejudice. In the late 1960s, grade school teacher Jane Elliot decided to teach her third-grade class an important lesson about prejudice. She believed that her students, who were all rural White children, could benefit from learning about prejudice from both sides of the fence.

One day in class, Elliot told her students that she had recently heard that scientists had determined that brown-eyed people were inferior to blue-eyed people. She told the class that brown-eyed people were less intelligent, trustworthy, and

YOU REVIEW The Learning of a Prejudice Against People Who Are Homeless

Type of Learning	Situation	Outcome
Classical conditioning	On the subway, Marlita is aggressively confronted (US) by a person who appears homeless (CS). The person yells incoherently at Marlita for no apparent reason. During the encounter, Marlita feels fear (UR/CR).	After the encounter, Marlita feels fear when encountering people who are homeless. Marlita has been classically conditioned to feel negative emotions in response to people who are homeless.
Operant conditioning	On a school trip to the city, Bobbi sees a person who is homeless sleeping on the sidewalk and begins to make fun of the person (behavior). All of Bobbi's friends laugh when they see Bobbi behaving this way (reinforcement).	Bobbi is more likely to make fun of people who are homeless in the future because Bobbi has been reinforced for doing so. Bobbi's friends have operantly conditioned Bobbi's prejudiced, discriminatory behavior.
Observational learning	Growing up, Jackie heard others frequently say that people who are homeless are just lazy people who do not want to work for a living.	Jackie is likely to model the prejudices against people who are homeless that were modeled by others during childhood.

nice than the "superior" blue-eyed people. To make the group differences very salient, Elliot had all the brown-eyed children wear brown cloth collars over their clothing so they could be immediately identified as members of the "inferior" group of students.

Within hours of her announcement concerning eye color, Elliot had created a strong prejudice in her classroom. The blue-eyed children made fun of the brown-eyed children. The blue-eyes called the brown-eyes names, ostracized them, and in general treated them cruelly. A fight even occurred on the playground as a result of the prejudice. In less than a day, Elliot turned a peaceful, egalitarian classroom into a hotbed of prejudice and discrimination (Monteith & Winters, 2002). Elliot's study showed the world how easily prejudice can be learned from others—especially when we learn it from those we look up to.

Admittedly, the environment Elliot created in her classroom was deliberately designed to create prejudice. What other types of environments may contribute to the development of prejudices? Can prejudice be developed within a family, for instance? Some evidence suggests that we do adopt the prejudices of our parents (Degner & Dalege, 2013; Dhont, Roets, & Van Hiel, 2013), especially when we perceive our parents as being supportive of us (Miklikowska, 2017). However, having prejudiced parents does not guarantee that we will become prejudiced. In one study that examined the match between parental values and those held by their children, it was found that children are most likely to have attitudes similar to those of their parents when the parents hold egalitarian beliefs. One reason for this is that parents who have high levels of internal motivation to respond in non-prejudicial ways tend to set higher non-prejudicial standards for their children. They expect their children to behave non-prejudicially and they experience more guilt when their children violate these standards (Scott, Shutts, & Devine, 2020).

On the other hand, when parents hold prejudicial attitudes, the match between their values and their children's values is less strong (Rohan & Zanna, 1996). It appears that when parents hold strong prejudices, the children may pick up these prejudices but later find that their peers do not reinforce them for holding such negative views. Because they are not reinforced and may even be punished by their peers for holding prejudices, they experience a decline in prejudice that distances them from their parents' values. But when parents hold egalitarian values, their children may pick up these values *and* be reinforced by their peers for having them. Their values

mark peterson/Corbis Historical/Getty Images

▲ Is this child likely to adopt the prejudices of their parents through modeling?

then remain more like those of their parents (Aronson et al., 2005). This line of research makes a powerful argument for teaching tolerance in schools and in society because if tolerance becomes prevalent in a culture, it may have the power to override what happens in the home. Furthermore, some evidence suggests that adolescents' attitudes may also impact those of their parents (Miklikowska, 2017). Perhaps teaching tolerance in the classroom may lead to greater tolerance at home.

10.3.4 Intergroup Dynamics and Prejudice

We all belong to certain groups: families, schools, clubs, states, countries, religions, and races. For Hongyong, the groups represented by her culture, her religion, and her family were an essential part of her life. The groups we belong to and the roles we play in them help define who we are as individuals and our connection to others (Gergen & Gergen, 1988; Halsam et al., 2014). Because we tend to identify with the groups to which we belong, we also tend to prefer the groups of which we are members (Roth & Steffens, 2014).

In-Group Bias: Us Versus Them

in-group bias our tendency to favor people who belong to the same groups that we do

out-group homogeneity [home-uh-juh-NEE-it-tee] bias our tendency to see out-group members as being pretty much all alike

We tend to like the people in our group a little more than we like the people who are not members. In other words, we exhibit an **in-group bias** (Hewstone, Rubin, & Willis, 2002). We tend to like our family members more than strangers. We like those who attend our school more than those who do not. We have a bias toward liking our country's citizens a little more than foreigners.

Think of the groups of spectators at a sporting event. Each group sits on its team's side, and at times the rivalry between the two sides erupts into name-calling and even aggression. If these same people met under other conditions in which their team affiliations were not obvious, such as at the grocery store or library, do you think they would be as likely to call each other names and fight? Probably not. Why do we sometimes allow our group affiliations to bias how we feel about and treat others? It appears to boil down to self-esteem.

We apparently derive some of our self-esteem from the groups of which we are members. In fact, just belonging to a social group has been shown to increase self-esteem (Haslam et al., 2016). Belonging to a group we perceive as good and desirable is especially likely to enhance self-esteem. For example, if you perceive your religion as the best religion, then belonging to this religious group increases your self-esteem. Unfortunately, one way to perceive your particular group as being good is to believe that other groups are not as good (Tajfel, 1982). When our group succeeds at something, we tend to be especially proud (Cialdini et al., 1976). For example, fans who strongly identify with a sports team are likely to *bask in the reflected glory* (BIRGing) of their team's victories, resulting in a boost to their own self-esteem (Ware & Kowalski, 2012). In the aftermath of President Barack Obama's 2008 election, there was an increase in Black mothers giving their children African-American sounding names. Furthermore, as a group, the mothers' levels of self-esteem tended to be positively correlated with the ethnic sound of their babies' names (Anderson-Clark & Green, 2017). Yet even in the absence of meaningful victory, we still tend to view our in-group members as superior to out-group members (Brewer, 1979; Molero et al., 2003; Tajfel, 1982).

The in-group bias tends to make us somewhat prejudiced against those who are not part of our social groups. Furthermore, the in-group bias tends to affect the way we perceive out-group members, causing us to see members of an out-group as being pretty much all alike. Researchers call this tendency the **out-group homogeneity bias** (Linville, Fischer, & Salovey, 1989; Rubin & Badea, 2012). Individual characteristics are perceived not to differ much from the stereotype that defines the group. So once we have knowledge about one member of an out-group, we tend to apply it to all people in that group (Quattrone & Jones, 1980).

It's not hard to see how learning and in-group bias can contribute to the development of prejudices. However, we do not hold strong prejudices for all out-groups and their members. For example, there are few hate crimes committed against librarians each year, but many are inspired by race, religion, sexual orientation, etc. Why would some out-groups be singled out for such ill-treatment? As we will see in our next section, competition for resources seems to be one reason why some groups come to be particularly disliked.

Conflict and Prejudice: It's Their Fault

realistic-conflict theory the theory that prejudice stems from competition for scarce resources

scapegoat an out-group that is blamed for many of society's problems

Realistic-conflict theory (Levine & Campbell, 1972) proposes that conflict among groups for resources motivates the development of prejudice. In the United States, immigrants are often the targets of prejudice because they are perceived as coming here "to steal jobs away from hard-working Americans" (Esses et al., 2001). Minority out-group members often play the role of **scapegoat**, the out-group members we blame for our problems, when times are hard (Allport, 1954/1979). This blaming of out-group members may help restore our sense of control when we experience hardships, such as unemployment (Bukowski et al., 2017). When we feel threatened, we are most likely to blame out-groups, which we perceive to be in competition with us for scarce resources, such as jobs. For example, a laid-off software engineer may blame their plight on highly educated immigrants coming from Asia, but not be tempted to blame agricultural workers immigrating from other parts of the world. In fact, if we perceive out-groups to be non-threatening and facing similar challenges as our own in-group, we may identify with them rather than blame them (Bukowski et al., 2018). In modern America, as you might expect, racial prejudice most often exists when groups are in direct competition for the same jobs (Simpson & Yinger, 1985).

Possibly the most famous study ever conducted on conflict and prejudice is Muzafer Sherif's (1906-1988) Robber's Cave experiment (Sherif et al., 1961). Sherif and his colleagues conducted this experiment in a naturalistic setting, a summer boys' camp at Robber's Cave State Park in Oklahoma (hence the experiment's nickname). The participants were described as normal, healthy, middle-class, White, Protestant, 11- to 12-year-old boys who attended Boy Scout camp at the park. Prior to participation in the camp, the boys were all strangers to one another.

As they arrived at the camp, the boys were randomly assigned to one of two cabins, the Eagles' cabin or the Rattlers' cabin. The cabins were situated fairly far apart to ensure that the two groups would not have much contact with each other. The boys in each group lived together, ate together, and spent much of their time together. Under these conditions of isolation from each other, the Eagles and the Rattlers became separate, tight-knit in-groups. Once each group bonded, the experimenters placed the Eagles and Rattlers together under conditions of conflict.

In this next phase, the experimenters had the Eagles and Rattlers compete with each other in sporting events. The winning group would get prizes that 12-year-old boys find attractive, such as pocketknives. The losers got nothing for their efforts except defeat. As a result of this competition, the Eagles and the Rattlers began to call each other names, sabotage each other's cabins and belongings, and even engage in physical violence against one another. In short, the Eagles hated the Rattlers, and the Rattlers hated the Eagles. A prejudice based on the relatively meaningless distinctions of being Eagles or Rattlers was fully developed in the boys. When the prejudice between the Eagles and Rattlers reached the point of physical violence, the experimenters stopped the competition between the boys and sought ways to reduce the prejudice that had developed.

10.3.5 Reducing Prejudice in the Real World

contact hypothesis the theory that contact between groups is an effective means of reducing prejudice between them

superordinate goal a goal that is shared by different groups

One of Sherif's strategies to reduce prejudice was to increase noncompetitive contact between the Eagles and the Rattlers (e.g., watching movies together). In fact, the idea that contact between groups is enough to reduce prejudice, the so-called **contact hypothesis**, has been around for quite some time (Lee & Humphrey, 1943, cited in Allport, 1954/1979). If people from different in-groups see a lot of each other, won't they realize that the prejudices that they hold about one another are unfounded and abandon them?

As Sherif found out, mere contact often does little to reduce prejudice (e.g., Poore et al., 2002). One reason contact doesn't work is that when people from different groups are thrown together, they tend to self-segregate (Binder et al., 2009). A drive through any big city illustrates this point. Neighborhoods are often well defined on the basis of ethnicity and race—even though people are legally free to live where they choose. Such segregation can prevent meaningful contact between groups from happening, precluding much chance of reducing prejudice.

To bring groups together in meaningful contact, they have to be motivated to really spend time together—not just occupy the same space. Not surprisingly, *cooperative contact,* in which the groups work together on a common task, has been shown to be more effective in reducing prejudice than merely forcing groups together (Pettigrew & Tropp, 2006). In fact, repeated cooperative contact can reduce both the conscious, explicit (Boccanfuso, White, & Maunder, 2020) and unconscious, implicit prejudices that we hold toward out-group members (Vezzali & Capozza, 2011).

After experimenting with increased contact between the Eagles and the Rattlers, Sherif and his colleagues (1961) tried facilitating cooperation between the two groups of boys. Sherif and his colleagues created *superordinate goals* for the Eagles and the Rattlers. A **superordinate goal** is a goal that both groups want to accomplish but cannot without the help of the other group. For instance, the researchers disrupted the water supply that both groups used by tampering with the water pipes. To reestablish water to the camp, the Eagles and Rattlers had to work together to find the source of the trouble. While they were trying to solve their mutual problem, the Eagles and Rattlers did not seem to have much time to hate one another. In another instance, a food supply truck broke down, and the two groups had to work together to push-start the truck. Without their combined efforts, both groups would have gone hungry.

After a series of such contacts, the prejudice between the groups began to dissolve, perhaps because the Eagles and Rattlers now saw themselves as part of the same group—the group that was trying to find food and water. Without clear lines between the boys, there was no basis for in-group or out-group bias or prejudice. The researchers noted that friendships began to form between individual Eagles and Rattlers, and as a whole, the Rattlers and Eagles began to cooperate, spend time together, and even share their money. The prejudice that was once so strong was dramatically reduced (Sherif, 1966).

Based in part on the results of the Robber's Cave study, researchers have attempted to outline the characteristics of the type of contact between groups that reduces prejudice. The most effective strategies are ones with the following factors:

- The different groups need each other.
- The different groups have a common, superordinate goal that requires everyone's effort to achieve.
- The different groups work shoulder to shoulder on an equal playing field to accomplish the goal.

- The contact is hospitable, informal, and free from negative emotional interaction.
- Contact with out-group members lasts for a significant period of time.
- The norms governing the contact situation promote harmony and mutual respect.

SeventyFour/Shutterstock.com

▲ Superordinate goals are an effective means of reducing prejudice. These people are likely to see themselves as members of the same in-group as they work together to accomplish their goals. As a result, they are likely to experience less prejudice toward one another.

One practical application of these conditions is called a *jigsaw classroom* (Aronson, 2000). A jigsaw classroom is one in which students from diverse ethnic groups are asked to work together on a project in a cooperative way. Each child is responsible for a different piece of the project, which forces the children to be interdependent. Because they must rely on each other, the children begin to focus more on the tasks at hand and less on their differences. According to psychologist Elliot Aronson (2000; 2011), 25 years of research on the outcomes of jigsaw classrooms consistently indicates that as participants begin to identify as members of the same in-group, prejudice and hostility among the children are reduced, and self-esteem and academic performance are increased. These findings further underscore the message of the Robber's Cave experiment—that cooperation rather than competition can work to lessen prejudice in the world.

Regardless of whether we base our impressions on a prejudice or on actual behavior, we tend to want to spend more time with people we like. This is the topic that we will tackle next as we look at what attracts us to others.

10.3 Quiz Yourself

1. **Kelly is a manager at a firm that has been troubled by considerable prejudice between its male and female employees. Kelly wants to institute a program that will reduce the level of prejudice between the sexes. Which of the following plans has the *best* chance of working?**
   a. Appoint opposite-sex managers to supervise workers.
   b. Have a "battle of the sexes" to see which sex can outperform the other on the job.
   c. Form work teams to solve company problems, and make sure that the teams contain both male and female members.
   d. Threaten to fire anyone who says or does anything prejudicial, and post this message around the workplace to ensure that everyone knows about the policy.

2. **Relative to in-group members, we tend to view out-group members as being ________.**
   a. less like us
   b. less favorable
   c. more homogeneous
   d. All of the above

3. **Which of the following is the *best* example of cooperative contact?**
   a. Teachers supervising students taking a math test
   b. A manager meeting with employees to discuss sales figures
   c. A police officer speaking to an elementary school class about the dangers of drugs
   d. A citizens' group meeting to find ways to reduce crime in their neighborhood

4. **To study the mechanics of prejudice, Dr. Williams spends 6 months sitting in 50 racially diverse college classrooms across the University System of Georgia. While in class, Dr. Williams records details of the interactions that occur between students of different races. What research method is Dr. Williams using?**
   a. A survey
   b. An experiment
   c. Case study
   d. Naturalistic observation

Answers 1. c; 2. d; 3. d; 4. d

10.4 Being Drawn to Others: The Nature of Attraction

The attitudes that we form about a person determine whether we will be attracted to this person as a friend or as a romantic partner. The affective component of the attitudes we hold about someone is particularly important. If a person produces positive emotional reactions in us, we are much more likely to find them attractive. Think about the people closest to you. How do you feel about your best friend or your significant other? We are betting that most of you generally feel positive emotions about those you love. Most of us do. When it comes to attraction, the most important question is: What makes us feel good about another person? Psychologists have identified several variables that affect attraction, including *proximity* and *exposure*, *similarity*, and *physical attractiveness*.

10.4.1 Proximity and Exposure: Attraction to Those Who Are Nearby

One of the most intriguing findings in the area of attraction concerns how much exposure we have to certain people and how the exposure affects our feelings of attraction for them. Recall from Chapter 5 that the more often we see a person or an object, the more we tend to like it. This trend, called the *mere exposure effect* (Lee, 2001; Zajonc, 1968), appears to be true for a variety of stimuli, including people (Moreland & Topolinski, 2010; Zebrowitz, White, & Wieneke, 2008).

Many studies have shown that we tend to be friends and lovers with those who live and work close to us (Clarke, 1952; Festinger, 1951; Festinger, Schachter, & Back, 1950; Ineichen, 1979; Segal, 1974). The more **proximity**, or physical closeness, we have to someone in our daily lives, the more exposure we have to them, and the more we tend to like them. For example, within an apartment building, the closer a person's apartment is to yours, the higher the probability that you will be friends with that person (Festinger, 1951). This is true even when apartments are assigned on a random basis, as you might find in university housing (Festinger et al., 1950). Attraction to those who live and work nearby seems to hold across cultures as well. Studies have found evidence supporting a relationship between proximity and liking in both Africa (Brewer & Campbell, 1976) and France (Maisonneuve, Palmade, & Fourment, 1952). But, is proximity enough to ensure attraction? Not necessarily. Other factors, such as how similar one's characteristics are to our own also matter.

proximity physical closeness

▼ People who work in close proximity to each other are more likely to become friends and lovers.

Kevin Jordan/DigitalVision/Getty Images

10.4.2 Similarity: Having Things in Common

Two old adages describe the people we tend to choose as friends or romantic partners. One says, "Birds of a feather flock together," and the other says, "Opposites attract." You probably know some couples who demonstrate both views of attraction. But what does the average person look for? Do we want someone who is similar to us, or are we looking for someone who is different to complement our personality?

Research on this issue indicates that, indeed, "birds of a feather flock together." When choosing a romantic partner, we tend to gravitate to people who are of similar age, socioeconomic status, education, intelligence, race, religion, attitudes, power, and physical attractiveness (Brehm, 1992; Browning et al., 1999; Hendrick & Hendrick, 1983). For example, it was after Hongyong discovered that she and Dukpil shared some similar attitudes that she began to feel real affection for him. Having things in common seems to be important in romantic relationships. Accordingly, similarity seems to predict attraction across a variety of cultures, including Mexico, India, and Japan (Byrne et al., 1971). Similarity also seems to be a factor in the friends we choose (Kandel, 1978; Newcomb, 1961; Rubin et al., 1994) and even in choosing which fictional characters we like in movies (Krause & Ricker, 2020).

Self-esteem may play a role in our preference for similar others. Being attracted to similar others may be motivated in part by a desire to maintain high self-esteem. After all, valuing similar others is, in a way, valuing one's self (Heine, Foster, & Spina, 2009). For example, in one study of people engaged in negotiations with a partner, more positive emotions were expressed by pairs that had similar personality characteristics relative to pairs that were dissimilar—even if the traits they shared were negative in nature (being disagreeable; Wilson et al., 2016).

It is also possible that we are attracted to similar others because finding ourselves attracted to dissimilar others might produce cognitive dissonance (Heider, 1958). For example, if you were attracted to someone who did not share your spiritual views, the conflict between your attitudes about the person and your attitudes about spirituality might produce dissonance. In the face of this dissonance, it might be easier to change your attitudes about the person (as opposed to your spirituality), lessening your attraction to them and reducing the dissonance. Overall, it is more reinforcing (see Chapter 6) to be attracted to those who share our attitudes.

10.4.3 The Importance of Physical Attractiveness

One of the first things we notice about a potential romantic partner is their physical attractiveness. Although standards of physical attractiveness vary across cultures (see • FIGURE 10.3), it is an important factor in determining our attraction to others. In a classic study that examined physical attractiveness and attraction in a blind-date scenario, physical attractiveness was the only factor found to predict whether a person wanted to go out on a second date (Walster et al., 1966). One reason physical attractiveness may be so important to us is that it may tell us something about a potential mate's underlying health. In one study, participants rated people who had fairly consistent reaction times (an indicator of how reliable one's central nervous system is) as being more attractive than people with higher reaction time variability (Butler et al., 2017).

Perhaps unsurprisingly, physical attractiveness seems to be important to heterosexuals of both sexes (Luo, 2009). Physical attractiveness also influences attraction for men and women in same-gender relationships (Felmlee, Orzechowicz, & Fortes, 2010). However, men seem to place particular emphasis on how attractive their potential romantic partners are (Jonason, 2009). This special emphasis that men place on physical attractiveness seems to hold for both homosexual and heterosexual men. Heterosexual and homosexual women, in contrast, place more importance on the psychological traits of their potential partners. For example, heterosexual women place more emphasis on a man's social status when choosing a mate (Alterovitz & Mendelsohn, 2009). So it seems that although physical attractiveness is important to women, it is not the most important aspect of a partner (Deaux & Hanna, 1984).

Although we may be attracted to good-looking people, we tend to be romantically involved with people whose level of physical attractiveness is comparable to our own. This tendency, called the **matching hypothesis**, seems to be true of both dating and married couples (Zajonc et al., 1987). Matching is so pervasive that we actually expect to date people at our same level of attractiveness (Montoya, 2008; Montoya & Horton, 2014).

matching hypothesis the theory that we are attracted to people whose level of physical attractiveness is similar to our own

FIGURE 10.3

Cultural Differences in Physical Attractiveness

Standards of physical attractiveness can vary across cultures. All of these people would be considered attractive in their respective cultures. Which of these people do you find attractive?

Yuri Arcurs/Alamy Stock Photo

ImageDB103/Alamy stock photo

Angelo Cavalli/Getty Images

GM Photo Images/Alamy Stock Photo

Interestingly, the influence of physical attractiveness on romantic relationships seems to be mirrored in our same-sex friendships. The matching hypothesis predicts that our same-sex friends will be, on average, about as attractive as we are (McKillip & Reidel, 1983). And although both men and women seem to choose their friends on the basis of their physical attractiveness, again men place more emphasis on this characteristic than do women (Berscheid et al., 1971; Feingold, 1988; Perlini, Bertolissi, & Lind, 1999). The importance of physical attractiveness in social relationships isn't surprising in light of findings that we tend to perceive attractive people more positively than unattractive people (Lemay, Clark, & Greenberg, 2010). Physical attractiveness often induces a *halo effect* in us, in that we tend to assume that people who look good must also possess other positive traits. For example, attractive people are perceived to be more interesting, sociable, kind, sensitive, and nurturing than unattractive people (Dion, Berscheid, & Walster, 1972). Participants even judged attractive people on an online dating site to have less chance of having a sexually transmitted infection (STI), suggesting they are perceived to be less risky sexual partners (Krishnamaturi, Davis, & Fischhoff, 2020). With all these perceived qualities, no wonder we want to be friends and lovers with attractive people!

However, another reason may also explain why we prefer attractive people. Perhaps being attracted to others is in part biological and instinctive. In an interesting study, researchers found that babies as young as 2 months old looked longer at attractive faces than they did at unattractive ones (Langlois et al., 1987), indicating that they preferred the attractive faces. Because it is hard to imagine that 2-month-old babies have had time to learn to be biased toward attractive people, these findings suggest that we are born with an instinctive preference for good-looking people. Indeed, research has suggested that we find faces to be attractive if they tend to be *symmetric*, *average* (nondistinctive), and have a *level of masculinity/femininity that is appropriate to the sex of the face* (Griffey & Little, 2013). Perhaps we evolved to be drawn to certain facial traits (e.g., symmetrical facial features) because they indicate good health (Bronstad, Langlois, & Russell, 2008; Butler et al., 2017). In terms of natural selection and evolution, it makes sense for us to be sexually attracted to people who are healthy and therefore able to facilitate our ability to produce offspring.

10.4.4 The "Chemistry" of Sex Drive, Love, and Romance

When it comes to love and romance, is there anything to the notion of "chemistry" between people? Perhaps. Neuroimaging studies suggest that many brain areas are involved in our complex feelings for our romantic partners (Acevedo et al., 2011; Takahashi et al., 2015). Furthermore, psychologists have identified three separate emotional systems involved in romantic relationships. *Sex drive* is our desire for sexual gratification. *Romantic attraction* is our physical and emotional desire for a specific person. Attachment is *companionate love*, or our desire to be close with our partner. Interestingly, psychologists have discovered that each of these emotional systems seems to be related to the action of different chemicals in the body. Sex drive is governed by hormones—in particular, estrogens and androgens (see Chapters 2 and 5). Experiencing romantic attraction is related to increased dopamine and norepinephrine, but lowered serotonin, in the brain. Experiencing attachment or love is associated with the action of other neurotransmitters and hormones, including neuropeptides, oxytocin, and vasopressin (Fisher, 2000; Takahashi et al., 2015).

Although the idea of "chemistry" in romance may have some merit, we are drawn to others for many reasons. Sexual attraction is just one of these reasons. Sometimes our desire to be with others serves a purpose other than romance, sex, and reproduction. In the next section, we will further explore our social nature by examining some of the reasons we are driven to be with others in the form of social groups.

goodluz/Shutterstock.com

▲ When it comes to romance, several chemicals in our bodies influence the sex drive, romantic attraction, and attachment we feel for others.

10.4 Quiz Yourself

1. **Based on the available psychological research, you are *most* likely to end up in a romantic relationship with ______________.**
   a. a neighbor who shares your values
   b. a person from another state who shares your values
   c. a fellow student who does not share your values
   d. a coworker who has opposite views

2. **Attractive people are assumed to be all of the following things, except ______________.**
   a. interesting
   b. sociable
   c. proud
   d. nurturant

3. **Which of the following statements is true?**
   a. Women are unconcerned with physical attractiveness when choosing a romantic partner.
   b. Women and men are equally interested in physical attractiveness when choosing a romantic partner.
   c. Only heterosexual men and women pay much attention to physical attractiveness when choosing a romantic partner.
   d. Men pay more attention to physical attractiveness when choosing a romantic partner.

Answers 1. a; 2. c; 3. d

10.5 Group Influence

Throughout our lifetime, we will belong to a multitude of groups—some of which we join and some of which we belong to by circumstance—families, communities, clubs, teams, professional organizations, and so on. For many of us, belonging to such groups is something that we value, but why? Psychologists suggest several potential explanations for why we join groups (Baumeister & Leary, 1995; Paulus, 1989). Groups may give us companionship, make us feel safe, make us feel proud, provide us with information, or help us achieve our goals in life. Regardless of why we join a group, once we do join, the group and its collective members then have the power to influence our behavior.

10.5.1 Social Forces Within Groups: Norms and Cohesiveness

Groups are characterized by the expectations and attitudes of their members. Group **norms** are the rules that guide the behavior of group members. Norms can be explicitly stated rules or unwritten expectations that members have for behavior within the group. Norms tell us how to dress, how to behave, how to interact with each other, and so on. Virtually every group has its own unique set of norms—each family, culture, workplace, and group of friends may have different expectations for how its members should behave. Norms can help ensure that societies run smoothly. For example, during the COVID-19 outbreak that began in 2019, the safety of everyone hinged in large part on people's willingness to conform to social distancing, handwashing, and mask-wearing norms set forth by health organizations (CDC, 2020b; WHO, 2020).

norms unwritten rules or expectations for how group members should behave

cohesiveness [coe-HEE-siv-ness] the degree to which members of a group value their group membership; cohesive groups are tight-knit groups

conformity behaving in accordance with group norms

In general, we do not like to break the norms of the groups to which we belong. When we do, we may face several unpleasant consequences. Group members may ridicule us or try to persuade us to change our behavior, or—perhaps most threatening—we might be thrown out or ostracized from the group. Recall that groups often fulfill social needs and give us a sense of security and identity. Because of these benefits, we often value our group memberships and wish to protect them. The degree to which members wish to maintain membership in the group is referred to as **cohesiveness**. In groups whose members have very positive attitudes about their membership in the group, cohesiveness is high, and the group tends to be close-knit. When cohesiveness is high, the pressure we feel to meet group norms is also high. The more we value our membership in a group, the less willing we are to risk losing that membership. Therefore, group cohesiveness helps ensure **conformity** within a group as group members modify their behavior to avoid breaking the group's norms (Crandall, 1988; Latané & L'Herrou, 1996; Schachter, 1951).

▼ Conforming to norms often makes societies run more smoothly. These people are conforming to the norm of wearing a mask during the COVID-19 pandemic that began in 2019.

Urban by Habit/Shutterstock.com

10.5.2 Conformity Within a Group

One of the most influential psychologists to formally study the process of conformity was Solomon Asch (1907–1996). During the 1950s, Asch conducted a series of classic experiments on conformity and the factors that make us more or less likely to conform in a given situation. Asch (1951) had male participants engage in a perceptual task with eight other men. The participants were unaware that the eight other men in the experiment were *confederates*, or actors posing as participants. Each participant, along with the eight confederates, was shown a series of lines and asked to match the length of a test line to one of three other comparison lines (● FIGURE 10.4). The experiment was set up so that the confederates made their judgments first. The participant heard all of the confederates in turn choose—aloud—the wrong line. By the time the true participant's turn came, they had heard all the others choose what was clearly the wrong line. A norm had formed in the group, the norm of choosing the wrong line. The dependent variable in Asch's study was whether the participant would conform to the norm or whether they would go with their own perception and choose the correct comparison line.

Asch found that 74% of his participants conformed at least once during the experiment. Apparently, many people can be easily made to conform at least some of the time. Only 26% of the men consistently stood by their convictions and refused to conform on any of the trials. Yet although Asch's experiments revealed that most people do conform at times, they also showed that few of us conform all the time. In fact, 95% of the men had at least one trial on which they refused to conform. Given that we often fail to conform, what circumstances make conformity more likely?

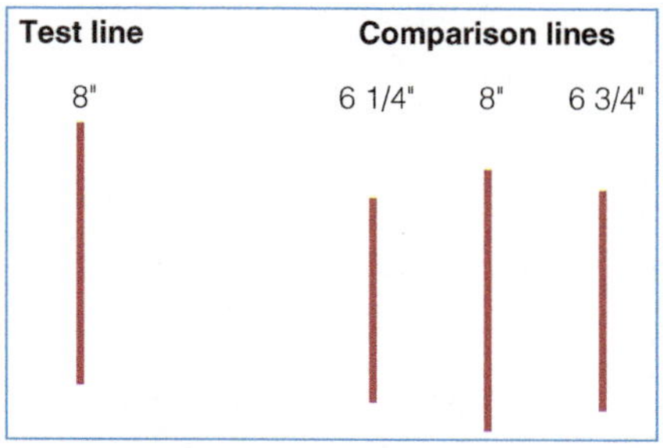

FIGURE 10.4

The Asch Procedure for Testing Conformity

In Asch's study, 74% of the subjects conformed and chose the 6¼-inch line as the match for the comparison line after hearing the confederates make this obviously incorrect choice.

Source: Based on Asch, 1951.

For starters, Asch found that as the *majority group* (the number of confederates who choose the wrong line) increased, so did the mens' tendency to conform. In one version of this experiment, Asch varied the number of confederates choosing the wrong line from 1 to 15 to see what effect the size of the majority would have on the men's level of conformity (Asch, 1955). You may be surprised to learn that Asch found that maximum conformity was reached in the men when only three confederates were present, suggesting that we do not need a large number of people to get us to conform. Others have studied this issue as well and found that we are most likely to conform if one or more these factors is present:

- We do not feel confident in our abilities (Cross et al., 2017).
- Cohesiveness is high in the group (Jovick, 1972).
- Our responses are made public (we are not anonymous; Tyson & Kaplowitz, 1977).
- The group has at least three members who are unanimous in their dedication to the norm (Asch, 1951).
- The idea that one should conform is itself a norm in our culture and/or we do not feel a personal need to be individuated (Bell & Baron, 2015; Boucher & Maslach, 2009).

Explaining Conformity: The Effects of Culture and Confidence

Asch showed us that conformity is rather easy to obtain, but why are we so willing to adhere to group norms? As part of his *debriefing* at the end of his experiments, Asch asked participants why they had chosen the wrong line. Their answers were interesting.

Some participants indicated that they chose the wrong line even though they knew it was wrong. This type of conformity, involving a change of behavior to fit a norm but no real attitude change or persuasion, is called **normative conformity**. The primary motive for normative conformity seems to be a desire to fit in with the group and be liked by others. This is one reason that cohesiveness tends to increase conformity. When we like being in the group, we want others to like us as well (Sakari, 1975). Research has shown that people in cultures that value individualism (such as the United States) are less likely to conform than are people from cultures that place more value on being part of a group (such as Japan; Bond & Smith, 1996; Killen, Crystal, & Watanabe, 2002; Takano & Sogon, 2008).

normative conformity conformity that occurs when group members change their behavior to meet group norms but are not persuaded to change their beliefs and attitudes

Interestingly, these differences in conformity that exist between collectivistic and individualistic cultures may not hold up in all situations. For example, researchers found increased conformity in people from collectivistic cultures in face-to-face interactions, but when examining interactions online, the cultural differences in conformity were not seen. It appears that conformity pressures in the cyberworld differ from those felt in face-to-face social interactions (Cinnirella & Green, 2007).

Although many of Asch's participants suggested that they conformed to be liked, some had other reasons for conforming. Some reported that they chose the wrong line because they became convinced that it was the correct choice. These participants were actually persuaded by the majority group. Recall that persuasion leads to attitude change. The way these participants perceived the lines and what they believed to be true about the lines changed as a function of the majority opinion. The majority opinion informed these participants of what the correct choice was. For this reason, conformity that results in actual attitude change is referred to as **informational conformity**. Informational conformity is heightened when people are unsure of their opinions and insecure about their abilities (Cacioppo & Petty, 1980).

informational conformity conformity that occurs when conformity pressures actually persuade group members to adopt new beliefs and/or attitudes

deindividuation [DEE-in-dih-vid-you-AY-shun] a state in which a person's behavior becomes controlled more by external norms than by the person's own internal values and morals

The Dark Side of Conformity: The Stanford Prison Experiment

In 1971, Stanford University psychologist Philip Zimbardo (b. 1933) set out to conduct an experiment on the effects of a prison setting on the behavior of prisoners and guards. Twenty-four healthy male participants were randomly assigned to play the role of either a prisoner or a guard in a mock prison set up in the basement of a campus building. All participants wore uniforms appropriate to their roles as guards or prisoners. The prisoners wore prison uniforms and were referred to by serial numbers rather than their names. The guards had dark sunglasses, wore khaki uniforms, and carried clubs.

The experiment was scheduled to last 2 weeks, with the prisoners remaining in the "prison" for the entire experiment. Within days, some very disturbing behavior began to emerge. The men assigned to play the guards became abusive toward the mock prisoners. The men assigned to play the prisoners became docile and depressed, allowing the so-called guards to abuse and manipulate them. The mock guards hooded the prisoners, called them names, and subjected them to a host of demeaning, humiliating activities. Their behavior got so out of hand that Zimbardo had to cancel the experiment before the end of the first week (Zimbardo, 1972).

▼ Nonconformists seem to enjoy violating the norms of the majority group.

Anthony Redpath/Getty Images

Why would 24 healthy young men behave so differently in such a short time? One possibility is that young men who might be tempted to sign up for a study on prison life might be higher in traits that would support such abusive behavior to begin with (Carnahan & McFarland, 2007). Another possibility is that participants were just behaving as they thought the experimenter wanted them to behave in the situation, and as a result, their behavior was not truly genuine (Griggs, 2014a). Criticisms such as these make it difficult to draw firm conclusions about the causes of the participants' behavior.

However, it is also possible that the participants' behavioral reactions were genuine. Zimbardo argued that the participants' behavior was affected by the fact that they were isolated from the outside world and the norms of society. Within the prison-like setting, a new set of norms sprang up—ones that called for the guards to be abusive and the prisoners to be submissive. **Deindividuation** may have also contributed to the abusive behavior. In deindividuation, a person's behavior becomes controlled more by external norms than by the person's own internal values and morals (Singer, Brush, & Lublin, 1965; Vilanova et al., 2017). In short, the roles that the men were playing may have become stronger determinants of their behavior than their own attitudes and beliefs. Several factors present in the experimental setting may have aided the deindividuation process:

- All participants wore uniforms, which heightened their anonymity.
- All participants were "playing" an assigned social role. As "actors," the participants' behavior was more controlled by their roles and their ideas about how prison guards and prisoners typically behave than it was by their own internal values and beliefs.
- The guards hid behind dark glasses, which heightened their anonymity.
- The prisoners were referred to by numbers, not names, which made them seem less human.
- The experiment was conducted in a basement, away from the outside world and its norms.
- There was no strong leader who argued for fair treatment of the prisoners.

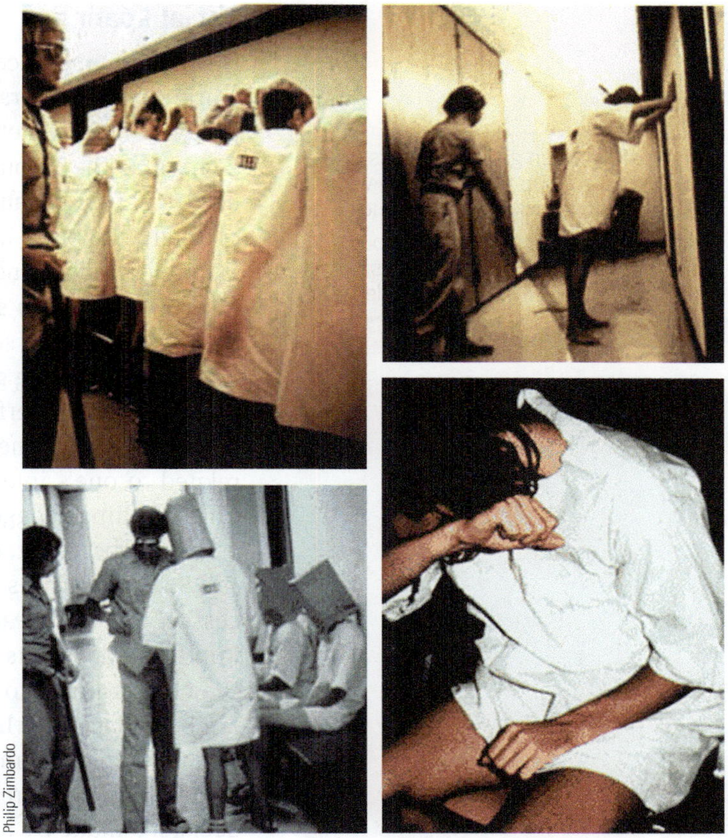

Philip Zimbardo

▲ Phillip Zimbardo's Stanford prison experiment shows that when we become deindividuated, we lose track of our own internal values and beliefs, and our behavior comes under the control of the group's norms. When deindividuated, we may find ourselves doing things we never thought we would do.

When deindividuation occurs, dangerous things can happen. All it takes is for a few people to begin behaving badly, and even good people may blindly conform to this new norm of behavior. Sometimes being part of a group can be problematic, but working in a group can also enhance our performance. We'll explore both possibilities further in the next section.

10.5.3 Is Working in a Group Better Than Working Alone?

Have you ever heard that "many hands make light work"? Or "two heads are better than one"? Such sayings extol the virtues of working in groups. Do we really accomplish more when we are part of a group?

In the late 1800s, psychologist Norman Triplett observed that people seem to perform tasks faster when they perform in the presence of others. For example, bicyclers seem to ride faster when riding along with other cyclists than they do when riding alone (Triplett, 1898). This enhanced performance when others are present is called **social facilitation**. Over the last century, social facilitation has been demonstrated in humans and many other species across a wide variety of situations (Aiello & Douthitt, 2001; Halfmann, Bredehöft, & Häusser, 2020).

social facilitation performing better on a task in the presence of others than you would if you were alone

But do we always perform better when others are around? Not always. For example, when we perform unfamiliar or complex tasks, having others around is likely to impede performance (Zajonc, 1965). For many of us, giving a speech is an example of an unfamiliar task that becomes more daunting when others are present. And many of us can think of times when we "choked" in front of others despite the fact that we could recite our speech perfectly when alone. Today, social facilitation researchers seek to explain the complex interplay of situational, task, and personality factors that result in either enhanced or impaired performance in front of others (Aiello & Douthitt, 2001; see also Snyder, Anderson-Henley, & Arciero, 2012).

social loafing when group members exert less effort on a group task than they would if they were performing the task alone

groupthink a situation in which a group fixates on one decision and members blindly assume that it is the correct decision

Social Loafing

Having an audience can affect performance, but what happens when we are working with others? How does working toward a common goal affect individual performance? Sometimes **social loafing** occurs when group members fail to work as hard as they would if they were working alone (Harkins, 1987). Social loafing occurs in part because group members perceive that others will not hold them accountable for their individual performance (Pearsall, Christian, & Ellis, 2010). For example, if everyone receives the same grade for a group project, some members may be tempted to slack off in hopes that other members will pick up the slack. One way to reduce social loafing is to encourage individual effort as well as teamwork by rewarding group members for both the quality of the group's output and their individual performance (Pearsall et al., 2010). Individual differences in the degree to which one is mindful and places value on morality are also negatively related to one's intention to engage in social loafing (Mihelič & Culiberg, 2019). These findings suggest that helping people develop prosocial characteristics such as being observant, selfless, and ethical may reduce social loafing.

So many hands only *sometimes* make light work. What about cognitive processes? Are two heads better than one? We often seek out others when we have important decisions to make. We form committees to set policy for organizations. We choose juries to try court cases. The assumption is that important decisions are best placed in the hands of many. Ironically, psychological research indicates that in some instances, our faith in the wisdom of groups may be misplaced. Group decisions are not necessarily better, more effective, or more logical than decisions made by individuals.

Groupthink

One factor that can contribute to poor group decisions is known as **groupthink**. Groupthink occurs when a group fixates on one decision and members assume that it must be the correct one without carefully examining other alternatives (Janis, 1982). When groupthink occurs, the group does not weigh all of the options, often resulting in disastrous decisions. For example, some groups that have opposed public health mandates (i.e., staying at home, wearing masks, and social distancing) during the COVID-19 pandemic may have experienced groupthink in reaching these decisions (Forsyth, 2020).

Group isolation, group cohesiveness, strong dictatorial leadership, and stress within the group have all been implicated as factors that promote groupthink (Forsyth, 2020; Janis, 1985, 2007). Sometimes groups must work in *isolation* because the issues they are dealing with are secret or confidential. At other times, groups may choose to self-isolate for any number of reasons, for example not wishing to engage with dissenting opinions. Regardless of the reason, an isolated group cannot get information from or call on outside sources; they can only consider solutions that are generated within the group. Because the group cannot consider all possible solutions, some potentially good solutions may be overlooked, and groupthink is more likely.

Group *cohesiveness* also contributes to groupthink. As we have seen, when a group is very cohesive, members highly value their membership in the group. When this is the case, the group's norms become powerful influences on the members' behavior. In a cohesive group, members may be hesitant to voice their objections to the prevailing group attitude because they do not want to "rock the boat." When members hesitate to voice objections, groupthink becomes more likely and potentially poor decisions are not adequately critiqued and rejected (Packer, 2009).

For the same reason, a *dictatorial group leader* would also facilitate groupthink. When members are afraid to disagree with a leader, they tend to go along with the leader's position, and groupthink is more likely (Janis, 2007; Shafer & Crichlow, 1996). If a group wants to make good decisions, thoughtful critique of all ideas should be encouraged rather than discouraged in the group.

A final reason for groupthink is *stress*. When a group is making decisions under some form of duress, they may not behave in as logical a manner as they would if they were not stressed. Time pressure is one such stressor that can contribute to groupthink. When a group has a very short time in which to generate a solution to some problem, they are less likely to be able to examine all possible options, and groupthink becomes more likely.

In our next section, we will look at how others can influence our judgment and behavior by making requests and demands that challenge us to respond appropriately.

10.5 Quiz Yourself

1. **When Hongyong behaved submissively even though she wanted to speak her mind because she didn't want to violate the norms of her culture, her behavior was an example of ___________.**
   a. deindividuation
   b. consistency
   c. cognitive dissonance
   d. conformity
2. **Bill is working on a group project for psychology class. To Bill's dismay, some of the group members haven't contributed very much to the project, leaving Bill to do most of the work. Which of the following *best* explains Bill's situation?**
   a. Deindividuation
   b. Social facilitation
   c. Social loafing
   d. Fundamental attribution error
3. **What do groupthink and deindividuation have in common?**
   a. They both involve persuasion.
   b. They both are more common in individualistic cultures.
   c. They both involve cognitive dissonance.
   d. They both involve conformity.

Answers 1. d; 2. c; 3. d

10.6 Requests and Demands: Compliance and Obedience

Imagine that you answer the phone one evening and hear a telemarketer on the other end. After the caller identifies themself as a telemarketer, they ask you to contribute to the local police organization. Would you agree to contribute, or would you refuse? Now compare this situation with a similar one. This time, you answer the phone and hear a police officer on the other end. After identifying themself as a local officer, they ask you to contribute to the police organization. Would you be more inclined to agree to the officer's request? Many people would, but why? What makes these two situations different?

One difference is the source of the request. A police officer represents an authority figure to many people. Many of us would perceive a request coming from an authority figure to be more of a *demand* for **obedience**. On the other hand, we are less likely to be intimidated by a telemarketer, and therefore we would likely

obedience yielding to a demand

compliance yielding to a simple request

foot-in-the-door compliance increasing compliance by first asking people to give in to a small request, which then paves the way for compliance with a second, larger request

perceive their request as just that, a simple *request* for **compliance**. Although the differences between compliance and obedience situations may appear to be subtle, they can have great implications for how we respond.

10.6.1 Compliance Techniques: Getting People to Say "Yes"

Compliance situations are very common in life. For instance, salespeople try to get us to agree to buy their products. Doctors ask us to follow their instructions. Spouses ask their partners to do household chores. Given that pressures to comply are inescapable, psychologists are interested in identifying successful compliance techniques and the reasons that make them work well. Marketers and other professionals also want to understand compliance so that they can create more effective campaigns for changing public behavior—for example, to increase sales (Weyant, 1996), to get online consumers to divulge personal information for marketing purposes (Melumad & Meyer, 2020), or to follow a doctor's orders for the taking of prescribed medications (Holt et al., 2014). It's a good idea for us to become familiar with compliance techniques, because others will be using them on us. Let's look at a few of the more popular ones, beginning with *foot-in-the-door.*

Foot-in-the-Door Compliance

Suppose a friend asks to borrow a dollar, and you comply. Later, if that same friend asks to borrow $5, would it be harder to refuse the request because you had previously lent them the dollar? Research on compliance suggests that it would. Once a person gets a foot in the door, so to speak, by getting us to comply with a small request, it seems to open the way to getting us to comply with another, larger request. In a classic experiment on **foot-in-the-door compliance**, researchers approached some homes and asked the person answering the door to sign a petition to promote safe driving. The researchers also selected other homes in the neighborhood to participate in the study but did not approach them at this time. Two weeks later, the researchers returned to the neighborhood and approached the homes they had previously visited as well as the homes that were not visited on the first day. This time, the researchers asked if they could put up a huge billboard that said "Drive Carefully" in the front yard. The data showed that those people who had complied with the first request to sign the petition were more likely to comply with the request for the billboard (Freedman & Fraser, 1966). Similarly, researchers in Israel found that people who had previously signed a petition for a specific charity were more likely to agree to donate money to the charity at a later date (Schwarzwald, Bizman, & Raz, 1983). It appears that giving in to a small request paves the way for us to give in to a larger request.

Sharkshock/Shutterstock.com

▲ Compliance techniques such as foot-in-the-door can be used to influence our behavior. Agreeing to display these signs may pave the way for future campaign contributions.

One explanation for foot-in-the-door's effectiveness is that our general desire to behave in a consistent fashion makes it hard for us to refuse subsequent requests. When you give in to the initial small request, your self-image changes ever so slightly. Having already complied, you are now the type of person who complies with requests made by this person or group. Because your self-image has changed, you now feel compelled to behave consistently with this new self-image. Recall that to not act in accordance with one's attitudes would likely produce cognitive dissonance. So when the person or group makes a subsequent request, to deny it would mean going against one's self-image and perhaps feeling dissonance. Therefore, compliance is more likely.

Recently, the dissonance explanation of foot-in-the-door has been called into question. Researchers in New Zealand demonstrated a foot-in-the-door like effect in pigeons. Since it is hard to imagine pigeons experiencing psychological conflicts and dissonance, this may indicate that other processes underlie the foot-in-the-door effect (Bartonicek & Colombo, 2020). Whatever its cause, when a clever manipulator gets a person to give in on a small matter, it does indeed seem to lead to a greater chance of future compliance (Cialdini, 2001; Girandola, 2002; Pascual et al., 2013).

Door-in-the-Face Compliance

In **door-in-the-face compliance**, a very large request is followed by a smaller target request. For example, researchers asked college students whether they would agree to commit to volunteering 2 hours a week for the next 2 years in a program to help juvenile delinquents. As you might guess, all the students declined. Then the researchers asked if the students would be willing to volunteer to take the juveniles to the zoo for a couple of hours. A full 50% of the students agreed to take the trip to the zoo after they had refused to volunteer weekly. This number was significantly higher than the 17% of students in a control group who agreed after being asked only whether they would take the trip to the zoo (Cialdini et al., 1975). It appears that if we figuratively "slam the door" in the face of a person's request, we are more likely to comply if they make a more reasonable or smaller request later (for review, see Feeley, Anker, & Aloe, 2012).

door-in-the-face compliance increasing compliance by first asking people to give in to a very large request and then, after they refuse, asking them to give in to a smaller request

reciprocity [reh-cih-PRAH-cih-tee] a strong norm that states that we should treat others as they treat us

One explanation for door-in-the-face compliance centers on the *perceptual contrast* between the two requests. After the extremity of the first request, the second, smaller request may seem more reasonable to you than if it had been the only request you received (Cialdini et al., 1975).

Another explanation for door-in-the-face compliance centers on **reciprocity**, a very strong norm in many cultures that requires that we return others' behavior (Lecat, Hilton, & Crano, 2009; Mowen & Cialdini, 1980). For example, if we are nice, others should be nice to us. If we are mean, others may be mean in return. Reciprocity explains in part why we feel more obligated to comply in a door-in-the-face situation than with a single request. In a door-in-the-face situation, after you refuse the initial request, the requester then concedes the initial position and makes a more reasonable request. Because the requester has made a concession, we feel as though we must reciprocate and also make a concession. The easiest way to do this is to comply with the second request. If we don't make this concession, then we may feel as if we are breaking an important social norm.

Finally, some researchers (O'Keefe & Figge, 1997) propose that emotion plays a role in compliance. When we turn down the initial large request, we feel negative emotions, such as guilt. Because we do not enjoy feeling bad, we look for a way to reduce these negative emotions. With the opportunity to comply when a second, more reasonable, request is presented, we are more likely to comply to relieve our guilt and make ourselves feel better (Millar, 2002).

Low-Balling and That's-Not-All

Salespeople often use compliance techniques to increase sales. If you think about it, salespeople are in fact asking us to do something. They are asking us to buy

low-balling increasing compliance by first getting the person to agree to a deal and then changing the terms of the deal to be more favorable to yourself

that's-not-all increasing compliance by sweetening the deal with additional incentives

destructive obedience obedience to immoral, unethical demands that cause harm to others

their products. One technique that is a favorite among salespeople is **low-balling**, or increasing compliance by first getting the person to agree to a deal and then changing the terms of the deal to be more favorable to the salesperson (Burger & Caputo, 2015; Cialdini et al., 1978). For example, a salesperson might offer you a car for $16,750, which you agree to pay. Then, when you go to sign the contract, you find that several charges have been added on, bringing the price up to $17,435. Because you agreed to the original price ($16,750), you are more likely to agree to the $17,435.

This technique works, in part, because we have given our word that we will purchase the car, and we don't like to break promises. We are also likely to be happy to be buying the car, and $17,435 doesn't seem like that much more than $16,750 (perceptual contrast). So, we comply.

If we do quibble about the additional money, the salesperson might also try the **that's-not-all** technique by sweetening the deal with additional incentives (Burger, 1986, 2011). They might throw in some new floor mats or some free car washes to get us to sign. These incentives will not be worth $685, but they might still get us to comply. That's-not-all works, in part, on the norm of reciprocity. The salesperson does something nice for you, and you are supposed to reciprocate by saying yes.

Many salespeople are professional compliance experts. Even if you know about compliance techniques, they can still work on you. If you feel pressured, it might be best to leave the situation before doing something that you will regret.

10.6.2 Obedience: Doing What We Are Told to Do

The research on compliance shows that we are fairly likely to give in to simple requests from others. Given this, how do we respond when others *demand* our obedience?

In many instances, obedience is a good thing. For instance, we want people to obey the laws of our society; otherwise, chaos would ensue. However, sometimes we are asked to do things that we know are wrong—things that may even cause harm to others. In these instances, if we give in to the demands, we would be engaging in what psychologists call **destructive obedience**. Recall from Chapter 1 the controversial work of Yale psychologist Stanley Milgram (1933–1984). In the 1960s, Milgram set out to discover just how likely the average person is to engage in destructive obedience. Milgram ran an ad in a New Haven, Connecticut, newspaper that solicited participants for an experiment that would investigate the role of punishment in learning. In actuality, the experiment would measure the participants' willingness to obey an order to administer a very painful electric shock to another person. The participants weren't told this until *after* the experiment was over. As far as the participants knew, they were participating in a study on learning, not obedience.

In all, 40 men participated in Milgram's first study (Milgram, 1963). These men ranged from 20 to 50 years of age, and they represented a variety of professions, including teachers, engineers, and postal clerks. All of the men were paid $4.50 (approximately $30 in today's money) for their participation *before* the experiment began.

When they arrived at the lab, the participants were told that they would be playing the role of a teacher in the experiment. As the teacher, their job would be to administer electric shocks, using an apparatus that delivered shocks ranging from 15 volts to 450 volts, to a participant playing the role of the learner (● FIGURE 10.5). The learner was supposed to learn a list of words, and the teachers were told that the purpose of the experiment was to see whether the shocks would improve the learner's rate of learning. In actuality, the learner was a confederate, an actor who only pretended to be shocked, but the participants did not know this until after the experiment ended.

During the procedure, the experimenter, a 31-year-old high school biology teacher dressed in a lab coat, stood slightly behind the seated teacher. Throughout the experiment, the teacher and learner communicated via an intercom system, but they did not have visual contact. The teacher was instructed to read a list of words to the learner over the intercom, and then to listen as the learner recalled the words from memory. Every time the learner made a mistake, the teacher was told to deliver a shock to the learner by flipping one of the switches on the apparatus. The procedure began with the 15-volt switch, and the teacher was instructed to move progressively up the scale toward the 450-volt switch as the learner made more and more mistakes.

FIGURE 10.5

The Apparatus Used by Milgram in His Famous Obedience Studies

How far would you go before you refused to obey?

Milgram was primarily interested in seeing how far up the scale the teachers would go before they refused to obey orders to shock the learner further. At the 300-volt mark, the learner began to pound on the wall as if in great pain, protesting the continued shocking. At this point, most participants began to question the experimenter as to whether they should continue to shock the learner, who was obviously in pain. The teachers began to show clear signs of distress, including shaking, stuttering, sweating, nervous laughter, and biting their lips and fingernails. The teachers often protested verbally and indicated that they didn't feel good about continuing to shock the learner.

In response to such displays and protests, the experimenter calmly prodded the participants to continue with the procedure. The experimenter never yelled. They never made verbal or physical threats. They never threatened to take away their $4.50. The experimenter merely requested that the participants continue following orders. The strongest statement by the experimenter was "You have no other choice, you must go on" (Milgram, 1963, p. 374).

After the 315-volt mark, the learner fell completely silent and unresponsive, as if they had lost consciousness or was injured. Because the learner missed all the words on the trial by not responding, the experimenter instructed the teacher to continue delivering the shocks. At this point, it is likely that the teacher believed that they were being asked to shock an injured—or even unconscious—man! What would you do in this situation? What do you think the teachers did?

The results of Milgram's study were nothing short of shocking (Burger, 2014). A full 65% of the teachers continued to shock the learner all the way up to the 450-volt mark. Despite believing the learner to be ill or worse, most of the teachers continued to follow the experimenter's orders. Even Stanley Milgram was surprised by his findings. Prior to the experiment, Milgram had surveyed psychology students and behavioral science professionals to get a feel for how many participants they thought would go all the way to 450 volts (Milgram, 1963, 1974). Most people believed that only 1% to 3% would. The results showed, of course, a very different picture. Approximately 65% of the participants did go all the way to 450 volts, and no participant refused to obey before the 300-volt mark had been reached!

As you might imagine, Milgram's findings generated a great deal of skepticism. Some people questioned whether the participants in Milgram's (1963) study were abnormal in some way. This is predictable as the *fundamental attribution error* would lead people to assume that an abnormal and socially undesirable behavior (i.e., delivering 450 volts of shock to a defenseless man) must be attributable to an underlying abnormality in one's personality. So, to answer such skepticism and to further investigate the variables that affect the rate of obedience, Milgram repeated his procedure with different participants. He replicated the study in another town (Bridgeport, CT) and found similar results (Milgram, 1965). Milgram also conducted the study using female participants and again found high rates of obedience (Milgram, 1974).

Other researchers have since replicated Milgram's findings. High school students were found to be even more willing to obey orders (Rosenhan, 1969). Cross-cultural research in other Western cultures has also yielded high rates of obedience using Milgram's procedure (Triandis, 1994). However, a partial replication of Milgram's study (Burger, 2009) has sparked a debate over whether societal changes since the 1960s have made people less obedient. Could it be that relative to their grandparents, the young people of today would be less likely to follow orders to hurt others?

Variations: Obedience 5 Decades After Milgram

Today, most institutions will not allow researchers to use Milgram's experimental procedure because of concerns over the amount of distress it would cause participants and the possibility that it might violate the ethical rule of doing no harm to research participants (see Chapter 1). Reluctance to replicate Milgram's study has largely left open the question of how people today would react when asked to obey destructive commands. Given that Millennials (people born after 1980) are thought to be more self-focused and assertive than the relatively conformist Baby Boomers (people born between 1945 and 1964), would they be more likely to assert themselves by disobeying destructive orders (Twenge, 2009)?

Psychologist Jerry Burger (2009) found a way to address this question. Burger modified Milgram's procedure to reduce the amount of stress it causes participants and therefore make the procedure more ethical. In his so-called *150-volt solution,* participants are first carefully screened to eliminate those who are likely to experience psychological harm during the study; second, the participants are asked to go only to 150 volts—not the 450 volts used in Milgram's studies (Miller, 2009). Using this less stressful, more ethical procedure, Burger found that his participants were just as likely as Milgram's participants to obey at the 150-volt level (Burger, 2009).

▼ Have things changed since the 1960s when Milgram conducted his original studies? Are young people today as willing to engage in destructive obedience as their grandparents were? Today, would research participants go all the way to 450 volts?

Rawpixel.com/Shutterstock.com

However, Burger's sample of participants was very different from the sample Milgram used. For example, Milgram used only males in his original study. Burger had both male and female participants (Twenge, 2009). When the data were reanalyzed using only the male participants, the results showed that nearly twice as many males disobeyed in 2009 (33.3%) as did in Milgram's original study (17.5%). Although this difference did not reach statistical significance, some researchers argue that it at least suggests that obedience may be decreasing (Twenge, 2009). Clearly, more research is needed to determine whether this is true. Perhaps Burger's 150-volt solution will prove to be a valuable tool in these investigations (Miller, 2009).

Factors that Affect Obedience

Regardless of whether destructive obedience has decreased somewhat over the generations or not, it appears that Milgram's results were not accidents. Unfortunately, even today, many people seem willing to follow orders to hurt others (Burger, 2009). What accounts for this tendency?

One factor that contributed to the high rate of obedience in the Milgram studies was the presence of a *perceived authority figure*. During the procedure, the experimenter, dressed in a lab coat and looking official, stood close by the participant and issued orders to deliver the shocks. Authority figures work in two ways to ensure obedience. First, the fact that the authority figure is ultimately in charge may seem to relieve the person following orders from responsibility for their actions. A person can always tell themself that they were only following orders. Second, the presence of official-looking authority figures tends to intimidate us, and we are therefore more likely to obey their orders (Bushman, 1988). Sometimes it makes sense to be intimidated by authority figures because some authority figures have true power (e.g., police officers). If you perceive that authority figures can observe your behavior and that you may suffer negative consequences for disobeying, you might obey out of fear alone.

In later experiments, Milgram found that he could reduce obedience in his participants by increasing the physical distance between the experimenter and the teacher. If the experimenter was not physically present to watch the teacher's behavior, the teachers were much less likely to obey the orders to shock the participant. ● TABLE 10.2 summarizes some of the later experimental manipulations that Milgram (1965) used to test variables that affect rates of obedience. From Table 10.2, you can see that when the experimenter telephoned his orders to the teachers, obedience dropped to 27.5%.

Another reason for the high rates of obedience in Milgram's studies is the *timing of the requests* made by the experimenter. When the participants arrived at the lab, they very quickly found themselves faced with orders from an authority figure to shock another human being. Because the orders began almost immediately after the participants arrived, they did not have much time to think about

TABLE 10.2 Some Experimental Conditions in Milgram's Experiments and Their Resultant Rates of Obedience

Experimental Manipulation	Percentage of Participants Who Obeyed All the Way to the 450-Volt Level
The learner was seated in the same room with the teacher.	40%
The teacher had to hold the learner's hand down on the shock plate.	30%
The experimenter delivered orders by telephone instead of in person.	27.5%
The teacher was tested with two confederates who pretended to be participants also playing the role of teacher. Halfway through the experiment, the two confederates refused to shock the learner any further.	10% of participants continued to obey after the confederates refused to further shock the learner.
The teacher was tested with two confederates who pretended to be participants also playing the role of teacher. One of the confederates was the one who actually flipped the switch to shock the learner. The real participant only played an auxiliary role in shocking the learner.	92.5%
Female participants played the role of teacher.	65%

Source: Milgram, 1965.

their actions (Burger, 2014). As we saw earlier, when we do not have time to think things through, we are more susceptible to persuasive attempts.

Another factor that contributed to high rates of obedience was the fact that the shock levels were increased incrementally. In essence, Milgram's procedure was a textbook example of foot-in-the-door compliance in action. The first orders were for the teachers to deliver a 15-volt shock, a mere tingle compared to the final shock level of 450 volts. Few people would have qualms about following an order to deliver an almost painless shock, so why not obey? What the participants did not know was by obeying the order to deliver the 15-volt shock, they were paving the way for their own obedience to further orders to shock the learner. Every time the participants obeyed an order to shock, it became harder for them to refuse to continue. Some have likened this type of incremental obedience to standing on a **slippery slope**. Once you begin to obey, it's like beginning to slide down the slope. The farther you go, the more momentum you gain, and the harder it is to stop obeying. If Milgram's procedure had begun with an order to deliver the potentially dangerous shock of 450 volts, it is unlikely that he would have obtained such high rates of obedience.

slippery slope the use of foot-in-the-door compliance in an obedience situation to get people to obey increasing demands

psychological distance the degree to which one can disassociate oneself from the consequences of their actions

Another factor that affects obedience is the **psychological distance** we feel between our actions and the results of those actions. In Milgram's first experiment (Milgram, 1963), the teacher could not see the learner during the procedure. In this type of condition, psychological distance is large, meaning that it was relatively easy for the teachers to not think about the consequences of their actions. If you don't think about the consequences of your actions, then you don't have to consciously come to terms with and take responsibility for those actions. This allows you to obey even in situations in which your actions may harm others.

In one dramatic experiment, Milgram had the teacher and learner sit side by side during the procedure. In this variation of the experiment, the teacher had to reach over and hold the learner's hand down on the shock plate. As you might guess, this procedure dramatically reduced the psychological distance for the teacher. It's hard to dissociate yourself from the consequences of your actions when you're actually touching your victim. Under these conditions, only 30% of the participants delivered the maximum 450-volt shock. Note, however, that although obedience was cut in half by reducing the psychological distance, obedience was *not* eliminated. Almost one-third of participants still continued to obey the experimenter, even under these conditions.

A final reason that people may exhibit destructive obedience may reside in the people themselves. In his replication of Milgram's work, Jerry Burger recorded the comments of the participants for later analysis. Burger found some interesting trends. For example, he found that participants who refused to obey were more likely to have expressed a sense of *personal responsibility* than the participants who obeyed to the end of the experiment. Those participants who expressed concern for the learner were also more reluctant to continue to obey, but their reluctance was *not* great enough for them to ultimately disobey (Burger, Girgis, & Manning, 2011). These data suggest that a sense of *personal responsibility* and *concern for others* may be traits that serve to reduce our tendency to engage in destructive obedience. Further research will be needed to fully investigate the effects of these traits.

Despite the controversy generated by Milgram's studies, his work remains one of the most powerful statements ever made about human behavior. Aside from demonstrating our obedience to authority, Milgram's work also brings up some important and perhaps frightening questions about basic human nature. For instance, how can psychologists explain the tendency of some people to behave aggressively? We will look at this issue next.

10.6 Quiz Yourself

1. **You want your friend to lend you $50. If you want to use the door-in-the-face compliance technique to ensure that your friend will comply with your request, what should you do?**
   a. First ask for $1,000 before asking for the $50.
   b. First ask for $10 before asking for the $50.
   c. Wash your friend's car before you ask for the $50.
   d. Tell your friend that you will pay the money back in 1 week.
2. **In Milgram's original experiment, what was the dependent variable?**
   a. The level of distress experienced by the "teachers"
   b. The number of times the "teachers" complained about shocking the "learner"
   c. The maximum intensity of shock the participants gave to the "learner"
   d. The minimum intensity of shock the participants gave to the "learner"
3. **Which of the following compliance techniques *best* explains Milgram's findings in his study on obedience?**
   a. Foot-in-the-door
   b. Door-in-the-face
   c. Reciprocity
   d. Low-balling
4. **During the COVID-19 pandemic, some state governments passed laws or issued executive orders requiring the use of face masks in public. This is *best* an example of attempting to achieve which of the following in citizens?**
   a. Compliance
   b. Obedience
   c. Conformity
   d. Persuasion

Answers 1. *a*; 2. *c*; 3. *a*; 4. *b*

10.7 Aggression: Hurting Others

Psychologists define **aggression** as an action that is intended to cause harm to another person who does not want to be harmed (Baron & Richardson, 1992; Brehm, Kassin, & Fein, 2002; Huesmann, 1994). Aggressive acts can be classified as *instrumental* or *hostile*. **Instrumental aggression** is aimed at achieving some goal. For example, a child may hit a playmate to distract them so the child can grab their toy. **Hostile aggression** is motivated solely by a desire to hurt others. For example, a bully may punch another child on the playground just to see the child cry.

aggression an action that is intended to cause harm to another person who does not want to be harmed

instrumental aggression aggression that is used to facilitate the attainment of a goal

hostile aggression aggression that is meant to cause harm to others

Although both types of aggression are widespread in many cultures, the overall prevalence of aggression varies across cultures. Among developed countries, the United States is considered to be an aggressive society (Osterman et al., 1994). Watch the evening news any day of the week, and you will see abundant evidence of this in the daily crime reports. In 2018, there were 367,651 violent crimes reported in the United States or 383.4 violent crimes for every 100,000 people. However, these data are incomplete, representing only 38% of the U.S. population as many law-enforcement agencies do not report crime data at the federal level (FBI, 2020a).

Besides the almost daily reports of violent crime in the United States, it appears that even noncriminals have aggression on their minds. Researchers surveyed 312 college students at a U.S. university about whether they had ever thought about killing someone. Fully 73% of male students and 66% of female students reported that they had (Kenrick & Sheets, 1993)! Furthermore, the tendency to think about being aggressive towards others has been shown to be stable and trait-like in adolescents (Murray et al., 2016). What could account for such findings? Could aggressive feelings be more natural than we like to think?

10.7.1 Biological Theories of Aggression

It has been widely documented that among many species, including humans, males tend to be more aggressive than females (Sysoeva et al., 2010). In 2018, males accounted for 87.8% of those arrested for murder and nonnegligent manslaughter charges (FBI, 2020b). Because males have more of the hormone testosterone in

▲ Instrumental aggression is aimed at achieving some goal. The older child is being aggressive to obtain a toy.

their bodies, researchers have long suspected that testosterone and aggressive behavior are related. But the research on the relationship between aggression and testosterone has yielded a somewhat confusing picture. Sometimes higher levels of testosterone are associated with higher levels of aggression in animals (Müller, Moe, & Groothuis, 2014; Wagner, Beuving, & Hutchinson, 1980), but sometimes they are not (Eaton & Resko, 1974). Likewise, human studies sometimes show a correlation between testosterone levels and aggression (Dabbs & Morris, 1990; Sánchez-Martín et al., 2011; Van Goozen, Frijda, & de Poll, 1994), but sometimes they fail to find a clear relationship (Coccaro et al., 2007; Turanovic, Pratt, & Piquero, 2017). A recent *meta-analysis* of the research on the link between testosterone and aggression in humans found that testosterone was generally only weakly associated with aggression for males, but not for females (Geniole et al., 2020).

Even if the correlation between testosterone and aggressive behavior were more consistent in the literature, it would still be difficult to determine the actual cause(s) of aggressive behavior. Recall that *correlation* does not imply *causation* (see Chapter 1). In fact, despite finding correlations between testosterone levels and aggression, Geniole and colleagues (2020) did not find evidence of a causal link between testosterone and aggression in their meta-analysis. One possible explanation for these findings is that higher levels of testosterone are associated with muscularity and strength, which may simply give one the physical ability to be a bully. Some researchers have found that in adolescent boys, aggression is correlated with physical size but not correlated with levels of testosterone (Tremblay et al., 1998).

A Possible Role for Serotonin

Research has suggested that another chemical, serotonin (see Chapter 2), may also play a role in the regulation of aggressive behavior (for a review, see Cupaioli et al., 2020; Duke et al., 2013; Libersat & Pflueger, 2004). Researchers measured levels of the neurotransmitter serotonin in the bloodstream of three groups of people: survivors of suicide attempts, people institutionalized since childhood for aggressive behavior, and a normal control group (Marazzitti et al., 1993). They found that the suicide survivors and the aggressive patients had lower levels of serotonin than those in the normal control group.

Researchers also found that giving healthy participants an antidepressant that increases serotonin made them less likely to take action that would financially harm other players in a monetary game. This change in behavior seemed to stem from the participants becoming more empathetic and therefore more averse to harming others (Crockett et al., 2010).

Low levels of serotonin are associated with conditions such as obsessive-compulsive disorders, in which the person has difficulty controlling their behavior and feels compelled to repeat certain actions (see Chapter 13). If we extend this thinking to the relationship between serotonin and aggression, we can speculate that people with lower levels of serotonin may have difficulty in controlling their aggressive impulses toward themselves (as in suicide) and toward others (as in the institutionalized patients). However, the link between serotonin and aggression may be more complex than originally thought. For example, one study found that *selective serotonin reuptake inhibiting drugs* (SSRIs; see Chapter 2) tend to reduce aggression in male hamsters and increase aggression in female hamsters, suggesting sex differences in the biochemistry of aggression (Terranova et al., 2016). A recent study in Sweden found that for a small minority of people taking SSRI drugs, treatment with SSRIs was associated with higher risk of committing violent crimes, particularly in participants under the age of 34. However, no causal conclusions could be drawn from this study, and it should be noted that most (nearly 97%) of the people taking SSRIs in the study did not commit violent crimes (Lagerberg et al., 2020). Clearly, more research is needed.

Childhood Abuse and Aggression

Another connection between biology and aggression comes from research into the backgrounds of incarcerated criminals. During the 1980s and 1990s, psychiatrist Dorothy Otnow Lewis interviewed more than 100 murderers in an attempt to discover whether they had experienced abuse as children (Lewis, 1992). During these interviews, Lewis discovered that an overwhelming majority of these murderers had suffered extreme abuse during childhood. In particular, many had suffered severe head injuries as a result of the abuse, which led Lewis and her colleagues to hypothesize that the murderers' aggressive tendencies may have resulted from brain damage (Lewis et al., 2004).

Using some of the techniques for studying the brain that we discussed in Chapter 2 (such as EEG, MRI, and fMRI), researchers have found that childhood abuse and neglect correlate with having structural abnormalities in the amygdala, hippocampus, corpus callosum, left frontal lobe, left temporal lobe, and cerebellum (Teicher, 2002). A correlation between damage in the area of the frontal lobe adjoining the limbic system and agitated/aggressive behavior in people with mild cognitive impairment and Alzheimer's disease has also been seen (Trzepacz et al., 2013).

Virtually no one would disagree that an end to child abuse would be good for society. Aside from a possible link between the physical damage caused by child abuse and later aggression, psychologists have other reasons to fear the destructive influence of child abuse. An aggressive model, such as an aggressive, punitive parent or a violent TV character, can teach a child to be aggressive.

10.7.2 Learning Theories of Aggression

In Chapter 6, we described Albert Bandura's *Bobo doll* experiments, in which children who watched an adult model beat up a plastic Bobo doll were likely to mimic the model's aggression when later left alone with the doll (Bandura, Ross, & Ross, 1963). After being exposed to an aggressive model, the children acquired new and aggressive behaviors. Many psychologists believe that aggression is often learned through this type of *observational learning*. This is a bit concerning, given the frequency with which Americans are exposed to violence on television. A review of studies conducted over a 40-year period found that nearly 70% of prime-time shows contain violence (Weaver, Zelenkauskaite, & Samson, 2012), and even commercials portray violence at an alarming rate (Cheong & Combs, 2016).

Exposure to such violent media may also impact us on a cognitive level. For example, researchers found that having recently watched violent media is associated with having subsequent violent dreams (Van den Bulck et al., 2016). One model of aggression, the **cognitive neoassociation theory**, proposes that cues present during an aggressive event can become associated in memory with the thoughts and emotions experienced during that event (Anderson & Bushman, 2002; Berkowitz, 1990; 2012). For example, if you see many instances (real or televised) in which people use guns to shoot and hurt those who have humiliated them, you may begin to associate concepts from these events in your memory. You

cognitive neoassociation theory proposes that cues present during an aggressive event can become associated in memory with the thoughts and emotions experienced during that event may begin to associate guns with anger, hurt, fear, and humiliation; or you may begin to associate conflict with shooting. Because these concepts become tightly linked in memory, activation of one of them can *prime* other related concepts and cause them to become active. In other words, merely seeing a gun may cause you to have aggressive thoughts. Being humiliated may activate feelings of anger and the desire to use a gun to retaliate against those who hurt you. Indeed, research participants have been shown to have aggressive thoughts after simply being shown pictures of weapons (Anderson, Benjamin, & Bartholow, 1998).

Maltreatment in childhood may also lead to aggressive thought patterns. For example, a tendency to *ruminate* or mentally fixate on things that make one angry and a *hostile attribution bias* or the tendency to perceive that others are motivated by hostile intent both help explain the correlation found between childhood maltreatment and later aggression. Children who have been maltreated seem to be more likely to perceive others as being generally hostile. If one perceives others to be motivated by hostile intent, they are more likely to become angry when others provoke them—even if the provocation was innocent. Once angry, they may then ruminate or replay the provocation in their mind, increasing the likelihood that they will behave aggressively (Zhu, Chen, & Xia, 2020). So, what types of situations are likely to provoke anger?

10.7.3 Situations That Promote Aggressive Behavior

frustration-aggression hypothesis the idea that frustration causes aggressive behavior

One key factor in aggression appears to be frustration. According to the **frustration-aggression hypothesis** (Dollard et al., 1939), when we become frustrated, we activate a motive to harm other people or objects. These motives are likely to be directed at those people or objects that we perceive to be the source of our frustration. Most physically abusive parents never intend to threaten or harm their children. But in the heat of the moment, some parents take out their frustration on their children. One study of fathers with 3-year-old children found that the more parenting stress a father was under, the more likely they were to use physical punishment on their child (S. J. Lee et al., 2011). Likewise, parents in high-stress situations—such as extreme poverty—who do not have good coping skills are most at risk for becoming abusive (Garbarino, 1997; see also Guterman et al., 2013). Recall from Chapter 5 that motives drive and catalyze behavior. Consequently, when we are frustrated, our chances of behaving aggressively increase. Therefore, during stressful, frustrating situations, we have to be on guard for possible aggressive behavior in ourselves and in others.

10.7 Quiz Yourself

1. Which neurotransmitter has been implicated as possibly playing a role in aggressive behavior?
   a. Testosterone
   b. Serotonin
   c. Dopamine
   d. Estrogen

2. Road rage incidents are more likely to occur in heavy traffic. This fact can *best* be explained as due to the increase in ________ that occurs among drivers in heavy traffic.
   a. frustration
   b. fatigue
   c. fear
   d. anxiety

3. Little Sabina wants to play with Brandi's doll, but Brandi will not let Sabina have the doll. So Sabina hits Brandi and takes the doll away while Brandi cries. Sabina's behavior is *best* characterized as an example of ________.
   a. hostile aggression
   b. instrumental aggression
   c. biological aggression
   d. learned aggression

Answers 1. b; 2. a; 3. b

10.8 Choosing to Help Others: Prosocial Behavior

By now you might be thinking that humans are pretty rotten creatures. We seem to be easily biased against others, easily influenced by others, aggressive, and even easily convinced to do real harm to others. But it is also true that humans often engage in **prosocial behavior**, or behavior that helps others. Recall how Hongyong engaged in prosocial behavior when she used *ch'iryo* to heal others of their ailments. In doing so, Hongyong not only helped others, she also helped herself. But, helping need not involve some sort of benefit. Sometimes we demonstrate **altruism**, or a willingness to help others without considering any possible benefit for ourselves. Just as we have the capacity for violence, we also have the capacity for kindness and compassion.

prosocial behavior behavior that helps others

altruism helping another without being motivated by self-gain

helping behavior another term for altruism

10.8.1 The Murder of Kitty Genovese

As is sometimes the case, the psychological study of altruism, or **helping behavior**, was prompted by the murder of Kitty Genovese in New York City on March 13, 1964. Kitty Genovese, age 28, was returning to her apartment in Queens at 3:20 a.m. when she was approached and stabbed by a man in a prolonged assault that lasted 30 minutes. Early reports suggested that during the attack, Kitty's screams were heard by 38 of her neighbors. Yet Kitty did not get the help she needed, and she died from her injuries. A *New York Times* article that reported the murder claimed that although 38 people witnessed Kitty's murder, none of them called the police until after she was dead (Gansberg, 1964). As you might imagine, people reacted with shock and outrage to this news. Further reports of interviews with some of the witnesses only increased the controversy. Some of the witnesses explained their inaction by saying, "I didn't want to get involved." Even a man who finally did call the police first called a friend for advice because he was so afraid of getting involved (Mohr, 1964).

Today, some people allege that these early reports misrepresented some of the facts of the case and overstated the witnesses' apathy (Lurigio, 2015). For example, most of the 38 "witnesses" may not have been in a position to actually see the attack; they may have only heard some vague commotion on the street. It is also possible that some witnesses may have tried to call the police immediately after Kitty was attacked but for unknown reasons the calls were ineffective (De May, 2006). Perhaps we will never know exactly how the witnesses, many of whom have since passed away, actually responded that night. However, what is certain is how the public perceived the situation back in 1964—they perceived that the witnesses were apathetic and callous. What is also certain is that examples of apparent bystander apathy have periodically reappeared in the decades since Kitty's murder. When they do, people once again express outrage that such a thing can happen in a civilized society (Livingston, 2010).

Soon after Kitty's murder and the uproar that followed, researchers Bibb Latané and John Darley (1969) set out to determine which factors influence whether we help others in need. They found that apathy or lack of concern is not the reason that people fail to help in situations like the Genovese murder. They also discovered that deciding whether to help someone is not necessarily a single decision, nor is it a simple decision to make. In fact, they identified 5 steps to deciding whether or not to help. First, you must notice that something out of the ordinary is occurring. Second, you must correctly interpret the situation as one that requires your aid. It is very possible that some of those who heard Kitty Genovese's cries did not realize that they were anything other than the normal sounds of a New York City street at night. Third, you must feel that you have a responsibility to intervene in the situation. Some of the 38 witnesses may have believed that someone else was coming to Kitty's aid. Fourth, you must decide how to help the person in distress. If you don't know what to do, you cannot offer help to someone in need. Finally, you must implement your helping strategy, and actually help the person in need.

10.8.2 The Bystander Effect

bystander effect the idea that the more witnesses there are to an emergency, the less likely any one of them is to offer help

diffusion of responsibility the idea that responsibility for taking action is diffused across all the people witnessing an event

pluralistic ignorance the idea that we use the behavior of others to help us determine whether a situation is an emergency requiring our help; if no one else is helping, we may conclude that help isn't needed

Because deciding to help is a multistep process, failure can occur at any of the five steps. Early studies of helping behavior focused on responsibility and the thought processes that might contribute to one person feeling responsible to help another in need. Latané and Darley proposed what they called the **bystander effect**. As the number of bystanders increases in an emergency situation, the probability that any one of the bystanders will actually intervene *decreases*.

To test their theory, Latané and Darley conducted a number of experiments (Latané & Darley, 1969). In one study, participants worked on a questionnaire either alone or in the presence of two other people. Halfway through the questionnaire, smoke began to filter into the room through a wall vent, as if there were a fire nearby. The dependent variable in the study was whether the participant got up to investigate the source of the smoke and how quickly they did so. The results of this experiment supported the idea of the bystander effect. When participants were in the room alone, most of them got up to investigate the source of the smoke. When there were two other people in the room, only a few of the participants got up to investigate. It appears that even when you may be helping yourself, the presence of other bystanders can reduce your tendency to help. Why would this be the case?

One explanation for the bystander effect is **diffusion of responsibility**, or the idea that all bystanders share equally in the responsibility for helping in an emergency. Each of the 38 witnesses would thus have borne only a small fraction of the responsibility for helping Kitty Genovese. As the number of bystanders decreases, the amount of responsibility any one bystander bears increases. When you are the only witness, you bear all of the responsibility for helping. So, what can you do if you need help and there are several bystanders present? You can reduce the bystander effect by clearly identifying one bystander and requesting their help. By singling out one person, you eliminate the diffusion of responsibility, placing all of the responsibility on that one person. Remembering this could save your life someday!

Diffusion of responsibility is not the only factor that prevents people from helping others. Another possible explanation for a bystander's failure to help is **pluralistic ignorance**, or the failure of a group of witnesses to perceive there is a problem that requires their help (Latané & Darley, 1969). When the witnesses saw the others doing nothing to help Kitty, this lack of action on the part of others may have caused each individual to inaccurately perceive that Kitty did not need help (Sexton, 1995). In other words, when we see that others are not interpreting a situation as an emergency, we are less likely to interpret the situation as an emergency, and therefore we are less likely to help.

Researchers now believe that the number of witnesses to an emergency is only one factor that influences helping. Several other variables that have been shown to influence helping behavior are summarized in ● TABLE 10.3. As you read through Table 10.3, you'll notice that, unfortunately, not all people are equally likely to receive help.

10.8.3 Choosing to Help

Although Kitty did not receive the help she needed in time, there are many examples of people who have helped others both in heroic ways and through simple, everyday acts of kindness, such as helping an elderly neighbor up the stairs or donating money to a charity. When the COVID-19 pandemic impacted the world,

TABLE 10.3 Variables That Affect Helping Behavior

Variable	Description
Level of bystander's hurry (Darley & Batson, 1973)	Bystanders who are in a hurry are less likely to stop and help someone in distress.
Bystander's relationship to other bystanders (Gottlieb & Carver, 1980)	When bystanders expect to interact with each other in the future, they are more likely to help a stranger in need.
Relationship between victim and bystander (Katz et al., 2015; Kogut & Ritov, 2011; Zelin, Walker, & Johnson, 2019)	A bystander is more likely to help a victim they know.
Bystander's perceived ambiguity (Solomon, Solomon, & Maiorca, 1982)	If the situation is ambiguous, bystanders will tend to see it as a nonemergency and therefore be less likely to help.
Bystander's fear for own safety (Tobin, Davey, & Latkin, 2005)	If bystanders are afraid they will be harmed in some way (e.g., arrested), they are less likely to help.
Bystander's prejudice against the victim or belief that the victim is an out-group member (Saucier, McManus, & Smith, 2010)	Bystanders who are prejudiced against the victim or see the victim as an out-group member are less likely to help.
Victim's level of dependency (Bornstein, 1994)	Bystanders are more likely to help a victim they perceive to be dependent—for example, a child.
Victim's responsibility for own plight (DePalma et al., 1999)	Bystanders are less likely to help if they perceive the emergency to be the victim's own fault.
Bystander's characteristics (e.g., gender, height/weight, and self-defense training; Brewster & Tucker, 2016)	Bystanders who feel physically competent to intervene are more likely to do so.

many people engaged in altruistic behavior by self-isolating, wearing masks, and so on. Some of this behavior may have been motivated by self-concern, but concern for others is also a reason for taking such precautions (Cheng, Lam, & Leung, 2020). In a study of Chinese university students conducted during the pandemic, students who were high in altruism experienced more negative emotion than those low in altruism, suggesting deep concern for the threat COVID-19 posed for others. However, they were also unable to do much to help others, which may

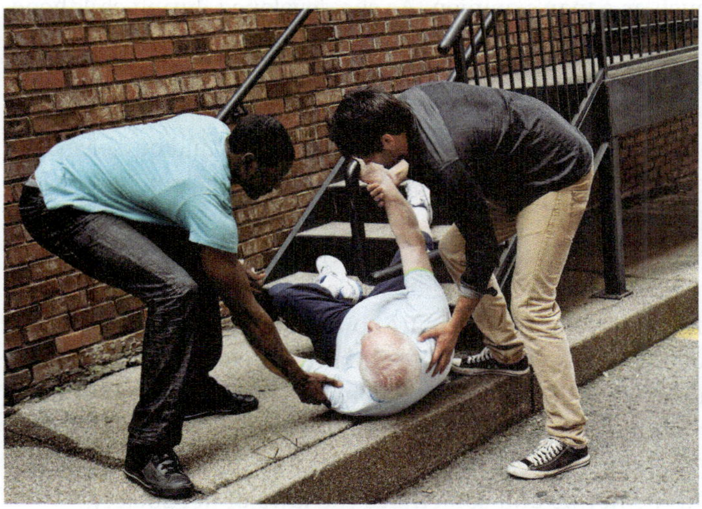

brittak/E+/Getty Images

MediaNews Group/Reading Eagle via Getty Images/Getty Images

▲ Humans often come to the aid of others in both big and small ways. When helping does not occur, it is often due to factors other than a callous lack of concern for others.

have further deepened their distress (Yi et al., 2020). This may be just one of many reasons that mental health issues, such as anxiety and depressive symptoms, have worsened during the pandemic (Fitzpatrick, Harris, & Drawve, 2020).

Many factors can prevent us from helping. However failing to help is usually *not* out of a sense of apathy or cruelty, but rather out of misunderstanding, confusion, feelings of helplessness, or fear. Perhaps by becoming aware of the factors that affect our tendency to help others we can find ways to make the world a more altruistic place.

10.8 Quiz Yourself

1. **What did Darley and Latané conclude about the witnesses in the Kitty Genovese murder case?**
   a. Many of the witnesses were uncaring people, and that is why they failed to help.
   b. The witnesses were too busy doing other things to stop and help Kitty.
   c. Many of the witnesses did not help because they assumed that someone else would help.
   d. Fear was the best explanation for why the witnesses did not help.
2. **Recently, one of the authors was sitting in her office when the fire alarms in her building went off. To her amazement, everyone seemed to ignore the alarms, and no one evacuated the building until security forced them to leave. Which of the following best explains their reluctance to leave the building?**
   a. Diffusion of responsibility
   b. Apathy
   c. Pluralistic ignorance
   d. A lack of conformity
3. **If you are ever the victim of an accident and there are many witnesses, what should you do to help ensure that one of the witnesses helps you?**
   a. Scream for help.
   b. Remain quiet so as not to scare the witnesses.
   c. Single out one of the witnesses, and request that they help you.
   d. Yell "Fire!"

Answers 1. c; 2. c; 3. c

10.9 Integrating Psychology: The Big Picture

The life of Hongyong Baek illustrates many of the processes that social psychologists study. The *attitudes* she held about herself as a woman were influenced in large part by the *stereotypes* and *prejudices* that many in her culture held about women at the time—for example, that women should be obedient to men and that a woman's opinion was not worth as much as a man's opinion. As she developed during childhood, many of these cultural ideas became imprinted in her mind. Yet, as she continued to develop throughout adulthood, her attitudes also changed over time; showing us that as we are exposed to new experiences, processes such as *persuasion* and *cognitive dissonance* can change the attitudes we hold about the world and ourselves.

Despite an arranged marriage to a man she barely knew, the *similarity* of attitudes she shared with her husband led Hongyong to fall in love with him. For a period of time, she reveled in her role as wife and mother, and when her husband began to wander, she *attributed* his infidelity to her lack of *attractiveness* as a woman.

Throughout her life, Hongyong felt pressure to *conform* to the norms of her culture. In her traditional Korean culture, these norms often called for *compliance* and *obedience*. However, at times, Hongyong failed to conform, comply, and obey. She went against her husband's wishes. She smuggled opium. She spoke her mind. She considered abandoning her child under desperate circumstances. All these behaviors violated the norms and sometimes the laws of her society.

Yet she also met society's expectations in many ways. She cared for her husband and children. She worked at several honest professions. She educated herself.

She tried to help others with her practice of *ch'iryo*. She searched for decades until she found the son she had lost in the chaos of the war. In many ways, Hongyong engaged in *prosocial behavior*.

Like Hongyong, you too are affected by others. All of us feel social pressures toward persuasion, conformity, compliance, obedience, and so on. Many of us have dealt with prejudice, aggression, love, and the need to help others. We can't escape these forces, for we are social beings. Yet, despite the social influences we all feel, we are still individuals. For Hongyong, her determined and independent personality may have helped drive her to overcome some of the pressures and challenges that she faced in life. In our next chapter, we will examine how psychologists study and understand personality. As you read Chapter 11, think about Hongyong and all that she experienced. Also, think of the ways that you have been influenced by others and how your own unique personality has guided your behavior in the social world.

Studying the Chapter

Key Terms

actor/observer bias (446)
aggression (475)
altruism (479)
attitudes (436)
attribution (443)
aversive racism (449)
bystander effect (480)
central route to persuasion (440)
cognitive consistency (439)
cognitive dissonance theory (439)
cognitive neoassociation theory (477)
cohesiveness (462)
collectivistic cultures (445)
compliance (468)
conformity (462)
contact hypothesis (456)
deindividuation (464)
destructive obedience (470)
diffusion of responsibility (480)
discrimination (449)
door-in-the-face compliance (469)
foot-in-the-door compliance (468)
frustration-aggression hypothesis (478)
fundamental attribution error (445)
groupthink (466)
helping behavior (479)
hostile aggression (475)
impression formation (443)
individualistic cultures (445)
informational conformity (464)
in-group bias (454)
instrumental aggression (475)
low-balling (470)
matching hypothesis (459)
normative conformity (463)
norms (462)
obedience (467)
out-group homogeneity bias (454)
peripheral route to persuasion (440)
persuasion (440)
pluralistic ignorance (480)
prejudice (448)
prosocial behavior (479)
proximity (458)
psychological distance (474)
realistic-conflict theory (455)
reciprocity (469)
scapegoat (455)
self-serving bias (446)
situational attribution (443)
slippery slope (474)
social cognition (435)
social facilitation (465)
social influence (435)
social loafing (466)
social psychology (436)
stereotype (448)
stereotype threat (449)
superordinate goal (456)
that's-not-all (470)
trait attribution (443)

What Do You Know? Assess Your Understanding

Test your retention and understanding of the material by answering the following questions.

1. Which of the following is *not* an attitude?
   a. Liking rap music
   b. Believing that honesty is the best policy
   c. Believing that Atlanta is the capital of Georgia
   d. All of the above are attitudes.

2. When Hongyong tried to convince her husband that smuggling opium was a good idea, she was attempting to employ which technique of social influence?
   a. Cognitive dissonance
   b. Persuasion
   c. Conformity
   d. Compliance

3. If you are in the market for a new car, you should process television ads from car dealers on the ______ route to persuasion.
   a. central
   b. peripheral
   c. cognitive
   d. emotional

4. Which of the following is *least* likely to affect persuasion?
   a. How distracted the audience members are
   b. How intelligent the audience members are
   c. How attractive the audience members are
   d. The mood of the audience members

5. Assuming that your professor is a happy person because they were smiling today in class is most likely an example of ______.
   a. cognitive dissonance
   b. the fundamental attribution error
   c. the actor/observer bias
   d. the in-group/out-group bias

6. Believing that your roommate is to blame for your poor performance on your history exam is most likely an example of ______.
   a. a trait attribution
   b. the fundamental attribution error
   c. the actor/observer bias
   d. the self-serving bias

7. Dr. Jones wants to test the hypothesis that being with one's own in-group (as opposed to being in the company of out-group members) increases the likelihood that one will express having racial prejudices. To test this hypothesis, Dr. Jones interviews White participants in the presence of White confederates and Black participants in the presence of Hispanic confederates. In conducting this study, Dr. Jones has inadvertently introduced a confounding variable. What is it?
   a. Participant race
   b. Confederate race
   c. Experimenter race
   d. There are no confounds in this study.

8. Jane Elliott's study of prejudice in brown-eyed and blue-eyed grade school students showed us that ______.
   a. prejudices are already present in us
   b. prejudices develop easily in us
   c. prejudices develop slowly over time
   d. children do not form prejudices as easily as adults do

9. When Mary says, "All men hate to ask for directions," Mary is most likely exhibiting the ______.
   a. out-group homogeneity bias
   b. in-group/out-group bias
   c. actor-observer bias
   d. fundamental attribution error

10. Muzafer Sherif's study of the Eagles and Rattlers indicated that ______ is the most useful way to reduce prejudice.
    a. punishment
    b. mere contact with out-group members
    c. cooperative contact between groups
    d. competition between groups

11. Living and working in close proximity to someone is likely to increase our liking for that person because of ______.
    a. in-group/out-group bias
    b. the mere exposure effect
    c. similarity
    d. the out-group homogeneity effect

12. Being in love with someone is associated with increased ______ in the brain.
    a. dopamine
    b. serotonin
    c. GABA
    d. acetylcholine

13. Immediately after a famous actor wears Cooldog brand jeans in a movie, the Cooldog company sees sales of its jeans increase by 500%. This sales increase is most likely the result of ______.
    a. compliance
    b. conformity
    c. mere exposure
    d. obedience

14. Sasha loves to knit. Compared to working alone, Sasha seems to get more done when knitting with other knitters. Sasha's experience is most likely an example of ______.
    a. informational conformity
    b. social loafing
    c. social facilitation
    d. the self-serving bias

15. Which of the following would be *least* likely to reduce the risk of groupthink in a group?
    a. Having a strong group leader
    b. Allowing ample time for discussion of ideas
    c. Allowing visitors to attend group meetings
    d. Having low cohesiveness

16. The destructive obedience that Stanley Milgram demonstrated in his experiments is *most* closely related to which of the following social psychological phenomena?
   a. Realistic conflict
   b. Attribution
   c. Foot-in-the-door compliance
   d. The frustration-aggression hypothesis

17. Which of the following has *not* been linked to aggressive behavior?
   a. Low serotonin levels
   b. High testosterone
   c. Frustration
   d. High norepinephrine levels

18. The bystander effect predicts that you are *most* likely to receive help from an individual when they ______.
   a. are the only witness to your plight
   b. are one of many witnesses to your plight
   c. are knowledgeable about helping
   d. are a compassionate person

19. Altruism is helping someone ______.
   a. without concern for your own gain
   b. because you expect a reward
   c. because you are afraid you'll be sued if you fail to help
   d. because other people are watching

20. Pluralistic ignorance prevents helping because ______.
   a. everyone decides that someone else is responsible for helping
   b. no one knows how to help
   c. no one recognizes that help is needed
   d. no one cares enough to help

Answers: 1. c; 2. b; 3. a; 4. c; 5. b; 6. d; 7. a; 8. b; 9. a; 10. c; 11. b; 12. a; 13. b; 14. c; 15. a; 16. c; 17. d; 18. a; 19. a; 20. c

Use It or Lose It: Applying Psychology

1. Given what you have learned about obedience and compliance, what precautions would you urge people to take if they wanted to make themselves less vulnerable to requests and demands from others?

2. Pretend you have just been appointed to a committee at your place of work. Your mission is to develop a strategic plan that will take your company into the future. What precautions would you take to ensure that your group does not develop groupthink?

3. Pretend you are an advertising account executive working for a new client. Using your knowledge of persuasion, design a television ad campaign to sell a new type of dishwashing detergent called Squeeky Clean Suds. Then justify to your client why your plan should be successful.

4. Pretend you are a community leader in a racially divided community. Design a program to reduce racial tensions among your community's citizens. Then explain why your plan should work.

5. Keep a log of the attributions you make in a single day. How often did you use the heuristics discussed in this chapter? How often did you engage in careful attributions?

6. Find an article from an online newspaper that discusses an instance in which someone committed an act of altruism. Then find an article that describes an emergency in which no one came to the aid of the victim. Compare and contrast the two situations in terms of the variables that affect helping behavior. Do these situations fit with what you have learned about helping behavior? If not, how do they differ?

Critical Thinking About the Science of Psychology

In section 10.5.2, you read about Asch's famous studies on conformity. After reviewing these studies in that section, answer the following questions:

1. Given the research design Asch used, what type of conclusion can be legitimately drawn concerning the size of the majority and conformity?

2. What is a weakness in Asch's research design? Explain.

3. Do you see any ethical problems with Asch's procedure? Why or why not?

Are You Getting the Big Picture?

monkeybusinessimages/iStock/Getty Images

Social psychology is the study of how we think and behave in social situations. **Social cognition** refers to the ways in which we think about ourselves and others.

10.1 Evaluating the World: Attitudes

Jim West/Alamy stock photo

- **Attitudes** are evaluative beliefs that we hold about things in our world.
- Attitudes develop through learning processes, including classical conditioning, operant conditioning, and observational learning or modeling.
- Attitudes sometimes predict how we will behave in certain situations.
- **Cognitive dissonance** results from a lack of **cognitive consistency**; it motivates us to change either our attitudes or our behavior.
- **Persuasion** occurs when someone makes a direct attempt to change our attitudes.
- We tend to be most persuaded by people who appear to be attractive, credible, and expert.
- Typically, people are easier to persuade when they are processing on the **peripheral route** rather than the **central route.**

10.2 Forming Impressions of Others

- In forming impressions of others, we make **trait** or **situational attributions** when we assign cause to their behavior.
- The **fundamental attribution error** (also known as the *correspondence bias*) is the tendency to overuse trait explanations during attribution.
- The **actor/observer bias** and the **self-serving bias** are two other sources of mistaken or biased attributions.

10.3 Prejudice: Why Can't We All Just Get Along?

Justin Berken/Shutterstock.com

- **Prejudices** are negatively biased **stereotypes** that are applied to all members of a social group regardless of the members' individual characteristics.
- Like most attitudes, prejudices are learned.
- Intergroup dynamics such as **in-group bias** and **out-group homogeneity bias** often play a role in prejudice.
- The **contact hypothesis** states that mere contact between in-group and out-group members can reduce prejudice. Cooperative contact and **superordinate goals** have been shown to be more effective in reducing prejudice.

10.4 Being Drawn to Others: The Nature of Attraction

- Some of the factors that affect our attraction to others include **proximity**, similarity of their attitudes and characteristics to ours, physical attractiveness, and the biochemical processes in our bodies.

10.5 Group Influence

Anthony Redpath/Getty Images

- **Conformity** is the tendency to behave in ways that are consistent with the **norms** or expectations of a group.
- In **normative conformity**, we conform just to avoid breaking norms. In **informational conformity**, we conform because we are persuaded by conformity pressure to believe the group's stance is correct.
- Conformity is influenced by such factors as majority group size, unanimity of the majority group, anonymity, group cohesion, and self-esteem.
- **Social facilitation** occurs when we perform better in the presence of others, but sometimes working with others can lead to **social loafing** as group members decrease their effort.
- **Groupthink** occurs when groups working under conditions of isolation, high **cohesiveness**, stress, and dictatorial leadership make poor decisions after failing to examine all possible solutions to a problem.

10.6 Requests and Demands: Compliance and Obedience

Sharkshock/Shutterstock.com

- **Compliance** is giving in to a simple request.
- In **foot-in-the-door compliance**, one is more likely to yield to a second larger request after having already complied with a first, smaller request.
- In **door-in-the-face compliance**, one is more likely to yield to a second, smaller request after having refused an earlier large request.
- **Reciprocity**, or feeling obligated to return others' favors, is a major reason why we comply.
- **Obedience** is giving in to a demand. Factors that make us more likely to obey orders, even when they direct us to behave destructively, include: the presence of an authority figure; the foot-in-the door compliance of the **slippery slope**; and increased **psychological distance.**

10.7 Aggression: Hurting Others

- **Aggression** is causing harm or injury to someone who does not wish to be harmed.
- **Instrumental aggression** is goal-directed aggression; **hostile aggression** is aimed solely at hurting others.
- Potential causes of aggression include high levels of testosterone, a lack of serotonin, brain damage caused by child abuse, observational learning or modeling the aggression of others, **cognitive neoassociation theory**, and the **frustration-aggression hypothesis.**

10.8 Choosing to Help Others: Prosocial Behavior

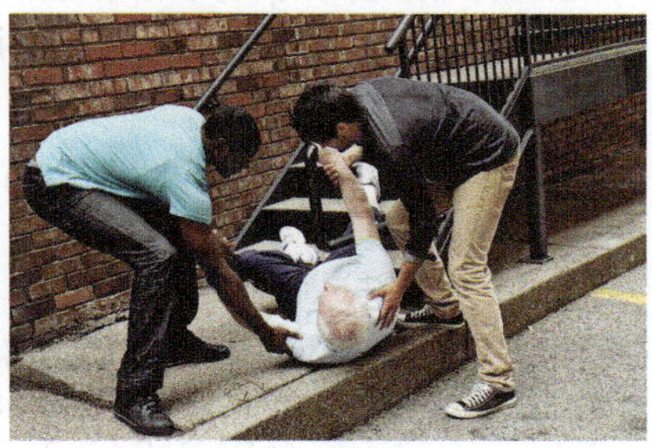

brittak/E+/Getty Images

- **Helping behavior**, or **altruism**, is the tendency to help others in need with little concern for our own gain.
- One of the factors affecting helping behavior is the **bystander effect**, in which **diffusion of responsibility** reduces the likelihood of obtaining help when there are many witnesses. **Pluralistic ignorance** may also prevent witnesses from perceiving the situation as an emergency.

Learning Objectives

11.1 Discuss Freud's perspective on personality, describing how his levels of awareness, psychosexual stages, and personality structures interact to generate behavior. (APA 1.1, 1.2)

11.1 Discuss neo-Freudian perspectives on personality, indicating their differences from and similarities to Freud's theory. (APA 1.1, 1.2)

11.1 Indicate the strengths and weaknesses of the psychoanalytic approach in explaining personality. (APA 1.2, 2.1)

11.2 Define traits, and apply the various trait approaches to understanding personality (Allport, Cattell, Eysenck, and the five factor theory). (APA 1.1, 1.2, 1.3)

11.2 Discuss genetic contributions to personality, and address whether personality is consistent and stable over time. (APA 1.2, 1.3, 2.1)

11.2 Indicate the strengths and weaknesses of the trait approach in explaining personality. (APA 1.2, 2.1)

11.3 Describe social cognitive approaches to personality, such as Bandura's reciprocal determinism and Rotter's locus of control. (APA 1.1, 1.2)

11.3 Indicate the strengths and weaknesses of the social cognitive approach in explaining personality. (APA 1.2, 2.1)

11.4 Define self-actualization, and describe how the humanistic views of Maslow and Rogers propose that it can be achieved. (APA 1.1, 1.2)

11.4 Indicate the strengths and weaknesses of the humanistic approach in explaining personality. (APA 1.2, 2.1)

11.5 Compare and contrast the advantages and disadvantages of using personality inventories, projective tests, and rating scales to measure personality. (APA 1.3, 2.1, 2.4, 5.5)

11.5 Describe the purpose of direct observation and the clinical interview in assessing personality. (APA 1.1, 1.3, 5.5)

Fancy/Alamy Stock Photo

11 Personality

Chapter Outline

In the previous two chapters, we outlined how social and developmental processes contribute to variations in behavior across people. This chapter extends that discussion by examining personality. **Personality** is the unique collection of attitudes, emotions, thoughts, habits, impulses, and behaviors that define how a person typically behaves across situations. Hongyong Baek's story at the opening of this part illustrated a complex and rich array of personalities within one family. Hongyong Baek was willful, curious, and insecure about her appearance. Her husband, Dukpil, was compromising, resourceful, and sociable. Some of the children were more outgoing and independent, whereas others were quieter and more unassuming. Perhaps your family is similarly varied, seeming like a cast of actors put together for an off-Broadway play! How can we understand these similarities and differences in personality? That is the focus of this chapter as we explore this critical question: how do we develop our personalities, and how stable—or changeable—are they?

Psychologists do not agree on a single, specific answer to this question—personality is difficult to define, difficult to measure, and influenced by many factors (Schultz & Schultz, 2005). As such, four dominant scientific perspectives have emerged to explain our personalities: the *psychoanalytic approach,* the *trait approach,* the *social cognitive approach,* and the *humanistic approach*. No single approach can explain all facets of personality in all people, and each perspective has advantages and disadvantages. As we describe each approach, consider your own ideas about personality. Do you think you inherit your personality, or is it formed through experiences? Examining such ideas speaks to whether you think personality is stable and consistent over time or whether it can change. It also will help you connect the material to your experiences and current way of thinking. ■

▲ The psychoanalytic perspective on personality originated with Sigmund Freud. Freud saw personality as the product of driving forces within a person that were often conflicting and sometimes unconscious.

11.1 The Psychoanalytic Approach: Sigmund Freud and the Neo-Freudians

The **psychoanalytic perspective** on personality originated with Sigmund Freud (1856–1939). We introduced his approach to understanding behavior in Chapter 1. Freud practiced medicine, specializing in "nervous diseases." However, soon after beginning private practice, Freud moved away from physical explanations of nervous disorders and focused more on investigating psychological causes of these disorders. His ideas about personality were based on case studies of his patients, his reading of literature, and his own self-analysis. Freud saw personality as the product of driving forces within a person that were often conflicting and sometimes unconscious. As we saw in Chapter 4, Freud believed that dreams were one of the ways these unconscious forces expressed themselves. Freud's theory is unique in that it strongly emphasizes unconscious aspects of personality.

11.1.1 Freud's Levels of Awareness

Freud (1940/1964) proposed that human personality operates at three different levels of awareness or consciousness and that each level of awareness influences behavior. Freud viewed consciousness as being like an iceberg (● FIGURE 11.1). When we look at behavior, all we usually see is the tip of the iceberg, or the **conscious level**: the thoughts, perceptions, and explanations of behavior of which the person is aware. The major portion of the iceberg, according to Freud, is below the surface. These impulses, memories, and thoughts are unseen but have a huge impact on personality. Because so large a portion of one's personality lies below the surface of consciousness, or awareness, Freud believed, any explanation of personality and behavior must focus on these unconscious forces.

Your conscious level, as previously stated, includes any memories, thoughts, or urges of which you are currently aware. You know you want to download a new hit song, or you know that it is important to read this chapter and study for the test next week. But the things you could potentially be aware of at any one time are infinite, and you cannot hold more than a couple of thoughts, urges, and memories in consciousness at any one time. So, according to Freud, it is necessary to have a holding place for easily accessible memories, thoughts, or impulses of which you could become aware. This is the role of the **preconscious level**.

The **unconscious level** contains all those inaccessible thoughts, impulses, memories, and behaviors of which you are unaware. However, although you are unaware of them, they always influence your behavior. Consider a 4-year-old boy who stops his parents from hugging or inserts himself between them to prevent them from kissing. According to Freud, he is not aware that this behavior stems from a need or wish to bond with his mother, yet it is still influencing his behavior.

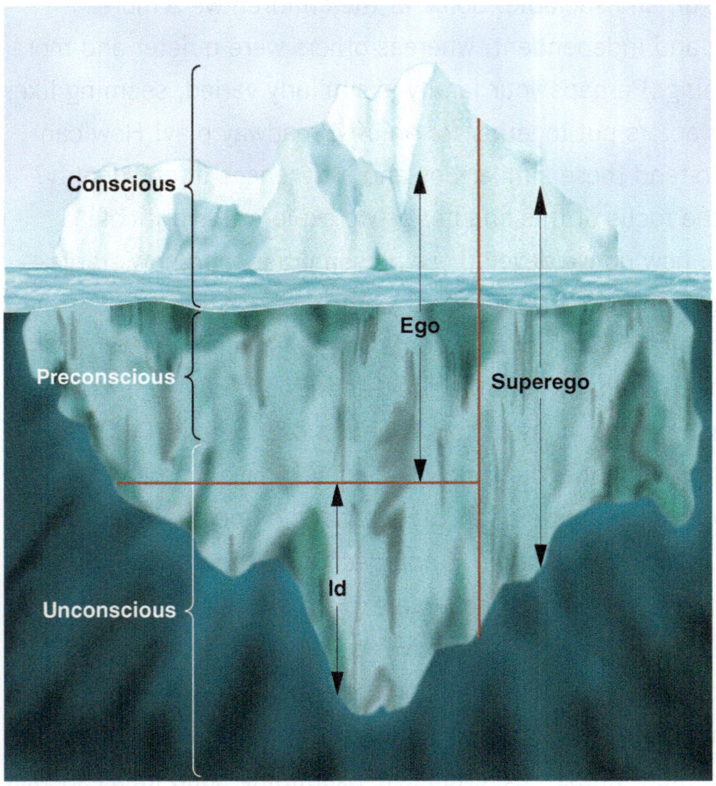

FIGURE 11.1

Iceberg Analogy of Freud's Levels of Awareness

In Freud's "iceberg" analogy of the mind, the id and parts of the ego and superego are submerged below the water in the unconscious. Most of the ego and some of the superego also operate in the conscious and preconscious.

11.1.2 Freud's Structure of Personality

To Freud (1940/1964), human personality is an energy system comprising three major personality structures: the *id*, the *ego*, and the *superego*. At birth, all of the energy of the personality is contained within a structure called the **id**. The id is an unconscious energy force that seeks pleasure and gratification. Hungry infants cry for food or because they are wet or tired. The id operates according to the **pleasure principle**; it drives people to feel good and to maximize pleasure and gratification, and to avoid pain. Freud saw the impulses driving the id as *sexual* and *aggressive* in nature. In this way, he viewed humans as very similar to animals—unconsciously and selfishly motivated by basic sexual and aggressive instincts. Such basic instincts ensure and promote the survival of the individual, and therefore the survival of the species as a whole.

When we grow and begin to interact with our environment, we realize that our demands cannot always be immediately fulfilled. For example, when a baby's cry for food is not met every time, the baby has encountered reality. As a result, part of the energy of the id becomes directed to a second personality structure, the **ego**. The ego acts as a negotiator between the instinctual needs of the id and the demands of membership in human society. Children learn that their id demands can be fulfilled only when they behave appropriately. The ego operates according to the **reality principle**. It realizes that the desires of the id can be met only by acting in ways that are acceptable and appropriate in that reality or environment. Suppose a 4-year-old wants something to eat. Do they immediately cry like a baby? Not typically. The 4-year-old with a functioning ego may have already tested the method of crying and knows that it is not a good plan of action to get food. They will probably ask for something to eat and be willing to wait (at least for a little while) for a caregiver to prepare it. We see the ego functioning in the child's ability to delay the desire for food. But the ego's job is still to fulfill the instinctual demands of the id—the unseen force beneath the tip of the iceberg (see Figure 11.1).

As the child continues to grow, parents and other important people impart their values and standards of behavior to the child. Parents convey the right and wrong ways to feel, think, and behave. The child incorporates these standards as the energy of the personality further divides into a third personality structure. The **superego** typically emerges during the resolution of the *phallic stage* (discussed shortly) and represents our moral conscience. Our superego judges the rightness or wrongness of our actions. When we have the sense that we did something wrong, our superego is talking. The moral directives of the superego must also be taken into account by the ego. Just like id demands, superego demands must be met realistically by the ego in order to function in society.

The energy that these three personality components use is fluid. For Freud, personality is a dynamic, or active, process. The id, ego, and superego are not fixed entities but rather parts of our personality that serve different functions. A healthy personality will have developed a strong ego that appropriately releases and controls instinctual energy. However, problems may arise in personality functioning if id energy or superego energy overwhelms the functioning of the ego.

Mel Yates/The Image Bank/Getty Images

▲ According to Freud, it is a child's superego that drives feelings of guilt after wrongdoing.

personality the unique collection of attitudes, emotions, thoughts, habits, impulses, and behaviors that define how a person typically behaves across situations

psychoanalytic [psi-co-an-uh-LIH-tic] perspective a personality approach developed by Sigmund Freud that sees personality as the product of driving forces within a person that are often conflicting and sometimes unconscious

conscious [CON-shus] level the level of consciousness that holds all the thoughts, perceptions, and impulses of which we are aware

preconscious [pre-CON-shus] level the level of consciousness that holds thoughts, perceptions, and impulses of which we could potentially be aware

unconscious [un-CON-shus] level the level of awareness that contains all the inaccessible thoughts, perceptions, and impulses of which we are unaware

id the unconscious part of the personality that seeks pleasure and gratification

pleasure principle the basis on which the id operates; the urge to feel good and maximize gratification

ego the part of the personality that attempts to meet the demands of the id in a socially appropriate way

reality principle the basis on which the ego operates; finding socially appropriate means to fulfill id demands

superego the part of the personality that represents your moral conscience

FIGURE 11.2

Freud's Personality Structures

According to Freud, adult behavior results from the interaction among the three personality structures of the id, ego, and superego.

To Freud, all adult behaviors are a reflection of the interplay among these three structures (● FIGURE 11.2). When examining behavior, we see only the functioning of the ego, but this ego is simultaneously being influenced by the unconscious demands of the id and the superego. *Freudian slips* illustrate this interaction. A Freudian slip is the expression of an unconscious impulse from the id before the ego controls the impulse. The ego may then state that it did not mean to say something and corrects the slip to conform to socially approved behavior. For example, one might say to a rival businessperson at a meeting, "Would you like to hit in this chair?" instead of "Would you like to *sit* in this chair?" and then quickly correct the error. Freud would assert that what "slipped out" was meant. It just hadn't yet been socially screened by the ego.

You can see that the demands of the id and the superego are often in direct opposition to one another. This internal conflict sometimes overwhelms the ego, creating *anxiety*. According to Freud, the ego handles this anxiety by using **defense mechanisms** (A. Freud, 1936). Defense mechanisms, discussed more thoroughly in Chapter 12, protect the ego by reducing the anxiety it feels when faced with the conflicting demands of the id and the superego. We all make use of these *emotional coping mechanisms*, as they are now familiarly called. We tend to use those defense mechanisms that have been previously reinforced or that successfully reduce anxiety. For example, if you *rationalized* or justified behavior (see Chapter 12) as a child, you would probably continue to use this defense mechanism as an adult.

defense mechanisms processes used to protect the ego by reducing the anxiety it feels when faced with the conflicting demands of the id and the superego

Consider this part's case story. From a psychoanalytic perspective, Hongyong's business endeavors would be related to her efforts to cope with her husband's unfaithfulness. Emotionally, Hongyong would feel anger at this betrayal. It is normal to feel anger when a loved one cheats, to be mad at them for betraying one's trust. We cannot direct our anger toward its true source if our culture sees this behavior as unacceptable. We may also feel it is wrong to be angry with someone we love. So Hongyong's superego would attempt to squelch her anger, but the energy of those feelings would still need an outlet. Hongyong's ego satisfied both the id and the superego by using the defense mechanism called *sublimation* (see Chapter 12). She directed her anger into something more productive—a successful restaurant that perhaps would also serve to keep her husband busy and away from other women.

Differences in personality, then, arise from internal energy conflicts among the id, ego, and superego (called *intrapsychic conflicts*). Freud further believed that personality is shaped by differences in how we resolve psychosexual stages of development.

11.1.3 Freud's Psychosexual Stages of Development

According to Freud (1940/1964), personality develops through a series of five *psychosexual stages*. These stages represent a complex interaction between natural shifts of pleasure from one part of the body to another and the environmental factors that influence how we handle these sensual desires. From birth through adolescence, children must resolve numerous unconscious conflicts that arise from sensual pleasure associated with stimulation of certain body parts, or what Freud called *erogenous zones*. For example, the infant nursing (from the mother's breast or from a bottle) derives a great deal of sensual pleasure from the feel of the nipple on their lips, and the satisfaction in reducing the sensation of hunger that the milk brings. However, the pleasure received from any erogenous zone must be balanced with parental restrictions (or permissiveness) placed on one's behavior. This creates an internal struggle, or "conflict," that significantly influences the resulting personality. Freud uses the term *psychosexual* to refer to the psychological significance of these sexual drives in the formation of a healthy personality. Because environmental circumstances vary in terms of how we are parented or how we respond to these socialization experiences, the result is individual differences in personality. Let's take a brief look at each of Freud's psychosexual stages.

oral stage Freud's first psychosexual stage of development, which occurs during the first 18 months of life, in which the handling of the child's feeding experiences influences personality development

anal stage Freud's second psychosexual stage, which occurs from approximately 18 months to 3 years of age, in which the parents' regulation of the child's biological urge to expel or retain feces influences personality development

phallic [FAH-lick] stage Freud's third psychosexual stage of development, which occurs between 3 and 6 years of age, in which little boys experience the Oedipus complex and little girls the Electra complex

Oedipus [ED-uh-puss] complex in the male, an unconscious sexual urge for the mother that develops during the phallic psychosexual stage

Electra complex in the female, an unconscious sexual urge for the father that develops during the phallic psychosexual stage

Oral Stage

The **oral stage** lasts from birth until approximately 18 months of age. The mouth, tongue, and lips are the erogenous zones, or focus of pleasure. Babies receive pleasure from sucking, licking, biting, and chewing.

Anal Stage

The **anal stage** lasts from approximately 18 months to 3 years. The anus and rectum are the erogenous zones. Freud viewed production of feces as a creative act. The toddler typically feels quite proud of them, either holding feces in or spreading them around. How the parent then responds to this or how the parent attempts to control this production through toilet-training practices is the key to adequately resolving this stage.

Phallic Stage

During the **phallic stage**, from 3 to 6 years of age, the genitals are the primary erogenous zone, and children receive pleasure from self-stimulation. This stage is particularly important for personality development, since it represents the time when the **Oedipus complex** and the **Electra complex** occur. Freud believed that at this age, young children develop unconscious sexual urges for the parent of the other sex. The child wants to bond with the parent of the other sex as the child sees the parents bonding. Using the terms *Oedipus* and *Electra* from two ancient Greek tragedies, Freud believed that at this psychosexual stage, little boys unconsciously fall in love with their mothers and experience hostile feelings toward their fathers much as Oedipus (unknowingly) married his mother and killed his father. Like Electra, little girls unconsciously fall in love with their fathers and feel jealousy toward their mothers. Children at this age may prevent their parents from hugging or be jealous of the parents' spending time alone together. Children then resolve these complexes by identifying with and behaving more like the same-sex parent. A young boy may start to imitate the way his father eats, or a young girl may mimic the way her mother brushes her hair. The child incorporates the values and standards of the same-sex parent, thus ending the rivalry. The child's psychic energy is then redirected to the growth of the superego.

Ryan McVay/Photodisc/Getty Images

▲ Parents' toilet-training practices influence a toddler's attempt to resolve the anal psychosexual stage, according to Freud.

▲ According to Freud, the genital stage of psychosexual development unconsciously motivates teens to interact with potential sexual partners.

Latency Stage

The **latency stage** occurs from age 6 until puberty. During the latency stage, sexual impulses are pushed into the background. The child's energy focuses on other demands of the environment, most noticeably school and peer relations. Sexuality reappears at puberty as reflected in the final psychosexual stage, the genital stage.

Genital Stage

The **genital stage** begins with puberty. The genitals again become the source of pleasure, as the adolescent must revisit the sexual urges that first appeared during the phallic stage. Recall that during the phallic stage, children developed unconscious attractions to the other-sex parent. Recognizing now that the sexual love for the parent cannot be fulfilled, the adolescent seeks resolution of the genital stage by transferring this love to an other-sex mate. Consequently, for Freud, adult heterosexual intimate relations reflect the unconscious desire to choose a mate in the image of one's other-sex parent. If during the phallic stage the child develops unconscious attractions to the same-sex parent, then during the genital stage, homosexual intimate relations arise from transferring love to a same-sex partner.

latency [LATE-an-see] stage Freud's fourth psychosexual stage of development, which occurs from around age 6 to puberty, in which the child's sexuality is suppressed due to widening social contacts with school, peers, and family

genital stage Freud's final psychosexual stage of development, which begins at puberty, in which sexual energy is transferred toward peers of the other sex (heterosexual orientation) or same sex (homosexual orientation)

personal unconscious according to Jung, the part of the unconscious that consists of forgotten memories and repressed experiences from one's past

collective unconscious according to Jung, the part of the unconscious that contains images and material universal to people of all time periods and cultures

archetypes [ARE-kuh-types] according to Jung, mental representations or symbols of themes and predispositions to respond to the world in a certain way that are contained in the collective unconscious

Variations in Personality and Fixations

As Freud saw it, all children develop through these predictable stages, which are primarily sexual but are psychologically significant in forming a healthy personality. Successfully resolving these stages entails receiving an optimal amount of gratification at each stage—not too much and not too little. A child who receives too much satisfaction at one stage may be reluctant to move on to the next stage. Too little satisfaction may result in frustration for the child, who may continue to seek gratification instead of moving on. These examples of inadequate resolution of a stage result in what Freud called a *fixation*. Those who fixate at one stage remain stuck, and their personalities remain immature or underdeveloped. Part of the personality remains focused on the concerns of this stage.

For Freud, problems in adult personality reflect these unresolved issues or fixations from childhood. For example, a person whose oral urges were not adequately satisfied in infancy would develop an *oral fixation*. An oral fixation might be expressed in the adult behaviors of overeating, nail biting, constantly chewing on pens or pencils, or boasting. More serious behaviors reflecting oral fixations include smoking, alcoholism, and binge eating. Fixation at the anal stage may express itself in the adult personality as *anal-retentiveness* or *anal-expulsiveness*. Being overly neat, stingy, or orderly (anal-retentive) or being excessively sloppy, generous, or carefree (anal-expulsive) both result from inadequate resolution of the anal stage, according to Freud. These are just two examples of how fixations might manifest themselves in an adult personality.

11.1.4 Neo-Freudian Theories Explaining Variations in Personality: Carl Jung, Alfred Adler, and Karen Horney

Freud's work created much controversy among professionals in the developing field of psychology. Many physicians and psychologists were initially intrigued by Freud's ideas but had their differences with aspects of his theory and eventually separated from Freud. These *neo-Freudians* agreed with Freud that unconscious conflicts were important to understanding personality, but they placed less emphasis on the role of the instinctual impulses of sex and aggression in motivating behavior. We have already introduced one neo-Freudian, Erik Erikson, whose theory of *psychosocial development* we discussed in Chapter 9. His eight stages described the influence of the environment on the developing ego over the life span. Three other examples of neo-Freudian theories are presented here, in the ideas of Carl Jung, Alfred Adler, and Karen Horney.

▲ Carl Jung divided the unconscious into the personal unconscious (forgotten memories and repressed experiences) and the collective unconscious (the collected images and ideas from the earliest development of the human psyche).

Carl Jung and the Collective Unconscious

Carl Jung (1875–1961) was a student of Freud's who came to reject his ideas about personality, particularly the sexual aspects of his theory. Like Freud, Jung maintained that personality was a function of the interplay between conscious and unconscious processes. However, Jung (1917/1967) divided the unconscious into the *personal unconscious* and the *collective unconscious*. The **personal unconscious**, much like Freud's unconscious, consisted of forgotten memories and repressed experiences. The **collective unconscious** is universal to all people of all time periods and cultures. The collective unconscious represents the collected images and ideas from the earliest development of the human psyche.

In particular, the collective unconscious includes **archetypes**, mental representations or symbols of themes and predispositions to respond to the world in a certain way. According to Jung, two of the major archetypes of the personality are the *anima* and the *animus*, the female and male aspects of each person. Among the other archetypes Jung identified are the *persona* and the *shadow*. The persona is the appearance we present to the world, the role or character we assume when relating to others, such as the martyr, the rebel, or the teacher. The shadow includes those negative tendencies or qualities of the self that a person tries to deny or hide from the world. Jung's emphasis on the collective unconscious, and his belief that spiritual and religious drives are just as important as sexual ones, continues to draw attention. He also stressed the importance of enduring personality traits such as *introversion* and *extraversion* (discussed shortly).

▲ Children's small stature and dependence on parents create inferiority feelings that motivate them toward achievement, according to Adler.

Alfred Adler and the Inferiority Complex

Alfred Adler (1870–1937) also began as a student of Freud's but disagreed with his emphasis on aggressive and sexual urges as the major force in personality development. Adler (1928) believed that it is the child's desire to overcome feelings of helplessness and to master the environment that directs behavior. In the world of adults, children are small and helpless and feel inadequate and weak. Children have to be bathed by a parent and hold a parent's hand when crossing the street. These feelings of inferiority motivate the child—and later the adult—toward achievement. For Adler, personality develops from our attempts to compensate for inferiority feelings. Moderate feelings of inferiority will result in constructive achievement and creative growth, but deep feelings of inferiority will impede positive growth and development and result in an *inferiority complex*.

Adler also emphasized the importance of birth order as a factor in personality development. He argued that firstborns, middle-borns, and youngest children grow up in differing family environments and are not necessarily treated the same by parents. These different experiences are likely to affect personality development. Adler's ideas have resulted in hundreds of studies on the effects of birth order. These studies have generally not found any reliable relationships between birth order and personality (Damian & Roberts, 2015; Rohrer, Egloff, & Schmukle, 2017).

Bettmann/Getty Images

▲ Karen Horney argued that culture plays a larger role in personality development than does biology and suggested that family environments and disturbances in early relationships lead to basic anxiety in children. Children cope with this basic anxiety by pursuing love, power, prestige, or detachment.

basic anxiety according to Horney, the feeling of helplessness that develops in children from early relationships

Yet people generally believe that birth order influences personality, which may then actually encourage those in various birth ranks to differ in their personalities (Herrera et al., 2003).

Karen Horney, Basic Anxiety, and Culture

Although Karen Horney (1885–1952) agreed with Freud on the significance of early childhood in personality development, she rejected his belief that this development arose from instinctual conflicts. Instead, Horney (1937, 1939) suggested that family environments and disturbances in early relationships lead to **basic anxiety**, or a feeling of helplessness in children. Children cope with this basic anxiety by pursuing love, power, prestige, or detachment. Horney further argued, in contrast to Freud, that culture plays a larger role in personality development than biology and instinct. For Horney, personality is not merely the result of psychosexual conflicts, as Freud would argue, but rather is influenced by all the events and people in the culture that make a child feel unsafe and unloved, giving rise to basic anxiety.

11.1.5 Contributions and Criticisms of the Psychoanalytic Approach

Freud's contributions to psychology have been immense (Erwin, 2002). He is regarded as one of the most influential thinkers of the 20th century (Gedo, 2002). His presence is still felt among the general public through literature, arts, and the movies. His theory on dreams stimulated much research on the nature of sleep. His notion of defense mechanisms was extensively elaborated on by his daughter, Anna Freud (1895–1982), and his focus on coping and well-being sparked interest and research in health psychology. His ideas are evident in tests designed to measure personality (discussed later in this chapter) and in therapy approaches to help people with mental health problems (Chapter 14). Freud's basic notion of the unconscious influencing our behavior also has merit. Research in the area of cognitive neuroscience does support *unconscious* or *implicit cognition*—thought processes that occur outside conscious awareness that potentially influence judgments and behavior (Atas et al., 2014; Bargh & Morsella, 2008; Brinke, Stimson, & Carney, 2014; Dehaene, 2018).

Furthermore, Freud was one of the first to see the importance of early development in later adult behavior (Gedo, 2002). In the early 1900s, children were seen as mini-adults. People did not believe as strongly as we do now that how infants and children are treated influences their adult behavior. Although we know that infancy and childhood experiences do not *determine* adult behavior, as Freud asserted, his emphasis on the importance of these early years was a critical departure from accepted beliefs at that time. Through his psychosexual stages, Freud placed much emphasis on explaining the developmental nature of personality, probably more so than any other theorist. His views on sexuality and the impact of culture on sexuality continue to influence research (Hartmann, 2009; Person, 2005).

Freud's perspective has been criticized on several counts, however. First, many believe that Freud placed too much emphasis on sexual and aggressive instincts. His perspective shines very little light on environmental and social conditions that may affect personality functioning. We have just noted how many neo-Freudians diverged from Freud on this point, creating alternate views of the ego and personality that take our interactions with others into account (Horgan, 1996). His ideas and themes have also been attacked for their focus on male development and their perpetuation of the idea of male superiority (Person, 1990).

Much more problematic are Freud's methods of data collection and the fact that his theories cannot be readily tested experimentally (Crews, 1996). His theories are based almost entirely on case study research and his own self-analysis. His observations may not have been objective, and his case studies involved patients who were diagnosed with nervous disorders. What his patients told him may not have been accurate, and their statements were not corroborated by other sources. These issues make it difficult to generalize Freud's observations. Scientifically testing Freud's theoretical concepts is also quite challenging. Measuring the unconscious is difficult if participants are unaware of these impulses. It is equally difficult to measure psychosexual stages of development. For this reason, we cannot confirm Freud's theory with data, but we also cannot disprove it. Thus, it remains a possible explanation of personality functioning, though not as popular as it was in the past. Freud's ideas have not been supported by data from other cultures, possibly because his theories reflect the Western cultural value of individualism. They may not apply in collectivist cultures that emphasize the importance of the group (Matsumoto, 1994).

11.1 Quiz Yourself

1. **The psychoanalytic perspective emphasizes the influence of _____ on personality.**
   a. unconscious desires
   b. traits
   c. self-actualization
   d. environmental factors
2. **Your memories of your high school graduation or first date reside at the level of the _____ consciousness.**
   a. aconscious
   b. preconscious
   c. unconscious
   d. subconscious
3. **Maria often feels guilty when she engages in even the slightest offensive behavior. Freud would say that Maria has a strong _____.**
   a. id
   b. ego
   c. superego
   d. collective unconscious
4. **Neo-Freudian Alfred Adler emphasized _____ as motivators of personality development.**
   a. fears
   b. basic anxiety
   c. archetypes
   d. feelings of inferiority
5. **One of the major criticisms of Freud's theory concerns its _____.**
   a. overemphasis on environmental and cognitive factors in explaining behavior
   b. difficulty in being experimentally tested and validated
   c. emphasis on the conscious
   d. assumption that all people are good

Answers 1. a; 2. b; 3. c; 4. d; 5. b

11.2 The Trait Approach: Consistency and Stability in Personality

A second major perspective on personality is called the **trait approach**. The trait approach, like the psychoanalytic approach, focuses on internal aspects of personality. Whereas the psychoanalytic approach attempts to explain personality by focusing on unconscious forces, the trait perspective describes personality and emphasizes its biological aspects. Trait theory assumes that we all have internal **traits**, or tendencies to behave in a certain way across most situations. These traits remain relatively stable as we age and explain why individuals generally behave the same way

trait approach a personality perspective that attempts to describe personality by emphasizing internal, biological aspects of personality called traits

traits tendencies to behave in a certain way across most situations across a variety of situations. Yet because people differ in the degree to which they possess various traits, we develop unique personalities. We will describe four major approaches to understanding these personality traits in the theories of Gordon Allport, Raymond Cattell, Hans Eysenck, and Costa and McCrae's five factor theory.

11.2.1 Gordon Allport's Trait Theory

Psychologist Gordon Allport (1897–1967) believed that three types of traits help us understand a person's uniqueness: *central traits, secondary traits,* and *cardinal traits* (Allport, 1961). **Central traits** are those tendencies we have across most situations; they are the core qualities your friends would state if they were asked to describe you. For example, if you are friendly in most situations, then friendly would be considered a central trait. We all have central traits, but the specific qualities

central traits according to Allport, the tendencies we have to behave in a certain way across most situations

sensation seekers people who by trait tend to seek out arousing activities

Psychology Applies to Your World

Are You a Sensation Seeker?

ONE TRAIT OF PARTICULAR INTEREST to psychologists is that of *sensation seeking*. Some people seem to crave arousal, seeking out higher levels of arousal than the rest of us. In fact, sometimes they seek out levels of arousal that the rest of us would find aversive or unpleasant. These people are what psychologists call **sensation seekers**; they habitually tend to seek out high levels of physiological arousal by engaging in intensely stimulating experiences (Zuckerman, 1978, 1994). Some sensation seekers pursue daring activities such as mountain climbing, skydiving, bungee jumping, and fast driving, whereas others may be stimulated by engaging in problem behaviors such as drug use, aggression, or delinquency (Akbari, Lankarani, Heydari et al., 2019; Lynne-Landsman et al., 2011; Meil et al., 2016).

One theory that seeks to explain the causes of sensation seeking looks at biological differences in the brains of sensation seekers. Psychologist Marvin Zuckerman (1928–2018) found that sensation seekers tend to have low levels of a substance called *monoamine oxidase*, or *MAO* (Zuckerman & Kuhlman, 2000). MAO is an enzyme that breaks down neurotransmitters like serotonin, dopamine, and norepinephrine (Chapter 2). One of these neurotransmitters, dopamine, seems to be responsible for motivating us to obtain rewards. The low level of MAO in the brains of sensation seekers may mean that they experience more dopamine activity than other people. Without MAO to break it down, the dopamine would remain in the synapse longer, continuing to stimulate the neuron. This increased dopamine action may be related to sensation seekers' motivation to experience reward from intense arousal.

▲ According to psychologist Marvin Zuckerman, some people are high in the trait of sensation seeking. They engage in highly energizing and stimulating activities such as skydiving and extreme sports.

Research examining brain region responses to highly arousing stimuli between individuals high and low in sensation seeking supports this view. Individuals high in sensation seeking tend to show more activation in brain regions associated with reward and risk and tend to show less inhibition or the ability to regulate this activation compared to those low in sensation seeking (Joseph et al., 2009; Norbury & Husain, 2015; Rao, Zhou, Zheng et al., 2018). What causes these brain differences? Research suggests that multiple dopamine genes that we inherit may be at the heart of sensation-seeking behavior (Derringer et al., 2010). To get a feel for your level of sensation seeking, take the questionnaire in ● Table 11.1.

that are considered a central trait may differ from person to person. Hongyong was generally driven and industrious, two examples of her central traits.

Secondary traits describe how we behave in certain situations; they are tendencies that are less consistent and more situation-specific. Many of us behave aggressively in certain situations, such as when we are frustrated or when we see others behave aggressively. Again, we all have secondary traits, but whether a specific quality is considered a secondary trait may differ from person to person.

Cardinal traits describe how we behave across all situations. Allport considered these a very basic and permanent element of our personalities—but he had difficulty finding cardinal traits in all people that he studied. Consequently, the validity of cardinal traits became suspect. Recall from Chapter 6 on learning and Chapter 10 on social psychology the powerful effect the environment can have on our behavior. This effect often makes us behave differently across situations.

secondary traits according to Allport, the tendencies we have that are less consistent and describe how we behave in certain situations

cardinal traits according to Allport, those dominant elements of our personalities that drive all of our behaviors

TABLE 11.1 Brief Sensation-Seeking Questionnaire

Answer "true" or "false" to each item listed below by circling *T* or *F*. A "true" means that the item expresses your preference most of the time. A "false" means that you do not agree that the item is generally true for you. After completing the test, score your responses according to the instructions that follow the test items.

T	F	1. I would really enjoy skydiving.
T	F	2. I can imagine myself driving a sports car in a race and loving it.
T	F	3. My life is very secure and comfortable—the way I like it.
T	F	4. I usually like emotionally expressive or artistic people, even if they are sort of wild.
T	F	5. I like the idea of seeing many of the same warm, supportive faces in everyday life.
T	F	6. I like doing adventurous things and would have enjoyed being a pioneer in the early days of this country.
T	F	7. A good photograph should express peacefulness creatively.
T	F	8. The most important thing in living is fully experiencing all emotions.
T	F	9. I like creature comforts when I go on a trip or vacation.
T	F	10. Doing the same things each day really gets to me.
T	F	11. I love snuggling in front of a fire on a wintry day.
T	F	12. I would like to try several types of drugs as long as they didn't harm me permanently.
T	F	13. Drinking and being rowdy really appeals to me on weekends.
T	F	14. Rational people try to avoid dangerous situations.
T	F	15. I prefer figure A to figure B.

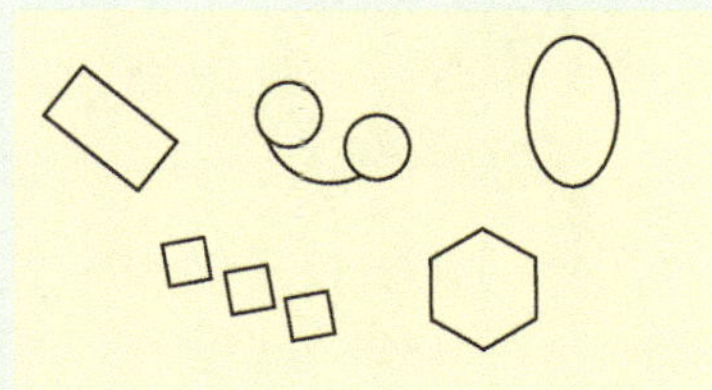

A

B

Give yourself 1 point for answering "true" to the following items: 1, 2, 4, 6, 8, 10, 12, and 13. Also give yourself 1 point for answering "false" to the following items: 3, 5, 7, 9, 11, 14, and 15. Add up your points, and compare your total to the following norms: 11–15, high sensation seeker; 6–10, moderate sensation seeker; 1–5, low sensation seeker. Bear in mind that this is a shortened version of the Sensation Seeking Scale and that it provides only a rough approximation of your status on this personality trait.

Source: A. F. Grasha & D. S. Kirschenbaum (1986). *Adjustment and Competence: Concepts and Applications*. St. Paul, MN: West Publishing.

▲ Using factor analysis, Raymond Cattell reduced the number of core personality traits to 16 basic traits, referred to as source traits.

surface traits basic traits that describe people's personalities, according to Cattell

source traits universal tendencies that underlie and are at the core of surface traits, according to Cattell

Allport's goal in describing traits was to understand the behavior of a specific individual. Other research focused on identifying and understanding core or universal traits that direct the behavior of people in general, relying heavily on the use of statistics. This set the stage for Raymond Cattell's statistical analysis of personality traits.

11.2.2 Raymond Cattell's Factor Analytic Trait Theory

Raymond Cattell (1905–1998) attempted to document relationships among traits using a sophisticated statistical technique called *factor analysis* (Cattell, 1943). In contemporary factor analysis, the possible traits that could be used to describe people are entered into a computer program; then the program groups related traits into factors. In this way, Cattell reduced the number of personality traits that could be used to describe all people.

Cattell's research (1965) originally yielded 36 **surface traits** that could describe personality. He then hypothesized that there must be common underlying factors that account for the 36 surface traits. Cattell referred to these factors or dimensions as **source traits**. Source traits are basic, broad, and relatively universal tendencies at the core of our personalities. We may differ in the amount or quality of these traits, but they are present in everyone's personality to some degree. Through subsequent analysis and research, Cattell identified 16 source traits (● TABLE 11.2). However, Cattell's 16 source traits did not easily lend themselves to research. Research led by British psychologist Hans Eysenck would further reduce the number.

11.2.3 Hans Eysenck Narrows the Traits: The PEN Model

Building on Cattell's factor analytic studies, Eysenck and Rachman (1965) found two factors that they believed measured people's key characteristics: *introversion/*

TABLE 11.2 Cattell's 16 Personality Factors

Factor	Description (Extremes of Each Factor from Low to High Levels)
Warmth	Reserved ---------- Warm
Reasoning	Less intelligent ---------- More intelligent
Emotional stability	Easily upset ---------- Emotionally stable
Dominance	Submissive ---------- Dominant
Liveliness	Serious ---------- Expressive
Rule consciousness	Nonconforming ---------- Conforming
Social boldness	Shy ---------- Venturesome
Sensitivity	Tough-minded ---------- Sensitive
Vigilance	Trusting ---------- Suspicious
Abstractedness	Practical ---------- Imaginative
Privateness	Open ---------- Shrewd
Apprehension	Unworried ---------- Worried
Openness to change	Conservative ---------- Experimenting
Self-reliance	Dependent ---------- Self-sufficient
Perfectionism	Undisciplined ---------- Precise
Tension	Relaxed ---------- Tense

extraversion and *emotional stability/neuroticism*. Introversion and extraversion define where a person's energy is directed. **Introversion** means that the person's energy is directed inward. This tendency could include being rigid, reliable, sober, or controlled. **Extraversion** means that the person's energy is directed outward. This tendency could include being easygoing, lively, or excitable.

Emotional stability and neuroticism refer to control over one's emotions. Being even-tempered and calm are traits that include more control over emotions and represent **emotional stability**, whereas moody and touchy describe traits that represent **neuroticism** (unstable emotions). We all are somewhere on the introversion/extraversion scale and somewhere on the emotional stability/neuroticism continuum; however, we all differ in the degree to which we express the two factors (● FIGURE 11.3).

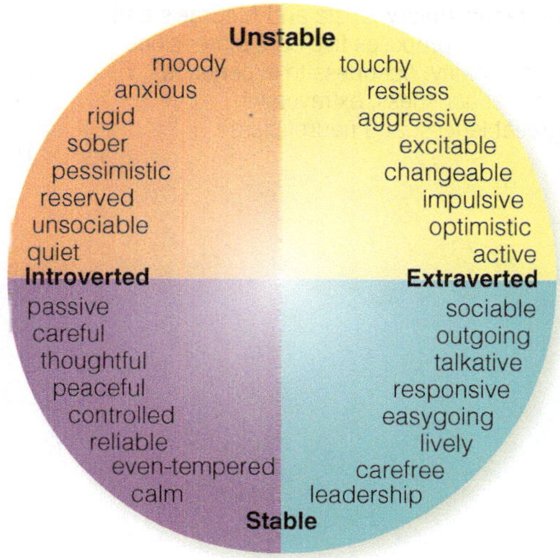

FIGURE 11.3

Eysenck's Trait Theory

British psychologist Hans Eysenck arrived at two universal traits using factor analysis. The stable–unstable axis defines one's emotionality; the introverted–extraverted axis defines the degree to which a person's energy is directed inward or outward. The traits in each quadrant indicate where they are placed with respect to these two factors.

In the 1970s, Hans Eysenck (1916–1997), in collaboration with his wife, Sybil Eysenck (b. 1927), added a third dimension called *psychoticism* to the model (Eysenck & Eysenck, 1969, 1976). **Psychoticism** includes tendencies toward recklessness, disregard for common sense and cultural norms, inconsideration, hostility, anger, and impulsivity. Eysenck originally characterized impulsivity as a dimension of extraversion. However, once the dimension of psychoticism was added, he moved this trait from extraversion to psychoticism. Eysenck's three-factor model of personality is referred to as the PEN (psychoticism, extraversion, neuroticism) model (● TABLE 11.3).

The Neurobiology of Extraversion and Introversion

Eysenck (1967, 1982, 1991) proposed that introverts inherit the tendency toward higher levels of physical arousal than extraverts. Introverts are more likely to avoid social situations because such experiences will elevate their arousal and lead to overstimulation and discomfort. Hence, they are more likely than extraverts to turn inward and become introverted. Extraverts, by contrast, seek out stimulating environments to increase their naturally lower arousal levels. Research has generally supported Eysenck's *arousal theory*; several studies confirm that introverts tend to show higher levels of physical arousal than extraverts (Beauducel, Brocke, & Leue, 2006; Bullock & Gilliland, 1993; Kumari et al., 2004; LeBlanc, Ducharme, & Thompson, 2004; Wei et al., 2014). Another prominent explanation of introversion and extraversion is the *reward-processing theory*. It suggests that extraverts' brains are more sensitive to both rewards and dopamine functioning, which leads them to gravitate to more stimulating social activities (Cohen et al., 2005; Depue & Collins, 1999; Depue & Fu, 2013; Smillie, 2013). Future research on the neuroscience of personality traits will further expand our knowledge in this area.

introversion [in-tro-VER-shun] personality traits that involve energy directed inward, such as being calm or peaceful

extraversion [ex-tra-VER-shun] personality traits that involve energy directed outward, such as being easygoing, lively, or excitable

emotional stability having control over one's emotions

neuroticism [nur-RAH-tuh-siz-um] the degree to which one is emotionally unstable

psychoticism [psi-COT-uh-siz-um] the degree to which one is hostile, nonconforming, impulsive, and aggressive

TABLE 11.3 Eysenck's PEN Model

Psychoticism	Extraversion	Neuroticism
Aggressive	Sociable	Anxious
Assertive	Optimistic	Depressed
Impulsive	Expressive	Guilt feelings
Manipulative	Active	Moody
Tough-minded	Dominant	Obsessive
Hostile	Lacking reflection	Tense

five factor theory Costa and McCrae's trait theory that proposes five core dimensions to personality: openness to experience, conscientiousness, extraversion, agreeableness, and neuroticism

11.2.4 The Five Factor Trait Theory

Currently, the most widely accepted trait theory derived from factor analysis is Paul Costa (b. 1942) and Robert McCrae's (b. 1949) (1992) **five factor theory**. This theory proposes five core dimensions that can be measured along a continuum in all people.

- *Openness to experience*: the degree to which one is thoughtful and rational in considering new ideas and experiences. People who score high in openness to experience tend to be imaginative, creative, and curious, and to prefer variety and novelty; those who score low in openness to experience prefer routine and familiarity and are less likely to consider new ideas or try new things.
- *Conscientiousness*: the degree to which one is aware of and attentive to other people, to the details of a task, or to both. People who are high in conscientiousness tend to be hardworking, ambitious, reliable, and self-controlled, whereas individuals low on this dimension are more often described as unreliable, lazy, and spontaneous.
- *Extraversion*: the degree to which one's energy is directed inward or outward. People high in extraversion are talkative and sociable and prefer to be around others. At the other end of the continuum are people low in extraversion (introverts), who are quiet, reserved, and more comfortable on their own.
- *Agreeableness*: the degree to which one gets along well with others and acts unselfishly. Being easy going, altruistic, and trusting are traits characteristic of one high in agreeableness. At the other end of the spectrum are people who are less concerned with other people and tend to be unfriendly, antagonistic, and suspicious (low agreeableness).
- *Neuroticism*: the degree to which one is emotionally stable or unstable. People high in neuroticism are temperamental, worrisome, and pessimistic. People who score low on this factor tend to be more even-tempered and calmer.

These five dimensions appear in all cultures and in other species such as chimpanzees and bonobos, suggesting that these five factors may represent universal personality components (Katigbak et al., 2002; McCrae & Costa, 1998; Weiss et al., 2015; Yamagata et al., 2006). An easy way to remember the five factors is with the acronym OCEAN. Each letter in OCEAN stands for one of the five factors: O= openness to experience; C= conscientiousness; E= extraversion; A= agreeableness; and N= neuroticism.

You Review: Summary of Trait Theories compares the four trait theories. Notice that the main difference in these theories is the number of source traits that are proposed. Allport's theory proposes three types, Eysenck's theory proposes three, Cattell's theory proposes 16, and Costa and McCrae's model proposes five.

YOU REVIEW Summary of the Trait Theories

Theorist/Theory	Method of Collection	Results
Allport	Subjectively collected traits	Three trait levels: central, secondary, and cardinal
Cattell	Factor analysis	36 surface traits; 16 source traits
Eysenck's PEN model	Factor analysis	Three basic traits labeled PEN: psychoticism, extraversion, and neuroticism
Costa & McCrae's five factor theory	Factor analysis	Five basic traits that form the acronym OCEAN: openness to experience, conscientiousness, extraversion, agreeableness, and neuroticism

11.2.5 Genetic Contributions to Personality

The trait perspective assumes that people have internal dispositions to behave consistently across situations. Thus, some researchers have speculated that we inherit some aspects of our personalities. Recall that newborn infants do show differences in behavior that we refer to as *temperament* (see Chapter 9), that these temperamental differences appear strongly related to genes (Braungart et al., 1992; Plomin et al., 2008), and that they are quite stable over time (Jaffari-Bimmel et al., 2006; Kopala-Sibley, Olino, Durbin et al., 2018; Majdandzic & van den Boom, 2007; McCrae et al., 2000; Rothbart, Ahadi, & Evans, 2000). As we saw in this part's case study, Hongyong had a difficult temperament that was relatively stable at least through childhood. It seems possible that other characteristics or personality dispositions are also inherited.

Researchers in the field of **behavioral genetics** study the degree to which personality traits are influenced by genetics and hereditary factors. One way to study genetic contributions—the nature side of personality—is to look at children who are adopted. On the one hand, because adopted children have fewer genes in common with their adoptive family members, any similarities in personality characteristics between these children and their adoptive parents are likely due to learning or modeling. On the other hand, because these children have more genes in common with their biological parents but do not share a family environment, any similarities to them are likely due to genetics. These research studies have found more personality similarities between adoptive children and their biological parents (Carey & DiLalla, 1994) suggesting that personality traits are moderately heritable.

behavioral genetics field of study that examines the influence of genetics and hereditary factors on personality traits

Another method for investigating the contribution of genes—or nature—is to study identical twins. Research on identical twins provides even more compelling evidence that at least *some* personality tendencies may be inherited (Bouchard, 2004; Vukasovic & Bratko, 2015; Weiss, Bates, & Luciano, 2008). Identical twins reared in separate environments appeared to show remarkable similarities in behavior years later when they were reunited (Bouchard et al., 1990; Holden, 1980; Lykken et al., 1992). One of the more famous separated pairs is James Springer and James Lewis, known as the "Jim twins." Both drove Chevrolets and chain-smoked Salem cigarettes. They both worked as sheriff's deputies and listed stock car racing, carpentry, and mechanical drawing as interests and hobbies (Holden, 1980). Studies have indeed found more similarities between the personalities of identical twins than of nonidentical (fraternal) twins (Buss, 1995; Laceulle et al., 2013; Montag et al., 2016; Plomin et al., 2008). Such evidence supports a genetic component in the personalities we exhibit.

Other research on the heritability of personality traits in a domain called *personality neuroscience* has focused on genes that direct neurotransmitter functioning, specifically serotonin and dopamine. For example, several studies have found an association between the *serotonin transporter gene* and anxiety-related personality traits (Hayden et al., 2007; Madsen et al., 2016; Sen, Burmeister, & Ghosh, 2004). This gene influences the levels of serotonin in the brain and may account for differences in anxiety levels from person to person. Other studies have investigated the relationship between a *dopamine receptor gene* and the personality trait of novelty seeking (He, Martin, Zhu, & Lie, 2018; Jonsson et al., 2003; Munafo et al., 2008; Norbury & Husain, 2015; Schinka, Letsch, & Crawford, 2002). Such results suggest a complex interaction among one's biology, the environment, and personality. Human behavior is the product of many genes working simultaneously, together with multiple environmental

▲ Studies have found more similarities between identical twins' personalities than between nonidentical twins' personalities, suggesting a modest genetic component in the personalities that we exhibit.

and developmental events (Barlow et al., 2014; Chabris et al., 2015; Hamer, 2002). Unraveling these connections and influences will keep scientists very busy in the years ahead.

11.2.6 Stability and Change in Personality

The trait approach assumes not only that traits are inherited but also that these internal tendencies are consistent and stable over time. What does the research indicate? Research does support the stability of *some* personality traits over the course of adulthood (see Costa, McCrae, & Löckenhoff, 2019, for review). However, age, culture, and gender are important when considering stability and change in personality.

Diversity: The Influence of Age, Culture, and Gender on Personality

After the age of 30, changes in personality traits are smaller than in childhood and young adulthood (Costa & McCrae, 1997; McCrae, 2009; Roberts, Walton, & Viechtbauer, 2006; Spengler, Gottschling, & Spinath, 2012; Terracciano, Costa, & McCrae, 2006). As a part of the developmental process, children, adolescents, and young adults experiment with new identities and ways of behaving. They may adopt new values and attitudes or revise existing ones (McAdams & Olson, 2010). Changes in personality, therefore, are more frequent during these periods.

Some studies suggest that at least for some traits, there is a consistency from childhood to adulthood (Edmonds et al., 2013; Roberts, Caspi, & Moffitt, 2001). For example, McCrae and colleagues (2002) found stability in the traits of extraversion, agreeableness, and conscientiousness from age 12 to age 18. The trait of neuroticism also appears to remain relatively stable across childhood and early adulthood before decreasing as people age (Barlow et al., 2014). Hampson and Goldberg (2006) found stability for the traits of extraversion and conscientiousness from elementary school to midlife. Another study (Robins et al., 2001) found consistency in the five factor personality traits when following the same people from the beginning to the end of their college years.

However, research on U.S. and cross-cultural samples also suggests gradual and modest *changes* in personality even during the course of adulthood. People generally become more conscientious, agreeable, and emotionally stable, slightly less open to experience, and less extraverted across adulthood (Bleidorn, 2015; Bleidorn et al., 2013; Carducci, 2009; Chopik & Kitayama, 2018; Jackson et al., 2012; Laceulle et al., 2013; Ludtke, Trautwein, & Husemann, 2009; Roberts & Mroczek, 2008). For example, despite being headstrong as a child, Hongyong learned to temper her willfulness and became more accommodating in her marriage and her businesses as she got older.

Age differences in personality have also been investigated in other cultures, and a similar picture has emerged. Data from 62 nations over five continents (the Americas, Australia, Africa, Asia, and Europe) are consistent with findings on the five factor model of personality in U.S. samples (Bleidorn et al., 2013; Chopik & Kitayama, 2018; McCrae, 2009; McCrae et al., 1999, 2000). Older men and women in these cultures also tended to be modestly lower in extraversion and neuroticism and somewhat higher in agreeableness and conscientiousness. Such findings appear to support the universality of *some* personality traits. These societies differ dramatically in language, culture, and historical experiences from one another and from the experiences of many people in the United States. Yet the cultural differences seemed to have little impact on age differences in personality traits.

person–situation interaction the influence of the situation on the stability of traits; when in the same situation, we display similar behavior, but when the situation is different, behavior may change

Gender differences in personality traits also show evidence of both stability and change. Across cultures and for both college-age and older adult samples, females report themselves to be higher in neuroticism, extraversion, agreeableness, and openness to feelings, whereas males report themselves higher in assertiveness and openness to ideas (Costa, Terracciano, & McCrae, 2001; McCrae, 2009; Schmitt et al., 2008; Weisberg, DeYoung, & Hirsh, 2011). Parental reports also confirm gender differences in neuroticism by mid-adolescence (Soto, 2016). Yet these personality traits varied more *within* each gender than they did between genders. Gender differences in neuroticism and extraversion also become smaller over time as men and women age (Carducci, 2009; Srivastava et al., 2003). Moreover, the research demonstrates that not all youth and adults change at the same rate over their lives. Some people's traits may be stable, whereas other people's traits may change (Barlow et al., 2014; Mroczek & Spiro, 2003; Roberts & Mroczek, 2008; Soto & Tackett, 2015). Why personality change occurs for some people and not others is a question that continues to be researched.

The Influence of the Environment on Traits

Situational factors also influence the stability and consistency of traits. Many of us display the same trait (behave the same way) when faced with similar circumstances—that is, when the environmental cues are the same. However, when the situation is different, our behavior may change. This relationship among traits, situations, and behavior is referred to as the **person–situation interaction** (Mischel & Shoda, 1995). For example, the students of one of the authors of this textbook are always surprised to hear that she has a fear of public speaking. They see her speak every week in class with little anxiety. They know that she has been teaching for more than 30 years. From such knowledge, they predict that she would not fear public speaking in other situations, such as at an academic conference or at a community function. But in these different situations, she is extremely anxious, panicked, and nauseated at the thought of speaking in front of a group. The cues of the two different situations evoke different behaviors and reactions. Thus, our traits do not always predict how we will behave across different situations. Discovering how loved ones will behave in specific situations is just as important as knowing their traits (Friesen & Kammrath, 2011).

How do psychologists reconcile these seemingly contradictory findings? Psychologists recognize that personality is both stable *and* changeable. Some traits are probably more consistent across the life span and from culture to culture, whereas others are more easily influenced by one's biology, society, gender, environment, and daily situations (Costa, McCrae & Löckenhoff, 2019; Fleeson, 2004; Soto & Tackett, 2015). Such flexibility enables individuals to face developmental changes and challenges throughout their lives.

Tyler Olson/Shutterstock.com

Tyler Olson/Shutterstock.com

▲ Often our personality interacts with our environment. A behavior we display in one context (texting on our cell phone when the teacher is not looking) may not be the same behavior we exhibit at other times (being studious and engaged when the teacher is attentive).

11.2.7 Contributions and Criticisms of the Trait Approach

The trait perspective has contributed to our understanding of personality by providing psychologists with a common vocabulary to describe people's personalities. Because this common language facilitates communication within the field, the trait approach has been particularly useful in the area of personality assessment, a topic we will turn to shortly. Knowing a person's tendencies or traits also helps psychologists predict future behavior. These predictions, however, will be influenced by the nature of the situation (J. A. Johnson, 1997). The assumptions of the trait perspective—that traits are internal and stable—have also fueled research investigating the biological aspects of personality and the consistency and stability of personality traits across the life span.

However, the objective of personality research is to uncover how we differ from one another. Although the trait perspective does a good job of *describing* people's personalities, it is criticized for not *explaining* why we behave in a particular way (Digman, 1997; McCabe & Fleeson, 2012). Critics further argue that it portrays personality too simplistically and fails to reflect its complexity and depth (Block, 1995; Epstein, 1994; Gladwell, 2004). Can everyone really be reduced to 3, 5, or 16 dimensions? Can we cleanly divide personality into biological and environmental components without taking into account the complex interactions among them? We have also seen the trait perspective's shortcomings in predicting people's behavior across different situations (Wiggins, 1997). This should not be surprising, though, given the powerful influence of situational forces on behavior.

11.2 Quiz Yourself

1. **The trait perspective attempts to describe ____**
   a. person–situation interactions
   b. a person's key characteristics
   c. cultural influences on personality
   d. factor analysis
2. **Terrence is outgoing in most situations. Allport would describe this tendency in Terrence as a ____**
   a. source trait
   b. secondary trait
   c. cardinal trait
   d. central trait
3. **Which of the following is *not* considered one of the five factor traits of personality?**
   a. Achievement
   b. Extraversion
   c. Conscientiousness
   d. Agreeableness
4. **Research on the stability of personality traits over the life span suggests that in general after age ____ changes in one's personality traits are small.**
   a. 12
   b. 20
   c. 30
   d. 50
5. **Malcolm is hostile, aggressive, and impulsive. According to Eysenck, Malcolm is high in ____**
   a. conscientiousness
   b. neuroticism
   c. psychoticism
   d. introversion

Answers 1. b; 2. d; 3. a; 4. c; 5. c

11.3 The Social Cognitive Approach: The Environment and Patterns of Thought

social cognitive approach a personality perspective that emphasizes the influence of one's thoughts and social experiences in formulating personality

The **social cognitive approach** sees personality as influenced by both the environment and one's thoughts. Although Freud focused on how unconscious forces influence behavior, and the trait perspective investigates internal tendencies, the social cognitive approach looks at the characteristic ways a person perceives and interprets events in the environment. For example, the person who assumes that others are unlikely to treat them fairly is more likely to have a quarrelsome personality than a person who tends to assume that things generally happen for the best. These patterns of thought are established through our interactions with and observations of other people. Two examples of this approach are Albert Bandura's *reciprocal determinism* and Julian Rotter's *locus of control theory.*

reciprocal determinism [ree-SIP-pra-cull dee-TER-min-iz-um] according to Bandura, the mutual interaction among one's behavior, thoughts, and environment determines personality

self-efficacy [self-EF-fuh-kah-see] the expectation that one has for success in a given situation

11.3.1 Reciprocal Determinism: Albert Bandura's Interacting Forces

Albert Bandura (b. 1925) speculates that personality is the product of three interacting forces: *environment, behavior,* and *thoughts* (Bandura, 1986). Bandura called the mutual interaction among these three factors **reciprocal determinism** (● FIGURE 11.4). We choose to place ourselves in certain environments, and these environments then influence our behavior and the way we think. However, the way we think—our attributions, goals, values, and perceptions—may guide which environments we choose to be in as well as the behavior we exhibit (Dweck, 2008). Our behavior, in turn, may change the environment as well as the way we think. All three variables influence each other in a *reciprocal* manner.

Jon Brenneis/The LIFE Images Collection/Getty Images

▲ Albert Bandura speculates that personality is the product of reciprocal determinism, or the mutual interaction among one's environment, behavior, and thoughts.

For example, when we were children, we were placed in a family environment that modeled specific child-rearing techniques. We tend to think that everything we experienced in our home was normal, and that these same experiences occurred everywhere else, too. We tend to think that everyone else grew up with the parental discipline style we had. When we ourselves have children, if we have not learned anything different, we tend to behave in the same way toward our children. The family environment and our understanding of the way we were raised have now influenced our own parenting behavior.

A critical cognitive element in this interplay is what Bandura (1997) termed **self-efficacy**, or one's expectation of success in a given situation. Self-efficacy can differ across different domains in one's life. People with high self-efficacy in a certain domain believe that they will be successful in that domain. Approaching a situation with this belief is more likely to result in actual success. In contrast, people with low self-efficacy in a particular domain are more likely to approach a task believing that they won't succeed at it. This mindset then decreases their chance of succeeding by causing them to give up too easily or to not even really try in the first place.

Let's return to our previous example. If you believe that you will be a successful parent by using the same discipline techniques that your parents used with you, you will be more likely to use such measures. If such practices are successful—in other words, your children behave as you would like—you feel even better as a parent. However, if you do not believe that you will be a successful parent, you may constantly change the methods you use to discipline your children. Such inconsistency will make it even less likely that your children will behave the way you want, which only reinforces your lack of confidence in your parenting ability.

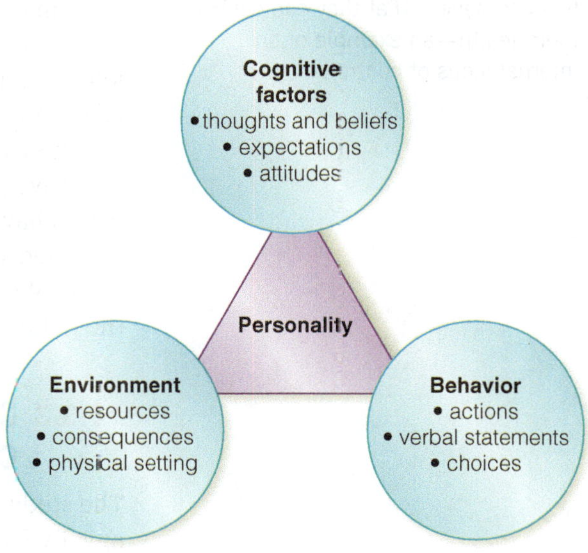

FIGURE 11.4

Bandura's Reciprocal Determinism

Albert Bandura speculates that the mutual interaction among our behavior, thoughts (cognitive factors), and environment determines our personalities.

11.3.2 Julian Rotter's Locus of Control: Internal and External Expectations

locus [LOW-cus] of control according to Rotter, the expectation of control we have over the outcome of an event; an internal locus means we expect some degree of personal control, whereas an external locus means we expect little personal control

Julian Rotter (1916–2014) provides another example of a social cognitive approach to personality. His theory (Rotter, 1982) is referred to as **locus of control**, or *location of control*. Rotter believed that we all have expectations regarding how much control we have over the outcome of an event. These expectations fall on a continuum from internal to external. For example, you probably enter the testing room on exam day already expecting to do well, average, or poorly on the exam. This is your expectation of the event. Some people attribute the outcome of an event to internal forces, such as hard work. If you expect to do well on an exam because you studied hard, you are exhibiting an *internal locus of control*. As an "internal," you are attributing the outcome of the event to factors within your control. However, other people attribute the outcome of an event to external forces, such as good luck, fate, or environmental factors. If you believe you will do well on the exam because the course or test is easy or because the professor likes you, these expectations demonstrate an *external locus of control*. As an "external," you attribute the outcome to factors outside your control. Not surprisingly, internals tend to have higher academic achievement than externals. Externals tend to believe that only fate or the luck of a sympathetic teacher will get them a good grade, and so they tend not to study as much as internals (Schultz & Schultz, 2005).

Image Source Plus/Alamy stock photo

▲ People who exercise may be more likely to believe that they can control their health—an example of an internal locus of control.

Rotter suggests that these varying expectations of control lead to differences in personality. Think about your health. Who would be more likely to exercise regularly and maintain a healthy lifestyle? Externals are more likely to attribute their weight, health, or medical condition to fate. "What will be, will be" could be their motto. They may feel that when their time is up, their time is up. Internals, however, tend to believe that they can control their health and are therefore more likely to exercise, follow doctors' directions, get regular checkups, and eat wisely, behaviors that actually contribute to better health (Phares, 1991; Ryon & Gleason, 2014; Strickland, 1989).

In examining this part's case study, how would Bandura's and Rotter's social cognitive perspectives explain Hongyong's personality? They would probably see her as having an internal locus of control and a strong sense of self-efficacy. She expected to succeed in business, in her marriage, and in learning to read and write. She was determined to get her family to freedom and to find her son despite the political and cultural upheaval around her.

11.3.3 Contributions and Criticisms of the Social Cognitive Approach

The study of social cognition has made major contributions to the field of psychology. By focusing on cognitive processes such as thinking, expectations, and other mental events that influence our behavior, it has expanded our conceptualization and understanding of personality. This knowledge in turn has stimulated an enormous amount of research, as we saw in the second part of this text that examined how cognition influences behavior. Our knowledge of memory, attributions, and problem solving stem directly from this perspective, which easily lends itself to research, specifically experimental testing. Objectively measuring social and cognitive processes is easier than measuring unconscious forces or biological tendencies. Despite these contributions, the social cognitive approach to personality has been criticized for not addressing biological, unconscious, and emotional factors that influence personality (Liebert & Spiegler, 1998). It has also been criticized for not specifying the exact nature of personality development.

11.3 Quiz Yourself

1. The social cognitive perspective emphasizes the influence of _____ on personality.
a. unconscious impulses
b. internal control
c. self-actualization and self-esteem
d. the environment and patterns of thoughts

2. Dylan is sure he will do poorly on his next psychology exam. Dylan often thinks this way in regard to his academic studies. Bandura would say that Dylan has _____
a. low self-actualization
b. low self-efficacy
c. an external locus of control
d. reciprocal determinism

3. Juanita believes that finding a job is a matter of being in the right place at the right time. Rotter would classify Juanita as having _____
a. low self-efficacy
b. low determinism
c. an internal locus of control
d. an external locus of control

Answers 1. d; 2. b; 3. d

11.4 The Humanistic Approach: Free Will and Self-Actualization

The fourth and final personality perspective we will discuss is the **humanistic approach**. Humanistic psychology viewed itself as a "third force" in American psychology, following psychoanalytic and behavioral views. The humanistic approach emphasizes the individual, personal choice, and free will in shaping personality. The individual is seen as an active participant in their growth as a person. The humanistic view further assumes that humans have a built-in drive toward fulfilling their own natural potential. The attainment of this potential is referred to as **self-actualization**. Two well-known humanistic theorists have charted somewhat different paths to achieving self-actualization. One is Abraham Maslow, whose *hierarchy of needs theory* was introduced in Chapter 5. The other is Carl Rogers and his *self theory*.

humanistic approach a personality perspective that emphasizes the individual, personal choice, and free will in shaping personality; assumes that humans have a built-in drive toward fulfilling their own natural potentia

self-actualization [self-ack-shu-lih-ZAY-shun] the fulfillment of one's natural potential

11.4.1 Abraham Maslow and the Hierarchy of Needs Theory

Recall from Chapter 5 that Maslow (1908–1970) believed that the pathway to achieving self-actualization was in the form of a hierarchy, with physical or biological needs at the bottom and more psychological or social needs at the top (Maslow, 1968, 1970, 1971). According to Maslow, a person must satisfy lower-level needs before higher-level needs can be attained. At the bottom of the hierarchy are basic physiological needs, such as the need for food and water. Without food and water, we cannot proceed to the next rung of the ladder. At this next level, safety becomes the concern: the need to be free from harm and to feel secure. Once this safety need is met, the person focuses on psychological needs, such as feeling a sense of belongingness (the need to fit in), feeling esteem or respect from others, and meeting cognitive and aesthetic needs. Once these needs have been satisfied, self-actualization

REUTERS/Alamy stock photo

▲ People who meet the criteria for self-actualization, such as the late Nelson Mandela, might actually deprive themselves of lower-level needs (remaining imprisoned) in favor of higher needs (the right to criticize one's government).

can be attained. Maslow estimated that only one person in 10 operates from self-actualization needs. While in Chapter 5 we discussed how Maslow's theory relates to motivation, here we are revisiting Maslow's theory as it applies to personality and explaining why people may consistently behave the way they do.

Unfortunately, Maslow's hierarchy does not explain why some people would deprive themselves of lower food and safety needs in favor of higher needs, such as esteem or self-actualization. For example, Nelson Mandela preferred to remain imprisoned in South Africa for many years than to lose his right to criticize the apartheid government. Maslow's hierarchy has also been criticized for not capturing the power of culture in influencing and shaping human needs (Kesebir, Graham, & Oishi, 2010). Some critics contend that Maslow's hierarchy is just too simple a view of motives and personality (Kenrick et al., 2010; Neher, 1991). Another view of self-actualization is Carl Rogers's self theory.

11.4.2 Carl Rogers and Self Theory

Carl Rogers (1902–1987) believed that understanding human personality required an understanding of how people view themselves and how they interpret events around them (Rogers, 1942, 1951, 1961, 1970, 1980). He believed that human beings naturally strive for fulfillment and enhancement, a built-in motive that he referred to as the **actualizing tendency**.

actualizing [ACK-shu-lies-ing] tendency according to Rogers, the natural drive in humans to strive for fulfillment and enhancement

self-concept one's perception or image of their abilities and uniqueness

The Development of Self-Concept

Rogers's proposed actualizing tendency is set at birth and moves the infant to recognize that they are separate from the parent and an independent being. The infant begins to experience the self as "I" or "me." This self gradually evolves into the person's self-concept. **Self-concept** is our perception or image of our abilities and our uniqueness. At first one's self-concept is simple and concrete, as in the 4-year-old who describes themselves as a person with brown hair or the 3-year-old who states in one moment that they are happy but 5 minutes later that they are sad. As we grow older, these self-perceptions become more comprehensive and differentiated as we learn more about ourselves. For example, a 15-year-old is more likely to describe themselves in terms of their academic abilities, athletic abilities, social abilities, and talents. For example, the teenager may say, "I'm a decent second baseman, a B student, and I have a lot of friends."

Underlying Rogers's actualizing tendency is an *organismic valuing process*. Experiences that maintain or enhance the person are valued, and therefore are preferred and liked. Experiences that do not maintain or enhance the person are not valued, and therefore are rejected (Sheldon, Arndt, & Houser-Marko, 2003). An infant's valuing process is direct and simple. We know as infants what we like and what we dislike. We value food because it reduces the sensation of hunger. We value being held in a parent's arms because it makes us feel secure. However, such an internal evaluation of our values is soon influenced by our social interactions and cultural environments and by our basic need for love and acceptance (Fulmer et al., 2010; Markus & Kitayama, 2010; McAdams, 2013).

Michael Rougier/Time & Life Pictures/Contributor/Getty Images

▲ Carl Rogers believed that understanding human personality requires an understanding of how people view themselves and how they interpret events around them.

As children, we come to realize that other important people in our lives (such as parents, teachers, siblings, or other relatives) also place value on our experiences. They communicate to us the "right" and "wrong" ways to think, feel, and behave. Cultural, racial, and gender norms may become especially powerful influences on our behavior. Because we desire their love and affection, we incorporate these messages into our valuing process. Experiences that meet these imposed values tend to be incorporated into our self-concept. For example, if a parent has communicated to a child that good grades are valued and the child gets good grades, the child may describe themselves as a good student. A child may come home every day from school reporting on how well they did in school. This accomplishment gives the child the opportunity to gain acceptance and love from the parent. Conversely, suppose the child does not get good grades at school. This child may hide test scores from their parents for fear of being rejected and unloved. This example illustrates the enormous influence of others' standards and values on our self-concepts. We may no longer listen to our own internal valuing system but pay more attention to the views and values of loved ones and our society. Our worth and regard are now judged on the basis of the imposed opinions, judgments, and values of others, rather than our own internal organismic valuing process. We have come to see ourselves as others see us.

The Value of Unconditional Positive Regard

What determines the degree to which we "listen" to, or incorporate, these parental and societal norms and standards? For Rogers, it is the degree of **unconditional positive regard**, or acceptance and love with no strings attached, that we receive from others. Our good points as well as bad points are accepted. People accept us and love us for who we are. This does not mean that a person's *actions* always receive approval. For example, suppose a youngster kicks the dog because the dog chewed a cherished toy. A parent can express displeasure at the child's actions, yet still let the child know that the angry behavior is understood and that the child is still loved by the parent despite the behavior. However, if the parent attacks the child's self, calling the child "bad," the parent has now communicated *conditional positive regard*. The child will believe that feeling angry is wrong because feeling angry will lose the parent's love and acceptance. In other words, unconditional positive regard communicates respect for a person's thoughts and feelings.

unconditional positive regard acceptance and love of another's thoughts and feelings without expecting anything in return

On the one hand, if a child experiences unconditional positive regard, especially during the early years of life, they are less likely to lose contact with the organismic valuing process established at birth. In this way, the child grows into an adult who chooses to act, feel, or think on the basis of their inner evaluations, taking into consideration the effect of their behavior on others. For Rogers, this represented a healthy personality. On the other hand, if a child experiences primarily conditional positive regard during these years, they are more likely to develop a self-concept that is based on how others see them and disregard the inner guiding voice in their behavior. Such people think, act, or behave in a certain way in hope of ensuring the continued love and acceptance of others. They believe that if they don't meet certain self-imposed expectations, their parents will not love them anymore. These perceptions, whether accurate or not, impede our ability to fulfill our potential, according to Rogers. In such situations, healthy development of the personality is hindered, and psychological discomfort may occur (Assor, Roth, & Deci, 2004).

Let's take one more look at Hongyong Baek from a humanistic perspective. Growing up female in the Korean culture, during a time of political and cultural upheaval, potentially influenced Hongyong's perception of reality and the evaluation of her self-concept. Others' opinions and judgments (such as her husband's) affected her view of herself. Moreover, her struggle at times to fulfill basic biological, security, and belongingness needs may have influenced the attainment of higher psychological needs. Her self-concept influenced her experiences and behaviors.

AnnGaysorn/Shutterstock.com

▲ The approval (or disapproval) we receive from others influences our self-concept, according to Rogers

11.4.3 Contributions and Criticisms of the Humanistic Approach

Many humanistic ideas have been incorporated into individual, family, and group therapy approaches, as we will see in Chapter 14. The humanistic approach has encouraged many people to become more aware of themselves and their interactions with others. However, the humanistic perspective has been criticized for its seemingly naïve and optimistic assumption that all people are good and are motivated toward attaining self-actualization. Critics argue that all people are not necessarily good and that humanists underestimate the capacity for evil in some individuals (Coffer & Appley, 1964; Ellis, 1959). Equally problematic is the difficulty in validating through experiments many of the humanistic concepts such as actualizing tendency, organismic valuing process, and unconditional positive regard (Burger, 2004). The major source of data for Rogers's self theory has been under scrutiny as well, as it was derived from clients' self-statements. How reliable and valid are such statements? It's possible that clients did not always present their "true" selves to Rogers and that as a listener, Rogers was biased. As a result, humanistic psychology has not become as major a force in psychology as Maslow once hoped—although many consider the emergence of *positive psychology* (see Chapter 12) a rebirth of humanistic goals and its enduring legacy (Diener, Oishi, & Lucas, 2003).

11.4 Quiz Yourself

1. **The humanistic perspective emphasizes the influence of _____ on personality.**
   a. unconscious impulses
   b. internal traits
   c. an actualizing tendency
   d. environmental and cognitive factors
2. **Maslow's hierarchy of needs theory would have the most difficulty explaining which one of the following?**
   a. A teenager shopping for the "right" clothes to wear to school
   b. A starving child stealing food at the grocery store
   c. A person who lives in a dangerous part of town trying to find a job that makes them feel important
   d. A successful business person with a satisfying relationship searching for spiritual fulfillment
3. **Which of the following elements does Rogers believe promotes the fulfillment of one's potential?**
   a. Unconditional positive regard
   b. Esteem
   c. Sympathy
   d. Adaptability

Answers 1. c; 2. c; 3. a

11.5 Scientifically Measuring Personality

We have described four different approaches to personality. Each perspective tends to employ certain tools to measure or assess personality. The results of these tests can be used in clinical settings to inform therapists about their clients' behavior, as well as in research to explore variations in personalities across individuals.

As with any tool or measuring device, it is important that the test be *reliable* and *valid*. **Reliability** refers to the consistency of a measurement tool. If we were to assess your height as an adult with a tape measure, we would want to get a consistent reading every time we measured your height. Personality tests also need to be reliable, or yield similar results over time. This reliability will not be perfect as we are not consistent in our behavior at all times. However, personality tests should report similar trends if they are reliable.

reliability the degree to which a test yields consistent measurements over time

validity the degree to which a test measures what it claims to measure

Measurement tools like personality tests also need to be valid. **Validity** refers to the ability of a test to measure what it says it is measuring. If a test states that it is measuring your intelligence and it does so by measuring your foot size, this test would not be valid. There is no relationship between foot size and intelligence. Notice that this test would be reliable (i.e., yield a consistent measurement over time), but

Psychology Works!

iStock.com/ferrantraite

Understanding personality can be beneficial to many careers. Employment recruiters, hiring managers, and other human resource personnel are increasingly using personality tests to assess potential job candidates and find the best "fit" for a specific position. Understanding what different tests measure, their reliability, how to interpret the test's findings, and how personality traits can be both stable and changeable are all crucial skills in these professions. So, learning about personality works!

it does not measure what we think of as intelligence. Therefore, personality tests should measure what we believe personality to be.

Each of the four major perspectives has developed its own way of measuring personality. These measures include *personality inventories, projective tests, rating scales,* and *clinical interviews.*

11.5.1 Personality Inventories: Mark Which One Best Describes You

Personality inventories are objective paper-and-pencil or computerized self-report forms. You are typically asked to indicate how well a statement describes you or to answer true or false to a specific statement. Perhaps you have completed a personality questionnaire for a potential job or on an online dating site? In college settings, many students have completed the *Myers-Briggs Personality Inventory.* This test assesses an individual's personality on four different dimensions. In clinical settings, the most frequently used personality inventory is the **Minnesota Multiphasic Personality Inventory (MMPI-2)**.

The MMPI-2 is a 567-item true/false questionnaire that takes about 1 hour to complete. The questions describe a wide range of behaviors (● TABLE 11.4). The purpose of the MMPI-2 is to identify problem areas of functioning in an individual's

personality inventories objective paper-and-pencil or computerized self-report forms that measure personality on several dimensions or traits

Minnesota Multiphasic [mul-tee-FAZE-ick] Personality Inventory (MMPI-2) a personality inventory that is designed to identify problem areas of functioning in an individual's personality

TABLE 11.4 Sample MMPI-2 Items

I have trouble with my bowel movements.	T	F
I do not sleep well.	T	F
At parties, I sit by myself or with one other person.	T	F
A lot of people have it in for me.	T	F
In school, I was frequently in trouble for acting up.	T	F
I am anxious most of the time.	T	F
I hear strange things that others do not hear.	T	F
I am a very important person.	T	F

projective test a less structured and subjective personality test in which an individual is shown an ambiguous stimulus and is asked to describe what they see

Rorschach [ROAR-shock] Inkblot Test a projective personality test consisting of 10 ambiguous inkblots in which a person is asked to describe what they see; the person's responses are then coded for consistent themes and issues

Thematic Apperception [thee-MAT-ick ap-per-SEP-shun] Test (TAT) a projective personality test consisting of a series of pictures in which the respondent is asked to tell a story about each scene; the responses are then coded for consistent themes and issues

FIGURE 11.5

Sample Rorschach Inkblot

After being shown an inkblot like this one, the person indicates what they see on the card.

FIGURE 11.6

Sample Thematic Apperception Test (TAT) Card

In taking the TAT, a person is asked to tell a story about a scene such as this one.

personality. It is organized into 10 groups of items, called *clinical scales*. These scales measure patterns of responses or traits associated with specific mental health disorders such as depression, paranoia, and schizophrenia. A person's response patterns are reviewed to see whether they resemble the pattern of responses from groups of people who have these disorders. Interpreting the MMPI-2 involves comparing the test taker's responses to those of the "norming" population.

As part of its construction, the MMPI-2 was given to thousands of people, called a *norming group*. Individuals in the norming group included people who had no mental health disorders and people who had particular disorders. In this way, the test constructors could see how frequently someone without the disorder would respond "true" to these items and how frequently someone with the mental health disorder would respond "true." The first group established the average, or *normal*, number of items for each of these clinical scales, whereas the second group gave an indication of what would be considered problematic functioning. A psychologist or mental health professional is interested in examining any areas of your personality that fall outside the normal range. These areas would be considered problem areas of your personality and might suggest issues for therapy.

Another widely used personality inventory is the *California Psychological Inventory (CPI)*. The CPI contains 434 true/false items, including 194 from the original MMPI. Unlike the MMPI, the CPI was developed to measure positive traits such as sociability, independence, and responsibility in healthy individuals. The CPI norming groups did not contain people who had been diagnosed with mental health problems.

One of the main problems with self-report measures such as the MMPI-2 and CPI is the test taker's honesty or truthfulness. For this reason, both the MMPI-2 and CPI contain *validity scales* to assess the truthfulness of the individual's responses.

11.5.2 Projective Tests: Tell Me What You See

Another type of tool used to measure personality, the **projective test**, is less structured than the personality inventory. When taking this test, you are shown an ambiguous image and then asked to describe what you see or to tell a story about the picture. Such tests rely on the idea that whatever stories, motives, or explanations you offer reflect your own issues and concerns, projected onto the image.

One of the most famous projective tests is the **Rorschach Inkblot Test**. The Rorschach test consists of 10 inkblots on cards. As each card is presented, you indicate what images you see. Your responses are then coded according to specific guidelines to decrease subjectivity and enhance the validity of the results. A sample card is shown in • FIGURE 11.5.

Another widely used projective test is the **Thematic Apperception Test (TAT)**. In the TAT, you are shown images that are not as ambiguous as inkblots yet still allow for a variety of interpretations. You are asked to tell a story about the image, and your responses are then coded for any consistent themes, emotions, or issues. An image like those used in the TAT is depicted in • FIGURE 11.6. After being shown this image, a client might relate the following story: "It's a picture of a young man who has been waiting several hours at a park for his partner to arrive. He is tired, anxious, and angry. He is hoping that nothing bad has happened to his partner. He is also hoping that he wasn't stood up."

The purpose of projective tests is similar to that of personality inventories. Psychologists and other mental health professionals want to pinpoint healthy and unhealthy areas of functioning in the individual being tested. However, unlike personality inventories, projective tests are derived from the psychoanalytic perspective; the images and stories described are thought to reflect underlying unconscious urges and desires. Because projective tests are more subject to the interpretation of the clinician than are personality inventories, coding systems have been devised to decrease variation in interpretation and increase their reliability in measuring personality. Projective tests are most useful for identifying themes in a person's life or for delineating an individual's problem-solving style.

11.5.3 Rating Scales and Direct Observation

A third type of tool used by psychologists to measure personality is the *rating scale*. Rating scales are formatted similarly to checklists. You check off the statements or behaviors that most apply to you. Because the person being evaluated may not answer the statements truthfully, teachers, parents, partners, and clinicians can also complete rating scales on the person being evaluated. These alternate perspectives minimize the self-distortions that are associated with self-report instruments.

Psychologists may also rely on directly observing a client's behavior and interactions with others to assess personality. Closely watching how you behave in particular situations can be helpful in determining what happens before and after your responses. Such information is particularly important to clinicians who favor a social cognitive approach and who want to understand the social or environmental factors that may be influencing problem behavior.

Engage Yourself!

Psychologists may find rating scales on self-esteem and self-concept useful for understanding how a person perceives reality and feels about themselves. Take a moment to complete the self-esteem scale provided in ● TABLE 11.5.

TABLE 11.5 Rosenberg Self-Esteem Scale

Below is a list of statements dealing with your general feelings about yourself. If you Strongly Agree, circle *SA*. If you Agree with the statement, circle *A*. If you Disagree, circle *D*. If you Strongly Disagree, circle *SD*.

		Strongly Agree	Agree	Disagree	Strongly Disagree
1.	I feel that I'm a person of worth, at least on an equal plane with others.	SA	A	D	SD
2.	I feel that I have a number of good qualities.	SA	A	D	SD
3.	All in all, I am inclined to feel that I am a failure.	SA	A	D	SD
4.	I am able to do things as well as most other people.	SA	A	D	SD
5.	I feel I do not have much to be proud of.	SA	A	D	SD
6.	I take a positive attitude toward myself.	SA	A	D	SD
7.	On the whole, I am satisfied with myself.	SA	A	D	SD
8.	I wish I could have more respect for myself.	SA	A	D	SD
9.	I certainly feel useless at times.	SA	A	D	SD
10.	At times I think I am no good at all.	SA	A	D	SD

Scoring:
For items 1, 2, 4, 6, 7 Strongly Agree = 3; Agree = 2; Disagree = 1; Strongly Disagree = 0
For items 3, 5, 8, 9, 10 Strongly Agree = 0; Agree = 1; Disagree = 2; Strongly Disagree = 3
The scale ranges from 0 to 30, with 30 indicating the highest score possible. There are no discrete cutoff points for high and low self-esteem. Higher scores indicate more positive feelings toward the self while lower scores indicate more negative feelings toward the self.

Source: Rosenberg, M. (1989). *Society and the Adolescent Self-image.* Middletown, CT: Wesleyan University Press.

clinical interview the initial meeting between a client and a clinician in which the clinician asks questions to identify the difficulty in functioning that the person is experiencing

11.5.4 Clinical Interviews

One tool used by most mental health professionals to assess personality is the **clinical interview**. This interview, which typically takes place during the first meeting between the client and the clinician, involves the clinician asking the client questions to identify the client's difficulty in functioning. The format and length of the interview, as well as the questions that are asked during the interview, may differ from clinician to clinician. These differences again relate to the alternate views on personality that were discussed in this chapter. For example, a clinician who favors the social cognitive approach is more likely to ask specific questions about social situations and patterns of thought. This clinician may want to know what you were thinking about prior to, during, and after a particular behavior occurred. A humanist is more likely to focus on the client's interpretation and perception of reality. The focus of any clinical interview, however, is to identify as clearly as possible the difficulty in functioning that the person is experiencing. This difficulty is often given a name, or *diagnosis*. The exact nature of these diagnoses is covered in Chapter 13.

11.5 Quiz Yourself

1. **The major disadvantage of self-report instruments such as the MMPI-2 and the CPI is ____.**
   a. the subjective interpretation of the results by the clinician
   b. the respondents may not tell the truth
   c. the scoring criteria are very vague and unreliable
   d. there are no norms to compare one's responses against
2. **Tamara goes to see a clinical psychologist. The psychologist asks her to look at some vague pictures and report what she sees. Most likely Tamara is taking a ____.**
   a. personality inventory
   b. projective test
   c. rating scale
   d. clinical interview
3. **When one goes to a clinical psychologist or mental health therapist, the first session is most likely to involve ____.**
   a. validity testing
   b. a physical examination
   c. hypnosis
   d. a clinical interview

Answers 1. b; 2. b; 3. d

11.6 Integrating Psychology: The Big Picture

This chapter presented four different views of personality: the *psychoanalytic perspective*, the *trait approach*, the *social cognitive perspective*, and the *humanistic approach*. Rather than debating which of these perspectives is "right," many psychologists prefer instead to see these viewpoints as complementary. Just as a photographer may take the same picture from many different angles, psychologists, too, like to understand personality from varying viewpoints. When taken together, these theories provide a much more complex and richer view of the forces that make us unique than any single perspective could do.

These complementary perspectives also underscore the necessity in understanding and integrating the different areas of contemporary psychology. Reconsider all the potential forces that influenced Hongyong's Baek's personality. Biologically, she may have inherited traits and drives that motivated her to succeed at business and have the fortitude to move her family to freedom. Her cognitive processes helped her solve problems and learn how to read and write, despite being raised at a time when women did not learn these skills. Yet Hongyong fulfilled the valued cultural roles as mother and wife while still finding meaning in her life with her *ch'iryo* practice. However, her journey was not without challenges as she battled health problems and depression when she lost her son and then after her husband's death. Such challenges illustrate the importance of understanding physical and mental health processes—our next and last foundation of psychology to explore.

Studying the Chapter

Key Terms

actualizing tendency (510)
anal stage (493)
archetypes (495)
basic anxiety (496)
behavioral genetics (503)
cardinal traits (499)
central traits (498)
clinical interview (516)
collective unconscious (495)
conscious level (490)
defense mechanisms (492)
ego (491)
Electra complex (493)
emotional stability (501)
extraversion (501)
five factor theory (502)
genital stage (494)
humanistic approach (509)
id (491)
introversion (501)
latency stage (494)
locus of control (508)
Minnesota Multiphasic Personality Inventory (MMPI-2) (513)
neuroticism (501)
Oedipus complex (493)
oral stage (493)
personal unconscious (495)
personality (489)
personality inventories (513)
person–situation interaction (505)
phallic stage (493)
pleasure principle (491)
preconscious level (490)
projective test (514)
psychoanalytic perspective (490)
psychoticism (501)
reality principle (491)
reciprocal determinism (507)
reliability (512)
Rorschach Inkblot Test (514)
secondary traits (499)
self-actualization (509)
self-concept (510)
self-efficacy (507)
sensation seekers (498)
social cognitive approach (506)
source traits (500)
superego (491)
surface traits (500)
Thematic Apperception Test (TAT) (514)
traits (497)
trait approach (497)
unconditional positive regard (511)
unconscious level (490)
validity (512)

What Do You Know? Assess Your Understanding

Test your retention and understanding of the material by answering the following questions.

1. Which perspective suggests that human beings have genetic dispositions to behave in a certain way across situations?
   a. Psychoanalytic perspective
   b. Trait perspective
   c. Humanistic perspective
   d. Social cognitive perspective

2. Meera's friends describe her as warm and giving across most situations. According to Allport, warm and giving are ______ of Meera's.
   a. central traits
   b. source traits
   c. cardinal traits
   d. primary traits

3. Which personality perspective emphasizes the influence of unconscious forces on personality?
   a. Psychoanalytic perspective
   b. Trait perspective
   c. Humanistic perspective
   d. Social cognitive perspective

4. Timothy feels very confident about his writing abilities. Bandura would say that Timothy has high ______ for his writing.
   a. extraversion
   b. self-efficacy
   c. determinism
   d. self-concept

5. Even though her mother told her not to, Gretchen had a second piece of chocolate cake. Which personality structure, according to Freud, motivated Gretchen's behavior?

a. Superego
b. Ego
c. Id
d. The preconscious

6. Which of the following is *not* one of the traits of the five factor theory?

a. Openness to experience
b. Extraversion
c. Conformity
d. Agreeableness

7. Defense mechanisms are used to handle intrapsychic conflict between which two personality structures?

a. Id and ego
b. Id and superego
c. Ego and superego
d. The ego and the preconscious

8. Which theory examines the influence of one's environment, behaviors, and thoughts on personality?

a. Hierarchy of needs
b. Locus of control
c. Self theory
d. Reciprocal determinism

9. The Oedipus and Electra complexes occur during which psychosexual stage?

a. Phallic
b. Latency
c. Anal
d. Genital

10. People generally become more ______ and less ______ across adulthood.

a. neurotic; introverted
b. emotionally stable; extraverted
c. extraverted; conscientious
d. open to experience; agreeable

11. Melinda believes that hard work and determination have led to her successful career. According to Rotter, Melinda has a(n) ______.

a. positive self-concept
b. external locus of control
c. internal locus of control
d. overactive superego

12. You take a personality test in which you are asked to indicate how well a statement describes you. Most likely you are taking which of the following personality tests?

a. MMPI-2
b. IQ test
c. Rorschach Inkblot Test
d. TAT

13. Your long-term memories most likely reside in which level of consciousness?

a. Unconscious
b. Subconscious
c. Preconscious
d. Conscious

14. Wally is described as moody, tense, and anxious. According to Eysenck, Wally is high in ______.

a. extraversion
b. neuroticism
c. fearfulness
d. psychoticism

15. Marley is in high school and very much wants to be a part of the in-crowd. According to Maslow, Marley is trying to fulfill ______ needs.

a. peer
b. safety
c. belongingness
d. esteem

16. Donny's parent is very upset when his grades slip below a B level. Donny feels that he must make good grades in order to receive his parent's love and acceptance. According to Rogers, Donny perceives ______ from his parent.

a. unconditional positive regard
b. conditional positive regard
c. actualizing tendency
d. self-actualization

17. Shanique takes a self-esteem test in which she is asked to count to 10 and identify pictures of animals. This personality test most lacks ______.

a. validity
b. reliability
c. consistency
d. norming

18. In what way did Karen Horney agree with Freud on personality development?

a. Development arises from instinctual conflicts.
b. Personality is the result of psychosexual conflicts.
c. Culture plays a large role in personality development.
d. Early childhood is a significant time for personality development.

19. The humanistic approach has been criticized for ______.

a. not detailing personality development
b. relying too heavily on experimental data
c. its optimistic view that all people are good
d. All of the above

20. Which of the following is *not* a contribution of the psychoanalytic perspective?

a. Stimulated research on sleep and dreaming
b. Stimulated research on coping and health
c. Created personality tests and therapy approaches
d. Stimulated experimentation on learning and perception

Answers: 1. b; 2. a; 3. a; 4. b; 5. c; 6. c; 7. b; 8. d; 9. a; 10. b; 11. c; 12. a; 13. c; 14. b; 15. c; 16. b; 17. a; 18. d; 19. c; 20. d

Use It or Lose It: Applying Psychology

1. Which theory of personality do you find most compelling, and why?

2. Using one of the personality perspectives discussed in this chapter, analyze the personality of a favorite television or movie character.

3. How has your personality changed over the years? How has it remained the same? What theory or theories can best explain these changes and consistencies?

4. How would you go about constructing a personality test? How does the structure of your test relate to your perspective on personality?

5. Try to describe your personality in detail from each of the four perspectives discussed in this chapter.

Critical Thinking About the Science of Psychology

In Section 11.2.6, you read about a study conducted by Weisberg, DeYoung & Hirsch (2011) investigating gender differences in personality traits. 892 males and 1751 females completed questions designed to assess the five factor theory. Females reported higher extraversion, neuroticism, and agreeableness than males. Given this information, answer the following questions:

1. What type of research method was used?

2. What goal of psychology are the researchers addressing?

3. What was/were the dependent measure(s) in the study?

4. Distinguish between the sample and the population in this study.

Are You Getting the Big Picture?

Fancy/Alamy Stock Photo

Personality is the unique collection of attitudes, emotions, thoughts, habits, impulses, and behaviors that define how a person typically behaves across situations.

11.1 The Psychoanalytic Approach: Sigmund Freud and the Neo-Freudians

- Emphasizes unconscious aspects of personality. It proposes that personality operates at the **conscious**, **preconscious**, and **unconscious** levels.

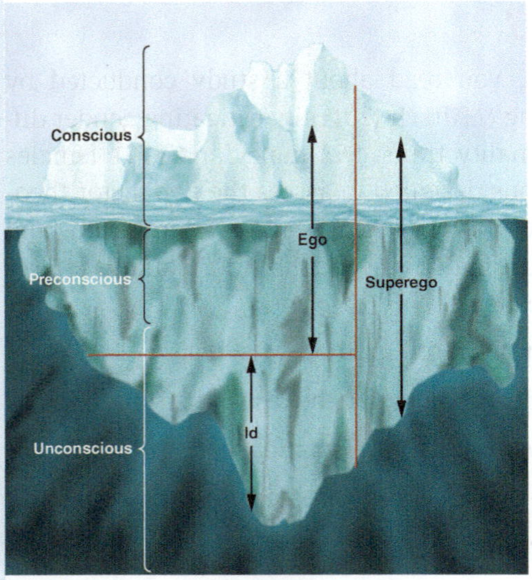

- According to Freud, personality is comprised of the unconscious **id** that operates according to the **pleasure principle**, the conscious **ego** that operates according to the **reality principle**, and the moral directives of the **superego**.
- For Freud, personality develops through a series of five psychosexual stages (**oral**, **anal**, **phallic**, **latency**, **genital**) that represent a complex interaction between natural sexual urges and our socialization experiences.
- Neo-Freudians such as Jung, Adler, and Horney placed less emphasis on the role of instinctual impulses in motivating behavior.

Hulton Archive/Getty Images

11.2 The Trait Approach: Consistency and Stability in Personality

- Attempts to describe personality by identifying the internal **traits**, or tendencies that we have across most situations.
- Allport classified traits into three types: **central**, **cardinal**, and **secondary** traits.
- Cattell's factor analysis of traits yielded 16 **source traits** that could be measured in everyone. Eysenck proposed three universal traits in his PEN model: **psychoticism**, **extraversion**, and **neuroticism**.
- Costa and McCrae's **five factor theory** proposes five core universal traits: openness to experience, conscientiousness, extraversion, agreeableness, and neuroticism (OCEAN).
- Research suggests a complex interaction between genes and the environment in producing personality. Some traits remain stable over the course of adulthood, but situational factors also influence the consistency of traits.

Ashley Cooper/Alamy stock photo

11.3 The Social Cognitive Approach: The Environment and Patterns of Thought

- Evaluates environmental and cognitive factors that influence personality.
- Bandura's **reciprocal determinism** suggests that personality is due to the mutual interaction among one's environment, behaviors, and thoughts. A critical cognitive element is **self-efficacy**, or the expectation one has for success in a given situation.
- Rotter believes that one's **locus of control**, or one's expectations of whether the outcome of an event is due to internal or external forces, influences personality.
- The **social cognitive approach** is comprehensive, has many applications, and is easily tested experimentally.

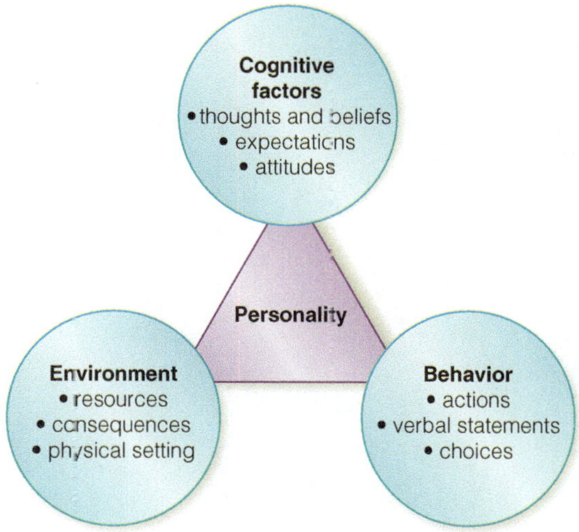

11.4 The Humanistic Approach: Free Will and Self-Actualization

- Emphasizes one's drive toward uniqueness and **self-actualization**.
- Maslow believed that the pathway to self-actualization lies in fulfilling a hierarchy of needs, with physical needs at the bottom and psychological needs at the top.
- Rogers's self theory emphasizes how one's **self-concept**, or perception of self, is influenced by the standards and values of others, most notably the degree to which we perceive and receive **unconditional positive regard** from others.
- The **humanistic approach** promotes self-awareness and positive interactions with others, and its ideas have been incorporated into several therapy approaches.

Michael Rougier/Time & Life Pictures/Contributor/Getty Images

11.5 Scientifically Measuring Personality

- Tools that assess personality should be **reliable** and **valid**.
- **Personality inventories** such as the **MMPI-2** and CPI are objective paper-and-pencil or computerized self-report forms that can reliably describe a person's traits if answered honestly.
- **Projective tests** such as the **Rorschach Inkblot Test** and the **Thematic Apperception Test (TAT)** are less structured tests in which a person is shown an ambiguous image and asked to describe it. According to the psychoanalytic perspective, a person's responses are believed to reflect underlying unconscious concerns.
- Psychologists may also use rating scales and direct observation to measure behaviors and interactions with others.
- The focus of the **clinical interview** is to identify the difficulty in functioning that a person is experiencing.

Part 4

Foundations in Physical and Mental Health

The final foundation of psychology focuses on *physical* and *mental health*. It emphasizes a "biopsychosocial" approach that highlights how biological, psychological, and social factors contribute to both physical and mental health behaviors. The term *biopsychosocial* underscores how interrelated these factors are in understanding a person's physical and mental functioning. Part 4 includes three topics: health, mental health disorders, and mental health therapies. Chapter 12 introduces **health psychology** and **positive psychology**, the study of how people's behavior influences their physical and psychological health for better and for worse, and the behaviors that lead to meaningful and productive lives. This chapter examines how stress, coping, personality, and lifestyles influence our health and well-being. Chapter 13 outlines the major **mental health disorders** such as depressive disorders, anxiety disorders, and schizophrenia. It includes the main symptoms of these disorders as well as our current understanding of what contributes to such problems. Chapter 14 explores therapy. **Therapy** consists of techniques that are used to help people with mental health or interpersonal problems. Because all of us sometimes experience difficulty in functioning, these topics offer much psychological research that will be relevant to your day-to-day living. It will help you realize how some of your personal habits, thoughts, or daily actions may be problematic, and hopefully will enable you to change them and enhance your personal well-being. To illustrate, consider for a moment the following story.

THE BIG PICTURE

THE UPS AND DOWNS OF LIFE

When most adolescents enter adulthood, especially when they come from privilege, it is thought of as a carefree, exciting time in life. It is often considered a time to go to college, enter the workforce or both, and discover and nurture one's talents and ambitions. But this is often not the case for young people who struggle with mental health issues. Emily's teenage years centered around mental health institutions. Her childhood was not entirely unhappy. By outward appearances, her early childhood was enriched with music, literature, and engaging activities. But inwardly, Emily felt emotionally neglected by her parents. Emily's father, a professor of economics, was tense, intellectual, judgmental, easily angered, and focused on work and achievement. Her mother was often sad and depressed, and often abused alcohol.

Emily gained her parents' attention by being disobedient and acting out. She was an underachiever at school, had difficulty learning, and spent hours in detention for misbehavior. Her father called her careless

In this Part:

and clumsy. Her mother was embarrassed by her. Her behavior and academic performance were unacceptable to her achievement-oriented parents—children of immigrant parents who cut their religious and cultural ties to achieve the "American dream." Emily was curious about religion, but it was scorned by her parents. She felt awkward, fat, and hopeless, and spent more and more time reading or alone. Emily had difficulty fitting in and felt like a misfit. She experienced unprecedented rages and panic, developing a spastic colon and rapid heartbeat. She regarded herself as the difficult child, the family scapegoat, and an outcast at school. She felt forgotten and was hungry for spiritual and emotional connections.

Emily Fox Gordon

Emily Fox Gordon

In the eighth grade, Emily was sent to Dr. V., a therapist, following another incident at school in which she angrily chased another student with what school administrators described as an intention to inflict physical harm. In these therapy sessions, Emily would lie down on a couch while Dr. V. remained silent in a chair. Not knowing what to do, Emily remained silent as well, listening to Dr. V. steadily scribbling on a notepad. After a year, Emily's family moved, and she continued therapy to deal with her rage and panic. She was sent to see Dr. H. There, Emily sat on a couch and Dr. H. remained silent in a nearby chair, knitting a sweater. After a year of listening to the click-clacking of knitting needles, therapy with Dr. H. was terminated.

Emily's problems at home and school continued. She was kicked out of several private schools for misbehavior and truancy. She often snuck out of her parents' house at night to hang out with two brothers who were also social outcasts. They would stay out half the night smoking cigarettes and roaming the town. On one of these occasions, at 16, Emily's father found her at an unchaperoned party with a boy in a dark room, where they were kissing and groping one another. Her father dragged her out of the party and drove her home. Furious with her parents, Emily broke an aspirin jar and, using a piece of the glass, scratched her wrists in a half-hearted suicide attempt. Her parents sent her to see another therapist, Dr. G.

Therapy with Dr. G. was different from what Emily had experienced before. She sat facing him and was encouraged to talk freely about her dreams, stress, and problems, while Dr. G. looked for themes threaded through her discussions. She saw Dr. G. on and off through her high school years. After she again attempted suicide at age 18, Dr. G. recommended an inpatient facility for Emily. She was placed in the highly regarded Austen Riggs treatment center in Massachusetts. Her intelligence was measured and she was given the Rorschach Inkblot test. During her interview she stated she felt detached and disengaged. Emily was diagnosed as having an anxiety problem with borderline personality trends. She stayed at Riggs for three years, one year as an inpatient and another two years as an outpatient in residential apartments.

As an inpatient, Emily was told when to eat and sleep, and she attended group meetings. If she did not get her assigned chores done or go to bed at the appropriate time, she lost privileges. Patients received medication at regular intervals. Her first therapist in the hospital was considerably different from her previous therapists. He took walks with Emily, drank wine with her and her roommate, and on one occasion put his arm around her waist. On the one hand, Emily craved his affection and attention; but on the other hand, she knew he was becoming inappropriately attached to her, and so she searched for a new therapist. She was fortunate enough to find Dr. Leslie Farber.

Dr. Farber's approach seemed radically different. He emphasized the presence of will in human behavior, and he communicated to Emily that he believed in her and her value. He shared with Emily anecdotes about his own life that were similar to her experiences and feelings. He treated her with warmth and understanding rather than aloofness or pity. He challenged her personal beliefs and highlighted her negative self-remarks. Emily felt as if she was being treated as a fellow human being. At Dr. Farber's urging, Emily studied for and passed her GED certification. She completed a few courses at the local college. Yet she still had times of difficulty while an outpatient. She would hang out at the local bar, drink heavily, and wait to be picked up by men. She had many sexual partners. When Dr. Farber moved to New York to set up a practice, Emily followed. She found an apartment and a job and continued to meet with Dr. Farber. Through many years and many therapy sessions, Dr. Farber helped Emily "recover" her life and discover her "best self."

In her adulthood, Emily married, gave birth to a daughter, and went on to earn a bachelor's and a master's degree in English. She taught English at a local college and joined women's writing groups. She reentered therapy in her adulthood to cope with her emotional anger, neediness, and marital conflict, and at this time was diagnosed with depression. Since ending therapy, Emily has realized writing as a way to make sense of her thoughts, history, and the world. She has written four books and has taught writing workshops at several U.S. universities.

Courtesy of Emily Fox Gordon

▲ Emily Fox Gordon's novel, *Mockingbird Years*, highlights how biological, psychological, and social factors can influence our ability to function in a healthy or unhealthy way.

As you can see, Emily experienced many stressors and did not effectively cope with them. Despite having money, she did not always receive effective help to learn positive ways of coping. Her journey, detailed in one of her books, *Mockingbird Years: A Life In and Out of Therapy* (2000), highlights how biological, psychological, and social factors can influence our ability to function in a healthy or unhealthy way. As you read the chapters in this part, you will gain a deeper understanding of how stress and coping impact our physical and psychological health, the criteria for various mental health disorders, and the therapy techniques that can improve our functioning. As you are on this journey, think about your own behaviors. How do you cope with stress? How did you learn to do so? How might gaining insight into difficulty in functioning improve your own physical and mental health? By understanding stress and coping, mental health disorders, and therapy as an intersection of biological, psychological, and social factors, you will hopefully be able to recognize healthy and unhealthy patterns of functioning in yourself and the people around you, learn how to successfully cope with the difficult times, and be better able to weather the ups and downs of life. ■

Learning Objectives

12.1 Define stress and discriminate among the four types of stressors. (APA 1.1, 1.3)

12.1 Define resilience and describe key factors in its expression. (APA 1.1, 1.3)

12.1 Distinguish among the four types of conflict situations and give examples of each. (APA 1.2, 1.3)

12.2 Discuss the role of cognitive appraisal in the biological stress response. (APA 1.2, 5.1)

12.2 Explain the HPA axis and how the body responds to stress and how this physiological response may vary in males and females. (APA 1.1, 2.5, 3.2, 3.3)

12.2 Discuss how the stress response influences immunity to disease. (APA 1.2, 2.1, 5.1)

12.3 Distinguish between problem-focused and emotion-focused coping styles, providing examples of each. (APA 1.1, 1.2, 1.3)

12.3 Describe positive and adaptive ways to manage and cope with stress and explain how these techniques influence the stress response and one's health and well-being. (APA 1.3, 5.1)

12.4 Discriminate among Type A, Type B, Type C, and Type D personalities, and critically examine the research on the relationship between these personality types and health and well-being. (APA 1.1, 2.1, 3.2)

12.4 Define learned helplessness and explain its influence on health and well-being. (APA 1.1, 1.3, 5.1)

12.4 Explain the three factors of a hardy personality and its relationship to stress and positive coping. (APA 1.2, 3.2)

12.5 Identify health-defeating behaviors and describe how alcohol use and smoking negatively influence health and well-being. (APA 1.2, 1.3, 5.1)

12.5 Discriminate among the various sexually transmitted infections, understanding their causes, modes of transmission, and treatment options. (APA 1.1, 1.2, 3.3)

12.5 Identify health-promoting behaviors, and apply how physical activity, eating habits, and sleep influence health and well-being. (APA 1.3, 5.1)

12.5 Identify the factors that contribute to happiness and well-being. (APA 1.3, 3.2, 3.3)

Kathleen Finlay/Masterfile

12 Health, Stress, and Positive Psychology

In this chapter, we'll explore the fields of **health psychology** and **positive psychology.** Health psychologists study how a person's behavior, thoughts, personality, and attitudes influence one's health for better and for worse. Positive psychology seeks to discover and promote those factors that contribute to happiness and well-being. In this regard, health and well-being are seen as the result of the interaction among biological, psychological, and social forces highlighting a "biopsychosocial" approach introduced in the part opening (Brannon & Feist, 2004; S. E. Taylor, 2003). The main topics of this chapter center around stress and coping. We saw in this part's case study how the stress of Emily's home life and her difficulty at school, combined with her ineffective ways of coping, influenced her thoughts, behavior, and feelings of well-being. Because all of us cope with stress on a daily basis, this chapter offers much psychological research that will be relevant to your day-to-day living. We hope that you will be able to apply the information in this chapter to Emily's story as well as your own life and realize how personal habits, thoughts, and daily actions influence your physical and psychological health. Hopefully, this analysis will encourage you to live a healthier and happier life! ■

Chapter Outline

12.1 What Is Stress? Stress and Stressors

You are running late for school and your car breaks down—today of all days, when you have a major project due in one course and a midterm in another. Or maybe you're a working parent, trying to get the kids off to school in the morning, when your youngest can't find her shoes and the dog just got into the garbage. Perhaps you have just fallen in love and have decided to make the relationship more serious. Or maybe you have grown dissatisfied with your relationship and are contemplating ending it. All of these situations have one thing in common: they all include *stress*, an inevitable and unavoidable fact of life.

health psychology the subfield of psychology that investigates the relationship between people's behaviors and their health

positive psychology the subfield of psychology that seeks to discover and promote those factors that contribute to happiness and well-being

stress any event or environmental stimulus (stressor) that we respond to because we perceive it as challenging or threatening

life events changes in one's life, good or bad, that require readjustment

Stress is difficult to define because it is perceived and experienced differently from one person to the next. In simplest terms, **stress** can be defined as any event or environmental stimulus (stressor) that we respond to because we perceive it as challenging or threatening. This definition implies three aspects to stress. First, we all encounter *stressors*—stimuli in our lives that we perceive as challenges or threats, such as traffic, an approaching midterm exam, or a hurricane. Second, our *reactions* to these stressors include physiological and behavioral changes. Third, by perceiving and then reacting, we *cope* with the challenges or threats (successfully or not, as we will see). Consequently, stress is a psychological state, uniquely perceived by the individual, accompanied by predictable physical and behavioral changes in response to environmental change or threat, that forces the person to react or cope with the change. As you can see, stress is complex and multidimensional.

Briefly reflect on an ordinary day in your life. You probably perceive many events or stimuli as provoking or annoying: a long line at the fast-food drive-through, a confrontation with your boss, or the need to do several errands in a limited amount of time. There probably have also been events in your life that you found to be particularly trying or traumatic, such as the death of a loved one, an unplanned pregnancy, termination from your job, or dealing with the COVID-19 pandemic. Stressors come in all shapes and sizes. Emily's story illustrated several stressors: difficulty at school, conflicts with her father, and frequent changes in schools and therapists. Psychological research classifies these stressors into four types:

- Major life events
- Catastrophes and trauma
- Daily hassles
- Conflict

Let's take a look at how each of these stressors is defined and explore the impact that they have on our health and well-being.

Image Source/Getty Images

▲ Life events, both good and bad, can be perceived as stressful and require us to adjust to them.

12.1.1 Life Events: Change Is Stressful

How do we know which events in our life qualify as major, rather than minor, stressors when they all feel stressful? Believe it or not, psychologists have tried to measure this difference. Pioneering research by Thomas Holmes and Richard Rahe in 1967 set out to measure the impact of particular stressors on people's physical health. They asked a large sample group to rate **life events**, or changes in one's living, both good and bad, that require us to adjust to them. In other words, which life events did the respondents perceive as more or less stressful? From these ratings, Holmes and Rahe (1967) developed the *Social Readjustment Rating Scale* (SRRS), reprinted in ● TABLE 12.1.

TABLE 12.1 Holmes and Rahe's Social Readjustment Rating Scale

Rank	Life Event	Life Change Units	Rank	Life Event	Life Change Units
1	Death of spouse	100	23	Son or daughter leaving home	29
2	Divorce	73	24	Trouble with in-laws	29
3	Marital separation	65	25	Outstanding personal achievement	28
4	Jail term	63	26	Spouse begins or stops work	26
5	Death of a close family member	63	27	Begin or end school	26
6	Personal injury or illness	53	28	Change in living conditions	25
7	Marriage	50	29	Revision of personal habits	24
8	Fired at work	47	30	Trouble with boss	23
9	Marital reconciliation	45	31	Change in work hours or conditions	20
10	Retirement	45	32	Change in residence	20
11	Change in health of family member	44	33	Change in school	20
12	Pregnancy	40	34	Change in recreation	19
13	Sex difficulties	39	35	Change in church activities	19
14	Gain of new family member	39	36	Change in social activities	18
15	Business readjustment	39	37	Take out loan less than $20,000	17
16	Change in financial state	38	38	Change in sleeping habits	16
17	Death of a close friend	37	39	Change in number of family get-togethers	15
18	Change to different line of work	36	40	Change in eating habits	15
19	Change in number of arguments with spouse	35	41	Vacation	13
20	Take out mortgage or loan for major purchase	31	42	Christmas	12
21	Foreclosure of mortgage or loan	30	43	Minor violation of the law	11
22	Change in responsibilities at work	29			

Note: In Holmes and Rahe's Social Readjustment Rating Scale, each major life event is assigned a numerical value. The higher the number, the more stressful the life event is perceived to be. Add up the life change units for all those events you have experienced in the past year. Then compare your total to the standards indicated in the text.

Source: From T. H. Holmes & R. H. Rahe (1967), "The Social Readjustment Rating Scale," in the *Journal of Psychosomatic Research*, Vol. 11, No. 2, pp. 213–218. Copyright © 1967 Elsevier Science

Holmes and Rahe assigned each major life event a numerical value, referred to as a *life change unit*. The higher the number, the more stressful this life event was rated by Holmes and Rahe's sample. Notice that the life events on the scale include positive as well as negative changes—for example, marriage, a new family member, and outstanding personal achievement. However, it is not just experiencing one of these events that is at issue. Rather, it is reacting to several of these events within a year that Holmes and Rahe found may influence one's physical health.

Engage Yourself! Take a moment to look at the Social Readjustment Rating Scale (Table 12.1). Add up the life change units for all those events you have experienced in the last year. Compare your total to the standards devised by Holmes and Rahe.

0–150	No significant problems
150–199	Mild life crisis
200–299	Moderate life crisis
300 or more	Major life crisis

Holmes and Rahe (1967) found that the higher people scored on the SRRS, the more prone they were to illness. Of those who scored within the mild life crisis range, 37% had experienced deteriorated health. This figure rose to 51% for those whose scores indicated they were experiencing a moderate life crisis, and 79% for those in the major life crisis range. Follow-up studies have supported Holmes and Rahe's findings (Gruen, 1993; Scully, Tosi, & Banning, 2000). If you scored high on the scale, you may want to consider adjusting your lifestyle in ways that reduce your chances of becoming ill. However, keep in mind that these are correlations and, as we discussed in Chapter 1, correlation does not mean causation. Life events do not directly cause illness, but they may make a person more vulnerable to illness and disease.

Subsequent research (Pearlin, 1993) evaluating Holmes and Rahe's scale indicates that the impact of these life changes is not simply a matter of how many of them one experiences. We need to take several other variables into account, including these:

- The voluntary or involuntary nature of the life change
- How desirable or undesirable the life change is perceived to be
- Whether the life change is scheduled or unscheduled

For example, when Emily's family moved, she had to change schools. This can be considered involuntary because she did not decide to move her family, undesirable as she would have to make new friends, and unforeseeable from a child's perspective. Consider as another example a couple about to break up. Typically, the partner who initiates the breakup feels less stress after telling the other person of their decision. In this context, the breakup is seen as voluntary, desirable, and scheduled. At the same time, the other person may experience increased stress, as the dissolution of the relationship is involuntary (not of the partner's choosing), undesirable, and unscheduled. As this example illustrates, the amount of stress one experiences when faced with life changes may vary across people. We can consider Holmes and Rahe's scale as a rough index of how susceptible some people may be to illness, given the number of major stressors the person encounters.

You may have noticed that the scale has very few life events that are likely to be experienced by college students and younger people. The SRRS has been criticized for not adequately defining stress events among younger age groups. Yet research supports the notion that major changes—such as the breakup of a relationship, academic pressure, or even college itself—may influence the physical and psychological health of college students (Crandall, Preisler, & Aussprung, 1992; Mohr et al., 2014). This is important, because perceived stress also seems to predict how well students perform academically. High levels of perceived stress in college and medical students correlate with lower grade point averages (Maville & Huerta, 1997; Rice et al., 2015; Sohail, 2013). For example, in one survey of college students (ACHA, 2017), stress and anxiety were the most frequent reasons given for academic problems. You may find that the Undergraduate Stress Questionnaire (● TABLE 12.2) includes more of the stressors that you typically

TABLE 12.2 Undergraduate Stress Questionnaire

Have any of the following stressful events happened to you at any time during the past semester? If any has, check the space next to it. If an item has not occurred, leave it blank. Stressful life events are listed in descending order of severity. Students with more checkmarks are more likely to need health care than students with fewer checkmarks.

____ 1. Death (family member or friend)
____ 2. Had a lot of tests
____ 3. It's finals week
____ 4. Applying to graduate school
____ 5. Victim of a crime
____ 6. Assignments in all classes due the same day
____ 7. Breaking up with boy/girlfriend
____ 8. Found out boy/girlfriend cheated on you
____ 9. Lots of deadlines to meet
____ 10. Property stolen
____ 11. You have a hard upcoming week
____ 12. Went into a test unprepared
____ 13. Lost something (especially wallet)
____ 14. Death of a pet
____ 15. Did worse than expected on test
____ 16. Had an interview
____ 17. Had projects, research papers due
____ 18. Did badly on a test
____ 19. Parents getting a divorce
____ 20. Dependent on other people
____ 21. Having roommate conflicts
____ 22. Car/bike broke down, flat tire
____ 23. Got a traffic ticket
____ 24. Missed your menstrual period and waiting
____ 25. Thoughts about future
____ 26. Lack of money
____ 27. Dealt with incompetence at the Registrar's Office
____ 28. Thought about unfinished work
____ 29. No sleep
____ 30. Sick, injury
____ 31. Had a class presentation
____ 32. Applying for a job
____ 33. Fought with boy/girlfriend
____ 34. Working while in school
____ 35. Arguments, conflict of values with friends
____ 36. Bothered by not having family's social support
____ 37. Performed poorly at a task
____ 38. Can't finish everything you need to do
____ 39. Heard bad news
____ 40. Had confrontation with an authority figure
____ 41. Maintaining a long-distance boy/girlfriend
____ 42. Crammed for a test
____ 43. Feel unorganized
____ 44. Trying to decide on major
____ 45. Feel isolated
____ 46. Parents controlling with money
____ 47. Couldn't find a parking space
____ 48. Noise disturbed you while trying to study
____ 49. Someone borrowed something without your permission
____ 50. Had to ask for money
____ 51. Ran out of ink while printing
____ 52. Erratic schedule
____ 53. Can't understand your professor
____ 54. Trying to get into your major or college
____ 55. Registration for classes
____ 56. Stayed up late writing a paper
____ 57. Someone you expected to call did not
____ 58. Someone broke a promise
____ 59. Can't concentrate
____ 60. Someone did a "pet peeve" of yours
____ 61. Living with boy/girlfriend
____ 62. Felt need for transportation
____ 63. Bad haircut today
____ 64. Job requirements changed
____ 65. No time to eat
____ 66. Felt some peer pressure
____ 67. You have a hangover
____ 68. Problems with your computer
____ 69. Problem getting home when drunk
____ 70. Used a fake I.D.
____ 71. No sex in a while
____ 72. Someone cut ahead of you in line
____ 73. Checkbook didn't balance
____ 74. Had a visit from a relative and entertained him/her
____ 75. Decision to have sex on your mind
____ 76. Spoke with a professor
____ 77. Change of environment (new doctor, dentist, etc.)
____ 78. Exposed to upsetting TV show, book, or movie
____ 79. Got to class late
____ 80. Holiday
____ 81. Sat through a boring class
____ 82. Favorite sports team lost

Source: C. S. Crandal et al., "Measuring Life Event Stress in the Lives of College Students: The Undergraduate Stress Questionnaire (USQ)," *in Journal of Behavioral Medicine, 15*(6), pp. 627–662, © 1992.

face than does Holmes and Rahe's SRRS. It was specifically designed to measure life event stress in college students. Undergraduates who have experienced many of these life events are more likely to report physical symptoms and are less likely to report a positive mood (Crandall et al., 1992). It may therefore provide a more accurate assessment of your stress level and hence your susceptibility to physical illness and/or emotional distress.

12.1.2 Catastrophes & Trauma

Unexpected traumatic events or *catastrophes* that almost all people perceive as threats also qualify as stressors. Catastrophes may affect one's physical and mental health (Bonanno et al., 2010). After catastrophic events such as floods, earthquakes, hurricanes, tornadoes, or fires, people are generally more likely to experience depression or anxiety (McKinzie, 2018; Neria, Nandi, & Galea, 2008; North & Pfefferbaum, 2013).

We have for a long time recognized the stress of war on soldiers, as evidenced by the pattern of symptoms that some soldiers experience when they return called *posttraumatic stress disorder (PTSD)*. Soldiers often experience nightmares, flashbacks, and vivid memories as they relive their war experiences. They may evidence intense startle responses to loud noises and have difficulty concentrating and getting along with others. Sexual assault victims report similar physical and psychological symptoms that may meet the criteria for a specific type of PTSD referred to as *rape trauma syndrome*—more evidence that unexpected events may take their toll on one's physical and psychological health. The rapid emergence of the COVID-19 pandemic has created considerable stress and distress for many people leading psychologists to coin the term, *COVID stress syndrome*. COVID stress syndrome is characterized mainly by worry over contracting the disease but also with worry about finances, intrusive thoughts and images about COVID-19, compulsive checking and reassurance-seeking regarding potential COVID-19 threats, and fear of foreigners carrying the infection (Taylor et al., 2020). Traumatic events and catastrophes are often involuntary, undesirable, and unscheduled, in that we typically don't have a lot of time to prepare for them; it is relatively easy to see how they might influence our health and well-being. We'll discuss PTSD in more detail in Chapter 13.

Do catastrophes or traumatic events always affect physical and mental health negatively? Not necessarily. Some people exposed to disaster may show chronic dysfunction, yet many others show remarkable *resilience* (discussed shortly), experiencing only temporary distress (Bonanno et al., 2010). Moreover, research has documented a potential positive effect of stressful life experiences for *some* people, referred to as *posttraumatic growth* or *benefit-finding*. People report that these events have changed their lives in positive ways, such as building stronger relationships with others, emphasizing enjoyment in life, and initiating positive changes in physical and emotional health behaviors (Bower, Moskowitz, & Epel, 2009; Mancini, Littleton, & Grills, 2016; Updegraff, Silver, & Holman, 2008). Research suggests that one important factor in making meaning out of traumatic experiences includes trying to understand the event as opposed to unwanted and uncontrollable thinking about the event (Kamijo & Yukawa, 2018; Wozniak et al., 2019), although there could be other variables that have yet to be investigated. It seems that for some people, a severe life-threatening event provides an opportunity to reevaluate their lives and prompts them to initiate positive changes.

Tony Arruza/Getty Images

▲ Unexpected catastrophes or traumatic events also cause stress and can influence one's physical and mental health.

12.1.3 Daily Hassles: Little Things Add Up!

When psychologists evaluate the relationship among stress, health, and well-being, they not only measure life changes and analyze the influence of catastrophes; they also evaluate the impact of everyday irritations and frustrations. These **daily hassles** also appear to play a role in our health and life satisfaction. At times these irritants add to the stress of major life changes and catastrophic events, such as the daily planning for a wedding or getting stuck in traffic during an evacuation due to a natural disaster. But for most of us, the routine annoyances and frustrations we experience on a daily basis are stressful in themselves. Can you think of any examples of daily hassles? Waiting in lines, lack of money, losing your wallet, or fights with loved ones are a few examples that may come to mind. Such daily hassles may in fact be the most significant source of stress, placing a great burden on our physical and mental health and on our relationships and sexual functioning (Charles et al., 2013; Hamilton & Julian, 2014; Lazarus, 1990; Repetti, Wang, & Saxbe, 2009). As the number of daily hassles increases, our physical and mental health tends to decrease (O'Connor et al., 2008; Sim, 2000). However, whether we perceive these frustrations as stressful is of prime importance in determining our susceptibility to illness. Some people easily shrug off these annoyances, whereas others find them particularly distressing such that the lingering negative emotions may also be detrimental to our health (Leger, Charles, & Almeida, 2018). Emily faced several daily hassles in school that she found upsetting and frustrating—difficulty learning, interactions with peers—which contributed to her upset stomach and rapid heartbeat.

Rubberball/Mike Kemp/Getty Images

▲ Everyday irritations and frustrations increase our stress level and can influence our physical health and well-being.

daily hassles the everyday irritations and frustrations that individuals face

Variations in Stress

Gender, race, age, socioeconomic status, sexual orientation, and education all seem to influence our perception of stressors (Almeida, 2005; Dunkel Schetter et al., 2013; Hamilton & Julian, 2014; Neubauer, Smyth, & Sliwinski, 2019; Taylor, 2002). Women are more likely than men to perceive stress from concerns about money, having a lot of things to do, health concerns, and trouble relaxing. In general, younger people report more daily hassles in their lives and perceive them to be more stressful than older people. Those with more money and more education also report lower levels of perceived stress from daily hassles than do those with lower income and less education. Although people who make more money and have more education may lead full and hectic lives, they generally perceive that they have more control over their lives and report having more fun. They are less likely to experience daily hassles concerning their own health, illness of a family member, trouble relaxing, problems at work, and exposure to excessive noise than are people with less education and lower incomes.

Racial and ethnic differences also appear in reports on daily hassles. African Americans are more likely than Hispanic or European Americans to report economic hassles, exposure to noise, feeling lonely, and invasion of personal privacy as frequent day-to-day hassles. Hispanic Americans are more likely than European or African Americans to report problems with aging parents as a hassle of daily living. Some minorities and immigrants may experience *acculturative stress,* or the difficulties associated with adapting to a new culture (Hovey, 2000; Torres et al., 2012).

Prejudice, stigma and discrimination are unique sources of stress for members of racial and sexual minority groups termed *minority stress* and members of lower-income groups (called *social-class discrimination*) (Bernstein et al., 2011; Burton, Wang & Pachankis, 2018; D'Anna et al., 2010; Dunkel Schetter et al., 2013; Fuller-Rowell et al.,

2012; Landor & McNeil-Smith, 2019; D. J. Levy et al., 2016; Lewis & Van Dyke, 2018; McClure et al., 2010; Padela & Heisler, 2010). Anticipating being discriminated against or interpreting others' behaviors as discriminatory can increase stress in some people. They worry that their behavior will be interpreted in a way that confirms negative stereotypes. Such situations are potentially stressful and can influence people's physical and mental health. For example, lesbian, gay, and bisexual adults who experience high levels of minority stress report more health problems and poorer overall health than those who experience less minority stress (Hatzenbuehler, 2014; Lick, Durso, & Johnson, 2013). Such research illustrates the impact that our interactions with others can have on our physical and mental well-being.

Resilience

As we have seen, considerable evidence indicates that major life events, catastrophes, trauma, and daily stressors can have negative effects on physical and mental health. However, we also have reason to believe that under the right conditions, facing adversity can build **resilience** or adapting well to significant stressors. Resilience essentially conveys "bouncing back" from adversity.

resilience the capacity to adapt well to significant stressors

Consider children who live in poverty, those who immigrate to another country, and/or those children who experience adverse life experiences such as abuse, neglect, household substance abuse, or parental incarceration. These are significant sources of stress that may be accompanied by housing problems, limited access to health care, fewer educational and employment opportunities, and/or limited economic resources for food, shelter, or the common necessities of life. Children who are raised in poor families or those who experience early-life adversity tend to have elevated rates of medical problems later in adulthood (Agahi, Shaw, & Fors, 2014; Cohen et al., 2010; Ortiz, 2019). Yet, remarkably, some of these children stay in good physical and mental health later in life and have high academic achievement despite their exposure to such challenges. What accounts for their resilience? The answer is quite complex.

Key factors in resilience may be related to biopsychosocial factors or multiple levels of influence. For example, a child's temperament, intelligence, or internal locus of control (Chapter 11) may play a role. Family factors such as social support and maternal warmth and nurturance may buffer children from the harmful effects of poverty (Miller et al., 2011). Positive peer relations and school adjustment and engagement also help youth adapt (Motto-Stefanidi, 2019). Some research suggests that successfully recovering from significant stress especially early in life may strengthen neural networks in our bodies such that we are less vulnerable or tougher to subsequent stressors later in life. In contrast, chronic, uncontrollable stress in childhood may weaken neural networks and alter immune system functioning such that one is more vulnerable to physical and mental health disorders in adulthood (Fagundes et al., 2013; Russell et al., 2014). Specific social-cognitive skills such as emotion recognition, optimism, and attention-shifting, also may be shaped by childhood adversity that allow one to successfully navigate future stressors (Ellis, Bianchi, Griskevicius, & Frankenhuis, 2017). For example, psychologist Edith Chen (2012) and her colleagues (Chen, McLean, & Miller, 2015; Chen & Miller, 2012) propose that some individuals from low socioeconomic conditions may develop *"shift-and-persist"* strategies that reduce their physical responses to the chronic stress they face, which then lessens their susceptibility to chronic disease. *Shifting* involves accepting stressors as uncontrollable and less threatening to reduce their emotional impact. *Persisting* involves enduring by finding meaning when times get tough and remaining optimistic about one's future.

Several investigations also suggest that experiencing moderate cumulative adversity is related to resilience. That is, both people who are sheltered from experiencing adversity and those who experience a high amount of lifetime adversity are more likely to report poorer physical and mental health and well-being compared to people who experience some or a moderate amount of lifetime adversity (Seery, 2011; Seery et al., 2013; Shapero et al., 2015). Similar to the shift-and-persist model, Seery and his colleagues speculate that perhaps some adversity allows a person to generate the necessary biopsychosocial resources to prepare for subsequent stressors. Future research will hopefully shed more light on the nature and development of resilience.

12.1.4 Conflict: Approach and Avoidance

conflict situation in which a person must choose between two or more needs, desires, or demands

approach-approach conflict situation in which a person must choose between two likable events

Conflict, or having to choose between two or more needs, desires, or demands, can also place stress on us. Should you take the required science course or the required math course? Should you wear the blue or the gray suit to the job interview? Whether we perceive these options as positive or negative results in four basic forms of conflict (● FIGURE 12.1):

1. *Approach–approach conflicts.* The easiest conflict to resolve, and therefore the conflict that is accompanied by the least amount of perceived stress, is the **approach-approach conflict**, in which a person must choose between two likable, or positive, events. Choosing between seeing an old friend who is passing through town or going out with someone you've been hoping to spend time with is an example of an approach-approach conflict. A more stressful approach-approach example could be liking and being challenged in your job and being offered another attractive and challenging position in the same company. In this type of conflict, you really can't lose because both options are favorable.

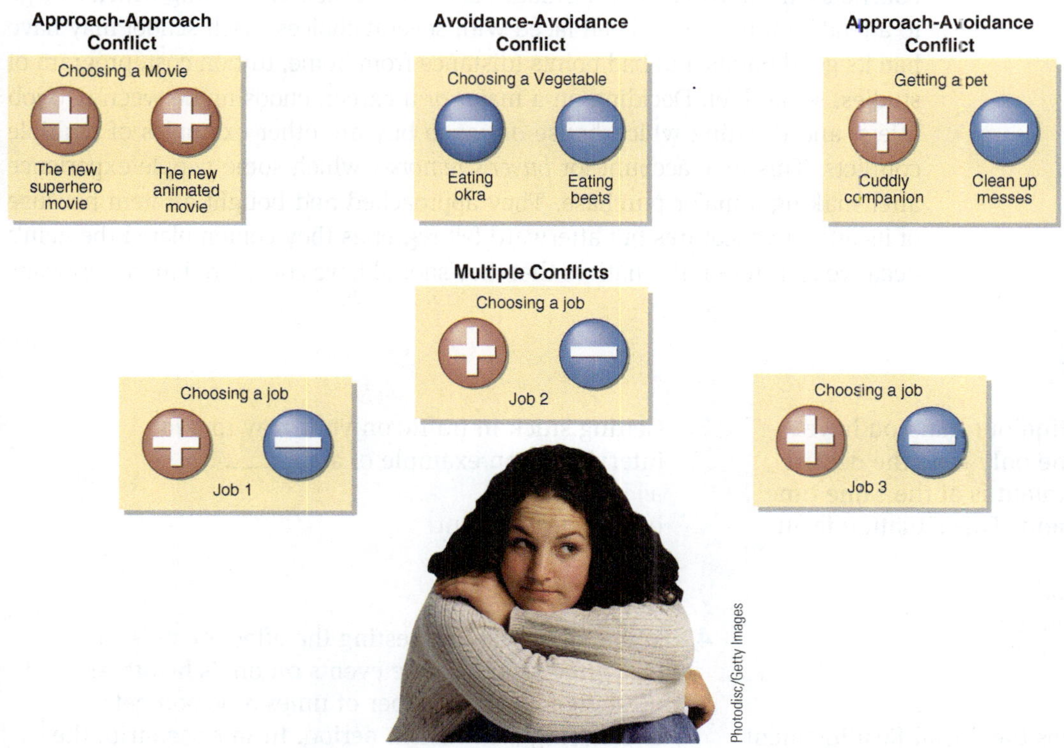

FIGURE 12.1

Four Common Conflict Situations

In an approach-approach conflict, a person must choose between two appealing choices—in this example, two movies one would like to see. In an avoidance-avoidance conflict, a person must choose between two undesirable choices—in this example, two disliked vegetables. In an approach-avoidance conflict, a person faces a decision that has both positive and negative features—in this example, owning a pet that cuddles yet also makes messes. Multiple approach-avoidance conflicts involve several choices that have both positive and negative qualities—in this example, choosing among three jobs.

avoidance-avoidance conflict a situation in which a person must choose between two undesirable events

approach-avoidance conflict a situation in which a person is faced with a desire or need that has both positive and negative aspects

multiple approach-avoidance conflicts situations that involve several choices, each of which has positive and negative features

2. *Avoidance–avoidance conflicts.* The opposite of the approach-approach conflict is the **avoidance-avoidance conflict**, in which a person has to choose between two undesirable, or negative, events. For example, do you spend the morning in line to register your car, or do you get your car towed because the registration has expired? Because both options in an avoidance-avoidance conflict are unappealing, many people remain undecided and inactive, or "frozen." They don't do anything. Consequently, avoidance-avoidance conflicts are accompanied by a greater degree of perceived stress than are approach-approach conflicts.
3. *Approach-avoidance conflicts.* Another stressful conflict to resolve is the **approach-avoidance conflict**, in which a person is faced with a desire or need that has both positive and negative qualities. The individual is drawn to the situation because of its positive features (approach), but is also repelled by and would rather not experience the negative aspects of the situation (avoidance). Emily's stay at Austen Riggs had elements of an approach-avoidance conflict. It gave Emily the opportunity to improve her mental health functioning, but at the same time limited her freedom. Or think of a home fire with your dog trapped inside the burning structure. You don't want to lose your lifelong friend and therefore want to save the dog, but attempting to do so may put your own life at risk. As with avoidance-avoidance conflicts, these situations may immobilize people so that they cannot make a decision or resolve the conflict, which leads to the experience of stress.
4. *Multiple conflicts.* In real life, many conflicts involve several alternatives, each with both positive and negative features. These **multiple approach-avoidance conflicts** can contribute to the amount of stress we feel. In deciding which college to attend, you may have been faced with several choices. Each school may have had its good points and bad points (distance from home, tuition cost, program of studies, social life). Deciding on a major or a career, choosing between two job offers, and deciding which house or car to buy are other examples of multiple conflicts. This may account for *buyer's remorse,* which some people experience after making a major purchase. They approached and bought an item because of its attractive features but afterward felt regret as they contemplated the item's negative features or alternatives that they should have considered more seriously.

12.1 Quiz Yourself

1. You go to the dentist and find out that you have to get a tooth extracted. The only time the dentist can schedule your appointment is at the same time as a traffic court appointment. This situation is an example of a(n) ______.
   a. approach-approach conflict
   b. approach-avoidance conflict
   c. avoidance-avoidance conflict
   d. multiple conflict
2. Which of the following does the Social Readjustment Rating Scale consider the most stressful major life event for adults?
   a. A jail term
   b. Death of a spouse
   c. Divorce
   d. Pregnancy
3. Getting stuck in traffic on your way to a job interview is an example of a ______.
   a. daily hassle
   b. major life event
   c. catastrophe
   d. stress response
4. You are a researcher testing the effect of stress as measured by major life events on one's health as measured by the number of times a person gets sick during a 12-month period. In this scenario, the independent variable is the ______.
   a. number of times a person gets sick
   b. 12-month period
   c. people
   d. number of major life events

Answers 1. c; 2. b; 3. a; 4. d

12.2 The Stress Response

Now that we have looked at the types of stressors that may influence physical and mental health, we will examine the second feature of stress: the reactions that accompany stress. This analysis will further your understanding of the relationship among stress, health, and well-being.

12.2.1 Cognitive Appraisal: Assessing Stress

We all experience stressors, especially daily hassles. We all wait in lines, sit in traffic, and pay bills. Yet not all of us interpret these events as equally stressful. Some people view giving blood as less stressful than others do. You may feel excited about giving a speech, whereas others cringe at the same prospect. Some people may view social-distancing during the COVID-19 outbreak as an opportunity to focus on self-care while others are stressed by the isolation. Therefore, the first step in experiencing stress is how you think about or interpret an event or situation. Our initial interpretation of an event is called our **primary appraisal** (Lazarus, 1991, 1993). This primary appraisal can be irrelevant, positive, or stressful.

primary appraisal [uh-PRAY-zull] our initial interpretation of an event as irrelevant, positive, or stressful

If your primary appraisal of an event is *irrelevant,* you interpret the situation as unrelated to your happiness or safety. For example, the number of students in a particular course you are taking may not make a difference to you one way or another. Class size may be appraised as not relevant to your performance in the class, and therefore viewed as not stressful. Primary appraisals also can be *positive.* For example, you may take a class in which there are a small number of students and view this situation as something good. Again, we typically don't feel much stress in situations such as these. However, when we appraise a situation as *stressful,* we believe it will require a great deal of our emotional and psychological resources. For example, you may view a small class size as stressful if you fear speaking in front of a group and are expected to participate in class discussion.

Our primary appraisal of an event as stressful can lead to positive or negative emotions that either increase or decrease our perceived stress levels (Barlow, 2002; Bovin & Marx, 2011). How much stress we experience will depend on whether we see the situation as a threat, a harm, or a challenge. If we appraise a stressful event as *threatening,* we believe that the situation will cause us some harm in the future. When we interpret an event in this manner, we typically feel fear, anxiety, or anger—negative emotions that increase our stress levels and decrease our performance (Gildea, Schneider, & Shebilske, 2007; Moore et al., 2013; Williams et al., 2017). For example, having to give an oral presentation on a project later in the term may be perceived as threatening by some students. They may fear negative evaluations by the professor or other students or be anxious that their voice will crack or that they will stammer. If we appraise an event as *harmful,* we believe it will do us some damage or injury. For example, one of the authors of your textbook appraised putting holiday lights up on her house as stressful because she believed that getting on the roof of her house would lead to injury. Again, such appraisals typically lead to feelings of fear and anxiety that increase our feelings of stress. However, situations can also be appraised as *challenging,* as a means toward personal growth or personal gain. For example, taking a new job may be appraised as an opportunity for career growth, or getting married may be appraised as an opportunity to deepen and expand the nature of an intimate relationship. Challenge appraisals typically elicit positive emotions such as excitement and happiness, and are therefore perceived as less stressful.

Not all primary appraisals break down easily into the categories of threat, harm, or challenge. A situation or event may involve a combination of appraisals. For example, starting a relationship, finding a job, and having a baby are complex

▲ Do you perceive an oral presentation as a threat or a challenge? A primary appraisal of threat will make you feel more stressed than viewing it as a challenge.

situations that may involve appraisals of both threat and challenge. Also, the appraisal process is a personal one. Not everyone appraises the same situation in the same manner. For example, some students may perceive course exams as threats, whereas other students may see them as challenges. Culture also influences the appraisal of everyday experiences. In individualistic cultures such as the United States, personal control and mastery are emphasized. In contrast, in collectivistic cultures such as China, connectedness with others is emphasized and perceived control is less valued. Consequently, a lack of perceived control may be associated with more psychological distress for those individuals from individualistic cultures than for those from collectivistic cultures (Bernardi & Jobson, 2019).

Once you appraise a situation or event as a threat or a challenge, you must evaluate what can be done to cope with or manage the stressor, referred to as **secondary appraisal** (Lazarus & Folkman, 1984). In secondary appraisal, people take into account the resources available to cope with the stressor. It includes an assessment of how they might cope, if that strategy or behavior will be successful in managing the stressor, and the likelihood that they can actually produce the necessary coping behaviors and strategies (discussed later in the chapter). Primary appraisals of threat or challenge interact with secondary appraisals of coping options to influence one's overall feelings of stress. If these appraisals lead to feelings of stress, your body changes to deal with the stressor.

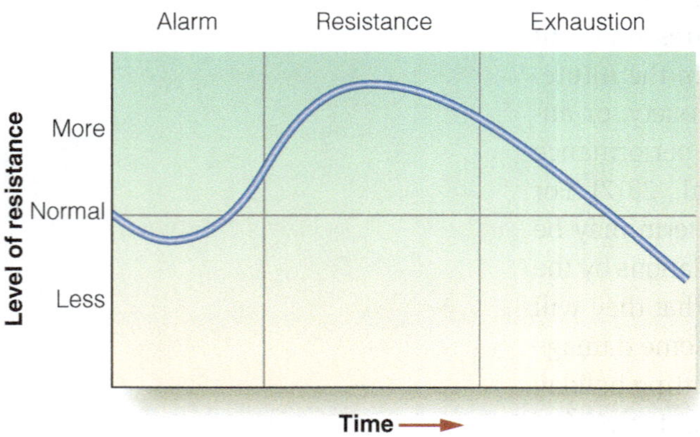

FIGURE 12.2

General Adaptation Syndrome

According to Hans Selye, the biological stress response consists of three phases. In the alarm reaction, the body releases chemicals to deal with a stressor. These chemicals lower the body's resistance. In the resistance stage, the body shores up additional resources to cope with the stressor. If the stressor persists, the body enters the exhaustion stage, in which bodily resources dwindle and we function at less than normal. Wear and tear on the body begin.

12.2.2 Selye's General Adaptation Syndrome: The Body's Response to Stress

Many of us recognize stressful situations because of the bodily reactions that accompany them. For example, if you perceive giving a speech as a stressor, then when faced with doing so, you may feel shaky, perspire more, feel your heart race, or even experience difficulty breathing. You may experience these same reactions when accepting an award or before an important job interview. These reactions are a part of a general bodily pattern termed the **general adaptation syndrome (GAS)** (Selye, 1976). ● FIGURE 12.2 shows the GAS as three phases that we all experience when we perceive a stressor in the environment: an initial *alarm reaction, resistance,* and *exhaustion.*

Alarm Reaction and the HPA Axis

The **alarm reaction** consists of those bodily responses that are immediately triggered when we initially appraise an event as stressful. It is much like the car alarm that goes off the moment an intruder tries to open the car door. In the body, this involves activation of the nervous system and the endocrine system.

Recall from Chapter 2 that the peripheral nervous system includes the somatic and autonomic divisions. The autonomic division includes two systems: the parasympathetic branch, which

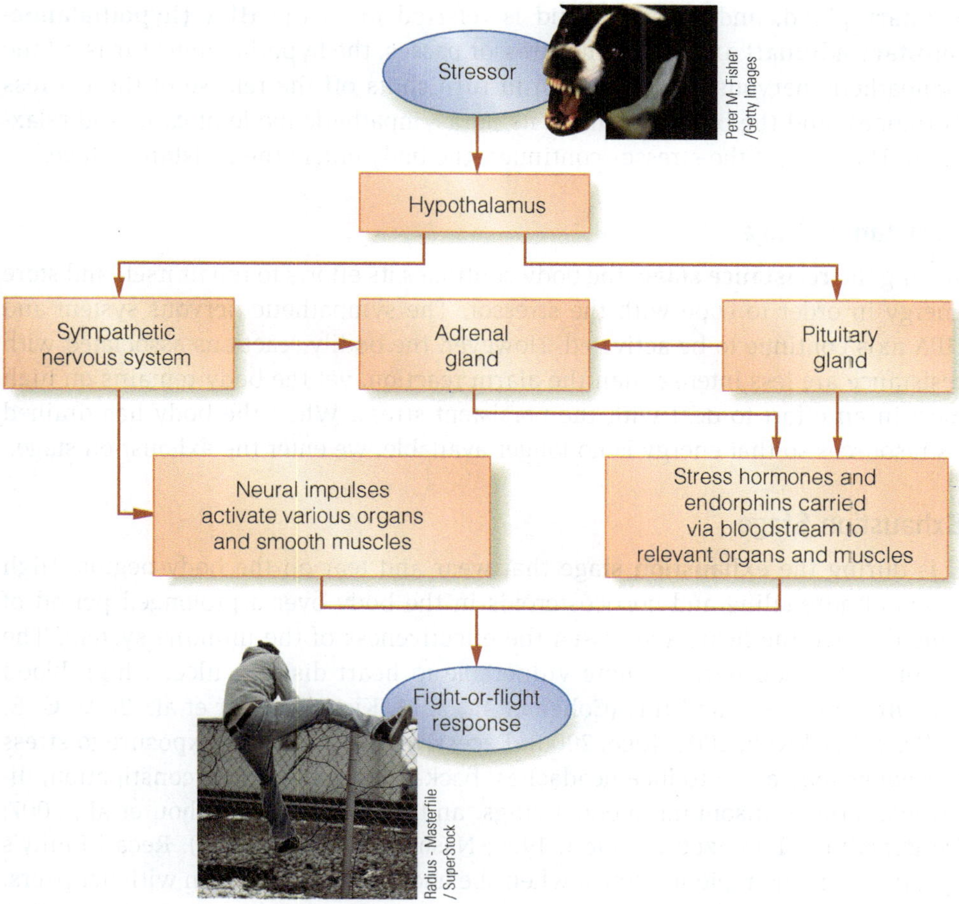

FIGURE 12.3

Biological Pathway of the Stress Response – The HPA Axis

When we perceive an event as stressful, the hypothalamus in the brain activates two systems: the sympathetic branch of the nervous system and the pituitary gland of the endocrine system. The nervous system sends neural messages to the major glands, organs, and muscles to prepare for fight or flight. At the same time, neural messages act vate the adrenal gland to secrete the stress hormone, adrenaline. The pituitary gland sends hormonal messages to the adrenal gland to secrete the stress hormones, corticosteroids, while at the same time releasing endorphins, the body's natural painkillers. The combined effects of the stress hormones and endorphins prepare our bodies to face stressors.

operates when we are calm and relaxed; and the sympathetic nervous system, our fight-or-flight mechanism that prepares us to face a threat in the environment. This sympathetic branch of the nervous system is at the heart of the stress response.

When a person perceives a threat in the environment—or what we have now referred to as a stressor—a distress signal is sent to the hypothalamus in the brain (● Figure 12.3). The hypothalamus activates the sympathetic nervous system. In turn, the sympathetic nervous system works in conjunction with the endocrine (or hormonal) system to prepare the body to deal with the stressor. It stimulates the adrenal gland to secrete the stress hormone, *adrenaline*. At the same time, the hypothalamus stimulates the pituitary gland to release endorphins, the body's natural painkillers, and to send messages to the adrenal gland to secrete the stress hormones, corticosteroids. These hormones travel to the major organs (liver, heart, and lungs) to prepare the body for fight or flight. Our heart rate and blood pressure increase, our lungs expand, and our liver releases stored sugars that can be used for energy. The body continues to expend these resources for as long as the stressor persists. This complex interaction between the hypothalamus,

secondary appraisal an evaluation of resources available to cope with a stressor

general adaptation syndrome (GAS) the general physical responses we experience when faced with a stressor

alarm reaction the first phase of the general adaptation syndrome, characterized by immediate activation of the nervous and endocrine systems

HPA (hypothalamic-pituitary-adrenal) axis the major system that controls the stress response involving the hypothalamus, pituitary gland, and adrenal gland

resistance stage the second phase of the general adaptation syndrome, in which the nervous and endocrine systems continue to be activated

exhaustion stage the third and final phase of the general adaptation syndrome, in which bodily resources are drained and wear and tear on the body and well-being begins

pituitary gland, and adrenal gland is referred to as the **HPA (hypothalamic-pituitary-adrenal) axis**. Once the stressor passes, the hypothalamus turns off the sympathetic nervous system, which in turn shuts off the release of these stress hormones, and the body returns to its parasympathetic mode of calm and relaxation. However, if the stressor continues, the body enters the resistance stage.

Resistance Stage

During the **resistance stage**, the body continues its efforts to repair itself and store energy in order to cope with the stressor. The sympathetic nervous system and HPA axis continue to be activated. However, the bodily reactions associated with resistance are less intense than the alarm reaction, yet the body remains on high alert in an effort to deal with the persistent stress. When the body has drained its resources so that energy is no longer available, we enter the exhaustion stage.

Exhaustion Stage

It is during the **exhaustion stage** that wear and tear on the body begins. High levels of adrenaline and corticosteroids in the body over a prolonged period of time damage the heart and lessen the effectiveness of the immune system. The result is that you become more vulnerable to heart disease, ulcers, high blood pressure, and colds and flus (Cohen et al., 2012; Kiecolt-Glaser et al., 2002; G. E. Miller & Blackwell, 2006; Rice, 2000). Excessive and prolonged exposure to stress hormones may also produce headaches, backaches, indigestion, constipation, diarrhea, fatigue, insomnia, mood swings, and muscle tension (Chou et al., 2007; De Benedittis, Lorenzetti, & Pieri, 1990; Nash & Thebarge, 2006). Recall Emily's spastic colon and rapid heartbeat when she had difficulty fitting in with her peers. Exposure in early life to high stress hormone levels may also adversely program the HPA axis and trigger changes in the brain that may negatively influence one's physical and mental health (Vyas et al., 2016).

12.2.3 Gender and the Stress Response

Evidence suggests that women and men do not respond physiologically to stress in exactly the same way. Although both males and females have the necessary fight-or-flight response, adult males may produce higher corticosteroid levels when under stress compared to adult females (Kajantie & Phillips, 2006; Kudielka & Kirschbaum, 2005; Wang et al., 2007), perhaps because of their naturally higher levels of testosterone (Girdler, Jamner, & Shapiro, 1997). These higher steroid levels in males, combined with the male's evolutionary role as protector, hunter, and aggressor, may motivate men to be more likely to fight or confront a threat when under stress.

In contrast, female responses to stress may be better characterized as "tend and befriend" rather than fight or flight (S. E. Taylor et al., 2000; Youssef et al., 2018). In response to stress or threat, women are more likely to come together in groups, seek social support, and care for offspring. These behaviors may be related to the hormone *oxytocin,* which is released in response to at least some stressors and tends to have a calming effect on the fight-or-flight response. Estrogen, which is naturally higher in adult females than adult males, seems to enhance the effects of oxytocin, whereas testosterone seems to reduce its effects. Consequently, the enhanced effects of oxytocin in females, combined with the female's evolutionary role as child nurturer and gatherer, may motivate women to be more likely to seek social contact when under threat or stress (S. E. Taylor, 2006). Perhaps Emily's frequent sexual affairs were a way to connect with others when she was under stress. This is not to say that men do not or cannot tend and befriend, or that women do not or cannot fight or flee. Each gender just may be more specifically adapted to one response or the other in times of stress.

12.2.4 Stress and the Immune System: Resistance to Disease

As we have seen, our body's reaction to stress, particularly during the exhaustion phase, can influence the effectiveness of our immune system. Researchers' interest in the connection between the immune system and stress has generated a new field of study called **psychoneuroimmunology**, which investigates the connections among psychology (behaviors, thoughts, and emotions), the nervous system, and immune system functioning. The immune system is our body's best defense against illness because it fights and destroys bacteria, viruses, and other foreign substances that may invade our bodies. If this system is impaired, as in the case of prolonged stress, we are more prone to illness and disease (Fagundes, Glaser, & Kiecolt-Glaser, 2013; Kiecolt-Glaser, 2009; Vyas et al., 2016; Webster Marketon & Glaser, 2008).

psychoneuroimmunology [sigh-ko-nur-o-im-ya-NAH-la-gee] the field of study that investigates the connections among psychology (behaviors, thoughts and, emotions), the nervous system, and immune system functioning

immunosuppression [im-mew-no-suh-PREH-shun] the reduction in activity of the immune system

The corticosteroids and endorphins that are released into our bloodstream during the stress response actually reduce and dampen the activity of our immune system. This effect is referred to as **immunosuppression**. Consequently, turning on our stress response, which ensures our ability to survive immediate danger, comes at the expense of our immune system, our long-term survival mechanism.

Much research supports the notion that stress suppresses the functioning of the immune system, which then increases the chances of developing infections such as the common cold (Anderson, 2003; Cohen et al., 2012; Kiecolt-Glaser et al., 2002; Rice, 2000). During final exam time and other periods of academic pressure, students show a weakened immune system (Chandrashekara et al., 2007; Gilbert et al., 1996). This may explain why you catch a cold or are more likely to experience allergies and sinus infections during finals week or when you have several projects or papers due at the same time. Immunosuppression also occurs in both men and women following the death of a spouse or partner (Beem et al., 1999; Schleifer et al., 1983) and in people going through separation and divorce (Kiecolt-Glaser & Glaser, 1992; Kiecolt-Glaser et al., 2003). People who are caregivers for someone with a terminal disease or dementia experience chronic stress that also results in immunosuppression (Damjanovic et al., 2007; Vitaliano, Young, & Zhang, 2004). Lower socioeconomic status, childhood adversity, and family chaos can also influence the normal functioning of the HPA axis in children, which may increase their risk of later health problems (Bower, Crosswell, & Slavich, 2014; Chen, Cohen, & Miller, 2010; Fagundes & Way, 2014; Zilioli et al., 2016).

More serious, though, is the correlation among stress, the immune system, and cancer. Most people's initial reaction to a cancer diagnosis is panic, anger, or depression—negative emotions that activate the stress response and momentarily retard immune system functioning (Ader, 2001; Fagundes, Murdock, Chirinos, & Green, 2017). Moreover, our response and attitude toward having cancer may influence the eventual spread and fatality of the disease. For example, emotional distress in breast cancer patients is associated with a lower survival rate (Luecken & Compas, 2002; Osborne et al., 2004). Patients who express their emotions about the disease—both positive and negative—tend to have a higher chance of survival than patients who hold in their emotions (Conley, Bishop, & Andersen, 2016; Lehto et al., 2006; Reynolds et al., 2000). Similarly, cancer patients with an optimistic attitude who are determined to beat the disease often outlive patients with a less positive attitude (Carver et al., 2000; Shen, McCreary, & Myers, 2004). Notice that this research does not say that stress *causes* cancer, but rather that stress may influence the rate at which cancer cells grow. If your immune system is functioning at reduced levels during times of chronic stress, it is less available to fight these life-threatening cells.

Psychology Works!

Monkey Business Images/Shutterstock

Students going into any health-related or medical field would do well to study the psychological concepts presented in this chapter. As we have seen, there is an intimate connection among one's thoughts and emotions and the functioning and health of one's body. The stressors a patient is experiencing as well as their coping mechanisms and resources is important for understanding and treating health issues as they may underlie a patient's symptoms. Health and medical professionals can be instrumental in reducing health-defeating behaviors and recommending those behaviors that promote health and well-being. Knowledge of stress, health, and positive psychology can help prevent disease and improve a patient's quality of life.

We are by no means saying that surviving or not surviving cancer is totally up to the individual. The onset, course, and magnitude of cancer in patients are influenced by variables that include one's genetics, the type of cancer, when it is detected, social support, and the treatments available. Our attitudes about developing cancer and receiving cancer treatment and how we regulate our emotions during these time periods are just two factors among many to consider when examining the connection between stress and health. There is virtually no scientific evidence that one's mental state *causes* cancer or that one's mental state *cures* cancer. We look to future research to fill in the blanks and make our knowledge more complete.

12.2 Quiz Yourself

1. You are more vulnerable to illness during which stage of Selye's stress response model?
   a. Alarm reaction
   b. Resistance
   c. Rejuvenation
   d. Exhaustion

2. Immunosuppression refers to ______.
   a. the activation of the immune system when we are faced with a stressor
   b. a reduction in the activity of the immune system
   c. the immune system's ability to survive immediate danger
   d. the release of endorphins and corticosteroids to help the immune system function

3. Eniesha was shopping at the mall when she heard a person yelling angrily close by. Eniesha turned around to see who was yelling and saw that two adults were arguing. So Eniesha went back to her shopping. In psychological terms, Eniesha just ______.
   a. made a primary appraisal
   b. made a secondary appraisal
   c. had an avoidance-avoidance conflict
   d. experienced stress

4. The stress response experienced by women may be better characterized as ______, *primarily* due to the hormone called ______.
   a. "tend and befriend"; oxytocin
   b. "tend and befriend"; estrogen
   c. "fight or flight"; oxytocin
   d. "fight or flight"; estrogen

Answers 1. d; 2. b; 3. a; 4. a

12.3 Coping with Stress

Think of the exam or exams you will take for this course. Does your body evidence the telltale signs of the stress response when thinking about your exam? What do you do when faced with a stressor like this? Are you likely to react emotionally, becoming very anxious and worrying about what the test will be like? Are you likely to tackle the stressor directly, focusing all your energy on studying and preparing for the exam? Or do you simply ignore your stress, hoping for a postponement or cancellation of the exam? Maybe you experience some of these reactions.

Whatever you do to manage an event or stimulus that you perceive as threatening is part of **coping**. How we cope with stress influences the way stress affects our physical and emotional well-being. We will discuss two broad types of strategies for coping: *problem-focused coping* and *emotion-focused coping* (Folkman & Lazarus, 1988). Some research suggests that females are somewhat more likely to use emotion-focused strategies and males are somewhat more likely to use problem-focused coping, but these gender differences are dependent on the nature of the stressor (Craciun, 2013; Howerton & Van Gundy, 2009; Matud, 2004; Ptacek, Smith, & Dodge, 1994; Tamres, Janicki, & Helgeson, 2002). Anyone may use one or both types of coping when faced with a stressor. Each has its benefits and costs (Lazarus & Folkman, 1984; Roth & Cohen, 1986).

coping the behaviors that we engage in to manage stressors

problem-focused coping behaviors that aim to control or alter the environment that is causing stress

12.3.1 Problem-Focused Coping: Change the Situation

Problem-focused coping is aimed at controlling or altering the environment that is causing the stress and includes strategies such as planning and active coping. For example, problem-focused coping strategies during the COVID-19 pandemic may include wearing a mask when in the company of others, frequent handwashing, making several plans for childcare, or using technology to connect with loved ones to reduce feelings of isolation. As another example, let's say that you are working while going to school and your boss just increased your work hours. You now feel that you don't have enough time for school or your social life. A problem-focused approach to coping with this increased workload might be finding another job without as many required hours or reducing the number of credit hours you are taking in school. Both of these strategies are aimed at changing the situation to reduce the amount of perceived stress. One benefit of either of these problem-focused coping strategies would be elimination of the perceived stressor. At the same time, you benefit by experiencing more control over your environment, which may also enhance your self-esteem. However, it is also possible that you have misdiagnosed the problem, which is a cost of problem-focused coping. Maybe the number of work hours isn't affecting your college work as much as your motivation or your social schedule is. You may actually increase your long-term level of stress by choosing an inappropriate course of action. For example, reducing your college hours increases the time it will take to complete your college education. Alternately, changing jobs may result in lower wages, making it more difficult to pay for your education and living expenses.

Generally, problem-focused coping tends to be most useful when we feel that we can actually do something about a situation (Folkman & Moskowitz, 2000; Haines et al., 2016; Troy, Shallcross, & Mauss, 2013). Under these circumstances, problem-focused coping is more likely to lead to a more positive health outcome (Largo-Wight, Peterson, & Chen, 2005; Penley, Tomaka, & Wiebe, 2002; Smith & Dust, 2006). However, when we do not feel that a situation is controllable, we often rely more on emotion-focused coping strategies (Lazarus, 1993).

▲ Taking your anger out on someone to relieve stress is an example of emotion-focused coping.

12.3.2 Emotion-Focused Coping: Change Your Reaction

Emotion-focused coping is aimed at controlling your internal, subjective, emotional reactions to stress. You either express your emotions or alter the way you feel or think in order to reduce your perceived stress. Stressors activate a variety of emotions, including anxiety, worry, guilt, shame, jealousy, envy, and anger. Because these emotions are usually experienced as unpleasant, we are motivated to release, reduce, or avoid them. Recall from this part's case study Emily's emotion-focused coping. Her anger, panic, and depression were typical ways in which she reacted to the stress in her life. Or suppose that you are anticipating the arrival of your partner at a party where you planned to meet, and your partner is already an hour late. The stress of this situation not only activates the physical sensations that we have discussed previously but also triggers emotional reactions. You may be angry with your partner because you feel purposely ignored. You may take this anger out on a friend, or turn all of your emotional energy into being the life of the party. Conversely, you may experience anxiety and worry, fearing that something harmful has happened to your partner. When your partner arrives, you may express your anger by complaining about their lateness or ignoring the partner altogether, or by being especially loving and attentive. Either way, your coping behavior is directed at regulating the unpleasant emotions of anger, anxiety, or worry that you are experiencing.

We attempt to lessen the effects of these negative emotions in two ways: by engaging in *cognitive reappraisal* and by using psychological *defense mechanisms*. **Cognitive reappraisal** (also called positive reappraisal or reframing) is an active and conscious process in which we alter our interpretation of the stressful event in order to reduce negative feelings. In the previous example, you have appraised your partner's lateness in a negative manner (as being ignored or something bad has happened). These appraisals have led to feelings of anger and anxiety. You can reappraise or reinterpret the lateness in a more realistic manner—your partner got caught in traffic or had to work late. These reappraisals are less likely to lead to negative emotional states. Thus, cognitive reappraisal can be an emotionally constructive and positive way of coping with a stressful event (Gross, Halperin, & Porat, 2013; Jamieson, Mendes, & Nock, 2013; Ray, Wilhelm, & Gross, 2008; Torrence & Connelly, 2019; Troy et al., 2010). In one study, positive reappraisal even led to less immunosuppression during a chronic stress period (Koh et al., 2006). Cognitive reappraisal is effective for regulating negative emotions when the perceived stressor is uncontrollable—when the only thing a person can control is their emotions. For example, during the COVID-19 pandemic, many families had to cope with their children participating in distance learning while at the same time working from home. Such a shift in one's daily life may create anxiety and distress. However, reframing the situation as an opportunity to spend more time with loved ones and become more active in your child's education may alleviate one's negative emotions.

emotion-focused coping behaviors aimed at controlling the internal emotional reactions to a perceived stressor

cognitive reappraisal [re-uh-PRAY-zull] an active and conscious process in which we alter our interpretation of a stressful event in order to reduce negative feelings

defense mechanisms unconscious, emotional strategies that are engaged in to reduce anxiety and maintain a positive self-image

A more automatic and unconscious way in which we lessen the effects of our emotions is by using **defense mechanisms**. Sigmund Freud was one of the first theorists to identify psychological defense mechanisms. Recall Freud's ideas on personality and coping in Chapter 11. Freud suggested that we use coping strategies unconsciously to reduce our anxiety and maintain a positive self-image and self-esteem. Because of these features, we now consider these defense mechanisms emotion-focused coping strategies. We use them to avoid or reduce the emotions associated with a stressor, but they do not necessarily eliminate the source of stress. For example, you might use the defense mechanism of *displacement* to deal with your anger toward a boss, a parent, or a significant other. You take your anger out on a friend by yelling at them, or on an object by throwing it against the wall. Afterward, you may *feel* better, but it does not resolve the issue that made you angry in the first place. The stressor is still present and may resurface again in the future.

Everyone uses defense mechanisms from time to time. Some of these defense mechanisms are adaptive. Directing your anger into a more constructive activity such as washing your car is more productive than hurting someone else (see "Sublimation" in ● TABLE 12.3). Other defense mechanisms, especially when we use them to excess, can prevent us from developing effective ways of coping. For example, the student who fails to study for a test may decide that their roommate who plays video games is at fault. Such a defense on the part of the student does not promote an adaptive way of coping with failure. The more common defense mechanisms are displayed in Table 12.3. See if you can identify the defense mechanisms that you tend to use.

TABLE 12.3 Common Defense Mechanisms

Defense Mechanism	Definition	Examples
Denial	Refusing to accept or acknowledge the reality of a situation or idea	Going out partying the night before an exam denies how this behavior will affect your exam performance. Having unprotected sex denies the possibility of an unwanted pregnancy or contracting an STI.
Rationalization	Devising a plausible reason or motive to explain one's behavior	You rationalize your excessive consumption of alcohol by saying it makes you more sociable or improves your personality.
Reaction formation	Engaging in a behavior or attitude that is at the opposite extreme of one's true motive or impulse	One student pulls the ponytail of another student, behaving aggressively to cover up the opposite emotion—liking the student. When you see someone at the store whom you dislike, you approach and say warmly, "Hi. How have you been? You look great!"
Regression	Returning to an earlier stage of development in one's behavior, thinking, or attitudes	Adults who throw tantrums, pout, or whine are engaging in childlike behaviors. An older child may react to the birth of a sibling by wetting the bed or sucking their thumb again.
Sublimation	Directing emotions into an activity that is more constructive and socially acceptable	Some people exercise or clean their room when they are angry or upset. Others direct their emotions into writing, sculpting, music, or painting.
Repression	Excluding wishes, impulses, ideas, or memories from consciousness	A person may forget the details of an accident, crime, or other situation associated with trauma or harm.
Projection	Attributing one's own ideas, feelings, or attitudes to other people	You accuse another student of flattering the professor to get special treatment when in reality it is you who engages in this behavior. A person in a relationship may accuse their partner of wanting to date other people when this is their own desire.
Displacement	Directing emotions toward a less threatening source	You yell at your partner after an argument with your boss. An athlete throws objects or kicks the bench after a missed play.

The use of defense mechanisms involves costs and benefits. The main reason we use them is to restore our self-image. We also benefit because defense mechanisms reduce anxiety. They may also give us the confidence to handle additional stressors. However, the benefits of defense mechanisms are typically outweighed by the costs. Defense mechanisms often inhibit our ability to resolve a problem. Using our emotions to cope with stressors may impede our functioning in other daily activities—Emily's rages and panic often distanced her further from her friends and family. Most important, using defense mechanisms keeps us in a state of unawareness as to the true source of any stress-related physical or emotional symptoms. Given these disadvantages, why do we continue to use defense mechanisms? Basically, they are easier and produce quicker results in reducing our feelings of anxiety. Unfortunately, these advantages are often at the expense of our health and well-being, as we may experience more distress and negative moods over the long run (Langford et al., 2017; Littleton et al., 2007; O'Brien, Terry, & Jimmieson, 2008).

Emotion-focused coping is not *always* maladaptive. Intentionally expressing one's emotions in reaction to a stressor can be beneficial depending on the stressor, the environment, and the person (Bonanno & Burton, 2013; Stanton & Low, 2012; Tullett, Teper, & Inzlicht, 2011). Writing in a journal or expressing feelings with friends often helps people manage their responses to stressors—our next topic of discussion.

12.3.3 Managing Stress: Applying the Research

Because stress affects our physical and psychological health, considerable research has addressed what strategies may reduce our risk of physical and mental illness. These techniques all focus on changing one or more aspects of the stress response. Many of these methods address both problem-focused and emotion-focused coping:

- *Exercise*. Some form of regular aerobic exercise, such as swimming, walking, or dancing, can be an effective strategy for reducing physical stress reactions (Huang et al., 2013; Langreth, 2000; Stear, 2003). Exercise reduces negative emotions such as depression and anxiety that we often feel in response to stress (Brugman & Ferguson, 2002; Kandola et al., 2018; Long & van Stavel, 1995; Stubbs et al., 2017). Exercise raises energy levels, strengthens the heart, and lowers muscle tension. We sleep more soundly after exercise and also feel better as the body increases its production of natural mood elevators like serotonin and endorphins (Chapter 2).
- *Relax*. One of the most successful nonchemical ways to manage stress is through the application of relaxation techniques. Such methods may include **progressive relaxation training**, in which you learn to alternately tense and then relax each muscle group of the body in a systematic fashion. This activity gives you an awareness of when and where you feel tension when you're under stress. You then learn to manage and control the tension that you feel by relaxing on command. Other relaxation techniques may include regular massages, mindfulness meditation, yoga, deep breathing exercises, engaging in a hobby, or listening to music. Daily use of relaxation procedures are effective in lessening symptoms of asthma, insomnia, headaches, rheumatoid arthritis, high blood pressure, chronic pain conditions, intestinal problems, and chronic anxiety (Astin, 2004; Fumal & Schoenen, 2008; J. W. Hughes et al., 2013; Lebovits, 2007; McCallie, Blum, & Hood, 2006; Meyer et al., 2016; Ostelo et al., 2007).

progressive relaxation training a stress management technique in which a person learns how to systematically tense and relax muscle groups in the body

Relaxation techniques have also been helpful in reducing anxiety and stress levels of cancer patients, medical students, and assembly-line workers (Isa et al., 2013; Kim, Na, & Hong, 2016; Sundram, Dahlui, & Chinna, 2016; Wild et al., 2014).

Leonora Hamill/Getty Images

▲ Having close relationships with others helps us weather stress.

- *Develop social support.* As social animals, humans are motivated to maintain social connections with others. Having friends, a shoulder to cry on, or someone to discuss an issue or trying event with are all examples of **social support**—having close and positive relationships with others. Social support buffers the effects of stress and reduces appraisals of threat (Algoe, 2019; Diener & Seligman, 2004; Hornstein & Eisenberger, 2018; Lee & Dik, 2016; Slatcher & Selcuk, 2017; Uchino, 2009). Family stability, a partner's support, or simply having friends to confide in is related to a longer life span, as well as a longer survival rate for those with cancer or heart disease (Cohen & Janicki-Deverts, 2009; Holt-Lunstad, 2018; Holt-Lunstad, Smith, & Layton, 2010; Slatcher & Selcuk, 2017). Even giving social support to others appears to buffer the effects of stress (Brown et al., 2003; Inagaki & Orehek, 2017; Raposa, Laws, & Ansell, 2016). Social support also may act to decrease the release of stress hormones and reduce stress-induced immune responses and susceptibility to infections (S. Cohen et al., 2015; Eisenberger et al., 2007; Fagundes et al., 2011; Pietromonaco, DeBuse, & Powers, 2013). Yet cultural norms influence the appropriateness of seeking and using social support networks. For example, Asians and Asian Americans are less likely to ask directly for emotional support in times of distress as it is more likely to be viewed negatively in their culture. They benefit more from social support when it is unsolicited or received without directly asking for it (Kim, Sherman, & Taylor, 2008; Mojaverian & Kim, 2013; Sherman, Kim, & Taylor, 2009).

  The impact of social support on health can also be seen in the research on loneliness and social isolation. Feeling lonely or socially rejected, as Emily did, has a major impact on health and well-being (DeWall & Bushman, 2011; Hawkley & Cacioppo, 2010; Holt-Lunstad et al., 2015; Jaremka et al., 2013; Leigh-Hunt et al., 2017). Higher levels of loneliness, smaller social networks, or experiencing social rejection have been found to be associated with higher levels of cortisol (a corticosteroid secreted during the stress response), a lower antibody response to flu shots, and poorer immune system functioning. High levels of cortisol are not good for one's health. Poor antibody response means the body's immune system produces fewer protective antibodies and puts the person at greater risk for illness (Pressman et al., 2005).

social support having close and positive relationships with others

- *Be spiritual.* Spiritual faith, prayer, church or temple membership, and strong value systems may promote physical health and well-being for *some* people (Inzlicht & Tullett, 2010; McCullough et al., 2000; McIntosh et al., 2011; Miller & Thoresen, 2003; Powell, Shahabi, & Thoresen, 2003). Spirituality often means having a purpose in life, self-awareness, and connectedness with self, others, and a larger community. Having a purpose in life is associated with a longer life span (Cohen, Bavishi, & Rozanski, 2016; Hill & Turiano, 2014). Religiousness is typically defined as participation in an institutionalized doctrine. For example,

Kelly Foreman/Shutterstock.com

▲ The stress management technique of guided imagery involves using your mind to achieve a state of relaxation. Whenever you feel stressed, you focus on a pleasant, calming environment like the image shown here, to relieve bodily tensions and promote relaxation.

guided imagery a technique in which you focus on a pleasant, calming image to achieve a state of relaxation when you feel stressed

several studies have found that prayer and spirituality are associated with reduced symptoms of distress in cancer patients (Laubmeier, Zakowski, & Bair, 2004; Lynn, Yoo, & Levine, 2014; Taylor & Outlaw, 2002). Religiousness and spirituality have also been shown to be associated with reduced symptoms in people with mental health problems (Corrigan et al., 2003; Lorenz, Doherty, & Casey, 2019; McClintock, Lau, & Miller, 2016). One study found a relationship between prayer and better health, but only among less educated and, to a lesser extent, lower-income people (Banthia et al., 2007). Recall Emily's desire for spiritual and emotional connections; resources that may have helped her well-being.

Religion, spirituality, and health are correlated. We cannot conclude that religiousness or spirituality *causes* better health and well-being. Which, if any, specific religious or spiritual factors enhance or undermine health and well-being remains unclear (Jordan et al., 2014). One must also consider the importance of religion and spirituality within one's culture (Masters & Hooker, 2013). Many of the studies define religion and spirituality in a variety of ways (Hill & Pargament, 2003; Schreiber & Brockopp, 2012). As more sound research is conducted, psychologists may be able to uncover the distinct contribution of religion and spirituality to health and well-being.

- *Imagine a calm environment.* **Guided imagery** is a technique in which you learn to use your mind to achieve a state of relaxation. You imagine that you are in a safe, pleasant, calming environment, perhaps walking along a beach or in a forest. You maintain your focus on this image as you feel the tensions associated with stress leave your body. As with progressive relaxation, you become trained to automatically summon up the soothing image when you feel stressed. For some people, guided imagery is just as effective as the relaxation techniques discussed previously (Astin, 2004; Varvogli & Darviri, 2011). Can you think of your own image, scene, or memory that would provide these benefits for you? How does your body feel as you think about it?
- *Be mindful and meditate.* As discussed in Chapter 4, *mindfulness meditation* is where a person intentionally focuses and pays attention to and experiences what is going on in the moment—their emotions, thoughts, and/or bodily sensations—without judgment. The person sits in a comfortable position with their eyes closed and silently focuses their attention on a specially assigned word that creates a resonant sound or on a bodily state such as one's breathing. Mindfulness-based practices in the form of yoga, Zen, or transcendental meditation may reduce tension and anxiety caused by stress (Creswell & Lindsay, 2014; Gu et al., 2015; Holzel et al., 2011; Hughes et al., 2013; Paul et al., 2007). Mindfulness may help regulate attention and enhance body awareness such that we are better able to cognitively reappraise and process our emotions (Verdonk et al., 2020). Meditation appears to decrease heart rate, respiration, and oxygen consumption (Carrington, 1993; Tang et al., 2009). Some studies have also found that meditation can improve mood, lessen tiredness, and enhance immune system response (Fan et al., 2010; Moyer et al., 2011; Rosenkranz et al., 2013; Solberg, Halvorsen, & Holen, 2000). However, the studies designed to evaluate these outcomes have major limitations and methodological issues. Mindfulness encompasses such a large number of practices that a universally accepted definition of mindfulness and its features has not been reached. As a result, assessing and measuring its therapeutic effects is quite challenging (Breedvelt, Amanvermez, Harrer et al., 2019; Levine, Lang, Bairey-Merz et al., 2017). Isolating the key element common to the different

meditation and mindfulness practices may help us draw more solid conclusions on their specific physical and mental health benefits (Van Dam et al., 2018; Xiong & Doraiswamy, 2009).

- *Be optimistic.* Simply expecting good things to happen promotes resilience and positive health and is associated with a longer life span (Dantzer, Cohen, Russo, & Dinan, 2018; Lee et al., 2019). For example, in a study on first-year law students, those students who endorsed optimistic beliefs, such as believing they could succeed and having confidence about their abilities, had better immune system functioning at mid-semester than did students with a more pessimistic outlook (Segerstrom & Sephton, 2010). Optimists report lower stress levels and fewer symptoms of depression, and have fewer stress-related physical complaints (Finkelstein et al., 2007; Liu, Pu, & Hou, 2016; Pritchard, Wilson, & Yamnitz, 2007). Optimists also evidence lower levels of the stress hormone, cortisol, upon awakening than pessimists (Endrighi, Hamer, & Steptoe, 2011; Jobin, Wrosch, & Scheier, 2014). Cancer and heart disease patients with an optimistic attitude often show a better response to treatment than patients with a less positive attitude (Carver et al., 2000; Kim et al., 2017; Shen et al., 2004). Focusing on the half of the glass that is full is better for your physical and mental health than focusing on the half that is empty.
- *Laugh.* Laughter promotes relaxation, which may explain why good-humored people perceive less stress when faced with life's challenges (Lefcourt, 2001; Lefcourt & Davidson-Katz, 1991; Martin & Kuiper, 2016). Laughter may buffer stress by reducing blood pressure, increasing deep breathing, boosting the immune system, increasing feelings of well-being, and raising energy levels (Bennett et al., 2003; Christie & Moore, 2005). Any one or all of these factors may be responsible for the positive health effects. Even hearing laughter or smiling through stress has been linked to lowered levels of heart rate during stress response recovery (Fujiwara & Okamura, 2018; Kraft & Pressman, 2012), giving credence to the saying "Grin and bear it."
- *Manage your time wisely.* Many of us experience stress because we feel that there is not enough time to accomplish all the tasks, errands, and work that we have established for ourselves. Feelings of time pressure can negatively influence our health and well-being (Menzies, 2005). One way to minimize the stress resulting from such pressures is to organize your time better. Keeping a daily planner, electronic calendar, or formal time schedule to record your obligations, commitments, and deadlines for study, work, and leisure activities can ease tension. Keeping a formal time schedule also allows you to evaluate the number and importance of your commitments. One of the most common time management mistakes that college students make is not allowing enough time to study all of the assigned material (Buehler, Griffin, & Ross, 1994; Jacobs & Hyman, 2013). The key to effective time management is to treat each responsibility—whether work, study, or play—as a serious commitment.

By using these methods, you have the opportunity to reduce the ill effects of stress on your physical and mental health right now, as well as the cumulative effect of stress on your body and mind in the future. However, if you sometimes feel that you cannot manage the stress in your life, or you aren't coping well with your stressors, then it may be time to seek professional help. Chapter 14 describes the different types of mental health professionals who can help us cope more effectively.

12.3 Quiz Yourself

1. Organizing your time better would be best classified as a(n) ______ coping skill.
   a. problem-focused
   b. emotion-focused
   c. avoidance-focused
   d. encounter-focused

2. It is common for young children to react to the birth of a sibling by regressing to earlier behaviors such as sucking their thumb again or wanting to feed from a bottle. Such behaviors exemplify ______ coping skills.
   a. problem-focused
   b. emotion-focused
   c. avoidance-focused
   d. encounter-focused

3. Which of the following is the *least* effective stress management technique?
   a. Guided imagery
   b. Physical exercise
   c. Defense mechanisms
   d. Relaxation techniques

Answers 1. a; 2. b; 3. c

12.4 Personality, Health, and Well-Being

Psychologists have also been interested in how personality influences our physical health and well-being. A number of personality dimensions have been related to health—specifically, to the functioning of our cardiovascular and immune systems (Segerstrom, 2000; T. W. Smith, 2006). We consider three such avenues of research here: the *Type A personality, learned helplessness,* and the *hardy personality.*

12.4.1 Type A Personality: Ambition, Drive, and Competitiveness

Type A personality a personality that is aggressive, ambitious, and competitive

Type B personality a personality characterized by patience, flexibility, and an easygoing manner

Type C personality a personality that is cautious, serious, sensitive to criticism, and results oriented, and that suppresses negative emotions such as anger

Type D personality a personality characterized by negative emotions and social inhibition

Take a moment to look at ● TABLE 12.4. Which of these descriptions most accurately reflects your personality? Would you consider yourself more of a **Type A personality**, a person who is aggressive, competitive, and driven to achieve? Do you characterize yourself as more of a **Type B personality**, a person who is more relaxed, easygoing, patient, and flexible? Do you consider yourself more like a **Type C personality**, describing a person who is cautious, careful, overly patient and nice, and who avoids conflict and suppresses negative emotions such as anger? Or would you characterize yourself more as a **Type D personality**, someone who always expects the worst to happen, worries much, is often sad, and avoids social interactions with others? Emily's father probably fit the Type A description more than the Type B, Type C, or Type D.

At one time, having a Type A personality was considered a risk factor for heart disease. Cardiologists Meyer Friedman and Ray Rosenman (1974) were the first to examine the connection between personality and heart disease. They suspected that personality or behavior patterns might play a role in the lives of men who were more likely to develop heart disease or more likely to die from a heart attack. To test their idea, the researchers gathered a sample of 3,000 men between the ages of 35 and 59 with no known health problems. Each man was interviewed, and based on his behavior during the interview, each was designated as a Type A personality, a Type B personality, or somewhere in between. A label of Type A or Type B was given to those men who very much exemplified those traits listed in Table 12.4. The majority of the sample fell somewhere in between, but in comparing the two types, Friedman and Rosenman found that over the next decade, those with Type A personalities were two to three times more likely to experience

TABLE 12.4 The ABCDs of Personality: Which Type Are You?

Type A	Type B	Type C	Type D
 iStock.com/repinanatoly	 StockLite/Shutterstock.com	 UpperCut Images/Alamy stock photo	 Ollyy/Shutterstock.com
Competitive	Easygoing	Cautious	Distressed
Verbally aggressive	Calm	Careful	Worrisome
Overcommitted to achieving	Relaxed	Detached	Isolated
Impatient	Patient	Introspective	Irritated
Hostile attitude when frustrated	Trusting	Sensitive to criticism	Sad
Sense of time urgency	Good-natured	Serious	Lonely
Workaholic	Lower need for achievement	Results oriented	Fear of rejection and disapproval
Easily angered	Supportive	Suppressed emotion	Suppressed emotion

a heart attack. Keep in mind that the majority of the sample could not easily be categorized as either Type A or Type B.

Friedman and Rosenman's landmark study stimulated additional research on how personality factors may place people at risk for disease. However, subsequent research on the connection between Type A personality and the risk of heart disease has not been able to replicate these results (Booth-Kewley & Friedman, 1987; T. Q. Miller et al., 1991). Later research attempted to isolate which specific aspects of the Type A personality might predispose a person to heart problems. The key features include anger, mistrust, and hostility. People who are frequently angry, suspicious, bitter, antagonistic, and distrustful of others seem more likely to experience heart-related health problems and have a shorter life span (Deary, Weiss, & Batty, 2010; Mommersteeg & Pouwer, 2012; Roberts et al., 2007; Smith et al., 2004). People with a Type A personality who do not show these specific behaviors appear to be no more at risk for heart disease than their Type B counterparts. However, while the negative effect of expressing anger on health is quite robust in the United States, it may not apply to all cultures. For example, in Japan expressing anger is linked to reduced health risk (Kitayama & Park, 2017; Kitayama et al., 2015).

Research on the Type C or "cancer-prone" personality has proceeded in a similar fashion. That is, at one time, having a Type C personality was suggested as a major factor in the development of cancer, specifically breast cancer in women (see Scheier & Bridges, 1995, for review). Subsequent research suggested that the suppression or denial of anger, one specific aspect of the Type C personality, may put a woman more at risk for breast cancer. However, such studies suggest weak relationships between not expressing one's negative emotions and the risk of breast cancer (Bleiker et al., 2008; Butow et al., 2000). Several large-scale studies indicate little evidence for a so-called cancer-prone personality, including breast cancer (Jokela et al., 2014; Nakaya et al., 2010; Sawada et al., 2016).

Research on the Type D or "distressed" personality suggests that the combination of negative emotions (anxiety, worry, and sadness) and social inhibition (withdrawal, difficulty making friends) may put one at increased risk of heart problems, high blood pressure, and depression (Compare et al., 2014; Denollet et al., 2013; Kupper & Denollet, 2007). Unlike the Type A person who expresses their negative emotions, the Type D person doesn't have an outlet for their negative emotions. People with Type D personalities show higher stress hormone levels especially in social situations (Bibbey et al., 2015; Kupper & Denollet, 2007), which as we have seen has the potential to negatively influence one's long term health and well-being.

12.4.2 Learned Helplessness: I Can't Do It

Do you believe that you have no control over stressful life events? Do you believe that even your best efforts will result in failure? When you blame yourself for any failure you experience, are you more likely to attribute your failure to a specific factor—you're just not good at soccer—or to a more global feature—you're just too uncoordinated to do any athletic activity? These questions illustrate the key features of a personality factor called **learned helplessness**, in which people develop a passive response to stressors based on their exposure to previously uncontrolled, negative events.

learned helplessness a passive response to stressors based on exposure to previously uncontrolled, negative events

Learned helplessness was first demonstrated in dogs in a psychological laboratory (Seligman & Maier, 1967). The dogs were placed in a cage that was equipped with an electrified grid. When the dogs received a shock they could not escape from, after repeated trials, the dogs' escape responses slowly decreased. Recall from Chapter 6 that this decrease in responding is called *extinction*. Even when they were later given the opportunity to escape the shock, the dogs remained in the cage. The dogs had learned to be helpless. Experiments using human participants (not using shock) have produced similar results (Hiroto, 1974; W. R. Miller & Seligman, 1975). Consequently, when previous experiences lead you to believe that you cannot fix the problems facing you, you may approach new situations with this perceived lack of control and passively endure whatever comes your way (Dweck, Chiu, & Hong, 1995; Peterson, Maier, & Seligman, 1993). You are likely to view stressors as threats rather than as challenges. As a result, your levels of stress increase, and you are more likely to develop stress-related physical illnesses (Overmier, 2002; Stern, Dhanda, & Hazuda, 2009). Remember Emily's failures at school and her resulting feelings of hopelessness. It is possible that her attitude of learned helplessness contributed to her emotional distress.

Digital Vision./Getty Images

▲ If you fail an exam, do you go and get help, or do you just assume that you'll never understand the material and withdraw from the class? Expecting to fail and believing you have no control over the outcome of events are key qualities of learned helplessness.

Research supports the notion that college students who feel helpless are less likely to persist and more likely to give up easily; as a result, they are more likely to earn poor grades and report unhappiness (Fazio & Palm, 1998; Krejtz & Nezlek, 2016; McKean, 1994). Adults and adolescents (like Emily) who react to stress by feeling at a loss to do anything about the situation are more prone to depression and other stress problems (Diener et al., 2009; Rotenberg et al., 2012; Waschbusch et al., 2003). Learned helplessness has also been documented in children with a history of reading failure (Fowler & Peterson, 1981). It can develop in elderly people in assisted living facilities who are not given choices about their daily activities and routines (Seligman, 1989). In all these situations, the *expectation* of failure and lack of control is what influences one's perceived level of stress, one's subsequent response to stress, and ultimately, one's mental and physical health.

hardy personality a personality, high in the traits of commitment, control, and challenge, which appears to be associated with strong stress resistance

12.4.3 The Hardy Personality: Control, Commitment, and Challenge

Do you view stressors as challenges or as threats? For example, do you try out for the tennis team to see if you can make it, or do you simply not try out at all for fear of failing? Do you stay committed to the pursuit of your goals and values? If you fail an exam, do you get help, or do you just assume that you'll never understand the material and withdraw from the class? Do you believe that your actions influence the outcome of a situation? Your answers to these questions outline three factors that appear to be related to health and well-being: challenge, commitment, and control.

- The tendency to see life as a series of *challenges*
- A sense of personal *commitment* to self, work, family, and other values
- A perception of *control* over life and work

These "three Cs" taken together were labeled by psychologists Salvatore Maddi and Suzanne Kobasa (1984) as the **hardy personality**.

This term resulted from Kobasa's (1982) research on upper-level executives and attorneys who had experienced considerable stress over a three-year period. Those who exemplified hardy traits were less likely to get ill during this time of stress. Even Type A people who scored high on measures of hardiness were less likely to get ill than Type A people who scored low on hardiness. This observation led Kobasa to conclude that hardiness traits may decrease stress levels, thereby decreasing one's chances of developing illness.

Psychological research confirms that hardy people seem to be unusually resistant to stress (Bonanno, 2004; Maddi, 2005). Although related to resilience (bouncing back from stress), hardiness is a general style of functioning that enables a person to turn stressors into opportunities for personal growth and change. Hardy people endorse a positive worldview in which stressors are appraised as challenges rather than threats, so they feel less potential harm from them. Notice that these qualities are in direct contrast to learned helplessness. This positive attitude appears to promote more problem-focused coping, enabling such people to handle conflict better and be more willing to rely on the help of others when weathering stress (Maddi et al., 2006; Scheir & Carver, 1992). Hardy people also report higher levels of personal satisfaction with their work (Rush, Schoel, & Barnard, 1995) and show greater immune system responses to bacteria (Dolbier et al., 2001).

s_bukley/Shutterstock.com

▲ After surviving being kidnapped and held captive for 9 months at the age of 14, Elizabeth Smart still perceives life as a challenge. She testified against her kidnappers and is now an activist fighting human trafficking and sex crimes against children. She exemplifies the three traits of a hardy personality.

What does all this research on personality tell us? First, we can recognize that how one expresses negative emotions such as anger and hostility may influence one's mental and physical health. Frequent anger and hostility as well as suppressing one's negative emotions may not promote good health. Similarly, negative cognitions such as expecting failure or a lack of control may not be good for our well-being. In contrast, the three Cs of hardiness—a sense of control, being comfortable with challenge, and maintaining commitment—appear to be most beneficial to our ability to deal with stress and therefore most advantageous to our mental and physical health.

12.4 Quiz Yourself

1. **Donald is described by his friends as easygoing, calm, and patient. Donald would most likely be classified as a ______.**
   a. Type A personality
   b. Type B personality
   c. Type C personality
   d. Type D personality
2. **Which of the following personality factors has been strongly linked to depression and other stress problems?**
   a. Type A traits
   b. Type B traits
   c. Hardiness
   d. Learned helplessness
3. **After working on a project for more than 3 years, Zilmarie is told by her boss to redesign the project in a new way. Zilmarie considers such a task a challenge and commits to the new project with gusto. Zilmarie is probably high on which personality dimension?**
   a. Type A personality
   b. Type D personality
   c. Hardiness
   d. Type C personality

Answers 1. *b;* 2. *d;* 3. *c*

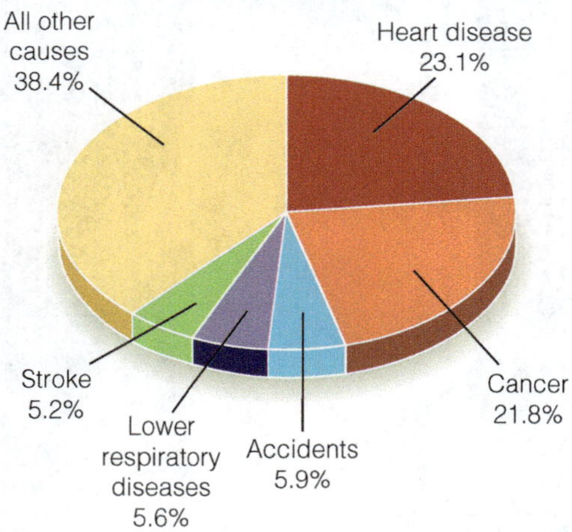

FIGURE 12.4

Leading Causes of Death in the United States

In 2017, heart disease, cancer, accidents, respiratory diseases, and stroke were the top five causes of death in the United States. The top two causes of death, heart disease and cancer, were the same for males and females and for Whites, Blacks, and American Indians; for Asian/Pacific Islanders, cancer was the leading cause of death with heart disease second. Many of these deaths could have been prevented by engaging in better health practices.

Source: *National Vital Statistics Report*, Vol. 68, No. 6, 2019.

12.5 Lifestyle, Health, and Well-Being

Psychologists also examine voluntary lifestyle choices and environmental factors that may play a role in our susceptibility to mental illness and physical disease as well as those lifestyle choices that can benefit our physical and mental health and contribute to happiness and well-being (Li, Pan, Wang et al., 2018; Ruark, 2009; Wallis, 2005).

12.5.1 Health-Defeating Behaviors

We already have seen that high levels of stress may increase your chances of illness. Some of these events may or may not be under your control. Psychologists define **health-defeating behaviors** as those behaviors that increase the chance of illness, disease, or death. They include risky behaviors such as driving at excessive speeds or while texting, carrying a weapon, or being a passenger in a car with a driver who is under the influence of drugs or alcohol. Risky behaviors endanger your health because you place yourself in a situation in which you have a higher risk of physical injury.

In fact, many of the leading causes of death are related to unsafe health practices (● FIGURE 12.4, Heron, 2019). Four of the top five leading causes of death—heart disease, cancer, lower respiratory diseases, and stroke—have been linked to personal habits that damage our health. We will examine behavior patterns, usually engaged in over a long period of time, that are controllable and that seriously put your physical and mental health at risk. These behaviors include alcohol consumption, smoking or vaping, distracted driving, and unsafe sex practices that can lead to contracting a sexually transmitted infection (STI). Notice that Emily engaged in many of these health-defeating behaviors.

health-defeating behaviors behaviors that increase the chance of illness, disease, or death

Alcohol

Recall from Chapter 4 the specific effects that alcohol has on the body and brain. These effects can be seen within a larger context by examining the social and physical ramifications of alcohol abuse on people's health and well-being. Consider that the majority of manslaughter convictions, assaults, and domestic violence incidents involve alcohol (Abbey, 2002; Abramsky et al., 2011). Nearly half of all U.S. highway deaths involve alcohol. Fetal alcohol syndrome (FAS), caused by a mother's excessive ingestion of alcohol during pregnancy, is the leading preventable cause of intellectual disability. In one national survey (Miech et al., 2019), 13.8% of high school seniors admitted to binge drinking in the past two weeks, despite being underage. For college students, the rate is even higher.

Alcohol abuse not only leads to social problems but is also associated with major health problems, including heart disease, stroke, cancer, liver disease, memory blackouts, and erectile dysfunction in males. These data convey the drastic impact that alcohol abuse has on our nation's health and suggest that alcohol should be used only in moderation, if at all.

Smoking & Vaping

Another easily preventable behavior is cigarette smoking and vaping. Recall from Chapter 4 that nicotine affects several neurotransmitters in the brain that act as stimulants, increasing arousal, feelings of pleasure and reward, and metabolic rate, which is why smokers tend to be thinner than nonsmokers. However, in high doses, nicotine causes vomiting, diarrhea, sweating, and dizziness. Most first-time users report nausea and dizziness from smoking cigarettes or vaping. Yet users quickly develop nicotine dependence (J. E. Rose et al., 2007).

In some developing countries, smoking is the norm. In the United States, nicotine use has declined over the past 50 years, yet, 15.8% of adult men and 13.2% of adult women continue to smoke cigarettes regularly (Wang, Asman, Gentzke et al., 2018) and an estimated 3.7% of adults use electronic nicotine delivery systems to vape nicotine (Schoenborn & Gindi, 2015). American Indian/Alaska Native and multiracial adults have the highest rates of tobacco use (Centers for Disease Control and Prevention [CDC], 2015a). Rates are lower among adults aged 65 and older, perhaps because many longtime smokers die (CDC, 2009). Level of education and income level also differentiate smokers from nonsmokers, with people living below poverty level and people with lower levels of education having higher smoking rates (Wetter et al., 2005).

Many adolescents experiment with smoking or vaping in middle and high school. Although only roughly 4% of high school seniors are daily cigarette smokers 26.5% report current vaping (Miech et al., 2019). As such, e-cigarettes are becoming the most commonly used tobacco product among teenagers. Many of these young people are aware of the health hazards associated with smoking and vaping, yet they begin anyway. Teens often perceive vaping as less harmful and easier to conceal than cigarettes, even though there are still many unknowns about vaping such as what chemicals are in the vapors and how they influence health in the long term.

Nicotine use is related to both biological and environmental factors. On the side of biology, there is considerable evidence that specific genes and gene combinations are involved in nicotine dependence (Erblich et al., 2005; Kremer et al., 2005; Ling et al., 2004). However, social pressure may also be a factor. For example, peer pressure and curiosity are often cited as reasons why young people start smoking cigarettes or vaping (Hayes & Plowfield, 2007; Perikleous et al., 2018). Seeing their favorite celebrities smoke, or even watching movies in which many characters smoke, also glamorizes smoking (Cin et al., 2007; Distefan, Pierce & Gilpin, 2004; Heatherton & Sargent, 2009; Pierce, 2005). Celebrities are also used in promotional and social media advertising of e-cigarettes targeted at teens (Grana & Ling, 2014). For this reason, many antismoking programs are aimed at teenagers, because this seems to be the prime age when smoking and vaping begin. Health officials have determined that the cost of treating the health problems associated with smoking and vaping far outweighs the cost of prevention programs.

Unsafe Sex and the Risk of Sexually Transmitted Infections (STIs)

sexually transmitted infections (STIs) infections that are passed from one person to another primarily through sexual contact

Sexually transmitted infections (**STIs**) are infections that are passed from one person to another, usually through sexual contact. However, some STIs may be spread by nonsexual contact as well as from a female to her fetus. Many STIs often have no symptoms, so they are unknowingly passed from one person to the next. There is also a social stigma attached to those infected with an STI. Such negative perceptions may prevent people from openly discussing their condition with medical personnel, partners, and other loved ones.

Psychology Applies to Your World

Technology's Influence on Health and Well-Being

TECHNOLOGY HAS THE POTENTIAL for great benefit and great harm to our physical and psychological health. On the plus side, social networking sites, e-mail, and text messaging can reduce loneliness and offer companionship and social support that can help combat stress, improve well-being and lead to a longer life. Such benefits are more likely to occur when they are used in a way that enhances existing relationships, builds new social connections, or fosters a deeper understanding of people's thoughts and feelings (Clark, Algoe, & Green, 2018; Hobbs et al., 2016; Nowland, Necka, & Cacioppo, 2018; Waytz & Gray, 2018). The Internet provides instant access to health information and resources that can reduce stress and worry. Fitness video games, trackers, and apps offer a fun, enjoyable, and often inexpensive way to remain physically active.

However, social media and smartphone use also have their drawbacks. The Internet may produce information overload or give contradictory or unreliable health information that creates stress and worry (Abbott, 2010; Jungmann et al., 2020). Being inundated with constant communication 24/7 creates stress and can make it more difficult to relax. Feeling like you are being left out of a social loop can create social anxiety. People may disengage from loved ones and pay more attention to the person on the phone or on the computer than to the people who are actually present. Passively viewing profiles, videos, or Instagram feeds do not meaningfully connect us to others. Such disengagement and passive social media use rob us of the psychological benefits linked to social participation and connection, making us feel more isolated (Clark et al., 2018; Kushlev, Dwyer, & Dunn, 2019; Waytz & Gray, 2018). Repeated social comparison to others may make us feel that others live better lives than we do, which is more likely to negatively influence self-esteem and mental health (Clark et al., 2018). Several studies suggest that teens and young adults who spend more time on digital media compared to less frequent users report lower levels of happiness and life satisfaction including more stress, anxiety, depressive symptoms, and loneliness (Twenge, 2019; Twenge et al., 2018). Other studies report either mixed or no effects of digital media on adolescents' psychological well-being (Heffer et al., 2019; Jensen et al., 2019).

In addition to psychological well-being, technology use may also influence our physical health. After prolonged cell phone use, people may notice aching, burning, numbness, or tingling in the forearm and hand called "cell phone elbow" (Darowish, Lawton, & Evans, 2009). It is associated with people who use their cell phones for extended periods while holding their neck crooked and elbow bent. It can aggravate a

Risk Factors for STIs Women, teenagers, men who have sex with men, and some ethnic groups are more likely to have an STI in the United States. Young people between the ages of 15 and 24 are most at risk (CDC, 2019). Young people are at increased risk because they engage in many high-risk sexual behaviors, such as having multiple partners and engaging in unprotected sexual intercourse. Women are at higher risk for contracting an STI than men because the warm, moist environment of the vagina renders women more susceptible to infection (Bolton, van der Straten, & Cohen, 2008). Younger women are especially vulnerable, because viruses and bacteria can more easily invade immature cervical cells than mature ones (Parker-Pope, 2002). According to data from the CDC (2010, 2015c), higher rates of STIs are found among gay and bisexual men, and all ethnic minority populations except Asians/Pacific Islanders when compared to European Americans.

Engaging in certain sexual behaviors also puts one at a higher risk for contracting an STI. High-risk sexual behaviors include oral-genital sex without a condom or dental dam, semen in the mouth, and vaginal or anal intercourse without a condom (Hatcher et al., 1994). Sex with multiple partners, as Emily evidenced, also increases one's chances of contracting an STI. Moreover, some STIs are contracted through non-sexual means. Certain forms of drug use increase the risk, as sharing contaminated needles can directly transmit organisms such as HIV. An infected pregnant woman also risks transmitting the infection to her fetus and causing serious birth defects.

painful and disabling condition called *cubital tunnel syndrome,* or the compression of the ulnar nerve near the elbow. Similarly, irritation and compression of the median nerve in the wrist, known as *carpal tunnel syndrome,* can result from repetitive work such as uninterrupted computer typing and frequent mouse use, depending on the frequency of use and wrist position of the user (Rempel, Keir, & Bach, 2008). Excessive texting uses short little motions that do not effectively use the muscles. This action can lead to painful cramping in the thumbs, hands, or joints, popularly called "BlackBerry thumb" or "teenager tendonitis" (Gordon, 2008). Staring at computer, tablet, or cell phone screens for long periods can lead to dry eyes, eye irritation, redness, blurred vision, and eye strain, a condition referred to as *computer vision syndrome* and that can cause headaches, pain, and fatigue (Blehm et al., 2005; Gowrisankaran & Sheedy, 2015). Perhaps one of the most dangerous behaviors that has resulted from technology use is an increase in distracted driving.

Eight people are killed each day in the United States due to distracted driving—activities like eating, texting, or using a cell phone while driving (NHTSA, 2019). People do not turn off their connection to the outside world when they get into their cars. Despite many states prohibiting handheld cellphone use while driving, 52% of U.S. drivers reported talking on a phone, and 32% reported sending or receiving a text while driving (AAA Foundation for Traffic Safety, 2019). Yet, our brains are not capable of fully concentrating on two things simultaneously. Text messaging and conversing on either a handheld or hands-free cell phone while driving slows reaction time more than being drunk or high (Drews et al., 2009; Haque & Washington, 2014; Leung et al., 2012; Strayer, Drews, & Crouch, 2006). Text messaging takes drivers' eyes off the road for the longest time (an average of 4.6 seconds) compared to drivers talking on a cell phone and those not using a phone (Olson et al., 2009). Drivers who are text messaging show more missed lane changes and more variability in lane position and following distances (Hosking, Young, & Regan, 2009). Driving safely is keeping your eyes and your mind on the road. Text messaging while driving compromises both.

Sean Locke Photography/Shutterstock.com

▲ Texting and driving is a health-defeating behavior, increasing one's chances of injury or death.

STIs can cause irreparable damage. Left untreated, STIs can cause pelvic inflammatory disease (PID), chronic pelvic pain, and infertility in women (CDC, 2019). They can also result in arthritis, heart problems, brain damage, and even death. The financial cost to our health care system is enormous, while the human cost to partners, families, and infected persons is incalculable. It's a cost that does not necessarily have to be paid, as many STIs are easily treated and prevented.

Types of STIs There are three basic categories of STIs: bacterial infections, viral infections, and parasitic infections.

Bacterial infections include *chlamydia, gonorrhea,* and *syphilis*. Bacteria are microorganisms or germs that can quickly reproduce and cause disease in the body. Chlamydia, gonorrhea, and syphilis are transmitted primarily through vaginal, anal, or oral sexual activity. If present in the vagina, these infections also can be transmitted from a mother to a newborn during delivery. An unusual discharge and sore or painful urination are common symptoms of these infections. However, many people show no symptoms during the early stages and therefore do not seek treatment until more serious symptoms develop. Antibiotics are typically used to treat bacterial infections (Cates, 1998).

Viral infections include *genital herpes, human papillomavirus (HPV),* and *HIV/AIDS*. Viruses are incapable of reproducing on their own. They invade a normal cell and direct that cell to make new viral copies. These copies then invade other healthy cells, causing infection. Many of the symptoms of these infections can be treated, but the virus remains in the body and is yours for life. Most people with genital herpes or HPV do not initially develop symptoms or health problems. When symptoms do occur in genital herpes, noticeable sores appear. Similarly, most people who become infected with any of the more than 40 strains of HPV do not know they have it. However, certain types of HPV can cause *genital warts,* small bumps, or groups of bumps, usually in the genital area. It is estimated that most sexually active people will get infected with HPV at some point in their lives, making it the most common STI in the United States (CDC, 2014). A vaccine can be administered to young females to protect them from four types of HPV that cause most cervical cancers and genital warts. The vaccine also protects young males against two HPV types that cause most genital warts. The vaccine is most effective when a person completes the treatment before becoming sexually active.

Being HIV-positive means that a person has been infected with the human immunodeficiency virus (HIV). In HIV/AIDS, the HIV attacks the immune system, resulting in mild flu-like symptoms that may then disappear for years before developing into a full-blown case of AIDS. Although symptoms may not be present, a person still carries the virus and is therefore capable of transmitting it to a partner during sexual activity. HIV/AIDS can also be contracted through the exchange of contaminated blood or passed to a fetus during pregnancy or to an infant during breastfeeding. People with HIV are more likely to be gay, bisexual, or other men who have sex with men; and are more likely to be African American (CDC, 2018). However, anyone—regardless of age, income, race, or sexual orientation—can contract HIV. Treatment to suppress HIV/AIDS infection typically consists of a steady regime of antiretroviral drugs to slow the disease's progression.

Eye of Science/Science Source

▲ Pubic lice are often called "crabs" because of the organism's resemblance to a crab.

Parasitic infections include *pubic lice* and *scabies*. A parasite lives off another organism or host. Pubic lice, or "crabs," survive by feeding on human blood. Scabies are tiny mites that burrow under the skin and lay eggs. Both infections can be spread through sexual contact or by contact with infested towels, linens, or clothing. The most common symptom is intense itching in the genital area. Parasitic infections are typically treated with a solution that kills the lice or mites and their eggs. It is important to carefully reexamine the body four to seven days after treatment to ensure that all the eggs have been killed. Towels, linens, and clothing also need to be treated to prevent reinfection. You Review: Sexually Transmitted Infections (STIs) shows the main types of sexually transmitted infections, modes of transmission, symptoms, and treatment.

YOU REVIEW Sexually Transmitted Infections (STIs)

STI	Transmission Modes	Symptoms	Treatments
Bacterial			
Chlamydia	Vaginal, oral, or anal sexual activity, or from an infected mother to her newborn during vaginal birth	In females: frequent and painful urination, lower abdominal pain, and vaginal discharge. In males: burning or painful urination, and slight penis discharge. However, many people show no symptoms.	Antibiotics
Gonorrhea	Vaginal, oral, or anal sexual activity, or from an infected mother to her newborn during vaginal birth	In females: increased vaginal discharge, burning urination, or irregular menstrual bleeding (many women show no early symptoms). In males: yellowish, thick penile discharge, or burning urination.	Antibiotics
Syphilis	Vaginal, oral, or anal sexual activity, or by touching an infected chancre or sore	A hard, round, painless chancre or sore appears at site of infection within 2–4 weeks.	Penicillin or other antibiotics for penicillin-allergic patients
Viral			
Genital herpes	Vaginal, oral, or anal sexual activity	Painful, reddish blisters around the genitals, thighs, or buttocks, and for females on the vagina or cervix. Other symptoms may include burning urination, flu-like symptoms, or vaginal discharge in females.	No cure, although certain drugs can provide relief and help sores heal
HPV	Vaginal, oral, or anal sexual activity	Some strains cause painless warts to appear in the genital area or anus; other strains may cause abnormal cell changes in the cervix.	Vaccine, cryotherapy (freezing), acid burning, or surgical removal of warts
HIV/AIDS	Sexual contact, infusion with contaminated blood, or from mother to child during pregnancy, childbirth, or breast feeding.	May develop flu-like symptoms that may disappear for many years before developing full-blown AIDS. AIDS symptoms include fever, weight loss, fatigue, diarrhea, and susceptibility to infection.	No cure; treatment includes a combination of antiretroviral drugs
Parasites			
Pubic lice	Sexual contact or contact with infested linens or toilet seats	Intense itching in hairy regions of the body, especially the pubic area	Prescription shampoos or nonprescription medications
Scabies	Sexual contact or contact with infested linens or toilet seats	Intense itching, reddish lines on skin, welts, and pus-filled blisters in affected area	Prescription shampoos

12.5.2 Health-Promoting Behaviors

health-promoting behaviors behaviors that decrease the chance of illness, disease, or death

Psychologists define **health-promoting behaviors** as those that decrease the chance of illness, disease, or death. Throughout this chapter we have indicated behaviors that you can engage in that appear to be related to better physical and mental health. Three additional behaviors that benefit the body and mind are *physical activity, healthy eating,* and *getting enough sleep.* Regular physical activity, healthful eating habits, and a good night's sleep promote a longer and healthier life.

Physical Activity

Physical activity improves physical and mental health. Such activity may include taking the stairs instead of the elevator at school or at work; parking farther away from stores when shopping; or walking or biking to campus instead of driving. Most health experts recommend moderate physical activity for at least 30 minutes a day. Moderate physical activity includes walking briskly, swimming, cycling, or jogging— aerobic activities that stimulate heart and lung functioning.

In addition to combating stress, physical activity helps us live longer, improves mental health, and positively affects memory and cognition (Cassilhas, Tufik, & de Mello, 2016; Collins et al., 2009; Lee et al., 2011; Williams & Kemper, 2010). Exercise reduces negative emotions such as depression and anxiety that we often feel in response to stress (Kandola et al., 2018; Stubbs et al., 2017). Engaging in regular physical activity also protects against cardiovascular disease, some kinds of cancer, and bone density loss, and can help with weight control (Bassuk & Manson, 2010; Huang et al., 2013; Slattery et al., 2010). Regular exercise is one of the most critical elements in any weight-loss program. Another important factor is eating right.

Eating Right

Being overweight or obese is associated with a higher risk of several types of health problems, such as type 2 diabetes, sleep apnea, migraine headaches, heart disease, and some cancers. It can also shorten one's life span (Li et al., 2018; National Research Council, 2011). Even perceiving oneself as overweight is associated with declines in physical health and impaired well-being (Daly, Robinson, & Sutin, 2017). Healthful eating when combined with physical activity can decrease one's risk of disease and death.

Eating right means choosing foods that are nutritious and healthy. Nutritious foods such as fruits, vegetables, and grains are high in vitamins, minerals, and fiber. Processed foods and foods high in sugar, salt, oil, or fat (like fast food) increase cholesterol, which contributes to the development of heart problems (Phelan et al., 2009). One should strive to eat well-balanced meals that meet one's nutritional needs and include a variety of foods from each of the major food groups.

Eating right also means eating breakfast. Breakfast is your first chance to refuel your body to prepare it for the day's activities. Regularly eating a healthy breakfast is associated with increased attention span, less risk of chronic diseases, and living a longer life (Hoyland, Dye, & Lawton, 2009; Schoenborn, 1986). Eating a healthy breakfast also makes us less likely to overeat later in the day.

Getting Enough Sleep

As we saw in Chapter 4, adults and teenagers require at least 8 hours of sleep a night, yet few of us achieve this. Why is getting enough sleep so important? For one, doing so enhances your immune system. When you deprive your body of sleep, your natural immune responses are reduced (Ruiz et al., 2012; Wright et al., 2015).

The right amount of sleep also activates chemicals that influence your emotions and enhance mood. If you are deprived of sleep, you are more likely to be irritable, cranky, and unhappy, in addition to being tired (Lemola, Ledermann, & Friedman, 2013; Short et al., 2013). Sleep offers many benefits to our functioning and ensures that we will be healthy, alert, and happy.

Soul/Getty Images

▲ People who are happy are healthier and live longer.

12.5.3 Happiness and Well-Being

Healthy living promotes happiness and life satisfaction. So, it is fitting to end this chapter by investigating what makes people happy. Research typically measures happiness by asking people how satisfied they are with their lives. This is referred to as *subjective well-being*. People who score high on measures of subjective well-being live longer and healthier lives (Boehm et al., 2016; Chida & Steptoe, 2008; Kushlev et al., 2020; Xu & Roberts, 2010). The factors that contribute to happiness nicely summarize much of the research that this chapter has explored:

- *Social relationships*. People who are happy have close, strong, and positive relationships with others. Higher well-being is associated with social rather than solitary pursuits that involve meaningful conversations with others (Algoe, 2019; Diener et al., 2018; Mehl et al., 2010; Mogilner, 2010; Rohrer et al., 2018; Rook, 2015). Strong ties increase subjective well-being and help moderate the ill effects of stress. Emily's loneliness and lack of connections with others often made her depressed and unhappy.
- *Cognitive patterns*. People think in ways that contribute to happiness. Happy people view stressors as opportunities rather than as threats, engage in more intentional positive activities such as expressing gratitude and thinking optimistically, and remember positive experiences rather than dwelling on negative ones (Lyubomirsky & Layous, 2013; Sin & Lyubomirsky, 2009). Across much of the world, people who state that their lives have purpose or meaning report higher subjective well-being than those without it (Jebb et al., 2020).
- *Temperament*. Good and bad events happen to everyone and influence levels of happiness. However, individuals differ in their ability to adapt to these events. People who bounce back from negative events by using positive emotions to cope can more easily reset their point of being happy to the same or a new adjusted level. This ability may stem from inherited differences in temperament and thus be greatly influenced by genetics.
- *Wealth*. Can money buy happiness? Only to a small extent. In poor societies, people who have more money report higher levels of happiness. However, once people rise above poverty level in terms of wealth, money doesn't buy more happiness. Income level shows only a weak to modest relationship with subjective well-being (Aknin, Norton, & Dunn, 2009; C. Anderson et al., 2012; Boyce et al., 2017; Diener et al., 2018). However, income loss and economic troubles may be related to lower well-being (Boyce et al., 2013; Sutin et al., 2013). Moreover, valuing money above relationships, love, and personal satisfaction is negatively associated with happiness (Bauer et al., 2012). How one spends their money may also be important to consider. People who spend

money on others or who spend their discretionary income on products that reflect who they are as individuals report more happiness (Dunn, Aknin, & Norton, 2014; Matz, Gladstone, & Stillwell, 2016; O'Brien & Kassirer, 2019).

- *Culture.* One's feeling of happiness is also influenced by the values that characterize one's society. Cultural norms dictate whether happiness and positive emotions are important and what constitutes a good life. Individualistic cultures endorse the value of personal happiness, whereas collectivistic cultures aspire to less happiness, value group identity and view positive emotions as transitory or of brief duration (Hornsey et al., 2018; Miyamoto & Ma, 2011). These differing definitions of happiness influence how people in a culture pursue happiness. People from collectivistic cultures place a greater emphasis on social engagement, connectedness, and family well-being. In contrast, people in individualistic cultures are less likely to emphasize social engagement in pursuing happiness. As a result, people in the United States (an individualistic culture) who pursue happiness may experience *lower* well-being compared to people in collectivistic cultures, especially if they spend less time with family and friends or helping others (Ford et al., 2015). This should not be surprising given that the first variable we mentioned as contributing to happiness is social relationships.

Future research will help us discover more about the nature of happiness and life satisfaction. This knowledge will enable psychologists to continue their efforts at understanding stress, preventing illnesses, and promoting lifelong well-being.

12.5 Quiz Yourself

1. Which of the following is *not* a health-promoting behavior?
   a. Viewing stressors as challenges rather than as threats
   b. Perceiving events as controllable
   c. Relying exclusively on one defense mechanism for coping
   d. Engaging in problem-focused coping

2. Pedro has experienced an intense, burning sensation during urination and a thick, yellowish penile discharge. Pedro most likely has which STI?
   a. Gonorrhea
   b. Genital herpes
   c. Genital warts
   d. HPV

3. Which of the following people is most likely to report being the happiest?
   a. Haifa, who is extremely wealthy, has a few close friends, and focuses on negative experiences
   b. Sam, who is moderately wealthy, optimistic, and adapts well to negative events
   c. Agustin, who is moderately wealthy, optimistic, and lives in a war-torn nation
   d. All of these would report similar levels of happiness

4. Which one of the following statements is *true*?
   a. Collectivistic cultures most value personal happiness.
   b. Higher well-being is associated with solitary pursuits.
   c. Skipping breakfast helps to focus one's attention.
   d. Income level has only a modest correlation with happiness.

Answers 1. c; 2. a; 3. b; 4. d

12.6 Integrating Psychology: The Big Picture

This chapter explored the topics of health, stress, and positive psychology—topics that are bound to be relevant to you. Notice how the information in this chapter emphasizes a *biopsychosocial* approach. The physical aspect of the stress response, the HPA axis, and the functioning of our immune systems constitute biological elements that influence our physical and mental health. What we perceive as stressors and how we cope with stress, as well as our personality, illustrate psychological factors involved in our general health and feelings of well-being. How we deal with different social, cultural, and environmental types of stressors such as major life events, daily hassles, and catastrophes also influences our health and happiness.

Think about Emily's story from the part opener. Her negative emotional responses of rage and panic often resulted in a spastic colon and elevated heart rate—biological effects from how she coped with stress. Her learned helplessness and negative self-evaluations only contributed to her difficulty in functioning. Acting out, smoking, drinking excessively, and sex with multiple partners were not effective means of coping with the emotional neglect she felt from those around her. Even despite a privileged background, Emily lacked social support, optimism, and other forms of positive and adaptive coping techniques, even from some of her therapists. Once she established a trusting and respectful relationship with Dr. Farber, she was able to make some progress toward her "best self."

Think about how the information in this chapter might apply to you. Examine the ways in which you handle stress. Do you spend a significant amount of your time on social media, gaming, or watching television, drinking alcohol, smoking, vaping, exercising, or using drugs? Are these methods adaptive or maladaptive? Do you experience any stress-related symptoms such as headaches, backaches, muscle tension, anxiety, or upset stomach? How might your coping style be influencing your health and well-being? What stress management techniques do you use and could you adopt more positive and adaptive ones? Are there any improvements that you could make in your personality or lifestyle that would enhance your health and happiness, and how might you begin to make these changes? Addressing issues such as these will help you master the material and hopefully will make you pause for a moment to contemplate how your health and well-being may be improved for today and for the future.

Studying the Chapter

Key Terms

alarm reaction (538)
approach-approach conflict (535)
approach-avoidance conflict (536)
avoidance-avoidance conflict (536)
cognitive reappraisal (544)
conflict (535)
coping (543)
daily hassles (533)
defense mechanisms (544)
emotion-focused coping (544)
exhaustion stage (540)
general adaptation syndrome (GAS) (538)
guided imagery (548)
hardy personality (553)
health psychology (527)
health-defeating behaviors (554)
health-promoting behaviors (560)
HPA (hypothalamic-pituitary-adrenal) axis (540)
immunosuppression (541)
learned helplessness (552)
life events (528)
multiple approach-avoidance conflicts (536)
positive psychology (527)
primary appraisal (537)
problem-focused coping (543)
progressive relaxation training (546)
psychoneuroimmunology (541)
resilience (534)
resistance stage (540)
secondary appraisal (538)
sexually transmitted infections (STIs) (556)
social support (547)
stress (528)
Type A personality (550)
Type B personality (550)
Type C personality (550)
Type D personality (550)

What Do You Know? Assess Your Understanding

Test your retention and understanding of the material by answering the following questions.

1. Which of the following events is likely to produce the most stress for the average person?
   a. Losing your job after months of talk about a buyout
   b. Losing your job without any warning
   c. Quitting your job to look for a different line of work
   d. Keeping your job after others have lost their jobs due to downsizing

2. Which of the following is *not* considered a major life event?
   a. Marriage
   b. Losing your job
   c. Buying a home
   d. Being late to work

3. The adrenal gland secretes which two hormones during the stress response?
   a. Adrenaline and corticosteroids
   b. Adrenaline and GABA
   c. Corticosteroids and insulin
   d. Insulin and GABA

4. Cecilia feels stressed from her full-time job and taking care of her two children. Cecilia finds a more flexible job that allows her to spend more time with her children. Which style of coping does Cecilia's behavior illustrate?
   a. Emotion-focused
   b. Problem-focused
   c. Defensive
   d. Both a and c

5. Which of the following behaviors promotes health and well-being?
   a. Perceiving events as controllable
   b. Engaging in defense mechanisms
   c. Expecting failure
   d. All of these help your health

6. Ryan can't decide whether to vacation in the mountains or at the beach. Ryan is experiencing a(n)______.
   a. approach-avoidance conflict
   b. approach-approach conflict
   c. avoidance-avoidance conflict
   d. multiple approach-avoidance conflict

7. Matresha is driving when a van pulls out in front of her and almost causes an accident. Matresha's heart begins to pound, and her blood pressure shoots up. Matresha is likely in the ______ phase of the general adaptation syndrome.
   a. alarm
   b. resistance
   c. exhaustion
   d. final

8. A weakened immune system and vulnerability to disease are most likely to occur in which stage of the general adaptation syndrome?
   a. Alarm
   b. Resistance
   c. Exhaustion
   d. Resilience

9. Jariel is a workaholic. He never takes a vacation. He won't even speak to friends and family on the phone when they call him at work. He is often angry and impatient with others and expresses his frustration to them. What type of personality does Jariel appear to have?
   a. Type A
   b. Type B
   c. Type C
   d. Type D

10. April recently lost her high-paying job. While talking to a friend about her job loss, she told the friend that she was looking forward to finding a job in a new field. April appears to be *most* exhibiting the hardy trait of ______.
    a. challenge
    b. commitment
    c. control
    d. resistance

11. Which of the following is *not* an effective means of managing stress?
    a. Exercise
    b. Relaxation techniques
    c. Talking to friends
    d. Being spontaneous with your time

12. Tom views his new job as a positive and challenging change. Tom's appraisal of stress in this situation is most likely to elicit the emotion of ______.
    a. anger
    b. fear
    c. excitement
    d. anxiety

13. Lucinda believes she has no control over what happens to her. She expects failure and often feels stressed out. What type of personality does Lucinda appear to have?
    a. Learned helplessness
    b. Type C personality
    c. Type A personality
    d. Type B personality

14. Which of the following is an accurate statement concerning the relationship between stress and the immune system?
    a. Stress always decreases the effectiveness of our immune system.
    b. Stress always increases the effectiveness of our immune system.
    c. If stress disrupts normal immune system functioning, we increase our vulnerability to illness and disease.
    d. If stress disrupts normal immune system functioning, we decrease our vulnerability to illness and disease.
15. Hurricane Dorian's destructive path through the Bahamas in 2019 powerfully illustrates the stressful nature of ______.
    a. daily hassles
    b. major life events
    c. catastrophes
    d. both a and b
16. Jeffrey has been feeling like he has the flu. He also has noticed reddish bumps around his genital area. Jeffrey most likely has which STI?
    a. Gonorrhea
    b. Genital herpes
    c. Syphilis
    d. Chlamydia
17. Which of the following is *not* a factor that contributes to happiness?
    a. Social support
    b. Cultural norms
    c. Wealth
    d. Eating breakfast
18. Florangel feels really stressed. Her child was up most of the night coughing. She has a major project due for her Economics course, and she is not sure if she will have enough money to pay her monthly bills. Florangel's high stress level is most due to ______.
    a. major life events
    b. daily hassles
    c. catastrophes
    d. approach-approach conflict
19. When Alexandra gets in a fight with her partner, she stomps her feet, covers her ears, and refuses to listen. Alexandra's behavior *best* illustrates the defense mechanism called ______.
    a. regression
    b. repression
    c. reaction formation
    d. displacement
20. The research on personality and health investigates if any specific personality traits are associated with specific health conditions. This is an example of ______ research.
    a. case study
    b. naturalistic
    c. correlational
    d. experimental

Answers: 1. b; 2. d; 3. a; 4. b; 5. a; 6. b; 7. a; 8. c; 9. a; 10. a; 11. d; 12. c; 13. a; 14. c; 15. c; 16. b; 17. d; 18. b; 19. a; 20. c

Use It or Lose It: Applying Psychology

1. What defense mechanisms do you think are more often employed by people who engage in health-defeating behaviors? Provide examples to illustrate and support your answer.
2. Using your own behavior, give an example of each of the following defense mechanisms: projection, denial, reaction formation, displacement, and sublimation.
3. Using your own behavior, give an example of each of the conflict situations discussed in the section on stress and stressors in this chapter. How did you respond to each of these situations? Indicate whether your response reflected a problem-focused coping strategy or an emotion-focused coping strategy.
4. Develop a formal time schedule to better manage your time. First create a chart showing all the hours in a day and all the days of the week. Block out all those times that are already committed, such as sleeping, class time, work, and daily chores. Now allocate a specific amount of time to study for your classes and to exercise. Follow this plan for a week to see whether you need to make any modifications. Provide an analysis of your time use.

Critical Thinking About the Science of Psychology

As we saw in Section 12.1, Holmes and Rahe (1967) found a correlation between people's score on the Social Readjustment Rating Scale and their likelihood of illness. Review their research and then answer the following questions:

1. What type of correlation did Holmes and Rahe find?
2. What specifically were the variables in their study?
3. What conclusion can be drawn from this correlation and which goal of psychology does it relate to?

Are You Getting the Big Picture?

Kathleen Finlay/Masterfile

Health psychologists study how people's behavior influences their health for better and for worse. **Positive psychology** seeks to discover and promote those factors that contribute to happiness and well-being.

12.1 What Is Stress? Stress and Stressors

- **Stress** is any event or environmental stimulus (stressor) that we respond to because we perceive it as challenging or threatening.
- *Catastrophes*, trauma, and significant **life events**, such as the death of a loved one or a new job, are major stressors. Everyday frustrations—called **daily hassles**—are less serious stressors, but can have a negative effect on physical and mental health.
- **Resilience** or adapting well to significant stressors may be a protective factor for some people who experience chronic stress.
- **Conflict** also produces stress.

Rubberball/Mike Kemp/Getty Images

12.2 The Stress Response

- If our initial interpretation or **primary appraisal** of an event is one of stress, we may view it as a threat, as harmful, or merely as a challenge.
- Our body responds to stress in a three-phase **general adaptation syndrome:**
  - The **alarm reaction** consists of those bodily responses, including the nervous system and endocrine system (**HPA axis**), that are immediately triggered when we initially appraise an event as stressful.
  - In the **resistance stage**, the body shores up additional energy to cope with the stressor, but the bodily reactions are less intense than during the alarm reaction.
  - In the **exhaustion phase**, wear and tear on the body begins, causing serious damage if stress continues over an extended period of time.
- The corticosteroids and endorphins that are released into our body during the stress response dampen the activity of our immune system (**immunosuppression**), making us more vulnerable to health problems.

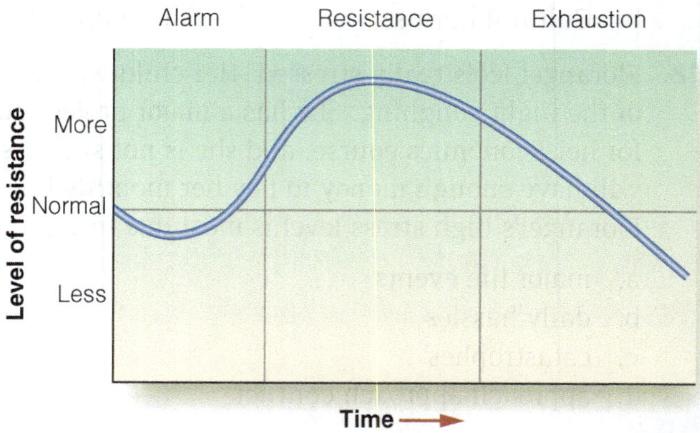

12.3 Coping with Stress

- **Coping** is how we manage a threatening event or stimulus.
- **Problem-focused coping** controls or alters the environment that caused the stress. It is most useful when we feel that we can do something about the stressor.
- **Emotion-focused coping** controls our internal, subjective, emotional responses to stress. We alter the way we feel or think in order to reduce stress.
- **Defense mechanisms** are unconscious coping strategies that allow us to reduce our anxiety and maintain a positive self-image and self-esteem.
- A number of strategies can be used to reduce stress and promote well-being in one's life, including exercise, **social support**, **guided imagery**, *mindfulness-based practices*, laughter, and time management.

Leonora Hamill/Getty Images

12.4 Personality, Health, and Well-Being

- A person with a **Type A personality** is aggressive, competitive, and driven to achieve; a person with a **Type B personality** is relaxed, easygoing, patient, and flexible; a person with a **Type C personality** is careful and patient and suppresses negative emotions such as anger; a **Type D personality** worries, is sad, and avoids social interactions. The Type A personality trait of hostility is related to a higher incidence of heart disease. The Type D personality may put one at greater risk for heart problems.
- **Learned helplessness** results from believing that you have no control over stressful life events. You view stressors as threats, your level of stress increases, and you are more likely to develop stress-related illnesses.
- The **hardy personality** is resistant to stress; it includes characteristics such as
  - A tendency to see life as a series of *challenges*;
  - A sense of personal *commitment* to self, work, family, and other values;
  - A perception of *control* over one's life and work.

12.5 Lifestyle, Health and Well-Being

- **Health-defeating behaviors**, such as alcohol and substance abuse, smoking and vaping, distracted driving, and unsafe sex, increase the chance of illness, disease, or death.
- **Sexually transmitted infections** are passed from one person to another primarily through sexual contact. Young people are at greater risk for contracting STIs because they are more likely to engage in high-risk sexual behaviors.
- **Health-promoting behaviors** decrease the chance of illness, disease, or death. Regular physical activity, healthful eating, and getting enough sleep promote a longer and healthier life.

Soul/Getty Images

- Happiness and *subjective well-being* are related to a strong social support network, an optimistic outlook, economic resources, temperament, and cultural values.

Learning Objectives

13.1 Define a mental health disorder and identify and apply the criteria that psychologists use for determining dysfunctional behavior. (APA 1.1, 1.2, 1.3)

13.1 Indicate the lifetime and annual prevalence rates of mental health disorders by development, gender, and ethnicity. (APA 1.1, 1.3, 2.5)

13.1 Compare and contrast the varying perspectives on explaining mental health disorders including the biopsychosocial perspective. (APA 1.2, 2.1)

13.2 Identify the structure of the *DSM* model, and explain the research on its strengths and weaknesses. (APA 1.1, 2.1, 3.3)

13.3 Describe the components of excessive anxiety and distinguish among the symptoms of anxiety, obsessive-compulsive, and trauma-related disorders. (APA 1.1, 1.2)

13.3 Discuss research on the biopsychosocial factors that contribute to anxiety, obsessive-compulsive, and trauma-related disorders. (APA 2.1, 2.5)

13.4 Distinguish among the symptoms of the various dissociative disorders, and describe their link to stressful or traumatic events. (APA 1.1, 1.3)

13.4 Distinguish among the symptoms of the various somatic symptom and related disorders, and discuss their link to health anxiety. (APA. 1.1, 1.2)

13.5 Distinguish between the symptoms of the depressive and bipolar disorders. (APA 1.1, 1.3)

13.5 Describe common misconceptions that people hold about suicide. (APA 1.3)

13.5 Discuss research on the biopsychosocial factors that play a role in depressive and bipolar disorders. (APA 1.2, 2.1, 2.5)

13.5 Explain the role of biopsychosocial factors in women's higher vulnerability to depression. (APA 1.3, 2.1, 2.5)

13.6 Describe the typical onset and prognosis for schizophrenia and its variation by age, gender, social class, and ethnicity. (APA 1.1, 2.5)

13.6 Identify and discriminate among the positive and negative symptoms of schizophrenia. (APA 1.1, 1.2)

13.6 Discuss the research on our current understanding of the causes of schizophrenia. (APA 2.1, 2.5)

13.7 Discriminate among the different types of personality disorders. (APA 1.1, 1.2)

badahos/Shutterstock.com

13 Mental Health Disorders

This chapter outlines several major categories of mental health disorders and explains the symptoms used to diagnose particular disorders. For each type of disorder, we will consider the possible reasons why a person behaves this way. Although the research presented may seem overwhelming at times, keep in mind that these explanations are closely tied to topics with which you are already familiar. For example, many of the symptoms of mental health disorders are physical in nature, involving brain functioning, neurotransmitters, hormones, and genetics—biological factors that were introduced in Chapter 2. Many of the symptoms also relate to psychological concepts such as learning, cognition, and emotions—again, topics that have been addressed in previous chapters. Furthermore, we will see that certain disorders are more common among certain segments of the population. Your familiarity with previous discussions on gender, race, social class, personality, development, and culture will assist you in understanding these sociocultural factors and individual variations that influence mental health. ■

Chapter Outline

BSIP SA/Alamy stock photo

▲ Autism spectrum disorder, typically diagnosed in childhood, is characterized by challenges in social communication.

13.1 What Is a Mental Health Disorder?

There is no simple test that a person can take to uncover a mental health disorder. As such, mental health professionals define a **mental health disorder** as a dysfunction in thinking (cognition), emotions, and/or social behavior that impairs functioning and is not culturally expected (Insel et al., 2010; Sanislow et al., 2011). Recall from this part's case study that Emily's difficulty in functioning would meet these criteria. Her rage, panic, and suicide attempts were emotional responses that impaired her functioning and were not typical behaviors for her circumstances. Let's look more closely at how this definition distinguishes typical behavior from dysfunctional behavior:

1. *Not typical or culturally expected*. If we judge typical as what most people do, then engaging in a behavior less or more frequently than others would be atypical. For example, it is considered crucial for survival to ingest a minimum amount of food per day. People who engage in this behavior a lot less than most people—as in the case of people with anorexia—would qualify as atypical. Persons with autism spectrum disorder engage in social communication and social interaction far less than most people. As such, their behavior may be considered atypical. Atypical can also mean engaging in a behavior that most people do not. For example, believing that you are from another planet or galaxy is a thought that most people do not have.

   Also implied in this definition is whether the behavior violates social and cultural norms of how people are supposed to behave. However, it is extremely important to emphasize that social norms vary widely across cultures, within cultures, and across historical times. What is considered socially acceptable in Los Angeles, California, may be considered unacceptable in Keokuk, Iowa. Similarly, what was deemed unacceptable in the 1950s may be considered acceptable today. For example, changing views on homosexuality in part influenced the American Psychiatric Association to remove homosexuality from its list of mental health disorders in 1973. The Chinese Psychiatric Association did not do so until 2001. Because social norms vary so widely, judging dysfunctional behavior on this aspect alone is especially problematic.
2. *Distress*. A mental health disorder causes great personal distress to the individual or those around them. Often people seek treatment when a behavior causes such emotional or physical pain. Alternatively, a person with a mental health disorder may cause distress in others through chronic lying or violence.
3. *Dysfunction*. In defining a mental health disorder, psychologists consider whether a behavior interferes with a person's ability to function. Can the person hold a job, go to school, or form close relationships? The more difficulty a person has in functioning in everyday life, the more likely their behavior is considered to meet criteria for a mental health disorder.

13.1.1 Prevalence of Mental Health Disorders

In 2017, there were an estimated 19% of Americans 18 and older with a mental health disorder in the past year (SAMHSA, 2018). Lifetime prevalence estimates are quite a bit higher, with close to half of U.S. adults meeting the criteria for a mental health disorder at some time in their lives (Kessler et al., 2009; see ● FIGURE 13.1). And yet, this may be a conservative estimate, as many people who have difficulty functioning may not want or have access to mental health services (SAMHSA, 2018).

Mental health disorders are the leading cause of disability worldwide (Whiteford et al., 2015). Although there is little overall gender difference in the lifetime risk of a mental health disorder, adult females were more likely than adult

mental health disorder a dysfunction in thinking (cognition), emotions, and/or social behavior that impairs functioning and is not culturally expected

psychopathology the scientific study of mental health disorders males to have both any mental health disorder (22.3% vs. 15.1%) and a serious mental health disorder (5.7% vs. 3.3%) in the last year (SAMHSA, 2018). Moreover, males and females do show differences in the types of mental health disorders they are more likely to experience (Eaton et al., 2012; NCS-R, 2007; see ● FIGURE 13.2). However, these gender differences may in part reflect clinician bias in diagnosis as well as the finding that females are more likely than males to use mental health services (Center for Behavioral Health Statistics & Quality, 2016; Jane et al., 2007; SAMHSA, 2018). Among U.S. teens, data from national surveys indicate that 22% were likely to experience a mental health disorder with severe impairment or distress at some time in their lives (Merikangas et al., 2010). Suicide, although not always related to a mental health disorder, consistently remains as the 10th leading cause of death in the United States (CDC, 2020c; Kochanek et al., 2016). Consequently, it is likely that you or someone close to you will at some time experience psychological distress or a mental health disorder.

Stress during the COVID-19 pandemic has also created a mental health burden of increasing concern. Research suggests that infected patients are more likely to show posttraumatic stress symptoms; health-care workers are more susceptible to depressive and anxiety symptoms as well as sleep disturbances; and people with preexisting mental health problems are more likely to experience a worsening of symptoms (Vindegaard & Benros, 2020). An American Psychiatric Association poll in March of 2020 indicated that nearly half of Americans were anxious about contracting COVID-19 and 62% of Americans were anxious about loved ones contracting the virus. Additional cited worries included finances, running out of supplies, and the economy. Social distancing, isolation, and economic hardship may serve to increase feelings of anxiety, loneliness, and depressed mood. Being familiar with psychology's current understanding of such behavior may help you manage such a situation.

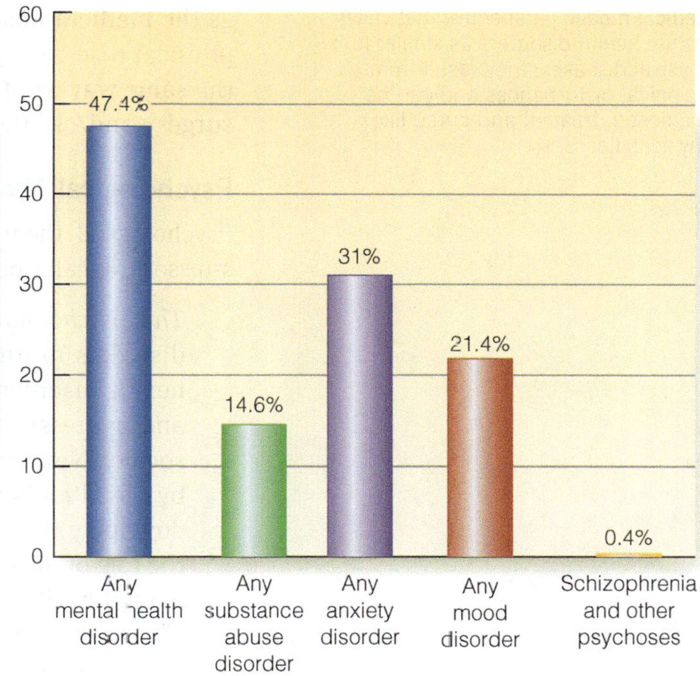

FIGURE 13.1

Lifetime Prevalence of Mental Health Disorders

Close to half of U.S. adults will be diagnosed with a mental health disorder at some time in their lives.

Source: Kessler et al., 2009.

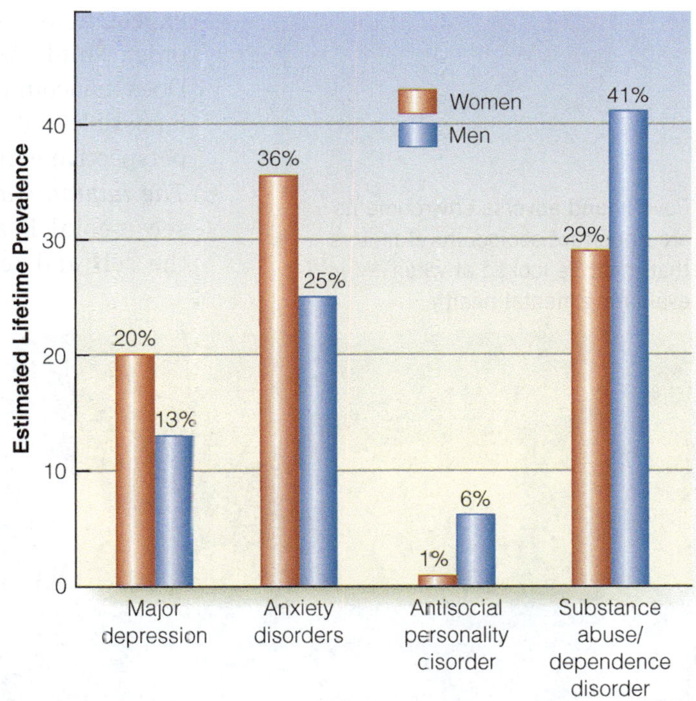

FIGURE 13.2

Prevalence of Depression, Anxiety, Substance Abuse, and Antisocial Personality Disorder in Women and Men

Males and females differ in the types of mental health disorders they are more likely to experience.

Source: National Comorbidity Survey Replication data, Table 1. Updated 2007. http://www.hcp.med.harvard.edu/ncs

13.1.2 Explaining Mental Health Disorders: Perspectives Revisited

Psychopathology is the scientific study of mental health disorders. Today, Western cultures lean toward three main models or approaches for understanding abnormal behavior: *biological theories, psychological theories,* and *social* or *cultural theories.*

Biological Theories: The Medical Model

Biological theories attribute mental health disorders to some physical process: genetics, an imbalance in hormones or neurotransmitters, or some brain or bodily dysfunction. The biological perspective is also known

medical model perspective that views mental health disorders as similar to physical diseases; they result from biological disturbances and can be diagnosed, treated, and cured like physical illnesses

as the **medical model** because mental health disorders are viewed as similar to physical diseases. Therefore, they can be diagnosed, treated, or cured in much the same way as other physical illnesses by prescribing medications or through surgery and/or other medical procedures.

Psychological Theories: Internal and External Influences

Psychological theories attribute mental health disorders to internal or external stressors. Recall from Chapter 11 on personality that four perspectives predominate:

- *The psychoanalytic perspective*. This perspective attributes mental health disorders to unresolved unconscious conflicts. According to Freud, mental health disorders result from the conflict between the unconscious sexual and aggressive instinctual desires of the id and the outward demands of society. Newer theories, referred to as *psychodynamic theories* and developed by Freud's followers such as Alfred Adler and Karen Horney (see Chapter 11), downplay the role of sexual and aggressive instincts and instead emphasize the role of the ego and interpersonal relationships in maintaining or restoring mental health.
- *The social learning perspective*. Learning theorists explain difficulty in functioning as a result of the same learning processes that produce functional behavior—classical conditioning, operant conditioning, and observational learning (see Chapter 6). A person's responses to stimuli in the environment and the consequences of these behaviors are what lead to problematic behavior. A person's past learning and modeling along with current experiences can explain mental health disorders.
- *The cognitive perspective*. This perspective emphasizes the role of thoughts, expectations, assumptions, and other mental processes in mental health disorder. Think about the little voice inside you that comments on your behavior. Does it encourage you to do well, or does it criticize you for your stupidity? Is it possible that such internal messages influence your behavior? The cognitive perspective maintains that they do.
- *The humanistic perspective*. Humanists like Carl Rogers (see Chapter 11) see mental health disorders as resulting from a distorted perception of the self and reality. When people lose touch with their personal values and their sense of self, or when they fail to fulfill their basic biological and psychological needs, they cannot attain self-actualization. Instead, they experience personal distress and are more likely to engage in maladaptive behavior.

▼ Poverty and adverse environments are important sociocultural factors that must be looked at when evaluating mental health.

Owen Franken/The Image Bank Unreleased/Getty Images

Sociocultural Theories: The Individual Varies in Context

Sociocultural theories emphasize social or cultural factors that may play a role in mental health. Such a perspective argues that internal biological and psychological processes can be understood only in the context of the larger society and culture that shape and influence people's behavior. Mental health disorders, therefore, can only be fully understood when social factors such as age, race, gender, social roles, and socioeconomic status are taken into account. In addition, social conditions such as poverty, discrimination, and environmental stressors must be looked at when evaluating mental health (Evans & Cassells, 2014; Zvolensky et al., 2010).

A Biopsychosocial Model: Integrating Perspectives

Despite decades of research, no single theory or perspective is correct. It is only by integrating all the perspectives that our explanations of mental health disorders become comprehensive. We often hear in the popular press and in television commercials that a mental health disorder such as depression or anxiety is caused by "a specific gene" or "a chemical imbalance." But such reports are too simplistic to explain the complexity of mental illness. Most mental health disorders result from a combination of biological, psychological, and social factors (hence the name of the *biopsychosocial model*); they do not have just one cause.

For example, as we will soon see, research on people diagnosed with major depressive disorder suggests changes in brain chemistry—a biological factor. They also are likely to engage in a negative pattern of thinking, a psychological factor. In addition, major depression is more likely to be diagnosed in women—in part, a sociocultural factor. Current research in psychology focuses on understanding how these forces operate together, much as the pieces of a jigsaw puzzle fit together.

13.1 Quiz Yourself

1. **Susan will only eat soup with a fork. By which criteria can Susan's behavior be considered atypical?**
   a. Danger to others
   b. Violates social norms
   c. Distress
   d. All of the above
2. **What is the likelihood that you or someone close to you will be diagnosed with a mental health disorder sometime in your life?**
   a. About 15%
   b. About 25%
   c. About 50%
   d. About 75%
3. **Dr. Kwan believes that Ken's difficulty in functioning has resulted from a distorted sense of self and a loss of personal values. Dr. Kwan is adopting which psychological perspective?**
   a. Humanistic
   b. Psychoanalytic
   c. Social learning
   d. Cognitive

Answers 1. *b*; 2. *c*; 3. *a*

13.2 The *DSM* Model for Classifying Abnormal Behavior

In 1952, the American Psychiatric Association published a book listing the symptoms that must be shown in order for a person to be diagnosed with a specific mental health disorder. Emily, featured in this part's case study, was diagnosed as having an anxiety problem with borderline personality trends. More than 65 years later, the ***Diagnostic and Statistical Manual of Mental Disorders (DSM)*** is in its fifth edition, published in 2013. This most recent edition, known as the *DSM-5*, lists specific and concrete criteria for diagnosing nearly 300 disorders in children, adolescents, and adults. Here we outline the general structure of the *DSM* and describe its strengths and weaknesses.

Diagnostic and Statistical Manual of Mental Disorders (DSM) a book published by the American Psychiatric Association that lists the diagnostic criteria for close to 300 mental health disorders

13.2.1 The Structure of the *DSM*

The *DSM-5* includes 20 major categories of mental health disorders. Many of these disorders are the focus of this chapter and are listed in ● TABLE 13.1. It also indicates the length of time that a person must show these symptoms to qualify for a diagnosis. These criteria require that the symptoms interfere with the person's ability to function, adopting the definition of a mental health disorder described at the start of this chapter and that is accepted by many professionals today. However, the current version of the *DSM* does not speculate as to the causes of the individual's behavior—it is *atheoretical*. This atheoretical position underscores the complex biopsychosocial nature of the causes of mental illness. Moreover, because the *DSM-5* is relatively new, some of the research described therein is derived from individuals who met the diagnostic criteria from previous editions of the *DSM*.

TABLE 13.1 *DSM-5* Major Categories of Disorders

Major Category	Some Included Disorders
Neurodevelopmental Disorders	• Intellectual Disabilities • Communication Disorders • Autism Spectrum Disorders • Attention-Deficit/Hyperactivity Disorder • Specific Learning Disorder • Motor Disorders
Schizophrenia Spectrum and Other Psychotic Disorders	• Delusional Disorder • Brief Psychotic Disorder • Schizophrenia • Schizoaffective Disorder
Bipolar and Related Disorders	• Bipolar I Disorder • Bipolar II Disorder • Cyclothymic Disorder
Depressive Disorders	• Major Depressive Disorder • Persistent Depressive Disorder • Premenstrual Dysphoric Disorder
Anxiety Disorders (see You Review)	• Separation Anxiety Disorder • Social Anxiety Disorder (Social Phobia) • Panic Disorder • Generalized Anxiety Disorder • Specific Phobia
Obsessive-Compulsive and Related Disorders (see You Review)	• Obsessive-Compulsive Disorder • Body Dysmorphic Disorder • Hoarding Disorder
Trauma- and Stressor-Related Disorders (see You Review)	• Reactive Attachment Disorder • Posttraumatic Stress Disorder • Acute Stress Disorder

TABLE 13.1 *DSM-5* Major Categories of Disorders (*Continued*)

Major Category	Some Included Disorders
Dissociative Disorders (see Table 13.2)	• Dissociative Identity Disorder • Dissociative Amnesia • Depersonalization/Derealization Disorder
Somatic Symptom and Related Disorders (see Table 13.3)	• Somatic Symptom Disorder • Conversion Disorder • Illness Anxiety Disorder
Feeding and Eating Disorders (see Chapter 5)	• Binge Eating Disorder • Anorexia Nervosa • Bulimia Nervosa
Elimination Disorders	• Enuresis • Encopresis
Sleep-Wake Disorders (see Chapter 4)	• Insomnia Disorder • Central Sleep Apnea • Restless Legs Syndrome
Sexual Dysfunctions	• Erectile Disorder • Female Orgasmic Disorder • Genito-Pelvic Pain/Penetration Disorder
Gender Dysphoria	• Gender Dysphoria
Disruptive, Impulse-Control, and Conduct Disorders	• Oppositional Defiant Disorder • Conduct Disorder • Kleptomania
Substance-Related and Addictive Disorders (see Chapter 4)	• Alcohol-Related Disorders • Opioid-Related Disorders • Stimulant-Related Disorders • Gambling Disorder
Neurocognitive Disorders	• Delirium • Major and Mild Neurocognitive Disorders
Personality Disorders (see Table 13.4)	• Paranoid Personality Disorder • Antisocial Personality Disorder • Borderline Personality Disorder • Unspecified Personality Disorder
Paraphilic Disorders	• Voyeuristic Disorder • Fetishistic Disorder • Sexual Sadism Disorder
Other Mental Disorders	• Unspecified Mental Disorder

Source: Reprinted with permission from the *Diagnostic and Statistical Manual of Mental Disorders, Fifth Edition*, Copyright 2013. American Psychiatric Association.

13.2.2 How Good Is the *DSM* Model?

How *reliable* and *valid* is the *DSM* model? Recall from Chapter 11 that *reliability* refers to the consistency of a measurement system. We would expect two different clinicians to give a similar judgment or a consistent rating when presented with the same symptoms. Similar diagnoses should also be made when different people exhibit the same symptoms.

Validity refers to how well a rating system does what it was intended to do; it refers to the accuracy of the test. We would expect that the *DSM* model should be accurate in diagnosing people who are having difficulty functioning. In addition, it should be accurate in the label it applies to a person's condition. People who are depressed should be diagnosed as depressed, and people addicted to drugs should be diagnosed as having a substance-related disorder.

The numerous revisions of the *DSM* have attempted to improve its reliability and validity based on sound scientific data. As a result, the reliability and validity for many of the diagnostic categories have improved (T.A. Brown et al., 2001; Hasin et al., 2006; Lahey et al., 2004). However, disagreement exists as to whether the *DSM-5* has improved its diagnostic reliability over previous editions (Lieblich et al., 2015; Regier et al., 2013), as very few changes were made to diagnosing the personality disorders. This is potentially problematic, as the reliability of the personality disorders was considered low, calling into question the validity of diagnosing the personality disorders (Clark, 2007; Falkum, Pedersen, & Karterud, 2009; Widiger & Trull, 2007).

Having a standard system such as the *DSM* does not guarantee an accurate diagnosis. Making diagnostic judgments usually involve some subjectivity and personal bias on the part of the clinician, as people's symptoms often do not fit neatly into one category. Moreover, certain symptoms may be listed as a part of several disorders. As a result, sometimes people meet the criteria for more than one disorder, and can be diagnosed with both, a situation called *comorbidity*. Biases having to do with gender, race, or culture—whether conscious or unconscious—can also skew a diagnosis (Jane et al., 2007; Oltmanns & Powers, 2012; Skodol & Bender, 2003; Widiger & Chaynes, 2003).

Critics of the *DSM* model also point out the possible negative effects of labeling someone with a mental health disorder (Baumann, 2007; Grover, 2005). A diagnostic label may serve as a *self-fulfilling prophecy*, encouraging a person to behave in a way that is consistent with the disorder. Remember how Emily's father called her careless and clumsy, which only contributed to Emily's feelings of awkwardness. Others in the person's environment may also treat the person in a way that encourages the symptoms of the disorder. We as a society tend to treat people with any diagnostic label negatively which creates a *stigma* or mark of disapproval, perhaps increasing their maladaptive functioning through prejudice and discrimination and decreasing their likelihood of seeking treatment (Corrigan, Druss, & Perlick, 2014). Such negative treatment and social stigma may persist even after the person's behavior returns to normal (Rosenhan, 1973; Szasz, 1987).

The *DSM* model is not perfect and can provide only a general description of the problem a person is experiencing. It does not consider the uniqueness of each individual, nor can it tell us how this person will behave in the future. Yet the *DSM* provides a useful framework and common language for clinicians and researchers to diagnose and study people with mental health problems. Having a common language also allows researchers to more effectively study the possible underlying causes of mental health disorders. Keep in mind the advantages and criticisms of the *DSM* system as we review some of the more prevalent and more complicated mental health disorders.

Psychology Works!

monkeybusinessimages/iStock/Getty Images

The mental health field is extensive and includes a variety of careers: licensed social workers, licensed professional counselors, couple and family therapists, addiction counselors, psychiatric nurses, community service managers, applied behavior analysts, and of course psychologists, to name a few. In all of these professions, individuals are trained to assess and diagnose mental health disorders. They learn the nature of the *DSM* and the symptoms of specific mental health disorders as well as the biopsychosocial nature of mental health so that they can understand all the factors that may play a role in a person's difficulty in functioning. They may work in direct patient care with children, teenagers, and/or adults while others may perform research on mental health. As you can see, a degree in the mental health field offers many career options.

13.2 Quiz Yourself

1. **The purpose of the *DSM* is to _____.**
   a. explain the causes of mental health disorders
   b. describe the symptoms of mental health disorders
   c. indicate the frequency of mental health disorders
   d. prescribe treatment methods for mental health disorders
2. **The *DSM* model most emphasizes which aspect of the definition of a mental health disorder?**
   a. Atypical
   b. Violation of social norms
   c. Inability to function
   d. Mental insanity
3. **Which of the following is *true* about diagnosis?**
   a. A diagnostic system is valid if two different clinicians give a similar judgment or a consistent rating when presented with the same symptoms.
   b. The *DSM-5* has eliminated the problem of comorbidity.
   c. A diagnostic label may serve as a self-fulfilling prophecy.
   d. The *DSM-5* guarantees accurate diagnoses.

Answers 1. *b*; 2. *c*; 3. *c*

13.3 Anxiety, Obsessive-Compulsive, and Trauma-Related Disorders: It's Not Just "Nerves"

We all experience anxiety from time to time. Many students are anxious when they have to make an oral presentation. Other people are nervous when they have to meet new people or fly in an airplane. In these examples, however, the anxiety tends to decrease once the situation is over. People with excessive anxiety are different in that the intensity, duration, frequency, and/or rationality of their fear are out of proportion to the situation or occur without apparent triggers or signals of danger and seriously interfere with their ability to function. We saw in this part's case study how Emily's panic caused distress and difficulty in coping.

13.3.1 Components of Excessive Anxiety

Typically, excessive anxiety can be characterized by four components: *physical, cognitive, emotional,* and *behavioral*. These components interact powerfully, creating an unpleasant experience of fear or dread, although there may not be a specific fear-producing stimulus present.

The *physical* components of anxiety include dizziness, elevated heart rate and blood pressure, muscle tension, sweating palms, and dry mouth. These physical symptoms stem from the activation of the sympathetic nervous system (see Chapter 2). The hormonal system is also activated as adrenaline is released into the bloodstream. Recall that this process is referred to as the fight-or-flight response. This fight-or-flight response occurs every time we perceive a threat in our environment.

People with excessive anxiety have concerns that are unrealistic and out of proportion to the amount of harm that could occur. *Cognitive* components of anxiety may include worrying, fearing loss of control, exaggerating (in one's mind) the danger of a situation, exhibiting paranoia, or being extremely wary and watchful of people and events. These thoughts may lead to *emotional* reactions such as a sense of dread, terror, panic, irritability, or restlessness. These thoughts and emotions propel the person to behave in ways meant to cope with the anxiety.

Coping with excessive anxiety may include *behaviors* such as escaping or fleeing from the situation; behaving aggressively; "freezing," which results in being unable to move; or avoiding the situation in the future. Again, these symptoms are so intense that they disrupt the quality of the person's life and cause significant distress.

13.3.2 Types of Excessive Anxiety Disorders

Anxiety disorders are one of the more common mental health disorders. Approximately 19% of Americans over 18 years of age are diagnosed with an anxiety disorder in a given year (Kessler et al., 2009; NCS-R, 2007) (see ● FIGURE 13.3). However, results from the 2008–2012 Mental Health Surveillance Study (MHSS) conducted by the Substance Abuse and Mental Health Services Administration (SAMHSA) are significantly lower at 5.7% perhaps due to different interview and assessment methods (Karg et al., 2014). Yet both estimates found women have consistently higher rates of anxiety disorders than do men (Karg et al., 2014).

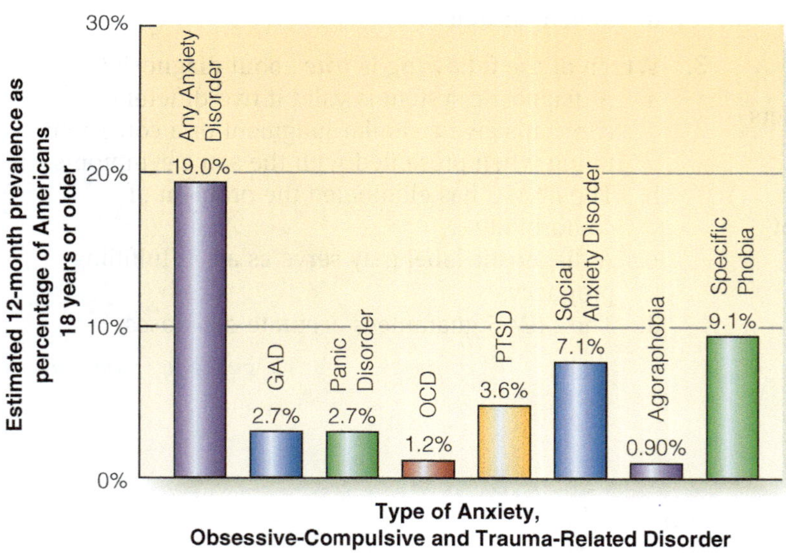

FIGURE 13.3

Prevalence of Anxiety, Obsessive-Compulsive, and Trauma-Related Disorders in a Given Year

Among adults 18 years of age or older, social anxiety disorder and specific phobia are the most commonly diagnosed disorders in any given year, because the age of onset is typically earlier for these disorders than for the other excessive anxiety disorders.

Source: National Comorbidity Survey Replication data, Table 2. Updated 2007. http://www.hcp.med.harvard.edu/ncs

Lifetime risk of an anxiety disorder for people aged 13 or older is estimated at 29%, with White Americans having a higher lifetime risk than African Americans, Hispanic Americans, and Asian Americans (Asnaani et al., 2010; Kessler et al., 2012). Anxiety disorders typically begin in childhood or adolescence and are highly *comorbid*, meaning that the anxiety disorder occurs along with another mental health disorder (Copeland et al., 2014; Kessler et al., 2010). Recall that Emily's anxiety was evident by the early teen years, and she was diagnosed as having not just an anxiety disorder but also borderline personality disorder.

We will discuss three *DSM-5* categories of disorders characterized by excessive anxiety: anxiety disorders, obsessive-compulsive disorders, and trauma-related disorders. The anxiety disorders include *generalized anxiety disorder, panic disorder, agoraphobia, specific phobia,* and *social anxiety disorder.* The obsessive-compulsive disorders include *obsessive-compulsive disorder* and *hoarding disorder. Posttraumatic stress disorder* is a trauma-related disorder.

Generalized Anxiety Disorder (GAD)

Some people are anxious all the time in almost all situations. These individuals may be diagnosed with **generalized anxiety disorder (GAD)**. Symptoms of GAD include excessive anxiety, worry, and difficulty in controlling such worries. The person may be easily fatigued, restless, and irritable, and may experience difficulty concentrating or sleeping (American Psychiatric Association, 2013). People with GAD chronically worry not only about major issues, such as which car or house to buy, their children's health, or their job performance, but also about minor issues such as being late, wearing the right outfit, or what to make for dinner. It is estimated that about 2% to 4% of American adults experience GAD in any given year (Karg et al., 2014; Kessler et al., 2005b; Ruscio et al., 2017) with 8% to 14% meeting the criteria for the disorder some time in their lives (Moffitt et al., 2010; Ruscio et al., 2017). White Americans are at higher risk of GAD than African Americans, Hispanic Americans, and Asian Americans (Asnaani et al., 2010).

generalized anxiety disorder (GAD) an anxiety disorder characterized by chronic, constant worry in almost all situations

panic disorder an anxiety disorder characterized by intense fear and anxiety in the absence of danger that is accompanied by strong physical symptoms

agoraphobia [agg-or-uh-FOE-bee-uh] an anxiety disorder characterized by excessive fear of being in places from which escape might be difficult or where help might not be available if one were to experience panic

Panic Disorder and Agoraphobia

Imagine that you are attending a party given by a good friend. When you arrive at the party, a feeling of panic suddenly overwhelms you. Your heart begins to pound, you hear ringing in your ears, your skin feels tingly and numb, and it becomes harder and harder to breathe. These are common symptoms that occur during a *panic attack,* a short but intense episode of severe anxiety. As many as 30% of adults in the United States report occasional panic attacks that do not interfere with their daily functioning (Kessler et al., 2006). However, when panic attacks are more common, and a person begins to fear having panic attacks to the extent that it interferes with their ability to function, a diagnosis of **panic disorder** may be given (American Psychiatric Association, 2013).

It is estimated that between 1% and 5% of people will develop panic disorder at some time in their lives (Grant et al., 2006; Karg et al., 2014). It typically develops in late adolescence or early adulthood and is two to four times as common in women as in men (Grant et al., 2006; Karg et al., 2014; Sawchuk et al., 2017). White Americans and Native Americans tend to have a higher prevalence rate of panic disorder than do African Americans, Asian Americans, and Hispanic Americans (Asnaani et al., 2010; Breslau et al., 2006; Grant et al., 2006).

People with panic disorder often feel so overwhelmed by the feelings of panic that they think they are having a heart attack or a seizure. They may believe that they are "going crazy" or going to die, and many seek medical attention to find out what is wrong with them. The panic attacks may occur frequently or only sporadically. Most people with panic disorder cannot identify any specific thing that might have triggered the attack. However, when a panic attack occurs, the same situation may then trigger a future attack. Emily's teenage behavior was probably most consistent with panic disorder.

Fear of having another panic attack may lead to **agoraphobia**, or fear of being in places from which escape may be difficult or where help may not be available if one were to experience panic (American Psychiatric Association, 2013). People affected with agoraphobia avoid any place—the mall, the grocery store, or the movie

▲ For many college students, taking a test is an anxiety-producing event.

theater—in which they believe a panic attack may occur. Such fears can leave people housebound for years. At least 75% of those who are diagnosed with agoraphobia are women (Barlow, 2002).

Specific Phobia and Social Anxiety Disorder

All of us have fears. Some of us get anxious when we think of or see a snake or a spider. Others may fear public speaking or eating in public. As children, we may have been afraid of the dark or the dentist. These are common fears. However, when our fears become so intense that they cause severe anxiety, possibly even panic attacks that interfere with our ability to function, then a diagnosis of *specific phobia* or *social anxiety disorder* is made (American Psychiatric Association, 2013).

A **specific phobia** involves a persistent fear and avoidance of a specific object or situation—animals, heights, bridges—or other specific stimuli. They are one of the most common disorders worldwide, affecting approximately 7.4% of the world population (Wardenaar et al., 2017). Lifetime prevalence is estimated at 12% in the United States, 7% in Mexico, and 3.4% in Japan to name just a few (Wardenaar et al., 2017). Specific phobias typically begin in childhood (Kessler et al., 2005a; Wardenaar et al., 2017) and are more common in females (Karg et al., 2014; Wardenaar et al., 2017).

Social anxiety disorder (social phobia) includes an irrational, persistent fear of being negatively evaluated by others in a social situation. A person with social anxiety disorder may have an extreme fear of rejection, embarrassment, or humiliation. This disorder may include fear of public speaking, fear of eating or undressing in front of others, or fear of meeting new people. The person endures intense anxiety or avoids these social situations such that their functioning is impaired (American Psychiatric Association, 2013). It is estimated that 1% to 12% of American adults will experience social anxiety disorder at some time in their lives (Karg et al., 2014; NCS-R, 2007; Stein et al., 2017). Social anxiety disorder tends to develop in the early preschool years and in adolescence, and it is somewhat more likely to develop in women than in men (Bogels et al., 2010; Kessler et al., 2005a; Lang & Stein, 2001; Stein et al., 2017). White Americans tend to have a higher lifetime risk of social anxiety disorder than do African Americans, Hispanic Americans, and Asian Americans (Asnaani et al., 2010). On average, social anxiety disorder is also more prevalent in high-income countries (Stein et al., 2017). People with specific phobia and social anxiety disorder typically recognize that their fears are irrational, but they cannot stop the overwhelming anxiety they feel when faced with the feared object or situation.

Obsessive-Compulsive Disorder (OCD) and Hoarding Disorder

Obsessions are recurrent thoughts or images that intrude on a person's consciousness or awareness. **Compulsions** are repetitive behaviors that a person feels a strong urge to perform. All of us experience intrusive thoughts and strong urges. For example, on your way to school or work, the thought pops into your head that you left the stove on, and you start worrying about a house fire. What do you do? Many of us feel compelled to turn the car around to check that everything is okay. However, what if this scenario occurred every time you got in the car, and you felt compelled to check each time? In such a case, you might be diagnosed with **obsessive-compulsive disorder (OCD)**.

Obsessive-compulsive disorder is a disorder in which a person experiences recurrent obsessions or compulsions or both that they feel cannot be controlled

specific phobia an anxiety disorder characterized by persistent fear and avoidance of a specific object or situation

social anxiety disorder (social phobia) an anxiety disorder characterized by an irrational, persistent fear of being negatively evaluated by others in a social situation

obsessions recurrent thoughts or images that intrude on a person's awareness

compulsions repetitive behaviors that a person feels a strong urge to perform

obsessive-compulsive disorder (OCD) a disorder involving a pattern of unwanted intrusive thoughts and/or the urge to engage in repetitive actions that interferes with a person's functioning

(American Psychiatric Association, 2013). Obsessions often center on dirt and contamination, doing harm to oneself or others, sexual thoughts, or repeated doubts (such as not having locked the house). Common compulsions include cleaning, checking, counting things, or arranging and straightening things in a particular fashion. The compulsions are often performed with the hope of preventing the obsessive thoughts or making them go away. However, performing these "rituals" provides only temporary relief. Not performing the rituals increases the person's anxiety.

Recurrent obsessions cause great personal distress, and compulsions can be time-consuming and in some cases harmful—as when a person washes their hands so frequently that they bleed. It is estimated that between 1% and 3% of individuals will develop OCD at some time in their lives; in the United States, the rates are higher among European Americans than among Hispanic Americans and African Americans (Calamari et al., 2012; Kessler et al., 2005b; Leckman et al., 2010).

WR Publishing/Alamy Stock Photo

▲ In hoarding disorder a person keeps large amounts of items that others consider excessive or worthless such that it interferes with their safety and/or ability to function.

Hoarding disorder is characterized by persistent difficulty in throwing away possessions, even when the item is of very little value. The person's compulsion to hoard impairs their ability to function, yet having to part with or discard their possessions causes significant distress and anxiety. As a result, the person's living environment becomes cluttered, unusable, and in some cases even hazardous (American Psychiatric Association, 2013). It is estimated that between 2% and 5% of the population engage in hoarding, with nearly equal numbers of males and females (Frost, Steketee, & Tolin, 2012; Iervolino et al., 2009; Postlethwaite, Kellett, & Mataix-Cols, 2019).

Posttraumatic Stress Disorder (PTSD)

Excessive anxiety can also develop following a traumatic event as in the case of **posttraumatic stress disorder (PTSD)**. PTSD develops after exposure to a terrifying event or ordeal in which grave physical harm occurred or was threatened. Traumatic events may include the following:

- Violent personal assaults such as rape, physical abuse, or sexual abuse
- Natural or human-caused disasters such as an earthquake, a hurricane, a terrorist attack, or an outbreak of an infectious disease
- Military combat
- Events that anyone might experience—the sudden, unexpected death of a loved one or witnessing a violent crime or a deadly traffic accident

A diagnosis of PTSD requires that the person repeatedly reexperience the ordeal in the form of distressing memories, nightmares, frightening thoughts, or flashback episodes, especially when exposed to situations that are similar to the original trauma. For example, a car backfire might trigger a flashback to a combat trauma or being the victim of an armed robbery. Anniversaries of the event also can trigger symptoms. At the same time, they persistently avoid situations, thoughts, or memories that are associated with the trauma. In addition, people diagnosed with PTSD may experience emotional numbness or withdrawal from themselves or others such that they lose interest in usual activities or are regarded as distant and emotionally unavailable. Finally, people with PTSD are always on guard and alert to any real or imagined potential threats in their environments—showing *hypervigilance*, having difficulty concentrating, or having difficulty sleeping (American Psychiatric Association, 2013). They may experience depression, anxiety, irritability,

hoarding disorder an obsessive-compulsive-related disorder characterized by persistent difficulty in discarding possessions such that they accumulate and clutter living areas, causing significant distress and impairment in functioning

posttraumatic stress disorder (PTSD) a trauma-related disorder, characterized by distressing memories, emotional numbness, and hypervigilance, that develops after exposure to a traumatic event

Mike Goldwater/Alamy Stock Photo

▲ Exposure to a trauma can lead to the development of PTSD.

or outbursts of anger; physical symptoms such as headaches, dizziness, or chest pain; or feelings of intense guilt. For some people, such symptoms can seriously disrupt the ability to work or to meet social, professional, and family obligations.

Although the majority of people exposed to trauma respond with resilience, nearly 5% of U.S. adults experience PTSD in a given year with elevated rates among Native Americans (Goldstein et al., 2016). More females than males experience PTSD following exposure to a trauma, typically sexual or physical assault (Goldstein et al., 2016; Karg et al., 2014; Liu et al., 2017; Zinzow et al., 2012).

Women's higher PTSD risk has been attributed to a number of variables that reinforce the biopsychosocial perspective on mental health disorders. For example, sex differences in the responses of the *amygdala,* the brain structure that mediates fear, have been documented (Keiser et al., 2017; Stevens & Hamann, 2012). Moreover, compared to men, women are more likely to feel threatened and perceive a low sense of control—psychological factors that may influence the risk of PTSD (Olff et al., 2007). Women are more likely to be victims of sexual abuse and experience these traumas at younger ages than men—social factors that also play a role in PTSD (Olff et al., 2007; Zinzow et al., 2012).

Soldiers (male or female) are also at high risk for developing PTSD, as military conflict is a source of trauma (Creamer et al., 2011). Studies of U.S. military personnel in Iraq and Afghanistan indicate problems in mental health, most notably PTSD (Cameron, Sturdivant, & Baker, 2019; Felker et al., 2008; Sundin et al., 2010, 2014), with one study estimating the prevalence of PTSD among a nationwide study of U.S. veterans at 13.5% (Dursa et al., 2014). Soldiers high in *catastrophic thinking* (exaggerated thoughts about worst-case outcomes) or those who faced four or more combat stressors such as high combat intensity are more likely to develop PTSD (Seligman et al., 2019).

You Review: Symptoms of Some of the Anxiety, Obsessive-Compulsive, and Trauma-Related Disorders summarizes those disorders that we have discussed.

13.3.3 Research Explaining Anxiety, Obsessive-Compulsive, and Trauma-Related Disorders

What causes the disorders characterized by excessive anxiety? Research on people with excessive anxiety suggests biological, psychological, and sociocultural factors may contribute to such behavior, underscoring the biopsychosocial nature of mental health disorders presented at the beginning of the chapter.

Biology: Neurotransmitters, Genetics, and the Brain

Problems in the regulation of several neurotransmitters has been linked to excessive anxiety. This may involve norepinephrine, serotonin, or GABA, although the serotonin system has been implicated to some degree in most anxiety disorders, PTSD, and OCD (see Bandelow et al., 2017 for review; Goddard et al., 2010; Kuzelova, Ptacek, & Milan, 2010; Maia & Cano-Colino, 2015; Mellman et al., 2009).

Although anxiety disorders are not based on a single gene, a genetic predisposition to excessive anxiety may exist. Children of parents with anxiety disorders have a greater risk for anxiety disorders than children of parents with no mental health disorders (Micco et al., 2009). Recall that Emily's father was described as tense and keyed-up, so it is possible that Emily inherited a tendency to be anxious

YOU REVIEW Symptoms of Some of the Anxiety, Obsessive-Compulsive, and Trauma-Related Disorders

Anxiety Disorders	Symptoms
Generalized Anxiety Disorder	Excessive worry for at least 6 months about a number of events accompanied by physical symptoms such as muscle tension, difficulty concentrating, and irritability that impair a person's functioning
Panic Disorder	Recurrent abrupt experiences of unexpected intense fear accompanied by physical symptoms such as heart palpitations, shortness of breath, or dizziness (panic attacks) followed by 1 month of either persistent worry over additional panic attacks or behavior designed to avoid panic attacks that interfere with a person's functioning
Specific Phobia	Persistent fear of a specific object or situation that is excessive and unreasonable, lasts for 6 months or more, and interferes with a person's functioning
Social Anxiety Disorder (Social Phobia)	Persistent fear of one or more social situations in which the person is possibly judged by others that is excessive and unreasonable, lasts for 6 months or more, and interferes with a person's functioning
Agoraphobia	Excessive and unreasonable anxiety about two or more of the following: public transportation, open spaces, enclosed spaces, being in a crowd or outside the home alone, that the person avoids because of fear of no escape or help if panic-like symptoms develop; lasts for 6 months or more, and interferes with a person's functioning
Trauma-Related Disorder	**Symptoms**
Posttraumatic Stress Disorder	Exposure to a traumatic event during which one feels helplessness or fear followed by recurrent and intrusive memories or nightmares of the event, avoidance of stimuli associated with the event, numbing of emotions, and increased arousal that impair the person's functioning
Obsessive-Compulsive and Related Disorders	**Symptoms**
Obsessive-Compulsive Disorder	Presence of recurrent, persistent, intrusive thoughts or images (obsessions), and/or repetitive behaviors or mental acts that a person feels driven to perform (compulsions) to reduce distress or to prevent some event from happening. The thoughts or behaviors are time-consuming and interfere with a person's functioning.
Hoarding Disorder	Persistent difficulty discarding possessions such that they accumulate and clutter living areas, causing significant distress and impairment in functioning

herself. Even relatives of a person (siblings, aunts, uncles) with an anxiety disorder are more likely to have one compared with relatives of someone without a disorder (Hanna, 2000). Twin and family studies have found high heritability especially for panic disorder and OCD (Mosing et al., 2009; Nicolini et al., 2009; Wittchen et al., 2010). Having a fearful temperament in infancy also has been linked to the development of anxiety symptoms, although not all fearful babies become anxious (Buss & McDoniel, 2016).

Other studies have focused on specific brain areas that are involved in anxiety and fear. As stated previously, our fear response is coordinated by the amygdala, a small structure deep inside the limbic system of the brain that also plays a role in our emotional memories. Neuroimaging studies on people with GAD and PTSD suggest an overactive amygdala that may contribute to their heightened level of anxiety and memory-related symptoms (Etkin et al., 2010; Hettema et al., 2012; Sadeh et al., 2014; Shin et al., 2011). Abnormalities involving another part of the limbic system called the *cingulate cortex* has also been implicated in panic disorder, OCD, and social anxiety disorder (Bruhl, Delsignore, Komossa, & Weidt, 2014; Goddard, 2017; McGovern & Sheth, 2017). Neural pathways that connect the prefrontal cortex to the part of the forebrain called the *striatum* has been investigated as a possible factor in OCD (Bandelow et al., 2017; Choi et al., 2007; Milad & Rauch, 2012; Snyder et al., 2015). These circuits regulate our thoughts and behaviors and allow us to break out of habits, make decisions, and plan for the future—tasks that are impaired in people with OCD.

Psychological Factors: Learning and Cognition

Psychological factors also help in explaining excessive anxiety. For example, specific phobias can be learned in the same way that Watson and Rayner were able to condition Little Albert to fear a white rat (see Chapter 6; Field, 2006). A neutral stimulus (the phobic object) gets paired with a stimulus that naturally elicits fear. So, when a thunderstorm gets paired with a loud noise (thunder) that naturally evokes fear, we learn to be fearful of thunderstorms.

Conditioning processes also may play a role in panic disorder. Neutral stimuli that are present during an initial panic attack may then become conditioned stimuli that trigger panic symptoms on subsequent occasions. These conditioned stimuli are then thought to generalize to other neutral stimuli, resulting in a variety of cues that evoke panic symptoms (Lissek et al., 2010).

Direct experience is not always necessary to develop a specific phobia. We may acquire fears simply by observing or hearing about others' negative experiences (Kelly & Forsyth, 2007). How many of us have come face to face with a bear? But after hearing someone's account on the news or seeing Internet videos of people's encounters, we may also now fear bears. Negative reinforcement is a learning process that helps explain compulsions. If you engage in a certain behavior following an anxiety-provoking obsession, your anxiety is often reduced. The next time the obsession occurs, you feel more compelled to engage in the behavior so that you can reduce your anxiety (Barlow, 2002). Learning and conditioning theories have also been useful in understanding PTSD. Sights, sounds, or images of the trauma all become conditioned stimuli that trigger the fear reaction.

Cognitive research suggests that our thinking processes play a role in developing excessive anxiety. In particular, people who perceive situations and objects as uncontrollable, unpredictable, dangerous, and disgusting are more vulnerable to excessive anxiety disorders. They are more sensitive to and allocate more attention to potential threats in their environments (Armfield, 2006; Newman et al., 2013; Shechner & Bar-Haim, 2016).

People with disorders marked by excessive anxiety also may have the tendency to process more negative information rather than positive or neutral information about an event (Everaert & Joormann, 2019; Fox, Cahill, & Zougkou, 2010; Hertel & Brozovich, 2010; Kleim et al., 2014). For example, studies suggest that people with panic disorder sometimes misinterpret their bodily sensations, thinking they are beginning a panic attack. Their negative and catastrophic thinking then heightens their anxiety (Clark & Beck, 2010; Craske & Barlow, 2001). People diagnosed with GAD tend to interpret ambiguous situations in a threatening manner, anticipating that something bad will happen to them and that they will feel out of control. While driving in a car, they may worry that they will get lost or in an accident. These worries become constant and almost automatic in their thought processes (Beck, 1997; Hirsch, Beale, Grey, & Liness, 2019; Riskind et al., 2000).

The shattering of common cognitive beliefs about life may bring on PTSD. An unpredictable trauma—such as a rape, an earthquake, or an automobile accident—may make us question our assumptions that the world is safe and just and that events happen for a reason. It dispels our illusion of control and invincibility, and our assumption that bad things only happen to bad people (Edmondson et al., 2011; Janoff-Bulman, 1992).

Sociocultural Variations: Stress, Gender, and Culture

Sociocultural factors must also be considered when explaining the development of disorders characterized by excessive anxiety. For example, in cultures experiencing rapid social change, war, or viral pandemics such as COVID-19, people are more likely to exhibit anxiety symptoms than are people in more stable countries (Asmundson et al., 2020; Compton et al., 1991). Similarly, people who had adverse childhood experiences such as abuse or violence or who have had other previous traumatic or stressful experiences are more likely to develop excessive anxiety disorders (Berntsen et al., 2012; Green et al., 2010; Li, D'Arcy, & Meng, 2016; Ogle et al., 2013).

Available social support from family, friends, or the community also makes a difference; people with emotional support may function better following a traumatic event than those who are isolated or rely on more problematic coping strategies such as avoidance or drug use (Friedman, 2009; La Greca et al., 2010). In this part's case study, Emily's difficulty with learning at school, high expectations for success, and social rejection at home could be sociocultural factors that contributed to her feelings of anxiety. We have also seen that White Americans and women are more likely than other ethnic groups and men to be diagnosed with an anxiety disorder. More research will have to examine the role of gender and culture in the experience of excessive anxiety before we fully understand their influence.

13.3 Quiz Yourself

1. **Marilu is anxious and nervous all the time. She constantly worries over her family, her job, and her schoolwork. Which disorder best describes Marilu's behavior?**
   a. Panic disorder
   b. Generalized anxiety disorder
   c. Specific phobia
   d. Obsessive-compulsive disorder
2. **Learning theories suggest that obsessive-compulsive disorder is the result of _____.**
   a. reinforcement processes
   b. faulty cognitions
   c. low self-esteem
   d. unconscious impulses
3. **Abdul was involved in a four-car pileup on the interstate 8 months ago. Since then, he has been having nightmares and flashback episodes of the accident. He has difficulty concentrating and has withdrawn from his family and friends. Abdul would most likely be diagnosed with which disorder?**
   a. Panic disorder
   b. Posttraumatic stress disorder
   c. Social anxiety disorder
   d. Generalized anxiety disorder

Answers 1. *b*; 2. *a*; 3. *b*

13.4 Dissociative and Somatic Symptom and Related Disorders: Other Forms of Anxiety?

Dissociative and *somatic symptom and related disorders* are quite rare in the general population but often are of much interest to students. Here we outline the general nature of these disorders and the factors that may a play a role in their development.

dissociative [dih-SO-shee-tive] disorders mental health disorders marked by a loss of awareness of some part of one's self or one's surroundings that seriously interferes with the person's ability to function

dissociative identity disorder (DID) a disorder in which two or more identities coexist within the same individual

13.4.1 Dissociative Disorders: Loss of Self or Awareness

To *dissociate* means to break or pull apart. Thus, the **dissociative disorders** involve a loss of awareness of some part of our self, our surroundings, or what is going on around us. Mild dissociative experiences are common (Aderibigbe, Bloch, & Walker, 2001; Hunter, Sierra, & David, 2004). For instance, have you ever driven somewhere and on arrival did not remember driving there? Have you ever missed a part of a conversation but can tell from the speaker's demeanor that you appeared to have been listening the whole time? Have you ever appeared attentive in class while you were daydreaming about your plans for the weekend? All of these are common, everyday dissociative experiences.

However, when loss of awareness becomes more extreme, a diagnosis of a dissociative disorder may apply. Such extreme dissociation is typically linked to severe stress, a history of trauma, or a series of emotionally traumatic events (Dalenberg et al., 2012; Isaac & Chand, 2006; Kihlstrom, 2001; Ural et al., 2015). ● TABLE 13.2 provides a brief description of the dissociative disorders listed in the *DSM-5*. Here we will confine our discussion to perhaps the most controversial and fascinating one, *dissociative identity disorder*.

Dissociative identity disorder (DID) involves the existence of two or more separate identities in the same individual (American Psychiatric Association, 2013). The separate identities—referred to as alters (for alternate identities)—may or may not be known to the "core," or "host," identity—the person who asks for treatment. Each identity has its own perceptions, thoughts, mannerisms, speech characteristics, and gestures. Each alter appears to have a specific function. For example, one alter may arise to deal with romantic relationships, whereas another alter deals with academic work. The alter identities may be of different ages, gender, or ethnicities. The majority of people diagnosed with DID are women. It is estimated that approximately 1% of the general population experience DID (Brand et al., 2016).

Frequent blackouts or episodes of amnesia are common in people with dissociative identity disorder. They may notice money missing from their bank accounts that they don't remember spending, or find objects in their home that they do not recognize. Self-mutilating behavior is also common in people with this disorder. They may repeatedly burn or cut themselves and have a history of suicide attempts (Foote et al., 2008; Webermann et al., 2016). Often, they have been previously diagnosed with other disorders such as major depressive disorder, PTSD, a substance-related disorder, borderline personality disorder, or schizophrenia, especially if they have reported hearing voices (Brand et al., 2016; Dorahy et al., 2014; Loewenstein & Putnam, 2004; Rodewald et al., 2011; Ross, Ferrell, & Schroeder, 2014).

TABLE 13.2 Types of Dissociative Disorders

Disorder	Major Features
Depersonalization disorder	Frequent episodes in which the person feels detached from their own mental state or body that causes significant distress or impairs functioning
Dissociative amnesia	Memory loss of important personal information, not due to substance use or brain injury that causes significant distress or impairs functioning. May occur with or without *dissociative fugue*, in which a person unexpectedly travels away from home with memory loss of identity or other personal information.
Dissociative identity disorder	Two or more separate identities in the same individual that cause significant distress or impaired functioning

One striking similarity among people with DID is their backgrounds. Almost all have documented evidence of or report experiencing chronic, horrific, childhood physical and/or sexual abuse at the hands of loved ones (Brand et al., 2016; Dorahy et al., 2014; Ellason, Ross, & Fuchs, 1996; Ross & Ness, 2010). Many clinicians believe that in an attempt to deal with such trauma, these people defensively dissociate, developing alter identities that can protect them from experiencing such events in life or in memory. People with DID are also highly susceptible to hypnosis (Kihlstrom, 2005; Kihlstrom, Glisky, & Angiulo, 1994). Thus, the ability to dissociate may have become an effective coping mechanism early in life (Spiegel et al., 2011). Moreover, traumatic experiences disrupt the normal sleep-wake cycle and these disruptions increase one's vulnerability to dissociative symptoms (van der Kloet et al., 2012).

As you can see, explaining the occurrence of DID is highly debated. Some psychologists even question the validity of dissociative identity disorder (Kihlstrom, 2005; Piper & Merskey, 2004). There has been a great increase in the number of reported cases since 1980 (American Psychiatric Association, 2000a), and it is more frequently diagnosed in the United States (Boysen, 2011), although studies on patients with DID have been conducted in 16 countries, contradicting this claim (Brand et al., 2016). Verifying the claims of amnesia and blackouts are difficult, and people with DID have often been diagnosed with other mental health disorders (Loewenstein & Putnam, 2004; Rodewald et al., 2011; Ross et al., 2014). Some believe that DID may represent an extreme form of posttraumatic stress disorder, since a subset of people with PTSD do experience dissociative symptoms, especially those who have experienced repeated sexual trauma (Terhune & Cardena, 2015; Wolf et al., 2012). Thus, a *dissociative-PTSD subtype* has been included in the *DSM-5*. Future research may help us better understand the nature of both dissociation and its relationship to PTSD.

13.4.2 Somatic Symptom and Related Disorders: "Doctor, I'm Sure I'm Sick"

Somatic means "related to the body." The **somatic symptom and related disorders** involve physical complaints for which there is no apparent physical cause. The physical symptoms are real to the person, but physicians can find no medical reason why the individual is experiencing such symptoms. For example, a person may complain of constant hip pain. Numerous medical tests are completed, but there is no apparent physical cause for the hip ache. Because no physical cause can be found, it is assumed that psychological distress underlies the physical problem. In Emily's case, we saw that her anxiety often caused her to have a spastic colon—a somatic symptom related to her emotional distress. ● TABLE 13.3 describes the somatic symptom and related disorders listed in the *DSM-5*. Our discussion in this section will focus on one of them, *illness anxiety disorder*.

somatic [so-MAA-tic] symptom and related disorders mental health disorders marked by physical complaints that have no apparent physical cause

TABLE 13.3 Types of Somatic Symptom and Related Disorders

Disorder	Major Features
Conversion disorder	One or more symptoms affecting voluntary motor or sensory functioning, but no physical cause can be found; causes significant distress or impaired functioning
Somatic symptom disorder	Six months of persistent physical complaints with excessive thoughts, feelings, or behaviors related to the symptoms that cause distress or disrupt one's life. The person has sought medical attention, but no physical cause can be found.
Illness anxiety disorder	Persistent worry over having a serious illness for at least 6 months. The person may frequently seek or rarely use medical care.

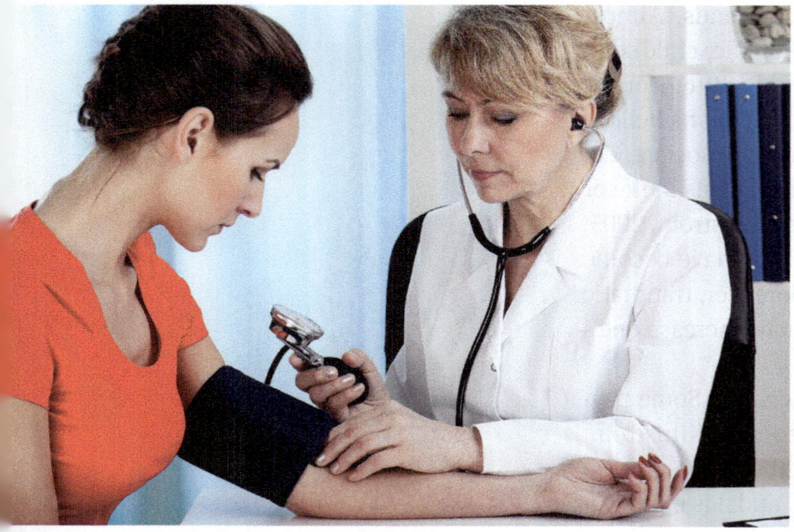

ESB Professional/Shutterstock.com

▲ Somatic symptom and related disorders involve physical complaints with no apparent physical cause. Numerous medical tests may be completed, but no physical cause can be found for the patient's complaint.

In **illness anxiety disorder**, a person believes that they have a serious medical illness despite evidence to the contrary (American Psychiatric Association, 2013). Many of us know someone who frequently complains about physical ailments. However, people with illness anxiety disorder are convinced that they have a serious illness, not just one or two specific symptoms. People with illness anxiety disorder may undergo extensive medical testing by several doctors to confirm the existence of their illness. When a doctor suggests that they may have a mental health problem, people with illness anxiety disorder are likely to seek out another physician rather than seek mental health counseling (Kirmayer & Looper, 2007). Alternatively, others with the disorder may believe they have a serious illness but refuse to seek medical attention. People with illness anxiety disorder often have a family history of depression or anxiety, leading some researchers to speculate that this disorder is an intense form of health anxiety related to panic disorder and obsessive-compulsive disorder (Abramowitz & Moore, 2007; Gropalis et al., 2012; Scarella et al., 2016). Illness anxiety disorder has an estimated prevalence between 1% and 5% in the general population (American Psychiatric Association, 2000a).

13.4 Quiz Yourself

1. **Dissociative disorders involve _____.**
   a. disruptions in movement
   b. physical symptoms without any physical cause
   c. a splitting off of one's conscious mind
   d. a numbness or paralysis in some part of the body

2. **Alphonsia has recurrent abdominal pain. Her doctors have conducted numerous medical tests and can find no physical cause for her symptom. Alphonsia appears to have a(n) _____.**
   a. anxiety disorder
   b. somatic symptom and related disorder
   c. dissociative disorder
   d. obsessive-compulsive disorder

3. **What do the dissociative and somatic symptom and related disorders have in common?**
   a. They both occur more frequently in men than in women.
   b. They both involve a preoccupation with the body.
   c. They both include a loss of identity.
   d. They both may represent alternate expressions of anxiety.

Answers 1. c; 2. b; 3. d

13.5 Depressive and Bipolar Disorders: A Change in Mood

Depressive and bipolar disorders involve a significant change in a person's emotional state or mood. This change may include feeling depressed (*depressive disorders*) or extremely elated for an extended time (*bipolar disorders*). Like anxiety disorders, depressive and bipolar disorders are also likely to have a high rate of comorbidity, or coexist with another mental health disorder.

Many of us experience sadness, but typically this period of sadness lasts only a few days. For depressive disorders, the mood change is persistent and interferes significantly with a person's ability to function. Also, normal periods of sadness are usually brought on by environmental events—the loss of a loved one, the breakup of a relationship, or a disappointment in one's life. People diagnosed with depressive disorders are sad over a longer period, sometimes in the absence of such external events or long after most people would have adjusted to such changes.

illness anxiety disorder a somatic symptom and related disorder in which the person persistently worries over having a serious illness, without any evident physical basis

Depressive and bipolar disorders can be devastating to personal relationships and to the ability to work or go to school. Recall that later in adulthood Emily was diagnosed with depression. Her emotional neediness and anger negatively impacted her marital relationship. Many people think that the symptoms are not "real" and that the person should be able to "snap out of it." These inaccurate beliefs may cause shame and stigma, which discourages people from seeking appropriate treatment. Fortunately, Emily reentered therapy to address her disorder.

13.5.1 Depressive Disorders: A Change to Sadness

The *DSM-5* indicates several depressive disorders. Here we discuss two types: *major depressive disorder* and *persistent depressive disorder.*

Major Depressive Disorder

A diagnosis of **major depressive disorder** requires that a person experience either depressed mood or loss of interest or pleasure in one's usual activities plus at least four other symptoms of depression for a period of at least 2 weeks. These symptoms must be severe enough that they interfere with the person's ability to function but not be due to a general medical condition or the effects of a substance (drug abuse or medication) (American Psychiatric Association, 2013). The other symptoms of depression may include these:

major depressive disorder a depressive disorder involving sadness, feelings of worthlessness, loss of interest in one's usual activities, and changes in bodily activities such as sleep and appetite that persists for at least 2 weeks

Physical and Behavioral Symptoms

- Change in sleep patterns—either sleeping too much (hypersomnia) or too little (insomnia)
- Change in appetite—either eating too much (resulting in weight gain) or too little (resulting in weight loss)
- Change in motor functioning—either moving slowly and sluggishly or appearing agitated in movement
- Fatigue, or loss of energy

Cognitive Symptoms

- Inability to concentrate or difficulty in making decisions
- Exaggerated feelings of worthlessness or guilt
- Thoughts of suicide (see Psychology Applies to Your World)

Major depressive disorder may occur as a single episode or as repeated episodes over the course of years. Some episodes may be so severe that the person requires hospitalization, especially in the presence of frequent suicide attempts or *delusions* (believing something that most people would agree is not true) and *hallucinations* (perceiving things that are not there). Approximately 7% of adults in the United States experience a major depressive episode in a given year (Center for Behavioral Health Statistics and Quality, 2018).

martin-dm/E+/Getty Images

▲ Major depressive disorder is marked by physical, behavioral, and cognitive symptoms, in addition to depressed mood.

Psychology Applies to Your World

Suicide Facts and Misconceptions

SUICIDAL THOUGHTS ARE ONE SYMPTOM of depressive and bipolar disorders. Research suggests that nearly 90% of all people who commit suicide have some diagnosable mental health disorder, commonly a depressive or bipolar disorder or a substance-related disorder (Borges et al., 2010). Suicide is the tenth leading cause of death in the United States (higher than homicide). Among 15- to 34-year-olds, it was the second-leading cause of death; among 35- to 54-year-olds, it was the fourth-leading cause of death. Among 10- to 14-year-olds, suicide was the third-leading cause of death. However, these rates are probably grossly underestimated given the negative stigma attached to suicide in the United States (CDC, 2020c; Kochanek et al., 2016).

Women are two to three times more likely than men to *attempt* suicide, but four times as many men actually kill themselves, in part because of the means chosen (Curtin, Warner, & Hedegaard, 2016; Kung et al., 2008). Men tend to shoot, hang, or stab themselves. Women are more likely to choose less lethal means, such as drug overdoses. This gender difference appears in many countries across the world (Weissman et al., 1999; Welch, 2001) except China, where more women commit suicide than men (Phillips, Li, & Zhang, 2002). As seen in ● FIGURE 13.4, in the United States, Whites and American Indian/Alaska Natives have higher rates of suicide than other ethnic groups (Curtin & Hedegaard, 2019; Stone et al., 2017). Veterans and sexual minorities are also at high suicide risk (Stone et al., 2017; U.S. Department of Veterans Affairs, 2019). As we saw in the case study, Emily had made several suicide attempts. Because many of us will encounter or already have encountered someone who is suicidal, let's take a moment to dispel some of the more common misconceptions concerning suicide.

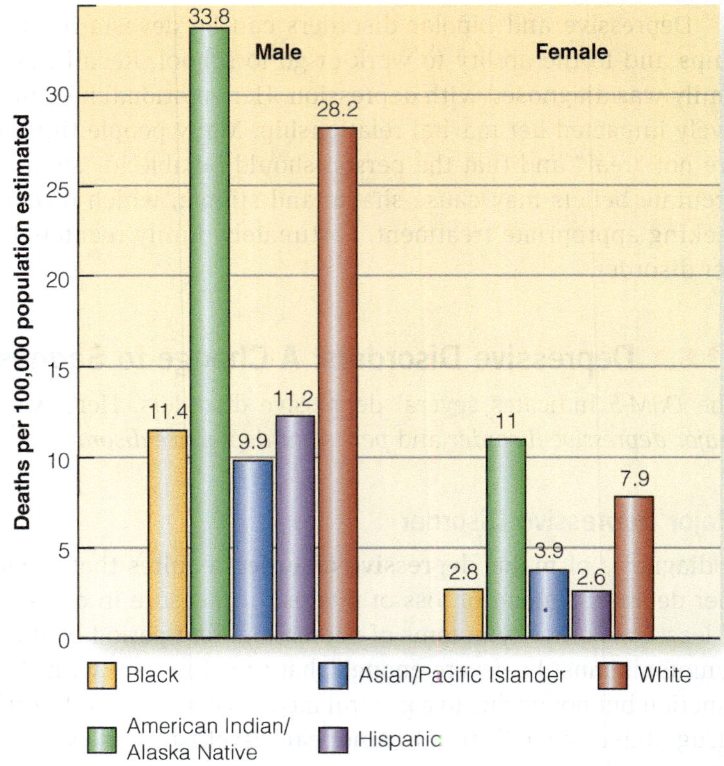

FIGURE 13.4

U.S. Death Rates for Suicide by Gender and Ethnicity

Although women attempt suicide more often, men across all ethnic groups are more likely to commit suicide.

Source: Curtin, S. C., & Hedegaard, H. (2019). Suicide rates for females and males by race and ethnicity: United States, 1999 and 2017. *NCHS Health E-Stat.*

Misconception #1: People who talk of suicide will not kill themselves.

Although most people who talk of suicide do not go on to attempt suicide, people who commit suicide typically have

Persistent Depressive Disorder

persistent depressive disorder a depressive disorder that is a less severe but more chronic form of major depressive disorder

Persistent depressive disorder is a less severe but more chronic form of major depressive disorder. The person seems sad and downcast over a longer time. A diagnosis of persistent depressive disorder requires the symptom of depressed mood plus at least two other symptoms of depression for a period of at least 2 years (American Psychiatric Association, 2013). Persistent depressive disorder generally begins in childhood, adolescence, or early adulthood. Typically, the symptoms of persistent depressive disorder are not severe enough to require hospitalization. However, many people with persistent depressive disorder eventually experience expressed their intentions at some time to family members or friends before their attempt (Ortega & Karch, 2010; Shneidman, 1987). They may have talked about "going away" or be preoccupied in general with the notion of death. Therefore, any talk of suicide should be taken seriously. A person who is suicidal should not be left alone. You may need to contact a mental health professional, call 911, or call a suicide crisis hotline in your area.

Misconception #2: If you ask someone who is depressed whether they have thoughts of suicide, it will only plant the idea of suicide in their head.

Asking direct questions about a person's plan for suicide is the only way to assess the person's risk for committing suicide. Bringing up the subject can also give the person an opportunity to talk about their problems. People who have a concrete plan in mind for when or how they will end their life are more likely to attempt suicide than those whose plans are less specific (Nock et al., 2008; SAMHSA, 2009b).

Misconception #3: People who have unsuccessfully attempted suicide will not try again.

In the United States from 2003 to 2007, among women aged 15 to 44 who committed suicide, 37% had a history of suicide attempts (Ortega & Karch, 2010). Similarly, among adolescents, a previous history of suicide attempts is the single best predictor of future suicide attempts and completions (Lewinsohn, Rohde, & Seeley, 1994; Liu & Spirito, 2019; Miranda et al., 2014). Therefore, a previous suicide attempt puts adolescents and young and middle-aged women in particular at a higher risk for future suicide attempts.

Misconception #4: A better mood means the risk of suicide is gone.

Suicide does not typically happen when a person is in the depths of a deep depression. Rather, suicide attempts are more likely to occur when people with depression have energy and can make decisions. This energy makes it appear to loved ones that the person is getting better and is therefore at a lower risk of suicide, when sometimes a better mood can indicate an increased risk of suicide. Although the person may have thoughts of suicide for a while, the time between actually deciding to attempt suicide and actually making the attempt often occurs quickly—usually within an hour but could be as short as five minutes (Millner, Lee, & Nock, 2017).

Misconception #5: Only people who are depressed attempt suicide.

Although suicidal thoughts are a symptom of depression and people who are depressed are 30 times more likely to commit suicide than are individuals who are not depressed (Joiner, 2010), people with other serious mental health disorders, including bipolar disorder, substance-related disorders, dissociative disorders, borderline personality disorder, and schizophrenia, are also at risk for suicide (DeVylder et al., 2015; Foote et al., 2008; Soloff & Chiapetta, 2012; Yalch et al., 2014). According to findings from the World Health Organization (WHO) World Mental Health Surveys, the strongest predictors of suicide attempts in developed countries are depressive and bipolar disorders, whereas in developing countries, they are substance use, PTSD, and impulse control disorders (Nock et al., 2009).

A number of other events and situations also increase one's risk of suicide, including economic hardship, serious illness, problems with a partner or the loss of a relationship, childhood sexual or physical abuse, and access to firearms (Anestis & Anestis, 2015; Borges et al., 2010; Bruffaerts et al., 2010; Karch et al., 2009; Ortega & Karch, 2010). Suicide occurs among people who have mental health disorders as well as those who face environmental stressors. The majority of suicide attempts are expressions of extreme distress and helplessness, not just "harmless" bids for attention.

a major depressive episode (Klein, Lewinsohn, & Seeley, 2001; Klein, Shankman, & Rose, 2006). Approximately 1.7% of adults experience persistent depressive disorder in a given year (Karg et al., 2014).

Individual Variations in Depression

Worldwide, depression is projected as the single most burdensome disease in terms of disability (World Health Organization, 2017). In the United States, almost 21% of adults experience an episode of depression at some time in their lives, and nearly 11% experienced a major depressive episode in the last year (Hasin et al., 2018).

Yet, symptoms of depression can vary from one person to another so that not all people with depression will "look" the same (Monroe & Anderson, 2015). As we will soon see, the cause(s) of someone's depression may also differ.

Depression also appears to be related to age, gender, and ethnicity. Although major depressive disorder can develop at any age, the majority of people who experience a major depressive episode do so in early adulthood (Hasin et al., 2018; Rohde et al., 2013; SAMHSA, 2015a). People between 15 and 24 years of age are at high risk for experiencing a major depressive episode, whereas adults aged 60 or older experience the lowest rates of major depressive episodes (Hasin et al., 2018; Merikangas et al., 2010; SAMHSA, 2015a). Women are twice as likely as men to experience both mild and more severe depression, a difference found in many different countries, ethnic groups, and across adolescent and adult age groups (Bradley & Hopcroft, 2007; Hasin et al., 2018; Karg et al., 2014; Pratt & Brody, 2014; Rohde et al., 2013; Salk, Hyde, & Abramson, 2017; Schuch et al., 2014). Adolescent females between the ages of 13 and 15 are particularly susceptible to depression as are people who live in poverty (Hasin et al., 2018; Salk, Hyde, & Abramson, 2017). African Americans, Asian Americans, and Hispanic Americans appear to have a lower lifetime and 12-month risk for a major depressive disorder compared to White Americans and Native Americans (Hasin et al., 2018).

Unfortunately, only about half of people with depression receive some form of professional or nonprofessional treatment (such as support chat rooms or groups) (Hasin et al., 2018). In one study, only 51% of participants who met the criteria for major depressive disorder during the prior year received some type of treatment for it. African Americans and Mexican Americans were least likely to receive any care (Gonzalez et al., 2010). In another national survey, just 35% of people with severe depression reported seeing a mental health professional in the past year (Pratt & Brody, 2014).

bipolar disorder a bipolar-related disorder characterized by mania or mania and depression that interferes with a person's ability to function

mania a period of abnormally excessive energy and elation

cyclothymic [sigh-clo-THIGH-mik] disorder a bipolar-related disorder that is a less severe but more chronic form of bipolar disorder

13.5.2 Bipolar-Related Disorders: The Presence of Mania

The *DSM-5* includes several diagnoses under bipolar-related disorders. Here we will discuss two of them: *bipolar disorder* and *cyclothymic disorder*.

Bipolar disorder involves a shift in mood between two states, or *poles*. One of these shifts is to a depressed state, with symptoms similar to those of major depressive disorder. The person feels sad, lacks self-worth, and may show changes in sleeping and eating over a 2-week period. The second mood change is to the opposite extreme—to a "high" or euphoric state, called **mania**. Mania involves a persistently elevated mood *and* increased activity or energy that is present most of the day, nearly every day for at least 1 week. During a manic episode, people feel elated and have high self-esteem, have a decreased need for sleep, are more talkative than usual, and are highly distractible. Much energy is directed at achieving goals, although many projects may be started and few finished. People in this state have an inflated sense of self, feeling confident and able to accomplish anything. This may result in delusional thinking or hallucinations. Also, their boundless energy often results in more impulsive and risk-taking behaviors. When such symptoms of mania, or mania and depression, interfere with a person's ability to function, a diagnosis of bipolar disorder is appropriate (American Psychiatric Association, 2013).

DFree/Shutterstock.com

▲ Singer Demi Lovato sought treatment after being diagnosed with bipolar disorder.

Cyclothymic disorder is a less severe but more chronic form of bipolar disorder. In cyclothymic disorder, a person alternates between milder periods of mania and more moderate depression for at least 2 years (American Psychiatric Association, 2013). The person functions reasonably well during the mild mania but is likely to be more impaired during the depressive phase.

Bipolar spectrum disorders are less common than depressive disorders, with approximately 2.4% of adult Americans experiencing an episode of bipolar disorder at some time in their lives (Rowland & Marwaha, 2018). Men are just as likely as women to be diagnosed with bipolar disorder. The median age of onset for bipolar disorder is late adolescence and early adulthood (Merikangas et al., 2011; Rowland & Marwaha, 2018).

13.5.3 Research Explaining Depressive and Bipolar Disorders

What causes depressive and bipolar-related disorders? Not surprisingly, research has identified biological, psychological, and sociocultural factors that may contribute to them. Again, this highlights the biopsychosocial nature of mental health.

Biological Factors: Genes, Neurotransmitters, Stress Hormones, and Brain Structures

Several biological factors have been investigated as contributing to depressive and bipolar disorders: *genes*, *neurotransmitters*, *stress hormones*, and *specific brain areas*.

Genes The evidence from family history studies and twin studies suggests that these disorders may be genetically transmitted, especially in the case of bipolar disorder, although no individual gene has been identified. For example, first-degree relatives (parent, child, or sibling) of persons with bipolar disorder are much more likely to develop the disorder than are relatives of people without the disorder (Perlis et al., 2006; Saunders et al., 2008). Similarly, if an identical twin is diagnosed as having bipolar disorder, the other identical twin has a higher probability of developing the disorder than if they were fraternal twins (Kieseppa et al., 2014; McGuffin et al., 2003; Wallace, Schneider, & McGuffin, 2002).

The evidence for genetic factors in major depressive disorder is less clear. The trend toward genetic transmission is present, particularly in women and when the depression begins early in life (Abkevich et al., 2003; Ebmeier et al., 2006; Mosing et al., 2009). Emily's mother was often sad and depressed, perhaps increasing Emily's chances of inheriting depression as an adult. Specific regions of chromosomes also have been identified that may contribute to one's risk for depressive and bipolar disorders (Barbu et al., 2019; Duric et al., 2010; Hayden et al., 2010; Holmans et al., 2007; Kuzelova et al., 2010; Levinson et al., 2007).

Neurotransmitters The malfunctioning of certain neurotransmitters has also been linked to depressive and bipolar disorders, specifically serotonin and norepinephrine (Carver, Johnson, & Joormann, 2009; Goddard et al., 2010; Kambeitz & Howes, 2015). Antidepressant drugs that act on serotonin and norepinephrine to relieve the symptoms of depression seem to offer evidence for the role of these neurotransmitters in depression. Similarly, abnormalities in the neurotransmitters norepinephrine, dopamine, and glutamate have been investigated as possible factors for proneness to mania in bipolar disorder (Ashok et al., 2017; Carlson et al., 2006; Cousins, Butts, & Young, 2009; Gigante et al., 2012; Keck, McElroy, & Arnold, 2001). Unstable circadian rhythm functions may also influence the functioning of these neurotransmitters (Bullock & Murray, 2014).

Stress Hormones The connection between depression and hormones has also been studied. Hormones regulate functions such as sleep, appetite, sexual desire, and pleasure. Symptoms of depression relate to these bodily functions (McClung, 2007). Of particular interest to psychologists is the link between stress hormones and depression. When stress hormones are released, they tend to inhibit the activity of brain neurotransmitters that are related to mood. Hence, repeated activation of the *HPA axis* stress system may lay the groundwork for depression (Gillespie & Nemeroff, 2007; Gotlib, Joormann, & Foland-Ross, 2014; Saveanu & Nemeroff, 2012). Excessive levels of stress hormones have also been linked to the shrinkage of certain brain areas that may be related to depression (Belleau, Treadway & Pizzagalli, 2019; Kunugi et al., 2010; Sheline, 2000).

Brain Structures Other studies have focused on brain areas that are involved in depression, specifically abnormal functioning of the prefrontal cortex and limbic system (Belleau et al., 2019; Gotlib et al., 2014; Saveanu & Nemeroff, 2012; Thase, 2010). Recall from Chapter 2 that the prefrontal cortex is involved in planning, attention, working memory, problem solving, and goal-oriented behavior. The limbic system includes the amygdala and hippocampus, structures that regulate emotion, memory, motivation, and mood.

Research is also investigating how connections in the brain *between* the cortex and the limbic system may be associated with depressive symptoms (Gotlib & Hamilton, 2008; Gotlib et al., 2014). Studies by Helen Mayberg and her colleagues (1997, 1999, 2005) as well as others have suggested a consistent relationship between depression and dysfunction in an area of the brain's cortex called the *subgenual cingulate*, also known as *Brodmann's area 25* (Dobbs, 2006; Drevets, Savitz, & Trimble, 2008; Tripp et al., 2011). Overactivity in this area allows negative emotions to overwhelm the thinking part of the brain. Additional evidence for this brain region's role in depression comes from treatment studies. Effective antidepressant treatment reduces abnormal activation in this area in people who are depressed (Fu et al., 2004). Using electrodes to reduce activity in this area has also been moderately successful in alleviating symptoms in people with treatment-resistant depression (symptoms that do not respond to at least one trial of antidepressant medication) (Hamani et al., 2009; Kito, Hasegawa, & Koga, 2011; Mayberg et al., 2005).

Research on the biological factors that may contribute to depressive and bipolar disorders indicates a complex relationship among genes, neural activity, hormones, and brain functioning (Dannlowski et al., 2007; Gotlib et al., 2014; Kraft et al., 2007). Future technologies may assist us in sorting out the precise relationship among them.

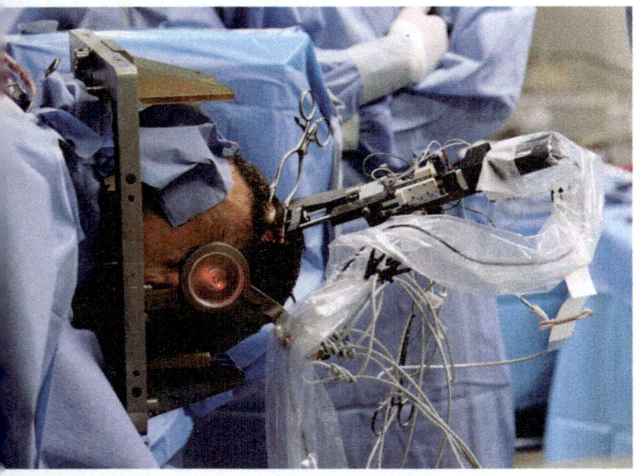

Ian HANNING/REA/Redux

▲ Deep brain stimulation involves implanting electrodes in the part of the brain that affects mood. This surgery has been moderately successful in alleviating depression in clinical trials in participants with treatment-resistant depression.

Psychological Factors: Early Adverse Life Events, Learned Helplessness, and Negative Thinking

Psychological factors also help in explaining depressive and bipolar disorders, especially depression. Specifically, psychologists have examined how *negative life events*, *learned helplessness*, and *negative patterns of thinking* may put one more at risk for depression.

Early Adverse Life Events Psychoanalytic theory suggests that depression is linked to unresolved childhood issues of abandonment, rejection, and loss that result in self-blame, self-hatred, and other symptoms of depression (Freud, 1917). Some research is consistent with this view. A history of early adverse experiences and childhood maltreatment such as insecure attachments, abuse, separations, and losses can make one vulnerable to depression (Green et al., 2010; Li et al., 2016; McLaughlin et al., 2010; Nederhof, Ormel, & Oldehinkel, 2014). Emily's childhood feelings of parental neglect coincide with this viewpoint. While it is possible that early feelings of abandonment and rejection may play a role in depression, it is also possible that such early stressful life events may adversely affect brain chemistry and immune system responses that contribute to depression (Belleau et al., 2019; Heim et al., 2008; Hennessy, Schiml-Webb, & Deak, 2009; Vrshek-Schallhorn et al., 2014).

Learned Helplessness Another psychological explanation of depression is **learned helplessness**, which involves the belief that you cannot control the outcome of events or what is going to happen (see Chapter 12). Therefore, you do not respond even when your response could lead to success. Initial evidence for learned helplessness came from studies in which dogs were administered controllable shock, uncontrollable shock, or no shock (Overmier & Seligman, 1967; Seligman & Maier, 1967). The dogs in the controllable shock situation had to learn to jump a barrier in order to turn off the shock. They quickly learned this behavior. The dogs in the uncontrollable shock situation could not turn off the shock. Later, when the dogs that had been in the uncontrollable shock situation were given the opportunity to jump the barrier to avoid the shock, they failed to respond. They had *learned* to be helpless and just sat there taking the shock *even when they could escape it*. Such research suggests that people who are depressed may respond similarly—they do not take steps to solve or even prevent problems when such action could be helpful, because they believe that life is uncontrollable (Ilgen & Hutchison, 2005).

learned helplessness the belief that one cannot control the outcome of events

ruminative [RUE-muh-nay-tive] coping style the tendency to persistently focus on how one feels without attempting to do anything about one's feelings

cognitive distortions thoughts that tend to be pessimistic and negative

Negative Thinking Research by Susan Nolen-Hoeksema (1959–2013) and her colleagues (Nolen-Hoeksema, 2001, 2002; Nolen-Hoeksema, Larson, & Grayson, 1999; Nolen-Hoeksema et al., 2007; Nolen-Hoeksema, Wisco, & Lyubomirsky, 2008) suggests that coping styles play a role in depression. People who are depressed are more likely to engage in what is called a **ruminative coping style**. To ruminate means to focus on your thoughts. People who are depressed spend a lot of time thinking about their depression and why they are depressed. They tend not to do anything about their depression or its causes but rather remain focused on repetitively analyzing their feelings and concerns. This focus makes it more likely that they will become more severely depressed and also stay depressed longer. Many studies support an association among rumination, negative mood, and vulnerability to depression (Aldao, Nolen-Hoeksema, & Schweizer, 2010; Huffziger, Reinhard, & Kuehner, 2009; Joormann, 2010; Joormann, Levens, & Gotlib, 2011; Joorman & Vanderlind, 2014; Marchetti, Koster, & De Raedt, 2013; McIntosh, Gillanders, & Rodgers, 2010).

Research also highlights the role of negative thinking patterns and attributions in the development of depression. If you have ever been around someone who is "down," or depressed, you realize that their thoughts tend to be pessimistic and negative. People who are depressed are more likely to engage in negative thinking errors, called **cognitive distortions**, according to classic research by Aaron Beck (1967, 1976). For example, people who are depressed tend to reject positive experiences and attend more to the negative aspects of a situation (Hsu & Davison, 2017). They interpret ambiguous material in a negative manner and are more likely to recall negative events and information, relative to positive information (Everaert, Bronstein, Cannon, & Joormann, 2018; Everaert & Joormann, 2019; Joormann, Waugh, & Gotlib, 2015). Beck believes that these

Andrew Sacks/The New York Times/Redux Pictures

▲ Susan Nolen-Hoeksema (1959–2013) was a Yale University professor and researcher who focused on women's mental health, with a special emphasis on how rumination influences women's vulnerability to depression.

people engage in a negative view so automatically that they may not even realize their errors in thinking.

Engage Yourself!

To help you understand the impact of negative thinking errors on mood, try this demonstration. Before you go to bed tonight, write down how you feel generally—for example, happy, sad, or stressed. Tomorrow, carry a notepad or tablet around with you all day. Every time you have a positive thought or experience, write it down. At the end of the day, again write down how you feel generally. It is likely that noting positive feelings all day will create a more positive overall feeling. If we had asked you to note negative thoughts for an entire day, how do you think that would affect your outlook on your day?

Research on the *attributions* of people who are depressed further supports Beck's model. An attribution is assigning a cause to behavior (see Chapter 10). People who are depressed tend to feel undeserving of positive outcomes and attribute negative environmental events to factors within themselves (Alloy, Abramson, & Francis, 1999; Kaiser et al., 2018; Wood et al., 2009). For instance, failing an exam is interpreted to mean that one is stupid, will always be stupid, and will probably fail more exams. A relationship breakup is interpreted to mean that one is not lovable and will always be unlovable. These negative attributions and cognitive distortions appear related to depressed mood (Abramson et al., 2002; Gibb et al., 2004; Moore & Fresco, 2007). Beck (2008) has suggested that early adverse experiences combined with biological vulnerabilities (genetics and neurochemistry) may influence the development of these cognitive deficits in people who are depressed. The negative cognitions then influence the interpretation and processing of future stressors as well as neurochemistry and brain activation, creating a vicious cycle of biopsychosocial factors and the maintenance of depression (Foland-Ross et al., 2013).

Sociocultural Variations: Social Status, Stress, and Gender

Sociocultural factors must also be considered when explaining depressive and bipolar disorders. Depression is more likely among people of lower social status (Blazer et al., 1994; Pratt & Brody, 2014), especially those from adverse neighborhoods (Cutrona, Wallace, & Wesner, 2006). As we have seen, a considerable body of research also documents a consistent relationship between major stressful life events and the onset of depression, especially among people who are genetically predisposed to depression (Belleau et al., 2019; Green et al., 2010; Hammen, 2009; Monroe & Reid, 2009; Nederhof et al., 2014; S. E. Taylor et al., 2006). Explaining such differences is further complicated by the worldwide gender difference in depression. As we have noted, women are more likely to be diagnosed with depression than men.

13.5.4 Gender and Depression

Biopsychosocial forces that are unique to women may explain their higher vulnerability to depressive disorders (see • FIGURE 13.5; Gorman, 2006; Mendle, Eisenlohr-Moul, & Kiesner, 2016; Nolen-Hoeksema & Hilt, 2013). We have already seen that the genetic risk of depression appears stronger in women than in men. Research has also investigated—over many years and many studies—the relationship between the female ovarian hormones, estrogen and progesterone, and mood in an effort to understand pathways to depression. However, it is not as simple as saying ovarian hormones *cause* depression. Research suggests that women's estrogen and progesterone levels may influence the functioning of the neurotransmitters serotonin and dopamine, which play a central role in mood. However, researchers don't yet understand the precise actions by which estrogen and progesterone influence serotonin functioning (Hughes et al., 2009; Krolick, Zhu, & Shi, 2018; Lu et al., 2003; Parker & Brotchie, 2004; Steiner, Dunn, & Born, 2003). Similarly, some argue that stress hormones differentially contribute to gender differences in depression (Gordon et al., 2016; Parker & Brotchie, 2010; Young & Korszun, 2010).

Psychological factors unique to women must also be considered when examining gender differences in depression. For example, females are more likely than males to engage in a ruminative coping style (Li, DiGiuseppe, & Froh, 2006; Lopez, Driscoll, & Kistner, 2009; Nolen-Hoeksema, 2001; Papadakis et al., 2006). That is, women tend to focus on how they feel and to fret about their feelings. Even co-rumination, or excessively talking about problems with friends, though offering women social support, can also amplify or increase their depressive symptoms (Byrd-Craven et al., 2008; Rose, Carlson, & Waller, 2007; Spendelow, Simonds, & Avery, 2017). In contrast, men are more likely to engage in some activity to take their minds off their feelings, to withdraw, or to abuse drugs (Nolen-Hoeksema & Hilt, 2013). As Nolen-Hoeksema and her colleagues (1999) put it, "Women think and men drink."

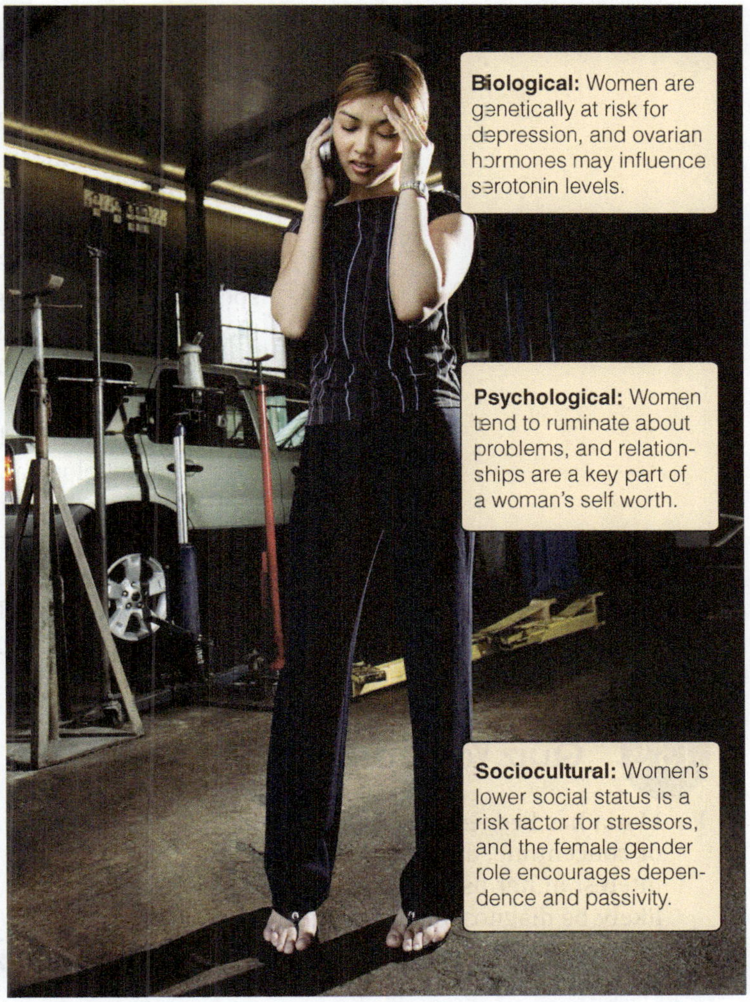

Masterfile

FIGURE 13.5

Women and Depression

Biopsychosocial forces unique to women may explain their higher vulnerability to depressive disorders.

Women are also more likely to have an interpersonal orientation that puts them at risk for depression (Mazure, Keita, & Blehar, 2002). Relationships are more important to a woman's sense of self-worth than they are to a man's. As a result, women are more likely to silence their own demands in order to maintain a positive relationship and are more likely to place their needs secondary to those of others. This relational style may also predispose women to depression.

Tied to these biological and psychological factors are the social circumstances that women face. Women are at a disadvantage in society: They earn less and have less power than men. They report less satisfaction with work and family and are more likely to be victims of discrimination, sexual abuse, and poverty (Heim et al., 2009; Klonoff, Landrine, & Campbell, 2000; Koss & Kilpatrick, 2001). Negative life events such as these foster feelings of uncontrollability and helplessness, perceptions that are intimately connected to depressive disorders (Browne, 1993; Ilgen & Hutchison, 2005). Traditional gender roles also discourage women from being masterful, independent, and assertive and encourage them to be dependent and passive. These prescribed roles may increase women's feelings of uncontrollability and helplessness (Barlow, 2002).

Although rates of depression are higher in women, approximately 15% of U.S. men will experience a major depressive disorder sometime in their lives (Hasin et al., 2018). We have also seen that men are at a much higher risk for committing suicide than women. Yet, some men may not express the symptoms of depression in the same manner as women. Although men may report the physical symptoms of depression—fatigue, sleep problems, and loss of interest in their usual activities—men are less likely to cry and express sadness and are more likely to hide their feelings, be irritable, lash out at others, and abuse alcohol. Male gender-role socialization encourages men to be strong and in control, which may discourage men from admitting and expressing emotional distress as well as deterring men from seeking help when experiencing depression (Cochran & Rabinowitz, 2000; Seidler et al., 2016; Tang et al., 2014).

For both men and women, depression is a complex behavior affected by biological, psychological, and sociocultural variables. Each of us probably has some biological vulnerability to either depressive or bipolar disorders. However, social and psychological factors may act to protect us from such vulnerability or, alternatively, make us more likely to express this vulnerability (Beck & Bredemeier, 2016; Gotlib, Goodman & Humphreys, 2020). Research continues to explore the exact role these factors play. People's lives depend on it.

13.5 Quiz Yourself

1. Maria has been sad for 3 weeks. She can't sleep, eat, or concentrate, and is constantly crying. She has lost interest in her usual activities. Maria would most likely be diagnosed with which disorder?

a. Bipolar disorder
b. Cyclothymic disorder
c. Major depressive disorder
d. Persistent depressive disorder

2. People who are depressed are more likely to engage in ____ or repetitively analyzing their feelings and concerns.

a. cognitive distortions
b. rumination
c. pessimism
d. negative attributions

3. Which of the following statements about suicide is *true*?

a. People who talk of suicide are often just looking for attention and will not kill themselves.
b. Among adolescents, previous suicide attempts are a predictor of future attempts.
c. A better mood means the risk of suicide is gone.
d. Only people who are depressed commit suicide.

4. Which of the following statements about women's higher vulnerability to depression is *false*?

a. Women are more likely to have higher levels of estrogen and progesterone, which cause depression.
b. Women are more likely to experience negative life events that may lead to feelings of helplessness.
c. Women are more likely to have an interpersonal orientation that puts them at risk for depression.
d. Women are more likely to focus on how they feel, which may increase feelings of depression.

Answers 1. c; 2. b; 3. b; 4. a

13.6 Schizophrenia: Disintegration

schizophrenia [skit-suh-FREE-nee-uh] a severe mental health disorder characterized by disturbances in thought, perceptions, emotions, and behavior

Schizophrenia is a chronic, disabling mental health disorder that affects roughly 1% of the general population worldwide (Ho, Black, & Andreasen, 2003; Lieberman, Stroup, & Perkins, 2012). It involves the disintegration of one's personality.

Is schizophrenia the same thing as dissociative identity disorder? No. Dissociative identity disorder, as previously discussed, involves the existence of several *intact* identities within a person. In schizophrenia, the one identity is no longer intact, or held together and connected. If we think of someone's identity as a related set of cognitive, emotional, perceptual, and motor behaviors, then in schizophrenia we see the disconnection among these identity elements. As these elements lose their connections with one another, the person loses their connection with reality. This results in impaired functioning.

13.6.1 Individual Variations: Onset, Gender, Ethnicity, Social Class, and Prognosis

Symptoms of schizophrenia typically appear in adolescence or young adulthood. In some cases, the symptoms come on gradually; in others, they appear more abruptly. Schizophrenia affects men and women with equal frequency, although it typically appears earlier in men than in women. Men tend to develop the disorder in their late teens or early 20s, and women are generally affected in their 20s or early 30s (American Psychiatric Association, 2000a). This gender difference may be related to hormonal and sociocultural factors. The hormone estrogen may protect women by lessening abnormal brain development associated with schizophrenia (Canuso & Pandina, 2007; Seeman, 2008, 2018). In addition, women's higher social competence and more extensive social networks may delay the onset of the disorder (Combs & Mueser, 2007; Hooley, 2010). Perhaps because of the earlier onset, men with schizophrenia tend to be more chronically impaired (Grossman et al., 2008; Ho et al., 2003).

Schizophrenia and other psychotic disorders are diagnosed more often in African Americans, Latino American/Hispanic, and Asian Americans. However, this difference may be due to racial bias and cultural insensitivity (Barnes, 2004; Bresnahan et al., 2007; Schwartz & Blankenship, 2014). Once diagnosed, racial and ethnic disparities in quality of care are also evident, with Blacks and Latinos receiving lower quality of care relative to Whites (Horvitz-Lennon et al., 2015). Schizophrenia also is more prevalent in lower socioeconomic groups (Escobar, 1993; Kirkbride et al., 2007).

Most people with schizophrenia have difficulty functioning throughout their adult lives, losing opportunities for careers and relationships (Hooley, 2010; Jobe & Harrow, 2010). Several factors contribute to this difficulty in functioning: the negative stigma that a schizophrenia diagnosis brings, the lack of public understanding, and media portrayals of people with schizophrenia as criminally violent. Although people diagnosed with schizophrenia are more likely to commit a violent crime, their increased risk of violence is significantly associated with male sex, being single, refusing to accept treatment, substance abuse and duration of illness—variables that are also associated with violent crime in healthy individuals—particularly male sex and substance abuse (Fazel, Gulati et al., 2009; Fazel, Långström et al., 2009; Ghoreishi et al., 2015; Soyka et al., 2007). Many people with schizophrenia are not violent toward others but are withdrawn and prefer to be left alone (Steadman et al., 1998).

Although there currently is no cure, a diagnosis of schizophrenia does not necessarily mean progressive deterioration in functioning, as most people believe. Rather, for reasons not yet understood, schizophrenic symptoms and episodes tend to decrease as a person ages. However, recovery is very much related to social factors such as economic and social support, adherence to medication, and substance abuse (Eaton et al., 1998; Harrow et al., 2005; Jablensky, 2000; Medrano et al., 2018). Most people with schizophrenia continue to experience difficulties throughout their lives (Jobe & Harrow, 2010).

Gary Leonard/Corbis Entertainment/Getty Images

▲ Nathaniel Ayers, a promising musician, left the Juilliard School when he developed schizophrenia, a severe mental health disorder marked by disordered thoughts, perceptions, emotions, and/or motor behavior.

delusions thoughts or beliefs that a person believes to be true but that most people would agree are not true

hallucinations perceiving something that does not exist in reality

disorganized speech a positive symptom of schizophrenia in which one's speech lacks association between one's ideas and the events that one is experiencing

disordered behavior a positive symptom of schizophrenia that includes inappropriate or unusual behavior such as silliness, catatonic excitement, or catatonic stupor

13.6.2 Symptoms of Schizophrenia

Schizophrenia may express itself in many forms, depending on which symptoms are present. People diagnosed with schizophrenia show two or more of the following symptoms nearly every day during a 1-month period with continued disturbance for at least 6 months; and one of the symptoms must be *delusions, hallucinations,* or *disorganized speech* (discussed shortly). These symptoms are not due to substance use or a medical condition, and they interfere with the person's ability to function (American Psychiatric Association, 2013). Symptoms of schizophrenia fall into two broad categories: positive and negative symptoms.

Positive Symptoms of Schizophrenia

Positive symptoms of schizophrenia represent an excess or distortion of normal functions and are more obvious signs of a break with reality called *psychosis*. They include *delusions, hallucinations, disorganized speech,* and *grossly disorganized* or *catatonic behavior*.

- **Delusions** are thoughts and beliefs that the person believes to be true but that most people would agree, have no basis in reality. For example, *persecutory delusions* involve beliefs about being followed or watched, usually by agents of authorities such as the Federal Bureau of Investigation (FBI) or the government. *Grandiose delusions* involve beliefs about being a famous or special person. For instance, a person with schizophrenia may believe that they are the president of France. People with schizophrenia may also hold *delusions of reference* (believing that others are talking about them) or *delusions of thought control* (believing that their thoughts are controlled by another person or force).
- People who are diagnosed with schizophrenia also may experience **hallucinations**, in which the person sees, hears, tastes, smells, or feels something that others do not perceive. In schizophrenia, hearing voices or other sounds (called *auditory hallucinations*) is the most common altered perception, followed by *visual hallucinations* (seeing things that aren't there). The hallucinations may tell the person to perform certain acts or may be frightening in nature.
- The speech of individuals with schizophrenia is often disorganized in a variety of ways that impair effective communication. **Disorganized speech** (*formal thought disorder*) involves a lack of associations between ideas and events. Because the ideas of people with schizophrenia lack connection, we refer to this disconnection as *loose associations*. Their ideas seem unrelated to one another, and their speech is often characterized as a *word salad* (words seem tossed together without any apparent syntax or organization). They may be saying a lot, but what they say is not communicating anything clearly to the receiver.
- **Disordered behavior** may also characterize some people with schizophrenia. This may take the form of unusual, odd, or repetitive behaviors and gestures. Head banging, finger flapping, or tracing a pattern over and over again are examples. Childlike silliness, inappropriate sexual behavior (such as public masturbation), or difficulty maintaining hygiene may be present. Some people with schizophrenia may show an absence of all motor behaviors, remaining totally motionless and rigid for hours on end and

Grunnitus Studio/Science Source

▲ In a catatonic stupor, the person may remain in a "posed" position for hours on end.

resisting efforts to be moved. Such behavior is referred to as a **catatonic stupor**. Other people with schizophrenia may show **catatonic excitement**, in which they are suddenly agitated, fidgety, shouting, swearing, or moving around rapidly.

catatonic [cat-uh-TAWN-ick] stupor a positive symptom of schizophrenia marked by disorder in motor behavior involving immobility

catatonic excitement a positive symptom of schizophrenia marked by disorder in motor behavior involving excited agitation

blunted affect a negative symptom of schizophrenia involving lack of emotional expression

alogia [uh-LO-jeeuh] a negative symptom of schizophrenia involving decreased quality and/or quantity of speech

avolition [aa-vuh-LISH-un] a negative symptom of schizophrenia marked by the inability to follow through on one's plans

Negative Symptoms of Schizophrenia

Negative symptoms of schizophrenia represent a restriction or absence of normal functions. These include *blunted affect, alogia,* and *avolition* (American Psychiatric Association, 2013). Approximately 25% of persons with schizophrenia display these symptoms (C. I. Cohen et al., 2013; Ho et al., 2003).

- *Affect,* in psychological terms, refers to expressing emotions. Some people with schizophrenia show **blunted affect**, or a lack of emotional expression. They appear passive, with immobile facial expressions. Their vocal tone does not change even when the conversation is emotional in tone. They do not respond to events in their environment with any emotion. Their speech lacks the inflection that usually communicates a speaker's mood.
- **Alogia**, also called *poverty of speech,* refers to decreased quality and/or quantity of speech. The person with schizophrenia gives brief and empty replies.
- **Avolition** is the inability to follow through on one's plans. A person with schizophrenia may seem apathetic, sitting for long periods of time, showing little interest in their usual activities.

Many people with schizophrenia exhibit both positive and negative symptoms. People with schizophrenia who show predominantly positive symptoms tend to have a less severe course of the disorder and respond better to medication than those who show predominately negative symptoms (Kendler et al., 1994; Kutscher, 2008; Remington et al., 2016). Such findings have led researchers to believe that positive symptoms of schizophrenia may have a different cause than negative symptoms.

13.6.3 Research Explaining Schizophrenia: Genetics, the Brain, and the Environment

To date, biological factors account for the strongest evidence in the development of schizophrenia, although environmental factors must also be considered. It is likely that environmental conditions interact with biological factors to make a person either more or less susceptible to the illness. Biological research has focused on three main areas: *genetics, brain abnormalities,* and the malfunctioning of *specific neurotransmitters* in the brain. Environmental research has focused on prenatal and development factors, as well as the role of family and the environment.

A Strong Genetic Factor

Family, twin, and adoption studies have routinely demonstrated a high heritability of schizophrenia (N.C. Allen et al., 2008; Chou et al., 2017; Levy et al., 2010; NIMH Genetics Workgroup, 1998). As ● FIGURE 13.6 shows, although the incidence of schizophrenia in the general population is around 1%, the more genetically similar a person is to someone with schizophrenia, the more likely they will also develop the disorder (Cardno & Gottesman, 2000). In identical

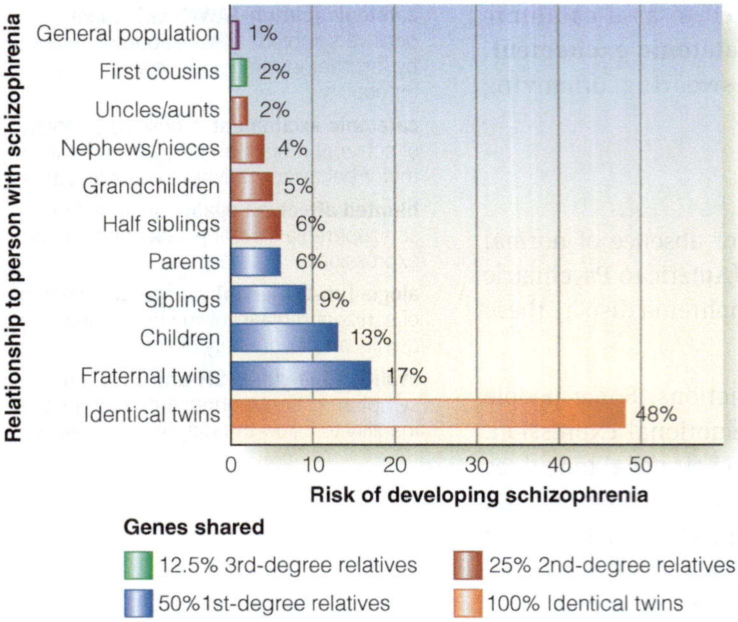

FIGURE 13.6

Risk of Schizophrenia and Genetic Relatedness

The incidence of schizophrenia in the general population is around 1%. However, the more closely one is genetically related to a person with schizophrenia, the higher the risk of developing the disorder.

Source: Reprinted by permission of Irving I. Gottesman.

twin pairs, if one twin develops schizophrenia, the other twin has about a 48% chance of developing the disorder. However, in fraternal twins (who are not genetically identical), the probability is only 17%. Adoption studies show a similar pattern (Tienari et al., 2003; Tienari, Wahlberg, & Wynne, 2006). Adopted children who have biological parents with schizophrenia are 10 times more likely to develop the disorder than are adopted children whose biological parents are not diagnosed with schizophrenia.

Despite these results, it is unlikely that a single gene is responsible for the disorder; if it were, the heritability rates would be higher. Research has therefore moved toward exploring several chromosomal regions that may work together to increase a person's vulnerability to schizophrenia, as well as altered gene expressions that may give rise to brain abnormalities (Nicodemus et al., 2010; Pogue-Geile & Yokley, 2010; Schizophrenia Working Group of the Psychiatric Genomics Consortium, 2014; Shi et al., 2009; Sinkus et al., 2013; E. Walker et al., 2010). The exact nature of these pathways has yet to be identified.

Another genetic explanation for schizophrenia stems from a modest association between advanced paternal age and an increased risk of schizophrenia. That is, some people with schizophrenia are more likely to have had older fathers (45 years or older) at birth. Such an association has led to the hypothesis that mutations in male sperm cells (which are more likely to occur as a male ages) may be in part a genetic mechanism for schizophrenia in at least some people (Byrne et al., 2003; Dalman & Allebeck, 2002; Malaspina et al., 2001; Taylor et al., 2019; Torrey et al., 2009). However, it is also possible that an unknown third factor is associated with both delayed fatherhood and schizophrenia (Ek et al., 2015; Petersen, Mortensen, & Pedersen, 2011).

The Brain: Neurotransmitters and Structural Abnormalities

A second area of research on the development of schizophrenia looks at neurotransmitters and abnormalities in certain brain structures. Two of the most influential hypotheses concerning the neurobiology underlying schizophrenia involve dopamine and glutamate. It was originally believed that schizophrenia was caused by excess activity of the neurotransmitter dopamine in the brain. The drugs that are prescribed for schizophrenia, called *phenothiazines,* reduce dopamine activity in the brain and are typically more effective in reducing the positive symptoms of schizophrenia. However, many people with schizophrenia do not respond to treatment with phenothiazines. One of the newer drugs used to treat schizophrenia, called *clozapine,* blocks different dopamine receptors than the phenothiazines do, clearly indicating that dopamine is involved, but in a more complex way (Conklin & Iacono, 2002; Grace, 2010; Howes, McCutcheon, & Stone, 2015).

Other research suggests a potential role for the neurotransmitter glutamate (Coyle, 2006; Grace, 2010; Hu et al., 2015). Drugs such as PCP and ketamine (see Chapter 4) that block the action of glutamate can cause research participants who have not been diagnosed with schizophrenia, to exhibit cognitive impairments and negative symptoms similar to those found in people with schizophrenia (Deakin et al., 2008). Current research is focused on how glutamate and dopamine dysfunction may interact to contribute to the development of schizophrenia (Anticevic, Murray, & Barch, 2015; McCutcheon, Krystal, & Howes, 2020). Obviously, the relationship between neurotransmitters and schizophrenia remains a complex one.

Given that cognitive deficits are a core feature of schizophrenia and cognition is related to interactions among various brain regions, abnormalities in certain brain structures have also been investigated for their links to schizophrenia. The most consistent abnormality found in people with schizophrenia is enlarged ventricles (see photos) (Jaaro-Peled et al., 2010; Kuo & Pogue-Geile, 2019; Lieberman et al., 2001; Mitelman et al., 2005). A *ventricle* is a fluid-filled cavity in the brain. Enlarged ventricles reduce the overall size of the brain, which in turn may contribute to the development of schizophrenia. Brain dysfunction in the frontal and temporal lobes has also been implicated in the development of schizophrenia (Brugger & Howes, 2017; Haut et al., 2015; Karlsgodt, Sun, & Cannon, 2010; Wolf et al., 2007). The frontal lobe is responsible for language, emotions, and social behavior, and the temporal lobe plays an important role in memory. The symptoms of schizophrenia (disordered speech, blunted affect, and catatonic behavior) are associated with these brain areas.

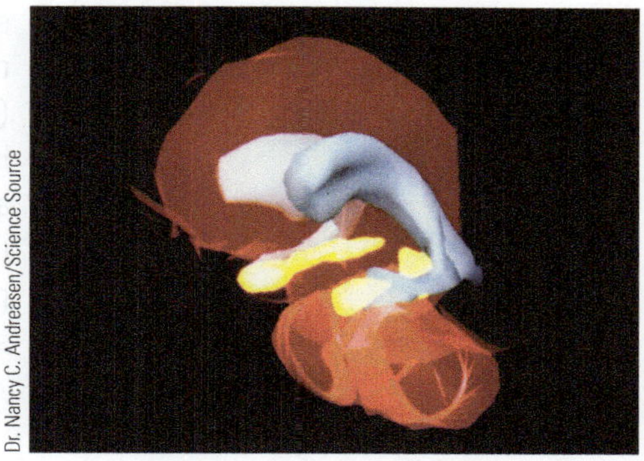

Dr. Nancy C. Andreasen/Science Source

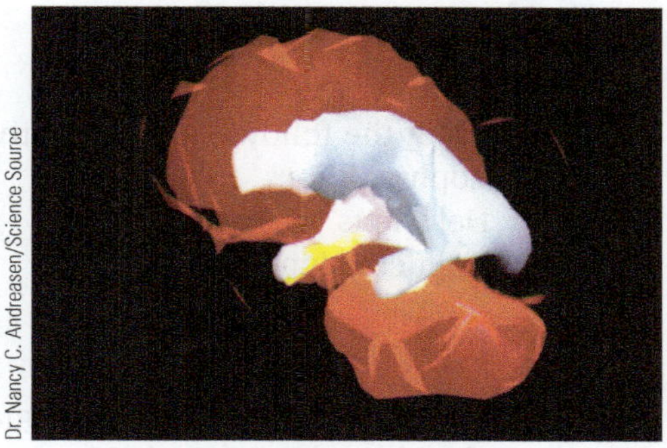

Dr. Nancy C. Andreasen/Science Source

▲ The most consistent brain abnormality that has been found in people diagnosed with schizophrenia is enlarged ventricles. Shown here are 3-D magnetic resonance images (MRI) of the brain of a person with schizophrenia (bottom) and the brain of a person without schizophrenia (top). The hippocampus (yellow, at center) is shrunken and the fluid-filled ventricles (white) are enlarged in the brain of the person with schizophrenia.

Prenatal and Developmental Factors

How do people with schizophrenia develop these neurochemical or brain abnormalities? In addition to possible hereditary factors, these abnormalities have been linked to factors of pregnancy and birth such as birth complications, maternal diabetes, low birth weight, prenatal maternal stress, and the mother's exposure to prenatal viruses (A. S. Brown et al., 2004; King, St-Hilaire, & Heidkamp, 2010; Seeman, 2018; Walder et al., 2014; E. Walker et al., 2010), although many other causes could exist. It is theorized that a genetic predisposition to schizophrenia interacts with prenatal environmental agents such as a maternal virus or poor nutrition, causing changes in normal brain development. Then, as the brain reaches maturation (during adolescence), a natural trimming away of brain synapses occurs. It is hypothesized that in people with schizophrenia, the brain trims away too many synapses, resulting in the expression of the disorder in the teenage years. Symptoms of schizophrenia are particularly likely to appear if the person has a strong genetic disposition or if environmental circumstances have encouraged the expression of the disorder in those with even a mild genetic link (Barch, Cohen, & Csernansky, 2014; Fatemi & Folson, 2009; Rapoport et al., 2005; Walder et al., 2014).

The Role of Family and Environment

Two critical factors that appear to contribute to the onset and course of schizophrenia are family support and exposure to stressful living conditions. Studies on the families of people with schizophrenia have found that the quality of family communications and interactions may predict the onset of schizophrenia in people who are genetically at high risk (Hooley, 2010; Walder et al., 2014). The quality of family interactions may also influence whether future psychotic episodes are triggered. Families that are critical, harsh, hostile, and poor communicators may make a high-risk person more susceptible to the disorder (Hooley, 2007; Schlosser et al., 2010; Walder et al., 2014). Chronic stress from living a low-income lifestyle or within a family with poor communication also appears to influence future relapses (Ventura et al., 2000). Although it appears that family and lifestyle do not *cause* schizophrenia, they are critical factors in people's susceptibility to the disorder and must be taken into account when designing prevention or treatment programs for those with schizophrenia.

13.6 Quiz Yourself

1. **Which of the following is a negative symptom of schizophrenia?**
   a. Delusions
   b. Hallucinations
   c. Alogia
   d. Catatonic stupor
2. **The most consistent brain abnormality found among people with schizophrenia is _____.**
   a. a small frontal lobe
   b. a small temporal lobe
   c. enlarged ventricles
   d. an enlarged frontal lobe
3. **Loose associations and word salad characterize which symptom of schizophrenia?**
   a. Disorganized speech
   b. Avolition
   c. Delusions
   d. Blunted affect

Answers 1. c; 2. c; 3. a

13.7 Personality Disorders: Maladaptive Patterns of Behavior

personality disorders mental health disorders marked by maladaptive behaviors that have been stable over a long period and across many situations

The **personality disorders** consist of long-standing patterns of malfunctioning. All of us have personality quirks. Some people may be excessively neat. Others may be somewhat suspicious and mistrustful of others. However, these traits do not necessarily qualify someone for a personality disorder. In personality disorders, the person's emotions, thoughts, and behavior result in persistent distress to oneself or others and interfere with one's ability to function. As we saw in this part's case study, Emily was diagnosed as having borderline personality trends indicating that her personality was contributing to her difficulty in functioning.

People with personality disorders also can be diagnosed with any of the mental health disorders previously discussed, and they typically seek treatment for these disorders or because someone else has a problem with their behavior and encourages them to undergo therapy. Individuals with a personality disorder often don't see a problem with their behavior and, therefore, seldom seek treatment on their own. It is estimated that as many as 10% of adults in the United States meet the criteria for at least one personality disorder (Grant et al., 2004; Lenzenweger et al., 2007; Sansone & Sansone, 2011b). Worldwide, about 8% of adults may have a diagnosable personality disorder (Winsper et al., 2020). The *DSM-5* lists 10 personality disorders, and space considerations prohibit a

TABLE 13.4 Types of Personality Disorders

Disorder	Major Features
Cluster A: Odd or Eccentric Disorders	
Paranoid personality disorder	Excessive suspicion and mistrust of others
Schizoid personality disorder	Lack of desire to form close relationships with others; emotional detachment and coldness toward others
Schizotypal personality disorder	Considered a mild version of schizophrenia. The person shows inappropriate social and emotional behavior, and unusual thoughts and speech.
Cluster B: Dramatic, Emotional, or Erratic Disorders	
Antisocial personality disorder	Chronic pattern of impulsive behavior; violates rights of others and does not show remorse or guilt for actions
Borderline personality disorder	Instability in mood, self-concept, and interpersonal relationships
Histrionic personality disorder	Intense need for attention; always wants to be the center of attention; excessively dramatic behavior; rapidly changing moods
Narcissistic personality disorder	Preoccupation with own sense of importance and view of self as above others; typically ignores the needs and wants of others
Cluster C: Anxious or Fearful Disorders	
Avoidant personality disorder	Intense and chronic anxiety over being negatively evaluated by others, so avoids social interactions
Dependent personality disorder	Excessive need to be cared for by others; denies own thoughts and feelings and clings to others
Obsessive-compulsive personality disorder	Pattern of rigid and perfectionist behavior; preoccupied with details, rules, order, and routine; experiences upset when routine is disrupted. (This is not the same as the disorder OCD.)

discussion of all of them, but we give a brief description of them in TABLE 13.4. Here we will confine our discussion to two: *antisocial personality disorder* and *borderline personality disorder*.

13.7.1 Antisocial Personality Disorder: Impulsive and Dangerous

People who are impulsive and disregard the rights of others without showing any remorse or guilt are diagnosed with **antisocial personality disorder** (American Psychiatric Association, 2013). *Antisocial* in this context does not mean shy or unsociable, but rather indicates harmful acts against (anti) others (social). People who have antisocial personalities lack impulse control and often act hastily and recklessly with little concern for the consequences of their behavior. They are irresponsible, blame others for their problems, and frequently have difficulty maintaining social relationships. They repeatedly lie and may manipulate others into doing what they want. Such antisocial or harmful behavior has often been present since childhood or adolescence (Loney et al., 2007).

antisocial personality disorder a personality disorder marked by a pattern of impulsivity and disregard for and violation of the rights of others with no remorse or guilt for one's actions

FBI/Hulton Archive/Getty Images

▲ Andrew Cunanan murdered famous clothing designer Gianni Versace after killing several others. He was described by many as a charming and bright young man.

It is one of the more common personality disorders, and men are three to five times more likely than women to be diagnosed with this disorder (Grant et al., 2004; Hasin & Grant, 2015; Lenzenweger, 2008).

People with antisocial personality disorder are more often sent to prison than to treatment. However, this does not mean that all criminals have antisocial personality disorder. Although antisocial behavior is highly correlated with delinquency and criminal behavior, not all criminals are antisocial. One of the key features distinguishing the two is the lack of remorse and guilt for one's actions. A person can commit armed robbery yet afterward regret their actions. A person who is antisocial does not experience such regret or remorse. People with antisocial personality disorder may not be violent. They may be "con artists," and more of them may live outside prison than in it. They may function successfully in business, politics, or entertainment (Stout, 2005).

What causes antisocial personality disorder? Some research suggests biological factors. Twin studies, adoption studies, and family studies suggest a genetic influence (Hicks et al., 2004; Moffitt, 2005). For example, family members of people with antisocial personality disorder have higher rates of the disorder than the general population. Other research suggests low levels of the neurotransmitter serotonin (Baskin-Sommers, 2016; Moffitt et al., 1998); deficits in brain areas that control impulsivity, attention, and decision making (Kiehl et al., 2006; Raine, 2008; Raine et al., 2011; Waller et al., 2019); elevated levels of the hormone testosterone (van Honk & Schutter, 2007); and low arousal of the nervous system (Raine, 1997; Raine et al., 2000).

However, psychological and social variables cannot be ruled out. People with antisocial personality disorder often experience conflict-filled childhoods. Their parents may be neglectful, inconsistent in discipline, harsh, hostile, or less warm. As a result, they often learn to expect such treatment from others and adopt a mistrustful and aggressive stance toward others (Afifi et al., 2011; Dishion & Patterson, 1997; Feinberg et al., 2007). In all likelihood, a complex interplay of neural, genetic, and environmental factors best explains the development of antisocial personality disorder (Arias et al., 2011; Baskin-Sommers, 2016; Fowles & Dindo, 2009; Raine, 2008).

13.7.2 Borderline Personality Disorder: Living on Your Fault Line

borderline personality disorder (BPD) a personality disorder marked by a pattern of instability in mood, relationships, self-image, and behavior

Borderline personality disorder (**BPD**) is characterized by instability in moods, interpersonal relationships, self-image, and behavior (American Psychiatric Association, 2013). This key feature of instability often disrupts a person's relationships, career, and identity. Their unstable emotions result in intense bouts of anger, depression, or anxiety that may occur for hours or for days. Their unstable self-concepts are reflected in extreme insecurity at some times and exaggerated feelings of importance at other times. This instability may prompt frequent changes in goals, jobs, friendships, and values because people with borderline personalities lack a clear definition of themselves. They have little idea of who they are. Their interpersonal relationships are also characterized by instability. They may admire, idealize, and cling to loved ones at first; but when conflict occurs, feelings of abandonment and rejection surface, and their feelings quickly turn to anger and dislike. They then seek out new friends or loved ones, and the cycle repeats itself. People with this disorder often feel unworthy, bad, or empty inside. At times of extreme insecurity and depression, self-injury and suicide attempts are common (D. W. Black et al., 2004; Soloff & Chiapetta, 2012). Notice how much of Emily's problems in her teenage years match these symptoms. Her emotions often vacillated between rage and panic. Her feelings of inadequacy often made her feel insecure and unlovable, and she had several suicide attempts.

Like Emily, people with BPD are often diagnosed with other mental health disorders such as major depression, substance-related disorder, or anxiety (Eaton et al., 2011). It is estimated that approximately 2% to 6% of the population could be diagnosed with BPD at some point in their lives, and it is diagnosed slightly more often in young women than in men (Torgersen, 2012; Zanarini et al., 2012). Extensive mental health services are often needed to treat people diagnosed with BPD.

As we have seen with many of the mental health disorders we have discussed in this chapter, interactions among neurobiological and environmental factors (emphasizing the biopsychosocial approach) may best explain BPD (Winsper et al., 2016). Low levels of serotonin are related to impulsive behaviors (Ni et al., 2007; Siever & Koenigsberg, 2000). Difficulty in regulating emotions may be related to abnormal brain functioning (Leichsenring et al., 2011; L. M. Williams et al., 2006). However, many people diagnosed with BPD report a history of adverse life events such as abuse or neglect, making environment a probable factor as well (Bornovalova et al., 2006; Leichsenring et al., 2011). For example, in one study (Zanarini, 2000), a large percentage of patients diagnosed with BPD reported having been sexually abused. Such social stressors may impede normal attachment patterns, identity development, and the ability to express appropriate emotions.

13.7 Quiz Yourself

1. **Which of the following is *not* a feature of antisocial personality disorder?**
   a. Lack of remorse
   b. Shyness and unsociability
   c. Poor impulse control
   d. Disregard for the rights of others

2. **Felicia is extremely insecure and lacks a clear sense of identity. She often clings to new friends and then hates them a month later. She has an intense fear of abandonment and rejection. Felicia's behavior *best* fits which personality disorder?**
   a. Narcissistic
   b. Antisocial
   c. Borderline
   d. Paranoid

3. **Personality disorders ______.**
   a. do not coexist with other mental health disorders such as depression or anxiety
   b. generally appear in early or middle adulthood
   c. are stable patterns of malfunctioning
   d. do not pose any threat to others

Answers 1. b; 2. c; 3. c

13.8 Integrating Psychology: The Big Picture

In this chapter, we have provided examples of disorders from nine of the major categories of mental health disorders listed in the *DSM-5*. Although research continues into the exact origins of each disorder, we have seen that in many cases, a person's biological vulnerability appears to combine with psychological and sociocultural factors—learning experiences, thinking patterns, development, family interactions, cultural attitudes, gender roles—to trigger the onset of the disorder.

Such an interaction of variables is helpful in understanding Emily's difficulty in functioning. Biologically, Emily may have been genetically predisposed to anxiety and depression, because her father was a tense and driven man while her mother was often sad and depressed. Yet, psychological variables such as learning, cognitions, and emotions also need to be considered. Emily could have been modeling her parents' coping mechanisms. We also saw that Emily's delinquent and disruptive behavior was often a way for her to get parental attention. In addition, her negative cognitions and feelings of parental and peer rejection could have also contributed to her psychological distress. Such stress could have further affected her biological functioning. Traditional female gender roles that perhaps went against a family culture of high expectations for achievement are sociocultural variables that could have further compounded Emily's problems, especially as she evidenced difficulty in learning. Only by integrating and examining all these variables can we achieve a comprehensive picture of Emily's behavior.

Like Emily, many people with mental health disorders seek help in the form of therapy. So, keep the symptoms of these disorders in mind. It will assist you in mastering the material of the next chapter, where we explore the different therapies psychologists, mental health professionals, and psychiatrists use to treat mental health disorders.

Studying the Chapter

Key Terms

agoraphobia (579)
alogia (601)
antisocial personality disorder (605)
avolition (601)
bipolar disorder (592)
blunted affect (601)
borderline personality disorder (BPD) (606)
catatonic excitement (601)
catatonic stupor (601)
cognitive distortions (595)
compulsions (580)
cyclothymic disorder (592)
delusions (600)
Diagnostic and Statistical Manual of Mental Disorders (DSM) (573)
disordered behavior (600)
disorganized speech (600)
dissociative disorders (586)
dissociative identity disorder (DID) (586)
generalized anxiety disorder (GAD) (579)
hallucinations (600)
hoarding disorder (581)
illness anxiety disorder (588)
learned helplessness (595)
major depressive disorder (589)
mania (592)
medical model (572)
mental health disorder (570)
obsessions (580)
obsessive-compulsive disorder (OCD) (580)
panic disorder (579)
persistent depressive disorder (590)
personality disorders (604)
posttraumatic stress disorder (PTSD) (581)
psychopathology (571)
ruminative coping style (595)
schizophrenia (598)
social anxiety disorder (social phobia) (580)
somatic symptom and related disorders (587)
specific phobia (580)

What Do You Know? Assess Your Understanding

Test your retention and understanding of the material by answering the following questions.

1. Allison can't help feeling sad most of the time. It upsets her that she can't be happy and seem "normal." Allison's behavior *best* fits which criterion of a mental health disorder?
   a. Violation of social norms
   b. Personal distress
   c. Danger to others
   d. All of the above

2. If a person had "stage fright" or fear of public speaking to the degree that it interfered with their ability to function, these would be examples of which mental health disorder?
   a. Specific phobia
   b. Social anxiety disorder
   c. Major depressive disorder
   d. Agoraphobia

3. Dr. Sanchez believes that mental health disorders are the result of irrational assumptions and negative thinking patterns. Dr. Sanchez views mental illness from a ______ perspective.
   a. social learning
   b. biological
   c. psychoanalytic
   d. cognitive

4. Julissa repeatedly complains about stomach pains and nausea. Numerous medical tests and procedures cannot find a physical cause for Julissa's symptoms. Julissa may be diagnosed with what type of mental health disorder?
   a. A depressive disorder
   b. An anxiety disorder
   c. A somatic symptom and related disorder
   d. A dissociative disorder

5. Alogia and avolition represent ______ symptoms of schizophrenia.
   a. positive
   b. negative
   c. neutral
   d. undifferentiated

6. Some clinicians question the validity of dissociative identity disorder, suggesting that it represents an extreme form of which mental health disorder?
   a. Bipolar disorder
   b. Panic disorder
   c. Generalized anxiety disorder
   d. Posttraumatic stress disorder

7. Men are more likely than women to be diagnosed with ______.
   a. anxiety disorders
   b. substance-related disorders
   c. depressive disorders
   d. schizophrenia

8. A young woman reports frequent blackouts, consistently receives phone calls and mail addressed to a person with a different name, and often finds items in her closet that she cannot remember buying. This woman is most likely to be diagnosed with which type of mental health disorder?

a. A dissociative disorder
b. A somatic symptom and related disorder
c. Obsessive-compulsive disorder
d. Borderline personality disorder

9. Which mental health disorder is characterized by delusions, hallucinations, incoherent thought and speech, and inappropriate emotions?

a. Dissociative identity disorder
b. Schizophrenia
c. Panic disorder
d. Generalized anxiety disorder

10. For the last month, Dimitri has been sad, has felt worthless, has been losing weight, can't concentrate, and constantly feels tired. Dimitri is most likely to be diagnosed with which mental health disorder?

a. Bipolar disorder
b. Major depressive disorder
c. Cyclothymic disorder
d. Persistent depressive disorder

11. Jayne was shopping at the local mall when all of a sudden her chest felt tight, she couldn't catch her breath, her heart began to pound, and she felt shaky and dizzy. Since that day, Jayne has had several more episodes like this. They always strike without warning and in different types of situations. It is most likely that Jayne has ______.

a. generalized anxiety disorder
b. bipolar disorder
c. panic disorder
d. agoraphobia

12. Which of the following symptoms distinguishes bipolar disorder from major depressive disorder?

a. Mania
b. Alogia
c. Apathy
d. Delusions

13. Betta is always worried. She worries that her kids will get sick. She worries that she will lose her job. She worries that her spouse will get cancer. Sometimes she is worried without even knowing why she is worried. Betta is most likely to be diagnosed with ______.

a. posttraumatic stress disorder
b. obsessive-compulsive disorder
c. generalized anxiety disorder
d. agoraphobia

14. Which personality disorder is characterized by instability in moods, interpersonal relationships, self-image, and behavior?

a. Histrionic
b. Narcissistic
c. Antisocial
d. Borderline

15. The *DSM* is an abbreviation for ______.

a. *Disorders and Statistics for Mental Health*
b. *Diagnostic and Statistical Manual of Mental Disorders*
c. *Dimensions and Symptoms of Mental Disorders*
d. *Disorders and Symptoms of Mental Health Disorders*

16. Which brain structure is *most* involved in anxiety and fear?

a. Frontal lobe
b. Temporal lobe
c. Hippocampus
d. Amygdala

17. When depressed, Katelyn constantly thinks about her depression and why she is depressed. This often results in Katelyn being even more depressed. Katelyn's behavior is most consistent with ______.

a. learned helplessness
b. negative attributions
c. a ruminative coping style
d. compulsions

18. When neuroscientists perform brain imaging studies on people with mental health disorders, it is possible that medications the participant has taken for the disorder could influence the results. This is referred to as a potential ______ of the study.

a. correlation
b. confound
c. double-blind
d. anomaly

19. Ozzie always wants to be the center of attention and is excessively dramatic. His moods rapidly change. Which personality disorder *best* fits Ozzie's behavior?

a. Histrionic personality disorder
b. Antisocial personality disorder
c. Schizoid personality disorder
d. Borderline personality disorder

20. Sociocultural theories emphasize the role of ______ in explaining mental health disorders.

a. negative thoughts
b. unconscious conflicts
c. unrealistic self-images
d. environmental stressors

Answers: 1. b; 2. b; 3. d; 4. c; 5. b; 6. d; 7. b; 8. a; 9. b; 10. b; 11. c; 12. a; 13. c; 14. d; 15. b; 16. d; 17. c; 18. b; 19. a; 20. d

Use It or Lose It: Applying Psychology

1. What behaviors do you believe would be considered atypical in every culture and society (present and past) and in all situations? Are these behaviors symptoms of any of the disorders discussed in this chapter? How does this list help or hinder psychologists' understanding of mental health?
2. Which disorders would people be most likely AND least likely to seek treatment for, and why? How might this differ by gender, age, or ethnicity?
3. Create a program that would best address the treatment and care of people diagnosed with schizophrenia.
4. After reading this chapter, what factors appear to be most linked to mental health and illness? What can our society do to improve mental health?
5. Which mental health disorders do you think young adults are most at risk for, and why? Be sure to consider biopsychosocial factors in formulating your response.

Critical Thinking About the Science of Psychology

Researchers have routinely applied magnetic resonance imaging (MRI) to explore differences in the brains of people with schizophrenia relative to the brains of people without schizophrenia. As stated in Section 13.6.3, one of the most consistent findings to emerge from such studies is enlarged brain ventricles in people with schizophrenia. In a typical study, all participants undergo an MRI of the brain and then the volume of the ventricles are measured. The measures taken from the participants with schizophrenia are then compared to the participants without schizophrenia to see if there is a statistical difference. Given this information, answer the following questions:

1. Which group serves as the experimental group?
2. Which group serves as the control group?
3. What is the dependent variable?
4. Can cause and effect conclusions be made from these studies? Why or why not?

Are You Getting the Big Picture?

13.1 What Is a Mental Health Disorder?

- A **mental health disorder** is a dysfunction in thinking (cognition), emotions, and/or social behavior that impairs functioning and is not culturally expected.
- Mental health disorders result from a combination of biological, psychological, and social factors (*biopsychosocial perspective*). They do not have just one cause.

badahos/Shutterstock.com

13.2 The *DSM* Model for Classifying Abnormal Behavior

- The ***Diagnostic and Statistical Manual of Mental Disorders (DSM)***, currently in its fifth edition, is an *atheoretical* system that describes specific criteria for a diagnosis of a mental health disorder.
- Labeling someone with a mental health disorder can create *stigma* and have negative effects, because it may encourage the person to behave in a way that is consistent with the disorder.

13.3 Anxiety, Obsessive-Compulsive, and Trauma-Related Disorders

- **Generalized anxiety disorder** is characterized by excessive anxiety, worry, and difficulty in controlling such worries. **Panic disorder** is characterized by recurrent panic attacks or the persistent fear of having a panic attack. **Specific phobia** is a persistent fear of an object, and **social anxiety disorder** is a persistent fear of being negatively evaluated by others in a social situation.
- In **obsessive-compulsive disorder**, a person experiences recurrent **obsessions, compulsions,** or both that cannot be controlled. **Hoarding disorder** involves persistent difficulty in throwing away possessions, even when the items are of very little value.
- **Posttraumatic stress disorder** develops after exposure to a terrifying event. The person experiences distressing memories, nightmares, thoughts, or flashback episodes of the event that interfere with functioning.

WR Publishing/Alamy Stock Photo

- Potential biopsychosocial factors for anxiety, obsessive-compulsive, and trauma-related disorders include:
  - Biological factors (genetics, neurotransmitter imbalances, and brain dysfunction)
  - Psychological factors such as conditioning and maladaptive cognitions
  - Social factors such as rapid social change, stress, low social status, and gender

13.4 Dissociative and Somatic Symptom and Related Disorders: Other Forms of Anxiety?

- **Dissociative disorders** are characterized by a loss of awareness of some part of the self. In **dissociative identity disorder**, separate multiple identities exist in the same person. It is believed to be related to severe stress or a series of emotionally traumatic events.
- **Somatic symptom and related disorders** are characterized by physical complaints or symptoms with no apparent physical cause, as in **illness anxiety disorder**. Psychological distress appears to underlie the physical complaints of these disorders.

13.5 Depressive and Bipolar Disorders: A Change in Mood

- Depressive and bipolar disorders are characterized by a significant change in one's emotional state or mood over an extended period.
- In **major depressive disorder**, the person experiences extreme or chronic sadness or loss of pleasure.
- **Bipolar disorder** involves symptoms of **mania** or mania and depression.
- Potential biopsychosocial factors explaining depressive and bipolar disorders include:
  - Biological factors such as genetics, neurotransmitter imbalances, stress hormones, and brain dysfunction
  - Psychological factors such as unresolved issues of loss and rejection, **learned helplessness**, **ruminative coping style**, **cognitive distortions**, and pessimistic attributions
  - Social factors such as lower social status, stressful life events, and gender

martin-dm/Getty Images

13.6 Schizophrenia: Disintegration

- **Schizophrenia** is a chronic mental health disorder characterized by positive symptoms (**delusions**, **hallucinations**, **disorganized speech**, **catatonic stupor**, or **catatonic excitement**), and/or negative symptoms (**blunted affect**, **alogia**, **avolition**).
- Potential causes of schizophrenia are primarily biological, including genetics, dopamine and glutamate activity, and abnormal brain functioning. However, family support and stressful living conditions may influence the course of the disorder.

Grunnitus Studio/Science Source

13.7 Personality Disorders: Maladaptive Patterns of Behavior

- The **personality disorders** consist of long-standing patterns of malfunctioning typically evident in childhood or adolescence.
- People who are impulsive and disregard the rights of others without showing any remorse or guilt are diagnosed with **antisocial personality disorder**.
- **Borderline personality disorder** is characterized by instability in moods, interpersonal relationships, self-image, and behavior.
- Personality disorders are related to biological factors (genetics, neurotransmitters, abnormal brain functioning) and psychosocial factors (inconsistent parenting practices, gender, conflict-filled childhood).

FBI/Hulton Archive/Getty Images

Learning Objectives

14.1 Distinguish between psychotherapy and biomedical therapy, and describe the trained professionals who are qualified to give each. (APA 1.1, 5.5)

14.1 Describe the ethical principles that psychotherapists must follow when conducting therapy. (APA 3.1)

14.1 Identify when a person should consider seeking therapy. (APA 1.3)

14.2 Describe the aim of psychoanalytic therapies, and distinguish between traditional and modern psychoanalysis. (APA 1.1, 1.2)

14.3 Describe the aim of humanistic therapy and the three key characteristics of client-centered therapy. (APA 1.1, 1.2)

14.4 Describe how classical conditioning processes are used in therapy. (APA 1.1, 1.2, 1.3)

14.4 Discuss how operant conditioning techniques are used in therapy. (APA 1.1, 1.3)

14.5 Describe the aim of cognitive therapy approaches and distinguish between Ellis's rational-emotive therapy and Beck's cognitive therapy. (APA 1.1, 1.2)

14.6 Describe the advantages and disadvantages of group therapy and identify types of group therapy. (APA 1.1, 1.2, 1.3)

14.7 Examine the complexity of conducting research on the effectiveness of psychotherapy. (APA 1.2, 2.1, 2.5)

14.7 Define eclectic therapy and give some examples of it. (APA 1.1, 1.3)

14.7 Describe the factors that contribute to effective psychotherapy. (APA 1.2, 1.3, 3.2)

14.7 Describe how technology has influenced the delivery of psychotherapy. (APA 1.3, 2.1, 3.1)

14.8 Distinguish the treatment effects and side effects of antianxiety drugs, antipsychotic drugs, antidepressants, and antimanic drugs. (APA 1.2, 1.3)

14.8 Describe noninvasive brain stimulation procedures (TMS and ECT). (APA 1.2)

14.8 Describe emerging alternatives in biomedical therapy including neurosurgery for mental disorder. (APA 1.1, 1.3)

Laurence Mouton/Getty Images

14 Mental Health Therapies

Therapy consists of techniques that are used to help people with mental health or interpersonal problems. All therapies attempt to change a person's behavior. However, the techniques that are used differ, because each therapy approach stems from one of the main theoretical perspectives introduced in Chapter 1 and explained in more detail in subsequent chapters. We saw in this part's case study that Emily's therapists did not conduct treatment with her in the same way. This chapter explores the principal approaches to therapy that are common today. We will begin by defining therapy, examining who is qualified to give it, and addressing when it is appropriate for a person to seek therapy. ■

Chapter Outline

14.1 Providing Psychological Assistance

Mental health professionals today use two broad forms of therapy to help people who are having difficulty functioning: *psychotherapy* and *biomedical therapy*. Many people, like Emily in this part's case study, receive therapy that combines both approaches.

14.1.1 Psychotherapy versus Biomedical Therapy

therapy techniques that are used to help people with mental health disorders or interpersonal problems

psychotherapy the use of psychological principles and techniques to treat mental health disorders

biomedical therapy the use of medications or other medical interventions to treat mental health disorders

Psychotherapy is the use of psychological principles and techniques to treat the symptoms of mental health disorders, such as major depressive disorder, or to treat interpersonal problems, such as troubled relationships. *Psychotherapy* is a general term that encompasses many different forms of therapy. However, all psychotherapies are based on the central assumption that underlying psychological factors such as emotions, cognitions, behavior, or relationships are at the root of interpersonal problems and mental illness. In contrast, **biomedical therapy** uses medications or other medical interventions to treat the symptoms of mental health problems. Biomedical therapy assumes that biological factors, such as abnormal brain functioning or chemistry, are at the root of mental illness.

As we saw in Chapter 13 on mental health disorders, both assumptions are supported by substantial research. Indeed, American attitudes toward both psychotherapy and biomedical therapy have become more favorable over the years. For example, Ramin Mojtabai (2007; Mojtabai et al., 2016) compared data on adults' attitudes toward seeking mental health services from two large representative surveys of the U.S. population, one from 1990 to 1992 and one from 2001 to 2003. Compared to the earlier survey, participants from the more recent survey reported being more willing to seek professional help for a mental health problem, more comfortable talking with a professional about their problems, and less likely to report feeling embarrassed if others discovered they were seeking help for mental health issues. Attitudes of younger participants improved more than attitudes of middle-aged participants.

Research has also assessed U.S. adult attitudes toward psychiatric medications (Mojtabai, 2009; Schomerus et al., 2014). Most participants expected benefits from psychiatric medications and were likely to say that medications help people deal with day-to-day stress, make it easier to deal with family and friends, and help people feel better about themselves. Participants were also likely to report a willingness to take medications for personal problems, depression, panic attacks, and to cope with life stresses.

Stigma and negative attitudes toward mental health services can influence a person to deny symptoms or delay treatment (Corrigan, Druss, & Perlick, 2014). An analysis of U.S. news stories about mental illness from 1995 to 2014 found that media reports more often focused on mass shootings by people with mental illness rather than describing successful treatment or recovery from mental health problems (McGinty et al., 2016). Fortunately, as these studies suggest, attitudes toward psychotherapy and medications appear to be improving, at least in the United States.

14.1.2 Who Is Qualified to Give Therapy?

Trained professionals administer psychotherapy and biomedical therapy. A variety of educational and experiential backgrounds characterize psychotherapists (● TABLE 14.1). These include clinical psychologists, psychoanalysts, licensed professional counselors or social workers, and marital or family therapists. A master's degree is the minimum educational requirement for any of these professions, and some require doctorate-level degrees. Many therapists receive training in specialty

TABLE 14.1 Types of Mental Health Professionals

Profession	Education	Training
Clinical Psychologist	• College degree • Graduate school in clinical psychology to earn a doctorate (PhD or PsyD; requires 5–8 years after college degree)	Supervised research and/or training in psychotherapy techniques, psychological testing, and the diagnosis of mental health disorders
Counseling Psychologist	• College degree • Graduate school in counseling psychology or education to earn a doctorate (PhD or EdD; requires 4–6 years after college degree)	Supervised training in assessment, counseling, and therapy techniques
Licensed Professional Counselor	• College degree • Graduate school to earn a master's degree in counseling (requires 3–5 years after college degree)	Supervised training in assessment, counseling, and therapy techniques
Licensed Social Worker	• College degree • Graduate school in social work to receive a master's degree (MSW; requires 3–5 years after college degree)	Supervised training in a social service agency or a mental health center; may or may not include training in psychotherapy
Couple or Family Therapist	• College degree • Graduate school to receive a master's degree in counseling, psychology, or social work (requires 3–5 years after college degree)	Supervised training in family and couple therapy; may also include training in individual psychotherapy methods
Psychiatrist	• College degree • Medical school to receive a medical degree (MD or DO) and then specialize in psychiatry (requires 5–10 years after college degree)	Training in the diagnosis and prevention of mental health disorders with a focus on pharmaceutical treatment approaches; may include training in psychotherapy methods

areas or in specific forms of psychotherapy. For example, a *psychoanalyst* is trained in Freud's methods of treatment. Therapists' backgrounds often include internships in which they have been supervised in administering treatment. In addition, most states require licensing and/or certification of mental health professionals.

Typically only licensed psychiatrists or other medical doctors can legally administer biomedical therapies. Certification as a psychiatrist requires completion of medical school before specializing in psychiatry. In general, a psychiatrist is the only mental health professional who can prescribe medication. However, the right of clinical psychologists to prescribe medications has long been a topic of hot debate. As of this writing, only five states, Louisiana, Illinois, Iowa, Idaho, and New Mexico, currently grant prescription privileges to clinical psychologists who have completed additional training. Similarly, the Armed Forces, the Indian Health Service, and the National Health Services Corps all give psychologists prescribing privileges after they complete specialized training in *psychopharmacology*.

14.1.3 Ethical Standards for Psychotherapists

In addition to being adequately trained and educated, mental health professionals are required to behave ethically and according to certain professional standards when conducting treatment. These are not legal statutes but rather standards established by the American Psychological Association (APA, 2002) indicating how psychotherapists should behave toward their clients. Violations of these standards should be reported to professional review boards that oversee the licensing of

Pormezz/Shutterstock.com

▲ Psychotherapists are ethically bound to provide culturally sensitive, competent treatment.

psychotherapists. Four essential ethical principles are *competent treatment*, *informed consent*, *confidentiality*, and *appropriate interactions*.

Culturally Sensitive, Competent Treatment and Informed Consent

The primary responsibility of the clinician toward a client is to provide *appropriate* and *adequate treatment*. Such a guideline prevents clinicians from merely warehousing clients in a treatment center, a practice that was common in previous decades and centuries. When providing treatment, psychotherapists must get *informed consent* from their clients. This guideline involves fully informing clients of the nature of treatment and the details of their participation, including any potential side effects or consequences of treatment. These requirements are especially critical if any experimental types of treatment will be used. Additionally, clinicians must possess the necessary training to provide *culturally sensitive* and competent care to clients from diverse backgrounds including age, gender, race, ethnicity, religion, sexual orientation, disability, language, or socioeconomic status.

Confidentiality

Psychotherapists must respect the *confidentiality* of their communications with clients. They do not repeat to family members or friends any client discussions that occur within the context of therapy. Consultations with other professionals are permitted only when the client has agreed. Using client stories or experiences in a published work is not permitted without the express permission of the client. This ensures trust within the therapist-client relationship.

However, there are exceptions to this guideline. One exception occurs when the therapist believes that the client should be committed to a treatment facility. In this circumstance, the therapist will have to break confidentiality to convince a court that the client is a danger to themselves. Another exception to maintaining confidentiality occurs when others might be in danger. For example, if during therapy a client expresses violent intent toward another person, therapists are legally required to inform the potential victim of this potential harm. In addition, if a therapist suspects child abuse, partner abuse, or elder abuse, they are legally required to report such cases to the appropriate authorities.

Appropriate Interactions

Therapists must *interact appropriately* with clients for successful therapy to occur. For example, psychotherapists are forbidden from becoming sexually or romantically involved with any client, and are not to socialize with their clients. Psychotherapists do not drink alcohol with their clients or engage in intimate demonstrations of affection such as an arm around the waist. The behavior of Emily's first therapist in the hospital was inappropriate and therefore unethical. Psychotherapists are not to go into business with clients or establish any other form of social relationship that would impede the course of therapy. Unfortunately, when therapists are depicted in movies and on television, they often do not maintain these ethical standards. Such media portrayals confuse the public as to the appropriate behavior of therapists.

Psychology Applies to Your World

When Does One Need to Consider Therapy?

PEOPLE SEEK THERAPY for a variety of reasons. Many come to therapy because they are in distress from one of the many mental health disorders discussed in Chapter 13. Their behavior is maladaptive, or they are experiencing difficulty functioning in everyday life. They may be dealing with symptoms of depression, extreme anxiety, or schizophrenia. Others who seek treatment have a history of mental health problems and exhibit significant symptoms of a disorder. Some people are legally mandated to receive outpatient therapy by the court system. Most states also have laws that detail when a person can be *involuntarily committed* or forced to receive inpatient mental health treatment against their will. In the United States and many other countries, the criteria for involuntary commitment to a psychiatric facility often involve being judged as incapacitated by a mental health disorder and/or an imminent danger to oneself or others.

Although healthcare reform has reduced the number of uninsured individuals, an estimated 45% of U.S. adults with mental health problems had not received mental health services in the past year. About one out of four adults with a mental health problem report that they cannot get the treatment they need. The primary barrier to care was cost. Other barriers included lack of insurance or inadequate insurance, an inability to afford care after insurance has paid, not knowing where to go for services, and the belief that they could handle the problem without treatment (Center for Behavioral Health Statistics and Quality, 2018). People with mental health problems are more likely to receive therapy if they have some type of insurance and are educated. Females are more likely than males, and multiracial and white groups are more likely than other ethnic groups to use mental health services (Center for Behavioral Health Statistics and Quality, 2018; see ● FIGURE 14.1).

You do not have to be diagnosed with a mental health disorder in order to benefit from psychotherapy. Millions of people seek professional help to cope with other life problems. For example, couples and families in conflict may consider counseling to deal with their troubled relationships. People who have experienced major life transitions such as divorce, unemployment, retirement, or the death of a loved one may seek therapy to help them adjust to these changes.

You may want to consider therapy if you feel helpless, sad, blue, or anxious for a prolonged period, or if such feelings do not improve despite several efforts to change them. You also may want to consider therapy if you are having difficulty carrying out your everyday activities. Therapy may also be useful if you want to make decisions differently, improve the functioning of important relationships, or change your life to feel more satisfied.

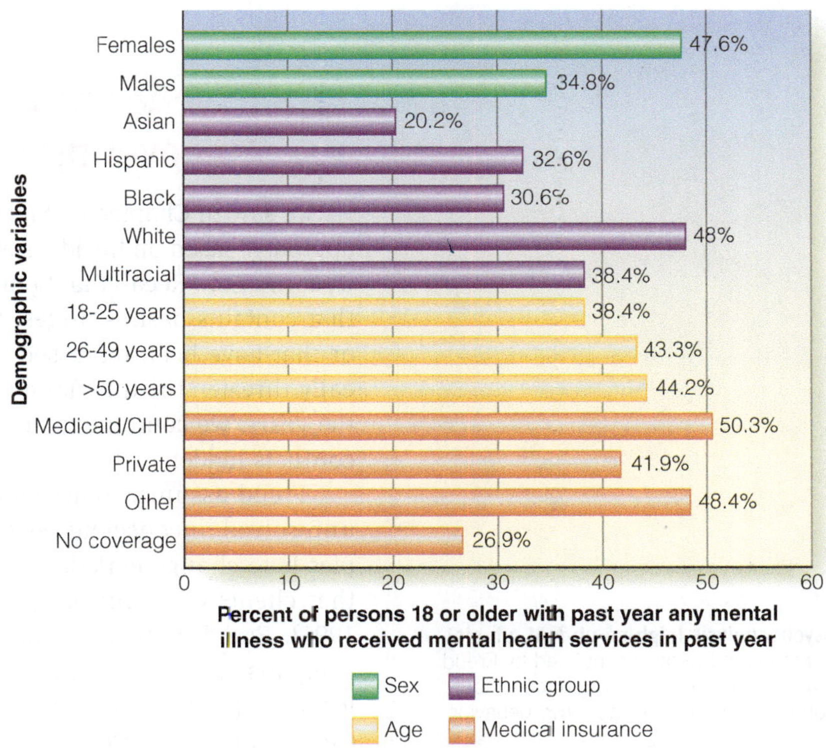

FIGURE 14.1

Who Uses Therapy?

People who have a mental health disorder are more likely to use mental health services if they have some type of health insurance. Therapy is also more likely to be used by females, and white and multiracial groups, and people older than 25 years.

Source: Center for Behavioral Health Statistics and Quality. (2018). *2017 National Survey on Drug Use and Health.* Rockville, MD: SAMHSA.

14.1.4 Seeking Therapy

How do you find a therapist? Talk to family and friends for recommendations, use directories on the Internet, consult your local or state psychological association, or inquire at your community mental health center. Your place of worship, physician, or local college may also be a useful resource for finding a therapist.

Given the many therapeutic approaches, which one should you choose? The next five sections of this chapter describe the main psychotherapy approaches. After reading about them, you may find that you are more comfortable with the philosophy, goals, and techniques of some over others. This information will assist you in understanding the nature of therapy, and in choosing a therapist if the need ever arises.

14.1 Quiz Yourself

1. **Psychotherapy should be considered when ______.**
   a. you get in trouble with your boss
   b. you are having difficulty functioning in some aspect of your life
   c. you have physical problems
   d. All of the above
2. **Michael is seeing a social worker to help him with his interpersonal problems. Michael is undergoing ______.**
   a. psychiatric counseling
   b. medical treatment
   c. psychotherapy
   d. biomedical therapy
3. **Which of the following professionals is *most* likely to prescribe medication as a form of therapy?**
   a. Clinical psychologist
   b. Social worker
   c. Biological psychologist
   d. Psychiatrist

Answers 1. b; 2. c; 3. d

14.2 Psychoanalytic Therapies: Uncovering Unconscious Conflicts

As we saw in Chapter 11, Sigmund Freud originally developed the psychoanalytic approach based on his ideas about different levels of consciousness and personality formation. Recall that Freud theorized that each of us has an unconscious level that contains desires, urges, thoughts, and memories of which we are unaware or that have been repressed or hidden. These unconscious conflicts psychologically threaten the functioning of the ego by causing us distress and anxiety. Over the years, we continue to defend our ego by erecting more barriers to keep these conflicts hidden.

Freud assumed that symptoms of mental health disorders stem from these unresolved unconscious issues. Consequently, the goal of psychoanalytic therapies is to change maladaptive behavior by uncovering unconscious conflicts so that clients can gain *insight* into the real source of their problems (Wolitzky, 1995). Freud named this approach **psychoanalysis**. Professionals who administer this type of therapy are called *psychoanalysts*. Here we will describe two forms of psychoanalysis: *traditional psychoanalysis* and the more modern *psychodynamic approach*.

psychoanalysis [sigh-co-uh-NAL-uh-sis] a method of therapy formulated by Freud that focuses on uncovering unconscious conflicts that drive maladaptive behavior

14.2.1 Traditional Psychoanalysis

▲ In traditional psychoanalysis, the client lies down on a couch away from the therapist so that the client may freely associate and express whatever comes to mind.

In traditional psychoanalysis as developed by Freud, the client lies down on a couch and talks about their concerns. It is the psychoanalyst's job to listen carefully and attentively to the client and discover what unconscious conflicts, themes, or concerns may be affecting the person. The first two therapists that Emily went to adopted this approach. Uncovering unconscious conflicts is not an easy task. Therefore, the psychoanalyst uses several methods to help clients gain insight and uncover critical issues from their pasts (Freud, 1949). These methods include *free association*, *dream analysis*, and *interpretation*. The psychoanalyst also observes the client's behaviors for clues as to unconscious conflicts. Two examples of client behaviors that give such clues are *resistance* and *transference*.

Free association involves talking freely about a subject without censoring any thoughts. The client is fully awake and is asked to talk about a specific topic. The client says whatever comes to mind. The psychoanalyst makes very few comments during free association, instead focusing on important themes or issues that may be revealed.

Dream analysis is a tool that some psychoanalysts use to reveal unconscious conflicts (Pesant & Zadra, 2004). Dreams do not directly represent unconscious conflicts but rather are made up of symbols that reflect these underlying unconscious impulses (see Chapter 4). It is the psychoanalyst's job to decipher the true meaning, or *latent content*, of these dreams and thereby reveal important unconscious issues. Recall from this part's case study that one of Emily's therapists was very interested in the content of her dreams and would attempt to find the themes embedded within them.

Free association and dream analysis provide the psychoanalyst with information on the unconscious workings of the client's mind. The psychoanalyst can then make interpretations to the client. **Interpretations** are the psychoanalyst's views on the themes and issues that may be influencing the client's behavior. These interpretations may help the client gain insight into their problems.

However, if the client is not psychologically ready to deal with these issues, they may resist these interpretations. **Resistance** occurs when a client behaves in such a way as to deny or avoid certain topics or issues. A client may resist a psychoanalyst's interpretation because it is too close to the truth and therefore creates anxiety. Clients may miss appointments or arrive late as a way of resisting the revealing nature of the therapy session. Clients may laugh or joke about topics that are actually quite painful for them. These resistant behaviors provide the psychoanalyst an additional clue as to the unconscious conflicts affecting the client.

The process of **transference** also provides a clue to a client's unconscious conflicts. Freud (1949) believed that at some point during therapy, clients would unconsciously react to the therapist as if the therapist were their parent, friend, sibling, or romantic partner. Freud termed this unconscious reaction *transference* because the client was unknowingly transferring feelings and emotions toward a loved one onto the therapist. The psychoanalyst can explore such instances of transference to reveal how the dynamics of clients' relationships may be influencing their behavior.

In traditional psychoanalysis uncovering unconscious conflicts often took years and called for as many as five sessions per week. Its long-term nature made it increasingly impractical and expensive for the average person due to the growing involvement of the health insurance industry. The development of other psychotherapies as well as the advent of drug therapy (discussed later) also led to a decrease in the popularity of traditional psychoanalysis (Henry et al., 1994). Hence, psychoanalysis was forced to move in a new direction.

free association a technique in psychoanalysis in which the client says whatever comes to mind

dream analysis a technique in psychoanalysis in which the therapist examines the hidden symbols in a client's dreams

interpretations the psychoanalyst's views on the themes and issues that may be influencing the client's behavior

resistance a process in psychoanalysis whereby the client behaves in such a way as to deny or avoid sensitive issues

transference a process in psychoanalysis in which the client unconsciously reacts to the therapist as if the therapist were a parent, friend, sibling, or romantic partner

14.2.2 Modern Psychoanalysis

psychodynamic therapy modern psychoanalysis delivered in a shorter time that focuses less on the client's past and more on current problems and the nature of interpersonal relationships

Modern psychoanalysis, often referred to as **psychodynamic therapy**, or *short-term dynamic therapy*, is evident in many different forms. Such therapies are consistent with the views of Freud and the psychoanalytic approach. They continue to rely on the therapist's interpretations of the client's feelings and behavior, and on identifying instances of transference and resistance. However, modern psychoanalysis tends to focus less on the client's past. Current problems and the nature of interpersonal relationships are seen as more important in improving the client's behavior. The therapist also plays a more direct role, rapidly interviewing and questioning the client to uncover unconscious issues and themes in a shorter time. Then the therapist and client agree to focus on a limited set of problems that are seen as causing the client the most trouble. For example, in *interpersonal therapy*, extensive attention is given to the client's relationships and interpersonal behaviors that seem to be the most important in the onset and/or maintenance of depression. Modern psychoanalysis tends to be more short term, lasting no more than a few months, and appears to be effective in improving clients' symptoms (Abbass, Town, & Driessen, 2011; Fonagy, 2015; Jakobsen et al., 2012; Levi et al., 2016; Shedler, 2010; Slavin-Mulford et al., 2011; Steinert et al., 2017).

14.2 Quiz Yourself

1. The goal of psychoanalysis is to change behavior by ____.
   a. uncovering unconscious conflicts so that the client can gain insight into the source of their problems
   b. uncovering negative cognitive patterns that impede the client's ability to function
   c. examining environmental conditions and how they influence the client's responses
   d. providing the client with unconditional support and love so that they make adaptive and healthy behavioral choices
2. Song often arrives late for her psychoanalysis appointments and sometimes forgets her appointments altogether. Her psychoanalyst might interpret Song's behavior as a sign of ____.
   a. transference
   b. challenge interpretation
   c. resistance
   d. free association
3. Modern psychoanalysis differs from traditional psychoanalysis in that ____.
   a. it is shorter in duration
   b. it is focused less on the client's past and more on present relationships and issues
   c. the therapist is more direct
   d. All of the above

Answers 1. a; 2. c; 3. d

14.3 Humanistic Therapy: Facilitating Self-Actualization

As we have just seen, problems with psychoanalysis forced it to move in a new direction that resulted in briefer psychodynamic therapies that were still connected to the ideas of Freud. However, some psychoanalysts departed radically from these views and developed different forms of therapy. One example is *humanistic therapy*.

14.3.1 The Aim of Humanistic Therapy Approaches

The *humanistic approach* focuses less on unconscious forces and more on the conscious actions we take in controlling our behavior. Even though Dr. Farber was a trained psychoanalyst, his belief in Emily's value and his emphasis on her free will exemplify this humanistic perspective. In Emily's words:

> Dr. Farber was both far humbler than his more conventional colleagues and far bolder. He was humbler because he approached his patients as a whole human being. . . . He was bolder because . . . he committed himself to a risky, open-ended friendship and to all the claims of responsibility that friendship entails. (Gordon, 2000, p. 125)

Humanists emphasize that behavior is driven not by unconscious impulses, but by how we interpret the world and our awareness of our feelings. The only way to understand a person's behavior, therefore, is to connect with and understand the person's worldview. Humanism further assumes that people will naturally strive toward personal growth and achievement of their full potential when raised in a positive and accepting environment. When a person holds distorted perceptions or lacks self-awareness, mental health problems arise, preventing the person from becoming *self-actualized*. Yet people are capable of healing themselves, if only the right environment is provided. The therapist's role is to create this safe environment for self-exploration and facilitate the journey toward self-fulfillment (Greenberg & Rice, 1997). One of the most influential and best known of the humanistic therapies is *client-centered therapy*.

iStock.com/Prostock-Studio

▲ In humanistic therapy, therapist and client sit face-to-face as they work together in solving the client's problems.

14.3.2 Client-Centered Therapy: Three Key Ingredients

Disillusioned with the goals, methods, and assumptions of psychoanalysis, Carl Rogers (1902–1987) developed a different therapy approach that exemplifies the humanistic perspective. Whereas Freud saw the analyst as all-knowing and responsible for client change, Rogers believed that the therapist should serve more as a facilitator or coach to help move the client in the direction of change. Such a viewpoint resulted in **client-centered therapy**, or *person-centered therapy*. As the names imply, in client-centered therapy the focus and direction of therapy comes from the person, or client. The client decides what to talk about, without interpretation or judgment from the therapist. The therapist, according to Rogers (1951, 1980, 1986), creates a positive and accepting environment to facilitate self-awareness and personal growth by providing three key characteristics: *empathy*, *genuineness*, and *unconditional positive regard*.

client-centered therapy a humanistic psychotherapy approach developed by Carl Rogers that emphasizes the use of empathy, genuineness, and unconditional positive regard to help the client reach their potential

empathy the ability of a therapist to understand a client's feelings and thoughts without being judgmental

Empathy: Understanding the Client

Are you a good listener? Do friends and family frequently confide in you? If so, then you may possess *empathy*. According to Rogers, **empathy** is the ability to understand a client's feelings and thoughts without being judgmental. The therapist does not express disapproval toward the client but rather indicates understanding of the client's feelings. Conveying empathy involves actively listening to the client—making eye contact, nodding as the client speaks, and assuming an interested and attentive pose. Empathy also involves *reflection*. The therapist restates, repeats, or summarizes the thoughts and feelings that they hear the client express. Reflected statements communicate to the client the active attention of the therapist and mirror the client's perceptions and views of reality. Consider this example of empathy and reflection from Irvin Yalom's work, *Love's Executioner and Other Tales of Psychotherapy* (1989, p. 29).

> Client: I believe he is intentionally trying to drive me to suicide. Does that sound like a crazy thought?
>
> Therapist: I don't know if it's crazy, but it sounds like a desperate and terribly painful thought.

Notice in this example that the therapist does not judge the client's thoughts as crazy and reflects the emotions underlying the statement of suicide. Ideally, empathy and reflection will help clients see themselves and their problems more clearly, promoting a realistic self-image and greater self-acceptance.

Genuineness: Sharing Thoughts, Feelings, and Experiences

genuineness the ability of a therapist to openly share their thoughts and feelings with a client

unconditional positive regard the ability of a therapist to accept and value a person for who they are, regardless of their faults or problems

A second key therapist quality in client-centered therapy is *genuineness*. **Genuineness** is the ability to openly share one's thoughts and feelings with others. The therapist expresses their true feelings and thoughts to the client and does not hide behind the mask of being the "professional," "doctor," or authority figure. The therapist self-discloses a fair amount to the client, which allows the client to see the therapist as a real, living person. Such disclosure also creates an open environment that promotes trust and an honest expression of thoughts and feelings. Rogers believed that such an environment would model to the client how relationships can be built on a foundation of trust and honesty. Emily learned such a lesson from Dr. Farber. His genuineness made her believe he truly cared about her well-being.

Unconditional Positive Regard: Valuing the Client

The third key quality in client-centered therapy, *unconditional positive regard*, was introduced in the chapter on personality (see Chapter 11). Recall that Rogers defined **unconditional positive regard** as the ability to accept and value a person for who they are, regardless of their faults or problems. Rogers believed that receiving unconditional positive regard in one's childhood is a key factor in healthy personality adjustment. A therapist who offers unconditional positive regard to a client does not indicate shock, dismay, or disapproval to any client statements. Instead, the therapist communicates caring and respect toward the client regardless of what the client says.

This does not mean that the therapist has to personally *agree* with everything the client states. Rather, the therapist's job is to reflect the client's feelings and thoughts in order to further the client's self-knowledge and enable the client to solve problems in their own way. Unconditional positive regard enables the client to believe that they have value and are competent at making decisions. Such attitudes foster self-confidence and self-acceptance that lead to healthier growth choices.

For Rogers, a therapist who demonstrates all three qualities—empathy, genuineness, and unconditional positive regard—establishes a positive and nurturing environment. A person feels accepted, understood, and valued. These feelings help the client self-explore a more realistic self-image and perception of the world. This in turn removes the obstacles to personal growth so that self-actualization can be realized.

Does client-centered therapy work? Compared to no-treatment control groups, people in client-centered therapy do change their behavior (Greenberg & Rice, 1997; Hill & Nakayama, 2000). Compared to more structured therapy approaches, client-centered therapy is equally effective, at least for moderately distressed individuals (Stiles et al., 2006, 2008).

14.3 Quiz Yourself

1. **The goal of humanistic therapy is to change behavior by _____.**
   a. confronting unconscious conflicts through therapist interpretations
   b. uncovering negative thoughts that cause the client anxiety and distress
   c. examining stimuli in the environment and how they influence the client's responses
   d. providing the client with a safe environment for self-exploration and facilitating the journey toward self-fulfillment
2. **Which of the following is *not* one of the elements used in client-centered therapy to help the client achieve self-fulfillment?**
   a. Genuineness
   b. Free association
   c. Unconditional positive regard
   d. Empathy
3. **Marcos is receiving client-centered therapy. His therapist openly shares his thoughts and feelings with Marcos, relating his own experiences that are similar to those of Marcos's. Marcos's therapist is exhibiting which quality of client-centered therapy?**
   a. Genuineness
   b. Reflection
   c. Unconditional positive regard
   d. Empathy

Answers 1. d; 2. b; 3. a

14.4 Behavior Therapies: Learning Healthier Behaviors

Psychoanalytic and humanistic therapies focus on internal reflection by the client. In contrast, **behavior therapy** focuses directly on changing current problem behaviors rather than delving into the client's past. Behavior therapies, also called *behavior modification*, consist of techniques and methods that use learning principles to change problem behavior. Chapter 6 described the learning processes of classical conditioning and operant conditioning. The behavioral perspective relies on these principles to modify behavior. Recall that the *behavioral perspective* assumes that behavior is a result of environmental variables such as stimuli and consequences in the environment. It further assumes that people learn maladaptive behavior in the same way that they learn adaptive behavior. So, changing behavior involves changing the environmental circumstances that seem to elicit and maintain negative behavior. Learning principles that focus on *extinction* are used to stop disruptive behaviors. Similarly, learning principles that focus on *shaping* or acquiring behaviors are used to replace undesirable behaviors with more adaptive ones.

behavior therapy therapy that applies the principles of classical and operant conditioning to help people change maladaptive behaviors

Behavior therapy can take many forms. Here we discuss two broad categories of behavior therapy: *classical conditioning techniques* and *operant conditioning techniques*.

14.4.1 Applying Classical Conditioning Techniques in Therapy: Exposure and Aversion

Some behavior therapies rely on the principles of classical conditioning outlined in Chapter 6. Briefly, classical conditioning occurs when stimuli in the environment become associated so that both produce the same response. For example, as a child, one of the authors was bitten by a dog twice within a 2-year period. In both instances, the dog was a German shepherd. Following those incidents, she developed an intense fear of large dogs. Her dog-biting experiences became associated with pain, so that now she feared pain from all large dogs and routinely avoided them. Her fear was a learned behavior. Behavior therapy would focus on having her unlearn her response to large dogs. Three behavior therapy techniques that rely on classical conditioning principles are *systematic desensitization*, *flooding*, and *aversion therapy*.

Systematic Desensitization: Relax and Have No Fear

systematic desensitization [sis-tuh-MAT-ick dee-sen-sih-tuh-ZAY-shun] a behavior therapy technique that uses a gradual, step-by-step process to replace fear or anxiety with an incompatible response of relaxation and positive emotion

anxiety hierarchy a list that orders, according to the degree of fear, the situations or items that trigger anxiety; the list starts with the least frightening images and progresses to the most distressing

One effective tool for treating phobias and anxiety is systematic desensitization (Wolpe, 1958). **Systematic desensitization** involves replacing a fear or anxiety response with an incompatible response of relaxation and positive emotion. Anxiety and relaxation are *competing responses*. You cannot feel both at the same time; you can only feel one or the other. So, the aim of systematic desensitization is to have a client learn how to relax and then slowly and systematically introduce the feared object, situation, or thought while the client maintains a positive state of pleasure or relaxation. An early example of systematic desensitization was an experiment by Mary Cover Jones (1897–1987; 1924) in which she treated a 3-year-old's fear of rabbits. The child, Peter, sat at a distance from a caged rabbit while eating one of his favorite foods. The cage was gradually moved closer to Peter until he was able to play with the rabbit and not experience any fear. Jones had countered Peter's negative emotional reaction of fear with a positive one of pleasure from the food.

Systematic desensitization is accomplished in three basic steps. First, the client is trained in *progressive muscle relaxation*. As discussed in Chapter 12, this method involves alternately tensing and relaxing different muscle groups, beginning with the head and working down to the toes, so that the client learns to distinguish when muscles are tense and when they are relaxed.

Engage Yourself! Try progressive muscle relaxation training on your own. Close your eyes and take deep breaths for a minute. Then tighten your jaw muscles and clench your teeth. Hold the tension for a few moments and then relax and take several deep breaths. Do the same for your eyes, forehead, neck, and shoulders, alternating between tensing your muscles and then relaxing them. You will be pleasantly surprised by how a few minutes of this procedure can reduce tension and promote relaxation.

Once the client has learned progressive relaxation, the client and therapist develop an anxiety hierarchy. An **anxiety hierarchy** (● FIGURE 14.2) is a list of situations or items that trigger a client's anxiety or fear. The items on the hierarchy start with the least anxiety-provoking situations or items and progress to the most distressing.

In the third step, progressive relaxation and the anxiety hierarchy are combined. Relaxation is paired with each item in the hierarchy. As the client becomes able to imagine a feared situation and remain relaxed, the next item in the hierarchy is addressed. Over several therapy sessions, this systematic process continues until the client has become desensitized to all items in the hierarchy.

You may be skeptical at this point, unconvinced that thinking about a feared stimulus is similar to actually encountering the object or situation. This skepticism

An Anxiety Hierarchy for Systematic Desensitization

Degree of fear	
5	I'm standing on the balcony of the top floor of an apartment tower.
10	I'm standing on a stepladder in the kitchen to change a light bulb.
15	I'm walking on a ridge. The edge is hidden by shrubs and treetops.
20	I'm sitting on the slope of a mountain, looking out over the horizon.
25	I'm crossing a bridge 6 feet above a creek. The bridge consists of an 18-inch-wide board with a handrail on one side.
30	I'm riding a ski lift 8 feet above the ground.
35	I'm crossing a shallow, wide creek on an 18-inch-wide board, 3 feet above water level.
40	I'm climbing a ladder outside the house to reach a second-story window.
45	I'm pulling myself up a 30-degree wet, slippery slope on a steel cable.
50	I'm scrambling up a rock, 8 feet high.
55	I'm walking 10 feet on a resilient, 18-inch-wide board which spans an 8-foot-deep gulch.
60	I'm walking on a wide plateau, 2 feet from the edge of a cliff.
65	I'm skiing an intermediate hill. The snow is packed.
70	I'm walking over a railway trestle.
75	I'm walking on the side of an embankment. The path slopes to the outside.
80	I'm riding a chair lift 15 feet above the ground.
85	I'm walking up a long, steep slope.
90	I'm walking up (or down) a 15-degree slope on a 3-foot-wide trail. On one side of the trail the terrain drops down sharply; on the other side is a steep upward slope.
95	I'm walking on a 3-foot-wide ridge. The slopes on both sides are long and more than 25 degrees steep.
100	I'm walking on a 3-foot-wide ridge. The trail slopes on one side. The drop on either side of the trail is more than 25 degrees.

FIGURE 14.2

Sample Anxiety Hierarchy

An anxiety hierarchy like the one shown here is used during systematic desensitization. This hierarchy was developed for a person who had a fear of heights.

From K. E. Rudestam, *Methods of Self Change: An ABC Primer*, © 1980 Wadsworth. Reprinted with permission of the author.

is somewhat warranted, so once the client has mastered the mental images, behavior therapists can extend systematic desensitization to a simulated or actual environment. For many fears, this is when systematic desensitization is most effective (Antony & Barlow, 2002). For example, flight simulators can be used to help desensitize people to a fear of flying. Combining systematic desensitization with the actual situation, called *in vivo exposure*, is a very effective tool in treating a variety of anxiety disorders (Barlow et al., 2015; Foa et al., 2013; Meyerbroeker et al., 2013; Wechsler et al., 2019).

Virtual reality computer technology also can be used to simulate a feared situation. Virtual reality bridges the gap between imagining feared stimuli in a therapist's office and in vivo exposure in the field by simulating a feared situation. The client wears a head-mounted display with small video monitors and stereo earphones that integrate visual and auditory cues to immerse the client in a computer-generated virtual environment. For example, a person with a fear of flying may be exposed to stimuli that simulate sitting in a plane and hearing the plane's engines revving for takeoff. A person with a fear of public speaking may experience simulation of standing at a podium. The therapist can control the images the client receives while monitoring heart rate, respiration, and skin temperature to assess the client's fear responses during the session (Bender, 2004).

Virtual reality exposure therapy has become an increasingly common, effective treatment for people with excessive anxiety disorders such as specific phobias, social anxiety disorders, and panic disorders, and trauma-related disorders

BORIS HORVAT/AFP/Getty Images

▲ Virtual reality exposure therapy allows clients to experience their fears in a simulated, nonthreatening environment.

such as PTSD (Bouchard et al., 2017; Carl et al., 2019; de Carvalho, Freire, & Nardi, 2010; Gerardi et al., 2010; McLay et al., 2010; Motraghi et al., 2014; Rothbaum, Rizzo, & Difede, 2010; Wechsler et al., 2019).

Flooding: Facing Our Fears

Another exposure behavior therapy that relies on classical conditioning processes is flooding. In **flooding** (also called *prolonged exposure (PE) therapy*), the client remains exposed to the feared object, situation, or image for an extended time period (1–2 hours) until their anxiety decreases. Recall from Chapter 6 that this is a process called *extinction*, in which the conditioned stimulus (CS) (the feared item) is presented by itself until it no longer produces the conditioned response (CR) of anxiety and fear. In contrast to systematic desensitization, flooding starts with the *most* feared item or situation rather than the least distressing item. In addition, instead of relaxing, the client is told to experience the fear fully and is prevented from escaping the situation or engaging in any other anxiety-avoiding behaviors. Whatever terrible consequences the client imagined would happen do not occur, and their anxiety decreases.

Flooding can be an effective and efficient way to reduce anxiety and fear (Dixon, Ahles, & Marques, 2016; Foa & McLean, 2016; McNeil & Kyle, 2009). A client's anxiety subsides rather quickly; however, relapses (return of the fear) are common (Escobar, 2008; Ginsberg et al., 2014). This should not be surprising if you recall the concept of *spontaneous recovery*, in which the conditioned response (anxiety) can reappear after it has been extinguished. For this reason, flooding is often used in combination with other therapy techniques (Corey, 2009). Because of the discomfort associated with flooding, it is ethically imperative that clients be fully informed and prepared for flooding treatment.

Aversion Therapy: We Won't Do Something If We Dislike It

Do you bite your nails? As a child, did you suck your thumb? Did loved ones try to get you to stop such behaviors? Many parents put a foul-tasting or spicy liquid such as Tabasco sauce on their child's nails or thumb to stop nail biting or thumb sucking. These parents may not know that they are performing *aversion therapy*, another example of a behavior therapy that relies on classical conditioning principles. **Aversion therapy** involves pairing an unpleasant stimulus (foul or spicy taste) with a specific undesirable behavior such as biting one's fingernails. Ideally, the aversive stimulus becomes associated with the undesirable response so that the person is less likely to engage in the response again.

Aversive conditioning occurs frequently in everyday life. Food poisoning is a prime example. If a particular food has ever made you sick, normally it will be months or even years before you touch that food again. The food (stimulus) becomes associated with being sick (response) so that you avoid it at all costs. Therapists use this knowledge to treat a variety of undesirable habits and behaviors. For example, an aversion therapy method for treating alcohol use disorder involves taking a drug called Antabuse (Cannon & Baker, 1981). Antabuse interacts

flooding a behavior therapy technique in which a client is exposed to a feared object or situation for a prolonged period until their anxiety extinguishes

aversion [uh-VER-shun] therapy a behavior therapy technique in which a specific behavior is paired with an unpleasant stimulus in order to reduce its occurrence with alcohol, causing nausea and vomiting. If a person with alcohol use disorder drinks while using Antabuse, it makes them ill. The unwanted stimulus (alcohol) becomes associated with the response of feeling ill and nauseated. The person with alcohol use disorder learns to avoid alcohol in order to avoid the associated unpleasant response. Unfortunately, the person with alcohol use disorder can also simply avoid taking the medication, thereby nullifying the effectiveness of the procedure.

In clinical trials, Antabuse has demonstrated mixed results in helping people abstain from alcohol use. When Antabuse is given under supervision and in conjunction with a drug that specifically reduces alcohol cravings, its effectiveness on short-term abstinence and days until relapse is improved (Barth & Malcolm, 2010; Brewer, Streel, & Skinner, 2017; B. A. Johnson, 2008; Jorgensen, Pedersen, & Tonnesen, 2011; Krampe & Ehrenreich, 2010; Skinner et al., 2014).

An alternative form of aversion therapy is called **covert sensitization therapy**. In this procedure, graphic imagery is used to create unpleasant associations with specific stimuli. For example, a person who smokes cigarettes may have to repeatedly imagine black and diseased lungs when faced with the stimulus of a cigarette. At this point, you may be disturbed by the knowledge that therapists use such unpleasant procedures in treatment. Keep in mind, though, that therapists are ethically bound to get informed consent from clients. Clients are informed of the procedure and must agree before such a method can be used.

covert sensitization [co-VERT sen-sih-tuh-ZAY-shun] therapy a milder form of aversion therapy in which graphic imagery is used to create unpleasant associations with specific stimuli

14.4.2 Applying Operant Conditioning Techniques in Therapy

Although systematic desensitization, flooding, and aversion therapy rely on classical conditioning principles, some behavior therapies rely on the principles of operant conditioning outlined in Chapter 6. Briefly, operant conditioning focuses on the consequences of a behavior. It assumes that reinforced behavior will be maintained and punished behavior will be extinguished. For instance, in the previous example in which one of your authors developed a fear of large dogs, recall that following the dog-biting episodes she responded by avoiding large dogs. The consequence of this response was reinforcing—it reduced her fear. She learned that the next time she encountered a large dog, avoiding it would quickly rid her of any anxiety.

Changing undesirable behavior, therefore, involves changing the consequences of a behavior. These changes can be accomplished in a variety of ways (Kazdin, 2013).

- *Positive reinforcement.* Positive reinforcement is used to encourage or maintain a behavior. For example, every time a child complies with a parental request, verbal praise follows. After the child's compliance increases, verbal praise need not occur every single time.
- *Nonreinforcement and Extinction.* To discourage unwanted behavior, any reinforcers of the behavior are removed. For instance, to discourage a child from throwing tantrums at home, the child's parent ignores the behavior so that no attention (even negative attention, such as a reprimand) reinforces the behavior. If a reinforcer does not follow a behavior, the behavior will occur less frequently. Eventually the behavior will be eliminated or extinguished. However, keep in mind that often the unwanted behavior will increase before it goes away, because a person is expecting the reinforcer. The child's tantrums will initially be longer or more frequent in an attempt to get a reaction from the parent. Misbehavior may also continue because all subtle forms of reinforcement have not been eliminated. For example, consider

▲ Children's tantrums can be eliminated if their inappropriate behavior is not reinforced. However, keep in mind that the child's tantrums will initially get worse as the child attempts to get a reaction from loved ones.

what happens when the same child acts up in school. Although the teacher may scold or reprimand the child, the child still receives a form of attention, and therefore the behavior may not subside. Even if the teacher ignores the child's misbehavior, classmates may reinforce the behavior by laughing and paying attention to them.

- *Punishment*. Sometimes punishment is used to decrease undesirable behaviors. Recall that punishment occurs when an undesired behavior is immediately followed by a negative or unpleasant consequence such as loss of a privilege. But also remember the side effects of punishment. It can produce negative emotions such as anger or fear, or negative behaviors such as avoidance. For these reasons, punishment is used sparingly.
- *Shaping*. Recall from Chapter 6 that shaping involves positively reinforcing each successive attempt at a behavior. It is used to teach a person new, desired behaviors. For example, shaping may be used to teach children with autism spectrum disorder how to speak. If the child makes a "t" sound to say toy, this attempt is reinforced. Shaping has also been successfully used to teach people with intellectual and developmental disabilities self-help skills, such as washing their faces or brushing their teeth.
- *Token economy*. A **token economy** involves reinforcing people with tokens, or symbolic rewards, for desired behavior. Because not everyone is influenced by the same reinforcer, tokens—such as chips, points, or stars—are given each time a person engages in a desired behavior. These tokens can then be exchanged for a variety of reinforcers such as food, privileges, goods, phone time, and so on.

You may recall having had a treasure chest or goody box in elementary school. Students who had acquired a certain number of points or tokens could visit the prize box at the end of the week. Today, your consumer behavior may be unknowingly reinforced by a token economy. Many credit card companies, restaurants, and retail stores offer points for purchases. These points can then be exchanged for merchandise, food, or future discounts. Airlines do the same thing with frequent flyer points. Their aim is to increase your consumption of their services.

The same principle can be used in hospitals, halfway houses, prisons, substance abuse treatment centers, and other institutional settings. People earn tokens for desired behavior and constructive activities, and then exchange them for passes, free time, snacks, access to television, or private rooms. Recall that Emily's behavior in the Riggs treatment center was monitored in this fashion. To receive privileges, she had to get her chores done and go to bed at the appropriate time. In some institutions, patients may lose or be charged tokens for undesired behavior such as fighting, noncompliance, or not completing their chores. A token economy can be a very effective tool for treating children with intellectual disabilities and autism spectrum disorders, and for managing behavior in a group setting (Jowett Hirst, Dozier, & Payne, 2016; Matson & Boisjoli, 2009; Mottram & Berger-Gross, 2004; Park & Lee, 2012).

token economy a behavior therapy technique in which people are reinforced with tokens for desired behavior; the tokens can then be exchanged for what is reinforcing to the individuals

Although behavior therapies have been very successful in treating a variety of psychological and behavioral problems, particularly in children, they do not address the thoughts and perceptions that often accompany behavior. For this reason, behavioral strategies have been increasingly used in conjunction with cognitive therapy, our next topic of discussion.

14.4 Quiz Yourself

1. **Behavior therapies change behavior by _____.**
   a. examining unconscious conflicts and replacing them with subconscious memories
   b. focusing on negative cognitive patterns that impede the client's ability to function
   c. examining and then changing the environmental circumstances that seem to elicit and maintain negative behavior
   d. identifying the client's worldview to facilitate the journey toward self-fulfillment
2. **Celia goes to a therapist to try to reduce her fear of driving. The therapist teaches Celia how to relax and then has her imagine those aspects of driving that make her fearful while maintaining her relaxed mode. Celia is most likely undergoing _____.**
   a. aversion therapy
   b. a token economy
   c. systematic desensitization
   d. client-centered therapy
3. **Which of the following is a therapy approach based on the principles of classical conditioning?**
   a. A token economy
   b. Shaping
   c. Positive reinforcement
   d. Aversion therapy

Answers 1. c; 2. c; 3. d

14.5 Cognitive Therapies: Changing Thoughts

Many mental health disorders such as anxiety and depression may stem from negative and distorted thought patterns. *Cognitive therapies* focus on changing these maladaptive patterns of thinking and perceiving, and replacing them with more adaptive ways of interpreting events. Two of the most widely used cognitive therapies are Albert Ellis's *rational-emotive therapy* and Aaron Beck's *cognitive therapy.*

rational-emotive therapy a cognitive therapy approach created by Albert Ellis that focuses on changing the irrational beliefs that are believed to impede mental health

14.5.1 Ellis's Rational-Emotive Therapy: Reinterpret One's Viewpoint

Developed by Albert Ellis (1913–2007; 1973, 1995), **rational-emotive therapy** is based on the premise that many mental health problems stem from how people think about and interpret events in their lives. It is not the actual event that causes the emotional upset, but rather the person's *interpretation* of the event that results in emotional distress. Specifically, rational-emotive therapy identifies the client's faulty or irrational beliefs that lead to self-defeating behaviors, anxiety, depression, anger, or other mental health problems. Research supports Ellis's notion that people who think more irrationally experience more psychological distress (Hyland et al., 2014; Nieuwenhuijsen et al., 2010; Taghavi et al., 2006; Turner, 2016; Ziegler & Smith, 2004).

Ellis identified common irrational beliefs (1991) that often impede people's functioning (see ● TABLE 14.2). Identifying such irrational beliefs is the first step in rational-emotive therapy. For example, one client may have an excessive need for approval because they believe that they "must be loved by everyone." Another client may irrationally believe that there is a "right" solution for every problem and become frustrated or depressed because a problem recurs. Once these beliefs have been identified, the therapist challenges their validity. The therapist

Courtesy of Albert Ellis Institute

▲ Albert Ellis developed rational-emotive therapy to deal with clients' faulty or irrational beliefs that lead to self-defeating behaviors such as anxiety, depression, or anger.

TABLE 14.2 Examples of Irrational Assumptions

1. I must be loved by or approved of by everyone.
2. I must be competent and achieving in all things I do; otherwise I am worthless.
3. Some people are bad and should be severely blamed and punished for it. I should be extremely upset over the wrongdoings of others.
4. It is awful and upsetting when things are not the way I would like them to be.
5. Unhappiness is caused by external events, and I cannot control my bad feelings and emotional reactions.
6. If something unpleasant happens, I should dwell on it.
7. Avoiding difficulties, rather than facing them, will make you happy.
8. Always rely on someone who is stronger than you.
9. Your past will always affect your present life.
10. There is a perfect solution for every problem, and it is awful and upsetting if this solution is not found.

confronts and disputes these fallacies in a logical and persuasive manner, pushing the client to recognize that such beliefs are irrational and unhealthy. The therapist might make statements such as "What evidence do you have to support this belief?" or "In what other ways could this evidence be interpreted?" Additionally, the client may be asked "What is the worst thing that could happen?" and "If that happened, what could you do?" Asking such questions forces clients to consider alternative viewpoints, face their fears and anxieties, and explore possible problem-solving methods.

After a client's irrational beliefs have been recognized and refuted, they can then be replaced with more realistic and rational beliefs. These beliefs may be reflected in such statements as "Not everyone will like me, but that is okay and not a measure of my worth" or "There are several ways to solve a problem, and if one approach fails, I can try another."

Rational-emotive therapy is a very direct and confrontational approach. Admitting that our way of thinking is irrational and unhealthy and radically changing our interpretation of events in our lives is not an easy task. Yet despite these obstacles, rational-emotive therapy has generally been effective in treating depressive, bipolar, and excessive anxiety disorders (David et al., 2008, 2018; Lewinsohn et al., 1990; Sava et al., 2009).

14.5.2 Beck's Cognitive Therapy: Replace Negative Thoughts

A second illustration of focusing on thought patterns in therapy is Aaron Beck's (b. 1921) **cognitive therapy**. Noticing that many of his clients who were depressed expressed a negative view of themselves and the world almost habitually, Beck turned his attention to the role cognitions play in emotional distress. He developed a cognitive therapy based on the principle that distorted thinking, in the form of **cognitive distortions** and negative, automatic thought patterns, leads to depression, anxiety, and low self-esteem (Beck et al., 1979). For example, do you ever make critical remarks to yourself such as "Oh, I am so stupid" or "I am such an idiot"? Recall Emily's declarations that she was fat, awkward, and a misfit. Such personal negative statements depress mood and lower self-esteem. Beck believed that such maladaptive patterns could be

cognitive therapy a cognitive therapy approach created by Aaron Beck that focuses on uncovering negative automatic thought patterns that impede mental health

cognitive distortions distorted thinking patterns, such as overgeneralization or all-or-none thinking, that, according to Aaron Beck, lead to depression, anxiety, and low self-esteem identified and changed, resulting in more adaptive behavior. ● TABLE 14.3 illustrates some of the more common cognitive distortions that Beck identified in people who are depressed.

Beck's cognitive therapy is not as confrontational in its approach as rational-emotive therapy. Rather, Beck (1991) saw the client and therapist as a collaborative team, working together to identify and evaluate the accuracy and biases of the client's thought patterns. At first, the therapist teaches the client how to recognize and keep track of negative automatic thoughts, such as "I never do anything right" or "I always fail at whatever I do." The therapist and client then test the validity or accuracy of these thoughts. For example, a client may be asked to list all the tasks assigned to them in a week and then indicate whether each task was completed. The therapist hopes that such an exercise will not only point out the inaccuracy of the client's beliefs, but also teach the client how to evaluate negative automatic thoughts in the future. We saw that as a part of therapy, Dr. Farber would often highlight Emily's negative thought patterns as a way of improving her self-image.

Cognitive therapy, like rational-emotive therapy, has been very effective in treating depressive, bipolar, and excessive anxiety disorders (David et al., 2008; Gibbons et al., 2010). In some studies, it has been just as effective as drugs (Sava et al., 2009). More important, clients who have adopted new and more adaptive patterns of thinking are less likely to become depressed in the future—a benefit that drugs cannot provide (Jarrett et al., 2001; Teasdale et al., 2001).

▲ Aaron Beck developed cognitive therapy based on the principle that distorted thinking and negative, automatic thought patterns lead to depression, anxiety, and low self-esteem.

TABLE 14.3 Examples of Cognitive Distortions

Cognitive Error	Description	Example
All-or-nothing thinking	Seeing each event as completely good or bad, right or wrong, a success or a failure	"If I don't get this job, I am a failure."
Arbitrary inference	Concluding that something negative will happen or is happening even though there is no evidence to support it	"My neighbors did not say hello to me. They must be mad at me."
Disqualifying the positive	Rejecting positive experiences	"Anyone can paint. It's no big deal."
Emotional reasoning	Assuming that negative emotions are accurate without questioning them	"I feel fat, so I must be fat."
Labeling	Placing a negative, global label on a person or situation	"I can't do anything right, so why should I try?"
Magnification and minimization	Overestimating the importance of negative events and underestimating the impact of positive events	"In my job evaluation, my boss said I need to work on my time management skills. My boss only said I was a productive worker and good team manager to be nice."
Overgeneralization	Applying a negative conclusion from one event to other unrelated events and areas of one's life	"I messed up on my math test, so I won't do well in history or Spanish. I should drop out of school."
Personalization	Attributing negative events to oneself without reason	"My parents are in a bad mood because I'm an idiot."
Selective abstraction	Focusing on a single, irrelevant, negative aspect of a situation while ignoring more relevant and important aspects of the situation	"It doesn't matter that I got a raise and a promotion. I now have to go to work an hour earlier."

cognitive-behavioral therapy (CBT) a range of treatment approaches to alter faulty cognitions and maladaptive behaviors

Currently, the elements of cognitive therapy are often combined with the techniques of behavioral therapy (discussed previously) and called **cognitive-behavioral therapy** (**CBT**). Some argue it is the "gold standard" of therapy (David, Cristea, & Hofmann, 2018) as it is the most well-researched and strongest evidence-based psychological treatment for youth and adults with obsessive-compulsive, trauma-related, anxiety and depressive disorders, and chronic pain (Baker, McFall, & Shoham, 2008; Ehde, Dillworth, & Turner, 2014; Higa-McMillan, Francis, Rith-Najarian, & Chorpita, 2016; Hofmann & Smits, 2008; Lack, 2012; Lang et al., 2011; Lopez & Basco, 2015; Miskovic et al., 2011; Olatunji et al., 2013; Paintain & Cassidy, 2018; Silverman et al., 2019; Weersing et al., 2017). It is also effective in treating eating disorders and substance-related disorders (Baker et al., 2008; Ricca et al., 2010; Schmidt et al., 2007; Turner et al., 2016). CBT has also been successfully used to help treat a number of medical problems such as diabetes and irritable bowel syndrome (Beck, 2019).

You Review: Psychotherapy Approaches contrasts the goals and therapeutic techniques of the psychotherapy approaches we have discussed in this chapter.

YOU REVIEW Psychotherapy Approaches

Psychological Perspective	Therapy Approaches	Therapy Goals	Therapy Techniques
Psychoanalytic	Traditional psychoanalysis and modern psychodynamic therapy	Insights and resolution regarding unconscious conflicts	Free association, dream analysis, interpretation
Humanistic	Client-centered therapy	Acceptance of genuine self and personal growth	Genuineness, empathy, and unconditional positive regard
Behavioral/ Learning	Exposure therapy, behavior modification	Eliminate maladaptive behaviors and acquire adaptive behaviors	Systematic desensitization, flooding, aversion therapy, shaping, reinforcement, extinction, token economy
Cognitive	Rational-emotive therapy, cognitive therapy	Reduce negative thinking and irrational beliefs; develop more realistic thinking	Challenge irrational beliefs, record negative automatic thoughts

14.5 Quiz Yourself

1. Svetlana goes to a therapist who focuses on her negative automatic statements. Svetlana is most likely undergoing what type of therapy?
a. Rational-emotive therapy
b. Cognitive therapy
c. Systematic desensitization
d. Client-centered therapy

2. The goal of cognitive therapy approaches is to change behavior by _____.
a. uncovering unconscious conflicts so that the client can gain insight into the source of their problems
b. uncovering negative cognitive patterns that impede the client's ability to function
c. changing reinforcers in the environment that seem to elicit negative behavior
d. examining the client's self-awareness to increase self-exploration and facilitate self-actualization

3. The cognitive therapies have been most effective in treating which type of disorders?
a. Schizophrenia
b. Personality disorders
c. Depressive disorders
d. Autism Spectrum disorders

Answers 1. b; 2. b; 3. c

14.6 Group Therapy: Strength in Numbers

The psychotherapies we have described so far focus on a one-to-one relationship between a client and a therapist. This is known as *individual psychotherapy*. However, therapy can be administered to many people at one time with one or more therapists, in a process called **group therapy**. Group therapy approaches are often used in psychiatric facilities, group homes, the military, addiction centers, and mental health units. They are also frequently offered by community mental health centers and outpatient treatment programs. Emily attended many group meetings, not only at the hospital as an inpatient but also as an outpatient at the community center. Group therapy often centers on one type of problem (such as substance use or depressive disorder) or is offered for a specific type of client (such as people who have experienced intimate partner violence, teenagers, or caregivers for people with Alzheimer's disease). Group therapy may be administered by any of the different types of professionals discussed at the beginning of this chapter.

group therapy therapy that is administered to more than one person at a time

family therapy therapy that focuses on creating balance and restoring harmony to improve the functioning of the family as a whole system

14.6.1 The Benefits of Group Therapy

Group therapy has several distinct advantages over individual therapy (Dies, 1993; Yalom & Leszcz, 2005). First, group therapy tends to be less expensive than individual therapy. The cost of one or more therapists is shared by several people. However, clients do receive less one-on-one or individualized treatment in a group therapy setting. Second, group therapy offers therapists a view into the client's social interactions with others. Because many people receive therapy to address interpersonal problems, group therapy offers a safe mini-environment in which to explore new social behaviors or to understand how our interactions with others may be impeding our mental health.

Group therapy also enables clients to recognize that they are not the only ones struggling with difficulties. Group members can offer acceptance, trust, and support for someone who is having problems. They can offer ideas or suggestions for solving problems and can learn from one another. Studies on group therapy have found it to be generally comparable in outcomes to individual psychotherapy for some mental health disorders (Barrera et al., 2013; Mulcahy et al., 2010; Schwartze et al., 2019).

14.6.2 The Nature and Types of Group Therapy

Group therapy, like individual psychotherapy, can take many forms. Any one of the four approaches previously described can be used for treating groups of people. For example, group cognitive-behavioral therapy can be used to reduce people's fear of flying. Group interpersonal psychotherapy can be used to improve people's interpersonal relations. Three unique forms of group therapy are *family therapy*, *couple therapy*, and *self-help groups*.

Jon Bradley/Getty Images

▲ Group therapy can be a less expensive alternative to individual psychotherapy.

Family Therapy: The Whole System

In **family therapy**, the family unit is the group. Often families come to therapy with an "identified patient," such as a misbehaving or rebellious teenager. Yet the focus of family therapy is not just on the functioning of the individual but, rather, on

▲ The goal of family therapy is to improve the functioning of the family system.

the functioning of the family as a whole system. The goal of family therapy is to create balance and restore harmony within the family system to improve its functioning. If one person in the family is having problems, these problems are seen as a symptom of disharmony within the family unit (Lebow & Gurman, 1995).

Think of your own family for a moment. All members of a family have roles, expectations, or labels placed on them, usually at a very young age. One member of the family may be considered "the brain." Another family member may be viewed as "the peacemaker." These roles are not spoken but rather are communicated through our interactions with our family members. If a family member does not conform to their assigned role, the rest of the family system will be disrupted. Many times we try to make family members behave in a way that is consistent with our expectations of their perceived roles. Do you ever feel that your family does not know the "real" you? Have you ever tried to step out of your assigned role, only to find family members so concerned or shaken by your new behavior that it is easier to just go back to your old pattern of behaving? If so, you have experienced the power of the family system.

Family therapists view the "identified patient" as merely the focus for problems in the family system. Rather than simply treating the individual, they explore and analyze the interactions and communications between family members. They address sources of conflict and note how unspoken rules or expected roles may be interfering with healthy family functioning. Although Emily never underwent family therapy, in her book she acknowledges how a family therapist might have viewed her situation: "A family therapist would have identified me as the family scapegoat, the child designated to 'act out' the conflicts between my tense, driven father and my incipiently alcoholic mother" (Gordon, 2000, p. 63).

couple therapy therapy that focuses on improving communication and intimacy between two people in a committed relationship

Couple Therapy: Improving Communication and Securing Attachment

Couple therapy focuses on improving communication and intimacy between two people in a committed relationship. The unspoken rules that couples use to communicate and the ways in which they miscommunicate, are identified and addressed. The couple therapist then replaces ineffective or unhealthy patterns of communicating with more adaptive ones (Gurman & Jacobson, 2002). For example, each partner is encouraged to paraphrase what the other has said to confirm that the correct message has been heard. Criticism and derogatory labels or names are discouraged. These are just two examples of the "new rules" therapists suggest to improve communication and intimacy within couples.

A specific form of couple therapy is *emotionally focused therapy* (*EFT*). EFT, developed by Les Greenberg and Sue Johnson (1988), helps couples identify, manage, and ultimately transform negative, reactive emotions that arise when a couple is in conflict and a person's attachment to their loved one is uncertain or threatened. Research on EFT suggests positive impact on alleviating couple distress (Greenberg, Warwar, & Malcolm, 2010; Johnson & Williams-Keeler, 1998;

Lebow et al., 2012; MacIntosh & Johnson, 2008; Makinen & Johnson, 2006), and improving attachment and relationship satisfaction (Burgess Moser et al., 2016; Wiebe et al., 2017).

Self-Help Groups: Helping Each Other Cope

Self-help groups are composed of people who share the same problem and meet to help one another. Self-help groups differ from other forms of group therapy in that they may be organized and led by nonprofessionals. Self-help organizations are becoming increasingly popular, and you, a family member, or a friend may have attended one of their meetings. It is estimated that 1.1% of the U.S. population received support from a mental health self-help group in the past year (SAMHSA, 2009b). Self-help groups can be found for anything from grief and eating disorders to people who have a loved one dealing with a substance-related disorder. The main purpose of these groups is to offer social support and help one another cope, but they often provide useful information and advice as well.

Monkey Business Images/Shutterstock.com

▲ Self-help groups offer social support and often complement professional mental health treatment.

self-help groups groups comprised of people who share the same problem and meet to help one another

The format and purpose of self-help groups vary widely. For example, group meetings may be highly structured or conducted more loosely. Many self-help groups adopt a 12-step program format originated by the well-known Alcoholics Anonymous (AA). Such a format includes admitting that you have a problem and that you are powerless over the problem. It encourages people to seek strength from a "greater power," to admit one's shortcomings, and to make amends to people they have harmed. Although such 12-step programs are not therapy, mental health professionals often encourage clients to participate in such groups to receive additional emotional support and encouragement. Such groups can increase a client's adherence to treatment, encourage drug abstinence, and reduce the severity of mental health symptoms (Donovan et al., 2013; Kaskutas, 2009; Markowitz, 2015; Sussman, 2010). However, research has been unable to specify what elements of self-help groups make them effective or what types of people they benefit most. For many people, mental health self-help groups complement professional mental health treatment (SAMHSA, 2009b).

14.6 Quiz Yourself

1. **Which of the following is *not* an advantage of group therapy approaches?**
   a. Less expensive
   b. More individual attention
   c. Focus on interpersonal interactions
   d. None of the above

2. **The main goal of family therapy is to _____.**
   a. fix the person with the most problems
   b. improve communication between the parents
   c. create harmony and balance within the family unit
   d. understand the past problems of the family

3. **Many self-help groups, such as Alcoholics Anonymous and Narcotics Anonymous, assume that a critical factor in improving one's mental health is _____.**
   a. social support
   b. physical health
   c. financial status
   d. medication

Answers 1. b; 2. c; 3. a

14.7 Effective Psychotherapy: Do Treatments Work?

After reading about all these different forms of psychotherapy, you may be asking yourself, "Does psychotherapy work? And if it does work, which approach is the best?" Researchers analyzing the effectiveness of therapy have asked themselves similar questions. As we shall soon see, the answers to these questions are neither simple nor straightforward. Many factors influence and contribute to the effectiveness of therapy.

14.7.1 Conducting Research on Therapy's Effectiveness

To answer the question "Does psychotherapy work?" research typically compares clients who are receiving therapy with clients who are receiving a placebo treatment or no treatment at all. Such studies generally suggest that psychotherapy has positive effects and is better than a placebo treatment or no treatment at all. They also suggest that the different approaches—*psychodynamic, humanistic, behavioral*, and *cognitive*—produce relatively equivalent results in terms of client improvement (Baker et al., 2008; Chambless & Ollendick, 2001; Shedler, 2010; Steinert et al., 2017). This finding has been termed the *Dodo Bird verdict* after the Dodo Bird in *Alice in Wonderland* who, following the race, stated, "Everyone has won, and all must have prizes." The Dodo Bird verdict implies that it doesn't matter which therapy approach a therapist selects because all are equivalent in effectiveness.

Other research suggests that certain forms of therapy work better for certain types of mental health disorders (Chambless & Ollendick, 2001; Crits-Christoph, 1997; Tolin, 2010). For example, panic disorder and obsessive-compulsive and related disorders may respond best to cognitive-behavioral therapy, whereas phobias may respond best to behavioral methods (Allen et al., 2010; Ponniah, Magiati, & Hollon, 2013; Roshanaei-Moghaddam et al., 2011).

Some evidence suggests that psychotherapy can even alter the functioning of the brain. For example, A. L. Brody and colleagues (1998) took positron emission tomography (PET) scans of persons with obsessive-compulsive disorder before and after receiving 2 months of behavioral therapy. Metabolic activity of the brain decreased in the clients following treatment. Excessive activity in certain areas of the brain may in part explain the intrusive and uncontrollable obsessions that inundate people with this disorder. It appears that psychotherapy, like medication, can reduce these faulty signals. Neuroimaging studies on people with other mental health disorders (panic disorder, major depressive disorder, specific phobias, PTSD, substance use disorders) have also documented changes in brain metabolism following psychotherapy treatment (Beauregard, 2007; Dichter, Felder, & Smoski, 2010; Felmingham et al., 2007; Frewen, Dozois, & Lanius, 2008; Zilverstand et al., 2016).

Conducting research on therapy's effectiveness is quite complex. First, think about the selection of participants for such a study. It is hard to find people who all have the same disorder to the same degree, and many people like Emily in the part case study may be diagnosed with symptoms of more than one disorder (*comorbidity*). Such differences in symptoms introduce potential sampling problems into the research. Next, think about the administration of the *independent variable*. In an experiment, therapists would be trained to deliver a very specific type of therapy. To ensure consistency among therapists, deviations from these methods would not be allowed. As you might imagine, this is much different from the way treatment is administered in the real world (Chambless & Hollon, 1998).

In addition, it is difficult to design a "no treatment" control group. Add to these issues the problem of defining what a good outcome is and how it will be measured, the *dependent variable* (Lilienfeld et al., 2014; Westen & Bradley, 2005). Do we rely on the therapist's judgment of improvement, the client's self-report of well-being, significant others' reports of mental health functioning or some other measure? And what if these assessments don't agree (Marsh, Zeveney, & De Los Reyes, 2020)? How long should the client be free of symptoms for treatment to be considered effective? Although you may not feel that such research questions are important to you, the results of such studies are important to health insurance companies. They use this research to determine the most cost-effective and efficient means of treatment. Consequently, outcome research may indirectly affect you or a loved one in the future.

14.7.2 Eclectic Therapy: CBT, MBCT, and EMDR

Perhaps a more appropriate question to ask about therapy is "Which treatment is most effective for this person, with this problem, under these circumstances?" Such a personalized approach to treatment is becoming more common as many therapists are adopting an *eclectic approach* to treatment (Kopta et al., 1999). An **eclectic therapy** approach involves an integrated and diverse use of therapeutic methods. We have already introduced one such integration called cognitive-behavioral therapy (CBT) where the elements of cognitive therapy are combined with the techniques of behavioral therapy. Two additional examples include *mindfulness-based cognitive therapy (MBCT)* and *eye-movement desensitization and reprocessing therapy (EMDR)*.

Mindfulness-based cognitive therapy (MBCT) initially conceived as a method to prevent relapse in people with recurrent depression (Teasdale, Segal, & Williams, 1995), integrates mindfulness-based interventions such as mindfulness meditation and breathing exercises with cognitive-behavioral therapy. Studies suggest it is just as effective as drugs in preventing depressive relapse (Kuyken et al., 2015; Piet & Hougaard, 2011; Segal et al., 2010). As such, MBCT is now officially endorsed by the American Psychiatric Association for preventing relapse in individuals who have had three or more previous episodes of depression. MBCT has been extended to other problems and populations such as anxiety disorders, chronic pain, and substance use disorders to name a few. Research suggests moderate effectiveness in reducing symptoms of anxiety, depression, and pain and insufficient or mixed evidence for substance abuse (Goldberg et al., 2018; Goyal et al., 2014; Van Dam et al., 2018). More research is needed before we understand for what physical and mental health disorders, and in which individuals, MBCT is definitively helpful.

Eye movement desensitization and reprocessing (EMDR) therapy (Shapiro, 1991) is an eclectic therapy approach recommended by the American Psychiatric Association (2004) as an effective treatment for trauma. The client's distressing memories are identified, along with positive beliefs the client will need to cope with future stressful situations. The client then focuses on the most vivid image of the trauma while simultaneously attending to another stimulus for 20 to 30 seconds, such as moving one's eyes back and forth or tapping one's fingers. The client is directed to notice whatever thoughts, feelings, or images come to mind. This process is repeated until the client's distress is reduced. The client then focuses on the positive belief while engaging in the dual attention task (Shapiro, 2001). EDMR therapy appears to be effective in reducing symptoms of PTSD (L. Chen et al., 2015; Kemp, Drummond, & McDermott, 2010; Nijdam et al., 2012; Ponniah & Hollon, 2009; Watts et al., 2013). EMDR therapy also has shown promise as a

eclectic [ee-KLECK-tick] therapy approach therapy that incorporates an integrated and diverse use of therapeutic methods

mindfulness-based cognitive therapy (MBCT) an eclectic therapy approach to prevent relapse in people with recurrent depression that integrates mindfulness meditation and breathing exercises with cognitive-behavioral therapy

eye movement desensitization and reprocessing (EMDR) therapy an eclectic therapy approach to treat trauma in which the client attends to emotionally disturbing images while simultaneously focusing on an external stimulus

GARO/PHANIE/AGE Fotostock

▲ EMDR therapy is an eclectic therapy approach designed to reduce distress in people who have experienced trauma.

treatment option for people with chronic pain or obsessive-compulsive disorder (Nazari et al., 2011; Tesarz et al., 2014). However, the sample sizes of these studies are small. The quality of systematic reviews on EDMR therapy's effectiveness has also been questioned (Opheim et al., 2019). Further replication of EMDR therapy's effectiveness for these disorders is warranted.

14.7.3 Factors That Contribute to Effective Psychotherapy

Although research has provided mixed results on the question "Which psychotherapy is most effective?" evidence suggests that all successful psychotherapies share certain common elements, even when the specific methods used differ greatly. The term **therapeutic alliance** describes the interactive and collaborative relationship between the client and the therapist. The nature and development of this relationship can influence the effectiveness of therapy (Lorenzo-Luaces, Derubeis, & Webb, 2014; Norcross & Wampold, 2011; Watson, Schein, & McMullen, 2010).

therapeutic alliance [thair-uh-PEW-tick uh-LIE-unce] the interactive and collaborative relationship between the client and the therapist

Therapists contribute to a successful alliance in many ways. First, the therapist establishes a positive relationship with the client. This involves creating an atmosphere of mutual respect and trust. Clients who trust their therapist are more likely to believe that they will benefit from therapy. The clients, therefore, are more likely to engage in the therapy process by revealing important information about themselves and by trying the new skills, behaviors, or techniques that the therapist suggests. Second, effective therapists are empathetic and warm, evidencing a caring attitude toward the client and the ability to listen (Norcross & Wampold, 2011; Teyber & McClure, 2000; Vitinius et al., 2018). Third, effective therapists offer an explanation or interpretation of why the client is having a problem and encourage clients to confront painful emotions (Ingram, Hayes, & Scott, 2000; Snyder et al., 2000).

Finally, effective therapists provide *culturally sensitive* treatment by adapting psychotherapy to the client's cultural background (Smith, Rodriguez, & Bernal, 2011; Thomas, Solorzano, & Cobb, 2007). Given that most providers of mental health services come from the majority culture and clients may be members of minority cultures, it is important to the success of therapy that therapists acknowledge and understand the experiences and values of diverse ethnocultural populations in the United States (Pedersen, 2002; White, Gibbons, & Schamberger, 2006; Yasui, Pottick, & Chen, 2017). Otherwise, therapists may unintentionally introduce bias (based on race, gender, sexual orientation, or social class) into therapist-client interactions, making empathy and trust more difficult to achieve (Draguns, 2002; Vasquez, 2007).

Therapist characteristics are not the only determinant of a successful alliance. Client attitudes and behaviors also make a difference (Kwan, Dimidjian, & Rizvi, 2010; Leon et al., 1999; Lorenzo-Luaces et al., 2014; Vitinius et al., 2018). Clients who are motivated and committed to therapy tend to experience more positive results. Those who are actively involved in the therapy process and optimistic about the benefits of therapy also fare better. Moreover, clients who can express their feelings and thoughts and who are more psychologically mature experience more gains from therapy. Clients who have no previous history of mental health disorders also tend to benefit more. The social environment of the client is also important. Clients who have supportive loved ones and stable, rather than chaotic, living conditions tend to benefit more from therapy.

Notice that none of these characteristics is specific to any one of the therapy approaches we have described. So, if you or a loved one is in need of a therapist, it is important to find a therapist and an approach that make you comfortable. Believing in the therapist and their approaches will establish a positive therapeutic alliance, thereby enhancing the effectiveness of your therapy.

14.7.4 The Effectiveness and Ethics of Technology in the Delivery of Psychotherapy

The rapid development of computer technology, smartphones, and the Internet has influenced psychotherapy in the form of *behavioral intervention technologies* (*BITs*) (Kazdin & Blase, 2011; Schueller, Munoz, & Mohr, 2013; C. B. Taylor & Luce, 2003). Computer-based programs can now be used to administer personality assessments such as the MMPI-2. Smartphones can be used to collect data from clients on their thoughts, behaviors, and mood, allowing clinicians and people in general to become more aware of their behavior across many situations. Text therapy apps such as Talkspace and BetterHelp allow one to message licensed mental health professionals. Videoconferencing and Skype can provide a link to therapists for clients who live too far away for face-to-face meetings. These are just some of the technological tools that can enhance the delivery of psychotherapy.

The Internet also has produced mental health treatment called *cybertherapy* and *e-health interventions* through e-mail, real-time online counseling, professionally assisted chat rooms, self-help groups, and mental health information and education sites. However, technology-assisted treatments present a number of professional and ethical issues (Hilgart et al., 2012; Spriggs, 2009; Stoll, Müller, & Trachsel, 2019). Online mental health services lack the close, personal contact of face-to-face interactions. Establishing a therapeutic alliance is more difficult when you cannot

iStock.com/SDI Productions

▲ Videoconferencing can provide mental health services to people who live a long distance away, such as in large rural areas.

hear the tone of someone's voice or read their body language and facial expressions. Yet, several studies and reviews suggest roughly equivalent ratings between face-to-face therapy and internet interventions (Berger, 2017; Preschl, Maercker, & Wagner, 2011; Wehmann et al., 2020). Online counselors may or may not have adequate training or be appropriately licensed. Client confidentiality is of great concern because information on the Internet can be easily accessed.

Despite these concerns, the effectiveness of these programs shows promise. For example, the U.S. Department of Veteran Affairs (VA) mental health care facilities have launched multiple technology-assisted programs to help treat close to 2 million veterans with encouraging results (Brief et al., 2013; Morland et al., 2010; Tuerk et al., 2010). Evidence-based technology-assisted interventions have been shown to reduce symptoms in people with anxiety, depressive, and substance-related disorders as well as insomnia (Carlbring et al., 2011; Carroll et al., 2008; Cavanagh et al., 2009; Klein et al., 2010; Mohr et al., 2010; Munoz et al., 2016; Rogers et al., 2017; Sander, Rausch, & Baumeister, 2016). Many of these programs are intensive, requiring user engagement over weeks or months and often employ cognitive-behavioral strategies. However, more research is needed to better understand for which people technology-assisted treatments work best, especially in the real world outside of research settings (Fleming et al., 2018; Griffiths, Calear, & Banfield, 2009; Shoham & Insel, 2011). At this time, technology and the Internet appear to be promising and impactful resources that may help broaden the reach of mental health services to people who otherwise might not have access (Stoll et al., 2019; Teachman, 2014).

14.7 Quiz Yourself

1. Which of the following statements about the effectiveness of psychotherapy is ***true***?
   a. Cognitive therapy is considerably more effective than other forms of therapy.
   b. Psychoanalysis is considerably more effective than other forms of therapy.
   c. The main types of therapy appear to be equally effective.
   d. Receiving therapy appears to be no more effective than no therapy.
2. Which of the following is an element associated with successful therapy?
   a. Free association
   b. Chaotic living conditions of the client
   c. Being forced to receive therapy
   d. A positive therapist-client relationship
3. An eclectic therapy approach refers to ____.
   a. an integrated and diverse use of therapeutic methods
   b. a reliance on free association and interpretation
   c. a mutual bond of respect and warmth between the therapist and client
   d. deepening the client's knowledge of psychology

Answers 1. c; 2. d; 3. a

14.8 Biomedical Therapies: Applying Neuroscience

Now that we have described psychological treatments for mental health disorders, it is time to turn our attention to biomedical approaches. The two dominant biomedical approaches are *drug therapy* and *brain stimulation procedures*.

14.8.1 Drug Therapies: Chemically Altering the Brain

psychopharmacology [sigh-co-farm-uh-KAH-lo-gee] the use of medications to treat mental health problems

Today, the most common biomedical therapy used to treat mental health problems is medication. Recall that medications are generally prescribed by physicians or psychiatrists who have extensive training in **psychopharmacology**, or the use of drugs to treat mental health problems. Medications are generally not prescribed

Psychology Works!

Monkey Business Images/Shutterstock.com

Because pharmacists prepare and dispense medical drugs for physical and mental health problems every day, it is necessary that they are knowledgeable about biomedical therapies. Pharmacists filling prescriptions for people with mental health problems can explain to people what the medication is being used for, how to properly take the medication, and how long it may take to see a decrease in symptoms. Pharmacists can also educate people on the possible side effects they may experience. Pharmacists also need to inform people of how drugs prescribed for physical health conditions may influence mental health or the cumulative effects of multiple drugs on mental health, as people often may be taking more than one prescribed drug. These are just a few examples of how knowledge about biomedical therapies can help those on a pharmacy career path.

by psychologists. As with any prescribed medication, side effects can occur and must be considered in any treatment plan.

Medication cannot cure a mental health disorder. Rather, it reduces the symptoms of the disorder while the person is taking the medication. Often, therefore, medications are prescribed jointly with psychotherapy. The medication stabilizes the person sufficiently so that psychological issues can be addressed. Here we present the major types of medications that are prescribed for specific mental health disorders.

Antianxiety Drugs: Reduce Tension

antianxiety medications minor tranquilizers such as Valium that are prescribed to reduce tension and anxiety

As the name implies, **antianxiety medications** are sedatives prescribed to reduce tension and anxiety. The best-known antianxiety drugs are the *benzodiazepines* such as *Valium*, *Ativan*, and *Xanax*. These medications reduce tension, relax the muscles, and promote sleep by depressing the central nervous system. They influence the functioning of three neurotransmitters: GABA, serotonin, and norepinephrine (see Chapter 2). They are fast-acting drugs, calming feelings of anxiety within an hour or so. These medications are useful in treating people who are diagnosed with generalized anxiety disorder, social anxiety disorder, panic disorder, posttraumatic stress disorder, agoraphobia, and insomnia (Barlow, 2002; Nardi et al., 2010; Offidani et al., 2013).

The benzodiazepines are highly addictive if taken over a long period. People quickly build up a tolerance to these medications, requiring higher and higher dosages to achieve a reduction in anxiety. If dependence does occur, the person must be gradually weaned from the drug, because abrupt withdrawal can be life threatening. Withdrawal symptoms can include tremors, irritability, insomnia, tingling sensations, a return of intense anxiety, and in rare cases even seizures and paranoia.

A second drawback of taking benzodiazepines is the effect on cognitive and motor functioning. As a depressant drug, the benzodiazepines reduce coordination, alertness, and reaction time (van Laar, Volkerts, & Verbaten, 2001). These impairments can affect a person's ability to drive a car or perform tasks at work or school. These effects are even more severe, including possible death, when alcohol is used with these medications.

Finally, *relapse rates* for patients taking benzodiazepines are high. This means that many people taking these drugs experience the anxiety symptoms again when they discontinue treatment or are taken off the drugs. The drugs appear to provide only short-term relief from anxiety symptoms. Long-term benefits are more likely when benzodiazepine treatment is combined with cognitive-behavioral therapies or antidepressant medication (Roy-Byrne, 2014).

Because of the disadvantages of benzodiazepine treatment, a nonbenzodiazepine drug, called *buspirone* (trade name BuSpar), is sometimes prescribed to treat anxiety, particularly generalized anxiety disorder and social anxiety disorder (Chessick et al., 2006; Halaby, Haddad, & Naja, 2015; Loane & Politis, 2012; Mokhber et al., 2010). A modest success, buspirone has a lower risk of dependence, but it takes considerably longer for the drug to reduce anxiety. The person must take this medication for several days or weeks before a noticeable reduction in anxiety symptoms is achieved.

Antipsychotic Drugs: Reduce Symptoms of Psychosis

Over the centuries, many medical treatments had been unsuccessful in treating psychotic symptoms, especially in people diagnosed with schizophrenia. Such treatments included brain surgery (lobotomy), insulin injections, and shock treatment. Because these treatments were ineffective, most people with schizophrenia were merely warehoused in mental hospitals. Then, in the 1950s, *chlorpromazine* (trade name *Thorazine*) was discovered as an effective drug in treating psychosis, or a loss of touch with reality. As Thorazine and the numerous drugs that followed, such as *Mellaril* and *Haldol*, were the first drugs to effectively reduce psychosis for some people, they are referred to as *conventional* or *first-generation antipsychotic medications*.

antipsychotic medications major tranquilizers such as Haldol that are prescribed to relieve psychotic symptoms such as delusions and hallucinations

tardive dyskinesia [TAR-div dis-kuh-NEE-juh] a possible long-term side effect of conventional antipsychotic medications involving involuntary motor movements of the mouth, tongue, and face

Antipsychotic medications are major tranquilizers prescribed to relieve psychotic symptoms such as agitation, delusions, disordered thinking, and hallucinations. They may be prescribed for people with schizophrenia, bipolar disorder, major depressive disorder, or substance-related disorders when such individuals have lost touch with reality. These drugs appear to work by reducing the action of the neurotransmitter dopamine in the brain (Sanyal & vanTol, 1997). Recall that dopamine has long been suspected as a major link in understanding psychotic behavior (see Chapter 13).

Although conventional antipsychotic drugs dramatically decreased the number of patients in mental hospitals for several decades, they are effective for only 60% of persons who try them (American Psychiatric Association, 2000b). They are more effective in treating the positive symptoms of schizophrenia, such as delusions (false beliefs) and hallucinations (hearing voices), than the negative symptoms, such as blunted affect (lack of emotional reactions), alogia (poverty of speech), and avolition (lack of motivation) (see Chapter 13). The conventional antipsychotic medications also have significant side effects, including sleepiness, dry mouth, blurred vision, weight change, drooling, constipation, sexual dysfunction, and depression. Motor side effects also occur, including tremors, spasms, frozen facial expressions, and motor agitation, causing people with schizophrenia to pace. These motor side effects often look like Parkinson's disease. This should not be surprising given that Parkinson's disease has been related to a reduced functioning of dopamine in the brain, precisely the effect of conventional antipsychotic medications.

Long-term use of such drugs can lead to an irreversible motor disorder called **tardive dyskinesia** that involves involuntary motor movements of the mouth, tongue, and face. People experiencing this side effect may repeatedly smack their lips, stick out their tongues, puff out their cheeks, or make other odd facial movements. It is estimated that this serious side effect occurs in 10% to 20% of people with long-term use of conventional antipsychotic drugs (Chakos et al., 1996; Oosthuizen et al., 2003).

Newer drugs, called *atypical antipsychotics* or *second-generation antipsychotics*, have renewed hope of successfully treating people with schizophrenia. These drugs mostly influence the action of serotonin and to a lesser extent the action of dopamine in the brain and cause less serious side effects and a lower incidence of tardive dyskinesia (Meltzer, 2013). They are effective in reducing both the positive and negative symptoms of schizophrenia (Lieberman et al., 2003; Lindenmayer et al., 2007; Macfadden et al., 2010). Side effects include sedation, nausea, headaches, seizures, dizziness, and an increased risk of sleep apnea (Rishi et al., 2010), but for people who do not respond to conventional antipsychotic medications, these newer drugs can be a lifesaver. As a result, they have become the most commonly used antipsychotic drugs in clinical practice. Examples of such drugs include *clozapine, risperidone,* and *aripiprazole*. Atypical antipsychotic medications are approved by the Food and Drug Administration (FDA) for treatment of schizophrenia and bipolar disorder (to treat manic episodes) and as augmentation for major depressive disorder and autism spectrum disorders (Cipriani et al., 2011; Maher & Theodore, 2012).

Antidepressant Drugs: Mood, Compulsions, and Cravings

Antidepressants Antidepressants are prescribed to alter mood and alleviate the symptoms of major depressive disorder. Antidepressants have also been effective in treating people with obsessive-compulsive disorder, panic disorder, eating disorders, and drug cravings (Barlow, 2002). There are many different classes of antidepressants. Here we describe three: *tricyclics, MAO inhibitors*, and the *reuptake inhibitors*.

antidepressants medications prescribed to alleviate the symptoms of depression, eating disorders, drug cravings, some anxiety disorders, and obsessive-compulsive disorder

Tricyclics Tricyclic antidepressants, such as *Tofranil* and *Elavil*, elevate mood and reduce the symptoms of depression by influencing the action of norepinephrine and serotonin in the brain (Stahl, 1998). However, it takes from 4 to 8 weeks on such medication before noticeable relief from depression occurs. Tricyclics are effective in relieving depressive symptoms in 60% to 85% of people who are depressed (Arroll et al., 2005; Fawcett, 1994). As with any drug, tricyclics have a number of side effects, including dry mouth, weight gain, dizziness, blurred vision, constipation, and sexual dysfunction. The tricyclics can also be fatal in overdose amounts, which is why they are seldom prescribed to patients who are suicidal.

MAO Inhibitors The monoamine oxidase (MAO) inhibitors, such as *Nardil* and *Parnate*, are antidepressants that elevate mood by blocking the enzyme, *monoamine oxidase* which breaks down serotonin, norepinephrine, and dopamine. As a result, the levels of these neurotransmitters increase in the brain (Stahl & Felker, 2008). They are just as effective as the tricyclic antidepressants but are less frequently prescribed because of their more serious side effects (Fava & Rosenbaum, 1995). These include lowered blood pressure, liver damage, and weight gain. These drugs also interact with substances high in an amino acid called *tyramine*. Tyramine is present in common foods such as cheese and smoked meats, liquids such as draft beer and soy sauce, and even over-the-counter (OTC) medications. This interaction can produce a sudden rise in blood pressure that is potentially fatal. You may have noticed the caution statements on the back of any OTC cold medication stating that it is not to be used by a person who is taking an MAO inhibitor. Yet MAO inhibitors may be more effective for treatment-resistant or severe depression than the newer antidepressants (Ionescu et al., 2015; Parker et al., 2001).

selective serotonin reuptake inhibitors (SSRIs) antidepressant drugs that inhibit the reuptake of the neurotransmitter serotonin, thereby improving mood

antimanic medications drugs that are prescribed to alleviate manic symptoms of bipolar disorder

lithium a naturally occurring mineral salt prescribed to control manic symptoms in people with bipolar disorder; it influences several neurotransmitters in the brain, including glutamate, serotonin, and dopamine

Reuptake Inhibitors: SSRIs & SNRIs Currently, the most frequently prescribed antidepressant medications are the **selective serotonin reuptake inhibitors (SSRIs)** such as *Prozac*, *Lexapro*, and *Zoloft*. Recall from Chapter 2 that reuptake is the process whereby the neurotransmitters that are left over in the synapse are recycled back into the presynaptic neuron. SSRIs elevate mood by leaving the neurotransmitter serotonin in the synapse longer. They have several advantages over other types of antidepressants.

The side effects of SSRIs are less severe and are not fatal in overdose. These include increased nervousness, headaches, insomnia, nausea, stomach cramps, decreased sexual drive, and sexual dysfunction (Fisher, Kent, & Bryant, 1995; Michelson et al., 2000). Some of these side effects may diminish after a few weeks of treatment. Another antidepressant, *Wellbutrin*, is similar to the SSRIs but influences the norepinephrine and dopamine systems. It does not decrease one's sexual drive and is therefore sometimes used in combination with SSRI drugs to elevate mood while lessening the sexual side effects (Leuchter et al., 2008; Zisook et al., 2006). SSRIs are also useful in treating excessive anxiety disorders, obsessive-compulsive disorders, PTSD, eating disorders, and substance-related disorders, especially alcohol use disorder (Lenze et al., 2009; Romanelli et al., 2014; van Apeldoorn et al., 2010). For all of these reasons, the SSRIs are quite popular.

Another type of antidepressant that acts as a reuptake inhibitor is the *serotonin and norepinephrine reuptake inhibitors* (*SNRIs*), such as *Cymbalta and Effexor XR*. These drugs elevate mood by leaving *both* serotonin and norepinephrine in the synapse longer. They are just as effective as the SSRIs in treating depression and anxiety disorders but also may be prescribed for chronic pain conditions. Their side effects are similar to those of the SSRIs (Sansone & Sansone, 2014; Stahl et al., 2005).

There is considerable debate over the effectiveness of antidepressants, specifically the reuptake inhibitors, compared to placebos in treating major depressive disorder. Some research suggests beneficial effects (Arroll et al., 2005; Cipriani et al., 2018; Garnock-Jones & McCormack, 2010; Gartlehner et al., 2017; Stewart et al., 2012), while other research suggests modest to insignificant effects (Fournier et al., 2010; Jakobsen et al., 2017; Kirsch et al., 2008). Accordingly, the clinical benefits of antidepressants are unclear. In addition, antidepressant medication has been associated with an increased risk of suicidal thoughts and behaviors in children, adolescents, and adults aged 18 to 24 years, especially in the first few months of treatment (FDA Public Health Advisory, 2004). Consequently, all antidepressants in the United States carry a warning of increased suicidality for children, adolescents, and young adults.

Antimanic Drugs: Mood Stabilizers

The **antimanic medications** are prescribed to alleviate manic symptoms of bipolar disorder. The first mood-stabilizing drug approved by the FDA was **lithium**, a naturally occurring mineral salt. Lithium has the advantage of controlling both manic and depressive symptoms in people with bipolar disorder, although it is far more effective in treating mania (Amsterdam & Shults, 2010; Nivoli, Murru, & Vieta, 2010; Yalin & Young, 2020; Young et al., 2010). For this reason, people with bipolar disorder may be prescribed antidepressant drugs in addition to lithium to stabilize their moods. Lithium achieves its effect by influencing several neurotransmitters in the brain: glutamate, serotonin, and dopamine (Dixon & Hokin, 1998). It is taken even when people have no symptoms of mania to prevent future manic episodes.

Research on the effectiveness of lithium treatment is challenging, because there is extreme variability in people's absorption of lithium. Some people absorb lithium rather quickly and can therefore tolerate only small dosages, whereas others absorb the chemical more slowly. Lithium dosage amounts, therefore, vary considerably from one person to the next. Too little lithium can lead to manic episodes, whereas too much can lead to lithium poisoning, causing vomiting, nausea, slurred speech, and impaired muscle coordination. For any one person, the difference between the correct, or "therapeutic," amount of lithium and a toxic amount is a very fine line. For this reason, lithium levels must be carefully monitored in people with bipolar disorder.

Lithium, like all the drugs discussed so far, also has side effects, including nausea, vomiting, diarrhea, blurred vision, reduced concentration, weight gain, and increased risk of diabetes and kidney problems (Maj et al., 1997). It can also lead to birth defects if taken by pregnant women during their first trimester.

For those people with bipolar disorder who do not respond to lithium or who cannot tolerate its side effects, other drug options are available. For example, *anticonvulsant drugs* such as carbamazepine (*Tegretol*) and valproate (*Depakote*) are effective in treating severe mania and produce fewer side effects than lithium. *Valproate* is also a frequently prescribed mood-stabilizing drug. However, the anticonvulsant drugs are less effective than lithium in preventing suicide (Goodwin & Goldstein, 2003; Tondo & Baldessarini, 2009; Yalin & Young, 2020). The anticonvulsant drugs can also cause birth defects when taken by pregnant women. However, when compared to placebo, both lithium and the anticonvulsant drugs have been shown to be effective treatments for bipolar disorder (Bauer et al., 2016; Bowden et al., 2010; Cipriani et al., 2013; Woo et al., 2014; Yalin & Young, 2020).

The effectiveness of medications for treating bipolar disorder is further complicated by patient compliance (Sachs & Rush, 2003). Some people with bipolar disorder miss the euphoric feelings of the manic state and, against the advice of their physicians, go off their medications when they are feeling better. They often believe that they can control their symptoms without medication. For example, in one large study of patients with bipolar disorder receiving treatment in VA settings, almost 50% did not take their medications as prescribed (Sajatovic et al., 2007). Unfortunately, manic symptoms often return, thus requiring a recalibration of appropriate medication levels.

You Review: Drug Therapy and Mental Health Disorders summarizes which medications are typically prescribed for specific mental health disorders.

YOU REVIEW Drug Therapy and Mental Health Disorders

Medication Type	Type of Drug	Examples	Symptoms Treated
Antianxiety drugs	Benzodiazepines Nonbenzodiazepines	Valium, Xanax, Ativan BuSpar	Anxiety and tension; insomnia
Antipsychotic drugs	Conventional antipsychotics	Thorazine, Mellaril, Haldol	Psychotic symptoms such as agitation, delusions, disordered thinking, and hallucinations
	Atypical antipsychotics	Clozaril, Risperdal, Zyprexa, Seroquel	Psychotic symptoms such as agitation, delusions, disordered thinking, and hallucinations; negative symptoms of schizophrenia
Antidepressant drugs	Tricyclics MAO inhibitors Selective serotonin reuptake inhibitors (SSRIs) Serotonin norepinephrine reuptake inhibitors (SNRIs)	Elavil, Tofranil Nardil, Parnate, Marplan Prozac, Paxil, Zoloft, Lexapro, Celexa, Abilify Cymbalta, Effexor XR	Depressed mood; excessive anxiety disorders; eating disorders; substance-related disorders; obsessive-compulsive disorder
Antimanic drugs	Lithium Anticonvulsants	Lithium carbonate Tegretol, Depakote	Relieves manic symptoms; prevents future manic episodes

14.8.2 Noninvasive Brain Stimulation Procedures: TMS and ECT

Some people with mental health disorders evidence *treatment resistance*. That is, despite psychotherapy and/or drug therapy, their symptoms do not improve. In cases such as these, directly stimulating the brain has produced promising and unexpected results. Two such procedures include *transcranial magnetic stimulation* and *electroconvulsive therapy*.

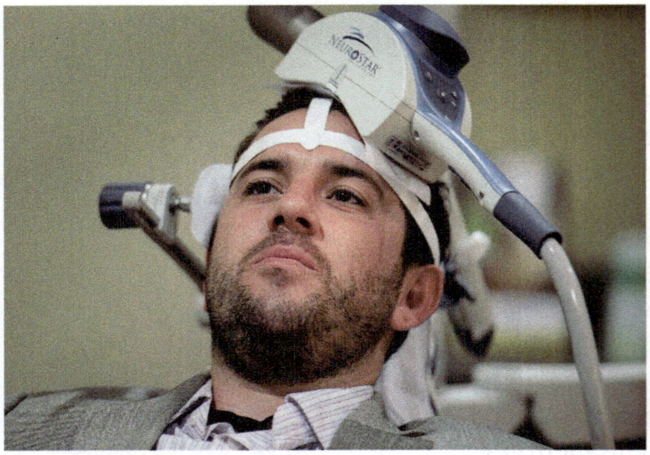

Tribune Content Agency LLC/Alamy Stock Photo

▲ Transcranial magnetic stimulation (TMS) is a biomedical therapy that uses magnetic impulses to stimulate brain neurons to ease symptoms of depression.

Transcranial Magnetic Stimulation (TMS): Stimulating Neurons

Transcranial magnetic stimulation (**TMS**) uses brief magnetic impulses to stimulate brain neurons to ease symptoms of depression. In TMS, an electromagnetic coil is placed against the forehead, near an area of the brain involved in regulating mood. Short electromagnetic pulses are administered, which pass through the skull to stimulate neurons in the brain. As the pulses are administered, the person will feel a slight tapping on the head. The strength of the pulse is equivalent to that of an MRI scan. A typical session lasts 30 to 60 minutes and the therapy is typically repeated daily over 4 to 6 weeks. Common side effects include headaches, lightheadedness, and scalp discomfort. TMS is an approved treatment for major depressive disorder for people who have not responded to at least one antidepressant medication, for treatment-resistant obsessive-compulsive disorder, and for pain associated with migraine headaches.

Research on the effectiveness of TMS in treating depression has produced mixed results. Some studies suggest an effect (Dunner et al., 2014; Fitzgerald et al., 2003; Gaynes et al., 2011; Slotema et al., 2010); some have found an effect only for distinct subtypes of depression (Downar et al., 2014; Ren et al., 2014), and others suggest that TMS's effectiveness is tied to other variables such as the coil type, location, or positioning method, frequency and duration of pulses, depth and width of brain stimulation, length of treatment period, and its use alone or in conjunction with medication (Aleman, 2013; Brunoni et al., 2017; Luber et al., 2017; Mutz et al., 2019; Xie, Chen, & Wei, 2013). TMS as a potential intervention for treatment-resistant OCD also shows promise (Carmi et al., 2018, 2019). More research is needed to understand the most effective use of TMS.

Electroconvulsive Therapy (ECT): Inducing a Brief Seizure

Although still highly controversial, **electroconvulsive therapy** (**ECT**) consists of a series of treatments, (as an inpatient or outpatient) in which electrical current is passed through the brain, causing a seizure. It can be effective in treating people with severe depression. After administration of anesthesia and a muscle relaxant, metal electrodes are placed on the head of the now unconscious patient. A current of 70 to 130 volts is passed through one side of the brain for roughly one-half second. A seizure occurs, causing the patient to have muscle tremors for about 1 minute. Violent convulsions do not occur because of the administration of the muscle relaxant prior to the procedure. The patient undergoes this procedure about every other day for 6 to 12 sessions. It is a quick and painless medical procedure.

Many students are appalled and even frightened by ECT. It seems so archaic and primitive. These are natural and common reactions. However, keep in mind that ECT is not the first treatment for depression, but rather a last resort. It is administered to patients who are depressed and are not responding to psychotherapy or drug therapy and remain in a severely depressed state. These patients may be suicidal or even

transcranial magnetic stimulation (TMS) a biomedical treatment approach in which electromagnetic impulses stimulate brain neurons; used for treatment-resistant major depressive disorder, obsessive-compulsive disorder, and for pain from migraine headaches

electroconvulsive therapy (ECT) a series of treatments in which electrical current is passed through the brain, causing a seizure; used to alleviate severe depression psychotic. For these patients, ECT may be the only form of treatment that is effective (Nemeroff, 2007).

ECT is effective for people who are severely depressed, or who are considered treatment-resistant, and it is very effective in treating psychotic depression or depression combined with hallucinations and delusions (J. J. Chen et al., 2017; Damm et al., 2010; Gaynes et al., 2011; Kellner et al., 2010; Merkl, Heuser, & Bajbouj, 2009; Mutz et al., 2019; Ren et al., 2014). It also relieves depression faster than drug therapy. Most patients improve within a few days. It is not currently understood how ECT lifts depression. It is speculated that the seizure may alter the functioning of specific brain structures, of neurotransmitters in the brain, or both (Abbott et al., 2014; S. M. Taylor, 2008; Yatham et al., 2010). Identifying the precise effect of shock on all brain functions is rather like finding a needle in a haystack, but research continues to investigate the effect of ECT on depression.

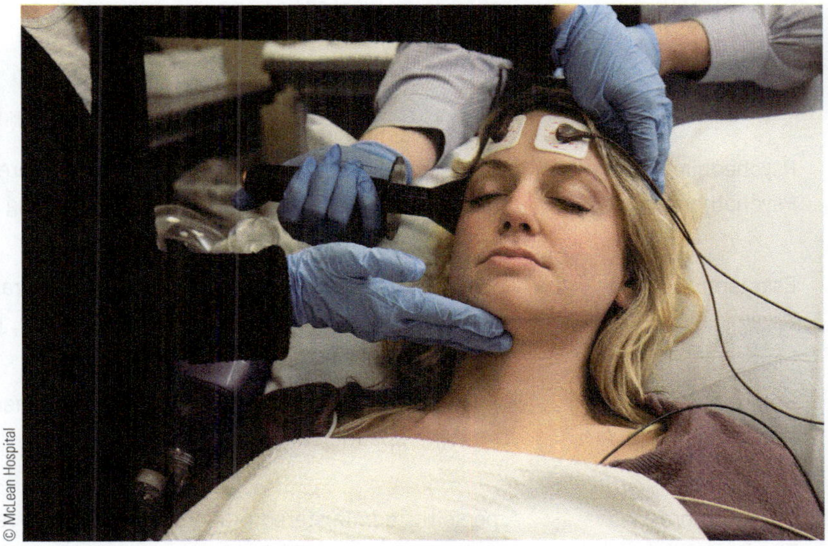

▲ Electroconvulsive therapy (ECT) is a last-resort treatment option administered to patients who are depressed and are not responding to psychotherapy or drug therapy and remain in a severely depressed state.

ECT does have its drawbacks. It can lead to cognitive impairments, such as memory loss, learning difficulties, or disturbances in verbal abilities. A second concern in using ECT is the high relapse rate. Many ECT patients relapse into depression. The period of greatest risk of relapse is the first 6 months after treatment (Jelovac, Kolshus, & McLoughlin, 2013). Despite ECT's short-term effectiveness, these concerns—as well as people's fears about administering electrical shock to the brain—continue to make ECT a very controversial treatment approach.

14.8.3 Cutting-Edge Biomedical Treatments: Emerging Alternatives

Mental health disorders affect millions of U.S. adults each year. The majority of these people, if they receive appropriate treatment, will return to productive lives. Yet, for a very small minority, their disorders are severely disabling over a prolonged period of time and they have not responded to standard psychotherapy and/or biomedical treatments. For these few, emerging alternatives in biomedical therapy can be a life saver.

Space considerations prohibit a detailed discussion of each technique but • Table 14.4 describes some of these cutting-edge trends and the symptoms that they are designed to treat. Notice that some are drug therapies (see Garcia-Romeu et al., 2016 for review) and others are what are referred to as **neurosurgery for mental disorder (NMD)**. Such neurosurgery involves surgically altering the brain to alleviate symptoms in someone with a mental health disorder (see Barrett, 2017 for review). For example, a neurosurgeon may lesion (destroy) a small target area of the brain to reduce severe symptoms of obsessive-compulsive disorder. Research suggests that approximately 25% to 30% of patients who have undergone this procedure improve significantly (Patel et al., 2013; Read & Greenberg, 2009; Shah et al., 2008). Similarly, implanting deep brain stimulators in people with severe cases of obsessive-compulsive disorder also shows promising results and has received FDA approval as a "humanitarian device exemption" moving it toward limited clinical use (Blomstedt et al., 2013; Huff et al., 2010; Read & Greenberg, 2009; Shah et al., 2008). Keep in mind, however, that such procedures are experimental, performed very infrequently, and only as a last resort after all standard methods of treatment have been exhausted.

neurosurgery for mental disorder a biomedical treatment approach involving surgically altering the brain to alleviate symptoms in someone with a mental health disorder

TABLE 14.4 Emerging Biomedical Therapy Techniques

Treatment	Description	Potential Symptoms Treated
	Drug Therapies	
Psychedelic-Assisted Psychotherapy	Drugs such as LSD or psilocybin (mushrooms) are administered in a medically supervised psychotherapeutic setting embedded within ongoing psychotherapy sessions.	Substance use, anxiety, major depression, OCD
Esketamine Nasal Spray	Approved by the FDA and taken along with an oral antidepressant, a nasal spray containing the anesthetic, ketamine, is self-administered under the supervision of a health care provider.	Depression
Ketamine-Assisted Psychotherapy (KAP)	Ketamine, an anesthetic, is administered in a medically supervised psychotherapeutic setting.	Depression, bipolar disorder, suicidal behavior, PTSD, OCD, chronic pain
Burst Suppression Therapy	A person is administered propofol anesthesia to reach 80% burst-suppression on an EEG indicating a severe reduction in brain activity. The person is maintained there for 15 minutes after which the propofol is discontinued and the person is allowed to awaken.	Depression
MDMA-Assisted Psychotherapy	Prescribed doses of MDMA are administered a few times (not every time) within a medically supervised psychotherapeutic setting.	PTSD
	Neurosurgery	
Deep Brain Stimulation	Electrodes are surgically implanted in a specific brain area (based on the disorder) and connected to a pacemaker-like pulse generator implanted in the chest that typically provides continuous electrical stimulation.	Depression, OCD
Vagus Nerve Stimulation	An FDA approved procedure that involves stimulating the vagus nerve in the neck via electrical shocks from a pacemaker-like pulse generator implanted in the chest.	Depression
Gamma-Knife Surgery	Delivers highly focused radiation deep within the brain to lesion or destroy targeted brain areas.	OCD, depression, substance use
Cingulotomy	Specialized laser systems or a gamma knife are used to create small lesions in all or parts of the cingulate gyrus.	OCD, depression, substance use
Anterior Capsulotomy	Specialized laser systems or a gamma knife are used to create small lesions in the anterior limb of the internal capsule (separates the caudate nucleus and lenticular nucleus in the brain).	OCD, depression

14.8 Quiz Yourself

1. Electroconvulsive therapy is most effective for the treatment of _____.
   a. schizophrenia
   b. panic attacks
   c. severe depression
   d. bipolar disorder
2. Which of the following is the most serious side effect of taking conventional antipsychotic medication?
   a. Rebound anxiety
   b. Physical dependence
   c. Hallucinations
   d. Tardive dyskinesia
3. Prozac is what type of antidepressant drug?
   a. SSRI
   b. MAO inhibitor
   c. Tricyclic
   d. Benzodiazepine

Answers 1. c; 2. d; 3. a

14.9 Integrating Psychology: The Big Picture

This chapter has outlined the major types of psychotherapies and biomedical therapies. We have seen that each therapeutic approach stems from one of the main theoretical perspectives introduced in the beginning of this textbook: *biological*, *psychoanalytic*, *cognitive*, *behavioral*, and *humanistic*. The aim of all therapies is to improve a person's ability to function, yet some focus on altering biology (drug therapy), while others focus on psychological factors (cognitions, emotions, learning) or one's social relationships and interpersonal functioning. We have also seen that therapy is generally effective, regardless of the specific techniques endorsed and that in many cases using an eclectic approach that combines *biopsychosocial* methods can be very effective. Of course, the effectiveness of therapy also will be related to the characteristics of the therapist and the client, as was illustrated by Emily and Dr. Farber's therapeutic alliance.

We hope that you have enjoyed your journey through *What Is Psychology? Foundations, Applications, and Integration*. We have provided you with a *foundation* of psychological concepts and research that we encourage you to *apply* to your life. Remember that behavior and mental processes are never due to just one cause and that there is a complicated interaction among biological, psychological, and social variables that best explains behavior, and this explanation may vary from individual to individual. Acknowledging this *integration* and complexity will further your understanding of not only your behavior but also the behavior of those around you. Good luck!

Studying the Chapter

Key Terms

antianxiety medications (643)
antidepressants (645)
antimanic medications (646)
antipsychotic medications (644)
anxiety hierarchy (626)
aversion therapy (628)
behavior therapy (625)
biomedical therapy (616)
client-centered therapy (623)
cognitive-behavioral therapy (CBT) (634)
cognitive distortions (632)
cognitive therapy (632)
couple therapy (636)
covert sensitization therapy (629)
dream analysis (621)
eclectic therapy approach (639)
electroconvulsive therapy (ECT) (648)
empathy (623)
eye movement desensitization and reprocessing (EMDR) therapy (639)
family therapy (635)
flooding (628)
free association (621)
genuineness (624)
group therapy (635)
interpretations (621)
lithium (646)
mindfulness-based cognitive therapy (MBCT) (639)
neurosurgery for mental disorder (NMD) (649)
psychoanalysis (620)
psychodynamic therapy (622)
psychopharmacology (642)
psychotherapy (616)
rational-emotive therapy (631)
resistance (621)
selective serotonin reuptake inhibitors (SSRIs) (646)
self-help groups (637)
systematic desensitization (626)
tardive dyskinesia (644)
therapeutic alliance (640)
therapy (615)
token economy (630)
transcranial magnetic stimulation (TMS) (648)
transference (621)
unconditional positive regard (624)

What Do You Know? Assess Your Understanding

Test your retention and understanding of the material by answering the following questions.

1. Most psychotherapists hold at least a(n) ______ degree and in most states hold an appropriate license or certificate.
   a. bachelor's
   b. associate's
   c. master's
   d. doctorate

2. Which of the following is *not* an ethical guideline of psychotherapists?
   a. Inform the client of the nature of the treatment.
   b. Never break the confidentiality of communications with client.
   c. Interact appropriately with clients.
   d. Provide adequate treatment.

3. ______ uses techniques such as free association and dream analysis to uncover hidden conflicts.
   a. Psychoanalysis
   b. Cognitive therapy
   c. Behavior therapy
   d. Client-centered therapy

4. Which psychotherapy would use systematic desensitization to treat a person with a specific phobia?
   a. Psychoanalysis
   b. Cognitive therapy
   c. Behavior therapy
   d. Client-centered therapy

5. In which psychotherapy does the therapist challenge the illogical beliefs of the client?
   a. Behavior therapy
   b. Rational-emotive therapy
   c. Client-centered therapy
   d. Psychodynamic therapy

6. Dr. Ramon expresses genuineness and empathy to the client. Dr. Ramon is most likely engaging in ______.
   a. psychoanalysis
   b. cognitive therapy
   c. behavior therapy
   d. client-centered therapy

7. Dr. Andrews reinforces appropriate client behavior and ignores inappropriate behavior. Dr. Andrews is engaging in ______.
   a. psychoanalysis
   b. cognitive therapy
   c. behavior therapy
   d. client-centered therapy

8. Dr. Shu reflects the client's thoughts and feelings so that the client's problems can be better understood. Dr. Shu is engaging in ______.
   a. behavior modification
   b. client-centered therapy
   c. rational-emotive therapy
   d. free association

9. Which type of therapy pairs an unpleasant stimulus with the problem behavior in the hopes of reducing its occurrence?
   a. Aversion therapy
   b. Systematic desensitization
   c. Token economy
   d. Client-centered therapy

10. Dr. Tyler teaches the client how to recognize negative automatic thought patterns. Dr. Tyler is engaging in ______.
    a. rational-emotive therapy
    b. systematic desensitization
    c. cognitive therapy
    d. psychodynamic therapy

11. Which of the following is *not* a benefit of group therapy?
    a. It is less expensive than individual psychotherapy.
    b. Therapists can view clients' social interactions.
    c. It offers more one-on-one treatment.
    d. It provides social support from others experiencing the same problem.

12. Dr. Mendel encourages Maurice to paraphrase what his partner says to confirm that he has understood the comment. It is most likely that Maurice is engaged in ______.
    a. psychoanalysis
    b. family therapy
    c. couple therapy
    d. drug therapy

13. Which of the following reflects a potential problem related to the *dependent variable* when evaluating the effectiveness of therapy?
    a. Finding people who have the same disorder to the same degree
    b. Relying on the client's self-report of improvement
    c. Designing a no treatment control group
    d. Training therapists to deliver a specific type of therapy

14. Dr. Garfield and the client have an interactive and collaborative relationship, commonly referred to as a(n) ______.
    a. eclectic approach
    b. therapeutic alliance
    c. psychotherapeutic effect
    d. transference
15. Which of the following is a disadvantage of cybertherapy?
    a. The increased client confidentiality
    b. Provides clients who live far away from therapists access to mental health services
    c. Lacks the close personal contact of face-to-face interactions
    d. It costs more than face-to-face therapy
16. Juanita has been diagnosed with generalized anxiety disorder. A psychiatrist is most likely to prescribe ______ to treat Juanita's symptoms.
    a. lithium
    b. Xanax
    c. Prozac
    d. clozapine
17. Conventional antipsychotic medications affect which neurotransmitter?
    a. Endorphins
    b. Glutamate
    c. GABA
    d. Dopamine
18. Craig has been diagnosed with schizophrenia and has been prescribed Thorazine to reduce delusions and hallucinations. Which of the following side effects might Craig experience from taking this medication long-term?
    a. Loss of sense of smell
    b. Tardive dyskinesia
    c. Fluid retention and rash
    d. Kidney problems
19. Electroconvulsive therapy has been shown to be particularly effective for the treatment of ______.
    a. schizophrenia
    b. severe depression
    c. panic disorder
    d. obsessive-compulsive disorder
20. Which of the following medications has been associated with an increased risk of suicidal thoughts and behaviors in children and adolescents?
    a. Antianxiety drugs
    b. Lithium
    c. SSRI drugs
    d. Antipsychotic drugs

Answers: 1. c; 2. b; 3. a; 4. c; 5. b; 6. d; 7. c; 8. b; 9. a; 10. c; 11. c; 12. c; 13. b; 14. b; 15. c; 16. b; 17. d; 18. b; 19. b; 20. c

Use It or Lose It: Applying Psychology

1. Compare and contrast psychoanalysis and client-centered therapy. What qualities do they have in common? What are their major differences?
2. Which psychotherapy approach do you find the most appealing, and why? Which psychotherapy approach do you find the least appealing, and why?
3. What can the critical components of therapy effectiveness teach us about resolving our own problems? How might these components be useful in group therapy approaches?
4. What are the advantages and disadvantages of using drug therapy to treat mental health problems?
5. Think about a behavior or problem that you have had or are having. Apply a behavior therapy method to change this behavior. What would the behavior and the method be, and how would you go about changing the behavior?

Critical Thinking About the Science of Psychology

Research evaluating the effectiveness of psychotherapy (Section 14.7) typically compares participants who are receiving therapy with participants who are receiving a placebo treatment or no treatment at all. Given this information, answer the following questions:

1. What research method is being used by these studies?
2. What is the independent variable in these types of studies?
3. What is the dependent variable in these types of studies?

Are You Getting the Big Picture?

Therapy consists of techniques that are used to help people with mental health or interpersonal problems.

Laurence Mouton/Getty Images

14.1 Providing Psychological Assistance

- **Psychotherapy** is administered by clinical psychologists, licensed counselors, social workers, and therapists.
- Psychotherapists abide by ethical standards of *confidentiality, competent treatment* that is *culturally sensitive*, *informed consent*, and *appropriate interactions*.
- You should consider therapy if you feel helpless, sad, or nervous for a prolonged period of time or if such feelings do not improve despite several efforts to change them.

iStock.com/FatCamera

14.2 Psychoanalytic Therapies

- Traditional **psychoanalysis** has clients gain insight into the underlying source of their problems. Modern **psychodynamic therapy** also relies on the therapist's **interpretations** of the client's feelings and behaviors but places more emphasis on current problems and interpersonal relations and less on the client's past.

wavebreakmedia/Shutterstock.com

14.3 Humanistic Therapy

- Humanistic therapy such as **client-centered therapy** connects with and understands the client's worldview. The therapist offers **genuineness**, **empathy**, and **unconditional positive regard** to encourage self-exploration and self-fulfillment.

Pormezz/Shutterstock.com

14.4 Behavior Therapies

- **Behavior therapies** use learning principles to change maladaptive behavior.
  - Classical conditioning therapies use techniques such as **systematic desensitization**, *virtual reality exposure therapy*, **flooding**, and **aversion therapy** to change the client's responses to stimuli.
  - Operant conditioning therapies use techniques such as shaping, extinction, positive reinforcement, and **token economies** to change behavior.

BORIS HORVAT/AFP/Getty Images

14.5 Cognitive Therapies

- In cognitive therapies, maladaptive patterns of thinking and perceiving are replaced with more adaptive ways of interpreting events.
  - In **rational-emotive therapy**, the therapist confronts, questions, and challenges the validity of client's irrational beliefs.
  - In **cognitive therapy**, the therapist identifies and tracks negative automatic thoughts and has the client test the accuracy of these **cognitive distortions**.

Courtesy of Beck Institute for Cognitive Therapy and Research

14.6 Group Therapy

- The goal of **group therapy** is to improve the functioning and interactions among individuals, couples, families, or other groups.
- Group therapy tends to be less expensive than individual therapy and offers a safe mini-environment in which to explore new social behaviors or to understand how our interactions with others may be impeding our mental health.

Monkey Business Images/Shutterstock.com

14.7 Effective Psychotherapy: Do Treatments Work?

- Generally, the different psychotherapy approaches produce relatively equivalent results in terms of client improvement.
- A personalized approach to treatment is becoming more common as many therapists adopt an **eclectic therapy approach** that involves an integrated and diverse use of therapeutic methods. Examples include **cognitive-behavioral therapy (CBT)**, **mindfulness-based cognitive therapy (MBCT)**, and **eye-movement desensitization and reprocessing therapy (EMDR)**.
- *Behavioral intervention* and *e-health technologies* as well as *cybertherapy* are tools that can enhance the delivery of psychotherapy, yet present ethical considerations.

GARO/PHANIE/Age Fotostock

14.8 Biomedical Therapies

- **Biomedical therapies** are administered by psychiatrists and other medical professionals.
- The most common biomedical therapy is **psychopharmacology**, or the use of medications to treat mental health problems. Drug therapies influence brain neurotransmitters to alter behavior.
  - **Antianxiety medications** are prescribed to reduce tension and anxiety.
  - **Antipsychotic medications** are prescribed to relieve psychotic symptoms such as agitation, delusions, disordered thinking, and hallucinations.
  - **Antidepressants** are prescribed for depressive, bipolar, and anxiety disorders, eating disorders, substance-related disorders, and obsessive-compulsive disorder.
  - **Antimanic medications** are used primarily to treat mania.
- More controversial biomedical therapies include noninvasive brain stimulation procedures such as **transcranial magnetic stimulation (TMS)** and **electroconvulsive therapy (ECT)**, and **neurosurgery for mental disorder**.

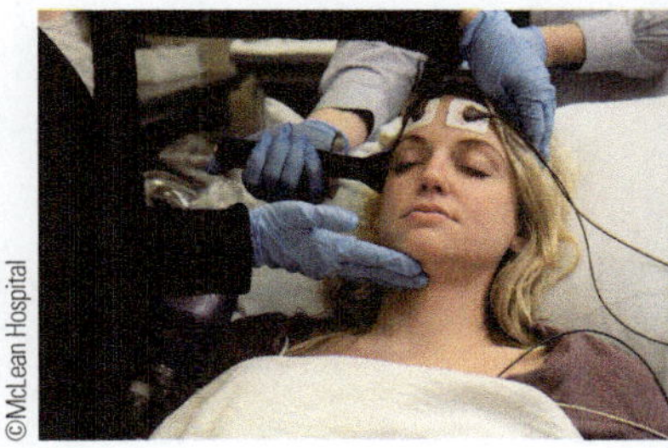

©McLean Hospital

A Statistics in Psychology

Learning Objectives

A.1 Define the terms data and statistics, and explain how they are used in science. (APA 2.4)

A.1 Describe the different types of graphs and distributions used in statistical analyses, including frequency distributions, frequency polygons, histograms, and scatter plots. (APA 2.4)

A.2 Calculate and interpret the different measures of central tendency used in statistics: the mean, median, and mode. (APA 2.4)

A.3 Calculate and interpret the different measures of variability used in statistics: the range, variance, and standard deviation. (APA 2.4)

A.4 Explain what a normal and standard normal distribution are. (APA 2.4)

A.5 Calculate and interpret a *z* score and a correlation coefficient. (APA 2.4)

A.6 Explain the logic behind inferential statistics, hypothesis testing, and statistical significance. (APA 2.4)

Appendix Outline

A.1 Using Statistics to Describe Data

As you learned in Chapter 1, psychology is the scientific study of behavior and mental processes. Psychologists develop hypotheses about behavior and mental processes and then test these hypotheses using experiments, case studies, surveys, naturalistic observations, or other research methods. In the course of their research, psychologists collect a variety of information, or **data**, from their research participants.

data information gathered in scientific studies

Imagine that you are a health psychologist interested in whether the legal drinking age in a country affects the rate of underage drinking in that society. More specifically, you might ask questions like these: "Does having a lower legal drinking age encourage drinking among 15-year-olds? And if so, does the legal drinking age equally affect both male and female 15-year-olds?" To see whether such relationships exist, you must first collect data on the number of 15-year-olds who drink in particular countries, along with each country's legal drinking age (see ● TABLE A.1).

Take a moment to look at the data in Table A.1. By just looking at the table, can you tell whether a relationship exists between the percentage of 15-year-old students who drink and a country's minimum legal drinking age? If you cannot, you are in good company—it's impossible to tell from just a table whether the

TABLE A.1 Percentage of Students Who Report Drinking Alcohol Weekly at Age 15, Selected Countries

Country	Minimum Legal Drinking Age	% Males	% Females
Austria	16	39	23
Belgium	16	38	22
Canada	18	22	17
Czech Republic	18	32	19
Denmark	15	46	38
England	18	47	36
Estonia	18*	21	10
Finland	18	11	8
France	16	31	15
Germany	16	29	22
Greece	16*	52	31
Greenland	18	13	10
Hungary	16	29	11
Ireland	18	27	12
Israel	18	26	10
Latvia	18	28	12
Lithuania	21	16	9
Northern Ireland	18	33	20
Norway	18	16	12
Poland	18	20	8
Portugal	16	29	9
Russia	18	28	24
Scotland	18	37	33
Slovakia	18	32	16
Sweden	18	17	11
Switzerland	16	19	9
United States	21	23	15
Wales	18	53	36

Source: Except where noted, data taken from Kaul, C. (2002). *Statistical Handbook on the World's Children* (p. 447). Westport, CT: Oryx Press.

*Data from http://www2.potsdam.edu/alcohol-info/LegalDrinkingAge.html#worlddrinkingages

statistics a type of applied mathematics used to describe data and test hypotheses

graph a visual depiction of data

frequency distribution a graph of data that plots the frequency of data points on the *y*-axis and the data points themselves on the *x*-axis

data support one's hypothesis. Instead, psychologists must use a type of applied mathematics, called **statistics**, to describe and analyze their data. Only then can a researcher determine what the data say about their hypothesis.

A.1.1 Graphs: Depicting Data Visually

Take another look at the data in Table A.1. Where would you start if you wanted to see whether the legal drinking age is related to drinking rates among 15-year-olds? Well, have you ever heard that *a picture is worth a thousand words*? One way to start would be to create a **graph**, or pictorial representation, of the data. Psychologists use many different types of graphs to help analyze their data. One of the more common graphs is a **frequency distribution**. A graph of a frequency distribution is a two-dimensional illustration that plots how frequently certain events occur. For example, it might be useful to see the frequency, or rate, at which countries have set certain minimum drinking ages. This information could be depicted using several types of graphs to illustrate the frequency distribution; two of the more common ones are a **frequency polygon** (a line graph) and a **histogram** (a bar graph). ● FIGURE A.1 shows the frequency distribution of legal drinking age depicted in a frequency polygon; ● FIGURE A.2 shows the same frequency distribution using a histogram. By looking at either one of these graphs, we can see that most of these selected governments have set their minimum drinking age below 21 and that the most commonly set drinking age is 18.

An even more useful type of graph for this investigation would be a **scatter plot**. In a scatter plot, two variables are plotted as a function of each other. For example, we could plot the percentage of 15-year-old drinkers as a function of the country's minimum drinking age. ● FIGURE A.3 shows such plots separately for males and females. By looking at the scatter plots in Figure A.3, you can get a

frequency polygon a line graph that is used to illustrate a frequency distribution

histogram a bar graph that is used to illustrate a frequency distribution

scatter plot a graph of data that plots pairs of data points, with one data point on the *x*-axis and the other on the *y*-axis

FIGURE A.1

Frequency Polygon

Frequency polygon showing the frequency distribution for minimum drinking age in 28 countries (data from Table A.1).

FIGURE A.2

Histogram

Histogram showing the frequency distribution for minimum drinking age in 28 countries (data from Table A.1).

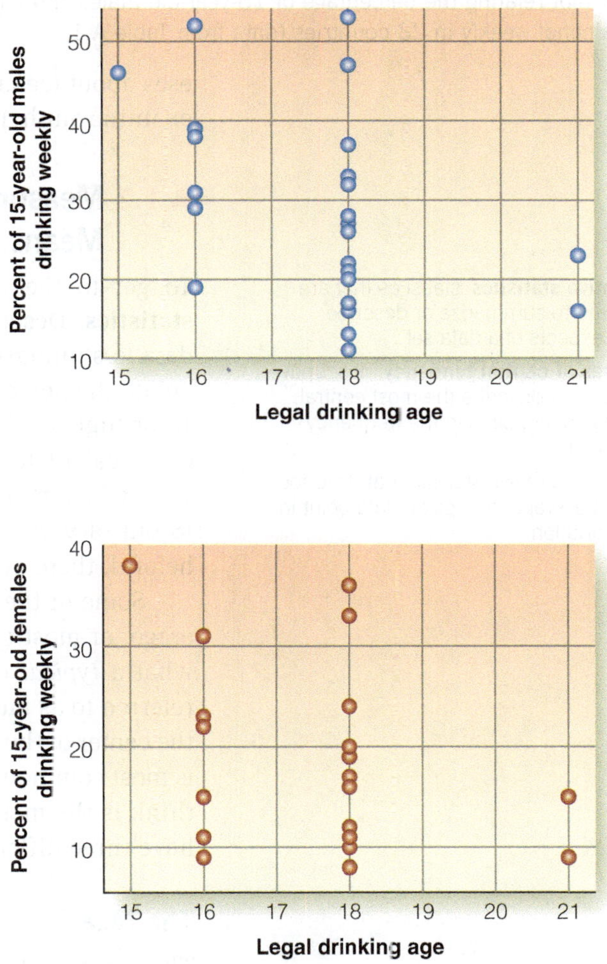

FIGURE A.3

Drinking at Age 15 as a Function of Minimum Legal Drinking Age

Scatter plots of the percentage of 15-year-olds who drink weekly as a function of minimum legal drinking age in 28 countries (data from Table A.1).

very crude picture of the relationship between drinking age and the rate of underage drinking at age 15. Looking at Figure A.3, as the minimum drinking age decreases, does the rate of underage drinking increase? Do these data confirm or discount our hypothesis that lowering the drinking age encourages underage drinking? Although it is true that countries with a minimum drinking age of 16 or younger have relatively high levels of underage drinking, there are also a number of countries with a minimum drinking age of 18 that have high levels of underage drinking by 15-year-olds.

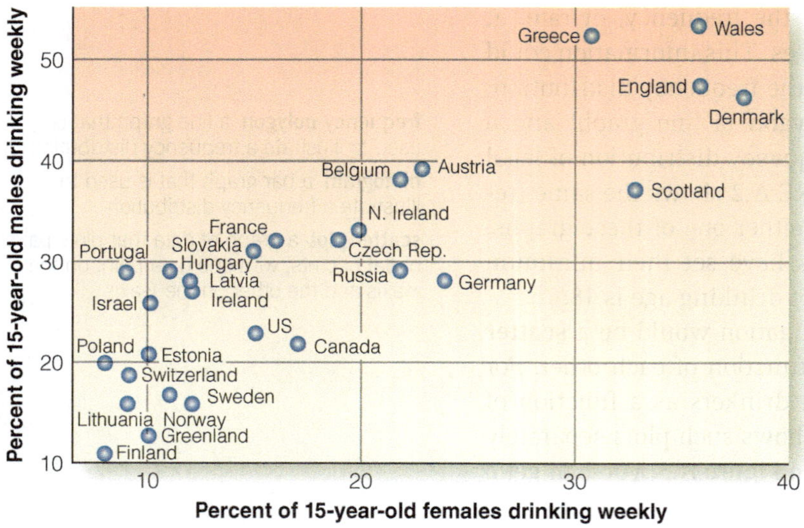

FIGURE A.4

Drinking at Age 15 of Males Versus Females

Scatter plot relating the percentage of 15-year-old males and females who drink alcohol weekly in 28 countries (data from Table A.1).

● FIGURE A.4 is another scatter plot, this time relating male and female rates of drinking. It appears from this graph that as more males drink, more females also engage in drinking—but if you look closely at the scatter plot, this isn't *always* true. Therefore, these plots only give us a crude picture of the relationship between our variables. It's impossible to say for sure whether our hypotheses about teenage drinking have merit simply by looking at these plots. To truly examine our hypotheses, we will have to delve deeper into our statistical analysis.

A.1.2 Measures of Central Tendency: Means, Medians, and Modes

descriptive statistics statistics that are calculated to summarize or describe certain aspects of a data set

measures of central tendency descriptive statistics that describe the most central, or typical, data points in the frequency distribution

mean a descriptive statistic that describes the most average, or typical, data point in the distribution

To get to the heart of the matter, we are going to have to use **descriptive statistics**. Descriptive statistics are numerical values that are calculated on the data to summarize and describe the data as a whole. For example, you could calculate the percentage of these 28 countries that have a minimum drinking age of 18 or higher. This percentage would be 19 of the 28 countries, or 67.9%. Or you could calculate the percentage of countries with a minimum drinking age under 18 in which more than 25% of their male sample indicated that they drank weekly (8 out of 9 countries, or 88.9%). Although such percentages can sometimes be helpful, there are other, better statistical methods to use in this situation.

Some of the most useful descriptive statistics are those that describe the average, or most typical, entry in a data set—in other words, a statistic that shows what a *typical* country's legal drinking age is. These measures are collectively referred to as **measures of central tendency** because they tell us something about the center of the frequency distribution (in this case, what minimum drinking age is most common, or most typical). Look again at Figures A.1 and A.2. What do you think is the most common minimum drinking age? To answer this question, we have three different measures of central tendency: the *mean*, *median*, and *mode*.

The Mean

The **mean** is the average of a distribution. To calculate the mean, you add up all of the data points and then divide the total by the number of data points. This formula can be expressed with this equation:

$$\bar{X} = \frac{\Sigma X}{N}$$

where

$\overline{X}$ = the symbol for the mean;

Σ = a mathematical symbol that means to sum up the items that follow it;

X = the individual data points in the distribution;

N = the total number of data points or scores in the distribution.

The calculations for the average minimum drinking age and the average percentages of males and females who drink weekly at age 15 are shown in • TABLE A.2.

median a descriptive statistic that identifies the center of the frequency distribution; 50% of the scores are above and 50% are below this point in the distribution

outliers unusual data points that are at the extremes of the frequency distribution and either far above or below the mean

The Median

Another measure of central tendency is the **median**, or the score that is at the center of a frequency distribution. To find the median, you must first list all of the scores in ascending order. Once this is done, simply find the score that is at the center of this ordered list of scores. The calculation of the median legal drinking age is shown in • FIGURE A.5. As you can see by comparing Figure A.5 and Table A.2, the median and the mean are not the same number. This shows one advantage of the median over the mean.

The mean is highly affected by unusual scores, or **outliers**, in the distribution. In this case, one country, Denmark, has an unusually low drinking age of 15. Although Denmark's minimum drinking age of 15 does not differ very much from the more common limit of 16, Denmark is the only country to set the age this low, and this outlying score works to lower the mean somewhat. However, because the median is simply the center score of the distribution, it is unaffected by unusual scores. So whereas the mean drinking age is 17.5, the median drinking age is somewhat higher at 18.

When a distribution contains outliers, the median is the better choice for measuring central tendency. This is especially true for situations in which the outliers are more extreme than in our drinking-age example. For instance, assume that in a class of 10 students, 9 students score a 75 on an exam, and 1 student scores a 15. The mean for the class would be 69, but the median would be 75. That's a difference of more than half a letter grade between these two measures of central tendency, with the median more accurately reflecting how most students scored on the exam.

TABLE A.2 Average Minimum Drinking Age and Average Percentage of Students Who Report Drinking Alcohol Weekly at Age 15, Selected Countries

Country	Minimum Legal Drinking Age	% Males	% Females
Austria	16	39	23
Belgium	16	38	22
Canada	18	22	17
Czech Republic	18	32	19
Denmark	15	46	38
England	18	47	36
Estonia	18*	21	10
Finland	18	11	8
France	16	31	15
Germany	16	29	22
Greece	16*	52	31
Greenland	18	13	10
Hungary	16	29	11
Ireland	18	27	12
Israel	18	26	10
Latvia	18	28	12
Lithuania	21	16	9
Northern Ireland	18	33	20
Norway	18	16	12
Poland	18	20	8
Portugal	16	29	9
Russia	18	28	24
Scotland	18	37	33
Slovakia	18	32	16
Sweden	18	17	11
Switzerland	16	19	9
United States	21	23	15
Wales	18	53	36
ΣX	491	814	498
$\overline{X} = \frac{\Sigma X}{N}$	491/28 = 17.5	814/28 = 29.1	498/28 = 17.8

Source: Except where noted, data taken from Kaul, C. (2002). *Statistical Handbook on the World's Children* (p. 447). Westport, CT: Oryx Press.

*Data from http://www2.potsdam.edu/alcohol-info/LegalDrinkingAge.html#worlddrinkingages

First take all of the minimum legal drinking ages for the countries and list them in ascending order:

15, 16, 16, 16, 16, 16, 16, 16, 16, 18, 18, 18, 18, 18, 18, 18, 18, 18, 18, 18, 18, 18, 18, 18, 18, 18, 21, 21

Now find the score at the center of this distribution. In this case, because there is an even number of scores ($N = 28$) the center of this distribution would be between the 14th and 15th score in the list. Therefore, to find the median or X_{50}, we would average the 14th and 15th score:

$$(18 + 18)/2 = 18$$

$$X_{50} = 18$$

FIGURE A.5

Calculation of the Median Legal Drinking Age

The Mode

The final measure of central tendency is the **mode,** or the most frequent score in the distribution. If you look again at Figure A.1 (or Figure A.2), you will see that the most frequent, or most common, drinking age is 18. Therefore, like the median, the mode is also 18. The mode is an especially useful measure of central tendency when the data being examined are not numerical (for example, the most typical car color in the student parking lot).

Measures of central tendency tell us something about the most representative scores at the center of the frequency distribution, but they do not tell us anything about the range, or breadth, of the scores in the distribution. To determine this characteristic of the distribution, we will have to look at *measures of variability*.

A.1.3 Measures of Variability: Analyzing the Distribution of Data

Variability refers to the degree to which the individual scores of the distribution tend to *differ* from the central tendency of the distribution. In other words, variability measures how spread out the frequency distribution is. Look back at Figure A.1. As we just saw, the mean drinking age is 17.5. As you would expect, most of the scores in the frequency distribution are clustered around 18, but that does not mean that *all* of the scores are close in value to 18. Some scores are as low as 15, and some are as high as 21. Measures of variability tell us about the degree to which these more extreme scores differ from the mean. The simplest measure of variability is the **range** of the distribution, or the difference between the highest and lowest values in the distribution. In this case, the range of drinking ages would be $21 - 15 = 6$ years.

Although the range is a measure of variability, it is fairly crude in that it doesn't really tell us the degree to which most scores differ from the mean. Another measure of variability, called the **variance**, takes into account the difference between the individual scores of the distribution and the mean of the distribution. The first step to calculating the variance is to calculate the mean of the distribution. The next step is to calculate the **sum of squares** of the distribution. Here, *squares* refers to the difference between each score in the distribution and the mean of the distribution, with this difference being taken to the second power (i.e., squared, or multiplied by itself). So, the sum of squares (*SS*) can be calculated using the following equation:

$$SS = \Sigma(X - \bar{X})^2$$

Once you have calculated *SS*, to calculate the variance (S^2), simply divide by the total number of scores minus one ($N - 1$). The formula to the right is a *computational formula* that is easier to calculate by hand as it will not involve decimals. Both formulae will give the same answer if correctly used.

$$S^2 = \frac{\Sigma(X - \bar{X})^2}{N - 1} = \frac{N\Sigma X^2 - (\Sigma X)^2}{N(N - 1)}$$

Another measure of variability is the **standard deviation** (*S*), or the square root of the variance:

$$S = \sqrt{\frac{\Sigma(X - \bar{X})^2}{N - 1}} = \sqrt{\frac{N\Sigma X^2 - (\Sigma X)^2}{N(N - 1)}}$$

mode a measure of central tendency that identifies the most common, or frequent, score in the distribution

range a measure of variability that is the difference between the high score and the low score of the distribution

variance a measure of variability that shows on average how much the scores vary from the mean

sum of squares the sum of the squared errors, or deviations, from the mean for the scores in the distribution; the numerator of the variance equation

standard deviation a measure of variability equal to the square root of the variance; often used to gauge the degree to which an individual score deviates from the mean of a distribution

***z* score** a measure of relative standing that measures the distance of a score from the mean of the distribution in standard deviation units

normal distribution a bell-shaped, symmetric frequency distribution

All three measures of variability indicate the degree to which the scores in the distribution are dispersed. The higher these measures are, the more dispersion, or spread, there is among the scores. Although it may be difficult to see why you would want to know the variability of a distribution, one reason is that you can use the standard deviation as a ruler, or guideline, for judging how atypical or typical a score in the distribution is.

To see how this works, take a look at ● FIGURE A.6. Figure A.6 shows the calculation of the standard deviation for the male drinking percentages across the 28 countries. As you can see, the standard deviation for the distribution of male drinking scores is 11.24. We can use this figure to gauge how unusual a specific score in the distribution is. Using the standard deviation and the mean of the distribution, we can calculate a ***z* score**, which expresses the degree to which an individual score differs from the mean of the distribution in terms of the standard deviation of the distribution.

$$Z_x = \frac{X - \bar{X}}{S}$$

For example, in Germany, 29% of 15-year-old males drink weekly. This means that Germany's score would be

$$Z_x = (29 - 29.1)/11.24 = -.009.$$

Germany's *z* score indicates that the percentage of German 15-year-old males who drink is far less than one standard deviation below the mean of 29.1 for all of the 28 countries. This is illustrated graphically in ● FIGURE A.7.

Now look at the figure reported for Wales. In Wales, 53% of the 15-year-old males surveyed were drinking. Wales's *z* score of 2.13 indicates that their score of 53% is more than 2 standard deviations above the mean. This indicates that Wales's experience is not very typical of the average country's experience with male underage drinking at age 15. Wales *seems* to have a bigger problem with this issue than the average country does, but is this deviation from the mean enough of a problem to worry about? To answer this, we have to assess the probability that a given country would have a particular percentage of its young men drinking alcohol on a weekly basis. Luckily, we might be able to do this.

Country $N = 28$	X = Percentage of 15-Year-Old Males Drinking Alcohol	X^2
Austria	39	1521
Belgium	38	1444
Canada	22	484
Czech Republic	32	1024
Denmark	46	2116
England	47	2209
Estonia	21	441
Finland	11	121
France	31	961
Germany	29	841
Greece	52	2704
Greenland	13	169
Hungary	29	841
Ireland	27	729
Israel	26	676
Latvia	28	784
Lithuania	16	256
Northern Ireland	33	1089
Norway	16	256
Poland	20	400
Portugal	29	841
Russia	28	784
Scotland	37	1369
Slovakia	32	1024
Sweden	17	289
Switzerland	19	361
United States	23	529
Wales	53	2809
	$\sum X = 814$	$\sum X^2 = 27{,}072$
	$(\sum X)^2 = 814^2 = 662{,}596$	

$$S = \sqrt{\frac{N\sum X^2 - (\sum X)^2}{N(N-1)}} = \sqrt{\frac{28(27{,}072) - 662\ 596}{28(28-1)}} = \sqrt{\frac{95{,}420}{756}} = 11.24$$

Legend: $\bar{X}$ = the mean; S^2 = the sample variance; S = the standard deviation; $\sum$ = a symbol that means sum up the items that follow; N = the total number of scores or data points

FIGURE A.6

Calculation of the Standard Deviation for the Percentage of Males Drinking Weekly at Age 15

A.1.4 Normal and Standard Normal Distributions

Many variables, such as height, weight, IQ, and so on, have a **normal distribution**. In other words, if you measured these characteristics for a very large number of people and plotted them in a frequency distribution, the resulting graph would

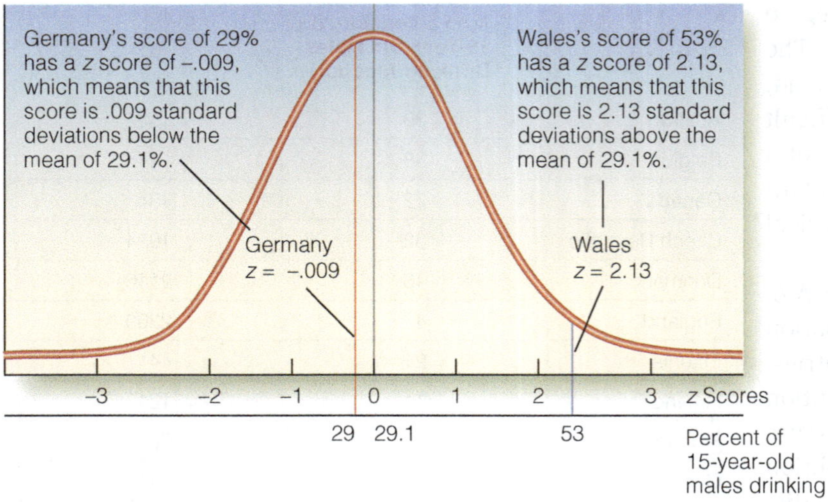

FIGURE A.7

z Scores for Germany and Wales

The mean, or average, percentage of 15-year-old males who drank was 29.1% and the standard deviation was 11.24 across the 28 countries. This figure shows the individual *z* scores for the percentage of 15-year-old males drinking in Germany and Wales. *Z* scores indicate how many standard deviations away from the mean a particular score falls. As you can see, Germany has a slightly below average percentage of 15-year-old male drinkers, with a raw score of 29% and a *z* score of −.009. Wales is quite a bit above average in its male underage drinking, with a raw score of 53% and a *z* score of 2.13.

be bell-shaped and symmetrical, like the one in Figure A.7. If we assume that drinking behavior is normally distributed, then we can also assume that if we calculated the *z* scores for all of the different countries and plotted them in a frequency distribution, that distribution of *z* scores would also be a normal distribution, with $\bar{Z} = 0, S = 1$.

When a distribution of *z* scores is normal in shape, it is referred to as the **standard normal distribution**. The great thing about the standard normal distribution is that we know exactly what percentage of the distribution falls between any two scores, as shown in • FIGURE A.8. As you can see, 68.26% of the *z* scores should fall within the range of *z* scores from −1 to +1, whereas only 0.26% of the scores will be below a *z* score of −3 or above a *z* score of +3. The probability that a country would have a *z* score of +2.13 or higher is on the order of a mere 1.7%. So, indeed, Wales seems to have some possible cause for concern here, because the number of 15-year-old males consuming alcohol on a weekly basis is unusual compared to other countries.

standard normal distribution The standard normal distribution is a symmetric, bell-shaped distribution of *z* scores with ($\bar{Z} = 0$, $S = 1$) for which we know the exact area under the curve

correlation coefficient the average product of *z* scores calculated on pairs of scores; describes the degree to which the scores in the pairs are linearly related

A.1.5 The Correlation Coefficient: Measuring Relationships

Take a look again at Figure A.4, the scatter plot for underage drinking in males versus females in the 28 countries. Do you notice anything interesting about this scatter plot? Don't the data points of the scatter plot tend to fall along a line that slopes up to the right of the graph? Doesn't this seem to indicate that there might be a linear relationship between the percentage of 15-year-old males and females drinking alcohol in a country? As one sex drinks more, doesn't the other seem to generally follow suit? To examine the degree to which such a relationship might exist, psychologists would use yet another statistic to describe these data—the **correlation coefficient**. Simply put, the correlation coefficient measures the degree to which pairs of data points fall along a straight line on a scatter plot. The formulae for the correlation coefficient are

$$r = \frac{\Sigma Z_x Z_y}{N} = \frac{N\Sigma XY - (\Sigma X)(\Sigma Y)}{\sqrt{[N\Sigma X^2 - (\Sigma X)^2][N\Sigma Y^2 - (\Sigma Y)^2]}}$$

where

r = the correlation coefficient;

z_x = the *z* score for one of the variables in a pair;

z_y = the *z* score for the other variable of the pair;

N = the total number of pairs of scores;

X and Y refer to the pairs of scores for the variables being correlated.

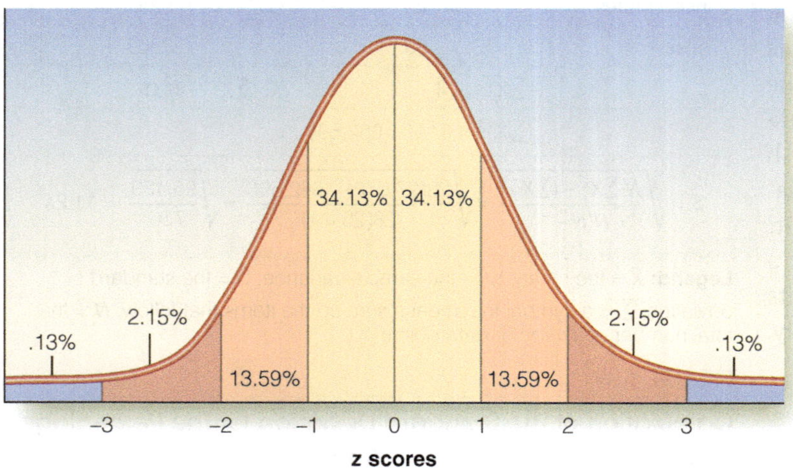

FIGURE A.8

The Standard Normal Distribution of z Scores

The standard normal distribution is a symmetric, bell-shaped distribution of *z* scores with $\bar{Z} = 0$, $S = 1$. The *z* score is the number of standard deviations from the mean that the score is.

The correlation coefficients that can be calculated with this formula have a possible range of $-1 \leq r \leq +1$. See ● FIGURE A.9 for an interpretation of these values. As you can see, an r value of 0 (Figure A.9a) indicates no linear relationship between the two variables. As r approaches either -1 (Figure A.9b) or $+1$ (Figure A.9c), the linear relationship between the two variables becomes stronger. Positive r values indicate a *direct* relationship between the variables—as one variable increases, so does the other. Negative r values indicate an *indirect* relationship between the variables—as one variable increases, the other decreases.

Now let's return to our question of a relationship between the percentage of males and females in a particular country who at age 15 drink weekly. Although the formula for r may look scary, if you calculate each piece and then plug these numbers into the computational formula, it is not that bad, we promise! ● FIGURE A.10 shows the calculation of the correlation coefficient for these data using the computational formula. As you can see, there is a strong positive correlation ($r = .87$) between the percentage of males and females who drink alcohol weekly at age 15. This makes sense, because one might expect many of the factors that influence male underage drinking in a country to influence females similarly. One might think that one of these factors would be the legal drinking age in the country—that countries with a younger drinking age would have a higher percentage of 15-year-olds drinking alcohol illegally.

The data, however, do not fully support this hypothesis. In our sample, the correlation between legal drinking age and the percentage of males drinking at 15 is $r = -.412$. This moderately negative correlation indicates that countries with a lower legal drinking age tend to have higher rates of males drinking illegally at age 15. However, such a clear relationship was not found for females. Therefore, we can conclude that having a lower drinking age is *related* to higher rates of drinking at age 15 for males only. Recall from Chapter 1 that correlation does not imply causation here. We cannot say that a lower drinking age *causes* males to drink at 15. We can only say that the two variables are related in a linear fashion.

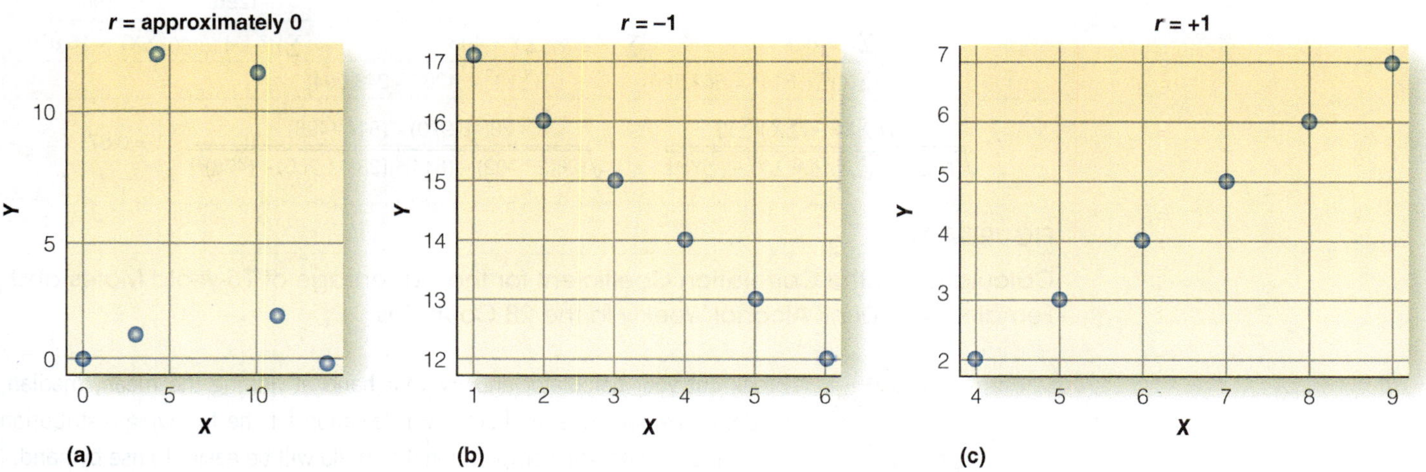

FIGURE A.9

The Correlation Coefficient (r)

Graphic depictions of different values of the correlation coefficient: (a) r = approximately 0; (b) $r = -1$; (c) $r = +1$.

Country N = 28	X = Percentage of 15-yr-old Males Drinking Alcohol	X^2	Y = Percentage of 15-yr-old Females Drinking Alcohol	Y^2	XY
Austria	39	1521	23	529	897
Belgium	38	1444	22	484	836
Canada	22	484	17	289	374
Czech Republic	32	1024	19	361	608
Denmark	46	2116	38	1444	1748
England	47	2209	36	1296	1692
Estonia	21	441	10	100	210
Finland	11	121	8	64	88
France	31	961	15	225	465
Germany	29	841	22	484	638
Greece	52	2704	31	961	1612
Greenland	13	169	10	100	130
Hungary	29	841	11	121	319
Ireland	27	729	12	144	324
Israel	26	676	10	100	260
Latvia	28	784	12	144	336
Lithuania	16	256	9	81	144
Northern Ireland	33	1089	20	400	660
Norway	16	256	12	144	192
Poland	20	400	8	64	160
Portugal	29	841	9	81	261
Russia	28	784	24	576	672
Scotland	37	1369	33	1089	1221
Slovakia	32	1024	16	256	512
Sweden	17	289	11	121	187
Switzerland	19	361	9	81	171
United States	23	529	15	225	345
Wales	53	2809	36	1296	1908
	$\sum X = 814$	$\sum X^2 = 27$	$\sum Y = 498$	$\sum Y^2 = 11{,}260$	$\sum XY = 16{,}970$
	$(\sum X)^2 = 814^2 = 662{,}596$		$(\sum Y)^2 = 498^2 = 248{,}004$		

$$r = \frac{N\sum XY - (\sum X)(\sum Y)}{\sqrt{[N\sum X^2 - (\sum X)^2][N\sum Y^2 - (\sum Y)^2]}} = \frac{28(16{,}970) - (814)(498)}{\sqrt{[28(27{,}702) - (814)^2][28(11{,}260) - (498)^2]}} = 0.87$$

FIGURE A.10

Calculation of the Correlation Coefficient for the Percentage of 15-yr-old Males and Females Who Drink Alcohol Weekly in the 28 Countries

Engage Yourself!

Break out your calculator and try your hand at finding the mean, median, mode, range, variance, and standard deviation for the following distribution of numbers. *Hint*: The computational formula will be easier to use by hand.

Distribution: 10, 21, 11, 5, 10, 13, 13, 19, 7, 2, 10

Answers: Mean=11; median=10; mode=10; range=19; standard deviation=5.55

A.2 Using Statistics to Draw Conclusions

inferential statistics statistics that psychologists use in hypothesis testing to tell them when they should reject or accept their hypotheses about the population

significant results are considered significant when there is a very small chance (usually less than 5%) of finding those results given the assumption that the null hypothesis is true

null hypothesis (H_0) the hypothesis that contains a statement of what we do not believe is true about our variables in the population

alternative hypothesis (H_1) the hypothesis that contains a statement of what we do believe is true about our variables in the population

Inferential statistics are statistics for testing hypotheses about data. In short, inferential statistics help psychologists judge whether observed differences in their data are large enough to be **significant** or meaningful. To illustrate this issue, let's look at the difference in the average rate of drinking for males and females across the 28 countries (see Table A.2). The mean percentage of males drinking at 15 is 29.1%, but the mean percentage of females who report drinking at 15 is only 17.8%. Thus, it appears that males and females are not equally likely to drink at age 15. But is this difference (29.1 − 17.8 = 11.3) large enough to convince us that males really differ from females in their underage drinking? Is it possible that these data are merely a fluke or coincidence? How big a difference must we see between the sexes before we can say that our results are *significant*? These are the questions that inferential statistics tackle.

The first step to understanding inferential statistics is to understand the nature of hypotheses. In all studies that use inferential statistics, the researcher sets forth two hypotheses. The first one, called the **null hypothesis** (H_0), is a statement of what the researcher does not believe to be true about the variables. The second one, called the **alternative hypothesis** (H_1), is a statement of what the researcher *does* believe to be true about the variables. In our example, these would be

$$H_0\text{: } \mu_{\text{males}} = \mu_{\text{females}}$$
$$H_1\text{: } \mu_{\text{males}} \neq \mu_{\text{females}}$$

where

$\mu_{\textbf{males}}$ = the mean percent of males drinking in the entire population of all 15-year-old males;

$\mu_{\textbf{females}}$ = the mean percent of females drinking in the entire population of all 15-year-old females.

In other words, we do *not* believe that the rate of drinking is the same for males and females across the world at age 15. Rather, we believe that 15-year-old males drink at a different rate than 15-year-old females. Although it may seem odd, the way that scientists proceed from this point is to try to show that the null hypothesis is correct. Rather than directly testing the notion set forth in the alternative hypothesis, we instead test the hypothesis that contains the statement of what we do *not* believe to be true about our variables. So for the moment, we will assume that there is no difference between the rates of drinking for males and females at age 15. We will analyze our data to see whether they support this notion or whether we must reject this null hypothesis in favor of the alternative hypothesis that at age 15, males and females do indeed differ in their rates of drinking alcohol.

To test the null hypothesis, we must determine the probability of finding our results (that 29.1% of males and 17.8% of females were drinking), given the *assumption* that there is no real difference between the males and females when it comes to drinking at age 15. This is where a standard distribution comes in handy. If we can calculate a statistic on our data for which we know the distribution and the probabilities of obtaining certain values of the statistic, then we can determine how likely or unlikely it would be to get our results simply by accident or chance. In a sense, we did this earlier when we looked at the probability of finding that Wales had a rate of drinking for males that was 2.13 standard deviations above the mean. When we found that the probability of Wales having a z score of 2.13 was only about

1.7%, we were then fairly confident that the rate of male drinking in Wales was significantly different from most of the other countries. So, how low a probability is low enough for us to say that our results are significant? Generally speaking, psychologists are comfortable dealing with results that have probabilities less than 5%, although in some cases the significance level might be placed at a lower percentage.

Going back to our current example, the question now is this: "Is there a 5% or less probability of finding that 29.1% of the males and 17.8% of the females in our sample drink, if there is indeed *no* difference between 15-year-old males and females in the population at large?" If we find that the probability of obtaining our results is less than 5%, then we can safely conclude that our null hypothesis is likely incorrect, and we should *reject* it in favor of the alternative hypothesis. If we find that the probability of obtaining our results is greater than 5%, then we must accept our null hypothesis and admit that we were likely wrong in formulating our alternative hypothesis.

So how do we go about finding the probability of our results? Unfortunately, a detailed explanation of how we would determine this probability is beyond the scope of this text. If you ever take a statistics class, you will learn how this number is determined. However, so as not to leave you in suspense, we will tell you how the story ends. If the null hypothesis is true and there is no difference between male and female drinking in the population, the probability of finding our results (that 29.1% of males and 17.8% of females drink at age 15) is close to 0. This means that it is highly unlikely that males and females drink equally at age 15, and we can safely reject our null hypothesis in favor of the alternative hypothesis.

A.3 Summary

We hope that this appendix has helped you get a very basic understanding of how psychologists use statistics. Statistics are the major tool through which we as scientists judge the validity of our research results. Without statistics, we would have no way to separate the flukes and coincidences of life from the true, meaningful differences that exist in the world. We use statistics to describe our data, and in doing so, we use graphs or plots to visually depict data. We use measures of central tendency, such as the mean, median, and mode, to describe the center, or most typical, score in a frequency distribution. We use measures of variability, such as the range, variance, or standard deviation, to describe the dispersion, or spread, of the scores within the frequency distribution.

Another descriptive statistic that is commonly used is the correlation coefficient. The correlation coefficient describes the degree to which two variables are linearly related. A linear relationship between variables indicates that as one variable changes in magnitude, the other variable also experiences some change. The range of the correlation coefficient is $-1 \leq r \leq +1$. Positive correlations indicate a direct relationship between the variables: as one variable increases, so does the other. Negative correlations indicate an indirect relationship between the variables: as one variable increases, the other tends to decrease. As the correlation coefficient approaches −1 and +1, the described relationship between the variables is stronger or more linear.

Statistics are also used to test hypotheses about variables in the population being studied using a representative sample. When statistics are used to test hypotheses and thus to draw inferences about the population, they are referred to as inferential statistics. In testing hypotheses, researchers always set up two competing hypotheses. The null hypothesis contains a statement of what the researcher does not believe about the variables. The alternative hypothesis contains a statement of what the researcher believes to be true about the variables. The researcher then uses inferential statistics to test the null hypothesis.

To do this, the researcher must calculate some statistic on the data in the sample, and this statistic must be one for which we know what its distribution looks like. For instance, if the variable being studied is normally distributed in the population, then one could calculate *z* scores on the data and know that the distribution of these *z* scores in the population would be the standard normal distribution. The standard normal distribution is a bell-shaped, symmetric curve that has a mean of 0 and a standard deviation of 1. Because we know the shape, mean, and variance of the standard normal distribution, we also know exactly how much of the distribution falls between any two *z* scores. This allows us to determine the exact probability of obtaining any particular *z* score in our data.

In practice, *z* scores are not used very often to test hypotheses because psychologists frequently study more than one variable, and *z* scores can help us determine only the probability of obtaining a single data point in a sample. Therefore, psychologists often use other inferential statistics. The principle is still the same, however. You calculate an inferential statistic with a known distribution on your sample data. Next, you use the distribution to determine the probability of obtaining this particular value of the statistic, given the assumption that the null hypothesis is true. If the probability of obtaining this value of the inferential statistic when the null hypothesis is true is less than 5%, then you can safely say that within an acceptable margin of error, it appears that the null hypothesis is not true and it should be rejected in favor of the alternative hypothesis. In other words, your results are significant, and your data support your hypothesis.

In conclusion, please realize that this appendix has just skimmed the surface of what statistics is all about. All psychologists must undergo fairly extensive training in statistics before completing their degrees so that they have all the tools they need to test hypotheses about mental processes and behavior.

Studying the Appendix

Key Terms

alternative hypothesis (H_1) (667)
correlation coefficient (664)
data (657)
descriptive statistics (660)
frequency distribution (658)
frequency polygon (659)
graph (658)
histogram (659)
inferential statistics (667)
mean (660)
measures of central tendency (660)
median (661)
mode (662)
normal distribution (663)
null hypothesis (H_0) (667)
outliers (661)
range (662)
scatter plot (659)
significant (667)
standard deviation (662)
standard normal distribution (664)
statistics (658)
sum of squares (662)
variance (662)
***z* score** (663)

What Do You Know? Assess Your Understanding

Test your retention and understanding of the material by answering the following questions.

1. ________ are bits of knowledge gathered in scientific studies.

a. Statistics
b. Data
c. Hypotheses
d. Correlations

2. If we want to know if a person's height is a good predictor of their shoe size, which statistic(s) would be the most useful?

a. The mean
b. The mode
c. The correlation coefficient
d. A *z* score

3. If you want to describe the most common pet in America, after surveying 20,000 people to determine the type(s) of pet(s) they own, you should calculate the ________ of your data.

a. mean
b. median
c. mode
d. variance

4. A small company employs 10 people. At this company, three employees earn $20,000 a year, four employees earn $17,000, two employees earn $21,000, and the president earns $210,000 a year. Which of the following measures of central tendency is the most appropriate measure for accurately depicting the typical salary at this company?

a. Mean
b. Median
c. Mode
d. Variance

5. The mean of the standard normal distribution is equal to ________.

a. 0
b. 2
c. 3
d. −1

6. Which of the following statistics would be most useful for describing how the grades in a psychology course differ across the students in the class?

a. Mean
b. Variance
c. Correlation coefficient
d. *z* score

7. A *z* score of 2.66 means that the raw score in question is ________ the mean of the distribution.

a. 1.33 standard deviations below
b. 1.33 standard deviations above
c. 2.66 standard deviations below
d. 2.66 standard deviations above

8. Assuming that IQ scores are normally distributed, what percentage of the population can be expected to score 2 or more standard deviations above the mean on an IQ test?

a. 2.28%
b. 5.36%
c. 8.77%
d. 52.35%

9. The hypothesis that psychologists actually test is called the ________ hypothesis.

a. true
b. null
c. alternative
d. testable

10. A ________ distribution is a bell-shaped, symmetric frequency distribution.

a. normal
b. histogram
c. scatter plot
d. frequency polygon

Answers: 1. b; 2. c; 3. c; 4. b; 5. a; 6. b; 7. d; 8. a; 9. b; 10. a

B Applying Psychology in the Workplace

Originally authored by KATHY A. HANISCH, Iowa State University

Updated and edited by ELLEN PASTORINO

Learning Objectives

B.1 Define industrial and organizational psychology and discuss the value of work in people's lives. (APA 1.1, 1.2, 5.1, 5.5)

B.1 Describe the different types of jobs available. (APA 1.1, 1.3)

B.2 Explain how employers decide which job applicants to hire. (APA 1.2, 1.3, 5.1)

B.3 Describe how new employees become socialized to their work and organization through culture, groups, leadership, and performance appraisal. (APA 1.2, 1.3, 3.2, 5.1, 5.5)

B.4 Detail how employee satisfaction is influenced by employees' attitudes and behaviors at work. (APA 1.2, 1.3, 5.1)

Appendix Outline

industrial and organizational (I/O) psychology the study of people's behavior at work using psychological principles

Psychologists who study people's behavior at work using psychological principles are called *industrial* and *organizational psychologists*, and their field of study is **industrial and organizational (I/O) psychology**. I/O psychologists study employee selection, performance appraisal, training, job design, communication, work stress, motivation, leadership, groups and teams, organizational culture/climate, human factors, job attitudes, well-being, and work behavior. This appendix will introduce you to the field of I/O psychology. You will experience many of the topics discussed here when you seek, obtain, and keep a job.

B.1 Industrial and Organizational Psychology

You have applied for a job, submitted your résumé, and taken a series of tests. You have been interviewed by your potential supervisor and been given a tour of the company. You now find yourself sitting across from the co-owners, who have just offered you a position. They tell you that their organization is a great place to work. As evidence, they tell you that no one has quit in the last 5 years and that employees are rarely absent. They also tell you that they have flexible policies. You can work whatever hours you like and take vacation whenever you want. And if you decide to work for them, you'll have access to spending cash as well as keys to the company.

You try to maintain your composure. You'd heard interesting things about this company but didn't really believe them. Finally, the co-owners ask you what you are worth, indicating they will pay you whatever you wish. Now you're really dumbfounded and wonder what the catch is, but sit quietly while they talk about other issues. Does this sound too good to be true? Wouldn't this be ideal?

Almost this exact scenario played out in an organization owned and managed by an Oakland appliance dealer in the 1970s. His name was Arthur Friedman, and he had decided to change how he ran his business. Art, as reported in the *Washington Post* (Koughan, 1975), announced at one of his staff meetings that employees could work the hours they wanted, be paid what they thought they were worth, take vacation time when they wanted, and help themselves to petty cash if they were in need of spending money. New employees would be allowed to set their own wages, too. As you might imagine, the employees weren't sure how to take this news. It was reported that no one said anything during the meeting when Art first described his plan (Koughan, 1975).

When asked why he was changing his business practices, Art replied, "I always said that if you give people what they want, you get what you want. You have to be willing to lose, to stick your neck out. I finally decided that the time had come to practice what I preached" (Koughan, 1975). In the final analysis, Art's experiment worked. The organization was profitable. Friedman signed union contracts without reading them (the employees didn't need a union with Art in charge). Employees didn't quit, they didn't steal from the company, and they were rarely absent. Net profits increased, and the company was a success. The employees realized that to make the organization work and remain in business, they had to be reasonable in their requests and behavior (Koughan, 1975).

A present-day company with some enticing work perks is SAS, one of the largest privately held software companies in the world. It has consistently been rated as one of the best employers to work for by *Forbes* and *Fortune* magazines. Included among its many perks are first-class medical, dental, and vision care, unlimited sick days, free health care with an on-site medical center that has a $4.5 million budget (it still saves the company $5 million a year; Kaplan, 2010), subsidized child care and cafeteria, free fitness center, swimming pool, and summer camps for employees' children. The company encourages a 35-hour work week and allows for flexible scheduling. In addition, SAS has an on-site billiards hall, sauna, manicurist, and hair salon, and offers massages. The company also has picnics and other family events (which employees and their families want to attend) as well as snacks (fruit, donuts, and candy) on different days. In addition to these benefits, SAS rewards innovation and risk taking while supporting the growth of its employees both personally and professionally (www.sas.com).

Organizations like SAS and Art Friedman's company are interesting because of how they deal with their employees and how that treatment affects the employees' behaviors. This interest is what is at the heart of industrial and organizational psychology. I/O psychology studies human behavior in work settings.

Adam Berry/Bloomberg/Getty Images

▲ Jim Goodnight is the cofounder and has been CEO of SAS since incorporation in 1976. His organization has consistently been rated as one of the best companies to work for by *Forbes* and *Fortune* magazines.

B.1.1 Work in Our Lives

You have learned about work since you were a small child. You may have asked where your parent was going when you went to day care or why your parent left the house before 8 a.m. and did not return until after 5 p.m. You likely "played" at different jobs by dressing up as an astronaut, a firefighter, a teacher, a chef, or a construction worker. As you got older, other information about work may have come from your friends, other family members, school, and the media. In high school, more education and a part-time job may have given you additional details about the meaning of work. As you pursue a college degree, you may receive information about the work and jobs available in your chosen field through classes, service learning, internships, or other job or research experiences.

Work is an important part of life for many people. We often ask people we meet what they "do," which translates into "What is your job and whom do you work for?" Many people identify with their work because they spend so much of their waking lives at work. Work is important because it provides many of the things people need and value. Income from work provides us with the money necessary to satisfy our basic needs for food, shelter, and security (for example, health care or retirement income), while the "leftover" money provides us with discretionary funds to use as we see fit. These funds may be used to buy a round of golf, an iPad, or a fancy place to live; to support charities or attend athletic or fine art performances; or to save for college. Essentially, money, typically from work, provides us with a standard of living that varies from person to person depending on our income and how we choose to spend it. In addition, work provides much more. It provides a source of social interactions and friendships, independence, a sense of accomplishment, satisfaction, a reason to get up in the morning, happiness, a sense of identity, recognition, and prestige (see ● Table B.1).

Although most researchers and practitioners agree that money and recognition are nearly universal motivators (R. E. Clark, 2003), many of the things we value or seek from work vary from person to person. For example, the prestige of a job may not be important to you, but it might be important to your best friend. Perhaps you will want your work to provide you with a sense of accomplishment or be a source of social interactions, while those attributes may not be valued by another person. It is important to understand what you want from your work as well as what a job can provide.

From an employer's perspective, it is useful to determine what employees want, because satisfied employees will be more likely than dissatisfied employees to work to meet organizational goals. Part of a supervisor's job is to ascertain what employees value, because those values can be used to motivate employees to perform well in their jobs.

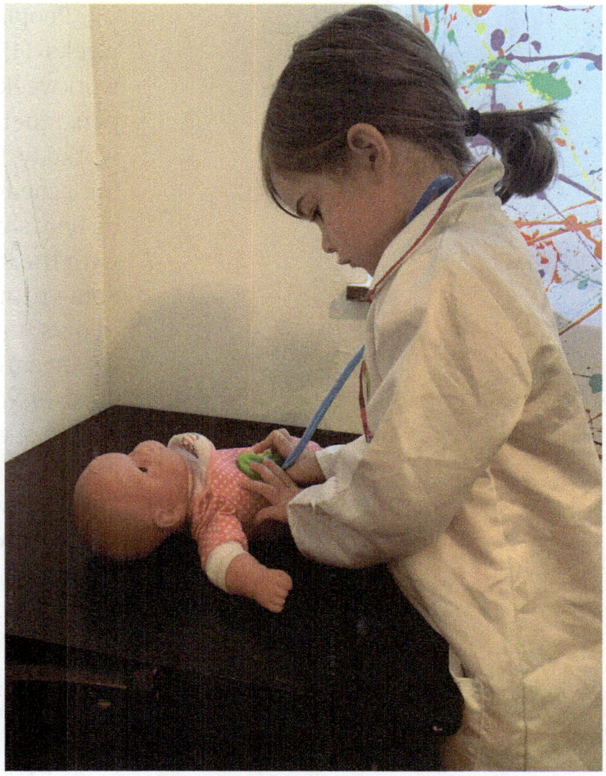

Carmen Compton

▲ Children learn about work through play and dress-up.

TABLE B.1 Jobs with the Highest and Lowest Prestige*

Job Description	Percentage Rating Job as has Prestige or a Great Deal of Prestige
Highest Prestige	
Doctor	90%
Scientist	83%
Firefighter	80%
Military Officer	78%
Engineer	76%
Lowest Prestige	
Public Relations (PR) Consultant	31%
Real Estate Agent/Broker	32%
Videogame Developer/Designer	37%
Stockbroker	39%
Politician	40%

Sources: www.harrispoll.com, 2015

*It is interesting to note that some of the professions with the highest prestige (firefighter) are not considered high-paying jobs, while some of those with the least prestige (stockbroker, real estate agent) are associated with fame or high earning potential or both. It appears that the polled individuals do not equate money and fame with high prestige; they appear to be unique concepts.

B.1.2 Types of Jobs

There are many types of work, in many types of jobs, in many different organizational settings. These settings include multinational conglomerates; public and private companies; nonprofits; federal, state, and local government organizations; and home businesses.

People in the United States work a variety of schedules, from extended workweeks (45 to 99 hours) to standard workweeks (35 to 44 hours) to part-time workweeks (fewer than 35 hours). Some people, such as police officers, medical personnel, and factory workers, work shifts other than the typical 8 a.m. to 5 p.m. workday because of the nature of their jobs. Others are offered flexible working schedules that best fit their lives as long as they work the required number of hours and accomplish the work. Telecommuting has become more common with the increase in appropriate technology and due to the coronavirus pandemic. Some people work for virtual organizations that use communication technologies to outsource the majority of their functions.

Regardless of the type of job or your work schedule, you will likely spend most of your waking hours in some type of employment for many years. Many people spend their weekends working, too. Because work is critical to who we are and what we do, studying the psychological principles and some of the topics examined by I/O psychologists will provide you with information that may be useful to you in your future careers.

B.1 Quiz Yourself

1. **Nearly all people value ____ and ____ from their work.**

a. money; prestige
b. prestige; social interactions
c. money; recognition
d. satisfaction; prestige

2. **Which of the following would an I/O psychologist be least likely to study?**

a. Leadership
b. Life satisfaction
c. Employee selection
d. Performance appraisal

Answers 1. c; 2. b

B.2 Selecting Employees: The Hiring Process

Industrial and organizational psychologists first became involved in the process of selecting employees when the U.S. government needed help selecting and placing officers and soldiers in World War I (Aamodt, 2010). Psychologists used mental ability tests to determine who would become officers and who would be in the infantry. The process many employers now use to hire employees is very detailed, typically consisting of five components: *job analysis, testing, legal issues, recruitment*, and the *selection decision*.

B.2.1 Job Analysis

job analysis the identification of the critical elements of a job, including tasks, skills required, and working conditions

Job analysis is the identification of the critical elements of a job. I/O psychologists have helped devise effective strategies for determining three basic aspects of any job: (1) What tasks and behaviors are essential to the job? (2) What knowledge, skills, abilities, and other characteristics (KSAOs) are needed to perform the job? (3) What are the conditions (such as stress, safety, and temperature) under which the job is performed? A job analysis can be conducted in many ways. An analyst (an I/O psychologist, human resources (HR) employee, manager, or outside consultant) may interview current employees, have them complete questionnaires, observe people in the job, or talk to people knowledgeable about the job (Gael, 1988).

The information from a job analysis is used in many types of personnel functions. These include employee selection, performance appraisal, training, and HR planning. Within the hiring process, job analysis is used to write job descriptions; to determine what tests might be used to assess the relevant knowledge, skills, and abilities of job applicants; and to assist in meeting legal requirements that affect the selection process.

B.2.2 Testing

You are familiar with tests and taking tests. **Tests** are defined here as the measurement of carefully chosen samples of behavior. These include the standard paper-and-pencil or computerized tests used to measure specific skills or abilities in a class, or more general abilities as in the SAT or ACT. They also include personality assessments (see Chapter 11) such as conscientiousness and honesty tests, since conscientiousness and agreeableness have been found to be personality attributes important for success across many jobs (Sackett & Walmsley, 2014). In addition, *work samples*, in which applicants do a replica of the work they will be asked to do on the job, are useful tests (Scott & Reynolds, 2010). Tests are vital to the success of organizations. They are used to determine differences between people. The goal of these tests is to help employers choose the person best suited for the job and the organization. Regardless of the type of test or how it is administered, the reliability and validity of a test are very important (see Chapter 11).

tests the measurements of carefully chosen samples of behavior

unstructured interviews informal, unplanned interviews conducted by an untrained interviewer using random questions and no scoring key

structured interviews interviews conducted by a trained interviewer using standardized questions, a specific question order, and a predetermined scoring or answer key

Another type of test is the *employee interview*. Nearly all organizations use some type of interview in their selection of employees (Salgado, Viswesvaran, & Ones, 2003). Even though interviews are often viewed as subjective, more than 85 years of research has provided evidence regarding when interviews are useful and when they are not.

Selection interviews can be broadly classified as *unstructured* and *structured*. **Unstructured interviews** are informal and unplanned. They are conducted by an untrained interviewer, with random questions and no scoring key. Some typical questions asked during an unstructured interview are listed in ● TABLE B.2. **Structured interviews** are conducted by a trained interviewer. They have standardized questions, a specific question order, and a predetermined scoring or answer key. Examples of structured interview questions are listed in ● Table B.3. Structured interviews, based on a job analysis, have greater reliability and validity than unstructured interviews (Huffcutt et al., 2001; Macan, 2009). However, they are still likely to be influenced by a candidate's verbal skills, attractiveness, and impression management tactics (Huffcutt, 2011).

TABLE B.2 Typical Unstructured Interview Questions

1. Tell me about yourself.
2. Describe your ideal job.
3. Why do you want to work here?
4. What are your goals?
5. Why did you leave (or why are you leaving) your job?
6. What accomplishment are you most proud of and why?
7. What can you do for us that other candidates can't?
8. What are three positive things your last boss would say about you?
9. What salary are you seeking?
10. If you were an animal, which one would you want to be?

Sources: Indeed.com, 2020; C. Martin, 2006, Monster.com.

TABLE B.3 Structured Behavior-Based Interview Questions

1. Tell me in specific details about a time when you had to deal with a difficult customer.
2. Give me an example of a time when you had to make a decision without a supervisor present.
3. Give me a specific example of when you demonstrated initiative in an employment setting.
4. Give me an example of a time when you had to work with a team.
5. Describe a time when you had to be creative at solving a problem.

Source: Adapted from The Job Centre, Niagara College Canada, 2005, http://jobs.niagarac.on.ca/.

B.2.3 Legal Issues

Title VII of the Civil Rights Act of 1964 the law that prohibits discrimination based on race, color, religion, sex, and national origin, and extends to sexual orientation and transgender status

One of the most important pieces of legislation regarding employment, and specifically the hiring of employees, is **Title VII of the Civil Rights Act of 1964** (Equal Employment Opportunity Commission, 2002). Title VII "prohibits discrimination based on race, color, religion, sex, and national origin," known as the "Big 5." In 2020, the U.S. Supreme Court extended Title VII protections from workplace discrimination based on sexual orientation and transgender status. Providing protection for people helps to ensure that they have equal employment opportunities. Exceptions to this provision include national security, seniority systems, and *bona fide occupational qualifications (BFOQs)*.

BFOQs permit organizations to discriminate in hiring persons in a protected class if the qualification is determined to be reasonably necessary to the operation of the business. For example, women can be discriminated against when hiring someone to model men's swimwear, and vice versa. It is reasonably necessary to the marketing and selling of swimwear that organizations hire men to model male swimwear and women to model female swimwear; sex is a BFOQ. It is not reasonably necessary, however, that a secretary in a church who does secretarial work and not church or religious work believe in the same religion as the church that employs them; religion in this case could not be used as a BFOQ.

It is important for employers to abide by laws that protect people against discrimination because the costs of litigation can be very high, both monetarily and in terms of an organization's reputation. This protection applies to discrimination based not only on the Big 5, covered under the Civil Rights Act, but also on other characteristics such as age (Age Discrimination in Employment Act, 1967) and disability (Americans with Disabilities Act, 1990). Employment law in the United States is meant to protect and provide equal opportunities for all individuals.

Legal issues in employment vary in different countries, however. The advertisement shown in ● Figure B.1 for a bookkeeper in Johannesburg, South Africa would not be legal in the United States. It specifies that the applicant must be female, which would be illegal under Title VII of the Civil Rights Act. It also

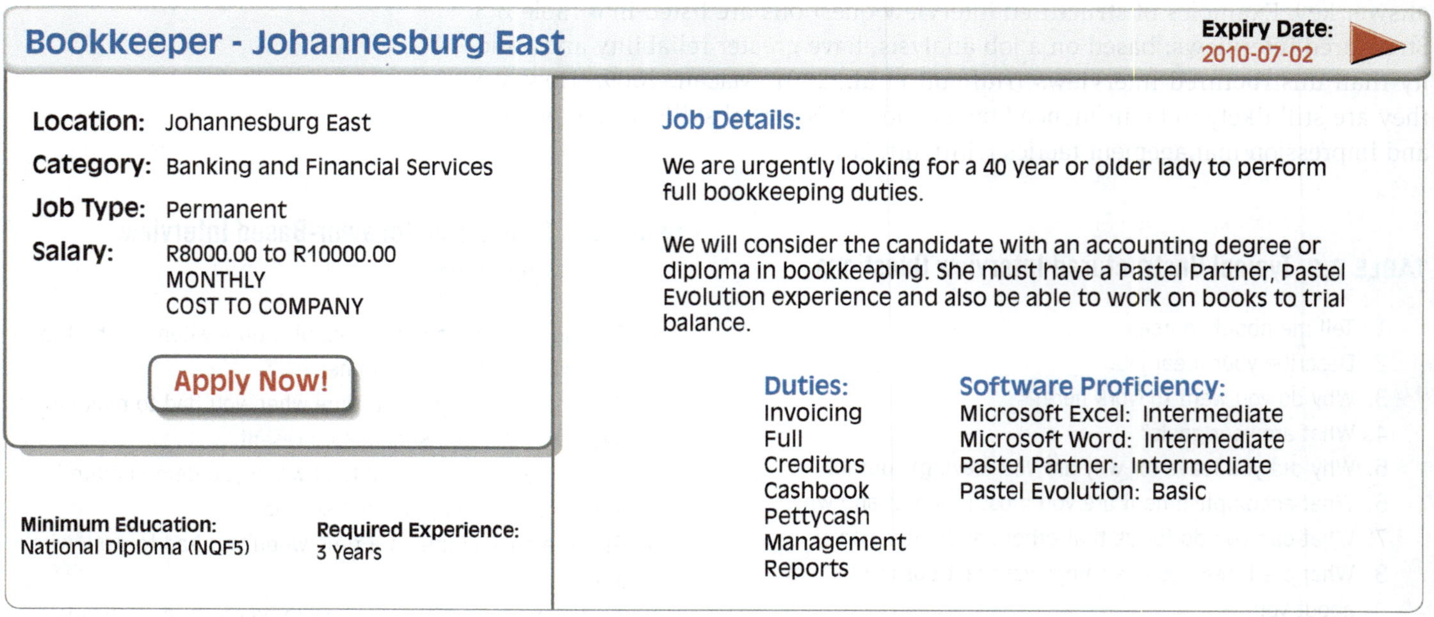

FIGURE B.1

This advertisement for a bookkeeper in Johannesburg, South Africa would be illegal in the U.S. under Title VII of the Civil Rights Act.

specifies age 40 or older, which would be illegal in some states that protect younger individuals against age discrimination. U.S. federal law prohibits discrimination based on age once a person reaches the age of 40 (Age Discrimination in Employment Act). The employer is seeking an older woman, which is likely not related to expected job performance; people younger than 40 could perform just as well in the job of a bookkeeper.

Employment legislation offers fair treatment for people looking for a job. In the United States, organizations with several employees are required to abide by the employment laws. These laws make the U.S. job market fairer than in many other countries.

B.2.4 Recruitment

The process organizational managers use to identify potential employees for a job is called **recruitment**. Depending on the job, a manager or owner may recruit from inside the company or seek someone outside the organization. The owner or manager may advertise on the company website or on a website such as Indeed.com or SimplyHired.com for specific types of jobs. In addition, websites like Monster.com and CareerBuilder.com link potential employees and employers in a variety of jobs and locations. Other recruitment sources include college career centers, newspapers, radio and television advertisements, trade magazines, professional publications, and employee referrals.

recruitment the process organizations use to identify potential employees for a job

Research suggests that employees recruited through inside sources such as employee referrals or rehires work for the organization longer and have better job performance than those recruited through outside sources including advertisements, employment agencies, or recruiters (Zottoli & Wanous, 2000). Studies have supported the idea that those recruited using inside sources receive more accurate information about the job than those recruited through external sources (Conrad & Ashworth, 1986; McManus & Baratta, 1992). In effect, the new employees receive realistic job previews.

A survey of the 50 best small and medium organizations to work for in the United States found that 92% use employee referrals, and that nearly 30% of all hires were referred by a current employee (NAS, 2012; Pomeroy, 2005). Because of their effectiveness, some companies provide rewards to employees who recommend an applicant who is hired. These rewards include cash, vacations, and prizes such as televisions and free house cleaning services for a year (R. Stewart et al., 1990). Typically, the new employee must work for the organization a set period of time before the referring employee can receive the award (R. Stewart et al., 1990). Unfortunately, relying on internal networks can contribute to gender and minority disparities in hiring, especially for higher-level jobs (Fernandez & Rubineau, 2019; Gibbs et al., 2016; Glass & Minnotte, 2010).

After applicants have submitted either a résumé or an application, someone from the organization such as the HR manager or supervisor, or a "bot" (a software application that screens résumés for the right qualifications and skills before a human sees them), will determine which applicants should be considered further. In that process, the supervisor may make telephone inquiries of previous employers or other references and conduct criminal background checks.

Employers also may use social networking sites such as Facebook, LinkedIn, and Twitter to learn about and even seek job candidates (Brown & Vaughn, 2011). On these sites, employers have found promising candidates reporting on their own drug use, sexual exploits, and drinking, as well as posting inappropriate photographs and bad-mouthing their previous employer (Haefner, 2009).

Louis Quail/Getty Images

▲ Based on this photo, would you hire this job candidate?

In addition to identifying risky behavior patterns, managers are using social networking sites to determine whether applicants would fit in well with the company culture and to evaluate their professionalism (Hargis, 2008). Some applicants feel this is an invasion of privacy and actually lowers the applicant's attraction to the organization (Stoughton, Thompson, & Meade, 2015). At any rate, it would be wise to closely look at any publicly accessible information before a job search and to establish privacy settings for any material that you do not want a potential employer to see. Legislation in many states prohibits employers from requiring passwords to access social media sites.

B.2.5 Making the Decision

When selecting employees, employers are looking for a good match between the employee and the organization. They would like to match the requirements for excellent performance in the job with the person's knowledge, skills, abilities, personality, and motivation for the job. They attempt to accomplish this by using the different types of tests discussed earlier.

Researchers have posited two groups of factors that determine an employee's performance in a job. They are the "*can-do*" and the "*will-do*" *factors* (Schmitt et al., 2003). "**Can-do" factors** include an employee's knowledge, skills, and abilities that determine the maximum performance an employee can exhibit. "**Will-do" factors** include personality traits, personal values, and motivations an employee is willing to exert for the organization. Personality factors such as conscientiousness, emotional stability, and need for achievement as well as integrity have been classified as important "will-do" factors in performance (Ones, Dilchert, & Viswesvaran, 2007; Schmitt et al., 2003). A person's "can-do" and "will-do" factors may change as they move from organization to organization. Once a person is selected, the important process of being accepted and socialized into the organization at all levels, including a work group or team, begins.

"can-do" factors factors that include an employee's knowledge, skills, and abilities that determine their maximum job performance

"will-do" factors factors that include personality traits, personal values, and motivations that an employee is willing to exert for the organization and that influence their normal or typical job performance

B.2 Quiz Yourself

1. **Asking employees to describe their job is one way of conducting a ____.**
   a. job evaluation
   b. job analysis
   c. performance appraisal
   d. job review
2. **Zachary is usually a conscientious and hardworking employee, but the company has hired a new boss who is really lazy and doesn't motivate the employees. It is likely that Zachary's ____ will be compromised in this situation.**
   a. try-to factors
   b. will-do factors
   c. can-do factors
   d. must-do factors
3. **Alexander, a television reporter, wants access to the women's locker room right after the basketball game to conduct interviews with the team members. The women's team lets female reporters in to interview them but wants Alexander to wait until after they have showered and changed. Alexander argues he needs to be treated the same as the female reporters. What would be the likely outcome if this issue goes before a court?**
   a. The women's team would win because sex is a BFOQ in this case.
   b. The women's team would win because they can discriminate against Alexander because they don't like his reporting style.
   c. Alexander would win because the women's team members can't discriminate against him because they don't like his reporting style.
   d. Alexander would win because sex is not a BFOQ in this case.

Answers 1. b; 2. b; 3. d

B.3 Socializing Employees: Culture, Groups, Leadership, and Performance Appraisal

When you report for your first day of work in an organization, you will need to learn many things to be successful in your job. The process of learning these things is called **organizational socialization**, which has been defined as "the process by which organizational members become a part of, or are absorbed into, the culture of the organization" (Jablin, 1982, p. 255). Organizational socialization consists of people learning how the organization operates by using information provided by management, coworkers, observation, and company handbooks, websites, or memos.

organizational socialization the process by which members of an organization become a part of, or are absorbed into, the culture of the organization

mentoring the pairing of a current and often long-term employee (the mentor) with a new employee

organizational culture the shared cognitive assumptions and beliefs of an organization

organizational climate the behavioral norms of an organization

Often, one of the first things an employee encounters on the job is new employee orientation training that focuses on the goals and expectations of the organization. These clearly help to set the expectations and culture of the organization. Other common types of training in organizations are diversity and harassment training. These training programs are usually required company-wide to ensure that all employees are aware of the policies of the organization; they also are used by organizations to try to prevent and correct harassment problems in an attempt to limit liability in harassment complaints (Equal Employment Opportunity Commission, 2010).

Supervisors and coworkers are also important sources of socialization information. **Mentoring** is a form of training in which a current and often long-term employee (the mentor) is paired with a new employee. The mentor's role is to help the new employee adapt to the job by assisting with advice or resources. The mentor may provide information about how the organization works, career advancement opportunities, and how performance is evaluated. Good mentoring helps new employees become successful on the job and learn the formal and informal rules of the organization (Aamodt, 2010).

Research suggests that both mentors and those they mentor often benefit from the relationship. For example, in one study of health care employees, it was found that those who were mentored reported higher salaries, greater promotion rates, and more positive career success than those who did not receive mentoring (Allen, Lentz, & Day, 2006). Employees who have been mentored experience more effective socialization and better compensation, advancement, career satisfaction, job satisfaction, job involvement, and organizational commitment than those with no mentoring (Eby et al., 2013; Greenhaus, 2003).

B.3.1 Organizational Culture and Climate

Organizational culture includes the shared assumptions and beliefs of the organization. These cognitions then influence the **organizational climate**, or actions and behaviors of the people in the group or organization (Schein, 1985). These behaviors are considered the norm for the organization; they represent the "normal behaviors" expected from its members. Because culture and climate generally operate in unison, our discussion will refer to these elements collectively as *culture* (Ostroff, Kinicki, & Tamkins, 2003). Organizational culture is important because it lets employees know what is expected of them and affects how they think and behave. Culture is often determined by the founders of the organization and may be modified over time by the successes and failures of an organization. See ● FIGURE B.2 for factors that affect organizational culture.

FIGURE B.2
Several factors affect the organizational culture of an organization.

Some organizations, such as SAS, have cultures that appear to have been successful from the start, as suggested by low turnover and organizational profitability. Several case studies have described organizations that have successfully changed their culture from poor to better or great. Remember Art Friedman from the beginning of this appendix? He allowed his employees to set their own wages and decide the hours they worked; he also required employees to belong to the union. After Friedman made these changes, employee grumbling stopped (Koughan, 1975). The organizational culture changed, resulting in better morale, increased productivity, and employee longevity. No one wanted to quit working in a culture where the employees got to make their own decisions that affected the organization's bottom line.

Finding an organizational culture that fits your working style will have consequences for your attitudes, performance, and tenure in an organization. *Work teams* and the *leadership* of an organization have a large influence on the culture of an organization.

B.3.2 Groups and Teams

work teams/groups two or more employees who together perform organizationally relevant tasks, share one or more common goals, interact socially, and exhibit task interdependencies

leadership a social influence process in which a person steers others toward a goal

Work teams/groups can be defined as two or more employees who have common goals, have tasks that are interdependent, interact socially, and work on relevant organizational tasks within specific requirements and rules (Kozlowski & Bell, 2003). Just as there can be a culture in an organization, groups or teams also exhibit cultures that may encourage or discourage certain types of work-related behaviors and attitudes. These cultures then form the basis for the socialization of new group or team members (Kozlowski, 2018).

Although most organizations provide formal means of socializing new employees (e.g., new employee orientation training), the group or team dynamics have immediate and direct effects on employees' socialization (Anderson & Thomas, 1996). The outcomes of organization socialization and work group socialization may be different. Teams may have leaders or may be self-managing. Self-managing teams tend to show better productivity, an increase in work quality, improved quality of life for employees, decreased absenteeism, and decreased turnover than teams with leaders (Cohen & Ledford, 1994; Stewart, Courtright, & Barrick, 2012). When teams fail, often the failure is linked to the team leader, who may be too autocratic, wielding too much power or influence, or too lax and providing too little monitoring. As a result, the team does not realize the autonomy and control levels it needs to be successful (Langfred, 2004; G. L. Stewart & Manz, 1995). Shared leadership is positively related to the performance of self-managing teams (McIntyre & Foti, 2013; Wang, Waldman, & Zhang, 2014).

B.3.3 Leadership

Leadership is the art of getting someone else to do something you want done because he wants to do it.

—Dwight D. Eisenhower

Leadership has many definitions, including one person influencing another person or a team toward a goal (Bryman, 1996). Leadership has received a lot of research attention in industrial/organizational psychology. Yet it is still difficult to describe how to make or select the ideal or best leader. Many theories exist, and most have been useful in helping us understand what makes a good leader and how to improve leadership style.

Personality plays a role in many leadership theories. Certainly, it is an important aspect of successful or unsuccessful leaders. Kirkpatrick and Locke's (1991) review suggests that drive, honesty and integrity, self-confidence, cognitive abilities, and knowledge are associated with successful leaders. Leaders with poor cognitive abilities and social skills and those who are indecisive, low in self-confidence and self-esteem, dishonest, and lacking in ambition tend to be less successful (Kaplan, Drath, & Kofodimos, 1991; Oreg & Berson, 2018).

Kevin Winter/Getty Images Entertainment/Getty Images

▲ Oprah Winfrey is a modern-day charismatic leader. She is probably best known as host for 25 years of *Oprah*. In addition, she has started a television network (OWN), established *O* magazine, and created multiple charity groups, donating millions of dollars across the globe.

Art Friedman's integrity likely made him a successful leader. He decided to give employees what he would want, providing them with the capabilities to make major decisions that could either make or break the organization. In his case, he created a self-managing group that had no need for external assistance from unions or other entities. As a result, Friedman demonstrated the *transformational leadership* approach (Bass, 1990). **Transformational leadership** is characterized by high ethical standards, inspirational motivation, intellectual stimulation, and individual consideration—all clearly evident in Friedman's leadership style.

Jim Goodnight, the CEO and cofounder of SAS, has the philosophy that you should "treat employees like they make a difference and they will" (https://www.sas.com/en_us/careers.html). Undoubtedly, his philosophy is working because SAS has continued to grow and has remained profitable. Other indicators include the company's consistent ranking by *Forbes* and *Fortune* magazines as one of the best employers to work for, employee turnover of 6.5% compared to the software industry average of more than 14%, and an employee absence rate of only 4.79 days per year (there is no limit). Goodnight wants a balanced work and personal life for his employees, so they work 35-hour workweeks with many of them setting their own hours. He wants his employees to work well during their 7-hour days, so his company tries to take care of inconveniences by having many services on-site. Employees rave about how great it is to work at SAS (Kaplan, 2010).

transformational leadership characterized by high ethical standards, inspirational motivation, intellectual stimulation, and individual consideration

performance appraisals the evaluations or reviews of employees' job performance

Leaders today must contend with information-based team environments requiring the capacity for sifting large amounts of information coming from computer networks (Avolio, Kahai, & Dodge, 2000). The widely varying working environments that result from global competition require leaders to be adaptable (Mann, 1959), capable of handling stress (Goleman, 1998), knowledgeable about competitors and products (Kirkpatrick & Locke, 1991), and able to solve complex problems quickly (Zaccaro et al., 2000). Leaders in organizations today also need to be concerned with HR planning (the hiring and maintenance of an employee workforce) and the appropriate evaluation of employee performance to ensure their organizations will be competitive and profitable in the ensuing years.

B.3.4 Performance Appraisal

Performance appraisals are the evaluations or reviews of employees' performance. Employees should continually be told about their job performance, both the good and the bad, by their employers. Formal employee performance appraisals are times for management to systematically evaluate employee performance and productivity on the job, set performance goals, and directly convey information about the culture of the organization (Fletcher & Perry, 2001). Performance appraisals are important for many reasons, including (1) determining areas of employees' work needing improvement and areas to be complimented, (2) effectively managing

▲ Performance review meetings should be conducted in a distraction-free, neutral location with a prepared and trained employer.

employee raises and promotions, (3) dealing with unproductive employees in a fair and appropriate manner that may include termination, and (4) assisting in workforce planning that may be particularly important in difficult economic times but should be done routinely to have the best employees in the organization.

Performance appraisals vary in frequency, with some organizations evaluating new employees 30 or 60 days after hire, while others evaluate new employees' performance 3 or 6 months after hire. Once an employee has been working for an organization for one year, most organizations formally evaluate performance annually or semiannually (Aamodt, 2010). A typical performance review consists of some type of form that is filled out by the employee's supervisor; some organizations have both the employee and the employer fill out the same form to allow them to compare their views of the employee's performance. This is followed by a meeting between the manager and the employee to discuss the employee's performance. This meeting should be held in a neutral, distraction-free location with an appropriate amount of time for discussion.

Because the performance appraisal will often clearly define the most important components of employees' jobs and help shape the culture of the organization, it is recommended that employers provide performance appraisal forms to new employees when they are hired or on their first day of work. This will send a clear message to the employees about the work that is valued by the organization and about whether they will be evaluated according to criteria set by management (this may suggest a more collaborative or cooperative culture) or will be appraised relative to their coworkers (this may suggest a more competitive culture). It is in the best interest of both the employer (for performance management) and the employee (as a road map to success) that the job performance requirements be known at the time of hire. Once employees are hired who can complete the work tasks and be effective in the organization (i.e., they have the ability to do the job), then their attitudes become important, because their attitudes will directly influence their work behaviors.

B.3 Quiz Yourself

1. Spencer, a new employee of the company, has learned most of the behaviors required to do the job effectively. This would illustrate that Spencer has learned the _____ of the organization.

a. organizational climate
b. organizational culture
c. transformational culture
d. transformational climate

2. Performance appraisals are important because they _____.

a. help define the culture of the organization
b. provide employees needed information on their job performance
c. aid employers in determining the type of training needed by their employees
d. All of the above

(Continued)

3. Carol is part of a successful self-managing team in an organization that produces handcrafted furniture. Compared to her coworkers in traditional-leader teams, Carol and her work team should have _____.

a. better productivity, lower work quality, and a decrease in absenteeism
b. an increase in work quality, decrease in work quantity, and better quality of life
c. an increase in absenteeism, lower work quality, and higher work quantity
d. better productivity, better work quality, and a better quality of life

Answers 1. b; 2. d; 3. d

B.4 Employee Satisfaction: Attitudes and Behaviors at Work

One of the most important factors influencing whether you will be motivated to do a good job hinges on your *attitudes* and *behaviors* at work. The causes and consequences of work attitudes have been extensively researched. Some of the outcomes of attitudes include work behaviors such as volunteering for a project, helping out a coworker, quitting, absenteeism, tardiness, early retirement, and performance.

attitudes at work satisfaction with the work itself, pay and benefits, supervision, coworkers, promotion opportunities, working conditions, and job security

job satisfaction the positive or negative feelings associated with a job

B.4.1 Attitudes at Work

Attitudes at work are many and varied. In general, you can be satisfied or dissatisfied with the tasks and conditions at work, the people in your work environment, and the rewards you get from work. Employee satisfaction is important because it has been shown to be related to employee behaviors at work (Judge et al., 2001; Ziegler & Schlett, 2016). Two of the most commonly studied work attitudes are *job satisfaction* and *organizational commitment*.

Job Satisfaction

The positive or negative feelings associated with a job define **job satisfaction** (Thurstone, 1931). Some of the ways organizations can create satisfied employees include flexible working hours, professional growth opportunities, meaningful work, autonomy, job security, a good supervisor, good benefits, competitive pay, opportunities for promotion, respect, recognition, and being part of something or being included (Allan et al., 2018; Borgogni et al., 2010; Cranny, Smith, & Stone, 1992; Hackman & Oldham, 1976). It is important to note that what makes one worker satisfied may not make another worker satisfied. For some people, interesting work is paramount. Others place higher emphasis on having coworkers they like. Still others feel that the pay and benefits they receive are most important. Virtually all employees value recognition (some acknowledgment of their work), respect, and being part of the organization. These rewards are all inexpensive and typically require very little time to implement. Just as in selection, a match between what you want and what the organization can provide will result in a successful outcome for both parties.

Christopher Robbins/Getty Images

▲ Employees report higher job satisfaction and productivity if they are allowed privileges such as listening to music while they work.

Engage Yourself!

One measure often used to assess employee work attitudes, and specifically different facets of job satisfaction, is the *Job Descriptive Index* (JDI; P. C. Smith, Kendall, & Hulin, 1969). This index has been improved based on years of research (e.g., Balzer et al., 1997;

TABLE B.4 Work on Present Job

Think of the work you do at present. How well does each of the following words or phrases describe your job? In the blank beside each word or phrase below, write:
Y for "Yes" if it describes your work
N for "No" if it does not describe your work
? if you cannot decide

____1. Fascinating	____6. Creative	____11. Tiring	____16. Simple
____2. Routine	____7. Respected	____12. Healthful	____17. Repetitive
____3. Satisfying	____8. Uncomfortable	____13. Challenging	____18. Gives sense of accomplishment
____4. Boring	____9. Pleasant	____14. Too much to do	
____5. Good	____10. Useful	____15. Frustrating	
Scoring Key:			
1. Y=3, N=0, ?=1;	6. Y=3, N=0, ?=1;	11. Y=0, N=3, ?=1;	16. Y=0, N=3, ?=1;
2. Y=0, N=3, ?=1;	7. Y=3, N=0, ?=1;	12. Y=3, N=0, ?=1;	17. Y=0, N=3, ?=1;
3. Y=3, N=0, ?=1;	8. Y=0, N=3, ?=1;	13. Y=3, N=0, ?=1;	18. Y=3, N=0, ?=1
4. Y=0, N=3, ?=1;	9. Y=3, N=0, ?=1;	14. Y=0, N=3, ?=1;	
5. Y=3, N=0, ?=1;	10. Y=3, N=0, ?=1;	15. Y=0, N=3, ?=1;	

To interpret your score on the work scale, 27 is considered the neutral value (Balzer et al., 1997). Values considerably higher would be evaluated as very satisfied; values considerably lower would be evaluated as very dissatisfied with the work on your present job.

Hanisch, 1992). The JDI measures five facets of satisfaction: Work on Present Job, Supervisor, Coworkers, Present Pay, and Opportunities for Promotion. Try filling out the JDI Work on Present Job scale in • TABLE B.4.

Organizational Commitment

Employee commitment to an organization is related to employee retention within the organization. There are three types of organizational commitment: *affective, normative,* and *continuance* (Meyer & Allen, 1991). Meyer and Allen define **affective commitment** as an employee's emotional attachment to the organization that makes the employee want to stay in the organization. **Normative commitment** is based on feelings of obligation. **Continuance commitment** results when an employee remains with a company because of the high cost of losing organizational membership, including monetary (e.g., pension benefits) and social (such as friendships) costs. Meyer and Herscovitch (2001) argue that employees have an organizational commitment profile at any given time in their job, with high or low values on each of the three types of commitment. In other words, an employee may have high scores on normative and continuance commitment, but be lower on affective commitment. Depending on the profile, the employee may engage in different behaviors such as quitting or helping out the organization.

affective commitment an employee's emotional attachment to the organization

normative commitment commitment to the organization based on feelings of obligation

continuance commitment remaining with an organization because of the high cost (monetary or social or both) of losing organizational membership

Students may experience these different types of commitment to their college. Affective commitment occurs when a student feels an emotional attachment to their college because they really like the school, including classes, the football team, and the town. Normative commitment might be evidenced by a student whose parent attended that college and who feels obligated to do the same regardless of whether it is the best school for them. Staying at a college because your friends are there and you have already paid for 2 years would typify acting under continuance commitment. The three levels of commitment could be represented as a commitment profile for a student.

Organizational commitment is related to job satisfaction. Employees who are satisfied with their job are more committed to their organization than are those who are less satisfied (Mosedeghrad, Ferlie, & Rosenberg, 2008; Mueller et al., 1994). Other correlates of organizational commitment include trust in one's supervisor and HR practices that are supportive of employees (Arthur, 1994). The organizational commitment of Friedman's employees was very high, as evidenced by no turnover in 5 years; the low turnover at SAS also supports strong organizational commitment by its employees.

B.4.2 Behaviors at Work

Employers want their employees to engage in behaviors that will make them successful in the job, because their success helps the organization meet its goals, including earning profits and fulfilling its mission. Employees have control over two aspects of their work: their time and their effort (Naylor, Pritchard, & Ilgen, 1980). Employees that both attend work instead of being late or absent and exert effort while at work are important to performance and productivity. Positive behaviors such as *organizational citizenship behaviors* generally help an organization meet its goals, whereas negative behaviors such as *organizational withdrawal* and *counterproductive behaviors* detract from goal attainment.

Organizational Citizenship Behaviors

Organizational citizenship behaviors (OCBs), or prosocial behaviors, are often described as extra-role behaviors because they are behaviors not specifically required by the job and not usually evaluated during performance reviews. These behaviors go beyond what is expected by the organization (C. A. Smith, Organ, & Near, 1983). Examples include staying late to finish a project, mentoring a new employee, volunteering for work, and helping a coworker. Some reasons why people engage in organizational citizenship behaviors are job satisfaction, high job autonomy, a positive organizational culture, high agreeableness (as a personality dimension; Witt et al., 2002), and high conscientiousness (Borman et al., 2001). OCBs have positive consequences for the organization and for employees in their day-to-day interactions with others in the organization.

Organizational Withdrawal and Counterproductive Behaviors

Unhappy employees cause problems for organizations because they sometimes engage in behaviors that researchers refer to as *organizational withdrawal* and *counterproductive behaviors*. **Organizational withdrawal** has been defined as behaviors employees use to avoid their work (**work withdrawal**) or their job (**job withdrawal**) (Hanisch, 1995; Hanisch & Hulin, 1990, 1991). Examples of work withdrawal are being absent from work, leaving work early, arriving to work late, missing meetings, and using work equipment for personal use without permission. Examples of job withdrawal are quitting one's job, transferring to another department within an organization, and retiring.

College students are familiar with withdrawal behaviors when it comes to certain college courses. For example, in some classes it may be difficult to maintain your attention, and you may find yourself taking a nap in class or texting with a friend during lecture. You may even look for legitimate reasons not to attend class,

organizational citizenship behaviors (OCBs) employee behaviors that go beyond what is expected by the organization

organizational withdrawal work withdrawal or job withdrawal

work withdrawal behaviors employees use to avoid their work (e.g., lateness, absenteeism)

job withdrawal behaviors employees use to avoid their job (e.g., quitting, retiring) such as offering to fill in for another employee at work or deciding to attend an optional session for another class.

counterproductive behaviors intentional behaviors on the part of an organizational member viewed by the organization as contrary to its legitimate interests

Counterproductive behaviors, although similar in some ways to withdrawal behaviors, are defined as "any intentional behavior on the part of an organizational member viewed by the organization as contrary to its legitimate interests" (Sackett & DeVore, 2001, p. 145). An example of a counterproductive behavior would be an intentional violation of safety procedures that puts the employee and the organization at risk. Other examples of counterproductive behavior are theft, destruction of property, unsafe behavior, poor attendance, drug use, and inappropriate physical actions such as attacking a coworker.

B.4.3 Relation Between Attitude and Behavior

Organizational citizenship behaviors are positively related to job satisfaction and organizational commitment. In other words, employees with good attitudes and who feel committed to their organization are more likely to do positive things to assist the organization (LePine, Erez, & Johnson, 2002; Riketta, 2008). Research suggests that those employees who demonstrate organizational citizenship behaviors are less likely to engage in counterproductive behaviors (Dalal, 2005). Some research indicates a negative association between job satisfaction and specific withdrawal or counterproductive behaviors such as absenteeism and job withdrawal (Falkenburg & Schyns, 2007; Hackett, 1989; Hanisch & Hulin, 1990).

Employers need to evaluate their work environment and benefit packages and make modifications where necessary to ensure that they have employees who are satisfied and committed. Art Friedman made modifications in the work environment of his organization that resulted in high satisfaction and commitment among his employees. To help with the inconvenience of going to the doctor, SAS built an on-site medical center for employees and their families; there is no charge unless you fail to show up for an appointment (Kaplan, 2010). Employees need to learn how to seek out satisfying work and perks that will result in their commitment to the organization. Satisfaction and commitment facilitate OCBs and decrease withdrawal and counterproductive behaviors. Together the right employee attitudes and behaviors will lead to successful organizational functioning.

B.4 Quiz Yourself

1. Quitting one's job would be an example of ______.
   a. normative commitment
   b. job withdrawal
   c. organizational citizenship behavior
   d. work withdrawal

2. ______ would be an example of an organizational citizenship behavior, whereas ______ would be an example of a counterproductive behavior.
   a. Mentoring a new employee; engaging in safe work practices`
   b. Being late; staying late to help a coworker
   c. Missing a meeting; being late for work
   d. Volunteering to serve on a committee; physically attacking your supervisor

3. Gordon's organizational commitment has been decreasing in the last year. Which of the following is Gordon *most* likely to do if his organizational commitment doesn't improve soon?
   a. Quit
   b. Be absent
   c. Ask for a raise
   d. Steal from the organization

Answers 1. b; 2. d; 3. a

B.5 Summary

This appendix has described the role of I/O psychologists in the workplace, including job analysis, employee recruitment and selection, organizational culture, performance appraisal, and the effect of employees' work attitudes on their work behaviors.

Now that you have an understanding of the process organizations use to hire successful employees, you have some of the tools necessary to help you in your search for a job. You have also learned about the appropriate matches you might strive for in seeking employment that will make your work with an organization fulfilling for both you and the company.

If you enjoyed learning about I/O psychology and think it might be a possible career for you, education and employment opportunities may interest you. Most I/O psychologists earn a master's or doctoral degree from a graduate school. This may take an additional 2 to 5 years beyond a bachelor's degree. Job opportunities are varied and often lucrative. For example, people with master's degrees in I/O psychology may work for an organization in its HR office or conduct research on the best ways to train its employees. They may also work for the government, be employed in a consulting firm, or start their own consulting firm after obtaining some experience in the workplace. Those who earn a doctoral degree may secure the same types of jobs as those with master's degrees, but will typically be paid more for their expertise. In addition, they may work for a university or college teaching courses or conducting research on topics of their choosing, or both. I/O psychology is an excellent career choice for many students interested in business who wish to have an impact on the work lives of employees.

Studying the Appendix

Key Terms

What Do You Know? Assess Your Understanding

Test your retention and understanding of the material by answering the following questions.

1. Industrial and organizational psychologists may be employed in _____.
   a. organizations
   b. universities
   c. government agencies
   d. All of the above

2. On an employee's first day working for the Campbell Company, they will most likely be required to attend _____.
   a. diversity training
   b. safety training
   c. employee orientation training
   d. job rotation training

3. Mentoring of new employees, in general, has been found to have positive outcomes or consequences for _____.
   a. both the mentor and the employee
   b. the mentor
   c. the employee
   d. organizations with autocratic leaders
4. Structured interviews are better than unstructured interviews because they are _____.
   a. easier to conduct
   b. more valid and reliable
   c. liked better by job applicants
   d. less time-consuming
5. Giving new employees a copy of their performance appraisal forms would be important in helping to _____.
   a. determine employees' organizational citizenship behaviors
   b. shape the culture and climate of the organization
   c. determine employees' organizational withdrawal behaviors
   d. increase affective commitment
6. SAS has company picnics and provides tickets to rodeos and the circus to help employees with the process of _____.
   a. organizational withdrawal
   b. organizational socialization
   c. organizational transformation
   d. organizational productivity
7. Todd stays late to help a coworker who has gotten behind on a project. Todd is exhibiting which type of behavior?
   a. Work withdrawal
   b. Productive behavior
   c. Organizational citizenship behavior
   d. Job withdrawal
8. The employees of SAS believe they have a great place to work with a fair employer and a trusting environment. In I/O psychology terms, they have a positive _____.
   a. organizational culture
   b. organizational climate
   c. work-group climate
   d. transformational leader
9. Terry has been offered a position in another company that pays better and has a more liberal leave policy than the current company. Terry is having a hard time deciding whether to accept the position because the current company allowed a lot of time off to care for Terry's parent. Terry's decision-making problem is likely due to _____.
   a. normative commitment
   b. occupational commitment
   c. affective commitment
   d. continuance commitment
10. Howard refers Lucille for a position in the organization. Based on research on employee referral programs, Lucille should _____.
   a. be more satisfied with the job
   b. be a poor performer
   c. file fewer grievances with the company
   d. stay longer with the organization

Answers: 1. d; 2. c; 3. a; 4. b; 5. b; 6. b; 7. c; 8. a; 9. a; 10. d

GLOSSARY

absolute threshold the minimum intensity of a stimulus at which participants can identify its presence 50% of the time

accommodation [uh-com-muh-DAY-shun] Chap. 3: the process through which the lens is stretched or squeezed to focus light on the retina; Chap. 9: the process by which a schema is changed, modified, or created anew in order to understand something new in the environment

acetylcholine [uh-see-til-COE-leen] (ACh) a neurotransmitter related to muscle movement and perhaps consciousness, learning, and memory

acquisition the process of learning a conditioned response or behavior

action potential a neural impulse fired by a neuron when it reaches −55 mv

activation-synthesis theory suggests that dreams do not have symbolic meaning, but are the by-product of the brain's random firing of neural impulses during REM sleep

actor/observer bias our tendency to make the fundamental attribution error when judging others, while being less likely to do so when making attributions about ourselves

actualizing [ACK-shu-lies-ing] tendency according to Rogers, the natural drive in humans to strive for fulfillment and enhancement

adrenal cortex the outside part of the adrenal gland that plays a role in the manufacture and release of androgens, and therefore influences sexual characteristics

adrenal [uh-DREEN-ull] medulla the center part of the adrenal gland that plays a crucial role in the functioning of the sympathetic nervous system

affective commitment an employee's emotional attachment to the organization

affective component of emotion the subjective experience of what you are feeling during the emotion

affective heuristic a heuristic in which we make quick judgements about people and things based on whether or not we have an immediate positive or negative emotional reaction to them

aggression an action that is intended to cause harm to another person who does not want to be harmed

agoraphobia [agg-or-uh-FOE-bee-uh] an excessive anxiety disorder characterized by fear of being in places from which escape might be difficult or where help might not be available if one were to experience panic

alarm reaction the first phase of the general adaptation syndrome, characterized by immediate activation of the nervous and endocrine systems

algorithm [AL-go-rih-thum] a method of solving a particular problem that always leads to the correct solution

all-or-none law all action potentials are equal in strength; once a neuron begins to fire an action potential, it fires all the way down the axon

alogia [uh-LO-jeeuh] a negative symptom of schizophrenia involving decreased quality and/or quantity of speech

alternative hypothesis (H_1) the hypothesis that contains a statement of what we do believe is true about our variables in the population

altruism helping another without being motivated by self-gain

amplitude a physical property of some energies that corresponds to the height of wave peaks

amygdala [uh-MIG-duh-luh] a part of the limbic system that plays a role in the emotions of fear and aggression

anal stage Freud's second psychosexual stage, which occurs from approximately 18 months to 3 years of age, in which the parents' regulation of the child's biological urge to expel or retain feces influences personality development

androgens [ANN-dro-jens] a class of male hormones that regulate many aspects of sexuality and are found in both males and females

anorexia [an-or-EX-ee-uh] nervosa an eating disorder in which a person has an intense fear of gaining weight, even though they are actually underweight; this irrational fear motivates the person to lose unhealthy amounts of weight through self-starvation

anterograde [an-TARE-oh-grade] amnesia an inability to store new declarative memories in long-term memory

antianxiety medications minor tranquilizers such as Valium that are prescribed to reduce tension and anxiety

antidepressants medications prescribed to alleviate the symptoms of depression, eating disorders, drug cravings, some anxiety disorders, and obsessive-compulsive disorder

antimanic medications drugs that are prescribed to alleviate manic symptoms of bipolar disorder

antipsychotic medications major tranquilizers such as Haldol that are prescribed to relieve psychotic symptoms such as delusions and hallucinations

antisocial personality disorder a personality disorder marked by a pattern of impulsivity and disregard for and violation of the rights of others with no remorse or guilt for one's actions

anxiety hierarchy a list that orders, according to the degree of fear, the situations or items that trigger anxiety; the list starts with the least frightening images and progresses to the most distressing

approach-approach conflict a situation in which a person must choose between two likable events

approach-avoidance conflict a situation in which a person is faced with a desire or need that has both positive and negative aspects

archetypes [ARE-kuh-types] according to Jung, mental representations or symbols of themes and predispositions to respond to the world in a certain way that are contained in the collective unconscious

assimilation [uh-sim-uh-LAY-shun] the process by which an existing schema is used to understand something new in the environment

association cortex areas of the cortex involved in the association or integration of information from the motor-sensory areas of the cortex

attachment an emotional bond between an infant and someone or something; an infant's first attachment with their caretaker is typically established by 8 or 9 months

attention conscious awareness; can be focused on events that are taking place in the environment or inside our minds

attitudes evaluative beliefs that we hold about things in our world

attitudes at work satisfaction with the work itself, pay and benefits, supervision, coworkers, promotion opportunities, working conditions, and job security

attribution the act of assigning cause to behavior

auditory cortex a region of cortex found in the temporal lobe that governs the processing of auditory information in the brain

auditory nerve the nerve that carries information from the inner ear to the brain

authoritarian [ah-thor-uh-TARE-ee-an] parent a parenting style characterized by high levels of control and low levels of affection

authoritative [ah-thor-uh-TAY-tive] parent a parenting style characterized by moderate levels of control and affection

autobiographical memory memory for our past that gives us a sense of personal history

autonomic nervous system the branch of the peripheral nervous system that primarily governs involuntary organ functioning and actions in the body

availability heuristic a heuristic in which we use the ease with which we can recall instances of an event to help us estimate the frequency of the event

aversion [uh-VER-shun] therapy Chap. 6: a type of therapy that uses classical conditioning to condition people to avoid certain stimuli; Chap. 14: a behavior therapy technique in which a specific behavior is paired with an unpleasant stimulus in order to reduce its occurrence

aversive racism a proposed form of subtle racism in which European Americans feel aversive emotions around African Americans, which may lead them to discriminate against African Americans

avoidance-avoidance conflict a situation in which a person must choose between two undesirable events

avolition [aa-vuh-LISH-un] a negative symptom of schizophrenia marked by the inability to follow through on one's plans

axon [AXE-on] a long tail-like structure growing out of the cell body of a neuron that carries action potentials that convey information from the cell body to the synapse

babbling the combinations of vowel and consonant sounds uttered by infants beginning around 4 months

basic anxiety according to Horney, the feeling of helplessness that develops in children from early relationships

basic emotions a proposed set of innate emotions that are common to all humans and from which other higher-order emotions may derive

basic level category the intermediate level of categorization that seems to be the level that we use most to think about our world

basilar membrane the structure in the cochlear duct that contains the hair cells, which convert sound waves into neural impulses

behavior modification using the principles of learning to modify problematic behaviors

behavior therapy therapy that applies the principles of classical and operant conditioning to help people change maladaptive behaviors

behavioral genetics field of study that examines the influence of genetics and hereditary factors on personality traits

behavioral perspective an approach that focuses on external, environmental influences on behavior

behaviorism Chap. 1: a psychological perspective that emphasizes the study of observable stimuli, responses, and consequences; Chap. 6: a school of thought in psychology that emphasizes the study of observable behavior over the study of the mind

bereavement [bee-REEVE-munt] the experience of losing a loved one

binge eating disorder (BED) an eating disorder characterized by recurrent episodes of binge eating, as in bulimia nervosa, but without regular use of compensatory measures to avoid weight gain

binocular [bye-NOCK-you-lar] depth cues depth cues that utilize information from both eyes

biological perspective an approach that focuses on physical causes of behavior

biological preparedness a genetic tendency to learn certain responses very easily

biomedical therapy the use of medications or other medical interventions to treat mental health disorders

bipolar disorder a bipolar-related disorder characterized by mania or mania and depression that interferes with a person's ability to function

bisexuals people who are sexually attracted to members of both sexes

blindspot the point where the optic nerve leaves the retina (the optic disk), where there are no rods or cones

blunted affect a negative symptom of schizophrenia involving lack of emotional expression

borderline personality disorder (BPD) a personality disorder marked by a pattern of instability in mood, relationships, self-image, and behavior

bottom-up perceptual processing perception that is not guided by prior knowledge or expectations

brightness the intensity of light; it corresponds to the amplitude of the light waves

Broca's aphasia [ah-FAYZ-yah] a condition resulting from damage to Broca's area of the brain that leaves the person unable to produce speech

Broca's [BRO-kuz] area a region in the left frontal lobe that plays a role in the production of speech

bulimia nervosa an eating disorder in which a person alternately binges on large quantities of food and then engages in some inappropriate compensatory behavior to avoid weight gain

bystander effect the idea that the more witnesses there are to an emergency, the less likely any one of them is to offer help

"can-do" factors factors that include an employee's knowledge, skills, and abilities that determine their maximum job performance

Cannon-Bard theory a theory of emotion that states that emotions originate in the brain, not the body

cardinal traits according to Allport, those dominant elements of our personalities that drive all of our behaviors

case study an in-depth observation of one or a few participants or settings

catatonic excitement a positive symptom of schizophrenia marked by disorder in motor behavior involving excited agitation

catatonic [cat-uh-TAWN-ick] stupor a positive symptom of schizophrenia marked by disorder in motor behavior involving immobility

causal hypothesis an educated guess about how one variable will influence another variable

cell body the part of the neuron that contains the nucleus and DNA

central executive the attention-controlling component of working memory

central nervous system (CNS) the brain and the spinal cord

central route to persuasion a style of thinking in which the person carefully and critically evaluates persuasive arguments and generates counterarguments; the central route requires motivation and available cognitive resources

central traits according to Allport, the tendencies we have to behave in a certain way across most situations

centration the act of focusing on only one aspect or feature of an object

cerebellum a hindbrain structure that plays a role in balance, muscle tone, and coordination of motor movements

cerebral cortex the thin, wrinkled outer covering of the brain in which high-level processes such as thinking, planning, language, interpretation of sensory data, and coordination of sensory and motor information take place

cerebral hemispheres the right and left sides of the brain that to some degree govern different functions in the body

cholecystokinin [coe-lih-cyst-oh-KYE-nin] (CCK) a hormone released by the small intestines that plays a role in hunger regulation

chunking a means of using one's limited short-term memory resources more efficiently by combining small bits of information to form larger bits of information, or chunks

circadian [sir-KAY-dee-un] rhythm changes in bodily processes that occur repeatedly on approximately a 24- to 25-hour cycle

classical conditioning learning that occurs when a neutral stimulus is repeatedly paired with an unconditioned stimulus; because of this pairing, the neutral stimulus becomes a conditioned stimulus with the same power as the unconditioned stimulus to elicit the response in the organism

client-centered therapy a humanistic psychotherapy approach developed by Carl Rogers that emphasizes the use of empathy, genuineness, and unconditional positive regard to help the client reach their potential

clinical interview the initial meeting between a client and a clinician in which the clinician asks questions to identify the difficulty in functioning that the person is experiencing

closure a Gestalt principle of perception that states that when we look at a stimulus, we tend to see it as a closed shape rather than lines

cochlea [COCK-lee-uh] the curled, fluid-filled tube in the inner ear that contains the basilar membrane

coding system a system of encoding in which memories can be stored in memory using a visual, acoustic (with sound), verbal, or semantic (in terms of meaning) format

cognition Chap. 1: mental processes such as reasoning and problem solving; Chap. 8: the way in which we use and store information in memory

cognitive-behavioral therapy (CBT) a range of treatment approaches to alter faulty cognitions and maladaptive behaviors

cognitive consistency the idea that we strive to have attitudes and behaviors that do not contradict one another

cognitive dissonance theory a theory that predicts that we will be motivated to change our attitudes and/or our behaviors to the extent that they cause us to feel cognitive dissonance, an uncomfortable physical state

cognitive distortions Chap. 13: thoughts that tend to be pessimistic and negative; Chap. 14: distorted thinking patterns, such as overgeneralization or all-or-none thinking, that, according to Aaron Beck, lead to depression, anxiety, and low self-esteem

cognitive map a mental representation of the environment that is formed through observation of one's environment

cognitive-mediational theory a theory of emotion that states that our cognitive appraisal of a situation determines what emotion we will feel in the situation

cognitive neoassociation theory proposes that cues present during an aggressive event can become associated in memory with the thoughts and emotions experienced during that event

cognitive perspective an approach that focuses on how mental processes influence behavior

cognitive reappraisal [re-uh-PRAY-zull] an active and conscious process in which we alter our interpretation of a stressful event in order to reduce negative feelings

cognitive therapy a cognitive therapy approach created by Aaron Beck that focuses on uncovering negative automatic thought patterns that impede mental health

cohesiveness [coe-HEE-siv-ness] the degree to which members of a group value their group membership; cohesive groups are tight-knit groups

collective unconscious according to Jung, the part of the unconscious that contains images and material universal to people of all time periods and cultures

collectivistic cultures cultures, like many Asian cultures, in which group accomplishments are valued over individual accomplishments

color blindness a condition in which a person cannot perceive one or more colors because of altered cone activity in the retina

compliance yielding to a simple request

compulsions repetitive behaviors that a person feels a strong urge to perform

concepts mental categories that contain related bits of information

concrete operations Piaget's third stage of cognitive development, characterized by logical thought

conditioned response (CR) the response that is elicited by a conditioned stimulus

conditioned stimulus (CS) a stimulus that elicits a conditioned response in an organism

cones the cells of the retina that are sensitive to specific colors of light and send information to the brain concerning the colors we are seeing

confidentiality the ethical principle that researchers do not reveal which data were collected from which participant

confirmation bias a tendency to interpret people's behavior in a way that supports our expectations

conflict a situation in which a person must choose between two or more needs, desires, or demands

conformity behaving in accordance with group norms

confounding variables factors other than the independent variable that affect the dependent measure

conscious [CON-shus] level the level of consciousness that holds all the thoughts, perceptions, and impulses of which we are aware

consciousness [CON-shis-nus] Chap. 4: feelings, thoughts, and aroused states of which we are aware; Chap. 7: an organism's awareness of its own mental processes and/or its environment

conservation the understanding that an object retains its original properties even though it may look different

constructive memory memory that utilizes knowledge and expectations to fill in the missing details in retrieved memory traces

contact hypothesis the theory that contact between groups is an effective means of reducing prejudice between them

contiguity [con-teh-GYU-eh-tee] the degree to which two stimuli occur close together in time

contingency [con-TINGE-en-see] the degree to which the presentation of one stimulus reliably predicts the presentation of the other stimulus

continuance commitment remaining with an organization because of the high cost (monetary or social or both) of losing organizational membership

continuity hypothesis suggests that dreaming is a way of coping with daily problems and issues

continuous reinforcement a schedule of reinforcement in which the organism is reinforced for every instance of the desired response

control group the group of participants who do not receive the manipulation that is being tested

cooing the vowel sounds made by infants beginning at 2 months

coping the behaviors that we engage in to manage stressors

cornea [COR-nee-ah] the clear, slightly bulging outer surface of the eye that both protects the eye and begins the focusing process

corpus callosum [COR-puss cal-OH-sum] a thick band of neurons that connects the right and left hemispheres of the brain

correlation [cor-ruh-LAY-shun] the relationship between two or more variables

correlation coefficient the average product of z scores calculated on pairs of scores; describes the degree to which the scores in the pairs are linearly related

counterconditioning removing a classically conditioned response by conditioning a new, incompatible response to the unconditioned stimulus

counterproductive behaviors intentional behaviors on the part of an organizational member viewed by the organization as contrary to its legitimate interests

couple therapy therapy that focuses on improving communication and intimacy between two people in a committed relationship

covert sensitization [co-VERT sen-sih-tuh-ZAY-shun] therapy a milder form of aversion therapy in which graphic imagery is used to create unpleasant associations with specific stimuli

creativity the ability to combine mental elements in new and useful ways

critical thinking thought processes used to evaluate and analyze information and apply it to other situations

crystallized intelligence Chap. 8: our accumulation of knowledge; Chap. 9: abilities that rely on knowledge, expertise, and judgment

cue-dependent forgetting a type of forgetting that occurs when one cannot recall information in a context other than the context in which it was encoded

cultural bias the degree to which a test puts people from other cultures at an unfair disadvantage because of the culturally specific nature of the test items

cycle a physical characteristic of energy defined as a wave peak and the valley that immediately follows it

cyclothymic [sigh-clo-THIGH-mik] disorder a bipolar-related disorder that is a less severe but more chronic form of bipolar disorder

daily hassles the everyday irritations and frustrations that individuals face

dark adaptation the process through which our eyes adjust to dark conditions after having been exposed to bright light

data information gathered in scientific studies

debriefing the ethical principle that participants be fully informed of the nature of the study after participating in research involving deception

decay theory a theory of forgetting that proposes that memory traces that are not routinely activated in long-term memory will degrade

decibels [DESS-uh-bells] (dB) the unit of measurement used to describe the loudness of a sound

decision making making a choice from among a series of alternatives

declarative memory a type of long-term memory encompassing memories that are easily verbalized, including episodic and semantic memories

deductive reasoning reasoning from the general to the specific

defense mechanisms Chap. 11: processes used to protect the ego by reducing the anxiety it feels when faced with the conflicting demands of the id and the superego; Chap. 12: unconscious, emotional strategies that are engaged in to reduce anxiety and maintain a positive self-image

deindividuation [DEE-in-dih-vid-you-AY-shun] a state in which a person's behavior becomes controlled more by external norms than by the person's own internal values and morals

delay of gratification learning to forego immediate reinforcement in favor of waiting for a later, sometimes larger, reinforcement

delusions thoughts or beliefs that a person believes to be true but that most people would agree are not true

dendrites [DEN-drights] branchlike structures on the head of the neuron that receive incoming signals from other neurons in the nervous system

dependent variable the variable in an experiment that measures any effect of the manipulation

depressants drugs that inhibit or slow down normal neural functioning

dermis the inner layer of the skin

descriptive statistics statistics that are calculated to summarize or describe certain aspects of a data set

destructive obedience obedience to immoral, unethical demands that cause harm to others

development changes in behavior or abilities or both

***Diagnostic and Statistical Manual of Mental Disorders* (*DSM*)** a book published by the American Psychiatric Association that lists the diagnostic criteria for close to 300 mental health disorders

dialectical reasoning or thinking an advanced type of reasoning that emerges, in part, from cultural influences. When examining opposing or contradictory statements, dialectical reasoning does not assume that one statement is necessarily true and the other is therefore necessarily false. Rather, both statements are assumed to have the potential to be at least partially true, and logic, reason, and discourse are used in an attempt to fully understand the opposing views.

diffusion of responsibility the idea that responsibility for taking action is diffused across all the people witnessing an event

discrimination the behavioral expression of a prejudice

dishabituation [DIS-huh-bit-chew-AYE-shun] responding to a stimulus to which one has been habituated

disordered behavior a positive symptom of schizophrenia that includes inappropriate or unusual behavior such as silliness, catatonic excitement, or catatonic stupor

disorganized speech a positive symptom of schizophrenia in which one's speech lacks association between one's ideas and the events that one is experiencing

display rules cultural rules governing when it is and isn't appropriate to display certain emotions

dissociative [dih-SO-shee-tive] disorders mental health disorders marked by a loss of awareness of some part of one's self or one's surroundings that seriously interfere with the person's ability to function

dissociative identity disorder (DID) a disorder in which two or more identities coexist within the same individual

DNA the chemical found in the nuclei of cells that contains the genetic blueprint that guides development in the organism

door-in-the-face compliance increasing compliance by first asking people to give in to a very large request and then, after they refuse, asking them to give in to a smaller request

dopamine [DOPE-uh-mean] a neurotransmitter that plays a role in reward, movement, motivation, learning, and attention

double-blind studies experiments in which neither the experimenters nor the participants know to which group (experimental or control) participants have been assigned

Down syndrome a genetic birth disorder resulting from an extra 21st chromosome, characterized by distinct facial features and a greater likelihood of heart defects and intellectual disability

dream analysis a technique in psychoanalysis in which the therapist examines the hidden symbols in a client's dreams

drive an uncomfortable internal state that motivates us to reduce this discomfort through our behavior

drive reduction theories theories of motivation that propose that people seek to reduce internal levels of drive

dualistic [do-uhl-LIS-tik] thinking reasoning that divides situations and issues into right and wrong categories

eclectic [ee-KLECK-tic] approach an approach that integrates and combines several perspectives when explaining behavior

eclectic [ee-KLECK-tick] therapy approach therapy that incorporates an integrated and diverse use of therapeutic methods

ego the part of the personality that attempts to meet the demands of the id in a socially appropriate way

egocentrism [ee-go-SEN-trih-zum] the belief that everyone thinks as you do

elaborative rehearsal forming associations or links between information one is trying to learn and information already stored in long-term memory so as to facilitate the transfer of this new information into long-term memory

Electra complex in the female, an unconscious sexual urge for the father that develops during the phallic psychosexual stage

electroconvulsive therapy (ECT) a series of treatments in which electrical current is passed through the brain, causing a seizure; used to alleviate severe depression

embryonic [em-bree-AH-nik] stage the second stage of prenatal development, lasting from the 3rd through the 8th week

emerging adulthood the transitional period between late adolescence and the mid-20s when young people have left adolescence but have not yet assumed adult roles and responsibilities

emotion a complex reaction to some internal or external event that involves physiological reactions, behavioral reactions, facial expressions, cognition, and affective responses

emotion-focused coping behaviors aimed at controlling the internal emotional reactions to a perceived stressor

emotional stability having control over one's emotions

empathy the ability of a therapist to understand a client's feelings and thoughts without being judgmental

encoding the act of inputting information into memory

endocrine [EN-doe-crin] glands the organs of the endocrine system that produce and release hormones into the blood

endocrine [EN-doe-crin] system a chemical system of communication in the body that uses chemical messengers, called hormones, to affect organ function and behavior

endorphins [in-DOOR-fins] neuromodulators that act as natural painkillers

enuresis [en-your-REE-sus] a condition in which a person over the age of 5 shows an inability to control urination during sleep

epidermis the outer layer of the skin

episodic [epp-uh-SOD-ick] memory memory for the recent events in our lives

erogenous [eh-ROJ-en-ous] zones areas of the skin that are sensitive to touch

estrogens [ESS-tro-jens] a class of female sex hormones that regulate many aspects of sexuality

estrus [ESS-truss] in most mammals, a period of "being in heat" in which the female is receptive to males' attempts to mate with her

evolutionary perspective an approach that focuses on how evolution and natural selection influence behavior

excitation when a neurotransmitter makes the postsynaptic cell more positive inside, it becomes more likely to fire an action potential

excitement phase the first stage of the sexual response cycle, in which males get erections and females produce vaginal lubrication

exemplars [ig-ZEM-plar] a mental representation of an actual instance of a member of a category

exhaustion stage the third and final phase of the general adaptation syndrome, in which bodily resources are drained and wear and tear on the body and well-being begins

experiment a research method that is used to test causal hypotheses

experimental group the group of participants who receive the manipulation that is being tested

explicit memory the conscious use of memory

extinction the removal of a conditioned response

extinction burst a temporary increase in a behavioral response that occurs immediately after extinction has begun

extrasensory perception (ESP) also known as *psi*, the ability to acquire information about the world without using the known senses

extraversion [ex-tra-VER-shun] personality traits that involve energy directed outward, such as being easygoing, lively, or excitable

extrinsic motivation motivation that comes from outside the person

eye movement desensitization and reprocessing (EMDR) therapy an eclectic therapy approach to treat trauma in which the client attends to emotionally disturbing images while simultaneously focusing on an external stimulus

facial feedback hypothesis a theory that states that our emotional state is affected by the feedback our brain gets from facial muscles

family therapy therapy that focuses on creating balance and restoring harmony to improve the functioning of the family as a whole system

feature detection theory a theory of perception that proposes that we have specialized cells in the visual cortex, feature detectors, that fire only when they receive input that indicates we are looking at a particular shape, color, angle, or other visual feature

fetal alcohol syndrome (FAS) a birth condition resulting from the mother's chronic use of alcohol during pregnancy, characterized by facial and limb deformities and intellectual disability

fetal stage the third stage of prenatal development, from the 9th week through the 9th month

figure-ground a Gestalt principle of perception that states that when we perceive a stimulus, we visually pull the figure part of the stimulus forward while visually pushing backward the background, or ground, part of the stimulus

fine motor skills motor behaviors involving the small muscles of the body

five factor theory Costa and McCrae's trait theory that proposes five core dimensions to personality: openness to experience, conscientiousness, extraversion, agreeableness, and neuroticism

fixed interval schedule a schedule of reinforcement in which the organism is reinforced for the first desired response in an *x*th interval of time

fixed ratio schedule a schedule of reinforcement in which the organism is reinforced for every *x*th instance of the desired response

flashbulb memory an unusually detailed and seemingly accurate memory for an emotionally charged event

flooding a behavior therapy technique in which a client is exposed to a feared object or situation for a prolonged period until their anxiety extinguishes

fluid intelligence Chap. 8: the speed and efficiency with which we learn new information and solve problems; Chap. 9: abilities that rely on information-processing skills such as reaction time, attention, and working memory

foot-in-the-door compliance increasing compliance by first asking people to give in to a small request, which then paves the way for compliance with a second, larger request

forebrain the brain structures, including the limbic system, thalamus, hypothalamus, and cortex, that govern higher-order mental processes

forgetting curve a graph of the amount of learned information that is forgotten over time

formal concepts concepts that are based on learned, rigid rules that define certain categories of things

formal operations Piaget's final stage of cognitive development, characterized by the ability to engage in abstract thought

free association a technique in psychoanalysis in which the client says whatever comes to mind

frequency a physical characteristic of energy defined as the number of cycles that occur in a given unit of time

frequency distribution a graph of data that plots the frequency of data points on the *y*-axis and the data points themselves on the *x*-axis

frequency polygon a line graph that is used to illustrate a frequency distribution

frequency theory a theory that proposes that our brain decodes pitch directly from the frequency at which the hair cells of the basilar membrane are firing

frontal lobe the cortical area directly behind the forehead that plays a role in thinking, planning, decision making, language, and motor movement

frustration-aggression hypothesis the idea that frustration causes aggressive behavior

functional fixedness being able to see objects only in their familiar roles

functionalism an early psychological perspective concerned with how behavior helps people adapt to their environment

fundamental attribution error our tendency to overuse trait information when making attributions about others

gamma amino butyric [GAM-ma uh-MEAN-oh bee-you-TREE-ick] acid (GABA) the body's chief inhibitory neurotransmitter, which plays a role in regulating arousal and pain

gate control theory of pain a theory of pain that proposes that tiny neural networks in the spinal cord block pain signals from a particular part of the body when they receive additional neural signals from intense tactile stimulation being applied to the same part of the body

gender permanence the understanding that one's gender will not change

gender roles society's expectations for how males and females should behave

gender-schema theory the idea that gender roles are acquired through modeling and reinforcement processes that work together with a child's mental abilities

general adaptation syndrome (GAS) the general physical responses we experience when faced with a stressor

general intelligence (*g*) a general level of intelligence that underlies our separate abilities

generalizability [jen-er-uh-lies-uh--BILL-uh-tee] how well a researcher's findings apply to other individuals and situations

generalized anxiety disorder (GAD) an anxiety disorder characterized by chronic, constant worry in almost all situations

genes strands of DNA found in the nuclei of all living cells

genital stage Freud's final psychosexual stage of development, which begins at puberty, in which sexual energy is transferred toward peers of the other sex (heterosexual orientation) or same sex (homosexual orientation)

genotype [JEAN-oh-type] inherited genetic pattern for a given trait

genuineness the ability of a therapist to openly share their thoughts and feelings with a client

germinal stage the first stage of prenatal development, from conception to 14 days

Gestalt [gush-TALLT] approach a psychological school of thought originating in Germany that proposed that the whole of a perception must be understood rather than trying to deconstruct perception into its parts

ghrelin [GRELL-in] a hunger-stimulating hormone produced by the stomach

glia [GLEE-uh] cells brain cells that provide important support functions for the neurons and are involved in the formation of myelin

glucose the form of sugar that the body burns as fuel

glutamate [GLUE-tuh-mate] the chief excitatory neurotransmitter in the brain, found at more than 50% of the synapses in the brain

glycogen [GLIE-co-jen] a starchy molecule that is produced from excess glucose in the body; it can be thought of as the body's stored energy reserves

gonads [GO-nads] endocrine glands that directly affect sexual reproduction by producing sperm (testes) or eggs (ovaries)

good continuation a Gestalt principle of perception that states that we have a preference for perceiving stimuli that seem to follow one another as part of a continuing pattern

grammar the rules that govern the sentence structure in a particular language

graph a visual depiction of data

grief one's emotional reaction to the death of a loved one

gross motor skills motor behaviors involving the large muscles of the body

group therapy therapy that is administered to more than one person at a time

groupthink a situation in which a group fixates on one decision and members blindly assume that it is the correct decision

guided imagery a technique in which you focus on a pleasant, calming image to achieve a state of relaxation when you feel stressed

gustation [gus-TAY-shun] the sense of taste

habituation [huh-bit-chew-AYE-shun] the tendency of an organism to ignore repeated stimuli

hair cells neurons that grow out of the basilar membrane and convert sound waves into neural impulses

hallucinations perceiving something that does not exist in reality

hallucinogens [huh-LOO-sin-no-gens] drugs that simultaneously excite and inhibit normal neural activity, thereby causing distortions in perception

hardy personality a personality, high in the traits of commitment, control, and challenge, which appears to be associated with strong stress resistance

health psychology the subfield of psychology that investigates the relationship between people's behaviors and their health

health-defeating behaviors behaviors that increase the chance of illness, disease, or death

health-promoting behaviors behaviors that decrease the chance of illness, disease, or death

helping behavior another term for altruism

heterosexuals people who are sexually attracted primarily to members of the other sex

heuristic [hyur-RISS-tick] a shortcut or rule of thumb that may or may not lead to a correct solution to the problem

hierarchy of needs Maslow's theory that humans are motivated by different needs, some of which take precedence over others

hindbrain a primitive part of the brain that comprises the medulla oblongata, pons, and cerebellum

hippocampus [HIP-po-CAM-puss] a part of the brain that plays a role in the transfer of information from short- to long-term memory

histogram a bar graph that is used to illustrate a frequency distribution

hoarding disorder an obsessive-compulsive related disorder characterized by persistent difficulty in discarding possessions such that they accumulate and clutter living areas, causing significant distress and impairment in functioning

homeostasis [hoe-mee-oh-STAY-suss] an internal state of equilibrium in the body

homophobia prejudicial attitudes against homosexuals and homosexuality

homosexuals people who are sexually attracted primarily to members of the same sex

hormones the chemical messengers of the endocrine system

hostile aggression aggression that is meant to cause harm to others

HPA (hypothalamic-pituitary-adrenal) axis the major system that controls the stress response involving the hypothalamus, pituitary gland, and adrenal gland

hue the color of light; it corresponds to the light's wavelength

humanism a psychological perspective that emphasizes the personal growth and potential of humans

humanistic approach a personality perspective that emphasizes the individual, personal choice, and free will in shaping personality; assumes that humans have a built-in drive toward fulfilling their own natural potential

humanistic perspective an approach that focuses on how peoples' view of themselves and the world influence behavior

hypnosis a state of relaxation and heightened suggestibility

hypothalamus [high-poe-THAL-uh-muss] a part of the forebrain that plays a role in maintaining homeostasis in the body, involving sleep, body temperature, sexual behavior, thirst, and hunger; also the point where the nervous system intersects with the endocrine system

hypothesis an educated guess

id the unconscious part of the personality that seeks pleasure and gratification

illness anxiety disorder a somatic symptom and related disorder in which the person persistently worries over having a serious illness, without any evident physical basis

ill-structured problems problems for which algorithms are not known

imaginary audience the belief held by adolescents that everyone is watching what they do

immunosuppression [im-mew-no-suh-PREH-shun] the reduction in activity of the immune system

implicit memory the unconscious use of memory

impression formation the way that we understand and make judgments about others

in-group bias our tendency to favor people who belong to the same groups that we do

incentives goals or desires that we are motivated to fulfill

incubation [in-cue-BAY-shun] a period of not thinking about a problem that helps one solve the problem

independent variable the variable in an experiment that is manipulated

individualistic cultures cultures, like many Western cultures, in which individual accomplishments are valued over group accomplishments

inductive reasoning reasoning from the specific to the general

industrial and organizational (I/O) psychology the study of people's behavior at work using psychological principles

inferential statistics statistics that psychologists use in hypothesis testing to tell them when they should reject or accept their hypotheses about the population

informational conformity conformity that occurs when conformity pressures actually persuade group members to adopt new beliefs and/or attitudes

informed consent the ethical principle that research participants be told about various aspects of the study, including any risks, before agreeing to participate

in-group bias our tendency to favor people who belong to the same groups that we do

inhibition when a neurotransmitter makes the postsynaptic cell more negative inside, it becomes less likely to fire an action potential

inner ear the innermost portion of the ear that includes the cochlea

insight Chap. 6: a sudden realization about how to solve a problem that occurs after an organism has studied the problem for a period of time; Chap. 8: a new way of looking at a problem that leads to a sudden understanding of how to solve it

insomnia a sleep disorder in which a person cannot get to sleep and/or stay asleep

instinctive drift the tendency for an animal who has been conditioned to perform a certain behavior to abandon learned behavioral response in favor of a more instinctive response

instincts innate impulses from within a person that direct or motivate behavior

Institutional Review Board (IRB) a committee that reviews research proposals to ensure that ethical standards have been met

instrumental aggression aggression that is used to facilitate the attainment of a goal

insulin [IN-suh-lin] a hormone produced by the pancreas that facilitates the movement of glucose from the blood into the cells of the body

intelligence abilities that enable you to adapt to your environment and behave in a goal-directed way

intelligence quotient (IQ) one's mental age divided by one's chronological age times 100

interactionism the perspective that our genes and environmental influences work together to determine our characteristics

interpretations the psychoanalyst's views on the themes and issues that may be influencing the client's behavior

intrinsic motivation motivation that comes from within the person

introspection observing one's own thoughts, feelings, or sensations

introversion [in-tro-VER-shun] personality traits that involve energy directed inward, such as being calm or peaceful

intuition believing that something is true independent of any reasoning process

ions [EYE-ons] charged particles that play an important role in the firing of action potentials in the nervous system

James-Lange theory a theory of emotion that defines an emotion as a unique pattern of physiological arousal

job analysis identification of the critical elements of a job, including tasks, skills required, and working conditions

job satisfaction the positive or negative feelings associated with a job

job withdrawal behaviors employees use to avoid their job (e.g., quitting, retiring)

judgment the act of estimating the probability of an event

just noticeable difference (jnd) the minimum change in intensity of a stimulus that participants can detect 50% of the time

kinesthesis [kin-ess-THEE-sis] the ability to sense the position of our body parts in relation to one another and in relation to space

knowledge information stored in our long-term memory about the world and how it works

language a well-developed, syntactical verbal system for representing the world

latency [LATE-an-see] stage Freud's fourth psychosexual stage of development, which occurs from around age 6 to puberty, in which the child's sexuality is suppressed due to widening social contacts with school, peers, and family

latent content according to Freud, the symbolic meaning of a dream

latent learning learning that cannot be directly observed in an organism's behavior

lateral hypothalamus (LH) a region of the hypothalamus once thought to be the hunger center in the brain

law of effect a principle discovered by E. L. Thorndike, which states that behaviors that lead to positive consequences will be strengthened and behaviors that lead to negative consequences will be weakened

leadership a social influence process in which a person steers others toward a goal

learned helplessness Chap. 12: a passive response to stressors based on exposure to previously uncontrolled, negative events; Chap. 13: the belief that one cannot control the outcome of events

learning a relatively permanent change in behavior, or behavior potential, as a result of experience

lens the part of the eye that lies behind the pupil and focuses light rays on the retina

leptin a hormone released by fat cells in the body that plays a role in hunger regulation

levels-of-processing model a model that predicts that information that is processed deeply and elaboratively will be best retained in and recalled from long-term memory

libido [leh-BEE-doe] one's physical desire, or drive, to have sex

life events changes in one's life, good or bad, that require readjustment

light adaptation the process through which our eyes adjust to bright light after having been exposed to darkness

limbic system a system of structures, including the amygdala and hippocampus, that govern certain aspects of emotion, motivation, and memory

lithium a naturally occurring mineral salt prescribed to control manic symptoms in people with bipolar disorder; it influences several neurotransmitters in the brain, including glutamate, serotonin, and dopamine

lock-and-key theory a theory that proposes that olfactory receptors are excited by odor molecules in a way that is similar to the way in which neurotransmitters excite receptor sites

locus [LOW-cus] of control according to Rotter, the expectation of control we have over the outcome of an event; an internal locus means we expect some degree of personal control, whereas an external locus means we expect little personal control

long-term memory (LTM) a system of memory that works to store memories for a long time, perhaps even permanently

loudness the psychophysical property of sound that corresponds to the amplitude of a sound wave

low-balling increasing compliance by first getting the person to agree to a deal and then changing the terms of the deal to be more favorable to yourself

maintenance rehearsal repeating information over and over again to keep it in short-term memory for an extended period of time

major depressive disorder a depressive disorder involving sadness, feelings of worthlessness, loss of interest in one's usual activities, and changes in bodily activities such as sleep and appetite that persists for at least 2 weeks

mania a period of abnormally excessive energy and elation

manifest content according to Freud, what the dreamer recalls on awakening

matching hypothesis the theory that we are attracted to people whose level of physical attractiveness is similar to our own

mean a descriptive statistic that describes the most average, or typical, data point in the distribution

measures of central tendency descriptive statistics that describe the most central, or typical, data points in the frequency distribution

median a descriptive statistic that identifies the center of the frequency distribution; 50% of the scores are above and 50% are below this point in the distribution

medical model perspective that views mental health disorders as similar to physical diseases; they result from biological disturbances and can be diagnosed, treated, and cured like physical illnesses

meditation a practice whereby a person focuses their attention on a singular source such as a word, bodily sensation, or object for a period of time

medulla oblongata [meh-DOO-luh ob-LONG-ga-ta] a part of the hindbrain that controls basic, life-sustaining functions such as respiration, heart rate, and blood pressure

melatonin [mel-uh-TONE-in] a hormone in the body that facilitates sleep

memory the storage, processing, and retrieval of information in the mind

memory consolidation the stabilization and long-term storage of memory traces in the brain

memory theory suggests that dreams are a way to consolidate information and get rid of trivial details in our memories

memory traces the stored code that represents a piece of information that has been encoded into memory

menarche [MEN-ar-kee] a female's first menstruation

menopause the period when a female stops menstruating and is no longer fertile

mental age the age that reflects the child's mental abilities in comparison to the average child of the same age

mental health disorder a dysfunction in thinking (cognition), emotions, and/or social behavior that impairs functioning and is not culturally expected

mental representations memory traces that represent objects, events, people, and so on that are not present at the time

mental set the tendency to habitually use methods of problem solving that have worked for you in the past

mentoring the pairing of a current and often long-term employee (the mentor) with a new employee

mere exposure effect the idea that the more one is exposed to something, the more one grows to like it

meta-analyses research procedures that combine the findings from a number of scientific studies on the same question or topic to establish the reliability of the findings, observe any overall trends, and to resolve any discrepancies among the research studies

microsleep a brief episode of sleep that occurs in the midst of a wakeful activity

midbrain the brain structure that connects the hindbrain with the forebrain

middle ear the part of the ear behind the ear drum and in front of the oval window, including the hammer, anvil, and stirrup

mindfulness meditation a practice where a person intentionally focuses and pays attention to and experiences what is going on in the moment–their emotions, thoughts, and/or sensations–without judgment

mindfulness-based cognitive therapy (MBCT) an eclectic therapy approach to prevent relapse in people with recurrent depression that integrates mindfulness meditation and breathing exercises with cognitive-behavioral therapy

Minnesota Multiphasic [mul-tee-FAZE-ick] Personality Inventory (MMPI-2) a personality inventory that is designed to identify problem areas of functioning in an individual's personality

misinformation effect the distortion of memory that occurs when people are exposed to misinformation

mode a measure of central tendency that identifies the most common, or frequent, score in the distribution

monocular depth cues depth cues that require information from only one eye

moral reasoning how you decide what is right and what is wrong

morphemes [MORE-feems] the smallest units of sound in a language that have meaning

motive a tendency to desire and seek out positive incentives or rewards and to avoid negative outcomes

motor neurons neurons that transmit commands from the brain to the muscles of the body

multiple approach-avoidance conflicts situations that involve several choices, each of which has positive and negative features

multiple intelligences the idea that we possess different types of intelligence rather than a single, overall level of intelligence

myelin [MY-eh-lynn] a fatty, waxy substance that insulates portions of some neurons in the nervous system

myelin sheath [MY-eh-lynn SHEEth] the discontinuous segments of myelin that cover the outside of some axons in the nervous system

narcolepsy [NAR-co-lep-see] a rare sleep disorder in which a person falls asleep during alert times of the day

natural concepts concepts that develop naturally as we live our lives and experience the world

natural selection the cornerstone of Darwin's theory of evolution, which states that genes for traits that allow an organism to be reproductively successful will be selected or retained in a species and genes for traits that hinder reproductive success will not be selected and therefore will die out in a species

naturalistic observations research studies conducted in an environment in which the behavior typically occurs

nature-nurture debate/issue the degree to which biology (nature) or the environment (nurture) contributes to a person's development

negative correlation a relationship in which increases in one variable correspond to decreases in the other variable

negative feedback loop a system of feedback in the body that monitors and adjusts our motivation level so as to maintain homeostasis

negative punishment weakening a behavior by removing something pleasant from the organism's environment

negative reinforcement strengthening a behavior by removing something unpleasant from the environment of the organism

neodissociation [knee o dis-so-see-AYE-shun] theory Hilgard's proposal that hypnosis involves two simultaneous states: a hypnotic state and a hidden observer

neonate a newborn during the first 28 days of life

nervous system an electrochemical system of communication within the body that uses cells called neurons to convey information

neuromodulators [NUR-oh-MOD-yoo-lay-tors] chemicals in the nervous system that affect neural signaling without directly changing the resting potential of the postsynaptic cell

neurons [NUR-ons] cells in the nervous system that transmit information

neuropeptide Y a powerful hunger stimulant

neuroplasticity [NUR-o-plas-TI-city] the nervous system's ability to rewire its structures as a result of experience

neuroscience [NUR-o-SCI-ence] Chap. 1: a field of science that investigates the relationships between the nervous system and behavior/mental processes; Chap. 2: the study of how the brain and nervous system affect mental processes and behavior

neurosurgery for mental disorder a biomedical treatment approach involving surgically altering the brain to alleviate symptoms in someone with a mental health disorder

neuroticism [nur-RAH-tuh-siz-um] the degree to which one is emotionally unstable

neurotransmitters [NUR-oh-TRANS-mitt-ers] chemical messengers that carry neural signals across the synapse

neutral stimulus (NS) a stimulus that does not naturally elicit the unconditioned response in an organism

night terrors very frightening non-REM sleep episodes

nightmares brief scary REM dreams that are often remembered

non-REM sleep the relaxing state of sleep in which the person's eyes do not move

norepinephrine [nor-ep-in-EF-rin] (NOR) a neurotransmitter that plays a role in regulating sleep, arousal, and mood

norms unwritten rules or expectations for how group members should behave

normal distribution a bell-shaped, symmetric frequency distribution

normative commitment commitment to the organization based on feelings of obligation

normative conformity conformity that occurs when group members change their behavior to meet group norms but are not persuaded to change their beliefs and attitudes

null hypothesis (H_0) the hypothesis that contains a statement of what we do not believe is true about our variables in the population

obedience yielding to a demand

obesity having a body mass index of 30 or over

object permanence the understanding that an object continues to exist even when it is not present

observational learning learning through observation and imitation of others' behavior

obsessions recurrent thoughts or images that intrude on a person's awareness

obsessive-compulsive disorder (OCD) a disorder involving a pattern of unwanted intrusive thoughts and/or the urge to engage in repetitive actions that interferes with a person's functioning

occipital [ox-SIP-it-ull] lobe the cortical area at the back of the brain that plays a role in visual processing

Oedipus [ED-uh-puss] complex in the male, an unconscious sexual urge for the mother that develops during the phallic psychosexual stage

olfaction the sense of smell

olfactory epithelium [ole-FACT-uh-ree epp-ith-THEEL-ee-um] a special piece of skin at the top of the nasal cavity that contains the olfactory receptors

operant conditioning a type of learning in which the organism learns through the consequences of its behavior

opiates [OH-pee-ates] painkilling drugs that depress some brain areas and excite others

opponent-process theory the idea that we have dual-action cells beyond the level of the retina that signal the brain when we see one of a pair of colors

optic chiasm the point in the brain where the optic nerve from the left eye meets the optic nerve from the right eye

optic nerve the structure that conveys visual information away from the retina to the brain

oral stage Freud's first psychosexual stage of development, which occurs during the first 18 months of life, in which the handling of the child's feeding experiences influences personality development

organizational citizenship behaviors (OCBs) employee behaviors that go beyond what is expected by the organization

organizational climate the behavioral norms of an organization

organizational culture the shared cognitive assumptions and beliefs of an organization

organizational socialization the process by which members of an organization become a part of, or are absorbed into, the culture of the organization

organizational withdrawal work withdrawal or job withdrawal

orgasm phase the third stage of the sexual response cycle, in which the pelvic and anal muscles contract

orienting reflex the tendency of an organism to orient its senses toward unexpected stimuli

out-group homogeneity [home-uh-juh-NEE-it-tee] bias our tendency to see out-group members as being pretty much all alike

outer ear the outermost parts of the ear, including the pinna, auditory canal, and surface of the ear drum

outliers unusual data points that are at the extremes of the frequency distribution, either far above or below the mean

ovaries the organs in a female's body that produce eggs, or ova

overextension when a child uses one word to symbolize all manner of similar instances (e.g., calling all birds parakeet)

overweight having a body mass index of 25–29.9

panic disorder an anxiety disorder characterized by intense fear and anxiety in the absence of danger that is accompanied by strong physical symptoms

papillae [puh-PILL-ee] bumps on the tongue that many people mistake for taste buds

parasympathetic nervous system the branch of the autonomic nervous system most active during times of normal functioning

parietal [puh-RYE-it-ull] lobe the cortical area on the top sides of the brain that play a role in touch and certain cognitive processes

partial reinforcement a schedule of reinforcement in which the organism is reinforced for only some instances of the desired response

perception the process through which we interpret sensory information

perceptual set a general readiness to perceive something in a particular manner

performance appraisals the evaluations or reviews of employees' job performance

peripheral nervous system (PNS) all of the nervous system except the brain and the spinal cord

peripheral route to persuasion a style of thinking in which the person does not carefully and critically evaluate persuasive arguments or generate counter-arguments; the peripheral route ensues when one lacks motivation and/or available cognitive resources

permissive parent a parenting style characterized by low levels of control or discipline

persistent depressive disorder a depressive disorder that is a less severe but more chronic form of major depressive disorder

person-situation interaction the influence of the situation on the stability of traits; when in the same situation, we display similar behavior, but when the situation is different, behavior may change

personal fable the belief held by adolescents that they are unique and special

personal unconscious according to Jung, the part of the unconscious that consists of forgotten memories and repressed experiences from one's past

personality the unique collection of attitudes, emotions, thoughts, habits, impulses, and behaviors that define how a person typically behaves across situations

personality disorders mental health disorders marked by maladaptive behaviors that have been stable over a long period and across many situations

personality inventories objective paper-and-pencil or computerized self-report forms that measure personality on several dimensions or traits

persuasion a type of social influence in which someone tries to change our attitudes

phallic [FAH-lick] stage Freud's third psychosexual stage of development, which occurs between 3 and 6 years of age, in which little boys experience the Oedipus complex and little girls the Electra complex

phenotype [FEEN-oh-type] an actual characteristic that results from interaction of the genotype and environmental influences

pheromones [FAIR-uh-moans] airborne chemicals that are released from glands and detected by the vomeronasal organs in some animals and perhaps humans

phonemes [FOE-neems] the smallest units of sound in a language

photopigments light-sensitive chemicals that create electrical charges when they come into contact with light

pitch the psychophysical property of sound that corresponds to the frequency of a sound wave

pituitary [peh-TOO-uh-tare-ee] gland the master gland of the endocrine system that controls the action of all other glands in the body

place theory a theory that proposes that our brain decodes pitch by noticing which region of the basilar membrane is most active

placebo effect a measurable change in participants' behavior due to the expectation or belief that a treatment will have certain effects

plateau phase the second stage of the sexual response cycle, in which excitement peaks

pleasure principle the basis on which the id operates; the urge to feel good and maximize gratification

pluralistic ignorance the idea that we use the behavior of others to help us determine whether a situation is an emergency requiring our help; if no one else is helping, we may conclude that help isn't needed

pons a hindbrain structure that plays a role in respiration, consciousness, sleep, dreaming, facial movement, sensory processes, and the transmission of neural signals from one part of the brain to another

population of interest the entire universe of animals or people that could be studied

positive correlation a relationship in which increases in one variable correspond to increases in the other variable

positive psychology Chap. 1: the study of factors that contribute to happiness, positive emotions, and well-being; Chap. 12: the subfield of psychology that seeks to discover and promote those factors that contribute to happiness and well-being

positive punishment weakening a behavior by adding something unpleasant to the organism's environment

positive reinforcement strengthening a behavior by adding something pleasant to the environment of the organism

postformal thought the idea that a correct solution (or solutions) may vary, depending on the circumstances

postsynaptic neuron [post-sin-AP-tic NUR-on] the neuron that is receiving the signal at a synapse in the nervous system

posttraumatic stress disorder (PTSD) a trauma-related disorder, characterized by distressing memories, emotional numbness, and hypervigilance, that develops after exposure to a traumatic event

pragmatics the rules of conversation in a particular culture

preconscious [pre-CON-shus] level the level of consciousness that holds thoughts, perceptions, and impulses of which we could potentially be aware

prediction an expected outcome of how variables will relate

predictive hypothesis an educated guess about the relationships among variables

prejudice a largely negative stereotype that is unfairly applied to all members of a group regardless of their individual characteristics

preoperational stage Piaget's second stage of cognitive development, characterized by the use of symbols and illogical thought

presynaptic neuron [pre-sin-AP-tic NUR-on] the neuron that is sending the signal at a synapse in the nervous system

primacy effect the tendency for people to recall words from the beginning of a list better than words that appeared in the middle of the list

primary appraisal [uh-PRAY-zull] our initial interpretation of an event as irrelevant, positive, or stressful

primary drives drives that motivate us to maintain homeostasis in certain biological processes in the body

primary motor area a strip of cortex at the back of the frontal lobe that governs the execution of motor movement in the body

primary reinforcer a reinforcer that is reinforcing in and of itself

primary somatosensory [so-MAT-oh-SEN-sor-ee] area a strip of cortex at the front of the parietal lobe that governs the sense of touch

private speech Vygotsky's term describing the behavior of young children who talk to themselves to guide their own actions

primary visual area a region of cortex found in the back of the occipital lobe that processes visual information in the brain

proactive interference a type of forgetting that occurs when older memory traces inhibit the retrieval of newer memory traces

problem-focused coping behaviors that aim to control or alter the environment that is causing stress

procedural memory long-term memory for skills and behaviors

progressive relaxation training a stress management technique in which a person learns how to systematically tense and relax muscle groups in the body

projective test a less structured and subjective personality test in which an individual is shown an ambiguous stimulus and is asked to describe what they see

prosocial behavior behavior that helps others

prototypes our concepts of the most typical members of a category

proximity Chap. 3: a Gestalt principle of perception that states that we tend to group close objects together during perception; Chap. 10: physical closeness

pseudopsychology psychological information or conclusions that sound scientific but have not been systematically tested using the scientific method

psychoactive drugs substances that influence the brain and thereby the individual's behavior

psychoanalysis [sigh-co-uh-NAL-uh-sis] a method of therapy formulated by Freud that focuses on uncovering unconscious conflicts that drive maladaptive behavior

psychoanalytic [psi-co-an-uh-LIH-tic] perspective a personality approach developed by Sigmund Freud that sees personality as the product of driving forces within a person that are often conflicting and sometimes unconscious

psychoanalytic theory Sigmund Freud's view that emphasizes the influence of unconscious desires and conflicts on behavior

psychodynamic perspective an approach that focuses on internal unconscious mental processes, motives, and desires that may explain behavior

psychodynamic therapy modern psychoanalysis delivered in a shorter time that focuses less on the client's past and more on current problems and the nature of interpersonal relationships

psychological distance the degree to which one can disassociate oneself from the consequences of their actions

psychology the scientific study of behavior and mental processes

psychoneuroimmunology [sigh-ko-nur-o-im-ya-NAH-la-gee] the field of study that investigates the connections among psychology (behaviors, thoughts, emotions), the nervous system, and immune system functioning

psychopathology the scientific study of mental health disorders

psychopharmacology [sigh-co-farm-uh-KAH-lo-gee] the use of medications to treat mental health problems

psychophysics the study of how the mind interprets the physical properties of stimuli

psychotherapy the use of psychological principles and techniques to treat mental health disorders

psychoticism [psi-COT-uh-siz-um] the degree to which one is hostile, nonconforming, impulsive, and aggressive

puberty [PEW-bur-tee] the process of sexual maturation

punishment the weakening of a response that occurs when a behavior leads to an unpleasant consequence

pupil the hole in the iris through which light enters the eye

quasi-experiment a research study that is not a true experiment because participants are not randomly assigned to the different conditions

random assignment a method of assigning participants in which they have an equal chance of being placed in any group or condition of the study

range a measure of variability that is the difference between the high score and the low score of the distribution

rational-emotive therapy a cognitive therapy approach created by Albert Ellis that focuses on changing the irrational beliefs that are believed to impede mental health

realistic-conflict theory the theory that prejudice stems from competition for scarce resources

reality principle the basis on which the ego operates; finding socially appropriate means to fulfill id demands

reasoning drawing conclusions about the world based on certain assumptions

recall a type of retrieval process in which the probe or cue does not contain much information

recency effect the tendency for people to recall words from the end of a list better than words that appeared in the middle of the list

reciprocal determinism [ree-SIP-pra-cull dee-TER-min-iz-um] according to Bandura, the mutual interaction among one's behavior, thoughts, and environment determines personality

reciprocity [reh-cih-PRAH-cih-tee] a strong norm that states that we should treat others as they treat us

recognition a type of retrieval process in which the probe or cue contains a great deal of information, including the item being sought

reconstructive memory memory that is based on the retrieval of memory traces that contain the actual details of events we have experienced

recruitment the process organizations use to identify potential employees for a job

reflex an automatic response to a specific environmental stimulus

refractory period Chap. 2: a brief period of time after a neuron has fired an action potential during which the neuron is inhibited and unlikely to fire another action potential; Chap. 5: a time during the resolution phase in which males are incapable of experiencing another orgasm or ejaculation

reinforcement the strengthening of a response that occurs when the response leads to a pleasant consequence

relativistic [rell-uh-tah-VIS-tik] thinking the idea that in many situations there is not necessarily one right or wrong answer

reliability the degree to which a test yields consistent measurements over time

REM behavior disorder a condition in which normal muscle paralysis does not occur, leading to violent movements during REM sleep

REM rebound the loss of REM sleep is recouped by spending more time in REM on subsequent nights

REM sleep an active state of sleep in which the person's eyes move

representativeness heuristic a heuristic in which we rely on the degree to which something is representative of a category, rather than the base rate, to help us judge whether or not it belongs in the category

repression a type of forgetting proposed by Sigmund Freud in which memories for events, desires, or impulses that we find threatening are pushed into an inaccessible part of the mind called the unconscious

resilience the capacity to adapt well to significant stressors

resistance a process in psychoanalysis whereby the client behaves in such a way as to deny or avoid sensitive issues

resistance stage the second phase of the general adaptation syndrome, in which the nervous and endocrine systems continue to be activated

resolution phase the final stage of the sexual response cycle, in which the body returns to homeostasis

response an organism's reaction to a stimulus

response set theory of hypnosis asserts that hypnosis is not an altered state of consciousness, but a cognitive set to respond appropriately to suggestions

resting metabolic rate the rate at which we burn energy in our bodies when resting

resting potential the potential difference that exists in the neuron when it is resting (approximately −70 mv in mammals)

restless legs syndrome (RLS) a neurological movement disorder occurring primarily at night in which a person has unpleasant sensations in the legs and an irresistible urge to move them to relieve the discomfort

reticular formation a part of the midbrain that regulates arousal and plays an important role in attention, sleep, and consciousness

retina the structure at the back of the eye that contains cells that convert light into neural signals

retinal disparity a binocular depth cue that uses the difference in the images projected on the right and left retinas to inform the brain about the distance of a stimulus

retrieval the process of accessing information in memory and pulling it into consciousness

retroactive interference a type of forgetting that occurs when newer memory traces inhibit the retrieval of older memory traces

retrograde amnesia an inability to recall previously stored declarative memories from long-term memory

reuptake the process through which neurotransmitters are recycled back into the presynaptic neuron

rods the light-sensitive cells of the retina that pick up any type of light energy and convert it to neural signals

Rorschach [ROAR-shock] Inkblot Test a projective personality test consisting of 10 ambiguous inkblots in which a person is asked to describe what they see; the person's responses are then coded for consistent themes and issues

ruminative [RUE-muh-nay-tive] coping style the tendency to persistently focus on how one feels without attempting to do anything about one's feelings

sample the portion of the population of interest that is selected for a study

saturation the purity of light; light that consists of a single wavelength produces the richest or most saturated color

scaffolding [SKAH-fol-ding] a process in which adults initially offer guidance and support in helping a child to reason, solve a problem, or master a task; as the child becomes more proficient and capable, the adult helps less and less until the child can master the task on their own

scapegoat an out-group that is blamed for many of society's problems

scatter plot a graph of data that plots pairs of data points, with one data point on the *x*-axis and the other on the *y*-axis

schedule of reinforcement the frequency and timing of the reinforcements that an organism receives

schema [SKEE-ma] Chap. 7: an organized, generalized knowledge structure in long-term memory; Chap. 9: a mental idea, concept, or thought

schizophrenia [skit-suh-FREE-nee-uh] a severe mental health disorder characterized by disturbances in thought, perceptions, emotions, and behavior

scientific method a systematic process used by psychologists for testing hypotheses about behavior

secondary appraisal an evaluation of resources available to cope with a stressor

secondary drives learned drives that are not directly related to biological needs

secondary reinforcer a reinforcer that is reinforcing only because it leads to a primary reinforcer

secondary traits according to Allport, the tendencies we have that are less consistent and describe how we behave in certain situations

selective serotonin reuptake inhibitors (SSRIs) antidepressant drugs that inhibit the reuptake of the neurotransmitter serotonin, thereby improving mood

self-actualization [self-ack-shu-lih-ZAY-shun] the fulfillment of one's natural potential

self-concept one's perception or image of their abilities and uniqueness

self-determination theory a theory of motivation that proposes that as we pursue the fulfillment of basic needs, we experience different types of motivation that come from both the self and the outside world

self-efficacy [self-EF-fuh-kah-see] the expectation that one has for success in a given situation

self-help groups groups comprised of people who share the same problem and meet to help one another

self-serving bias our tendency to make attributions that preserve our own self-esteem—for example, making trait attributions for our successes and situational attributions for our failures

semantic encoding encoding memory traces in terms of the meaning of the information being stored

semantic memory long-term, declarative memory for conceptual information

sensation the process through which our sense organs convert environmental energy such as light and sound into neural signals

sensation seekers people who by trait tend to seek out arousing activities

sensitive periods in prenatal development, times when genetic and environmental agents are most likely to cause birth defects

sensorimotor stage Piaget's first stage of cognitive development, in which infants form schemas through their senses and motor abilities

sensory memory a system of memory that very briefly stores sensory impressions so that we can extract relevant information from them for further processing

sensory neurons neurons that transmit information from the sense organs to the central nervous system

separation anxiety the fear an infant expresses when separated from the primary caretaker

serotonin [ser-uh-TOE-nin] a neurotransmitter that plays a role in many different behaviors, including sleep, arousal, mood, eating, and pain perception

set point a particular weight that our body seeks to maintain

sexual arousal a heightened state of sexual interest and excitement

sexual desire one's motivation and interest in engaging in sexual activity

sexual orientation one's sexual attraction for members of the same and/or other sex

sexually transmitted infections (STIs) infections that are passed from one person to another primarily through sexual contact

shaping using operant conditioning to build a new behavior in an organism by reinforcing successive approximations of the desired response

short-term memory (STM) a system of memory that is limited in both capacity and duration; in the three stages model of memory, short-term memory is seen as the intermediate stage between sensory memory and long-term memory

signal detection theory states that our ability to detect the presence of a stimulus is affected by more than just the intensity of that stimulus. Factors such as fatigue, motivation, and attention may also affect these judgments

significant results are considered significant when there is a very small chance (usually less than 5%) of finding those results given the assumption that the null hypothesis is true

similarity a Gestalt principle of perception that states that we tend to group like objects together during perception

situational attribution an attribution that assigns the cause of a behavior to some characteristic of the situation or environment in which the behavior occurs

Skinner box device created by B. F. Skinner to study operant behavior in a compressed time frame; in a Skinner box, an organism is automatically reinforced or punished for engaging in certain behaviors

sleep apnea [APP-nee-uh] a sleep disorder in which a person stops breathing during sleep

sleep disorder a disturbance in the normal pattern of sleeping

sleepwalking a sleep disorder in which a person is mobile and may perform actions during non-REM slow-wave sleep

slippery slope the use of foot-in-the-door compliance in an obedience situation to get people to obey increasing demands

social anxiety disorder (social phobia) an anxiety disorder characterized by an irrational, persistent fear of being negatively evaluated by others in a social situation

social cognition the area of social psychology that deals with the ways in which we think about other people and ourselves

social cognitive approach a personality perspective that emphasizes the influence of one's thoughts and social experiences in formulating personality

social facilitation performing better on a task in the presence of others than you would if you were alone

social influence social pressures that serve to modify our thoughts and/or behavior

social loafing when group members exert less effort on a group task than they would if they were performing the task alone

social psychology the branch of psychology that studies how we think and behave in social situations

social support having close and positive relationships with others

sociocultural perspective an approach that focuses on societal and cultural factors that may influence behavior

somatic nervous system the branch of the peripheral nervous system that governs sensory and voluntary motor action in the body

somatic [so-MAA-tic] symptom and related disorders mental health disorders marked by physical complaints that have no apparent physical cause

source traits universal tendencies that underlie and are at the core of surface traits, according to Cattell

specific phobia an anxiety disorder characterized by a persistent fear and avoidance of a specific object or situation

split brain a brain with its corpus callosum severed; sometimes done to control the effects of epilepsy in people who do not respond to other therapies

spontaneous recovery during extinction, the tendency for a conditioned response to reappear and strengthen over a brief period of time before re-extinguishing

standard deviation a measure of variability equal to the square root of the variance; often used to gauge the degree to which an individual score deviates from the mean of a distribution

standard normal distribution a bell-shaped, symmetric distribution of z scores with ($\bar{Z} = 0, S = 1$) for which we know the exact area under the curve

standardized test a test that uses a standard set of questions, procedures, and scoring methods for all test takers

statistics a type of applied mathematics used to describe data and test hypotheses

stereotype a schema for a particular group of people

stereotype threat a phenomenon in which fears of being discriminated against elicit stereotype-confirming behaviors

stimulants drugs that speed up normal brain functioning

stimulus any object or event that is perceived by our senses

stimulus discrimination responding only to a particular stimulus

stimulus generalization responding in a like fashion to similar stimuli

storage the place where information is retained in memory

stranger anxiety the distress an infant expresses when faced with unfamiliar people

stress any event or environmental stimulus (stressor) that we respond to because we perceive it as challenging or threatening

structuralism an early psychological perspective concerned with identifying the basic elements of experience

structured interviews interviews conducted by a trained interviewer using standardized questions, a specific question order, and a predetermined scoring or answer key

subliminal perception when the intensity of a stimulus is below the participant's absolute threshold and the participant is not consciously aware of the stimulus

subordinate category the lowest level of categorization, which contains concepts that are less general and more specific than those at the basic level

substance use disorder a condition in which a person cannot control their drug use and continues to use a drug despite negative social, occupational, and health consequences, risky use, as well as evidence of tolerance or withdrawal

sum of squares the sum of the squared errors, or deviations, from the mean for the scores in the distribution; the numerator of the variance equation

superego the part of the personality that represents your moral conscience

superordinate category the highest, most general level of a concept

superordinate goal a goal that is shared by different groups

suprachiasmatic [sue-pra-kigh-as-MAT-ick] nucleus (SCN) a group of brain cells located in the hypothalamus that signal other brain areas when to be aroused and when to shut down

surface traits basic traits that describe people's personalities, according to Cattell

surveys research methods that ask a large group of people about their attitudes, beliefs, and/or behaviors

symbolic thinking the understanding that objects can be represented with symbols such as bodily gestures or language

sympathetic nervous system the branch of the autonomic nervous system most active during times of danger or stress

synapse [SIN-aps] the connection formed between two neurons when the axon bulb of one neuron comes into close proximity with the dendrite of another neuron

systematic desensitization [sis-tuh-MAT-ick dee-sen-sih-tuh-ZAY-shun] a behavior therapy technique that uses a gradual, step-by-step process to replace fear or anxiety with an incompatible response of relaxation and positive emotion

tardive dyskinesia [TAR-div dis-kuh-NEE-juh] a possible long-term side effect of conventional antipsychotic medications involving involuntary motor movements of the mouth, tongue, and face

taste aversion classical conditioning that occurs when an organism pairs the experience of nausea with a certain food and becomes conditioned to feel ill at the sight, smell, or idea of the food

taste buds the sense organs for taste that are found between the papillae on the tongue

telegraphic speech two-word sentences that children begin to utter at 20 to 26 months

temperament a person's general pattern of attention, arousal, and mood that is evident at birth

temporal [TEM-por-ull] lobe the cortical area directly below the ears that plays a role in auditory processing and language

teratogen [tur-RAH-tuh-jun] an environmental substance that has the potential to harm the developing organism

tests the measurements of carefully chosen samples of behavior

testes the organs in a male's body that produce both sperm and testosterone

testosterone a male hormone that plays a role in many aspects of sexuality, including sexual desire

thalamus [THAL-uh-muss] a part of the forebrain that functions as a sensory relay station

that's-not-all increasing compliance by sweetening the deal with additional incentives

THC (tetrahydrocannabinol) [tet-rah-high-dro-can-NAH-bin-all] the active ingredient in marijuana that affects learning, short-term memory, coordination, emotion, and appetite

Thematic Apperception [thee-MAT-ick ap-per-SEP-shun] Test (TAT) a projective personality test consisting of a series of pictures in which the respondent is asked to tell a story about each scene; the responses are then coded for consistent themes and issues

theory an explanation of why and how a behavior occurs

therapeutic alliance [thair-uh-PEW-tick uh-LIE-unce] the interactive and collaborative relationship between the client and the therapist

therapy techniques that are used to help people with mental health disorders or interpersonal problems

thinking the use of knowledge to accomplish some sort of goal

threat simulation theory (TST) suggests that dreaming is an ancient biological defense mechanism that allows us to repeatedly simulate potentially threatening situations so that we can rehearse our responses to these events

threshold of excitation the potential difference at which a neuron will fire an action potential (−55 mv in humans)

tip of the tongue phenomenon knowing that you know a piece of information, even though you cannot recall it at the moment

Title VII of the Civil Rights Act of 1964 the law that prohibits discrimination based on race, color, religion, sex, and national origin, and extends to sexual orientation and transgender status

token economy Chap. 6: a system of operant conditioning in which participants are reinforced with tokens that can later be cashed in for primary reinforcers; Chap. 14: a behavior therapy technique in which people are reinforced with tokens for desired behavior; the tokens can then be exchanged for what is reinforcing to the individuals

tolerance a condition in which after repeated use, more of a drug is needed to achieve the same effect

top-down perceptual processing perception that is guided by prior knowledge or expectations

traits tendencies to behave in a certain way across most situations

trait approach a personality perspective that attempts to describe personality by emphasizing internal, biological aspects of personality called traits

trait attribution an attribution that assigns the cause of a behavior to the traits and characteristics of the person being judged

transcranial magnetic stimulation (TMS) a biomedical treatment approach in which electromagnetic impulses stimulate brain neurons; used for treatment-resistant major depressive disorder, obsessive-compulsive disorder, and for pain from migraine headaches

transference a process in psychoanalysis in which the client unconsciously reacts to the therapist as if the therapist were a parent, friend, sibling, or romantic partner

transformational leadership characterized by high ethical standards, inspirational motivation, intellectual stimulation, and individual consideration

triarchic [tri-ARK-ic] theory of intelligence a theory that proposes that intelligence is composed of analytical, practical, and creative abilities that help us adapt to our environment

trichromatic [try-crow-MAT-ick] theory of color vision the idea that color vision is made possible by the presence of three different types of cones in the retina that react, respectively, to red, green, or blue light

two-factor theory of emotion a theory that states that emotions result when we cognitively interpret our physiological reactions in light of the situation

Type A personality a personality that is aggressive, ambitious, and competitive

Type B personality a personality characterized by patience, flexibility, and an easygoing manner

Type C personality a personality that is cautious, serious, sensitive to criticism, and results oriented, and that suppresses negative emotions such as anger

Type D personality a personality characterized by negative emotions and social inhibition

unconditional positive regard Chap. 11: acceptance and love of another's thoughts and feelings without expecting anything in return; Chap. 14: the ability of a therapist to accept and value a person for who they are regardless of their faults or problems

unconditioned response (UR) the response that is elicited by an unconditioned stimulus

unconditioned stimulus (US) a stimulus that naturally elicits a response in an organism

unconscious [un-CON-shus] level the level of awareness that contains all the inaccessible thoughts, perceptions, and impulses of which we are unaware

underextension when a child inappropriately restricts the use of a word to a particular case (e.g., using the word cat to describe only the family pet)

unstructured interviews informal, unplanned interviews conducted by an untrained interviewer using random questions and no scoring key

validity the degree to which a test measures what it claims to measure

variable interval schedule a schedule of reinforcement in which the organism is reinforced for the first desired response in an average *x*th interval of time

variable ratio schedule a schedule of reinforcement in which the organism is reinforced on average for every *x*th instance of the desired response

variance a measure of variability that shows on average how much the scores vary from the mean

ventromedial [ven-tro-MEE-dee-al] hypothalamus (VMH) a region of the hypothalamus that plays an indirect role in creating a feeling of satiety

vestibular [ves-STIB-you-lar] sense the sense of balance

visible spectrum the spectrum of light that humans can see

volley theory a theory that proposes that our brain decodes pitch by noticing the frequency at which groups of hair cells on the basilar membrane are firing

wavelength a physical property of some energies that corresponds to the distance between wave peaks

Weber's [VAY-bers] law psychological principle that states that for each of our five senses, the amount of change in the stimulus that is necessary to produce a jnd depends on the intensity at which the stimulus is first presented

well-structured problems problems for which there are clear pathways to the solutions

Wernicke's aphasia [ah-FAYZ-yah] a condition resulting from damage to Wernicke's area of the brain that leaves a person unable to comprehend speech

Wernicke's [WURR-neh-kees] area a region of the left temporal lobe that plays a role in the comprehension of speech

Whorfian [WORE-fee-un] hypothesis or the linguistic relativity hypothesis the theory that one's language can directly determine or influence one's thoughts

"will-do" factors factors that include personality traits, personal values, and motivations that an employee is willing to exert for the organization and that influence their normal or typical job performance

withdrawal symptoms physical or behavioral effects that occur after a person stops using a drug

work teams/groups two or more employees who together perform organizationally relevant tasks, share one or more common goals, interact socially, and exhibit task interdependencies

work withdrawal behaviors employees use to avoid their work (e.g., lateness, absenteeism)

working memory a multifaceted component of long-term memory that contains a central executive, an episodic buffer, a phonological loop, and a visuospatial sketch pad; the function of working memory is to access, move, and process information that we are currently using

***z* score** a measure of relative standing that measures the distance of a score from the mean of the distribution in standard deviation units

zone of proximal development (ZPD) according to Vygotsky, the gap between what a child is already able to do and what they are not yet capable of doing without help

zygote [ZIE-goat] a fertilized egg

REFERENCES

AAA Foundation for Traffic Safety. (2019). *2018 Traffic Safety Culture Index*. Author.

Aamodt, M. G. (2010). *Industrial/organizational psychology: An applied approach*. Thomson Wadsworth.

Abad, V. C., & Guilleminault, C. (2004). Review of rapid eye movement behavior sleep disorders. *Current Neurology Neuroscience Reports, 4,* 157–163.

Abar, B., Carter, K. L., & Winsler, A. (2009). The effects of maternal parenting style and religious commitment on self-regulation, academic achievement, and risk behavior among African-American parochial college students. *Journal of Adolescence, 32,* 259–273.

Abbass, A., Town, J., & Driessen, E. (2011). The efficacy of short-term psychodynamic psychotherapy for depressive disorders with comorbid personality disorder. *Psychiatry, 74,* 58–71.

Abbey, A. (2002). Alcohol-related sexual assault: A common problem among college students. *Journal of Studies on Alcohol, 14,* 118–128.

Abbott, C. C., Gallegos, P., Rediske, N., Lemke, N. T., & Quinn, D. K. (2014). A review of longitudinal electroconvulsive therapy: Neuroimaging investigations. *Journal of Geriatric Psychiatry and Neurology, 27,* 33–46.

Abbott, R. (2010). Delivering quality-evaluated healthcare information in the era of Web 2.0: Design implication for Intute: Health and Life Sciences. *Health Informatics Journal, 16,* 5–14.

Abboub, N., Nazzi, T., & Gervain, J. (2016). Prosodic grouping at birth. *Brain and Language, 162,* 46–59. doi:10.1016/j.bandl.2016.08.002

ABC News. (2004). *American Sex Survey.* https://abcnews.go.com/images/Politics/959a1AmericanSexSurvey.pdf.

Abdulla Alabbasi, A. M., A. Ayoub, A. E., & Ziegler, A. O. (2020). Are gifted students more emotionally intelligent than their non-gifted peers? A meta-analysis. *High Ability Studies*. https://doi.org/10.1080/13598139.2020.1770704

Abkevich, V., Camp, N. J., Hensel, C. H., Neff, C. D., Russell, D. L., Hughes, D. C., . . . Stone, S. (2003). Predisposition locus for major depression at chromosome 12q22–12q23.2. *American Journal of Human Genetics, 73,* 1271–1281.

Abramowitz, J. S., & Moore, E. L. (2007). An experimental analysis of hypochondriasis. *Behaviour Research and Therapy, 45,* 413–424.

Abrams, J. A., Javier, S. J., Maxwell, M. L., Belgrave, F. Z., & Nguyen, A. B. (2016). Distant but relative: Similarities and differences in gender role beliefs among African American and Vietnamese American women. *Cultural Diversity & Ethnic Minority Psychology, 22*(2), 256-267. doi:10.1037/cdp0000038.

Abramson, L. Y., Alloy, L. B., Hankin, B. L., Haeffel, G. J., MacCoon, D. G., & Gibb, B. E. (2002). Cognitive vulnerability: Stress models of depression in a self-regulatory and psychobiological content. In I. H. Gotlib & C. L. Hammen (Eds.), *Handbook of depression* (pp. 268–294). Guilford Press.

Acevedo, B. P., Aron, A., Fisher, H. E., & Brown, L. L. (2011). Neural correlates of long-term intense romantic love. *Social Cognitive and Affective Neuroscience, 7*(2), 145-159. doi:10.1093/scan/nsq092.

Ackerman, J. P., Riggins, T., & Black, M. M. (2010). A review of the effects of prenatal cocaine exposure among school-aged children. *Pediatrics, 125,* 554–565.

Ackerman, P. L. (2014). Adolescent and adult intellectual development. *Current Directions in Psychological Science, 23,* 246–251.

Ackerman, R. A., Kashy, D. A., Donnellan, M. B., Neppi, T., Lorenz, F. O., & Conger, R. D. (2013). The interpersonal legacy of a positive family climate in adolescence. *Psychological Science, 24,* 243–250.

Ackermann, S., & Rasch, B. (2014). Differential effects of non-REM and REM sleep on memory consolidation? *Current Neurology and Neuroscience Reports, 14,* 430.

Ackley, D. (2016). Emotional intelligence: A practical review of models, measures, and applications. *Consulting Psychology Journal: Practice and Research, 68*(4), 269–286. doi:10.1037/cpb0000070

Adachi, T., Fujino, H., Nakae, A., Mashimo, T., & Sasaki, J. (2014). A meta-analysis of hypnosis for chronic pain problems: A comparison between hypnosis, standard care, and other psychological interventions. *International Journal of Clinical and Experimental Hypnosis, 62,* 1–28.

Adam, E. K. (2006). Transactions among adolescent trait and state emotion and diurnal and momentary cortisol activity in naturalistic settings. *Psychoneuroendocrinology, 31,* 664–679.

Adamaszek, M., D'Agata, F., Ferrucci, R., Habas, C., Keulen, S., Kirkby, K. C., . . . Verhoven, J. (2016). Consensus paper: Cerebellum and emotion. *The Cerebellum, 16*(2), 552–576. doi:10.1007/s12311-016-0815-8

Ader, R. (2001). Psychoneuroimmunology. *Current Directions in Psychological Science, 10,* 94–98.

Aderibigbe, Y. A., Bloch, R. M., & Walker, W. R. (2001). Prevalence of depersonalization and derealization experiences in a rural population. *Social Psychiatry and Psychiatric Epidemiology, 36,* 63–69.

Adler, A. (1928). *Understanding human nature.* Allen & Unwin.

Administration on Aging (AOA). (2011). *A profile of older Americans: 2011.* U.S. Department of Health and Human Services. http://www.aoa.gov

Adólfsdóttir, S., Wollschlaeger, D., Wehling, E., & Lundervold, A. J. (2016). Inhibition and switching in healthy aging: A longitudinal study. *Journal of the International Neuropsychological Society, 23(1), 90–97.* doi:10.1017/S1355617716000898

Adolph, K. E., Karasik, L. B., & Tamis-Lemonda, C. S. (2009). Moving between cultures: Cross-cultural research on motor development. In M. Bornstein (Ed.), *Handbook of cross-cultural developmental science, Vol. 1. Domains of development across cultures* (pp. 61–88). Erlbaum.

Adolphs, R. (2002). Neural systems for recognizing emotion. *Current Opinion in Neurobiology, 12,* 169–177.

Adolphs, R., Tranel, D., & Damasio, A. R. (1998). The human amygdala in social judgment. *Nature, 393,* 470–474.

Afifi, T. O., Mather, A., Boman, J., Fleisher, W., Enns, M. W., MacMillan, H., & Sareen, J. (2011). Childhood adversity and personality disorders: Results from a nationally representative population-based study. *Journal of Psychiatric Research, 45,* 814–822.

Afifi, T. O., Mota, N., MacMillan, H. L., & Sareen, J. (2013). Harsh physical punishment in childhood and adult physical health. *Pediatrics, 132,* 333–340. doi:10.1542/peds.2012-4021.

Agahi, N., Shaw, B. A., & Fors, S. (2014). Social and economic conditions in childhood and the progression of functional health problems from midlife into old age. *Journal of Epidemiology and Community Health, 68,* 734–740.

Aghajanian, G. K. (1994). Serotonin and the action of LSD in the brain. *Psychiatric Annala, 24,* 137–141.

Aiello, J. R., & Douthitt, E. A. (2001). Social facilitation from Triplett to electronic performance monitoring. *Group Dynamics: Theory, Research, and Practice, 5,* 163–180.

Ainsworth, M. D., Blehar, M. C., Waters, E., & Wall, S. (1978). *Patterns of attachment: A psychological study of the strange situation.* Erlbaum.

Aït-Aïssa, S., de Gannes, F. P., Taxile, M., Billaudel, B., Hurtier, A., Haro, E., . . . Lagroye, I. (2013). In situ expression of heat-shock proteins and 3-nitrotyrosine in brains of young rats exposed to a Wi-Fi signal in utero and in early life. *Radiation Research, 179(6),* 707–716. doi:10.1667/RR2995.1

Aknin, L. B., Norton, M. I., & Dunn, E. W. (2009). From wealth to well-being? Money matters, but less than people think. *Journal of Positive Psychology, 4,* 523–527.

Albarracín, D., Kumkale, G. T., & Poyner-Del Vento, P. (2017). How people can become persuaded by weak messages presented by credible communicators: Not all sleeper effects are created equal. *Journal of Experimental Social Psychology, 68,* 171–180. doi:10.1016/j.jesp.2016.06.009

Albouy, G., King, B. R., Maquet, P., & Doyon, J. (2013). Hippocampus and striatum: Dynamics and interaction during acquisition and sleep-related motor sequence memory consolidation. *Hippocampus, 11,* 985–1004. doi:10.1002/hipo.22183

Albouy, G., Sterpenich, V., Balteau, E., Vandewalle, G., Desseilles, M., Dang-Vu, T., . . . Degueldre, C. (2008). Both the hippocampus and striatum are involved in consolidation of motor sequence memory. *Neuron, 58,* 261–272.

Aldalur, A., & Schooler, D. (2019). Culture and deaf women's body image. *Journal of Deaf Studies and Deaf Education, 24*(1), 11–24. https://doi.org/10.1093/deafed/eny028

Aldao, A., Nolen-Hoeksema, S., & Schweizer, S. (2010). Emotion-regulation strategies across psychopathology: A meta-analytic review. *Clinical Psychology Review, 30,* 217–237.

Aldridge, M. A., Stillman, R. D., & Bower, T. G. R. (2001). Newborn categorization of vowel-like sounds. *Developmental Science, 4,* 220–232.

Aleman, A. (2013). Use of repetitive transcranial magnetic stimulation for treatment in psychiatry. *Clinical Psychopharmacology and Neuroscience, 11,* 53–59.

Alexander, G. M. (2003). An evolutionary perspective on sex-typed toy preferences: Pink, blue, and the brain. *Archives of Sexual Behavior, 32,* 7–14.

Alexander, G. M., Wilcox, T., & Woods, R. (2009). Sex differences in infants' visual interest in toys. *Archives of Sexual Behavior, 38,* 427–433.

Alexander, M., Ray, M. A., Hébert, J. R., Youngstedt, S. D., Zhang, H., Steck, S. E., . . . Burch, J. B. (2016). The National Veteran Sleep Disorder Study: Descriptive epidemiology and secular trends, 2000–2010. *Sleep, 39,* 1399–1410.

Algoe, S. B. (2019). Positive interpersonal processes. *Current Directions in Psychological Science, 28*(2), 183–188.

Allan, B. A., Dexter, C., Kinsey, R., & Parker, S. (2018). Meaningful work and mental health: Job satisfaction as a moderator. *Journal of Mental Health, 27*(1), 38–44. doi.org:10.1080/09638237.2016.1244718

Allen, L. B., White, K. S., Barlow, D. H., Shear, M. K., Gorman, J. M., & Woods, S. W. (2010). Cognitive-behavior therapy (CBT) for panic disorder: Relationship of anxiety and depression comorbidity with treatment outcome. *Journal of Psychopathology and Behavioral Assessment, 32,* 185–192.

Allen, N. C., Bagade, S., McQueen, M. B., Ioannidis, J. P., Kavvoura, F. K., Khoury, M. J., . . . Bertram, L. (2008). Systematic meta-analyses and field synopsis of genetic association studies in schizophrenia: The SzGene database. *Nature Genetics, 40,* 827–834.

Allen, R. J., Baddeley, A. D., & Hitch, G. J. (2014). Evidence for two attentional components in visual working memory. *Journal of Experimental Psychology: Learning, Memory, and Cognition, 40*(6), 1499–1509. doi:10.1037/xlm0000002

Allen, T. D., Lentz, E., & Day, R. (2006). Career success outcomes associated with mentoring others: A comparison of mentors and nonmentors. *Journal of Career Development, 32,* 272–285.

Allison, K. C., & Goel, N. (2018). Timing of eating in adults across the weight spectrum: Metabolic factors and potential circadian mechanisms. *Physiology & Behavior, 192,* 158–166. https://doi.org/10.1016/j.physbeh.2018.02.047

Alloy, L. B., Abramson, L. Y., & Francis, E. L. (1999). Do negative cognitive styles confer vulnerability to depression? *Current Directions in Psychological Science, 8,* 128–132.

Allport, G. W. (1961). *Pattern and growth in personality.* Holt, Rinehart, & Winston.

Allport, G. W. (1979). *The nature of prejudice.* Addison-Wesley. (Original work published 1954)

Almeida, D. M. (2005). Resilience and vulnerability to daily stressors assessed via diary methods. *Current Directions in Psychological Science, 14,* 64–68.

Al-Rasheed, A. S. (2015). An experimental study of gender and cultural differences in hue preference. *Frontiers in Psychology, 6,* 30. doi:10.3389/fpsyg.2015.00030

Alterovitz, S. S., & Mendelsohn, G. A. (2009). Partner preferences across the lifespan: Online dating by older adults. *Psychology and Aging, 24,* 513–517.

Aly, M., & Moscovitch, M. (2010). The effects of sleep on episodic memory in older and younger adults. *Memory, 18,* 327–334.

Alzahrani, T., Pena, I., Temesgen, N., & Glantz, S. A. (2018). Association between electronic cigarette use and myocardial infarction. *American Journal of Preventive Medicine, 55*(4), 455–461. doi:10.1016/j.amepre.2018.05.004

Amato, P. R. (1993). Children's adjustment to divorce: Theories, hypotheses, and empirical support. *Journal of Marriage and the Family, 55,* 23–38.

Amato, P. R. (2000). The consequences of divorce for adults and children. *Journal of Marriage and Family, 62,* 1269–1287.

Amato, P. R. (2010). Research on divorce: Continuing trends and new developments. *Journal of Marriage and Family, 72,* 650–666.

Amato, P. R., & Booth, A. (1996). A prospective study of divorce and parent-child relationships. *Journal of Marriage and Family, 58,* 356–365.

Amato, P. R., & DeBoer, D. D. (2001). The transmission of marital instability across generations: Relationship skills or commitment to marriage? *Journal of Marriage and Family, 63,* 1038–1051.

Ambrosius, U., Lietzenmaier, S., Wehrle, R., Wichniak, A., Kalus, S., Winkelmann, J., . . . Friess, E. (2008). Heritability of sleep electroencephalogram. *Biological Psychiatry, 64*(4), 344–348.

American Academy of Pediatrics. (2016). Media and young minds. *Pediatrics, 138*(5) e20162591. https://doi.org/10.1542/peds.2016-2591

American Association of Advertising Agencies. (2014). How many advertisements is a person exposed to in a day? https://ams.aaaa.org/eweb/upload/faqs/adexposures.pdf

American College Health Association (ACHA). (2017). *American College Health Association-National College Health Assessment II: Reference Group Executive Summary.* American College Health Association.

American College of Obstetricians and Gynecologists (ACOG). (2002). ACOG practice bulletin: Management of recurrent pregnancy loss, 24. *International Journal of Gynaecology and Obstetrics: The Official Organ of the International Federation of Gynaecology and Obstetrics, 78,* 179–190.

American Psychiatric Association. (2000a). *Diagnostic and statistical manual of mental disorders* (4th ed., Text Revision). Author.

American Psychiatric Association. (2000b). Substance use disorders: Alcohol, cocaine, opiods. In *Practice guidelines for the treatment of psychiatric disorders: Compendium 2000* (pp. 139–238). Author.

American Psychiatric Association. (2013). *Diagnostic and statistical manual of mental disorders* (5th ed.). Author.

American Psychiatric Association. (2020, March 25). "New Poll: COVID-19 impacting mental well-being: Americans feeling anxious, especially for loved ones; Older adults are less anxious." https://www.psychiatry.org/newsroom/news-releases/new-poll-covid-19-impacting-mental-well-being-americans-feeling-anxious-especially-for-loved-ones-older-adults-are-less-anxious

American Psychological Association (APA). (1975). *Council policy manual.* http://www.apa.org/about/governance/council/policy/index.aspx

American Psychological Association (APA). (1997). *Visions and transformations.* APA's Commission on Ethnic Minority Recruitment, Retention and Training in Psychology.

American Psychological Association (APA). (2000). *Women in academe: Two steps forward, one step back.* Author.

American Psychological Association (APA). (2002). Ethical principles of psychologists and code of conduct. *American Psychologist, 57,* 1060–1073.

American Psychological Association (APA). (2004). Resolution on sexual orientation and marriage. http://www.apa.org/releases/gaymarriage.html

American Psychological Association (APA). (2013). *APA guidelines for the undergraduate psychology major: Version 2.0.* http://www.apa.org/ed/precollege/undergrad/index.aspx

American Psychological Association (APA). (2014). *Strengthening the Common Core of the Introductory Psychology Course.* Author.

American Psychological Association (APA). (2016). By the numbers: How do undergraduate psychology majors fare? *Monitor on Psychology, 47,* 11.

Amoore, J. E. (1970). *Molecular basis of odor.* Thomas.

Amoroso, T., & Workman, M. (2016). Treating posttraumatic stress disorder with MDMA-assisted psychotherapy: A preliminary meta-analysis and comparison to prolonged exposure therapy. *Journal of Psychopharmacology, 30,* 595–600.

Amsterdam, J. D., & Shults, J. (2010). Efficacy and safety of long-term fluoxetine versus lithium monotherapy of bipolar II disorder: A randomized, double-blind, placebo substitution study. *American Journal of Psychiatry, 167,* 792–800.

Anderson, B. J., Greenwood, S. J., & McCloskey, D. (2010). Exercise as an intervention for the age-related decline in neural metabolic support. *Frontiers in Aging Neuroscience, 2,* 2–9. doi:10.3389/fnagi.2010.00030

Anderson, C. (2003). Social stress and support factors in susceptibility to the common cold. *APS Observer, 16,* 37.

Anderson, C. A., & Bushman, B. J. (2002). Human aggression. *Annual Review of Psychology, 53,* 27–51.

Anderson, C. A., Benjamin, A. J., & Bartholow, B. D. (1998). Does the gun pull the trigger? Automatic priming effects of weapon pictures and weapon names. *Psychological Science, 9,* 308–314.

Anderson, C., Kraus, M. W., Galinsky, A. D., & Keltner, D. (2012). The local-ladder effect:

Social status and subjective well-being. *Psychological Science, 23,* 764–771.

Anderson, J. R. (1974). Verbatim and propositional representation of sentences in immediate and long-term memory. *Journal of Verbal Learning and Verbal Behavior, 13,* 149–162.

Anderson, J. R. (2000). *Cognitive psychology and its applications* (5th ed.). Worth.

Anderson, M. C., & Hanslmayr, S. (2014). Neural mechanisms of motivated forgetting. *Trends in Cognitive Sciences, 18*(6), 279–292. doi:10.1016/j.tics.2014.03.002

Anderson, M. C., & Huddleston, E. (2012). Towards a cognitive neurobiological model of motivated forgetting. In R. F. Belli (Ed.), *True and false recovered memories: Toward a reconciliation of the debate.* (Vol. 58, pp. 53–120). Springer Science + Business Media.

Anderson, N., & Thomas, H. D. C. (1996). Work group socialization. In M. A. West (Ed.), *Handbook of work group psychology* (pp. 423–450). Wiley.

Anderson-Clark, T. N., & Green, R. J. (2017). Basking in reflected glory: The election of President Obama and naming behaviour. *Ethnic and Racial Studies, 40*(1), 63–76. https://doi.org/10.1080/01419870.2016.1178786

Andresen, G. V., Birch, L. L., & Johnson, P. A. (1990). The scapegoat effect on food aversions after chemotherapy. *Cancer, 66,* 1649–1653.

Andrews-Hanna, J. R., Snyder, A. Z., Vincent, J. L., Lustig, C., Head, D., Raichle, M. E., . . . Buckner, R. L. (2007). Disruptions of large-scale brain systems in advanced aging. *Neuron, 56,* 924–935.

Anestis, M. D., & Anestis, J. C. (2015). Suicide rates and state laws regulating access and exposure to handguns. *American Journal of Public Health, 105,* 2049–2058.

Anorexia and Related Eating Disorders (ANRED). (2008). Eating disorder statistics. http://www.anred.com

Anticevic, A., Murray, J. D., & Barch, D. M. (2015). Bridging levels of understanding in schizophrenia through computational modeling. *Clinical Psychological Science, 3,* 433–459.

Antony, M. M., & Barlow, D. H. (Eds.). (2002). *Handbook of assessment and treatment planning for psychological disorders.* Guilford Press.

Aoki, Y., Cortese, S., & Tansella, M. (2015). Neural bases of atypical emotional face processing in autism: A meta-analysis of fMRI studies. *World Journal of Biological Psychiatry, 16(5),* 291–300. doi:10.3109/15622975.2014.957719

APA Center for Workforce Studies. (2011) *2009 Doctorate Employment Survey.* Author. http://www.apa.org/workforce/publications/09-doc-empl/report.pdf

APA Center for Workforce Studies. (2015). *2005–2013: Demographics of the U.S. Psychology Workforce.* Author. http://www.apa.org/workforce/publications/13-demographics/index.aspx

Arendt, J. (2006). Melatonin and human rhythms. *Chronobiology International, 23,* 21–37.

Armfield, J. M. (2006). Cognitive vulnerability: A model of the etiology of fear. *Clinical Psychology Review, 26,* 746–768.

Armitage, R. (1995). The distribution of EEG frequencies in REM and NREM sleep stages in healthy young adults. *Sleep, 18,* 334–341.

Armstead, W. M., Riley, J., & Vavilala, M. S. (2016). Norepinephrine protects cerebral autoregulation and reduces hippocampal necrosis after traumatic brain injury via blockade of ERK MAPK and IL-6 in juvenile pigs. *Journal of Neurotrauma, 33*(19), 1761–1767. doi:10.1089/neu.2015.4290

Arnett, J. J. (2004). *Emerging adulthood: The winding road from the late teens through the twenties.* Oxford University Press.

Arnett, J. J. (2007). Emerging adulthood: What is it and what is it good for? *Child Development Perspectives, 1,* 68–73.

Arnett, J. J. (2010). Oh, grow up! Generational grumbling and the new life stage of emerging adulthood—Commentary on Trzesniewski & Donnellan (2010). *Perspectives on Psychological Science, 5,* 89–92.

Aronson, E. (1998). Dissonance, hypocrisy, and the self-concept. In E. Harmon-Jones & J. S. Mills (Eds.), *Cognitive dissonance theory: Revival with revisions and controversies* (pp. 103–126). American Psychological Association.

Aronson, E. (2000). The jigsaw strategy. *Psychology Review, 7,* 2.

Aronson, E. (2011). Reducing prejudice and building empathy in the classroom. In M. Gernsbacher, R. W. Pew, L. M. Hough, & J. R. Pomerantz (Eds.), *Psychology and the real world: Essays illustrating fundamental contributions to society* (pp. 230–236). Worth.

Aronson, E., Wilson, T. D., & Akert, R. M. (2005). *Social psychology* (5th ed.). Prentice Hall.

Aronson, J., Fried, C. B., & Good, C. (2002). Reducing the effects of stereotype threat on African American college students by shaping theories of intelligence. *Journal of Experimental Social Psychology, 38*(2), 113–125. https://doi.org/10.1006/jesp.2001.1491

Arroll, B., Macgillivray, S., Ogston, S., Reid, I., Sullivan, F., Williams, B., & Crombie, I. (2005). Efficacy and tolerability of tricyclic antidepressants and SSRIs compared with placebo for treatment of depression in primary care: A meta-analysis. *Annals of Family Medicine, 3,* 449–456.

Arthur, J. B. (1994). Effects of human resource systems on manufacturing performance and turnover. *Academy of Management Journal, 37,* 670-687.

Asch, S. E. (1951). Effects of group pressure upon modification and distortion of judgments. In H. Guetzkow (Ed.), *Groups, leadership, and men* (pp. 117–190). Carnegie.

Asch, S. E. (1955, November). Opinions and social pressure. *Scientific American,* 31–35.

Ashby, F. G., & Maddox, W. T. (2005). Human category learning. *Annual Review of Psychology, 56,* 149–178.

Ashok, A. H., Marques, T. R., Jauhar, S., Nour, M. M., Goodwin, G. M., Young, A. H., & Howes, O. D. (2017). The dopamine hypothesis of bipolar affective disorder: The state of the art and implications for treatment. *Molecular Psychiatry, 22*(5), 666–679. doi:10.1038/mp.2017.16

Ashtari, M., Cervellione, K. L., Hasan, K. M., Wu, J., McIlree, C., Kester, H., . . . Kumra, S. (2007). White matter development during late adolescence in healthy males: A cross-sectional diffusion tensor imaging study. *NeuroImage, 35,* 501–510.

Ashwin, C., Baron-Cohen, S., Wheelwright, S., O'Riordan, M., & Bullmore, E. T. (2006). Differential activation of the amygdala and the "social brain" during fearful face-processing in Asperger syndrome. *Neuropsychologia, 45,* 2–14.

Asmundson, G., Paluszek, M. M., Landry, C. A., Rachor, G. S., McKay, D., & Taylor, S. (2020). Do preexisting anxiety-related and mood disorders differentially impact COVID-19 stress responses and coping? *Journal of Anxiety Disorders, 74,* 102271. doi:10.1016/j.janxdis.2020.102271

Asnaani, A., Richey, J. A., Dimaite, R., Hinton, D. E., & Hofmann, S. G. (2010). A cross-ethnic comparison of lifetime prevalence rates of anxiety disorders. *The Journal of Nervous and Mental Disease, 198,* 551–555.

Association for Psychological Science (APS). (2016). Here, there, everywhere: Psychological scientists in schools of dentistry, computer science, law, and more. *APS Observer, 29,* 23–26.

Assor, A., Roth, G., & Deci, E. L. (2004). The emotional costs of parents' conditional regard: A self-determination theory analysis. *Journal of Personality, 72,* 47–88.

Astin, J. A. (2004). Mind-body therapies for the management of pain. *Clinical Journal of Pain, 20,* 27–32.

Atas, A., Faivre, N., Timmermans, B., Cleeremans, A., & Kouider, S. (2014). Nonconscious learning from crowded sequences. *Psychological Science, 25,* 113–119.

Athanasopoulos, P., & Casaponsa, A. (2020). The Whorfian brain: Neuroscientific approaches to linguistic relativity. *Cognitive Neuropsychology, 37,* 393-412. https://doi.org/10.1080/02643294.2020.1769050

Atherton, K. E., Nobre, A. C., Lazar, A. S., Wulff, K., Whittaker, R. G., Dhawan, V., . . . Butler, C. R. (2016). Slow wave sleep and accelerated forgetting. *Cortex: A Journal Devoted to the Study of the Nervous System and Behavior, 84,* 80–89. doi:10.1016/j.cortex.2016.08.013

Atkinson, J. W. (1983). Towards experimental analysis of human motivation in terms of motives, expectancies, and incentives. In J. W. Atkinson (Ed.), *Personality, motivation, and action: Selected papers* (pp. 81–97). Praeger. (Original work published 1958)

Atkinson, R. C., & Shiffrin, R. W. (1968). Human memory: A proposed system and its control processes. In K. Spence & J. Spence (Eds.), *The psychology of learning and motivation* (Vol. 2, pp. 89–195). Academic Press.

Aucoin, D. (2000, May 25). Feminist report says "sexist stereotypes" abound in prime time. *Oregonian,* E9.

Aughinbaugh, A., Robles, O., & Sun, H. (2013, October) Marriage and divorce: Patterns by gender, race, and educational attainment. *Monthly Labor Review,* U.S. Bureau of Labor Statistics. doi:10.21916/mlr.2013.32

Augustinack, J. C., van der Kouwe, A. J. W., Salat, D. H., Benner, T., Stevens, A. A., Annese, J., . . . Corkin, S. (2014). H.M.'s contributions to neuroscience: A review and autopsy studies. *Hippocampus, 24*(11), 1267–1286. doi:10.1002/hipo.22354

Augustine, G. J. (2012). Neurotransmitters and their receptors. In D. Purves, G. J. Augustine, D. Fitzpatrick, W. C. Hall, A. LaManita, & L. E. White (Eds.), *Neuroscience* (5th ed., pp. 109–140). Sinauer Associates.

Augustus-Horvath, C. L., & Tylka, T. L. (2011). The acceptance model of intuitive eating: A comparison of women in emerging adulthood, early adulthood, and middle adulthood. *Journal of Counseling Psychology, 58,* 110–125.

Aura, A., Laatikainen, T., Isoaho, H., Lazutkina, G., & Tossavainen, K. (2016). Adolescents' attitudes on smoking are related to experimentation with smoking, daily smoking and best friends' smoking in two Karelias in Finland and in Russia. *International Journal of Behavioral Medicine, 23*(6), 679-685. doi:10.1007/s12529-016-9566-7

Auyeung, B., Baron-Cohen, S., Ashwin, E., Knickmeyer, R., Taylor, K., Hackett, G., & Hines, M. (2009). Fetal testosterone predicts sexually differentiated childhood behavior in girls and in boys. *Psychological Science, 20,* 144–148.

Avalos, L. C., & Tylka, T. L. (2006). Exploring a model of intuitive eating with college women. *Journal of Counseling Psychology, 53,* 486–497.

Avolio, B. J., Kahai, S. S., & Dodge, G. (2000). E-leading in organizations and its implications for theory, research and practice. *Leadership Quarterly, 11,* 615–670.

Azar, B. (1998). A genetic disposition for certain tastes may affect people's food preferences. *American Psychological Association Monitor, 29*(1). http://www.apa.org/monitor/jan98/food.html

Azevedo, F. A., Carvalho, L. R., Grinberg, L. T., Farfel, J. M., Ferretti, R. E., Leite, R. E., . . . Herculano-Houzel, S. (2009). Equal numbers of neuronal and nonneuronal cells make the human brain an isometrically scaled-up primate brain. *Journal of Comparative Neurology, 513,* 532–541.

Baddeley, A. (2012). Working memory: Theories, models, and controversies. *Annual Review of Psychology, 63,* 1–29. doi:10.1146/annurev-psych-120710-100422

Baddeley, A., Allen, R. J., & Hitch, G. J. (2010). Investigating the episodic buffer. *Psychologica Belgica, 50*(3–4), 223–243. doi:10.5334/pb-50-3-4-223

Baddeley, A. D. (1986). *Working memory.* Clarendon Press.

Baddeley, A. D. (1992). Working memory. *Science, 255,* 556–559.

Baddeley, A. D. (2002). Is working memory still working? *European Psychologist, 7,* 85–97.

Baddeley, A. D., & Hitch, G. J. (1974). Working memory. In G. H. Bower (Ed.), *The psychology of learning and motivation* (Vol. 8, pp. 47–89). Academic Press.

Baddeley, A. D., & Hitch, G. J. (2017). Is the levels of processing effect language-limited? *Journal of Memory and Language, 92,* 1–13. doi:10.1016/j.jml.2016.05.001

Baddeley, A. D., Hitch, G. J., & Allen, R. J. (2019). From short-term store to multicomponent working memory: The role of the modal model. *Memory & Cognition, 47*(4), 575–588. https://doi.org/10.3758/s13421-018-0878-5

Bagshaw, S. M., Jr. (1985). The desensitisation of chronically motion sick aircrew in the Royal Air Force. *Aviation Space Environmental Medicine, 56,* 1144–1151.

Bahadur, N. (2013, December 16). 14 examples of everyday fat-shaming. *The Huffington Post.* http://www.huffingtonpost.com/2013/12/16/fatmicroaggressions-fat-shaming-tweets_n_4453060.html

Bahk, C. (2006). College students' perceived risk and anxiety after reading airplane crash news. *Psychological Reports, 99,* 107–110.

Bahrami Balani, A. (2020). Cross-modal information transfer and the effect of concurrent task-load. *Journal of Experimental Psychology: Learning, Memory, and Cognition, 46*(1), 104–116. https://doi.org/10.1037/xlm0000715

Bahrick, H. P. (1984). Semantic memory content in permastore: Fifty years of memory for Spanish learned in school. *Journal of Experimental Psychology: General, 113,* 1–24.

Bake, T., Edvardsson, C. E., Cummings, C. J., & Dickson, S. L. (2019). Ghrelin's effects on food motivation in rats are not limited to palatable foods. *Journal of Neuroendocrinology, 31*(7): e12665. https://doi.org/10.1111/jne.12665

Baker, T. B., Japuntich, S. J., Hogle, J. M., McCarthy, D. E., & Curtin, J. J. (2006). Pharmacologic and behavioral withdrawal from addictive drugs. *Current Directions in Psychological Science, 15,* 232–236.

Baker, T. B., McFall, R. M., & Shoham, V. (2008). Current status and future prospects of clinical psychology: Toward a scientifically principled approach to mental and behavioral health care. *Psychological Science in the Public Interest, 9,* 67–103.

Balsam, K. F., Rothblum, E. D., & Beauchaine, T. P. (2005). Victimization over the life span: A comparison of lesbian, gay, bisexual, and heterosexual siblings. *Journal of Consulting and Clinical Psychology, 73,* 477–487.

Baltes, P. B. (1997). On the incomplete architecture of human ontogeny: Selection, optimization, and compensation as foundation of developmental theory. *American Psychologist, 52,* 366–380.

Balzer, W. K., Kihm, J. A., Smith, P. C., Irwin, J. L., Bachiochi, P. D., Robie, C., . . . Parra, L. F. (1997). *Users' manual for the Job Descriptive Index (JDI, 1997 revision) and the Job in General Scales.* Bowling Green State University.

Bandelow, B., Baldwin, D., Abelli, M., Bolea-Alamanac, B., Bourin, M., Chamberlain, S. R., ... Riederer, P. (2017). Biological markers for anxiety disorders, OCD and PTSD: A consensus statement. Part II: Neurochemistry, neurophysiology and neurocognition. *The World Journal of Biological Psychiatry: The Official Journal of the World Federation of Societies of Biological Psychiatry, 18*(3), 162–214. doi:10.1080/15622975.2016.1190867

Banderali, G., Martelli, A., Landi, M., Moretti, F., Betti, F., Radaelli, G., . . . Verduci, E. (2015). Short and long term health effects of parental tobacco smoking during pregnancy and lactation: A descriptive review. *Journal of Translational Medicine, 13,* 327.

Bandura, A. (1965). Influence of model's reinforcement contingencies on the acquisition of imitative responses. *Journal of Personality and Social Psychology, 1,* 589–595.

Bandura, A. (1977). *Social learning theory.* Prentice Hall.

Bandura, A. (1986). *Social foundations of thought and action: A social cognitive theory.* Prentice Hall.

Bandura, A. (1997). *Self-efficacy: The exercise of control.* W. H. Freeman.

Bandura, A., Grusec, J. E., & Menlove, F. L. (1966). Observational learning as a function of symbolization and incentive set. *Child Development, 37,* 499–506.

Bandura, A., Ross, D., & Ross, S. (1961). Transmission of aggression through imitation of aggressive models. *Journal of Abnormal and Social Psychology, 63,* 575–582.

Bandura, A., Ross, D., & Ross, S. (1963). Imitation of film-mediated aggressive models. *Journal of Abnormal and Social Psychology, 66,* 3–11.

Bangasser, D. A., Waxler, D. E., Santollo, J., & Shors, T. J. (2006). Trace conditioning and the hippocampus: The importance of contiguity. *Journal of Neuroscience, 26,* 8702–8706.

Banich, M. T., & Heller, W. (1998). Evolving perspectives on lateralization of function. *Current Directions in Psychological Science, 74,* 1–2.

Banthia, R., Moskowitz, J. T., Acree, M., & Folkman, S. (2007). Socioeconomic differences in the effect of prayer on physical symptoms and quality of life. *Journal of Health Psychology, 12,* 249–260.

Baraas, R. C., Foster, D. H., Amano, K., & Nascimento, S. M. (2006). Anomalous judgments of surface color in natural scenes under different daylights. *Visual Neuroscience, 23,* 629–635.

Barakat, M., Carrier, J., Debas, K., Lungu, O., Fogel, S., Vandewalle, G., . . . Doyon, J. (2013). Sleep spindles predict neural and behavioral changes in motor sequence consolidation. *Human Brain Mapping, 34,* 2918–2928.

Barbee, J. G. (1993). Memory, benzodiazepines, and anxiety: Integration of theoretical and clinical perspectives. *Journal of Clinical Psychiatry, 54* (10 supplement), 86–101.

Barber, T. X. (2000). A deeper understanding of hypnosis: Its secrets, its nature, its essence. *American Journal of Clinical Hypnosis, 42,* 208–272.

Barbu, M. C., Zeng, Y., Shen, X., Cox, S. R., Clarke, T. K., Gibson, J. ... Whalley, H. C. (2019). Association of whole-genome and NETRIN1 signaling pathway-derived polygenic risk scores for major depressive disorder and white matter microstructure in the U.K. Biobank. *Biological Psychiatry. Cognitive Neuroscience and Neuroimaging, 4*(1), 91-100. doi:10.1016/j.bpsc.2018.07.006

Barch, D. M., Cohen, R., & Csernansky, J. G. (2014). Altered cognitive development in the siblings of individuals with schizophrenia. *Clinical Psychological Science, 2,* 138–151.

Bardone, A. M., Vohs, K. D., Abramson, L. Y., Heatherton, T. F., & Joiner, T. E., Jr. (2000). The confluence of perfectionism, body dissatisfaction, and low self-esteem predicts bulimic symptoms: Clinical implications. *Behavior Therapy, 31,* 265–280.

Barger, L. K., Lockley, S. W., Rajaratnam, S. M., & Landrigan, C. P. (2009). Neurobehavioral, health, and safety consequences associated with shift work in safety-sensitive professions. *Current Neurology and Neuroscience Reports, 9,* 155–164.

Bargh, J. A., & Morsella, E. (2008). The unconscious mind. *Perspectives on Psychological Science, 3,* 73–79.

Bar-Haim, Y., Ziv, T., Lamy, D., & Hodes, R. M. (2006). Nature and nurture in own-race face processing. *Psychological Science, 17,* 159–163.

Barker, J., Jones, M., & Greenlees, I. (2010). Assessing the immediate and maintained effects of hypnosis on self-efficacy and soccer wall-volley performance. *Journal of Sport and Exercise Psychology, 32,* 243–252.

Barlow, D. H. (Ed.). (2002). *Anxiety and its disorders: The nature and treatment of anxiety and panic* (2nd ed.). Guilford Press.

Barlow, D. H., Conklin, L. R., & Bentley, K. H. (2015). Psychological treatments for panic disorders, phobias, and social and generalized anxiety disorders. In P. E. Nathan & J. M. Gorman (eds.), *A guide to treatments that work, 4th ed.* (pp. 409–462). Oxford University Press.

Barlow, D. H., Ellard, K. K., Sauer-Zavala, S., Bullis, J. R., & Carl. J. R. (2014). The origins of neuroticism. *Perspectives on Psychological Science, 9,* 481–496.

Barnes, A. (2004). Race, schizophrenia, and admission to state psychiatric hospitals. *Administration and Policy in Mental Health, 31,* 241–252.

Barnes, C. M., & Drake, C. L. (2015). Prioritizing sleep health: Public health policy recommendations. *Perspectives on Psychological Science, 10,* 733–737.

Barnes, J., Dong, C. Y., McRobbie, H., Walker, N., Mehta, M., & Stead, L. F. (2010). Hypnotherapy for smoking cessation. *Cochrane Database of Systematic Reviews (Online), 6,* CD001008.

Baron, R. A., & Richardson, D. R. (1992). *Human aggression* (2nd ed.). Plenum Press.

Barrera, T. L., Mott, J. M., Hofstein, R. F., & Teng, E. J. (2013). A meta-analytic review of exposure in group cognitive behavioral therapy for posttraumatic stress disorder. *Clinical Psychology Review, 33,* 24–32.

Barrett, K. (2017). Psychiatric neurosurgery in the 21st century: Overview and the growth of deep brain stimulation. *BJPsych Bulletin, 41*(5), 281–286. doi:.10.1192/pb.bp.116.055772

Barsalou, L. W. (2008). Grounded cognition. *Annual Review of Psychology, 59,* 617–645.

Barth, K. S., & Malcolm, R. J. (2010). Disulfiram: An old therapeutic with new applications. *CNS and Neurological Disorders Drug Targets, 9,* 5–12.

Bartlett, F. C. (1932). *Remembering.* Cambridge University Press.

Bartonicek, A., & Colombo, M. (2020). Claw-in-the-door: Pigeons, like humans, display the foot-in-the-door effect. *Animal Cognition, 23,* 893–900. https://doi.org10.1007/s10071-020-01395-y

Bartoshuk, L. M. (2000). Comparing sensory experiences across individuals: Recent psychophysical advances illuminate genetic variation in taste perception. *Chemical Senses, 25,* 447–460.

Bartoshuk, L. M., & Beauchamp, G. K. (1994). Chemical senses. *Annual Review of Psychology, 45,* 419–449.

Bashash, M., Thomas, D., Hu, H., Martinez-Mier, E. A., Sanchez, B. N., Basu, N., ... Hernández-Avila, M. (2017). Prenatal fluoride exposure and cognitive outcomes in children at 4 and 6-12 years of age in Mexico. *Environmental Health Perspectives, 125*(9), 1–12. Health Source-Consumer Edition.

Baskin-Sommers, A. R. (2016). Dissecting antisocial behavior: The impact of neural, genetic, and environmental factors. *Clinical Psychological Science, 4,* 500–510.

Bass, B. M. (1990). From transactional to transformational leadership: Learning to share the vision. *Organizational Dynamics, 18,* 19–31.

Basseches, M. (1980). Dialectical schemata: A framework for the empirical study of the development of dialectical thinking. *Human Development, 23*(6), 400–421. doi:10.1159/000272600

Bassuk, S. S., & Manson, J. E. (2010). Physical activity and cardiovascular disease prevention in women: A review of the epidemiological evidence. *Nutrition, Metabolism, and Cardiovascular Diseases, 20,* 467–473.

Bates, B. L. (1994). Individual differences in response to hypnosis. In J. W. Rhue, S. J. Lynn, & I. Kirsch (Eds.), *Handbook of clinical hypnosis* (pp. 23–54). American Psychological Association.

Batsell, W. R., Jr. (2000). Augmentation: Synergistic conditioning in taste-aversion learning. *Current Directions in Psychological Science, 9,* 164–168.

Bauby, J. D. (1997). *The diving bell and the butterfly.* Vintage.

Bauer, M. A., Wilkie, J. E., Kim, J. K., & Bodenhausen, G. V. (2012). Cuing consumerism: Situational materialism undermines personal and social well-being. *Psychological Science, 23,* 517–523.

Bauer, M. S., Miller, C. J., Li, M., Bajor, L. A., & Lee, A. (2016). A population-based study of the comparative effectiveness of second-generation antipsychotics vs. older antimanic agents in bipolar disorder. *Bipolar Disorders, 18,* 481–489.

Baumann, A. E. (2007). Stigmatization, social distance and exclusion because of mental illness: The individual with mental illness as a "stranger." *International Review of Psychiatry, 19,* 131–135.

Baumeister, R. F. (2004). Gender and erotic plasticity: Sociocultural influences on the sex drive. *Sexual and Relationship Therapy, 19,* 133–139. doi:10.1080/14681990410001691343

Baumeister, R. F., & Bushman, B. J. (2017). *Social psychology and human nature, 4th ed.* Cengage Learning.

Baumeister, R. F., & Leary, M. R. (1995). The need to belong: The desire for interpersonal attachments as a fundamental human motivation. *Psychological Bulletin, 117,* 497–529.

Baumrind, D. (1964). Some thoughts on ethics of research: After reading Milgram's "Behavioral study of obedience." *American Psychologist, 19,* 421–423.

Baumrind, D. (1967). Child care practices anteceding three patterns of preschool behavior. *Genetic Psychology Monographs, 75,* 43–88.

Baumrind, D. (1971). Current patterns of parental authority. *Developmental Psychology Monograph, 4*(1, Pt. 2).

Baxter, J., Buchler, S., Perales, F., & Western, M. (2015). A life-changing event: First births and men's and women's attitudes to mothering and gender divisions of labor. *Social Forces, 93,* 989–1014. doi:10.1093/sf/sou103

Baxter, J., Hewitt, B., & Haynes, M. (2008). Life course transitions and housework: Marriage, parenthood, and time on housework. *Journal of Marriage and Family, 70*(2),259–272. doi:10.1111/j.1741-3737.2008.00479.x

Beatriz, E., & Salhi, C. (2019). Child discipline in low- and middle-income countries: Socioeconomic disparities at the household- and country-level. *Child Abuse & Neglect, 94,* 104023. https://doi.org/10.1016/j.chiabu.2019.104023

Beaty, R. E., Chen, Q., Christensen, A. P., Kenett, Y. N., Silvia, P. J., Benedek, M., & Schacter, D. L. (2020). Default network contributions to episodic and semantic processing during divergent creative thinking: A representational similarity analysis. *NeuroImage, 209,* 116499. https://doi.org/10.1016/j.neuroimage.2019.116499

Beauducel, A., Brocke, B., & Leue, A. (2006). Energetical bases of extraversion: Effort, arousal, EEG, and performance. *International Journal of Psychophysiology, 62,* 212–223.

Beauregard, M. (2007). Mind does really matter: Evidence from neuroimaging studies of emotional self-regulation, psychotherapy, and placebo effect. *Progress in Neurobiology, 81,* 218–236.

Beccia, A. L., Baek, J., Jesdale, W. M., Austin, S. B., Forrester, S., Curtin, C., & Lapane, K. L. (2019). Risk of disordered eating at the intersection of gender and racial/ethnic identity among U.S. high school students. *Eating Behaviors, 34,* 101299. https://doi.org/10.1016/j.eatbeh.2019.05.002

Beck, A. T. (1967). *Depression: Clinical, experimental, and theoretical aspects.* Harper & Row.

Beck, A. T. (1976). *Cognitive therapy and the emotional disorders.* International Universities Press.

Beck, A. T. (1991). Cognitive therapy: A 30-year retrospective. *American Psychologist, 46,* 368–375.

Beck, A. T. (1997). Cognitive therapy: Reflections. In J. K. Zeig (Ed.), *The evolution of psychotherapy: The third conference* (pp. 55–67). Brunner/Mazel.

Beck, A. T. (2008). The evolution of the cognitive model of depression and its neurobiological correlates. *American Journal of Psychiatry, 165,* 969–977.

Beck, A. T. (2019). A 60-year evolution of cognitive theory and therapy. *Perspectives on Psychological Science, 14*(1), 16–20.

Beck, A. T., & Bredemeier, K. (2016). A unified model of depression: Integrating clinical, cognitive, biological, and evolutionary perspectives. *Clinical Psychological Science, 4,* 596–619.

Beck, A. T., Rush, A. J., Shaw, B. F., & Emery, G. (1979). *Cognitive therapy of depression.* Guilford Press.

Beck, V. S., Boys, S., Rose, C., & Beck, E. (2012). Violence against women in video games: A prequel or sequel to rape myth acceptance? *Journal of Interpersonal Violence, 27*(15), 3016–3031. doi:10.1177/0886260512441078

Becker, C. B., & Stice, E. (2011). *Succeed, body image program-facilitator manual.* Oxford University Press.

Beckman, S., Eisen, E. A., Bates, M. N., Liu, S., Haegerstrom-Portnoy, G., & Hammond, S. K. (2016). Acquired color vision defects and hexane exposure: A study of San Francisco Bay area automotive mechanics. *American Journal of Epidemiology, 183*(11), 969–976. doi:10.1093/aje/kwv328

Beem, E. E., Hooijkaas, H., Cleiren, M. H., Schut, H. A., Garssen, B., Croon, M. A., . . . De Vries, M. J. (1999). The immunological and psychological effects of bereavement: Does grief counseling really make a difference? A pilot study. *Psychiatry Research, 85,* 81–93.

Bègue, L., Sarda, E., Gentile, D. A., Bry, C., & Roché, S. (2017). Video games exposure and sexism in a representative sample of adolescents. *Frontiers in Psychology, 8,* 466. doi:10.3389/fpsyg.2017.00466

Behme, C., & Deacon, S. H. (2008). Language learning in infancy: Does the empirical evidence support a domain specific language acquisition device? *Philosophical Psychology, 21,* 641–671.

Behrmann, M., & Plaut, D. C. (2015). A vision of graded hemispheric specialization. *Annals of The New York Academy of Sciences, 1359,* 30–46. doi:10.1111/nyas.12833

Békésy, G. von. (1960). *Experiments in hearing.* McGraw-Hill.

Belfort-DeAguiar, R., Seo, D., Naik, S., Hwang, J., Lacadie, C., Schmidt, C., ... Sherwin, R. (2016). Food image-induced brain activation is not diminished by insulin infusion. *International Journal of Obesity, 40*(11), 1679–1686. https://doi.org/10.1038/ijo.2016.152

Bell, A. R., Weinberg, M. S., & Hammersmith, S. K. (1981). *Sexual preference: Its development in men and women.* Indiana University Press.

Bell, N. J., & Baron, E. K. (2015). Resistance to peer influence during adolescence: Proposing a sociocultural-developmental framework. *New Ideas in Psychology, 39,* 53–62. doi:10.1016/j.newideapsych.2015.07.005

Belleau, E. L., Treadway, M. T., & Pizzagalli, D. A. (2019). The impact of stress and major depressive disorder on hippocampal and medial prefrontal cortex morphology. *Biological Psychiatry, 85*(6), 443–453. doi:10.1016/j.biopsych.2018.09.031

Belsky, J., & Rovine, M. (1990). Patterns of marital change across the transition to parenthood: Pregnancy to three years postpartum. *Journal of Marriage and Family, 52,* 5–19.

Bem, D. J. (2011). Feeling the future: Experimental evidence for anomalous retroactive influences on cognition and affect. *Journal of Personality and Social Psychology, 100,* 407–425. doi:10.1037/a0021524

Bem, D., Tressoldi, P., Rabeyron, T., & Duggan, M. (2016). Feeling the future: A meta-analysis of 90 experiments on the anomalous anticipation of random future events. Version 2. *F1000Research, 4,* 1188. doi:10.12688/f1000research.7177.2

Bem, S. L. (1981). Gender schema theory: A cognitive account of sex typing. *Psychological Review, 88,* 354–364.

Bender, E. (2004). Virtual reality treatment combats phobias, PTSD. *Psychiatric News, 39,* 45.

Benham, G., Woody, E. Z., Wilson, K. S., & Nash, M. R. (2006). Expect the unexpected: Ability, attitude, and responsiveness to hypnosis. *Journal of Personality and Social Psychology, 91,* 342–350.

Benjamin, L. T., Jr., Henry, K. D., & McMahon, L. R. (2005). Inez Beverly Prosser and the education of African Americans. *Journal of the History of the Behavioral Sciences, 41,* 43–62.

Bennett, M. P., Zeller, J. M., Rosenberg, L., & McCann, J. (2003). The effect of mirthful laughter on stress and natural killer cell activity. *Alternative Therapies in Health and Medicine, 9,* 38–45.

Bennett, W. I. (1990, December). Boom and doom. *Harvard Health Letter, 16,* 1–3.

Benzing, V., & Schmidt, M. (2019). The effect of exergaming on executive functions in children with ADHD: A randomized clinical trial. *Scandinavian Journal of Medicine & Science in Sports, 29*(8), 1243–1253. https://doi.org/10.1111/sms.13446

Berger, T. (2017). The therapeutic alliance in internet interventions: A narrative review and suggestions for future research. *Psychotherapy Research, 27*(5), 511-524. doi:10.1080/10503307.2015.1119908

Bergman, I., & Almkvist, O. (2013). The effect of age on fluid intelligence is fully mediated by physical health. *Archives of Gerontology and Geriatrics, 57*(1), 100–109. doi:10.1016/j.archger.2013.02.010

Berk, L. E., & Spuhl, S. T. (1995). Maternal interaction, private speech, and task performance in preschool children. *Early Childhood Research Quarterly, 10,* 145–169.

Berkowitz, L. (1990). On the formation and regulation of anger and aggression: A cognitive-neoassociationistic analysis. *American Psychologist, 45,* 494–503.

Berkowitz, L. (2012). A cognitive-neoassociation theory of aggression. In P. A. M. Van Lange, A. W. Kruglanski, & E. T. Higgins (Eds.), *Handbook of theories of social psychology, Vol. 2* (pp. 99–117). SAGE Publications Ltd. doi:10.4135/9781446249222.n31

Berlau, D. J., Corrada, M. M., & Kawas, C. (2009). The prevalence of disability in the oldest-old is high and continues to increase with age: Findings from The 90+ Study. *International Journal of Geriatric Psychiatry, 24,* 1217–1225. doi:10.1002/gps.2248

Bernabe, C. S., Caliman, I. F., Truitt, W. A., Molosh, A. I., Lowry, C. A., Hay-Schmidt, A., Shekhar, A., & Johnson, P. L. (2020). Using loss- and gain-of-function approaches to target amygdala-projecting serotonergic neurons in the dorsal raphe nucleus that enhance anxiety-related and conditioned fear behaviors. *Journal of Psychopharmacology, 34*(4), 400–411. https://doi.orgdoi:10.1177/0269881119900981

Bernstein, K. S., Park, S. Y., Shin, J., Cho, S., & Park, Y. (2011). Acculturation, discrimination and depressive symptoms among Korean immigrants in New York City. *Community Mental Health Journal, 47,* 24–34.

Berntsen, D., Johannessen, K. B., Thomsen, Y. D., Bertelsen, M., Hoyle, R. H., & Rubin, D. C. (2012). Peace and war: Trajectories of posttraumatic stress disorder symptoms before, during, and after military deployment in Afghanistan. *Psychological Science, 23,* 1557–1565.

Berry, A. K. (2006). Helping children with nocturnal enuresis: The wait-and-see approach may not be in anyone's best interest. *American Journal of Nursing, 106,* 56–63.

Berry, M. S., Kangas, B. D., & Branch, M. N. (2012). Development of key-pecking, pause, and ambulation during extended exposure to a fixed-interval schedule of reinforcement. *Journal of Experimental Analysis of Behavior, 97,* 333–346.

Berscheid, E., Dion, K., Walster, E., & Walster, G. W. (1971). Physical attractiveness and dating choice: A test of the matching hypothesis. *Journal of Experimental Social Psychology, 7,* 173–189.

Berwick, R. C., Pietroski, P., Yankama, B., & Chomsky, N. (2011). Poverty of the stimulus revisited. *Cognitive Science, 35,* 1207–1242. doi:10.1111/j.1551-6709.2011.01189.x

Bezchlibnyk-Butler, K. Z., & Jeffries, J. J. (Eds.). (1998). *Clinical handbook of psychotropic drugs* (8th ed.). Hogrete & Huber.

Bhaskara, R. M., Brijesh, C. M., Ahmed, S., & Borges, R. M. (2009). Perception of ultraviolet light by crab spiders and its role in the selection of hunting sites. *Journal of Comparative Physiology A, Neuroethology, Sensory, Neural, and Behavioral Physiology, 195,* 409–417.

Bibbey, A., Carroll, D., Ginty, A. T., & Phillips, A. C. (2015). Cardiovascular and cortisol reactions to acute psychological stress under conditions of high versus low social evaluative threat: Associations with the type D personality construct. *Psychosomatic Medicine, 77,* 599–608.

Binder, J., Zagefka, H., Brown, R., Funke, F., Kessler, T., Mummendey, A., . . . Leyens, J. P. (2009). Does contact reduce prejudice or does prejudice reduce contact? A longitudinal test of the contact hypothesis among majority and minority groups in three European countries. *Journal of Personality and Social Psychology, 96,* 843–856.

Binet, A., & Simon, T. (1905). Méthodes nouvelles pour le diagnotics du niveau intéllectuel des anormaux. *L'Année Psychologique, 11,* 191–244.

Birak, K. S., Higgs, S., & Terry, P. (2011). Conditioned tolerance to the effects of alcohol on inhibitory control in humans. *Alcohol and Alcoholism, 46*(6), 686–693. https://doi.org/10.1093/alcalc/agr084

Biss, R. K., Campbell, K. L., & Hasher, L. (2013). Interference from previous distraction disrupts older adults' memory. *Journals of Gerontology: Series B: Psychological Sciences And Social Sciences, 68B,* 558–561.

Bissell, K., & Hays, H. (2011). Understanding anti-fat bias in children: The role of media and appearance anxiety in third to sixth graders' implicit and explicit attitudes toward obesity. *Mass Communication & Society, 14,* 113–140. doi:10.1080/15205430903464592

Black, D. W., Blum, N., Pfohl, B., & Hale, N. (2004) Suicidal behavior in borderline personality disorder: Prevalence, risk factors, prediction, and prevention. *Journal of Personality and Disorders, 18,* 226–239.

Black, L. S., deRegnier, R. A., Long, J., Georgieff, M. K., & Nelson, C. A. (2004). Electrographic imaging of recognition memory in 34–38 week gestation intrauterine growth restricted newborns. *Experimental Neurology, 190,* S72–S83.

Blacklivesmatter.com (2020). Black Lives Matter: About. https://blacklivesmatter.com/about/

Blackwell, L. S., Trzesniewski, K. H., & Dweck, C. S. (2007). Implicit theories of intelligence predict achievement across an adolescent transition: A longitudinal study and an intervention. *Child Development, 78*(1), 246–263. https://doi.org/10.1111/j.1467-8624.2007.00995.x

Blackwell, L. V., Snyder, L. A., & Mavriplis, C. (2009). Diverse faculty in STEM fields: Attitudes, performance, and fair treatment. *Journal of Diversity in Higher Education, 2,* 195–205.

Blanchard, B., Heurtaux, T., Garcia, C., Moll, N. M., Caillava, C., Grandbarbe, L. . . . Nait Oumesmar, B. (2013). Tocopherol derivative TFA-12 promotes myelin repair in experimental models of multiple sclerosis. *Journal of Neuroscience, 33,* 11633–11642. doi:10.1523/JNEUROSCI.0774-13.2013

Blanchard, R. (2008). Review and theory of handedness, birth order, and homosexuality in men. *Laterality, 13,* 51–70.

Blanchflower, D. G., & Oswald, A. J. (2008). Is well-being U-shaped over the life cycle? *Social Science & Medicine,* 66, 1733–1749.

Blane, H. T. (1988). Prevention issues with children of alcoholics. *British Journal of Addiction, 83,* 793–798.

Blazer, D G., Kessler, R. C., McGonagle, K. A., & Swartz, M. S. (1994). The prevalence and distribution of major depression in a national community sample: The National Comorbidity Study. *American Journal of Psychiatry, 151,* 979–986.

Blehm, C., Vishnu, S., Khattak, A., Mitra, S., & Yee, R. W. (2005). Computer vision syndrome: A review. *Survey of Ophthalmology, 50,* 253–262.

Bleidorn, W. (2015). What accounts for personality maturation in early adulthood? *Current Directions in Psychological Science, 24,* 245–252.

Bleidorn, W., Klimstra, T. A., Denissen, J., Rentfrow, P. J., Potter, J., & Gosling, S. D. (2013). Personality maturation around the world: A cross-cultural examination of social-investment theory. *Psychological Science, 24,* 2530–2540.

Bleiker, E. M., Hendriks, J. H., Otten, J. D., Verbeek, A. L., & van der Ploeg, H. M. (2008). Personality factors and breast cancer risk: A thirteen-year follow-up. *Journal of the National Cancer Institute, 100,* 213–218.

Blevins, J. E., & Baskin, D. G. (2010). Hypothalamic-brainstem circuits controlling eating. *Forum of Nutrition, 63,* 133–140.

Block, J. A. (1995). A contrarian view of the five-factor approach. *Psychological Bulletin, 117,* 187–215.

Blomstedt, P., Sjöberg, R. L., Hansson, M., Bodlund, O., & Hariz, M. I. (2013). Deep brain stimulation in the treatment of obsessive-compulsive disorder. *World Neurosurgery, 80,* e245–e253.

Bloom, F., Nelson, C. A., & Lazerson, A. (2001). *Brain, mind and behavior* (3rd ed.). Worth.

Boccanfuso, E., White, F. A., & Maunder, R. D., (2020). Reducing transgender stigma via an e-contact intervention. *Sex Roles: A Journal of Research.* https://doi.org/10.1007/s11199-020-01171-9

Bock, B. C., Dunsiger, S. I., Ciccolo, J. T., Serber, E. R., Wu, W. C., Sillice, M., & Marcus, B. H. (2019). Mediators of physical activity between standard exercise and exercise video games. *Health Psychology, 38* (12), 1107–1115. https://doi.org/10.1037/hea0000791

Boden, M. (1988). *Computer models of the mind. Computational approaches in theoretical psychology.* Cambridge University Press.

Boehm, J. K., Chen, Y., Williams, D. R., Ryff, C. D., & Kubzansky, L. D. (2016). Subjective well-being and cardiometabolic health: An 8–11 year study of midlife adults. *Journal of Psychosomatic Research, 85,* 1–8.

Boeri, M. W., Sterk, C. E., & Elifson, K. W. (2004). Rolling beyond raves: Ecstasy use outside the rave setting. *Journal of Drug Issues, 34,* 831–860.

Boerma, T., Hosseinpoor, A. R., Verdes, E., & Chatterji, S. (2016). A global assessment of the gender gap in self-reported health with survey data from 59 countries. *BMC Public Health, 16,* 675.

Bogaert, A. F., & Skorska, M. (2011). Sexual orientation, fraternal birth order, and the maternal immune hypothesis: A review. *Frontiers in Neuroendocrinology, 32*(2), 247–254. doi:10.1016/j.yfrne.2011.02.004

Bogels, S. M., Alden, L., Beidel, D. C., Clark, L. A., Pine, D. S., Stein, M. B., & Voncken, M. (2010). Social anxiety disorder: Questions and answers for the *DSM-V. Depression and Anxiety, 27,* 168–189.

Bogenschutz, M. P. (2013). Studying the effects of classic hallucinogens in the treatment of alcoholism: Rationale, methodology, and current research with psilocybin. *Current Drug Abuse Reviews, 6,* 17-29.

Bohnen, N. I., Muller, M. I., Kuwabara, H., Constantine, G. M., & Studenski, S. A. (2009). Age-associated leukoarasosis and cortical cholinergic deafferentation. *Neurology, 72,* 1411–1416.

Bolles, R. C. (1972). Reinforcement, expectancy, and learning. *Psychological Review, 79,* 394–409.

Bolton, M., van der Straten, A., & Cohen, C. (2008). Probiotics: Potential to prevent HIV and sexually transmitted infections in women. *Sexually Transmitted Diseases, 35,* 214–225.

Bonanno, G. A. (2004). Loss, trauma, and human resilience. *American Psychologist, 59,* 20–28.

Bonanno, G. A., & Burton, C. L. (2013). Regulatory flexibility: An individual differences perspective on coping and emotion regulation. *Perspectives on Psychological Science, 8,* 591–612.

Bonanno, G. A., Brewin, C. R., Kaniasty, K., & La Greca, A. M. (2010). Weighing the costs of disaster: Consequences, risks, and resilience in individuals, families, and communities. *Psychological Science in the Public Interest, 11,* 1–49.

Bond, R., & Smith, P. B. (1996). Culture and conformity: A meta-analysis of studies using Asch's (1952, 1956) line judgment task. *Psychological Bulletin, 119,* 111–137.

Bonilla-Silva, E. (2015). The structure of racism in color-blind, 'post-racial' America. *American Behavioral Scientist, 59*(11), 1358–1376. doi:10.1177/0002764215586826

Bonne, O., Vythilingam, M., Inagaki, M., Wood, S., Neumeister, A., Nugent, A. C., . . . Charney, D. S. (2008). Reduced posterior hippocampal volume in posttraumatic stress disorder. *Journal of Clinical Psychiatry, 69,* 1087–1091.

Bonte, M. (1962). The reaction of two African societies to the Mueller-Lyer illusion. *Journal of Social Psychology, 58,* 265–268.

Booth, A., & Amato, P. R. (2001). Parental pre-divorce relations and offspring post-divorce well-being. *Journal of Marriage and Family, 63,* 197–212.

Booth-Kewley, S., & Friedman, H. S. (1987). Psychological predictions of heart disease A quantitative review. *Psychological Bulletin, 101,* 343–362.

Bor, D., & Seth, A. K. (2012). Consciousness and the prefrontal parietal network: Insights from attention, working memory, and chunking. *Frontiers in Psychology, 3, ArtID* 63. doi:10.3389/fpsyg.2012.00063

Borges, G., Nock, M. K., Haro Abad, J. M., Hwang, I., Sampson, N. A., Alonso, J., . . . Kessler, R. C. (2010). Twelve-month prevalence of and risk factors for suicide attempts in the World Health Organization World Mental Health Surveys. *Journal of Clinical Psychiatry, 71,* 1617–1628.

Borgogni, L., Dello Russo, S., Petitta, L., & Vecchione, M. (2010). Predicting job satisfaction and job performance in a privatized organization. *International Public Management Journal, 13*(3), 275–296. doi:10.1080/10967494.2010.504114

Borman, G. D., Choi, Y., & Hall, G. J. (2020). The impacts of a brief middle-school self-affirmation intervention help propel African American and Latino students through high school. *Journal of Educational Psychology.* https://doi.org/10.1037/edu0000570

Borman, W. C., Penner, L. A., Allen, T. D., & Motowidlo, S. J. (2001). Personality predictors of citizenship performance. *International Journal of Selection and Assessment, 9,* 52–69.

Bornet, F. R., Jardy-Gennetier, A. E., Jacquet, N., & Stowell, J. (2007). Glycaemic response to foods: Impact on satiety and long-term weight regulation. *Appetite, 49,* 535–553.

Bornovalova, M. A., Gratz, K. L., Delany-Brumsey, A., Paulson, A. & Lejuez, C. W. (2006). Temperamental and environmental risk factors for borderline personality disorder among inner-city substance users in residential treatment. *Journal of Personality Disorders, 20,* 218–231.

Bornstein, M. H. (1985). On the development of color naming in young children: Data and theory. *Brain and Language, 26,* 72–93.

Bornstein, M. H., Putnick, D. L., Cote, L. R., Haynes, O. M., & Suwalsky, J. D. (2015). Mother-infant contingent vocalizations in 11 countries. *Psychological Science, 26*(8), 1272-1284. doi:10.1177/0956797615586796

Bornstein, R. F. (1994). Dependency as a social cue: A meta-analytic review of research on the dependency-helping relationship. *Journal of Research in Personality, 28,* 182–213. doi:10.1006/jrpe.1994.1015

Borst, G., & Kosslyn, S. M. (2008). Visual mental imagery and visual perception: Structural equivalence revealed by scanning processes. *Memory & Cognition, 36,* 849–862. doi:10.3758/MC.36.4.849

Borzekowski, D. L. G., & Pires, P. P. (2018). A six country study of young children's media exposure, logo recognition, and dietary preferences. *Journal of Children and Media, 12*(2), 143–158. https://doi.org/10.1080/17482798.2018.1425730

Bouchard, S., Dumoulin, S., Robillard, G., Guitard, T., Klinger, E., Forget, H., . . . Roucaut, F. X. (2017). Virtual reality compared with in vivo exposure in the treatment of social anxiety disorder: A three-arm randomised controlled trial. *The British Journal of Psychiatry, 210,* 276–283.

Bouchard, T. J. (2004). Genetic influence on human psychological traits: A survey. *Current Directions in Psychological Science, 13,* 148–151.

Bouchard, T. J., Lykken, D. T., McGue, M., Segal, N. L., & Tellegen, A. (1990). Sources of human psychological differences: The Minnesota study of twins reared apart. *Science, 250,* 223–228.

Boucher, H. C., & Maslach, C (2009). Culture and individuation: The role of norms and self-construals. *The Journal of Social Psychology, 149*(6), 677–693. doi:10.1080/00224540903366800

Boucher, H. C., & O'Dowd, M. C. (2011). Language and the bicultural dialectical self. *Cultural Diversity and Ethnic Minority Psychology, 17*(2), 211–216. doi:10.1037/a0023686

Bouchery, E. E., Harwood, H. J., Sacks, J. J., Simon, C. J., & Brewer, R. D. (2011). Economic costs of excessive alcohol consumption in the United States, 2006. *American Journal of Preventative Medicine, 41,* 516–524.

Boutwell, B. B., Young, J. T. N., & Meldrum, R. C. (2018). On the positive relationship between breastfeeding & intelligence. *Developmental Psychology, 54*(8), 1426–1433. https://doi.org/10.1037/dev0000537

Bovin, M. J., & Marx, B. P. (2011). The importance of the peritraumatic experience in defining traumatic stress. *Psychological Bulletin, 137,* 47–67.

Bowden, C. L., Mosolov, S., Hranov, L., Chen, E., Habil, H., Kongsakon, R., . . . Lin, H. N. (2010). Efficacy of valproate versus lithium in mania or mixed mania: A randomized, open 12-week trial. *International Clinical Psychopharmacology, 25,* 60–67.

Bower, B. (2003, November 8). Forgetting to remember: Emotion robs memory while reviving it. *Science News, 164,* 293.

Bower, J. E., Moskowitz, J. T., & Epel, E. (2009). Is benefit finding good for your health? Pathways linking positive life changes after stress and physical health outcomes. *Current Directions in Psychological Science, 18,* 337–341.

Bower, J. F., Crosswell, A. D., & Slavich, G. M. (2014). Childhood adversity and cumulative life stress: Risk factors for cancer-related fatigue. *Clinical Psychological Science, 2,* 108–115.

Bowlby, J. (1980). *Attachment and loss: Vol. 3. Loss: Sadness and depression.* Basic Books.

Boxer, P., Groves, C. L., & Docherty, M. (2015). Video games do indeed influence children and adolescents' aggression, prosocial behavior, and academic performance: A clearer reading of Ferguson (2015). *Perspectives on Psychological Science, 10*(5), 671–673. doi:10.1177/1745691615592239

Boyce. C. J., Daly, M., Hounkpatin, H. O., & Wood, A. M. (2017). Money may buy happiness, but often so little that it doesn't matter. *Psychological Science, 28,* 544–546.

Boyce, C. J., Wood, A. M., Banks, J., Clark, A. E., & Brown, G. D. (2013). Money, well-being, and loss aversion: Does an income loss have a greater impact on well-being than an equivalent income gain? *Psychological Science, 24,* 2557–2562.

Boysen, G. A. (2011). The scientific status of childhood dissociative identity disorder: A review of published research. *Psychotherapy and Psychosomatics, 80,* 329–334.

Bozarth, M. A., & Wise, R. A. (1984). Anatomically distinct opiate receptor fields mediate reward and physical dependence. *Science, 224,* 516–518.

Brackett, M. A., Rivers, S. E., Shiffman, S., Lerner, N., & Salovey, P. (2006). Relating emotional abilities to social functioning: A comparison of self-report and performance measures of emotional intelligence. *Journal of Personality and Social Psychology, 91,* 780–795.

Bradley, D. B., & Hopcroft, R. L. (2007). The sex difference in depression across 29 countries. *Social Forces, 85,* 1483–1507.

Bradley, R. H., & Corwyn, R. F. (2008). Infant temperament, parenting, and externalizing behavior in first grade: A test of the differential susceptibility hypothesis. *Journal of Child Psychology and Psychiatry and Allied Disciplines, 49,* 124–131.

Brady, S. S., & Matthews, K. A. (2006). Effects of media violence on health-related outcomes among young men. *Archives of Pediatrics & Adolescent Medicine, 160*(4), 341–347.

Brainerd, C. J., & Reyna, V. F. (2002). Recollection rejection: How children edit their false memories. *Developmental Psychology, 38,* 156–172.

Brand, B. L., Sar, V., Stavropoulos, P., Krüger, C., Korzekwa, M., Martínez-Taboas, A., & Middleton, W. (2016). Separating fact from fiction: An empirical examination of six myths about dissociative identity disorder. *Harvard Review of Psychiatry, 24*(4), 257–270. doi:10.1097/HRP.0000000000000100

Brannon, L., & Feist, J. (2004). *Health psychology: An introduction to behavior and health* (5th ed.). Wadsworth.

Brant, A. M., Munakata, Y., Boomsma, D. I., DeFries, J. C., Haworth, C. M., Keller, M. C., . . . Hewitt, J. K. (2013). The nature and nurture of high IQ: An extended sensitive period for intellectual development. *Psychological Science, 24,* 1487–1495.

Braungart, J. M., Plomin, R., DeFries, J. C., & Fulker, D. W. (1992). Genetic influence on tester-rated infant temperament as assessed by Bayley's Infant Behavior Record. *Developmental Psychology, 28,* 40–47.

Brehm, S. S. (1992). *Intimate relationships* (2nd ed.). McGraw-Hill.

Brehm, S. S., Kassin, S. M., & Fein, S. (2002). *Social psychology* (5th ed.). Houghton Mifflin.

Bremner, A. J., Bryant, P. E., & Mareschal, D. (2006). Object-centered spatial reference in 4-month-old infants. *Infant Behavior and Development, 29,* 1–10.

Bresnahan, M., Begg, M. D., Brown, A., Schaefer, C., Sohler, N., Insel, B., . . . Susser, E. (2007). Race and risk of schizophrenia in a U.S. birth cohort: Another example of health disparity? *International Journal of Epidemiology, 36,* 751–758.

Brewer, C., Streel, E., & Skinner, M. (2017). Supervised disulfiram's superior effectiveness in alcoholism treatment: Ethical, methodological, and psychological aspects. *Alcohol and Alcoholism, 52,* 213–219.

Brewer, M. B. (1979). In-group bias in the minimal intergroup situation: A cognitive-motivational analysis. *Psychological Bulletin, 86,* 307–324.

Brewer, M. B., & Campbell, D. T. (1976). *Ethnocentrism and intergroup attitudes: East African evidence.* Halstead.

Brewster, M., & Tucker, J. M. (2016). Understanding bystander behavior: The influence of and interaction between bystander characteristics and situational factors. *Victims & Offenders, 11*(3), 455–481. doi:10.1080/15564886.2015.1009593

Brick, J. (Ed.). (2008). *Handbook of the medical consequences of alcohol and drug abuse* (2nd ed.). Haworth Press/Taylor & Francis Group.

Brickman, A. M., Khan, U. A., Provenzano, F. A., Yeung, L. K., Suzuki, W., Schroeter, H., . . . Small, S. A. (2014). Enhancing dentate gyrus function with dietary flavanols improves cognition in older adults. *Nature Neuroscience, 17*(12), 1798–1803. doi:10.1038/nn.3850

Brief, D. J., Rubin, A., Keane, T. M., Enggasser, J. L., Roy, M., Helmuth, E., . . . Rosenbloom, D. (2013). Web intervention for OEF/OIF veterans with problem drinking and PTSD symptoms: A randomized clinical trial. *Journal of Consulting and Clinical Psychology, 81,* 890–900.

Brighina, F., Cosentino, G., & Fierro, B. (2016). Habituation or lack of habituation: What is really lacking in migraine? *Clinical Neurophysiology, 127*(1), 19–20. doi:10.1016/j.clinph.2015.05.028

Brinke, L. T., Stimson, D., & Carney, D. R. (2014). Some evidence for unconscious lie detection. *Psychological Science, 25,* 1098–1105.

Britt, G. C., & McCance-Katz, E. F. (2005). A brief overview of the clinical pharmacology of "club drugs." *Substance Use & Misuse, 40,* 1189–1201.

Broberg, D. J., & Bernstein, I. L. (1987). Candy as a scapegoat in the prevention of food aversions in children receiving chemotherapy. *Cancer, 60,* 2344–2347.

Brochu, P. M., Pearl, R. L., Puhl, R. M., & Brownell, K. D. (2014). Do media portrayals of obesity influence support for weight-related medical policy? *Health Psychology, 33,* 197–200. doi:10.1037/a0032592

Brockmeyer, T., Anderle, A., Schmidt, H., Febry, S., Wünsch-Leiteritz, W., Leiteritz, A., & Friederich, H. C. (2018). Body image related negative interpretation bias in anorexia nervosa. *Behaviour Research and Therapy, 104,* 69–73. https://doi.org/10.1016/j.brat.2018.03.003

Brody, A. L., Saxena, S., Schwartz, J. M., Stoessel, P. W., Maidment, K., Phelps, M. E., & Baxter, L. R., Jr. (1998). FDG-PET predictors of response to behavioral therapy and pharmacotherapy in obsessive compulsive disorder. *Psychiatry Research: Neuroimaging, 84,* 1–6.

Bronstad, P. M., Langlois, J. H., & Russell, R. (2008). Computational models of facial attractiveness judgments. *Perception, 37,* 126–142.

Brookoff, D., O'Brien, K. K., Cook, C. S., Thompson, T. D., & Williams, C. (1997). Characteristics of participants in domestic violence: Assessment at the scene of domestic assault. *JAMA, 277,* 1369–1373.

Brotto, L. A., Petkau, A., Labrie, F., & Basson, R. (2011). Predictors of sexual desire disorders in women. *Journal of Sexual Medicine, 8,* 742–753. doi:10.1111/j.1743-6109.2010.02146.x

Brown, A. (2011). Media use by children younger than 2 years. *Pediatrics, 128*(5), 1040–1045. doi:10.1542/peds.2011-1753

Brown, A. D., & Curhan, J. R. (2013). The polarizing effect of arousal on negotiation. *Psychological Science, 24,* 1928–1935.

Brown, A. S., Begg, M. D., Gravenstein, S., Schaefer, C. A., Wyatt, R. J., Bresnahan, M., . . . Susser, E. S. (2004). Serological evidence of prenatal influenza in the etiology of schizophrenia. *Archives of General Psychiatry, 61,* 774–780.

Brown, B. B. (2004). Adolescents' relationship with peers. In R. Lerner & L. Steinberg (Eds.), *Handbook of adolescent psychology* (2nd ed., pp. 363–394). Wiley.

Brown, B. M., Peiffer, J. J., & Martins, R. N. (2013). Multiple effects of physical activity on molecular and cognitive signs of brain aging: Can exercise slow neurodegeneration and delay Alzheimer's disease? *Molecular Psychiatry, 18,* 864–874. doi:10.1038/mp.2012.162

Brown, C. S., & Stone, E. A. (2016). Gender stereotypes and discrimination: How sexism impacts development. *Advances in Child Development and Behavior, 50,* 105–133.

Brown, J. A. (1958). Some tests of the decay theory of immediate memory. *Quarterly Journal of Experimental Psychology, 10,* 12–21.

Brown, J. D., & Rogers, R. J. (1991). Self-serving attributions: The role of physiological arousal. *Personality and Social Psychology Bulletin, 17,* 501–506.

Brown, R., & Kulik, J. (1977). Flashbulb memories. *Cognition, 5,* 73–99.

Brown, S. L., Lee, G. R., & Bulanda, J. R. (2006). Cohabitation among older adults: A national portrait. *Journals of Gerontology, Series B: Psychological Sciences and Social Sciences, 61,* S71–S79.

Brown, S. L., Nesse, R. M., Vinokur, A. D., & Smith, D. M. (2003). Providing social support may be more beneficial than receiving it: Results from a prospective study of mortality. *Psychological Science, 14,* 320–327.

Brown, T. A., DiNardo, P. A., Lehman, C. L., & Campbell, L. A. (2001). Reliability of *DSM-IV* anxiety and mood disorders: Implications for the classification of emotional disorders. *Journal of Abnormal Psychology, 110,* 49–58.

Brown, V. R., & Vaughn, E. D. (2011). The writing on the (Facebook) wall: The use of social networking sites in hiring decisions. *Journal of Business and Psychology, 26,* 219–225.

Browne, A. (1993). Violence against women by male partners: Prevalence, outcomes, and policy implications. *American Psychologist, 48,* 1077–1087.

Browning, J. R., Kessler, D., Hatfield, E., & Choo, P. (1999). Power, gender, and sexual behavior. *Journal of Sex Research, 36,* 342–348.

Bruffaerts, R., Demyttenaere, K., Borges, G., Haro, J. M., Chiu, W. T., Hwang, I., . . . Nock, M. K. (2010). Childhood adversities as risk factors for onset and persistence of suicidal behavior. *British Journal of Psychiatry, 197,* 20–27.

Brugger, S. P., & Howes, O. D. (2017). Heterogeneity and homogeneity of regional brain structure in schizophrenia: A meta-analysis. *JAMA Psychiatry, 74*(11), 1104–1111. doi:.10.1001/jamapsychiatry.2017.2663

Brugman, T., & Ferguson, S. (2002). Physical exercise and improvements in mental health. *Journal of Psychosocial Nursing and Mental Health Services, 40,* 24–31.

Brühl, A. B., Delsignore, A., Komossa, K., & Weidt, S. (2014). Neuroimaging in social anxiety disorder: A meta-analytic review resulting in a new neurofunctional model. *Neuroscience & Biobehavioral Review, 47,* 260-280. doi:10.1016/j.neubiorev.2014.08.003.

Bruno, D., Koscik, R. L., Woodard, J. L., Pomara, N., & Johnson, S. C. (2018). The recency ratio as predictor of early MCI. *International Psychogeriatrics, 30*(12), 1883–1888. https://doi.org/10.1017/S1041610218000467

Bruno, D., Reichert, C., & Pomara, N. (2016). The recency ratio as an index of cognitive performance and decline in elderly individuals. *Journal of Clinical and Experimental Neuropsychology, 38*(9), 967–973. doi:10.1080/13803395.2016.1179721

Brunoni, A. R., Chaimani, A., Moffa, A. H., Razza, L. B., Gattaz, W. F., Daskalakis, Z. J., & Carvalho, A. F. (2017). Repetitive transcranial magnetic stimulation for the acute treatment of major depressive episodes: A systematic review with network meta-analysis. *JAMA Psychiatry, 74*(2), 143–152. doi:10.1001/jamapsychiatry.2016.3644

Bryman, A. S. (1996). The importance of context: Qualitative research and the study of leadership. *Leadership Quarterly, 7,* 353–370.

Brzezinski, A. (1997). Melatonin in humans. *New England Journal of Medicine, 336,* 186–195.

Buckingham-Howes, S., Berger, S. S., Scaletti, L. A., & Black, M. M. (2013). Systematic review of prenatal cocaine exposure and adolescent development. *Pediatrics, 131,* e1917–e1936.

Buckley, K. W. (1989). *Mechanical man: John Broadus Watson and the beginnings of behaviorism.* Guilford Press.

Bucur, B., & Madden, D. J. (2010). Effects of adult age and blood pressure on executive function and speed of processing. *Experimental Aging Research, 36,* 153–168.

Buczylowska, D., & Petermann, F. (2016). Age-related differences and heterogeneity in executive functions: Analysis of NAB executive functions module scores. *Archives of Clinical Neuropsychology, 31*(3), 254–262. doi:10.1093/arclin/acw005

Buehler, R., Griffin, D., & Ross, M. (1994). Exploring the "planning fallacy": Why people underestimate their task completion times. *Journal of Personality and Social Psychology, 67,* 366–381.

Buehner, M., Mangels, M., Krumm, S., & Ziegler, M. (2005). Are working memory and attention related constructs? *Journal of Individual Differences, 26,* 121–131.

Bufe, J., & Aslan, A. (2018). Desirable difficulties in spatial learning: Testing enhances subsequent learning of spatial information. *Frontiers in Psychology, 9,* 1701. https://doi.org/10.3389/fpsyg.2018.01701

Bukowski, M., de Lemus, S., Rodriguez-Bailón, R., & Willis, G. B. (2017). Who's to blame? Causal attributions of the economic crisis and personal control. *Group Processes & Intergroup Relations, 20*(6), 909–923. https://doi.org/10.1177/1368430216638529

Bukowski, M., Lemus, S., Rodríguez-Bailón, R., Willis, G. B., & Alburquerque, A. (2019). When lack of control enhances closeness to others: The case of unemployment and economic threat. *European Journal of Social Psychology, 49*(6), 1144–1160. https://doi.org/10.1002/ejsp.2563

Bulik, C. M., Flatt, R., Abbaspour, A., & Carroll, I. (2019). Reconceptualizing anorexia nervosa. *Psychiatry and Clinical Neurosciences, 73*(9), 518–525. https://doi.org/10.1111/pcn.12857

Bullock, B., & Murray, G. (2014). Reduced amplitude of the 24 hour activity rhythm: A biomarker of vulnerability to bipolar disorder? *Clinical Psychological Science, 2,* 86–96.

Bullock, W. A., & Gilliland, K. (1993). Eysenck's arousal theory of introversion–extraversion: A converging measures investigation. *Journal of Personality and Social Psychology, 64,* 113–123.

Buonfiglio, D., Tchio, C., Furigo, I., Donato, J. J., Baba, K., Cipolla-Neto, J., & Tosini, G. (2019). Removing melatonin receptor type 1 signaling leads to selective leptin resistance in the arcuate nucleus. *Journal of Pineal Research: Molecular, Biological, Physiological and Clinical Aspects of Melatonin, 67*(2), e12580. https://doi.org/10.1111/jpi.12580

Buonfiglio, M., Avanzini, G., Brighina, F., & Di Sabato, F. (2019). Hyperresponsivity in migraine: A network dysfunction or an analytic cognitive style-connected feature? *Neurological Sciences, 40*(2), 415–416. https://doi.org/10.1007/s10072-018-3593-x

Burdakov, D., Karnani, M. M., & Gonzalez, A. (2013). Lateral hypothalamus as a sensor-regulator in respiratory and metabolic control. *Physiology & Behavior, 121,* 117–124. doi:10.1016/j.physbeh.2013.03.023

Burdakov, D., Luckman, S. M., & Verkhratsky, A. (2005). Glucose-sensing neurons of the hypothalamus. *Philosophical Transactions of the Royal Society of London, Series B, Biological Sciences, 360,* 2227–2235.

Burgard, S. A. (2011). The needs of others: Gender and sleep interruptions for caregivers. *Social Forces, 89,* 1189–1215.

Burger, J. M. (1986). Increasing compliance by improving the deal: The that's-not-all technique. *Journal of Personality and Social Psychology, 51,* 277–283.

Burger, J. M. (2009). Replicating Milgram: Would people still obey today? *American Psychologist, 64,* 1–11.

Burger, J. M. (2011). Is that all there is? Reaction to the that's-not-all procedure. In R. M. Arkin (Ed.), *Most underappreciated: 50 prominent social psychologists describe their most unloved work* (pp. 213–216). Oxford University Press.

Burger, J. M. (2014). Situational features in Milgram's experiment that kept his participants shocking. *Journal of Social Issues, 70*(3), 489–500. doi:10.1111/josi.12073

Burger, J. M., & Caputo, D. (2015). The low-ball compliance procedure: A meta-analysis. *Social Influence, 10*(4), 214–220. doi:10.1080/15534510.2015.1049203

Burger, J. M., Girgis, Z. M., & Manning, C. C. (2011). In their own words: Explaining obedience to authority through an examination of participants' comments. *Social Psychological and Personality Science, 2,* 460–466. doi:10.1177/1948550610397632

Burgess Moser, M., Johnson, S. M., Dalgleish, T. L., Lafontaine, M. F., Wiebe, S. A., & Tasca, G. A. (2016). Changes in relationship-specific attachment in emotionally focused couple therapy. *Journal of Marital and Family Therapy, 42,* 231–245.

Burke, T. M., Markwald, R. R., Chinoy, E. D., Snider, J. A., Bessman, S. C., Jung, C.M., & Wright, K. P., Jr. (2013). Combination of light and melatonin time cues for phase advancing the human circadian clock. *Sleep, 36,* 1617–1624.

Burley, C. (2020). Suicide as a clinical feature of chronic traumatic encephalopathy: What is the evidence? *Aggression and Violent Behavior, 54.* https://doi.org/10.1016/j.avb.2020.101417

Burn, K., & Szoeke, C. (2016). Boomerang families and failure-to-launch: Commentary on adult children living at home. *Maturitas, 83,* 9–12.

Burns, M. N., Ryan, D. T., Garofalo, R., Newcomb, M. E., & Mustanski, B. (2015). Mental health disorders in young urban sexual minority men. *The Journal of Adolescent Health: Official Publication of the Society for Adolescent Medicine, 56*(1), 52–58. doi:10.1016/j.jadohealth.2014.07.018

Burt, C. D. B., Kemp, S., & Conway, M. (2008). Ordering the components of autobiographical events. *Acta Psychological, 127,* 36–45.

Bush, S. I., & Geer, J. H. (2001). Implicit and explicit memory of neutral, negative emotional, and sexual information. *Archives of Sexual Behavior, 30,* 615–631.

Bushman, B. J. (1988). The effects of apparel on compliance: A field experiment with a female authority figure. *Personality and Social Psychology Bulletin, 14,* 459–467.

Buss, D. M. (1995). Psychological sex differences. *American Psychologist, 50,* 164–168.

Buss, D.M. (2009). The great struggles of life: Darwin and the emergence of evolutionary psychology. *American Psychologist, 64,* 140–148.

Buss, K. A., & McDoniel, M. E. (2016). Improving the prediction of risk for anxiety development in temperamentally fearful children. *Current Directions in Psychological Science, 25,* 14–20.

Bussey, K., & Bandura, A. (1999). Social cognitive theory of gender development and differentiation. *Psychological Review, 106,* 676–713.

Bustin, G. M., Jones, D. N., Hansenne, M., & Quoidbach, J. (2015). Who does Red Bull give wings to? Sensation seeking moderates sensitivity to subliminal advertisement. *Frontiers in Psychology, 6,* 825. doi:10.3389/fpsyg.2015.00825

Butler, E. E., Saville, C. W. N., Ward, R., & Ramsey, R. (2017). Physical attraction to reliable, low variability nervous systems: Reaction time variability predicts attractiveness. *Cognition, 158,* 81–89. doi:10.1016/j.cognition.2016.10.012

Butow, P. N., Hiller, J. E., Price, M. A., Thackway, S. V., Kricker, A., & Tennant, C. C. (2000). Epidemiological evidence for a relationship between life events, coping style, and personality factors in the development of breast cancer. *Journal of Psychosomatic Research, 49,* 169–181.

Butt, M., Dwivedi, G., Khair, O., & Lip, G. Y. (2010). Obstructive sleep apnea and cardiovascular disease. *International Journal of Cardiology, 139,* 7–16.

Butts, S. F., & Seifer, D. B. (2010). Racial and ethnic differences in reproductive potential across the life cycle. *Fertility and Sterility, 93,* 681–690.

Byrd-Craven, J., Geary, D. C., Rose, A. J., & Ponzi, D. (2008). Co-ruminating increases stress hormone levels in women. *Hormones and Behavior, 53,* 489–492.

Byrne, D., Gouaux, C., Griffitt, W., Lamberth, J., Murakawa, N., Prasad, M. B., . . . Ramirez, M., III. (1971). The ubiquitous relationship: Attitude similarity and attraction: A cross-cultural study. *Human Relations, 24,* 201–207.

Byrne, M., Agerbo, E., Ewald, H., Eaton, W. W., & Mortensen, P. B. (2003). Parental age and risk of schizophrenia: A case-control study. *Archives of General Psychiatry, 60,* 673–678.

Cacioppo, J. T., & Petty, R. E. (1980). Sex differences in influenceability: Toward specifying the underlying processes. *Personality and Social Psychology Bulletin, 6,* 651–656.

Cacioppo, J. T., Hawkley, L. C., Kalil, A., Hughes, M. E., Waite, L., & Thisted, R. A. (2008). Happiness and the invisible threads of social connection: The Chicago Health, Aging, and Social Relations Study. In M. Eid & R. Larsen (Eds.), *The science of well-being* (pp. 195–219). Guilford Press.

Cain, A. S., Epler, A. J., Steinley, D., & Sher, K. J. (2010). Stability and change in patterns of concerns related to eating, weight, and shape in young adult women: A latent transition analysis. *Journal of Abnormal Psychology, 119,* 255–267.

Cain, W. S. (1988). Olfaction. In R. C. Atkinson, R. J. Herrnstein, G. Lindzey, & R. D. Luce (Eds.), *Steven's handbook of experimental psychology* (2nd ed., Vol. 1, pp. 409–459). Wiley.

Calamari, J. E., Chik, H. M., Pontarelli, N. K., & DeJong, B. L. (2012). Phenomenology and epidemiology of obsessive compulsive disorder. In G. Steketee (Ed.), *The Oxford handbook of obsessive compulsive and spectrum disorders* (pp. 11–47). Oxford University Press.

Caldera, Y. M., & Lindsey, E. W. (2006). Coparenting, mother-infant interaction, and infant-parent attachment relationships in two-parent families. *Journal of Family Psychology, 20,* 275–283.

Caldwell, J. A. (2012). Crew schedules, sleep deprivation, and aviation performance. *Current Directions in Psychological Science, 21,* 85–89.

Cameron, J. D., Goldfield, G. S., Riou, M.E., Finlayson, G. S., Blundell, J. E., & Doucet, E. (2016). Energy depletion by diet or aerobic exercise alone: Impact of energy deficit modality on appetite parameters. *The American Journal of Clinical Nutrition, 103*(4), 1008–1016. doi:10.3945/ajcn.115.115584

Cameron, K. L., Sturdivant, R. X., & Baker, S. P. (2019). Trends in the incidence of physician-diagnosed posttraumatic stress disorder among active-duty U.S. military personnel between 1999 and 2008. *Military Medical Research, 6*(1), 8. doi:10.1186/s40779-019-0198-5

Campos, B., Graesch, A. P., Repetti, R., Bradbury, T., & Ochs, E. (2009). Opportunity for interaction? A naturalistic observation study of dual-earner families after work and school. *Journal of Family Psychology, 23,* 798–807.

Cannon, D. S., & Baker, T. B. (1981). Emetic and electric shock alcohol aversion therapy: Assessment of conditioning. *Journal of Consulting and Clinical Psychology, 49,* 20–33.

Cannon, W. B. (1927). The James-Lange theory of emotions: A critical examination and an alternative theory. *American Journal of Psychology, 39,* 106–124.

Cano, M. E., & Knight, R. T. (2016). Behavioral and EEG evidence for auditory memory suppression. *Frontiers in Human Neuroscience, 10,* 133. doi:10.3389/fnhum.2016.00133

Canuso, C. M., & Pandina, G. (2007). Gender and schizophrenia. *Psychopharmacology Bulletin, 40,* 178–190.

Cappelletti, M., & Wallen, K. (2016). Increasing women's sexual desire: The comparative effectiveness of estrogens and androgens. *Hormones and Behavior, 78,* 178–193. https://doi.org/10.1016/j.yhbeh.2015.11.003

Caputo, F., Vignoli, T., Grignaschi, A., Cibin, M., Addolorato, G., & Bernardi, M. (2014). Pharmacological management of alcohol dependence: From mono-therapy to pharmacogenetics and beyond. *European Neuropsychopharmacology, 24*(2), 181–191. doi:10.1016/j.euroneuro.2013.10.004

Carbia, C., Corral, M., Caamaño-Isorna, F., & Cadaveira, F. (2020). Emotional memory bias in binge drinking women. *Drug and Alcohol Dependence, 209,* 107888. https://doi.org/10.1016/j.drugalcdep.2020.107888

Cardno, A. G., & Gottesman, I. I. (2000). Twin studies of schizophrenia: From bow-and-arrow concordances to Star Wars Mx and functional genomics. *American Journal of Medical Genetics, 97,* 12–17.

Cardozo, B. L., Bilukha, O. O., Gotway Crawford, C. A., Shaikh, I., Wolfe, M. I., Gerber, M. L., & Anderson, M. (2004). Mental health, social functioning, and disability in postwar Afghanistan. *Journal of the American Medical Association, 292,* 575–584.

Carducci, B. J. (2009). *The psychology of personality: Viewpoints, research, and applications* (2nd ed.). Wiley-Blackwell.

Carey, B. (2008). H.M., an unforgettable amnesiac, dies at age 82. *New York Times.* http://www.nytimes.com

Carey, G., & DiLalla, D. L. (1994). Personality and psychopathology: Genetic perspectives. *Journal of Abnormal Psychology, 103,* 32–43.

Carl, E., Stein, A. T., Levihn-Coon, A., Pogue, J. R., Rothbaum, B., Emmelkamp, P., ... Powers, M. B. (2019). Virtual reality exposure therapy for anxiety and related disorders: A meta-analysis of randomized controlled trials. *Journal of Anxiety Disorders, 61,* 27–36. doi:10.1016/j.janxdis.2018.08.003

Carlbring, P., Martin, L., Torngren, C. Linna, E., Eriksson, T., Sparthan, E., . . . Andersson, G. (2011). Individually-tailored, internet-based treatment for anxiety disorders: A randomized controlled trial. *Behaviour Research and Therapy, 49,* 18–24.

Carlisle, N. B., & Woodman, G. F. (2013). Reconciling conflicting electrophysiological findings on the guidance of attention by working memory. *Attention, Perception, & Psychophysics, 75,* 1330-1335. doi:10.3758/s13414-013-0529-7

Carlson, P. J., Singh, J. B., Zarate, C. A., Jr., Drevets, W. C., & Manji, H. K. (2006). Neural circuitry and neuroplasticity in mood disorders: Insights for novel therapeutic targets. *NeuroRx, 3,* 22–41.

Carlston, D. E., & Shovar, N. (1983). Effects of performance attributions on others' perceptions of the attributor. *Journal of Personality and Social Psychology, 44,* 515–525.

Carmi, L., Alyagon, U., Barnea-Ygael, N., Zohar, J., Dar, R., & Zangen, A. (2018). Clinical and electrophysiological outcomes of deep TMS over the medial prefrontal and anterior cingulate cortices in OCD patients. *Brain Stimulation, 11*(1), 158–165. doi:10.1016/j.brs.2017.09.004

Carmi, L., Tendler, A., Bystritsky, A., Hollander, E., Blumberger, D. M., Daskalakis, J., ... Zohar, J. (2019). Efficacy and safety of deep transcranial magnetic stimulation for obsessive-compulsive disorder: A prospective multicenter randomized double-blind placebo-controlled trial. *The American Journal of Psychiatry, 176*(11), 931–938. doi:10.1176/appi.ajp.2019.18101180

Carnahan, T., & McFarland, S. (2007). Revisiting the Stanford prison experiment: Could participant self-selection have led to the cruelty? *Personality and Social Psychology Bulletin, 33*(5), 603–614. doi:10.1177/0146167206292689

Carnethon, M. R., De Chavez, P. J., Zee, P. C., Kim, K. Y., Liu, K., Goldberger, J. J., . . . Knutson, K. L. (2016). Disparities in sleep characteristics by race/ethnicity in a population-based sample: Chicago Area Sleep Study. *Sleep Medicine, 18,* 50–55.

Carney, C. E., Edinger, J. D., Meyer, B., Lindman, L., & Istre, T. (2006). Daily activities and sleep quality in college students. *Chronobiology International, 23,* 623–637.

Carpenter, A. C., & Schacter, D. L. (2017). Flexible retrieval: When true inferences produce false memories. *Journal of Experimental Psychology: Learning, Memory, and Cognition, 43*(3), 335–349. doi:10.1037/xlm0000340

Carpenter, D. O. (2015). The microwave syndrome or electro-hypersensitivity: Historical background. *Reviews on Environmental Health, 30(4),* 217–222. doi:10.1515/reveh-2015-0016

Carreiro, A. L., Dhillon, J., Gordon, S., Jacobs, A. G., Higgins, K. A., McArthur, B. M., . . . Mattes, R. D. (2016). The macronutrients, appetite and energy intake. *Annual Review of Nutrition, 36,* 73–103. doi:10.1146/annurev-nutr-121415-112624

Carrington, P. (1993). Modern forms of meditation. In P. M. Lehrer & R. L. Woolfolk (Eds.), *Principles and practice of stress management* (2nd ed., pp. 139–168). Guilford Press.

Carroll, K. M., Ball, S. A., Martino, S., Nich, C., Babuscio, T. A., Nuro, K. F., . . .

Rounsaville, B. J. (2008). Computer-assisted delivery of cognitive-behavioral therapy for addiction: A randomized trial of CBT4CBT. *American Journal of Psychiatry, 165,* 793–795.

Carson, N., Rosenbaum, R. S., Moscovitch, M., & Murphy, K. J. (2019). Self-referential processing improves memory for narrative information in healthy aging and amnestic Mild Cognitive Impairment. *Neuropsychologia, 134,* 107179. https://doi.org/10.1016/j.neuropsychologia.2019.107179

Carter, R. S., & Wojtkiewicz, R. A. (2000). Parental involvement with adolescents' education: Do daughters or sons get more help? *Adolescence, 35,* 29–44.

Cartwright, R. D. (1993). Who needs their dreams? The usefulness of dreams in psychotherapy. *Journal of the American Academy of Psychoanalysis, 21,* 539–547.

Carver, C. S., Harris, S. D., Lehman, J. M., Durel, L. A., Antoni, M. H., Spencer, S. M., & Pozo-Kaderman, C. (2000). How important is the perception of personal control? Studies of early stage breast cancer patients. *Personality and Social Psychology Bulletin, 26,* 139–149.

Carver, C. S., Johnson, S. L., & Joormann, J. (2009). Two-mode models of self-regulation as a tool for conceptualizing effects of the serotonin system in normal behavior and diverse disorders. *Current Directions in Psychological Science, 18,* 195–199.

Casey, B. J., & Caudle, K. (2013). The teenage brain: Self-control. *Current Directions in Psychological Science, 22,* 82–87.

Casey, B. J., Giedd, J. N., & Thomas, K. M. (2000). Structural and functional brain development and its relation to cognitive development. *Biological Psychology, 54,* 241–257.

Cassidy, R. N., Tidey, J. W., Kahler, C. W., Wray, T. B., & Colby, S. M. (2015). Increasing the value of an alternative monetary reinforcer reduces cigarette choice in adolescents. *Nicotine & Tobacco Research, 17*(12), 1449-1455. doi:10.1093/ntr/ntv033

Cassilhas, R. C., Tufik, S., & de Mello, M. T. (2016). Physical exercise, neuroplasticity, spatial learning and memory. *Cellular and Molecular Life Sciences, 73*(5), 975–983.

Castel, A. D., Murayama, K., Friedman, M. C., McGillivray, S., & Link, I. (2013). Selecting valuable information to remember: Age-related differences and similarities in self-regulated learning. *Psychology and Aging, 28,* 232–242. doi:10.1037/a0030678

Cates, W., Jr. (1998). Reproductive tract infections. In R. A. Hatcher et al. (Eds.), *Contraceptive technology* (17th rev. ed., pp. 179–210). Ardent Media.

Cattell, N. R. (2006). *An introduction to mind, consciousness and language.* Continuum.

Cattell, R. B. (1943). The description of personality: Basic traits resolved into clusters. *Journal of Abnormal and Social Psychology, 38,* 476–506.

Cattell, R. B. (1963). Theory of fluid and crystallized intelligence: A critical experiment. *Journal of Educational Psychology, 54,* 1–22.

Cattell, R. B. (1965). *The scientific analysis of personality.* Penguin.

Cavanagh, K., Shapiro, D. A., Van Den Berg, S., Swain, S., Barkham, M., & Proudfoot, J. (2009). The acceptability of computer-aided cognitive behavioural therapy: A pragmatic study. *Cognitive Behaviour Therapy, 38,* 235–246.

Ceci, S. J. (1995). False beliefs: Some developmental and clinical considerations. In D. L. Schacter (Ed.), *Memory distortions* (pp. 91–125). Harvard University Press.

Cedernaes, J., Osorio R. S., Varga, A. W., Kam, K., Schiöth, H. B., & Benedict, C. (2017). Candidate mechanisms underlying the association between sleep-wake disruptions and Alzheimer's disease. *Sleep Medicine Reviews, 31,* 102–111.

Censor, N., Dayan, E., & Cohen, L. G. (2014). Cortico-subcortical neuronal circuitry associated with reconsolidation of human procedural memories. *Cortex, 58,* 281–288. doi:10.1016/j.cortex.2013.05.013

Center for Behavioral Health Statistics and Quality. (2015). *2014 National Survey on Drug Use and Health: Detailed Tables.* Substance Abuse and Mental Health Services Administration.

Center for Behavioral Health Statistics and Quality. (2018). *2017 National Survey on Drug Use and Health: Detailed Tables.* Substance Abuse and Mental Health Services Administration.

Center for Sexual Health Promotion. (2019). *National Survey of Sexual Health and Behavior.* https://nationalsexstudy.indiana.edu.

Centers for Disease Control and Prevention (CDC). (2009). Cigarette smoking among adults and trends in smoking cessation—United States, 2008. *Morbidity and Mortality Weekly Report, 58,* 1227–1232.

Centers for Disease Control and Prevention (CDC). (2010). Seroprevalence of herpes simplex virus type 2 among persons aged 14–49 years—United States, 2005–2008. *Morbidity and Mortality Weekly Report, 59,* 456–459.

Centers for Disease Control and Prevention (CDC). (2011a). Nonfatal traumatic brain injuries related to sports and recreation activities among persons aged ≤ 19 years—United States, 2001–2009. *Morbidity and Mortality Weekly Report, 60,* 1337–1342.

Centers for Disease Control and Prevention (CDC). (2011b). Unhealthy sleep-related behaviors—12 states, 2009. *Morbidity and Mortality Weekly Report, 60,* 233–238.

Centers for Disease Control and Prevention (CDC). (2014). *Genital HPV infection: CDC fact sheet.* U.S. Department of Health and Human Services.

Centers for Disease Control and Prevention (CDC). (2015a). Current cigarette smoking among adults—United States, 2005–2014. *Morbidity and Mortality Weekly Report, 64,* 1233–1240.

Centers for Disease Control and Prevention (CDC). (2015b). Prevalence of self-reported obesity among U.S. adults by state and territory. *Behavioral Risk Factor Surveillance System.* http://www.cdc.gov/obesity/data/prevalence-maps.html

Centers for Disease Control and Prevention (CDC). (2016a). *STD & HIV screening recommendations.* http://www.cdc.gov/std/prevention/screeningReccs.htm

Centers for Disease Control and Prevention (CDC). (2016b). National center for chronic disease prevention and health promotion, division of nutrition, physical activity, and obesity. Data, trend and maps. https://www.cdc.gov/nccdphp/dnpao/data-trends-maps/index.html.

Centers for Disease Control and Prevention (CDC). (2018). *HIV Surveillance Report, 2017, Vol. 29.* Department of Health and Human Services.

Centers for Disease Control and Prevention (CDC). (2019). *Sexually Transmitted Disease Surveillance 2018.* Department of Health and Human Services.

Centers for Disease Control and Prevention (CDC). (2020a). TBI-related emergency department visits, hospitalizations, and deaths (EDHDs). https://www.cdc.gov/traumaticbraininjury/data/tbi-edhd.html

Centers for Disease Control and Prevention (2020b). Coronavirus disease 2019. https://www.cdc.gov/coronavirus/2019-nCoV/index.html

Centers for Disease Control and Prevention. (2020c). Web-based Injury Statistics Query and Reporting System (WISQARS). National Center for Injury Prevention and Control. https://www.cdc.gov/injury/wisqars/index.html

Centers for Medicare and Medicaid Services (CMMS). (2004, July 16). *Medicare to fund obesity treatment.* CBS News. Available online at http://www.cbsnews.com/stories/2004/07/16/health/main630141.shtml?tag=mncol;lst;1

Cermak, L. S., Lewis, R., Butters, N., & Goodglass, H. (1973). Role of verbal mediation in performance of motor tasks by Korsakoff patients. *Perceptual and Motor Skills, 37,* 259–262.

Cernoch, J., & Porter, R. H. (1985). Recognition of maternal axillary odors by infants. *Child Development, 56,* 1593–1598.

Chabris, C. F., Lee, J. L., Cesarini, D., Benjamin, D. J., & Laibson, D. I. (2015). The fourth law of behavior genetics. *Current Directions in Psychological Science, 24,* 304–312.

Chaby, L. E., Sheriff, M. J., Hirrlinger, A. M., & Braithwaite, V. A. (2015). Can we understand how developmental stress enhances performance under future threat with the Yerkes-Dodson law? *Communicative & Integrative Biology, 8*(3), e1029689. doi:10.1080/19420889.2015.1029689

Chadwick, M. J., Bonnici, H. M., & Maguire, E. A. (2014). CA3 size predicts the precision of memory recall. *Proceedings of the National Academy of Sciences of the United States of America, 111*(29), 10720–10725. doi:10.1073/pnas.1319641111

Chadwick, S. B., Burke, S. M., Goldey, K. L., & van Anders, S. M. (2017). Multifaceted sexual desire and hormonal associations: Accounting for social location, relationship status, and desire target. *Archives of Sexual Behavior, 46*(8), 2445–2463. https://doi.org/10.1007/s10508-017-0959-8

Chakos, M. H., Alvir, J. M., Woerner, M., & Koreen, A. (1996). Incidence and correlates of tardive dyskinesia in first episode of schizophrenia. *Archives of General Psychiatry, 53,* 313–319.

Chaladze, G. (2016). Heterosexual male carriers could explain persistence of homosexuality in men: Individual-based simulations of an X-linked inheritance model. *Archives of Sexual Behavior, 45*(7), 1705–1711. doi:10.1007/s10508-016-0742-2

Chambers, D., & Reisberg, D. (1992). What an image depicts depends on what an image means. *Cognitive Psychology, 24,* 145–174.

Chambless, D. L., & Hollon, S. D. (1998). Defining empirically-supported therapies. *Journal of Consulting and Clinical Psychology, 66,* 7–18.

Chambless, D. L., & Ollendick, T. H. (2001). Empirically supported psychological interventions: Controversies and evidence. *Annual Review of Psychology, 52,* 685–716.

Chamorro-Premuzic, T., & Furnham, A. (2004). A possible model for understanding the personality-intelligence interface. *British Journal of Psychology, 95,* 249–264.

Champagne, F. A. (2010). Early adversity and development outcomes: Interaction between genetics, epigenetics, and social experiences across the life span. *Perspectives on Psychological Science, 5,* 564–574.

Champagne, F. A., & Mashoodh, R. (2009). Genes in context: Gene-environment interplay and the origins of individual differences in behavior. *Current Directions in Psychological Science, 18,* 127–131.

Chand, H. S., Muthumalage, T., Maziak, W., & Rahman, I. (2020). Pulmonary toxicity and the pathophysiology of electronic cigarette, or vaping product, use associated lung injury. *Frontiers in Pharmacology, 10,* 1619. doi:10.3389/fphar.2019.01619

Chandrashekar, J., Hoon, M. A., Ryba, N. J. P., & Zuker, C. S. (2006). The receptors and cells for mammalian taste. *Nature, 444,* 288–294.

Chandrashekara, S., Jayashree, K., Veeranna, H. B., Vadiraj, H. S., Ramesh, M. N., Shobha, A., . . . Vikram, Y. K. (2007). Effects of anxiety on TNF-a levels during psychological stress. *Journal of Psychosomatic Research, 63,* 65–69.

Chang, I. J., Pettit, R. W., & Katsurada, E. (2006). Where and when to spank: A comparison between U.S. and Japanese college students. *Journal of Family Violence, 21,* 281–286.

Chapman, S. J., & Benis, N. (2017). Ceteris non paribus: The intersectionality of gender, race, and region in the gender wage gap. *Women's Studies International Forum, 65,* 78–86. https://doi.org/10.1016/j.wsif.2017.10.001

Chaput, J. P., & Tremblay, A. A. (2009). The glucostatic theory of appetite control and the risk of obesity and diabetes. *International Journal of Obesity, 33,* 46–53. doi:10.1038/ijo.2008.221

Charles, S., & Carstensen, L. L. (2010). Social and emotional aging. *Annual Review of Psychology, 61,* 383–409.

Charles, S. T., Piazza, J. R., Mogle, J. M., Sliwinski, M. J., & Almeida, D. M. (2013). The wear and tear of daily stressors on mental health. *Psychological Science, 24,* 733–741.

Cheadle, S., Egner, T., Wyart, V., Wu, C., & Summerfield, C. (2015). Feature expectation heightens visual sensitivity during fine orientation discrimination. *Journal of Vision, 15*(14), 14. doi:10.1167/15.14.14

Cheah, C. S., Leung, C. Y., Tahseen, M., & Schuz, D. (2009). Authoritative parenting among immigrant Chinese mothers of preschoolers. *Journal of Family Psychology, 23,* 311–320.

Chen, A. C., Chang, R. Y., Besherat, A., & Baack, D. W. (2013). Who benefits from multiple brand celebrity endorsements? An experimental investigation. *Psychology & Marketing, 30*(10), 850-860. doi:10.1002/mar.20650

Chen, E. (2012). Protective factors for health among low-socioeconomic-status individuals. *Current Directions in Psychological Science, 21,* 189–193.

Chen, E., McLean, K. C., & Miller, G. E. (2015). Shift-and-persist strategies: Associations with socioeconomic status and the regulation of inflammation among adolescents and their parents. *Psychosomatic Medicine, 77,* 371–382.

Chen, E., & Miller, G. E. (2012). "Shift-and-persist" strategies: Why low socioeconomic status isn't always bad for health. *Perspectives on Psychological Science, 7,* 135–158.

Chen, E., Cohen, S., & Miller, G. E. (2010). How low socioeconomic status affects 2-year hormonal trajectories in children. *Psychological Science, 21,* 31–37.

Chen, J. J., Zhao, L. B., Liu, Y. Y., Fan, S. H., & Xie, P. (2017). Comparative efficacy and acceptability of electroconvulsive therapy versus repetitive transcranial magnetic stimulation for major depression: A systematic review and multiple-treatments meta-analysis. *Behavioural Brain Research, 320,* 30–36.

Chen, L., Zhang, G., Hu, M., & Liang, X. (2015). Eye movement desensitization and reprocessing versus cognitive-behavioral therapy for adult posttraumatic stress disorder: Systematic review and meta-analysis. *The Journal of Nervous and Mental Disease, 203,* 443–451.

Chen, L. W., Wu, Y., Neelakantan, N., Chong, M. F., Pan, A., & Van Dam, R. M. (2016). Maternal caffeine intake during pregnancy and risk of pregnancy loss: A categorical and dose-response meta-analysis of prospective studies. *Public Health Nutrition, 19*(7), 1233–1244.

Chen, S., & van Ours, J. C. (2018). Subjective well-being and partnership dynamics: Are same-sex relationships different? *Demography, 55*(6), 2299–2320. doi:10.1007/s13524-018-0725-0

Chen, S. T., Siddarth, P., Merrill, D. A., Martinez, J., Emerson, N. D., Liu, J., ... Small, G. W. (2018). FDDNP-PET tau brain protein binding patterns in military personnel with suspected chronic traumatic encephalopathy. *Journal of Alzheimer's Disease, 65*(1), 79–88. https://doi.org/10.3233/JAD-171152

Chen, S. X., Benet-Martínez, V., & Ng, J. C. K. (2014). Does language affect personality perception? A functional approach to testing the Whorfian hypothesis. *Journal of Personality, 82*(2), 130–143. doi:10.1111/jopy.12040

Chen, Y., Gao, X., Liu, Q., Zeng, L., Zhang, K., Mu, K., ... Mao, S. (2020). Alpha-asarone improves cognitive function of aged rats by alleviating neuronal excitotoxicity via $GABA_A$ receptors. *Neuropharmacology, 162,* 107843. https://doi.org/10.1016/j.neuropharm.2019.107843

Chen, Y. L., Su, M. C., Liu, W. H., Wang, C. C., Lin, M. C., & Chen, M. C. (2014). Influence and predicting variables of obstructive sleep apnea on cardiac function and remodeling in patients without congestive heart failure. *Journal of Clinical Sleep Medicine, 10,* 57–64.

Cheng, K. K., Lam, T. H., & Leung, C. C. (2020). Wearing face masks in the community during the COVID-19 pandemic: Altruism and solidarity. *Lancet (London, England),* S0140-6736(20)30918-1. https://doi.org/10.1016/S0140-6736(20)30918-1

Chengyang, L., Daqing, H., Jianlin, Q., Haisheng, C., Qingging, M., Jin, W., . . . Xi, Z. (2017). Short-term memory deficits correlate with hippocampal-thalamic functional connectivity alterations following acute sleep restriction. *Brain Imaging and Behavior, 11*(4), 954–963. doi:10.1007/s11682-016-9570-1

Cheong, Y., & Combs, J. (2016). An analysis of media violence in commercials aired during the telecasts of sports events. *Journal of Marketing Communications, 22*(6), 602–625. doi:10.1080/13527266.2014.930067

Cherry, K. E., Brown, J., Walker, E., Smitherman, E. A., Boudreaux, E. O., Volaufova, J., & Jazwinski, S. (2012). Semantic encoding enhances the pictorial superiority effect in the oldest-old. *Aging, Neuropsychology, and Cognition, 19,* 319–337. doi:10.1080/13825585.2011.619645

Chess, S., & Thomas, A. (1984). *Origins and evolution of behavior disorders: From infancy to early adult life.* Brunner/Mazel.

Chessick, C. A., Allen, M. H., Thase, M., Batista Miralha da Cunha, A. B., Kapczinski, F. F., de Lima, M.S., & dos Santos Souza, J. J. (2006). Azapirones for generalized anxiety disorder. *Cochrane Database of Systematic Reviews, 19,* CD006115.

Cheung, F. M., & Halpern, D. F. (2010). Women at the top: Powerful leaders define success as work + family in a culture of gender. *American Psychologist, 65,* 182–193.

Chiang, A. A. (2006). Obstructive sleep apnea and chronic intermittent hypoxia: A review. *Chinese Journal of Physiology, 49,* 234–243.

Chida, Y., & Steptoe, A. (2008). Positive psychological well-being and mortality: A quantitative review of prospective observational studies. *Psychosomatic Medicine, 70,* 741–756.

Childress, J. E., McDowell, E. J., Dalai, V. K., Bogale, S. R., Ramamurthy, C., Jawaid, A., . . . Schulz, P. E.. (2013). Hippocampal volumes in patients with chronic combat-related posttraumatic stress disorder: A systematic review. *Journal of Neuropsychiatry and Clinical Neurosciences, 25,* 12–25. doi:10.1176/appi.neuropsych.12010003

Childs, L. A. (2011). Assessing vestibular dysfunction. Exploring treatments of a complex condition. *Rehab Management, 23,* 24–25.

Child Trends. (2019). Dating. https://www.childtrends.org/indicators/dating.

Chipuer, H. M., Rovine, M. J., & Polmin, R. (1990). LISREL modeling: Genetic and environmental influences on IQ revisited. *Intelligence, 14,* 11–29.

Cho, J. R., Joo, E. Y., Koo, D. L., & Hong, S. B. (2013). Let there be no light: The effect of bedside light on sleep quality and background electroencephalographic rhythms. *Sleep Medicine, 14,* 1422–1425.

Choi, I., & Nisbitt, R. E. (1998). Situational salience and cultural differences in the correspondence bias and actor-observer bias. *Personality and Social Psychology Bulletin, 24,* 949–960.

Choi, J. S., Kim, S. H., Yoo, S. Y., Kang, D. H., Kim, C. W., Lee, J. M., . . . Kwon, J. S. (2007). Shape deformity of the corpus striatum in obsessive-compulsive disorder. *Psychiatry Research, 155,* 257–264.

Chollar, S. (1989, April). Dreamchasers. *Psychology Today,* 60–61.

Chomsky, N. (1957). *Syntactic structures* (1st edition.). Mouton.

Chomsky, N. (1965). *Aspects of the theory of syntax* (1st edition.). MIT Press.

Choromanska, K., Choromanska, B., Dabrowska, E., Baczek, W., Mysliwiec, P., Dadan, J., & Zalewska, A. (2015). Saliva of obese patients – is it different? *Postepy Higieny I Medycyny Doswiadczalnej (Online), 69,* 1190–1195.

Chory-Assad, R. M., & Tamborini, R. (2003). Television exposure and the public's perceptions of physicians. *Journal of Broadcasting and Electronic Media, 47,* 197–215.

Chou, I. J., Kuo, C. F., Huang, Y. S., Grainge, M. J., Valdes, A. M., See, L. C., ... Doherty,

M. (2017). Familial aggregation and heritability of schizophrenia and co-aggregation of psychiatric illnesses in affected families. *Schizophrenia Bulletin, 43*(5), 1070–1078. doi:10.1093/schbul/sbw159

Chou, R., Qaseem, A., Snow, V., Casey, D., Cross, J. T., Jr., Shekelle, P., & Owens, D. K. (2007). Diagnosis and treatment of low back pain: A joint clinical practice guideline from the American College of Physicians and the American Pain Society. *Annals of Internal Medicine, 147,* 478–491, W118–W120.

Chou, S. P., Dawson, D. A., Stinson, F. S., Huang, B., Pickering, R. P., Zhou, Y., & Grant, B. F. (2006). The prevalence of drinking and driving in the United States, 2001–2002: Results from the national epidemiological survey on alcohol and related conditions. *Drug and Alcohol Dependence, 83,* 137–146.

Chow, M., & Cao, M. (2016). The hypocretin/orexin system in sleep disorders: Preclinical insights and clinical progress. *Nature and Science of Sleep, 8,* 81–86.

Chrisman, S. P., Rivara, F. P., Schiff, M. A., Zhou, C., & Comstock, R. (2013). Risk factors for concussive symptoms 1 week or longer in high school athletes. *Brain Injury, 27,* 1–9. doi:10.3109/02699052.2012.722251

Christian, L. M. (2015). Stress and immune function during pregnancy: An emerging focus in mind-body medicine. *Current Directions in Psychological Science, 24,* 3–9.

Christie, W., & Moore, C. (2005). The impact of humor on patients with cancer. *Clinical Journal of Oncology Nursing, 9,* 211–218.

Chung, B. Y., Bignell, W., Jacklin, D. L., Winters, B. D., & Bailey, C. D. (2016). Postsynaptic nicotinic acetylcholine receptors facilitate excitation of developing CA1 pyramidal neurons. *Journal of Neurophysiology, 116*(5), 2043-2055. doi:10.1152/jn.00370.2016

Church, R. M., & Black, A. H. (1958). Latency of the conditioned heart rate as a function of the CS–US interval. *Journal of Comparative and Physiological Psychology, 51,* 478–482.

Cialdini, R. B. (2001). *Influence: Science and practice* (4th ed.). Allyn & Bacon.

Cialdini, R. B., Borden, R. J., Thorne, A., Walker, M. R., Freeman, S., & Sloan, L. R. (1976). Basking in the reflected glory: Three (football) field studies. *Journal of Personality and Social Psychology, 34,* 366–375.

Cialdini, R. B., Cacioppo, J. T., Bassett, R., & Miller, J. A. (1978). Low-ball procedure for producing compliance: Commitment then cost. *Journal of Personality and Social Psychology, 36,* 463–476.

Cialdini, R. B., Vincent, J. E., Catalan, J., Wheeler, D., & Darby, B. L. (1975). Reciprocal concessions procedure for inducing compliance: The door-in-the-face technique. *Journal of Personality and Social Psychology, 31,* 206–215.

Cin, S. D., Gibson, B., Zanna, M. P., Shumate, R., & Fong, G. T. (2007). Smoking in movies, implicit associations of smoking with the self, and intentions to smoke. *Psychological Science, 18,* 559–563.

Cinnirella, M., & Green, B. (2007). Does "cyber-conformity" vary cross-culturally? Exploring the effect of culture and communication medium on social conformity. *Computers in Human Behavior, 23,* 2011–2025. doi:10.1016/j.chb.2006.02.009

Cipriani, A., Barbui, C., Salanti, G., Rendell, J., Brown, R., Stockton, S., . . . Geddes, J. R. (2011). Comparative efficacy and acceptability of antimanic drugs in acute mania: A multiple-treatments meta-analysis. *Lancet, 378,* 1306–1315.

Cipriani, A., Furukawa, T. A., Salanti, G., Chaimani, A., Atkinson, L. Z., Ogawa, Y.,...Geddes, J. R. (2018). Comparative efficacy and acceptability of 21 antidepressant drugs for the acute treatment of adults with major depressive disorder: A systematic review and network meta-analysis. *Lancet, 391*(10128), 1357–1366. doi:10.1016/S0140-6736(17)32802-7

Cipriani, A., Reid, K., Young, A. H., Macritchie, K., & Geddes, J. (2013). Valproic acid, valproate and divalproex in the maintenance treatment of bipolar disorder. *The Cochrane Database of Systematic Reviews, 10,* CD003196.

Citirik, M., Acaroglu, G., Batman, C., & Zilelioglu, O. (2005). Congenital color blindness in young Turkish men. *Opthalmic Epidemiology, 12,* 133–137.

Citrome, L. (2015). A primer on binge eating disorder diagnosis and management. *CNS Spectrums, 20 Suppl 1,* 44–51. doi:10.1017/S1092852915000772

Claassen, J., Mazilescu, L., Thieme, A., Bracha, V., & Timmann, D. (2016). Lack of renewal effect in extinction of naturally acquired conditioned eyeblink responses, but possible dependency on physical context. *Experimental Brain Research, 234*(1), 151–159. doi:10.1007/s00221-015-4450-2

Clark, D. A., & Beck, A. T. (2010). Cognitive theory and therapy of anxiety and depression: Convergence with neurobiological findings. *Trends in Cognitive Sciences, 14,* 418–424.

Clark, J. L., Algoe, S. B., & Green, M. C. (2018). Social network sites and well-being: The role of social connection. *Current Directions in Psychological Science, 27*(1), 32–37.

Clark, K. B. (1950). *Effect of prejudice and discrimination on personality development.* Paper written for the White House Mid-Century Conference on Children and Youth.

Clark, K. B., & Clark, M. P. (1950). Emotional factors in racial identification and preference in Negro children. *Journal of Negro Education, 19,* 341–350.

Clark, L. A. (2007). Assessment and diagnosis of personality disorder: Perennial issues and emerging conceptualization. *Annual Review of Psychology, 58, 227–257.*

Clark, M. S., Lemay, E. P., Jr., Graham, S. M., Pataki, S. P., & Finkel, E. J. (2010). Ways of giving benefits in marriage: Norm use, relationship satisfaction, and attachment-related variability. *Psychological Science, 21,* 944–951.

Clark, R.E. (2003). Fostering the work motivation of individuals and teams. *Performance Improvement, 42(3),* 21-29.

Clarke, A. C. (1952). An examination of the operation of residential propinquity as a factor in mate selection. *American Sociological Review, 17,* 17–22.

Clemenson, G. D., & Stark, C. E. L. (2015). Virtual environmental enrichment through video games improves hippocampal-associated memory. *The Journal of Neuroscience, 35*(49), 16116–16125. https://doi.org/10.1523/JNEUROSCI.2580-15.2015

Clemenson, G. D., Stark, S. M., Rutledge, S. M., & Stark, C. E. L. (2020). Enriching hippocampal memory function in older adults through video games. *Behavioural Brain Research, 390,* 112667. https://doi.org/10.1016/j.bbr.2020.112667

Coccaro, E. F., Beresford, B., Minar, P., Kaskow, J., & Geracioti, T. (2007). CSF testosterone: Relationship to aggression, impulsivity, and venturesomeness in adult males with personality disorder. *Journal of Psychiatric Research, 41,* 488–492.

Cochran, S. V., & Rabinowitz, F. E. (2000). *Men and depression: Clinical and empirical perspectives.* Academic Press.

Coffer, C. N., & Appley, M. (1964). *Motivation: Theory and research.* Wiley.

Cohen, A. O., Breiner, K., Steinberg, L., Bonnie, R. J., Scott, E. S., Taylor-Thompson, K. . . . Casey, B. J. (2016). When is an adolescent an adult? Assessing cognitive control in emotional and nonemotional contexts. *Psychological Science, 27*(4), 549–562.

Cohen, C. I., Natarajan, N., Araujo, M., & Solanki, D. (2013). Prevalence of negative symptoms and associated factors in older adults with schizophrenia spectrum disorder. *American Journal of Geriatric Psychiatry, 21,* 100–107.

Cohen, M. X., Young, J., Baek, J., Kessler, C., & Ranganath, C. (2005). Individual differences in extraversion and dopamine genetics predict neural reward responses. *Cognitive Brain Research, 25,* 851–861.

Cohen, N. J. (1984). Preserved learning capacity in amnesia: Evidence for multiple memory systems. In L. R. Squire & N. Butters (Eds.), *Neuropsychology of memory* (pp. 83–103). Guilford Press.

Cohen, P., Kasen, S., Chen, H., Hartmark, C., & Gordon, K. (2003). Variations in patterns of developmental transitions in the emerging adulthood period. *Developmental Psychology, 39,* 657–669.

Cohen, R., Bavishi, C., & Rozanski, A. (2016). Purpose in life and its relationship to all-cause mortality and cardiovascular events: A meta-analysis. *Psychosomatic Medicine, 78*(2), 122–33. doi:10.1097/PSY.0000000000000274

Cohen, S., & Janicki-Deverts, D. (2009). Can we improve our physical health by altering our social networks? *Perspectives on Psychological Science, 4,* 375–378.

Cohen, S., Janicki-Deverts, D., Chen, E., & Matthews, K. A. (2010). Childhood socioeconomic status and adult health. *Annals of the New York Academy of Sciences, 1186,* 37–55.

Cohen, S., Janicki-Deverts, D., Doyle, W. J., Miller, G. E., Frank, E., Rabin, B. S., & Turner, R. B. (2012). Chronic stress, glucocorticoid receptor resistance, inflammation, and disease risk. *Proceedings of the National Academy of Sciences, 109*(16) 5995–5999. doi:10.1073/pnas.1118355109

Cohen, S., Janicki-Deverts, D., Turner, R. B., & Doyle, W. J. (2015). Does hugging provide stress-buffering social support? A study on susceptibility to upper respiratory infection and illness. *Psychological Science, 26,* 135–147.

Cohen, S. G., & Ledford, G. E., Jr. (1994). The effectiveness of self-managing teams: A quasi-experiment. *Human Relations, 47,* 13–43.

Colado, M. I., O'Shea, E., & Green, A. R. (2004). Acute and long-term effects of MDMA on cerebral dopamine biochemistry and function. *Psychopharmacology (Berlin), 173,* 249–263.

Colbert-White, E. N., Covington, M. A., & Fragaszy, D. M. (2011). Social context influences the vocalizations of a home-raised African grey parrot (*Psittacus erithacus erithacus*). *Journal of Comparative Psychology, 125,* 175–184.

Colbert-White, E. N., Hall, H. C., & Fragaszy, D. M. (2016). Variations in an African Grey parrot's speech patterns following ignored and denied requests. *Animal Cognition, 19*(3), 459–469. https://doi.org/10.1007/s10071-015-0946-1

Cole, R. E., Clark, H. L., Heileson, J., DeMay, J., & Smith, M. A. (2016). Normal weight status in military service members was associated with intuitive eating characteristic. *Military Medicine, 181*(6), 589–595. doi:10.7205/MILMED-D-15-00250

Coles, N. A., Larsen, J. T., & Lench, H. C. (2019). A meta-analysis of the facial feedback literature: Effects of facial feedback on emotional experience are small and variable. *Psychological Bulletin, 145*(6), 610–651. https://doi.org/10.1037/bul0000194

Coley, R. L. (2001). (In)visible men: Emerging research on low-income, unmarried, and minority fathers. *American Psychologist, 56*, 743–753.

Colley, A., Ball, J., Kirby, N., Harvey, R., & Vingelen, I. (2002). Gender-linked differences in everyday memory performance: Effort makes the difference. *Sex Roles: A Journal of Research, 47*, 577–582.

Collier, G., Hirsch, E., & Hamlin, P. H. (1972). The ecological determinants of reinforcement in the rat. *Physiology and Behavior, 9*, 705–716.

Collinger, J. L., Foldes, S., Bruns, T. M., Wodlinger, B., Gaunt, R., & Weber, D. J. (2013). Neuroprosthetic technology for individuals with spinal cord injury. *The Journal of Spinal Cord Medicine, 36*(4), 258–272. doi:10.1179/2045772313Y.0000000128

Collins, A. M., & Quillian, M. R. (1969). Retrieval time from semantic memory. *Journal of Verbal Learning and Verbal Behavior, 8*, 240–248.

Collins, A., Hill, L. E., Chandramohan, Y., Witcomb, D., Droste, S. K., & Reul, J. M. (2009). Exercise improves cognitive responses to stress through enhancement of epigenetic mechanisms and gene expression in the dentate gyrus. *PLoS One, 4*, e4330.

Collins, M. W., Field, M., Lovell, M. R., Iverson, G., Johnston, K. M., Maroon, J., . . . Foo, F. H. (2003). Relationship between postconcussion headache and neuropsychological test performance in high school athletes. *American Journal of Sports Medicine, 31*, 168–173.

Collins, W. A., & van Dulmen, M. (2006). Friendships and romance in emerging adulthood: Assessing distinctiveness in close relationships. In J. J. Arnett & J. L. Tanner (Eds.), *Emerging adults in America: Coming of age in the 21st century* (pp. 219–234). APA.

Colman, A. M. (2016). Race differences in IQ: Hans Eysenck's contribution to the debate in the light of subsequent research. *Personality and Individual Differences, 103*, 182–189. doi:10.1016/j.paid.2016.04.050

Cologan, V., Schabus, M., Ledoux, D., Moonen, G., Maquet, P., & Laureys, S. (2010). Sleep in disorders of consciousness. *Sleep Medicine Reviews, 14*, 97–105.

Combs, D. R., & Mueser, K. T. (2007). Schizophrenia. In M. Hersen, S. Turner, & D. Beidel (Eds.), *Adult psychopathology and diagnosis* (5th ed., pp. 234–285). Wiley.

Compare, A., Mommersteeg, P. M., Faletra, F., Grossi, E., Pasotti, E., Moccetti, T., & Auricchio, A. (2014). Personality traits, cardiac risk factors, and their association with presence and severity of coronary artery plaque in people with no history of cardiovascular disease. *The Journal of Cardiovascular Medicine* (Haverstown, MD), *15*, 423–430.

Compton, W. M., Helzer, J. E., Hwu, H., Yeh, E., McEvoy, L., Tipp, J. E., & Spitznagel, E. L. (1991). New methods in cross-cultural psychiatry: Psychiatric illness in Taiwan and the United States. *American Journal of Psychiatry, 148*, 1697–1704.

Conger, R. D., Schofield, T. J., Neppl, T. K., & Merrick, M. T. (2013). Disrupting intergenerational continuity in harsh and abusive parenting: The importance of a nurturing relationship with a romantic partner. *Journal of Adolescent Health, 53*, S11-S17.

Conklin, H. M., & Iacono, W. G. (2002). Schizophrenia: A neurodevelopmental perspective. *Current Directions in Psychological Science, 11*, 33–37.

Conley, C. C., Bishop, B. T., & Andersen, B. L. (2016). Emotions and emotion regulation in breast cancer survivorship. *Healthcare, 4*, 56.

Connelly, W. M., & Errington, A. C. (2012). Temporally selective firing of cortical and thalamic neurons during sleep and wakefulness. *Journal of Neuroscience, 32*, 7415–7417. doi:10.1523/JNEURO-SCI.1164-12.2012

Conrad, M. A., & Ashworth, S. D. (1986). *Recruiting source effectiveness: A meta-analysis and reexamination of two rival hypotheses.* Paper presented at the First Annual Meeting of the Society for Industrial and Organizational Psychology, Chicago.

Conway, B. R. (2009). Color vision, cones, and color-coding in the cortex. *Neuroscientist, 15*, 274–290.

Conway, M. A. (2009). Episodic memories. *Neuropsychologia, 47*, 2305–2313.

Cook, J. L., & Cook, G. (2005). *Child development: Principles and perspectives.* Allyn & Bacon.

Cooke, R., & Sheeran, P. (2004). Moderation of cognition-intention and cognition-behaviour relations: A meta-analysis of properties of variables from the theory of planned behaviour. *British Journal of Social Psychology, 43*, 159–186.

Cools, J., Schotte, D. E., & McNally, R. J. (1992). Emotional arousal and overeating in restrained eaters. *Journal of Abnormal Psychology, 69*, 390–400.

Cooper, J. A., Blanco, N. J., & Maddox, W. T. (2017). Framing matters: Effects of framing on older adults' exploratory decision-making. *Psychology and Aging, 32(1), 60-68.* doi:10.1037/pag0000146

Cooper, Z. D., & Haney, M. (2008). Cannabis reinforcement and dependence: Role of the cannabinoid CB1 receptor. *Addiction Biology, 13*, 188–195.

Copeland, W. E., Angold, A., Shanahan, L., & Costello, E. J. (2014). Longitudinal patterns of anxiety from childhood to adulthood: The Great Smoky Mountains Study. *Journal of the American Academy of Child and Adolescent Psychiatry, 53*, 21–33.

Copen, C. E., Daniels, K., & Mosher, W. D. (2013). First premarital cohabitation in the United States: 2006–2010 National Survey of Family Growth. *National Health Statistics Reports, 64*, 1–15.

Coren, S., Porac, C., Aks, D. J., & Morikawa, K. (1988). A method to assess the relative contribution of lateral inhibition to the magnitude of visual-geometric illusions. *Perception and Psychophysics, 43*, 551–558.

Coren, S., Ward, L. M., & Enns, J. T. (1999). *Sensation and perception* (5th ed.). Harcourt Brace.

Corey, G. (2009). *Theory and practice of counseling and psychotherapy* (8th ed.). Brooks/Cole.

Corkin, S. (1968). Acquisition of motor skill after bilateral medial temporal-lobe excision. *Neuropsychologia, 6*, 255–265.

Correll, J., Park, B., & Judd, E., Wittenbrink, B., Sadler, M. S., & Keesee, T. (2007). Across the thin blue line: Police officers and racial bias in the decision to shoot. *Journal of Personality and Social Psychology, 92*(6), 1006–1023. https://doi.org/10.1037/0022-3514.92.6.1006

Corrigan, P., McCorkle, B., Schell, B, & Kidder, K. (2003). Religion and spirituality in the lives of people with serious mental illness. *Community Mental Health Journal, 39*, 487–499.

Corrigan, P. W., Druss, B. G., & Perlick, D. A. (2014). The impact of mental illness stigma on seeking and participating in mental health care. *Psychological Science in the Public Interest, 15*, 37–70.

Corriveau, K. H., Min, G., & Kurkul, K. (2014). Cultural differences in children's learning from others. In E. J. Robinson & S. Einav (Eds.), *Trust and skepticism: Children's selective learning from testimony* (pp. 95–109). Psychology Press.

Cortesa, C. S., Hudac, C. M., & Molfese, D. L. (2019). Dynamic effects of habituation and novelty detection on newborn event-related potentials. *Brain and Language, 199*, 104695. https://doi.org/10.1016/j.bandl.2019.104695

Cosmides, L., & Tooby, J. (1996). Are humans good intuitive statisticians after all? Rethinking some conclusions from the literature on judgment under uncertainty. *Cognition, 58*, 1–73.

Costa, P. T., & McCrae, R. R. (1992). Multiple uses for longitudinal personality data. *European Journal of Personality, 6*, 85–102.

Costa, P. T., & McCrae, R. R. (1997). Longitudinal stability of adult personality. In R. Hogan, J. A. Johnson, & S. R. Briggs (Eds.), *Handbook of personality psychology* (pp. 269–290). Academic Press.

Costa, P. T., Terracciano, A., & McCrae, R. R. (2001). Gender differences in personality traits across cultures: Robust and surprising findings. *Journal of Personality and Social Psychology, 81*, 322–331.

Costello, F., & Watts, P. (2014). Surprisingly rational: Probability theory plus noise explains biases in judgment. *Psychological Review, 121*(3), 463–480. doi:10.1037/a0037010

Coumans, J. M. J., Danner, U. N., Hadjigeorgiou, C., Hebestreit, A., Hunsberger, M., Intemann, T., ... Adan, R. A. H. (2019). Emotion-driven impulsiveness but not decision-making ability and cognitive inflexibility predicts weight status in adults. *Appetite, 142*, 104367. https://doi.org/10.1016/j.appet.2019.104367

Cousins, D. A., Butts, K., & Young, A. H. (2009). The role of dopamine in bipolar disorder. *Bipolar Disorders, 11*, 787–806.

Coussons-Read, M. (2012). The psychoneuroimmunology of stress in pregnancy. *Current Directions in Psychological Science, 21*, 323–328.

Coutinho-Budd, J., & Freeman, M. R. (2013). Probing the enigma: Unraveling glial cell biology in invertebrates. *Current Opinion in Neurobiology, 23,* 1073–1079. doi:10.1016/j.conb.2013.07.002

Cowan, C. P., & Cowan, P. A. (2000). *When partners become parents: The big life change for couples.* Erlbaum.

Cowan, N. (2001). The magical number 4 in short-term memory: A reconsideration of mental storage capacity. *Behavioral and Brain Sciences, 24*(1), 87–185. doi:10.1017/S0140525X01003922

Coyle, J. T. (2006). Glutamate and schizophrenia: Beyond the dopamine hypothesis. *Cellular and Molecular Neurobiology, 26,* 365–384.

Crabbe, J. C., Harris, R. A., & Koob, G. F. (2011). Preclinical studies of alcohol binge drinking. *Annals of the New York Academy of Sciences, 1216,* 24–40.

Craciun, B. (2013). Coping strategies, self-criticism and gender factor in relation to quality of life. *Procedia-Social and Behavioral Sciences,* 78, 466–470. doi:10.1016/j.sbspro.2013.04.332

Craik, F. I. M., & Lockhart, R. S. (1972). Levels of processing: A framework for memory research. *Journal of Verbal Learning and Verbal Behavior, 11,* 671–684.

Crandall, C. S. (1988). Social contagion of binge eating. *Journal of Personality and Social Psychology, 55,* 588–598.

Crandall, C. S. (1991). Do heavy-weight students have more difficulty paying for college? *Personality and Social Psychology Bulletin, 17,* 606–611.

Crandall, C. S., Preisler, J. J., & Aussprung, J. (1992). Measuring life event stress in the lives of college students: The Undergraduate Stress Questionnaire (USQ). *Journal of Behavioral Medicine, 15,* 627–662.

Crane, M., & Markus, H. (1982). Gender identity: Benefits of a self-schema approach. *Journal of Personality and Social Psychology, 43,* 1195–1197.

Cranny, C. J., Smith, P. C., & Stone, E. F. (1992). *Job satisfaction: How people feel about their jobs and how it affects their performance.* Lexington Books.

Craske, M. G., & Barlow, D. H. (2001). Panic disorder and agoraphobia. In D. H. Barlow (Ed.), *Clinical handbook of psychological disorders* (3rd ed., pp. 1–59). Guilford Press.

Creamer, M., Wade, D., Fletcher, S., & Forbes, D. (2011). PTSD among military personnel. *International Review of Psychiatry, 23,* 160–165.

Creswell, J. D., & Lindsay, E. K. (2014). How does mindfulness training affect health? A mindfulness stress buffering account. *Current Directions in Psychological Science, 23,* 401–407.

Creswell, K. G., Chung, T., Clark, D. B., & Martin, C. S. (2014). Solitary alcohol use in teens is associated with drinking in responses to negative affect and predicts alcohol problems in young adulthood. *Clinical Psychological Science, 2,* 602–610.

Crews, F. (1996). The verdict on Freud. *Psychological Science, 7,* 63–68.

Crichton, G. E., Elias, M. F., & Alkerwi, A. (2016). Chocolate intake is associated with better cognitive function: The Maine-Syracuse Longitudinal Study. *Appetite, 100,* 126–132. doi:10.1016/j.appet.2016.02.010

Crick, F., & Mitchison, G. (1995). REM sleep and neural nets. *Behavioural Brain Research, 69,* 147–155.

Crits-Christoph, P. (1997). Limitations of the dodo bird verdict and the role of clinical trials in psychotherapy research: Comment on Wamplod et al. (1997). *Psychological Bulletin, 122,* 216–220.

Crocker, A., & Sehgal, A. (2010). Genetic analysis of sleep. *Genes and Development, 24,* 1220–1235.

Crockett, M. J., Clark, L., Hauser, M. D., & Robbins, T. W. (2010). Serotonin selectively influences moral judgment and behavior through effects on harm aversion. *Proceedings of the National Academy of Sciences, 107,* 17433–17438.

Croft, A., Schmader, T., Block, K., & Baron, A. S. (2014). The second shift reflected in the second generation: Do parents' gender roles at home predict children's aspirations? *Psychological Science, 25,* 1418–1428.

Crombag, H. S., & Robinson, T. E. (2004). Drugs, environment, brain, and behavior. *Current Directions in Psychological Science 13,* 107–111.

Cross, C. P., Brown, G. R., Morgan, T. J. H., & Laland, K. N. (2017). Sex differences in confidence influence patterns of conformity. *British Journal of Psychology, 108(4), 655-667.* doi:10.1111/bjop.12232

Cross, E. S., Mackie, E. C., Wolford, G., & Hamilton, A. F. de C. (2010). Contorted and ordinary body postures in the human brain. *Experimental Brain Research, 204,* 397–407. doi:10.1007/s00221-00902093-X

Crosscope-Happel, C. L. (2000). Male anorexia nervosa: A new focus. *Journal of Mental Health Counseling, 22,* 365.

Crowley, A. E., & Hoyer, W. D. (1994). An integrative framework for understanding two-sided persuasion. *Journal of Consumer Research, 20,* 561–574.

Crowley, S. J., Acebo, C., & Carskadon, M. A. (2007). Sleep, circadian rhythms, and delayed phase in adolescence. *Sleep Medicine, 8,* 602–612.

Croxford, J. L. (2003). Therapeutic potential of cannabinoids in CNS disease. *CNS Drugs, 17,* 179–202.

Croy, I., Bojanowski, V., & Hummel, T. (2013). Men without a sense of smell exhibit a strongly reduced number of sexual relationships, women exhibit reduced partnership security—A reanalysis of previously published data. *Biological Psychology, 92,* 292–294. doi:10.1016/j.biopsycho.2012.11.008

Crump, M. J. C., McDonnell, J. V., & Gureckis, T. M. (2013). Evaluating Amazon's Mechanical Turk as a tool for experimental behavioral research. *PLoS ONE, 8,* e57410. doi:10.1371/journal.pone.0057410

Cruz-Albarran, I. A., Benitez-Rangel, J. P., Osornio-Rios, R. A., & Morales-Hernandez, L. A. (2017). Human emotions detection based on a smart-thermal system of thermographic images. *Infrared Physics and Technology, 81,* 250–261.

Cuartas Arias, J. M. C., Palacio Acosta, C. A., Valencia, J. G., Montoya, G. J., Arango Viana, J. C., Nieto, O. C., . . . Ruiz-Linares, A. (2011). Exploring epistasis in candidate genes for antisocial personality disorder. *Psychiatric Genetics, 21,* 115–124.

Cuartas, J., Ward, K. P., Ma, J., & Grogan-Kaylor, A. (2020). Physical punishment and Colombian children and adolescents' cognitive and behavioral outcomes. *Journal of Applied Developmental Psychology, 68,* 101140. https://doi.org/10.1016/j.appdev.2020.101140

Cui, G., Wang, Y., Wang, X., Zheng, L., Li, L., Li, P. ,... Meng, X. (2020). Static and dynamic functional connectivity of the prefrontal cortex during resting-state predicts self-serving bias in depression. *Behavioural Brain Research, 379,* 112335. https://doi.org/10.1016/j.bbr.2019.112335

Cui, M., & Donnellan, M. B. (2009). Trajectories of conflict over raising adolescent children and marital satisfaction. *Journal of Marriage and Family, 71,* 478–494.

Cummings, E. M., & Miller-Graff, L. E. (2015). Emotional security theory: An emerging theoretical model for youths' psychological and physiological responses across multiple developmental contexts. *Current Directions in Psychological Science, 24,* 208–213.

Cunha, C., Guerreiro, M., de Mendonça, A., Oliveira, P., & Santana, I. (2012). Serial position effects in Alzheimer's disease, mild cognitive impairment, and normal aging: Predictive value for conversion to dementia. *Journal of Clinical and Experimental Neuropsychology, 34,* 841–852. doi:10.1080/13803395.2012.689814

Cupaioli, F. A., Zucca, F. A., Caporale, C., Lesch, K. P., Passamonti, L., & Zecca, L. (2020). The neurobiology of human aggressive behavior: Neuroimaging, genetic, and neurochemical aspects. *Progress in Neuro-Psychopharmacology & Biological Psychiatry,* 110059. Advance online publication. https://doi.org/10.1016/j.pnpbp.2020.110059

Curry, K., & Stasio, M. J. (2009). The effects of energy drinks alone and with alcohol on neuropsychological functioning. *Human Psychopharmacology, 24,* 473–481.

Curtin, S. C., & Hedegaard, H. (2019). *Suicide rates for females and males by race and ethnicity: United States, 1999 and 2017.* NCHS Health E-Stat.

Curtin, S. C., Warner, M., & Hedegaard, H. (2016). *Suicide rates for females and males by race and ethnicity: United States, 1999 and 2014.* NCHS Health E-Stat. CDC, National Center for Health Statistics.

Cutrona, C. E., Wallace, G., & Wesner, K. A. (2006). Neighborhood characteristics and depression: An examination of stress processes. *Current Directions in Psychological Science, 15,* 188–192.

Cvencek, D., Meltzoff, A. N., & Greenwald, A. G. (2011). Math-gender stereotypes in elementary school children. *Child Development, 82*(3), 766-79. doi:10.1111/j.1467-8624.2010.01529

Cyr, D., Head, M., Lim, E., & Stibe, A. (2018). Using the elaboration likelihood model to examine online persuasion through website design. *Information and Management, 55*(7), 807-821. http://dx.doi.org.proxygsu-ngal.galileo.usg.edu/10.1016/j.im.2018.03.009

D'Andrea, G., Ostuzzi, R., Bolner, A., Colavito, D., & Leon, A. (2012). Is migraine a risk factor for the occurrence of eating disorders? Prevalence and biochemical evidences. *Neurological Sciences: Official Journal of the Italian Neurological Society and of the Italian Society of Clinical Neurophysiology, 33*(Suppl 1), S71–76. doi:10.1007/s10072-012-1045-6

D'Anna, L. H., Ponce, N. A., & Siegel, J. M. (2010). Racial and ethnic health disparities: Evidence of discrimination's effects across the SEP spectrum. *Ethnicity and Health, 15,* 121–143.

Dabbs, J. M., Jr., & Morris, R. (1990). Testosterone, social class, and antisocial behavior in a sample of 4,462 men. *Psychological Science, 1,* 209–211.

Dalal, R. S. (2005). A meta-analysis of the relationship between organizational citizenship behavior and counterproductive work behavior. *Journal of Applied Psychology, 90,* 1241–1255.

Dalen, K., Bruaroy, S., Wentzel-Larsen, T., & Laegreid, L.M. (2009). Cognitive functioning in children prenatally exposed to alcohol and psychotropic drugs. *Neuropediatrics, 40,* 162–167.

Dalenberg, C. J., Brand, B. L., Gleaves, D. H., Dorahy, M. J., Loewenstein, R. J., Cardeña, E., . . . Spiegel, D. (2012). Evaluation of the evidence for the trauma and fantasy models of dissociation. *Psychological Bulletin, 138,* 550–588.

Dalman, C., & Allebeck, P. (2002). Paternal age and schizophrenia: Further support for an association. *American Journal of Psychiatry, 159,* 1591–1592.

Dalton, A. N., & Huang, L. (2014). Motivated forgetting in response to social identity threat. *Journal of Consumer Research, 40*(6), 1017–1038. doi:10.1086/674198

Daly, M., Robinson, E., & Sutin, A. R. (2017). Does knowing hurt? Perceiving oneself as overweight predicts future physical health and well-being. *Psychological Science, 28*(7), 872–881.

Damak, S., Rong, M., Yasumatsu, K., Kokrashvii, Z., Varadarajan, V., Zou, S., . . . Margolskee, R. F. (2003). Detection of sweet and umami taste in the absence of taste receptor T1r3. *Science, 301,* 850–851.

Damasio, H., Grabowski, T., Frank, R., Galaburda, A. M., & Damasio, A. R. (1994). The return of Phineas Gage: Clues about the brain from the skull of a famous patient. *Science, 264,* 1102–1105.

Damian, R. I., & Roberts, B. W. (2015). Settling the debate on birth order and personality. *Proceedings of the National Academy of Sciences of the United States of America, 112,* 14119–14120.

Damjanovic, A. K., Yang, Y., Glaser, R., Kiecolt-Glaser, J. K., Huy, N., Laskowski, B., . . . Weng, N. P. (2007). Accelerated telomere erosion is associated with a declining immune function of caregivers of Alzheimer's disease patients. *Journal of Immunology, 179,* 4249–4254.

Damm, J., Eser, D., Schule, C., Obermeier, M., Moeller, H. J., Rupprecht, R., & Baghai, T. C. (2010). Influence of age on effectiveness and tolerability of electroconvulsive therapy. *Journal of ECT, 26,* 282–288.

Damon, W. (1999). The moral development of children. *Scientific American, 281,* 73–78.

Dance, A. (2015). How online studies are transforming psychology research. *Proceedings of the Natural Academy of Sciences, 112,* 14399–14401.

Dang-Vu, T.T., Schabus, M., Desseilles, M., Sterpenich, V., Bonjean, M., & Maquet, P. (2010). Functional neuroimaging insights into the physiology of human sleep. *Sleep, 33,* 1589–1603.

Danhauer, J. L., Johnson, C. E., Byrd, A., DeGood, L., Meuel, C., Pecile, A., . . . Koch, L. L. (2009). Survey of college students on iPod and hearing health. *Journal of the American Academy of Audiology, 20,* 5–27.

Danielsdottir, S., O'Brien, K. S., & Ciao, A. (2010). Anti-fat prejudice reduction: A review of published studies. *Obesity Facts, 3,* 47–58.

Dank, M., Lachman, P., Zweig, J. M., & Yahner, J. (2014). Dating violence experiences of lesbian, gay, bisexual, and transgender youth. *Journal of Youth and Adolescence, 43*(5), 846–857. doi:10.1007/s10964-013-9975-8

Dannlowski, U., Ohrmann, P., Bauer, J., Kugel, H., Baune, B. T., Hohoff, C., . . . Suslow, T. (2007). Serotonergic genes modulate amygdale activity in major depression. *Genes, Brain and Behavior, 6,* 672–676.

Darchia, N., & Cervana, K. (2014). The journey through the world of adolescent sleep. *Reviews in the Neurosciences, 25,* 585–604.

Darley, J. M., & Batson, C. (1973). "From Jerusalem to Jericho": A study of situational and dispositional variables in helping behavior. *Journal of Personality and Social Psychology, 27,* 100–108. doi:10.1037/h0034449

Darowish, M., Lawton, J. N., & Evans, P. J. (2009). Q: What is cell phone elbow, and what should we tell our patients? *Cleveland Clinic Journal of Medicine, 76,* 306–308.

Darwin, C. (1936). *On the origin of species by means of natural selection.* Random House. (Original work published 1859)

Das, S., Barnwal, P., Ramasamy, A., Sen, S., & Mondal, S. (2016). Lysergic acid diethylamide: A drug of "use"? *Therapeutic Advances in Psychopharmacology, 6,* 214–228. doi:10.1177/2045125316640440

Dasen, P. R. (1994). Culture and cognitive development from a Piagetian perspective. In W. J. Lonner & R. Malpass (Eds.), *Psychology and culture* (pp. 141–150). Allyn & Bacon.

Dasgupta, A. M., Juza, D. M., White, G. M., & Maloney, J. F. (1995). Memory and hypnosis: A comparative analysis of guided memory, cognitive interviews, and hypnotic hyperamnesia. *Imagination, Cognition, and Personality, 14,* 117–130.

Dauvilliers, Y., Maret, S., & Tafti, M. (2005). Genetics of normal and pathological sleep in humans. *Sleep Medicine Review, 9,* 91–100.

David, D., Cotet, C., Matu, S., Mogoase, C., & Stefan, S. (2018). 50 years of rational-emotive and cognitive-behavioral therapy: A systematic review and meta-analysis. *Journal of Clinical Psychology, 74*(3), 304–318. doi:10.1002/jclp.22514

David, D., Cristea, I., & Hofmann, S. G. (2018). Why cognitive behavioral therapy is the current gold standard of psychotherapy. *Frontiers in Psychiatry, 9,* Article 4. doi:10.3389/fpsyt.2018.00004

David, D., Szentagotai, A., Lupu, V., & Cosman, D. (2008). Rational emotive behavior therapy, cognitive therapy, and medication in the treatment of major depressive disorder: A randomized clinical trial, posttreatment outcomes, and six-month follow-up. *Journal of Clinical Psychology, 64,* 728–746.

Davidson, R. J., Putnam, K. M., & Larson, C. L. (2000). Dysfunction in the neural circuitry of emotion regulation: A possible prelude to violence. *Science, 289,* 591–594.

Davies, G., Tenesa, A., Payton, A., Yang, J., Harris, S. E., Liewald, D., & . . . Deary, I. J. (2011). Genome-wide association studies establish that human intelligence is highly heritable and polygenic. *Molecular Psychiatry, 16*(10), 996-1005. doi:10.1038/mp.2011.85

Davies, I. R. L. (1998). A study of colour grouping in three languages: A test of the linguistic relativity hypothesis. *British Journal of Psychology, 89,* 433–452.

Davis, E. M., Kim, K., & Fingerman, K. L. (2018). Is an empty nest best?: Coresidence with adult children and parental marital quality before and after the Great Recession. *The Journals of Gerontology. Series B, Psychological Sciences and Social Sciences, 73*(3), 372–381. doi:10.1093/geronb/gbw022

Davis, K. C., George, W. H., Norris, J., Schacht, R. L., Stoner, S. A., Hendershot, C. S., & Kajumolo, K. F. (2009). Effects of alcohol and blood alcohol concentration limb on sexual risk-taking intentions. *Journal of Studies on Alcohol and Drugs, 70*(4), 499–507.

Davis, M., & Egger, M. D. (1992). Habituation and sensitization in vertebrates. In L. R. Squire, J. H. Byrne, L. Nadel, H. L. Roediger, D. L. Schacter, & R. F. Thompson (Eds.), *Encyclopedia of learning and memory* (pp. 237–240). Macmillan.

Davis, O. S., Haworth, C. M., & Plomin, R. (2009). Dramatic increase in heritability of cognitive development from early to middle childhood: An 8-year longitudinal study of 8,700 pairs of twins. *Psychological Science, 20,* 1301–1308.

Davis, P. J. (1999). Gender differences in autobiographical memory for childhood emotional experiences. *Journal of Personality and Social Psychology, 76,* 498–510.

Davis-Coelho, K., Waltz, J., & Davis-Coelho, B. (2000). Awareness and prevention of bias against fat clients in psychotherapy. *Professional Psychology: Research and Practice, 31,* 682–684.

Dawood, K., Bailey, J. M., & Martin, N. G. (2009). Genetic and environmental influences on sexual orientation. In Y. Kim & Y. Kim (Eds.), *Handbook of behavior genetics* (pp. 269–279). Springer Science + Business Media. doi:10.1007/978-0-387-76727-7_19

De Benedittis, G., Lorenzetti, A., & Pieri, A. (1990). The role of stressful life events in the onset of chronic primary headache. *Pain, 40,* 65–75.

De Carvalho, M. R., Freire, R. C., & Nardi, A. E. (2010). Virtual reality as a mechanism for exposure therapy. *World Journal of Biological Psychiatry, 11,* 220–230.

de Castro, J. M. (2002). The influence of heredity on self-reported sleep patterns in free-living humans. *Physiology and Behavior, 76,* 479–486.

De Goede, M., & Postma, A. (2015). Learning your way in a city: Experience and gender differences in configurational knowledge of one's environment. *Frontiers in Psychology, 6,* 402. doi:10.3389/fpsyg.2015.00402

De Houwer, J. (2019). Implicit bias is behavior: A functional-cognitive perspective on implicit bias. *Perspectives on Psychological Science, 14*(5), 835–840. https://doi.org/10.1177/1745691619855638

De Leersnyder, J., Boiger, M., & Mesquita, B. (2013). Cultural regulation of emotion: Individual, relational, and structural sources. *Frontiers in Psychology, 4,* 55. doi:10.3389/fpsyg.2013.00055

De Lisi, R., & Gallagher, A. M. (1991). Understanding gender stability and constancy in Argentinean children. *Merrill-Palmer Quarterly, 37,* 483–502.

De May, J. (2006). A critical review of the March 27, 1964, *New York Times* article that first broke the story. http://www.oldkewgardens.com/ss-nytimes-3.html

de Moura, F. B., Kohut, S. J., & Bergman, J. (2018). Limited modulation of the abuse-related behavioral effects of d-methamphetamine by disulfiram. *Experimental and Clinical Psychopharmacology, 26*(5), 497–502. https://doi.org/10.1037/pha0000222

de Tommaso, M., Difruscolo, O., Sardaro, M., Losito, L., Serpino, C., Pietrapertosa, A., . . . Lamberti, P. (2007). Influence of MTHFR genotype on contingent negative variation and MRI abnormalities in migraine. *Headache, 47,* 253–265.

de Tommaso, M., Sciruicchio, V., Ricci, K., Montemurno, A., Gentile, F., Vecchio, E., . . . Livrea, P. (2016). Laser-evoked potential habituation and central sensitization symptoms in childhood migraine. *Cephalalgia, 36*(5), 463–473. doi:10.1177/0333102415597527

Deak, G. O. (2006). Do children really confuse appearance and reality? *Trends in Cognitive Science, 10,* 546–550.

Deakin, J. F., Lees, J., McKie, S., Hallak, J. E., Williams, S. R., & Dursun, S. M. (2008). Glutamate and the neural basis of the subjective effects of ketamine: A pharmacomagnetic resonance imaging study. *Archives of General Psychiatry, 65,* 154–164.

DeAngelis, T. (2004). Size-based discrimination may be hardest on children. *American Psychological Association Monitor on Psychology, 35,* 62.

Deary, I. J., Weiss, A., & Batty, G. D. (2010). Intelligence, personality, and health outcomes. *Psychological Science in the Public Interest, 11,* 53–79.

Deaux, K., & Hanna, R. (1984). Courtship in the personals column: The influence of gender and sexual orientation. *Sex Roles, 11,* 363–375.

DeCasper, A. J., & Fifer, W. P. (1980). Of human bonding: Newborns prefer their mothers' voices. *Science, 208,* 1174–1176.

Deci, E. L., & Ryan, R. M. (1985). *Intrinsic motivation and self-determination in human behavior.* Plenum Press.

Deci, E. L., & Ryan, R. M. (2008). Self-determination theory: A macrotheory of human motivation, development, and health. *Canadian Psychology, 49,* 182–185.

Deemer, E. D., Lin, C., & Soto, C. (2016). Stereotype threat and women's science motivation: Examining the disidentification effect. *Journal of Career Assessment, 24*(4), 637–650. doi:10.1177/1069072715616064

Degner, J., & Dalege, J. (2013). The apple does not fall far from the tree, or does it? A meta-analysis of parent-child similarity in intergroup attitudes. *Psychological Bulletin, 139,* 1270–1304. doi:10.1037/a0031436

DeLoache, J. (2001). The symbol-mindedness of young children. In W. W. Hartup & R. A. Weinberg (Eds.), *Child psychology in retrospect and prospect* (Vol. 32, pp. 73–101). Erlbaum.

Demany, L., & Semal, C. (2005). The slow formation of a pitch percept beyond the ending time of a short tone burst. *Perception and Psychophysics, 67,* 1376–1383.

Dement, W. (1960). The effect of dream deprivation. *Science, 131,* 1705–1707.

Dement, W., & Kleitman, N. (1957). Cyclic variations in EEG during sleep and their relation to eye movements, body motility, and dreaming. *Electroencephalography and Clinical Neurophysiology, 9,* 673–690.

Demers, L. B., Hanson, K. G., Kirkorian, H. L., Pempek, T. A., & Anderson, D. R. (2013). Infant gaze following during parent–infant coviewing of baby videos. *Child Development, 84,* 591–603. doi:10.1111/j.1467-8624.2012.01868.x

Denis, M., & Cocude, M. (1999). On the metric properties of visual images generated from verbal descriptions: Evidence for the robustness of the mental scanning effect. *Journal of Cognitive Psychology, 9,* 353–379.

Denollet, J., Pedersen, S. S., Vrints, C. J., & Conraads, V. M. (2013). Predictive value of social inhibition and negative affectivity for cardiovascular events and mortality in patients with coronary artery disease. The type D personality construct. *Psychosomatic Medicine, 75,* 873–881.

Denson, T. F., Dixson, B. J. W., Tibubos, A. N., Zhang, E., Harmon-Jones, E., & Kasumovic, M. M. (2020). Violent video game play, gender, and trait aggression influence subjective fighting ability, perceptions of men's toughness, and anger facial recognition. *Computers in Human Behavior, 104,* 106175. https://doi.org/10.1016/j.chb.2019.106175

DePadilla, L., Miller, G. F., Jones, S. E., Peterson, A. B., & Breiding, M. J. (2018). Self-reported concussions from playing a sport or being physically active among high school students—United States. *Morbidity and Mortality Weekly, 67,* 682–685. doi:http://cx.doi.org/10.15585/mmwr.mm6724a3external icon.

DePalma, M., Madey, S. F., Tillman, T. C., & Wheeler, J. (1999). Perceived patient responsibility and belief in a just world affect helping. *Basic and Applied Social Psychology, 21,* 131–137. doi:10.1207/15324839951036470

Department of Housing and Urban Development (HUD). (2005). *Discrimination in metropolitan housing markets: National results from Phase 1, Phase 2, and Phase 3 of the housing discrimination study (HDS)* http://www.huduser.org/publications/hsgfin/hds.html

Depner, C. M., Stothard, E. R., & Wright, K. P., Jr. (2014). Metabolic consequences of sleep and circadian disorders. *Current Diabetes Reports, 14,* 507.

Depue, R. A., & Collins, P. F. (1999). Neurobiology of the structure of personality: Dopamine, facilitation of incentive motivation, and extraversion. *The Behavioral and Brain Sciences, 22,* 491–517.

Depue, R. A., & Fu, Y. (2013). On the nature of extraversion: Variation in conditioned contextual activation of dopamine-facilitated affective, cognitive, and motor processes. *Frontiers in Human Neuroscience, 7,* 288. doi:10.3389/fnhum.2013.00288

Deregowski, J. B. (2013). On the Muller-Lyer illusion in the carpentered world. *Perception, 42*(7), 790–792.

Derringer, J., Krueger, R. F., Dick, D. M., Saccone, S., Grucza, R. A., Agrawal, A., . . . Gene Environment Association Studies (GENEVA) Consortium (2010). Predicting sensation seeking from dopamine genes: A candidate-systems approach. *Psychological Science, 21,* 1282–1290.

Desombre, C., Anegmar, S., & Delelis, G. (2018). Stereotype threat among students with disabilities: The importance of the evaluative context on their cognitive performance. *European Journal of Psychology of Education, 33(2), 201-214.* doi:10.1007/s10212-016-0327-4

Desseilles, M., Dang-Vu, T. T., Sterpenich, V., Schwartz, S. (2011). Cognitive and emotional processes during dreaming: A neuroimaging view. *Consciousness and Cognition, 20,* 998–1008.

Deutsch, F. M. (2001). Equally shared parenting. *Current Directions in Psychological Science, 10,* 25–28.

Deutsch, J. A. (1990). Food intake. In E. M. Stricker (Ed.), *Handbook of behavioral neurobiology:* Vol. 10. *Neurobiology of food and fluid intake* (pp. 151–182). Plenum Press.

DeValois, R. L., & DeValois, K. K. (1975). Neural coding of color. In E. C. Carterette & M. P. Friedman (Eds.), *Handbook of perception* (pp. 117–166). Academic Press.

Devitt, A. L., Tippett, L., Schacter, D. L., & Addis, D. R. (2016). Autobiographical memory conjunction errors in younger and older adults: Evidence for a role of inhibitory ability. *Psychology and Aging, 31*(8), 927–942. doi:10.1037/pag0000129

DeVylder, J.E., Lukens, E.P., Link, B.G., & Lieberman, J.A. (2015). Suicidal ideation and suicide attempts among adults with psychotic experiences: Data from the Collaborative Psychiatric Epidemiology Surveys. *JAMA Psychiatry, 72,* 219–225.

DeWall, C. N., & Bushman, B. J. (2011). Social acceptance and rejection The sweet and the bitter. *Current Directions in Psychological Science, 20,* 256–260.

Dhont, K., Roets, A., & Van Hiel, A. (2013). The intergenerational transmission of need for closure underlies the transmission of authoritarianism and anti-immigrant prejudice. *Personality and Individual Differences, 54,* 779–784. doi:10.1016/j.paid.2012.12.016

Di Iorio, C. R., Watkins, T. J., Dietrich, M. S., Cao, A., Blackford, J. U., Rogers, B., . . . Cowan, R. L. (2012). Evidence for chronically altered serotonin function in the cerebral cortex of female 3, 4-methylenedioxymethamphetamine polydrug users. *Archives of General Psychiatry, 69*(4), 399–409.

Diamond, A., & Amso, D. (2008). Contributions of neuroscience to our understanding of cognitive development. *Current Directions in Psychological Science, 17,* 136–141.

Díaz-Mataix, L., Tallot, L., & Doyère, V. (2014). The amygdala: A potential player in timing CS–US intervals. *Behavioural Processes, 101,*112–122. doi.10.1016/j.beproc.2013.08.007

Dichter, G. S., Felder, J. N., & Smoski, M. J. (2010). The effects of brief behavioral activation therapy for depression on cognitive control in affective contexts: An fMRI investigation. *Journal of Affective Disorders, 126,* 236–244.

Dick, D. M., Meyers, J. L., Latendresse, S. J., Creemers, H. E., Lansford, J. E., Pettit, G. S., . . . Huizink, A. C. (2011). CHRM2, parental monitoring, and adolescent externalizing behavior: Evidence for gene–environment interaction. *Psychological Science, 22,* 481–489.

Dickens, W. T., & Flynn, J. R. (2006). Black Americans reduce the racial IQ gap. Evidence from standardization samples. *Psychological Science, 17,* 913–920.

Dickson, N., van Roode, T., Cameron, C., & Paul, C. (2013). Stability and change in same-sex attraction, experience, and identity by sex and age in a New Zealand birth cohort. *Archives of Sexual Behavior, 42,* 753–763. doi:10.1007/s10508-012-0063-z

Diekelmann, S., & Born, J. (2010). The memory function of sleep. *Nature Reviews: Neuroscience, 11,* 114–126.

Diener, C., Kuehner, C., Brusniak, W., Struve, M., & Flor, H. (2009). Effects of stressor controllability on psychophysiological, cognitive, and behavioral responses in patients with major depression and dysthymia. *Psychological Medicine, 39,* 77–86.

Diener, C. I., & Dweck, C. S. (1978). An analysis of learned helplessness: Continuous changes in performance, strategy, and achievement cognitions following failure. *Journal of Personality and Social Psychology, 36*(5), 451–462. https://doi.org/10.1037/0022-3514.36.5.451

Diener, E., & Seligman, M. E. (2004). Beyond money: Toward an economy of well-being. *Psychological Science in the Public Interest, 5,* 1–31.

Diener, E., Oishi, S., & Lucas, R. E. (2003). Personality, culture, and subjective well-being: Emotional and cognitive evaluations of life. *Annual Review of Psychology, 54,* 403–425.

Diener, E., Seligman, M. E. P., Choi, H., & Oishi, S. (2018). Happiest people revisited. *Perspectives on Psychological Science, 13*(2), 176–184.

Dies, R. R. (1993). Research on group psychotherapy: Overview and clinical applications. In A. Alonso & H. I. Swiller (Eds.), *Group therapy in clinical practice* (pp. 473–518). American Psychiatric Press.

Digman, J. M. (1997). Higher-order factors of the Big Five. *Journal of Personality and Social Psychology, 73,* 1246–1256.

Dill, K. E., & Thill, K. (2007). Video game characters and the socialization of gender roles: Young people's perceptions mirror sexist media depictions. *Sex Roles,* 57, 851–864. doi:10.1007/s11199-007-9278-1

Dindo, L., Brock, R. L., Aksan, N., Gamez, W., Kochanska, G., & Clark, L. A. (2017). Attachment and effortful control in toddlerhood predict academic achievement over a decade later. *Psychological Science, 28*(12), 1786–1795.

Dingfelder, S. F. (2010). How artists see. *Monitor on Psychology, 41,* p. 40.

Dinnella, C., Morizet, D., Masi, C., Danny, C., Depezay, L., Appleton, K. M., . . . Monteleone, E. (2016). Sensory determinants of stated liking for vegetable names and actual liking for canned vegetables: A cross-country study among European adolescents. *Appetite, 107,* 339–347. doi:10.1016/j.appet.2016.08.110

Dion, K. K., Berscheid, E., & Walster, E. (1972). What is beautiful is good. *Journal of Personality and Social Psychology, 24,* 285–290.

DiPatrizio, N. V., & Piomelli, D. (2012). The thrifty lipids: Endocannabinoids and the neural control of energy conservation. *Trends in Neurosciences, 35,* 403–411. doi:10.1016/j.tins.2012.04.006

Dishion, T. J., & Patterson, G. R. (1997). The timing and severity of antisocial behavior: Three hypotheses within an ecological framework. In D. M. Stoff, J. Breiling, & J. D. Maser (Eds.), *Handbook of antisocial personality disorder* (pp. 205–217). Wiley

Distefan, J. M., Pierce, J. P., & Gilpin, E. A. (2004). Do favorite movie stars influence adolescent smoking initiation? *American Journal of Public Health, 94,* 1239–1244.

Dixon, J. F., & Hokin, L. E. (1998). Lithium acutely inhibits and chronically up-regulates and stabilizes glutamate uptake by presynaptic nerve endings on mouse cerebral cortex. *Neurobiology, 95,* 8363–8368.

Dixon, L. E., Ahles, E., & Marques, L. (2016). Treating posttraumatic stress disorder in diverse settings: Recent advances and challenges for the future. *Current Psychiatry Reports, 18,* 108.

Dixon, M. J., Collins, K., Harrigan, K. A., Graydon, C., & Fugelsang, J. A. (2015). Using sound to unmask losses disguised as wins in multiline slot machines. *Journal of Gambling Studies, 31*(1), 183–196. doi:10.1007/s10899-013-9411-8

Do, J., & Schenk, S. (2013). Self-administered MDMA produces dose- and time-dependent serotonin deficits in the rat brain. *Addiction Biology, 18,* 441–447.

Dobbs, D. (2006). Turning off depression. *Scientific American, 17,* 26–31.

Dolan, P., Kudrna, L., & Stone, A. (2017). The measure matters: An investigation of evaluative and experience-based measures of wellbeing in time use data. *Social Indicators Research, 134*(1), 57–73. doi:10.1007/s11205-016-1429-8

Dolbier, C. L., Cocke, R. R., Leiferman, J. A., Steinhardt, M. A., Schapiro, S. J., Nehete, P. N., . . . Sastry, J. (2001). Differences in functional immune responses of high vs. low hardy healthy individuals. *Journal of Behavioral Medicine, 24,* 219–229.

Dollard, J., Doob, L., Miller, N., Mowrer, O. H., & Sears, R. R. (1939). *Frustration and aggression.* Yale University Press.

Dominowski, R. L., & Dallob, P. (1995). Insight and problem solving. In R. J. Sternberg & J. E. Davidson (Eds.), *The nature of insight* (pp. 33–62). MIT Press.

Domjan, M., & Purdy, J. E. (1995). Animal research in psychology: More than meets the eye of the general psychology student. *American Psychologist, 50,* 496–503.

Donaldson, C. D., Siegel, J. T., & Crano, W. D. (2020). Preventing college student nonmedical prescription stimulant use: Development of vested interest theory-based persuasive messages. *Addictive Behaviors, 108,* 106440. https://doi.org/10.1016/j.addbeh.2020.106440

Donoho, C. J., Crimmins, E. M., & Seeman, T. E. (2013). Marital quality, gender, and markers of inflammation in the MIDUS Cohort. *Journal of Marriage and the Family, 75*(1), 127–141. doi:10.1111/j.1741-3737.2012.01023.x

Donovan, D. M., Daley, D.C., Brigham, G. S., Hodgkins, C. C., Perl, H. I., Garrett, S. B., . . . Zammarelli, L. (2013). Stimulant abuser groups to engage in 12–step: A multisite trial in the National Institute on Drug Abuse Clinical Trials Network. *Journal of Substance Abuse Treatment, 44,* 103–114.

Dorahy, M. J., Brand, B. L., Sar, V., Kruger, C., Stavropoulos, P., Martínez-Taboas A., . . . Middleton W. (2014). Dissociative identity disorder: An empirical review. *The Australian and New Zealand Journal of Psychiatry, 48,* 402–417.

Doty, R. L. (2001). Olfaction. *Annual Review of Psychology,* 52, 423–452.

Dovidio, J. F., & Gaertner, S. L. (2000). Aversive racism. In M. P. Zanna (Ed.), *Advances in experimental social psychology* (Vol. 36, pp. 1–51). Academic Press.

Dovidio, J. F., & Gaertner, S. L. (2007). New directions in aversive racism research: Persistence and pervasiveness. In C. W. Esqueda (Ed.), *Nebraska Symposium on Motivation: Motivational aspects of prejudice and racism* (pp. 43-67). Springer.

Dovidio, J. F., Gaertner, S. L., & Pearson, A. R. (2017). Aversive racism and contemporary bias. In C. G. Sibley & F. K. Barlow (Eds.), *The Cambridge handbook of the psychology of prejudice.* (pp. 267–294). Cambridge University Press. https://doi.org/10.1017/9781316161579.012

Dovidio, J. F., Gaertner, S. L., & Saguy, T. (2015). Color-blindness and commonality: Included but invisible? *American Behavioral Scientist, 59*(11), 1518-1538. doi:10.1177/0002764215580591

Dovis, S., Van der Oord, S., Wiers, R. W., & Prins, P. M. (2013). What part of working memory is not working in ADHD? Short-term memory, the central executive and effects of reinforcement. *Journal of Abnormal Child Psychology, 41,* 901–917. doi:10.1007/s10802-013-9729-9

Downar, J., Geraci, J., Salomons, T. V., Dunlop, K., Wheeler, S., McAndrews, M. P., . . . Giacobbe, P. (2014). Anhedonia and reward-circuit connectivity distinguish nonresponders from responders to dorsomedial prefrontal repetitive transcranial magnetic stimulation in major depression. *Biological Psychiatry, 76*(3), 176–185.

Downs, E., & Smith, S. L. (2010). Keeping abreast of hypersexuality: A video game character content analysis. *Sex Roles,* 62, 721–733. doi:10.1007/s11199-009-9637-1

Draganova, R., Eswaran, H., Murphy, P., Lowery, C., & Preissi, H. (2007). Serial magnetoencephalographic study of fetal and newborn auditory discriminative evoked responses. *Early Human Development, 83,* 199–207.

Draguns, J. G. (2002). Universal and cultural aspects of counseling and psychotherapy. In P. B. Pedersen, J. G. Draguns, W. J. Lonner, & J. E. Trimble (Eds.), *Counseling across cultures* (5th ed., pp. 29–50). SAGE.

Drea, C. M. (2009). Endocrine mediators of masculinization in female mammals. *Current Directions in Psychological Science, 18,* 221–226.

Drevets, W.C., Savitz, J., & Trimble, M. (2008). The subgenual anterior cingulated cortex in mood disorders. *CNS Spectrums, 13,* 663–681.

Drew, P. D., & Kane, C. J. (2014). Fetal alcohol spectrum disorders and neuroimmune changes. *International Review of Neurobiology, 118,* 41–80. doi:10.1016/B978-0-12-801284-0.00003-8

Drews, F. A., Yazdani, H., Godfrey, C. N., Cooper, J. M., & Strayer, D. L. (2009). Text messaging during simulated driving. *Human Factors, 51,* 762–770.

Driver, H.S., & Taylor, S.R. (2000). Exercise and sleep. *Sleep Medicine Reviews, 4,* 387–402.

Druckman, D., & Bjork, R. A. (1994). *Learning, remembering, believing: Enhancing human performance.* National Academy Press.

Du, S., & Martinez, A. M. (2015). Compound facial expressions of emotion: From basic research to clinical applications. *Dialogues in Clinical Neuroscience, 17*(4), 443–455.

Duan, X., Dai, Q., Gong, Q., & Chen, H. (2010). Neural mechanism of unconscious perception of surprised facial expression. *Neuroimage, 52,* 401–407. doi:10.1016/j.neuroimage.2010.04.021

Duckitt, J. (1992). Psychology and prejudice: A historical analysis and integrative framework. *American Psychologist, 47,* 1182–1193.

Duckworth, T. S., Kreiner, D. S., Stark-Wroblewski, K., & Marsh, P. A. (2011). Effects of experiencing the eyewitness identification procedure on juror decisions. *Journal of Police and Criminal Psychology, 26,* 11–19. doi:10.1007/s11896-010-9071-X

Duke, A. A., Bègue, L., Bell, R., & Eisenlohr-Moul, T. (2013). Revisiting the serotonin–aggression relation in humans: A meta-analysis. *Psychological Bulletin, 139,* 1148–1172. doi:10.1037/a0031544

Dulas, M. R., & Duarte, A. (2016). Age-related changes in overcoming proactive interference in associative memory: The role of PFC-mediated executive control processes at retrieval. *NeuroImage, 132,* 116–128. doi:10.1016/j.neuroimage.2016.02.017

Dunkel Schetter, C., Schafer, P., Gaines Lanzi, R., Clark-Kauffman, E., Raju, T. N. K., & Hillemeier, M. M. (2013). Shedding light on the mechanisms underlying health disparities through community participatory methods: The stress pathway. *Perspectives on Psychological Science, 8,* 613–633.

Dunlop, R. A. (2016). The effect of vessel noise on humpback whale, Megaptera novaeangliae, communication behaviour. *Animal Behaviour, 111,* 13–21. doi:10.1016/j.anbehav.2015.10.002

Dunn, E. W., Aknin, L. B., & Norton, M. I. (2014). Prosocial spending and happiness: Using money to benefit others pays off. *Current Directions in Psychological Science, 23,* 41–47.

Dunner, D. L., Aaronson, S. T., Sackeim, H. A., Janicak, P. G., Carpenter, L. L., Boyadjis, T., . . . Demitrack, M. A. (2014). A multisite, naturalistic, observational study of transcranial magnetic stimulation for patients with pharmacoresistant major depressive disorder: Durability of benefit over a 1-year follow-up period. *Journal of Clinical Psychiatry, 75,* 1394–1401.

Duric, V., Banasr, M., Licznerski, P., Schmidt, H. D., Stockmeier, C. A., Simen, A. A., . . . Duman, R. S. (2010). A negative regulator of MAP kinase causes depressive behavior. *Nature Medicine, 16,* 1328–1332.

Durmer, J. S., & Dinges, D. F. (2005). Neurocognitive consequences of sleep deprivation. *Seminars in Neurology, 25,* 117–129.

Dursa, E. K., Reinhard, M. J., Barth, S. K., & Schneiderman, A. I. (2014). Prevalence of a positive screen for PTSD among OEF/OIF and OEF/OIF-era veterans in a large population-based cohort. *Journal of Traumatic Stress, 27,* 542–549.

Durston, S., Hulshoff Pol, H. E., Casey, B. J., Giedd, J. N., Buitelaar, J. K., & van Engeland, H. (2001). Anatomical MRI of the developing human brain: What have we learned? *Journal of the American Academy of Child and Adolescent Psychiatry, 40,* 1012–1020.

Duzel, E., van Praag, H., & Sendtner, M. (2016). Can physical exercise in old age improve memory and hippocampal function? *Brain, 139(3),* 662–673. doi:10.1093/brain/awv407

Dweck, C. S. (2006). *Mindset: The new psychology of success.* Ballantine Books.

Dweck, C. S. (2008). Can personality be changed? The role of beliefs in personality and change. *Current Directions in Psychological Science, 17,* 391–394.

Dweck, C. S., Chiu, C., & Hong, Y. (1995). Implicit theories and their role in judgments and reactions: A world from two perspectives. *Psychological Inquiry, 6,* 267–285.

Dweck, C. S., & Yeager, D. S. (2019). Mindsets: A view from two eras. *Perspectives on Psychological Science, 14*(3), 481–496. https://doi.org/10.1177/1745691618804166

Eagly, A. H., & Chaiken, S. (1975). An attribution analysis of communicator characteristics on opinion change: The case of communicator attractiveness. *Journal of Personality and Social Psychology, 32,* 136–144.

Eagly, A. H., & Wood, W. (2013). The nature–nurture debates: 25 years of challenges in understanding the psychology of gender. *Perspectives on Psychological Science, 8,* 340–357.

Eaton, A. H., & Resko, J. A. (1974). Plasma testosterone and male dominance in a Japanese macaque (Macca fuscata) troop compared with repeated measures of testosterone in laboratory males. *Hormones and Behavior, 5,* 251–259.

Eaton, N. R., Keyes, K. M., Krueger, R. F., Balsis, S., Skodol, A. E., Markon, K. E., Grant, B. F., & Hasin, D. S. (2012). An invariant dimensional liability model of gender differences in mental disorder prevalence: Evidence from a national sample. *Journal of Abnormal Psychology, 121*(1), 282–288. doi:10.1037/a0024780

Eaton, N. R., Krueger, R. F., Keyes, K. M., Skodol, A. E., Markon, K. E., Grant, B.F., & Hasin, D. S. (2011). Borderline personality disorder comorbidity: Relationship to the internalizing-externalizing structure of common mental disorders. *Psychological Medicine, 41,* 1041–1050.

Eaton, W. W., Thara, R., Federman, E., & Tien, A. (1998). Remission and relapse in schizophrenia: The Madras longitudinal study. *Journal of Nervous and Mental Disease, 186,* 357–363.

Ebbinghaus, H. (1910). *Abriss der psychologie.* Veit & Comp.

Ebbinghaus, H. (1913). *Memory: A contribution to experimental psychology* (H. Ruyer & C. E. Bussenius, Trans.). Teachers College, Columbia University. (Original work published in 1885)

Ebmeier, K. P., Donaghey, C., & Steele, J. D. (2006). Recent developments and current controversies in depression. *Lancet, 367,* 153–167.

Eby, L. T., Allen, T. D., Hoffman, B. J., Baranik, L. E., Sauer, J. B., Baldwin, S., . . . Evans, S. C. (2013). An interdisciplinary meta-analysis of the potential antecedents, correlates, and consequences of protégé perceptions of mentoring. *Psychological Bulletin, 139,* 441–476.

Eccles, J. S., & Wang, M. T. (2016). What motivates females and males to pursue careers in mathematics and science? *International Journal of Behavioral Development, 40*(2), 100–106. doi:10.1177/0165025415616201

Edenberg, H. J., & Foroud, T. (2006). The genetics of alcoholism: Identifying specific genes through family studies. *Addiction Biology, 11,* 386–396.

Edmonds, G. W., Goldberg, L. R., Hampson, S. E., & Barckley, M. (2013). Personality stability from childhood to midlife: Relating teachers' assessments in elementary school to observer- and self-ratings 40 years later. *Journal of Research in Personality, 47,* 505–513.

Edmondson, D., Chaidoir, S. R., Mills, M. A., Park, C. L., Holub, J., & Bartkowiak, J. M. (2011). From shattered assumptions to weakened worldviews: Trauma symptoms signal anxiety buffer disruption. *Journal of Loss & Trauma, 16,* 358–385.

Edosomwan, S. (2011). *Rural fair housing complaints and enforcement.* http://www.vtaffordablehousing.org/documents/resources/687_fairhousing2011.pdf

Egan, S. J., Watson, H. J., Kane, R. T., McEvoy, P., Fursland, A., & Nathan, P. R. (2013). Anxiety as a mediator between perfectionism and eating disorders. *Cognitive Therapy and Research, 37,* 905–913. doi:10.1007/s10608-012-9516-X

Egner, T., Jamieson, G., & Gruzelier, J. (2005). Hypnosis decouples cognitive control from conflict monitoring processes of the frontal lobe. *Neuroimaging, 27,* 969–978.

Egner, T., Monti, J. M., & Summerfield, C. (2010). Expectation and surprise determine neural population responses in the ventral visual stream. *Journal of Neuroscience, 29,* 16601–16608.

Ehde, D. M., Dillworth, T. M., & Turner, J. A. (2014). Cognitive-behavioral therapy for individuals with chronic pain: Efficacy, innovations, and directions for research. *American Psychologist, 69,* 153–166.

Eich, J. E. (1980). The cue-dependent nature of state-dependent retrieval. *Memory and Cognition, 8,* 157–173.

Eich, J. E., Weingartner, H., Stillman, R. C., & Gillin, J. C. (1975). State-dependent accessibility of retrieval cues in the retention of a categorized list. *Journal of Verbal Learning and Verbal Behavior, 14,* 408–417.

Einarsson, C., & Granstrom, K. (2004). Gender-biased interaction in the classroom: The influence of gender and age in the relationship between teacher and pupil. *Scandinavian Journal of Educational Research, 46,* 117–127.

Ein-Dor, T., & Hirschberger, G. (2016). Rethinking attachment theory: From a theory of relationships to a theory of individual and group survival. *Current Directions in Psychological Science, 25,* 223–227.

Eisen, S. V. (1979). Actor-observer differences in information inference and causal attribution. *Journal of Personality and Social Psychology, 37,* 261–272.

Eisenberger, N. I., Taylor, S. E., Gable, S. L., Hilmert, C. J., & Lieberman, M. D. (2007). Neural pathways link social support to attenuated neuroendocrine stress responses. *NeuroImage, 35,* 1601–1612.

Eisend, M. (2007). Understanding two-sided persuasion: An empirical assessment of theoretical approaches. *Psychology & Marketing, 24*(7), 615–640. doi:10.1002/mar.20176

Eiser, A. S. (2005). Physiology and psychology of dreams. *Seminars in Neurology, 25,* 97–105.

Ek, M., Wicks, S., Svensson, A. C., Idring, S., & Dalman, C. (2015). Advancing paternal age and schizophrenia: The impact of delayed fatherhood. *Schizophrenia Bulletin, 41,* 708–714.

Ekman, P. (1973). Cross-cultural studies of facial expression. In P. Ekman (Ed.), *Darwin and facial expression* (pp. 169–222). Academic Press.

Ekuni, R., Vaz, L. J., & Bueno, O. F. A. (2011). Levels of processing: The evolution of a framework. *Psychology & Neuroscience, 4*(3), 333–339. doi:10.3922/j.psns.2011.3.006

El Khoury, D., El-Rassi, R., Azar, S., & Hwalla, N. (2010). Postprandial ghrelin and PYY responses of male subjects on low carbohydrate meals to varied balancing proportions of proteins and fats. *European Journal of Nutrition, 49,* 493–500. doi:10.1007/s00394-010-0108-9

Eleazu, C. O. (2016). The concept of low glycemic index and glycemic load foods as panacea for type 2 diabetes mellitus: Prospects, challenges and solutions. *African Health Sciences, 16*(2), 468–479. doi:10.4314/ahs.v16i2.15

Elen, M., D'Heer, E., Geuens, M., & Vermeir, I. (2013). The influence of mood on attitude–behavior consistency. *Journal of Business Research, 66,* 917–923. doi:10.1016/j.jbusres.2011.12.011

Elfenbein, H. A., Beaupre, M., Levesque, M., & Hess, U. (2007). Toward a dialect theory: Cultural differences in the expression and recognition of posed facial expressions. *Emotion, 7,* 131–146.

Elkind, D. (1994). *A sympathetic understanding of the child: Birth to sixteen* (3rd ed.). Allyn & Bacon.

Elkind, D. (1998). *All grown up and no place to go* (Rev. ed.). Perseus Books.

Elkind, D., & Bowen, R. (1979). Imaginary audience behavior in children and adolescents. *Developmental Psychology, 15,* 38–44.

Ellason, J. W., Ross, C. A., & Fuchs, D. L. (1996). Lifetime Axis I and II comorbidity and childhood trauma history in dissociative identity disorder. *Psychiatry, 59,* 255–266.

Ellenbogen, J. M., Hu, P. T., Payne, J. D., Titone, D., & Walker, M. P. (2007). Human relational memory requires time and sleep. *Proceedings of the National Academy of Science U.S.A., 104,* 7723–7728.

Ellis, A. (1959). Requisite conditions for basic personality change. *Journal of Consulting Psychology, 23,* 538–540.

Ellis, A. (1973, February). The no cop-out therapy. *Psychology Today, 7,* 56–60, 62.

Ellis, A. (1991). *Reason and emotion in psychotherapy.* Carol Publishing.

Ellis, A. (1995). Changing rational-emotive therapy (RET) to rational emotive behavior therapy (REBT). *Journal of Rational-Emotive and Cognitive Behavior Therapy, 13,* 85–89.

Ellis, B. J., Bianchi, J., Griskevicius, V., & Frankenhuis, W. E. (2017). Beyond risk and protective factors: An adaptation-based approach to resilience. *Perspectives on Psychological Science, 12*(4), 561-587.

Ellithorpe, M. E., & Bleakley, A. (2016). Wanting to see people like me? Racial and gender diversity in popular adolescent television. *Journal of Youth and Adolescence, 45*(7), 1426–1437. doi:10.1007/s10964-016-0415-4

Emery, C. F., Finkel, D., & Pedersen, N. L. (2012). Pulmonary function as a cause of cognitive aging. *Psychological Science, 23,* 1024–1032.

End, C. M., Worthman, S., Mathews, M. B., & Wetterau, K. (2010). Costly cell phones: The impact of cell phone rings on academic performance. *Teaching of Psychology, 37*(1), 55–57. doi:10.1080/00986280903425912

Endrighi, R., Hamer, M., & Steptoe, A. (2011). Associations of trait optimism and diurnal neuroendocrine activity, cortisol responses to mental stress, and subjective stress measures in healthy men and women. *Psychosomatic Medicine, 73,* 672–678.

Epley, N., Savitsky, K., & Kachelski, R. A. (1999). What every skeptic should know about subliminal persuasion. *Skeptical Inquirer, 23,* 40–45.

Epping-Jordan, M. P., Watkins, S. S., Koob, G. F., & Markou, A. (1998). Dramatic decreases in brain reward function during nicotine withdrawal. *Nature, 393,* 76.

Epstein, R., & Phan, V. (2012). Which competencies are most important for creative expression? *Creativity Research Journal, 24,* 278–282. doi:10.1080/10400419.2012.726579

Epstein, S. (1994). Trait theory as personality theory: Can a part be as great as the whole? *Psychological Inquiry, 5,* 120–122.

Equal Employment Opportunity Commission. (2002, May 24). *Federal laws prohibiting job discrimination questions and answers.*

Equal Employment Opportunity Commission. (2010). *Sexual harassment charges EEOC and FEPAs combined: FY 1997–FY 2009.* Author.

Erblich, J., Lerman, C., Self, D. W., Diaz, G. A., & Bovbjerg, D. H. (2005). Effects of dopamine D2 receptor (DRD2) and transporter (SLC6A3) polymorphisms on smoking cue-induced cigarette craving among African-American smokers. *Molecular Psychiatry, 10,* 407–414.

Erfanian Saeedi, N., Blamey, P. J., Burkitt, A. N., & Grayden, D. B. (2016). Learning pitch with STDP: A computational model of place and temporal pitch perception using spiking neural networks. *PLoS Computational Biology, 12*(4), e1004860. doi:10.1371/journal.pcbi.1004860

Erikson, E. H. (1956). The problem of ego identity. *Journal of American Psychoanalysis Association, 4,* 56–121.

Erikson, E. H. (1958). *Young man Luther.* Norton.

Erikson, E. H. (1959). Identity and life cycle: Selected papers. *Psychological Issues, 1,* 1–171.

Erikson, E. H. (1963). *Childhood and society* (2nd ed.). Norton.

Erikson, E. H. (1968). *Identity, youth and crisis.* Norton.

Erikson, E. H. (1980). *Identity and the life cycle* (2nd ed.). Norton.

Eroglu, C., & Barres, B. A. (2010). Regulation of synaptic connectivity by glia. *Nature, 468,* 223–231.

Erwin, E. (Ed.). (2002). *The Freud encyclopedia: Theory, therapy, and culture.* Routledge.

Escobar, J. I. (1993). Psychiatric epidemiology. In A. C. Gaw (Ed.), *Culture, ethnicity, and mental illness* (pp. 43–73). American Psychiatric Press.

Espy, K. A., Riese, M. L., & Francis, D. J. (1997). Neurobehavior in preterm neonates exposed to cocaine, alcohol, and tobacco. *Infant Behavior and Development, 20,* 297–309.

Essed, N. H., van Staveren, W. A., Kok, F. J., & de Graaf, C. (2007). No effect of 16 weeks flavor enhancement on dietary intake and nutritional status of nursing home elderly. *Appetite, 48,* 29–36.

Esses, V. M., Dovidio, J. F., Jackson, L. M., & Armstrong, T. L. (2001). The immigration dilemma: The role of perceived group competition, ethnic prejudice, and national identity. *Journal of Social Issues, 57,* 389–412.

Etkin, A., Prater, K. E., Hoeft, F., Menon, V., & Schatzberg, A. F. (2010). Failure of anterior cingulated activation and connectivity with the amygdala during implicit regulation of emotional processing in generalized anxiety disorder. *American Journal of Psychiatry, 167,* 545–554.

Ettlinger, M., Lanter, J., & Van Pay, C. K. (2014). Learning to remember by learning to speak. *Developmental Psychology, 50,* 431–438. doi:10.1037/a0033317

Evans, A. T., & Clark, J. K. (2012). Source characteristics and persuasion: The role of self-monitoring in self-validation. *Journal of Experimental Social Psychology, 48,* 383–386. doi:10.1016/j.jesp.2011.07.002

Evans, G. W., & Cassells, R. C. (2014). Childhood poverty, cumulative risk exposure, and mental health in emerging adults. *Clinical Psychological Science, 2,* 287–296.

Everaert, J., & Joormann, J. (2019). Emotion regulation difficulties related to depression and anxiety: A network approach to model relations among symptoms, positive reappraisal, and repetitive negative thinking. *Clinical Psychological Science, 7*(6), 1304-1318.

Everaert, J., Bronstein, M. V., Cannon, T. D., & Joormann, J. (2018). Looking through tinted glasses: Depression and social anxiety are related to both interpretation biases and inflexible negative interpretations. *Clinical Psychological Science, 6*(4), 517-528.

Exelmans, L., Custers, K., & Van den Bulck, J. (2015). Violent video games and delinquent behavior in adolescents: A risk factor perspective. *Aggressive behavior, 41*(3), 267-279.

Eynon, R., Schroeder, M., & Fry J. (2009). New techniques in online research: Challenges for research ethics. *21st Century Society, 4,* 187–199.

Eysenck, H. J. (1967). *The biological basis of personality.* Charles C. Thomas.

Eysenck, H. J. (1982). *Personality, genetics, and behavior: Selected papers.* Praeger.

Eysenck, H. J. (1991). Dimensions of personality: 16, 5 or 3? Criteria for a taxonomic paradigm. *Personality and Individual Differences, 12,* 773–790.

Eysenck, H. J. (1995). *Genius: The natural history of creativity.* Cambridge University Press.

Eysenck, H. J., & Eysenck, S. B. G. (1969). *Personality structure and measurement.* Routledge.

Eysenck, H. J., & Eysenck, S. B. G. (1976). *Psychoticism as a dimension of personality.* Hodder and Stoughton.

Eysenck, H. J., & Rachman, S. (1965). *The causes and cures of neurosis: An introduction to modern behavior therapy based on learning theory and the principle of conditioning.* Knapp.

Fagan, J., Lyons, S., & Smyth, B. P. (2014). Content analysis of newspaper reports on alcohol-related deaths. *Alcohol and Alcoholism, 49*(4), 479–483. https://doi.org/10.1093/alcalc/agu015

Fagundes, C. P., Bennett, J. M., Derry, H. M., & Kiecolt-Glaser, J. K. (2011). Relationships and inflammation across the lifespan: Social developmental pathways to disease. *Social and Personality Psychology Compass, 5,* 891–903.

Fagundes, C. P., Glaser, R., & Kiecolt-Glaser, J. K. (2013). Stressful early life experiences and immune dysregulation across the lifespan. *Brain, Behavior, and Immunity, 27,* 8–12.

Fagundes, C. P., Murdock, K. W., Chirinos, D. A., & Green, P. A. (2017). Biobehavioral pathways to cancer incidence, progression, and quality of life. *Current Directions in Psychological Science, 26*(6), 548-553.

Fagundes, C. P., & Way, B. (2014). Early-life stress and adult inflammation. *Current Directions in Psychological Science, 23,* 277–283.

Fairbairn, C. E., Sayette, M. A., Aalen, O. O., & Frigessi, A. (2015). Alcohol and emotional contagion: An examination of the spreading of smiles in male and female drinking groups. *Clinical Psychological Science, 3,* 686–701.

Fairhurst, M. T., Loken, L., & Grossman, T. (2014). Physiological and behavioral responses reveal 9-month-old infants' sensitivity to pleasant touch. *Psychological Science, 25,* 1124–1131.

Falkenburg, K., & Schyns, B. (2007). Work satisfaction, organizational commitment and withdrawal behaviors. *Management Research News, 30,* 708–723.

Falkum, E., Pedersen, G., & Karterud, S. (2009). *Diagnostic and Statistical Manual of Mental Disorders, Fourth Edition,* paranoid personality disorder diagnosis: A unitary or a two-dimensional construct? *Comprehensive Psychiatry, 50,* 533–541.

Fan, Y., Tang, Y. Y., Ma, Y., & Posner, M. I. (2010). Mucosal immunity modulated by integrative meditation in a dose-dependent fashion. *Journal of Alternative and Complementary Medicine, 16,* 151–155.

Fatemi, S. H., & Folsom, T. D. (2009). The neurodevelopmental hypothesis of schizophrenia, revisited. *Schizophrenia Bulletin, 35*(3), 528–548. doi:10.1093/schbul/sbn187

Fattore, L. (2016). Synthetic cannabinoids: Further evidence supporting the relationship between cannabinoids and psychosis. *Biological Psychiatry, 79,* 539–548.

Fattore, L., & Fratta, W. (2011). Beyond THC: The new generation of cannabinoid designer drugs. *Frontiers in Behavioral Neuroscience, 5,* 1–12.

Fava, M., & Rosenbaum, J. F. (1995). Pharmacotherapy and somatic therapies. In E. E. Beckham & W. R. Leber (Eds.), *Handbook of depression* (2nd ed., pp. 280–301). Guilford Press.

Fawcett, J. (1994). Antidepressants: Partial response in chronic depression. *British Journal of Psychiatry, 165* (Suppl. 26), 37–41.

Fazel, S., Gulati, G., Linsell, L., Geddes, J. R., & Grann, M. (2009). Schizophrenia and violence: Systematic review and meta-analysis. *PLoS Medicine, 6,* e1000120.

Fazel, S., Långström, N., Hjern, A., Grann, M., & Lichtenstein, P. (2009). Schizophrenia, substance abuse, and violent crime. *JAMA, 301,* 2016–2023.

Fazio, N. M., & Palm, L. J. (1998). Attributional style, depression, and grade point averages of college students. *Psychological Reports, 83,* 159–162.

Fazio, R. H. (1989). On the power and functionality of attitudes: The role of attitude accessibility. In A. R. Pratkanis, S. J. Breckler, & A. G. Greenwald (Eds.), *Attitude structure and function* (pp. 153-180). Lawrence Erlbaum Associates.

FDA Public Health Advisory. (2004, October 15). *Suicidality in children and adolescents being treated with antidepressant medications.* www.fda.gov/cder/drug/antidepressants/SSRIPHA200410.htm

Federal Aviation Agency (FAA). (2016). 16S.4 Commercial air carrier fatality rate. *FY2016 Agency Scorecard.* https://www.faa.gov/about/plans_reports/Performance/quarter_scorecard/media/2016/q3/Commercial_Air_Carrier_Fatality_Rate.pdf

FBI. (2015a). 2015 hate crime statistics. *Uniform Crime Report, Table 1.* https://ucr.fbi.gov/hate-crime/2015/tables-and-data-declarations/1tabledatadecpdf

FBI. (2015b). 2015 crime in the United States. *Uniform Crime Report, Table 1.* https://ucr.fbi.gov/crime-in-the-u.s/2015/crime-in-the-u.s.-2015/offenses-known-to-law-enforcement/violent-crime

FBI. (2015c). 2015 crime in the United States. *Uniform Crime Report, Table 42.* https://ucr.fbi.gov/crime-in-the-u.s/2015/crime-in-the-u.s.-2015/tables/table-42

FBI. (2016). 2016 crime in the United States. *Uniform Crime Report.* https://ucr.fbi.gov/crime-in-the-u.s/2016/preliminary-semiannual-uniform-crime-report-januaryjune-2016/tables/table-1

FBI. (2017). Uniform crime reporting 2017 hate crime statistics. https://ucr.fbi.gov/hate-crime/2017

FBI. (2018a). Hate crime statistics, 2018. Uniform Crime Report. https://ucr.fbi.gov/hate-crime/2018/topic-pages/incidents-and-offenses.pdf

FBI. (2020a). Crime rates in the United States, 2008-2018. Crime Data Explorer. https://crime-data-explorer.fr.cloud.gov/explorer/national/united-states/crime

FBI. (2020b). Arrest offense counts in the United States-2018. Crime Data Explorer. https://crime-data-explorer.fr.cloud.gov/explorer/national/united-states/arrest

Feeley, T., Anker, A. E., & Aloe, A. M. (2012). The door-in-the-face persuasive message strategy: A meta-analysis of the first 35 years. *Communication Monographs, 79,* 316–343. doi:10.1080/03637751.2012.697631

Feeney, E., O'Brien, S., Scannell, A., Markey, A., & Gibney, E. R. (2011). Genetic variation in taste perception: Does it have a role in healthy eating? *Proceedings of the Nutrition Society, 70,* 135–143.

Feinberg, M. E., Button, T. M., Neiderhiser, J. M., Reiss, D., & Hetherington, E. M. (2007). Parenting and adolescent antisocial behavior and depression: Evidence of genotype 3 parenting environment interaction. *Archives of General Psychiatry, 64,* 457–465.

Feingold, A. (1988). Matching for attractiveness in romantic partners and same-sex friends: A meta-analysis and theoretical critique. *Psychological Bulletin, 104,* 226–235.

Feinstein, J. S., Adolphs, R., Damasio, A., & Tranel, D. (2011). The human amygdala and the induction and experience of fear. *Current Biology, 21,* 1–5.

Feldman, N. H., Griffiths, T. L., Goldwater, S., & Morgan, J. L. (2013). A role for the developing lexicon in phonetic category acquisition. *Psychological Review, 120,* 751–778. doi:10.1037/a0034245

Felker, B., Hawkins, E., Dobie, D., Gutierrez, J., & McFall, M. (2008). Characteristics of deployed Operation Iraqi Freedom military personnel who seek mental health care. *Military Medicine, 173,* 155–158.

Felmingham, K., Kemp, A., Williams, L., Das, P., Hughes, G., Peduto, A., & Bryant, R. (2007). Changes in anterior cingulated and amygdala after cognitive behavior therapy of posttraumatic stress disorder. *Psychological Science, 18,* 127–129.

Felmlee, D., Orzechowicz, D., & Fortes, C. (2010). Fairy tales: Attraction and stereotypes in same-gender relationships. *Sex Roles: A Journal of Research, 62*(3–4), 226–240. https://doi.org/10.1007/s11199-009-9701-x

Ferguson, C. J. (2015). Pay no attention to that data behind the curtain: On angry birds, happy children, scholarly squabbles, publication bias, and why betas rule metas. *Perspectives on Psychological Science, 10*(5), 683–691. doi:10.1177/1745691615593353

Fernandez, R. M., & Rubineau, B. (2019). Network recruitment and the glass ceiling: Evidence from two firms. *The Russell Sage Foundation Journal of the Social Sciences,* 5(3), 88–102. doi:10.7758/RSF.2019.5.3.05.

Ferreira, S. E., de Mello, M. T., Pompeia, S., & de Souza-Formigoni, M. L. (2006). Effects of energy drink ingestion on alcohol intoxication. *Alcoholism, Clinical and Experimental Research, 30,* 598–605.

Ferrucci, R., Brunoni, A. R., Parazzini, M., Vergari, M., Rossi, E., Fumagalli, M., . . . Priori, A. (2013). Modulating human procedural learning by cerebellar transcranial direct current stimulation. *The Cerebellum, 12,* 485–492. doi:10.1007/s12311-012-0436-9

Festinger, L. (1951). Architecture and group membership. *Journal of Social Issues, 1,* 152–163.

Festinger, L. (1957). *A theory of cognitive dissonance.* Row, Peterson.

Festinger, L., Schachter, S., & Back, K. (1950). *Social pressures in informal groups: A study of human factors in housing.* Stanford University Press.

Fichna, J., Janecka, A., Piestrzeniewicz, M., Costentin, J., & do Rego, J. C. (2007). Antidepressant-like effect of endomorphin-1 and endomorphin-2 in mice. *Neuropsychopharmacology, 32,* 813–821.

Fiedler, K., & Krueger, J. I. (2013). Afterthoughts on precognition: No cogent evidence for anomalous influences of consequent events on preceding cognition. *Theory & Psychology, 23,* 323–333.

Field, A. P. (2006). Is conditioning a useful framework for understanding the development and treatment of phobias? *Clinical Psychology Review, 26,* 857–875.

Field, T. M., Schanberg, S. M., Scafidi, F., Bauer, C. R., Vega-Lahr, N., Garcia, R., . . . Kuhn, C. M. (1986). Tactile/kinesthetic stimulation effects of preterm neonates. *Pediatrics, 77,* 654–658.

Fields, D. R. (2007). Sex and the secret nerve. *Scientific American Mind, 18,* 20–27.

Fiellin, D. A., Friedland, G. H., & Gourevitch, M. N. (2006). Opioid dependence: Rationale for and efficacy of existing and new treatments. *Clinical Infectious Diseases, 43*(Suppl.), S173–S177.

Figner, B., & Weber, E. U. (2011). Who takes risks when and why? Determinants of risk takings. *Current Directions in Psychological Science, 20,* 211–216.

Filbey, F. M., Aslan, S., Calhoun, V. D., Spence, J. S., Damaraju, E., Caprihan, A., & Segall, J. (2014). Long-term effects of marijuana use on the brain. *Proceedings of the National Academy of Sciences of the United States of America, 111,* 16913–16918. doi:10.1073/pnas.1415297111

Fillmore, K. M., Roach, E. L., & Rice, J. T. (2002). Does caffeine counteract alcohol-induced impairment? The ironic effects of expectancy. *Journal of Studies on Alcohol, 63,* 745–754.

Finch, C. E. (2001). Toward a biology of middle age. In M. E. Lachman (Ed.), *Handbook of midlife development* (pp. 77–108). Wiley.

Finkbeiner, N. W. B., Max, J. E., Longman, S., & Debert, C. (2016). Knowing what we don't know: Long-term psychiatric outcomes following adult concussion in sports. *The Canadian Journal of Psychiatry / La Revue Canadienne de Psychiatrie, 61*(5), 270–276. doi:10.1177/0706743716644953

Finkel, K. J., Searleman, A. C., Tymkew, H., Tanaka, C. Y., Saager, L., Safer-Zadeh, E., . . . Avidan, M. S. (2009). Prevalence of undiagnosed obstructive sleep apnea among adult surgical patients in an academic medical center. *Sleep Medicine, 10,* 753–758.

Finkelstein, D. M., Kubzansky, L. D., Capitman, J., & Goodman, E. (2007). Socioeconomic differences in adolescent stress: The role of psychological resources. *Journal of Adolescent Health, 40,* 127–134.

Finn, A. S., Kalra, P. B., Goetz, C., Leonard, J. A., Sheridan, M. A., & Gabrieli, J. D. E. (2016). Developmental dissociation between the maturation of procedural memory and declarative memory. *Journal of Experimental Child Psychology, 142,* 212–220. doi:10.1016/j.jecp.2015.09.027

Finn, R. (2003). Antabuse no panacea for alcoholism. *Clinical Psychiatry News, 31,* 6.

Finn, R. (2004). Functional MRI offers insights into working memory in Alzheimer's (greater whole-brain activation). *Internal Medicine News, 37,* 29.

Finnema, S. J., Nabulsi, N. B., Eid, T., Detyniecki, K., Lin, S. F., Chen, M. K., . . . Carson, R. E. (2016). Imaging synaptic density in the living human brain. *Science Translational Medicine, 8(348)*, 348–396. doi:10.1126/scitranslmed.aaf6667

Fiorentino, L., Marler, M., Stepnowsky, C., Johnson, S., & Ancoli-Israel, S. (2006). Sleep in older African Americans and Caucasians at risk for sleep-disordered breathing. *Behavioral Sleep Medicine, 4,* 164–178.

Fisher, B. S. (2009). The effects of question wording on rape estimates: Evidence from a quasi-experimental design. *Violence Against Women, 15,* 133–147.

Fisher, H. (2000). Lust, attraction, attachment, biology and evolution of the three primary emotional systems of mating, reproduction, and parenting. *Journal of Sex Education and Therapy, 25,* 96–102.

Fisher, H. E. (2004). *Why we love: The nature and chemistry of romantic love.* Holt.

Fisher, S., Kent, T. A., & Bryant, S. G. (1995). Postmarketing surveillance by patient self-monitoring: Preliminary data for sertraline versus fluoxetine. *Journal of Clinical Psychiatry, 56,* 288–296.

Fiske, M. (1980). Tasks and crises of the second half of life: The interrelationship of commitment, coping, and adaptation. In J. E. Birrent & R. B. Sloane (Eds.), *Handbook of mental health and aging* (pp. 337–373). Prentice-Hall.

Fiske, S. T., & Taylor, S. E. (2013). *Social cognition* (2nd ed.). SAGE.

Fitzgerald, P. B., Brown, T. L., Marston, N. A., Daskalakis, Z. J., De Castella, A., & Kulkarni, J. (2003). Transcranial magnetic stimulation in the treatment of depression: A double-blind placebo-controlled trial. *Archives of General Psychiatry, 60,* 1002–1008.

Fitzpatrick, D., & Mooney, R. D. (2012). Vision: The eye. In D. Purves, G. J. Augustine, D. Fitzpatrick, W. C. Hall, A. S. Lamantia, & L. E. White (Eds.), *Neuroscience* (5th ed., pp. 229–256). Sinauer Associates.

Fitzpatrick, K. M., Harris, C., & Drawve, G. (2020). Fear of COVID-19 and the mental health consequences in America. *Psychological Trauma: Theory, Research, Practice, and Policy, 12*(S1), S17–S21. https://doi.org/10.1037/tra0000924

Flanagin, A. J., & Waldeck, J. H. (2004). Technology use and organizational newcomer socialization. *Journal of Business Communication, 41,* 137–165.

Fleeson, W. (2004). Moving personality beyond the person-situation debate. *Current Directions in Psychological Science, 13,* 83–87.

Fleming, T., Bavin, L., Lucassen, M., Stasiak, K., Hopkins, S., & Merry, S. (2018). Beyond the trial: Systematic review of real-world uptake and engagement with digital self-help interventions for depression, low mood, or anxiety. *Journal of Medical Internet Research, 20*(6), e199. doi:10.2196/jmir.9275

Fletcher, C., & Perry, E. L. (2001). Performance appraisal and feedback: A consideration of national culture and a review of contemporary research and future trends. In N. Anderson, D. S. Ones, H. K. Sinangil, & C. Viswesvaran (Eds.), *Handbook of industrial, work and organizational psychology* (Vol. 1, pp. 127–144). SAGE.

Flieller, A. (1999). Comparison of the development of formal thought in adolescent cohorts aged 10 to 15 years (1967–1996 and 1972–1993). *Developmental Psychology, 35,* 1048–1058.

Flynn, J. R. (1999). Searching for justice: The discovery of IQ gains over time. *American Psychologist, 54*(1), 5–20. https://doi.org/10.1037/0003-066X.54.1.5

Flynn, J. R. (2018). Reflections about intelligence over 40 years. *Intelligence, 70,* 73–83. https://doi.org/10.1016/j.intell.2018.06.007

Flynn, J. R. (2019). Reservations about Rushton. *Psych, 1,* 35-43. doi:10.3390/psych1010003.

Foa, E. B., & McLean, C. P. (2016). The efficacy of exposure therapy for anxiety-related disorders and its underlying mechanisms: The case of OCD and PTSD. *Annual Review of Clinical Psychology, 12,* 1–28. doi:10.1146/annurev-clinpsy-021815-093533

Foa, E. B., McLean, C. P., Capaldi, S., & Rosenfield, D. (2013). Prolonged exposure vs supportive counseling for sexual abuse-related PTSD in adolescent girls: A randomized clinical trial. *Journal of the American Medical Association, 310,* 2650–2657.

Fogel, S. M., & Smith, C. T. (2011). The function of the sleep spindle: A physiological index of intelligence and a mechanism for sleep-dependent memory consolidation. *Neuroscience and Biobehavioral Reviews, 35,* 1154–1165.

Foland-Ross, L. C., Hamilton, J. P., Joormann, J., Berman, M. G., Jonides, J., & Gotlib, I. H. (2013). The neural basis of difficulties disengaging from negative irrelevant material in major depression. *Psychological Science, 24,* 334–344.

Folkman, S., & Lazarus, R. (1988). *Manual for the ways of coping questionnaire.* Consulting Psychologists Press.

Folkman, S., & Moskowitz, J. T. (2000). Stress, positive emotion, and coping. *Current Directions in Psychological Science, 9,* 115–118.

Fonagy, P. (2015). The effectiveness of psychodynamic psychotherapies: An update. *World Psychiatry, 14,* 137–150.

Foote, B., Smolin, Y., Neft, D. I., & Lipschitz, D. (2008). Dissociative disorders and suicidality in psychiatric outpatients. *Journal of Nervous and Mental Disease, 196,* 29–36.

Ford, B. Q., Dmitrieva, J. O., Heller, D., Chentsova-Dutton, Y., Grossmann, I., Tamir, M., . . . Mauss, I. B. (2015). Culture shapes whether the pursuit of happiness predicts higher or lower well-being. *Journal of Experimental Psychology: General, 144,* 1053–1062.

Ford, C. S., & Beach, F. A. (1951). *Patterns of sexual behavior.* Harper & Row.

Forsyth, D. R. (2020). Group-level resistance to health mandates during the COVID-19 pandemic: A groupthink approach. *Group Dynamics: Theory, Research, and Practice, 24*(3), 139-152. http://dx.doi.org/10.1037/gdn0000132

Fossum, I. N., Nordnes, L.T., Storemark, S. S., Bjorvatn, B., & Pallesen, S. (2014). The association between use of electronic media in bed before going to sleep and insomnia symptoms, daytime sleepiness, morningness, and chronotype. *Behavioral Sleep Medicine, 12*(5), 343-357.

Fournier, J. C., Derubeis, R. J., Hollon, S. D., Dimidijian, S. Amsterdam, J. D., Shelton, R. C., & Fawcett, J. (2010). Anti-depressant drug effects and depression severity: A patient-level meta-analysis. *JAMA, 303,* 47–53.

Fowler, J., & Peterson, P. (1981). Increasing reading persistence and altering attributional style of learned helpless children. *Journal of Educational Psychology, 73,* 251–260.

Fowles, D. C., & Dindo, L. (2009). Temperament and psychopathy: A dual-pathway model. *Current Directions in Psychological Science, 18,* 179–183.

Fox, E., Cahill, S., & Zougkou, K. (2010). Preconscious processing biases predict emotional reactivity to stress. *Biological Psychiatry, 67,* 371–377.

Frank, D. A., Jacobs, R. R., Beeghly, M., Augustyn, M., Bellinger, D., Cabral, H., & Heeren, T. (2002). Level of prenatal cocaine exposure and scores on the Bayley Scales of Infant Development: Modifying effects of caregiver, early intervention, and birth weight. *Pediatrics, 110,* 1143–1152.

Frank, M. C., Amso, D., & Johnson, S.P. (2014). Visual search and attention to faces during early infancy. *Journal of Experimental Child Psychology, 118,* 13–26.

Frankenberger, K. D. (2000). Adolescent egocentrism: A comparison among adolescents and adults. *Journal of Adolescence, 23,* 343–354.

Franklin, D. J., & Grossberg, S. (2017). A neural model of normal and abnormal learning and memory consolidation: Adaptively timed conditioning, hippocampus, amnesia, neurotrophins, and consciousness. *Cognitive, Affective & Behavioral Neuroscience, 17,* 24-76. doi:10.3758/s13415-016-0463-y

Franko, D. L., Keshaviah, A., Eddy, K. T., Krishna, M., Davis, M. C., Keel, P. K., & Herzog, D. B. (2013). Do mortality rates in eating disorders change over time? A longitudinal look at anorexia nervosa and bulimia nervosa. *The American Journal of Psychiatry, 170*(8), 917-925. doi:10.1176/appi.ajp 2013.12070868

Freedman, J. L., & Fraser, S. C. (1966). Compliance without pressure: The foot-in-the-door technique. *Journal of Experimental Social Psychology, 4,* 195–203.

Freud, A. (1936). *The ego and the mechanisms of defense.* Hogarth Press.

Freud, S. (1915). *Repression. In Freud's collected papers* (Vol. 4). Hogarth.

Freud, S. (1917). *Mourning and melancholia: Collected works.* Hogarth Press.

Freud, S. (1943). *A general introduction to psychoanalysis.* Garden City.

Freud, S. (1949). *An outline of psychoanalysis.* Norton.

Freud, S. (1954). An outline of psychoanalysis. In J. Strachey (Ed. and Trans.), *The standard edition of the complete psychological works of Sigmund Freud* (Vol. 23). Hogarth Press. (Original work published in 1940)

Freud, S. (1930). *The interpretation of dreams* (J. Strachey, Ed. and Trans.). Avon. (Original work published in 1900)

Freudenmann, R. W., Oxler, F., & Bernschneider-Reif, S. (2006). The origin of MDMA (ecstasy) revisited: The true story reconstructed from the original documents. *Addiction, 101,* 1241–1245.

Frewen, P. A., Dozois, D. J., & Lanius, R. A. (2008). Neuroimaging studies of psychological interventions for mood and anxiety disorders Empirical and methodological review. *Clinical Psychology Review, 28,* 228–246.

Friederici, A. D., Brauer, J., & Lohmann, G. (2011). Maturation of the language network: From inter- to intrahemispheric connectivities. *PLoS One, 6(6),* e20726. doi:10.1371/journal.pone.0020726

Friedman, M. (1990). Body fat and the metabolic control of food intake. *International Journal of Obesity, 14,* 53–67.

Friedman, M. J. (2009). Phenomenology of posttraumatic stress disorder and acute stress disorder. In M. M. Antony & M. B. Stein (Eds.), *Oxford handbook of anxiety and related disorders* (pp. 65–72). Oxford University Press.

Friedman, M., & Rosenman, R. (1974). *Type A behavior and your heart*. Knopf.

Frielingsdorf, H., Simpson, D. R., Thal, L. J., & Pizzo, D. P. (2007). Nerve growth factor promotes survival of new neurons in the adult hippocampus. *Neurobiology of Disease, 26,* 46–55.

Friesen, C. A., & Kammrath, L. K. (2011). What it pays to know about a close other: The value of if-then personality knowledge in close relationships. *Psychological Science, 22,* 567–571.

Frost, R. O., Steketee, G., & Tolin, D. F. (2012). Diagnosis and assessment of hoarding disorder. *Annual Review of Clinical Psychology, 8,* 219–242.

Fry, C., & Miller, P. (2002). *Victorian drug trends 2001: Findings from the illicit drug reporting system (IDRS).* National Drug and Alcohol Research Centre (NDARC) Technical Report No. 129. NDARC, University of New South Wales.

Fryar, C. D., Carroll, M. D., & Ogden, C. L. (2012). *Prevalence of obesity among children and adolescents: United States, trends 1963–1965 through 2009–2010.* Centers for Disease Control, National Center for Health Statistics. http://www.cdc.gov/nchs/data/hestat/obesity_child_09_10/obesity_child_09_10.htm

Fryar, C. D., Carroll, M. D., & Ogden, C. L. (2014). *Prevalence of overweight, obesity, and extreme obesity among adults: United States, 1960–1962 through 2011–2012.* Centers for Disease Control, National Center for Health Statistics. http://www.cdc.gov/nchs/data/hestat/obesity_adult_11_12/obesity_adult_11_12.pdf

Fu, C. H., Williams, S. C., Cleare, A. J., Brammer, M. J., Walsh, N. D., Kim, J., . . . Bullmore, E. T. (2004). Attentuation of the neural response to sad faces in major depression by antidepressant treatment: A prospective, event-related functional magnetic resonance imaging study. *Archives of General Psychiatry, 61,* 877–889.

Fujiwara, Y., & Okamura, H. (2018). Hearing laughter improves the recovery process of the autonomic nervous system after a stress-loading task: A randomized controlled trial. *Biopsychosocial Medicine, 12,* 22. doi:10.1186/s13030-018-0141-0

Fujiyama, R., & Toda, K. (2016). Functional effects of cold stimulation on taste perception in humans. *Odontology / The Society of the Nippon Dental University.* doi:10.1007/s10266-016-0263-4

Fuller-Rowell, T. E., Evans, G. W., & Ong, A. D. (2012). Poverty and health: The mediating role of perceived discrimination. *Psychological Science, 23,* 734–739.

Fulmer, C. A., Gelfand, M. J., Kruglanski, A. W., Kim-Prieto, C., Diener, E., Pierro, A., & Higgins, E. T. (2010). On "feeling right" in cultural contexts: How person-culture match affects self-esteem and subjective well-being. *Psychological Science, 21,* 1563–1569.

Fumal, A., & Schoenen, J. (2008). Tension-type headache: Current research and clinical management. *Lancet Neurology, 7,* 70–83.

Furnham, A., & Paltzer, S. (2010). The portrayal of men and women in television advertisements: An updated review of 30 studies published since 2000. *Scandinavian Journal of Psychology, 51,* 216–236. doi:10.1111/j.1467-9450.2009.00772.x

Furnham, A., Reeves, E., & Budhani, S. (2002). Parents think their sons are brighter than their daughters: Sex differences in parents' self-estimations and estimations of their children's multiple intelligences. *Journal of Genetic Psychology, 163,* 24–39.

Furnham, A., Wytykowska, A., & Petrides, K. V. (2005). Estimates of multiple intelligences: A study in Poland. *European Psychologist, 10,* 51–59.

Furumoto, L. (1989). The new history of psychology. In I. S. Cohen (Ed.), *The G. Stanley Hall lecture series* (Vol. 9, pp. 5–34). American Psychological Association.

Furuya-Kanamori, L., & Doi, S. A. R. (2016). Angry birds, angry children, and angry meta-analysts: A reanalysis. *Perspectives on Psychological Science, 11*(3), 408–414. doi:10.1177/1745691616635599

Gael, S. A. (1988). *The job analysis handbook for business, industry, and government* (Vols. 1 and 2). Wiley.

Gaertner, S. L., & Dovidio, J. F. (1986). The aversive form of racism. In J. F. Dovidio & S. L. Gaertner (Eds.), *Prejudice, discrimination, and racism* (pp. 61–89). Academic Press.

Gaertner, S. L., & Dovidio, J. F. (2005). Understanding and addressing contemporary racism: From aversive racism to the common ingroup identity model. *Journal of Social Issues, 61,* 615–639.

Gais, S., Lucas, B., & Born, J. (2006). Sleep after learning aids memory recall. *Learning and Memory, 13,* 259–262.

Galak, J., Leboeuf, R. A., Nelson, L. D., & Simmons, J. P. (2012). Correcting the past: Failures to replicate ψ. *Journal of Personality and Social Psychology, 6,* 933–948. doi:10.1037/a0029709

Galensky, T. L., Miltenberger, R. G., Stricker, J. M., & Garlinghouse, M. A. (2001). Functional assessment and treatment of mealtime behavior problems. *Journal of Positive Behavior Interventions, 3,* 211.

Gallerani, M., Manfredini, R., Dal Monte, D., Calo, G., Brunaldi, V., & Simona, C. (2001). Circadian differences in the individual sensitivity to opiate overdose. *Critical Care Medicine, 29,* 96–101.

Galliano, G. (2003). *Gender: Crossing boundaries.* Wadsworth.

Gallo, L. C., Troxel, W. M., Kuller, L. H., Sutton-Tyrell, K., Edmundowicz, D., & Matthews, K. A. (2003). Marital status, marital quality, and atherosclerotic burden in postmenopausal women. *Psychosomatic Medicine, 65,* 952–962.

Gallo, L. C., Troxel, W. M., Matthews, K. A., & Kuller, L. H. (2003). Marital status and quality in middle-aged women: Associations with levels and trajectories of cardiovascular risk factors. *Health Psychology, 22,* 453–463.

Gao, A. F., Keith, J. L., Gao, F., Black, S. E., Moscovitch, M., & Rosenbaum, R. S. (2020). Neuropathology of a remarkable case of memory impairment informs human memory. *Neuropsychologia, 140,* 107342. https://doi.org/10.1016/j.neuropsychologia.2020.107342

Galvan, A. Hare, T., Voss, H., Glover, G., & Casey, B. J. (2007). Risk-taking and the adolescent brain: Who is at risk? *Developmental Science, 10,* F8–F14.

Ganea, P. A., Fitch, A., Harris, P. L., & Kaldy, Z. (2016). Sixteen-month-olds can use language to update their expectations about the visual world. *Journal of Experimental Child Psychology, 151,* 65–76. doi:10.1016/j.jecp.2015.12.005

Ganea, P. A., Shutts, K., Spelke, E. S., & DeLoache, J. S. (2007). Thinking of things unseen: Infants' use of language to update mental representations. *Psychological Science, 18,* 734–739.

Gangestad, S. W., Thornhill, R., & Garver-Apgar, C. E. (2005). Adaptations to ovulation: Implications for sexual and social behavior. *Current Directions in Psychological Science, 14,* 312–316.

Gannon, J. R., & Walsh, T. J. (2016). Testosterone and sexual function. *The Urologic Clinics of North America, 43*(2), 217–222. doi:10.1016/j.ucl.2016.01.008

Gansberg, M. (1964, March 27). 37 who saw murder didn't call the police: Apathy at stabbing of Queens woman shocks inspector. *New York Times,* 1.

Ganzer, F., Bröning, Kraft, S., Sack, P. M., & Thomasius, R. (2016). Weighing the evidence: A systematic review on long-term neurocognitive effects of cannabis use in abstinent adolescents and adults. *Neuropsychological Review, 26,* 186–222.

Garaulet, M., Esteban, T. A., Lee, Y. C., Smith, C. E., Parnell, L. D., & Ordovás, J. M. (2012). SIRT1 AND CLOCK 3111T>C combined genotype is associated with evening preference and weight loss resistance in a behavioral therapy treatment for obesity. *International Journal of Obesity, 36,* 1436–1441. doi:10.1038/ijo.2011.270

Garaulet, M., Gómez-Abellán, P., Alburquerque-Béjar, J. J., Lee, Y. C., Ordovás, J. M., & Scheer, F. A. (2013). Timing of food intake predicts weight loss effectiveness. *International Journal of Obesity (London), 37,* 604–611. doi:10.1038/ijo.2012.229

Garaulet, M., & Gómez-Abellán, P. (2014). Timing of food intake and obesity: A novel association. *Physiology and Behavior, 134,* 44–50. doi:10.1016/j.physbeh.2014.01.001

Garaulet, M., Vera, B., Bonnet-Rubio, G., Gómez-Abellán, P., Lee, Y. C., & Ordovás, J. M. (2016). Lunch eating predicts weight-loss effectiveness in carriers of the common allele at PERILIPIN1: The ONTIME (Obesity, Nutrigenetics, Timing, Mediterranean) study. *The American Journal of Clinical Nutrition, 104*(4), 1160–1166. doi:10.3945/ajcn.116.134528

Garbarino, J. (1997). The role of economic deprivation in the social context of child maltreatment. In M. E. Helfer, R. S. Kempe, & R. D. Krugman (Eds.), *The battered child* (5th ed., pp. 49–60). University of Chicago Press.

Garcia, F., Serra, E., Garcia, O. F., Martinez, I., & Cruise, E. (2019). A third emerging stage for the current digital society? Optimal parenting styles in Spain, the United States, Germany, and Brazil. *International Journal of Environmental Research and Public Health, 16*(13), 2333. doi:10.3390/ijerph16132333

Garcia, J. (1992). Taste aversion and preference learning in animals. In L. R. Squire, J. H. Byrne, L. Nadel, H. L. Roediger, D. L. Schacter, & R. F. Thompson (Eds.), *Encyclopedia of learning and memory* (pp. 611–613). Macmillan.

Garcia, J., & Koelling, R. A. (1966). Relation of cue to consequence in avoidance learning. *Psychonomic Science, 4,* 123–124.

Garcia, J., Ervin, F. R., & Koelling, R. A. (1966). Learning with prolonged delay of reinforcement. *Psychonomic Science, 5,* 121–122.

Garcia, J., Kimeldorf, D. J., & Koelling, R. A. (1955). Conditioned taste aversion to saccharin resulting from exposure to

gamma radiation. *Science, 122,* 157–158. doi:10.1126/science.122.3179.1089
Garcia-Borreguero, D., Silber, M. H., Winkelman, J. W., Högl, B., Bainbridge, J., Buchfuhrer, M., . . . Allen, R. P. (2016). Guidelines for the first-line treatment of restless legs syndrome/Willis-Ekbom disease, prevention and treatment of dopaminergic augmentation: A combined task force of the IRLSSG, EURLSSG, and the RLS-foundation. *Sleep Medicine, 21,* 1–11.
Garcia-Romeu, A., Kersgaard, B., & Addy, P. H. (2016). Clinical applications of hallucinogens: A review. *Experimental and Clinical Psychopharmacology, 24*(4), 229–268. doi:10.1037/pha0000084
Gard, T., Taquet, M., Dixit, R., Hölzel, B. K., de Montjoye, Y. A., Brach, N., . . . Lazar, S. W. (2014). Fluid intelligence and brain functional organization in aging yoga and meditation practitioners. *Frontiers in Aging Neuroscience, 6, 76.* doi:10.3389/fnagi.2014.00076
Gardiner, H. W., Mutter, J. D., & Kosmitzki, C. (1998). *Lives across cultures: Cross-cultural human development.* Allyn & Bacon.
Gardner, H. (1983). *Frames of mind.* Basic Books.
Gardner, H. (1999). *Intelligence reframed: Multiple intelligences for the 21st century.* Basic Books.
Gardner, H. (2004). *Changing minds: The art and science of changing our own and other people's minds.* Harvard Business School Press.
Gardner, H., Kornhaber, M., & Chen, J. Q. (2018). The theory of multiple intelligences: Psychological and educational perspectives. In R. J. Sternberg (Ed.), *The nature of human intelligence.* (pp. 116–129). Cambridge University Press. https://doi.org/10.1017/9781316817049.009
Garnock-Jones, K. P., & McCormack, P. L. (2010). Escitalopram: A review of its use in the management of major depressive disorder in adults. *CNS Drugs, 24, 769–796.*
Gartlehner, G., Wagner, G., Matyas, N., Titscher, V., Greimel, J., Lux, L.,... Lohr, K. N. (2017). Pharmacological and non-pharmacological treatments for major depressive disorder: Review of systematic reviews. *BMJ Open, 7*(6), e014912. doi:10.1136/bmjopen-2016-014912
Gaskell, M. G., Warker, J., Lindsay, S., Frost, R., Guest, J., Snowden, R., & Stackhouse, A. (2014). Sleep underpins the plasticity of language production. *Psychological Science, 25,* 1457–1465.
Gaunt, R. (2006). Couple similarity and marital satisfaction: Are similar spouses happier? *Journal of Personality, 74,* 1401–1420.
Gawin, F. H. (1991). Cocaine addiction: Psychology and neurophysiology. *Science, 251,* 1580–1586.
Gawryszewski, V. P., & Monteiro, M. G. (2014). Mortality from diseases, conditions and injuries where alcohol is a necessary cause in the Americas, 2007–09. *Addiction, 109*(4), 570–577. https://doi.org/10.1111/add.12418
Gaynes, B. N., Lux, L. J., Lloyd, S. W., Hansen, R. A., Gartlehner, G., Keener, P., . . . Lohr, K. N. (2011). Nonpharmacologic interventions for treatment-resistant depression in adults. *Comparative Effectiveness Review,* No. 33. Agency for Healthcare Research and Quality.
Gazzaniga, M. S. (1967). The split brain in man. *Scientific American, 217,* 24–29.
Ge, X., Jin, R., Natsuaki, M. N., Frederick, X., Brody, G. H., Cutrona, C. E., & Simons, R. L. (2006). Pubertal maturation and early substance use risks among African American children. *Psychology of Addictive Behaviors, 20,* 404–414.
Gedo, J. E. (2002). The enduring scientific contributions of Sigmund Freud. *Perspective in Biology and Medicine, 45,* 200–212.
Gelade, G. (2002). Creative style, personality, and artistic endeavor. *Genetic, Social and General Psychology Monographs, 128,* 213–234.
Gelfand, S. A. (1981). *Hearing.* Marcel Dekker.
Geller, E. S., Russ, N. W., & Altomari, M. G. (1986). Naturalistic observations of beer drinking among college students. *Journal of Applied Behavior Analysis, 19,* 391–396.
Gelstein, S., Yeshurun, Y., Rozenkrantz, L., Shushan, S., Frumin, I., Roth, Y., . . . Sobel, N. (2011). Human tears contain a chemosignal. *Science, 331,* 226–230.
Geniole, S. N., Bird, B. M., McVittie, J. S., Purcell, R. B., Archer, J., & Carré, J. M. (2020). Is testosterone linked to human aggression? A meta-analytic examination of the relationship between baseline, dynamic, and manipulated testosterone on human aggression. *Hormones and Behavior, 123,* 104644. https://doi.org/10.1016/j.yhbeh.2019.104644
Genné-Bacon, E. A. (2014). Thinking evolutionarily about obesity. *The Yale Journal of Biology and Medicine, 87*(2), 99.
Gentile, D. A. (2015). What is a good skeptic to do? The case for skepticism in the media violence discussion. *Perspectives on Psychological Science, 10*(5), 674-676. doi:10.1177/1745691615592238
Geraerts, E., Lindsay, D. S., Merckelbach, H., Jelicic, M., Raymaekers, L., Arnold, M. M., & Schooler, J. W. (2009). Cognitive mechanisms underlying recovered-memory experiences of childhood sexual abuse. *Psychological Science, 20,* 92–98.
Gerardi, M., Cukor, J., Difede, J., Rizzo, A., & Rothbaum, B. O. (2010). Virtual reality exposure therapy for post-traumatic stress disorder and other anxiety disorders. *Current Psychiatry Reports, 12,* 298–305.
Gergen, K. J., & Gergen, M. M. (1988). Narrative and self as relationship. In L. Berkowitz (Ed.), *Advances in experimental social psychology* (Vol. 21, pp. 17–56). Academic Press.
Gerken, L. (2002). Early sensitivity to linguistic form. *Annual Review of Language Acquisition, 2,* 1–36.
German, C. L., Fleckenstein, A. E., & Hanson, G. R. (2014). Bath salts and synthetic cathinones: An emerging designer drug phenomenon. *Life Sciences, 97,* 2-8.
Germine, L. T., Duchaine, B., & Nakayama, K. (2011). Where cognitive development and aging meet: Face learning ability peaks after age 30. *Cognition, 118,* 201–210. doi:10.1016/j.cognition.2010.11.002
Gernsbacher, M. A. (1985). Surface information and loss in comprehension. *Cognitive Psychology, 17,* 324–363.
Gershoff, E. T. (2002). Corporal punishment by parents and associated child behaviors and experiences: A meta-analytic and theoretical review. *Psychological Bulletin, 128,* 539–579.
Gershoff, E. T. (2010). More harm than good: A summary of scientific research on the intended and unintended effects of corporal punishment on children. *Law and Contemporary Problems, 73,* 31–56.
Gershoff, E. T., Purtell, K. M., & Holas, I. (2015). *Corporal punishment in U.S. public schools: Legal precedents, current practices, and future policy.* Springer Science + Business Media.
Geschwind, N. (1975). The apraxias: Neural mechanisms of disorders of learned movements. *American Scientist, 63,* 188–195.
Geschwind, N., & Levitsky, W. (1968). Human brain: Left-right asymmetries in temporal speech region. *Science, 161,* 186–187.
Gheysen, F., Van Opstal, F., Roggeman, C., Van Waelvelde, H., & Fias, W. (2010). Hippocampal contribution to early and later stages of implicit motor sequence learning. *Experimental Brain Research, 202,* 795-807. doi:10.1007/s00221-010-2186-6
Ghoreishi, A., Kabootvand, S., Zangani, E., Bazargan-Hejazi, S., Ahmadi, A., & Khazaie, H. (2015). Prevalence and attributes of criminality in patients with schizophrenia. *Journal of Injury and Violence Research, 7,* 7–12.
Giancola, P. R., Josephs, R. A., Parrott, D. J., & Duke, A. A. (2010). Alcohol myopia revisited: Clarifying aggression and other acts of disinhibition through a distorted lens. *Perspectives on Psychological Science, 5,* 265–278.
Giannotti, F., & Cortesi, F. (2009). Family and cultural influences on sleep development. *Child and Adolescent Psychiatric Clinics of North America, 18,* 849–861.
Gibb, B. E., Alloy, L. B., Abramson, L. Y., Beevers, C. G., & Miller, I. W. (2004). Cognitive vulnerability to depression: A taxometric analysis. *Journal of Abnormal Psychology, 113,* 81–89.
Gibbons, C. J., Fournier, J. C., Stirman, S. W., Derubeis, R. J., Crits-Christoph, P., & Beck, A. T. (2010). The clinical effectiveness of cognitive therapy for depression in an outpatient clinic. *Journal of Affective Disorders, 125,* 169–176.
Gibbons, L. E., Carle, A. C., Mackin, R., Harvey, D., Mukherjee, S., Insel, P., . . . Crane, P. K. (2012). A composite score for executive functioning, validated in Alzheimer's Disease Neuroimaging Initiative (ADNI) participants with baseline mild cognitive impairment. *Brain Imaging and Behavior, 6,* 517-527. doi:10.1007/s11682-012-9176-1
Gibbs, K. D., Basson, J., Xierali, I. M., & Broniatowski, D. A. (2016). Decoupling of the minority PhD talent pool and assistant professor hiring in medical school basic science departments in the US. *eLife, 5,* e21393. doi.org:10.7554/eLife.21393
Gibbs, W. W. (1996). Gaining on fat. *Scientific American, 275,* 88–94.
Gibson, C., & Mumford, M. D. (2013). Evaluation, criticism, and creativity. Criticism content and effects on creative problem solving. *Psychology of Aesthetics, Creativity, and the Arts, 7,* 314-331.
Giedd, J. N. (2004). Structural magnetic resonance imaging of the adolescent brain. *Annals of the New York Academy of Sciences, 1021,* 77–85.
Gigante, A. D., Bond, D. J., Lafer, B., Lam, R. W., Young, L. T., & Yatham, L. N. (2012). Brain glutamate levels measured by magnetic resonance spectroscopy in patients with bipolar disorder: A meta-analysis. *Bipolar Disorders, 14,* 478–487.
Gilbert, D. G., Stunkard, M. E., Jensen, R. A., & Detwiler, F. R. J. (1996). Effects of exam stress on mood, cortisol, and immune functioning. *Personality and Individual Differences, 21,* 235–246.

Gilbertson, M. W., Shenton, M. E., Ciszewski, A., Kasai, K., Lasko, N. B., Orr, S. P., . . . Pitman, R. K. (2002). Smaller hippocampal volume predicts pathologic vulnerability to psychological trauma. *Nature Neuroscience, 5,* 1242–1247.

Gildea, K. M., Schneider, T. R., & Shebilske, W. I. (2007). Appraisals and training performance on a complex laboratory task. *Human Factors, 49,* 745–758.

Gillam, B. (1980). Geometrical illusions. *Scientific American, 242,* 102–111.

Gillespie, C. F., & Nemeroff, C. B. (2007). Corticotropin-releasing factor and the psychobiology of early-life stress. *Current Directions in Psychological Science, 16,* 85–89.

Gilligan, C. F. (1982). *In a different voice.* Harvard University Press.

Gillund, G., & Shiffrin, R. M. (1984). A retrieval model for both recognition and recall. *Psychological Review, 91,* 1–67.

Ginsberg, G. S., Becker, E. M., Keeton, C. P., Sakolsky, D., Piacentini, J., Albano, A. M., . . . Kendall, P. C. (2014). Naturalistic follow-up of youths treated for pediatric anxiety disorders. *JAMA Psychiatry, 71,* 310–318.

Girandola, F. (2002). Sequential requests and organ donation. *Journal of Social Psychology, 142,* 171–178.

Girdler, S. S., Jamner, L. D., & Shapiro, D. (1997). Hostility, testosterone and vascular reactivity to stress: Effects of sex. *International Journal of Behavioral Medicine, 4,* 242–263.

Giret, N., Péron, F., Lindová, J., Tichotová, L., Nagle, L., Kreutzer, M., . . . Bovat, D. (2010). Referential learning of French and Czech labels in African grey parrots (*Psittacus erithacus*): Different methods yield contrasting results. *Behavioural Processes, 85,* 90–98.

Gitelson, I. B., & McDermott, D. (2006). Parents and their young adult children: Transitions to adulthood. *Child Welfare League of America, 85,* 853–866.

Giurfa, M. (2021). Learning of sameness/difference relationships by honey bees: Performance, strategies and ecological context. *Current Opinion in Behavioral Sciences, 37,* 1–6.

Givens, B. (1995). Low doses of ethanol impair spatial working memory and reduce hippocampal theta activity. *Alcoholism: Clinical and Experimental Research, 19,* 763–767.

Gladwell, M. (2004, September 20). Annals of psychology: Personality plus. *New Yorker,* pp. 42–48.

Glanzer, M., & Cunitz, A. R. (1966). Two storage mechanisms in free recall. *Journal of Verbal Learning and Verbal Behavior, 5,* 351–360.

Glass, C., & Minnotte, K. L. (2010). Recruiting and hiring women in STEM fields. *Journal of Diversity in Higher Education, 3*(4), 218–229.

Glenberg, A. M., Smith, S. M., & Green, C. (1977). Type I rehearsal: Maintenance and more. *Journal of Verbal Learning and Verbal Behavior, 16,* 339–352.

Glenn, N. D., Uecker, J., & Love, R. W. B. (2010). Later first marriage and marital success. *Social Science Research, 39,* 787–800.

Global Initiative to End All Corporal Punishment of Children. (2016). *States which have prohibited all corporal punishment.* http://www.endcorporalpunishment.org/progress/prohibiting-states/

Global Initiative to End All Corporal Punishment of Children. (2020). *Global Progress.* https://endcorporalpunishment.org/global-progress/

Goddard, A. W. (2017). The neurobiology of panic: A chronic stress disorder. *Chronic Stress, 1,* 2470547017736038. doi:10.1177/2470547017736038

Goddard, A. W., Ball, S. G., Martinez, J., Robinson, M. J., Yang, C. R., Russell, J. M , & Shekhar, A. (2010). Current perspectives of the roles of the central norepinephrine system in anxiety and depression. *Depression and Anxiety, 27,* 339–350.

Godden, D. R., & Baddeley, A. D. (1975). Context dependent memory in two natural environments: On land and underwater. *British Journal of Psychology, 66,* 325–332.

Gola, M., Wordecha, M., Marchewka, A., & Sescousse, G. (2016). Visual sexual stimuli—cue or reward? A perspective for interpreting brain imaging findings on human sexual behaviors. *Frontiers in Human Neuroscience, 10,* 402. doi:10.3389/fnhum.2016.00402

Goldberg, S. B., Tucker, R. P., Greene, P. A., Davidson, R. J., Wampold, B. E., Kearney D. J., & Simpson, T. L. (2018). Mindfulness-based interventions for psychiatric disorders: A systematic review and meta-analysis. *Clinical Psychology Review, 59,* 52–60. doi:10.1016/j.cpr.2017.10.011

Goldin, C. (2014). A grand gender convergence: Its last chapter. *American Economic Review, 104,* 1091–1119.

Goldstein, R. B., Smith, S. M., Chou, S. P., Saha, T. D., Jung, J., Zhang, H., ... Grant, B. F. (2016). The epidemiology of *DSM-5* posttraumatic stress disorder in the United States: Results from the National Epidemiologic Survey on Alcohol and Related Conditions-III. *Social Psychiatry and Psychiatric Epidemiology, 51*(8), 1137–1148. doi:10.1007/s00127-016-1208-5

Goleman, D. (1982, March). Staying up: The rebellion against sleep's gentle tyranny. *Psychology Today,* 24–35.

Goleman, D. (1995). *Emotional intelligence.* Bantam.

Goleman, D. (1998). *Working with emotional intelligence.* Bloomsbury.

Goleman, D., Boyatzis, R. E., & McKee, A. (2002). *Primal leadership: Realizing the power of emotional intelligence.* Harvard Business School Press.

Gonzalez, H. M., Vega, W. A., Williams, D. R., Tarraf, W., West, B. T., & Neighbors, H. W. (2010). Depression care in the United States: Too little for too few. *Archives of General Psychiatry, 67,* 37–46.

Good, J. J., Woodzicka, J. A., & Wingfield, L. C. (2010). The effects of gender stereotypic and counterstereotypic textbook images on science performance. *Journal of Social Psychology, 150,* 132–147.

Goodwin, F. K., & Goldstein, M. A. (2003). Optimizing lithium treatment in bipolar disorder: A review of the literature and clinical recommendations. *Journal of Psychiatric Practice, 9,* 333–343.

Goodwin, P. Y., Mosher, W. D., & Chandra, A. (2010). Marriage and cohabitation in the United States: A statistical portrait based on cycle 6 (2002) of the National Survey of Family Growth. *Vital Health Statistics, 23,* 1–45.

Goranson, A., Ritter, R. S., Waytz, A. Norton, M. I., & Gray, K. (2017). Dying is unexpectedly positive. *Psychological Science, 28*(7), 988–999.

Gorchoff, S. M., John, O. P., & Helson, R. (2008). Contextualizing change in marital satisfaction during middle age. *Psychological Science, 19,* 1194–1200.

Gordon, E. F. (2000). *Mockingbird years: A life in and out of therapy.* Basic Books.

Gordon. J. L., Eisenlohr-Moul, T. A., Rubinow, D. R., Schrubbe, L., & Girdler, S. S. (2016). Naturally occurring changes in estradiol concentrations in the menopause transition predict morning cortisol and negative mood in perimenopausal depression. *Clinical Psychological Science, 4,* 919–935.

Gordon, S. (2008, June 15). Beware the "Blackberry thumb." *U.S. News & World Report.* http://health.usnews.com

Gorman, J. M. (2006). Gender differences in depression and response to psychotropic medication. *Gender Medicine, 3,* 93–109.

Gorrell, S., & Murray, S. B. (2019). Eating disorders in males. *Child and Adolescent Psychiatric Clinics of North America, 28*(4), 641–651. https://doi.org/10.1016/j.chc.2019.05.012

Gosling, A. L., Buckley, H. R., Matisoo-Smith, E., & Merriman, T. R. (2015). Pacific populations, metabolic disease and "just-so stories": A Critique of the "thrifty genotype" hypothesis in Oceania. *Annals of Human Genetics, 79*(6), 470–480. doi:10.1111/ahg.12132

Gosling, S. D., & Johnson, A. J. (2010). *Advanced methods for conducting online behavioral research.* APA Books.

Gosling, S. D., & Mason, W. (2015). Internet research in psychology. *Annual Review of Psychology, 3,* 877–902.

Gothe, N. P. (2020). Examining the effects of light versus moderate to vigorous physical activity on cognitive function in African American adults. *Aging & Mental Health,* 1-7. https://doi.org/10.1080/13607863.2020.1768216

Gotlib, I. H., Goodman, S. H., & Humphreys, K. L. (2020). Studying the intergenerational transmission of risk for depression: Current status and future directions. *Current Directions in Psychological Science, 29*(2), 174-179.

Gotlib, I. H., & Hamilton, J. P. (2008). Neuroimaging and depression: Current status and unresolved issues. *Current Directions in Psychological Science, 17,* 159–163.

Gotlib, I. H., Joormann, J., & Foland-Ross, L. C. (2014). Understanding familial risk for depression: A 25-year perspective. *Perspectives on Psychological Science, 9,* 94–108.

Gottlieb, G., Wahlsten, D., & Lickliter, R. (1998). The significance of biology for human development: A developmental psychobiological systems view. In W. Damon & R. M. Lerner (Eds.), *Handbook of child psychology* (Vol. 1, pp. 233–273). Wiley.

Gottlieb, J., & Carver, C. S. (1980). Anticipation of future interaction and the bystander effect. *Journal of Experimental Social Psychology, 16,* 253–260. doi:10.1016/0022-1031(80)90068-2

Gottman, J. (1999a). *The marriage clinic.* Norton.

Gottman, J. (1999b). *The seven principles of making marriage work.* Crown.

Gotts, S. J., Jo, H., Wallace, G. L., Saad, Z. S., Cox, R. W., & Martin, A. (2013). Two distinct forms of functional lateralization in the human brain. *PNAS: Proceedings of the National Academy of Sciences of the United States of America, 110,* E3435–E3444.

Gouin, K., Murphy, K., & Shah, P. S. (2011). Effects of cocaine use during pregnancy on low birthweight and preterm birth: Systematic review and metaanalyses. *American Journal of Obstetrics and Gynecology, 204,* 340.e1–340.e12.

Gowrisankaran, S., & Sheedy, J. E. (2015). Computer vision syndrome: A review. *Work, 52,* 303–314.

Goyal, M., Singh, S., Sibinga, E. M., Gould, N. F., Rowland-Seymour, A., Sharma, R.…. Haythornthwaite, J. A. (2014). Meditation programs for psychological stress and well-being: A systematic review and meta-analysis. *JAMA Internal Medicine, 174*(3), 357–368. doi:10.1001/jamainternmed.2013.13018

Graber, J. A., Brooks-Gunn, J., & Warren, M. P. (2006). Pubertal effects on adjustment in girls: Moving from demonstrating effects to identifying pathways. *Journal of Youth and Adolescence, 35,* 413–423.

Grace, A. A. (2010). Ventral hippocampus, interneurons, and schizophrenia: A new understanding of the pathophysiology of schizophrenia and its implications for treatment and prevention. *Current Directions in Psychological Science, 19,* 232–237.

Gradari, S., Pérez-Domper, P., Butler, R. G., Martínez-Cué, C., de Polavieja, G. G., & Trejo, J. L. (2016). The relationship between behavior acquisition and persistence abilities: Involvement of adult hippocampal neurogenesis. *Hippocampus, 26*(7), 857–874. doi:10.1002/hipo.22568

Graf, P., & Schacter, D. L. (1985). Implicit and explicit memory for new associations in normal and amnesiac subjects. *Journal of Experimental Psychology: Learning, Memory, and Cognition, 11,* 501–518.

Graffin, N. F., Ray, W. J., & Lundy, R. (1995). EEG concomitants of hypnosis and hypnotic susceptibility. *Journal of Abnormal Psychology, 104,* 123–131.

Graham, K. S., Simons, J. S., Pratt, K. H., Patterson, K., & Hodges, J. R. (2000). Insights from semantic dementia on the relationship between episodic and semantic memory. *Neurpsychologia, 38,* 313–324.

Graham, R., Devinsky, O., & LaBar, K. S. (2007). Quantifying deficits in the perception of fear and anger in morphed facial expressions after bilateral amygdala damage. *Neuropsychologia, 45,* 42–54.

Grana, R. A., & Ling, P. M. (2014). "Smoking revolution": A content analysis of electronic cigarette retail websites. *American Journal of Preventive Medicine, 46*(4), 395–403. doi:10.1016/j.amepre.2013.12.010

Grand, J. A. (2017). Brain drain? An examination of stereotype threat effects during training on knowledge acquisition and organizational effectiveness. *Journal of Applied Psychology, 102*(2), 115–150. doi:10.1037/apl0000171

Grant, B. F., Hasin, D. S., Stinson, F. S., Dawson, D. A., Chou, S. P., Ruan, W. J., & Pickering, R. P. (2004). Prevalence, correlates, and disability of personality disorders in the United States: Results from the National Epidemiologic Survey on Alcohol and Related Conditions. *Journal of Clinical Psychiatry, 65,* 948–958.

Grant, B. F., Hasin, D. S., Stinson, F. S., Dawson, D. A., Goldstein, R. B., Smith, S., . . . Saha, T. D. (2006). The epidemiology of *DSM-IV* panic disorder and agoraphobia in the United States: Results from the National Epidemiologic Survey on Alcohol and Related Conditions. *Journal of Clinical Psychiatry, 67,* 363–374.

Grant, J. E., & Phillips, K. A. (2004). Is anorexia nervosa a subtype of body dysmorphic disorder? Probably not, but read on. . . . *Harvard Review of Psychiatry, 12,* 123–126.

Grasso, D. J., Henry, D., Kestler, J., Nieto, R., Wakschlag, L. S., & Briggs-Gowan, M. J. (2016). Harsh parenting as a potential mediator of the association between intimate partner violence and child disruptive behavior in families with young children. *Journal of Interpersonal Violence, 31*(11), 2102–2126. doi:10.1177/0886260515572472

Green, J. G., McLaughlin, K. A., Berglund, P. A., Gruber, M. J., Sampson, N. A., Zaslavsky, A. M., & Kessler, R. C. (2010). Childhood adversities and adult psychiatric disorders in the National Comorbidity Survey Replication I: Associations with first onset of *DSM-IV* disorders. *Archives of General Psychiatry, 67,* 113–123.

Green, J. P., & Lynn, S. J. (2000). Hypnosis and suggestion-based approaches to smoking cessation: An examination of the evidence. *International Journal of Clinical and Experimental Hypnosis, 48,* 195–224.

Greenberg, L. S., & Johnson, S. M. (1988). *Emotionally focused therapy for couples.* Guilford Press.

Greenberg, L. S., & Rice, L. N. (1997). Humanistic approaches to psychotherapy. In P. L. Wachtel & S. B. Messer (Eds.), *Theories of psychotherapy: Origins and evolution* (pp. 97–129). American Psychological Association.

Greenberg, L., Warwar, S., & Malcolm, W. (2010) Emotion-focused couples therapy and the facilitation of forgiveness. *Journal of Marital and Family Therapy, 36,* 28–42.

Greenfield, P. (1997). You can't take it with you: Why ability assessments don't cross cultures. *American Psychologist, 52,* 1115–1124.

Greenhaus, J. H. (2003). Career dynamics. In W. C. Borman, D. R. Ilgen, & R. J. Klimoski (Eds.), *Handbook of psychology: Industrial and organizational psychology* (Vol. 12, pp. 519–540). Wiley.

Greenwald, A. G., & Krieger, L. H. (2006). Implicit bias: Scientific foundations. *California Law Review, 94*(4), 945-967.

Greenwald, A. G., McGhee, D. E., & Schwartz, J. L. K. (1998). Measuring individual differences in implicit cognition: The Implicit Association Test. *Journal of Personality and Social Psychology, 74*(6), 1464–1480. https://doi.org/10.1037//0022-3514.74.6.1464

Greer, G. R., & Tolbert, R. (1998). A method of conducting therapeutic sessions with MDMA. *Journal of Psychoactive Drugs, 30,* 371–379.

Gregg, R. A., & Rawls, S. M. (2014). Behavioral pharmacology of designer cathinones: A review of the preclinical literature. *Life Sciences, 97,* 27–30.

Gregory, C. K., Meade, A. W., & Thompson, L. F. (2013). Understanding Internet recruitment via signaling theory and the elaboration likelihood model. *Computers in Human Behavior, 29*(5), 1949–1959. doi:10.1016/j.chb.2013.04.013

Greitemeyer, T. (2020). The police officer's dilemma: The relationship between violent video game play and responses in a first-person shooter task. *Journal of Media Psychology: Theories, Methods, and Applications, 32*(2), 82–88. https://doi.org/10.1027/1864-1105/a000260

Griest, S. E., Folmer, R. L., & Martin, W. H. (2007). Effectiveness of "Dangerous Decibels," a school-based hearing loss prevention program. *American Journal of Audiology, 16,* S165–S181.

Griffey, J. F., & Little, A. C. (2013). Similarities in human visual and declared measures of preference for opposite-sex faces. *Experimental Psychology, 18,* 1-9. doi:10.1027/1618-3169/a000248

Griffiths, K. M., Calear, A. L., & Banfield, M. (2009). Systematic review on Internet Support Groups (ISGs) and depression: Do ISGs reduce depressive symptoms? *Journal of Medical Internet Research, 11,* e40.

Griffiths, S., Murray, S. B., & Touyz, S. (2013). Drive for muscularity and muscularity-oriented disordered eating in men: The role of set shifting difficulties and weak central coherence. *Body Image, 10*(4), 636–639. doi:10.1016/j.bodyim.2013.04.002

Griggs, R. A. (2014a). Coverage of the Stanford prison experiment in introductory psychology textbooks. *Teaching of Psychology, 41*(3), 195-203.

Griggs, R. A. (2014b). The continuing saga of Little Albert in introductory psychology textbooks. *Teaching of Psychology, 41*(4), 309–317. doi:10.1177/0098628314549702

Grinspoon, L., Bakalar, J. B., Zimmer, L., & Morgan, J. P. (1997). Marijuana addiction. *Science, 277,* 751–752.

Grivetti, L. E. (2000). Food prejudices and taboos. In K. E. Kipple & K. C. Ornelas (Eds.), *The Cambridge world history of food* (Vol. 1, pp. 1495–1513). Cambridge University Press.

Gropalis, M., Bleichhardt, G., Witthoft, M., & Hiller, W. (2012). Hypochondriasis, somatoform disorders, and anxiety disorders: Sociodemographic variables, general psychopathology, and naturalistic treatment effects. *Journal of Nervous and Mental Disease, 200,* 406–412.

Gross, J. J., Halperin, E., & Porat, R. (2013). Emotion regulation in intractable conflicts. *Current Directions in Psychological Science, 22,* 423–429.

Grossman, L. S., Harrow, M., Rosen, C., Faull, R., & Strauss, G. P. (2008). Sex differences in schizophrenia and other psychotic disorders: A 20-year longitudinal study of psychosis and recovery. *Comprehensive Psychiatry, 49,* 523–529.

Grossman, M. I., & Stein, L. F. (1948). Vagotomy and the hunger-producing action of insulin in man. *Journal of Applied Physiology, 1,* 263–269.

Grossman, R. P., & Till, B. D. (1998). The persistence of classically conditioned brand attitudes. *Journal of Advertising, 27,* 23–31.

Grossmann, I., Karasawa, M., Izumi, S., Na, J., Varnum, M. E., Kitayama, S., & Nisbett, R. E. (2012). Aging and wisdom: Culture matters. *Psychological Science, 23,* 1059–1066.

Grover, S. (2005). Reification of psychiatric diagnoses as defamatory: Implications for ethical clinical practice. *Ethical Human Psychology and Psychiatry, 7,* 77–86.

Gruen, R. J. (1993). Stress and depression: Toward the development of integrative models. In L. Goldberger & S. Breznitz (Eds.), *Handbook of stress: Theoretical and clinical aspects* (pp. 550–569). Free Press.

Grysman, A., Fivush, R., Merrill, N. A., & Graci, M. (2016). The influence of gender and gender typicality on autobiographical memory across event types and age groups. *Memory & Cognition, 44*(6), 856–868. doi:10.3758/s13421-016-0610-2

Grysman, A., & Hudson, J. A. (2010). Abstracting and extracting: Causal coherence and the development of the life story. *Memory, 18,* 565–580.

Grysman, A., & Hudson, J. A. (2013). Gender differences in autobiographical memory:

Developmental and methodological considerations. *Developmental Review, 33,* 239–272. doi:10.1016/j.dr.2013.07.004

Grysman, A., Merrill, N., & Fivush, R. (2017). Emotion, gender, and gender typical identity in autobiographical memory. *Memory, 25*(3), 289–297. https://doi.org/10.1080/09658211.2016.1168847

Gu, J., Strauss, C., Bond, R., & Cavanagh, K. (2015). How do mindfulness-based cognitive therapy and mindfulness-based stress reduction improve mental health and well-being? A systematic review and meta-analysis of mediation studies. *Clinical Psychological Review, 37,* 1–12.

Gugger, J. J., & Wagner, M. L. (2007). Rapid eye movement sleep behavior disorder. *Annals of Pharmacotherapy, 41,* 1833–1841.

Guilford, J. P. (1967). *The nature of human intelligence.* McGraw-Hill.

Guilleminault, C., Palombini, L., Pelayo, R., & Chervin, R. D. (2003). Sleepwalking and sleep terrors in prepubertal children: What triggers them? *Pediatrics, 111,* e17–e25.

Guisinger, S. (2003). Adapted to flee famine: Adding an evolutionary perspective on anorexia nervosa. *Psychological Review, 110,* 745–761.

Guo, M., Li, C., Lei, Y., Xu, S., Zhao, D., & Lu, X.Y. (2017). Role of the adipose PPARϒ-adiponectin axis in susceptibility to stress and depression/anxiety-related behaviors. *Molecular Psychiatry, 22*(7), 1056–1068. https://doi.org/10.1038/mp.2016.225

Gurman, A. S., & Jacobson, N. S. (Eds.). (2002). *Clinical handbook of couple therapy* (3rd ed.). Guilford Press.

Gustavson, C. R., & Garcia, J. (1974, August). Pulling a gag on the wily coyote. *Psychology Today,* pp. 68–72.

Gustavson, D. E., Lurquin, J. H., Michaelson, L. E., Barker, J. E., Carruth, N. P., von Bastian, C. C., & Miyake, A. (2020). Lower general executive function is primarily associated with trait worry: A latent variable analysis of negative thought/affect measures. *Emotion, 20*(4), 557–571. https://doi.org/10.1037/emo0000584

Guterman, N. B., Tabone, J. K., Bryan, G. M., Taylor, C. A., Napoleon-Hanger, C., & Banman, A. (2013). Examining the effectiveness of home-based parent aide services to reduce risk for physical child abuse and neglect: Six-month findings from a randomized clinical trial. *Child Abuse & Neglect, 37,* 566–577. doi:10.1016/j.chiabu.2013.03.006

Ha, T., Overbeek, G., & Engels, R. C. (2010). Effects of attractiveness and social status on dating desire in heterosexual adolescents: An experimental study. *Archives of Sexual Behavior, 39,* 1063–1071.

Haba-Rubio, J., Marti-Soler, H., Marques-Vidal, P., Tobback, N., Andries, D., Preisig, M., . . . Heinzer, R. (2016). Prevalence and determinants of periodic limb movements in the general population. *Annals of Neurology, 79*(3), 464–474.

Haber, D. (1994). *Health promotion and aging.* Springer.

Habibi, A. A., Kemp, C., & Xu, Y. (2020). Chaining and the growth of linguistic categories. *Cognition, 202,* 104323. doi:10.1016/j.cognition.2020.104323

Hackett, R. D. (1989). Work attitudes and employee absenteeism: A synthesis of the literature. *Journal of Occupational Psychology, 62,* 235–248.

Hackley, C. (2007). Marketing psychology and the hidden persuaders. *The Psychologist, 20*(8), 488–490.

Hackman, J. R., & Oldham, G. R. (1976). Motivation through the design of work: A test of a theory. *Organizational Behavior and Human Performance, 16,* 250–279.

Hadjikhani, N., Kveraga, K., Naik, P., & Ahlfors, S. P. (2009). Early (M170) activation of face-specific cortex by face-like objects. *Neuroreport, 20,* 403–407.

Haefner, R. (2009, June). More employers screening candidates via social networking sites. Careerbuilder.com

Hagenauer, M. H., & Lee, T. M. (2012). The neuroendocrine control of the circadian system: Adolescent chronotype. *Frontiers in Neuroendocrinology, 33,* 211–229.

Haidt, J. (2008). Morality. *Perspectives on Psychological Science, 1,* 65–72.

Haie, L., & Do, D. P. (2007). Racial differences in self-reports of sleep duration in a population-based study. *Sleep, 30,* 1096–1103.

Haines, S. J., Gleeson, J., Kuppens, P., Hollenstein, T., Ciarrochi, J., Labuschagne, I., . . . Koval, P. (2016). The wisdom to know the difference: Strategy-situation fit in emotion regulation in daily life is associated with well-being. *Psychological Science, 27,* 1651–1659.

Haith, M. M., & Benson, J. B. (1998). Infant cognition. In W. Damon & R. M. Lerner (Eds.), *Handbook of child psychology* (Vol 1, pp. 235–246). Wiley.

Hakuta, K. (1999). The debate on bilingual education. *Developmental and Behavioral Pediatrics, 20,* 36–37.

Hakuta, K., Bialystok, E., & Wiley, E. (2003). Critical evidence: A test of the critical-period hypothesis for second-language acquisition. *Psychological Science, 14,* 31–38.

Halaby, A., Haddad, R. S., & Naja, W. J. (2015). Non-antidepressant treatment of social anxiety disorder: A review. *Current Clinical Pharmacology, 10,* 126–30.

Halbrook, Y. J., O'Donnell, A. T., & Msetfi, R. M. (2019). When and how video games can be good: A review of the positive effects of video games on well-being. *Perspectives on Psychological Science, 14*(6), 1096–1104. https://doi.org/10.1177/1745691619863807

Hales, C. M., Carroll, M., Fryar, C. D., & Ogden, C. L. (2017). Prevalence of obesity among adults and youth: United States, 2015–2016. *National Center for Health Statistics Brief No. 288.* NCHS.

Halfmann, E., Bredehöft, J., & Häusser, J. A. (2020). Replicating roaches: A preregistered direct replication of Zajonc, Heingartner, and Herman's (1969) social-facilitation study. *Psychological Science, 31*(3), 332–337. https://doi.org/10.1177/0956797620902101

Halim, M. L., Ruble, D., Tamis-LeMonda, C., & Shrout, P. E. (2013). Rigidity in gender-typed behaviors in early childhood: A longitudinal study of ethnic minority children. *Child Development, 84,* 1269–1284

Halim, M. L., Ruble, D. N., Tamis-LeMonda, C. S., Zosuls, K. M., Lurye, L. E., & Greulich, F. K. (2014). Pink frilly dresses and the avoidance of all things "girly": Children's appearance rigidity and cognitive theories of gender development. *Developmental Psychology, 50,* 1091–1101.

Halpern, D. F. (1996). Public policy implications of sex differences in cognitive abilities. *Psychology, Public Policy and Law, 2*(3/4), 564.

Halpern, D. F., & LeMay, M. L. (2000). The smarter sex: A critical review of sex-differences in intelligence. *Educational Psychology Review, 12,* 229–246.

Halpern, D. F., Benbow, C. P., Geary, D. C., Gur, R. C., Hyde, J. S., & Gernsbacher, M. A. (2007). The science of sex differences in science and mathematics. *Psychological Science in the Public Interest, 8,* 1–51.

Halpern, J. H., & Pope, H. G., Jr. (2003). Hallucinogen persisting perception disorder: What do we know after 50 years? *Drug and Alcohol Dependence, 69,* 109–119.

Halpern, M. (2016). How children learn their mother tongue: They don't. *Journal of Psycholinguistic Research, 45*(5), 1173–1181. doi:10.1007/s10936-015-9378-y

Hamani, C., Mayberg, H., Snyder, B., Giacobbe, P., Kennedy, S., & Lozano, A. M. (2009). Deep brain stimulation of the subcallosal cingulated gyrus for depression: Anatomical location of active contacts in clinical responders and a suggested guideline for targeting. *Journal of Neurosurgery, 111,* 1209–1215.

Hamel, R., & Elshout, J. (2000). On the development of knowledge during problem solving. *Journal of Cognitive Psychology, 12,* 289–322.

Hamer, D. (2002). Genetics. Rethinking behavior genetics. *Science, 298,* 71–72.

Hamilton, C. E. (2000). Continuity and discontinuity of attachment from infancy through adolescence. *Child Development, 71,* 690–694.

Hamilton, L. D., & Julian, A. M. (2014). The relationship between daily hassles and sexual function in men and women. *Journal of Sex & Marital Therapy, 40,* 379–395.

Hamlat, E. J., Snyder, H. R., Young, J. F., & Hankin, B. L. (2019). Pubertal timing as a transdiagnostic risk for psychopathology in youth. *Clinical Psychological Science, 7*(3), 411-429. doi:10.1177/2167702618810518

Hammen, C. (2009). Adolescent depression: Stressful interpersonal contexts and risk for recurrence. *Current Directions in Psychological Science, 18,* 200–204.

Hampson, S. E., & Goldberg, L. R. (2006). A first large cohort study of personality trait stability over the 40 years between elementary school and midlife. *Journal of Personality and Social Psychology, 91,* 763–779.

Hanisch, K. A. (1992). The Job Descriptive Index revisited: Questions about the question mark. *Journal of Applied Psychology, 77,* 377–382.

Hanisch, K. A. (1995). Behavioral families and multiple causes: Matching the complexity of responses to the complexity of antecedents. *Current Directions in Psychological Science, 4,* 156–162.

Hanisch, K. A., & Hulin, C. L. (1990). Job attitudes and organizational withdrawal: An examination of retirement and other voluntary withdrawal behaviors. *Journal of Vocational Behavior, 37,* 60–78.

Hanisch, K. A., & Hulin, C. L. (1991). General attitudes and organizational withdrawal: An evaluation of a causal model. *Journal of Vocational Behavior, 39,* 110–128.

Hanna, G. H. (2000). Clinical and family-genetic studies of childhood obsessive-compulsive disorder. In W. K. Goodman, M. V. Rudofer, & J. D. Maser (Eds.), *Obsessive-compulsive disorder: Contemporary issues in treatment* (pp. 87–103). Erlbaum.

Hanson, G., & Venturelli, F. J. (1998). *Drugs and society* (5th ed.). Jones and Bartlett.

Haque, M. M., & Washington, S. (2014). A parametric duration model of the reaction time of drivers distracted by mobile phone conversations. *Accident, Analysis and Prevention, 62,* 42–53.

Harari, G. M., Lane, N. D., Wang, R., Crosier, B. S., Campbell, A. T., & Gosling, S. D. (2016). Using smartphones to collect behavioral data in psychological science: Opportunities, practical considerations, and challenges. *Perspectives on Psychological Science, 11,* 838–854.

Hargis, M. (2008, November 5). Social networking sites dos and don'ts. CNN.com. http://www.cnn.com/2008/LIVING/worklife/11/05/cb.social.networking/index.html

Harkins, S. G. (1987). Social loafing and social facilitation. *Journal of Experimental Social Psychology, 23,* 1–18.

Harlow, H. F., & Zimmerman, R. (1959). Affectional responses in the infant monkey. *Science, 130,* 421–432.

Harlow, J. M. (1869). *Recovery from the passage of an iron bar through the head.* David Clapp & Son. (Reprinted from *Publications of the Massachusetts Medical Society, 2(3),* 327–347, 1868).

Harrigan, W. J., & Commons, M. L. (2015). Replacing Maslow's needs hierarchy with an account based on stage and value. *Behavioral Development Bulletin, 20*(1), 24–31. doi:10.1037/h0101036

Harris, A., & Seckl, J. (2011). Glucocorticoids, prenatal stress and the programming of disease. *Hormones and Behavior, 59,* 279–289.

Harris, B. (2020). Journals, referees, and gatekeepers in the dispute over Little Albert, 2009–2014. *History of Psychology, 23*(2), 103–121. https://doi.org/10.1037/hop0000087

Harris, J. D. (1943). Habituatory response decrement in the intact organism. *Psychological Bulletin, 40,* 385–422.

Harrow, M., Grossman, L. S., Jobe, T. H., & Hernener, E. S. (2005). Do patients with schizophrenia ever show periods of recovery? A 15-year multi-follow-up study. *Schizophrenia Bulletin, 31,* 723–734.

Hart, B., Risley, T.R., & Kirby, J. R. (1997). Meaningful differences in the everyday experience of young American children. *Canadian Journal of Education, 22*(3), 323.

Hartmann, A. S., Thomas, J. J., Greenberg, J. L., Matheny, N. L., & Wilhelm, S. (2014). A comparison of self-esteem and perfectionism in anorexia nervosa and body dysmorphic disorder. *The Journal of Nervous and Mental Disease, 202*(12), 883–888. doi:10.1097/NMD.0000000000000215

Hartmann, U. (2009). Sigmund Freud and his impact on our understanding of male sexual dysfunction. *Journal of Sexual Medicine, 6,* 2332–2339.

Hartshorne, J. K., & Germine, L. T. (2015). When does cognitive functioning peak? The asynchronous rise and fall of different cognitive abilities across the lifespan. *Psychological Science, 26,* 433–443.

Hasin, D., Hatzenbuehler, M. L., Keyes, K., & Ogburn, E. (2006). Substance use disorders: *Diagnostic and Statistical Manual of Mental Disorders,* fourth edition (*DSM-IV*) and *International Classification of Diseases,* tenth edition (*ICD-10*). *Addiction, 101*(Suppl. 1), 59–75.

Hasin, D. S., & Grant, B. F. (2015). The National Epidemiologic Survey on Alcohol and Related Conditions (NESARC) Waves 1 and 2: Review and summary of findings. *Social Psychiatry and Psychiatric Epidemiology, 50,* 1609–1640.

Hasin, D. S., Sarvet, A. L., Meyers, J. L., Saha, T. D., Ruan, W. J., Stohl, M., & Grant, B. F. (2018). Epidemiology of adult *DSM-5* major depressive disorder and its specifiers in the United States. *JAMA Psychiatry, 75*(4), 336–346. doi:10.1001/jamapsychiatry.2017.4602

Haslam, C., Cruwys, T., Haslam, S. A., Dingle, G., & Chang, M. X. L. (2016). GROUPS 4 HEALTH: Evidence that a social-identity intervention that builds and strengthens social group membership improves mental health. *Journal of Affective Disorders, 194,* 188–195. doi:10.1016/j.jad.2016.01.010

Haslam, C., Haslam, S. A., Knight, C., Gleibs, I., Ysseldyk, R., & McCloskey, L. (2014). We can work it out: Group decision-making builds social identity and enhances the cognitive performance of care residents. *British Journal of Psychology, 105*(1), 17-34. doi:10.1111/bjop.12012

Hasselmo, M. E. (2010). Consciousness and neural time travel. In E. Perry, D. Collerton, F. LeBeau, & H. Ashton (Eds.), *New horizons in the neuroscience of consciousness* (pp. 73–80). Benjamins.

Hassett, J. M., Siebert, E. R., & Wallen, K. (2008). Sex differences in rhesus monkey toy preferences parallel those of children. *Hormones and Behavior, 54,* 359–364.

Hastings, E. C., Karas, T. L., Winsler, A., Way, E., Madigan, A., & Tyler, S. (2009). Young children's video/computer game use: Relations with school performance and behavior. *Issues in Mental Health Nursing, 30,* 638–649.

Hatcher, R., Trussell, J., Stewart, F., Stewart, G., Kowal, D., Guest, F., . . . Policar, M. S. (1994). *Contraceptive technology* (16th ed.). Irvington.

Hatfield, G., & Allred, S. (2012). *Visual experience: Sensation, cognition, and constancy.* Oxford University Press. doi:10.1093/acprof:oso/9780199597277.001.0001

Hatzenbuehler, M. L. (2014). Structural stigma and the health of lesbian, gay, and bisexual populations. *Current Directions in Psychological Science, 23,* 127–132.

Hatzigeorgiadis, A., Zourbanos, N., Galanis, E., & Theodorakis, Y. (2011). Self-talk and sports performance: A meta-analysis. *Psychological Science, 6,* 348–356.

Hausner, H., Nicklaus, S., Issanchou, S., Mølgaard, C., & Møller, P. (2010). Breast-feeding facilitates acceptance of a novel dietary flavor compound. *Clinical Nutrition, 29,* 141–148.

Haut, K. M., van Erp, T. G. M., Knowlton, B., Bearden, C. E., Subotnik, K., Ventura, J., . . . Cannon, T. D. (2015). Contributions of feature binding during encoding and functional connectivity of the medial temporal lobe structures to episodic memory deficits across the prodromal and first-episode phases of schizophrenia. *Clinical Psychological Science, 3,* 159–174.

Havermans, R. C., & Jansen, A. (2007). Increasing children's liking of vegetables through flavour-flavour learning. *Appetite, 48*(2), 259–262.

Hawco, C., Armony, J. L., & Lepage, M. (2013). Neural activity related to self-initiating elaborative semantic encoding in associative memory. *Neuroimage, 67,* 273–282. doi:10.1016/j.neuroimage.2012.11.004

Hawkley, L. C., & Cacioppo, J. T. (2010). Loneliness matters: A theoretical and empirical review of consequences and mechanisms. *Annals of Behavioral Medicine, 40,* 218–227.

Hawley, D. F., & Leasure, J. (2012). Region-specific response of the hippocampus to chronic unpredictable stress. *Hippocampus, 22,* 1333–1349. doi:10.1002/hipo.20970

Hayden, E. P., Dougherty, L. R., Maloney, B., Durbin, C. E., Olino, T. M., Nurnberger, J. I., . . . Klein, D. N. (2007). Temperamental fearfulness in childhood and the serotonin transporter promoter region polymorphism: A multimethod association study. *Psychiatric Genetics, 17,* 135–142.

Hayden, E. P., Klein, D. N., Dougherty, L. R., Olino, T. M., Dyson, M. W., Durbin, C. E. . . . Singh, S. M. (2010). The role of brain-derived neurotrophic factor genotype, parental depression, and relationship discord in predicting early-emerging negative emotionality. *Psychological Science, 21,* 1678–1685.

Hayes, E. R., & Plowfield, L. A. (2007). Smoking too young: Students' decisions about tobacco use. *American Journal of Maternal Child Nursing, 32,* 112–116.

Hayes, J. R. (1989). *The complete problem solver* (2nd ed). Erlbaum.

Hays, N. P., & Roberts, S. B. (2008). Aspects of eating behaviors: "Disinhibition" and "restraint" are related to weight gain and BMI in women. *Obesity, 16,* 52–58.

Hayward, M. D., Schaich-Borg, A., Pintar, J. E., & Low, M. J. (2006). Differential involvement of endogenous opioids in sucrose consumption and food reinforcement. *Pharmacology Biochemistry and Behavior, 85,* 601–611.

Heatherton, T. F., & Sargent, J. D. (2009). Does watching smoking in movies promote teenage smoking? *Current Directions in Psychological Science, 18,* 63–67.

Hebb, D. O. (1955). Drives and the CNS (conceptual nervous system). *Psychological Review, 62,* 243–255.

Hedden, T., & Park, D. C. (2003). Contributions of source and inhibitory mechanisms to age-related retroactive interference in verbal working memory. *Journal of Experimental Psychology: General, 132,* 93–122.

Hedden, T., & Yoon, C. (2006). Individual differences in executive processing predict susceptibility to interference in verbal working memory. *Neuropsychology, 20,* 511–528.

Heider, F. (1946). Attitudes and cognitive organization. *Journal of Psychology, 21,* 107–112.

Heider, F. (1958). *The psychology of interpersonal relations.* Wiley.

Heilman, M. E., & Kram, K. E. (1983). Male and female assumptions about colleagues' views of their competence. *Psychology of Women Quarterly, 7,* 329–337.

Heim, C., Bradley, B., Mietzko, T. C., Deveau, T. C., Musselman, D. L., Nemeroff, C. B., . . . Binder, E. B. (2009). Effect of childhood trauma on adult depression and neuroendocrine function: Sex-specific moderation by CRH receptor 1 gene. *Frontiers in Behavioral Neuroscience, 3,* 41.

Heim, C., Newport, D. J., Mietzko, T., Miller, A. H., & Nemeroff, C. B. (2008). The link between childhood trauma and depression: Insights from HPA axis studies in humans. *Psychoneuroendocrinology, 33,* 693–710.

Hein, S., Tan, M., Aljughaiman, A., & Grigorenko, E. L. (2015). Gender differences and school influences with respect to three indicators of general intelligence: Evidence from Saudi Arabia. *Journal of Educational Psychology, 107*(2), 486–501. doi:10.1037/a0037519

Heine, S. J. (2008). *Cultural psychology.* Norton.

Heine, S. J., Foster, J. B., & Spina, R. (2009). Do birds of a feather universally flock together? Cultural variation in the similarity-attraction effect. *Asian Journal of Social Psychology, 12,* 247–258.

Heiser, P., Dickhaus, B. Schreiber, W., Clement, H. W., Hasse, C., Hennig, J., . . . Opper, C. (2000). White blood cells and cortisol after sleep deprivation and recovery sleep in humans. *European Archives of Psychiatry and Clinical Neuroscience, 250,* 16–23.

Hejmadi, A., Davidson, R. J., & Rozin, P. (2000). Exploring Hindu Indian emotion expressions. *Psychological Science, 11,* 183–187.

Hélie, S., & Sun, R. (2010). Incubation, insight, and creative problem solving: A unified theory and connectionist model. *Psychological Review, 117,* 994–1024.

Helland, M. S., von Soest, T., Gustavson, K., Røysamb, E., & Mathiesen, K. S. (2014). Long shadows: A prospective study of predictors of relationship dissolution over 17 child-rearing years. *BMC Psychology, 2,* 40.

Helmholtz, H. L. F. von. (1930). *The sensations of tone* (A. J. Ellis, Trans.). Longmans, Green. (Original work published in 1863)

Helmuth, L. (2001). From the mouths (and hands) of babes. *Science, 293,* 1758–1759.

Helwig, C. C. (1997). Making moral cognition respectable (again): A retrospective review of Lawrence Kohlberg. *Contemporary Psychology, 42,* 191–195.

Helzer, J. E., & Canino, G. J. (Eds.). (1992). *Alcoholism in North America, Europe, and Asia.* Oxford University Press.

Hendrick, C., & Hendrick, S. S. (1983). *Liking, loving, and relating.* Brooks/Cole.

Hennessy, D. A., & Jakubowski, R. (2007). The impact of perspective and anger on the actor-observer bias among automobile drivers. *Traffic Injury Prevention, 8,* 115–122.

Hennessy, M. B., Schiml-Webb, P. A., & Deak, T. (2009). Separation, sickness, and depression: A new perspective on an old animal model. *Current Directions in Psychological Science, 18,* 227–231.

Henry, L. A., Messer, D., Luger-Klein, S., & Crane, L. (2012). Phonological, visual, and semantic coding strategies and children's short-term picture memory span. *Quarterly Journal of Experimental Psychology, 65,* 2033–2053. doi:10.1080/17470218.2012.672997

Henry, W. P., Strupp, H. H., Schacht, T. E., & Gaston, L. (1994). Psychodynamic approaches. In A. E. Bergin & S. L. Garfield (Eds.), *Handbook of psychotherapy and behavior change* (4th ed., pp. 143–189). Wiley.

Herbenick, D., Fu, T. J., Owens, C., Bartelt, E., Dodge, B., Reece, M., & Fortenberry, J. D. (2019). Kissing, cuddling, and massage at most recent sexual event: Findings from a U.S. Nationally representative probability sample. *Journal of Sex & Marital Therapy, 45*(2), 159–172. https://doi.org/10.1080/0092623X.2018.1494648

Herbenick, D., Reece, M., Schick, V., Sanders, S. A., Dodge, B., & Fortenberry, J. D. (2010). Sexual behavior in the United States: Results from a national probability sample of men and women ages 14–94. *Journal of Sexual Medicine, 7* (Suppl. 5), 255–265. doi:10.1111/j.1743-6109.2010.02012.x

Herbert, B. M., Blechert, J., Hautzinger, M., Matthias, E., & Herbert, C. (2013). Intuitive eating is associated with interoceptive sensitivity: Effects on body mass index. *Appetite, 70,* 22–30. doi:10.1016/j.appet.2013.06.082

Herculano-Houzel, S. (2011). Not all brains are made the same: New views on brain scaling in evolution. *Brain, Behavior and Evolution, 78,* 22–36. doi:10.1159/000327318

Herman, L. M., & Uyeyama, R. J. (1999). The dolphin's grammatical competency: Comments on Kako (1999). *Animal Learning and Behavior, 27,* 18–23.

Herman, L. M., Kuczaj, S. A., II, & Holder, M. D. (1993). Responses to anomalous gestural sequences by a language-trained dolphin: Evidence for processing of semantic relations and syntactical information. *Journal of Experimental Psychology: General, 122,* 184–194.

Heron, M. (2019). Deaths: Leading causes for 2017. *National Vital Statistics Reports, 68,* No 6. National Center for Health Statistics.

Herrera, N. C., Zajonc, R. B., Wieczorkowska, G., & Cichomski, B. (2003). Beliefs about birth rank and their reflection in reality. *Journal of Personality and Social Psychology, 85,* 142–150.

Herrnstein, R., & Murray, C. (1994). *The bell curve.* Free Press.

Hertel, P. T., & Brozovich, F. (2010). Cognitive habits and memory distortions in anxiety and depression. *Current Directions in Psychological Science, 19,* 155–160.

Hertzog, C., Kramer, A. F., Wilson, R. S., & Lindenberger, U. (2008). Enrichment effects on adult cognitive development: Can the functional capacity of older adults be preserved and enhanced? *Psychological Science in the Public Interest, 9,* 1–65.

Hesse, E., & Main, M. (2006). Frightened, threatening, and dissociative parental behavior in low-risk samples: Description, discussion, and interpretations. *Development and Psychopathology, 18,* 309–343.

Hesslinger, V. M., & Carbon, C.-C. (2016). #TheDress: The role of illumination information and individual differences in the psychophysics of perceiving white-blue ambiguities. *I-Perception, 7*(2), article ID 2041669516645592. doi:10.1177/2041669516645592

Hettema, J. M., Kettenmann, B., Ahluwalia, V. McCarthy, C., Kates, W. R., Schmitt, J. E., . . . Fatouros, P. (2012). Pilot multimodal twin imaging study of generalized anxiety disorder. *Depression and Anxiety, 29,* 202–209.

Hewstone, M., Rubin, M., & Willis, H. (2002). Intergroup bias (social prejudice). *Annual Review of Psychology, 53,* 575–604.

Hicks, B. M., Krueger, R. F., Iacono, W. G., McGue, M., & Patrick, C. J. (2004). Family transmission and heritability of externalizing disorders: A twin-family study. *Archives of General Psychiatry, 61,* 922–928.

Higa-McMillan, C. K., Francis, S. E., Rith-Najarian, L., & Chorpita, B. F. (2016). Evidence base update: 50 years of research on treatment for child and adolescent anxiety. *Journal of Clinical Child and Adolescent Psychology, 45*(2), 91-113. doi:10.1080/15374416.2015.1046177

Higbee, K. L., & Clay, S. L. (1998). College students' beliefs in the ten-percent myth. *Journal of Psychology, 132,* 469–476.

Higuchi, S., & Saito, T. (2013). Reduction in alcohol consumption: Therapeutic goal in alcohol dependence treatment [Abstract]. *Nihon Arukoru Yakubutsu Igakkai Zasshi, 48,* 17–31.

Hikosaka, O., Nakamura, K., Sakai, K., & Nakamura, H. (2002). Central mechanisms of motor skill learning. *Current Opinion in Neurobiology, 12,* 217–222.

Hilgard, E. R. (1977). *Divided consciousness: Multiple controls in human thought and action.* Wiley.

Hilgard, E. R. (1992). Divided consciousness and dissociation. *Consciousness and Cognition, 1,* 16–31.

Hilgard, E. R., Morgan, A. H., & MacDonald, H. (1975). Pain and dissociation in the cold pressor test: A study of "hidden reports" through automatic key-pressing and automatic talking. *Journal of Abnormal Psychology, 84,* 280–289.

Hilgart, M., Thorndike, F. P., Pardo, J., & Ritterband, L. M. (2012). Ethical issues of web-based interventions and online therapy. In M. M. Leach, M. J. Stevens, G. Lindsay, A. Ferrero, & Y. Korkut (Eds.), *The Oxford handbook of international psychological ethics* (pp. 426–464). Oxford University Press.

Hill, C. E., & Nakayama, E. Y. (2000). Client-centered therapy: Where has it been and where is it going? A comment on Hathaway (1948). *Journal of Clinical Psychology, 56,* 861–875.

Hill, P. C., & Pargament, K. I. (2003). Advances in the conceptualization and measurement of religion and spirituality. Implications for physical and mental health research. *American Psychologist, 58,* 64–74.

Hill, P. L., & Turiano, N. A. (2014). Purpose in life as a predictor of mortality across adulthood. *Psychological Science, 25,* 1482–1486.

Hill-Soderlund, A. L., & Braungart-Rieker, J. M. (2008). Early individual differences in temperamental reactivity and regulation: Implications for effortful control in early childhood. *Infant Behavior and Development, 31,* 386–397.

Himmerich, H., Hotopf, M., Shetty, H., Schmidt, U., Treasure, J., Hayes, R. D., ... Chang, C.-K. (2019). Psychiatric comorbidity as a risk factor for mortality in people with anorexia nervosa. *European Archives of Psychiatry and Clinical Neuroscience, 269*(3), 351–359. https://doi.org/10.1007/s00406-018-0937-8

Hines, M., Constantinescu, M., & Spencer, D. (2015). Early androgen exposure and human gender development. *Biology of Sex Differences, 6,* 3. doi:10.1186/s13293-015-0022-1

Hingson, R. W., Heeren, T., Zakocs, R. C., Kopstein, A., & Wechsler, H. (2002). Magnitude of alcohol-related mortality and morbidity among U.S. college students ages 18-24. *Journal of Studies on Alcohol, 63*(2), 136–144. https://doi.org/10.15288/jsa.2002.63.136

Hingston, S. T., & Noseworthy, T. J. (2020). On the epidemic of food waste: Idealized prototypes and the aversion to misshapen fruits and vegetables. *Food Quality and Preference, 86,* 103999. doi:10.1016/j.foodqual.2020.103999

Hiroto, D. S. (1974). Locus of control and learned helplessness. *Journal of Experimental Psychology, 102,* 187–193.

Hirsch, C. R., Beale, S., Grey, N., & Liness, S. (2019). Approaching cognitive behavior therapy for generalized anxiety disorder from a cognitive process perspective. *Frontiers in Psychiatry, 10,* 796. doi:10.3389/fpsyt.2019.00796

Hirsch, M. S., Conway, B., D'Aquila, R. T., Johnson, V. A., Brun-Vezinet, F., Clotet, B., . . . Richman, D. D. (1998). Antiretroviral drug resistance testing in adults with HIV infection: Implications for clinical management. *Journal of the American Medical Association, 279,* 1984–1991.

Hirschberger, G., Srivastava, S., Marsh, P., Cowan, C. P., & Cowan, P. A. (2009).

Attachment, marital satisfaction, and divorce during the first fifteen years of parenthood. *Personal Relationships, 16,* 401–420.

Hirshkowitz, M., Moore, C. A., & Minhoto, G. (1997). The basics of sleep. In M. R. Pressman & W. C. Orr (Eds.), *Understanding sleep: The evaluation and treatment of sleep disorders* (pp. 11–34). American Psychological Association.

Hirshkowitz, M., Whiton, K., Albert, S. M., Alessi, C., Bruni, O., DonCarlos, L., … Hillard, A. (2015). National Sleep Foundation's sleep time duration recommendations: Methodology and results summary. *Sleep Health, 1*(1), 40-43.

Hirst, W., & Phelps, E. A. (2016). Flashbulb memories. *Current Directions in Psychological Science, 25*(1), 36–41. doi:10.1177/0963721415622487

Hirst, W., Phelps, E. A., Buckner, R. L., Budson, A. E., Cuc, A., Gabrieli, J. E., . . . Vaidya, C. J. (2009). Long-term memory for the terrorist attack of September 11: Flashbulb memories, event memories, and the factors that influence their retention. *Journal of Experimental Psychology: General, 138,* 161–176. doi:10.1037/a0015527

Hirst, W., Phelps, E. A., Meksin, R., Vaidya, C. J., Johnson, M. K., Mitchell, K. J., . . . Olsson, A. (2015). A ten-year follow-up of a study of memory for the attack of September 11, 2001: Flashbulb memories and memories for flashbulb events. *Journal of Experimental Psychology: General, 144*(3), 604–623. doi:10.1037/xge0000055

Hively, K., & El-Alayli, A. (2014). "You throw like a girl:" The effect of stereotype threat on women's athletic performance and gender stereotypes. *Psychology of Sport and Exercise, 15,* 48–55. doi:10.1016/j.psychsport.2013.09.001

Ho, B. C., Black, D. W., & Andreasen, N. C. (2003). Schizophrenia and other psychotic disorders. In R. E. Hales & S. C. Yudofsky (Eds.), *Textbook of clinical psychiatry* (4th ed., pp. 379–438). American Psychiatric Publishing.

Hobbs, W. R., Burke, M., Christakis, N. A., & Fowler, J. H. (2016). Online social integration is associated with reduced mortality risk. *Proceedings of the National Academy of Sciences of the United States of America, 113,* 12980–12984.

Hobson, J. A., & McCarley, R. W. (1977). The brain as a dream state generator: An activation-synthesis hypothesis of the dream process. *American Journal of Psychiatry, 134,* 1335–1348.

Hobson, J. A., Pace-Schott, E., & Stickgold, R. (2000). Dreaming and the brain: Toward a cognitive neuroscience of conscious states. *Behavioral and Brain Sciences, 23,* 783–842.

Hodson, G., Dovidio, J. F., & Gaertner, S. L. (2002). Processes in racial discrimination: Differential weighting of conflicting information. *Personality and Social Psychology, 28,* 460–471.

Hodson, G., Dovidio, J. F., & Gaertner, S. L. (2010). The aversive form of racism. In J. Chin (Ed.), *The psychology of prejudice and discrimination: A revised and condensed edition* (pp. 1-13). Praeger/ABC-CLIO.

Hodson, N. A., & Linden, R. W. A. (2006). The effect of monosodium glutamate on parotid salivary flow in comparison to the response to representatives of the other four basic tastes. *Physiology and Behavior, 89,* 711–717.

Hoeft, F., Gabrieli, J. D., Whitfield-Gabrieli, S., Haas, B. W., Bammer, R., Menon, V., & Spiegel, D. (2012). Functional brain basis of hypnotizability. *Archives of General Psychiatry, 69,* 1064–1072.

Hofmann, S. G., & Smits, J. A. (2008). Cognitive-behavioral therapy for adult anxiety disorders: A meta-analysis of randomized placebo-controlled trials. *Journal of Clinical Psychiatry, 69,* 621–632.

Holden, C. (1980, November). Twins reunited. *Science, 80,* 55–59.

Holland, A. J., Sicotte, N., & Treasure, J. (1988). Anorexia nervosa: Evidence of a genetic basis. *Journal of Psychosomatic Research, 32,* 561–571.

Hollos, M., & Richards, F. A. (1993). Gender-associated development of formal operations in Nigerian adolescents. *Ethos, 21,* 24–52.

Holmans, P., Weissman, M. M., Zubenko, G. S., Scheftner, W. A., Crowe, R. R., Depaulo, J. R., . . . Levinson, D. F. (2007). Genetics of recurrent early-onset major depression (GenRED): Final genome scan report. *American Journal of Psychiatry, 164,* 248–258.

Holmes, T. H., & Rahe, R. H. (1967). The Social Readjustment Rating Scale. *Journal of Psychosomatic Research, 11,* 213–218.

Holmqvist, J. L., Hill, T., & Lang, A. (2009). Effects of aggression replacement training in young offender institutions. *International Journal of Offender Therapy and Comparative Criminology, 53,* 74–92.

Holt, E. W., Rung, A. L., Leon, K. A., Firestein, C., & Krousel-Wood, M. (2014). Medication adherence in older adults: A qualitative study. *Educational Gerontology, 40,* 198–211. doi:10.1080/03601277.2013.802186

Holt-Lunstad, J. (2018). Why social relationships are important for physical health: A systems approach to understanding and modifying risk and protection. *Annual Review of Psychology, 69,* 437-458.

Holt-Lunstad, J., Birmingham, W., & Jones, B. Q. (2008). Is there something unique about marriage? The relative impact of marital status, relationship quality, and network social support on ambulatory blood pressure and mental health. *Annals of Behavioral Medicine, 35,* 239–244.

Holt-Lunstad, J., Smith, T. B., Baker, M., Harris, T., & Stephenson, D. (2015). Loneliness and social isolation as risk factors for mortality: A meta-analytic review. *Perspectives on Psychological Science, 10,* 227–237.

Holt-Lunstad, J., Smith, T. B., & Layton, J. B. (2010). Social relationships and mortality risk: A meta-analytic review. *PLoS Medicine, 7,* e1000316.

Holzel, B. K., Lazar, S. W., Gard, T., Schuman-Olivier, Z., Vago, D. R., & Ott, U. (2011). How does mindfulness meditation work? Proposing mechanisms of action from a conceptual and neural perspective. *Perspectives on Psychological Science, 6,* 537–559.

Homberg, J. R., Olivier, J. D. A., VandenBroeke, M., Youn, J., Ellenbroek, A. K., Karel, P., . . . Ellenbroek, B. A. (2016). The role of the dopamine D1 receptor in social cognition: Studies using a novel genetic rat model. *Disease Models and Mechanisms 9*(10), 1147–1158. doi:10.1242/dmm.024752

Hong, Y., Chiu, C., Dweck, C. S., Lin, D. M.S., & Wan, W. (1999). Implicit theories, attributions, and coping: A meaning system approach. *Journal of Personality and Social Psychology, 77*(3), 588–599. https://doi.org/10.1037/0022-3514.77.3.588

Hood, D. C , & Finkelstein, M. A. (1986). Sensitivity to light. In K. R. Boff, L. Kaufman, & J. P. Thomas (Eds.), *Handbook of perception and human performance* (pp. 5.1–5.66). Wiley.

Hooley, J. M. (2007). Expressed emotion and relapse of psychopathology. *Annual Review of Clinical Psychology, 3,* 329–352.

Hooley, J. M. (2010). Social factors in schizophrenia. *Current Directions in Psychological Science, 19,* 238–242.

Hopthrow, T., Hooper, N., Mahmood, L., Meier, B. P., & Weger, U. (2017). Mindfulness reduces the correspondence bias. *The Quarterly Journal of Experimental Psychology, 70*(3), 351–360. doi:10.1080/17470218.2016.1149498

Horgan, D. D. (1995). *Achieving gender equity: Strategies for the classroom.* Allyn & Bacon.

Horgan, J. (1996, December). Why Freud isn't dead. *Scientific American,* pp. 106–111.

Horiguchi, H., Winawer, J., Dougherty, R. F., & Wandell, B. A. (2013). Human trichromacy revisited. *PNAS: Proceedings of the National Academy of Sciences of the United States of America, 110,* E260–E269. doi:10.1073/pnas.1214240110

Horn, J. L. (1982). The aging of human abilities. In B. B. Wolman (Ed.), *Handbook of developmental psychology* (pp. 847–870). Prentice-Hall.

Horn, J. L., Donaldson, G., & Engstrom, R. (1981). Apprehension, memory, and fluid intelligence decline through the "vital years" of adulthood. *Research on Aging, 3,* 33–84.

Hornboll, B. Macoveanu, J., Rowe, J., Elliott, R., Paulson, O. B., Siebner, H. R., & Knudsen, G. M. (2013). Acute serotonin 2A receptor blocking alters the processing of fearful faces in the orbitofrontal cortex and amygdala. *Journal of Psychopharmacology, 27,* 903–914.

Horne, J. A., & Staff, L. H. E. (1983). Exercise and sleep: Body-heating effects. *Sleep, 6,* 36–46.

Horney, K. (1937). *The neurotic personality of our time.* Norton.

Horney, K. (1939). *New ways in psychoanalysis.* Norton.

Hornsey, M. J., Bain, P. G., Harris, E. A., Lebedeva, N., Kashima, E. S., Guan, Y., … Blumen, S. (2018). How much is enough in a perfect world? Cultural variation in ideal levels of happiness, pleasure, freedom, health, self-esteem, longevity, and intelligence. *Psychological Science, 29*(9), 1393-1404.

Hornstein, E. A., & Eisenberger, N. I. (2018). A social safety net: Developing a model of social-support figures as prepared safety stimuli. *Current Directions in Psychological Science, 27*(1), 25-31.

Hornyak, M., Feige, B., Riemann, D., & Voderholzer, U. (2006). Periodic leg movements in sleep and periodic limb movement disorder: Prevalence, clinical significance and treatment. *Sleep Medicine Reviews, 10,* 169–177.

Horton, C. L., & Malinowski, J. E. (2015). Autobiographical memory and hyperassociativity in the dreaming brain: Implications for memory consolidation in sleep. *Frontiers in Psychology, 6,* 874.

Horváth, K., & Plunkett, K. (2016). Frequent daytime naps predict vocabulary growth in early childhood. *Journal of Child Psychology and Psychiatry, 57*(9), 1008–1017. doi:10.1111/jcpp.12583

Horvitz-Lennon, M., Volya, R., Garfield, R., Donohue, J. M., Lave, J. R., & Normand,

S. L. T. (2015). Where you live matters: Quality and racial/ethnic disparities in schizophrenia care in four state medicaid programs. *Health Services Research, 50,* 1710–1729.

Hosking, S. G., Young, K. L., & Regan, M. A. (2009). The effects of text messaging on young drivers. *Human Factors, 51,* 582–592.

Hovey, J. D. (2000). Psychosocial predictors of depression among Central American immigrants. *Psychological Reports, 86,* 1237–1240.

Hovland, C. I., & Weiss, W. (1951). The influence of source credibility on communication effectiveness. *Public Opinion Quarterly, 15,* 635–650.

Howard, D. J. (2019). A dual process theory explanation for door-in-the-face effectiveness. *Basic and Applied Social Psychology, 41*(5), 273–286. https://doi.org/10.1080/01973533.2019.1648265

Howe, M. L. (2000). *The rate of early memories.* American Psychological Association.

Howerton, A., & Van Gundy, K. (2009). Sex differences in coping styles and implications for depressed mood. *International Journal of Stress Management, 16*(4), 333-350.

Howes, O., McCutcheon, R., & Stone, J. (2015). Glutamate and dopamine in schizophrenia: An update for the 21st century. *Journal of Psychopharmacology* (Oxford, England), *29,* 97–115.

Howland, J., Rohsenow, D. J., Arnedt, J. T., Bliss, C. A., Hunt, S. K., Calise, T. V., . . . Gottlieb, D. J. (2011). The acute effects of caffeinated versus non-caffeinated alcoholic beverage on driving performance and attention/reaction time. *Addiction, 106,* 335–341.

Hoyland, A., Dye, L., & Lawton, C. L. (2009). A systematic review of the effect of breakfast on the cognitive performance of children and adolescents. *Nutrition Research Reviews, 22,* 220–243.

Hsu, K. J., & Davison, G. C. (2017). Compounded deficits: The association between neuropsychological impairment and attention biases in currently depressed, formerly depressed, and never depressed individuals. *Clinical Psychological Science, 5,* 286–298.

Hu, J., Chiang, L. Y., Koch, M., & Lewin, G. R. (2010). Evidence for a protein tether involved in somatic touch. *EMBO Journal, 29,* 855–867. doi:10.1038/emboj.2009.398

Hu, T., Zhang, D., & Ran, G. (2016). Self-serving attributional bias among Chinese adolescents. *Personality and Individual Differences, 91,* 80–83. doi:10.1016/j.paid.2015.10.008

Hu, W., MacDonald, M. L., Elswick, D. E., & Sweet, R. A. (2015). The glutamate hypothesis of schizophrenia: Evidence from human brain tissue studies. *Annals of the New York Academy of Sciences, 1338,* 38–57.

Huang, C. J., Webb, H. E., Zourdos, M. C., & Acevedo, E. O. (2013). Cardiovascular reactivity, stress, and physical activity. *Frontiers in Physiology, 4,* 314.

Hubel, D. H. (1995). *Eye, brain, and vision.* Scientific American Library.

Huber, D., Henrich, G., & Gündel, H. (2005). Psychophysiological response patterns of migraine patients in two habituation tests. *Headache: The Journal of Head and Face Pain, 45,* 1375–1387.

Hudson, A. J. (2009). Consciousness: Physiological dependence on rapid memory access. *Frontiers in Bioscience, 14,* 2779–2800.

Hudson, S., & Ramsey, J. (2011). The emergence and analysis of synthetic cannabinoids. *Drug Testing & Analysis, 3,* 466–478.

Huesmann, L. R. (Ed.). (1994). *Aggressive behavior: Current perspectives.* Plenum Press.

Huff, N. C., Hernandez, J. A., Blanding, N. Q., & LaBar, K. S. (2009). Delayed extinction attenuates conditioned fear renewal and spontaneous recovery in humans. *Behavioral Neuroscience, 123,* 834–843.

Huff, W., Lenartz, D., Schormann, M., Lee, S. H., Kuhn, J., Koulousakis, A., . . . Sturm, V. (2010). Unilateral deep brain stimulation of the nucleus accumbens in patients with treatment-resistant obsessive-compulsive disorder: Outcomes after 1 year. *Clinical Neurology and Neurosurgery, 112,* 137–143.

Huffcutt, A. I. (2011). An empirical review of the employment interview construct literature. *International Journal of Selection and Assessment, 19*(1), 62-81. doi: 10.1111/j.1468-2389.2010.00535.x

Huffcutt, A. I., & Arthur, W., Jr. (1994). Hunter and Hunter (1984) revisited: Interview validity for entry-level jobs. *Journal of Applied Psychology, 79,* 184–190.

Huffcutt, A. I., Conway, J. M., Roth, P. L., & Stone, N. J. (2001). Identification and meta-analytic assessment of psychological constructs measured in employment interviews. *Journal of Applied Psychology, 86,* 897–913.

Huffziger, S., Reinhard, I., & Kuehner, C. (2009). A longitudinal study of rumination and distraction in formerly depressed inpatients and community controls. *Journal of Abnormal Psychology, 118,* 746–756.

Hughes, D. J., Furnham, A., & Batey, M. (2013). The structure and personality predictors of self-rated creativity. *Thinking Skills and Creativity, 9,* 76–84. doi:10.1016/j.tsc.2012.10.001

Hughes, J., Smith, T. W., Kosterlitz, H. W., Fothergill, L. A., Morgan, B. A., & Morris, H. R. (1975). Identification of two related pentapeptides from the brain with potent opiate agonist activity. *Nature, 258,* 577–579.

Hughes, J. W., Fresco, D. M., Myerscough, R., van Dulmen, M. H., Carlson, L. E., & Josephson, R. (2013). Randomized controlled trial of mindfulness-based stress reduction for prehypertension. *Psychosomatic Medicine, 75,* 721–728.

Hughes, M. E., & Waite, L. J. (2009). Marital biography and health at mid-life. *Journal of Health and Social Behavior, 50,* 344–358.

Hughes, Z. A., Liu, F., Marquis, K., Muniz, L., Pangalos, M. N., Ring, R. H., . . . Brandon, N. J. (2009). Estrogen receptor neurobiology and its potential for translation into broad spectrum therapeutics for CNS Disorders. *Current Molecular Pharmacology, 2,* 215–236.

Hulbert, A. (2003). Colour vision: Primary visual cortex shows its influence. *Current Biology, 13,* R270–R272.

Hull, C. L. (1943). *Principles of behavior.* Appleton-Century-Crofts.

Human Rights Campaign. (2019). Hate crimes state maps of laws and policies. https://www.hrc.org/state-maps/hate-crimes#

Hummel, M., & Unterwald, E. M. (2002). D1 dopamine receptor: A putative neurochemical and behavioral link to cocaine action. *Journal of Cell Physiology, 191,* 17–27.

Hunt, R. R. (2002). How effective are pharmacologic agents for alcoholism? *Journal of Family Practice, 51,* 577.

Hunter, E. C., Sierra, M., & David, A. S. (2004). The epidemiology of personalization and derealisation: A systematic review. *Social Psychiatry and Psychiatric Epidemiology, 39,* 9–18.

Hupp, J. M., Smith, J. L., Coleman, J. M., & Brunell, A. B. (2010). That's a boy's toy: Gender-typed knowledge in toddlers as a function of mother's marital status. *Journal of Genetic Psychology, 171,* 389–401.

Hurlstone, M. J., Hitch, G. J., & Baddeley, A. D. (2014). Memory for serial order across domains: An overview of the literature and directions for future research. *Psychological Bulletin, 140,* 339–373. doi:10.1037/a0034221

Hurvich, L. M., & Jameson, D. (2000). An opponent-process theory of color vision. In S. Yantis (Ed.), *Visual perception: Essential readings* (pp. 129–144). Psychology Press. (Original work published 1957)

Huttenlocher, P. R. (2002). *Neural plasticity: The effects of environment on the development of the cerebral cortex.* Harvard University Press.

Hyde, J. S., & McKinley, N. M. (1997). Gender differences in cognition: Results from meta-analyses. In P. J. Caplan, M. Crawford, J. S. Hyde, & J. T. E. Richardson (Eds.), *Gender differences in human cognition* (pp. 30–51). Oxford University Press.

Hyde, J. S., Fenneman, E., & Lamon, S. (1990). Gender differences in mathematics performance: A meta-analysis. *Psychological Bulletin, 107,* 139–155.

Hyland, P., Shevlin, M., Adamson, G., & Boduszek, D. (2014). The organization of irrational beliefs in posttraumatic stress symptomology: Testing the predictions of REBT theory using structural equation modelling. *Journal of Clinical Psychology, 70,* 48–59.

Idogho, J. A., & Osuya, O. (2020). Teaching emotional intelligence through drama: A report of the UNIBEN consultancy primary II pupils project. *Gender & Behaviour, 18*(2), 15707–15718.

Iervolino, A. C., Perroud, N., Rullana, M. A., Guipponi, M., Cherkas, L., Collier, D. A., & Mataix-Cols, D. (2009). Prevalence and heritability of compulsive hoarding: A twin study. *American Journal of Psychiatry, 166,* 1156–1161.

Igarashi, H., Hooker, K., Coehlo, & Manoogian, M. M. (2013). "My nest is full": Intergenerational relationships at midlife. *Journal of Aging Studies, 27,* 102–112.

Iidaka, T., Anderson, N. D., Kapur, S., Cabeza, S., & Craik, F. I. M. (2000). The effect of divided attention on encoding and retrieval in episodic memory revealed by positron emission tomography. *Journal of Cognitive Neuroscience, 12,* 267.

Ikonomidou, C., Bittigau, P., Ishimaru, M. J., Wozniak, D. F., Koch, C., Genz, K., . . . Olney, J. W. (2000). Ethanol-induced apoptotic neurodegeneration and fetal alcohol syndrome. *Science, 287,* 1056–1060.

Ilgen, M. A., & Hutchison, K. E. (2005). A history of major depressive disorder and the response to stress. *Journal of Affective Disorders, 86,* 143–150.

Inagaki, T. K., & Orehek, E. (2017). On the benefits of giving social support: When, why, and how support providers gain by caring for others. *Current Directions in Psychological Science, 26,* 109–113

Incollingo Rodriguez, A. C., White, M. L., Standen, E. C., Mann, T., Wells, C. R., & Tomiyama, A. J. (2019). Body mass index and educational inequality: An update of Crandall (1995). *Stigma and Health, 4*(3), 357–363. https://doi.org/10.1037/sah0000149

Ineichen, B. (1979). The social geography of marriage. In M. Cook & G. Wilson (Eds.), *Love and attraction* (pp. 145–149). Pergamon Press.

Infante-Rivard, C., Fernandez, A., Gauthier, R., David, M., & Rivard, G. E. (1993). Fetal loss associated with caffeine intake before and during pregnancy. *Journal of the American Medical Association, 270,* 2940–2943.

Ingram, R. E., Hayes, A., & Scott, W. (2000). Empirically supported treatments: A critical analysis. In C. R. Snyder & R. E. Ingram (Eds.), *Handbook of psychological change: Psychotherapy processes and practices for the 21st century* (pp. 40–60). Wiley.

Innes, C. R., Poudel, G. R., & Jones, R. D. (2013). Efficient and regular patterns of nighttime sleep are related to increased vulnerability to microsleeps following a single night of sleep restriction. *Chronobiology International, 30,* 1187–1196.

Innis, N. K. (1979). Stimulus control of behavior during postreinforcement pause of FI schedules. *Animal Learning and Behavior, 7,* 203–210.

Inostroza, M., & Born, J. (2013). Sleep for preserving and transforming episodic memory. *Annual Review of Neuroscience, 36,* 79–102.

Insel, T., Cuthbert, B., Garvey, M., Heinssen, R., Pine, D., Quinn, K., . . . Wang, P. (2010). Research domain criteria (RDoC): Toward a new classification framework for research on mental disorders. *American Journal of Psychiatry, 167,* 748–751.

Inzlicht, M., & Ben-Zeev, T. (2000). A threatening intellectual environment: Why females are susceptible to experiencing problem-solving deficits in the presence of males. *Psychological Science, 11,* 365–371.

Inzlicht, M., & Tullett, A. M. (2010). Reflecting on God: Religious primes can reduce neurophysiological response to errors. *Psychological Science, 21,* 1184–1190.

Ionescu, D. F., Rosenbaum, J. F., & Alpert, J. E. (2015). Pharmacological approaches to the challenge of treatment-resistant depression. *Dialogues in Clinical Neuroscience, 17*(2), 111–126.

Isa, M. R., Moy, F. M., Abdul Razack, A. H., Zainuddin, Z. M., & Zainal, N. Z. (2013). Impact of applied progressive deep muscle relation training on the level of depression, anxiety and stress among prostate cancer patients: A quasi-experimental study. *Asian Pacific Journal of Cancer Research, 14,* 2237–2242.

Isaac, M., & Chand, P. K. (2006). Dissociative and conversion disorders: Defining boundaries. *Current Opinion in Psychiatry, 19,* 61–66.

Isenberg, N., Silbersweig, D., Engelien, A., Emmerich, S., Malavade, K., Beattie, B., . . . Stern, E. (1999). Linguistic threat activates the human amygdala. *Proceedings of the National Academy of Sciences, USA, 96,* 10456–10459.

Iso, H., Simoda, S., & Matsuyama, T. (2006). Environmental change during postnatal development alters behavior, cognitions, and neurogenesis of mice. *Behavioural Brain Research, 179,* 90–98.

Iverson, L. (2003). Cannabis and the brain. *Brain, 126,* 1252–1270.

Izac, S. M. (2006). Basic anatomy and physiology of sleep. *American Journal of Electroneurodiagnostic Technology, 46,* 18–38.

Jaaro-Peled, H., Ayhan, Y., Pletnikov, M. V., & Sawa, A. (2010). Review of pathological hallmarks of schizophrenia: Comparison of genetic models with patients and nongenetic models. *Schizophrenia Bulletin, 36,* 301–313.

Jablensky, A. (2000). Epidemiology of schizophrenia: The global burden of disease and disability. *European Archives of Psychiatry and Clinical Neuroscience, 250,* 274–285.

Jablin, F. M. (1982). Organizational communication: An assimilation approach. In M. E. Rolff & C. R. Berger (Eds.), *Social cognition and communication* (pp. 255–286). SAGE.

Jackson, J. B., Miller, R. B., Oka, M., & Henry, R. G. (2014). Gender differences in marital satisfaction: A meta-analysis. *Journal of Marriage and Family, 76,* 105-129. doi:10.1111/jomf.12077

Jackson, J. L., Thoemmes, F., Jonkmann, K., Ludtke, O., & Trautwein, U. (2012). Military training and personality trait development: Does the military make the man, or does the man make the military? *Psychological Science, 23,* 270–277.

Jackson, P. A., Pialoux, V., Corbett, D., Drogos, L., Erickson, K., Eskes, G. A., & Poulin, M. J. (2016). Promoting brain health through exercise and diet in older adults: A physiological perspective. *The Journal of Physiology, 594,* 4485–4498.

Jackson, S., & Blake, R. (2010). Neural integration of information specifying human structure from form, motion, and depth. *Journal of Neuroscience, 30,* 838–848.

Jacobs, L. F., & Hyman, J. S. (2013). *The secrets of college success.* 2nd ed. Jossey-Bass.

Jacoby, L. L., Debner, J. A., & Hay, J. F. (2001). Proactive interference, accessibility bias, and process dissociations: Valid subjective reports of memory. *Journal of Experimental Psychology: Learning, Memory, and Cognition, 27,* 686–700.

Jadack, R. A., Hyde, J. S., Moore, C. F., & Keller, M. L. (1995). Moral reasoning about sexually transmitted diseases. *Child Development, 66,* 167–177.

Jaffari-Bimmel, N., Juffer, F., van Ijzendoorn, M. H., Bakermans-Kranenburg, M. J., & Mooijaart, A. (2006). Social development from infancy to adolescence: Longitudinal and concurrent factors in an adoption sample. *Developmental Psychology, 42,* 1143–1153.

Jaffee, S., & Hyde, J. (2000). Gender differences in moral orientation: A meta-analysis. *Psychological Bulletin, 126,* 703–726.

Jain, G., Gaeth, G. J., Nayakankuppam, D., & Levin, I. P. (2020). Revisiting attribute framing: The impact of number roundedness on framing. *Organizational Behavior and Human Decision Processes, 161,* 109–119.

Jain, V., Srivastava, I., Palchaudhuri, S., Goel, M., Sinha-Mahapatra, S. K., & Dhingra, N. K. (2016). Classical photoreceptors are primarily responsible for the pupillary light reflex in mouse. *PLoS ONE, 11*(6), e0157226. doi:10.1371/journal.pone.0157226

Jaint, N., Verma, P., Mittal, S., Singh, A. K., & Munjal, S. (2010). Gender based alteration in color perception. *Indian Journal of Physiological Pharmacology, 54,* 366–370.

Jairam, D., Kiewra, K. A., Rogers-Kasson, S., Patterson-Hazley, M., & Marxhausen, K. (2014). SOAR versus SQ3R: A test of two study systems. *Instructional Science, 42*(3), 409–420. https://doi.org/10.1007/s11251-013-9295-0

Jakobsen, J. C., Hansen, J. L., Simonsen, E., & Gluud, C. (2012). The effect of adding psychodynamic therapy to antidepressants in patients with major depressive disorder: A systematic review of randomized clinical trials with meta-analyses and trial sequential analyses. *Journal of Affective Disorders, 137,* 4–14.

Jakobsen, J. C., Katakam, K. K., Schou, A., Hellmuth, S. G., Stallknecht, S. E., Leth-Møller, K.,... Gluud, C. (2017). Selective serotonin reuptake inhibitors versus placebo in patients with major depressive disorder. A systematic review with meta-analysis and Trial Sequential Analysis. *BMC Psychiatry, 17*(1), 58. doi:10.1186/s12888-016-1173-2

James, L., James, S. M., & Villa, B. J. (2016). The reverse racism effect: Are cops more hesitant to shoot black than white suspects? *Criminology and Public Policy, 15*(2), 457-479. doi:10.1111/1745-9133.12483

James, W. (1884). What is an emotion? *Mind, 9,* 188–205.

James, W. (1890). *The principles of psychology.* Holt.

Jamieson, J. P., Mendes, W. B., & Nock, M. K. (2013). Improving acute stress responses: The power of reappraisal. *Current Directions in Psychological Science, 22,* 51–56.

Jane, J. S., Oltmanns, T. F., South, S. C., & Turkheimer, E. (2007). Gender bias in diagnostic criteria for personality disorders: An item response theory analysis. *Journal of Abnormal Psychology, 116,* 166–175.

Janis, I. L. (1982). *Victims of groupthink* (2nd ed.). Houghton Mifflin.

Janis, I. L. (1985). Sources of error in strategic decision making. In J. M. Pennings (Ed.), *Organizational strategy and change* (pp. 157–197). Jossey-Bass.

Janis, I. L. (2007). Groupthink. In R. P. Vecchio (Ed.), *Leadership: Understanding the dynamics of power and influence in organizations* (2nd ed., pp. 157–169). University of Notre Dame Press.

Janoff-Bulman, R. (1992). *Shattered assumptions: Toward a new psychology of trauma.* Maxwell Macmillan International.

Janowitz, H., & Grossman, M. (1950). Hunger and appetite: Some definitions and concepts. *Journal of Mount Sinai Hospital, 16,* 231–240.

Jaremka, L. M., Fagundes, C. P., Peng, J., Bennett, J. M., Glaser, R., Malarkey, W. B., & Kiecolt-Glaser, J. K. (2013). Loneliness promotes inflammation during acute stress. *Psychological Science, 24,* 1089–1097.

Jaremka, L. M., Fagundes, C. P., Peng, J., Belury, M. A., Andridge, R. R., Malarkey, W. B., & Kiecolt-Glaser, J. K. (2015). Loneliness predicts postprandial ghrelin and hunger in women. *Hormones and Behavior, 70,* 57–63. doi:10.1016/j.yhbeh.2015.01.011

Jarrett, R. B., Kraft, D., Doyle, J., Foster, B. M., Eaves, G. G., & Silver, P.C. (2001). Preventing recurrent depression using cognitive therapy with and without a continuation phase. *Archives of General Psychiatry, 58,* 381–388.

Jedziewski, M. K., Ewbank, D. C., Wang, H., & Trojanowski, J. Q. (2010). Exercise and cognition: Results from the national Long Term Care Survey. *Alzheimer's and Dementia: The Journal of the Alzheimer's Association, 6,* 448–455.

Jelovac, A., Kolshus, E., & McLoughlin, D. M. (2013). Relapse following successful electroconvulsive therapy for major depression: A meta-analysis. *Neuropsychopharmacology, 38*, 2467–2474.

Jenkins, J. M., & Astington, J. W. (1996). Cognitive factors and family structure associated with theory of mind development in young children. *Developmental Psychology, 32*, 70–78.

Jensen, M. P., Ehde, D. M., Gertz, K. J., Stoelb, B. L., Dillworth, T. M., Hirsh, A. T., . . . Kraft, G. H. (2011). Effects of self-hypnosis training and cognitive restructuring on daily pain intensity and catastrophizing in individuals with multiple sclerosis and chronic pain. *International Journal of Clinical and Experimental Hypnosis, 59*, 45–63.

Jiang, H., Liang, J., Wang, H., & Sun, P. (2016). The interplay of emotions, elaboration, and ambivalence on attitude-behavior consistency. *Journal of Consumer Behaviour, 15*(2), 126–135. doi:10.1002/cb.1551

Jiang, H., White, M. P., Greicius, M. D., Waelde, L. C., & Spiegel, D. (2016). Brain activity and functional connectivity associated with hypnosis. *Cerebral Cortex*, 1–11. doi:10.1093/cercor/bhw220

Jiang, J., Schmajuk, N., & Egner, T. (2012). Explaining neural signals in human visual cortex with an associative learning model. *Behavioral Neuroscience, 126*, 575–581. doi:10.1037/a0029029

Jiang, T., Soussignan, R., Carrier, E., & Royet, J.-P. (2019). Dysfunction of the mesolimbic circuit to food odors in women with anorexia and bulimia nervosa: A fMRI study. *Frontiers in Human Neuroscience, 13*, 117. https://doi.org/10.3389/fnhum.2019.00117

Jobe, T. H., & Harrow, M. (2010). Schizophrenia course, long-term outcome, recovery, and prognosis. *Current Directions in Psychological Science, 19*, 220–225.

Jobin, J., Wrosch, C., & Scheier, M. F. (2014). Associations between dispositional optimism and diurnal cortisol in a community sample: When stress is perceived as higher than normal. *Health Psychology, 33*, 382–391.

Johansson, O., & Redmayne, M. (2016). Exacerbation of demyelinating syndrome after exposure to wireless modem with public hotspot. *Electromagnetic Biology and Medicine, 35*(4), 393–397. doi:10.3109/15368378.2015.1107839

Johns, B. T., & Dye, M. (2019). Gender bias at scale: Evidence from the usage of personal names. *Behavior Research Methods, 51*(4), 1601-1618. doi:10.3758/s13428-019-01234-0

Johnson, B. A. (2008). Update on neuropharmacological treatments for alcoholism: Scientific basis and clinical findings. *Biochemical Pharmacology, 75*, 34–56.

Johnson, D., Wyeth, P., & Sweetser, P. (2014). Creating good lives through computer games. In F. A. Huppert & C. L. Cooper (Eds.), *Interventions and policies to enhance well-being* (pp. 485–510). Wiley-Blackwell.

Johnson, J. A. (1997). Units of analysis for the description and explanation of personality. In R. Hogan, J. Johnson, & S. Briggs (Eds.), *Handbook of personality psychology* (pp. 3–93). Academic Press.

Johnson, M. K., Hashtroudi, S., & Lindsay, D. S. (1993). Source monitoring. *Psychological Bulletin, 114*, 3–28.

Johnson, S. M., & Williams-Keeler, L. (1998). Creating healing relationships for couples dealing with trauma: The use of emotionally focused marital therapy. *Journal of Marital and Family Therapy, 24*, 25–40.

John-Steiner, V., & Mahn, H. (1996). Sociocultural approaches to learning and development: A Vygotskian framework. *Educational Psychologist, 31*, 191–206.

Johnston, L. D., O'Malley, P. M., Miech, R. A., Bachman, J. G., & Schulenberg, J. E. (2016). *Monitoring the future: National survey results on drug use, 1975-2015; Overview, key findings on adolescent drug use.* Institute for Social Research, The University of Michigan.

Joiner, T. (2010). *Myths about suicide.* Harvard University Press.

Jokela, M., Batty, G. D., Hintsa, T., Elovainio, M., Hakulinen, C., & Kivimäki, M. (2014). Is personality associated with cancer incidence and mortality? An individual-participant meta-analysis of 2156 incident cancer cases among 42,843 men and women. *British Journal of Cancer, 110*(7), 1820–1824. doi:10.1038/bjc.2014.58

Jolicoeur, P., & Kosslyn, S. M. (1985). Demand characteristics in image scanning experiments. *Journal of Mental Imagery, 9*, 41–49.

Joliot, A. E. (2001). A comparative study of body image satisfaction and attitudes among American, Israeli, Spanish, and Brazilian college women (United States). *Dissertation Abstracts International: B. The Physical Sciences and Engineering, 61*, 55–67.

Jonason, P. K. (2009). The value of physical attractiveness in romantic partners: Modeling biological and social variables. *Journal of Social Psychology, 149*, 229–240.

Jones, E. E. (1979). The rocky road from acts to dispositions. *American Psychologist, 34*, 107–117.

Jones, E. E., & Nesbitt, R. E. (1971). *The actor and the observer: Divergent perceptions of the causes of behavior.* General Learning Press.

Jones, S. A., & Wilson, A. E. (2009). The horizon line, linear perspective, interposition, and background brightness as determinants of the magnitude of the pictorial moon illusion. *Attention, Perception, & Psychophysics, 71*, 131–142.

Jones, S., & Dindia, K. (2004). A meta-analytic perspective on sex equity in the classroom. *Review of Educational Research, 74*, 443–471.

Jonsson, E. G., Burgert, E., Crocq, M. A., Gustavsson, J. P., Forslund, K., Mattila-Evenden, M., . . . Bergman, H. (2003). Association study between dopamine D3 receptor gene variant and personality traits. *American Journal of Medical Genetics, 117B*, 61–65.

Joormann, J. (2010). Cognitive inhibition and emotion regulation in depression. *Current Directions in Psychological Science, 19*, 161–166.

Joormann, J., Levens, S. M., & Gotlib, I. H. (2011). Sticky thoughts: Depressions and rumination are associated with difficulties manipulating emotional material in working memory. *Psychological Science, 22*, 979–983.

Joorman, J., & Vanderlind, W. M. (2014). Emotion regulation in depression: The role of biased cognition and reduced cognitive control. *Clinical Psychological Science, 2*, 402–421.

Joorman, J., Waugh, C. E., & Gotlib, I.H. (2015). Cognitive bias modification for interpretation in major depression: Effects on memory and stress reactivity. *Clinical Psychological Science, 3*, 126–139.

Jordan, A. S., & McEvoy, R. D. (2003). Gender differences in sleep apnea: Epidemiology, clinical presentation and pathogenic mechanisms. *Sleep Medical Review, 7*, 377–389.

Jordan, G., Deeb, S. S., Bosten, J. M., & Mollon, J. D. (2010). The dimensionality of color vision in carriers of anomalous trichromacy. *Journal of Vision, 10*, 12. doi:10.1167/10.8.12

Jordan, K. D., Masters, K. S., Hooker, S. A., Ruiz, J. M., & Smith, T. W. (2014). An interpersonal approach to religiousness and spirituality: Implications for health and well-being. *Journal of Personality, 82* (5), 418-431.

Jorgensen, C. H., Pedersen, B., & Tonnesen, H. (2011). The efficacy of disulfiram for the treatment of alcohol use disorder. *Alcoholism, Clinical and Experimental Research, 35*, 1749–1758.

Jorgensen, G. (2006). Kohlberg and Gilligan: Duet or duel? *Journal of Moral Education, 35*, 179–196.

Joseph, J. E., Liu, X., Jiang, Y., Lynam, D., & Kelly, T. H. (2009). Neural correlates of emotional reactivity in sensation seeking. *Psychological Science, 20*, 215–223.

Joule R. V., & Azdia, T. (2003). Cognitive dissonance, double forced compliance, and commitment. *European Journal of Social Psychology, 33*, 565–571.

Jovick, R. L. (1972). Cohesiveness-conformity relationship and conformity instrumentality. *Psychological Reports, 30*(2), 404–406. doi:10.2466/pr0.1972.30.2.404

Jowett Hirst, E. S., Dozier, C. L., & Payne, S. W. (2016). Efficacy of and preference for reinforcement and response cost in token economies. *Journal of Applied Behavior Analysis, 49*(2), 329–345. doi:10.1002/jaba.294

Judge, T. A., Thoresen, C. J., Bono, J. E., & Patton, G. K. (2001). The job satisfaction-job performance relationship: A qualitative and quantitative review *Psychological Bulletin, 127*, 376–407.

Julien, R. M. (1995). *A primer of drug action.* Freeman.

Jung, C. G. (1967). The psychology of the unconscious. In H. Read, M. Fordham, & G. Adler (Eds.), *Collected works of C. G. Jung* (Vol. 7). Princeton University Press. (Original work published in 1917)

Jusienė, R., Rakickienė, L., Breidokienė, R., & Laurinaitytė, I. (2020). Executive function and screen-based media use in preschool children. *Infant and Child Development, 29*(1), e2173. https://doi.org/10.1002/icd.2173

Kaelberer, M. M., & Bohórquez, D. V. (2018). The now and then of gut-brain signaling. *Brain Research, 1693*(Part B), 192–196. https://doi.org/10.1016/j.brainres.2018.03.027

Kahneman, D., & Tversky, A. (1973). On the psychology of prediction. *Psychological Review, 80*, 237–251.

Kahneman, D., & Tversky, A. (1984). Choices, values, and frames. *American Psychologist, 39*, 341–350.

Kahol, K., Leyba, M. J., Deka, M., Deka, V., Mayes, S., Smith, M., . . . Panchanathan, S. (2008). Effect of fatigue on psychomotor and cognitive skills. *American Journal of Surgery, 195*, 195–204.

Kaiser, R. H., Snyder, H. R., Goer, F., Clegg, R., Ironside, M., & Pizzagalli, D. A. (2018). Attention bias in rumination and depression:

Cognitive mechanisms and brain networks. *Clinical Psychological Science, 6*(6), 765–782.

Kajantie, E., & Phillips, D. I. (2006). The effects of sex and hormonal status on the physiological response to acute psychosocial stress. *Psychoneuroendocrinology, 31,* 151–178.

Kako, E. (1999). Elements of syntax in the systems of three language-trained animals. *Animal Learning and Behavior, 27,* 1–14.

Kaldenbach, F., Bleckmann, H., & Kohl, T. (2016). Responses of infrared-sensitive tectal units of the pit viper crotalus atrox to moving objects. *Journal of Comparative Physiolology A, Neuroetholology Sensory Neural and Behavioral Physiology, 202(6),* 389–398. doi:10.1007/s00359-016-1076-1

Kalish, R. A. (1985). The social context of death and dying. In R. H. Binstock & E. Shanas (Eds.), *Handbook of aging and the social sciences* (2nd ed., pp. 149–170). Van Nostrand Reinhold.

Kambeitz, J. P., & Howes, O. D. (2015). The serotonin transporter in depression: Meta-analysis of in vivo and post mortem findings and implications for understanding and treating depression. *Journal of Affective Disorders, 186,* 358–366.

Kamijo, N., & Yukawa, S. (2018). The role of rumination and negative affect in meaning making following stressful experiences in a Japanese sample. *Frontiers in Psychology, 9,* 2404. doi:10.3389/fpsyg.2018.02404

Kamins, M. L., & Dweck, C. S. (1999). Person versus process praise and criticism: Implications for contingent self-worth and coping. *Developmental Psychology, 35*(3), 835–847. https://doi.org/10.1037/0012-1649.35.3.835

Kandel, D. B. (1978). Similarity in real-life adolescent friendship pairs. *Journal of Personality and Social Psychology, 36,* 306–312.

Kandler, C., Riemann, R., Angleitner, A., Spinath, F. M., Borkenau, P., & Penke, L. (2016). The nature of creativity: The roles of genetic factors, personality traits, cognitive abilities, and environmental sources. *Journal of Personality and Social Psychology, 111*(2), 230–249. doi:10.1037/pspp0000087

Kandola, A., Vancampfort, D., Herring, M., Rebar, A., Hallgren, M., Firth, J., & Stubbs, B. (2018). Moving to beat anxiety: Epidemiology and therapeutic issues with physical activity for anxiety. *Current Psychiatry Reports, 20*(8), 63. doi:10.1007/s11920-018-0923-x

Kanny, D., Liu, Y., & Brewer, R. D. (2011). Binge drinking—the United States, 2009. *Morbidity and Mortality Weekly, 60,* 101–104.

Kanoy, K., Ulku-Steiner, B., Cox, M., & Burchinal, M. (2003). Marital relationship and individual psychological characteristics that predict physical punishment of children. *Journal of Family Psychology, 17,* 20–28.

Kant, R. M. N., Wong-Chung, A., Evans, E. H., Stanton, E. C., & Boothroyd, L. G. (2019). The impact of a dissonance-based eating disorders intervention on implicit attitudes to thinness in women of diverse sexual orientations. *Frontiers in Psychology, 10,* 2611. https://doi.org/10.3389/fpsyg.2019.02611

Kanwisher, N. (2003). The ventral visual pathway in humans: Evidence from fMRI. In L. M. Chalupa & J. S. Werner (Eds.), *The visual neuroscience* (pp. 1179–1190). MIT Press.

Kaplan, C. A., & Simon, H. A. (1990). In search of insight. *Cognitive Psychology, 22,* 374–419.

Kaplan, D. A. (2010, January 22). SAS: A new no. 1 best employer. *Fortune.* http://money.cnn.com/2010/01/21/technology/sas_best_companies.fortune

Kaplan, R. E., Drath, W. H., & Kofodimos, J. R. (1991). *Beyond ambition: How driven managers can lead better and live better.* Jossey-Bass.

Kaplan, R. M., & Saccuzzo, D. P. (1989). *Psychological testing: Principles, applications, and issues.* Brooks/Cole.

Kapur, S., Craik, F. I. M., Tulving, E., Wilson, A. A., Houle, S., & Brown, G. M. (1994). Neuroanatomical correlates of encoding in episodic memory. *Proceedings of the National Academy of Sciences, USA, 91,* 2008–2011.

Karg, R. S., Bose, J., Batts, K. R., Forman-Hoffman, V. L., Liao, D., Hirsch, E., . . . Hedden, S. L. (2014). *Past year mental disorders among adults in the United States: Results from the 2008-2012 Mental Health Surveillance Study.* CBHSQ Data Review. Substance Abuse and Mental Health Services Administration, Center for Behavioral Health Statistics and Quality.

Karlsgodt, K. H., Sun, D., & Cannon, T. D. (2010). Structural and functional brain abnormalities in schizophrenia. *Current Directions in Psychological Science, 19,* 226–231.

Karni, A., Tanne, D., Rubenstein, B. S., Askenasy, J. J. M., & Sagi, D. (1994). Dependence on REM sleep of overnight improvement of a perceptual skill. *Science, 265,* 679–682.

Kashubeck-West, S., Whiteley, A. M., Vossenkemper, T., Robinson, C., & Deitz, C. (2017). Conflicting identities: Sexual minority, transgender, and gender nonconforming individuals navigating between religion and gender–sexual orientation identity. In K. A. DeBord, A. R. Fischer, K. J. Bieschke, R. M. Perez (Eds.), *Handbook of sexual orientation and gender diversity in counseling and psychotherapy* (pp. 213–238). American Psychological Association.

Kaskutas, L. A. (2009). Alcoholics anonymous effectiveness: Faith meets science. *Journal of Addictive Diseases, 28,* 145–157.

Katigbak, M. S., Church, A. T., Guanzon-Lapena, M. A., Carlota, A. J., & del Pilar, G. H. (2002). Are indigenous personality dimensions culture specific? Philippine inventories and the Five-Factor model. *Journal of Personality and Social Psychology, 82,* 89–101.

Kattner, F., & Green, C. S. (2019). Enhanced early visual processing after evaluative conditioning. *Acta Psychologica, 197,* 1–9. https://doi.org/10.1016/j.actpsy.2019.04.009

Katz, J., Pazienza, R., Olin, R., & Rich, H. (2015). That's what friends are for: Bystander responses to friends or strangers at risk for party rape victimization. *Journal of Interpersonal Violence, 30*(16), 2775–2792. https://doi.org/10.1177/0886260514554290

Katz-Wise, S. L., Priess, H. A., & Hyde, J. S. (2010). Gender-role attitudes and behavior across the transition to parenthood. *Developmental Psychology, 46,* 18–28.

Kaufman, A. S., Kaufman, J. C., Liu, X., & Johnson, C. K. (2009). How do educational attainment and gender relate to fluid intelligence, crystallized intelligence, and academic skills at ages 22–90 years? *Archives of Clinical Neuropsychology, 24,* 153–163.

Kaufman, L., & Rock, L. (1989). The moon illusion thirty years later. In M. Hershenson (Ed.), *The moon illusion* (pp. 193–234). Erlbaum.

Kavushansky, A., Kritman, M., Maroun, M., Klein, E., Richter-Levin, G., Hui, K., & Ben-Shachar, D. (2013). *b*-endorphin degradation and the individual reactivity to traumatic stress. *European Neuropsychopharmacology, 23,* 1779–1788. doi:10.1016/j.euroneuro.2012.12.003

Kazdin, A. E. (1977). *The token economy: A review and evaluation.* Plenum Press.

Kazdin, A. E. (2013). *Behavior modification in applied settings.* Waveland Press.

Kazdin, A. E., & Blase, S. L. (2011). Rebooting psychotherapy research and practice to reduce the burden of mental illness. *Perspectives on Psychological Science, 6,* 21–37.

Keck, P. E., Jr., McElroy, S. L., & Arnold, L. M. (2001). Bipolar disorder. *Medical Clinics of North America, 85,* 645–661.

Keel, P. K., & Klump, K. L. (2003). Are eating disorders culture-bound syndromes? Implications for conceptualizing their etiology. *Psychological Bulletin, 129,* 747–769.

Keiser, A. A., Turnbull, L. M., Darian, M. A., Feldman, D. E., Song, I., & Tronson, N. C. (2017). Sex differences in context fear generalization and recruitment of hippocampus and amygdala during retrieval. *Neuropsychopharmacology, 42,* 397–407.

Keller, C. (2001). Effect of teachers' stereotyping on students' stereotyping of mathematics as a male domain. *Journal of Social Psychology, 141,* 165–173.

Keller, H. (2013). Attachment and culture. *Journal of Cross-Cultural Psychology, 44,* 175–194.

Keller, H. (2017). Culture and development: A systematic relationship. *Perspectives on Psychological Science, 12*(5), 833-840.

Keller, J. (2007). Stereotype threat in classroom settings: The interactive effect of domain identification, task difficulty and stereotype threat on female students' math performance. *British Journal of Educational Psychology, 77,* 323–338. doi:10.1348/000709906X113662

Keller, J., & Dauenheimer, D. (2003). Stereotype threat in the classroom: Dejection mediates the disrupting threat effect of women's math performance. *Personality and Social Psychology Bulletin, 29,* 371–381.

Kellner, C. H., Knapp, R., Husain, M. M., Rasmussen, K., Sampson, S., Cullum, M., . . . Petrides, G. (2010). Bifrontal, bitemporal and right unilateral electrode placement in ECT: a randomised trial. *British Journal of Psychiatry, 196,* 226–234.

Kelly, D. J., Ge, L., Liu, S., Quinn, P. C., Slater, A. M., Lee, K., . . . Pascalis, O. (2007). Cross-race preferences for same-race faces extend beyond the African versus Caucasian contrast in 3-month-old infants. *Infancy, 11,* 87–95.

Kelly, M. M., & Forsyth, J. P. (2007). Observational fear conditioning in the acquisition and extinction of attentional bias for threat: An experimental evaluation. *Emotion, 7,* 324–335.

Kelman, C. A. (2001). Egocentric language in deaf children. *American Annals of the Deaf, 146,* 276–279.

Kelsch, W., Sim, S., & Lois, C. (2010). Watching synaptogenesis in the adult brain. *Annual Review of Neuroscience, 33,* 131–149.

Keltner, D., Sauter, D., Tracy, J., & Cowen, A. (2019). Emotional expression: Advances in basic emotion theory. *Journal of Non-Verbal Behavior, 43*(2), 133–160.

Kemp, M., Drummond, P., & McDermott, B. (2010). A wait-list controlled pilot study of eye movement desensitization and reprocessing (EMDR) for children with posttraumatic stress disorder (PTSD) symptoms from motor vehicle accidents. *Clinical Child Psychology and Psychiatry, 15,* 5–25.

Kendler, K. S., McGuire, M., Gruenberg, A. M., & Walsh, D. (1994). Outcome and family study of the subtypes of schizophrenia in the west of Ireland. *American Journal of Psychiatry, 151,* 849–856.

Kendrick, C., Sliwinski, J., Yu, Y., Johnson, A., Fisher, W., Kekecs, Z., & Elkins, G. (2016). Hypnosis for acute procedural pain: A critical review. *The International Journal of Clinical and Experimental Hypnosis, 64,* 75–115.

Kennedy, K., & Hellmich, N. (2011). Medicare to pay for obesity prevention, *USA Today,* online http://usatoday30.usatoday.com/news/health/healthcare/story/2011-11-29/Medicare-to-pay-for-obesity-prevention/51478232/1

Kennedy, T. D., Flach, Y., Detullio, D., Millen, D. H., Englebert, N., & Edmonds, W. A. (2019). Exploring emotional intelligence and IQ as predictors of success of foster care alumni. *Journal of Child and Family Studies, 28*(12), 3286–3295. https://doi.org/10.1007/s10826-019-01503-8

Kenrick, D. T., & Sheets, V. (1993). Homicidal fantasies. *Ethology and Sociobiology, 14,* 231–246.

Kenrick, D. T., Griskevicius, V., Neuberg, S. L., & Schaller, M. (2010). Renovating the pyramid of needs: Contemporary extensions built upon ancient foundations. *Perspectives on Psychological Science, 5,* 292–314.

Kerns, K. A., Abraham, M. M., Schlegelmilch, A., & Morgan, T. A. (2007). Mother-child attachment in later middle childhood: Assessment approaches and associations with mood and emotion regulation. *Attachment and Human Development, 9,* 33–53.

Kesebir, S., Graham, J., & Oishi, S. (2010). A theory of human needs should be human-centered: Commentary on Kenrick et al. (2010). *Perspectives on Psychological Science, 5,* 315–319.

Kessler, R. C., Aguilar-Gaxiola, S., Alonso, J., Chatterji, S., Lee, S., Ormel, J., Ustün, T. B., & Wang, P. S. (2009). The global burden of mental disorders: An update from the WHO World Mental Health (WMH) surveys. *Epidemiologia e psichiatria sociale, 18*(1), 23–33. doi:10.1017/s1121189x00001421

Kessler, R. C., Berglund, P. A., Demler, O., Jin, R., & Walters, E. E. (2005a). Lifetime prevalence and age-of-onset distributions of *DSM-IV* disorders in the National Comorbidity Survey Replication (NCS-R). *Archives of General Psychiatry, 62,* 593–602.

Kessler, R. C., Chiu, W. T., Demler, O., & Walters, E. E. (2005b). Prevalence, severity, and comorbidity of twelve-month *DSM-IV* disorders in the National Comorbidity Survey Replication (NCS-R). *Archives of General Psychiatry, 62,* 617–627.

Kessler, R. C., Chiu, W. T., Jin, R., Ruscio, A. M., Shear, K., & Walters, E. E. (2006). The epidemiology of panic attacks, panic disorder, and agoraphobia in the National Comorbidity Survey Replication. *Archives of General Psychiatry, 63,* 415–424.

Kessler, R. C., Petukhova, M., Sampson, N. A., Zaslavsky, A. M., & Wittchen, H. U. (2012). Twelve-month and lifetime prevalence and lifetime morbid risk of anxiety and mood disorders in the United States. *International Journal of Methods in Psychiatric Research, 21,* 169–184.

Kessler, R. C., Ruscio, A. M., Shear, K., & Wittchen, H. U. (2010). Epidemiology of anxiety disorders. *Current Topics in Behavioral Neurosciences, 2,* 21–35.

Kessler, Y., & Meiran, N. (2006). All updateable objects in working memory are updated whenever any of them are modified: Evidence from the memory updating paradigm. *Journal of Experimental Psychology: Learning, Memory, and Cognition, 32,* 570–585.

Khatami, R., Luca, G., Baumann, C.R., Bassetti, C.L., Bruni, O., Canellas, F., . . . European Narcolepsy Network. (2016). The European narcolepsy network (EU-NN) database. *Journal of Sleep Research, 25,* 356–364.

Kibbe, M. M., & Leslie, A. M. (2011). What do infants remember when they forget? Location and identity in 6-month-olds' memory for objects. *Psychological Science, 22,* 1500–1505.

Kiecolt-Glaser, J. K. (2009). Psychoneuroimmunology: Psychology's gateway to the biomedical future. *Perspectives on Psychological Science, 4,* 367–369.

Kiecolt-Glaser, J. K., & Glaser, R. (1992). Psychoneuroimmunology: Can psychological interventions modulate immunity? *Journal of Consulting and Clinical Psychology, 60,* 569–575.

Kiecolt-Glaser, J. K., Bane, C., Glaser, R., & Malarkey, W. B. (2003). Love, marriage, and divorce: Newlywed's stress hormones foreshadow relationship changes. *Journal of Consulting and Clinical Psychology, 71,* 176–188.

Kiecolt-Glaser, J. K., McGuire, L., Robles, T. F., & Glaser, R. (2002). Emotions, morbidity, and mortality: New perspectives from psychoneuroimmunology. *Annual Review of Psychology, 53,* 83–107.

Kiehl, K. A., Bates, A. T., Laurens, K. R., Hare, R. D., & Liddle, P. F. (2006). Brain potentials implicate temporal lobe abnormalities in criminal psychopaths. *Journal of Abnormal Psychology, 115,* 443–453.

Kieseppa, T., Partonen, T., Haukka, J., Kaprio, J., & Lonnqvist, J. (2014). High concordance of bipolar I disorder in a nationwide sample of twins. *American Journal of Psychiatry, 161,* 1814–1821.

Kihlstrom, J. F. (2001). Dissociative disorders. In H. E. Adams & P. B. Sutker (Eds.), *Comprehensive handbook of psychopathology* (pp. 259–276). Academic/Plenum.

Kihlstrom, J. F. (2005). Dissociative disorders. *Annual Review of Clinical Psychology, 1,* 227–253.

Kihlstrom, J. F., Glisky, M. L., & Angiulo, M. J. (1994). Dissociative tendencies and dissociative disorders. *Journal of Abnormal Psychology, 103,* 117–124.

Killen, M., Crystal, D. S., & Watanabe, H. (2002). Japanese and American children's evaluations of peer exclusion, tolerance of differences, and prescriptions for conformity. *Child Development, 73,* 1788–1802.

Kim, E. S., Hagan, K. A., Grodstein, F., DeMeo, D. L., De Vivo, I., & Kubzansky, L. D. (2017). Optimism and cause-specific mortality: A prospective cohort study. *American Journal of Epidemiology, 185*(1), 21-29. doi:10.1093/aje/kww182

Kim, H. S., Sherman, D. K., & Taylor, S. E. (2008). Culture and social support. *American Psychologist, 63,* 518–526.

Kim, H., & Chung, R. H. (2003). Relationship of recalled parenting style to self-perception in Korean American college students. *Journal of Genetic Psychology, 164,* 481–492.

Kim, K., Na, Y. K., & Hong, H. S. (2016). Effects of progressive muscle relaxation therapy in colorectal cancer patients. *Western Journal of Nursing Research, 38*(8), 959–973.

Kim, N. (2012). Oculomotor effects in the size-distance paradox and the moon illusion. *Ecological Psychology, 24,* 122–138.

Kimura, D. (2000). *Sex and cognition.* MIT Press.

King, B. M. (2006). The rise, fall, and resurrection of the ventromedial hypothalamus in the regulation of feeding behavior and body weight. *Physiology and Behavior, 87,* 221–244.

King, D. (2016). Poverty of stimulus arguments and behaviourism. *Behavior and Philosophy, 43,* 38–61.

King, S., St-Hilaire, A., & Heidkamp, D. (2010). Prenatal factors in schizophrenia. *Current Directions in Psychological Science, 19,* 209–213.

King, S. L., & Janik, V. M. (2013). Bottlenose dolphins can use learned vocal labels to address each other. *PNAS Proceedings of the National Academy of Sciences of the United States of America, 110*(32), 13216–13221. https://doi.org/10.1073/pnas.1304459110

Kinnish, K. K., Strassberg, D. S., & Turner, C. W. (2005). Sex differences in the flexibility of sexual orientation: A multidimensional retrospective assessment *Archives of Sexual Behavior, 34,* 173–183.

Kinomura, S., Larsson, J., Gulyas, B., & Roland, P. E. (1996). Activation by attention of the human reticular formation and thalamic intralaminar nuclei. *Science, 271,* 512–515.

Kinsey, A. C., Pomeroy, W. B., & Martin, C. E. (1948). *Sexual behavior in the human male.* Saunders.

Kinsey, A. C., Pomeroy, W. B., Martin, C. E., & Gebhard, P. H. (1953). *Sexual behavior in the human female.* Saunders.

Kirkbride, J. B., Morgan, C., Fearon, P., Dazzan, P., Murray, R. M., & Jones, P. B. (2007). Neighborhood-level effects on psychoses: Re-examining the role of context. *Psychological Medicine, 37,* 1413–1425.

Kirkpatrick, S. A., & Locke, E. A. (1991). Leadership: Do traits matter? *Academy of Management Executive, 5,* 48–60.

Kirmayer, L. J., & Looper, K. J. (2007). Somatoform disorders. In M. Hersen, S. M. Turner, & D. C. Beidel (Eds.), *Adult psychopathology and diagnosis* (5th ed., pp. 410–472). Wiley.

Kirsch, I. (1994). Cognitive-behavioral hypnotherapy. In J. W. Rhue, S. J. Lynn, & I. Kirsch (Eds.), *Handbook of clinical hypnosis* (pp. 151–172). American Psychological Association.

Kirsch, I. (2000). The response set theory of hypnosis. *American Journal of Clinical Hypnosis, 42,* 274–292.

Kirsch, I., & Lynn, S. J. (1995). The altered state of hypnosis. *American Psychologist, 50,* 846–858.

Kirsch, I., & Lynn, S. J. (1997). Hypnotic involuntariness and the automaticity of everyday life. *American Journal of Clinical Hypnosis, 40,* 329–348.

Kirsch, I., Montgomery, G., & Sapirstein, G. (1995). Hypnosis as an adjunct to cognitive behavioral psychotherapy: A meta-analysis. *Journal of Consulting and Clinical Psychology, 63,* 214–220.

Kisilevsky, B. S., Hains, S. M., Lee, K., Xie, X., Huang, H., Ye, H. H., . . . Wang, Z. (2003). Effects of experience on fetal voice recognition. *Psychological Science, 14,* 220–224.

Kitayama, S., & Park, J. (2017). Emotion and biological health: The socio-cultural moderation. *Current Opinion in Psychology, 17,* 99–105. doi:10.1016/j.copsyc.2017.06.016

Kitayama, S., Park, J., Boylan, J. M., Miyamoto, Y., Levine, C. S., Markus, H. R., . . . Ryff, C. D. (2015). Expression of anger and ill health in two cultures: An examination of inflammation and cardiovascular risk. *Psychological Science, 26,* 211–220.

Kito, S., Hasegawa, T., & Koga, Y. (2011). Neuroanatomical correlates of therapeutic efficacy of low-frequency right prefrontal transcranial magnetic stimulation in treatment-resistant depression. *Psychiatry and Clinical Neurosciences, 65,* 175–182.

Kizilirmak, J. M., Galvao Gomes da Silva, J., Imamoglu, F., & Richardson-Klavehn, A. (2016). Generation and the subjective feeling of "aha!" are independently related to learning from insight. *Psychological Research, 80*(6), 1059–1074. doi:10.1007/s00426-015-0697-2

Kleim, B., Graham, B., Fihosy, S., Stott, R., & Ehlers, A. (2014). Reduced specificity in episodic future thinking in posttraumatic stress disorder. *Clinical Psychological Science, 2,* 165–173.

Klein, B., Mitchell, J., Abbott, J., Shandley, K., Austin, D., Gilson, K., . . . Redman, T. (2010). A therapist-assisted cognitive behavior therapy internet intervention for posttraumatic stress disorder: Pre-, post- and 3-month follow-up results from an open trial. *Journal of Anxiety Disorders, 24,* 635–644.

Klein, D. N., Lewinsohn, P. M., & Seeley, J. R. (2001). A family study of major depressive disorder in a community sample of adolescents. *Archives of General Psychiatry, 58,* 13–21.

Klein, D. N., Shankman, S. A., & Rose, S. (2006). Ten-year prospective follow-up study of the naturalistic course of dysthymic disorder and double depression. *American Journal of Psychiatry, 163,* 872–880.

Klein, S. B. (1987). *Learning.* McGraw-Hill.

Klein, S. B., & Markowitsch, H. J. (2015). The nature of the semantic/episodic memory distinction: A missing piece of the "working through" process. *Behavioral and Brain Sciences, 38,* e9. https://doi.org/10.1017/S0140525X14000181

Klein, T. W., & Newton, C. A. (2007). Therapeutic potential of cannabinoid-based drugs. *Advances in Experimental Medicine and Biology, 601,* 395–413.

Klemfuss, J. Z., Milojevich, H. M., Yim, I. S., Bush, E. B., & Quas, J. A. (2013). Stress at encoding, context at retrieval, and children's narrative content. *Journal of Experimental Child Psychology, 116,* 693–706.

Klöckener, T., Hess, S., Belgardt, B., Paeger, L., Verhagen, L. W., Husch, A., . . . Brüning, J. C. (2011). High-fat feeding promotes obesity via insulin receptor/PI3K-dependent inhibition of SF-1 VMH neurons. *Nature Neuroscience, 14,* 911–918. doi:10.1038/nn.2847

Klonoff, E. A., Landrine, H., & Campbell, R. (2000). Sexist discrimination may account for well-known gender differences in psychiatric symptoms. *Psychology of Women Quarterly, 24,* 93–99.

Kobasa, S. C. (1982). Commitment and coping in stress resistance among lawyers. *Journal of Personality and Social Psychology, 42,* 707–717.

Köbe, T., Witte, A. V., Schnelle, A., Lesemann, A., Fabian, S., Tesky, V. A., . . . Flöel, A. (2016). Combined omega-3 fatty acids, aerobic exercise and cognitive stimulation prevents decline in gray matter volume of the frontal, parietal and cingulate cortex in patients with mild cognitive impairment. *NeuroImage, 131,* 226–238. doi:10.1016/j.neuroimage.2015.09.050

Kocab, A., Senghas, A., & Snedeker, J. (2016). The emergence of temporal language in Nicaraguan sign language. *Cognition, 156,* 147–163. doi:10.1016/j.cognition.2016.08.005

Koch, K., Reess, T. J., Rus, O. G., & Zimmer, C. (2015). Extensive learning is associated with gray matter changes in the right hippocampus. *NeuroImage, 125,* 627–632.

Kochanek, K. D., Murphy, S. L., Xu, J. Q., & Tejada-Vera, B. (2016). *Deaths: Final data for 2014. National Vital Statistics Reports, 65,* no 4. National Center for Health Statistics.

Kochanska, G. (1995). Children's temperament, mothers' discipline, and security of attachment: Multiple pathways to emerging internalization. *Child Development, 66,* 597–615.

Kogan, A., Impett, E. A., Oveis, C., Hui, B., Gordon, A. M., & Keltner, D. (2010). When giving feels good: The intrinsic benefits of sacrifice in romantic relationships for the communally motivated. *Psychological Science, 21,* 1918–1924.

Kogut, T., & Ritov, I. (2011). The identifiable victim effect: Causes and boundary conditions. In D. M. Oppenheimer & C. Y. Olivola (Eds.), *The science of giving: Experimental approaches to the study of charity* (pp. 133–145). Psychology Press.

Koh, K. B., Choe, E., Song, J. E., & Lee, E. H. (2006). Effect of coping on endocrinoimmune functions in different stress situations. *Psychiatry Research, 143,* 223–234.

Kohlberg, L. (1969). Stage and sequence: The cognitive-developmental approach to socialization. In D. A. Goslin (Ed.), *Handbook of socialization theory and research* (pp. 347–480). Rand McNally.

Kohlberg, L., Levine, C., & Hewer, A. (Eds.). (1983). *Moral stages: A current formulation and a response to critics (Contributions to human development, Vol. 10).* Basel, Switzerland: Karger.

Köhler, W. (1925). *The mentality of apes.* Harcourt Brace.

Koles, Z. J., Lind, J. C., & Flor-Henry, P. (2010). Gender differences in brain functional organization during verbal and spatial cognitive challenges. *Brain Topography, 23,* 199–204. doi:10.1007/s10548-009-0119-0

Koller, M., Floh, A., Zauner, A., & Rusch, T. (2013). Persuasibility and the self—Investigating heterogeneity among consumers. *Australasian Marketing Journal (AMJ), 21*(2), 94–104. doi:10.1016/j.ausmj.2013.02.004

Kollmayer, M., Schultes, M. T., Schober, B., Hodosi, T., & Spiel, C. (2018). Parents' judgments about the desirability of toys for their children: Associations with gender role attitudes, gender-typing of toys, and demographics. *Sex Roles, 79*(5), 329–341. doi:10.1007/s11199-017-0882-4

Komisaruk, B. R., & Whipple, B. (2011). Non-genital orgasms. *Sexual and Relationship Therapy, 26,* 356–372. doi:10.1080/14681994.2011.649252

Komisaruk, B. R., Wise, N., Frangos, E., Birbano, W., & Allen, K. (2011). An fMRI video animation time-course analysis of brain regions activated during self-stimulation to orgasm in women. *Society for Neuroscience,* 495.03.

Koob, G. F., & Volkow, N. D. (2016). Neurobiology of addiction: A neurocircuitry analysis. *Lancet Psychiatry, 3(8),* 760–773. doi:10.1016/S2215-0366(16)00104-8

Koolschijn, P. C., & Crone, E. A. (2013). Sex differences and structural brain maturation from childhood to early adulthood. *Developmental Cognitive Neuroscience, 5,* 106–118.

Kopelman, P. G. (2000). Obesity as a medical problem. *Nature, 404,* 635–643.

Kopp, S. J., Sockol, L. E., & Multhaup, K. S. (2020). Age-related differences in flashbulb memories: A meta-analysis. *Psychology and Aging, 35*(4), 459–472. https://doi.org/10.1037/pag0000467

Kopta, S. M., Lueger, R. J., Saunders, S. M., & Howard, K. I. (1999). Individual psychotherapy outcome and process research: Challenges leading to greater turmoil or a positive transition? *Annual Review of Psychology, 50,* 441–469.

Koss, M. P., & Kilpatrick, D. G. (2001). Rape and sexual assault. In E. Gerrity (Ed.), *The mental health consequences of torture* (pp. 177–193). Kluwer Academic/Plenum Press.

Kosslyn, S. M. (1994). *Image and brain: The resolution of the imagery debate.* MIT Press.

Kosslyn, S. M., Ball, T. M., & Reiser, B. J. (2004). Visual images preserve metric spatial information: Evidence from studies of image scanning. In D. A. Balota & E. J. Marsh (Eds.), *Cognitive psychology: Key readings* (pp. 239–253). Psychology Press. (Original work published in 1978)

Kosten, T. R., Wu, G., Huang, W., Harding, M. J., Hamon, S. C., Lappalainen, J., & Nielsen, D. A. (2013). Pharmacogenetic randomized trial for cocaine abuse: Disulfiram and dopamine â-hydroxylase. *Biological Psychiatry, 73,* 219–224. doi:10.1016/j.biopsych.2012.07.011

Kotnik, P., Fischer Posovszky, P., & Wabitsch, M. (2015). Endocrine and metabolic effects of adipose tissue in children and adolescents. *Slovenian Journal of Public Health, 54*(2), 131–138. doi:10.1515/sjph-2015-0020

Koughan, M. (1975, February 23). Arthur Friedman's outrage: Employees decide their pay. *Washington Post.*

Kowalski, K. (2003). The emergence of ethnic and racial attitudes in preschool-aged children. *Journal of Social Psychology, 143,* 677–690.

Kozlowski, S. W. J. (2018). Enhancing the effectiveness of work groups and teams: A reflection. *Perspectives on Psychological Science, 13*(2), 205-212.

Kozlowski, S. W., & Bell, B. S. (2003). Work groups and teams in organizations. In W. C. Borman, D. R. Ilgen, & R. J. Klimoski (Eds.), *Handbook of psychology: Industrial and organizational psychology* (Vol. 12, pp. 333–375). Wiley.

Kraft, J. B., Peters, E. J., Slager, S. L., Jenkins, G. D., Reinalda, M. S., McGrath, P. J., & Hamilton, S. P. (2007). Analysis of association between the serotonin transporter and antidepressant response in a large clinical sample. *Biological Psychiatry, 61,* 734–742.

Kraft, T. L., & Pressman, S. D. (2012). Grin and bear it: The influence of manipulated facial expression on the stress response. *Psychological Science, 23,* 1372–1378.

Kraha, A., & Boals, A. (2011). Parents and vehicle purchases for their children: A surprising source of weight bias. *Obesity, 19,* 541–545.

Kramer, A. F., & Colcombe, S. (2018). Fitness effects on the cognitive function of older adults: A meta-analytic study—revisited. *Perspectives on Psychological Science, 13*(2), 213-217.

Krampe, H., & Ehrenreich, H. (2010). Supervised disulfiram as adjunct to psychotherapy in alcoholism treatment. *Current Pharmaceutical Design, 16,* 2076–2090.

Krause, R. J., & Rucker, D. D. (2020). Can bad be good? The attraction of a darker self. *Psychological Science, 31*(5), 518–530. https://doi.org/10.1177/0956797620909742

Kraut, R. E. (1982). Social presence, facial feedback, and emotion. *Journal of Personality and Social Psychology, 42,* 853–863.

Krautbauer, K. H., & Drossel, C. (2018). Cancer-related eating problems. In A. Maragakis & W. T. O'Donohue (Eds.), *Principle-based stepped care and brief psychotherapy for integrated care settings* (pp. 89–97). Springer International Publishing. https://doi.org/10.1007/978-3-319-70539-2_9

Kreibig, S. D. (2010). Autonomic nervous system activity in emotion: A review. *Biological Psychology, 84,* 394–421. doi:10.1016/j.biopsycho.2010.03.010

Kreibig, S. D., Samson, A. C., & Gross, J. J. (2015). The psychophysiology of mixed emotional states: Internal and external replicability analysis of a direct replication study. *Psychophysiology, 52*(7), 873–886. https://doi.org/10.1111/psyp.12425

Krejtz, I., & Nezlek, J. B. (2016). It's Greek to me: Domain specific relationships between intellectual helplessness and academic performance. *The Journal of Social Psychology, 156,* 664–668.

Kremer, I., Bachner-Melman, R., Reshef, A., Broude, L., Nemanov, L., Gritsenko, I., . . . Ebstein, R. P. (2005). Association of the serotonin transporter gene with smoking behavior. *American Journal of Psychiatry, 162,* 924–930.

Krishnamurti, T., Davis, A. L., & Fischhoff, B. (2020). Inferring sexually transmitted infection risk from attractiveness in online dating among adolescents and young adults: Exploratory study. *Journal of Medical Internet Research, 22*(6), e14242. https://doi.org/10.2196/14242

Kristenson, H. H. (1992). Long-term Antabuse treatment of alcohol-dependent patients. *Acta Psychiatrica Scandinavica, 86* (Suppl. 369), 41–45. doi:10.1111/j.1600-0447.1992.tb03314.X

Krolick, K. N., Zhu, Q., & Shi, H. (2018). Effects of estrogens on central nervous system neurotransmission: Implications for sex differences in mental disorders. *Progress in Molecular Biology and Translational Science, 160,* 105–171. doi.org/10.1016/bs.pmbts.2018.07.008

Krongold, M., Cooper, C., & Bray, S. (2017). Modular development of cortical gray matter across childhood and adolescence. *Cerebral Cortex, 27*(2), 1125–1136. doi:10.1093/cercor/bhv307

Kropp, P., Siniatchkin, M., & Gerber, W.D. (2002). On the pathophysiology of migraine—Links for "empirically based treatment" with neurofeedback. *Applied Psychophysiology and Biofeedback, 27,* 203–213.

Krystal, J. H., Staley, J., Mason, G., Petrakis, I. L., Kaufman, J., Harris, R. A., . . . Lappalainen, J. (2006). Gamma-aminobutyric acid type A receptors and alcoholism: Intoxication, dependence, vulnerability, and treatment. *Archives of General Psychiatry, 63,* 957–968.

Kryukov, V. I. (2012). Towards a unified model of Pavlovian conditioning: Short review of trace conditioning models. *Cognitive Neurodynamics, 6,* 377–398. doi:10.1007/s11571-012-9195-z

Ksir, C., & Hart, C. L. (2016). Cannabis and psychosis: A critical overview of the relationship. *Current Psychiatry Reports, 18,* 12.

Kubota, J. T., Mojdehbakhsh, R., Raio, C., Brosch, T., Uleman, J. S., & Phelps, E. A. (2014). Stressing the person: Legal and everyday person attributions under stress. *Biological Psychology, 103,* 117–124. doi:10.1016/j.biopsycho.2014.07.020

Kübler-Ross, E. (1969). *On death and dying.* Macmillan.

Kübler-Ross, E. (1974). *Questions and answers on death and dying.* Macmillan.

Kudielka, B. M., & Kirschbaum, C. (2005). Sex differences in HPA axis responses to stress: A review. *Biological Psychology, 69,* 113–132.

Kuhbandner, C., Lichtenfeld, S., & Pekrun, R. (2011). Always look on the broad side of life: Happiness increases the breadth of sensory memory. *Emotion, 11,* 958–964. doi:10.1037/a0024075

Kuhn, D., & Crowell, A. (2011). Dialogic argumentation as a vehicle for developing young adolescents' thinking. *Psychological Science, 22,* 545–552.

Kumada, T., Jiang, Y., Cameron, D. B., & Komuro, H. (2007). How does alcohol impair neuronal migration? *Journal of Neuroscience Research, 85,* 465–470.

Kumari, V., ffytche, D. H., Williams, S. C., & Gray, J. A. (2004). Personality predicts brain responses to cognitive demands. *Journal of Neuroscience, 24,* 10636–10641.

Kung, H. S., Hoyert, D. L., Xu, J., & Murphy, S. L. (2008). Deaths: Final data for 2005. *National Vital Statistics Reports, 56*(10).

Kunstman, J. W., & Plant, E. A. (2008). Racing to help: Racial bias in high emergency helping situations. *Journal of Personality and Social Psychology, 95,* 1499–1510.

Kuntsche, E., Knibbe, R., Gmel, G., & Engels, R. (2006). Who drinks and why? A review of socio-demographic, personality, and contextual issues behind drinking motives in young people. *Addictive Behaviors, 31,* 1844–1857.

Kunugi, H., Hori, H., Adachi, N., & Numakawa, T. (2010). Interface between hypothalamic-pituitary-adrenal axis and brain-derived neurotrophic factor in depression. *Psychiatry and Clinical Neurosciences, 64,* 447–459.

Kuo, S. S., & Pogue-Geile, M. F. (2019). Variation in fourteen brain structure volumes in schizophrenia: A comprehensive meta-analysis of 246 studies. *Neuroscience and Biobehavioral Reviews, 98,* 85–94. doi:10.1016/j.neubiorev.2018.12.030

Kupper, N., & Denollet, J. (2007). Type D personality as a prognostic factor in heart disease: Assessment and mediating mechanisms. *Journal of Personality Assessment, 89,* 265–276.

Kurdek, L. A. (1999). The nature and predictors of the trajectory of change in marital quality for husbands and wives over the first 10 years of marriage. *Developmental Psychology, 35,* 1283–1296.

Kushlev, K., Dwyer, R., & Dunn, E. W. (2018). The social price of constant connectivity: Smartphones impose subtle costs on well-being. *Current Directions in Psychological Science, 28*(4), 347-352.

Kutscher, E. C. (2008). Antipsychotics. In K. T. Mueser & D. V. Jeste (Eds.), *Clinical handbook of schizophrenia* (pp. 159–167). Guilford Press.

Kuyken, W., Hayes, R., Barrett, B., Byng, R., Dalgleish, T., Kessler, D., ...Byford, S. (2015). Effectiveness and cost-effectiveness of mindfulness-based cognitive therapy compared with maintenance antidepressant treatment in the prevention of depressive relapse or recurrence (PREVENT): A randomised controlled trial. *Lancet, 386*(9988), 63–73. doi:10.1016/S0140-6736(14)62222-4

Kuyper, L., & Bos, H. (2016). Mostly heterosexual and lesbian/gay young adults: Differences in mental health and substance use and the role of minority stress. *Journal of Sex Research, 53*(7), 731–741. doi:10.1080/00224499.2015.1071310

Kuyper, L., & Fokkema, T. (2011). Minority stress and mental health among Dutch LGBs: Examination of differences between sex and sexual orientation. *Journal of Counseling Psychology, 58,* 222–233. doi:10.1037/a0022688

Kuzelova, H., Ptacek, R., & Milan, M. (2010). The serotonin transporter gene (5-HTT) variant and psychiatric disorders: Review of current literature. *Neuroendocrinology Letters, 31,* 5.

Kuznekoff, J. H., Munz, S., & Titsworth, S. (2015). Mobile phones in the classroom: Examining the effects of texting, Twitter, and message content on student learning. *Communication Education, 64*(3), 344–365. https://doi.org/10.1080/03634523.2015.1038727

Kwan, B. M., Dimidjian, S., & Rizvi, S. L. (2010). Treatment preference, engagement, and clinical improvement in pharmacotherapy versus psychotherapy for depression. *Behaviour Research and Therapy, 48,* 799–804.

La Greca, A. M., Silverman, W. K., Lai, B., & Jaccard, J. (2010). Hurricane-related exposure experiences and stressors, other life events, and social support: Concurrent and prospective impact on children's persistent posttraumatic stress symptoms. *Journal of Consulting and Clinical Psychology, 78,* 794–805.

La Mela, C., Maglietta, M., Caini, S., Casu, G. P., Lucarelli, S., Mori, S., & Ruggiero, G. M. (2015). Perfectionism, weight and shape concerns, and low self-esteem: Testing a model to predict bulimic symptoms. *Eating Behaviors, 19,* 155–158. doi:10.1016/j.eatbeh.2015.09.002

Lacayo, A. (1995). Neurologic and psychiatric complications of cocaine abuse. *Neuropsychiatry, Neuropsychology, and Behavioral Neurology, 8,* 53–60.

Laceulle, O. M., Ormel, J., Aggen, S. H., Neale, M. C., & Kendler, K. S. (2013). Genetic and environmental influences on the longitudinal structure of neuroticism: A trait-state approach. *Psychological Science, 24,* 1780–1790.

Lachman, M. E., Teshale, S., & Agrigoroaei, S. (2015). Midlife as a pivotal period in the life course: Balancing growth and decline at the crossroads of youth and old age. *International Journal of Behavioral Development, 39*(1), 20–31. doi:10.1177/0165025414533223

Lack, C. W. (2012). Obsessive-compulsive disorder: Evidence-based treatments and future directions for research. *World Journal of Psychiatry, 2,* 86–90.

Laeng, B., Bloem, I. M., D'Ascenzo, S., & Tommasi, L. (2014). Scrutinizing visual images: The role of gaze in mental imagery and memory. *Cognition, 131*(2), 263–283. doi:10.1016/j.cognition.2014.01.003

Lagerberg, T., Fazel, S., Molero, Y., Franko, M. A., Chen, Q., Hellner, C., Lichtenstein, P., & Chang, Z. (2020). Associations between selective serotonin reuptake inhibitors and violent crime in adolescents, young, and older adults—A Swedish register-based study. *European Neuropsychopharmacology, 36*, 1–9. https://doi.org/10.1016/j.euroneuro.2020.03.024

Lahera, G., Ruiz-Murugarren, S., Fernandez-Liria, A., Saiz-Ruiz, J., Buck, B. E., & Penn, D. L. (2016). Relationship between olfactory function and social cognition in euthymic bipolar patients. *CNS Spectrums, 21*(1), 53–59. doi:10.1017/S1092852913000382

Lahey, B. B., Pelham, W. E., Loney, J., Kipp, H., Ehrhardt, A., Lee, S. S., . . . Massetti, G. (2004). Three-year predictive validity of *DSM-IV* attention deficit hyperactivity disorder in children diagnosed at 4–6 years of age. *American Journal of Psychiatry, 161*, 2014–2020.

Lakens, D., Hilgard, J., & Staaks, J. (2016). On the reproducibility of meta-analyses: Six practical recommendations. *BioMedCentral Psychology, 4*, 24. doi:10.1186/s40359-016-0126-3

Lambeth, G. S., & Hallett, M. (2002). Promoting healthy decision making in relationships: Developmental interventions with young adults on college and university campuses. In C. L. Atkinson & D. R. Atkinson (Eds.), *Counseling across the lifespan: Prevention and treatment* (pp. 209–226). SAGE.

Lamidi, E. O., Manning, W. D., & Brown, S. L. (2015). *Change in the stability of first premarital cohabitation, 1980–2009.* Paper presented at the annual meeting of the Population Association of America, 2014.

Lancet, D. Ben-Arie, N., Cohen, S., Gat, U., Gross-Isseroff, R., Horn-Saban, S., . . . Walker, N. (1993). Olfactory receptors: Transduction diversity, human psychophysics and genome analysis. In D. Chadwick, J. Marsh, & J. Goode (Eds.), *The molecular basis of smell and taste transduction* (pp. 131–146). Wiley.

Landabaso, M. A., Iraurgi, I., Sanz, J., Calle, R., Ruiz de Apodaka, J., Jimenez-Lerma, J. M., & Gutierrez-Fraile, M. (1999). Naltrexone in the treatment of alcoholism: Two-year follow up results. *European Journal of Psychiatry, 13*, 97–105.

Landor, A. M., & McNeil-Smith, S. (2019). Skin-tone trauma: Historical and contemporary influences on the health and interpersonal outcomes of African Americans. *Perspectives on Psychological Science, 14*(5), 797-815.

Lang, A. J., & Stein, M. B. (2001). Social phobia: Prevalence and diagnostic threshold. *Journal of Clinical Psychiatry, 62*(Suppl. 1), 5–10.

Lang, R., Mahoney, R., El Zein, F., Delaune, E., & Amidon, M. (2011). Evidence to practice: Treatment of anxiety in individuals with autism spectrum disorders. *Neuropsychiatric Disease and Treatment, 7*, 27–30.

Lange, T., Dimitrov, S., Fehm, H. L., Westermann, J., & Born, J. (2006). Shift of monocyte function toward cellular immunity during sleep. *Archives of Internal Medicine, 166*, 1695–1700.

Langford, D. J., Cooper, B., Paul, S., Humphreys, J., Keagy, C., Conley, Y. P., ... Dunn, L. B. (2017). Evaluation of coping as a mediator of the relationship between stressful life events and cancer-related distress. *Health Psychology, 36*(12), 1147–1160. doi:10.1037/hea0000524

Langfred, C. (2004). Too much of a good thing? Negative effects of high trust and individual autonomy in self-managing teams. *Academy of Management Journal, 47*, 385–399.

Langlois, J. H., Roggman, L. A., Casey, R. J., Ritter, J. M., Rieser-Danner, L. A., & Jenkins, V. Y. (1987). Infant preferences for attractive faces: Rudiments of a stereotype? *Developmental Psychology, 23*, 363–369.

Langreth, R. (2000, May 1). Every little bit helps: How even moderate exercise can have a big impact on your health. *Wall Street Journal*, p. R5.

Lansford, J. E. (2009). Parental divorce and children's adjustment. *Perspectives on Psychological Science, 4*, 140–152.

Lanska, M., Olds, J. M., & Westerman, D. L. (2014). Fluency effects in recognition memory: Are perceptual fluency and conceptual fluency interchangeable? *Journal of Experimental Psychology: Learning, Memory, and Cognition, 40*, 1–11. doi:10.1037/a0034309

LaPiere, R. T. (1934). Attitudes versus actions. *Social Forces, 13*, 230-237.

Largo-Wight, E., Peterson, P. M., & Chen, W. W. (2005). Perceived problem solving, stress, and health among college students. *American Journal of Health Behavior, 29*, 360–370.

Larkin, M. (1998). On the trail of human pheromones. *Lancet, 351*, 809.

Lassman, D. J., McKie, S., Gregory, L. J., Lal, S., D'Amato, M., Steele, I., . . . Thompson, D. G. (2010). Defining the role of cholecystokinin in the lipid-induced human brain activation matrix. *Gastroenterology, 138*, 1514–1524.

Latané, B., & Darley, J. (1969). Bystander "apathy." *American Scientist, 57*, 244–268.

Latané, B., & L'Herrou, T. (1996). Spatial clustering in the conformity game: Dynamic social impact in electronic groups. *Journal of Personality and Social Psychology, 70*, 1218–1230.

Lattal, K., & Lattal, K. A. (2012). Facets of Pavlovian and operant extinction. *Behavioural Processes, 90*, 1–8. doi:10.1016/j.beproc.2012.03.009

Laubmeier, K. K., Zakowski, S. G., & Bair, J. P. (2004). The role of spirituality in the psychological adjustment to cancer. A test of the transactional model of stress and coping. *International Journal of Behavioral Medicine, 11*, 48–55.

Laudanski, J., Zheng, Y., & Brette, R. (2014). A structural theory of pitch. *eNeuro, 1*(1), ENEURO.0033-14.2014. doi:10.1523/ENEURO.0033-14.2014

Lavner, J. A., & Bradbury, T. N. (2010). Patterns of change in marital satisfaction over the newlywed years. *Journal of Marriage and Family, 72*, 1171–1187.

Lavoie, C., & Desrochers, S. (2002). Visual habituation at five months: Short-term reliability of measures obtained with a new polynomial regression criterion. *Journal of Genetic Psychology, 163*, 261–271.

Lazarus, R. S. (1990). Theory-based stress measurement. *Psychological Inquiry, 1*, 3–13.

Lazarus, R. S. (1991). Cognition and motivation in emotion. *American Psychologist, 46*, 352–367.

Lazarus, R. S. (1993). From psychological stress to the emotions: A history of changing outlooks. *Annual Review of Psychology, 44*, 1–21.

Lazarus, R. S. (1995). Vexing research problems inherent in cognitive-mediational theories of emotion—and some solutions. *Psychological Inquiry, 6*, 183–197.

Lazarus, R. S., & Folkman, S. (1984). *Stress, appraisal, and coping.* Springer.

Leader, L. R. (2016). The potential value of habituation in the fetus. In N. Reissland & B. S. Kisilevsky (Eds.), *Fetal development: Research on brain and behavior, environmental influences, and emerging technologies* (pp. 189–209). Springer Science + Business Media.

Leaper, C., & Brown, C. S. (2014). Sexism in schools. *Advances in Child Development and Behavior, 47*, 189–223.

Leaper, C., & Friedman, C. K. (2007). The socialization of gender. In J. E. Grusec & P. D. Hastings (Eds.), *Handbook of socialization: Theory and research* (pp. 561–587). Guilford Press.

Leary, C., Kelley, M., Morrow, J., & Mikulka, P. (2008). Parental use of physical punishment as related to family environment, psychological well-being, and personality in undergraduates. *Journal of Family Violence, 23*, 1–7.

LeBlanc, J., Ducharme, M. B., & Thompson, M. (2004). Study on the correlation of the autonomic nervous system response to a stressor of high discomfort with personality traits. *Physiology of Behavior, 82*, 647–652.

Lebovits, A. (2007). Cognitive-behavioral approaches to chronic pain. *Primary Psychiatry, 14*, 48–54.

Lebow, J. L., & Gurman, A. S. (1995). Research assessing couple and family therapy. *Annual Review of Psychology, 46*, 27–57.

Lebow, J. L., Chambers, A. L., Christensen, A., & Johnson, S. M. (2012). Research on the treatment of couple distress. *Journal of Marital and Family Therapy, 38*, 145–168.

Lecanuet, J. P., Manera, S., & Jacquet, A. Y. (2002, April). *Fetal cardiac responses to maternal sentences, to playback of these sentences, and to their recordings by another woman's voice.* Paper presented at the XIII International Conference on Infant Studies, Toronto, Ontario, Canada.

Lecat, B., Hilton, D. J., & Crano, W. D. (2009). Group status and reciprocity norms: Can the door-in-the-face effect be obtained in an out-group context? *Group Dynamics: Theory, Research, and Practice, 13*, 178–189. doi:10.1037/a0014956

Leckman, J. F., Denys, D., Simpson, H. B., Mataix-Cols, D., Hollander, E., Saxena, S., . . . Stein, D. J. (2010). Obsessive-compulsive disorder: A review of the diagnostic criteria and possible subtypes and dimensional signifiers for *DSM-V. Depression and Anxiety, 27*, 507–527.

Lee, A. Y. (2001). The mere exposure effect: An uncertainty reduction explanation revisited. *Personality and Social Psychology Bulletin, 27*, 1255–1266.

Lee, C. S., & Dik, B. J. (2016). Associations among stress, gender, sources of social support, and health in emerging adults. *Stress and Health, 33(4), 378-388.* doi:10.1002/smi.2722

Lee, D. C., Sui, X., Ortega, F. B., Kim, Y. S., Church, T. S., Winett, R. A., . . . Blair, S. N. (2011). Comparisons of leisure-time physical activity and cardiorespiratory fitness as predictors of all-cause mortality in men and women. *British Journal of Sports Medicine, 45*, 504-510.

Lee, D. M., Nazroo, J., O'Connor, D. B., Blake, M., & Pendleton, N. (2016). Sexual health and well-being among older men and women in England: Findings from the English Longitudinal Study of Ageing. *Archives of Sexual Behavior, 45*(1), 133-44. doi:10.1007/s10508-014-0465-1.

Lee, H. (1997). *Still life with rice*. Touchstone.

Lee, H. J., Lee, J. O., Lee, Y. W., Kim, S. A., Seo, I. H., Han, J. A., ... Kim, H. S. (2019). LIF, a novel myokine, protects against amyloid-beta-induced neurotoxicity via Akt-mediated autophagy signaling in hippocampal cells. *International Journal of Neuropsychopharmacology, 22*(6), 402–414. https://doi.org/10.1093/ijnp/pyz016

Lee, L. O., James, P., Zevon, E. S., Kim, E. S., Trudel-Fitzgerald, C., Spiro, A., Grodstein, F., & Kubzansky, L. D. (2019). Optimism is associated with exceptional longevity in 2 epidemiologic cohorts of men and women. *Proceedings of the National Academy of Sciences of the United States of America, 116*(37), 18357-18362. doi:10.1073/pnas.1900712116

Lee, S. J., Perron, B. E., Taylor, C. A., & Guterman, N. B. (2011). Parental psychosocial characteristics and corporal punishment in their 3-year-old children. *Journal of Interpersonal Violence, 26*, 71–87.

Leehr, E. J., Schag, K., Brinkmann, A., Ehlis, A. C., Fallgatter, A. J., Zipfel, S., . . . Dresler, T. (2016). Alleged approach-avoidance conflict for food stimuli in binge eating disorder. *PloS One, 11*(4), e0152271. doi:10.1371/journal.pone.0152271

Lefcourt, H. M. (2001). The humor solution. In C. R. Snyder (Ed.), *Coping with stress: Effective people and processes* (pp. 68–92). Oxford University Press.

Lefcourt, H. M., & Davidson-Katz, K. (1991). The role of humor and the self. In C. R. Synder & D. R. Forsyth (Eds.), *Handbook of social and clinical psychology: The health perspective* (pp. 41–56). Pergamon Press.

Leger, K. A., Charles, S. T., & Almeida, D. M. (2018). Let it go: Lingering negative affect in response to daily stressors is associated with physical health years later. *Psychological Science, 29*(8), 1283-1290.

Lehto, U. S., Ojanen, M., Dyba, T., Aromaa, A., & Kellokumpu-Lehtinen, P. (2006). Baseline psychosocial predictors of survival in localized breast cancer. *British Journal of Cancer, 94*, 1245–1252.

Lei, L., & South, S. J. (2016). Racial and ethnic differences in leaving and returning to the parental home: The role of life course transitions, socioeconomic resources, and family connectivity. *Demographic Research, 34*, 109–142.

Leibowitz, S. F. (1991). Brain neuropeptide Y: An integrator of endocrine, metabolic, and behavioral processes. *Brain Research Bulletin, 27*, 333–337.

Leichsenring, F., Leibing, E., Kruse, J., New, A. S., & Leweke, F. (2011). Borderline personality disorder. *Lancet, 377*, 74–84.

Leigh-Hunt, N., Bagguley, D., Bash, K., Turner, V., Turnbull, S., Valtorta, N., & Caan, W. (2017). An overview of systematic reviews on the public health consequences of social isolation and loneliness. *Public Health, 152*, 157–171. doi:10.1016/j.puhe.2017.07.035

Leite, N. C., de Paula, F., Borck, P. C., Vettorazzi, J. F., Branco, R. C. S., Lubaczeuski, C., . . . Carneiro, E. M. (2016). Protein malnutrition potentiates the amplifying pathway of insulin secretion in adult obese mice. *Scientific Reports, 6*, 33464. doi:10.1038/srep33464

Lekander, M., Andreasson, A. N., Kecklund, G., Ekman, R., Ingre, M., Akerstedt, T., & Axelsson, J. (2013). Subjective health perception in healthy young men changes in response to experimentally restricted sleep and subsequent recovery sleep. *Brain, Behavior, and Immunity, 34*, 43–46.

Lekic, S. (2013, September 30). U.S. Navy dolphins help clean up seabed off of Croatia resort town. *Stars and Stripes*, https://www.stripes.com/news/navy/us-navy-dolphins-help-clean-up-seabed-off-of-croatia-resort-town-1.244200

Lelièvre-Desmas, M., Chollet, S., Abdi, H., & Valentin, D. (2015). Becoming a beer expert: Is simple exposure with feedback sufficient to learn beer categories? *Acta Psychologica, 161*, 95–103. doi:10.1016/j.actpsy.2015.08.003

Lemay, E. P., Clark, M. S., & Greenberg, A. (2010). What is beautiful is good because what is beautiful is desired: Physical attractiveness stereotyping as projection of interpersonal goals. *Personality and Social Psychology Bulletin, 36*, 339–353.

Lemola, S., Ledermann, T., & Friedman, E. M. (2013). Variability of sleep duration is related to subjective sleep quality and subjective well-being: An actigraphy study. *PLoS One, 8*, e71292.

Lenhart, A., Smith, A., & Anderson, M. (2015). *Teens, technology and romantic relationships*. Pew Research Center.

Lent, R., Azevedo, F. A., Andrade-Moraes, C. H., & Pinto, A. V. (2012). How many neurons do you have? Some dogmas of quantitative neuroscience under revision. *European Journal of Neuroscience, 35*, 1–9. doi:10.1111/j.1460-9568.2011.07923.x

Lenze, E. J., Rollman, B. L., Shear, M. K., Dew, M. A., Pollock, B. G., Ciliberti, C., . . . Reynolds, C. F. (2009). Escitalopram for older adults with generalized anxiety disorder: A randomized controlled trial. *Journal of the American Medical Association, 301*, 295–303.

Lenzenweger, M. F. (2008). Epidemiology of personality disorders. *Psychiatric Clinics of North America, 31*, 395–403.

Lenzenweger, M. F., Lane, M., Loranger, A., & Kessler, R. (2007). *DSM-IV* personality disorders in the National Comorbidity Survey Replication. *Biological Psychiatry, 62*, 553–564.

Leon, S. C., Kopta, S. M., Howard, K. I., & Lutz, W. (1999). Predicting patients' responses to psychotherapy: Are some more predictable than others? *Journal of Consulting and Clinical Psychology, 67*, 698–704.

Leopold, D. A., & Rhodes, G. (2010). A comparative view of face perception. *Journal of Comparative Psychology, 124*, 233–251.

LePine, J. A., Erez, A., & Johnston, D. E. (2002). The nature and dimensionality of organizational citizenship behavior: A critical review and a meta-analysis. *Journal of Applied Psychology, 87*, 52–65.

Lester, B. M., Andreozzi, L., & Appiah, L. (2004). Substance use during pregnancy: Time for policy to catch up with research. *Harm Reduction Journal, 1*, 5–49.

Leuchter, A. F., Lesser, I. M., Trivedi, M. H., Rush, A. J., Morris, D. W., Warden, D., . . . Stewart, J. W. (2008). An open pilot study of the combination of escitalopram and bupropion-SR for outpatients with major depressive disorder. *Journal of Psychiatric Practice, 14*, 271–280.

Leung, N. T. Y., Tam, H. M. K., Chu, L. W., Kwok, T. C. Y., Chan, F., Lam, L. C. W., . . . Lee, T. M. C. (2015). Neural plastic effects of cognitive training on aging brain. *Neural Plasticity, 2015*, 535618. doi:10.1155/2015/535618

Leung, S., Croft, R. J., Jackson, M. L., Howard, M. E., & McKenzie, R. J. (2012). A comparison of the effect of mobile phone use and alcohol consumption on driving simulation performance. *Traffic Injury Prevention, 13*, 566–574.

Levenson, R. W., Ekman, P., & Friesen, W. V. (1990). Voluntary facial action generates emotion-specific nervous system activity. *Psychophysiology, 27*, 363–384.

Levin, B. E. (2010). Developmental gene × environment interactions affecting systems regulating energy homeostasis and obesity. *Frontiers in Neuroendocrinology, 31*(3), 270–283. https://doi.org/10.1016/j.yfrne.2010.02.005

Levin, B. E., & Routh, V. H. (1996). Role of the brain in energy balance and obesity. *American Journal of Physiology, 271*, R491–R500.

Levine, B., Turner, G. R., Tisserand, D., Hevenor, S. J., Graham, S. J., & McIntosh, A. R. (2004). The functional neuroanatomy of episodic and semantic autobiographical remembering: A prospective functional MRI study. *Journal of Cognitive Neuroscience, 16*, 1633–1646.

Levine, R. A., & Campbell, D. T. (1972). *Ethnocentrism: Theories of conflict, ethnic attitudes, and group behavior.* Wiley.

Levinson, D. F., Evgrafov, O. V., Knowles, J. A., Potash, J. B., Weissman M. M., Scheftner, W. A., . . . Holmans, P. (2007). Genetics of recurrent early-onset major depression (GenRED): Significant linkage on chromosome 15q25–q26 after fine mapping with single nucleotide polymorphism markers. *American Journal of Psychiatry, 164*, 259–264.

Levitt, A. G., & Utmann, J. G. A. (1992). From babbling towards the sound systems of English and French: A longitudinal two-case study. *Journal of Child Language, 19*, 19–40.

Levy, B. R., & Myers, L. M. (2004). Preventive health behaviors influenced by self-perceptions of aging. *Preventive Medicine, 39*, 625–629.

Levy, B. R., Slade, M. D., Kunkel, S. R., & Kasl, S. V. (2002). Longevity increased by positive self-perceptions of aging. *Journal of Personality and Social Psychology, 83*, 261–270.

Levy, D. J., Heissel, J. A., Richeson, J. A., & Adam, E. K. (2016). Psychological and biological responses to race-based social stress as pathways to disparities in educational outcome. *The American Psychologist, 71*, 455–473.

Levy, D. L., Coleman, M. J., Sung, H., Ji, F., Matthysse, S., Mendell, N. R., & Titone, D. (2010). The genetic basis of thought disorder and language and communication disturbances in schizophrenia. *Journal of Neurolinguistics, 23*, 176.

Levy, G. D., Taylor, M. G., & Gelman, S. A. (1995). Traditional and evaluative aspects of flexibility in gender roles, social conventions, moral rules, and physical laws *Child Development, 66*, 515–531.

Levy-Shiff, R. (1994). Individual and contextual correlates of marital change across the transition to parenthood. *Developmental Psychology, 30*, 591–601.

Lewinsohn, P. M., Clark, G. N., Hops, H., & Andrews, J. (1990). Cognitive-behavioral treatment for depressed adolescents. *Behavior Therapy, 21,* 385–401.

Lewinsohn, P. M., Rohde, P., & Seeley, J. R. (1994). Psychosocial risk factors for future adolescent suicide attempts. *Journal of Consulting and Clinical Psychology, 62,* 297–305.

Lewis, B. A., Minnes, S., Short, E.J., Min, M. O., Wu, M., Lang, A., . . . Singer, L. T. (2013). Language outcomes at 12 years for children exposed prenatally to cocaine. *Journal of Speech, Language, and Hearing Research, 56,* 1662–1676.

Lewis, D. O. (1992). From abuse to violence: Psychophysiological consequences of maltreatment. *Journal of the American Academy of Child and Adolescent Psychiatry, 31,* 383–391.

Lewis, D. O., Yeager, C. A., Blake, P., Bard, B., & Strenziok, M. (2004). Ethics questions raised by the neuropsychiatric, neuropsychological, educational, developmental, and family characteristics of 18 juveniles awaiting execution in Texas. *Journal of the American Academy of Psychiatry and the Law, 32,* 408–429.

Lewis, T. T., & Van Dyke, M. E. (2018). Discrimination and the health of African Americans: The potential importance of intersectionalities. *Current Directions in Psychological Science, 27*(3), 176–182.

Lewis-Peacock, J. A., Drysdale, A. T., & Postle, B. R. (2015). Neural evidence for the flexible control of mental representations. *Cerebral Cortex, 25*(10), 3303–3313. doi:10.1093/cercor/bhu130

Leyhe, T., Müller, S., Milian, M., Eschweiler, G. W., & Saur, R. (2009). Impairment of episodic and semantic autobiographical memory in patients with mild cognitive impairment and early Alzheimer's disease. *Neuropsychologia, 47,* 2464–2469. doi:10.1016/j.neuropsychologia.2009.04.018

Li, B. J., & Lwin, M. O. (2016). Player see, player do: Testing an exergame motivation model based on the influence of the self avatar. *Computers in Human Behavior, 59,* 350–357. doi:10.1016/j.chb.2016.02.034

Li, B. Y., Tang, H. D., & Chen, S. D. (2016). Retrieval deficiency in brain activity of working memory in amnesic mild cognitive impairment patients: A brain event-related potentials study. *Frontiers in Aging Neuroscience, 8,* 54. doi:10.3389/fnagi.2016.00054

Li, C. E., DiGiuseppe, R., & Froh, J. (2006). The roles of sex, gender, and coping in adolescent depression. *Adolescence, 41,* 409–415.

Li, G., Ji, G., Hu, Y., Liu, L., Jin, Q., Zhang, W., ... Wang, G.-J. (2019). Reduced plasma ghrelin concentrations are associated with decreased brain reactivity to food cues after laparoscopic sleeve gastrectomy. *Psychoneuroendocrinology, 100,* 229–236. https://doi.org/10.1016/j.psyneuen.2018.10.022

Li, J., Gao, W., Yu, L., Zhu, S., & Cao, F. (2017). Breast-related stereotype threat contributes to a symptom cluster in women with breast cancer. *Journal of Clinical Nursing, 26*(9-10), 1395–1404. doi:10.1111/jocn.13698

Li, M., D'Arcy, C., & Meng, X. (2016). Maltreatment in childhood substantially increases the risk of adult depression and anxiety in prospective cohort studies: Systematic review, meta-analysis, and proportional attributable fractions. *Psychological Medicine, 46,* 717–730.

Li, N., Papandonatos, G. D., Calafat, A. M., Yolton, K., Lanphear, B. P., Chen, A., & Braun, J. M. (2019). Identifying periods of susceptibility to the impact of phthalates on children's cognitive abilities. *Environmental Research, 172,* 604–614..

Li, S., Lindenberger, U., Hommel, B., Aschersleben, G., Prinz, W., & Baltes, P. B. (2004). Transformations in the couplings among intellectual abilities and constituent cognitive processes across the life span. *Psychological Science, 15,* 155–163.

Li, Y., Pan, A., Wang, D. D., Liu, X., Dhana, K., Franco, O. H.... Hu, F. B. (2018). Impact of healthy lifestyle factors on life expectancies in the U.S. population. *Circulation, 138*(4), 345–355. doi:10.1161/CIRCULATIONAHA.117.032047

Li, Y., Xiao, X., Ma, W., Jiang, J., Qiu, J., & Zhang, Q. (2013). Electrophysiological evidence for emotional valence and competitive arousal effects on insight problem solving. *Brain Research, 153, 8,* 61–72. doi:10.1016/j.brainres.2013.09.021

Libersat, F., & Pflueger, H. J. (2004). Monoamines and the orchestration of behavior. *BioScience, 54,* 17–25.

Lick, D.J., Durso, L.E., & Johnson, K. L. (2013). Minority stress and physical health among sexual minorities. *Perspectives on Psychological Science, 8,* 521–548.

Lieberman, J. A., Stroup, T. S., & Perkins, D. O. (2012). *Essentials of schizophrenia.* American Psychiatric Publishing.

Lieberman, J., Chakos, M., Wu, H., Alvir, J., Hoffman, E., Robinson, D., & Bilder, R. (2001). Longitudinal study of brain morphology in first episode schizophrenia. *Biological Psychiatry, 49,* 487–499.

Lieberman, J., Tollefson, G., Tohen, M., Green, A. I., Gur, R. E., Kahn, R., . . . HGDH Study Group (2003). Comparative efficacy and safety of atypical and conventional antipsychotic drugs in first-episode psychosis: A randomized, double-blind trial of olanzapine versus haloperidol. *American Journal of Psychiatry, 160,* 1396–1404.

Liebert, R. M., & Spiegler, M. D. (1998). *Personality: Strategies and issues* (8th ed.), Brooks/Cole.

Lieblich, S. M., Castle, D. J., Pantelis, C., Hopwood, M., Young, A. H., & Everall, I. P. (2015). High heterogeneity and low reliability in the diagnosis of major depression will impair the development of new drugs. *British Journal of Psychiatry Open, 1,* e5–e7.

Lien, Y., Chu, R., Jen, C., & Wu, C. (2006). Do Chinese commit neither fundamental attribution error nor ultimate attribution error? *Chinese Journal of Psychology, 48,* 163–181.

Lilienfeld, S. O., Lynn, S. J., Ruscio, J., & Beyerstein, B. L. (2011). *50 great myths of popular psychology: Shattering widespread misconceptions about human behavior.* Wiley-Blackwell.

Lilienfeld, S. O., Ritschel, L. A., Lynn, S. J., Cautin, R. L., & Latzman, R. D. (2014). Why ineffective psychotherapies appear to work: A taxonomy of causes of spurious therapeutic effectiveness. *Perspectives on Psychological Science, 9,* 355–387.

Liljeholm, M., Dunne, S., & O'Doherty, J. P. (2015). Differentiating neural systems mediating the acquisition vs expression of goal-directed and habitual behavioral control. *European Journal of Neuroscience, 41*(10), 1358–1371. https://doi.org/10.1111/ejn.12897

Lin, I. F., Brown, S. L., Wright, M. R., & Hammersmith, A. M. (2018). Antecedents of gray divorce: A life course perspective. *The Journals of Gerontology. Series B, Psychological Sciences and Social Sciences, 73*(6), 1022–1031. doi:10.1093/geronb/gbw164

Lin, J. Y., Arthurs, J., & Reilly, S. (2017). Conditioned taste aversions: From poisons to pain to drugs of abuse. *Psychonomic Bulletin & Review, 24*(2), 335–351. doi:10.3758/s13423-016-1092-8

Lincoln, A. E., Caswell, S. V., Almquist, J. L., Dunn, R. E., Norris, J. B., & Hinton, R. Y. (2011). Trends in concussion incidence in high school sports: A prospective 11-year study. *American Journal of Sports Medicine, 39,* 958–963. doi:10.1177/0363546510392326

Lindau, S. T., Schumm, L. P., Laumann, E. O., Levinson, W., O'Muircheartaigh, C. A., & Waite, L. J. (2007). A study of sexuality and health among older adults in the United States. *New England Journal of Medicine, 357,* 762–774.

Lindenmayer, J. P., Khan, A., Iskander, A., Abad, M. T., & Parker, B. (2007). A randomized controlled trial of olanzapine versus haloperidol in the treatment of primary negative symptoms and neurocognitive deficits in schizophrenia. *Journal of Clinical Psychiatry, 68,* 368–379.

Ling, D., Niu, T., Feng, Y., Xing, H., & Xu, X. (2004). Association between polymorphism of the dopamine transporter gene and early smoking onset: An interaction risk on nicotine dependence. *Journal of Human Genetics 49,* 35–39.

Linhares, J. M., Pinto, P. D., & Nascimento, S. M. (2008). The number of discernable colors in natural scenes. *Journal of the Optical Society of America, 25,* 2918–2924.

Lino, M., Kuczynski, K., Rodriguez, N., and Schap, T. (2017). *Expenditures on Children by Families, 2015.* Miscellaneous Publication No. 1528-2015. U.S. Department of Agriculture, Center for Nutrition Policy and Promotion.

Linville, P. W., Fischer, G. W., & Salovey, P. (1989) Perceived distributions of characteristics on in-group and out-group members: Empirical evidence and a computer simulation. *Journal of Personality and Social Psychology, 57,* 165–188.

Liossi, C., White, P., & Hatira, P. (2006). Randomized clinical trial of local anesthetic versus a combination of local anesthetic with self-hypnosis in the management of pediatric procedure-related pain. *Health Psychology, 25,* 307–315.

Lippa, R. (2003). Handedness, sexual orientation, and gender-related personality traits in men and women. *Archives of Sexual Behavior, 32,* 103–114.

Lissek, S., Rabin, S., Heller, R. E., Lukenbaugh, D., Geraci, M., Pine, D. S., & Grillon, C. (2010). Overgeneralization of conditioned fear as a pathogenic marker of panic disorder. *American Journal of Psychiatry, 167,* 47–55.

Littleton, H., Horsley, S., John, S., & Nelson, D. V. (2007). Trauma coping strategies and psychological distress: A meta-analysis. *Journal of Trauma and Stress, 20,* 977–988.

Liu, B., Pu, J., & Hou, H. (2016). Effect of perceived stress on depression of Chinese "Ant Tribe" and the moderating role of dispositional optimism. *Journal of Health Psychology, 21,* 2725–2731.

Liu, H., Petukhova, M. V., Sampson, N. A., Aguilar-Gaxiola, S., Alonso, J., Andrade, L. H., ... World Health Organization World Mental Health Survey Collaborators (2017). Association of *DSM-IV* posttraumatic stress disorder with traumatic experience type and history in the World Health Organization World Mental Health Surveys. *JAMA*

Psychiatry, 74(3), 270–281. doi:10.1001/jamapsychiatry.2016.3783

Liu, H., & Waite, L. (2014). Bad marriage, broken heart? Age and gender differences in the link between marital quality and cardiovascular risks among older adults. *Journal of Health and Social Behavior, 55*(4), 403–423. doi:10.1177/0022146514556893

Liu, H., Wang, F., & Yang, X. (2015). More dialectical thinking, less creativity? The relationship between dialectical thinking style and creative personality: The case of China. *PLoS ONE, 10*(4). doi:10.1371journal.pone.0122926

Liu, R. T., & Spirito. A. (2019). Suicidal behavior and stress generation in adolescents. *Clinical Psychological Science, 7*(3), 488-501.

Liu, S., Xiao, W. S., Xiao, N. G., Quinn, P. C., Zhang, Y., Chen, H., . . . Lee, K. (2015). Development of visual preference for own- versus other-race faces in infancy. *Developmental Psychology, 51*(4), 500-511.

Livingston, I. (2010, April 24). Stabbed hero dies as more than 20 people stroll past him. *New York Post.* http://nypost.com/2010/04/24/stabbed-hero-dies-as-more-than-20-people-stroll-past-him/

Livingstone, M. S., Lafer-Sousa, R., & Conway, B. R. (2011). Stereopsis and artistic talent: Poor stereopsis among art students and established artists. *Psychological Science, 22*(3), 336–338. doi:10.1177/0956797610397958

Loane, C., & Politis, M. (2012). Buspirone: What is it all about? *Brain Research, 1461,* 111–118.

Lockenhoff, C. E., De Fruyt, F., Terracciano, A., McCrae, R. R., De Bolle, M., Costa, P.T., Jr., . . . Yik, M. (2009). Perceptions of aging across 26 cultures and their culture-level associates. *Psychology and Aging, 24,* 941–954.

Lockhart, R. S., & Craik, F. I. M. (1990). Levels of processing: A retrospective commentary on a framework for memory research. *Canadian Journal of Psychology, 44,* 87–112.

Loersch, C., Durso, G. O., & Petty, R. E. (2013). Vicissitudes of desire: A matching mechanism for subliminal persuasion. *Social Psychological and Personality Science, 4,* 624–631. doi:10.1177/1948550612471975

Loewenstein, R. J., & Putnam, F. W. (2004). The dissociative disorders. In B. J. Sadock, & V. A. Sadock (Eds.), *Posttraumatic stress disorder: DSM-IV and beyond* (8th ed., pp. 1844–1901). Williams & Wilkins.

Loewenstein, W. R. (1960). Biological transducers. *Scientific American, 203,* 98–108.

Loftus, E. F. (1979). *Eyewitness testimony.* Harvard University Press.

Loftus, E. F. (2000). Remembering what never happened. In E. Tulving (Ed.*), Memory, consciousness, and the brain* (pp. 106–118). Psychology Press.

Loftus, E. F., & Davis, D. (2006). Recovered memories. *Annual Review of Clinical Psychology, 2,* 469–498.

Loftus, E. F., & Palmer, J. C. (1974). Reconstruction of automobile destruction: An example of the interaction between language and memory. *Journal of Verbal Learning and Verbal Behavior, 13,* 585–589.

Loftus, E. F., & Zanni, G. (1975). Eyewitness testimony: The influence of the wording of a question. *Bulletin of the Psychonomic Society, 5,* 86–88.

Logie, R. H. (1999). State of the art: Working memory. *Psychologist, 12,* 174–178.

Logie, R. H., Della Sala, S., Wynn, V., & Baddeley, A. D. (2000, November). *Division of attention in Alzheimer's disease.* Paper presented at the Psychonomics Society meeting.

Logue, A. W. (1979). Taste aversion and the generality of the laws of learning. *Psychological Bulletin, 86,* 276–296.

Logue, A. W., Ophir, I., & Strauss, K. E. (1981). The acquisition of taste aversions in humans. *Behavior Research and Therapy, 19,* 319–333.

Lombardo, C., Ballesio, A., Gasparrini, G., & Cerolini, S. (2019). Effects of acute and chronic sleep deprivation on eating behaviour. *Clinical Psychologist, 24,* 64-72. https://doi.org/10.1111/cp.12189

Lomenick, J. P., Melguizo, M. S., Mitchell, S. L., Summar, M. L., & Anderson, J. W. (2009). Effects of meals high in carbohydrate, protein, and fat on ghrelin and peptide YY secretion in prepubertal children. *Journal of Clinical Endocrinology and Metabolism, 94* 4463–4471.

Loney, B. R., Taylor, J., Butler, M. A., & Iacono, W. G. (2007). Adolescent psychopathy features: 6-year temporal stability and the prediction of externalizing symptoms during the transition to adulthood. *Aggressive Behavior, 33,* 242–252.

Long, B. C., & van Stavel, R. (1995). Effects of exercise training on anxiety: A meta-analysis. *Journal of Applied Sport Psychology, 7,* 167–189.

Long, N., Readdy, T., & Raabe, J. (2014). What motivates firefighters to exercise? A mixed-methods investigation of self-determination theory constructs and exercise behavior. *Sport, Exercise, and Performance Psychology, 3*(3), 203–218. doi:10.1037/spy0000012

Longstreth, W. T., Jr., Koepsell, T. D., Ton, T. G., Hendrickson, A. F., & van Belle, G. (2007). The epidemiology of narcolepsy. *Sleep, 30,* 13–26.

Lopez Cascales, J. J., Oliveira Costa, S. D., de Groot, B. L., & Walters, D. E. (2010). Binding of glutamate to the umami receptor. *Biochemical Chemistry, 152,* 139–144.

Lopez, C. M., Driscoll, K. A., & Kistner, J. A. (2009). Sex differences and response styles: Subtypes of rumination and associations with depressive symptoms. *Journal of Clinical Child and Adolescent Psychology, 38,* 27–35.

Lopez, M. A., & Basco, M. A. (2015). Effectiveness of cognitive behavioral therapy in public mental health: Comparison to treatment as usual for treatment-resistant depression. *Administration and Policy in Mental Health, 42,* 87–98.

Loprinzi, P. D., & Davis, R. E. (2016). Secular trends in parent-reported television viewing among children in the United States, 2001–2012. *Child: Care, Health and Development, 42*(2), 288–291. doi:10.1111/cch.12304

Loprinzi, P. D., Frith, E., & Crawford, L. (2020). The effects of acute exercise on retroactive memory interference. *American Journal of Health Promotion, 34*(1), 25–31. https://doi.org/10.1177/0890117119866138

Lorenz, F. O., Wickrama, K. A., Conger, R. D., & Elder, G. H., Jr. (2006). The short-term and decade-long effects of divorce on women's midlife health. *Journal of Health and Social Behavior, 47,* 111–125.

Lorenz, L., Doherty, A., & Casey, P. (2019). The role of religion in buffering the impact of stressful life events on depressive symptoms in patients with depressive episodes or adjustment disorder. *International Journal of Environmental Research and Public Health, 16*(7), 1238. doi:10.3390/ijerph16071238

Lorenzo-Luaces, L., Derubeis, R. J., & Webb, C. A. (2014). Client characteristics as moderators of the relation between the therapeutic alliance and outcome in cognitive therapy for depression. *Journal of Consulting and Clinical Psychology, 82,* 368–373.

Loughnan, S., Haslam, N., Sutton, R. M., & Spencer, B. (2014). Dehumanization and social class: Animality in the stereotypes of "white trash," "chavs," and "bogans." *Social Psychology, 45,* 54–61. doi:10.1027/1864-9335/a000159

Lourenco, O., & Machado, A. (1996). In defense of Piaget's theory: A reply to 10 common criticisms. *Psychological Review, 103,* 143–164.

Loveless, A. S., & Holman, T. B. (2007). *The family in the new millennium: The place of family in human society.* Praeger.

Lowe, S. R., Dillon, C. O., Rhodes, J. E., & Zwiebach, L. (2013). Defining adult experiences: Perspectives of a diverse sample of young adults. *Journal of Adolescent Research, 28,* 31–68.

Lowis, M. J., Edwards, A. C., & Burton, M. (2009). Coping with retirement: Well-being, health, and religion. *Journal of Psychology, 143,* 427–448.

Lu, H., Xu, F., Rodrigue, K. M., Kennedy, K. M., Cheng, Y., Flicker, B., . . . Park, D. C. (2011). Alterations in cerebral metabolic rate and blood supply across the adult lifespan. *Cerebral Cortex, 21(6),* 1426–1434. doi:10.1093/cercor/bhq224

Lu, N. Z., Eshleman, A. J., Janowsky, A., & Bethea, C. L. (2003). Ovarian steroid regulation of serotonin reuptake transporter (SERT) binding, distribution, and function in female macaques. *Molecular Psychiatry, 8,* 353–360.

Luber, B. M., Davis, S., Bernhardt, E., Neacsiu, A., Kwapil, L., Lisanby, S. H., & Strauman, T. J. (2017). Using neuroimaging to individualize TMS treatment for depression: Toward a new paradigm for imaging-guided intervention. *NeuroImage, 148,* 1–7.

Lucas, R. E. (2005). Time does not heal all wounds: A longitudinal study of reaction and adaptation to divorce. *Psychological Science, 16,* 945–950.

Luders, E., Thompson, P. M., Kurth, F., Hong, J., Phillips, O. R., Wang, Y., . . . Toga, A. W. (2013). Global and regional alterations of hippocampal anatomy in long-term meditation practitioners. *Human Brain Mapping, 34,* 3369–3375. doi:10.1002/hbm.22153

Ludtke, O., Trautwein, U., & Husemann, N. (2009). Goal and personality trait development in a transitional period: Assessing change and stability in personality development. *Personality and Social Psychology Bulletin, 35,* 428–441.

Luecken, L. J., & Compas, B. E. (2002). Stress, coping, and immune function in breast cancer. *Annals of Behavioral Medicine, 24,* 336–344.

Luhmann, M., Hofmann, W., Eid, M., & Lucas, R. E. (2012). Subjective well-being and adaptation to life events: A meta-analysis. *Journal of Personality and Social Psychology, 102,* 592–615.

Lumer, E. D., Friston, K. J., & Rees, G. (1998). Neural correlates of perceptual rivalry in the human brain. *Science, 280,* 1930–1934.

Lundberg, S., Pollak, R. A., & Stearns, J. (2016). Family inequality: Diverging patterns in marriage, cohabitation, and childbearing. *The Journal of Economic Perspectives, 30,* 79–102.

Luo, S. (2009). What leads to romantic attraction: Similarity, reciprocity, security, or beauty? Evidence from a speed-dating study. *Journal of Personality, 77,* 933–964.

Lurigio, A. J. (2015). Crime narratives, dramatizations, and the legacy of the Kitty Genovese murder: A half century of half truths. *Criminal Justice and Behavior, 42*(7), 782–789. doi:10.1177/0093854814562954

Lussier, K. (2019). Of Maslow, motives, and managers: The hierarchy of needs in American business, 1960–1985. *Journal of the History of the Behavioral Sciences, 55*(4), 319-341. https://doi.org/10.1002/jhbs.21992

Ly, H. G., Dupont, P., Van Laere, K., Depoortere, I., Tack, J., & Van Oudenhove, L. (2016). Differential brain responses to gradual intragastric nutrient infusion and gastric balloon distension: A role for gut peptides? *NeuroImage, 144*(A), 101–112. doi10.1016/j.neuroimage.2016.09.032

Lykken, D. T., McGue, M., Tellegen, A., & Bouchard, T. J. (1992). Emergenesis. *American Psychologist, 47,* 1565–1567.

Lynn, B., Yoo, G.J., & Levine, E.G. (2014). "Trust in the Lord": Religious and spiritual practices of African American breast cancer survivors. *Journal of Religion and Health, 53*(6), 1706–1716. doi:10.1007/s10943-013-9750-x

Lynn, S. J. (1997). Automaticity and hypnosis: A sociocognitive account. *International Journal of Clinical and Experimental Hypnosis, 45,* 239–250.

Lynn, S .J., Laurence, J. R., & Kirsch, I. (2015). Hypnosis, suggestion, and suggestibility: An integrative model. *The American Journal of Clinical Hypnosis, 57,* 314–329.

Lynne-Landsman, S. D., Graber, J. A., Nichols, T. R., & Botvin, G. J. (2011). Is sensation seeking a stable trait or does it change over time? *Journal of Youth and Adolescence, 40,* 48–58. doi:10.1007/s10964-010-9529-2

Lytton, H., & Romney, D. M. (1991). Parents' differential socialization of boys and girls: A meta-analysis. *Psychological Bulletin, 109,* 267–296.

Lyubomirsky, S., & Layous, K. (2013). How do simple positive activities increase well-being? *Current Directions in Psychological Science, 22,* 5762.

Macan, T. (2009). The employment interview: A review of current studies and directions for future research. *Human Resource Management Review, 19,* 203–218.

MacCann, C., & Roberts, R. D. (2013). Just as smart but not as successful: Obese students obtain lower school grades but equivalent test scores to nonobese students. *International Journal of Obesity, 37*(1), 40–46. doi:10.1038/ijo.2012.47

Macfadden, W., Bossie C. A., Turkoz, I., & Haskins, J. T. (2010). Risperidone long-acting therapy in stable patients with recently diagnosed schizophrenia. *International Clinical Psychopharmacology, 25,* 75–82.

Macintosh, H. B., & Johnson, S. (2008). Emotionally focused therapy for couples and childhood sexual abuse survivors. *Journal of Marital and Family Therapy, 34,* 298–315.

Mack, M. L., & Palmeri, T. J. (2015). The dynamics of categorization: Unraveling rapid categorization. *Journal of Experimental Psychology: General, 144*(3), 551–569. doi:10.1037/a0039184

Macmillan, M., & Lena M. L. (2010). Rehabilitating Phineas Gage. *Neuropsychological Rehabilitation, 20*(5), 641–658. doi:10.1080/09602011003760527

Maddi, S. R. (2005). On hardiness and other pathways to resilience. *American Psychologist, 60,* 261–262.

Maddi, S. R., & Kobasa, S. C. (1984). *The hardy executive: Health under stress.* Dorsey Press.

Maddi, S. R., Harvey, R. H., Khoshaba, D. M., Lu, J. L., Persico, M., & Brow, M. (2006). The personality construct of hardiness: III. Relationships with repression, innovativeness, authoritarianism, and performance. *Journal of Personality, 74,* 575–597.

Madsen, M. K., McMahon, B., Andersen, S. B., Siebner, H. R., Knudsen, G. M., & Fisher, P. M. (2016). Threat-related amygdala functional connectivity is associated with 5-HTTLPR genotype and neuroticism. *Social Cognitive and Affective Neuroscience, 11,* 140–149.

Maguire, E. A. (2014). Memory consolidation in humans: New evidence and opportunities. *Experimental Physiology, 99(3),* 471–486. doi:10.1113/expphysiol.2013.072157

Maguire, E. A., & Mullally, S. L. (2013). The hippocampus: A manifesto for change. *Journal of Experimental Psychology: General, 142,* 1180–1189. doi:10.1037/a0033650

Maguire, E. A., Woollett, K., & Spiers, H. J. (2006). London taxi drivers and bus drivers: A structural MRI and neuropsychological analysis. *Hippocampus, 16,* 1091–1101.

Mah, K., & Binik, Y. M. (2002). Do all orgasms feel alike? Evaluating the two-dimensional model of the orgasm experience across gender and sexual context. *Journal of Sex Research, 39,* 104–113.

Maher, A. R., & Theodore, G. (2012). Summary of the comparative effectiveness review on off- label use of atypical antipsychotics. *Journal of Managed Care Pharmacy, 18,* S1–S20.

Mahler, J. (2015, February 27). The white and gold (No, blue and black!) dress that melted the Internet. *New York Times.* New York City. http://www.nytimes.com/2015/02/28/business/a-simple-question-about-a-dress-and-the-world-weighs-in.html

Maia, T. V., & Cano-Colino, M. (2015). The role of serotonin in orbitofrontal function and obsessive-compulsive disorder. *Clinical Psychological Science, 3,* 460–482.

Maillot, P., Perrot, A., & Hartley, A. (2012). Effects of interactive physical-activity videogame training on physical and cognitive function in older adults. *Psychology and Aging, 27,* 589–600.

Main, M., & Solomon, J. (1990). Procedures for identifying infants as disorganized/disoriented during the Ainsworth Strange Situation. In M. Greenberg, D. Cicchetti, & M. Cummings (Eds.), *Attachment in the preschool years: Theory, research, and intervention* (pp. 121–160). University of Chicago Press.

Maisonneuve, J., Palmade, G., & Fourment, C. (1952). Selective choices and propinquity. *Sociometry, 15,* 135–140.

Maj, M., Pirozzi, R., Magliano, L., & Bartoli, L. (1997). Long-term outcome of lithium prophylaxis in bipolar disorder: A 5-year prospective study of 402 patients at a lithium clinic. *American Journal of Psychiatry, 155,* 30–55.

Majdandzic, M., & van den Boom, D. C. (2007). Multimethod longitudinal assessment of temperament in early childhood. *Journal of Personality, 75,* 121–168.

Majumder I., White J., & Irvine R. (2012). Antidepressant-like effects of ecstasy in subjects with a predisposition to depression. *Addictive Behaviors 37,* 1189–1192.

Makinen, J. A., & Johnson, S. M. (2006). Resolving attachment injuries in couples using emotionally focused therapy: Steps toward forgiveness and reconciliation. *Journal of Consulting and Clinical Psychology, 74,* 1055–1064.

Makino, H., & Jitsumori, M. (2007). Discrimination of artificial categories structured by family resemblances: A comparative study in people (Homo sapiens) and pigeons (Columba livia). *Journal of Comparative Psychology, 121,* 22–33.

Makris, N., Swaab, D. F., van der Kouwe, A., Abbs, B., Boriel, D., Handa, R. J., . . . Goldstein, J. M. (2013). Volumetric parcellation methodology of the human hypothalamus in neuroimaging: Normative data and sex differences. *Neuroimage, 69,* 1–10. doi:10.1016/j.neuroimage.2012.12.008

Malaspina, D., Harlap, S., Fennig, S., Heiman, D., Nahon, D., Feldman, D., & Susser, E. S. (2001). Advancing paternal age and the risk of schizophrenia. *Archives of General Psychiatry, 58,* 361–367.

Malina, R. M. (1990). Physical growth and performance during the transitional years (9–16). In R. Montemayor, G. R. Adams, & T. P. Gullotta (Eds.), *From childhood to adolescence: A transitional period?* (pp. 41–62). SAGE.

Mancini, A. D., Bonanno, G. A., & Clark, G. E. (2011). Stepping off the hedonic treadmill: Individual differences in response to major life events. *Journal of Individual Differences, 32,* 144–152.

Mancini, A. D., Littleton, H. L., & Grills, A. E. (2016). Can people benefit from acute stress? Social support, psychological improvement, and resilience after the Virginia Tech campus shootings. *Clinical Psychological Science, 4,* 401–417.

Mander, B. A., Winer, J. R., Jagust, W. J., & Walker, M. P. (2016). Sleep: A novel mechanistic pathway, biomarker, and treatment target in the pathology of Alzheimer's disease? *Trends in Neurosciences, 39,* 552–566.

Manigault, A. W., Shorey, R. C., Hamilton, K., Scanlin, M. C., Woody, A., Figueroa, W. S., France, C. R., & Zoccola, P. M. (2019). Cognitive behavioral therapy, mindfulness, and cortisol habituation: A randomized controlled trial. *Psychoneuroendocrinology, 104,* 276–285. https://doi.org/10.1016/j.psyneuen.2019.03.009

Mann, R. D. (1959). A review of the relationships between personality and performance in small groups. *Psychological Bulletin, 56,* 241–270.

Manning, W. D., Brown, S. L., & Stykes, J. B. (2016). Same-sex and different-sex cohabiting couple relationship stability. *Demography, 53*(4), 937–953. doi:10.1007/s13524-016-0490-x

Marañon, I., Echeburúa, E., & Grijalvo, J. (2004). Prevalence of personality disorders in patients with eating disorders: A pilot study using the IPDE. *European Eating Disorders Review, 12,* 217–222.

Marazzitti, D., Rotondo, A., Presta, S., Pancioloi-Guasagnucci, M. L., Palego, L., & Conti, L. (1993). Role of serotonin in human aggressive behavior. *Aggressive Behavior, 19,* 347–353.

Marchetti, I., Koster, E. H. W., & De Raedt, R. (2013). Rest-related dynamics of risk and protective factors for depression: A behavioral study. *Clinical Psychological Science, 1,* 443–451.

Marcia, J. E. (2002). Identity and psychosocial development in adulthood. *Identity, 2,* 7–28.

Markman, A. B., & Ross, B. H. (2003). Category use and category learning. *Psychological Bulletin, 129,* 592–613.

Markowitz F. E. (2015). Involvement in mental health self-help groups and recovery. *Health Sociology Review, 24*(2), 199–212. doi :10.1080/14461242.2015.1015149

Marks, D. F. (2010). IQ variations across time, race, and nationality: An artifact of differences in literacy skills. *Psychological Reports, 106,* 643–664.

Markus, H. R. (2013). Who am I? Race, ethnicity, and identity. In S .J. Ferguson (Ed.), *Race, gender, sexuality, and social class: Dimensions of inequality* (pp. 179–188). SAGE.

Markus, H. R., & Kitayama, S. (2010). Culture and selves: A cycle of mutual constitution. *Perspectives on Psychological Science, 5,* 420–430.

Markus, H., Crane, M., Bernstein, S., & Siladi, M. (1982). Self-schemas and gender. *Journal of Personality and Social Psychology, 42,* 38–50.

Marler, P. R., Duffy, A., & Pickert, R. (1986). Vocal communication in the domestic chicken: II. Is a sender sensitive to the presence and nature of a receiver? *Animal Behavior, 34,* 194–198.

Marques, J. F. (2010). The effect of visual deprivation on the organization of conceptual knowledge: Testing the grounded cognition hypothesis. *Experimental Psychology, 57,* 83–88.

Marsh, J. K., Zeveney, A. S., & De Los Reyes, A. (2020). Informant discrepancies in judgments about change during mental health treatments. *Clinical Psychological Science, 8*(2), 318-332.

Martin, C. L., & Halverson, C. F. (1981). A schematic processing model of sex typing and stereotyping in children. *Child Development, 52,* 1119–1134.

Martin, C. L., & Halverson, C. F. (1987). The role of cognition in sex role acquisition. In D. B. Carter (Ed.), *Current conceptions of sex roles and sex typing: Theory and research* (pp. 123–137). Praeger.

Martin, C. L., & Ruble, D. (2004). Children's search for gender cues: Cognitive perspectives on gender development. *Current Directions in Psychological Science, 13,* 67–70.

Martin, C. L., & Ruble, D. N. (2010). Patterns of gender development. *Annual Review of Psychology, 61,* 353–381.

Martin, G., & Pear, J. (2007). *Behavior modification: What it is and how to do it* (8th ed.). Prentice Hall.

Martin, G., England, G., Kaprowy, E., Kilgour, K., & Pilek, V. (1968). Operant conditioning of kindergarten-class behavior in autistic children. *Behavior Research and Therapy, 6,* 281–294.

Martinie, M., Milland, L., & Olive, T. (2013). Some theoretical considerations on attitude, arousal and affect during cognitive dissonance. *Social and Personality Psychology Compass, 7,* 680–688. doi:10.1111/spc3.1205

Martinie, M., Olive, T., & Milland, L. (2010). Cognitive dissonance induced by writing a counterattitudinal essay facilitates performance on simple tasks but not on complex tasks that involve working memory. *Journal of Experimental Social Psychology, 46,* 587–594. doi:10.1016/j.jesp.2009.10.018

Martorana, A., Mori, F., Esposito, Z., Kusayanagi, H., Monteleone, F., Codecà, C., . . . Koch, G. (2009). Dopamine modulates cholinergic cortical excitability in Alzheimer's disease patients. *Neuropsychopharmacology, 34,* 2323–2328.

Martuzzi, R., van der Zwaag, W., Farthouat, J., Gruetter, R., & Blanke, O. (2014). Human finger somatotopy in areas 3b, 1, and 2: A 7T fMRI study using a natural stimulus. *Human Brain Mapping, 35,* 213–226. doi:10.1002/hbm.22172

Marzoli, D., Custodero, M., Pagliara, A., & Tommasi, L. (2013). Sun-induced frowning fosters aggressive feelings. *Cognition and Emotion, 27,* 1513–1521. doi:10.1080/02699931.2013.801338

Mashal, N., & Faust, M. (2008). Right hemisphere sensitivity to novel metaphoric relations: Application of the signal detection theory. *Brain and Language, 104,* 103–112.

Maslow, A. (1968). *Toward a psychology of being* (2nd ed.). Van Nostrand.

Maslow, A. (1970). *Motivation and personality* (2nd ed.). Harper & Row

Maslow, A. (1971). *The farther reaches of human nature.* Viking.

Masters, K. S., & Hooker, S. A. (2013). Religiousness/spirituality, cardiovascular disease, and cancer: Cultural integration for health research and intervention. *Journal of Consulting and Clinical Psychology, 81,* 206–216.

Masters, W. H., & Johnson, V. E. (1966). *Human sexual response.* Little, Brown.

Masters, W. H., Johnson, V. E., & Kolodny, R. C. (1993). *Biological foundations of human sexuality.* Harpercollins College Division.

Mathew, R., Wilson, W., Blazer, D., & George, L. (1993). Psychiatric disorders in adult children of alcoholics: Data from the epidemiologic catchment area project. *American Journal of Psychiatry, 150,* 793–796.

Mathy, F., & Feldman, J. (2012). What's magic about magic numbers? Chunking and data compression in short-term memory. *Cognition, 122*(3), 346–362. doi:10.1016/j cognition.2011.11.003

Matlin, M. W., & Foley, H. J (1997). *Sensation and perception.* Allyn & Bacon.

Matson, J. L., & Boisjoli, J. A. (2009). The token economy for children with intellectual disability and/or autism: A review. *Research in Developmental Disabilities, 30,* 240–248.

Matsuda, L. A., Lolait, S. J., Brownstein, M. J., Young, A. C., & Bonner, T. I. (1990). Structure of a cannabinoid receptor and functional expression of the cloned cDNA. *Nature, 346,* 561–564.

Matsumoto, D. (1994). *People: Psychology from a cross-cultural perspective.* Brooks/Cole.

Matthes, J., Prieler, M., & Adam, K. (2016). Gender-role portrayals in television advertising across the globe. *Sex Roles, 75*(7), 314–327. doi:10.1007/s11199-016-0617-y

Matthews, B. R. (2015). Memory dysfunction. *CONTINUUM: Lifelong Learning in Neurology, 21*(3), 613–626.

Matud, M. P. (2004). Gender differences in stress and coping styles. *Personality and Individual Differences, 37,* 1401–1415.

Matynia, A., Nguyen, E., Sun, X., Blixt, F. W., Parikh, S., Kessler, J., . . . Gorin, M. B. (2016). Peripheral sensory neurons expressing melanopsin respond to light. *Frontiers in Neural Circuits, 10,* 60. doi:10.3389/fncir.2016.00060

Matz, S. C., Gladstone, J. J., & Stillwell, D. (2016). Money buys happiness when spending fits our personality. *Psychological Science, 27,* 715–725.

Maville, J., & Huerta, C. G. (1997). Stress and social support among Hispanic student nurses: Implications for academic achievement. *Journal of Cultural Diversity, 4,* 18–25.

Maxwell, J. C., & Spence, R. T. (2003). Profiles of club drug users in treatment. *Substance Use and Misuse, 40,* 1409–1426.

May, A. A., Liu, M., Woods, S. C., & Begg, D. P. (2016). CCK increases the transport of insulin into the brain. *Physiology & Behavior, 165,* 392–397. doi:10.1016/j.physbeh.2016.08.025

Mayberg, H. S. (1997). Limbic-cortical dysregulation: A proposed model of depression. *Journal of Neuropsychiatry & Clinical Neuroscience, 9,* 471–481.

Mayberg, H. S., Liotti, M., Brannan, S. K., McGinnis, S., Mahurin, R. K., Jerabek, P. A., . . . Fox, P. T. (1999). Reciprocal limbic-cortical function and negative mood: Converging PET findings in depression and normal sadness. *American Journal of Psychiatry, 156,* 675–682.

Mayberg, H. S., Lozano, A. M., Voon, V., McNeely, H. E., Seminowicz, D., Hamani, C., . . . Kennedy, S. H. (2005). Deep brain stimulation for treatment-resistant depression. *Neuron, 45,* 651–660.

Mayer, J. D., Salovey, P., Caruso, D. R., & Sitarenios, G. (2003). Measuring emotional intelligence with the MSCEIT V2.0. *Emotion, 3,* 97–105.

Mayer, R. E. (1983). *Thinking, problem solving, cognition.* Freeman.

Mazure, C. M., Keita, G. P., & Blehar, M. C. (2002). *Summit on women and depression: Proceedings and recommendations.* American Psychological Association.

Mazza, S., Gerbier, E., Gustin, M., Kasikci, Z., Koenig, O., Toppino, T. C., & Magnin, M. (2016). Relearn faster and retain longer: Along with practice, sleep makes perfect. *Psychological Science, 27*(10), 1321–1330. doi:10.1177/0956797616659930

Mazzella Ebstein, A. M., Sanzero Eller, L., Tan, K. S., Cherniss, C., Ruggiero, J. S., & Cimiotti, J. P. (2019). The relationships between coping, occupational stress, and emotional intelligence in newly hired oncology nurses. *Psycho-Oncology, 28*(2), 278–283. https://doi.org/10.1002/pon.4937

McAdams, D. P. (2013). The psychological self as actor, agent, and author. *Perspectives on Psychological Science, 8,* 272–295.

McAdams, D. P., & Guo, J. (2015). Narrating the generative life. *Psychological Science, 26,* 475–483.

McAdams, D. P., & Olson, B. D. (2010). Personality development: Continuity and change over the life course. *Annual Review of Psychology, 61,* 517–542.

McCabe, K. O., & Fleeson, W. (2012). What is extraversion for? Integrating trait and motivational perspectives and identifying the purpose of extraversion. *Psychological Science, 23,* 1498–1505.

McCallie, M. S., Blum, C. M., & Hood, C. J. (2006). Progressive muscle relaxation. *Journal of Human Behavior in the Social Environment, 13,* 51, 66.

McCann, U. D., Wilson, M. J., Sgambati, F. P., & Ricaurte, G. A. (2009). Sleep deprivation differentially impairs cognitive performance in abstinent methylenedioxymethamphetamine ("Ecstasy") users. *Journal of Neuroscience, 29,* 14050–14056.

McCarley, R. W. (1998). Dreams: Disguise of forbidden wishes or transparent reflections of a distinct brain state? *Annals of the New York Academy of Sciences, 843,* 116–133.

McClelland, D. C. (1987). *Human motivation*. Cambridge University Press.

McClintock, C. H., Lau, E., & Miller, L. (2016). Phenotypic dimensions of spirituality: Implications for mental health in China, India, and the United States. *Frontiers in Psychology, 7,* 1600.

McClung, C. A. (2007). Circadian genes, rhythms and the biology of mood disorders. *Pharmacology and Therapeutics, 114,* 222–232.

McClure, H. H., Snodgrass, J. J., Martinez, C. R., Jr., Eddy, J. M., Jimenez, R. A., & Isiordia, L. E. (2010). Discrimination, psychosocial stress, and health among Latin American immigrants in Oregon. *American Journal of Human Biology, 22,* 421–423.

McCormick, C., Rosenthal, C. R., Miller, T. D., & Maguire, E. A. (2017). Deciding what is possible and impossible following hippocampal damage in humans. *Hippocampus, 27*(3), 303–314. doi:10.1002/hipo.22694

McCrae, R. R. (2009, June). Cross-cultural research on the five-factor model of personality (Version 2). *Online Readings in Psychology and Culture* (Unit 6, Chapter 1/V2).

McCrae, R. R., & Costa, P. T. (1998). Personality trait structure as a human universal. *American Psychologist, 52,* 509–516.

McCrae, R. R., Costa, P. T., Ostendorf, F., Angleitner, A., Hrebickova, M., Avia, M. D., . . . Smith, P. B. (2000). Nature over nurture: Temperament, personality, and life span development. *Journal of Personality and Social Psychology, 78,* 173–186.

McCrae, R. R., Costa, P. T., Pedroso de Lima, M., Simoes, A., Ostendorf, F., Angleitner, A., . . . Piedmont, R. L. (1999). Age differences in personality across the adult life span: Parallels in five cultures. *Developmental Psychology, 35,* 466–477.

McCrae, R. R., Costa, P. T., Terracciano, A., Parker, W. D., Mills, C. J., De Fruyt, F., & Mervielde, I. (2002). Personality trait development from age 12 to age 18: Longitudinal, cross-sectional, and cross-cultural analyses. *Journal of Personality and Social Psychology, 83,* 1456–1468.

McCullough, M. E., Hoyt, W. T., Larson, D. S., Koenig, H. G., & Thoresen, C. (2000). Religious involvement and mortality: A meta-analytic review. *Health Psychology, 19,* 211–222.

McCusker, C. G., & Brown, K. (1990). Alcohol-predictive cues enhance tolerance to and precipitate "craving" for alcohol in social drinkers. *Journal of Studies on Alcohol, 51*(6), 494–499. https://doi.org/10.15288/jsa.1990.51.494

McCutcheon, R. A., Krystal, J. H., & Howes, O. D. (2020). Dopamine and glutamate in schizophrenia: Biology, symptoms and treatment. *World Psychiatry, 19*(1), 15– 33. doi:10.1002/wps.20693

McFalls, J. A., Jr. (1990). The risks of reproductive impairment in the later years of childbearing. *Annual Review of Sociology, 16,* 491–519.

McGehee, D. S., Heath, M. J. S., Gelber, S., Devay, P., & Role, L. W. (1995). Nicotine enhancement of fast excitation synaptic transmissions in CNS by presynaptic receptors. *Science, 269,* 1692–1696.

McGinty, E. E., Kennedy-Hendricks, A., Choksy, S., & Barry, C. L. (2016). Trends in news media coverage of mental illness in the United States: 1995–2014. *Health Affairs* (Project Hope), *35,* 1121–1129.

McGivern, R. F., Adams, B., Handa, R. J., & Pineda, J. A. (2012). Men and women exhibit a differential bias for processing movement versus objects. *PLoS ONE, 7*(3), e32238. doi:10.1371/journal.pone.0032238

McGovern, R. A., & Sheth, S. A. (2017). Role of the dorsal anterior cingulate cortex in obsessive-compulsive disorder: Converging evidence from cognitive neuroscience and psychiatric neurosurgery. *Journal of Neurosurgery, 126*(1), 132-147. doi:10.3171/2016.1.JNS15601

McGregor, G., Desaga, J. F., Ehlenz, K., Fischer, A., Heese, F., Hegele, A., . . . Lang, R. E. (1996). Radioimmunological measurement of leptin in plasma of obese and diabetic human subjects. *Endocrinology, 137,* 1501–1504.

McGuffin, P., Rijsdijk, F., Andrew, M., Sham, P., Katz, R., & Cardno, A. (2003). The heritability of bipolar affective disorder and the genetic relationship to unipolar depression. *Archives of General Psychiatry, 60,* 497–502.

McGuigan, N. (2013). The influence of model status on the tendency of young children to over-imitate. *Journal of Experimental Child Psychology, 116,* 962–969. doi:10.1016/j.jecp.2013.05.004

McHarg, G., Ribner, A. D., Devine, R. T., & Hughes, C. (2020). Infant screen exposure links to toddlers' inhibition, but not other EF constructs: A propensity score study. *Infancy, 25*(2), 205-222. https://doi.org/10.1111/infa.12325

McIntosh, D. N. (1996). Facial feedback hypotheses: Evidence, implications, and directions. *Motivation and Emotion, 20,* 121–147.

McIntosh, D. N., Poulin, M. J., Silver, R. C., & Holman, E. A. (2011). The distinct roles of spirituality and religiosity in physical and mental health after collective trauma: A national longitudinal study of responses to the 9/11 attacks. *Journal of Behavioral Medicine, 34,* 497–507.

McIntosh, E., Gillanders, D., & Rodgers, S. (2010). Rumination, goal linking, daily hassles and life events in major depression. *Clinical Psychology & Psychotherapy, 17,* 33–43.

McIntyre, H. H., & Foti, R. J. (2013). The impact of shared leadership on teamwork mental models and performance in self-directed teams. *Group Processes & Intergroup Relations, 16*(1), 46-57.

McKean, K. J. (1994). Using multiple risk factors to assess the behavioral, cognitive, and affective effects of learned helplessness. *Journal of Psychology, 128,* 177–183.

McKillip, J., & Reidel, S. L. (1983). External validity of matching on physical attractiveness for same and opposite sex couples. *Journal of Applied Social Psychology, 13,* 328–337.

McKim, W. A. (1997). *Drugs and behavior: An introduction to behavioral pharmacology* (3rd ed.). Prentice Hall.

McKinzie A. E. (2018). In their own words: Disaster and emotion, suffering, and mental health. *International Journal of Qualitative Studies on Health and Well-Being, 13*(1), 1440108. doi:10.1080/17482631.2018.1440108

McKnight-Eily, L. R., Liu, Y., Perry, G. S., Presley-Cantrell, L. R., Strine, T. W., Lu, H., & Croft, J. B. (2009). Perceived insufficient rest or sleep among adults—United States, 2008. *Morbidity and Mortality Weekly Report, 58,* 1175–1179.

McLaren, J. A., Silins, E., Hutchinson, D., Mattick, R. P., & Hall, W. (2010). Assessing evidence for a causal link between cannabis and psychosis: A review of cohort studies. *The International Journal on Drug Policy, 21,* 10–19.

McLaughlin Crabtree, V., & Williams, N. A. (2009). Normal sleep in children and adolescents. *Child and Adolescent Psychiatric Clinics of North America, 18,* 799–811.

McLaughlin, K. A., Green, J. G., Gruber, M. J., Sampson, N. A., Zaslavsky, A. M., & Kessler, R. C. (2010). Childhood adversities and adult psychiatric disorders in the National Comorbidity Survey Replication II: Associations with persistence of *DSM-IV* disorders. *Archives of General Psychiatry, 67,* 124–132.

McLay, R. N., McBrien, C., Wiederhold, M. D., & Wiederhold, B. K. (2010). Exposure therapy with and without virtual reality to treat PTSD while in the combat theater: A parallel case series. *Cyberpsychology, Behavior, and Social Networking, 13,* 37–42.

McManus, J. L., Saucier, D. A., O'Dea, C. J., & Bernard, D. L. (2019). Aversive affect versus racism as predictors of racial discrimination in helping. *Basic and Applied Social Psychology, 41*(4), 230–253. https://doi.org/10.1080/01973533.2019.1622545

McManus, M. A., & Baratta, J. E. (1992). *The relationship of recruiting source to performance and survival.* Paper presented at the annual meeting of the Society for Industrial and Organizational Psychology, Montreal.

McMillen, D. L., Smith, S. M., & Wells-Parker, E. (1989). The effects of alcohol, expectancy, and sensation seeking on driving risk taking. *Addictive Behaviors, 14,* 477–483.

McNeil, D. W., & Kyle, B. N. (2009). Exposure strategies. In S. Cormier, P. S. Nurius, & C. J. Osborn (Eds.), *Interviewing and change strategies for helpers: Fundamental skills and cognitive behavioral interventions* (6th ed., pp. 486–516). Brooks/Cole.

McNeill, B., Prieto, L., Niemann, Y., Pizarro, M., Vera, E., & Gomez, S. (2001). Current directions in Chicana/o psychology. *Counseling Psychologist, 29,* 5–17.

McNulty, J. K., Olson, M. A., Jones, R. E., & Acosta, L. M. (2017). Automatic associations between one's partner and one's affect as the proximal mechanism of change in relationship satisfaction: Evidence from evaluative conditioning. *Psychological Science, 28*(8), 1031-1040.

McRae, K. (2016). Cognitive emotion regulation: A review of theory and scientific findings. *Current Opinion in Behavioral Sciences, 10,* 119–124. doi:10.1016/j.cobeha.2016.06.004

McRae, K., Gross, J. J., Weber, J., Robertson, E. R., Sokol-Hessner, P., Ray, R. D., . . . Ochsner, K. N. (2012). The development of emotion regulation: An fMRI study of cognitive reappraisal in children, adolescents and young adults. *Social Cognitive and Affective Neuroscience, 7*(1), 11–22. doi:10.1093/scan/nsr093

McRae, K., Ochsner, K. N., Mauss, I. B., Gabrieli, J. J. D., & Gross, J. J. (2008). Gender differences in emotion regulation: An fMRI study of cognitive reappraisal. *Group Processes & Intergroup Relations, 11,* 143–162.

Medrano, S., Abdel-Baki, A., Stip, E., & Potvin, S. (2018). Three-year naturalistic study on early use of long-acting injectable antipsychotics in first episode psychosis. *Psychopharmacology Bulletin, 48*(4), 25–61.

Mega, C., Ronconi, L., & De Beni, R. (2014). What makes a good student? How emotions, self-regulated learning, and motivation contribute to academic achievement.

Journal of Educational Psychology, 106, 121–131. doi:10.1037/a0033546

Megías, J. L., Ryan, E., Vaquero, J. M. M., & Frese, B. (2007). Comparisons of traumatic and positive memories in people with and without PTSD profile. *Applied Cognitive Psychology, 21*(1), 117–130. https://doi.org/10.1002/acp.1282

Mehl, M. R., Vazire, S., Holleran, S. E., & Clark, C. S. (2010). Eavesdropping on happiness: Well-being is related to having less small talk and more substantive conversations. *Psychological Science, 21*, 539–541.

Meier, A. E., Fryling, M. J., & Wallace, M. D. (2012). Using high-probability foods to increase the acceptance of low-probability foods. *Journal of Applied Behavior Analysis, 45*, 149–153.

Meier, T. B., Bergamino, M., Bellgowan, P. S. F., Teague, T. K., Ling, J. M., Jeromin, A., & Mayer, A. R. (2016). Longitudinal assessment of white matter abnormalities following sports-related concussion. *Human Brain Mapping, 37*(2), 833–845. doi:10.1002/hbm.23072

Meil, W. M., LaPorte, D. J., Mills, J. A., Sesti, A., Collins, S. M., & Stiver, A. G. (2016). Sensation seeking and executive deficits in relation to alcohol, tobacco, and marijuana use frequency among university students: Value of ecologically based measures. *Addictive Behavior, 62*, 135–144.

Mellman, T. A., Alim, T., Brown, D. D., Gorodetsky, E., Buzas, B., Lawson, W. B., . . . Charney, D. S. (2009). Serotonin polymorphisms and posttraumatic stress disorder in a trauma exposed African American population. *Depression and Anxiety, 26*, 993–997.

Meltzer, H. Y. (2013). Update on typical and atypical antipsychotic drugs. *Annual Review of Medicine, 64*, 393–406.

Meltzer, L. J., & Mindell, J. A. (2006). Sleep and sleep disorders in children and adolescents. *Psychiatric Clinics of North America, 29*, 1059–1076.

Melumad, S., & Meyer, R. (2020). Full disclosure: How smartphones enhance consumer self-disclosure. *Journal of Marketing, 84*(3), 28–45. https://doi.org/10.1177/0022242920912732

Melzack, R., & Wall, P. D. (1965). Pain mechanisms: A new theory. *Science (New York, N.Y.), 150*(3699), 971–979.

Mendle, J. (2014). Beyond pubertal timing: New directions for studying individual differences in development. *Current Directions in Psychological Science, 23*, 215–219.

Mendle, J., Eisenlohr-Moul, T., & Kiesner, J. (2016). From menarche to menopause: Women's reproductive milestones and risk for psychopathology—An introduction to the special series. *Clinical Psychological Science, 4*, 859–866.

Mendle, J. & Ferrero, J. (2012). Detrimental psychological outcomes associated with pubertal timing in adolescent boys. *Developmental Review, 32*, 49–66.

Mendoza, J. S., Pody, B. C., Lee, S., Kim, M., & McDonough, I. M. (2018). The effect of cellphones on attention and learning: The influences of time, distraction, and nomophobia. *Computers in Human Behavior, 86*, 52–60. https://doi.org/10.1016/j.chb.2018.04.027

Menevis, I., & Özad, B. E. (2014). Do age and gender influence multiple intelligences? *Social Behavior and Personality, 42*(Supp), S9–S20. doi:10.2224/sbp.2014.42.0.S9

Mennella, J. A., & Beauchamp, G. K. (1991). Maternal diet alters the sensory qualities of human milk and nursling's behavior. *Pediatrics, 88*, 737–744.

Menz, M. M., Rihm, J. S., Salari, N., Born, J., Kalisch, R., Pape, H. C., . . . Büchel, C. (2013). The role of sleep and sleep deprivation in consolidating fear memories. *NeuroImage, 75*, 87–96.

Menzies, H. (2005). *No time: Stress and the crisis of modern life.* Douglas & McIntyre.

Mercimek Barış, Yavuz, A., Dönmez Onur, & Sak Uğur. (2020). Multitasking impairs learning from multimedia across gifted and non-gifted students. *Educational Technology, Research and Development, 68*(3), 995-1016. doi:http://dx.doi.org/10.1007/s11423-019-09717-9

Merikangas, K. R., He, J. P., Burstein, M., Swanson, S. A., Avenevoli, S., Cui, L., . . . Swendsen, J. (2010). Lifetime prevalence of mental disorder in U.S. adolescents: Results from the National Comorbidity Survey Replication—Adolescent Supplement (NCS-A). *Journal of the American Academy of Child and Adolescent Psychiatry, 49*, 980–989.

Merikangas, K. R., Jin, R., He, J. P., Kessler, R. C., Lee, S., Sampson, N. A., . . . Zarkov, Z. (2011). Prevalence and correlates of bipolar spectrum disorder in the World Mental Health Survey Initiative. *Archive of General Psychiatry, 68*, 241–251.

Merkl, A., Heuser, I., & Bajbouj, M. (2009). Antidepressant electroconvulsive therapy: Mechanism of action, recent advances and limitations. *Experimental Neurology, 219*, 20–26.

Messner, M., Reinhard, M., & Sporer, S. L. (2008). Compliance through direct persuasive appeals: The moderating role of communicator's attractiveness in interpersonal persuasion. *Social Influence, 3*, 67–83.

Meyer, B., Keller, A., Wöhlbier, H. G., Overath, C. H., Müller, B., & Kropp, P. (2016). Progressive muscle relaxation reduces migraine frequency and normalizes amplitudes of contingent negative variation (CNV). *The Journal of Headache and Pain, 17*, 37. doi:10.1186/s10194-016-0630-0

Meyer, J. P., & Allen, N. J. (1991). A three-component conceptualization of organizational commitment. *Human Resource Management Review, 1*, 61–89.

Meyer, J. P., & Herscovitch, L. (2001). Commitment in the workplace: Toward a general model. *Human Resource Management Review, 11*, 299–326.

Meyer, M., & Schoen, H. (2014). Response latencies and attitude-behavior consistency in a direct democratic setting: Evidence from a subnational referendum in Germany. *Political Psychology, 35*(3), 431–440. doi:10.1111/pops.12039

Meyer, P. (2016). Place de la testostérone dans le trouble du désir sexuel hypoactif chez la femme (Testosterone therapy in female hypoactive sexual desire disorder). *Revue medicale suisse, 12*(510), 540–543.

Meyer, T., Ikani, N., & Morina, N. (2019). Spatio-temporal associations with memory cues are linked to analogue traumatic intrusions. *Behaviour Research and Therapy, 123*, 103481. https://doi.org/10.1016/j.brat.2019.103481

Meyerbroeker, K., Morina, N., Kerkhof, G. A., & Emmelkamp, P. M. (2013). Virtual reality exposure therapy does not provide any additional value in agoraphobic patients: A randomized controlled trial. *Psychotherapy and Psychosomatics, 82*, 170–176.

Mez, J., Daneshvar, D. H., Abdolmohammadi, B., Chua, A. S., Alosco, M. L., Kiernan, P. T.,... McKee, A. C. (2020). Duration of American football play and chronic traumatic encephalopathy. *Annals of Neurology, 87*(1), 116–131. https://doi.org/10.1002/ana.25611

Mezulis, A. H., Abramson, L. Y., Hyde, J. S., & Hankin, B. L. (2004). Is there a universal positivity bias in attributions? A meta-analytic review of individual, developmental, and cultural differences in the self-serving attributional bias. *Psychological Bulletin, 130*, 711–747.

Micco, J. A., Henin, A., Mick, E., Kim, S., Hopkins, C. A., Biederman, J., & Hirshfeld-Becker, D. R. (2009). Anxiety and depressive disorders in offspring at high risk for anxiety: A meta-analysis. *Journal of Anxiety Disorders, 23*, 1158–1164.

Michael, G. A., Boucart, M., Degreef, J. F., & Goefroy, O. (2001). The thalamus interrupts top-down attentional control for permitting exploratory shiftings to sensory signals. *Neuroreport, 12*, 2041–2048.

Michalski, D., Kohout, J., Wicherski, M., & Hart, B. (2011). *2009 Doctorate Employment Survey.* APA Center for Workforce Studies.

Miech, R. A., Johnston, L. D., O'Malley, P. M., Bachman, J. G., Schulenberg, J. E., & Patrick, M. E. (2019). *Monitoring the Future National Survey Results on Drug Use, 1975–2018: Volume I, Secondary school students.* Institute for Social Research, The University of Michigan.

Migliore, M., Novara, G., & Tegolo, D. (2008). Single neuron binding properties and the magical number 7. *Hippocampus, 18*, 1122–1130.

Mihelič, K. K., & Culiberg, B. (2019). Reaping the fruits of another's labor: The role of moral meaningfulness, mindfulness, and motivation in social loafing. *Journal of Business Ethics, 160*(3), 713–727. https://doi.org/10.1007/s10551-018-3933-z

Miklikowska, M. (2017). Development of anti-immigrant attitudes in adolescence: The role of parents, peers, intergroup friendships, and empathy. *British Journal of Psychology, 108*(3), 626-648. doi:10.1111/bjop.12236

Milad, M. R., & Rauch, S. L. (2012). Obsessive-compulsive disorder: Beyond segregated corticostriatal pathways. *Trends in Cognitive Sciences, 16*, 43–51.

Milgram, S. (1963). Behavioral study of obedience. *Journal of Abnormal and Social Psychology, 67*, 371–378

Milgram, S. (1965). Some conditions of obedience and disobedience to authority. *Human Relations, 18*, 57–76.

Milgram, S. (1974). *Obedience to authority: An experimental view.* Harper & Row.

Millar, M. (2002). The effectiveness of the door-in-the-face compliance strategy on friends and strangers. *Journal of Social Psychology, 142*, 295–305.

Miller, A. G. (2009). Reflections on "Replicating Milgram." *American Psychologist, 64*, 20–27.

Miller, D. T., & Ross, M. (1975). Self-serving biases in the attribution of causality: Fact or fiction? *Psychological Bulletin, 82*, 213–225.

Miller, E. (1999). The pheromone androsterol: Evolutionary considerations. *Mankind Quarterly, 39*, 455–466.

Miller, G. E., & Blackwell, E. (2006). Turning up the heat: Inflammation as a mechanism linking chronic stress, depression, and heart disease. *Current Directions in Psychological Science, 15*, 269–272.

Miller, G. E., Lachman, M. E., Chen, E., Gruenewald, T. L., Karlamangla, A. S., & Seeman, T. E. (2011). Pathways to resilience: Maternal nurturance as a buffer against the effects of childhood poverty on metabolic syndrome at midlife. *Psychological Science, 22,* 1591–1599.

Miller, I. J., Jr., & Bartoshuk, L. M. (1991). Taste perception, taste bud distribution, and spatial relationships. In T. V. Gethell, R. L. Doty, L. M. Bartoshuk, & J. B. Snow, Jr. (Eds.), *Smell and taste in health and disease* (pp. 205–233). Raven.

Miller, N. S., & Gold, M. S. (1994). LSD and Ecstasy: Pharmacology, phenomenology, and treatment. *Psychiatric Annals, 24,* 131–133.

Miller, S., & Maner, J. K. (2010). Scent of a woman: Men's testosterone responses to olfactory ovulation cues. *Psychological Science, 21,* 276–283.

Miller, T. Q., Turner, C. W., Tindale, R. S., Posavac, E. J., & Dugoni, B. L. (1991). Reasons for the trend toward null findings in research on Type A behavior. *Psychological Bulletin, 110,* 469–485.

Miller, W. R., & Seligman, M. E. P. (1975). Depression and learned helplessness in man. *Journal of Abnormal Psychology, 84,* 228–238.

Miller, W. R., & Thoresen, C. E. (2003). Spirituality, religion, and health. An emerging research field. *American Psychologist, 58,* 24–35.

Milling, L. S., Reardon, J. M., & Carosella, G. M. (2006). Mediation and moderation of psychological pain treatments: Response expectancies and hypnotic suggestibility. *Journal of Consulting and Clinical Psychology, 74,* 253–262.

Millner, A. J., Lee, M. D., & Nock, M. K. (2017). Describing and measuring the pathway to suicide attempts: A preliminary study. *Suicide and Life-Threatening Behavior, 47,* 353-369.

Milner, B., Corkin, S., & Teuber, H. L. (1968). Further analysis of the hippocampal amnesiac syndrome: 14-year follow-up study of H. M. *Neuropsychologia, 6,* 215–234.

Milner, C. E., & Cote, K. A. (2009). Benefits of napping in healthy adults: Impact of nap length, time of day, age, and experience with napping. *Journal of Sleep Research, 18,* 272–281.

Milton, J., & Wiseman, R. (2001). Does psi exist? Reply to Storm and Ertel (2001). *Psychological Bulletin, 127,* 434–438.

Minda, J. P., & Smith, J. D. (2002). Comparing prototype-based and exemplar-based accounts of category learning and attentional allocation. *Journal of Experimental Psychology: Learning, Memory, and Cognition, 28,* 275–292.

Miner, A. E., Schurgin, M. W., & Brady, T. F. (2020). Is working memory inherently more "precise" than long-term memory? Extremely high fidelity visual long-term memories for frequently encountered objects. *Journal of Experimental Psychology: Human Perception and Performance, 46*(8), 813–830. https://doi.org/10.1037/xhp0000748

Minero, L. P., & Espinoza, R. K. E. (2016). The influence of defendant immigration status, country of origin, and ethnicity on juror decisions: An aversive racism explanation for juror bias. *Hispanic Journal of Behavioral Sciences, 38*(1), 55–74. doi:10.1177/0739986315620374

Minozzi, S., Davoli, M., Bargagli, A. M., Amato, L., Vecchi, S., & Perucci, C. A. (2010). An overview of systematic reviews on cannabis and psychosis: Discussing apparently conflicting results. *Drug and Alcohol Review, 29,* 304–317.

Mintz, A., & Wayne, C. (2014). Group decision making in conflict: From groupthink to polythink in the war in Iraq. In P. T. Coleman, M. Deutsch, & E. C. Marcus (Eds.), *The handbook of conflict resolution: Theory and practice, 3rd ed.* (pp. 331–352). Jossey-Bass.

Mintz, A., & Wayne, C. (2016). The polythink syndrome and elite group decision making. *Political Psychology, 37*(Suppl. 1), 3–21. doi:10.1111/pops.12319

Miranda, R., De Jaegere, E., Restifo, K., & Schaffer, D. (2014). Longitudinal follow-up study of adolescents who report a suicide attempt: Aspects of suicidal behavior that increase risk of a future attempt. *Depression and Anxiety, 31,* 19–26.

Mischel, W., & Shoda, Y. (1995). A cognitive-affective system theory of personality: Reconceptualizing situations, dispositions, dynamics, and invariance of personality structure. *Psychological Review, 102,* 246–268.

Miselis, R. R., & Epstein, A. N. (1970). Feeding induced by 2-deoxy-D-glucose injections into the lateral ventrical of the rat. *Physiologist, 13,* 262.

Miskovic, V., Moscovitch, D. A., Santesso, D. L., McCabe, R. E., Antony, M. M., & Schmidt, L. A. (2011). Changes in EEG cross-frequency coupling during cognitive behavioral therapy for social anxiety disorder. *Psychological Science, 22,* 507–516.

Mitelman, S. A., Buchsbaum, M. S., Brickman, A. M., & Shihabuddin, L. (2005). Cortical intercorrelations of frontal area volumes in schizophrenia. *Neuroimage, 27,* 753–770.

Mithoefer, M. C., Wagner, M. T., Mithoefer, A. T., Jerome, L., & Doblin, R. (2011). The safety and efficacy of {+/−}3,4-methylenedioxymethamphetamine-assisted psychotherapy in subjects with chronic, treatment-resistant posttraumatic stress disorder: The first randomized controlled pilot study. *Journal of Psychopharmacology, 25,* 439–452.

Mithoefer, M. C., Wagner, M. T., Mithoefer, A. T., Jerome, L., Martin, S. F., Yazar-Klosinski, B., . . . Doblin, R. (2013). Durability of improvement in post-traumatic stress disorder symptoms and absence of harmful effects or drug dependency after 3, 4-methylenedioxymethamphetamine-assisted psychotherapy: A prospective long-term follow-up study. *Journal of Psychopharmacology, 27,* 28–39.

Miyamoto, Y., & Ma, X. (2011). Dampening or savoring positive emotions: A dialectical cultural script guides emotion regulation. *Emotion, 11,* 1346-1357.

Miyauchi, S., Misaki, M., Kan, S., Fukunaga, T., & Koike, T. (2009). Human brain activity time-locked to rapid eye movements during REM sleep. *Experimental Brain Research, 192,* 657–667.

Mizushige, T., Inoue, K., & Fushiki, T. (2007). Why is fat so tasty? Chemical reception of fatty acid on the tongue. *Journal of Nutritional Science and Vitaminology, 53,* 1–4.

Moazzami, K., Lima, B. B., Sullivan, S., Shah, A., Bremner, J. D., & Vaccarino, V. (2019). Independent and joint association of obesity and metabolic syndrome with depression and inflammation. *Health Psychology, 38*(7), 586–595. https://doi.org/10.1037/hea0000764

Mobini, S., Chambers, L. C., & Yeomans, M. R. (2007). Effects of hunger state on flavour pleasantness conditioning at home: Flavour–nutrient learning vs. flavour–flavour learning. *Appetite, 48,* 20–28.

Moffitt, T. E. (2005). The new look of behavioral genetics in developmental psychopathology: Gene-environment interplay in antisocial behaviors. *Psychological Bulletin, 131,* 533–554.

Moffitt, T. E., Brammer, G. L., Caspi, A., Fawcet, J. P., Raleigh, M., Yuwiler, A., & Silva, P. (1998). Whole blood serotonin relates to violence in an epidemiological study. *Biological Psychiatry, 43,* 446–457.

Moffitt, T. E., Caspi, A., Taylor, A., Kokaua, J., Milne, B. J., Polanczyk, G., & Poulton, R. (2010). How common are common mental disorders? Evidence that lifetime prevalence rates are doubled by prospective versus retrospective ascertainment. *Psychological Medicine, 40,* 899–909.

Mogilner, C. (2010). The pursuit of happiness: Time, money, and social connection. *Psychological Science, 21,* 1348–1354.

Mohr, B. A., Guay, A. T., O'Donnell, A. B., & McKinlay, J. B. (2005). Normal, bound and nonbound testosterone levels in normally ageing men: Results from the Massachusetts Male Ageing Study. *Clinical Endocrinology, 62,* 64–73.

Mohr, C. (1964, March 28). Apathy is puzzle in Queens killing. *New York Times,* pp. 21, 40.

Mohr, C., Braun, S., Bridler, R., Chmetz, F., Delfino, J. P., Kluckner, V. J., . . . Stassen, H. H. (2014). Insufficient coping behavior under chronic stress and vulnerability to psychiatric disorders. *Psychopathology, 47*(4), 235-243. doi:10.1159/000356398

Mohr, D. C., Duffecy, J., Jin, L., Ludman, E. J., Lewis A., Begale, M., & McCarthy, M. (2010). Multimodal e-mental health treatment for depression: A feasibility trial. *Journal of Medical Internet Research, 12,* e48.

Mojaverian, T., & Kim, H. S. (2013). Interpreting a helping hand: Cultural variation in the effectiveness of solicited and unsolicited social support. *Personality & Social Psychology Bulletin, 39*(1), 88-99. doi:10.1177/0146167212465319

Mojtabai, R. (2007). Americans' attitudes toward mental health treatment seeking: 1990–2003. *Psychiatric Services, 58,* 642–651.

Mojtabai, R. (2009). Americans' attitudes toward psychiatric medications: 1998–2006. *Psychiatric Services, 60,* 1015–1023.

Mojtabai, R., Evans-Lacko, S., Schomerus, G., & Thornicroft, G. (2016). Attitudes toward mental health seeking as predictors of future help-seeking behavior and use of mental health treatments. *Psychiatric Services, 67,* 650–657.

Mokhber, N., Azarpazhooh, M. R., Khajehdaluee, M., Velayati, A., & Hopwood, M. (2010). Randomized, single-blind, trial of sertraline and buspirone for treatment of elderly patients with generalized anxiety disorder. *Psychiatry and Clinical Neurosciences, 64,* 128–133.

Molero, F., Navas, M. S., Gonzalez, J. L., Aleman, P., & Cuadrado, I. (2003). Paupers or riches: The perception of immigrants, tourists and ingroup members in a sample of Spanish children. *Journal of Ethnic and Migration Studies, 29,* 501–517.

Mommersteeg, P. M., & Pouwer, F. (2012). Personality as a risk factor for the metabolic syndrome: A systematic review. *Journal of Psychosomatic Research, 73,* 326–333.

Mongrain, V., Lavoie, S., Selmaoui, B., Paquet, J., & Dumont, M. (2004). Phase relationships between sleep–wake cycle and underlying circadian rhythms in Morningness–Eveningness. *Journal of Biological Rhythms, 19,* 248–257.

Monroe, S. M., & Anderson, S. F. (2015). Depression: The shroud of heterogeneity. *Current Directions in Psychological Science, 24,* 227–231.

Monroe, S. M., & Reid, M. W. (2009). Life stress and major depression. *Current Directions in Psychological Science, 18,* 68–72.

Montag, C., Hahn, E., Reuter, M., Spinath, F. M., Davis, K., & Panksepp, J. (2016). The role of nature and nurture for individual differences in primary emotional systems: Evidence from a twin study. *PLoS ONE, 11,* e0151405.

Monteith, M., & Winters, J. (2002, May–June). Why we hate. *Psychology Today, 35,* 44–51.

Montelius, C., Erlandsson, D., Vitija, E., Stenblom, E.-L., Egecioglu, E., & Erlanson-Albertsson, C. (2014). Body weight loss, reduced urge for palatable food and increased release of GLP-1 through daily supplementation with green-plant membranes for three months in overweight women. *Appetite, 81,* 295–304. https://doi.org/10.1016/j.appet.2014.06.101

Montemayor, R., & Ranganathan, C. (2012). Asian-Indian parents' attributions about the causes of child behavior: A replication and extension with parents from Chennai, India. *Journal of Genetic Psychology: Research and Theory on Human Development, 173,* 374–392. doi:10.1080/00221325.2011.614649

Monti-Bloch, L., Diaz-Sanchez, V., Jennings-White, C., & Berliner, D. L. (1998). Modulation of serum testosterone and autonomic function through stimulation of the male human vomeronasal organ (VNO) with pregna-4, 20-diene-3, 6-dione. *Journal of Steroid Biochemistry and Molecular Biology, 65,* 237–242.

Montoya, M. R. (2008). I'm hot, so I'd say you're not: The influence of objective physical attractiveness on mate selection. *Personality and Social Psychology Bulletin, 34,* 1315–1331.

Montoya, R. M., & Horton, R. S. (2014). A two-dimensional model for the study of interpersonal attraction. *Personality and Social Psychology Review, 18*(1), 59–86. doi:10.1177/1088868313501887

Moore, E. G. J. (1986). Family socialization and the IQ test performance of traditionally and transracially adopted black children. *Developmental Psychology, 22,* 317–326.

Moore, L. J., Wilson, M. R., Vine, S. J., Coussens, A. H., & Freeman, P. (2013). Champ or chump? Challenge and threat states during pressurized competition. *Journal of Sports & Exercise Psychology, 35,* 551–562.

Moore, M. T., & Fresco, D. M. (2007). Depressive realism and attributional style: Implications for individuals at risk for depression. *Behavior Therapy, 38,* 144–154.

Morehead, K., Dunlosky, J., & Rawson, K. A. (2019). How much mightier is the pen than the keyboard for note-taking? A replication and extension of Mueller and Oppenheimer (2014). *Educational Psychology Review, 31*(3), 753-780. https://doi.org/10.1007/s10648-019-09468-2

Moreland, R. L., & Topolinski, S. (2010). The mere exposure phenomenon: A lingering melody by Robert Zajonc. *Emotion Review, 2,* 329–339. doi:10.1177/1754073910375479

Moreno, M. A. (2015). Sleep terrors and sleepwalking: Common parasomnias of childhood. *JAMA Pediatrics, 169,* 704. doi:10.1001/jamapediatrics.2014.2140

Morie, K. P., Crowley, M. J., Mayes, L. C., & Potenza, M. N. (2019). Prenatal drug exposure from infancy through emerging adulthood: Results from neuroimaging. *Drug and Alcohol Dependence, 198,* 39–53. doi:10.1016/j.drugalcdep.2019.01.032

Morin, C. M., Vallieres, A., Guay, B., Ivers, H., Savard, J., Merette, C., . . . Baillargeon, L. (2009). Cognitive behavioral therapy, singly and combined with medication, for persistent insomnia: A randomized controlled trial. *Journal of the American Medical Association, 301,* 2005–2015.

Morland, L. A., Greene, C. J., Rosen, C. S., Foy, D., Reilly, P., Shore, J., . . . Frueh, B. C. (2010). Telemedicine for anger management therapy in a rural population of combat veterans with posttraumatic stress disorder: A randomized noninferiority trial. *Journal of Clinical Psychiatry, 71,* 855–863.

Morlock, R. J., Tan, M., & Mitchell, D. Y. (2006). Patient characteristics and patterns of drug use for sleep complaints in the United States: Analysis of National Ambulatory Medical Survey data, 1997–2002. *Clinical Therapeutics, 28,* 1044–1053.

Morris, M. W., & Peng, K. (1994). Culture and cause: American and Chinese attributions for social and physical events. *Journal of Personality and Social Psychology, 67,* 949–971. doi:10.1037/0022-3514.67.6.949

Morrison, P. D., Zois, V., McKeown, D. A., Lee, T. D., Holt, D. W., Powell, J. F., . . . Murray, R. M. (2009). The acute effects of synthetic intravenous Delta9-tetrahydrocannabinol on psychosis, mood and cognitive functioning. *Psychological Medicine, 39,* 1607–1616.

Morrow, E. M., Roffman, J.L., Wolf, D. H., & Coyle, J. T. (2008). Psychiatric neuroscience: Incorporating pathophysiology into clinical case formulation. In T. A. Stern, J. F., Rosenbaum, M. Fava, J. Biederman, & S. L. Rauch (Eds.). *Massachusetts General Hospital comprehensive clinical psychiatry.* Mosby-Elsevier.

Mosedeghrad, A., Ferlie, E., & Rosenberg, D. (2008). A study of the relationship between job satisfaction, organizational commitment and turnover intention among hospital employees. *Health Services Management Research, 21,* 211–227.

Mosing, M. A., Gordon, S. D., Medland, S. E., Statham, D. J., Nelson, E. C., Heath, A. C., . . . Wray, N. R. (2009). Genetic and environmental influences on the comorbidity between depression, panic disorder, agoraphobia, and social phobia: A twin study. *Depression and Anxiety, 26,* 1004–1011.

Motivala, S. J., & Irwin, M. R. (2007). Sleep and immunity: Cytokine pathways linking sleep and health outcomes. *Current Directions in Psychological Science, 16,* 21–25.

Motraghi, T. E., Seim, R. W., Meyer, E. C., & Morissette, S. B. (2014). Virtual reality exposure therapy for the treatment of posttraumatic stress disorder: A methodological review using CONSORT guidelines. *Journal of Clinical Psychology, 70,* 197–208.

Motti-Stefanidi, F. (2019). Resilience among immigrant youths: Who adapts well, and why? *Current Directions in Psychological Science, 28*(5), 510-517.

Moulton, S., & Kosslyn, S. (2008). Using neuroimaging to resolve the psi debate. *Journal of Cognitive Neuroscience, 20,* 182–192.

Mowen, J. C., & Cialdini, R. B. (1980). On implementing the door-in-the-face compliance technique in a business context. *Journal of Marketing Research, 17,* 253–258.

Moy, J., Petrie, T. A., Dockendorff, S., Greenleaf, C., & Martin, S. (2013). Dieting, exercise, and intuitive eating among early adolescents. *Eating Behaviors, 14,* 529–532. doi:10.1016/j.eatbeh.2013.06.014

Moyer, C. A., Donnelly, M. P. W., Anderson, J. C., Valek, K. C., Huckaby, S. J., Wiederholt, D. A., . . . Rice, B. L. (2011). Frontal electroencephalographic asymmetry associated with positive emotion is produced by very brief meditation training. *Psychological Science, 22,* 1277–1279.

Mroczek, D. K., & Spiro, A., III. (2003). Modeling intraindividual change in personality traits: Findings from the Normative Aging Study. *Journal of Gerontology: Psychological Sciences, 58B,* P153–P165.

Mrug, S., Elliott, M., Gilliland, M. J., Grunbaum, J. A., Tortolero, S. R., Cuccaro, P., & Schuster, M. (2008). Positive parenting and early puberty in girls: Protective effects against aggressive behavior. *Archives of Pediatrics and Adolescent Medicine, 162,* 781–786.

Mucherah, W., Owino, E., & McCoy, K. (2016). Grappling with the issue of homosexuality: Perceptions, attitudes, and beliefs among high school students in Kenya. *Psychology Research and Behavior Management, 9,* 253–262. doi:10.2147/PRBM.S112421

Mueller, A. S., James, W., Abrutyn, S., & Levin, M. L. (2015). Suicide ideation and bullying among U.S. adolescents: Examining the intersections of sexual orientation, gender, and race/ethnicity. *American Journal of Public Health, 105*(5), 980–985.

Mueller, C. M., & Dweck, C. S. (1998). Praise for intelligence can undermine children's motivation and performance. *Journal of Personality and Social Psychology, 75*(1), 33–52. https://doi.org/10.1037/0022-3514.75.1.33

Mueller, C. W., Boyer, E. M., Price, J. L., & Iverson, R. D. (1994). Employee attachment and noncoercive conditions of work: The case of dental hygienists. *Work and Occupations, 21,* 179–212.

Mueller, E. A., Wood, S. A., Hanoch, Y., Huang, Y., & Reed, C. L. (2020). Older and wiser: Age differences in susceptibility to investment fraud: The protective role of emotional intelligence. *Journal of Elder Abuse & Neglect, 32*(2), 152–172. https://doi.org/10.1080/08946566.2020.1736704

Mueller, P., & Oppenheimer, D. M. (2014). The pen is mightier than the keyboard: Advantages of longhand over laptop note taking. *Psychological Science, 25,* 1159-1168. doi:10.1177/0956797614524581

Mulcahy, R., Reay, E. E., Wilkinson, R. B., & Owen, C. (2010). A randomized control trial for the effectiveness of group interpersonal psychotherapy for postnatal depression. *Archives of Women's Mental Health, 13,* 125–139.

Müller, B. C. N., Gerasimova, A., & Ritter, S. M. (2016). Concentrative meditation influences creativity by increasing cognitive flexibility. *Psychology of Aesthetics, Creativity, and the Arts, 10*(3), 278–286. doi:10.1037/a0040335

Müller, M. S., Moe, B., & Groothuis, T. G. (2014). Testosterone increases siblicidal aggression in black-legged kittiwake chicks (*Rissa tridactyla*). *Behavioral Ecology and Sociobiology, 68,* 223–232. doi:10.1007/s00265-013-1637-z

Mulligan, N. W., & Besken, M. (2013). Implicit memory. In D. Reisberg (Ed.), *The Oxford handbook of cognitive psychology* (pp. 220–231). Oxford University Press. doi:10.1093/oxfordhb/9780195376746.013.0015

Mumford, M. D. (2003). Where have we been, where are we going? Taking stock in creativity research. *Creativity Research Journal, 15,* 107–120.

Mumme, D. L., & Fernald, A. (2003). The infant as onlooker: Learning from emotional reactions observed in a television scenario. *Child Development, 74,* 221–237.

Munafo, M. R., Yalcin, B., Willis-Owen, S. A., & Flint, J. (2008). Association of the dopamine D4 receptor (DRD4) gene and approach-related personality traits: Meta-analysis and new data. *Biological Psychiatry, 63,* 197–206.

Munoz, R. F., Bunge, E. L., Chen, K., Schueller, S. M., Bravin, J. I., Shaughnessy, E. A., & Perez-Stable, E. J. (2016). Massive open online interventions: A novel model for delivering behavioral-health services worldwide. *Clinical Psychological Science, 4,* 194–205.

Munson, C. (2006). *The effects of Leap Pad's text-to-speech support on kindergarten students' independent reading.* Unpublished master's thesis, University of Valdosta, Valdosta, Georgia. http://hdl.handle.net/10428/105

Murdoch, B. B., Jr. (1962). The serial position effect of free recall. *Journal of Experimental Psychology, 64,* 482–488.

Murillo-Rodriquez, E., Arais-Carrion, O., Sanguino-Rodriguez, K., Gonzalez-Arias, M., & Haro, R. (2009). Mechanisms of sleep-wake cycle modulation. *CNS Neurological Disorders Drug Treatment, 8,* 245–253.

Murphy, K., & Delanty, N. (2007). Sleep deprivation: A clinical perspective. *Sleep and Biological Rhythms, 5,* 2–14.

Murphy, K. J., Troyer, A. K., Levine, B., & Moscovitch, M. (2008). Episodic, but not semantic, autobiographical memory is reduced in amnestic mild cognitive impairment. *Neuropsychologia, 46*(13), 3116–3123. doi:10.1016/j.neuropsychologia.2008.07.004

Murphy, S. (2008). The loss of a child: Sudden death and extended illness perspectives. In M. S. Stroebe, R. O. Hansson, H. Schut, & W. Stroebe (Eds.), *Handbook of bereavement research and practice: Advances in theory and intervention* (pp. 375–395). American Psychological Association.

Murray, A., Faraoni, M., Castro, M., Alza, N., & Cavallaro, V. (2013). Natural AChE inhibitors from plants and their contribution to Alzheimer's disease therapy. *Current Neuropharmacology, 11,* 388–413. doi:10.2174/1570159X11311040004

Murray, A. L., Obsuth, I., Eisner, M., & Ribeaud, D. (2016). Shaping aggressive personality in adolescence: Exploring cross-lagged relations between aggressive thoughts, aggressive behaviour and self-control. *Personality and Individual Differences, 97,* 1–7. doi:10.1016/j.paid.2016.03.022

Murray, H. A. (1938). *Explorations in personality.* Oxford University Press.

Murray, S. B., & Touyz, S. W. (2012). Masculinity, femininity and male body image: A recipe for future research. *International Journal of Men's Health, 11,* 227–239. doi:10.3149/jmh.1103.227

Murray, S. L., Griffin, D. W., Derrick, J. L., Harris, B., Aloni, M., & Leder, S. (2011). Tempting fate or inviting happiness? Unrealistic idealization prevents the decline of marital satisfaction. *Psychological Science, 22,* 619–626.

Murray, S. O., Olshausen, B. A., & Woods, D. L. (2003). Processing shape, motion, and three-dimensional shape-from-motion in the human cortex. *Cerebral Cortex, 13,* 508–516.

Mutz, J., Vipulananthan, V., Carter, B., Hurlemann, R., Fu, C., & Young, A. H. (2019). Comparative efficacy and acceptability of non-surgical brain stimulation for the acute treatment of major depressive episodes in adults: Systematic review and network meta-analysis. *BMJ* (Clinical research ed.), *364,* l1079. doi.org/10.1136/bmj.l1079

Muurahainen, N. E., Kisileff, H. R., Lachaussee, J., & Pi-Sunyer, F. X. (1991). Effect of a soup preload on reduction of food intake by cholecystokinin in humans. *American Journal of Physiology, 260,* R672–R680.

Myers, D. G. (2000). The funds, friends, and faith of happy people. *American Psychologist, 55,* 56–67.

Myles, S., Lea, R. A., Ohashi, J., Chambers, G. K., Weiss, J. G., Hardouin, E., . . . Stoneking, M. (2011). Testing the thrifty gene hypothesis: The Gly482Ser variant in PPARGC1A is associated with BMI in Tongans. *BMC Medical Genetics, 12,* 10–10. doi:10.1186/1471-2350-12-10

Nacke, L. E., Nacke, A., & Lindley, C. A. (2009). Brain training for silver gamers: Effects of age and game form on effectiveness, efficiency, self-assessment, and gameplay experience. *Cyberpsychology and Behavior, 12,* 493–499.

Nadler, D. R., & Komarraju, M. (2016). Negating stereotype threat: Autonomy support and academic identification boost performance of African American college students. *Journal of College Student Development, 57*(6), 667–679. doi:10.1353/csd.2016.0039

Naegele, B., Thouvard, V., Pepin, J. L., Levy, P., Bonnet, C., Perret, J. E., . . . Feuerstein, C. (1995). Deficits of cognitive functions in patients with sleep apnea syndrome. *Sleep, 18,* 43–52.

Nagandia, K., & De, S. (2013). Restless legs syndrome: Pathophysiology and modern management. *Postgraduate Medical Journal, 89,* 402–410.

Nairne, J. S. (2002). Remembering over the short term: The case against the standard model. *Annual Review of Psychology, 53,* 53–81.

Nairne, J. S., & Pandeirada, J. N. S. (2010). Adaptive memory: Nature's criterion and the functionalist agenda. *The American Journal of Psychology, 123*(4), 381–390. doi:10.5406/amerjpsyc.123.4.0381

Nairne, J. S., & Pandeirada, J. N. S. (2016). Adaptive memory: The evolutionary significance of survival processing. *Perspectives on Psychological Science, 11*(4), 496–511. doi:10.1177/1745691616635613

Naish, P. L. (2010). Hypnosis and hemispheric asymmetry. *Consciousness and Cognition, 19,* 230–234.

Nakaya, N., Bidstrup, P. E., Saito-Nakaya, K., Frederiksen, K., Koskenvuo, M., Pukkala, E., ... Johansen, C. (2010). Personality traits and cancer risk and survival based on Finnish and Swedish registry data. *American Journal of Epidemiology, 172*(4), 377-85. doi:10.1093/aje/kwq046

Nam, B., Jun, H.-J., Fedina, L., Shah, R., & DeVylder, J. E. (2019). Sexual orientation and mental health among adults in four U.S. cities. *Psychiatry Research, 273,* 134–140. https://doi.org/10.1016/j.psychres.2018.12.092

Nardi, A. E., Freire, R. C., Valenca, A. M., Amrein, R., de Cerqueira, A. C., Lopes, F. L., . . . Versiani, M. (2010). Tapering clonazepam in patients with panic disorder after at least 3 years of treatment. *Journal of Clinical Psychopharmacology, 30,* 290–293.

Narvaez, D. (2010). Moral complexity: The fatal attraction of truthiness and the importance of mature moral functioning. *Perspectives on Psychological Science, 5,* 163–181.

NAS. (2012). Employee referrals: Trends in engagement and technology. *NAS Insights.* http://www.nasrecruitment.com/our-thinking/nas-insights

Naselaris, T., Olman, C. A., Stansbury, D. E., Ugurbil, K., & Gallant, J. L. (2015). A voxel-wise encoding model for early visual areas decodes mental images of remembered scenes. *NeuroImage, 105,* 215–228. doi:10.1016/j.neuroimage.2014.10.018

Nash, J. M., & Thebarge, R. W. (2006). Understanding psychological stress, its biological processes, and impact on primary headache. *Headache, 46,* 1377–1386.

Nash, M. (1987). What, if anything, is regressed about hypnotic age regression? A review of the empirical literature. *Psychological Bulletin, 102,* 42–52.

Nasiriavanaki, Z., ArianNik, M., Abbassian, A., Mahmoudi, E., Roufigari, N., Shahzadi, S., . . . Bahrami, B. (2015). Prediction of individual differences in risky behavior in young adults via variations in local brain structure. *Frontiers in Neuroscience, 9,* 359. doi:10.3389/fnins.2015.00359

Nassif, A., & Gunter, B. (2008). Gender representation in television advertisements in Britain and Saudi Arabia. *Sex Roles, 58,* 752–760.

National Comorbidity Survey Replication (NCS-R). (2007). http://www.hcp.med.harvard.edu/ncs

National Highway Traffic Safety Administration (NHTSA). (2013). *2012 Motor Vehicle Crashes: Overview.* Author.

National Highway Traffic Safety Administration (NHTSA). (2019). Distracted driving in fatal crashes, 2017. *Traffic Safety Facts Research Note,* Report No. DOT HS 812 700. Author.

National Institute of Alcohol Abuse and Alcoholism. (2004). NIAAA council approves definition of binge drinking. *NIAAA Newsletter, 3,* 3.

National Institute on Drug Abuse (NIDA). (2001). *Research report series: Hallucinogens and dissociative drugs.* NIH Publication Number 01-4209. Author.

National Institute on Drug Abuse (NIDA). (2006a). *Research report series: MDMA (Ecstasy) abuse.* NIH Publication Number 06-4728. Author.

National Institute on Drug Abuse (NIDA). (2006b). *Research report series: Methamphetamine abuse and addiction.* NIH Publication Number 06-4210. Author.

National Institutes of Health (NIH). (2016). *How are overweight and obesity diagnosed?* http://www.nhlbi.nih.gov/health/health-topics/topics/obe/diagnosis

National Research Council. (2011). *Explaining divergent levels of longevity in high-income countries.* National Academies Press.

National Safety Council. (2011). *Injury fact book, 2011 edition.* http://www.nsc.org/NSC%20Picture%20Library/News/web_graphics/Injury_Facts_37.pdf

National Science Board (NSB). (2016). *Science and Engineering Indicators 2016.* National Center for Science and Engineering Statistics.

National Science Board, National Science Foundation. (2020). *Science and Engineering Indicators 2020: The State of U.S. Science and Engineering.* NSB-2020-1. Alexandria, VA.

National Scientific Council on the Developing Child (NSCDC). (2007). *The timing and quality of early experiences combine to shape brain architecture: Working Paper No. 5.* http://developingchild.harvard.edu

National Sleep Foundation. (2004). *Summary findings: 2004 Sleep in America poll.* Author.

National Sleep Foundation. (2005). *Summary findings: 2005 Sleep in America poll.* Author.

National Sleep Foundation. (2010). *Summary findings: 2010 Sleep in America poll.* Author.

National Sleep Foundation. (2013). *International bedroom poll.* Author.

National Sleep Foundation. (2014). *Sleep in America poll: Sleep in the modern family.* The Foundation; : http://www.sleepfoundation.org/sleep-polls-data/sleep-in-america-poll/2014-sleep-in-the-modern-family

National Transportation Safety Board (NTSB). (2020). U.S. transportation fatalities in 2018—by mode. ntsb.gov/investigations/data/SiteAssets/Pages/Data_Stats/US-Transportation-fatalities-2018.pdf

Nave, K. A. (2010). Myelination and support of axonal integrity by glia. *Nature, 468,* 244–252.

Naylor, J. C., Pritchard, R. D., & Ilgen, D. R. (1980). *A theory of behavior in organizations.* Academic Press.

Nazari, H., Momeni, N., Jariani, M., & Tarrahi, M. J. (2011). Comparison of eye movement desensitization and reprocessing with citalopram in treatment of obsessive-compulsive disorder. *International Journal of Psychiatry in Clinical Practice, 15,* 270–274.

Nederhof, E., Ormel, J., & Oldehinkel, A.J. (2014). Mismatch or cumulative stress: The pathway to depression is conditional on attention style. *Psychological Science, 25,* 684–692.

Neher, A. (1991). Maslow's theory of motivation: A critique. *Journal of Humanistic Psychology, 31,* 89–112.

Neisewander, J. L., Cheung, T. C., & Pentkowski, N. S. (2014). Dopamine D3 and 5-HT1B receptor dysregulation as a result of psychostimulant intake and forced abstinence: Implications for medications development. *Neuropharmacology, 76*(Part B), 301–319. doi:10.1016/j.neuropharm.2013.08.014

Nel, E. C. (2019). The impact of workplace bullying on flourishing: The moderating role of emotional intelligence. *SAJIP: South African Journal of Industrial Psychology, 45,* 1–9.

Nelson, E. (2019). What Frege asked Alex the parrot: Inferentialism, number concepts, and animal cognition. *Philosophical Psychology, 33*(2), 206–227. https://doi.org/10.1080/09515089.2019.1688777

Nelson, K., & Fivush, R. (2004). The emergence of autobiographical memory: A social cultural developmental theory. *Psychological Review, 111,* 486–511.

Nelson, S. K., Kushlev, K., Dunn, E.W., & Lyubomirsky, S. (2014). Parents are slightly happier than nonparents, but causality still cannot be inferred: A reply to Bhargava, Kassam, and Loewenstein (2014). *Psychological Science, 25,* 303–304.

Nelson, S. K., Kushlev, K., English, T., Dunn, E. W., & Lyubomirsky, S. (2013). In defense of parenthood: Children are associated with more joy than misery. *Psychological Science, 24,* 3–10.

Nemeroff, C. B. (2007). The burden of severe depression: A review of diagnostic challenges and treatment alternatives. *Journal of Psychiatric Research, 41,* 189–206.

Nepocatych, S., Melson, C. E., Madzima, T. A., & Balilionis, G. (2019). Comparison of the effects of a liquid breakfast meal with varying doses of plant-based soy protein on appetite profile, energy metabolism and intake. *Appetite, 141,* 104322. https://doi.org/10.1016/j.appet.2019.104322

Neri, P. (2014). Semantic control of feature extraction from natural scenes. *The Journal of Neuroscience: The Official Journal of the Society for Neuroscience, 34*(6), 2374–2388. doi:10.1523/JNEUROSCI.1755-13.2014

Neria, Y., Nandi, A., & Galea, S. (2008). Post-traumatic stress disorder following disasters: A systematic review. *Psychological Medicine, 38,* 467–480.

Nestler, E. J., & Carlezon, W. A., Jr. (2006). The mesolimbic dopamine reward circuit in depression. *Biological Psychiatry, 59,* 1151–1159.

Nestor, L., Roberts, G., Garavan, H., & Hester, R. (2008). Deficits in learning and memory: Parahippocampal hyperactivity and frontocortical hypoactivity in cannabis users. *NeuroImage, 40,* 1328–1339.

Neubauer, A. B., Smyth, J. M., & Sliwinski, M. J. (2019). Age differences in proactive coping with minor hassles in daily life. *The Journals of Gerontology, Series B, Psychological Sciences and Social Sciences, 74*(1), 7-16. doi:10.1093/geronb/gby061.

Nevin, J. A. (2012). Resistance to extinction and behavioral momentum. *Behavioural Processes, 90,* 89–97.

Nevin, J. A., & Grace, R. C. (2005). Resistance to extinction in the steady state and in the transition. *Journal of Experimental Psychology: Animal Behavior Processes, 31,* 199–212.

Newcomb, T. M. (1961). *The acquaintance process.* Holt, Rinehart & Winston.

Newland, R. P., & Crnic, K. A. (2017). Developmental risk and goodness of fit in the mother-child relationship: Links to parenting stress and children's behaviour problems. *Infant and Child Development, 26*(2), e1980. doi:10.1002/icd.1980

Newman, M. G., Llera, S. J., Erickson, T. M., Przeworski, A., & Castonguay, L. G. (2013). Worry and generalized anxiety disorder: A review and theoretical synthesis of research on its nature, etiology, mechanisms, and treatment. *Annual Review of Clinical Psychology, 9,* 275–297.

Newmark, T. S., & Bogacki, D. F. (2005). The use of relaxation, hypnosis, and imagery in sport psychiatry. *Clinics in Sports Medicine, 24,* 973–977.

Ni, X., Sicard, T., Bulgin, N., Bismil, R., Chan, K., McMain, S., & Kennedy, J. L. (2007). Monoamine oxidase A gene is associated with borderline personality disorder. *Psychiatric Genetics, 17,* 153–157.

Nickel, F. T., Ott, S., Mohringer, S., Saake, M., Dorfler, A., Seifert, F., & Maihofner, C. (2014). Brain correlates of short-term habituation to repetitive electrical noxious stimulation. *European Journal of Pain (London, England), 18*(1), 56–66. doi:10.1002/j.1532-2149.2013.00339.x

Nicodemus, K. K., Callicott, J. H., Higier, R. G., Luna, A., Nixon, D. C., Lipska, B. K., . . . Weinberger, D. R. (2010). Evidence of statistical epistasis between DISC1, CIT and NDEL1 impacting risk for schizophrenia: Biological validation with functional neuroimaging. *Human Genetics, 127,* 441–452.

Nicolini, H., Arnold, P., Nestadt, G., Lanzagorta, N., & Kennedy, J. L. (2009). Overview of genetics and obsessive-compulsive disorder. *Psychiatry Research, 170,* 7–14.

Nicolosi, A., Laumann, E. O., Glasser, D. B., Moreira, E. D. J., Paik, A., & Gingell, C. (2004). Sexual behavior and sexual dysfunctions after age 40: The global study of sexual attitudes and behaviors. *Urology, 64*(5), 991–997. doi:10.1016/j.urology.2004.06.055

Niedzwienska, A. (2003). Gender differences in vivid memories. *Sex Roles: A Journal of Research, 49,* 321–331.

Nielsen, M., & Day, R. H. (1999). William James and the evolution of consciousness. *Journal of Theoretical and Philosophical Psychology, 19,* 90–113.

Nieuwenhuijsen, K., Verbeek, J. H., de Boer, A. G., Blonk, R. W., & van Dijk, F. J. (2010). Irrational beliefs in employees with an adjustment, a depressive, or an anxiety disorder: A prospective cohort study. *Journal of Rational-Emotive and Cognitive-Behavior Therapy, 28,* 57–72.

Nijdam, M. J., Gersons, B. P., Reitsma, J. B., de Jongh, A., & Olff, M. (2012). Brief eclectic psychotherapy v. eye movement desensitisation and reprocessing therapy for posttraumatic stress disorder: Randomised controlled trial. *British Journal of Psychiatry, 200,* 224–231.

Niki, C., Kumada, T., Maruyama, T., Tamura, M., & Muragaki, Y. (2019). Role of frontal functions in executing routine sequential tasks. *Frontiers in Psychology, 10,* 169. https://doi.org/10.3389/fpsyg.2019.00169

Nikolin, S., Loo, C. K., Bai, S., Dokos, S., & Martin, D. M. (2015). Focalised stimulation using high definition transcranial direct current stimulation (HD-tDCS) to investigate declarative verbal learning and memory functioning. *NeuroImage, 117,* 11–19. doi:10.1016/j.neuroimage.2015.05.019

NIMH Genetics Workgroup. (1998). *Genetics and mental disorders.* NIH Publication No. 98-4268. National Institute of Mental Health.

Nisbett, R. (1995). Race, IQ, and scientism. In Steven Fraser (Ed.), *The bell curve wars: Race, intelligence, and the future of America* (pp. 36–57). Basic Books.

Nisbett, R. E. (2013). Schooling makes you smarter: What teachers need to know about IQ. *American Educator, 37*(1), 10–19.

Nisbett, R. E., Aronson, J., Blair, C., Dickens, W., Flynn, J., Halpern, D. F., & Turkheimer, E. (2012). Intelligence: New findings and theoretical developments. *American Psychologist, 67,* 130–159. doi:10.1037/a0026699

Nishino, S. (2007). Narcolepsy: Pathophysiology and pharmacology. *Journal of Clinical Psychiatry, 68,* 9–15.

Nishino, S., & Okuro, M. (2010). Emerging treatments for narcolepsy and its related

disorders. *Expert Opinion on Emerging Drugs, 15,* 139–158.
Nivoli, A. M., Murru, A., & Vieta, E. (2010). Lithium: Still a cornerstone in the long-term treatment in bipolar disorder? *Neuropsychobiology, 62,* 27–35.
Noble, M., & Harding, G. E. (1963). Conditioning of rhesus monkeys as a function of the interval between CS and US. *Journal of Comparative and Physiological Psychology, 56,* 220–224.
Nock, M. K., Borges, G., Bromet, E. J., Cha, C. B., Kessler, R. C., & Lee, S. (2008). Suicide and suicidal behavior. *Epidemiologic Reviews, 30,* 133–154.
Nock, M. K., Hwang, I., Sampson, N., Kessler, R. C., Angermeyer, M., Beautrais, A., . . . Williams, D. R. (2009). Cross-national analysis of the associations among mental disorders and suicidal behavior: Findings from the WHO World Mental Health Surveys. *PLoS Medicine, 6,* e1000123.
Nolen-Hoeksema, S. (2001). Gender differences in depression. *Current Directions in Psychological Science, 10,* 173–176.
Nolen-Hoeksema, S. (2002). Gender differences in depression. In I. H. Gotlib & C. L. Hammen (Eds.), *Handbook of depression* (pp. 492–509). Guilford Press.
Nolen-Hoeksema, S., & Hilt, L. M. (2013). *Handbook of depression in adolescents.* Routledge.
Nolen-Hoeksema, S., Larson, J., & Grayson, C. (1999). Explaining the gender difference in depressive symptoms. *Journal of Personality and Social Psychology, 77,* 1061–1072.
Nolen-Hoeksema, S., Stice, E., Wade, E., & Bohon, C. (2007). Reciprocal relations between rumination and bulimic, substance abuse, and depressive symptoms in female adolescents. *Journal of Abnormal Psychology, 116,* 198–207.
Nolen-Hoeksema, S., Wisco, B. E., & Lyubomirsky, S. (2008). Rethinking rumination. *Perspectives on Psychological Science, 3,* 400–424.
Norbury, A., & Husain, M. (2015). Sensation-seeking: Dopaminergic modulation and risk for psychopathology. *Behavioural Brain Research, 288,* 79–93.
Norcross, J. C., & Wampold, B. E. (2011). Evidence-based therapy relationships: Research conclusions and clinical practices. *Psychotherapy, 48,* 98–102.
Nordin, S., Razani, J. L., Markison, S., & Murphy, C. (2003). Age-associated increases in intensity discrimination for taste. *Experimental Aging Research, 29,* 371–381.
North, C. S., & Pfefferbaum, B. (2013). Mental health response to community disasters: A systematic review. *JAMA, 310,* 507–518. doi:10.1001/jama.2013.107799
Nosofsky, R. M., & Zaki, S. R. (2002). Exemplar and prototype models revisited: Response strategies, selective attention, and stimulus generalization. *Journal of Experimental Psychology: Learning, Memory, and Cognition, 28,* 924–940.
Nottelmann, E. D., Inoff-Germain, G., Susman, E. J., & Chrousos, G. P. (1990). Hormones and behavior at puberty. In J. Bancroft & J. M. Reinisch (Eds.), *Adolescence and puberty* (pp. 88–123). Oxford University Press.
Novack, M. A., Congdon, E. L., Hemani-Lopez, N., & Goldin-Meadow, S. (2014). From action to abstraction: Using the hand to learn math. *Psychological Science, 25,* 903–910.
Novakova, M., Sladek, M., & Sumova, A. (2013). Human chronotype is determined in bodily cells under real-life conditions. *Chronobiology International, 30,* 607–617.
Nowicka, A., & Tacikowski, P. (2011). Transcallosal transfer of information and functional asymmetry of the human brain. *Laterality: Asymmetries of Body, Brain and Cognition, 16,* 35–74. doi:10.1080/13576500903154231
Nowland, R., Necka, E. A., & Cacioppo, J. T. (2018). Loneliness and social internet use: Pathways to reconnection in a digital world? *Perspectives on Psychological Science, 13*(1), 70-87.
Nummenmaa, L., Hietanen, J. K., Santtila, P., & Hyönä, J. (2012). Gender and visibility of sexual cues influence eye movements while viewing faces and bodies. *Archives of Sexual Behavior, 41,* 1439–1451.
Núñez, J. L., & León, J. (2016). The mediating effect of intrinsic motivation to learn on the relationship between student's autonomy support and vitality and deep learning. *The Spanish Journal of Psychology, 19,* E42. doi:10.1017/sjp.2016.43
Nusbaum, E. C., & Silvia, P. J. (2011). Are intelligence and creativity really so different? Fluid intelligence, executive processes, and strategy use in divergent thinking. *Intelligence, 39,* 36–45. doi:10.1016/j.intell.2010.11.002
Nuss, P. (2015). Anxiety disorders and GABA neurotransmission: A disturbance of modulation. *Neuropsychiatric Disease and Treatment, 11,* 165–175.
Nyberg, L., Marklund, P., Persson, J., Cabeza, R., Forkstam, C., Petersson, K. M., . . . Ingvar, M. (2003). Common prefrontal activations during working memory, episodic memory, and semantic memory. *Neuropsychologia, 41,* 371–377.
Nyer, P. U., & Dellande, S. (2010). Public commitment as a motivator for weight loss. *Psychology and Marketing, 27,* 1–12.
O'Brien, A., Terry, D. J., & Jimmieson, N. L. (2008). Negative affectivity and responses to work stressors: An experimental study. *Anxiety, Stress, and Coping, 21,* 55–83.
O'Brien, E., & Kassirer, S. (2019). People are slow to adapt to the warm glow of giving. *Psychological Science, 30*(2), 193-204.
O'Brien, E. L., & Hess, T. M. (2020). Differential focus on probability and losses between young and older adults in risky decision-making. *Aging, Neuropsychology, and Cognition, 27*(4), 532–552. https://doi.org/10.1080/13825585.2019.1642442
O'Brien, K. S., Hunter, J. A., Halberstadt, J., & Anderson, J. (2007). Body image and explicit and implicit anti-fat attitudes: The mediating role of physical appearance comparisons. *Body Image, 4,* 249–256. doi:10.1016/j.bodyim.2007.06.001
O'Brien, M. (1996). Child-rearing difficulties reported by parents of infants and toddlers. *Journal of Pediatric Psychology, 21,* 433–446.
O'Brien, M. C., McCoy, T. P., Rhodes, S. D., Wagoner, A., & Wolfson, M. (2008). Caffeinated cocktails: Energy drink consumption, high-risk drinking, and alcohol-related consequences among college students. *Academic Emergency Medicine, 15,* 453–460.
O'Bryan, M., Fishbein, H. D., & Ritchey, P. N. (2004). Intergenerational transmission of prejudice, sex role stereotyping, and intolerance. *Adolescence, 39,* 407–426.
O'Connor, D. B., Jones, F., Conner, M., McMillan, B., & Ferguson, E. (2008). Effects of daily hassles and eating style on eating behavior. *Health Psychology, 27,* S20–S31.
O'Keefe, D. J., & Figge, M. (1997). A guilt-based explanation of the door-in-the-face influence strategy. *Human Communication Research, 24,* 64–81.
O'Rourke, E. J., Halpern, L. F., & Vaysman, R. (2020). Examining the relations among emerging adult coping, executive function, and anxiety. *Emerging Adulthood, 8*(3), 209–225. https://doi.org/10.1177/2167696818797531
Ocklenburg, S., Ball, A., Wolf, C. C., Genç, E., & Güntürkün, O. (2015). Functional cerebral lateralization and interhemispheric interaction in patients with callosal agenesis. *Neuropsychology, 29(5),* 806–815. doi:10.1037/neu0000193
Oehen, P. Traber, R., Widmer, V., & Schnyder, U. (2013). A randomized, controlled pilot study of MDMA (+/- 3,4-methylenedioxymethamphetamine)-assisted psychotherapy for treatment of resistant, chronic post-traumatic stress disorder (PTSD). *Journal of Psychopharmacology, 27,* 40–52.
Oesch, S., Rüegg, C., Fischer, B., Degen, L., & Beglinger, C. (2006). Effect of gastric distension prior to eating on food intake and feelings of satiety in humans. *Physiology & Behavior, 87,* 903–910. doi:10.1016/j.physbeh 2006.02.003
Offidani, E., Guidi, J., Tomba, E., & Fava, G. A. (2013). Efficacy and tolerability of benzodiazepines versus antidepressants in anxiety disorders: A systematic review and meta-analysis. *Psychotherapy and Psychosomatics, 82,* 355–362.
Ogden, C. L., Carroll, M. D., Kit, B. K., & Flegal, K. M. (2013). *Prevalence of obesity among adults: United States, 2011–2012* (Data Brief, 131). Centers for Disease Control, National Center for Health Statistics. http://www.cdc.gov/nchs/data/databriefs/db131.pdf
Oginska, H., & Pokorski, J. (2006). Fatigue and mood correlates of sleep length in three age-social groups: School children, students, and employees. *Chronobiology International, 23,* 1317–1328.
Ogle, C. M., Rubin, D. C., Berntsen, D., & Siegler, I. C. (2013). The frequency and impact of exposure to potentially traumatic events over the life course. *Clinical Psychological Science, 1,* 426–434.
Ohayon, M. M., Mahowald, M. W., Dauvilliers, Y., Krystal, A. D., & Leger, D. (2012). Prevalence and comorbidity of nocturnal wandering in the U.S. adult general population. *Neurology, 78,* 1583–1589.
Olatunji, B. O., Davis, M. L., Powers, M. B., & Smits, J. A. (2013). Cognitive-behavioral therapy for obsessive-compulsive disorder: A meta-analysis of treatment outcome and moderators. *Journal of Psychiatric Research, 47,* 33–41
Olff, M., Langeland, W., Draijer, N., & Gersons, B. P. (2007). Gender differences in post-traumatic stress disorder. *Psychological Bulletin, 133,* 183–204.
Olson, R. L., Hanowski, R. J., Hickman, J. S., & Bocanegra, J. (2009). *Driver distraction in commercial vehicle operations.* Department of Transportation. Federal Motor Carrier Safety Administration report no. FMCSA-RRR-09-042. Virginia Tech Transportation Institute.
Oltmanns, T. F., & Powers, A. D. (2012). Gender and personality disorders. In T. A. Widiger (Ed.), *The Oxford Handbook of Personality*

Disorders (pp. 206–218). Oxford University Press.

Omalu, B. I., Hamilton, R. L., Kamboh, M. I., DeKosky, S. T., & Bailes, J. (2010). Chronic traumatic encephalopathy (CTE) in a National Football League player: Case report and emerging medicolegal practice questions. *Journal of Forensic Nursing, 6*(1), 40–46. https://doi.org/10.1111/j.1939-3938.2009.01064.x

Omar, H., McElderry, D., & Zakharia, R. (2003). Educating adolescents about puberty: What are we missing? *International Journal of Adolescent Medicine and Health, 15,* 79–83.

Ondersma, S. J., & Walker, C. E. (1998). Elimination disorders. In T. H. Ollendick & M. Hersen (Eds.), *Handbook of child psychopathology* (pp. 355–380). Plenum Press.

Ones, D. S., Dilchert, S., & Viswesvaran, C. (2007). In support of personality assessment in organizational settings. *Personnel Psychology, 60,* 995–1027.

Oosthuizen, P. P., Emsley, R. A., Maritz, J. S., Turner, J. A., & Keyter, N. (2003). Incidence of tardive dyskinesia in first-episode psychosis patients treated with low-dose haloperidol. *Journal of Clinical Psychiatry, 64,* 1075–1080.

Opheim, E., Andersen, P. N., Jakobsen, M., Aasen, B., & Kvaal, K. (2019). Poor quality in systematic reviews on PTSD and EMDR: An examination of search methodology and reporting. *Frontiers in Psychology, 10,* 1558. doi.org/10.3389/fpsyg.2019.01558

Ophir, Y., Sisso, I., Asterhan, C., Tikochinski, R., & Reichart, R. (2020). The Turker blues: Hidden factors behind increased depression rates among Amazon's Mechanical Turkers. *Clinical Psychological Science, 8*(1), 65-83.

Opree, S. J., Petrova, S., & Rozendaal, E. (2019). Investigating the unintended effects of television advertising among children in former-Soviet Bulgaria. *Journal of Children and Media, 14*(1), 1-17. https://doi.org/10.1080/17482798.2019.1644359

Oreg, S., & Berson, Y. (2018). The impact of top leaders' personalities: The processes through which organizations become reflections of their leaders. *Current Directions in Psychological Science, 27*(4), 241-248.

Orina, M. M., Collins, W. A., Simpson, J. A., Salvatore, J. E ., Haydon, K. C., & Kim, J. S. (2011). Developmental and dyadic perspectives on commitment in adult romantic relationships. *Psychological Science, 22,* 908–915.

Ornoy, A., & Ergaz, Z. (2010). Alcohol abuse in pregnant women: Effects on the fetus and newborn, mode of action and maternal treatment. *International Journal of Environmental Research and Public Health, 7,* 364–379.

Orr, J. M., Paschall, C. J., & Banich, M. T. (2016). Recreational marijuana use impacts white matter integrity and subcortical (but not cortical) morphometry. *NeuroImage: Clinical, 12,* 47–56. doi:10.1016/j.nicl.2016.06.006

Ortega, L. A., & Karch, D. (2010). Precipitating circumstances of suicide among women of reproductive age in 16 U.S. states, 2003–2007. *Journal of Women's Health, 19,* 5–7.

Ortiz, R. (2019). Building resilience against the sequelae of adverse childhood experiences: Rise up, change your life, and reform health care. *American Journal of Lifestyle Medicine, 13*(5), 470-479. doi:10.1177/1559827619839997.

Ortony, A., & Turner, T. J. (1990). What's basic about basic emotions? *Psychological Review, 97,* 315–331.

Osborne, R. H., Sali, A., Aaronson, N. K., Elsworth, G. R., Mdzewski, B., & Sinclair, A. J. (2004). Immune function and adjustment style: Do they predict survival in breast cancer? *Psychooncology, 13,* 199–210.

Ostelo, R. W. J. G., van Tulder, M. W., Vlaeyen, J. W. S., Linton, S. J., Morley, S. J., & Assendelft, W. J. J. (2007). Behavioural treatment for chronic low-back pain. *Cochrane Database of Systematic Reviews, 7,* CD002014. doi:10.1002/14651858.CD002014.pub3

Osterman, K., Bjorkqvist, K., Lagerspertz, K. M. J., Kaukiainen, A., Huesmann, L. R., & Fraczek, A. (1994). Peer and self-estimated aggression and victimization in 8-year-old children from five ethnic groups. *Aggressive Behavior, 20,* 411–428.

Ostroff, C., Kinicki, A. J., & Tamkins, M. M. (2003). Organizational culture and climate. In W. C. Borman, D. R. Ilgen, & R. J. Klimoski (Eds.), *Handbook of psychology: Industrial and organizational psychology* (Vol. 12, pp. 565–593). Wiley.

Oswalt, S. B., & Wyatt, T. J. (2011). Sexual orientation and differences in mental health, stress, and academic performance in a national sample of U.S. college students. *Journal of Homosexuality, 58,* 1255–1280. doi:10.1080/00918369.2011.605738

Oteri, A., Salvo, F., Caputi, A. P., & Calapai, G. (2007). Intake of energy drinks in association with alcoholic beverages in a cohort of students of the School of Medicine of the University of Messina. *Alcoholism, Clinical, and Experimental Research, 31,* 1677–1680.

Overman, W. H., Bachevalier, J., Schuhmann, E., & Ryan, P. (1996). Cognitive gender differences in very young children parallel biologically based cognitive gender differences in monkeys. *Behavioral Neuroscience, 110,* 673–684.

Overmier, J. B. (2002). On learned helplessness. *Integrative Physiological and Behavioral Science, 37,* 4–8.

Overmier, J. B., & Seligman, M. E. (1967). Effects of inescapable shock upon subsequent escape and avoidance responding. *Journal of Comparative and Physiological Psychology, 63,* 28–33.

Owens, A. (2018). Income segregation between school districts and inequality in students' achievement. *Sociology of Education, 91*(1), 1–27.

Owens, J. A. (2007). Sleep medicine. In R. M. Kliegman, R. E. Behrman, H. B. Jenson, & B. F. Stanton (Eds.), *Nelson textbook of pediatrics* (18th ed.). Saunders Elsevier.

Ozdemir Oz, A., Lane, J. F., & Michou, A. (2016). Autonomous and controlling reasons underlying achievement goals during task engagement: Their relation to intrinsic motivation and cheating. *Educational Psychology, 36*(7), 1157–1169. doi:10.1080/01443410.2015.1109064

Packer, D. J. (2009). Avoiding groupthink: Whereas weakly identified members remain silent, strongly identified members dissent about collective problems. *Psychological Science, 20,* 546–548.

Padela, A. I., & Heisler, M. (2010). The association of perceived abuse and discrimination after September 11, 2001, with psychological distress, level of happiness, and health status among Arab Americans. *American Journal of Public Health, 100,* 284–291.

Page, R. A., & Green, J. P. (2007). An update on age, hypnotic suggestibility, and gender: A brief report. *American Journal of Clinical Hypnosis, 49,* 283–287.

Paintain, E., & Cassidy, S. (2018). First-line therapy for post-traumatic stress disorder: A systematic review of cognitive behavioural therapy and psychodynamic approaches. *Counselling and Psychotherapy Research, 18*(3), 237–250. doi.org/10.1002/capr.12174

Paivio, A. (1982). The empirical case for dual coding. In J. Yuille (Ed.), *Imagery, cognition, and memory* (pp. 307–332). Erlbaum.

Paivio, A. (1986). *Mental representations: A dual coding approach.* Oxford University Press.

Palejwala, M. H., & Fine, J. G. (2015). Gender differences in latent cognitive abilities in children aged 2 to 7. *Intelligence, 48,* 96–108. doi:10.1016/j.intell.2014.11.004

Pallier, G. (March, 2003). Gender differences in the self-assessment of accuracy on cognitive tasks. *Sex Roles: A Journal of Research, 48*(5/6), 265–276.

Papadakis, A. A., Prince, R. P., Jones, N. P., & Strauman, T. J. (2006). Self-regulation, rumination, and vulnerability to depression in adolescent girls. *Development and Psychopathology, 18,* 815–829.

Parent, A. S., Teilmann, G., Juul, A., Skakkebaek, N. E., Toppari, J., & Bourguignon, J. P. (2003). The timing of normal puberty and the age limits of sexual precocity: Variations around the world, secular trends, and changes after migration. *Endocrine Reviews, 24,* 668–693.

Park, D. C., & McDonough, I. M. (2013). The dynamic aging mind: Revelations from functional neuroimaging research. *Psychological Science, 8,* 62–67

Park, J. S., & Lee, K. (2012). Modification of severe violent and aggressive behavior among psychiatric inpatients through the use of a short-term token economy. *Journal of Korean Academy of Nursing, 42,* 1062–1069.

Parker, E. S., Birnbaum, I. M., & Noble, E. P. (1976). Alcohol and memory: Storage and state dependency. *Journal of Verbal Learning and Verbal Behavior, 15,* 691–702.

Parker, G. B., & Brotchie, H. L. (2004). From diathesis to dimorphism: The biology of gender differences in depression. *Journal of Nervous and Mental Disorders, 192,* 210–216.

Parker, G. B., & Brotchie, H. L. (2010). Gender differences in depression. *International Review of Psychiatry, 22,* 429–436.

Parker, G. B., Roy, K., Wilhelm, K., & Mitchell, P. (2001). Assessing the comparative effectiveness of antidepressant therapies: A prospective clinical practice study. *Journal of Clinical Psychiatry, 62,* 117–125.

Parker-Pope, T. (2002, August 27). A new reason for teens to avoid sex: It could be harmful to their health. *Wall Street Journal,* D1.

Parkes, C. M. (1986). *Bereavement: Studies of grief in adult life* (2nd ed.). Tavistock.

Parkes, C. M. (1991). Attachment, bonding, and psychiatric problems after bereavement in adult life. In C. M. Parkes, J. Stevenson-Hinde, & P. Marris (Eds.), *Attachment across the life cycle* (pp. 268–292). Tavistock/Routledge.

Parkin, A. J., & Leng, N. R. C. (1993). *Neuropsychology of the amnesic syndrome.* Psychology Press.

Parks, T. E. (2013). On depth processing in the production of the Ponzo illusion: Two problems and a solution. *Perception, 42*(2), 242–244.

Parmley, M., & Cunningham, J. G. (2014). She looks sad, but he looks mad: The effects of age, gender, and ambiguity on emotion perception. *The Journal of Social Psychology, 154*(4), 323–338. doi:10.1080/00224545.2014.901287

Parolin, M., Simonelli, A., Mapelli, D., Sacco, M., & Cristofalo, P. (2016). Parental substance abuse as an early traumatic event. Preliminary findings on neuropsychological and personality functioning in young drug addicts exposed to drugs early. *Frontiers in Psychology, 7,* 887.

Parr, E. B., Coffey, V. G., & Hawley, J. A. (2013). "Sarcobesity": A metabolic conundrum. *Maturitas, 74,* 109–113. doi:10.1016/j.maturitas.2012.10.014

Parrott, A. C. (2014) The potential dangers of using MDMA for psychotherapy. *Journal of Psychoactive Drugs, 46(1),* 37–43.

Partnership Attitude Tracking Study (PATS). (2013). *The 2012 Partnership Attitude Tracking Study.* http://www.drugfree.org/wp-content/uploads/2013/04/PATS-2012-FULL-REPORT2.pdf

Pascalis, O., & Kelly, D. J. (2009). The origins of face processing in humans: Phylogeny and ontogeny. *Perspectives on Psychological Science, 4,* 200–209.

Pascual, A., Guéguen, N., Pujos, S., & Felonneau, M. (2013). Foot-in-the-door and problematic requests: A field experiment. *Social Influence, 8,* 46–53. doi:10.1080/15534510.2012.696038

Pasquet, P., Obeerti, B., El Ati, J., & Hladik, C. M. (2002). Relationships between threshold-based PROP sensitivity and food preferences of Tunisians. *Appetite, 39,* 167–173.

Passie, T., Halpern, J. H., Stichtenoth, D. O., Emrich, H. M., & Hintzen, A. (2008). The pharmacology of lysergic acid diethylamide: A review. *CNS Neuroscience & Therapeutics, 14,* 295–314.

Patel, R., & Titheradge, D. (2015). MDMA for the treatment of mood disorder: All talk no substance? *Therapeutic Advances in Psychopharmacology, 5(3),* 179–188. doi:10.1177/2045125315583786

Patel, S. R., Aronson, J. P., Sheth, S. A., & Eskandar, E. N. (2013). Lesion procedures in psychiatric neurosurgery. *World Neurosurgery, 80,* S31.e9–e16.

Pathania, R. (2015). Therapeutic potential of psychedelic agents. *British Journal of Psychiatry, 206(5),* 433. doi:10.1192/bjp.206.5.433

Patihis, L., Ho, L. Y., Tingen, I. W., Lilienfeld, S. O., & Loftus, E. F. (2014). Are the "memory wars" over? A scientist-practitioner gap in beliefs about repressed memory. *Psychological Science, 25,* 519–530.

Patrick, M. E., & Maggs, J. L. (2009). Does drinking lead to sex? Daily alcohol-sex behaviors and expectancies among college students. *Psychology of Addictive Behaviors, 23,* 472–481.

Patrick, M. E., & Maggs, J. L. (2014). Energy drinks and alcohol: Links to alcohol behaviors consequences across 56 days. *Journal of Adolescent Health, 54,* 454–459.

Patterson, C. J. (2006). Children of lesbian and gay parents. *Current Directions in Psychological Science, 15,* 241–244.

Paul, G., Elam, B., & Verhulst, S. J. (2007). A longitudinal study of students' perceptions of using deep breathing meditation to reduce testing stresses. *Teaching and Learning in Medicine, 19,* 287–292.

Paul Halpern, H., & Perry-Jenkins, M. (2016). Parents' gender ideology and gendered behaviour as predictors of children's gender-role attitudes: A longitudinal exploration. *Sex Roles, 74,* 527–542.

Paulson, R. M., Lord, C. G., Taylor, C. A., Brady, S. E., McIntyre, R. B., & Fuller, E. W. (2012). A matching hypothesis for the activity level of actions involved in attitude-behavior consistency. *Social Psychological and Personality Science, 3,* 40–47. doi:10.1177/1948550611408347

Paulson, S. E., & Sputa, C. L. (1996). Patterns of parenting during adolescence: Perceptions of adolescents and parents. *Adolescence, 31,* 369–381.

Paulus, P. B. (Ed.). (1989). *Psychology of group influence* (2nd ed.). Erlbaum.

Pause, B. M., Zlomuzica, A., Kinugawa, K., Mariani, J., Pietrowsky, R., & Dere, E. (2013). Perspectives on episodic-like and episodic memory. *Frontiers in Behavioral Neuroscience, 7,* 33. doi:10.3389/fnbeh.2013.00033

Pavlov, I. P. (1960). *Conditioned reflexes* (G. V. Anrep, Trans.). Dover. (Original work published in 1927)

Payne, J. D., & Kensinger, E. A. (2010). Sleep's role in the consolidation of emotional episodic memories. *Current Directions in Psychological Science, 19,* 290–295.

PDR.net (2016). *Disulfiram – Drug summary.* http://www.pdr.net/drug-summary/antabuse?druglabelid=681

Pearlin, L. I. (1993). The social contexts of stress. In L. Goldberger & S. Breznitz (Eds.), *Handbook of stress: Theoretical and clinical aspects* (2nd ed., pp. 303–315). Free Press.

Pearsall, M. J., Christian, M. S., & Ellis, A. P. (2010). Motivating interdependent teams: Individual rewards, shared rewards, or something in between? *Journal of Applied Psychology, 95,* 183–191.

Pearson, J., & Kosslyn, S. M. (2015). The heterogeneity of mental representation: Ending the imagery debate. *Proceedings of the National Academy of Sciences of the United States of America, 112*(33), 10089–10092. https://doi.org/10.1073/pnas.1504933112

Pearson, J., Naselaris, T., Holmes, E. A., & Kosslyn, S. M. (2015). Mental imagery: Functional mechanisms and clinical applications. *Trends in Cognitive Sciences, 19*(10), 590–602. https://doi.org/10.1016/j.tics.2015.08.003

Pebsworth, P., & Radhakrishna, S. (2020). Using conditioned taste aversion to reduce human-nonhuman primate conflict: A comparison of four potentially illness-inducing drugs. *Applied Animal Behaviour Science,* 225, 104948. https://doi.org/10.1016/j.applanim.2020.104948

Pedersen, D. M., & Wheeler, J. (1983). The Müller-Lyer illusion among Navajos. *Journal of Social Psychology, 121,* 3–6.

Pedersen, P. B. (2002). Ethics, competence, and other professional issues in culture-centered counseling. In P. B. Pedersen, J. G. Draguns, W. J. Lonner, & J. E. Trimble (Eds.), *Counseling across cultures* (5th ed., pp. 3–28). SAGE.

Peelen, M. V., Glaser, B., Vuilleumier, P., & Eliez, S. (2009). Differential development of selectivity for faces and bodies in the fusiform gyrus. *Developmental Science, 12,* F16–F25.

Pelleymounter, M. A., Cullen, M. J., Baker, M. B., Hecht, R., Winters, D., Boone, T., . . . Collins, F. (1995). Effects of the obese gene product on body weight regulation in ob/ob mice. *Science, 269,* 540–543.

Penaloza, A. A., & Calvillo, D. P. (2012). Incubation provides relief from artificial fixation in problem solving. *Creativity Research Journal, 24,* 338–344. doi:10.1080/10400419.2012.730329

Peng, F., Wang, L., Geng, Z., Zhu, Q., & Song, Z. (2016). A cross-sectional voxel-based morphometric study of age- and sex-related changes in gray matter volume in the normal aging brain. *Journal of Computer Assisted Tomography, 40(2),* 307–315. doi:10.1097/RCT.0000000000000351

Peng, K., & Nisbett, R. E. (1999). Culture, dialectics, and reasoning about contradiction. *American Psychologist, 54*(9), 741–754. doi:10.1037/0003-066X.54.9.741

Peng, S., Du, J., Jiang, H., Fu, Y., Chen, H., Sun, H., . . . Zhao, M. (2013). The dopamine receptor D1 gene is associated with the length of interval between first heroin use and onset of dependence in Chinese Han heroin addicts. *Journal of Neural Transmission, 120,* 1591–1598. doi:10.1007/s00702-013-1029-6

Penley, J. A., Tomaka, J., & Wiebe, J. S. (2002). The association of coping to physical and psychological health outcomes: A meta-analytic review. *Journal of Behavioral Medicine, 25,* 551–603.

Peppard, P. E., Young, T., Barnet, J. H., Palta, M., Hagen, E. W., & Hia, K. M. (2013). Increased prevalence of sleep-disordered breathing in adults. *American Journal of Epidemiology, 177,* 1006–1014.

Pepperberg, I. M. (1991). A communicative approach to animal cognition: A study of conceptual abilities of an African gray parrot. In C. A. Ristau (Ed.), *Cognitive ethology* (pp. 153–186). Erlbaum.

Pepperberg, I. M. (1993). Cognition and communication in an African gray parrot (*Psittacus erithacus*): Studies on a nonhuman, nonprimate, nonmammilian, subject. In H. L. Roitblat, L. M. Herman, & P. E. Nachtigall (Eds.), *Language and communication: Comparative perspectives* (pp. 221–248). Erlbaum.

Pepperberg, I. M. (1999). Rethinking syntax: A commentary on E. Kako's "Elements of syntax in the systems of three language-trained animals." *Animal Learning and Behavior, 27,* 15–17.

Pepperberg, I. M. (2017). Animal language studies: What happened? *Psychonomic Bulletin & Review 24*(1), 181–185. doi:10.3758/s13423-016-1101-y

Perez, M., Joiner, T. E., Jr., & Lewisohn, P. M. (2004). Is major depressive disorder or dysthymia more strongly associated with bulimia nervosa? *International Journal of Eating Disorders, 36,* 55–61.

Perikleous, E. P., Steiropoulos, P., Paraskakis, E., Constantinidis, T. C., & Nena, E. (2018). E-Cigarette use among adolescents: An overview of the literature and future perspectives. *Frontiers in Public Health, 6,* 86. doi:10.3389/fpubh.2018.00086

Perina, K. (2002). Hot on the trail of flashbulb memory. *Psychology Today, 35,* 15–16.

Perlini, A. H., Bertolissi, S., & Lind, D. L. (1999). The effects of women's age and physical appearance on evaluations of attractiveness and social desirability. *Journal of Social Psychology, 139,* 343–344.

Perlis, R. H., Brown, E., Baker, R. W., & Nierenberg, A. A. (2006). Clinical features of bipolar depression versus major depressive disorder in large multi-center trials. *American Journal of Psychiatry, 163,* 225–231.

Perry, E., Walker, M., Grace, J., & Perry, R. (1999). Acetylcholine in mind: A neurotransmitter correlate of consciousness? *Trends in Neurosciences, 22,* 273–280.

Perry, M., Kinoshita, M., Saldi, G., Huo, L., Arikawa, K., & Desplan, C. (2016). Molecular logic behind the three-way stochastic choices that expand butterfly colour vision. *Nature, 535(7611),* 280-284. doi:10.1038/nature18616

Perry, W. G., Jr. (1981). Cognitive and ethical growth. In A. Chickering (Ed.), *The modern American college* (pp. 76–116). Jossey-Bass.

Person, E. S. (1990). The influence of values in psychoanalysis: The case of female psychology. In C. Zanardi (Ed.), *Essential papers in psychoanalysis* (pp. 305–325). University Press.

Person, E. S. (2005). As the wheel turns: A centennial reflection on Freud's three essays on the theory of sexuality. *Journal of the American Psychoanalytic Association, 53,* 1257–1282.

Pesant, N., & Zadra, A. (2004). Working with dreams in therapy: What do we know and what should we do? *Clinical Psychology Review, 24,* 489–512.

Pesant, N., & Zadra, A. (2006). Dream content and psychological well-being: A longitudinal study of the continuity hypothesis. *Journal of Clinical Psychology, 62,* 111–121.

Petersen, L., Mortensen, P. B., & Pedersen, C. B. (2011). Paternal age at birth of first child and risk of schizophrenia. *American Journal of Psychiatry, 168,* 82–88.

Peterson, B. E., & Duncan, L. E. (2007). Midlife women's generativity and authoritarianism: Marriage, motherhood, and 10 years of aging. *Psychology and Aging, 22,* 411–419.

Peterson, C., Maier, S. F., & Seligman, M. E. P. (1993). *Learned helplessness: A theory for the age of personal control.* Oxford University Press.

Peterson, L. R., & Peterson, M. J. (1959). Short-term retention of individual verbal items. *Journal of Experimental Psychology, 58,* 193–198.

Petit, D., Pennestri, M., Paquet, J., Desautels, A., Zadra, A., Vitaro, F., . . . Montplaisir, J. (2015). Childhood sleepwalking and sleep terrors: A longitudinal study of prevalence and familial aggregation. *JAMA Pediatrics, 169,* 653–658. doi:10.1001/jamapediatrics.2015.127

Petitto, L. (2009). New discoveries from the bilingual brain and mind across the lifespan: Implications for education. *Mind, Brain, and Education, 3,* 185–197.

Petrides, K. V., Furnham, A., & Martin, G. N. (2004). Estimates of emotional and psychometric intelligence: Evidence for gender-based stereotypes. *Journal of Social Psychology, 144,* 149–162.

Petrovich, G. D. (2013). Forebrain networks and the control of feeding by environmental learned cues. *Physiology & Behavior, 121,* 10–18. doi:10.1016/j.physbeh.2013.03.024

Pettigrew, T. F., & Tropp, L. R. (2006). A meta-analytic test of intergroup contact theory. *Journal of Personality and Social Psychology, 90,* 751–783.

Petty, R. E., & Briñol, P. (2008). Persuasion: From single to multiple to metacognitive processes. *Perspectives on Psychological Science, 3,* 137–147.

Petty, R. E., & Cacioppo, J. T. (1986). *Communication and persuasion: Central and peripheral routes to attitude change.* Springer.

Petty, R. E., Cacioppo, J. T., & Goldman, R. (1981). Personal involvement as a determinant of argument-based persuasion. *Journal of Personality and Social Psychology, 41,* 847–855.

Petty, R. E., Fabrigar, L. R., & Wegener, D. T. (2003). Emotional factors in attitudes and persuasion. In R. J. Davidson, K. R. Scherer, & H. H. Goldsmith (Eds.), *Handbook of affective sciences* (pp. 752–772). Oxford University Press.

Pew Research Center. (2014, March). *Millennials in adulthood: Detached from institutions, networked with friends.* Author.

Pew Research Center. (2019). Same sex marriage around the world. https://www.pewforum.org/fact-sheet/gay-marriage-around-the-world/.

Pfaus, J. G. (2009). Pathways of sexual desire. *Journal of Sexual Medicine, 6,* 1506–1533.

Phares, E. J. (1991). *Introduction to personality* (3rd ed.). HarperCollins.

Phelan, S., Nallari, M., Daroch, F. E., & Wing, R. R. (2009). What do physicians recommend to their overweight and obese patients? *Journal of the American Board of Family Medicine, 22,* 115–122.

Phillips, M. R., Li, X., & Zhang, Y. (2002). Suicide rates in China, 1995–99. *Lancet, 359,* 835–840.

Piaget, J. (1929). *The child's conception of the world.* Harcourt Brace.

Piaget, J. (1952). *The origins of intelligence in children.* International Universities Press.

Pickering, G. J., Jain, A. K., & Bezawada, R. (2013). Super-tasting gastronomes? Taste phenotype characterization of foodies and wine experts. *Food Quality and Preference, 28,* 85–91. doi:10.1016/j.foodqual.2012.07.005

Pidoplichko, V. I., DeBiasi, M., Williams, J. T., & Dani, J. A. (1997). Nicotine activates and desensitizes midbrain dopamine neurons. *Nature, 390,* 401–404.

Pierce, J. P. (2005). Influence of movie stars on the initiation of adolescent smoking. *Pediatric Dentistry, 27,* 149.

Piet, J., & Hougaard, E. (2011). The effect of mindfulness-based cognitive therapy for prevention of relapse in recurrent major depressive disorder: A systematic review and meta-analysis. *Clinical Psychology Review, 31*(6), 1032–1040. doi.org/10.1016/j.cpr.2011.05.002

Pietromonaco, P. R., DeBuse, C. J., & Powers, S. I. (2013). Does attachment get under the skin? Adult romantic attachment and cortisol responses to stress. *Current Directions in Psychological Science, 22,* 63–68.

Pietschnig, J. (2016). The Flynn effect: Technology may be part of it, but is most certainly not all of it. *Measurement, 14*(2), 70.

Pietschnig, J., & Voracek, M. (2015). One century of global IQ gains: A formal meta-analysis of the Flynn effect (1909–2013). *Perspectives on Psychological Science, 10*(3), 282–306.. https://doi.org/10.1177/1745691615577701

Pietschnig, J., Voracek, M., & Formann, A. K. (2011). Female Flynn effects: No sex differences in generational IQ gains. *Personality and Individual Differences, 50*(5), 759–762. https://doi.org/10.1016/j.paid.2010.12.019

Pillar, G., & Lavie, P. (2011). Obstructive sleep apnea: Diagnosis, risk factors, and pathophysiology. *Handbook of Clinical Neurology, 98,* 383–399.

Pillemer, D. B., Wink, P., DiDonato, T. E., & Sanborn, R. L. (2003). Gender differences in autobiographical memory styles of older adults. *Memory, 11,* 525–532.

Pinedo, V. A. (2010). *Swinging '60s had nothing on the Noughties—Sex study.* http://www.reuters.com/assets/print?aid=USTRE62F23J20100316

Pinker, S. (1994). *The language instinct: How the mind creates language.* Morrow.

Pinna, B., Porcheddu, D., & Deiana, K. (2016). From grouping to coupling: A new perceptual organization in vision, psychology, and biology. *Frontiers in Psychology, 7,* 1051. doi:10.3389/fpsyg.2016.01051

Pinquart, M. (2017). Associations of parenting dimensions and styles with externalizing problems of children and adolescents: An updated meta-analysis. *Developmental Psychology, 53*(5), 873-932. doi:10.1037/dev0000295.

Pinto da Mota Matos, A., Alves Ferreira, J. G., & Haase, R. F. (2012). Television and aggression: A test of a mediated model with a sample of Portuguese students. *The Journal of Social Psychology, 152,* 75–91. doi:10.1080/00224545.2011.555645

Piper, A., & Merskey, H. (2004). The persistence of folly: A critical examination of dissociative identity disorder: Part I. The excesses of an improbable concept. *Canadian Journal of Psychiatry, 49,* 592–600.

Pirrallo, R. G., Loomis, C. C., Levine, R., & Woodson, B. T. (2012). The prevalence of sleep problems in emergency medical technicians. *Sleep & Breathing, 16,* 149–162.

Plancher, G., & Barrouillet, P. (2020). On some of the main criticisms of the modal model: Reappraisal from a TBRS perspective. *Memory & Cognition, 48*(3), 455–468. https://doi.org/10.3758/s13421-019-00982-w

Plazzi, B., Corsini, R., Provini, R., Pierangeli, G., Martinelli, P., Montagna, P., . . . Cortelli, P. (1997). REM sleep behavior disorders in multiple system atrophy. *Neurology, 48,* 1094–1097.

Pleyer, M., & Hartmann, S. (2019). Constructing a consensus on language evolution? Convergences and differences between biolinguistic and usage-based approaches. *Frontiers in Psychology, 10,* 1.

Plomin, R., DeFries, J. C., McClearn, G. E., & Rutter, M. (2008). *Behavioral genetics* (5th ed.). Freeman.

Plutchik, R. (1984). Emotions: A general psychoevolutionary theory. In K. R. Scherer & P. Ekman (Eds.), *Approaches to emotion* (pp. 197–219). Erlbaum.

Poe, G. R., Walsh, C. M., & Bjorness, T. E. (2010). Cognitive neuroscience of sleep. *Progress in Brain Research, 185,* 1–19.

Poelman, D., & Smet, P. F. (2010). Photometry in the dark: Time dependent visibility of low intensity light sources. *Optics Express, 18,* 26293–26299.

Pogue-Geile, M. F., & Yokley, J. L. (2010). Current research on the genetic contributors to schizophrenia. *Current Directions in Psychological Science, 19,* 214–219.

Polmin, R. (1994). The Emanuel Miller Memorial Lecture 1993: Genetic research and identification of environmental influences. *Journal of Child Psychology and Psychiatry, 35,* 817–834.

Poloskov, E., & Tracey, T. G. (2013). Internalization of U.S. female beauty standards as a mediator of the relationship between Mexican American women's acculturation and body dissatisfaction. *Body Image, 10,* 501–508. doi:10.1016/j.bodyim.2013.05.005

Polotsky, V. Y., & O'Donnell, C. P. (2007). Genomics of sleep-disordered breathing. *Proceedings of the American Thoracic Society, 4,* 121–126.

Pomeroy, A. (2005). 50 best small and medium places to work: Money talks. *HR Magazine, 50,* 44–65.

Pomeroy, W. (1965, May). Why we tolerate lesbians. *Sexology,* 652–654.

Ponniah, K., & Hollon, S. D. (2009). Empirically supported psychological treatments for adult acute stress disorder and posttraumatic stress disorder: A review. *Depression and Anxiety, 26,* 1086–1109.

Ponniah, K., Magiati, I., & Hollon, S. D. (2013). An update on the efficacy of psychological therapies in the treatment of obsessive-compulsive disorder in adults. *Journal of Obsessive-Compulsive and Related Disorders, 2,* 207–218.

Pontifex, M. B., Parks, A. C., O'Neil, P. C., Egner, A. R., Warning, J. T., Pfeiffer, K. A., & Fenn, K. M. (2014). Poorer aerobic fitness relates to reduced integrity of multiple memory systems. *Cognitive, Affective & Behavioral Neuroscience, 14*(3), 1132–1141. doi:10.3758/s13415-014-0265-z

Pool, E., Rehme, A. K., Fink, G. R., Eickhoff, S. B., & Grefkes, C. (2013). Network dynamics engaged in the modulation of motor behavior in healthy subjects. *Neuroimage, 82,* 68–76. doi:10.1016/j.neuroimage.2013.05.123

Pool, R. (2005, Fall/Winter). Motherese. *Research in Review Magazine*, Florida State University.

Poore, A. G., Gagne, F., Barlow, K. M., Lydon, J. E., Taylor, D. M., & Wright, S. C. (2002). Contact and the personal/group discrimination discrepancy in an Inuit community. *Journal of Psychology, 136,* 371–382.

Pope, H. G., & Yurgelun-Todd, D. (1996). The residual cognitive effects of heavy marijuana use in college students. *Journal of the American Medical Association, 275,* 521–527.

Porkka-Heiskanen, T., Strecker, R. E., Thakkar, M., Bjorkum, A. A., Greene, R. W., & McCarley, R. W. (1997). Adenosine: A mediator of the sleep-inducing effects of prolonged wakefulness. *Science, 276,* 1265–1268.

Porter, J. N., Collins, P. F., Muetzel, R. L., Lim, K. O., & Luciana, M. (2011). Associations between cortical thickness and verbal fluency in childhood, adolescence, and young adulthood. *NeuroImage, 55,* 1865–1877.

Porter, R. H. (1999). Olfaction and human kin recognition. *Genetica, 104,* 259–263.

Postlethwaite, A., Kellett, S., & Mataix-Cols, D. (2019). Prevalence of hoarding disorder: A systematic review and meta-analysis. *Journal of Affective Disorders, 256,* 309–316. doi:10.1016/j.jad.2019.06.004

Poulletier de Gannes, F., Haro, E., Hurtier, A., Taxile, M., Athane, A., Aït-Aïssa, S., . . . Lagroye, I. (2012). Effect of in utero Wi-Fi exposure on the pre- and postnatal development of rats. *Birth Defects Research Part B Developmental and Reproductive Toxicology, 95(2),* 130–136. doi:10.1002/bdrb.20346

Powell, L. H., Calvin, J. E., III, & Calvin, J. E., Jr. (2007). Effective obesity treatments. *American Psychologist, 62,* 234–246.

Powell, L. H., Shahabi, L., & Thoresen, C. E. (2003). Religion and spirituality: Linkages to physical health. *American Psychologist, 58,* 36–52.

Powers, T. L., & Jack, E. P. (2013). The influence of cognitive dissonance on retail product returns. *Psychology & Marketing, 30,* 724–735. doi:10.1002/mar.20640

Pratkanis, A. R. (1992). The cargo-cult science of subliminal persuasion. *The Skeptical Inquirer, 16,* 260–272.

Pratkanis, A. R., Epley, N., Savitsky, K., & Kachelski, R. A. (2007). Issue 12: Is subliminal persuasion a myth? In J. A. Nier (Ed.), *Taking sides: Clashing views in social psychology* (2nd ed., pp. 230–255). McGraw-Hill.

Pratt, L. A., & Brody, D. J. (2014). Depression in the U.S. household population, 2009–2012. NCHS data brief, no 172. National Center for Health Statistics.

Preis, M. A., Kröner-Herwig, B., Schmidt-Samoa, C., Dechent, P., & Barke, A. (2015). Neural correlates of empathy with pain show habituation effects. An fMRI study. *PLoS ONE, 10*(8), e0137056. doi:10.1371/journal.pone.0137056

Preschl, B., Maercker, A., & Wagner, B. (2011). The working alliance in a randomized controlled trial comparing online with face-to-face cognitive-behavioral therapy for depression. *BMC Psychiatry, 11,* 189. doi.org/10.1186/1471-244X-11-189

Prescott, C. A., Hewitt, J. K., Truett, K. R., Heath, A. C., Neale, M. C., & Eaves, L. J. (1994). Genetic and environmental influences on alcohol-related problems in a volunteer sample of older twins. *Journal of Studies on Alcohol, 55,* 184–202.

Pressman, S. D., Cohen, S., Miller, G. E., Barkin, A., Rabin, B. S., & Treanor, J. J. (2005). Loneliness, social network size, and immune response to influenza vaccination in college freshman. *Health Psychology, 24,* 297–306.

Preston, J. A. (2005, June). *Delaying a life: The consequences of career development for the Radcliffe class of 1950.* Paper presented at the IWPR's Eighth International Women's Policy Research Conference.

Price, C. A., & Balaswamy, S. (2009). Beyond health and wealth: Predictors of women's retirement satisfaction. *International Journal of Aging and Human Development, 68,* 195–214.

Price, W. F., & Crapo, R. H. (2002). *Cross-cultural perspectives in introductory psychology.* Wadsworth.

Prinzmetal, W., & Beck, D. M. (2001). The tilt-consistency theory of visual illusions. *Journal of Experimental Psychology: Human Perception and Performance, 27,* 206–217. doi:10.1037/0096-1523.27.1.206

Pritchard, M. E., Wilson, G. S., & Yamnitz, B. (2007). What predicts adjustment among college students? A longitudinal panel study. *Journal of American College Health, 56,* 15–21.

Prosser, I. B. (1933). *Non-academic development of Negro children in mixed and segregated schools.* Unpublished doctoral dissertation, University of Cincinnati.

Prosser, J. M., & Nelson, L. S. (2012). The toxicology of bath salts: A review of synthetic cathinones. *Journal of Medical Toxicology, 8,* 33–42.

Protzko, J., Aronson, J., & Blair, C. (2013). How to make a young child smarter: Evidence from the database of raising intelligence. *Perspectives on Psychological Science, 8*(1), 25-40.

Prutkin, J., Duffy, V. B., Etter, L., Fast, K., Gardner, E., Lucchina, L. A., . . . Bartoshuk, L. M. (2000). Genetic variation and inferences about perceived taste intensity in mice and men. *Physiology and Behavior, 69,* 161–173.

Ptacek, J. T., Smith, R. E., & Dodge, K. L. (1994). Gender differences in coping with stress: When stressor and appraisals do not differ. *Personality & Social Psychology Bulletin, 20,* 421–430.

Public Health England. (2014). *Public Health England (PHE) release local authority adult obesity data.* https://www.gov.uk/government/news/phe-release-local-authority-adult-obesity-data

Public Health England. (2019, March). Patterns and trends in adult obesity. https://www.gov.uk/guidance/phe-data-and-analysis-tools#obesity-diet-and-physical-activity.

Puhl, R. M. (2018). Stigma, discrimination, and obesity. In K. D. Brownell & B. T. Walsh (Eds.), *Eating disorders and obesity: A comprehensive handbook*, 3rd ed. (pp. 134–139). Guilford Press. http://libproxy.ung.edu/login?url=http://search.ebscohost.com/login.aspx?direct=true&db=psyh&AN=2017-08404-021&site=ehost-live

Puhl, R. M., Latner, J. D., O'Brien, K. S., Luedicke, J., Danielsdottir, S., & Salas, X. R. (2015). Potential policies and laws to prohibit weight discrimination: Public views from four countries. *The Milbank Quarterly, 93*(4), 691–731. doi:10.1111/1468-0009.12152

Purser, H., & Jarrold, C. (2010). Short- and long-term memory contributions to immediate serial recognition: Evidence from serial position effects. *The Quarterly Journal of Experimental Psychology, 63*(4), 679–693. https://doi.org/10.1080/17470210903067635

Pyke, K., & Johnson, D. (2003). Asian American women and racialized femininities: "Doing" gender across cultural worlds. *Gender and Society, 17,* 33–53.

Pylyshyn, Z. W. (2003). Return of the mental image: Are there really pictures in the brain? *Trends in Cognitive Science, 7,* 113–118.

Pylyshyn, Z. W. (2006). *Seeing and visualizing: It's not what you think.* MIT Press.

Pyun, Y. D. (2013). The effective use of hypnosis in schizophrenia: Structure and strategy. *International Journal of Clinical and Experimental Hypnosis, 61,* 388–400.

Qiu, J., Li, H., Jou, J., Liu, J., Luo, Y., Feng, T., . . . Zhang, Q. (2010). Neural correlates of the "aha" experiences: Evidence from an fMRI study of insight problem solving. *Cortex: A Journal Devoted to the Study of the Nervous System and Behavior, 46,* 397–403.

Quattrone, G. A., & Jones, E. E. (1980). The perception of variability within ingroups and outgroups: Implications for the law of small number. *Journal of Personality and Social Psychology, 38,* 141–152.

Querido, J. G., Warner, T. D., & Eyberg, S. M. (2002). Parenting styles and child behavior in African American families of preschool children. *Journal of Clinical Child and Adolescent Psychology, 31,* 272–277.

Quickfall, J., & Crockford, D. (2006). Brain neuroimaging in cannabis use: A review. *Journal of Neuropsychiatry and Clinical Neurosciences, 18,* 318–332.

Quigley, B. M., & Leonard, K. E. (2000). Alcohol and the continuation of early marital aggression. *Alcoholism: Clinical and Experimental Research, 24,* 1003–1010.

Quillian, L., Lee, J. J., & Honoré, B. (2020). Racial discrimination in the U.S. housing and mortgage lending markets: A quantitative review of trends, 1976-2016. *Race and Social Problems, 12*, 13-28. https://doi.org/10.1007/s12552-019-09276-x

Quinn, P. C., & Tanaka, J. W. (2007). Early development of perceptual expertise: Within-basic-level categorization experience facilitates the formation of subordinate-level category representations in 6- to 7-month-old infants. *Memory & Cognition, 35*, 1422–1431.

Rabkin, S. W., Boyko, E., Shane, F., & Kaufert, J. (1984). A randomized trial comparing smoking cessation programs utilizing behavior modification, health education, or hypnosis. *Addictive Behaviors, 9*, 157–173.

Raby, K. L., Cicchetti, D., Carlson, E. A., Cutuli, J. J., Englund, M. M., & Egeland, B. (2012). Genetic and caregiving-based contributions to infant attachment: Unique associations with distress reactivity and attachment security. *Psychological Science, 23*, 1016–1023.

Rahman, M. M., Callaghan, C. K., Kerskens, C. M., Sumantra, C., & O'Mara, S. M. (2016). Early hippocampal volume loss as a marker of eventual memory deficits caused by repeated stress. *Scientific Reports, 6*, 29127. doi:10.1038/srep29127

Rahman, Q. (2005). The neurodevelopment of human sexual orientation. *Neuroscience and Biobehavioral Reviews, 29*, 1057–1066.

Raine, A. (1997). Antisocial behavior and psychophysiology: A biological perspective. In D. M. Stoff, J. Breiling, & J. D. Maser (Eds.), *Handbook of antisocial personality disorder* (pp. 289–304). Wiley.

Raine, A. (2008). From genes to brain to antisocial behavior. *Current Directions in Psychological Science, 17*, 323–328.

Raine, A., Lencz, T., Bihrle, S., LaCasse, L., & Colletti, P. (2000). Reduced prefrontal gray matter volume and reduced autonomic activity in antisocial personality disorder. *Archives of General Psychiatry, 57*, 119–127.

Raine, A., Yang, Y., Narr, K. L., & Toga, A. W. (2011). Sex differences in orbitofrontal gray as a partial explanation for sex differences in antisocial personality. *Molecular Psychiatry, 16*, 227–236.

Rainville, P., Duncan, G. H., Price, D. D., Carrier, B., & Bushnell, M. C. (1997). Pain affect encoded in human anterior cingulate but not somatosensory cortex. *Science, 277*, 968–971.

Rajecki, D. W. (2012). Psychology baccalaureates at work: Major area subspecializations, earnings, and occupations. *Teaching of Psychology, 39*, 185–189.

Rajecki, D. W., & Borden, V. M. (2011). Psychology degrees: Employment, wage, and career trajectory consequences. *Perspectives on Psychological Science, 6*, 321–335.

Ram, S., Howland, M. A., Sandman, C. A., Davis, E. P., Glynn, L. M. (2019). Prenatal risk for autism spectrum disorder (ASD): Fetal cortisol exposure predicts child ASD symptoms. *Clinical Psychological Science, 7*(2), 349-361.

Ram, S., Seirawan, H., Kumar, S. K., & Clark, G. T. (2010). Prevalence and impact of sleep disorders and sleep habits in the United States. *Sleep & Breathing, 14*, 63–70.

Ramsey-Rennels, J. L., & Langlois, J. H. (2006). Infants' differential processing of female and male faces. *Current Directions in Psychological Science, 15*, 59–62.

Randall, J. G., Zimmer, C. U., O'Brien, K. R., Trump-Steele, R. C. E., Villado, A. J., & Hebl, M. R. (2017). *Weight discrimination in helping behavior. European Review of Applied Psychology / Revue Européenne de Psychologie Appliquée, 67*(3), 125–137. https://doi.org/10.1016/j.erap.2017.02.002

Randall, S., Johanson, C. E., Tancer, M., & Roehrs, T. (2009). Effects of acute 3, 4 methylenedioxymethamphetamine on sleep and daytime sleepiness in MDMA users: A preliminary study. *Sleep, 32*, 1513–1519.

Rando, T. A. (1995). Grief and mourning: Accommodating to loss. In H. Wass & R. A. Neimeyer (Eds.), *Dying: Facing the facts* (3rd ed., pp. 211–241). Taylor & Francis.

Ranganathan, M., & D'Souza, D. C. (2006). The acute effects of cannabinoids on memory in humans: A review. *Psychopharmacology (Berlin), 188*, 425–444.

Rao, V. T., Khan, D., Jones, R. G., Nakamura D. S., Kennedy, T. E., Cui, Q., . . . Antel, J. P. (2016). Potential benefit of the charge-stabilized nanostructure saline RNS60 for myelin maintenance and repair. *Scientific Reports, 6*, 125-141. doi:10.1038/srep30020

Rapoport, J. L., Addington, A. M., Frangou, S., & Psych, M. R. (2005). The neurodevelopmental model of schizophrenia: Update 2005. *Molecular Psychiatry, 10*, 434–449.

Raposa, E. B., Laws, H. B., & Ansell, E. B. (2016). Prosocial behavior mitigates the negative effects of stress in everyday life. *Clinical Psychological Science, 4*, 691–698.

Rappaport, V. J. (2008). Prenatal diagnosis and genetic screening: Integration into prenatal care. *Obstetrics and Gynecology Clinics of North America, 35*, 435–458.

Rastelli, F., Tallon-Baudry, C., Migliaccio, R., Toba, M. N., Ducorps, A., Pradat-Diehl, P., . . . Bartolomeo, P. (2013). Neural dynamics of neglected targets in patients with right hemisphere damage. *Cortex: A Journal Devoted to the Study of the Nervous System and Behavior, 49*, 1989–1996. doi:10.1016/j.cortex.2013.04.001

Rathbone, C. J., Moulin, C. A., Conway, M. A., & Holmes, E. A. (2012). Autobiographical memory and the self. In N. Braisby & A. Gellatly (Eds.), *Cognitive psychology* (2nd ed., pp. 546–576). Oxford University Press.

Rauchs, G., Bertran, F., Guillery-Girard, B., Desgranges, B., Kerrouche, N., Denise, P., . . . Eustache, F. (2004). Consolidation of strictly episodic memories mainly requires rapid eye movement sleep. *Sleep, 27*, 395–401.

Raven, J., & Raven, J. (2003). Raven Progressive Matrices. In R. S. McCallum (Ed.), *Handbook of nonverbal assessment* (pp. 223–237). Kluwer Academic/Plenum Publishers. https://doi.org/10.1007/978-1-4615-0153-4_11

Ray, R. D., Wilhelm, F. H., & Gross, J. J. (2008). All in the mind's eye? Anger rumination and reappraisal. *Journal of Personality and Social Psychology, 94*, 133–145.

Raz, A. (2005). Attention and hypnosis: Neural substrates and genetic associations of two converging processes. *International Journal of Clinical and Experimental Hypnosis, 53*, 237–258.

Raz, A., Fan, J., & Posner, M. I. (2006). Neuroimaging and genetic associations of attentional and hypnotic processes. *Journal of Physiology (Paris), 99*, 483–491.

Raz, N., Rodrigue, K. M., Kennedy, K. M., & Acker, J. D. (2007). Vascular health and longitudinal changes in brain and cognition in middle-aged and older adults. *Neuropsychology, 21*, 149–157.

Read, C. N., & Greenberg, B. D. (2009). Psychiatric neurosurgery 2009: Review and perspective. *Seminars in Neurology, 29*, 256–265.

Read, S., & Grundy, E. (2011). Mental health among older married couples: The role of gender and family life. *Social Psychiatry and Psychiatric Epidemiology, 46*, 331–341.

Reardon, S. F. (2016). *School district socioeconomic status, race, and academic achievement*. Stanford, CA: Center for Education Policy Analysis.

Reber, P. J. (2013). The neural basis of implicit learning and memory: A review of neuropsychological and neuroimaging research. *Neuropsychologia, 51*, 2026–2042. doi:10.1016/j.neuropsychologia.2013.06.019

Reckziegel, D., Raschke, F., Cottam, W. J., & Auer, D. P. (2016). Cingulate GABA levels inversely correlate with the intensity of ongoing chronic knee osteoarthritis pain. *Molecular Pain, 12*, 1–9. doi:10.1177/1744806916650690

Recio, G., Schacht, A., & Sommer, W. (2013). Classification of dynamic facial expressions of emotion presented briefly. *Cognition and Emotion, 27*, 1486–1494. doi:10.1080/02699931.2013.794128

Reder, L. M., Park., H., & Kieffaber, P. D. (2009). Memory systems do not divide on consciousness: Reinterpreting memory in terms of activation and binding. *Psychological Bulletin, 135*, 23–49.

Reece, M., Herbenick, D., Schick, V., Sanders, S., Dodge, B., & Fortenberry, J. D. (2010). Condom use rates in a national probability sample of males and females ages 14 to 94 in the United States. *Journal of Sexual Medicine, 7* (Suppl. 5), 266–276.

Regier, D. A., Narrow, W. E., Clarke, D. E., Kraemer, H. C., Kuramoto, S. J., Kuhl, E. A., & Kupfer, D. J. (2013). *DSM-5* field trials in the United States and Canada, Part II: Test-retest reliability of selected categorical diagnoses. *The American Journal of Psychiatry, 170*(1), 59–70.

Rehder, B., & Hoffman, A. B. (2005). Thirty-something categorization results explained: Selective attention, eyetracking, and models of category learning. *Journal of Experimental Psychology: Learning, Memory, and Cognition, 31*, 811–829.

Reichelt, A. C. (2016). Adolescent maturational transitions in the prefrontal cortex and dopamine signaling as a risk factor for the development of obesity and high fat/high sugar diet induced cognitive deficits. *Frontiers in Behavioral Neuroscience, 10*, 89. doi:10.3389%2Ffnbeh.2016.00189

Reichenberger, J., Kuppens, P., Liedlgruber, M., Wilhelm, F. H., Tiefengrabner, M., Ginzinger, S., & Blechert, J. (2018). No haste, more taste: An EMA study of the effects of stress, negative and positive emotions on eating behavior. *Biological Psychology, 131*, 54–62. doi:10.1016/j.biopsycho.2016.09.002

Reid, K. J., Baron, K. G., Lu, B., Naylor, E., Wolfe, L., & Zee, P. C. (2010). Aerobic exercise improves self-reported sleep and quality of life in older adults with insomnia. *Sleep Medicine, 11*, 934–940.

Reid, P., & Bing, V. (2000). Sexual roles of girls and women: An ethnocultural lifespan perspective. In C. Travis & J. White (Eds.), *Sexuality, society, and feminism* (pp. 141–166). American Psychological Association.

Reilly, A., Jones, D., Rey Vasquez, C., & Krisjanous, J. (2016). Confronting gender inequality in a business school. *Higher Education Research & Development, 35*(5), 1025-1038. doi:10.1080/07294360.2016.1138453

Reinisch, J. M. (1991). *The Kinsey Institute new report on sex: What you must know to be sexually literate.* St. Martin's Press.

Reisenzein, R. (1983). The Schachter theory of emotion: Two decades later. *Psychological Bulletin, 94,* 239–264.

Reite, M., Sheeder, J., Teale, P., Richardson, D., Adams, M., & Simon, J. (1995). MEG based brain laterality: Sex differences in normal adults. *Neuropsychologia, 33,* 1607–1616.

Remington, G., Foussias, G., Fervaha, G., Agid, O., Takeuchi, H., Lee, J., & Hahn, M. (2016). Treating negative symptoms in schizophrenia: An update. *Current Treatment Options in Psychiatry, 3,* 133–150. doi.org/10.1007/s40501-016-0075-8

Rempel, D. M., Keir, P. J., & Bach, J. M. (2008). Effect of wrist posture on carpal tunnel pressure while typing. *Journal of Orthopaedic Research, 26,* 1269–1273.

Ren, J., Li, H., Palaniyappan, L., Liu, H., Wang, J., Li, C., & Rossini, P. M. (2014). Repetitive transcranial magnetic stimulation versus electroconvulsive therapy for major depression: A systematic review and meta-analysis. *Progress in Neuro-psychopharmacology & Biological Psychiatry, 51,* 181–189.

Renoult, L., Davidson, P. R., Palombo, D. J., Moscovitch, M., & Levine, B. (2012). Personal semantics: At the crossroads of semantic and episodic memory. *Trends in Cognitive Sciences, 16,* 550–558. doi:10.1016/j.tics.2012.09.003

Renoult, L., Irish, M., Moscovitch, M., & Rugg, M. D. (2019). From knowing to remembering: The semantic-episodic distinction. *Trends in Cognitive Sciences, 23*(12), 1041-1057. https://doi.org/10.1016/j.tics.2019.09.008

Renoult, L., Tanguay, A., Beaudry, M., Tavakoli, P., Rabipour, S., Campbell, K., . . . Davidson, P. S. R. (2016). Personal semantics: Is it distinct from episodic and semantic memory? An electrophysiological study of memory for autobiographical facts and repeated events in honor of Shlomo Bentin. *Neuropsychologia, 83,* 242–256. doi:10.1016/j.neuropsychologia.2015.08.013

Rensink, R. A. (2014). Limits to the usability of iconic memory. *Frontiers in Psychology, 5, 971.* doi:10.3389/fpsyg.2014.00971

Repetti, R., Wang, S., & Saxbe, D. (2009). Bringing it all back home: How outside stressors shape families' everyday lives. *Current Directions in Psychological Science, 18,* 106–111.

Repovs, G., & Baddeley, A. (2006). The multi-component model of working memory: Explorations in experimental cognitive psychology. *Neuroscience, 139,* 5–21.

Rescorla, R. A. (1967). Pavlovian conditioning and its proper control procedures. *Psychological Review, 74,* 71–80.

Restuccia, D, Vollono, C., Virdis, D., Piero, I. D., Martucci, L., & Zanini, S. (2014). Patterns of habituation and clinical fluctuations in migraine. *Cephalalgia, 34,* 201–210. doi:10.1177/0333102413508241

Revenson, T. A., Griva, K., Luszczynska, A., Morrison, V., Panagopoulou, E., Vilchinsky, N., & Hagedoorn, M. (2016). Gender and caregiving: The costs of caregiving for women. In *Caregiving in the illness context* (pp. 48–63). Palgrave Macmillan. doi:10.1057/9781137558985.0008

Rex-Lear, M., Jensen-Campbell, L. A., & Lee, S. (2019). Young and biased: Children's perceptions of overweight peers. *Journal of Applied Biobehavioral Research, 24*(3), e12161. https://doi.org/10.1111/jabr.12161

Reyna, V. F., & Farley, F. (2006). Risk and rationality in adolescent decision making. *Psychological Science in the Public Interest, 7,* 1–44.

Reyngoudt, H., Paemeleire, K., Dierickx, A., Descamps, B., Vandemaele, P., De Deene, Y., & Achten, E. (2011). Does visual cortex lactate increase following photic stimulation in migraine without aura patients? A functional (1)H-MRS study. *Journal of Headache Pain, 12,* 295–302. doi:10.1007/s10194-011-0295-7

Reynolds, C. R., & Brown, R. T. (Eds.). (1984). *Perspectives on bias in mental testing.* Plenum Press.

Reynolds, J. R., & Burge, S. W. (2008). Educational expectations and the rise in women's post-secondary attainments. *Social Science Research, 37,* 485–499.

Reynolds, P., Hurley, S., Torres, M., Jackson, J., Boyd, P., & Chen, V.W. (2000). Use of coping strategies and breast cancer survival: Results from the Black/White Cancer Survival Study. *American Journal of Epidemiology, 152,* 940–949.

Reynolds, R. M. (2013). Glucocorticoid excess and the developmental origins of disease: Two decades of testing the hypothesis. *Psychoneuroendocrinology, 38,* 1–11.

Rhodes, N., & Wood, W. (1992). Self-esteem and intelligence affect influenceability: The mediating role of message reception. *Psychological Bulletin, 111,* 156–171.

Ribeiro, N., Gounden, Y., & Quaglino, V. (2020). A full night's sleep at home improves memory performance in an associative and relational learning task. *Dreaming, 30*(2), 171–188. https://doi.org/10.1037/drm0000130

Ricca, V., Castellini, G., Mannucci, E., Lo Sauro, C., Ravaldi, C., Rotella, C. M., & Faravelli, C. (2010). Comparison of individual and group cognitive behavioral therapy for binge eating disorder: A randomized, three-year follow-up study. *Appetite, 55,* 656–665.

Rice, K. G., Ray, M. E., Davis, D. E., DeBlaere, C., & Ashby, J. S. (2015). Perfectionism and longitudinal patterns of stress for STEM majors: Implications for academic performance. *Journal of Counseling Psychology, 62,* 718–731.

Rice, V. H. (Ed.). (2000). *Handbook of stress, coping and health.* SAGE.

Richardson, G. A., Goldschmidt, L., Leech, S., & Willford, J. (2011). Prenatal cocaine exposure: Effects on mother- and teacher-rated behavior problems and growth in school-age children. *Neurotoxicology and Teratology, 33,* 69–77.

Rieger, G., Gygax, L., & Bailey, J. M. (2008). Sexual orientation and childhood gender non-conformity: Evidence from home videos. *Developmental Psychology, 44,* 46–58.

Riemann, D., & Perlis, M. L. (2009). The treatments of chronic insomnia: A review of benzodiazepine receptor agonists and psychological and behavioral therapies. *Sleep Medicine Reviews, 13,* 205–214.

Rigaud, D., Jiang, T., Pennacchio, H., Bremont, M., & Perrin, D. (2014). Triggers of bulimia and compulsion attacks: Validation of the "Start" questionnaire. *L'Encephale, 40*(4), 323–329. doi:10.1016/j.encep.2013.06.008

Rihm, J. S., Menz, M. M., Schultz, H., Bruder, L., Schilbach, L., Schmid, S. M., & Peters, J. (2019). Sleep deprivation selectively upregulates an amygdala–hypothalamic circuit involved in food reward. *The Journal of Neuroscience, 39*(5), 888–899. https://doi.org/10.1523/JNEUROSCI.0250-18.2018

Rijsman, R. M., Schoolderman, L. F., Rundervoort, R. S., & Louter, M. (2014). Restless legs syndrome in Parkinson's disease. *Parkinsonism & Related Disorders, 20,* S5–S9.

Riketta, M. (2008). The causal relation between job attitudes and performance: A meta-analysis of panel studies. *Journal of Applied Psychology, 93,* 472–481.

Rinaudo, P., & Wang, E. (2012). Fetal programming and metabolic syndrome. *Annual Review of Physiology, 74,* 107–130.

Rindermann, H., & Baumesiter, A. E. E. (2015). Parents' SES vs. parental educational behavior and children's development: A reanalysis of the Hart and Risley study. *Learning and Individual Differences, 37,* 133-138.

Rinsky, J. R., & Henshaw, S. P. (2011). Linkages between childhood executive functioning and adolescent social functioning and psychopathology in girls with ADHD. *Child Neuropsychology, 4,* 1–23.

Riontino, L., & Cavallero, C. (2020). Individual differences in working memory efficiency modulate proactive interference after sleep deprivation. *Psychological Research.* https://doi.org/10.1007/s00426-020-01292-6

Rios Romenets, S., & Postuma, R. B. (2013). Treatment of restless legs syndrome. *Current Treatment Options in Neurology, 15,* 396–409.

Rishi, M. A., Shetty, M., Wolff, A., Amoateng-Adjepong, Y., & Manthous, C. A. (2010). Atypical antipsychotic medications are independently associated with severe obstructive sleep apnea. *Clinical Neuropharmacology, 33,* 109–113.

Riskind, J. H., Williams, N. L., Gessner, T. L., Chrosniak, L. D., & Cortina, J. M. (2000). The looming maladaptive style: Anxiety, danger, and schematic processing. *Journal of Personality and Social Psychology, 79,* 837–852.

Ritchie, S. J., Wiseman, R., & French, C. C. (2012). Failing the future: Three unsuccessful attempts to replicate Bem's 'retroactive facilitation of recall' effect. *PLoS One, 7(3),* e33423. doi:10.1371/journal.pone.0033423

Rivers, P. C. (1994). *Alcohol and human behavior.* Wiley.

Roberts, B. W., & Mroczek, D. (2008). Personality trait change in adulthood. *Current Directions in Psychological Science, 17,* 31–35.

Roberts, B. W., Caspi, A., & Moffitt, T. E. (2001). The kids are alright: Growth and stability in personality development from adolescence to adulthood. *Journal of Personality and Social Psychology, 81,* 670–683.

Roberts, B. W., Kuncel, N. R., Shiner, R., Caspi, A., & Goldberg, L. R. (2007). The power of personality: The comparative validity of personality traits, socioeconomic status, and cognitive ability for predicting important life outcomes. *Perspectives on Psychological Science, 2,* 313–345.

Roberts, B. W., Walton, K. E., & Viechtbauer, W. (2006). Patterns of mean-level change in personality traits across the life course: A meta-analysis of longitudinal studies. *Psychological Bulletin, 132,* 1–25.

Roberts, D. (2015). Can research on the genetics of intelligence be "socially neutral"? *The Hastings Center Report, 45*(5 Suppl), S50–S53. https://doi.org/10.1002/hast.499

Roberts, R. D., Schulze, R., O'Brien, K., MacCann, C., Reid, J., & Maul, A. (2006). Exploring the validity of the Mayer-Salovey-Caruso emotional intelligence test (MSCEIT) with established emotions measures. *Emotion, 6,* 663–669.

Roberts, R. E., Roberts, C. R., & Chan, W. (2006). Ethnic differences in symptoms of insomnia among adolescents. *Sleep, 29,* 359–365.

Robins, R. W., Fraley, R. C., Roberts, B. W., & Trzesniewski, K. H. (2001). A longitudinal study of personality change in young adulthood. *Journal of Personality, 69,* 617–640.

Robinson, N. M., Abbott, R. D., Berninger, V. W., & Busse, J. (1996). The structure of abilities in math-precocious young children: Gender similarities and differences. *Journal of Educational Psychology, 88,* 341–352.

Robinson-Cimpian, J. P., Lubienski, S. T., Ganley, C. M., & Copur-Gencturk, Y. (2014). Teachers' perceptions of students' mathematics proficiency may exacerbate early gender gaps in achievement. *Developmental Psychology, 50*(4), 1262-81. doi:10.1037/a0035073

Robles, T. F., & Kiecolt-Glaser, J. K. (2003). The physiology of marriage: Pathways to health. *Physiology and Behavior, 79,* 409–416.

Rockafellow, B. D., & Saules, K. K. (2006). Substance use by college students: The role of intrinsic versus extrinsic motivation for athletic involvement. *Psychology of Addictive Behavior, 20,* 279–287.

Rodewald, F., Wilhelm-Gosling, C., Emrich, H. M., Reddemann, L., & Gast, U. (2011). Axis-I comorbidity in female patients with dissociative identity disorder not otherwise specified. *Journal of Nervous and Mental Disease, 199,* 122–131.

Rogers, C. R. (1942). *Counseling and psychotherapy.* Houghton Mifflin.

Rogers, C. R. (1951). *Client-centered therapy: Its current practice, implications, and theory.* Houghton Mifflin

Rogers, C. R. (1961). *On becoming a person.* Houghton Mifflin.

Rogers, C. R. (1970). *Carl Rogers on encounter groups.* Harper & Row.

Rogers, C. R. (1980). *A way of being.* Houghton Mifflin.

Rogers, C. R. (1986). Client-centered therapy. In I. L. Kutash & A. Wolf (Eds.), *Psychotherapists' casebook* (pp. 197–208). Jossey-Bass.

Rogers, M. A., Lemmen, K., Kramer, R., Mann, J., & Chopra, V. (2017). Internet-delivered health interventions that work: Systematic review of meta-analyses and evaluation of website availability. *Journal of Medical Internet Research, 19*(3), e90. doi.org/10.2196/jmir.7111

Rogers, N. L., Szuba, M. P., Staab, J. P., Evans, D. L., & Dinges, D. F. (2001). Neuroimmunologic aspects of sleep and sleep loss. *Seminars in Clinical Neuropsychiatry, 6,* 295–307.

Rogoff, B., & Chavajay, P. (1995). What's become of research on the cultural basis of cognitive development? *American Psychologist, 50,* 859–873.

Rogol, A. D., Roemmich, J. N., & Clark, P. A. (2002). Growth at puberty. *Journal of Adolescent Health, 31,* 192–200.

Rohan, M. J., & Zanna, M. P. (1996). Value transmission in families. In C. Seligman & J. M. Olson (Eds.), *The psychology of values: The Ontario symposium* (Vol. 8, pp. 253–276). Erlbaum.

Rohde, P., Lewinsohn, P. M., Klein, D. N., Seeley, J. R., & Gau, J. M. (2013). Key characteristics of major depressive disorder occurring in childhood, adolescence, emerging adulthood, and adulthood. *Clinical Psychological Science, 1,* 41–53.

Rohrbach, L. A., Grana, R., Vernberg, E., Sussman, S., & Sun, P. (2009). Impact of Hurricane Rita on adolescent substance abuse. *Psychiatry, 72,* 222–237.

Rohrer, J. M., Richter, D., Brummer, M., Wagner, G. G., & Schmukle, S. C. (2018). Successfully striving for happiness: Socially engaged pursuits predict increases in life satisfaction. *Psychological Science, 29*(8), 1291-1298.

Roisman, G. I., Clausell, E., Holland, A., Fortuna, K., & Elieff, C. (2008). Adult romantic relationships as contexts of human development: A multimethod comparison of same-sex couples with opposite-sex dating, engaged, and married dyads. *Developmental Psychology, 44,* 91–101.

Rolls, E. T. (2000). The representation of umami tastes in the taste cortex. *Journal of Nutrition, 130,* 960–965.

Romanelli, R. J., Wu, F. M., Gamba, R., Mojtabai, R., & Segal, J. B. (2014). Behavioral therapy and serotonin reuptake inhibitor pharmacotherapy in the treatment of obsessive-compulsive disorder: A systematic review and meta-analysis of head-to-head randomized controlled trials. *Depression and Anxiety, 31*(8), 641-652.

Romano, E., Bell, T., & Norian, R. (2013). Corporal punishment: Examining attitudes toward the law and factors influencing attitude change. *Journal of Family Violence, 28,* 265–275. doi:10.1007/s10896-013-9494-0

Rook, K. S. (2015). Social networks in later life: Weighing positive and negative effects on health and well-being. *Current Directions in Psychological Science, 24,* 45–51.

Rooney, N. J., Bradshaw, J. W. S., & Robinson, I. H. (2001). Do dogs respond to play signals given by humans? *Animal Behavior, 61,* 715–722.

Ropero Peláez, F. J., & Taniguchi, S. (2016). The gate theory of pain revisited: Modeling different pain conditions with a parsimonious neurocomputational model. *Neural Plasticity, 2016,* 4131395. doi:10.1155/2016/4131395

Roquet, D., Foucher, J. R. Froehlig, P., Renard, F., Pottecher, J., Besancenot, H., . . . Kremer, S. (2016). Resting-state networks distinguish locked-in from vegetative state patients. *NeuroImage: Clinical, 12,* 16–22.

Rosch, E. (1973). Natural categories. *Cognitive Psychology, 4,* 328–350.

Rosch, E., Mervis, C. B., Gray, W. D., Johnson, D. M., & Boyes-Braem, P. (2004). Basic objects in natural categories. In D. A. Balota & E. J. Marsh (Eds.), *Cognitive psychology: Key readings* (pp. 448–471). Psychology Press.

Rose, A. J., & Smith, R. L. (2009). Sex differences in peer relationships. In K. H. Rubin, W. M. Bukowski, & B. Laursen (Eds.), *Handbook of peer interactions, relationships, and groups* (pp. 379–393). Guilford Press.

Rose, A. J., Carlson, W., & Waller, E. M. (2007). Prospective associations of co-rumination with friendship and emotional adjustment: Considering the socioemotional trade-offs of co-rumination. *Developmental Psychology, 43,* 1019–1031.

Rose, D. H., Slater, A., & Perry, H. (1986). Prediction of childhood intelligence from habituation in early infancy. *Intelligence, 10*(3), 251–263. doi:10.1016/0160-2896(86)90019-X

Rose, J. E., Behm, F. M., Salley, A. N., Bates, J. E., Coleman, R. E., Hawk, T. C., & Turkington, T. G. (2007). Regional brain activity correlates of nicotine dependence. *Neuropsychopharmacology, 32,* 2441–2452.

Rosén, M. (2017). Gender differences in broad and narrow ability dimensions: A confirmatory factor analytic approach. In M. Rosén, K. Yang Hansen, & U. Wolff (Eds.), *Cognitive abilities and educational outcomes: A festschrift in honour of Jan-Eric Gustafsson.* (pp. 61–88). Springer International Publishing. doi:10.1007/978-3-319-43473-5_4

Rosenblatt, P. C. (2008). Grief across cultures: A review and research agenda. In M. S. Stroebe, R. O. Hansson, H. Schut, & W. Stroebe (Eds.), *Handbook of bereavement research and practice: Advances in theory and intervention* (pp. 207–222). American Psychological Association.

Rosenhan, D. L. (1969). Some origins of the concerns for others. In P. Mussen & M. Covington (Eds.), *Trends and issues in developmental psychology* (pp. 134–153). Holt, Rinehart & Winston.

Rosenhan, D. L. (1973). On being sane in insane places. *Science, 179,* 250–258.

Rosenkranz, M. A., Davidson, R. J., Maccoon, D. G., Sheridan, J. F., Kalin, N. H., & Lutz, A. (2013). A comparison of mindfulness-based stress reduction and an active control in modulation of neurogenic inflammation. *Brain, Behavior, and Immunity, 27,* 174–184.

Roshanaei-Moghaddam, B., Pauly, M. C., Atkins, D. C., Baldwin, S. A., Stein, M. B., & Roy- Byrne, P. (2011). Relative effects of CBT and pharmacotherapy in depression versus anxiety: Is medication somewhat better for depression, and CBT somewhat better for anxiety? *Depression and Anxiety, 28,* 560–567.

Ross, C. A., Ferrell, L., & Schroeder, E. (2014). Co-occurrence of dissociative identity disorder and borderline personality disorder. *Journal of Trauma & Dissociation, 15,* 79–90.

Ross, C. A., & Ness, L. (2010). Symptom patterns in dissociative identity disorder patients and the general population. *Journal of Trauma and Dissociation, 11,* 458–468.

Ross, M. W. (1980). Retrospective distortion in homosexual research. *Archives of Sexual Behavior, 9,* 523–531.

Ross, W., & Vallée-Tourangeau, F. (2020). Catch that word: Interactivity, serendipity, and verbal fluency in a word production task. *Psychological Research,* https://doi.org/10.1007/s00426-019-01279-y.

Rotenberg, K. J., Costa, P., Trueman, M., & Lattimore, P. (2012). An interactional test of the reformulated helplessness theory of depression in women receiving clinical treatment for eating disorders. *Eating Behaviors, 13,* 264–266

Roth, J., & Steffens, M. C. (2014). When I becomes we: Associative self-anchoring drives implicit intergroup bias in minimal groups. *Social Psychology, 45*(4), 253–264. doi:10.1027/1864-9335/a000169

Roth, S., & Cohen, J. L. (1986). Approach, avoidance, and coping with stress. *American Psychologist, 41,* 813–819.

Roth, T. (2005). Prevalence, associated risks, and treatment patterns of insomnia. *Journal of Clinical Psychiatry, 66,* 10–13.

Roth, T., Krystal, A. D., & Lieberman, J. A., III. (2007). Long-term issues in the treatment of sleep disorders. *CNS Spectrum, 12,* 1–13.

Roth, T., Schwartz, J. R., Hirshkowitz, M., Erman, M. K., Dayno, J. M., & Arora, S. (2007). Evaluation of the safety of modafinil for treatment of excessive sleepiness. *Journal of Clinical Sleep Medicine, 3,* 595–602.

Rothbart, M. K., Ahadi, S. A., & Evans, D. E. (2000). Temperament and personality: Origins and outcomes. *Journal of Personality and Social Psychology, 78,* 122–135.

Rothbaum, B. O., Rizzo, A. S., & Difede, J. (2010). Virtual reality exposure therapy for combat-related posttraumatic stress disorder. *Annals of the New York Academy of Sciences, 1208,* 126–132.

Rothbaum, F., Rosen, K. S., Pott, M., & Beatty, M. (1995). Early parent-child relationships and later problem behaviour: A longitudinal study. *Merrill-Palmer Quarterly, 41,* 133–151.

Rothstein, H. R., & Bushman, B. J. (2015). Methodological and reporting errors in meta-analytic reviews make other meta-analysts angry: A commentary on Ferguson (2015). *Perspectives on Psychological Science, 10*(5), 677–679. doi:10.1177/1745691615592235

Rotter, J. (1982). *The development and application of social learning theory.* Praeger.

Rowe, T. (2006). Fertility and a woman's age. *Journal of Reproductive Medicine, 51,* 157–163.

Rowland, T. A., & Marwaha, S. (2018). Epidemiology and risk factors for bipolar disorder. *Therapeutic Advances in Psychopharmacology, 8*(9), 251–269. doi.org/10.1177/2045125318769235

Rowlett, J. K., Cook, J. M., Duke, A. N., & Platt, D. M. (2005). Selective antagonism of GABAA receptor subtypes: An in vivo approach to exploring the therapeutic and side effects of benzodiazepine-type drugs. *CNS Spectrums, 10,* 40–48.

Roy-Byrne, P. (2014). Treatment in nonresponsive patients with social anxiety: Back to the future with benzodiazepines. *American Journal of Psychiatry, 171,* 1–4.

Ruark, J. (2009, August 3). An intellectual movement for the masses: 10 years after its founding, positive psychology struggles with its own success. *Chronicle of Higher Education.*

Rubin, K. H., Lynch, D., Coplan, R., Rose-Krasnor, L., & Booth, C. L. (1994). "Birds of a feather . . .": Behavioral concordances and preferential personal attraction in children. *Child Development, 65,* 1778–1785.

Rubin, M., & Badea, C. (2012). They're all the same!. . . But for several different reasons: A review of the multicausal nature of perceived group variability. *Current Directions in Psychological Science, 21,* 367–372. doi:10.1177/0963721412457363

Ruble, D. N., Taylor, L. J., Cyphers, L., Greulich, F. K., Lurye, L. E., & Shrout, P. E. (2007). The role of gender constancy in early gender development. *Child Development, 78*(4), 1121-1136.

Ruderman, A. J. (1985). Dysphoric mood and overeating: A test of restraint theory's disinhibition hypothesis. *Journal of Abnormal Psychology, 94,* 78–85.

Rudgley, R. (1998). *The encyclopedia of psychoactive substances.* Little, Brown.

Rudner, M., Karlsson, T., Gunnarsson, J., & Rönnberg, J. (2013). Levels of processing and language modality specificity in working memory. *Neuropsychologia, 51,* 656–666. doi:10.1016/j.neuropsychologia.2012.12.011

Ruffman, T., Slade, L., & Redman, J. (2005). Young infants' expectations about hidden objects. *Cognition, 97,* B35–B43.

Ruiz, F. S., Andersen, M. L., Martins, R. C., Zager, A., Lopes, J. D., & Tufik, S. (2012). Immune alterations after selective eye movement or total sleep deprivation in healthy male volunteers. *Innate Immunity, 18,* 44–54.

Rumelhart, D. E. (1980). Schemata: The basic building blocks of cognition. In R. Spiro, B. Bruce, & W. Brewer (Eds.), *Theoretical issues in reading comprehension* (pp. 33–58). Erlbaum.

Ruscio, A. M., Hallion, L. S., Lim, C. C. W., Aguilar-Gaxiola, S., Al-Hamzawi, A., Alonso, J., ... Scott. K. M. (2017). Cross-sectional comparison of the epidemiology of *DSM-5* generalized anxiety disorder across the globe. *JAMA Psychiatry, 74*(5), 465–475. doi:10.1001/jamapsychiatry.2017.0056

Rush, M. C., Schoel, W. A., & Barnard, S. M. (1995). Psychological resiliency in the public sector: "Hardiness" and pressure for change. *Journal of Vocational Behavior, 46,* 17–39.

Rushton, J. P. (2012). No narrowing in mean Black–White IQ differences—Predicted by heritable *g. American Psychologist, 67,* 500–501. doi:10.1037/a0029614

Rushton, J. P., & Jensen, A. R. (2005). Thirty years of research on race differences in cognitive ability. *Psychology, Public Policy, and Law, 11,* 235–294.

Rushton, W. A. H. (1975). Visual pigments and color blindness. *Scientific American, 232,* 64–74.

Russell, C. J., & Keel, P. K. (2002). Homosexuality as a specific risk factor for eating disorders in men. *International Journal of Eating Disorders, 31,* 300–306.

Russell, V. A., Zigmond, M. J., Dimatelis, J. J., Daniels, W. M., & Mabandia, M. V. (2014). The interaction between stress and exercise, and its impact on brain function. *Metabolic Brain Disease, 29,* 255–260.

Rutherford, W. (1886). A new theory of hearing. *Journal of Anatomy and Physiology, 21,* 166–168.

Ryan, C. L., & Bauman, K. (2016). *Educational attainment in the United States: 2015.* U.S. Census Bureau.

Ryon, H. S., & Gleason, M. E. (2014). The role of locus of control in daily life. *Personality and Social Psychology Bulletin, 40,* 121–131.

Saadat, H., Drummond-Lewis, J., Maranets, I., Kaplan, D., Saadat, A., Wang, S. M., & Kain, Z. N. (2006). Hypnosis reduces preoperative anxiety in adult patients. *Anesthesia and Analgesia, 102,* 1394–1396.

Saalmann, Y. B., & Kastner, S. (2009). Gain control in the visual thalamus during perception and cognition. *Current Opinion in Neurobiology, 19,* 408–414. doi:10.1016/j.conb.2009.05.007

Sachs, G. S., & Rush, A. J. (2003). Response, remission, and recovery in bipolar disorders: What are the realistic treatment goals? *Journal of Clinical Psychiatry, 64*(Suppl. 6), 18–22.

Sachser, R. M., Haubrich, J., Lunardi, P. S., & de Oliveira Alvares, L. (2017). Forgetting of what was once learned: Exploring the role of postsynaptic ionotropic glutamate receptors on memory formation, maintenance, and decay. *Neuropharmacology, 112*(Part A), 94–103. doi:10.1016/j.neuropharm.2016.07.015

Sackett, P. R., & DeVore, C. J. (2001). Counterproductive behaviors at work. In N. Anderson, D. S. Ones, H. K. Sinangil, & C. Viswesvaran (Eds.), *Handbook of industrial, work and organizational psychology* (Vol. 1, pp. 145–165). SAGE.

Sackett, P. R., & Walmsley, P. T. (2014). Which personality attributes are most important in the workplace? *Perspectives on Psychological Science, 9,* 538–551.

Sadeh, N., Spielberg, J. M., Warren, S. L., Miller, G. A., & Heller, W. (2014). Aberrant neural connectivity during emotional processing associated with posttraumatic stress. *Clinical Psychological Science, 2,* 748–755.

Sadker, D. (2000). Gender equity: Still knocking at the classroom door. *Equity and Excellence in Education, 33,* 80–83.

Sadler, M. S., Correll, J., Park, B., & Judd, C. M. (2012). The world is not black and white: Racial bias in the decision to shoot in a multiethnic context. *Journal of Social Issues, 68*(2), 286-313. https://doi.org/10.1111/j.1540-4560.2012.01749.x

Sadler, W. A. (2000). *The third age: Six principles for growth and renewal after forty.* Perseus.

Sah, P., Faber, E. S. L., Lopez De Armentia, M., & Power, J. (2003). The aymgdaloid complex: Anatomy and physiology. *Physiological Reviews, 83,* 803–834.

Sajatovic, M., Valenstein, M., Blow, F., Ganoczy, D., & Ignacio, R. (2007). Treatment adherence with lithium and anticonvulsant medications among patients with bipolar disorder. *Psychiatric Services, 58,* 855–863.

Sakari, M. M. (1975). Small group cohesiveness and detrimental conformity. *Sociometry, 38,* 340–357.

Salend, S. J. (2001). *Creating inclusive classrooms: Effective and reflective practices,* Volume 1 (4th ed.). Prentice Hall.

Salgado, J. F., Viswesvaran, C., & Ones, D. (2003). Predictors used for personnel selection: An overview of constructs, methods and techniques. In N. Anderson, D. S. Ones, H. K. Sinangil, & C. Viswesvaran (Eds.), *Handbook of industrial, work and organizational psychology* (Vol. 1, pp. 166–199). SAGE.

Salk, R. H., Hyde, J. S., & Abramson, L. Y. (2017). Gender differences in depression in representative national samples: Meta-analyses of diagnoses and symptoms. *Psychological Bulletin, 143*(8), 783–822. https://doi.org/10.1037/bul0000102

Salthouse, T. A. (2012). Does the level at which cognitive change occurs change with age? *Psychological Science, 23,* 18–23.

Salvatore, J. E., Chun-Kuo, S. I., Steele, R. D., Simpson, J. A., & Collins, W. A. (2011). Recovering from conflict in romantic relationships: A developmental perspective. *Psychological Science, 22,* 376–383.

Samarel, N. (1995). The dying process. In H. Wass & R. A. Neimeyer (Eds.), *Dying: Facing the facts* (3rd ed., pp. 89–116). Taylor & Francis.

Sanada, M., Ikeda, K., Kimura, K., & Hasegawa, T. (2013). Motivation enhances visual working memory capacity through the modulation of central cognitive processes. *Psychophysiology, 50,* 864–871.

Sanaktekin, O. H., & Sunar, D. (2008). Persuasion and relational versus personal self-esteem: Does the message need to be one- or two-sided? *Social Behavior and Personality, 36,* 1315–1332.

Sánchez, R. C., Pérez, C. G., & Aránega, A. Y. (2020). General intelligence and emotional intelligence in senior management in the distribution sector: An applied analysis with synthetic indicators. *Psychology & Marketing, 37*(1), 6–14.

Sanchez-de-la-Torre, M., Campos-Rodriguez, F., & Barbe, F. (2013). Obstructive sleep apnea and cardiovascular disease. *The Lancet: Respiratory Medicine, 1,* 61–72.

Sanchez-Hucles, J. V., & Davis, D. D. (2010). Women and women of color in leadership. *American Psychologist, 65,* 171–181.

Sánchez-Martín, J. R., Azurmendi, A., Pascual-Sagastizabal, E., Cardas, J., Braza, F., Braza, P., . . . Muñoz, J. M. (2011). Androgen levels and anger and impulsivity measures as predictors of physical, verbal and indirect aggression in boys and girls. *Psychoneuroendocrinology, 36,* 750–760. doi:10.1016/j.psyneuen.2010.10.011

Sander, L., Rausch, L., & Baumeister, H. (2016). Effectiveness of internet-based interventions for the prevention of mental disorders: A systematic review and meta-analysis. *JMIR Mental Health, 3,* e38.

Sanders, J. D., Happe, H. K., Bylund, D. B., & Murrin, L. C. (2005). Development of the norepinephrine transporter in the rat CNS. *Neuroscience, 130,* 107–117.

Sanders, K. E., Osburn, S., Paller, K. A., & Beeman, M. (2019). Targeted memory reactivation during sleep improves next-day problem solving. *Psychological Science, 30*(11), 1616–1624.

Sanes, J. N., Dimitrov, B., & Hallett, M. (1990). Motor learning in patients with cerebellar dysfunction. *Brain, 113,* 103–120.

Sangrigoli, S., & de Schonen, S. (2004). Recognition of own-race and other-race faces by three-month-old infants. *Journal of Child Psychology and Psychiatry, 45,* 1219–1227.

Sanislow, C. A., Pine, D. S., Quinn, K. J., Kojak, M. J., Garvey, M. A., Heinssen, R. K., . . . Cuthbert, B. N. (2010). Developing constructs for psychopathology research: Research domain criteria. *Journal of Abnormal Psychology, 119,* 631–639.

Sansone, R. A., & Sansone, L. A. (2011a). Personality pathology and its influence on eating disorders. *Clinical Neuroscience, 8,* 14–18.

Sansone, R. A., & Sansone, L. A. (2011b). Personality disorders: A nation-based perspective on prevalence. *Innovations in Clinical Neuroscience, 8*(4), 13–18.

Sansone, R. A., & Sansone, L. A. (2014). Serotonin norepinephrine reuptake inhibitors: A pharmacological comparison. *Innovations in Clinical Neuroscience, 11*(3-4), 37–42.

Santelli, J. S., Lindberg, L. D., Abma, J., McNeeley, C. S., & Resnick, M. (2000). Adolescent sexual behavior: Estimates and trends from four nationally representative surveys. *Family Planning Perspectives, 32,* 156–165, 194.

Santoro, N., Worsley, R., Miller, K. K., Parish, S. J., & Davis, S. R. (2016). Role of estrogens and estrogen-like compounds in female sexual function and dysfunction. *The Journal of Sexual Medicine, 13*(3), 305–316. doi:10.1016/j.jsxm.2015.11.015

Sanyal, S., & vanTol, H. M. (1997). Review the role of dopamine D4 receptors in schizophrenia and anti-psychotic action. *Journal of Psychiatric Research, 31,* 219–232.

Sapolsky, R. M. (2000). The possibility of neurotoxicity in the hippocampus in major depression: A primer on neuron death. *Biological Psychiatry, 48,* 755–765.

Sapolsky, R. M. (2002). Chickens, eggs and hippocampal atrophy. *Nature Neuroscience, 5,* 1111–1113.

Sarker, M. R., Franks, S., & Caffrey, J. (2013). Direction of post-prandial ghrelin response associated with cortisol response, perceived stress and anxiety, and self-reported coping and hunger in obese women. *Behavioural Brain Research, 257,* 197–200 doi:10.1016/j.bbr.2013.09.046

Sárvári, M., Kalló, I., Hrabovszky, E., Solymosi, N., Rodolosse, A., Vastagh, C., . . . Liposits, Z. (2015). Hippocampal gene expression is highly responsive to estradiol replacement in middle-aged female rats. *Endocrinology, 156(7),* 2632–2645. doi:10.1210/en.2015-1109

Saskin, P. (1997). Obstructive sleep apnea: Treatment options, efficacy, and effects. In M. R. Pressman & W. C. Orr (Eds.), *Understanding sleep: The evaluation and treatment of sleep disorders* (pp. 283–297). American Psychological Association.

Saucier, D. A., McManus, J. L., & Smith, S. J. (2010). Discrimination against out-group members in helping situations. In S. Stürmer & M. Snyder (Eds.), *The psychology of prosocial behavior: Group processes, intergroup relations, and helping* (pp. 103–120). Wiley-Blackwell.

Saunders, E. H., Scott, L. J., McInnis, M. G., & Burmeister, M. (2008). Familiality and diagnostic patterns of subphenotypes in the National Institute of Mental Health bipolar sample. *American Journal of Medical Genetics Part B: Neuropsychiatric Genetics, 147B,* 18–26.

Saunders, N. L., & Summers, M. J. (2011). Longitudinal deficits to attention, executive and working memory in subtypes of mild cognitive impairment. *Neuropsychology, 25,* 237–248.

Sauter, D. A., Eisner, F., Ekman, P., & Scott, S. K. (2010). Cross-cultural recognition of basic emotions through nonverbal emotional vocalizations. *Proceedings of the National Academy of Sciences USA, 107,* 2408–2412.

Sava, F. A., Yates, B. T., Lupu, V., Szentagotai, A., & David, D. (2009). Cost-effectiveness and cost-utility of cognitive therapy, rational emotive behavioral therapy, and fluoxetine (Prozac) in treating depression: A randomized clinical trial. *Journal of Clinical Psychology, 65,* 36–52.

Savage-Rumbaugh, E. S. (1987). Communication, symbolic communication and language: Reply to Seidenberg and Petitto. *Journal of Experimental Psychology: General, 116,* 288–292.

Savage-Rumbaugh, E. S., McDonald, K., Sevcik, R., Hopkins, W., & Rupert, E. (1986). Spontaneous symbol acquisition and communicative use by pygmy chimpanzees (Pan paniscus). *Journal of Experimental Psychology: General, 115,* 211–235.

Saveanu, R. V., & Nemeroff, C. B. (2012). Etiology of depression: Genetic and environmental factors. *Psychiatric Clinics of North America, 35,* 51–71.

Savin-Williams, R. C. (2006). Who's gay? Does it matter? *Current Directions in Psychological Science, 15,* 40–44.

Savin-Williams, R. C., Joyner, K., & Rieger, G. (2012). Prevalence and stability of self-reported sexual orientation identity during young adulthood. *Archives of Sexual Behavior, 41,* 103–110. doi:1007/s10508-012-9913-y

Sawada, T., Nishiyama, T., Kikuchi, N., Wang, C., Lin, Y., Mori, M., ... Kikuchi, S. (2016). The influence of personality and perceived stress on the development of breast cancer: 20-year follow-up of 29,098 Japanese women. *Scientific Reports, 6,* 32559. doi:10.1038/srep32559

Sawchuk, C. N., Roy-Byrne, P., Noonan, C., Craner, J. R., Goldberg, J., Manson, S., Buchwald, D., & AI-SUPERPFP Team (2017). Panic attacks and panic disorder in the American Indian community. *Journal of Anxiety Disorders, 48,* 6–12. doi:10.1016/j.janxdis.2016.10.004

Sayette, M. A., Creswell, K. G., Dimoff, J. D., Fairbairn, C. E., Cohn, J. F., Heckman, B. W., . . . Moreland, R. L. (2012). Alcohol and group formation: A multimodal investigation of the effects of alcohol on emotion and social bonding. *Psychological Science, 23,* 869–878.

Sayette, M. A., Reichle, E. D., & Schooler, J. W. (2009). Lost in the sauce: The effects of alcohol on mind wandering. *Psychological Science, 20,* 747–752.

Sbarra, D. A. (2015). Divorce and health: Current trends and future directions. *Psychosomatic Medicine, 77*(3), 227–236. doi:10.1097/PSY.0000000000000168

Sbarra, D. A., Hasselmo, K., & Bourassa, K. J. (2015). Divorce and health: Beyond individual differences. *Current Directions in Psychological Science, 24,* 109–113.

Scarella, T. M., Laferton, J. A., Ahern, D. K., Fallon, B. A., & Barsky, A. (2016). The relationship of hypochondriasis to anxiety, depressive, and somatoform disorders. *Psychosomatics, 57*(2), 200–207. doi:10.1016/j.psym.2015.10.006

Schachter, S. (1951). Deviation, rejection, and communication. *Journal of Abnormal and Social Psychology, 46,* 190–207.

Schachter, S., & Singer, J. E. (1962). Cognitive, social, and physiological determinants of emotional state. *Psychological Review, 69,* 379–399.

Schacter, D. L., & Addis, D. R. (2007). The cognitive neuroscience of constructive memory: Remembering the past and imagining the future. *Philosophical Transactions of the Royal Society of London, Series B: Biological Sciences, 362,* 773–786.

Schacter, D. L., Alpert, N. M., Savage, C. R., Rauch, S. L., & Alpert, M. S. (1996). Conscious recollection and the hippocampal formation: Evidence from positron emission tomography. *Proceedings of the National Academy of Science, USA, 93,* 321–325.

Schaefer, L. M., Thibodaux, L. K., Krenik, D., Arnold, E., & Thompson, J. K. (2015). Physical appearance comparisons in ethnically diverse college women *Body Image, 15,* 153–157. doi:10.1016/j.bodyim.2015.09.002

Schag, K., Leehr, E. J., Martus, P., Bethge, W., Becker, S., Zipfel, S., & Giel, K. E. (2015). Impulsivity-focused group intervention to reduce binge eating episodes in patients with binge eating disorder: Study protocol of the randomised controlled IMPULS trial. *BMJ Open, 5*(12), e009445. doi:10.1136/bmjopen-2015-009445

Schaie, K. W. (1983). The Seattle longitudinal study: A 21-year exploration of psychometric intelligence in adulthood. In K. W. Schaie (Ed.), *Longitudinal studies of adult psychological development* (pp. 64–135). Guilford Press.

Schaie, K. W. (1994). The course of adult intellectual development. *American Psychologist, 49,* 304–313.

Schaie, K. W. (1996). *Intellectual development in adulthood: The Seattle longitudinal study.* Cambridge University Press.

Schaie, K. W., & Willis, S. L. (2000). A stage theory model of adult cognitive development revisited. In B. Rubinstein, M. Moss, & M. Kleban (Eds.), *The many dimensions of aging: Essays in honor of M. Powell Lawton* (pp. 173–191). Springer.

Schatz, P., Moser, R. S., Covassin, T., & Karpf, R. (2011). Early indicators of enduring symptoms in high school athletes with multiple previous concussions. *Neurosurgery, 68,* 1562–1567. doi:10.1227/NEU.0b013e31820e382e

Scheele, D., Striepens, N., Güntürkün, O., Deutschländer, S., Maier, W., Kendrick, K. M., & Hurlemann, R. (2012). Oxytocin modulates social distance between males and females. *The Journal of Neuroscience, 32,* 16074–16079. doi:10.1523/JNEUROSCI.2755-12.2012

Scheier, M. F., & Bridges, M. W. (1995). Person variables and health: Personality predispositions and acute psychological states as shared determinants for disease. *Psychosomatic Medicine, 57,* 255–268.

Schein, E. H. (1985). *Organizational leadership and culture: A dynamic view.* Jossey-Bass.

Scheir, M. F., & Carver, C. S. (1992). Effects of optimism on psychological and physical well-being: Theoretical overview and empirical update. *Cognitive Therapy and Research, 16,* 201–228.

Schellenberg, E. G. (2011). Examining the association between music lessons and intelligence. *British Journal of Psychology (London, England: 1953), 102*(3), 283–302. https://doi.org/10.1111/j.2044-8295.2010.02000.x

Scherf, K. S., Smyth, J. M., & Delgado, M. R. (2013). The amygdala: An agent of change in adolescent neural networks. *Hormones and Behavior, 64,* 298–313.

Schinka, J. A., Letsch, E. A., & Crawford, F. C. (2002). DRD4 and novelty seeking: Results of meta-analyses. *American Journal of Medical Genetics, 114,* 643–648.

Schizophrenia Working Group of the Psychiatric Genomics Consortium. (2014). Biological insights from 108 schizophrenia-associated genetic loci. *Nature, 511*(7510), 421–427. doi:10.1038/nature13595

Schleifer, S. J., Keller, S. E., Camerino, M., Thornton, J. C., & Stein, M. (1983). Suppression of lymphocyte stimulation following bereavement. *Journal of the American Medical Association, 250,* 374–377.

Schlesier-Stropp, B. (1984). Bulimia: A review of the literature. *Psychological Review, 95,* 247–257.

Schlosser, D. A., Zinberg, J. L., Loewy, R L., Casey-Cannon, S., O'Brien, M. P., Bearden, C. E., . . . Cannon, T. D. (2010). Predicting the longitudinal effects of the family environment on prodromal symptoms and functioning inpatients at-risk for psychosis. *Schizophrenia Research, 118,* 69–75.

Schmidt, B. P., Touch, P., Neitz, M., & Neitz, J. (2016). Circuitry to explain how the relative number of L and M cones shapes color experience. *Journal of Vision, 16*(8), 18. doi:10.1167/16.8.18

Schmidt, U., Lee, S., Beecham, J., Perkins, S., Treasure, J., Yi, I., . . . Eisler, I. (2007). A randomized controlled trial of family therapy and cognitive behavior therapy guided self-care for adolescent with bulimia nervosa and related disorders. *American Journal of Psychiatry, 164,* 591–598.

Schmidt-Hieber, C., Jonas, P., & Bischofberger, J. (2004). Enhanced synaptic plasticity in newly generated granule cells of the adult hippocampus. *Nature, 429,* 184–187.

Schmiedek, F., Lovden, M., & Lindenberger, U. (2013). Keeping it steady: Older adults perform more consistently on cognitive tasks than younger adults. *Psychological Science, 24,* 1747–1754.

Schmitt, D. P., Realo, A., Voracek, M., & Allik, J. (2008). Why can't a man be more like a woman? Sex differences in Big Five personality traits across 55 cultures. *Journal of Personality and Social Psychology, 94,* 168–182.

Schmitt, N., Cortina, J. M., Ingerick, M. J., & Wiechmann, D. (2003). Personnel selection and employee performance. In W. C. Borman, D. R. Ilgen, & R. J. Klimoski (Eds.), *Handbook of psychology: Industrial and organizational psychology* (Vol. 12, pp. 77–105). Wiley.

Schnepper, R., Richard, A., Wilhelm, F. H., & Blechert, J. (2019). A combined mindfulness–prolonged chewing intervention reduces body weight, food craving, and emotional eating. *Journal of Consulting and Clinical Psychology, 87*(1), 106–111. https://doi.org/10.1037/ccp0000361

Schoenborn, C. A. (1986). Health habits of U.S. adults, 1985: The "Alameda 7" revisited. *Public Health Reports, 101,* 571–580.

Schomerus, G., Matschinger, H., Baumeister, S. E., Mojtabai, R., & Angermeyer, M. C. (2014). Public attitudes towards psychiatric medication: A comparison between United States and Germany. *World Psychiatry, 13,* 320–321.

Schoppe-Sullivan, S. J., Mangelsdorf, S. C., Brown, G. L., & Sokolowski, M. S. (2007). Goodness-of-fit in family context: Infant temperament, marital quality, and early coparenting behavior. *Infant Behavior and Development, 30,* 82–96.

Schottenfeld, R. S., Chawarski, M. C., Cubells, J. F., George, T. P., Lappalainen, J., & Kosten, T. R. (2014). Randomized clinical trial of disulfiram for cocaine dependence or abuse during buprenorphine treatment. *Drug and Alcohol Dependence, 136,* 36–42.

Schredl, M. (2009). Dreams in patients with sleep disorders. *Sleep Medicine Reviews, 13,* 215–221.

Schreiber, J. A., & Brockopp, D. Y. (2012). Twenty-five years later—What do we know about religion/spirituality and psychological well-being among breast cancer survivors? A systematic review. *Journal of Cancer Survivorship, 6,* 82–94.

Schreiber, J., & Dixon, M. R. (2001). Temporal characteristics of slot machine play in recreational gamblers. *Psychological Reports, 89,* 67–72.

Schuch, J. J., Roest, A. M., Nolen, W. A., Penninx, B. W., & de Jonge, P. (2014). Gender differences in major depressive disorder: Results from the Netherlands study of depression and anxiety. *Journal of Affective Disorders, 156,* 156–163.

Schuckit, M. A., & Smith, T. L. (1997). Assessing the risk for alcoholism among sons of alcoholics. *Journal of Studies on Alcohol, 58,* 141–145.

Schueller, S. M., Munoz, R. F., & Mohr, D. C. (2013). Realizing the potential of behavioral intervention technologies. *Current Directions in Psychological Science, 22,* 478–483.

Schuh, K. J., & Griffiths, R. R. (1997). Caffeine reinforcement: The role of withdrawal. *Psychopharmacology, 130,* 320–326.

Schultz, D. P., & Schultz, S. E. (2005). *Theories of personality* (8th ed.). Wadsworth.

Schultz, D. P., & Schultz, S. E. (2012). *A history of modern psychology* (10th ed.) Wadsworth/Cengage Learning.

Schultz, D. P., & Schultz, S. E. (2016). *A history of modern psychology* (11th ed). Wadsworth/Cengage Learning.

Schumacher, J. E., Utley, J., Sutton, L., Horton, T., Hamer, T., You, Z., & Klapow, J. C. (2013). Boosting workplace stair utilization: A study of incremental reinforcement. *Rehabilitation Psychology, 58,* 81–86. doi:10.1037/a0031764

Schwartz, G., Kim, R. M., Kolundzjia, A. B., Rieger, G., & Sanders, A. R. (2010). Biodemographic and physical correlates of sexual orientation in men. *Archives of Sexual Behavior, 39,* 93–109.

Schwartz, M., O'Neal Chambliss, H., Brownell, K., Blair, S., & Billington, C. (2003). Weight bias among health professionals specializing in obesity. *Obesity Research, 11,* 1033–1039.

Schwartz, P. D., Maynard, A. M., & Uzelac, S. M. (2008). Adolescent egocentrism: A contemporary view. *Adolescence, 43,* 441–448.

Schwartz, R. C., & Blankenship, D. M. (2014). Racial disparities in psychotic disorder diagnosis: A review of empirical literature. *World Journal of Psychiatry, 4*(4), 133–140. doi.org/10.5498/wjp.v4.i4.133

Schwartze, D., Barkowski, S., Strauss, B., Knaevelsrud, C., & Rosendahl, J. (2019). Efficacy of group psychotherapy for posttraumatic stress disorder: Systematic review and meta-analysis of randomized controlled trials. *Psychotherapy Research, 29*(4), 415–431. doi:10.1080/10503307.2017.1405168

Schwarzwald, J., Bizman, A., & Raz, M. (1983). The foot-in-the-door paradigm: Effects of second request size on donation probability and donor generosity. *Personality and Social Psychology Bulletin, 9,* 443–450.

Scoboria, A., Mazzoni, G., & Kirsch, I. (2006). Effects of misleading questions and hypnotic memory suggestion on memory reports: A signal-detection analysis. *International Journal of Clinical and Experimental Hypnosis, 54,* 340–359.

Scollon, C. N., & Diener, E. (2006). Love, work, and changes in extraversion and neuroticism over time. *Journal of Personality and Social Psychology, 91,* 1152–1165.

Scott, J. C., & Reynolds, D. H. (Eds.). (2010). *Handbook of workplace assessment: Evidence-based practices for selecting and developing organizational talent* (1st ed.). Jossey-Bass.

Scott, K. E., Shutts, K., & Devine, P. G. (2020). Parents' expectations for and reactions to children's racial biases. *Child Development, 91*(3), 769-783. doi:10.1111/cdev.13231

Scott, T. R., & Plata-Salaman, C. R. (1991). Coding of taste quality. In T. V. Gethell, R. L. Doty, L. M. Bartoshuk, & J. B. Snow, Jr. (Eds.), *Smell and taste in health and disease* (pp. 345–368). Raven.

Scoville, W. B., & Milner, B. (1957). Loss of recent memory after bilateral hippocampal lesions. *Journal of Neurology, Neurosurgery, and Psychiatry, 20,* 11–19.

Scullin, M. K., & Bliwise, D. L. (2015). Sleep, cognition, and normal aging: Integrating a half century of multidisciplinary research. *Perspectives on Psychological Science, 10,* 97–137.

Scully, J. A., Tosi, H., & Banning, K. (2000). Life events checklist: Revisiting the social

readjustment rating scale after 30 years. *Educational and Psychological Measurement, 60,* 864–876.
Sedgh, G., Finer, L. B., Bankole, A., Eilers, M. A., & Singh, S. (2015). Adolescent pregnancy, birth, and abortion rates across countries: Levels and recent trends. *Journal of Adolescent Health, 56,* 223-230.
The See Jane 100: Gender and Race Representation in the Top 100 Family Films of 2017 (2018). *The Geena Davis Institute on Gender in Media.* https://seejane.org/wp-content/uploads/see-jane-100-report-2017.pdf
Seeman, M. V. (2008). Gender. In K. T. Mueser & D. V. Jeste (Eds.), *Clinical handbook of schizophrenia* (pp. 575–580). Guilford Press.
Seeman, M. V. (2018). Women who suffer from schizophrenia: Critical issues. *World Journal of Psychiatry, 8*(5), 125–136. doi:10.5498/wjp.v8.i5.125
Seeman, P. (2011). All roads to schizophrenia lead to dopamine supersensitivity and elevated dopamine d2high receptors. *CNS Neuroscience & Therapeutics, 17,* 118–132. doi:10.1111/j.1755-5949.2010.00162
Seery, M. D. (2011). Resilience: A silver lining to experiencing adverse life events? *Current Directions in Psychological Science, 20,* 390–394.
Seery, M. D., Leo, R. J., Lupien, S. P., Kondrak, C. L., & Almonte, J. L. (2013). An upside to adversity? Moderate cumulative lifetime adversity is associated with resilient responses in the face of controlled stressors. *Psychological Science, 24,* 1181–1189.
Segal, M. W. (1974). Alphabet and attraction: An unobtrusive measure of the effect of propinquity in a field setting. *Journal of Personality and Social Psychology, 30,* 654–657.
Segal, Z. V., Bieling, P., Young, T., MacQueen, G., Cooke, R., Martin, L., Bloch, R., & Levitan, R. D. (2010). Antidepressant monotherapy vs sequential pharmacotherapy and mindfulness-based cognitive therapy, or placebo, for relapse prophylaxis in recurrent depression. *Archives of General Psychiatry, 67*(12), 1256–1264. doi:10.1001/archgenpsychiatry.2010.168
Segerstrom, S. C. (2000). Personality and the immune system: Models, methods, and mechanisms. *Annals of Behavioral Medicine, 22,* 180–190.
Segerstrom, S. C., & Sephton, S. E. (2010). Optimistic expectancies and cell-mediated immunity: The role of positive affect. *Psychological Science, 21,* 448–455.
Seidler, R. D., Purushotham, A., Kim, S.-G., Ugurbil, K., Willingham, D., & Ashe, J. (2002). Cerebellum activation associated with performance change but not after motor learning. *Science (Washington), 296,* 2043–2046.
Seidler, Z. E., Dawes, A. J., Rice, S. M., Oliffe, J. L., & Dhillon, H. M. (2016). The role of masculinity in men's help-seeking for depression: A systematic review. *Clinical Psychology Review, 49,* 106–118.
Sekuler, R., McLaughlin, C., Kahana, M. J., Wingfield, A., & Yotsumoto, Y. (2006). Short-term visual recognition and temporal order memory are both well-preserved in aging. *Psychology and Aging, 21,* 632–637.
Sela, L., & Sobel, N. (2010). Human olfaction: A constant state of change blindness. *Experimental Brain Research, 205,* 13–29.
Seligman, M. E. P. (1970). On the generality of laws of learning. *Psychological Review, 77,* 406–418.
Seligman, M. E. P. (1989). *Helplessness.* Freeman.
Seligman, M. E. P., Allen, A. R., Vie, L. L., Ho, T. E., Scheier, L. M., Comum, R., & Lester, P. B. (2019). PTSD: Catastrophizing in combat as risk and protection. *Clinical Psychological Science, 7*(3), 516–529.
Seligman, M. E. P., & Csikszentmihalyi, M. (2000). Positive psychology: An introduction. *American Psychologist, 55,* 5–14.
Seligman, M. E. P., & Maier, S. F. (1967). Failure to escape traumatic shock. *Journal of Experimental Psychology, 74,* 1–9.
Selle, K., Brown, A. A., El-Alayli, A., & Ewen, S. (2019). Grandiose narcissists' public versus private attributions for a collaborative success. *Current Psychology: A Journal for Diverse Perspectives on Diverse Psychological Issues, 38*(2), 497–503. https://doi.org/10.1007/s12144-017-9628-2
Selye, H. (1976). *The stress of life.* McGraw-Hill.
Sen, S., Burmeister, M., & Ghosh, D. (2004). Meta-analysis of the association between a serotonin transporter promoter polymorphism (5-HTTLPR) and anxiety related personality traits. *American Journal of Medical Genetics, 127,* 85–89.
Senghas, A., & Coppola, M. (2001). Children creating language: How Nicaraguan sign language acquired a spatial grammar. *Psychological Science, 12,* 323–328.
Sepp, S., Howard, S. J., Tindall-Ford, S., Agostinho, S., & Paas, F. (2019). Cognitive load theory and human movement: Towards an integrated model of working memory. *Educational Psychology Review, 31*(2), 293-317. https://doi.org/10.1007/s10648-019-09461-9
Serrano, M. P., Herrero-Labrador, R., Futch, H. S., Serrano, J., Romero, A., Fernandez, A. F., . . . Martinez-Murillo, R. (2016). The proof-of-concept of ASS234: Peripherally administered ASS234 enters the central nervous system and reduces pathology in a male mouse model of Alzheimer's disease. *Journal of Psychiatry & Neuroscience: JPN, 41*(6), 150209.
Seshadri, K. G. (2016). The neuroendocrinology of love. *Indian Journal of Endocrinology and Metabolism, 20*(4), 558–563. doi:10.4103/2230-8210.183479
Sexton, J. (1995, July 25). Reviving Kitty Genovese case, and its passions. *New York Times,* pp. B1, B5.
Shadish, W. R., Cook, T. D., & Campbell, D. T. (2002). *Experimental and quasi-experimental designs for generalized causal inference.* Houghton Mifflin.
Shafer, M., & Crichlow, S. (1996). Antecedents of groupthink: A quantitative study. *Journal of Conflict Resolution, 40,* 415–435.
Shah, D. B., Pesiridou, A., Baltuch, G. H., Malone, D. A., & O'Reardon, J. P. (2008). Functional neurosurgery in the treatment of severe obsessive compulsive disorder and major depression: Overview of disease circuits and therapeutic targeting for the clinician. *Psychiatry, 5,* 24–33.
Shallenberger, R. S. (1993). *Taste chemistry.* Blackie.
Shallice, T., & Warrington, E.K. (1970). Independent functioning of verbal memory stores: A neuropsychological study. *Quarterly Journal of Experimental Psychology, 22,* 261–273.
Shamloo, Z. S., & Cox, W. M. (2010). The relationship between motivational structure, sense of control, intrinsic motivation and university students' alcohol consumption. *Addictive Behavior, 35,* 140–146.
Shanker, S. G., Savage-Rumbaugh, E. S., & Taylor, T. J. (1999). Kanzi: A new beginning. *Animal Learning and Behavior, 27,* 24–25.
Shapero, B. G., Hamilton, J. L., Stange, J. P., Liu, R. T., Abramson, L. Y., & Alloy, L. B. (2015). Moderate childhood stress buffers against depressive response to proximal stressors: A multi-wave prospective study of early adolescents. *Journal of Abnormal Child Psychology, 43*(8), 1403–1413. doi:10.1007/s10802-015-0021-z
Shapiro, F. (1991). Eye movement desensitization and reprocessing procedure: From EMD to EMD/R—a new treatment model for anxiety and related traumata. *Behavior Therapist, 14,* 133–135.
Shapiro, F. (2001). *Eye movement desensitization and reprocessing: Basic principles, protocols, and procedures* (2nd ed.). Guilford Press.
Sharafi, M., Hayes, J. E., & Duffy, V. B. (2013). Masking vegetable bitterness to improve palatability depends on vegetable type and taste phenotype. *Chemosensory Perception, 6*(1), 8–19. doi:10.1007/s12078-012-9137-5
Share, D. L., & Silva, P. A. (2003). Gender bias in IQ-discrepancy and post-discrepancy definitions of reading disability. *Journal of Learning Disabilities, 36,* 4–14.
Sharma, S., & Kavuru, M. (2010). Sleep and metabolism: An overview. *International Journal of Endocrinology, 2010,* 270832. doi:10.1155/2010/270832
Shavitt, S., Swan, S., Lowrey, T. M., & Wänke, M. (1994). The interaction of endorser attractiveness and involvement in persuasion depends on the goal that guides message processing. *Journal of Consumer Psychology, 3,* 137–162. doi:10.1016/S1057-7408(08)80002-2
Shaw, H., Ramirez, L., Trost, A., Randall, P., & Stice, E. (2004). Body image and eating disturbances across ethnic groups: More similarities than differences. *Psychology of Addictive Behaviors, 18,* 12–18.
Shea, A. K., & Steiner, M. (2008). Cigarette smoking during pregnancy. *Nicotine & Tobacco Research, 10,* 267–278.
Shechner, T., & Bar-Haim, Y. (2016). Threat monitoring and attention-bias modification in anxiety and stress-related disorders. *Current Directions in Psychological Science, 25,* 431–437.
Shedler, J. (2010). The efficacy of psychodynamic psychotherapy. *American Psychologist, 65,* 98–109.
Sheldon, K. M., Arndt, J., & Houser-Marko, L. (2003). In search of the organismic valuing process: The human tendency to move towards beneficial goal choices. *Journal of Personality, 71,* 835–869.
Sheline, Y. I. (2000). 3D MRI studies of neuroanatomic changes in unipolar major depression: The role of stress and medical comorbidity. *Biological Psychiatry, 48,* 791–800.
Shen, B. J., McCreary, C. P., & Myers, H. F. (2004). Independent and mediated contributions of personality, coping, social support, and depressive symptoms to physical functioning outcome among patients in cardiac rehabilitation. *Journal of Behavioral Medicine, 27,* 39–62.
Shepard, G. M. (2006). Smell images and the flavour system in the brain. *Nature, 444,* 316–321.
Shepard, R. N. (1978). The mental image. *American Psychologist, 33,* 125–137.
Sherif, M. (1966). *In common predicament: Social psychology of intergroup conflict and cooperation.* Houghton Mifflin.

Sherif, M., Harvey, O. J., White, J., Hood, W., & Sherif, C. (1961). *Intergroup conflict and cooperation: The Robber's Cave experiment*. University of Oklahoma Press.

Sherman, D. K., Kim, H. S., & Taylor, S. E. (2009). Culture and social support: Neural bases and biological impact. *Progress in Brain Research, 178*, 227–237.

Sherman, J. W., Gawronski, B., & Trope, Y. (Eds.) (2014). *Dual-process theories of the social mind*. Guilford Press.

Sherwin, B. B., & Gelfand, M. M. (1987). The role of androgen in the maintenance of sexual functioning in oophorectomized women. *Psychosomatic Medicine, 49*, 397–409.

Shi, J., Levinson, D. F., Duan, J., Sanders, A. R., Zheng, Y., Pe'er, I., . . . Gejman, P. V. (2009). Common variants on chromosome 6p22.1 are associated with schizophrenia. *Nature, 460*, 753–757.

Shimoff, E., Catania, A. C., & Matthews, B. A. (1981). Unstructured human responding: Sensitivity of low-rate performance to schedule contingencies. *Journal of Experimental Analysis of Behavior, 36*, 207–220.

Shin, L. M., Bush, G., Milad, M. R., Lasko, N. B., Brohawn, K. H., Hughes, K. C., . . . Pitman, R. K. (2011). Exaggerated activation of dorsal anterior cingulate cortex during cognitive interference: A monozygotic twin study of posttraumatic stress disorder. *American Journal of Psychiatry, 168*, 979–985.

Shiner, R. L., Masten, A. S., & Roberts, J. M. (2003). Childhood personality foreshadows adult personality and life outcomes two decades later. *Journal of Personality, 71*, 1145–1170.

Shinskey, J. L., & Munakata, Y. (2005). Familiarity breeds searching: Infants reverse their novelty preferences when reaching for hidden objects. *Psychological Science, 16*, 596–600.

Shintani, T., Hughes, C., Beckham, S., & O'Connor, H. (1991). Obesity and cardiovascular risk intervention through the ad libitum feeding of traditional Hawaiian diet. *American Journal of Clinical Nutrition, 53*, 1647S–1651S.

Shiraev, E., & Levy, D. (2010). *Cross-cultural psychology: Critical thinking and contemporary applications* (4th ed.). Allyn & Bacon.

Shneidman, E. S. (1987, March). At the point of no return. *Psychology Today*, 54–58.

Shoham, V., & Insel, T. R. (2011). Rebooting for whom? Portfolios, technology, and personalized intervention. *Perspectives on Psychological Science, 6*, 478–482.

Shors, T. J. (2014). The adult brain makes new neurons, and effortful learning keeps them alive. *Current Directions in Psychological Science, 23*, 311–318.

Short, M. A., Gradisar, M., Lack, L. C., & Wright, H. R. (2013). The impact of sleep on adolescent depressed mood, alertness, and academic performance. *Journal of Adolescence, 36*, 1025–1033.

Shreeram, S., He, J., Kalaydjian, A., Brothers, S., & Merikangas, K. R. (2009). Prevalence of enuresis and its association with attention-deficit/hyperactivity disorder among U.S. children: Results from a nationally representative study. *Journal of the American Academy of Child & Adolescent Psychiatry, 48*, 35–41.

Shulman, S., Scharf, M., Lumer, D., & Maurer, O. (2001). Parental divorce and young adult children's romantic relationships: Resolution of the divorce experience. *American Journal of Orthopsychiatry, 71*, 473–478.

Shuttleworth-Edwards, A. B. (2016). Generally representative is representative of none: Commentary on the pitfalls of IQ test standardization in multicultural settings. *The Clinical Neuropsychologist, 30*(7), 975–998. doi:10.1080/13854046.2016.1204011

Siegel, J. M. (2001). The REM sleep-memory consolidation hypothesis. *Science, 294*, 1058–1063.

Siegel, M. (2020). Racial disparities in fatal police shootings: An empirical analysis informed by critical race theory. *Boston Law Review, 100*, 1069-1092.

Siegel, S. (1984). Pavlovian conditioning and heroin overdose: Reports by overdose victims. *Bulletin of the Psychonomic Society, 22*(5), 428–430. https://doi.org/10.3758/BF03333867

Siegel, S. (1989). Pharmacological conditioning and drug effects. In A. J. Goudie & M. W. Emmett-Oglesby (Eds.), *Contemporary neuroscience. Psychoactive drugs: Tolerance and sensitization* (pp. 115–180). Humana Press. https://doi.org/10.1385/0-89603-148-9:115

Siegel, S. (2005). Drug tolerance, drug addiction, and drug anticipation. *Current Directions in Psychological Science, 14*, 296–300.

Siegel, S. (2011). The four-loko effect. *Perspectives on Psychological Science, 6*, 357–362.

Siegel, S., & Ellsworth, D. W. (1986). Pavlovian conditioning and death from apparent overdose of medically prescribed morphine: A case report. *Bulletin of the Psychonomic Society, 24*(4), 278–280. https://doi.org/10.3758/BF03330140

Siever, L. J., & Koenigsberg, H. W. (2000). The frustrating no-man's-land of borderline personality disorder. *Cerebrum: The Dana Forum on Brain Science, 2*(4).

Silva, C. E., & Kirsch, I. (1992). Interpretive sets, expectancy, fantasy proneness, and dissociation as predictors of hypnotic response. *Journal of Personality and Social Psychology, 63*, 847–856.

Silverman, W. K., Marin, C. E., Rey, Y., Kurtines, W. M., Jaccard, J., & Pettit, J. W. (2019). Group- versus parent-involvement CBT for childhood anxiety disorders: Treatment specificity and long-term recovery mediation. *Clinical Psychological Science, 7*(4), 840-855.

Silverstein, M. J., Faraone, S. V., Leon, T. L., Biederman, J., Spencer, T. J., & Adler, L. A. (2020). The relationship between executive function deficits and *DSM-5*-defined ADHD symptoms. *Journal of Attention Disorders, 24*(1), 41–51.

Sim, H. (2000). Relationship of daily hassles and social support to depression and antisocial behavior among early adolescents. *Journal of Youth and Adolescence, 29*, 647–659.

Simmler, L. D., Rickli, A., Hoener, M. C., & Liechti, M. E. (2013). Monoamine transporter and receptor interaction profiles of a new series of designer cathinones. *Neuropharmacology, 79C*, 152–160.

Simon, H. A. (1974). How big is a chunk? *Science, 183*, 482–488.

Simpson, G., & Yinger, J. M. (1985). *Racial and cultural minorities*. Plenum Press.

Simpson, J. (2017, August 25). *Finding brand success in the digital world*. Forbes Agency Council Post. https://www.forbes.com/sites/forbesagencycouncil/2017/08/25/finding-brand-success-in-the-digital-world/#470588b1626e

Simpson, J. A., Collins, W. A., & Salvatore, J. E. (2011). The impact of early interpersonal experience on adult romantic relationship functioning: Recent findings from the Minnesota Longitudinal Study of Risk and Adaptation. *Current Directions in Psychological Science, 20*, 355–359.

Simpson N. S., Gibbs, E. L., & Matheson, G. O. (2017). Optimizing sleep to maximize performance: Implications and recommendations for elite athletes. *Scandinavian Journal of Medicine and Science in Sports, 27*(3), 266–274. doi:10.1111/sms.12703

Sin, N. L., & Lyubomirsky, S. (2009). Enhancing well-being and alleviating depressive symptoms with positive psychology interventions: A practice friendly meta-analysis. *Journal of Clinical Psychology, 65*, 467–487.

Singer, J. E., Brush, C. A., & Lublin, S. C. (1965). Some aspects of deindividuation: Identification and conformity. *Journal of Experimental Social Psychology, 1*(4), 356–378. doi:10.1016/0022-1031(65)90015-6

Sinha, R., & Raut, S. (2016). Management of nocturnal enuresis – myths and facts. *World Journal of Nephrology, 5*, 328–338.

Sinha, R., Gu, P., Hart, R., & Guarnaccia, J. B. (2019). Food craving, cortisol and ghrelin responses in modeling highly palatable snack intake in the laboratory. *Physiology & Behavior, 208*, 112563. https://doi.org/10.1016/j.physbeh.2019.112563

Sinkus, M. L., Adams, C. E., Logel, J., Freedman, R., & Leonard, S. (2013). Expression of immune genes on chromosome 6p21.3-22.1 in schizophrenia. *Brain, Behavior, and Immunity, 32*, 51–62.

Sinnott, J. D. (1998). *The development of logic in adulthood: Postformal thought and its applications*. Plenum.

Sio, U. N., Kotovsky, K., & Cagan, J. (2017). Interrupted: The roles of distributed effort and incubation in preventing fixation and generating problem solutions. *Memory & Cognition, 45, 553-565*. doi:10.3758/s13421-016-0684-x

Sio, U. N., & Ormerod, T. C. (2009). Does incubation enhance problem solving? A meta-analytic review. *Psychological Bulletin, 135*, 94–120.

Skelton, C. (2006). Boys and girls in the elementary school. In C. Skelton, B. Francis, & L. Smulyan (Eds.), *The SAGE handbook of gender and education* (pp. 139–151). SAGE.

Skinner, A. L., Olson, K. R., & Meltzoff, A. N. (2020). Acquiring group bias: Observing other people's nonverbal signals can create social group biases. *Journal of Personality and Social Psychology, 119*(4), 824–838. https://doi.org/10.1037/pspi0000218

Skinner, B. F. (1938). *The behavior of organisms*. Appleton-Century-Crofts.

Skinner, B. F. (1953). *Science and human behavior*. Macmillan.

Skinner, B. F. (1958). Teaching machines. *Science, 128*, 969–977.

Skinner, M. D., Lahmek, P., Pham, H., & Aubin, H. J. (2014). Disulfiram efficacy in the treatment of alcohol dependence: A meta-analysis. *PLoS One, 9*, e87366.

Skodol, A. E., & Bender, D. S. (2003). Why are women diagnosed borderline more than men? *Psychiatry Quarterly, 74*, 349–360.

Skvortsova, A., Veldhuijzen, D. S., Kloosterman, I. E. M., Meijer, O. C., van Middendorp, H., Pacheco-Lopez, G., & Evers, A. W. M. (2019). Conditioned hormonal responses: A systematic review in animals and humans. *Frontiers in Neuroendocrinology, 52*, 206–218. https://doi.org/10.1016/j.yfrne.2018.12.005

Slagt, M., Dubas, J. S., Dekovic, M., & van Aken, M. A. (2016). Differences in sensitivity to parenting depending on child temperament: A meta-analysis. *Psychological Bulletin, 142,* 1068–1110.

Slameka, N. J. (1966). Differentiation versus unlearning of verbal associations. *Journal of Experimental Psychology, 71,* 822–828.

Slatcher, R. B., & Selcuk, E. (2017). A social psychological perspective on the links between close relationships and health. *Current Directions in Psychological Science, 26,* 16–21.

Slattery, M. L., Curtin, K., Wolff, R. K., Herrick, J. S., Caan, B. J., & Samowitz, W. (2010). Diet, physical activity, and body size associations with rectal tumor mutations and epigenetic changes. *Cancer Causes & Control, 21,* 1237–1245.

Slavin-Muldord, J., Hilsenroth, M., Weinberger, J., & Gold, J. (2011). Therapeutic interventions related to outcome in psychodynamic psychotherapy for anxiety disorder patients. *Journal of Nervous and Mental Disease, 199,* 214–221.

Slotema, C. W., Blom, J. D., Hoek, H. W., & Sommer, I. E. (2010). Should we expand the toolbox of psychiatric treatment methods to include repetitive transcranial magnetic stimulation (rTMS)? A meta-analysis of the efficacy of rTMS in psychiatric disorders. *Journal of Clinical Psychiatry, 71,* 873–884.

Slovic, P., Finucane, M., Peters, E., & MacGregor, D. G. (2002). Rational actors or rational fools: Implications of the affect heuristic for behavioral economics. *Journal of Socio-Economics, 31,* 329–342. doi:10.1016/S1053-5357(02)00174-9

Smetana, J. G., Campione-Barr, N., & Metzger, A. (2006). Adolescent development in interpersonal and societal contexts. *Annual Review of Psychology, 57,* 255–284.

Smillie, L. D. (2013). Extraversion and reward processing. *Current Directions in Psychological Science, 22,* 167–172.

Smith, C. (1995). Sleep states and memory processes. *Behavioural Brain Research, 69*(1–2), 137–145.

Smith, C. A., Organ, D. W., & Near, J. P. (1983). Organizational citizenship behavior: Its nature and antecedents. *Journal of Applied Psychology, 68,* 653–663.

Smith, D. E., & Cogswell, C. (1994). A cross-cultural perspective on adolescent girls' body perception. *Perceptual and Motor Skills, 78,* 744–746.

Smith, J. W., Frawley, P. J., & Polissar, N. L. (1997). Six- and twelve-month abstinence rates in inpatient alcoholics treated with either faradic aversion or chemical aversion compared with matched inpatients from a treatment registry. *Journal of Addictive Diseases, 16,* 5–24.

Smith, M. C., & Dust, M. C. (2006). An exploration of the influence of dispositional traits and appraisal on coping strategies in African American college students. *Journal of Personality, 74,* 145–174.

Smith, M. C., Coleman, S. R., & Gormezano, I. (1969). Classical conditioning of the rabbit's nictitating membrane response at backward, simultaneous, and forward CS–US intervals. *Journal of Comparative and Physiological Psychology, 69,* 226–231.

Smith, P. C., Kendall, L. M., & Hulin, C. L. (1969). *The measurement of satisfaction in work and retirement.* Rand McNally.

Smith, S. L., Choueiti, M., Prescott, A., & Pieper, K. (2012). Gender roles and occupations: A look at character attributes and job-related aspirations in film and television. *The Geena Davis Institute on Gender in Media.* https://seejane.org/wp-content/uploads/key-findings-gender-roles-2013.pdf

Smith, S. M., & Beda, Z. (2020). Old problems in new contexts: The context-dependent fixation hypothesis. *Journal of Experimental Psychology: General, 149*(1), 192–197. https://doi.org/10.1037/xge0000615

Smith, T., Brumskill, R., Johnson, A., & Zimmer, T. (2018). The impact of teacher language on students' mindsets and statistics performance. *Social Psychology of Education: An International Journal, 21*(4), 775–786. https://doi.org/10.1007/s11218-018-9444-z

Smith, T. B., Rodriguez, M. D., & Bernal, G. (2011). Culture. *Journal of Clinical Psychology, 67,* 166–175.

Smith, T. W. (2006). Personality as risk and resilience in physical health. *Current Directions in Psychological Science, 15,* 227–231.

Smith, T. W., Glazer, K., Ruiz, J. M., & Gallo, L. C. (2004). Hostility, anger, aggressiveness and coronary heart disease: An interpersonal perspective on personality, emotion, and health. *Journal of Personality, 72,* 1217–1270.

Snarey, J. (1995). In a communitarian voice: The sociological expansion of Kohlbergian theory, research, and practice. In W. M. Kurtines & J. L. Gewirtz (Eds.), *Moral development: An introduction* (pp. 109–134). Allyn & Bacon.

Snyder, A. L., Anderson-Hanley, C., & Arciero, P. J. (2012). Virtual and live social facilitation while exergaming: Competitiveness moderates exercise intensity. *Journal of Sport & Exercise Psychology, 34,* 252–259.

Snyder, C. R., Ilardi, S., Michael, S. T., & Cheavens, J. (2000). Hope theory: Updating a common process for psychological change. In C. R. Snyder & R. E. Ingram (Eds.), *Handbook of psychological change: Psychotherapy processes and practices for the 21st century* (pp. 128–153). Wiley.

Snyder, H. R., Kaiser, R. H., Warren, S. L., & Heller, W. (2015). Obsessive-compulsive disorders is associated with broad impairments in executive function: A meta-analysis. *Clinical Psychological Science, 3,* 301–330.

Sohail, N. (2013). Stress and academic performance among medical students. *Journal of the College of Physicians and Surgeons, 23,* 67–71.

Sohn, J. W., Oh, Y., Kim, K. W., Lee, S., Williams, K. W., & Elmquist, J. K. (2016). Leptin and insulin engage specific PI3K subunits in hypothalamic SF1 neurons. *Molecular Metabolism, 5*(8), 669–679. doi:10.1016/j.molmet.2016.06.004

Solberg, E. E., Halvorsen, R., & Holen, A. (2000). Effect of meditation on immune cells. *Stress Medicine, 16,* 185–190.

Solberg, L. (2010). Data mining on Facebook: A free space for researchers or an IRB nightmare? *University of Illinois Journal of Law, Technology & Policy, 2,* 311.

Soloff, P. H., & Chiapetta, L. (2012). Prospective predictors of suicidal behavior in borderline personality disorder at 6-year follow-up. *American Journal of Psychiatry, 169,* 484–490.

Solomon, L. Z., Solomon, H., & Maiorca, J. (1982). The effects of bystander's anonymity, situational ambiguity, and victim's status on helping. *Journal of Social Psychology, 117,* 285–294. doi:10.1080/00224545.1982.9713438

Somers, V. K., Phil, D., Dyken, M. E., Mark, A. L., & Abboud, F. M. (1993). Sympathetic-nerve activity during sleep in normal subjects. *New England Journal of Medicine, 328,* 303–307.

Somerville, L. H. (2013). The teenage brain: Sensitivity to social evaluation. *Current Directions in Psychological Science, 22,* 121–127.

Somerville, L. H., Jones, R. M., Ruberry, E. J., Dyke, J. P., Glover, G., & Casey, B. J. (2013). The medial prefrontal cortex and the emergence of self-conscious emotion in adolescence. *Psychological Science, 24,* 1554–1562.

Song, Y., Jordan, J. I., Shaffer, K. A., Wing, E. K., McRae, K., & Waugh, C. E. (2019). Effects of incidental positive emotion and cognitive reappraisal on affective responses to negative stimuli. *Cognition and Emotion, 33*(6), 1155–1168. https://doi.org/10.1080/02699931.2018.1541789

Soper, B., Milford, G. E., & Rosenthal, G. T. (1995). Belief when evidence does not support theory. *Psychology and Marketing, 12,* 415–422.

Soto, C. J. (2016). The little six personality dimensions from early childhood to early adulthood: Mean-level age and gender differences in parents' reports. *Journal of Personality, 84,* 409–422.

Soto, C. J., & Tackett, J. L. (2015). Personality traits in childhood and adolescence: Structure, development, and outcomes. *Current Directions in Psychological Science, 24,* 358–362.

Soyka, M., Graz, C., Bottlender, R., Dirschedl, P., & Schoech, H. (2007). Clinical correlates of later offences in schizophrenia. *Schizophrenia Research, 94,* 89–98.

Soyka, M., & Mutschler, J. (2016). Treatment-refractory substance use disorder: Focus on alcohol, opioids, and cocaine. *Progress in Neuro-Psychopharmacology & Biological Psychiatry, 70,* 148–161. doi:10.1016/j.pnpbp.2015.11.00

Soyka, M., Preuss, U. W., Hesselbrock, V., Zill, P., Koller, G., & Bondy, B. (2008). GABA-A2 receptor subunit gene (GABRA2) polymorphisms and risk for alcohol dependence. *Journal of Psychiatric Research, 42,* 184–191.

Spachtholz, P., Kuhbandner, C., & Pekrun, R. (2014). Negative affect improves the quality of memories: Trading capacity for precision in sensory and working memory. *Journal of Experimental Psychology: General, 143*(4), 1450–1456. doi:10.1037/xge0000012

Spanos, N. P. (1996). *Multiple identities and false memories: A sociocognitive perspective.* American Psychological Association.

Spanos, N. P., Burnley, M. C. E., & Cross, P. A. (1993). Response expectancies and interpretations as determinants of hypnotic responding. *Journal of Personality and Social Psychology, 65,* 1237–1242.

Spanou, E. E., & Morogiannis, F. F. (2010). The role of family and socio-cultural factors in the development of eating disorders. *Psychiatriki, 21,* 41–53.

Spearman, C. (1904). The proof and measurement of association between two things. *American Journal of Psychology, 15,* 72–101.

Spencer, J. A., & Fremouw, W. J. (1979). Binge eating as a function of restraint and weight classification. *Journal of Abnormal Psychology, 88,* 262–267.

Spendelow, J. S., Simonds, L. M., & Avery, R. E. (2017). The relationship between corumination and internalizing problems: A systematic review and meta-analysis. *Clinical Psychology & Psychotherapy, 24*(2), 512-527.

Spengler, M., Gottschling, J., & Spinath, F. M. (2012). Personality in childhood: A longitudinal behavior genetic approach. *Personality and Individual Differences, 53,* 411–416.
Spera, C., Wentzel, K. R., & Matto, H. C. (2009). Parental aspirations for their children's educational attainment: Relations to ethnicity, parental education, children's academic performance, and parental perceptions of school climate. *Journal of Youth and Adolescence, 38,* 1140–1152.
Spiegel, D., Loewenstein, R. J., Lewis-Fernandez, R., Sar, V., Simeon, D., Vermetten, E., . . . Dell, P. F. (2011). Dissociative disorders in *DSM-5. Depression and Anxiety, 28,* 824–852.
Spillmann, L. (2014). Receptive fields of visual neurons: The early years. *Perception, 43*(11), 1145–1176.
Spreng, R. N., & Turner, G. R. (2019). The shifting architecture of cognition and brain function in older adulthood. *Perspectives on Psychological Science, 14*(4), 523–542.
Spriggs, M. (2009). Consent in cyberspace: Internet-based research involving young people. *Monash Bioethics Review, 28,* 1–15.
Sprouse-Blum, A. S., Smith, G., Sugai, D., & Parsa, F. D. (2010). Understanding endorphins and their importance in pain management. *Hawaii Medical Journal, 69(3),* 70–71.
Squire, L. R. (1992). Memory and the hippocampus: A synthesis from findings with rats, monkeys, and humans. *Psychological Review, 99,* 195–232.
Squire, L. R., & Dede, A. J. O. (2015). Conscious and unconscious memory systems. *Cold Spring Harbor Perspectives in Biology, 7*(3), a021667. doi:10.1101/cshperspect.a021667
Squire, L. R., Knowlton, B., & Musen, G. (1993). The structure and organization of memory. *Annual Review of Psychology, 44,* 453–495.
Squire, L. R., Ojemann, J. G., Miezin, F. M., Petersen, S. E., Videen, T. O., & Raichle, M. E. (1992). Activation of the hippocampus in normal humans: A functional anatomical study of memory. *Proceedings of the National Academy of Science, USA, 89,* 1837–1841.
Sripada, R. K., & Rauch, S. A. M. (2015). Between-session and within-session habituation in prolonged exposure therapy for posttraumatic stress disorder: A hierarchical linear modeling approach. *Journal of Anxiety Disorders, 30,* 81–87. doi:10.1016/j.janxdis.2015.01.002
Srivastava, S., John, O. P., Gosling, S. D., & Potter, J. (2003). Development of personality in early and middle adulthood: Set in plaster or persistent change? *Journal of Personality and Social Psychology, 84,* 1041–1053.
Stacey, D., Clarke, T. K., & Schumann, G. (2009). The genetics of alcoholism. *Current Psychiatry Reports, 11,* 364–369.
Stahl, S. M. (1996). *Essential psychopharmacology.* Cambridge University Press.
Stahl, S. M. (1998). Basic psychopharmacology of antidepressants: Part I. Antidepressants have seven distinct mechanisms of action. *Journal of Clinical Psychiatry, 59*(Suppl. 4), 5–14.
Stahl, S. M., & Felker, A. (2008). Monoamine oxidase inhibitors: A modern guide to an unrequited class of antidepressants. *CNS Spectrums, 13*(10), 855–870. doi:10.1017/s1092852900016965
Stahl, S. M., Grady, M. M., Moret, C., & Briley, M. (2005). SNRIs: Their pharmacology, clinical efficacy, and tolerability in comparison with other classes of antidepressants. *CNS Spectrums, 10*(9), 732–747. doi:10.1017/s1092852900019726
Stalder, D. R. (2012). A role for social psychology instruction in reducing bias and conflict. *Psychology Learning & Teaching, 11,* 245–255.
Staniloiu, A., Kordon, A., & Markowitsch, H. J. (2020). Quo vadis 'episodic memory'?—Past, present, and perspective. *Neuropsychologia, 141,* 107362. https://doi.org/10.1016/j.neuropsychologia.2020.107362
Stanovich, K. E., & West, R. F. (1998). Individual differences in rational thought. *Journal of Experimental Psychology: General, 127,* 161–188.
Stanska, K., & Krzeski, A. (2016). The umami taste: From discovery to clinical use. *Otolaryngologia Polska = The Polish Otolaryngology, 70*(4), 10–15. doi:10.5604/00306657.1199991
Stanton, A. L., & Low, C.A. (2012). Expressing emotions in stressful contexts: Benefits, moderators, and mechanisms. *Current Directions in Psychological Science, 21,* 124–128.
Stanton, J. L. (2004). The end of TV advertising: Technologies allow consumers to miss what once were the bedrock of consumer product advertising. *Food Processing, 65,* 26.
Stawski, R. S., Almeida, D. M., Sliwinski, M. J., & Smyth, J. M. (2008). Reported exposure and emotional reactivity to daily stressors: The roles of adult age and global perceived stress. *Psychology and Aging, 23,* 52–61.
Steadman, H. J., Mulvey, E. P., Monahan, J., Robbins, P. C., Appelbaum, P. S., Grisso, T., . . . Silver, E. (1998). Violence by people discharged from acute psychiatric inpatient facilities and by others in the same neighborhoods. *Archives of General Psychiatry, 55*(5), 393–401.
Stear, S. (2003). Health and fitness: Series 1. The importance of physical activity on health. *Journal of Family Health Care, 13,* 10–13.
Steele, C. M. (1997). A threat in the air: How stereotypes shape the intellectual identities and performance of women and African-Americans. *American Psychologist, 52,* 613–629.
Steele, C. M., & Aronson, J. (1995). Stereotype threat and the intellectual test performance of African Americans. *Journal of Personality and Social Psychology, 69,* 797–811.
Stefflre, V., Castillo-Vales, V., & Morley, L. (1966). Language and cognition in Yucatan: A cross-cultural replication. *Journal of Personality and Social Psychology, 4,* 112–115.
Stein, D. J., Lim, C., Roest, A. M., de Jonge, P., Aguilar-Gaxiola, S., Al-Hamzawi, A., ... WHO World Mental Health Survey Collaborators (2017). The cross-national epidemiology of social anxiety disorder: Data from the World Mental Health Survey Initiative. *BMC Medicine, 15*(1), 143. doi:10.1186/s12916-017-0889-2
Steinberg, L., & Morris, A. S. (2001). Adolescent development. *Annual Reviews of Psychology, 52,* 83–110.
Steinberg, L., Lamborn, S. D., Dornbusch, S. M., & Darling, N. (1992). Impact of parenting practices on adolescent achievement: Authoritative parenting, school involvement, and encouragement to succeed. *Child Development, 63,* 1266–1281.
Steiner, M., Dunn, E., & Born, L. (2003). Hormones and mood: From menarche to menopause and beyond. *Journal of Affective Disorders, 74,* 67–83.
Steinert, C., Munder, T., Rabung, S., Hoyer, J., & Leichsenring, F. (2017). Psychodynamic therapy: As efficacious as other empirically supported treatments? A meta-analysis testing equivalence of outcomes. *The American Journal of Psychiatry, 174*(10), 943–953. doi:10.1176/appi.ajp.2017.17010057
Steinhausen, H. C., & Vollrath, M. (1993). The self-image of adolescent patients with eating disorders. *International Journal of Eating Disorders, 13,* 221–229.
Steinmayr, R., & Spinath, B. (2019). Why time constraints increase the gender gap in measured numerical intelligence in academically high achieving samples. *European Journal of Psychological Assessment, 35*(3), 392–402. https://doi.org/10.1027/1015-5759/a000400
Stenblom, E., Montelius, C., Östbring, K., Håkansson, M., Nilsson, S., Rehfeld, J. F., & Erlanson-Albertsson, C. (2013). Supplementation by thylakoids to a high carbohydrate meal decreases feelings of hunger, elevates CCK levels and prevents postprandial hypoglycaemia in overweight women. *Appetite, 68,* 118–123. doi:10.1016/j.appet.2013.04.022
Stephan, K. E., Marshall, J. C., Friston, K. J., Rowe, J. B., Ritzl, A., Zilles, K., . . . Fin, G. R. (2003). Lateralized cognitive processes and lateralized task control in the human brain. *Science, 301,* 384–386.
Stephens, C. E., Pear, J. J., Wray, L. D., & Jackson, G. C. (1975). Some effects of reinforcement schedules in teaching picture names to retarded children. *Journal of Applied Behavior Analysis, 8,* 435–447.
Stephens, N. M., & Levine, C. S. (2011). Opting out or denying discrimination? How the framework of free choice in American society influences perceptions of gender inequality. *Psychological Science, 22,* 1231–1236. doi:10.1177/0956797611417260
Steriade, M., & McCarley, R. W. (1990). *Brainstem control of wakefulness and sleep.* Plenum Press.
Stermer, P., & Burkley, M. (2015). Sex-box: Exposure to sexist video games predicts benevolent sexism. *Psychology of Popular Media Culture, 4,* 47–55. doi:10.1037/a0028397
Stern, K. N., & McClintock, M. K. (1998). Regulation of ovulation by human pheromones. *Nature, 392,* 177–179.
Stern, S. L., Dhanda, R., & Hazuda, H. P. (2009). Helplessness predicts the development of hypertension in older Mexican and European Americans. *Journal of Psychosomatic Research, 67,* 333–337.
Sternberg, R. J. (1985). *Beyond IQ: A triarchic theory of human intelligence.* Cambridge University Press.
Sternberg, R. J. (1997a). The concept of intelligence and its role in lifelong learning and success. *American Psychologist, 52,* 1030–1037.
Sternberg, R. J. (1997b). *Successful intelligence.* Plume.
Sternberg, R. J. (1999). *Handbook of creativity.* Cambridge University Press.
Sternberg, R. J. (2015). Successful intelligence: A model for testing intelligence beyond IQ tests. *European Journal of Education and Psychology, 8*(2), 76–84. doi:10.1016/j.ejeps.2015.09.004
Sternberg, R. J., Grigorenko, E. L., & Kidd, K. K. (2005). Intelligence, race, and genetics. *American Psychologist, 60,* 46–59.

Stevens, A., & Coupe, P. (1978). Distortions in judged spatial relations. *Cognitive Psychology, 10,* 422–437.

Stevens, J. S., & Hamann, S. (2012). Sex differences in brain activation to emotional stimuli: A meta-analysis of neuroimaging studies. *Neuropsychologia, 50,* 1578–1593.

Stewart, G. L., Courtright, S. H., & Barrick, M. R. (2012). Peer-based control in self-managing teams: Linking rational and normative influence with individual and group performance. *The Journal of Applied Psychology, 97*(2), 435–447. doi:10.1037/a0025303

Stewart, G. L., & Manz, C. C. (1995). Leadership for self-managing work teams: A typology and integrative model. *Human Relations, 48,* 347–370.

Stewart, J. A., Deliyannides, D. A., Hellerstein, D. J., McGrath, P. J., & Stewart, J. W. (2012). Can people with nonsevere major depression benefit from antidepressant medication? *Journal of Clinical Psychiatry, 73,* 518–525.

Stewart, R., Ellenburg, G., Hicks, L., Kremen, M., & Daniel, M. (1990). Employee references as a recruitment source. *Applied H.R.M. Research, 1(1),* 1–3.

Stickgold, R., & Walker, M. P. (2007). Sleep-dependent memory consolidation and reconsolidation. *Sleep Medicine, 8,* 331–343.

Stickgold, R., & Walker, M. P. (2013). Sleep-dependent memory triage: Evolving generalization through selective processing. *Nature Neuroscience, 16,* 139–145.

Stiles, W. B., Barkham, M., Mellor-Clark, J., & Connell, J. (2008). Effectiveness of cognitive-behavioural, person-centered, and psychodynamic therapies in UK primary-care routine practice: Replication in a larger sample. *Psychological Medicine, 38,* 677–688.

Stiles, W. B., Barkham, M., Twigg, E., Mellor-Clark, J., & Cooper, M. (2006). Effectiveness of cognitive-behavioural, person-centered, and psychodynamic therapies as practiced in UK National Health Service settings. *Psychological Medicine, 36,* 555–566.

Stine-Morrow, E. A., Parisi, J. M., Morrow, D. G., Greene, J., & Park, D. C. (2007). An engagement model of cognitive optimization through adulthood. *Journals of Gerontology, Series B: Psychological Sciences and Social Sciences, 62,* 62–69.

Stockhorst, U., de Fries, D., Steingrueber, H.-J., & Scherbaum, W. A. (2004). Insulin and the CNS: Effects on food intake, memory, and endocrine parameters and the role of intranasal insulin administration in humans. *Physiology & Behavior, 83*(1), 47–54. https://doi.org/10.1016/j.physbeh.2004.07.022

Stockhorst, U., Mahl, N., Krueger, M., Huenig, A., Schottenfeld-Naor, Y., Huebinger, A.,... Scherbaum, W. A. (2004). Classical conditioning and conditionability of insulin and glucose effects in healthy humans. *Physiology & Behavior, 81*(3), 375–388. https://doi.org/10.1016/j.physbeh.2003.12.019

Stoel-Gammon, C., & Otomo, K. (1986). Babbling development of hearing impaired and normal subjects. *Journal of Speech and Hearing Disorders, 51,* 33–41.

Stoll, J., Müller, J. A., & Trachsel, M. (2020). Ethical issues in online psychotherapy: A narrative review. *Frontiers in Psychiatry, 10,* 993. doi:10.3389/fpsyt.2019.00993

Stone, D. M., Holland, K. M., Bartholow, B., Crosby, A. E., Davis, S., & Wilkins, N. (2017). *Preventing suicide: A technical package of policies, programs, and practices.* National Center for Injury Prevention and Control, Centers for Disease Control and Prevention.

Storms, G., DeBoeck, P., & Ruts, W. (2001). Categorization of novel stimuli in well-known natural concepts. *Psychonomic Bulletin and Review, 8,* 377–384.

Storms, M. D. (1973). Videotape and the attribution process: Reversing actors' and observers' points of view. *Journal of Personality and Social Psychology, 27,* 165–175.

Stoughton, J. W., Thompson, L. F. & Meade, A. W. (2015). Examining applicant reactions to the use of social networking websites in pre-employment screening. *Journal of Business and Psychology, 30,* 73–88.

Stout, M. (2005). *The sociopath next door.* Broadway Books.

Stoyanov, G., Moneva, K., Sapundzhiev, N., & Tonchev, A. B. (2016). The vomeronasal organ—Incidence in a Bulgarian population. *The Journal of Laryngology and Otology, 130*(4), 344–347. doi:10.1017/S0022215116000189

Strassberg, Z., Dodge, K., Pettit, G. S., & Bates, J. E. (1994). Spanking in the home and children's subsequent aggression toward kindergarten peers. *Development and Psychopathology, 6,* 445–461.

Strauss, S., Swanepoel, D. W., Becker, P., Eloff, Z., & Hall, J. W. III (2014). Noise and age-related hearing loss: A study of 40 123 gold miners in South Africa. *International Journal of Audiology, 53 Suppl 2,* S66–S75. doi:10.3109/14992027.2013.865846

Strayer, D. L., Drews, F. A., & Crouch, D. J. (2006). A comparison of the cell phone driver and the drunk driver. *Human Factors, 48,* 381–391.

Strickland, B. R. (1989). Internal-external control expectancies: From contingency to creativity. *American Psychologist, 44,* 1–12.

Stright, A. D., Gallagher, K. C., & Kelley, K. (2008). Infant temperament moderates relations between maternal parenting in early childhood and children's adjustment in first grade. *Child Development, 79,* 186–200.

Strober, M., Freeman, R., Lampert, C., Diamond, J., & Kaye, W. (2000). Controlled family study of anorexia nervosa and bulimia nervosa: Evidence of shared liability and transmission of partial syndromes. *The American Journal of Psychiatry, 157*(3), 393–401. https://doi.org/10.1176/appi.ajp.157.3.393

Stroebe, M. (2001). Gender differences in adjustment to bereavement: An empirical and theoretical review. *Review of General Psychology, 5,* 62–83.

Stroebe, M., & Schut, H. (2015). Family matters in bereavement: Toward an integrative intra-interpersonal coping model. *Perspectives on Psychological Science, 10,* 873–879.

Stromquist, N. P. (2007). *The gender socialization process in schools: A cross-national comparison.* Paper commissioned for the EFA Global Monitoring Report, 2008, Education for all by 2015: Will we make it? 2008/ED/EFA/MRT/PI/71.

Strübel, J., & Petrie, T. A. (2020). Sexual orientation, eating disorder classification, and men's psychosocial well-being. *Psychology of Men & Masculinities, 21*(2), 190-200. https://doi.org/10.1037/men0000224

Stubbs, B., Vancampfort, D., Rosenbaum, S., Firth, J., Cosco, T., Veronese, N., Salum, G. A., & Schuch, F. B. (2017). An examination of the anxiolytic effects of exercise for people with anxiety and stress-related disorders: A meta-analysis. *Psychiatry Research, 249,* 102-108. doi:10.1016/j.psychres.2016.12.020

Su, K. G., Kim, H. M., & Martinez, V. (2020). Repeated group alternation as a programming strategy for essential tremor patients experiencing rapid habituation with deep brain stimulation treatment. *International Journal of Neuroscience,* 1–5. https://doi.org/10.1080/00207454.2020.1758083

Substance Abuse and Mental Health Services Administration (SAMHSA). (2006). *Results from the 2005 National Survey on Drug Use and Health: National findings.* Office of Applied Studies, NSDUH Series H-30, DHHS Publication No. SMA 06-4194.

Substance Abuse and Mental Health Services Administration (SAMHSA). (2009a). *The NSDUH Report: Suicidal thoughts and behaviors among adults.* Office of Applied Studies.

Substance Abuse and Mental Health Services Administration (SAMHSA). (2009b). *The NSDUH Report: Mental health support and self-help groups.* Office of Applied Studies.

Substance Abuse and Mental Health Services Administration (SAMHSA). (2012). *The NSDUH Report: State estimates of drunk and drugged driving.* Center for Behavioral Health Statistics and Quality.

Substance Abuse and Mental Health Services Administration (SAMHSA). (2013). *Results from the 2012 National Survey on Drug Use and Health: Summary of national findings,* NSDUH Series H-46, HHS Publication No. (SMA) 13-4795. Author.

Substance Abuse and Mental Health Services Administration (SAMHSA). (2015a). *Behavioral Health Barometer: United States, 2015.* HHS Publication No. SMA–16–Baro–2015. Author.

Substance Abuse and Mental Health Services Administration (SAMHSA). (2015b). *Results from the 2014 National Survey on Drug Use and Health,* HHS Publication No. SMA 15-4927, NSDUH Series H-50. Author.

Substance Abuse and Mental Health Services Administration (SAMHSA). (2018). *Key Substance Use and Mental Health Indicators in the United States: Results from the 2017 National Survey on Drug Use and Health (HHS Publication No. SMA 18-5068, NSDUH Series H-53).* Center for Behavioral Health Statistics and Quality, Substance Abuse and Mental Health Services Administration.

Sundin, J., Fear, N. T., Iversen, A., Rona, R. J., & Wessely, S. (2010). PTSD after deployment to Iraq: Conflicting rates, conflicting claims. *Psychological Medicine, 40,* 367–382.

Sundin, J., Herrell, R. K., Hoge, C. W., Fear, N. T., Adler, A. B., Greenberg, N., . . . Bliese, P. D. (2014). Mental health outcomes in U.S. and U.K. military personnel returning from Iraq. *British Journal of Psychiatry, 204,* 200–207.

Sundram, B. M., Dahlui, M., & Chinna, K. (2016). Effectiveness of progressive muscle relaxation therapy as a worksite health promotion program in the automobile assembly line. *Industrial Health, 54,* 204–214.

Super, D. E. (1957). *The psychology of careers.* Harper & Row.

Super, D. E. (1976). *Career education and the meanings of work.* U.S. Office of Education.

Super, D. E. (1980). A life-span, life-space approach to career development. *Journal of Vocational Behavior, 16,* 282–298.

Super, D. E. (1991). A life-span, life-space approach to career development. In D. Brown, L. Brooks, & Associates (Eds.),

Career choice and development: Applying contemporary theories to practice (2nd ed., pp. 197–261). Jossey-Bass.
Sussman, S. (2010). A review of Alcoholics Anonymous/Narcotics Anonymous programs for teens. *Evaluation and the Health Professions, 33,* 26–55.
Sussman, S., & Arnett, J. J. (2014). Emerging adulthood: Developmental period facilitative of the addictions. *Evaluation and the Health Professions, 37,* 147–155.
Sutin, A. R., Terracciano, A., Milaneschi, Y., An, Y., Ferrucci, L., & Zonderman, A. B. (2013). The effect of birth cohort on well-being: The legacy of economic hard times. *Psychological Science, 24,* 379–385.
Suzuki, K., Simpson, K. A., Minnion, J. S., Shillito, J. C., & Bloom, S. R. (2010). The role of gut hormones and the hypothalamus in appetite regulation. *Endocrine Journal, 57,* 359–372. doi:10.1507/endocrinj.K10E-077
Suzuki, K., Miyamoto, M., Miyamoto, T., & Hirata, K. (2015). Restless legs syndrome and leg motor restlessness in Parkinson's disease. *Parkinson's Disease, 2015,* 490938. doi:10.1155/2015/490938
Svaldi, J., Werle, D., Naumann, E., Eichler, E., & Berking, M. (2019). Prospective associations of negative mood and emotion regulation in the occurrence of binge eating in binge eating disorder. *Journal of Psychiatric Research, 115,* 61–68. https://doi.org/10.1016/j.jpsychires.2019.05.005
Swanson, L. M., Arnedt, J. T., Rosekind, M. R., Belenky, G., Balkin, T. J., & Drake, C. (2010). Sleep disorders and work performance: Findings from the 2008 National Sleep Foundation Sleep in America poll. *Journal of Sleep Research, 20,* 487–494. doi:10.1111/j.1365-2869.2010.00890.x
Sweet, T., & Welles, S. L. (2012). Associations of sexual identity or same-sex behaviors with history of childhood sexual abuse and HIV/STI risk in the United States. *JAIDS Journal of Acquired Immune Deficiency Syndromes, 59,* 400–408. doi:10.1097/QAI.0b013e3182400e75
Swift-Gallant, A., Coome, L. A., Aitken, M., Monks, D. A., & VanderLaan, D. P. (2019). Evidence for distinct biodevelopmental influences on male sexual orientation. *PNAS Proceedings of the National Academy of Sciences of the United States of America, 116*(26), 12787–12792. https://doi.org/10.1073/pnas.1809920116
Swinson, J., & Harrop, A. (2009). Teacher talk directed to boys and girls and its relationship to their behaviour. *Educational Studies, 35,* 515–524.
Symons, C. S., & Johnson, B. T. (1997). The self-reference effect in memory: A meta-analysis. *Psychological Bulletin, 121,* 371–394.
Sysoeva, O. V., Kulikova, M. A., Malyuchenko, N. V., Tonevitskii, A. G., & Ivanitskii, A. M. (2010). Genetic and social factors in the development of aggression. *Human Physiology, 36,* 40–46.
Szasz, T. S. (1987). *Insanity: The idea and its consequences.* Wiley.
Szentirmai, E., Yasuda, T., Taishi, P., Wang, M., Churchill, L., Bohnet, S., . . . Krueger, J. M. (2007). Growth hormone-releasing hormone: Cerebral cortical sleep-related EEG actions and expressions. *American Journal of Physiology: Regulatory, Integrative and Comparative Physiology, 293,* R922–R930.
Szkrybalo, J., & Ruble, D. N. (1999). "God made me a girl": Sex-category constancy judgments and explanations revisited. *Developmental Psychology, 35,* 392–402.
Szymanowicz, A., & Furnham, A. (2013). Gender and gender role differences in self- and other-estimates of multiple intelligences. *The Journal of Social Psychology, 153*(4), 399–423. doi:10.1080/00224545.2012.754397
Tager-Flusberg, H. (2005). Putting words together: Morphology and syntax in the preschool years. In J. B. Gleason (Ed.), *The development of language* (5th ed., pp. 148–190). Allyn & Bacon.
Taghavi, M. R., Goodarzi, M. A., Kazemi, H., & Ghorbani, M. (2006). Irrational beliefs in major depression and generalized anxiety disorder in an Iranian sample: A preliminary study. *Perceptual and Motor Skills, 102,* 187–196.
Tajfel, H. (1982). *Social identity and intergroup relations.* Cambridge University Press.
Takahashi, K., Mizuno, K., Sasaki, A. T., Wada, Y., Tanaka, M., Ishii, A., . . . Watanabe, Y. (2015). Imaging the passionate stage of romantic love by dopamine dynamics. *Frontiers in Human Neuroscience, 9,* 191. doi:10.3389/fnhum.2015.00191
Takano, Y., & Sogon, S. (2008). Are Japanese more collectivistic than Americans? Examining conformity in in-groups and the reference-group effect. *Journal of Cross-Cultural Psychology, 39,* 237–250.
Talamonti, D., Koscik, R., Johnson, S., & Bruno, D. (2020). Predicting early mild cognitive impairment with free recall: The primacy of primacy. *Archives of Clinical Neuropsychology, 35*(2), 133–142. https://doi.org/10.1093/arclin/acz013
Tam, C. S., Rigas, G., Heilbronn, L. K., Matisan, T., Probst, Y., & Talbot, M. (2016). Energy adaptations persist 2 years after sleeve gastrectomy and gastric bypass. *Obesity Surgery, 26*(2), 459–463. doi:10.1007/s11695-015-1972-4
Tamminen, J., Rastle, K., Darby, J., Lucas, R., & Williamson, V. J. (2017). The impact of music on learning and consolidation of novel words. *Memory, 25*(1), 107–121. doi:10.1080/09658211.2015.1130843
Tamres, L. K., Janicki, D., & Helgeson, V. S. (2002). Sex differences in coping behavior: A meta-analytic review and an examination of relative coping. *Personality and Social Psychology Review, 6,* 2–30.
Tan, R., & Goldman, M. S. (2015). Exposure to female fertility pheromones influences men's drinking. *Experimental and Clinical Psychopharmacology, 23*(3), 139–146. doi:10.1037/pha0000016
Tanaka-Arakawa, M. M., Matsui, M., Tanaka, C., Uematsu, A., Uda, S., Miura, K., . . . Noguchi, K. (2015). Developmental changes in the corpus callosum from infancy to early adulthood: A structural magnetic resonance imaging study. *PLoS One. 10(3),* e0118760. doi:10.1371/journal.pone.0118760
Tang, M. O., Oliffe, J. L., Galdas, P. M., Phinney, A., & Han, C. S. (2014). College men's depression-related help-seeking: A gender analysis. *Journal of Mental Health, 23,* 219–224.
Tang, Y. Y., Ma, Y., Fan, Y., Feng, H., Wang, J., Feng, S., . . . Fan, M. (2009). Central and autonomic nervous system interaction is altered by short-term meditation. *Proceedings of the National Academy of Sciences of the United States of America, 106,* 8865–8870.
Tanguy, S., Quarck, G., Etard, O., Gauthier, A., & Denise, P. (2008). Vestibulo-ocular reflex and motion sickness in figure skaters. *European Journal of Applied Physiology, 104,* 1031–1037.
Tanner-Smith, E. E. (2010). Negotiating the early developing body: Pubertal timing, body weight, and adolescent girls' substance use. *Journal of Youth and Adolescence, 39,* 1402–1416.
Taormina, R. J., & Gao, J. H. (2013). Maslow and the motivation hierarchy: Measuring satisfaction of the needs. *American Journal of Psychology, 126,* 155–177. doi:10.5406/amerjpsyc.126.2.0155
Taplin, C., Saddichha, S., Li, K., & Krausz, M. R. (2014). Family history of alcohol and drug abuse, childhood trauma, and age of first drug injection. *Substance Use & Misuse, 49,* 1311–1316.
Tashkin, D. P. (2005). Smoked marijuana as a cause of lung injury. *Monaldi Archives for Chest Disease, 63,* 92–100.
Tata, D. A., & Anderson, B. J. (2009). The effects of chronic glucocorticoid exposure on dendritic length, synapse numbers and glial volume in animal models: Implications for hippocampal volume reductions in depression. *Physiology and Behavior, 99,* 186–193.
Tauber, S. K., & Dunlosky, J. (2015). Monitoring of learning at the category level when learning a natural concept: Will task experience improve its resolution? *Acta Psychologica, 155,* 8–18. doi:10.1016/j.actpsy.2014.11.011
Taurah, L., Chandler, C., & Sanders, G. (2014). Depression, impulsiveness, sleep, and memory in past and present polydrug users of 3, 4-methylenedioxymethamphetamine (MDMA, ecstasy). *Psychopharmacology, 231,* 737–751.
Taylor, C. B., & Luce, K. H. (2003). Computer- and Internet-based psychotherapy interventions. *Current Directions in Psychological Science, 12,* 18–22.
Taylor, E. J., & Outlaw, F. H. (2002). Use of prayer among persons with cancer. *Holistic Nursing Practices, 16,* 46–60.
Taylor, H. (2002). Poor people and African Americans suffer the most stress from the hassles of daily living. *The Harris Poll #66.*
Taylor, J. L., Debost, J., Morton, S. U., Wigdor, E. M., Heyne, H. O., Lal, D., ... & Robinson, E. B. (2019). Paternal-age-related de novo mutations and risk for five disorders. *Nature Communications, 10*(1), 3043. doi:10.1038/s41467-019-11039-6
Taylor, S. E. (2003). *Health psychology* (5th ed.). McGraw-Hill.
Taylor, S. E. (2006). Tend and befriend: Biobehavioral bases of affiliation under stress. *Current Directions in Psychological Science, 15,* 273–277.
Taylor, S. E., Klein, L. C., Lewis, B. P., Gruenewald, T. L., Gurung, R. A., & Updegraff, J. A. (2000). Biobehavioral responses to stress in females: Tend-and-befriend, not fight-or-flight. *Psychological Review, 107,* 411–429.
Taylor, S. E., Way, B. M., Welch, W. T., Hilmert, C. J., Lehman, B. J., & Eisenberger, N. I. (2006). Early family environment, current adversity, the serotonin transporter promoter polymorphism, and depressive symptomatology. *Biological Psychiatry, 60,* 671–676.
Taylor, S. M. (2008). Electroconvulsive therapy, brain-derived neurotrophic factor, and possible neurorestorative benefit of the clinical application of electroconvulsive therapy. *Journal of ECT, 24,* 160–165.

Teachman, B. A. (2014). No appointment necessary: Treating mental illness outside the therapist's office. *Perspectives on Psychological Science, 9,* 85–87.

Teasdale, J. D., & Russell, M. L. (1983). Differential effects of induced mood on the recall of positive, negative, and neutral words. *British Journal of Clinical Psychology, 22,* 163–171.

Teasdale, J. D., Scott, J., Moore, R. G., Hayhurst, H., Pope, M., & Paykel, E. S. (2001). How does cognitive therapy prevent relapse in residual depression? Evidence from a controlled trial. *Journal of Consulting and Clinical Psychology, 69,* 347–357.

Teasdale, J. D., Segal, Z., & Williams, J. M. (1995). How does cognitive therapy prevent depressive relapse and why should attentional control (mindfulness) training help? *Behaviour Research and Therapy, 33*(1), 25–39. doi:10.1016/0005-7967(94)e0011-7

Tedeschi, P., Pearson, J. A., Bayly, D., & Fine, A. H. (2015). On call 24/7—The emerging roles of service and support animals. In A. H. Fine (Ed.), *Handbook on animal-assisted therapy: Foundations and guidelines for animal-assisted interventions,* 4th ed. (pp. 321–332). Elsevier Academic Press. https://doi.org/10.1016/B978-0-12-801292-5.00023-7

Teicher, M. H. (2002). Scars that won't heal: The neurobiology of child abuse. *Scientific American, 286,* 68–75.

Teitelbaum, P., & Epstein, A. N. (1962). The lateral hypothalamic syndrome: Recovery of feeding and drinking after lateral hypothalamic lesions. *Psychological Review, 69,* 74–90.

Teitelbaum, P., & Stellar, E. (1954). Recovery from failure to eat produced by hypothalamic lesions. *Science, 120,* 894–895.

Teixeira, P. J., Silva, M. N., Coutinho, S. R., Palmeira, A. L., Mata, J., Vieira, P. N., . . . Sardinha, L. B. (2010). Mediators of weight loss and weight loss maintenance in middle-aged women. *Obesity, 18,* 725–735.

Tenenbaum, H. R., & Leaper, C. (2003). Parent-child conversations about science: The socialization of gender inequities? *Developmental Psychology, 39,* 34–47.

te Nijenhuis, J., Willigers, D., Dragt, J., & van der Flier, H. (2016). The effects of language bias and cultural bias estimated using the method of correlated vectors on a large database of IQ comparisons between native Dutch and ethnic minority immigrants from non-Western countries. *Intelligence, 54,* 117–135.

ten Cate, C. (2017). Assessing the uniqueness of language: Animal grammatical abilities take center stage. *Psychonomic Bulletin & Review, 24, 91-96.* doi:10.3758/s13423-016-1091-9

Terhune, D. B., & Cardena, E. (2015). Dissociative subtypes in posttraumatic stress disorders and hypnosis: Neurocognitive parallels and clinical implications. *Current Directions in Psychological Science, 24,* 452–457.

Terhune, D. B., Cardena, E., & Lindgren, M. (2010). Dissociative tendencies and individual differences in high hypnotic suggestibility. *Cognitive Neuropsychology, 17,* 1–23.

Terman, L. M. (1916). *The measurement of intelligence: An explanation of and a complete guide for the use of the Stanford revision and extension of the Binet-Simon Intelligence Scale.* Houghton Mifflin.

Terracciano, A., Costa, P. T., & McCrae, R. R. (2006). Personality plasticity after age 30. *Personality and Social Psychology Bulletin, 32,* 999–1009.

Terrace, H. S. (2019). *Why chimpanzees can't learn language and only humans can.* Columbia University Press.

Terranova, J. I., Song, Z., Larkin, T. E. I., Hardcastle, N., Norvelle, A., Riaz, A., & Albers, H. E. (2016). Serotonin and arginine-vasopressin mediate sex differences in the regulation of dominance and aggression by the social brain. *PNAS Proceedings of the National Academy of Sciences of the United States of America, 113*(46), 13233–13238. doi:10.1073/pnas.1610446113

Terrion, J. L., & Aceti, V. (2012). Perceptions of the effects of clicker technology on student learning and engagement: A study of freshmen chemistry students. *Research in Learning Technology, 20*(2), 1–11.

Tesarz, J., Leisner, S., Gerhardt, A., Janke, S., Seidler, G. H., Eich, W., & Hartmann, M. (2014). Effects of eye movement desensitization and reprocessing (EMDR) treatment in chronic pain patients: A systematic review. *Pain Medicine, 15,* 247–263.

Testa, M., Quigley, B. M., & Leonard, K. E. (2003). Does alcohol make a difference? Within-participants comparison of incidents of partner violence. *Journal of Interpersonal Violence, 18,* 735–743.

Thase, M. E. (2010). The role of neurobiologic processes in treating depression. *Journal of Clinical Psychiatry, 71,* e28.

The Harris Poll (2016). *Harris polls in the news.* http://www.theharrispoll.com/in-the-news/harris-polls/Spanking.html

Thomas, A. R., Solorzano, L., & Cobb, H. C. (2007). Culturally responsive counseling and psychotherapy with children and adolescents. In H. Thompson Prout & D. T. Brown (Eds.), *Counseling and psychotherapy with children and adolescents* (4th ed., pp. 64–93). Wiley.

Thomas, A., & Chess, S. (1977). *Temperament and development.* Brunner/Mazel.

Thomas, A., & Chess, S. (1986). The New York longitudinal study: From infancy to early adult life. In R. Plomin & J. Dunn (Eds.), *The study of temperament: Changes, continuities, and challenges* (pp. 39–52). Erlbaum.

Thomas, C. P., Fullerton, C. A., Kim, M., Montejano, L., Lyman, D. R., Dougherty, R. H., . . . Delphin-Rittmon, M. E. (2014). Medication-assisted treatment with buprenorphine: Assessing the evidence. *Psychiatric Services, 65,* 158–170.

Thombs, D. L., O'Mara, R. J., Tsukamoto, M., Rossheim, M. E., Weiler, R. M., Merves, M. L., & Goldberger, B. A. (2010). Event-level analyses of energy drink consumption and alcohol intoxication in bar patrons. *Addictive Behaviors, 35,* 325–330.

Thompson, P. M., Giedd, J. N., Woods, R. P., MacDonald, D., Evans, A. C., & Togo, A. W. (2000, March 9). Growth patterns in the developing human brain detected by using continuum-mechanical tensor maps. *Nature, 404,* 190–193.

Thorndike, E. L. (1898). Animal intelligence: An experimental study of associative process in animals. *Psychological Review Monograph,* No. 8.

Thorndike, E. L. (1905). *The elements of psychology.* Seiler.

Thorpy, M. (2007). Therapeutic advances in narcolepsy. *Sleep Medicine, 8,* 427–440.

Thurber, C. A., & Walton, E. (2007). Preventing and treating homesickness. *Pediatrics, 119,* 192–201.

Thurstone, L. L. (1931). The measurement of social attitudes. *Journal of Abnormal and Social Psychology, 26,* 249–269.

Thurstone, L. L. (1938). *Primary mental abilities.* University of Chicago Press.

Tiedemann, J. (2002). Teachers' gender stereotypes as determinants of teacher perceptions in elementary school mathematics. *Educational Studies in Mathematics, 50,* 49–62.

Tienari, P., Wahlberg, K. E., & Wynee, L. C. (2006). Finnish Adoption Study of Schizophrenia: Implications for family interventions. *Families, Systems and Health, 24,* 442–451.

Tienari, P., Wynne, L. C., Laksy, K., Moring, J., Nieminen, P., Sorri, A., . . . Wahlberg, K. E. (2003). Genetic boundaries of the schizophrenia spectrum: Evidence from the Finnish Adoptive Family Study of Schizophrenia. *American Journal of Psychiatry, 160,* 1567–1594.

Till, B. D., Stanley, S. M., & Priluck, R. (2008). Classical conditioning and celebrity endorsers: An examination of belongingness and resistance to extinction. *Psychology & Marketing, 25,* 179–196. doi:10.1002/mar.20205

Tobin, K. E., Davey, M. A., & Latkin, C. A. (2005). Calling emergency medical services during drug overdose: An examination of individual, social and setting correlates. *Addiction, 100,* 397–404. doi:10.1111/j.1360-0443.2005.00975.

Tohidian, I. (2009). Examining linguistic relativity hypothesis as one of the main views on the relationship between language and thought. *Journal of Psycholinguist Research, 38,* 65–74.

Tolin, D. F. (2010). Is cognitive-behavioral therapy more effective than other therapies? A meta-analytic review. *Clinical Psychological Review, 30,* 710–720.

Tolman, E. C., & Honzik, C. H. (1930). "Insight" in rats. *University of California Publications in Psychology, 4,* 215–232.

Tomasello, M. (2000). Culture and cognitive development. *Current Directions in Psychological Science, 9,* 37–40.

Tomasi, D., & Volkow, N. D. (2012). Laterality patterns of brain functional connectivity: Gender effects. *Cerebral Cortex, 22,* 1455–1462. doi:10.1093/cercor/bhr230

Tommasi, M., Watkins, M., Orsini, A., Pezzuti, L., Cianci, L., & Saggino, A. (2015). Gender differences in latent cognitive abilities and education links with *g* in Italian elders. *Learning and Individual Differences, 37,* 276–282. doi:10.1016/j.lindif.2014.10.020

Torgersen, S. (2012). Epidemiology. In T. A. Widiger (Ed.), *The Oxford handbook of personality disorders* (pp. 186–205). Oxford University Press.

Tormala, Z. L., Briñol, P., & Petty, R. E. (2007). Multiple roles for sources credibility under high elaboration: It's all in the timing. *Social Cognition, 25,* 536–552.

Torrence, B. S., & Connelly, S. (2019). Emotion regulation tendencies and leadership performance: An examination of cognitive and behavioral regulation strategies. *Frontiers in Psychology, 10,* 1486. doi:10.3389/fpsyg.2019.01486

Torres, L., Driscoll, M. W., & Voell, M. (2012). Discrimination, acculturation, acculturative stress, and Latino psychological distress: A moderated mediational model.

Cultural Diversity and Ethnic Minority Psychology, 18, 17–25.

Torrey, E. F., Buka, S., Cannon, T. D., Goldstein, J. M., Seidman, L. J., Liu, T., . . . Yolken, R. H. (2009). Paternal age as a risk factor for schizophrenia: How important is it? *Schizophrenia Research, 114,* 1–5.

Tozios, C. J. I., & Fukuda, K. (2020). Indirect, but not direct, down-regulation of visual long-term memory encoding through strategic biasing of attentional allocation. *Journal of Experimental Psychology: General, 149*(7), 1294–1310. https://doi.org/10.1037/xge0000712

Traeen, B., Štulhofer, A., Jurin, T., & Hald, G. M. (2018). Seventy-five years old and still going strong: Stability and change in sexual interest and sexual enjoyment in elderly men and women across Europe. *International Journal of Sexual Health, 30*(4), 323-336. https://doi.org/10.1080/19317611.2018.1472704

Trace, S. E., Baker, J. H., Penas-Lledo, E., & Bulik, C. M. (2013). The genetics of eating disorders. *Annual Review of Clinical Psychology, 9,* 589–620. doi:10.1146/annurev-clinpsy-050212-185546

Trafimow, D., Armendariz, M. L., & Madsen, L. (2004). A test of whether attributions provide for self-enhancement or self-defense. *Journal of Social Psychology, 144,* 453–463.

Tramoni, E., Felician, O., Barbeau, E. J., Guedi, E., Guye, M., Bartolemei, F., . . . Ceccaldi, M. (2011). Long-term consolidation of declarative memory: Insight from temporal epilepsy. *Brain, 134,* 816–831.

Tremblay, R. E., Schaal, B., Boulerice, B., Arseneault, L., Soussignan, R. G., Paquette, D., . . . Laurent, D. (1998). Testosterone, physical aggression, dominance, and physical development in early adolescence. *International Journal of Behavioral Development, 22,* 753–777.

Triandis, H. C. (1994). *Culture and social behavior.* McGraw-Hill.

Triplett, N. (1898). The dynamogenic factors in pacemaking and competition. *American Journal of Psychology, 9,* 507–533.

Tripp, A., Kota, R. S., Lewis, D. A., & Sibille, E. (2011). Reduced somatostatin in subgenual anterior cingulate cortex in major depression. *Neurobiology of Disease, 42,* 116–124.

Troisi, J. R., II. (2003). Spontaneous recovery during, but not following, extinction of the discriminative stimulus effects of nicotine in rats: Reinstatement of stimulus control. *The Psychological Record, 53,* 579–592.

Troy, A. S., Wilhelm, F. H., Shallcross, A. J., & Mauss, I. B. (2010). Seeing the silver lining: Cognitive reappraisal ability moderates the relationship between stress and depressive symptoms. *Emotion, 10,* 783–795.

Troy, A. S., Shallcross, A. J., & Mauss, I. B. (2013). A person-by-situation approach to emotion regulation: Cognitive reappraisal can either help or hurt, depending on the context. *Psychological Science, 24,* 2505–2514.

Trzepacz, P. T., Yu, P., Bhamidipati, P. K., Willis, B., Forrester, T., Tabas, L., . . . Saykin, A. J. (2013). Frontolimbic atrophy is associated with agitation and aggression in mild cognitive impairment and Alzheimer's disease. *Alzheimer's & Dementia, 9*(5, Suppl), S95–S104. doi:10.1016/j.jalz.2012.10.005

Tucker, M. A., & Fishbein, W. (2009). The impact of sleep duration and subject intelligence on declarative and motor memory performance: How much is enough? *Journal of Sleep Research, 18,* 304–312.

Tucker-Drob, E. M., Briley, D. A., & Harden, K. P. (2013). Genetic and environmental influences on cognition across development and context. *Current Directions in Psychological Science, 22,* 349–355.

Tuerk, P. W., Yoder, M., Ruggiero, K. J., Gros, D. F., & Acierno, R. (2010). A pilot study of prolonged exposure therapy for posttraumatic stress disorder delivered via telehealth technology. *Journal of Traumatic Stress, 23,* 116–123.

Tullett, A. M., Teper, R., & Inzlicht, M. (2011). Confronting threats to meaning: A new framework for understanding responses to unsettling events. *Perspectives on Psychological Science, 6,* 447–453.

Tulving, E. (1972). Episodic and semantic memory. In E. Tulving & W. Donaldson (Eds.), *Organisation of memory* (pp. 381–403). Academic Press.

Tulving, E. (1974). Cue-dependent forgetting. *American Scientist, 62,* 74–82.

Tulving, E. (1983). *Elements of episodic memory.* Oxford University Press.

Turanovic, J. J., Pratt, T. C., & Piquero, A. R. (2017). Exposure to fetal testosterone, aggression, and violent behavior: A meta-analysis of the 2d:4d digit ratio. *Aggression and Violent Behavior, 33, 51–61.* doi:10.1016/j.avb.2017.01.008

Turati, C. (2004). Why faces are not special to newborns: An alternative account of the face preference. *Current Directions in Psychological Science, 13,* 5–8.

Turner, A. J., & Ortony, A. (1992). Basic emotions: Can conflicting criteria converge? *Psychological Review, 99,* 566–571.

Turner, H., Marshall, E., Wood, F., Stopa, L., & Waller, G. (2016). CBT for eating disorders: The impact of early changes in eating pathology on later changes in personality pathology, anxiety, and depression. *Behaviour Research & Therapy, 77,* 1–6.

Turner, M. J. (2016). Rational emotive behavior therapy (REBT), irrational and rational beliefs, and the mental health of athletes. *Frontiers in Psychology, 7,* 1423.

Tuyakova, U. Zh., Baizhumanova, B., & Alekeshova, L. B. (2020). Development of emotional intelligence among future social teachers using interactive educational technologies. *Talent Development & Excellence, 12*(1), 970–983.

Tversky, A., & Kahneman, D. (1974). Judgment under uncertainty: Heuristics and biases, *Science, 185,* 1124–1131.

Tversky, A., & Kahneman, D. (1980). Causal schemas in judgments under uncertainty. In M. Fishbein (Ed.), *Progress in social psychology* (pp. 49–72). Erlbaum.

Tversky, A., & Kahneman, D. (2004). The framing of decisions and the psychology of choice. In D. A. Balota & E. J. Marsh (Eds.), *Cognitive psychology: Key readings* (pp. 621–630). Psychology Press.

Twenge, J. M. (2009). Change over time in obedience: The jury's still out, but it might be decreasing. *American Psychologist, 64,* 28–31.

Twenge, J. M. (2017). *iGen: Why today's super-connected kids are growing up less rebellious, more tolerant, less happy – and completely unprepared for adulthood.* ATRIA Books.

Twenge, J. M. (2019). More time on technology, less happiness? Associations between digital-media use and psychological well-being. *Current Directions in Psychological Science, 28*(4), 372–379.

Tyson, H. L., & Kaplowitz, S. A. (1977). Attitudinal conformity and anonymity. *Public Opinion Quarterly, 41*(2), 226–234. doi:10.1086/268377

U.S. Census Bureau. (2010). *Current Population Survey, 2009. Annual Social and Economic Supplement.* U.S. Department of Commerce.

U.S. Census Bureau. (2012). U.S. Census Bureau projections show a slower growing, older, more diverse nation a half century from now. *U.S. Census Bureau Newsroom.* https://www.census.gov/newsroom/releases/archives/population/cb12-243.html

U.S. Census Bureau. (2015). *American community survey data on families and living arrangements: 2015: Adults (A table series).* U.S. Department of Commerce.

U.S. Census Bureau. (2018). *Current Population Survey, 2018. Annual Social and Economic Supplement.* U.S. Department of Commerce.

U.S. Department of Energy. (2007). The Human Genome Project information. http://www.ornl.gov/hgmis

U.S. Department of Health and Human Services. (2014). *The Health Consequences of Smoking—50 Years of Progress: A Report of the Surgeon General.* Centers for Disease Control and Prevention.

U.S. Department of Housing and Urban Development. (2012). Annual report on fair housing. https://www.hud.gov/sites/documents/2012-13ANNREPORT.PDF.

U.S. Department of Housing and Urban Development. (2017). Office of fair housing and equal opportunity annual report to congress. https://www.hud.gov/sites/dfiles/FHEO/images/FHEO_Annual_Report_2017-508c.pdf

U.S. Department of Veterans Affairs. (2019). *2019 National Veteran Suicide Prevention Annual Report.* Author.

U.S. Service Animals. (2020). *Emotional support cats: Benefits and how to register your cat.* https://usserviceanimals.org/blog/emotional-support-cats/#:~:text=Unfortunately%2C%20cats%20cannot%20be%20recognized,registered%20as%20emotional%20support%20animals.

Uchino, B. N. (2009). Understanding the links between social support and physical health: A life-span perspective with emphasis on the separability of perceived and received support. *Perspectives on Psychological Science, 4,* 236–255.

Udo, T., & Grilo, C. M. (2018). Prevalence and correlates of *DSM-5*–defined eating disorders in a nationally representative sample of U.S. adults. *Biological Psychiatry, 84*(5), 345–354. https://doi.org/10.1016/j.biopsych.2018.03.014

Ultan, R. (1969). Some general characteristics of interrogative systems. *Working Papers in Language Universals* (Stanford University), *1,* 41–63.

Umberson, D., Williams, K., Powers, D. A., Meichu, D. C., & Campbell, A. M. (2005). As good as it gets? A lifecourse perspective on marital quality. *Social Forces, 84,* 493–511.

Ünal, A., de Waard, D., Epstude, K., & Steg, L. (2013). Driving with music: Effects on arousal and performance. *Transportation Research Part F: Traffic Psychology and Behaviour, 21,* 52–65. doi:10.1016/j.trf.2013.09.004

UNICEF (United Nations Children's Fund). (2009). *State of the world's children*. Author.

Unsworth, N. (2017). Examining the dynamics of strategic search from long-term memory. *Journal of Memory and Language, 93,* 135–153. doi:10.1016/j.jml.2016.09.005

United Nations. (2017). *World Marriage Data 2017 (POP/DB/Marr/Rev2017)*. Department of Economic and Social Affairs, Population Division.

Updegraff, J. A., Silver, R. C., & Holman, E. A. (2008). Searching for and finding meaning in collective trauma: Results from a national longitudinal study of the 9/11 terrorist attacks. *Journal of Personality and Social Psychology, 95,* 709–722.

Ural, C., Belli, H., Akbudak, M., & Tabo, A. (2015). Childhood traumatic experiences, dissociative symptoms, and dissociative disorder comorbidity among patients with panic disorder: A preliminary study. *Journal of Trauma & Dissociation, 16,* 463–475.

Valensi, P., Doaré, L., Perret, G., Germack, R., Pariès, J., & Mesangeau, D. (2003). Cardiovascular vagosympathetic activity in rats with ventromedial hypothalamic obesity. *Obesity Research, 11,* 54–64.

Valenzuela, M., & Sachdev, P. (2009). Can cognitive exercise prevent the onset of dementia? Systematic review of randomized clinical trials with longitudinal follow-up. *American Journal of Geriatric Psychiatry, 17,* 179–187.

Valkenburg, P. M. (2015). The limited informativeness of meta-analyses of media effects. *Perspectives on Psychological Science, 10*(5), 680–682. doi:10.1177/1745691615592237

Vallée-Tourangeau, F., & Vallée-Tourangeau, G. (2020). Mapping systemic resources in problem solving. *New Ideas in Psychology, 59,* 100812.

Valli, K., & Revonsuo, A. (2009). The threat simulation theory in light of recent empirical evidence: A review. *American Journal of Psychology, 122,* 17–38.

Van Apeldoorn, F. J., Timmerman, M. E., Mersch, P. P., van Hout, W. J., Visser, S., van Dyck, R., & den Boer, J. A. (2010). A randomized trial of cognitive-behavioral therapy or selective serotonin reuptake inhibitor or both combined for panic disorder with or without agoraphobia: Treatment results through 1-year follow-up. *Journal of Clinical Psychiatry, 71,* 574–586.

Van Dam, N. T., van Vugt, M. K., Vago, D. R., Schmalzl, L., Saron, C. D., Olendzki, A., ... Meyer, D. E. (2018). Mind the hype: A critical evaluation and prescriptive agenda for research on mindfulness and meditation. *Perspectives on Psychological Science, 13*(1), 36–61. doi:10.1177/1745691617709589

Van den Broeck, A., Ferris, D. L., Chang, C., & Rosen, C. C. (2016). A review of self-determination theory's basic psychological needs at work. *Journal of Management, 42*(5), 1195–1229. doi:10.1177/0149206316632058

Van den Bulck, J. (2003). Text messaging as a cause of sleep interruption in adolescents: Evidence from a cross-sectional study. *Journal of Sleep Research, 12,* 263.

Van den Bulck, J. (2007). Adolescent use of mobile phones for calling and for sending text messages after lights out: Results from a prospective cohort study with a one-year follow-up. *Sleep, 30,* 1220–1223.

Van den Bulck, J., Çetin, Y., Terzi, Ö., & Bushman, B. J. (2016). Violence, sex, and dreams: Violent and sexual media content infiltrate our dreams at night. *Dreaming, 26*(4), 271–279. doi:10.1037/drm0000036

van der Kloet, D., Merckelbach, H., Giesbrecht, T., & Lynn, S.J. (2012). Fragmented sleep, fragmented mind: The role of sleep in dissociative symptoms. *Perspectives on Psychological Science, 7,* 159–175.

van der Meer, A. L. H., & van der Weel, F. R. (Ruud). (2017). Only three fingers write, but the whole brain works: A high-density EEG study showing advantages of drawing over typing for learning. *Frontiers in Psychology, 8,* 706. doi: 10.3389/fpsyg.2017.00706

Van Der Vorst, H., Engels, R. C. M. E., Meeus, W., & Dekovic´, M. (2006). The impact of alcohol-specific rules, parental norms about early drinking and parental alcohol use on adolescents' drinking behavior. *Journal of Child Psychology and Psychiatry, 47,* 1299–1306. doi:10.1111/j.1469-7610.2006.01680.x

van Goozen, S., Frijda, N., & de Poll, N. V. (1994). Anger and aggression in women: Influence of sports choice and testosterone administration. *Aggressive Behavior, 20,* 213–222.

Van Heteren, C. F., Boekkooi, P. F., Jongsma, H. W., & Nijhuis, J. G. (2000). Fetal learning and memory. *Lancet, 356,* 9236–9237.

van Honk, J., & Schutter, D. J. (2007). Testosterone reduces conscious detection of signals serving social correction: Implications for antisocial behavior. *Psychological Science, 18,* 663–667.

van Hooren, S. A., Valentijn, A. M., Bosma, H., Ponds, R. W., van Boxtel, M. P., & Jolles, J. (2007). Cognitive functioning in healthy older adults aged 64–81: A cohort study into the effects of age, sex, and education. *Neuropsychology, Development, and Cognition, Section B: Aging, Neuropsychology, and Cognition, 14,* 40–54.

Van Horn, J. D., Irimia, A., Torgerson, C. M., Chambers, M. C., Kikinis, R., & Toga, A.W. (2012). Mapping connectivity damage in the case of Phineas Gage. *PLoS One, 7*(5), e37454. doi:10.1371/journal.pone.0037454

van Ijzendoorn, M. H., & Sagi-Schwartz, A. (2008). Cross-cultural patterns of attachment: Universal and contextual dimensions. In J. Cassidy & P.R. Shaver (Eds.), *Handbook of attachment: Theory, research and clinical applications* (2nd ed., pp. 880–905). Guilford Press.

van Laar, M., Volkerts, E., & Verbaten, M. (2001). Subcronic effects of the GABA-agonist lorazepam and the 5-HT2A/2C antagonist ritanserin on driving performance, slow wave sleep and daytime sleepiness in healthy volunteers. *Psychopharmacology, 154,* 189–197.

van Solinge, H., & Henkens, K. (2005). Couples' adjustment to retirement: A multi-actor panel study. *Journals of Gerontology, Series B: Psychological Sciences and Social Sciences, 60,* S11–S20.

Vance, E. B., & Wagner, N. N. (1976). Written descriptions of orgasms: A study of sex differences. *Archives of Sexual Behavior, 5,* 87–98.

VandeVusse, L., Irland, J., Berner, M. A., Fuller, S., & Adams, D. (2007). Hypnosis for childbirth: A retrospective comparative analysis of outcomes in one obstetrician's practice. *American Journal of Clinical Hypnosis, 50,* 109–119.

Vandrey, R. G., Budney, A. J., Hughes, J. R., & Liguori, A. (2008). A within-subject comparison of withdrawal symptoms during abstinence from cannabis, tobacco, and both substances. *Drug and Alcohol Dependence, 92,* 48–54.

Vanini, G., & Baghdoyan, H. A. (2013). Extrasynaptic GABAA receptors in rat pontine reticular formation increase wakefulness. *Sleep: Journal of Sleep and Sleep Disorders Research, 36,* 337–343.

vanReekum, C., Johnstone, T., Etter, A., Wehrle, T., & Scherer, K. (2004). Psychophysiological response to appraisal dimensions in a computer game. *Cognition and Emotion, 18,* 663–688.

Vartanian, O., Martindale, C., & Kwiatkowski, J. (2003). Creativity and inductive reasoning: The relationship between divergent thinking and performance on Wason's 2-4-6 task. *The Quarterly Journal of Experimental Psychology, 56A,* 641–655.

Varvogli, L., & Darviri, C. (2011). Stress management techniques: Evidence-based procedures that reduce stress and promote health. *Health Science Journal,* 5, 74–78.

Vasquez, M. J. (2007). Cultural difference and the therapeutic alliance: An evidence-based analysis. *American Psychologist, 62,* 875–885.

Vassallo, S., Cooper, S. L., & Douglas, J. M. (2009). Visual scanning in the recognition of facial affect: Is there an observer sex difference? *Journal of Vision, 9,* 1–10.

Velez, J. A., Mahood, C., Ewoldsen, D. R., & Moyer-Gusé, E. (2014). Ingroup versus outgroup conflict in the context of violent video game play: The effect of cooperation on increased helping and decreased aggression. *Communication Research, 41*(5), 607–626. doi:10.1177/0093650212456202

Ventura, J., Nuechterlein, K. H., Subotnik, K. L., Hardesty, J. P., & Mintz, J. (2000). Life events can trigger depressive exacerbation in the early course of schizophrenia. *Journal of Abnormal Psychology, 109,* 139–144.

Vezzali, L., & Capozza, D. (2011). Reducing explicit and implicit prejudice toward disabled colleagues: Effects of contact and membership salience in the workplace. *Life Span and Disability, 14*(2), 139–162.

Vigezzi, P., Guglielmino, L., Marzorati, P., Silenzio, R., De Chiara, M., Corrado, F., . . . Cozzolino, E. (2006). Multimodal drug addiction treatment: A field comparison of methadone and buprenorphine among heroin- and cocaine-dependent patients. *Journal of Substance Abuse and Treatment, 31,* 3–7.

Vignovic, J. A., & Thompson L. (2010). Computer-mediated cross-cultural collaboration: Attributing communication errors to the person versus the situation. *Journal of Applied Psychology, 95,* 265–276. doi:10.1037/a001862

Vilanova, F., Beria, F. M., Costa, Â. B., & Koller, S. H. (2017). Deindividuation: From le bon to the social identity model of deindividuation effects. *Cogent Psychology, 4*(1), 1308104. https://doi.org/10.1080/23311908.2017.1308104

Vilensky, J. A. (2014). The neglected cranial nerve: Nervus terminalis (cranial nerve N). *Clinical Anatomy (New York, N.Y.), 27*(1), 46–53. doi:10.1002/ca.22130

Vindegaard, N., & Benros, M. E. (2020). COVID-19 pandemic and mental health consequences: Systematic review of the current evidence. *Brain, Behavior, and Immunity,* S0889-1591(20)30954-5. Advance online publication. doi:10.1016/j.bbi.2020.05.048

Vitaliano, P. P., Young, H. M., & Zhang, J. (2004). Is caregiving a risk factor for illness? *Current Directions in Psychological Science, 13,* 13–16.

Vitinius, F., Tieden, S., Hellmich, M., Pfaff, H., Albus, C., & Ommen, O. (2018). Perceived psychotherapist's empathy and therapy motivation as determinants of long-term therapy success: Results of a cohort study of short term psychodynamic inpatient psychotherapy. *Frontiers in Psychiatry, 9*, 660. doi.org/10.3389/fpsyt.2018.00660

Volkow, N. D., Wang, G. J., Fowler, J. S., Leonido-Yee, M., Franceschi, D., Sedler, M. J., . . . Miller, E. N. (2001). Association of dopamine transporter reduction with psychomotor impairment in methamphetamine abusers. *American Journal of Psychiatry, 158*, 377–382.

Volterra, A., & Steinhauser, C. (2004). Glial modulation of synaptic transmission in the hippocampus. *Glia, 47*, 249–257.

von Allmen, D., Wurmitzer, K., Martin, E., & Klaver, P. (2013). Neural activity in the hippocampus predicts individual visual short-term memory capacity. *Hippocampus, 23*, 606–615.

von Allmen, D. Y., Wurmitzer, K., & Klaver, P. (2014). Hippocampal and posterior parietal contributions to developmental increases in visual short-term memory capacity. *Cortex: A Journal Devoted to the Study of the Nervous System and Behavior, 59*, 95–102. doi:10.1016/j.cortex.2014.07.010

von Gontard, A., Schaumburg, H., Hollmann, E., Eiberg, H., & Rittig, S. (2001). The genetics of enuresis: A review. *Journal of Urology, 166*, 2438–2443.

Voorspoels, W., Vanpaemel, W., & Storms, G. (2008). Exemplars and prototypes in natural language concepts: A typicality-based evaluation. *Psychonomic Bulletin & Review, 15*, 630–637.

Voorspoels, W., Vanpaemel, W., & Storms, G. (2011). A formal ideal-based account of typicality. *Psychonomic Bulletin & Review, 18*, 1006–1014. doi:10.3758/s13423-011-0122-9

Voss, J. L., Federmeier, K. D., & Paller, K. A. (2012). The potato chip really does look like Elvis! Neural hallmarks of conceptual processing associated with finding novel shapes subjectively meaningful. *Cerebral Cortex, 22*, 2354–2364.

Vrshek-Schallhorn, S., Mineka, S., Zinbarg, R. E., Craske, M. G., Griffith, J. W., Sutton, J., . . . Adam, E. K.. (2014). Refining the candidate environment: Interpersonal stress, the serotonin transporter polymorphism, and gene-environment interactions in major depression. *Clinical Psychological Science, 2*, 235–248.

Vukasovic, T., & Bratko, D. (2015). Heritability of personality: A meta-analysis of behavior genetic studies. *Psychological Bulletin, 141*, 769–785.

Vyas, S., Rodrigues, A. J., Silva, J. M., Tronche, F., Almeida, O. F. X., Sousa, N., & Sotiropoulos, I. (2016). Chronic stress and glucocorticoids: From neuronal plasticity to neurodegeneration. *Neural Plasticity, 2016*, 6391686. doi:10.1155/2016/6391686

Vygotsky, L. S. (1978). *Mind in society: The development of higher mental process*. Harvard University Press.

Vygotsky, L. S. (1986). *Thought and language*. MIT Press.

Vygotsky, L. S. (1987). Thinking and speech. In R. W. Reiber & A. S. Carton (Eds.), *The collected works of L. S. Vygotsky: Vol. 11. Problems of general psychology* (pp. 37–285). Plenum Press. (Original work published in 1934)

Vytal, K., & Hamann, S. (2010). Neuroimaging support for discrete neural correlates of basic emotions: A voxel-based meta-analysis. *Journal of Cognitive Neuroscience, 22*, 2864–2885. doi:10.1162/jocn.2009.21366

Wadden, T. A., & Stunkard, A. J. (1987). Psychopathology and obesity. *Annals of the New York Academy of Sciences, 499*, 55–65.

Wade, N. J. (2010). Granit's retina. *Cortex: A Journal Devoted to the Study of the Nervous System and Behavior, 46*, 1070–1071.

Wade, T. D. (2007). Epidemiology of eating disorders: Creating opportunities to move the current classification paradigm forward. *International Journal of Eating Disorders, 40*, s27–s30.

Wadhera, D., Capaldi Phillips, E. D., & Wilkie, L. M. (2015). Teaching children to like and eat vegetables. *Appetite, 93*, 75–84. doi:10.1016/j.appet.2015.06.016

Wagner, A. F., & Vitousek, K. M. (2019). Personality variables and eating pathology. *Psychiatric Clinics of North America, 42*(1), 105–119. https://doi.org/10.1016/j.psc.2018.10.012

Wagner, D., Tkotz, S., Koester, P., Becker, B., Gouzoulis-Mayfrank, E., & Daumann, J. (2015). Learning, memory, and executive function in new MDMA users: A 2-year follow-up study. *Frontiers in Neuroscience, 9*, 445. doi:10.3389/fnins.2015.00445

Wagner, G. C., Beuving, L. J., & Hutchinson, R. R. (1980). The effects of gonadal hormone manipulations on aggressive target-biting in mice. *Aggressive Behavior, 6*, 1–7.

Wagner, M. F., Skowronski, John. J., Milner, J. S., Crouch, J. L., & Ammar, J. (2020). Exploring positive classical conditioning procedure effects on evaluations of children, thoughts about children, and behaviors toward children: Two experiments. *Psychological Reports, 123*(5), 1753–1784. https://doi.org/10.1177/0033294119894231

Walak, J., Szczepanik, M., Woszczak, M., & Józefowicz-Korczyn'ska, M. (2013). Impact of physiotherapy on quality of life improvement in patients with central vestibular system dysfunction [Abstract]. *Otolaryngol Polska, 67*, 11–17. doi:10.1016/j.otpol.2012.09.001

Walder, D. J., Faraone, S. V., Glatt, S. J., Tsuang, M. T., & Seidman, L. J. (2014). Genetic liability, prenatal health, stress, and family environment: Risk factors in the Harvard Adolescent Family High Risk for Schizophrenia study. *Schizophrenia Research, 157*, 142–148.

Waldinger, R. J., & Schulz, M. S. (2016). The long reach of nurturing family environments: Links with midlife emotion-regulatory styles and late-life security in intimate relationships. *Psychological Science, 27*, 1443–1450.

Waldron-Hennessey, R., & Sabatelli, R. M. (1997). The parental comparison level index: A measure for assessing parental rewards and costs relative to expectations. *Journal of Marriage and Family, 59*, 824–833.

Walker, B. R., Diefenbach, K. S., & Parikh, T. N. (2007). Inhibition within the nucleus tractus solitarius (NTS) ameliorates environmental exploration deficits due to cerebellum lesions in an animal model for autism. *Behavioural Brain Research, 176*, 109–120.

Walker, E., Shapiro, D., Esterberg, M., & Trotman, H. (2010). Neurodevelopment and schizophrenia: Broadening the focus. *Current Directions in Psychological Science, 19*, 204–208.

Walker, L. J (1995). Sexism in Kohlberg's moral psychology? In W. M. Kurtines & J. L. Gewirtz (Eds.), *Moral development: An introduction* (pp. 83–107). Allyn & Bacon.

Walker, L. J., & Taylor, J. H. (1991). Stage transitions in moral reasoning: A longitudinal study of developmental processes. *Developmental Psychology, 27*, 330–337.

Walker, M. P., & van der Helm, E. (2009). Overnight therapy? The role of sleep in emotional brain processing. *Psychological Bulletin, 135*, 731–748.

Wall, T. L., Luczak, S. E., & Hiller-Sturmhöfel, S. (2016) Biology, genetics, and environment: Underlying factors influencing alcohol metabolism. *Alcohol Research, 38*, 59–68.

Wallace, J., Schneider, T., & McGuffin, P. (2002). Genetics of depression. In I. H. Gotlib & C. L. Hammen (Eds.), *Handbook of depression* (pp. 169–191). Guilford Press.

Waller, R., Gard, A. M., Shaw, D. S., Forbes, E. E., Neumann, C. S., & Hyde, L. W. (2019). Weakened functional connectivity between the amygdala and the ventromedial prefrontal cortex is longitudinally related to psychopathic traits in low-income males during early adulthood. *Clinical Psychological Science, 7*(3), 628–635.

Wallis, C. (2005, January 9). The new science of happiness. *Time*. http://content.time.com/time/magazine/article/0,9171,1015832-1,00.html

Walster, E., Aronson, E., Abrahams, D., & Rottman L. (1966). Importance of physical attractiveness in dating behavior. *Journal of Personality and Social Psychology, 4*, 508–516.

Walters, S. T , Foy, B. D., & Castro, R. J. (2003). The agony of Ecstasy: Responding to growing MDMA use among college students. *Journal of American College Health, 51*, 139–141.

Wamsley, E. J. (2014). Dreaming and offline memory consolidation. *Current Neurology and Neuroscience Reports, 14*, 433.

Wang, D., Waldman, D. A., & Zhang, Z. (2014). A meta-analysis of shared leadership and team effectiveness. *The Journal of Applied Psychology, 99*(2), 181–198. doi:10.1037/a0034531

Wang, J., Korczykowski, M., Rao, H., Fan, Y., Pluta, J., Gur, R. C., . . . Detre, J. A. (2007). Gender difference in neural response to psychological stress. *Social Cognitive and Affective Neuroscience, 2*, 227–239.

Wang, S. H., Baillargeon, R., & Brueckner, L. (2004). Young infants' reasoning about hidden objects: Evidence from violation-of-expectation tasks with test trials only. *Cognition, 93*, 167–198.

Wang, W., & Parker, K. (2014). *Record share of Americans have never married: As values, economics and gender patterns change*. Pew Research Center.

Wang, Y., Nelson, L. D., LaRoche, A. A., Pfaller, A. Y., Nencka, A. S., Koch, K. M., & McCrea, M. A. (2016). Cerebral blood flow alterations in acute sport-related concussion. *Journal of Neurotrauma, 33*(13), 1227–1236. doi:10.1089/neu.2015.4072

Wanic, R., & Kulik, J. (2011). Toward an understanding of gender differences in the impact of marital conflict on health. *Sex Roles, 65*, 297–312.

Wanner, H. E (1968). *On remembering, forgetting, and understanding sentences: A study of the deep structure hypothesis*. Unpublished doctoral dissertation, Harvard University.

Warburton, D. M. (1995). Effects of caffeine on cognition and mood without caffeine abstinence. *Psychopharmacology, 119,* 66–70.

Ward, E. V., Berry, C. J., & Shanks, D. R. (2013). Age effects on explicit and implicit memory. *Frontiers in Psychology, 4,* 1–11. doi:10.3389/fpsyg.2013.00639

Wardenaar, K. J., Lim, C., Al-Hamzawi, A. O., Alonso, J., Andrade, L. H., Benjet, C., … de Jonge, P. (2017). The cross-national epidemiology of specific phobia in the World Mental Health Surveys. *Psychological Medicine, 47*(10), 1744–1760. doi:10.1017/S0033291717000174

Ware, A., & Kowalski, G. S. (2012). Sex identification and love of sports: BIRGing and CORFing among sport fans. *Journal of Sport Behavior, 35*(2), 223–237.

Warner, R., & Steel, B. (1999). Child rearing as a mechanism for social change: The relationship of child gender to parents' commitment to gender equity. *Gender and Society, 13,* 503–517.

Waschbusch, D. A., Sellers, D. P., LeBlanc, M., & Kelley, M. L. (2003). Helpless attributions and depression in adolescents: The roles of anxiety, event valence, and demographics. *Journal of Adolescence, 26,* 169–183.

Wasike, B. (2017). Persuasion in 140 characters: Testing issue framing, persuasion and credibility via Twitter and online news articles in the gun control debate. *Computers in Human Behavior, 66,* 179–190. doi:10.1016/j.chb.2016.09.037

Wasserman, E. A., & Miller, R. R. (1997). What's elementary about associative learning? *Annual Review of Psychology, 48,* 573–607.

Wasserman, G. S. (1978). *Color vision: An historical introduction.* Wiley.

Watson, J. B., & Rayner, R. (1920). Conditioned emotional reactions. *Journal of Experimental Psychology, 3,* 1–14.

Watson, J. C., Schein, J., & McMullen, E. (2010). An examination of clients' in-session changes and their relationship to the working alliance and outcome. *Psychotherapy Research, 20,* 224–233.

Watts, B. V., Schnurr, P. P., Mayo, L., Young-Xu, Y., Weeks, W. B., & Friedman, M. J. (2013). Meta-analysis of the efficacy of treatments for posttraumatic stress disorder. *Journal of Clinical Psychiatry, 74,* e541–e550.

Waytz, A., & Gray, K. (2018). Does online technology make us more or less sociable? A preliminary review and call for research. *Perspectives on Psychological Science, 13*(4), 473–491.

Weaver, A. J., Zelenkauskaite, A., & Samson, L. (2012). The (non)violent world of YouTube: Content trends in web video. *Journal of Communication, 62,* 1065–1083. doi:10.1111/j.1460-2466.2012.01675.x

Weaver, J. M., & Schofield, T. J. (2015). Mediation and moderation of divorce effects on children's behavior problems. *Journal of Family Psychology, 29*(1), 39–48. doi:10.1037/fam0000043

Weaver, R., Ferguson, C., Wilbourn, M., & Salamonson, Y. (2014). Men in nursing on television: Exposing and reinforcing stereotypes. *Journal of Advanced Nursing, 70,* 833–842.

Webb, W. B. (1983). Theories in modern sleep research. In A. Mayes (Ed.), *Sleep mechanisms and functions* (pp. 1–17). Van Nostrand Reinhold.

Webermann, A. R., Myrick, A. C., Taylor, C. L., Chasson, G. S., & Brand, B. L. (2016). Dissociative, depressive, and PTSD symptom severity as correlates of nonsuicidal self-injury and suicidality in dissociative disorder patients. *Journal of Trauma & Dissociation, 17,* 67–80.

Webster Marketon, J. I., & Glaser, R. (2008). Stress hormones and immune function. *Cellular Immunology, 252,* 16–26.

Wechsler, D. (1939). *The measurement of adult intelligence.* Williams & Wilkins.

Wechsler, T. F., Kümpers, F., & Mühlberger, A. (2019). Inferiority or even superiority of virtual reality exposure therapy in phobias? A systematic review and quantitative meta-analysis on randomized controlled trials specifically comparing the efficacy of virtual reality exposure to gold standard in vivo exposure in agoraphobia, specific phobia, and social phobia. *Frontiers in Psychology, 10,* 1758. doi:10.3389/fpsyg.2019.01758

Weener, E. F. (2012) *Personal flying: How safe do you want to be?* http://www.ntsb.gov/news/press_releases.html

Weersing, V. R., Jeffreys, M., Do, M. T., Schwartz, K. T., & Bolano, C. (2017). Evidence base update of psychosocial treatments for child and adolescent depression. *Journal of Clinical Child and Adolescent Psychology, 46*(1), 11–43. doi:10.1080/15374416.2016.1220310

Wegener, D. T., & Carlston, D. E. (2005). Cognitive processes in attitude formation and change. In D. Albarracín, B. T. Johnson, & M. P. Zanna (Eds.), *Handbook of attitudes* (pp. 493–542). Erlbaum.

Wehmann, E., Köhnen, M., Härter, M., & Liebherz, S. (2020). Therapeutic alliance in technology-based interventions for the treatment of depression: Systematic review. *Journal of Medical Internet Research, 22*(6), e17195. doi:10.2196/17195

Wei, L., Duan, X., Zheng, C., Wang, S., Gao, Q., Zhang, Z., . . . Chen, H. (2014). Specific frequency bands of amplitude low-frequency oscillation encodes personality. *Human Brain Mapping, 35,* 331–339.

Weidner, R., Plewan, T., Chen, Q., Buchner, A., Weiss, P. H., & Fink, G. R. (2014). The moon illusion and size-distance scaling—evidence for shared neural patterns. *Journal of Cognitive Neuroscience, 26*(8), 1871–1882. doi:10.1162/jocn_a_00590

Weiland, B. J., Thayer, R. E., Depue, B. E., Sabbineni, A., Bryan, A. D., & Hutchison, K. E. (2015). Daily marijuana use is not associated with brain morphometric measures in adolescents or adults. *The Journal of Neuroscience, 35,* 1505–1512. doi:10 1523/JNEUROSCI.2946-14.2015

Weisberg, Y. J., DeYoung, C. G., & Hirsh, J. B. (2011). Gender differences in personality across the ten aspects of the Big Five. *Frontiers in Psychology, 2,* 178.

Weiss, A., Bates, T. C., & Luciano, M. (2008). Happiness is a personal(ity) thing: The genetics of personality and well-being in a representative sample. *Psychological Science, 19*(3), 205–210.

Weiss, A., Staes, N., Pereboom, J. J. M., Inoue-Murayama, M., Stevens, J. M. G., & Eens, M. (2015). Personality in bonobos. *Psychological Science, 26,* 1430–1439.

Weissman, M. M., Bland, R. C., Canino, G. J., Greenwald, S., Hwu, H. G., Joyce, P. R., . . . Yeh, E. K. (1999). Prevalence of suicide ideation and suicide attempts in nine countries. *Psychological Medicine, 29,* 9–17.

Welch, S. S. (2001). A review of the literature on the epidemiology of parasuicide in the general population. *Psychiatric Services, 52,* 368–375.

Welford, A. T. (1987). Ageing. In R. L. Gregory (Ed.), *The Oxford companion to the mind* (pp. 13–14). Oxford University Press.

Wellman, H. M., Cross, D., & Watson, J. (2001). Meta-analysis of theory of mind development: The truth about false-belief. *Child Development, 72,* 655–684.

Wells, D. L., & Ott, C. A. (2011). The "new" marijuana. *Annals of Pharmacotherapy, 45,* 414–417.

Wells, G. L., & Olson, E. A. (2003). Eyewitness testimony. *Annual Review of Psychology, 54,* 277–295.

Wertheimer, M. (1923). Principles of perceptual organization (Abridged trans. by M. Wertheimer). In D. S. Beardslee & M. Wertheimer (Eds.), *Readings in perception* (pp. 115–137). Van Nostrand-Reinhold. (Original work published 1923, *Psychologische Forschung, 41,* 301–350)

West, M. R., Buckley, K., Krachman, S. B., & Bookman, N. (2018). Development and implementation of student social-emotional surveys in the CORE districts. *Journal of Applied Developmental Psychology, 55,* 119–129. https://doi.org/10.1016/j.appdev.2017.06.001

West, S. G. (2009). Alternatives to randomized experiments. *Current Directions in Psychological Science, 18,* 299–304.

Westen, D., & Bradley, R. (2005). Empirically supported complexity: Rethinking evidence-based practice in psychotherapy. *Current Directions in Psychological Science, 14,* 266–271.

Westermeyer, J. F. (2004). Predictors and characteristics of Erikson's life cycle model among men: A 32-year longitudinal study. *International Journal of Aging and Human Development, 58,* 29–48.

Wetter, D. W., Cofta-Gunn, L., Fouladi, R. T., Irvin, J. E., Daza, P., Mazas, C., . . . Gritz, E. R. (2005). Understanding the association among education, employment characteristics, and smoking. *Addictive Behaviors, 30,* 905–914.

Wever, E. G. (1970). *Theory of hearing.* Wiley. (Original work published in 1949)

Weyant, J. M. (1996). Application of compliance techniques to direct-mail requests for charitable donations. *Psychology and Marketing, 13,* 157–170.

Wheeler, D. S., & Miller, R. R. (2008). Determinants of cue interactions. *Behavioral Processes, 78,* 191–203.

Wheeler, M. A., Stuss, D. T., & Tulving, E. (1997). Toward a theory of episodic memory: The frontal lobes and autonoetic consciousness. *Psychological Bulletin, 121,* 331–354.

Whitbourne, S. K. (1996). *The aging individual.* Springer.

Whitbourne, S. K. (2001). The physical aging process in midlife: Interactions with psychological and sociocultural factors. In M. E. Lachman (Ed.), *Handbook of midlife development* (pp. 109–155). Wiley.

White, L. K., & Edwards, J. N. (1990). Emptying the nest and parental well-being: An analysis of national panel data. *American Sociological Review, 55,* 235–242.

White, T. M., Gibbons, M. B., & Schamberger, M. (2006). Cultural sensitivity and supportive expressive psychotherapy: An integrative approach to treatment. *American Journal of Psychotherapy, 60,* 299–316.

Whiteford, H. A., Ferrari, A. J., Degenhardt, L., Feigin, V., & Vos, T. (2015). The global burden of mental, neurological and substance use disorders: An analysis from the Global Burden of Disease Study 2010. *PLoS ONE, 10,* e0116820.

Whitton, S. W., & Whisman, M. A. (2010). Relationship satisfaction instability and depression. *Journal of Family Psychology, 24,* 791–794.

Whorf, B. L. (1956). *Language, thought, and reality: Selected writings of Benjamin Lee Whorf.* Wiley.

Wicherski, M., Michalski, D., & Kohout, J. (2009). *2007 Doctorate employment survey.* American Psychological Association.

Wickelgren, I. (1997). Marijuana: Harder than thought? *Science, 276,* 1967–1968.

Widiger, T. A., & Chaynes, K. (2003). Current issues in the assessment of personality disorders. *Current Psychiatry Reports, 5,* 28–35.

Widiger, T. A., & Trull, T. J. (2007). Plate tectonics in the classification of personality disorder: Shifting to a dimensional model. *American Psychologist, 62,* 71–83.

Wiebe, S. A., Johnson, S. M., Lafontaine, M. F., Burgess Moser, M., Dalgleish, T. L., & Tasca, G. A. (2017). Two-year follow-up outcomes in emotionally focused couple therapy: An investigation of relationship satisfaction and attachment trajectories. *Journal of Marital and Family Therapy, 43,* 227–244.

Wiechman Askay, S. & Patterson, D.R. (2007). Hypnotic analgesia. *Expert Review of Neuraltherapeutics, 7,* 1675-1683.

Wiggins, J. S. (1997). In defense of traits. In R. Hogan, J. Johnson, & S. Briggs (Eds.), *Handbook of personality psychology* (pp. 97–115). Academic Press.

Wijdicks, E. F. M., Atkinson, J. L. D., & Okazaki, H. (2001). Isolated medulla oblongata function after severe traumatic brain injury. *Journal of Neurology, Neurosurgery, and Psychiatry, 70,* 127.

Wikipedia (2019). List of dramatic television series with LGBT characters: 2010's. https://en.wikipedia.org/wiki/List_of_dramatic_television_series_with_LGBT_characters:_2010s

Wild, K., Scholz, M., Ropohl, A., Bräuer, L., Paulsen, F., & Burger, P. H. M. (2014). Strategies against burnout and anxiety in medical education—Implementation and evaluation of a new course on relaxation techniques (Relacs) for medical students. *PLoS ONE, 9,* e114967.

Wild, V., Graaf, C., & Jager, G. (2015). Efficacy of repeated exposure and flavour-flavour learning as mechanisms to increase preschooler's vegetable intake and acceptance. *Pediatric Obesity, 10*(3), 205–212.

Williams, J. A., Bartoshuk, L. M., Fillingim, R. B., & Dotson, C. D. (2016). Exploring ethnic differences in taste perception. *Chemical Senses, 41*(5), 449–456. doi:10.1093/chemse/bjw021

Williams, J. A., Zimmerman, F. J., & Bell J. F. (2013). Norms and trends of sleep time among U.S. children and adolescents. *Archives of Pediatric and Adolescent Medicine, 167,* 55–60. doi:10.1001/jamapediatrics.2013.423

Williams, J. M., & Galli, A. (2006). The dopamine transporter: A vigilant border control for psychostimulant action. *Handbook of Experimental Pharmacology, 175,* 215–232.

Williams, K. N., & Kemper, S. (2010). Interventions to reduce cognitive decline in aging. *Journal of Psychosocial Nursing and Mental Health Services, 48,* 1–10.

Williams, L. M., Sidis, A., Gordon, E., & Meares, R. A. (2006). "Missing links" in borderline personality disorder: Loss of neural synchrony relates to lack of emotion regulation and impulse control. *Journal of Psychiatry and Neuroscience, 31,* 181–188.

Williams, P. M., Goodie, J., & Motsinger, L. D. (2008). Treating eating disorders in primary care. *American Family Physician, 77,* 187–195.

Williams, S. E., Veldhuijzen van Zanten, J. J. C. S., Trotman, G. P., Quinton, M. L., & Ginty, A. T. (2017). Challenge and threat imagery manipulates heart rate and anxiety responses to stress. *International Journal of Psychophysiology, 117,* 111-118. doi:10.1016/j.ijpsycho.2017.04.011.

Wills, T. A., Pagano, I., Williams, R. J., & Tam, E. K. (2019). E-cigarette use and respiratory disorder in an adult sample. *Drug and Alcohol Dependence, 194,* 363–370. doi:10.1016/j.drugalcdep.2018.10.004

Wilson, G. T., Grilo, C. M., & Vitousek, K. M. (2007). Psychological treatment of eating disorders. *American Psychologist, 62,* 199–216.

Wilson, K. S., DeRue, D. S., Matta, F. K., Howe, M., & Conlon, D. E. (2016). Personality similarity in negotiations: Testing the dyadic effects of similarity in interpersonal traits and the use of emotional displays on negotiation outcomes. *Journal of Applied Psychology, 101*(10), 1405–1421. doi:10.1037/apl0000132

Wilson, N., Kariisa, M., Seth, P., Smith, H. IV, & Davis, N. L. (2020). Drug and opioid-involved overdose deaths — United States, 2017–2018. *Morbidity & Mortality Weekly Report, 69,* 290–297. doi:dx.doi.org/10.15585/mmwr.mm6911a4

Wilson, R. S., & Bennett, D. A. (2003). Cognitive activity and risk of Alzheimer's disease. *Current Directions in Psychological Science, 12,* 87–91.

Wiltink, J., Michal, M., Wild, P. S., Zwiener, I., Blettner, M., Münzel, T., . . . Beutel, M. E. (2013). Associations between depression and different measures of obesity (BMI, WC, WHtR, WHR). *BMC Psychiatry, 13,* 223. doi:10.1186/1471-244X-13-223

Winegard, B., Winegard, B., & Anomaly, J. (2020). Dodging Darwin: Race, evolution, and the hereditarian hypothesis. *Personality and Individual Differences, 160,* 109915. https://doi.org/10.1016/j.paid.2020.109915

Wingfield, A., & Kahana, M. J. (2002). The dynamics of memory retrieval in older adulthood. *Canadian Journal of Psychology, 56,* 187–199.

Winocur, G., Moscovitch, M., & Sekeres, M. J. (2013). Factors affecting graded and upgraded memory loss following hippocampal lesions. *Neurobiology of Learning and Memory, 106,* 351–364. doi:10.1016/j.nlm.2013.10.001

Winsper, C., Bilgin, A., Thompson, A., Marwaha, S., Chanen, A. M., Singh, S. P., Wang, A., & Furtado, V. (2020). The prevalence of personality disorders in the community: A global systematic review and meta-analysis. *The British Journal of Psychiatry: The Journal of Mental Science, 216*(2), 69–78. doi:10.1192/bjp.2019.166

Winsper, C., Marwaha, S., Lereya, S. T., Thompson, A., Eyden, J., & Singh, S. P. (2016). A systematic review of the neurobiological underpinnings of borderline personality disorder (BPD) in childhood and adolescence. *Reviews in the Neurosciences, 27,* 827–847.

Wirth, T., Ober, K., Prager, G., Vogelsang, M., Benson, S., Witzke, O., ... Schedlowski, M. (2011). Repeated recall of learned immunosuppression: Evidence from rats and men. *Brain, Behavior, and Immunity, 25*(7), 1444–1451. https://doi.org/10.1016/j.bbi.2011.05.011

Wise, S. M. (2000). *Rattling the cage: Toward legal rights for animals.* Perseus Books.

Wiseman, S., & Tulving, E. (1976). Encoding specificity: Relations between recall superiority and recognition failure. *Journal of Experimental Psychology: Human Learning and Memory, 2,* 349–361.

Witt, L. A., Kacmar, M., Carlson, D. S., & Zivnuska, S. (2002). Interactive effects of personality and organizational politics on contextual performance. *Journal of Organizational Behavior, 23,* 911–926.

Wittchen, H. U., Gloster, A.T., Beesdo-Baum, K., Fava, G., & Craske, M. G. (2010). Agoraphobia: A review of the diagnostic classificatory position and criteria. *Depression and Anxiety, 27,* 113–133.

Witzel, C. (2015). Commentary: An experimental study of gender and cultural differences in hue preference. *Frontiers in Psychology, 6,* 1840. doi:10.3389/fpsyg.2015.01840

Wolf, D. H., Gur, R. C., Valdez, J. N., Loughead, J., Elliott, M. A., Gur, R. E., & Ragland, J. D. (2007). Alterations of frontotemporal connectivity during word encoding in schizophrenia. *Psychiatry Research, 154,* 221–232.

Wolf, E. J., Miller, M. W., Reardon, A. F., Ryabchenko, K. A., Castillo, D., & Freund, R. (2012) A latent class analysis of dissociation and posttraumatic stress disorder: Evidence for a dissociative subtype. *Archives of General Psychiatry, 69,* 698–705.

Wolitzky, D. L. (1995). The theory and practice of traditional psychoanalytic psychotherapy. In A. S. Gurman & S. B. Messer (Eds.), *Essential psychotherapies* (pp. 12–54). Guilford.

Wolpe, J. (1958). *Psychotherapy by reciprocal inhibition.* Stanford University Press.

Woo, Y. S., Bahk, W. M., Jung, Y. E., Jeong, J. H., Lee, H. B., Won, S. H., . . . Min, K. J. (2014). One-year rehospitalization rates of patients with first-episode bipolar mania receiving lithium or valproate and adjunctive atypical antipsychotics. *Psychiatry and Clinical Neurosciences, 68*(6), 418-424.

Wood, E., Zivcakova, L., Gentile, P., Archer, K., De Pasquale, D., & Nosko, A. (2012). Examining the impact of off-task multitasking with technology on real-time classroom learning. *Computers & Education, 58*(1), 365–374. https://doi.org/10.1016/j.compedu.2011.08.029

Wood, J. V., Heimpel, S. A., Manwell, L. A., & Whittington, E. J. (2009). This mood is familiar and I don't deserve to feel better anyway: Mechanisms underlying self-esteem differences in motivation to repair sad moods. *Journal of Personality and Social Psychology, 96,* 363–380.

Woods, S. C. (2013). Metabolic signals and food intake. Forty years of progress. *Appetite, 71,* 440–444. doi:10.1016/j.appet.2013.08.016

Woods-Giscombé, C. L. (2010). Superwoman schema: African American women's beliefs on stress, strength, and health. *Qualitative Health Research, 20,* 668–683.

Woollett, K., Glensman, J., & Maguire, E. A. (2008). Non-spatial expertise and hippocampal gray matter volume in humans. *Hippocampus, 18,* 981–984.

Woollett, K., & Maguire, E. A. (2012). Exploring anterograde associative memory in London taxi drivers. *Neuroreport: For Rapid Communication of Neuroscience Research, 23,* 885–888. doi:10.1097/WNR.0b013e328359317e

World Health Organization (WHO). (2014). *Overweight (body mass index >=25) (age-standardized estimate) Data by country.* http://apps.who.int/gho/data/node.main.A897A?lang=en

World Health Organization (WHO). (2017). *Depression and Other Common Mental Disorders: Global Health Estimates.* Author. Licence: CC BY-NC-SA 3.0 IGO

World Health Organization (WHO). (2019). Health topics: Obesity. https://www.who.int/topics/obesity/en/.

World Health Organization (WHO). (2020). Coronavirus disease (COVID-19) advice for the public. https://www.who.int/emergencies/diseases/novel-coronavirus-2019/advice-for-public

Worthy, D. A., Gorlick, M. A., Pacheco, J. L., Schnyer, D. M., & Maddox, W. T. (2011). With age comes wisdom: Decision making in younger and older adults. *Psychological Science, 22,* 1375–1380.

Wozniak, J. D., Caudle, H. E., Harding, K., Vieselmeyer, J., & Mezulis, A. H. (2019). The effect of trauma proximity and ruminative response styles on posttraumatic stress and posttraumatic growth following a university shooting. *Psychological Trauma: Theory, Research, Practice, and Policy, 12*(3), 227–234. doi:10.1037/tra0000505.

Wright, K. P., Jr., Drake, A. L., Frey, D. J., Fleshner, M., Desouza, C. A., Gronfier, C., & Czeisler, C. G. (2015). Influence of sleep deprivation and circadian misalignment on cortisol, inflammatory markers, and cytokine balance. *Brain, Behavior, and Immunity, 47,* 24–34.

Wrightsman, L. S. (1994). *Adult personality development: Vol 1. Theories and concepts.* SAGE.

Wu, L., & Mo, L. (2011). Re-examining the classifying advantage and basic level effect. *Acta Psychologica Sinica, 43,* 143–151.

Wyman, M. F., Shiovitz-Ezra, S., & Parag, O. (2019). Ageism in informal care network members of older women. *International Psychogeriatrics, 31*(10), 1463–1472. https://doi.org/10.1017/S1041610218001977

Xie, J., Chen, J., & Wei, Q. (2013). Repetitive transcranial magnetic stimulation versus electroconvulsive therapy for major depression: A meta-analysis of stimulus parameter effects. *Neurological Research, 35,* 1084–1091.

Xie, T., Tong, L., McLane, M. W., Hatzidimitriou, G., Yuan, J., McCann, U., & Ricaurte, G. (2006). Loss of serotonin transporter protein after MDMA and other ring-substituted amphetamines. *Neuropsychopharmacology, 31,* 2639–2651.

Xiong, G. L., & Doraiswamy, P. M. (2009). Does meditation enhance cognition and brain plasticity? *Annals of the New York Academy of Sciences, 1172,* 63–69.

Xiong, Y., Mahmood, A., & Chopp, M. (2010). Neurorestorative treatments for traumatic brain injury. *Discovery Medicine, 10,* 434–442.

Xu, J., & Roberts, R. E. (2010). The power of positive emotions: It's a matter of life or death: Subjective well-being and longevity over 28 years in a general population. *Healthy Psychology, 29,* 9–19.

Xu, L., Sun, X., Lu, J., Tang, M., & Chen, J. D (2008). Effects of gastric electric stimulation on gastric distention responsive neurons and expressions of CCK in rodent hippocampus. *Obesity, 16,* 951–957.

Xu, Z., Shen, B., Taji, W., Sun, P., & Naya, Y. (2020). Convergence of distinct functional networks supporting naming and semantic recognition in the left inferior frontal gyrus. *Human Brain Mapping, 41*(9), 2389–2405. https://doi.org/10.1002/hbm.24953

Yackinous, C. A., & Guinard, J. (2002). Relation between PROP (6-n-propylthiouracil) taster status, taste anatomy and dietary intake measures for young men and women. *Appetite, 38,* 201–209.

Yalch, M. M., Hopwood, C. J., Fehon, D. C., & Grilo, C. M. (2014). The influence of borderline personality features on inpatient adolescent suicide risk. *Personality Disorders, 5,* 26–31.

Yalin, N., & Young, A. H. (2020). Pharmacological treatment of bipolar depression: What are the current and emerging options? *Neuropsychiatric Disease and Treatment, 16,* 1459–1472. doi:10.2147/NDT.S245166

Yalom, I. D. (1989). *Love's executioner and other tales of psychotherapy.* HarperCollins.

Yalom, I. D., & Leszcz, M. (2005). *The theory and practice of group psychotherapy* (5th ed.). Basic Books.

Yamagata, S., Suzuki, A., Ando, J., Ono, Y., Kijima, N., Yoshimura, K., . . . Jang, K. L. (2006). Is the genetic structure of human personality universal? A cross-cultural twin study from North America, Europe, and Asia. *Journal of Personality and Social Psychology, 90,* 987–998.

Yamawaki, R., Nakamura, K., Aso, T., Shigemune, Y., Fukuyama, H., & Tsukiura, T. (2017). Remembering my friends: Medial prefrontal and hippocampal contributions to the self-reference effect on face memories in a social context. *Human Brain Mapping, 38*(8), 4256–4269. https://doi.org/10.1002/hbm.23662

Yang, C. C., Wan, C. S., & Chiou, W. B. (2010). Dialectical thinking and creativity among young adults: A postformal operations perspective. *Psychological Reports, 106,* 79–92.

Yang, F. M., Grigorenko, A., Tommet, D., Farias, S. T., Mungas, D., Bennett, D. A., Jones, R. A., & Crane, P. K (2013). AD pathology and cerebral infarctions are associated with memory and executive functioning one and five years before death. *Journal of Clinical and Experimental Neuropsychology, 35,* 24–34. doi:10.1080/13803395.2012.740001

Yang, P. Y., Ho, K. H., Chen, H. C., & Chien, M. Y. (2012). Exercise training improves sleep quality in middle-aged and older adults with sleep problems: A systematic review. *Journal of Physiotherapy, 58,* 157–163.

Yao, M. Z., Mahood, C., & Linz, D. (2010). Sexual priming, gender stereotyping, and likelihood to sexually harass: Examining the cognitive effects of playing a sexually-explicit video game. *Sex Roles, 62,* 77–88.

Yardley, L., & Kirby, S. (2006). Evaluation of booklet-based self-management of symptoms in Ménière disease: A randomized controlled trial. *Psychosomatic Medicine, 68,* 762–769.

Yasui, M., Pottick, K. J., & Chen, Y. (2017). Conceptualizing culturally infused engagement and its measurement for ethnic minority and immigrant children and families. *Clinical Child and Family Psychology Review, 20*(3), 250–332. doi:10.1007/s10567-017-0229-2

Yasumoto, Y., Hashimoto, C., Nakao, R., Yamazaki, H., Hiroyama, H., Nemoto, T., . . . Oishi, K. (2016). Short-term feeding at the wrong time is sufficient to desynchronize peripheral clocks and induce obesity with hyperphagia, physical inactivity and metabolic disorders in mice. *Metabolism: Clinical and Experimental, 65*(5), 714–727. doi:10.1016/j.metabol.2016.02.003

Yatham, L. N., Liddle, P. F., Lam, R. W., Zis, A. P., Stoessl, A. J., Sossi, V., . . . Ruth, T. J. (2010). Effect of electroconvulsive therapy on brain 5-HT(2) receptors in major depression. *British Journal of Psychiatry, 196,* 474–479.

Yau, K. W., & Hardie, R. C. (2009). Phototransduction motifs and variations. *Cell, 139,* 246–264.

Yerkes, R. M., & Dodson, J. D. (1908). The relation of strength of stimulus to rapidity of habit-formation. *Journal of Comparative Neurology and Psychology, 18,* 459–482.

Yi, F., Min, Z., Zhizun, Y., Wen, G., Dan, D., & Zhihong, Q. (2020). When altruists cannot help: The influence of altruism on the mental health of university students during the COVID-19 pandemic. *Globalization and Health, 16,* 61. https://doi.org/10.1186/s12992-020-00587-y

Yim, M. H., Alkema, L., & Kantorova, V. (2017). National, regional and global trends in marriage and cohabiting unions: Estimates and projections of the proportion of women who are married or in a union by age. Poster presented at the Population Association of America Annual Conference, Chicago, Illinois. https://iussp.confex.com › ipc2017 › mediafile › Presentation › Paper4725

York, J. L., & Welte, J. W. (1994). Gender comparisons of alcohol consumption in alcoholic and nonalcoholic populations. *Journal of Studies on Alcohol, 55,* 743–750.

Young, A. H., McElroy, S. L., Bauer, M., Philips, N., Chang, W., Olausson, B., . . . EMBOLDEN I (Trial 001) Investigators (2010). A double-blind, placebo-controlled study of quetiapine and lithium monotherapy in adults in the acute phase of bipolar depression (EMBOLDEN I). *Journal of Clinical Psychiatry, 71,* 150–162.

Young, E., & Korszun, A. (2010). Sex, trauma, stress hormones, and depression. *Molecular Psychiatry, 15,* 23–28.

Young, J. K. (2010). Anorexia nervosa and estrogen: Current status of the hypothesis. *Neuroscience and Biobehavioral Reviews, 34,* 1195–1200. doi:10.1016/j.neubiorev.2010.01.015

Youssef, F. F., Bachew, R., Bissessar, S., Crockett, M. J., & Faber, N. S. (2018). Sex differences in the effects of acute stress on behavior in the ultimatum game. *Psychoneuroendocrinology, 96,* 126-131. doi:10.1016/j.psyneuen.2018.06.012.

Yu, F., Ryan, L. H., Schaie, K. W., Willis, S. L., & Kolanowski, A. (2009). Factors associated with cognition in adults: The Seattle longitudinal study. *Research in Nursing and Health, 32,* 540–550.

Yunker, G. W., & Yunker, B. D. (2002). Primal leadership (book). *Personnel Psychology, 55,* 1030–1033.

Zaalberg, R., Manstead, A. S. R., & Fischer, A. H. (2004). Relations between emotions, display rules, social motives, and facial behaviors. *Cognition and Emotion, 18*, 183–207.

Zaccaro, S. J., Mumford, M. D., Connelly, M., Marks, M., & Gilbert, J. A. (2000). Assessment of leader abilities. *Leadership Quarterly, 11*, 37–64.

Zack, E., Barr, R., Gerhardstein, P., Dickerson. K., & Meltzoff, A. N. (2009). Infant imitation from television using a novel touch screen technology. *British Journal of Developmental Psychology, 27*, 13–26.

Zadina, J. E., Hackler, L., Ge, L. J., & Kastin, A. J. (1997). A potent and selective endogeneous agonist for the u-opiate receptor. *Nature, 386*, 499–502.

Zadra, A., Desjardins, S., & Marcotte, E. (2006). Evolutionary function of dreams: A test of the threat simulation theory in recurrent dreams. *Consciousness and Cognition, 15*, 450–463.

Zahn-Waxler, C., & Robinson, J. (1995). Empathy and guilt: Early origins of feelings of responsibility. In J. P. Tangney & K. W. Fischer (Eds.), *Self-conscious emotions* (pp. 143–173). Guilford Press.

Zajenkowski, M. (2020). How do teenagers perceive their intelligence? Narcissism, intellect, well-being and gender as correlates of self-assessed intelligence among adolescents. *Personality and Individual Differences*, 109978. https://doi.org/10.1016/j.paid.2020.109978

Zajonc, R. B. (1965). Social facilitation. *Science, 149*, 269–274.

Zajonc, R. B. (1968). Attitudinal effects of mere exposure. *Journal of Personality and Social Psychology, 9*, 1–27.

Zajonc, R. B. (1980). Feeling and thinking: Preferences need no inferences. *American Psychologist, 35*, 151–175.

Zajonc, R. B., Adelmann, P. K., Murphy, S. T., & Neidenthal, P. M. (1987). Convergence in the physical appearance of spouse. *Motivation and Emotion, 11*, 335–346.

Zajonc, R. B., Murphy, S. T., & Inglehart, M. (1989). Feeling and facial efference: Implications of the vascular theory of emotions. *Psychological Review, 96*, 395–416.

Zamroziewicz, M. K., Paul, E. J., Zwilling, C. E., Johnson, E. J., Kuchan, M. J., Cohen, N. J., & Barbey, A. K. (2016). Parahippocampal cortex mediates the relationship between lutein and crystallized intelligence in healthy, older adults. *Frontiers in Aging Neuroscience, 8*, 297. doi:10.3389/fnagi.2016.00297

Zanarini, M. C. (2000). Childhood experiences associated with the development of borderline personality disorder. *Psychiatric Clinics of North America, 23*, 89–101.

Zanarini, M. C., Frankenburg, F. R., Reich, D. B., & Fitzmaurice, G. (2012). Attainment and stability of sustained symptomatic remission and recovery among patients with borderline personality disorder and axis II comparison subjects: A 16-year prospective follow-up study. *American Journal of Psychiatry, 169*, 476–483.

Zeamer, C., & Fox Tree, J. E. (2013). The process of auditory distraction: Disrupted attention and impaired recall in a simulated lecture environment. *Journal of Experimental Psychology: Learning, Memory, and Cognition, 39*, 1463–1472. doi:10.1037/a0032190

Zebrowitz, L. A., White, B., & Wieneke, K. (2008). Mere exposure and racial prejudice: Exposure to other-race faces increases liking for strangers from that race. *Social Cognition, 26*, 259–275.

Zee, P. C., & Manthena, P. (2007). The brain's master circadian clock: Implications and opportunities for therapy of sleep disorders. *Sleep Medicine Reviews, 11*, 59–70.

Zeidman, P., & Maguire, E. A. (2016). Anterior hippocampus: The anatomy of perception, imagination and episodic memory. *Nature Reviews Neuroscience, 17*(3), 173–182. doi:10.1038/nrn.2015.24

Ziegler, R., & Schlett, C. (2016). An attitude strength and self-perception framework regarding the bi-directional relationship of job satisfaction with extra-role and in-role behavior: The doubly moderating role of work centrality. *Frontiers in Psychology, 7*, 235. doi:10.3389/fpsyg.2016.00235

Zeitzer, J. M., Nishino, S., & Mignot, E. (2006). The neurobiology of hypocretins (orexins), narcolepsy and related therapeutic interventions. *Trends in Pharmacological Sciences, 27*, 368–374.

Zelin, A. I., Walker, R. V., & Johnson, D. M. (2019). Cornered at a bar: How victim clothing, alcohol intake, and relationship with bystander impact intention to help. *Violence Against Women, 25*(10), 1163–1190. https://doi.org/10.1177/1077801218809948

Zhang, B., & Wing, Y. K. (2006). Sex differences in insomnia: A meta-analysis. *Sleep, 29*, 85–93.

Zhang, L.Q., Yao, J., Gao, J., Sun, L., Wang, L.-T., & Sui, J.F. (2019). Modulation of eyeblink conditioning through sensory processing of conditioned stimulus by cortical and subcortical regions. *Behavioural Brain Research, 359*, 149–155. https://doi.org/10.1016/j.bbr.2018.10.035

Zhang, M., Ihme, K., & Drewitz, U. (2019). Discriminating drivers' emotions through the dimension of power: Evidence from facial infrared thermography and peripheral physiological measurements. *Transportation Research Part F: Traffic Psychology and Behaviour, 63*, 135–143. https://doi.org/10.1016/j.trf.2019.04.003

Zhang, T., Godara, P., Blanco, E. R., Griffin, R. L., Wang, X., Curcio, C. A., & Zhang, Y. (2015). Variability in human cone topography assessed by adaptive optics scanning laser ophthalmoscopy. *American Journal of Ophthalmology, 160*(2), 290–300.e1. doi:10.1016/j.ajo.2015.04.034

Zhang, Y., & Sharpee, T. O. (2016). A robust feedforward model of the olfactory system. *PLoS Computational Biology, 12*(4), e1004850. doi:10.1371/journal.pcbi.1004850

Zhao, L., & Brinton, R. D. (2007). Estrogen receptor alpha and beta differentially regulate intracellular Ca (2) dynamics leading to ERK phosphorylation and estrogen neuroprotection in hippocampal neurons. *Brain Research, 1172*, 48–59.

Zhou, J., Wang, E., Dovidio, J., & Yu, G. (2009). The effects of structural consistency on attitude-intention and attitude-behavior relationships. *Social Behavior and Personality, 37*(6), 781–790. doi:10.2224/sbp.2009.37.6.781

Ziegler, D. J., & Smith, P. N. (2004). Anger and the ABC model underlying rational-emotive behavior therapy. *Psychological Reports, 93*, 1009–1014.

Ziegler, M., Cengia, A., Mussel, P., & Gerstorf, D. (2015). Openness as a buffer against cognitive decline: The Openness-Fluid-Crystallized-Intelligence (OFCI) model applied to late adulthood. *Psychology and Aging, 30*(3), 573–588. doi:10.1037/a0039493

Zilioli, S., Slatcher, R. B., Chi, P., Li, X., Zhao, J., & Zhao, G. (2016). Childhood adversity, self-esteem, and diurnal cortisol profiles across the life span. *Psychological Science, 27*, 1249–1265.

Zilverstand, A., Parvaz, M. A., Moeller, S. J., & Goldstein, R. Z. (2016). Cognitive interventions for addiction medicine: Understanding the underlying neurobiological mechanisms. *Progress in Brain Research, 224*, 285–304.

Zimbardo, P. G. (1972, April). Psychology of imprisonment. *Transition/Society*, pp. 4–8.

Zinzow, H. M., Resnick, H. S., McCauley, J. L., Amstadter, A. B., Ruggiero, K. J., & Kilpatrick, D. G. (2012). Prevalence and risk of psychiatric disorders as a function of variant rape histories: Results from a national survey of women. *Social Psychiatry and Psychiatric Epidemiology, 47*, 893–902.

Zisook, S., Rush, A. J., Haight, B. R., Clines, D. C., & Rockett, C. B. (2006). Use of bupropion in combination with serotonin reuptake inhibitors. *Biological Psychiatry, 59*, 203–210.

Zottoli, M. A., & Wanous, J. P. (2000). Recruitment source research: Current status and future directions. *Human Resource Management Review, 10*, 435–451.

Zuckerman, M. (1978). The search for high sensation. *Psychology Today, 11*, 38–99.

Zuckerman, M. (1994). *Behavioral expressions and biosocial bases of sensation seeking.* Cambridge University Press.

Zuckerman, M., & Kuhlman, D. M. (2000). Personality and risk-taking: Common biosocial factors. *Journal of Personality, 68*, 999–1029.

Zvolensky, M. J., Vujanovic, A. A., Bernstein, A., & Leyro, T. (2010). Distress tolerance: Theory, measurement, and relations to psychopathology. *Current Directions in Psychological Science, 19*, 406–410.

NAME INDEX

B

F

H

I

J

M

O

Q

R

T

X

Y

Z

SUBJECT INDEX

Page numbers in bold indicate terms defined in the margins.